S0-AEC-224

SUBHASH C. JAIN
School of Business Administration
University of Connecticut

Marketing Planning & Strategy

Fourth Edition

COLLEGE DIVISION South-Western Publishing Co.
Cincinnati Ohio

3-3-95

Sponsoring Editor: Jeanne R. Busemeyer
Marketing Manager: Scott D. Person
Production Editor: Sue Ellen Brown
Cover Design: Tom Hubbard
Internal Design: Lesiak/Crampton Design
Production House: Custom Editorial Productions, Inc.

SS90DA

Library of Congress Cataloging-in-Publication Data

Jain, Subhash C.
Marketing planning & strategy / Subhash C. Jain. — 4th ed.
p. cm.
Includes bibliographical references and index.
ISBN 0-538-82648-7 (alk. paper)
1. Marketing—Management. I. Title. II. Title: Marketing planning and strategy.
HF5415.13.J35 1993
658.8′ 02—dc20 92-31418
CIP

Printed in the United States of America

1 2 3 4 5 6 MT 7 6 5 4 3 2

This book is printed on recycled, acid-free paper that meets Environmental Protection Agency standards.

With love to
my wife, Sadhna

Contents in Brief

Contents

Preface

In an era marked by the challenges of global competition, rapidly changing technology, new consumer needs, and shifting demographics, the development of strategic marketing skills is essential if companies are to survive, let alone prosper. Because unique strategic marketing moves are not often transparent to competitors and are nearly always difficult and time-consuming to copy, a focus on marketing strategy often yields significant advantage.

Marketing Planning and Strategy is a primer on strategic marketing. The book is intended for use in capstone marketing courses. The fourth edition contains two principal parts: text and cases. The text reviews the state of the art in marketing strategy, focusing on both research and concepts. The cases are comprehensive and integrative, most dealing with a broad range of marketing issues across varying strategic circumstances.

Today each company shares with all other companies the challenge of identifying and understanding the markets unfolding around it. Success will depend on the ability to perceive and understand these markets in all their subtlety, inconsistency, and rationality—in other words, in all their complexity. By choice, *Marketing Planning and Strategy* tries to illustrate and enrich this complexity so that students will approach the subject with the sophistication it deserves.

The book offers new ideas, new insights, and a reliable perspective on marketing strategy formulation. Topics of special interest include

- Determining what marketing strategy can realistically accomplish for a business
- Determining when a business needs to reformulate its marketing strategy
- Distinguishing marketing strategy from marketing management
- Identifying underlying factors that must be considered in developing marketing strategy
- Analyzing corporate perspective and measuring strengths and weaknesses
- Examining basic changes in America's social and industrial environments that have led to the new emphasis on marketing strategy
- Developing a mission statement that can advance marketing efforts
- Setting realistic marketing objectives
- Determining roles for different products of a business unit
- Employing portfolio techniques in strategy determination and resource allocation
- Organizing for successful strategy implementation
- Identifying the latest techniques for gathering information, undertaking strategic analysis, and formulating strategies

In recent years, to clearly delineate the role of marketing in strategy development, a new term, *strategic marketing,* has been coined. Marketing may be viewed in three ways: as marketing management, as marketing strategy or strategic marketing, and as corporate marketing. Marketing management deals with strategy implementation, usually at the product/market or brand level. Strategic marketing focuses on strategy formulation, whereas corporate marketing provides inputs for corporatewide strategy.

Strategy is commonly considered at the business unit level. At the heart of business unit strategy is marketing strategy, which becomes the basis of strategy in other functional areas. Integration of all functional strategies represents the business unit strategy. *Marketing Planning and Strategy* focuses on marketing strategy from the viewpoint of the business unit.

HALLMARKS OF THE FOURTH EDITION

This fourth edition presents a much more comprehensive treatment of the subject than previous editions. Developments in the field as evidenced by numerous journal articles, reports, and books on strategic marketing and the extension of my own thinking on the subject have enabled me to provide state-of-the-art coverage of the discipline.

Preparation of this new edition was guided by the following objectives:

- To provide emerging perspectives on strategic marketing
- To add material on global market strategies
- To bring in the international focus in developing marketing strategy
- To examine such emerging topics as product quality and service
- To strengthen the discussion on strategy implementation
- To include new cases reflecting a variety of strategic marketing situations
- To update concepts, illustrations, and statistics throughout

Accomplishment of these objectives led to a number of this edition's distinguishing features.

THE TEXT

Like the third edition, the fourth edition is based on current conceptual and research literature. The text follows a basic model to explain marketing strategy formulation. The text is organized according to this model, which focuses on company, competition, customer, environment, strengths and weaknesses, objectives and goals, strategy development, and strategy implementation. The fourth edition also contains several significant improvements:

- Current thoughts and concepts in marketing strategy formulation, based on constructs that have taken place in the field
- A new chapter on global market strategies to compete across national boundaries
- Discussion of problems and their solution for successful marketing strategy implementation

- Substantial revision of the chapters on market, product, pricing, distribution, and promotion strategies as well as those on strategic marketing, competitive analysis, environmental scanning, and portfolio analysis
- Updating of references to provide the most current perspectives on the subject

THE CASES

This edition includes 23 cases, of which 15 are new. The cases have been used at such schools as Harvard Business School, Stanford University, University of Western Ontario, and International Institute for Management Development. The cases included involve companies with which students will be familiar—Nike, Anheuser-Busch, Gillette, Benetton, Nissan Motor, Pizza Hut, Boise Cascade, Playboy, and Johnson Controls. Cases to illustrate each aspect of marketing strategy are included. Important improvements in cases include the following:

- An increased emphasis has been placed on including comprehensive and integrative cases that involve as many major strategy components as possible.
- New cases have been included, although the total number of cases has been kept to a manageable size.
- A concentrated effort has been made to include cases that cover the full spectrum of organizational size.
- The number of international cases has been increased to 10.
- One new case, Nissan Motor Co., Ltd., deals with European integration.
- Three cases about service organizations—one about insurance, one about an airline, and one about entertainment—have been included.

INSTRUCTOR'S MANUAL

The instructor's manual has been completely revised to provide in-depth analysis with a variety of new pedagogical aids: answers to the end-of-chapter discussion questions in the text; true/false, multiple-choice, and fill-in exam questions; suggested syllabi, solutions to cases, suggestions for further reading; and a list of additional cases. Significant improvements in the manual include the following:

- Careful revision of third edition test bank questions and the addition of new questions for each chapter
- Transparency masters
- Chapter outlines providing quick chapter reviews
- Comprehensive case notes

Assumptions about the audience significantly affect the style and content of a book. This book is intended primarily for advanced undergraduates and graduate students. Thus, the material has been developed from a classroom-tested conceptual framework. Many of the conceptual schemes included in the book have been reshaped and modified, based on feedback provided by many distinguished marketers. The experiences of a large number of companies have been drawn upon and are cited throughout the book as illustrations.

This book concentrates on areas of strategic importance only, especially those having significant implications and particular relevance for the making of policy decisions in competitive situations. Discussion of routine day-to-day decisions is intentionally avoided to keep the focus intact. The overall approach of this book is analytic rather than normative. This approach is necessary because strategy development is more an art than a science. In addition, strategy formulation is a highly complex process for which neat models and econometric equations, no matter how diligently worked out, do not suffice.

ACKNOWLEDGMENTS

A project of this nature cannot be completed without active support from different sources. I have been lucky in this respect to have received advice and assistance from many directions.

My colleagues at the University of Connecticut, especially Alan Andreasen, Michael Lubatkin, and John Clair Thompson, have contributed to the task of preparing this fourth edition in a variety of ways for which I am indebted to them. I acknowledge the valuable feedback provided by students at the University of Connecticut and Graduate School of Business Administration Zürich, who read early drafts of the text as part of their assignments during 1991.

A special mention of appreciation must go to Teresa Grusauskas for her valuable research assistance, to departmental secretary Mary Palmer and doctoral student Kiran Ahluwalia for their administrative support, and to Susan Levesque for typing portions of the manuscript. I am indebted to many writers and publishers for granting permission to include excerpts from their works or their cases, especially Harvard Business School; Graduate School of Business Administration, Stanford University; School of Business Administration, University of Western Ontario; International Institute for Management Development; North American Case Research Association; and the Planning Forum.

I wish to express gratitude to the following individuals for their permission to include cases written by them or under their supervision: Robert T. Davis, Stanford University; Fred W. Kniffen, University of Connecticut; H. Michael Hayes, University of Colorado at Denver; Tracy K. Short, Johnson Controls, Inc.; Erhard Karlheinz Valentin, Weber State College; Natalie Tabb Taylor, Babson College; Gordon McDougall, Wilfrid Laurier University; Douglas Snetsinger, University of Toronto; Jon Ozmun, Northern Arizona University; Robert McGlashan, University of Houston–Clear Lake; Tim Singleton, University of Houston–Clear Lake; Lew G. Brown, University of North Carolina at Greensboro; Richard Sharpe, University of Tennessee at Knoxville; Kyoichi Ikeo, Keio University, Japan; John A. Quelch, Harvard Business School; Patrick J. Kaufmann, Harvard Business School; James L. Heskett, Harvard Business School; Sergio Signorelli, Instituto Studi Direzionali SPA, Spain; C. Patrick Woodcock, University of Western Ontario; J. Michael Geringer, University of Western Ontario; H. Crookell, University of Western Ontario; Paul W. Beamish, University of Western Ontario; Peter Killing, University of Western Ontario; William Webb, University of Western Ontario.

Throughout the development of this fourth edition, a number of reviewers made important contributions, and at the same time, many colleagues provided insightful suggestions. All these individuals had an important influence on my thinking: C. P. Rao, University of Arkansas; John K. Ryans, Jr., Kent State University; Roberto Friedman, University of Georgia; Madhav P. Kacker, Iona College; Rajan Chandran, Temple University; Hugh E. Kramer, University of Hawaii; J. Krulis-Randa, Universität Zürich; Udo Koppelmann, Universität Zu Köln.

I owe a special word of gratitude to my former teacher, Professor Stuart U. Rich of the University of Oregon, who taught me what I know about marketing strategy, and to my former dean, Ronald J. Patten (now at DePaul University), who initially encouraged me to undertake this project.

I am indebted to the talented staff at South-Western Publishing Co., for their role in shaping the fourth edition. My editor, Jeanne Busemeyer, furnished excellent advice on the structure of the fourth edition. My production editor, Sue Ellen Brown, did a super job of seeing the book to completion. I also want to acknowledge Tom Hubbard's design work.

Finally, my gratitude must go to my wife and our children, who not only made it possible for me to live through the experience but gave me their support and inspiration in countless ways. This book belongs more to them than to me.

S.C.J.
Storrs, Connecticut
June 26, 1992

PART ONE
Introduction

CHAPTER 1

Marketing and the Concept of Planning and Strategy

We must plan for the future, because people who stay in the present will remain in the past.

ABRAHAM LINCOLN

Over the years marketers have been presented with a series of philosophical approaches to marketing decision making. One widely used approach is the *marketing concept approach,* which directs the marketer to develop the product offering, and indeed the entire marketing program, to meet the needs of the customer base. A key element in this approach is the need for information flow from the market to the decision maker. Another approach is the *systems approach,* which instructs the marketer to view the product not as an individual entity but as just one aspect of the customer's total need-satisfaction system. A third approach, the *environmental approach,* portrays the marketing decision maker as the focal point of numerous environments within which the firm operates and that affect the success of the firm's marketing program. These environments frequently bear such labels as legal-political, economic, competitive, consumer, market structure, social, technological, and international.

Indeed, these and other philosophical approaches to marketing decision making are merely descriptive frameworks that stress certain aspects of the firm's role vis-à-vis the strategic planning process. No matter what approach a firm follows, it needs a reference point for its decisions that is provided by the strategy and the planning process involved in designing the strategy. Thus the strategic planning process is the guiding force behind decision making, regardless of the framework one adopts. This relationship between the strategic planning process and approaches to marketing decision making is depicted in Exhibit 1-1.

Planning perspectives develop in response to needs that arise internally or that impinge on the organization from outside. During the 1950s and 1960s, growth was the dominant fact of the economic environment, and the planning processes developed during that time were typically geared to the discovery and exploitation of entrepreneurial opportunities. Decentralized planning was the order of the day. Top management focused on reviewing major investment proposals and approving annual operating budgets. Long-range corporate

EXHIBIT 1-1
Relationship between the Strategic Planning Process and Approaches to Marketing Decision Making

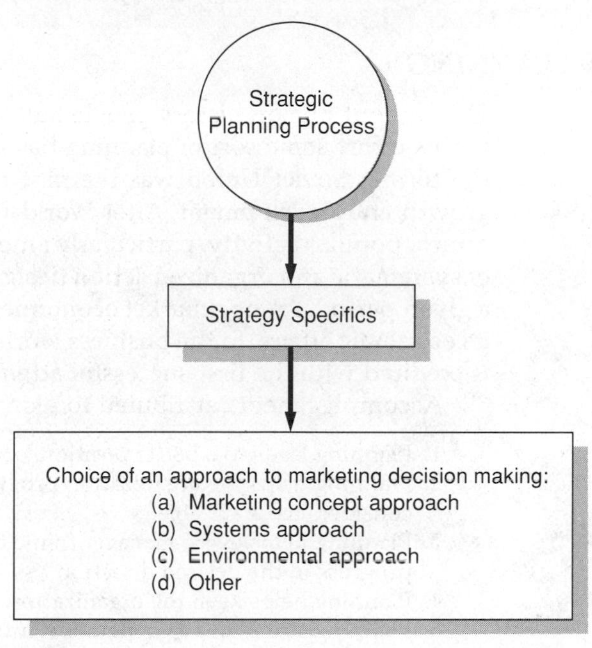

plans were occasionally put together, but they were primarily extrapolations and were rarely used for strategic decision making.

Planning perspectives changed in the 1970s. With the quadrupling of energy costs and the emergence of competition from new quarters, followed by a recession and reports of an impending capital crisis, companies found themselves surrounded by new needs. Reflecting these new management needs and concerns, a process aimed at more centralized control over resources soon pervaded planning efforts. Sorting out winners and losers, setting priorities, and conserving capital became the name of the game. A new era of strategic planning dawned over corporate America.[1]

The value of effective strategic planning is virtually unchallenged in today's business world. A majority of the *Fortune* 1000 firms in the United States, for instance, now have senior executives responsible for spearheading strategic planning efforts.

Strategic planning requires that company assets (i.e., resources) be managed to maximize financial return through the selection of a viable business in accordance with the changing environment. One very important component of strategic planning is the establishment of the product/market scope of a business. It is within this scope that strategic planning becomes relevant for marketers.[2] Thus as companies adopted and made progress in their strategic planning capabilities, a new strategic role for marketing emerged. In this strategic role, marketing concentrates on the markets to serve, the competition to be tackled, and the timing of market entry/exit.

CONCEPT OF PLANNING

Throughout human history people have tried to achieve specific purposes, and in this effort some sort of planning has always found a place. In modern times the former Soviet Union was the first nation to devise an economic plan for growth and development. After World War II, national economic planning became a popular activity, particularly among developing countries, with the goal of systematic and organized action designed to achieve stated objectives within a given period. Among market economies, France has gone furthest in planning its economic affairs. In the business world, Henri Fayol, the French industrialist, is credited with the first successful attempts at formal planning.

Accomplishments attributed to planning can be summarized as follows:

1. Planning leads to a better position, or standing, for the organization.
2. Planning helps the organization progress in ways that its management considers most suitable.
3. Planning helps every manager think, decide, and act more effectively and progress in the desired direction.
4. Planning helps keep the organization flexible.
5. Planning stimulates a cooperative, integrated, enthusiastic approach to organizational problems.
6. Planning indicates to management how to evaluate and check up on progress toward planned objectives.
7. Planning leads to socially and economically useful results.[3]

Planning in corporations emerged as an important activity in the 1960s. Several studies undertaken during that time showed that companies attached significant importance to planning. A Conference Board survey of 420 firms, for example, revealed that 85 percent had formalized corporate planning activity.[4] A 1983 survey by Coopers and Lybrand and Yankelovich, Skelly, and White confirmed the central role played by the planning function and the planner in running most large businesses.[5] Although the importance of planning had been acknowledged for some time, the executives interviewed in 1983 indicated that planning was becoming more important and was receiving greater attention.

Some companies that use formal planning believe that it improves profits and growth, finding it particularly useful in explicit objective setting and in monitoring results.[6] Certainly the current business climate is generating a new posture among executives, with the planning process being identified by eight out of ten respondents as a key to implementing the chief executive officer's (CEO) chosen strategy.[7] Today most companies insist on some sort of planning exercise to meet the rapidly changing environment. For many, however, the exercise is cathartic rather than creative.

Growth is an accepted expectation of a firm; however, it does not happen by itself. Growth must be carefully planned: questions such as how much, when, in which areas, where to grow, and who will be responsible for different tasks must be answered. Unplanned growth will be haphazard and may fail to provide desired levels of profit. Therefore, for a company to realize orderly growth, to maintain a high level of operating efficiency, and to achieve its goals fully, it must plan for the future systematically. Products, markets, facilities, personnel, and financial resources must be evaluated and selected wisely.

Today's business environment is more complex than ever. In addition to the keen competition that firms face from both domestic and overseas companies, a variety of other concerns, including environmental protection, employee welfare, consumerism, and antitrust action, impinge on business moves. Thus, it is desirable for a firm to be cautious in undertaking risks, which again calls for a planned effort.

Many firms pursue growth internally through research and development. This route to growth is not only time-consuming but also requires a heavy commitment of resources with a high degree of risk. In such a context, planning is needed to choose the right type of risk.

Since World War II, technology has had a major impact on markets and marketers. Presumably, the trend of accelerating technological change will continue in the future. The impact of technological innovations may be felt in any industry or in any firm. Therefore, such changes need to be anticipated as far in advance as possible in order for a firm to take advantage of new opportunities and to avoid the harmful consequences of not anticipating major new developments. Here again planning is significant.

Finally, planning is required in making a choice among the many equally attractive alternative investment opportunities a firm may have. No firm can afford to invest in each and every "good" opportunity. Planning, thus, is essential in making the right selection.

Planning for future action has been called by many different names: long-range planning, corporate planning, comprehensive planning, and formal planning. Whatever its name, the reference is obviously to the future.

Definition of Planning

Warren defines **planning** as

> essentially a process directed toward making today's decisions with tomorrow in mind and a means of preparing for future decisions so that they may be made rapidly, economically, and with as little disruption to the business as possible.[8]

Though there are as many definitions of planning as there are writers on the subject, Warren's emphasis on the future is the common thread underlying all planning theory. In practice, however, different meanings are attached to planning. Often a distinction is made between a *budget*—a yearly program of operations—and a *long-range plan*. Some people consider planning as something done by staff specialists, whereas budgeting is seen to fall within the purview of line managers.

It is necessary for a company to be clear about the nature and scope of planning that it intends to adopt. A definition of planning should then be based on what planning is supposed to be in an organization. It is not necessary for every company to engage in comprehensive planning of the same style. The basis of all planning should be to design courses of action to be pursued for achieving stated objectives such that opportunities are seized and threats are guarded against, but the exact planning posture must be custom-made (i.e., based on the decision-making needs of the organization).

Operations management, which emphasizes the current programs of an organization, and planning, which essentially deals with the future, are two intimately related activities. Operations management or budgeted programs should emerge as the result of planning. In the outline of a five-year plan, for example, years two through five may be described in general terms, but the activities of the first year should be budgeted and accompanied by detailed operational programs.

A distinction should also be made between planning and forecasting. Forecasting considers future changes in areas of importance to a company and tries to assess the impact of these changes on company operations. Planning takes over from there to set objectives and goals and develop strategy.

Briefly, no business, however small or poorly managed, can do without planning. Although planning per se may be nothing new for an organization, the current emphasis on it is indeed different. No longer just one of several important functions of the organization, planning's new role demands linkage of various parts of an organization into an integrated system. The emphasis has shifted from planning as an aspect of the organization to planning as the basis of all efforts and decisions, the building of an entire organization toward the achievement of designated objectives.

There is little doubt about the importance of planning. Planning departments are key in critiquing strategies, crystallizing goals, setting priorities, and maintaining control;[9] but to be useful, planning should be done properly. Planning just for the sake of it can be injurious; half-hearted planning can cause more problems than it solves. In practice, however, many business executives simply pay lip service to planning, partly because they find it difficult to incorporate planning into the decision-making process and partly because they are uncertain about how to adopt it.

Requisites for Successful Planning

If planning is to succeed, proper arrangements must be made to put it into operation. The Boston Consulting Group suggests the following concerns for effective planning:

- There is the matter of outlook, which can affect the degree to which functional and professional viewpoints, versus corporate needs, dominate the work of planning.
- There is the question of the extent of involvement for members of the management. Who should participate and to what extent?

- There is the problem of determining what part of the work of planning should be accomplished through joint effort and of how to achieve effective collaboration among participants in the planning process.
- There is the matter of incentive, of making planning an appropriately emphasized and rewarded kind of managerial work.
- There is the question of how to provide staff coordination for planning, which raises the issue of how a planning unit should be used in the organization.
- And there is the role of the chief executive in the planning process. What should it be?[10]

Though planning is conceptually rather simple, implementing it is far from easy. Successful planning requires a blend of many forces in different areas, not the least of which are behavioral, intellectual, structural, philosophical, and managerial. Achieving the proper blend of these forces requires making difficult decisions, as the Boston Consulting Group has suggested. Although planning is indeed complex, successful planning systems do have common fundamental characteristics despite differing operational details. First, it is essential that the CEO be completely supportive. Second, planning must be kept simple, in agreement with the managerial style, and unencumbered by detailed numbers and fancy equations. Third, planning is a shared responsibility, and it would be wrong to assume that the president or vice president of planning, staff specialists, or line managers could do it single-handedly. Fourth, the managerial incentive system should give due recognition to the fact that decisions made with long-term implications may not appear good in the short run. Fifth, the goals of planning should be achievable without excessive frustration and work load and with widespread understanding and acceptance of the process. Sixth, overall flexibility should be encouraged to accommodate changing conditions.

Initiating Planning Activities

There is no one best time for initiating planning activities in an organization; however, before developing a formal planning system, the organization should be prepared to establish a strong planning foundation. The CEO should be a central participant, spearheading the planning job. A planning framework should be developed to match the company's perspective and should be generally accepted by its executives. A manual outlining the work flow, information links, format of various documents, and schedules for completing various activities should be prepared by the planner. Once these foundations are completed, the company can initiate the planning process anytime.

Planning should not be put off until bad times prevail; it is not just a cure for poor performance. Although planning is probably the best way to avoid bad times, planning efforts that are begun when operational performance is at an ebb (i.e., at low or no profitability) will only make things worse, since planning efforts tend initially to create an upheaval by challenging the traditional patterns of decision making. The company facing the question of survival should concentrate on alleviating the current crisis.

Planning should evolve gradually. It is wishful thinking to expect full-scale planning to be instituted in a few weeks or months. Initial planning may be formalized in one or more functional areas; then, as experience is gained, a companywide planning system may be designed. IBM, a pioneer in formalized planning, followed this pattern. First, financial planning and product planning were attempted in the post-World War II period. Gradual changes toward increased formality were made over the years. Since 1966, increased attention has been given to planning contents, and a compatible network of planning data systems has been initiated. Corporatewide planning, which was introduced in the 1970s, forms the backbone of IBM's current global planning endeavors. Beginning in 1986, the company made several changes in its planning perspectives in response to the contingencies created by deteriorating performance.

Philosophies of Planning

In an analysis of three different philosophies of planning, Ackoff established the labels satisfying, optimizing, and adaptivizing.[11] Planning on the basis of the **satisfying** philosophy aims at easily achievable goals and molds planning efforts accordingly. This type of planning requires setting objectives and goals that are "high enough" but not as "high as possible." The satisfying planner, therefore, devises only one feasible and acceptable way of achieving goals, which may not necessarily be the best possible way. Under a satisfying philosophy, confrontations that might be caused by conflicts in programs are diffused through politicking, underplaying change, and accepting a fall in performance as unavoidable.

The philosophy of **optimizing** planning has its foundation in operations research. The optimizing planner seeks to model various aspects of the organization and define them as objective functions. Efforts are then directed so that an objective function is maximized (or minimized), subject to the constraints imposed by management or forced by the environment. For example, an objective may be to obtain the highest feasible market share; planning then amounts to searching for different variables that affect market share: price elasticity, plant capacity, competitive behavior, the product's stage in the life cycle, and so on. The effect of each variable is reduced to constraints on the market share. Then an analysis is undertaken to find out the optimum market share to target.

Unlike the satisfying planner, the optimizer endeavors, with the use of mathematical models, to find the best available course to realize objectives and goals. The success of an optimizing planner depends on how completely and accurately the model depicts the underlying situation and how well the planner can figure out solutions from the model once it has been built.

Ackoff considers the philosophy of **adaptivizing** planning as an innovative approach not yet popular in practice. To understand the nature of this type of planning, let us compare it to optimizing planning. In optimization the significant variables and their effects are taken for granted. Given these, an effort is made to achieve the optimal result. With an adaptivizing approach, on the other hand, planning may be undertaken to produce changes in the underlying relationships themselves and thereby create a desired future. Underlying relationships refer to an organization's internal and external environment and the dynamics of the values of the actors in these environments (i.e., how values relate to needs and to the satisfaction of needs, how changes in needs produce changes in values, and how changes in needs are produced).

CONCEPT OF STRATEGY

Strategy in a firm is

> the pattern of major objectives, purposes, or goals and essential policies and plans for achieving those goals, stated in such a way as to define what business the company is in or is to be in and the kind of company it is or is to be.[12]

Any organization needs strategy (a) when resources are finite, (b) when there is uncertainty about competitive strengths and behavior, (c) when commitment of resources is irreversible, (d) when decisions must be coordinated between far-flung places and over time, and (e) when there is uncertainty about control of the initiative.[13]

An explicit statement of strategy is the key to success in a changing business environment. Strategy provides a unified sense of direction to which all members of the organization can relate. Where there is no clear concept of strategy, decisions rest on either subjective or intuitive assessment and are made without regard to other decisions. Such decisions become increasingly unreliable as the pace of change accelerates or decelerates rapidly. Without a strategy, an organization is like a ship without a rudder going around in circles.[14]

Strategy is concerned with the deployment of potential for results and the development of a reaction capability to adapt to environmental changes. Quite naturally, we find that there are hierarchies of strategies: corporate strategy and business strategy. At the corporate level, strategy is mainly concerned with defining the set of businesses that should form the company's overall profile. **Corporate strategy** seeks to unify all the business lines of a company and point them toward an overall goal. At the business level, strategy focuses on defining the manner of competition in a given industry or product/market segment. A **business strategy** usually covers a plan for a single product or a group of related products. Today most strategic action takes place at the business unit level, where sophisticated tools and techniques permit the analysis of a business; the forecasting of such variables as market growth, pricing, and the impact of government regulation; and the establishment of a plan that can sidestep threats in an erratic environment from competitors, economic cycles, and social, political, and consumer changes.

Each functional area of a business (e.g., marketing) makes its own unique contribution to strategy formulation at different levels. In many firms, the marketing function represents the greatest degree of contact with the external environment, the environment least controllable by the firm. In such firms, marketing plays a pivotal role in strategy development.

In its strategic role, marketing consists of establishing a match between the firm and its environment. It seeks solutions to problems of deciding (a) what business the firm is in and what kinds of business it may enter in the future and (b) how the chosen field(s) of endeavor may be successfully run in a competitive environment by pursuing product, price, promotion, and distribution perspectives to serve target markets. In the context of strategy formulation, marketing has two dimensions: present and future. The present dimension deals with the existing relationships of the firm to its environments. The future dimension encompasses intended future relationships—in the form of a set of objectives—and the action programs necessary to reach those objectives. The following example illustrates the point.

McDonald's, the hamburger chain, has among its corporate objectives the goal of increasing the productivity of its operating units. Given the high proportion of costs in fixed facilities, McDonald's decided to increase facility utilization during off-peak hours, particularly during the morning hours. The program developed to accomplish these goals, the Egg McMuffin, was followed by a breakfast menu consistent with the limited product line strategy of McDonald's regular fare. In this example, the corporate goal of increased productivity led to the marketing perspective of breakfast fare (intended relationship), which was built over favorable customer attitudes toward the chain (existing relationship). Similarly, a new marketing strategy in the form of McDonald's Pizza (intended relationship) was pursued over the company's ability to serve food fast (existing relationship) to meet the corporate goal of growth.

Generally, organizations have identifiable existing strategic perspectives; however, not many organizations have an explicit strategy for the intended future. The absence of an explicit strategy is frequently the result of a lack of top management involvement and commitment required for the development of proper perspectives of the future within the scope of current corporate activities.

Marketing provides the core element for future relationships between the firm and its environment. It specifies inputs for defining objectives and helps formulate plans to achieve them.

CONCEPT OF STRATEGIC PLANNING

Strategy specifies direction. Its intent is to influence the behavior of competitors and the evolution of the market to the advantage of the strategist. It seeks to change the competitive environment. Thus a strategy statement includes a description of the new competitive equilibrium to be created, the cause-and-effect relationships that will bring it about, and the logic to support the course of action. Planning articulates the means of implementing strategy. A strategic plan specifies the sequence and the timing of steps that will alter competitive relationships.

The strategy and the strategic plan are quite different things. The strategy may be brilliant in content and logic; but the sequence and timing of the plan, inadequate. The plan may be the laudable implementation of a worthless strategy. Put together, strategic planning concerns the relationship of an organization to its environment. Conceptually, the organization monitors its environment, incorporates the effects of environmental changes into corporate decision making, and formulates new strategies. Exhibit 1-2 provides a scorecard to evaluate the viability of a company's strategic planning effort.

Companies that do well in strategic planning define their goals clearly and develop rational plans to implement them. In addition, they take the following steps to make their strategic planning effective:

- They shape the company into logical business units that can identify markets, customers, competitors, and the external threats to their business. These business units are managed semiautonomously by executives who operate under corporate financial guidelines and with an understanding of the unit's assigned role in the corporate plan.
- They demonstrate a willingness at the corporate level to compensate line managers on long-term achievements, not just the yearly bottom line; to fund research programs that could give the unit a long-term competitive edge; and to offer the unit the type of planning support that provides data on key issues and encourages and teaches sophisticated planning techniques.
- They develop at the corporate level the capacity to evaluate and balance competing requests from business units for corporate funds, based on the degree of risk and reward.

EXHIBIT 1-2
A Strategic Planning Scorecard

- Is our planning really strategic?

  Do we try to anticipate change or only project from the past?
- Do our plans leave room to explore strategic alternatives?

  Or do they confine us to conventional thinking?
- Do we have time and incentive to investigate truly important things?

  Or do we spend excessive planning time on trivia?
- Have we ever seriously evaluated a new approach to an old market?

  Or are we locked into the status quo?
- Do our plans critically document and examine strategic assumptions?

  Or do we not really understand the implications of the plans we review?
- Do we consistently make an attempt to examine consumer, competitor, and distributor responses to our programs?

  Or do we assume that changes will not affect the relationships we have seen in the past?

Source: Thomas P. Hustad and Ted J. Mitchell, "Creative Market Planning in a Partisan Environment," *Business Horizons,* March–April, 1982, p. 64. Copyright, 1982, by the Foundation for the School of Business at Indiana University. Reprinted by permission.

- They match shorter-term business unit goals to a long-term concept of the company's evolution over the next 15 to 20 years. Exclusively the CEO's function, effectiveness in matching business unit goals to the firm's evolution, may be tested by the board.

Strategic Planning—An Example

The importance of strategic planning for a company may be illustrated by the example of the Mead Corporation. The Mead Corporation is basically in the forest products business. More than 75 percent of its earnings are derived from trees, from the manufacture of pulp and paper, to the conversion of paperboard to beverage carriers, to the distribution of paper supplies to schools. Mead also has an array of businesses outside the forest products industry and is developing new technologies and businesses for its future, primarily in storing, retrieving, and reproducing data electronically. In short, Mead is a company growing in the industries in which it started as well as expanding into areas that fit the capabilities and style of its management.

Although Mead was founded in 1846, it did not begin to grow rapidly until around 1955, reaching the $1-billion mark in sales in the late 1960s. Unfortunately, its competitive position did not keep pace with this expansion. In 1972 the company ranked 12th among 15 forest products companies. Clearly, if Mead was to become a leading company, its philosophy, its management style and focus, and its sense of urgency—its whole corporate culture—had to change. The vehicle for that change was the company's strategic planning process.

When top managers began to discuss ways to improve Mead, they quickly arrived at the key question: What kind of performing company should Mead be? They decided that Mead should be in the top quartile of those companies with which it was normally compared. Articulation of such a clear and simple objective provided all levels of management with a sense of direction and with a frame of reference within which to make and test their own decisions. This objective was translated into specific long-term financial goals.

In 1972 a rigorous assessment of Mead's businesses was made. The results of this assessment were not comforting—several small units were in very weak competitive positions. They were substantial users of cash that was needed elsewhere in businesses where Mead had opportunities for significant growth. Mead's board decided that by 1977 the company should get out of certain businesses, even though some of those high cash users were profitable.

Setting goals and assessing Mead's mix of businesses were only the first steps. Strategic planning had to become a way of life if the corporate culture was going to be changed. Five major changes were instituted. First, the corporate goals were articulated throughout the company—over and over and over again.

Second, the management system was restructured. This restructuring was much easier said than done. In Mead's pulp and paper businesses, the culture expected top management to be heavily involved in the day-to-day operation of major facilities and intimately involved in major construction projects, a style that had served the company well when it was simply a producer of paper. By the early 1970s, however, Mead was simply too large and too diverse for such a hands-on approach. The nonpulp and paper businesses, which were managed with a variety of styles, needed to be integrated into a more balanced management system. Therefore, it was essential for top management to stay out of day-to-day operations. This decision allowed division managers to become stronger and to develop a greater sense of personal responsibility for their operations. By staying away from major construction projects, top managers allowed on-site managers to complete under budget and ahead of schedule the largest and most complex programs in the company's history.

Third, simultaneously with the restructuring of its management system, seminars were used to teach strategic planning concepts and techniques. These seminars, sometimes week-long sessions, were held off the premises with groups of 5 to 20 people at a time. Eventually, the top 300 managers in the company became graduates of Mead's approach to strategic planning.

Fourth, specific and distinctly different goals were developed and agreed upon for each of Mead's two dozen or so business units. Whereas the earlier Mead culture had charged each operation to grow in any way it could, each business unit now had to achieve a leadership position in its markets or, if a leadership position was not practical, to generate cash.

Finally, the board began to fund agreed-upon strategies instead of approving capital projects piecemeal or yielding to emotional pleas from favorite managers.

The first phase of change was the easiest to accomplish. Between 1973 and 1976, Mead disposed of 11 units that offered neither growth nor significant cash flow. Over $100 million was obtained from these divestitures, and that money was promptly reinvested in Mead's stronger businesses. As a result, Mead's mix of businesses showed substantial improvement by 1977. In fact, Mead achieved its portfolio goals one year ahead of schedule.

For the remaining businesses, developing better strategies and obtaining better operating performance were much harder to achieve. After all, on a relative basis, the company was performing well. With the exception of 1975, 1984, and 1989, the years from 1973 to 1990 set all-time records for performance. The evolution of Mead's strategic planning system and the role it played in helping the good businesses of the company improve their relative performance are public knowledge. The financial results speak for themselves. In spite of the divestitures of businesses with sales of over $500 million, Mead's sales grew at a compound rate of 9 percent from 1972 to reach $4.8 billion in 1990. In addition, by the end of 1990, Mead's return on total capital (ROTC) reached 11.8 percent. More important, among 15 forest product companies with which Mead is normally compared, it had moved from twelfth place in 1972 to second place in 1983, a position it continued to maintain in 1990. These were the results of using a strategic planning system as the vehicle for improving financial performance.

During the period from 1985 to 1990, Mead took additional measures to increase its focus in two areas: (a) its coated paper and board business and (b) its value-added, less capital-intensive businesses (the distribution and conversion of paper and related supplies and electronic publishing). Today Mead is a well-managed, highly focused, aggressive company. It is well positioned to be exceptionally successful in the 1990s, and beyond.

Strategic Planning—Emerging Perspectives

Many forces affected the way strategic planning developed in the 1970s and early 1980s. These forces included slower growth worldwide, intense global competition, burgeoning automation, obsolescence due to technological change, deregulation, an explosion in information availability, more rapid shifts in raw material prices, chaotic money markets, and major changes in macroeconomic and sociopolitical systems. As a result, destabilization and fluidity have become the norm in world business.

Today there are many, many strategic alternatives for all types of industries. Firms are constantly coming up with new ways of making products and getting them to market. Comfortable positions in industry after industry (e.g., in banking, telecommunications, airlines, automobiles) are disappearing, and barriers to entry are much more difficult to maintain. Markets are open, and new competitors are coming from unexpected directions.

To steadily prosper in such an environment, companies need new strategic planning perspectives. First, top management has to assume a more explicit role in strategic planning, dedicating a large amount of time to deciding how things ought to be instead of listening to analyses of how they are. Second, strategic planning has to become an exercise in creativity instead of an exercise in forecasting. Third, strategic planning processes and tools that assume that the future will be similar to the past must be replaced by a mindset obsessed with being first to recognize change and turn it into competitive advantage. Fourth, the role of the planner must change from being a purveyer of incrementalism to that of a crusader for action. Finally, strategic planning must be restored to the core of line management responsibilities.

These perspectives can be described along five action-oriented dimensions: managing a business for competitive advantage, viewing change as an opportunity, managing through people, shaping the strategically managed organization, and managing for focus and flexibility. Considering these dimensions can make strategic planning more relevant and effective.

Managing for Competitive Advantage. Organizations in a market economy are concerned with delivering a service or product in the most profitable way. The key to profitability is to achieve a sustainable competitive advantage based on superior performance relative to the competition. Superior performance requires doing three things better than the competition. First, the firm must clearly designate the product/market, based on marketplace realities and a true understanding of its strengths and weaknesses. Second, it must design a winning business system or structure that enables the company to outperform competitors in producing and delivering the product or service. Third, management must do a better job of managing the overall business system, by managing not only relationships within the corporation but also critical external relationships with suppliers, customers, and competitors.

Viewing Change as an Opportunity. A new culture should be created within the organization such that managers look to change as an opportunity and adapt their business system to continuously emerging conditions. In other words, change should not be viewed as a problem but as a source of opportunity, providing the potential for creativity and innovation.

Managing through People. Management's first task is to create a vision of the organization that includes (a) where the organization should be going, again based on a clear examination of the company's strengths and weaknesses; (b) what markets it should compete in; (c) how it will compete; and (d) major action programs required. The next task is to convert vision to reality—to develop the capabilities of the organization, to expedite change and remove obstacles, and to shape the environment. Central to both the establishment and execution of a corporate vision is the effective recruitment, development, and deployment of human resources. "In the end, management is measured by the skill and sensitivity with which it manages and develops people, for it is only through the quality of their people that organizations can change effectively."[15]

Shaping the Strategically Managed Organization.[16] Management should work toward developing an innovative, self-renewing organization that the future will demand. Organizational change depends on such factors as structure, strategy, systems, style, skills, staff, and shared values. Organizations that take an externally focused, forward-looking approach to the design of these factors have a much better chance of self-renewal than those whose perspective is predominantly internal and historical.

Managing for Focus and Flexibility. Today strategic planning should be viewed differently than it was viewed in the past. A five-year plan, updated annually, should be replaced by an ongoing concern for the direction the organization is taking. Many scholars describe an ongoing concern for the direction of the firm, that is, concern with what a company must do to become smart, targeted, and nimble enough to prosper in an era of constant change, as strategic thinking. The key words in this pursuit are focus and flexibility.

Focus means figuring out and building on what the company does best. It involves identifying the evolving needs of customers, then developing the key skills—often called the *core competence*—critical to serving them. It also means setting a clear, realistic mission and then working tirelessly to make sure that everyone in the company understands it. Flexibility means sketching rough scenarios of the future (i.e., bands of possibilities) and being ready to pounce on opportunities as they arise.

STRATEGIC BUSINESS UNITS (SBUs)

Frequent reference has been made in this chapter to the business unit, a unit comprising one or more products having a common market base whose manager has complete responsibility for integrating all functions into a strategy against an identifiable competitor. Usually referred to as a **strategic business unit (SBU)**, business units have also been called strategy centers, strategic planning units, or independent business units. The philosophy behind the SBU concept has been described this way:

> The diversified firm should be managed as a "portfolio" of businesses, with each business unit serving a clearly defined product-market segment with a clearly defined strategy.
>
> Each business unit in the portfolio should develop a strategy tailored to its capabilities and competitive needs, but consistent with the overall corporate capabilities and needs.
>
> The total portfolio of businesses should be managed by allocating capital and managerial resources to serve the interests of the firm as a whole—to achieve balanced growth in sales, earnings, and asset mix at an acceptable and controlled level of risk. In essence, the portfolio should be designed and managed to achieve an overall corporate strategy.[17]

Identification of Strategic Business Units

Since formal strategic planning began to make inroads in corporations in the 1970s, a variety of new concepts have been developed for identifying the opportunities of a corporation and for speeding up the process of strategy development. These newer concepts create problems of internal organization. In a dynamic economy, all functions of a corporation (e.g., research and development, finance, and marketing) are related. Optimizing certain functions instead of the company as a whole is far from adequate for achieving superior corporate performance. Such an organizational perspective leaves only the CEO in a position to think in terms of the corporation as a whole. Large corporations have tried many different structural designs to broaden the scope of the CEO in dealing with complexities. One such design is the profit center concept. Unfortunately, the profit center concept emphasizes short-term consequences; also, its emphasis is on optimizing the profit center instead of the corporation as a whole.

The SBU concept was developed to overcome the difficulties posed by the profit center type of organization. Thus the first step in integrating product/market strategies is to identify the firm's SBUs. This amounts to identifying natural businesses in which the corporation is involved. SBUs are not necessarily synonymous with existing divisions or profit centers. An SBU is composed of a product or product lines having identifiable independence from other products or product lines in terms of competition, prices, substitutability of product, style/quality, and impact of product withdrawal. It is around this configuration of products that a business strategy should be designed. In today's organizations, this strategy may encompass products found in more than one division. By the same token, some managers may find themselves managing two or more natural businesses. This does not necessarily mean that divisional boundaries need to be redefined; often an SBU can overlap divisions, and a division can include more than one SBU.

SBUs may be created by applying a set of criteria consisting of price, competitors, customer groups, and shared experience. To the extent that changes in a product's price entail a review of the pricing policy of other products may imply that these products have a natural alliance. If various products/markets of a company share the same group of competitors, they may be amalgamated into an SBU for the purpose of strategic planning. Likewise, products/markets sharing a common set of customers belong together. Finally, products/markets in different parts of the company having common research and development, manufacturing, and marketing components may be included in the same SBU. For purposes of illustration, consider the case of a large, diversified company, one division of which manufactures car radios. The following possibilities exist: the car radio division, as it stands, may represent a viable SBU; alternatively, luxury car radios with automatic tuning may constitute an SBU different from the SBU for standard models; or other areas of the company, such as the television division, may be combined with all or part of the car radio division to create an SBU.

Overall, an SBU should be established at a level where it can rather freely address (a) all key segments of the customer group having similar objectives; (b) all key functions of the corporation so that it can deploy whatever functional expertise is needed to establish positive differentiation from the competition in the eyes of the customer; and (c) all key aspects of the competition so that the corporation can seize the advantage when opportunity presents itself and, conversely, so that competitors will not be able to catch the corporation off balance by exploiting unsuspected sources of strength.

A conceptual question becomes relevant in identifying SBUs: How much aggregation is desirable? Higher levels of aggregation produce a relatively smaller and more manageable number of SBUs. Besides, the existing management information system may not have to be modified since a higher level of aggregation yields SBUs of the size and scope of present divisions or product groups. However, higher levels of aggregation at the SBU level permit only general notions of strategy that may lack relevance for promoting action at the operating level. For example, an SBU for medical care is probably too broad. It could embrace equipment, service, hospitals, education, self-discipline, even social welfare.

On the other hand, lower levels of aggregation make SBUs identical to product/market segments that may lack "strategic autonomy." An SBU for farm tractor engines would be ineffective because it is at too low a level in the organization to (a) consider product applications and customer groups other than farmers or (b) cope with new competitors who might enter the farm tractor market at almost any time with a totally different product set of "boundary conditions." Further, at such a low organizational level, one SBU may compete with another, thereby shifting to higher levels of management the strategic issue of which SBU should formulate what strategy.

The optimum level of aggregation, one that is neither too broad nor too narrow, can be determined by applying the criteria discussed above, then further refining it by using managerial judgment. Briefly stated, an SBU must look and act like a freestanding business, satisfying the following conditions:

1. Have a unique business mission, independent of other SBUs.
2. Have a clearly definable set of competitors.
3. Be able to carry out integrative planning relatively independently of other SBUs.
4. Be able to manage resources in other areas.
5. Be large enough to justify senior management attention but small enough to serve as a useful focus for resource allocation.

The definition of an SBU always contains gray areas that may lead to dispute. It is helpful, therefore, to review the creation of an SBU, halfway into the strategy development process, by raising the following questions:

- Are customers' wants well defined and understood by the industry and is the market segmented so that differences in these wants are treated differently?
- Is the business unit equipped to respond functionally to the basic wants and needs of customers in the defined segments?
- Do competitors have different sets of operating conditions that could give them an unfair advantage over the business unit in question?

If the answers give reason to doubt the SBU's ability to compete in the market, it is better to redefine the SBU with a view to increasing its strategic freedom in meeting customer needs and competitive threats.

The SBU concept may be illustrated with an example from Procter and Gamble.[18] For more than 50 years the company's various brands were pitted against each other. The Camay soap manager competed against the Ivory soap manager as fiercely as if each were in different companies. The brand management system that grew out of this notion has been used by almost every consumer-products company.

In the fall of 1987, however, Procter and Gamble reorganized according to the SBU concept (what the company called "along the category lines"). The reorganization did not abolish brand managers, but it did make them accountable to a new corps of mini-general managers who were responsible for an entire product line—all laundry detergents, for example. By fostering internal competition among brand managers, the classic brand management system established strong incentives to excel. It also created conflicts and inefficiencies as brand managers squabbled over corporate resources, from ad spending to plant capacity. The system often meant that not enough thought was given to how brands could work together. Despite these shortcomings, brand management worked fine when markets were growing and money was available. But now most packaged-goods businesses are growing slowly if at all, brands are proliferating, the retail trade is accumulating more clout, and the consumer market is fragmenting. Procter and Gamble reorganized along SBU lines to cope with this bewildering array of pressures.

Under Procter and Gamble's SBU scheme, each of its 39 categories of U.S. businesses, from diapers to cake mixes, is run by a category manager with direct responsibility. Advertising, sales, manufacturing, research, engineering, and other disciplines all report to the category manager. The idea is to devise marketing strategies by looking at categories and by fitting brands together rather than by coming up with competing brand strategies and then divvying up resources among them. The paragraphs that follow discuss how Procter and Gamble's reorganization impacted select functions.

Advertising. Procter and Gamble advertises Tide as the best detergent for tough dirt. But when the brand manager for Cheer started making the same claim, Cheer's ads were pulled after the Tide group protested. Now the category manager decides how to position Tide and Cheer to avoid such conflicts.

Budgeting. Brand managers for Puritan and Crisco oils competed for a share of the same ad budget. Now a category manager decides when Puritan can benefit from stepped-up ad spending and when Crisco can coast on its strong market position.

Packaging. Brand managers for various detergents often demanded packages at the same time. Because of these conflicting demands, managers complained that projects were delayed and nobody got a first-rate job. Now the category manager decides which brand gets a new package first.

Manufacturing. Under the old system, a minor detergent, such as Dreft, had the same claim on plant resources as Tide—even if Tide was in the midst of a big promotion and needed more supplies. Now a manufacturing staffer who helps to coordinate production reports to the category manager.

Problems in Creating SBUs

The notion behind the SBU concept is that a company's activities in a marketplace ought to be understood and segmented strategically so that resources can be allocated for competitive advantage. That is, a company ought to be able to answer three questions: What business am I in? Who is my competition? What is my position relative to that competition? Getting an adequate answer to the first question is often difficult. (Answers to the other two questions can be relatively easy.) In addition, identifying SBUs is enormously difficult in organizations that share resources (e.g., research and development or sales).

There is no simple, definitive methodology for isolating SBUs. Although the criteria for designating SBUs are clear-cut, their application is judgmental and problematic. For example, in certain situations, real advantages can accrue to businesses sharing resources at the research and development, manufacturing, or distribution level. If autonomy and accountability are pursued as ends in themselves, these advantages may be overlooked or unnecessarily sacrificed.

SUMMARY

This chapter focused on the concepts of planning and strategy. Planning is the ongoing management process of choosing the objectives to be achieved during a certain period, setting up a plan of action, and maintaining continuous surveillance of results so as to make regular evaluations and, if necessary, to modify the objectives and plan of action. Also described were the requisites for successful planning, the time frame for initiating planning activities, and various philosophies of planning (i.e., satisfying, optimizing, and adaptivizing).

Strategy, the course of action selected from possible alternatives as the optimum way to attain objectives, should be consistent with current policies and viewed in light of anticipated competitive actions.

The concept of strategic planning was also examined. Most large companies have made significant progress in the last 10 or 15 years in improving their strategic planning capabilities. Two levels of strategic planning were discussed: corporate and business unit level. Corporate strategic planning is concerned with the management of a firm's portfolio of businesses and with issues of firm-wide impact, such as resource allocation, cash flow management, government regulation, and capital market access. Business strategy focuses more narrowly on the SBU level and involves the design of plans of action and objectives based on analysis of both internal and external factors that affect each business unit's performance. An SBU is defined as a standalone business within a corporation that faces (an) identifiable competitor(s) in a given market.

In the 1990s, for strategic planning to be effective and relevant, the CEO must play a central role, not simply as the apex of a multilayered planning effort, but as a strategic thinker and corporate culture leader.

DISCUSSION QUESTIONS

1. Why is planning significant?
2. Is the concept of strategic planning relevant only to profit-making organizations? Can nonprofit organizations or the federal government also embrace planning?
3. Planning has always been considered an important function of management. How is strategic planning different from traditional planning?
4. What is an SBU? What criteria may be used to divide businesses into SBUs?
5. What are the requisites for successful strategic planning?
6. Differentiate between the planning philosophies of satisfying, optimizing, and adaptivizing.

NOTES

[1]Walter Kiechel III, "Corporate Strategists under Fire," *Fortune* (27 December 1982): 36.

[2]Paul F. Anderson, "Marketing, Strategic Planning and the Theory of the Firm," *Journal of Marketing* (Spring 1982): 24. See also Yoram Wind and Thomas S. Robertson, "Marketing Strategy: New Directions for Theory and Research," *Journal of Marketing* (Spring 1983): 12–25.

[3]David W. Ewing, *The Practice of Planning* (New York: Harper & Row, 1968), 9–14.

[4]James Brown, Saul S. Sands, and G. Clark Thompson, "The Status of Long Range Planning," *Conference Board Record* (September 1966): 11.

[5]*Business Planning in the Eighties: The New Competitiveness of American Corporations* (New York: Coopers & Lybrand, 1984).

[6]J. Scott Armstrong, "The Value of Formal Planning for Strategic Decisions: Review of Empirical Research," *Strategic Management Journal* 3 (1982): 197–211.

[7]C. Don Burnett, Dennis P. Yeskey, and David Richardson, "New Roles for Corporate Planners in the 1980's," *Journal of Business Strategy* (Spring 1984): 64–68.

[8]Kirby E. Warren, *Long Range Planning: The Executive Viewpoint* (Englewood Cliffs, NJ: Prentice-Hall, 1966), 5.

[9]See Lawrence C. Rhyne, "The Relationship of Strategic Planning to Financial Performance," *Strategic Management Journal* (1986): 423-36.

[10]*Perspectives on Corporate Planning* (Boston: Boston Consulting Group, 1968), 48.

[11]Russell L. Ackoff, *A Concept of Corporate Planning* (New York: John Wiley & Sons, 1970), 13.

[12]Kenneth R. Andrews, *The Concept of Corporate Strategy* (Homewood, IL: Dow Jones-Irwin, 1971), 28.

[13]Bruce D. Henderson, "The Concept of Strategy," in *A Special Commentary* (Boston: Boston Consulting Group, 1981), 3. See also Frederick W. Gluck, Stephen P. Kaufman, and A. Steven Walleck, "Strategic Management for Competitive Advantage," *Harvard Business Review* (July-August 1980): 154-61; and George S. Yip, "The Role of Strategic Planning in Consumer Marketing Businesses," Working Paper, Marketing Science Institute (April 1984): 3-7.

[14]Bruce D. Henderson, "The Origin of Strategy," *Harvard Business Review* (November-December 1989): 139-45.

[15]Fred Gluck, "A Fresh Look at Strategic Management," *Journal of Business Strategy* (Fall 1985): 18-21.

[16]For a detailed discussion on this topic, see chapter 11.

[17]William K. Hall, "SBU: Hot New Topic in the Management of Diversification," *Business Horizons* (February 1978): 17.

[18] "The Marketing Revolution at Procter & Gamble," *Business Week* (25 July 1988): 72.

CHAPTER 2
Strategic Marketing

Marketing is merely a civilized form of warfare in which most battles are won with words, ideas, and disciplined thinking.
ALBERT W. EMERY

In its strategic role, marketing focuses on a business's intentions in a market and the means and timing of realizing those intentions. The strategic role of marketing is quite different from marketing management, which deals with developing, implementing, and directing programs to achieve designated intentions. To clearly differentiate between marketing management and marketing in its new role, a new term—*strategic marketing*—has been coined to represent the latter. This chapter discusses different aspects of strategic marketing and examines how it differs from marketing management. Also noted are the trends pointing to the continued importance of strategic marketing. The chapter ends with a plan for the rest of the book.

CONCEPT OF STRATEGIC MARKETING

Exhibit 2-1 shows the role that the marketing function plays at different levels in the organization. At the corporate level, marketing inputs (e.g., competitive

EXHIBIT 2-1
Marketing's Role in the Organization

Organizational Level	*Role of Marketing**	*Formal Name*
Corporate	Provide customer and competitive perspective for corporate strategic planning	Corporate marketing
Business unit	Assist in the development of strategic perspective of the business unit to direct its future course	Strategic marketing
Product/market	Formulate and implement marketing programs	Marketing management

*Like marketing, other functions (finance, research and development, production, accounting, and personnel) plan their own unique role at each organizational level. The business unit strategy emerges from the interaction of marketing with other disciplines.

analysis, market dynamics, environmental shifts) are essential for formulating a corporate strategic plan. Marketing represents the boundary between the marketplace and the company, and knowledge of current and emerging happenings in the marketplace is extremely important in any strategic planning exercise. At the other end of the scale, marketing management deals with the formulation and implementation of marketing programs to support the marketing strategy. Marketing strategy is developed at the business unit level.

Within a given environment, marketing strategy deals essentially with the interplay of three forces known as the **strategic three Cs**: the customer, the competition, and the corporation. Marketing strategies focus on ways in which the corporation can differentiate itself effectively from its competitors, capitalizing on its distinctive strengths to deliver better value to its customers. A good marketing strategy should be characterized by (a) a clear market definition; (b) a good match between corporate strengths and the needs of the market; and (c) superior performance, relative to the competition, in the key success factors of the business.

Together the strategic three Cs form the marketing strategy triangle (see Exhibit 2-2). All three Cs—customer, corporation, and competition—are dynamic, living creatures with their own objectives to pursue. If what the customer wants does not match the needs of the corporation, the latter's long-term viability may be at stake. Positive matching of the needs and objectives of customer and corporation is required for a lasting good relationship. But such matching is relative, and if the competition is able to offer a better match, the corporation will be at a disadvantage over time. In other words, the matching of needs between customer and corporation must not only be positive, it must be better or stronger than the match between the customer and the competitor. When the corporation's approach to the customer is identical to that of the competition, the customer cannot differentiate between them. The result could be a price war that may satisfy the customer's but not the corporation's needs. **Marketing strategy**, in terms of these three key constituents, must be defined as an endeavor by a corporation to differentiate itself positively from its competitors, using its relative corporate strengths to better satisfy customer needs in a given environmental setting.

Based on the interplay of the strategic three Cs, formation of marketing strategy requires the following three decisions:

1. *Where to compete,* that is, it requires a definition of the market (for example, competing across an entire market or in one or more segments)
2. *How to compete,* that is, it requires a means for competing (for example, introducing a new product to meet a customer need or establishing a new image for an existing product)
3. *When to compete,* that is, it requires timing of market entry (for example, being first in the market or waiting until primary demand is established)

The concept of strategic marketing may be illustrated with reference to the establishment by General Mills of a chain of Italian restaurants, the Olive

EXHIBIT 2-2
Key Elements of Marketing Strategy Formulation

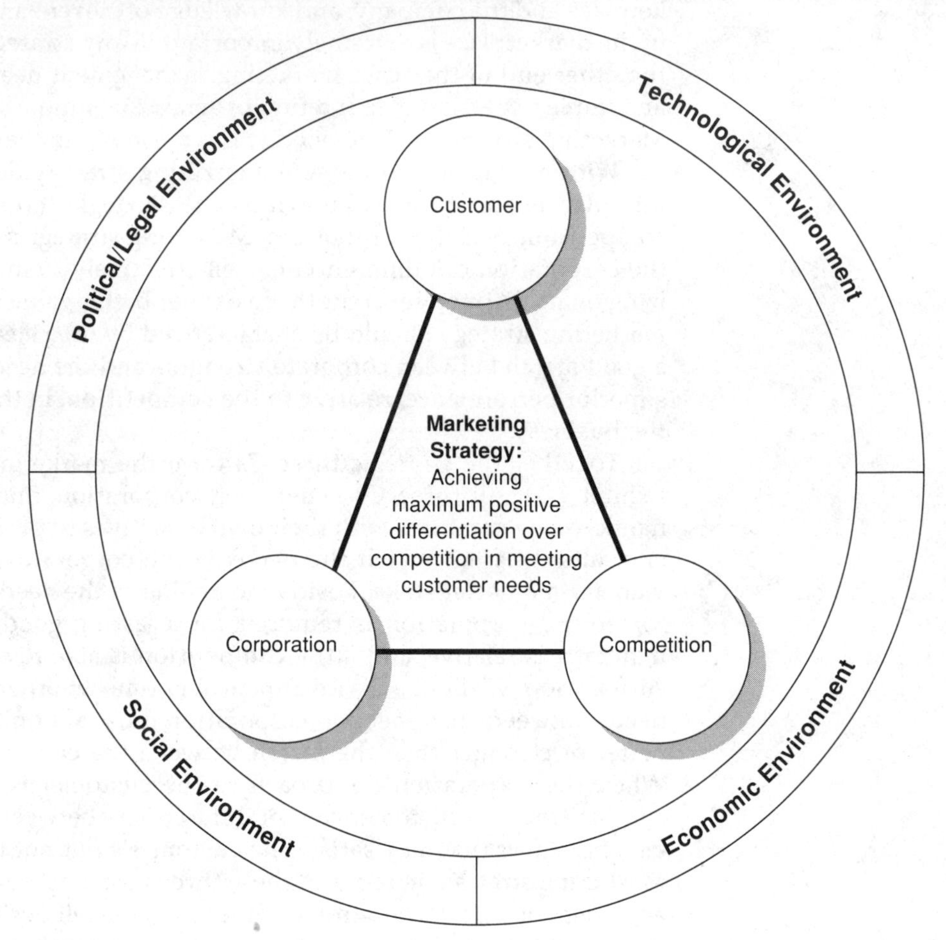

Garden.[1] In 1980, faced with unsteady performance of its restaurant division (mainly the Red Lobster chain), General Mills looked around for new opportunities. A chain of Italian restaurants looked attractive. Because of the long-accelerating trend toward eating out, restaurants' share of the total food market had been increasing, from $2.50 of every $10 spent on food in 1955 to $4 in 1980. Further, the company's research showed that consumers ranked Italian food as the most popular ethnic cuisine and indicated that it was in short supply. In 1980, compared with 17,000 oriental restaurants and 14,000 Mexican restaurants, the United States had only 11,800 Italian restaurants. General Mills delineated the following marketing strategy:

Market (where to compete)—open 10 to 12 restaurants annually for the next five years in areas popular for vacations
Means (how to compete)—cater to the mass market by offering an "Americanized" Italian fare for a price of about $10 for both food and wine
Timing (when to compete)—be cautious because starting a restaurant is risky.

According to the National Restaurant Association, about 50 percent of new restaurants fail in their first year; 65 percent within two years. General Mills itself had earlier failed in its attempt to run a Betty Crocker Treehouse chain, which served pie on elevated tables to the sound of tape-recorded bird chirping. Consequently, General Mills canvassed more than 1000 restaurants for recipes, interviewed 5000 consumers, and concocted more than 80 pots of spaghetti sauce before it settled on its final version, after three years of testing recipes.

General Mills based its marketing strategy decisions on extensive consumer research involving 5000 interviews. These interviews revealed that most consumers seemed to have only vague impressions of Italy. For example, men often mentioned gladiators, fountains, and Sophia Loren; women brought up hillside picnics and vineyards. People described Italian food as tasty and healthy but with too much basil and garlic; chocolate mousse (a French dessert) was ranked by consumers as the best Italian dessert. Based on these inputs, it became clear that authentic Italian food would not satisfy the American appetite. Therefore, the company's choice of an ethnic motif did not mean that eating at the Olive Garden would be a culinary adventure. General Mills lavished its time and money on creating an ambiance and a cuisine that was sort of Italian: people should think they are eating Italian food, but in reality, the food would be fully adapted to American taste.

General Mills's strategy emerged from a thorough consideration of the strategic three Cs. First, market entry was dictated by growing customer demand for restaurants. Second, the decision to enter the market was based on full knowledge of the competition, which included different types of ethnic and nonethnic restaurants. General Mills knew that the idea of a nationwide chain of Italian restaurants was hardly revolutionary. What was important and what would provide Olive Garden a differential advantage that competitors would find difficult to copy quickly was the creation of a real vision of Italian food being served in an Italian atmosphere. Third, the corporation's strength as an aggressive, successful marketer of packaged goods with experience in the restaurant business and adequate financial resources (initial start-up costs of $100 million) properly equipped it to seek entry into new fields. Finally, the environment (in this case, a trend toward eating out and a preference for fancy Italian food) substantiated the opportunity.

This strategy seems to have worked well for General Mills. In 1990 the typical Olive Garden had annual pretax earnings of at least $350,000 on sales of more than $2.8 million. Most of the 272 Olive Garden restaurants became profitable within six months of start-up.

ASPECTS OF STRATEGIC MARKETING

Strategic thinking represents a new perspective in the area of marketing. In this section we will examine the importance, characteristics, origin, and future of strategic marketing.

Importance of Strategic Marketing

Marketing plays a vital role in the strategic management process of the firm.[2] The experience of companies well versed in strategic planning indicates that failure in marketing can block the way to goals established by strategic planning. A prime example is provided by Texas Instruments, a pioneer in developing a system of strategic planning called the OST system. Marketing negligence forced Texas Instruments to withdraw from the digital watch business. When the external environment is stable, a company can successfully ride on its technological lead, manufacturing efficiency, and financial acumen. As the environment shifts, however, lack of marketing perspective makes the best-planned strategies treacherous. With the intensification of competition in the watch business and the loss of uniqueness of the digital watch, Texas Instruments began to lose ground. Its experience can be summarized as follows:

> The lack of marketing skills certainly was a major factor in the . . . demise of its watch business. T.I. did not try to understand the consumer, nor would it listen to the marketplace. They had the engineer's attitude.[3]

Philip Morris's success with Miller Beer illustrates how marketing's elevated strategic status can help in outperforming competitors. If Philip Morris had accepted the conventional marketing wisdom of the beer industry by basing its strategy on cost efficiencies of large breweries and competitive pricing, its Miller Beer subsidiary might still be in seventh place or lower. Instead, Miller Beer leapfrogged all competitors but Anheuser-Busch by emphasizing market and customer segmentation supported with large advertising and promotion budgets. A case of true strategic marketing, with the marketing function playing a crucial role in overall corporate strategy, Philip Morris relied on its corporate strengths and exploited its competitors' weaknesses to gain a leadership position in the brewing industry.

Indeed, marketing strategy is the most significant challenge that companies of all types and sizes face. As a study by Coopers and Lybrand and Yankelovich, Skelly, and White notes, "American corporations are beginning to answer a 'new call to strategic marketing,' as many of them shift their business planning priorities more toward strategic marketing and the market planning function."[4]

Characteristics of Strategic Marketing

Strategic marketing holds different perspectives from those of marketing management. Its salient features are described in the paragraphs that follow.

Emphasis on Long-Term Implications. Strategic marketing decisions usually have far-reaching implications. In the words of one marketing strategist, strategic marketing is a commitment, not an act. For example, a strategic marketing decision would not be a matter of simply providing an immediate delivery to a favorite customer but of offering 24-hour delivery service to all customers.

In 1980 the Goodyear Tire Company made a strategic decision to continue its focus on the tire business. At a time when other members of the industry were de-emphasizing tires, Goodyear opted for the opposite route.[5] This decision had wide-ranging implications for the company over the years. Looking back, Goodyear's strategy worked. Toward the end of the 1980s, it emerged as a globally dominant force in the tire industry.

The long-term orientation of strategic marketing requires greater concern for the environment. Environmental changes are more probable in the long run than in the short run. In other words, in the short run, one may assume that the environment will remain stable, but this assumption is not at all likely in the long run.

Proper monitoring of the environment requires strategic intelligence inputs. Strategic intelligence differs from traditional marketing research in requiring much deeper probing. For example, simply knowing that a competitor has a cost advantage is not enough. Strategically, one ought to find out how much flexibility the competitor has in further reducing price.

Corporate Inputs. Strategic marketing decisions require inputs from three corporate aspects: corporate culture, corporate publics, and corporate resources. **Corporate culture** refers to the style, whims, fancies, traits, taboos, customs, and rituals of top management that over time have come to be accepted as intrinsic to the corporation. **Corporate publics** are the various stakeholders with an interest in the organization. Typically customers, employees, vendors, governments, and society constitute an organization's stakeholders. **Corporate resources** include the human, financial, physical, and technological assets/experience of the company. Corporate inputs set the degree of freedom a marketing strategist has in deciding which market to enter, which business to divest, which business to invest in, etc. The use of corporatewide inputs in formulating marketing strategy also helps to maximize overall benefits for the organization.

Varying Roles for Different Products/Markets. Traditionally it has been held that all products exert effort to maximize profitability. Strategic marketing starts from the premise that different products have varying roles in the company. For example, some products may be in the growth stage of the product life cycle, some in the maturity stage, others in the introduction stage. Each position in the life cycle requires a different strategy and affords different expectations. Products in the growth stage need extra investment; those in the maturity stage should generate a cash surplus. Although conceptually this concept—different products serving different purposes—has been understood for many years, it has been articulated for real-world application only in recent years. The lead in this regard was provided by the Boston Consulting Group, which developed a portfolio matrix in which products are positioned on a two-dimensional matrix of market share and growth rate, both measured on a continuous scale from high to low.

The portfolio matrix essentially has two properties: (a) it ranks diverse businesses according to uniform criteria; (b) it provides a tool to balance a company's resources by showing which businesses are likely to be resource providers and which are resource users.[6]

The practice of strategic marketing seeks first to examine each product/market before determining its appropriate role. Further, different products/markets are synergistically related to maximize total marketing effort. Finally, each product/market is paired with a manager who has the proper background and experience to direct it.

Organizational Level. Strategic marketing is conducted primarily at the business unit level in the organization. At GE, for example, major appliances are organized into a separate business unit for which strategy is separately formulated. At Gillette Company, strategy for the Sensor razor is developed at the razor business unit level.

Relationship to Finance. Strategic marketing decision making is closely related to the finance function.[7] The importance of maintaining a close relationship between marketing and finance and, for that matter, with other functional areas of a business is nothing new. But in recent years, frameworks have been developed that make it convenient to simultaneously relate marketing to finance in making strategic decisions.[8]

Origin of Strategic Marketing

Strategic marketing did not originate systematically. As already noted, the difficult environment of the early 1970s forced managers to develop strategic plans for more centralized control of resources. It happened that these pioneering efforts at strategic planning had a financial focus. Certainly it was recognized that marketing inputs were required, but they were gathered as needed or were simply assumed. For example, most strategic planning approaches emphasized cash flow and return on investment, which of course must be examined in relation to market share. Perspectives on such marketing matters as market share, however, were either obtained on an ad hoc basis or assumed as constant. Consequently, marketing inputs, such as market share, became the result instead of the cause: a typical conclusion that was drawn was that market share must be increased to meet cash flow targets. The financial bias of strategic planning systems demoted marketing to a necessary but not important role in the long-term perspective of the corporation.

In a few years' time, as strategic planning became more firmly established, corporations began to realize that there was a missing link in the planning process. Without properly relating the strategic planning effort to marketing, the whole process tended to be static. Business exists in a dynamic setting, and by and large, it is only through marketing inputs that perspectives of changing social, economic, political, and technological environments can be brought into the strategic planning process.[9]

In brief, while marketing initially got lost in the emphasis on strategic planning, currently the role of marketing is better understood and has emerged in the form of strategic marketing.

Future of Strategic Marketing

A variety of factors point to an increasingly important role for strategic marketing in future years.[10] First, the battle for market share is intensifying in many industries as a result of declining growth rates. Faced with insignificant growth, companies have no choice but to grasp for new weapons to increase their share, and strategic marketing can provide extra leverage in share battles.

Second, deregulation in many industries is mandating a move to strategic marketing. Take, for example, the case of the airline, trucking, banking, and telecommunications industries. In the past, with territories protected and prices regulated, the need for strategic marketing was limited. With deregulation, it is an entirely different story. The prospect of Sears, Roebuck and Merrill Lynch as direct competitors would have been laughable as recently as eight years ago. Thus, emphasis on strategic marketing is no longer a matter of choice if these companies are to perform well.

Third, many packaged-goods companies are acquiring companies in hitherto nonmarketing-oriented industries and are attempting to gain market share through strategic marketing. For example, apparel makers, with few exceptions, have traditionally depended on production excellence to gain competitive advantage. But when marketing-oriented consumer-products companies purchased apparel companies, the picture changed. General Mills, through marketing strategy, turned Izod (the alligator shirt) into a highly successful business. Chesebrough-Pond's has done much the same with Health-Tex, making it the leading marketer of children's apparel.[11] On acquiring Columbia Pictures in 1982, the Coca-Cola Company successfully tested the proposition that it could sell movies like soft drinks. By using Coke's marketing prowess and a host of innovative financing packages, Columbia emerged as a dominant force in the motion picture business. It almost doubled its market share between 1982 and 1987 and increased profits by 20 percent annually.[12] Although in the last few years, Izod, Health-Tex, and Columbia Pictures have been sold, they fetched these marketing powerhouses huge prices for their efforts in turning them around.

Fourth, shifts in the channel structure of many industries have posed new problems. Traditional channels of distribution have become scrambled, and manufacturers find themselves using a mixture of wholesalers, retailers, chains, buying groups, and even captive outlets. In some cases, distributors and manufacturers' representatives are playing more important roles. In others, buying groups, chains, and cooperatives are becoming more significant. Because these groups bring greatly increased sophistication to the buying process, especially as the computer gives them access to more and better information, buying clout is being concentrated in fewer hands.

Fifth, competition from overseas companies operating both in the United States and abroad is intensifying. More and more countries around the world are developing the capacity to compete aggressively in world markets. Businesspeople in both developed and developing countries are aware of world market trends and are confident that they can reach new markets. Eager to improve their economic conditions and their living standards, they are willing to learn, adapt, and innovate. Thirty years ago, most American companies were confident that they could beat foreign competitors with relative ease. After all, they reasoned, we have the best technology, the best management skills, and the famous American "can do" attitude. Today competition from Europe, Japan, and elsewhere is seemingly insurmountable. To cope with worldwide competition, renewed emphasis on marketing strategy achieves significance.

Sixth, the fragmentation of markets—the result of higher per capita incomes and more sophisticated consumers—is another factor driving the increased importance of strategic marketing. In the United States, for example, the number of segments in the automobile market increased by one-third, from 18 to 24, during the period from 1978 to 1985 (i.e., two subcompact, two compact, two intermediate, four full size, two luxury, three truck, two van, and one station wagon in 1978 to two minicompact, two subcompact, two compact, two mid-sized, two intermediate, two luxury, six truck, five van, and one station wagon).[13] Many of these segments remain unserved until a company introduces a product offering that is tailored to that niche. The competitive realities of fragmented markets require strategic marketing capability to identify untapped market segments and to develop and introduce products to meet their requirements.

Seventh, in the wake of easy availability of base technologies and shortening product life cycles, getting to market quickly is a prerequisite for success in the marketplace. Early entrants not only can command premium prices, but they also achieve volume break points in purchasing, manufacturing, and marketing earlier than followers and, thus, gain market share. For example, in the European market, the first company to market car radios can typically charge 20 percent more for the product than a competitor who enters the market a year later.[14] In planning an early entry in the marketplace, strategic marketing achieves significance.

Eighth, the days are gone when companies could win market share by achieving cost and quality advantages in existing, well-defined markets. In the 1990s companies will need to conceive and create new and largely uncontested competitive market space. Corporate imagination and expeditionary policies are the keys that unlock new markets.[15] Corporate imagination involves going beyond served markets; that is, thinking about needs and functionalities instead of conventional customer-product grids; overturning traditional price/performance assumptions; and leading customers rather than following them. Creating new markets is a risky business; however, through expeditionary policies, companies can minimize the risk not by being fast followers but by the process of low-cost, fast-paced market incursions designed to reach the target market. To successfully develop corporate imagination and expeditionary policies, companies need strategic marketing.

Finally, demographic shifts in American society have created a new customer environment that makes strategic marketing an imperative.[16] In years past, the typical American family consisted of a working dad, a homemaker mom, and two kids. But the 1990 census revealed that only 26 percent of the 93.3 million households then surveyed fit that description. Of those families reporting children under the age of 18, 63 percent of the mothers worked full or part time outside the home, up from 51 percent in 1985 and 42 percent in 1980. Smaller households now predominate: more than 55 percent of all households comprise only one or two persons. Even more startling, and frequently overlooked, is the fact that 9.7 million households are now headed by singles. This fastest-growing segment of all—up some 60 percent over the previous decade—expanded mainly because of an increase in the number of men living alone. Some 24 percent of households now include people age 65 or older, a group that will grow rapidly. These statistics have strategic significance. The mass market has splintered, and companies can't sell their products they way they used to. The largest number of households may fall into the two-wage-earner grouping, but that group includes everyone from manicurists to Wall Street brokers, a group whose lifestyles and incomes are too diverse to qualify as a mass market. We may see every market breaking into smaller and smaller units, with unique products being aimed at defined segments.[17]

STRATEGIC MARKETING AND MARKETING MANAGEMENT

Strategic marketing focuses on choosing the right products for the right growth markets at the right time. It may be argued that these decisions are no different from those emphasized in marketing management. However, the two disciplines approach these decisions from different angles. For example, in marketing management, market segments are defined by grouping customers according to marketing mix variables. In the strategic marketing approach, market segments are formed to identify the group(s) that can provide the company with a sustainable economic advantage over the competition. To clarify the matter, Henderson labels the latter grouping a **strategic sector**. Henderson notes:

> A strategic sector is one in which you can obtain a competitive advantage and exploit it. . . . Strategic sectors are the key to strategy because each sector's frame of reference is competition. The largest competitor in an industry can be unprofitable in that the individual strategic sectors are dominated by smaller competitors.[18]

A further difference between strategic marketing and marketing management is that in marketing management the resources and objectives of the firm, however defined, are viewed as uncontrollable variables in developing a marketing mix. In strategic marketing, objectives are systematically defined at different levels after a thorough examination of necessary inputs. Resources are allocated to maximize overall corporate performance, and the resulting strategies are formulated with a more inclusive view. As Abell and Hammond have stated:

> A strategic market plan is not the same . . . as a marketing plan; it is a plan of all aspects of an organization's strategy in the market place. A marketing plan, in contrast, deals primarily with the delineation of target segments and the product, communication, channel, and pricing policies for reaching and servicing those segments—the so-called marketing mix.[19]

Marketing management deals with developing a marketing mix to serve designated markets. The development of a marketing mix should be preceded by a definition of the market. Traditionally, however, market has been loosely defined. In an environment of expansion, even marginal operations could be profitable; therefore, there was no reason to be precise, especially when considering that the task of defining a market is at best difficult. Besides, corporate culture emphasized short-term orientation, which by implication stressed a winning marketing mix rather than an accurate definition of the market.

To illustrate how problematic it can be to define a market, consider the laundry product Wisk. The market for Wisk can be defined in many different ways: the laundry detergent market, the liquid laundry detergent market, or the prewash-treatment detergent market. In each market, the product would have a different market share and would be challenged by a different set of competitors. Which definition of the market is most viable for long-term healthy performance is a question that strategic marketing addresses.

> A market can be viewed in many different ways, and a product can be used in many different ways. Each time the product-market pairing is varied, the relative competitive strength is varied, too. Many businessmen do not recognize that a key element in strategy is choosing the competitor whom you wish to challenge, as well as choosing the marketing segment and product characteristics with which you will compete.[20]

Exhibit 2-3 summarizes the differences between strategic marketing and marketing management. Strategic marketing differs from marketing management in many respects: orientation, philosophy, approach, relationship with the environment and other parts of the organization, and the management style required. For example, strategic marketing requires a manager to forgo short-term performance in the interest of long-term results. Strategic marketing deals with the business to be in; marketing management stresses running a delineated business.

For a marketing manager the question is: Given the array of environmental forces affecting my business, the past and the projected performance of the industry or market, and my current position in it, which kind of investments am I justified in making in this business? In strategic marketing, on the other hand, the question is rather: What are my options for upsetting the equilibrium of the marketplace and reestablishing it in my favor? Marketing management takes market projections and competitive position as a given and seeks to optimize within those constraints. Strategic marketing, by contrast, seeks to throw off those constraints wherever possible. Marketing management is deterministic.

EXHIBIT 2-3
Major Differences between Strategic Marketing and Marketing Management*

Point of Difference	*Strategic Marketing*	*Marketing Management*
Time frame	Long range; i.e., decisions have long-term implications	Day-to-day; i.e., decisions have relevance in a given financial year
Orientation	Inductive and intuitive	Deductive and analytical
Decision process	Primarily bottom-up	Mainly top-down
Relationship with environment	Environment condisered ever-changing and dynamic	Environment considered constant with occasional disturbances
Opportunity sensitivity	Ongoing to seek new opportunities	Ad hoc search for a new opportunity
Organizational behavior	Achieve synergy between different components of the organization, both horizontally and vertically	Pursue interests of the decentralized unit
Nature of job	Requires high degree of creativity and originality	Requires maturity, experience, and control orientation
Leadership style	Requires proactive perspective	Requires reactive perspective
Mission	Deals with what business to emphasize	Deals with running a delineated business

*These differences are relative, not opposite ends of a continuum.

Strategic marketing is opportunistic. Marketing management is deductive and analytical; strategic marketing is inductive and intuitive.

THE PROCESS OF STRATEGIC MARKETING—AN EXAMPLE

The process of strategic marketing planning, charted in Exhibit 2-4, may be illustrated with an SBU of the New England Products Company (a fictional name): health-related remedies. Headquartered in Hartford, Connecticut, NEPC is a worldwide manufacturer and marketer of a variety of food and nonfood products, including coffee, orange juice, cake mixes, toothpaste, diapers, detergents, and health-related remedies. The company conducts its business in

EXHIBIT 2-4
Process of Strategic Marketing

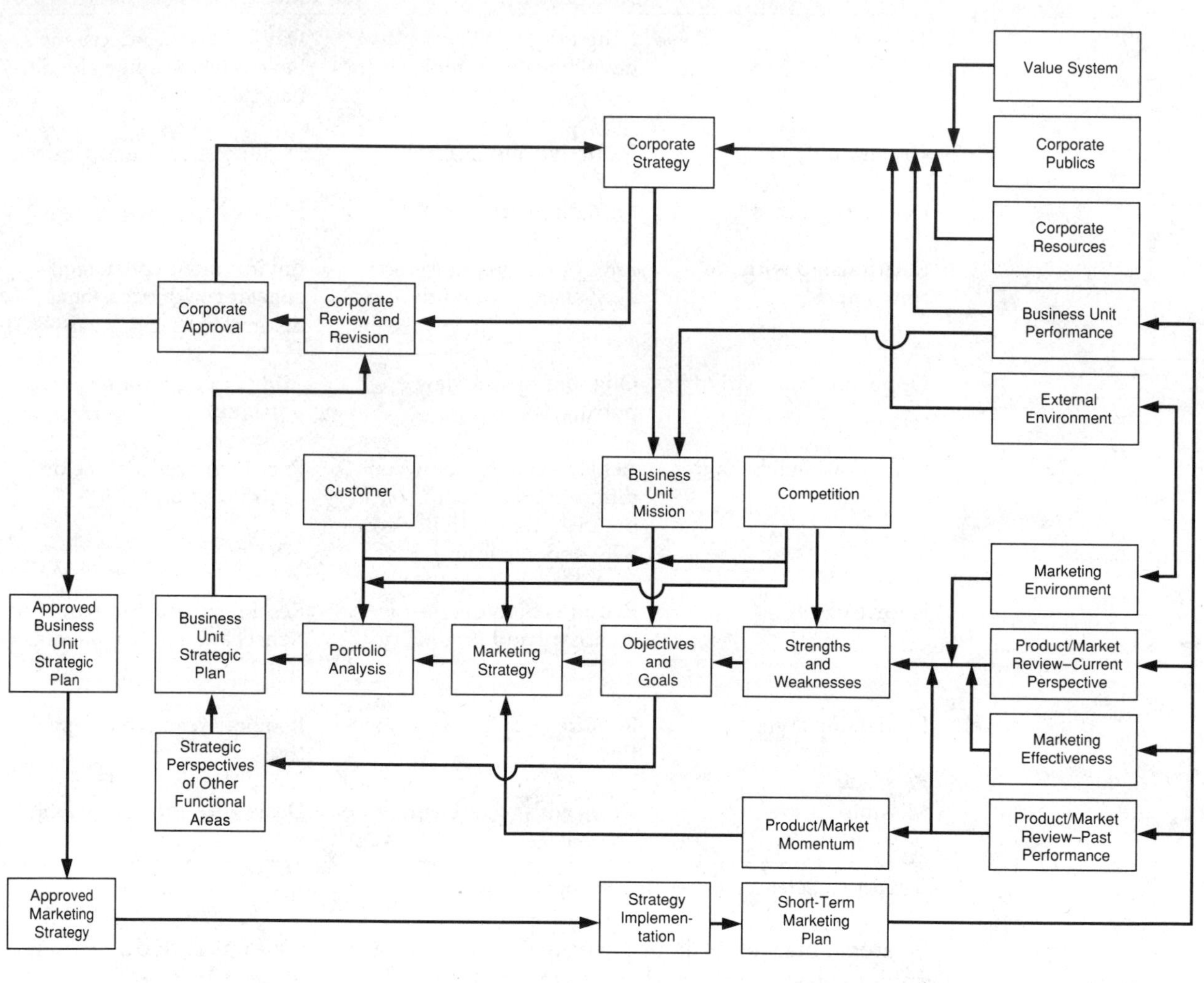

more than 100 countries, employs approximately 53,500 people, operates more than 140 manufacturing facilities, and maintains three major research centers. In 1990, the company's worldwide sales amounted to $24 billion.

Corporate Strategy

In 1986 the company's strategic plan established the following goals:

- To strengthen significantly the company's core businesses (i.e., toothpaste, diapers, and detergents)

- To view health care products as a critical engine of growth
- To boost the share of profits from health-related products from 20 percent to 30 percent over the next decade
- To divest those businesses not meeting the company's criteria for profitability and growth, thus providing additional resources to achieve other objectives
- To make an 18 percent return on total capital invested
- To a great extent, to depend on retained earnings for financing growth

This above strategy rested on the five factors, shown in Exhibit 2-4, that feed into corporate strategy:

Value system—always to be strong and influential in marketing, achieving growth through developing and acquiring new products for specific niches
Corporate publics—the willingness of NEPC stockholders to forgo short-term profits and dividends in the interest of long-term growth and profitability
Corporate resources—strong financial position, high brand recognition, marketing powerhouse
Business unit performance—health-related remedies sales, for example, were higher worldwide despite recessionary conditions
External environment—increased health consciousness among consumers

Business Unit Mission

The mission for one of NEPC's 34 business units, health-related remedies, emerged from a simultaneous review of corporate strategy, competitive conditions, customers' perspectives, past performance of the business unit, and marketing environment, as charted in Exhibit 2-4. The business unit mission for health-related remedies was delineated as follows:

- To consolidate operations by combining recent acquisitions and newly developed products and by revamping old products
- To accelerate business by proper positioning of products
- To expand the product line to cover the entire human anatomy

The mission for the business unit was translated into the following objectives and goals:

- To invest heavily to achieve $9 billion in sales by 1996, an increase of 109 percent over $4.4 billion in 1991
- To achieve a leadership position in the United States
- To introduce new products overseas as early as possible to preempt competition

Marketing objectives for different products/markets emerged from these overall business unit objectives. For example, the marketing objectives for a product to combat indigestion were identified as follows:

- To accelerate research to seek new uses for the product
- To develop new improvements in the product

Marketing Strategy

Marketing objectives, customer and competitive perspectives, and product/market momentum (i.e., extrapolation of past performance to the future) form the basis of marketing strategy. In the case of NEPC, the major emphasis of marketing strategy for health-related remedies was on positioning through advertising and on new product development. Thus the company decided to increase advertising support throughout the planning period and to broaden research and development efforts.

NEPC's strategy was based on the following rationale. Consumers are extremely loyal to health products that deliver, as shown by their willingness to resume buying Johnson & Johnson's Tylenol after two poisoning episodes. But while brand loyalty makes consumers harder to lure away, it also makes them easier to keep, and good marketing can go a long way in this endeavor. The company was able to enlarge the market for its indigestion remedy, which experts thought had hit maturity, through savvy marketing. NEPC used television advertising to sell it as a cure for overindulgence, which led to a 30 percent increase in business during 1986–91.

As NEPC pushes further into health products, its vast research and technological resources will be a major asset. NEPC spends nearly $600 million a year on research, and product improvements have always been an important key to the company's marketing prowess.

The overall strategy of the health-related remedies business unit was determined by industry maturity and the unit's competitive position. The industry was found to be growing, while the competitive position was deemed strong.

With insurers and the government trying to drive health care costs down, consumers are buying more and more over-the-counter nostrums. Advertisers are making health claims for products from cereal to chewing gum. As the fitness craze exemplifies, interest in health is higher than ever, and the aging of the population will accentuate these trends: people are going to be older, but they are not going to want to feel older. Thus the health-related remedies industry has a significant potential for growth. NEPC is the largest over-the-counter remedies marketer. As shown in the list below, it has products for different ailments. The company's combined strength in marketing and research puts it in an enviable position in the market.

Skin—NEPC produces the leading facial moisturizer. NEPC also leads the teenage acne treatment market. Work is now underway on a possible breakthrough antiaging product.

Mouth—After being on the market for 26 years, NEPC's mouthwash is the market leader. Another NEPC product, a prescription plaque-fighting mouthwash, may go over the counter, or it may become an important ingredient in other NEPC oral hygiene products.

Head—An NEPC weak spot, its aspirin holds an insignificant share of the analgesic market. NEPC may decide to compete with an ibuprofen-caffeine combination painkiller.

Chest—NEPC's medicated chest rub is an original brand in a stable that now includes cough syrup, cough drops, a nighttime cold remedy, and nasal spray. Other line extensions and new products are coming but at a fairly slow pace.

Abdomen—The market share for NEPC's indigestion remedy is up 20 percent in the last three years. Already being sold to prevent traveler's diarrhea, it may be marketed as an ulcer treatment. NEPC also dominates the over-the-counter bulk laxative market. New clinical research shows that its laxative may reduce serum cholesterol.

Bones—NEPC orange juice has a 10 percent share of the market. Orange juice with calcium is now being expanded nationwide and could be combined with a low-calorie version.

Briefly, these inputs, along with the business unit's goals, led to the following business unit strategy: to attempt to improve position, to push for share.

Portfolio Analysis. The marketing strategy for each product/market was reviewed using the portfolio technique (see chapter 10). By positioning different products/markets on a multifactor portfolio matrix (high/medium/low business strength and high/medium/low industry attractiveness), strategy for each product/market was examined and approved from the viewpoint of meeting business unit missions and goals. Following the portfolio analysis, the approved marketing strategy became a part of the business unit's strategic plan, which, when approved by top management, was ready to be implemented. As a part of implementation, an annual marketing plan was formulated and became the basis for operations managers to pursue their objectives.

Implementation of the Strategic Plan. A few highlights of the activities of the health-related remedies business unit during 1989–91 show how the strategic plan was implemented.

- Steps were taken to sell its laxative as an anticholesterol agent.
- The company won FDA permission to promote its indigestion remedy to doctors as a preventive for traveler's diarrhea. Company research has shown that it helps treat ulcers. Although some researchers have disputed this claim, the prospect of cracking the multibillion dollar ulcer treatment market is tantalizing.
- The company introduced its orange juice brand with calcium. The company sought and won the approval of the American Medical Women's Association for the product and put the group's seal on its containers.

STRATEGIC MARKETING IMPLEMENTATION

Strategic marketing has evolved by trial and error. In the 1980s, companies developed unique strategic marketing procedures, processes, systems, and models. Experience shows, however, that most companies' marketing strategies are burdened with undue complexity. They are bogged down in principles that produce similar responses to competition. Changes are needed to put speed and freshness into marketing strategy.

Failings in Strategic Marketing

The following are the common problems associated with marketing strategy formulation and implementation.[21]

1. **Too much emphasis on "where" to compete and not enough on "how" to compete.** Experience shows that companies have devoted a lot more attention to identifying markets in which to compete than to the means to compete in these markets. Information on where to compete is easy to obtain but seldom brings about sustainable competitive advantage. Further, "where" information is usually easy for competitors to copy. "How" information, on the other hand, is tough to get and tough to copy. It concerns the fundamental workings of the business and the company. For example, McDonald's motto, QSC & V, is a how-to-compete strategy—it translates into *quality* food products; fast, friendly *service*; restaurant *cleanliness*; and a menu that provides *value*. It is much more difficult to copy the "how" of McDonald's strategy than the "where."

   In the next era of marketing strategy, companies will need to focus on how to compete in entirely new ways. In this endeavor, creativity will play a crucial role. For example, a large insurance company substantially improved its business by making improvements in underwriting, claim processing, and customer service, a "how" strategy that could not be replicated by competitors forthwith.
2. **Too little focus on uniqueness and adaptability in strategy.** Most marketing strategies lack uniqueness. For example, specialty stores increasingly look alike because they use the same layout and stock the same merchandise. In the 1970s, when market information was scarce, companies pursued new and different approaches. But today's easy access to information often leads companies to follow identical strategies to the detriment of all.

   Ideas for uniqueness and adaptability may flow from unknown sources. Companies should, therefore, be sensitive and explore all possibilities. The point may be illustrated with reference to Arm and Hammer's advertising campaign that encouraged people to place baking soda in their refrigerators to reduce odors. The idea was suggested in a letter from a consumer. The introduction of that *unique* application for the product in the early 1970s caused sales of Arm and Hammer baking soda to double within two years.
3. **Inadequate emphasis on "when" to compete.** Because of the heavy emphasis on where and how to compete, many marketing strategies give inadequate attention to "when" to compete. Any move in the marketplace should be adequately timed. The optimum time is one that minimizes or eliminates competition and creates the desired impact on the market; in other words, the optimum time makes it easier for the firm to achieve its objectives. Timing also has strategy implementation significance. It serves as a guide for different managers in the firm to schedule their activities to meet the timing requirement.

   Decisions on timing should be guided by the following:

   a. *Market knowledge.* If you have adequate information, it is desirable to market readily; otherwise you must wait until additional information has been gathered.
   b. *Competition.* A firm may decide on an early entry to beat minor competition. If you face major competition, you may delay entry if necessary; for example, to seek additional information.

c. *Company readiness.* For a variety of reasons, the company may not be ready to compete. These reasons could be lack of financial resources, labor problems, inability to meet existing commitments, and others.

Decisions on timing have created large strategy problems because the best return on equity is often available to businesses requiring the highest levels of skill; these businesses, however, get the lowest return on those skills. Conversely, the best return on skills may be available to manufacturing businesses that require little skill. (For the measurement of return on skills, see chapter 11.)

Addressing the Problems of Strategic Marketing

Having the ability to do all the right things, however, is no guarantee that planned objectives will be realized. Any number of pitfalls may render the best strategies inappropriate. To counter the pitfalls, the following concerns should be addressed:

1. Develop attainable goals and objectives.
2. Involve key operating personnel.
3. Avoid becoming so engrossed in current problems that strategic planning is neglected and thus becomes discredited in the eyes of others.
4. Don't keep marketing strategy separate from the rest of the management process.
5. Avoid formality in strategy formulation that restrains flexibility and inhibits creativity.
6. Avoid creating a climate that is resistant to strategic planning.
7. Don't assume that strategy development can be delegated to a planner.
8. Don't overturn the strategy formulation mechanism with intuitive, conflicting decisions.

PLAN OF THE BOOK

Today's business and marketing managers are faced with a continuous stream of decisions, each with its own degree of risk, uncertainty, and payoff. These decisions may be categorized into two broad classes: operating and strategic. With reference to marketing, operating decisions are the domain of marketing management. Strategic decisions constitute the field of strategic marketing.

Operating decisions are those dealing with current operations of the business. The typical objective of these decisions in a business firm is profit maximization. During times of business stagnation or recession, as experienced in the early 1990s, efforts at profit maximization have typically encompassed a cost minimization perspective. Under these conditions, managers are pressured into shorter and shorter time horizons. All too frequently decisions are made regarding pricing, discounts, promotional expenditures, collection of marketing research information, inventory levels, delivery schedules, and a host of other areas with far too little regard for the long-term impact of the decision. As might be expected, a decision that may be optimal for one time period may not be optimal in the long run.

The second category of decision making, **strategic decisions,** deals with the determination of strategy: the selection of the proper markets and the products that best suit the needs of those markets. Although strategic decisions may represent a very small fraction of the multitude of management decisions, they are truly the most important as they provide the definition of the business and the general relationship between the firm and its environment. Despite their importance, the need to make strategic decisions is not always as apparent as the need (sometimes urgency) for successfully completing operating decisions.

Strategic decisions are characterized by the following distinctions:

1. They are likely to effect a significant departure from the established product market mix. (This departure might involve branching out technologically or innovating in other ways.)
2. They are likely to hold provisions for undertaking programs with an unusually high degree of risk relative to previous experience (e.g., using untried resources or entering uncertain markets and competitive situations where predictability of success is noticeably limited).
3. They are likely to include a wide range of available alternatives to cope with a major competitive problem, the scope of these alternatives providing for significant differences in both the results and resources required.
4. They are likely to involve important timing options, both for starting development work and for deciding when to make the actual market commitment.
5. They are likely to call for major changes in the competitive "equilibrium," creating a new operating and customer acceptance pattern.
6. They are likely to resolve the choice of either leading or following certain market or competitive advances, based on a trade-off between the costs and risks of innovating and the timing vulnerability of letting others pioneer (in the expectation of catching up and moving ahead at a later date on the strength of a superior marketing force).[22]

This book deals with strategic decisions in the area of marketing. Chapter 1 dealt with planning and strategy concepts and this chapter examined various aspects of strategic marketing. Chapters 3 through 6 deal with analysis of strategic information relative to company (e.g., corporate appraisal), competition, customer, and external environment. Chapter 7 focuses on the measurement of strategic capabilities, and chapter 8 concentrates on strategic direction via goals and objectives.

Chapters 9 and 10 are devoted to strategy formulation. Organization for strategy implementation and control is examined in chapter 11. The next five chapters, chapters 12 through 16, review major market, product, price, distribution, and promotion strategies. Chapter 17 discusses strategic techniques and models. The final chapter, chapter 18, focuses on global market strategy.

SUMMARY

This chapter introduced the concept of strategic marketing and differentiated it from marketing management. Strategic marketing focuses on marketing strategy, which is achieved by identifying markets to serve, competition to be tackled, and the timing of market entry/exit. Marketing management deals with developing a marketing mix to serve a designated market.

The complex process of marketing strategy formulation was described. Marketing strategy, which is developed at the SBU level, essentially emerges from the interplay of three forces—customer, competition, and corporation—in a given environment.

A variety of internal and external information is needed to formulate marketing strategy. Internal information flows both down from top management (e.g., corporate strategy) and up from operations management (e.g., past performance of products/markets). External information pertains to social, economic, political, and technological trends and product/market environment. The effectiveness of marketing perspectives of the company is another input in strategy formulation. This information is analyzed to identify the SBU's strengths and weaknesses, which together with competition and customer, define SBU objectives. SBU objectives lead to marketing objectives and strategy formulation. The process of marketing strategy development was illustrated with an example of a health-related product.

Finally, this chapter articulated the plan of this book. Of the two types of business decisions, operating and strategic, this book concentrates on strategic decision making with reference to marketing.

DISCUSSION QUESTIONS

1. Define strategic marketing. Differentiate it from marketing management.
2. What are the distinguishing characteristics of strategic marketing?
3. What emerging trends support the continuation of strategic marketing as an important area of business endeavor?
4. Differentiate between operating and strategic decisions. Suggest three examples of each type of decision from the viewpoint of a food processor.
5. How might the finance function have an impact on marketing strategy? Explain.
6. Adapt to a small business the process of marketing strategy formulation as presented in Exhibit 2-4.
7. Specify the corporate inputs needed to formulate marketing strategy.

NOTES

[1]Robert Johnson, "General Mills Risks Millions Starting Chain of Italian Restaurants," *Wall Street Journal*, 21 September 1987, p. 1.

[2]See Michael D. Hutt, Peter H. Reingen, and John R. Ronchetto, Jr., "Tracing Emergent Processes in Marketing Strategy Formation," *Journal of Marketing* (January 1988): 4-19.

[3]"When Marketing Failed at Texas Instruments," *Business Week* (22 June 1981): 91. See also Bro Uttal, "Texas Instruments Regroups," *Fortune* (9 August 1982): 40.

[4]*Business Planning in the Eighties: The New Competitiveness of American Corporations* (New York: Coopers & Lybrand, 1984).

[5]"Goodyear Feels the Heat," *Business Week* (7 March 1988): 26.

[6]For further discussion of the portfolio matrix, see chapter 10.

[7]See Robert W. Ruekert and Orville C. Walker, Jr., "Marketing's Interaction with Other Functional Units: A Conceptual Framework and Empirical Evidence," *Journal of Marketing* (January 1987): 1–19.

[8]See chapter 12.

[9]See George S. Day and Robin Wensley, "Marketing Theory with a Strategic Orientation," *Journal of Marketing* (Fall 1983): 50.

[10]See David W. Cravens, "Strategic Forces Affecting Marketing Strategy," *Business Horizons* (September–October 1986): 77–86; and Frederick E. Webster, Jr., "Marketing Strategy in a Slow Growth Economy," *California Management Review* (Spring 1986): 93–105.

[11]Edward G. Michaels, "Marketing Muscle: Who Needs It?" *McKinsey Quarterly* (Summer 1982): 37–55.

[12]Laura Landro, "Parent and Partners Help Columbia Have Fun at the Movies," *Wall Street Journal*, 7 December 1984, p. 1.

[13]T. Michael Nevens, Gregory L. Summe, and Bro Uttal, "Commercializing Technology: What the Best Companies Do," *Harvard Business Review* (May–June 1990): 154–63.

[14]Don G. Reinertsen, "Whodunit? The Search for New Product Killers," *Electronic Business* (July 1983): 62–66.

[15]Gary Hamel and C. K. Prahalad, "Corporate Imagination and Expeditionary Marketing," *Harvard Business Review* (July–August 1991): 81–92.

[16]Ken Dychtwald and Grey Gable, "American Diversity," *American Demographics* (July 1991): 75–77.

[17]Regis McKenna, "Marketing in an Age of Diversity," *Harvard Business Review* (September–October 1988): 88–95. Information was updated based on the company's 1990 annual report and a telephone interview with a company executive.

[18]Bruce D. Henderson, *Henderson on Corporate Strategy* (Cambridge, MA: Abt Books, 1981), 38.

[19]Derek F. Abell and John S. Hammond, *Strategic Market Planning* (Englewood Cliffs, NJ: Prentice-Hall, 1979), 9.

[20]Henderson, *Henderson on Corporate Strategy*, 4.

[21]This section draws heavily on Joel A. Bleeke, "Peak Strategies," *Across the Board* (February 1988): 45–80.

[22]J. Thomas Cannon, *Business Strategy and Policy* (New York: Harcourt, Brace & World, 1968), 20.

PART TWO

Strategic Analysis

CHAPTER 3
Corporate Appraisal

We that acquaint ourselves with every zone
And pass both tropics and behold the poles
When we come home are to ourselves unknown
And unacquainted still with our souls.

JOHN DAVIES

One important reason for formulating marketing strategy is to prepare the company to interact with the changing environment in which it operates. Implicit here is the significance of predicting the shape the environment is likely to take in the future. Then, with a perspective of the company's present position, the task ahead can be determined. Study of the environment is reserved for a later chapter. This chapter is devoted to corporate appraisal.

An analogy to corporate appraisal is provided by a career counselor's job. Just as it is relatively easy to make a list of the jobs available to a young person, it is simple to produce a superficial list of investment opportunities open to a company. With the career counselor, the real skill comes in taking stock of each applicant; examining the applicant's qualifications, personality, and temperament; defining the areas in which some sort of further development or training may be required; and matching these characteristics and the applicant's aspirations against various options. Well-established techniques can be used to find out most of the necessary information about an individual. Digging deep into the psyche of a company is more complex but no less important. Failure by the company in the area of appraisal can be as stunting to future development in the corporate sense as the misplacement of a young graduate in the personal sense.

How should the strategist approach the task of appraising corporate perspectives? What needs to be discovered? These and other similar questions are explored in this chapter.

MEANING OF CORPORATE APPRAISAL

Broadly, **corporate appraisal** refers to an examination of the entire organization from different angles. It is a measurement of the readiness of the internal culture of the corporation to interact with the external environment. Marketing strategists are concerned with those aspects of the corporation that have a direct bearing on corporatewide strategy because they must be referred to in defining the business unit mission. As shown in Exhibit 3-1, corporate publics, the value orientation of top management, corporate resources, the past performance of business units, and the external environment are all variables that affect the development of corporate strategy. Of these, the first four variables are discussed in this chapter.

Two important characteristics of strategic marketing are its concern with issues having far-reaching effects on the entire organization and change as an essential ingredient in its conduct. These characteristics make the process of marketing strategy formulation a difficult job and demand creativity and adaptability on the part of the organization. Creativity, however, is not everybody's forte. By the same token, adaptation to changing conditions may become a threat to existing styles, norms of behavior, and relationships.

> Success in the past always becomes enshrined in the present by the over-valuation of the policies and attitudes which accompanied that success. . . . With time these attitudes become embedded in a system of beliefs, traditions, taboos, habits, customs, and inhibitions which constitute the distinctive culture of that firm. Such cultures are as distinctive as the cultural differences between nationalities or the personality differences between individuals. They do not adapt to change very easily.[1]

Human history is full of instances of communities and cultures being wiped out over time for the apparent reason of failing to change with the times. In the

EXHIBIT 3-1
Scope of Corporate Appraisal

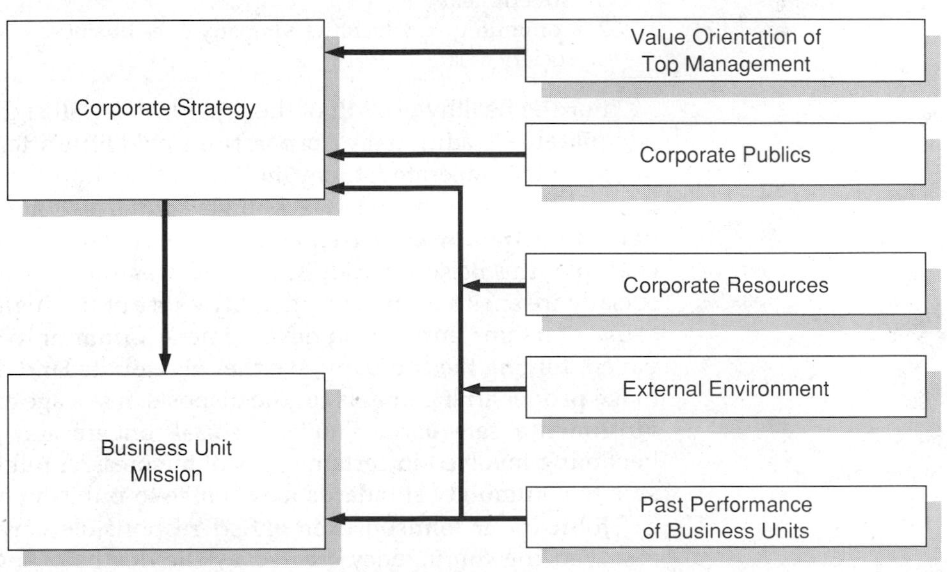

context of business, why is it that organizations like Xerox, R.J. Reynolds, Litton, and IBM, comparative newcomers among large organizations, are considered blue-chip companies? Why should United States Rubber and American Tobacco lag behind? Why are GE, Du Pont, and 3M continually ranked as "successful" companies? The outstanding common denominator in the success of companies is the element of change. When time demands that the perspective of an organization undergo a change, success is the outcome.

Obviously, the marketing strategist must take a close look at the perspectives of the organization before formulating future strategy. Strategies must bear a close relationship to the internal culture of the corporation if they are to be successfully implemented.

FACTORS IN APPRAISAL: CORPORATE PUBLICS

Business exists for people. Thus, the first consideration in the strategic process is to recognize the individuals and groups who have an interest in the fate of the corporation and the extent and nature of their expectations.

Meaning of Corporate Publics

The following groups generally constitute the interest-holders in business organizations:

1. Owners
2. Employees
3. Customers
4. Suppliers
5. Banking community and other lenders
6. Government
7. Community in which the company does business
8. Society at large

For the healthy growth of the organization, all eight groups must be served adequately.[2] Traditionally, corporations paid little attention to the communities in which they operated; today, however, the importance of service to community and to society is widely acknowledged. The community may force a company to refrain from activities that are detrimental to the environment. For example, the Boise Cascade Company was once denounced as harsh, stingy, socially insensitive, and considerably short of the highest ethical standards because of its unplanned land development. Community interests ultimately prevailed, forcing the company to either give up its land development activities or make proper arrangements for the disposal of sewage and to introduce other environmental safeguards. Similarly, social concern may prevent a company from becoming involved in certain types of business. A publishing company responsive to community standards may refuse to publish pornographic material.

Johnson & Johnson exemplified responsible corporate behavior when it resolved the contingency created by the deaths of seven individuals who had consumed contaminated Tylenol capsules.[3] Within a few days, the company instituted a total product recall at a cost of $50 million after taxes, despite the fact that the problem did not occur because of negligence on the part of the company. Subsequently, the company took the initiative to develop more effective packaging to prevent tampering in the future. The company's commitment to socially responsible behavior was reaffirmed when it quit producing capsules entirely after the tampering occurred again. Johnson & Johnson put the well-being of the customer ahead of profitability in resolving this tampering problem. In brief, the requirements and expectations of today's society must serve as basic ingredients in the development of strategy:

> Though profit and efficiency must remain central values within the culture, they must be balanced by other values that help define the limits of activities designed to achieve those objectives and by values describing other important ethical and socially responsible behaviors. Without the integration of concerns about ethics and social responsibility at the very beginning of the marketing planning process, as well as throughout the process, the organizational culture may not provide the checks and balances needed to develop ethical and socially responsible marketing programs.[4]

It was mainly a social concern that led Control Data Corporation to locate four new plants in depressed inner cities, a far-from-easy move. For example, to counter absenteeism at one of its inner city plants in Minneapolis, the company had to send a lawyer with a book of bail bonds to the city jail every Monday morning. With time, things at the plant worked out. As Control Data's chairman at the time, William C. Norris, put it: "By whatever criteria are used to measure these plants—tenure, absenteeism, profitability—they are equal to or better than the company's conventional operations."[5]

Corporate Response to Different Publics

Historically, a business organization considered its sole purpose to be economic gain, concerning itself with other spheres of society only when required by law or self-interest or when motivated by philanthropy or charity. Charity was merely a celebration of a corporation's good fortune that it desired to share with "outsiders" or a display of pity for the unfortunate.[6] Indirectly, of course, even this rather uninspired notion of charity gave the company a good name and thus served a public relations function. In slack times, a company reduced its activities in all areas, instituting both inside cost-cutting measures and the lowering of commitments to all publics other than stockholders. Such a perspective worked well until the mid-1960s;[7] however, with economic prosperity almost assured, different stakeholders have begun to demand a more equitable deal from corporations.

Concern over environmental pollution by corporations, for example, has become a major issue in both the public and the private sector. Similarly, customers expect products to be wholesome; employees want opportunities for advancement and self-improvement; the community hopes that the corporation would assume some of its concerns, such as unemployment among minorities. Society now expects business corporations to help in resolving social problems.

In brief, the role of the corporation has shifted from that of an economic institution solely responsible to its stockholders to that of a multifaceted force owing its existence to different stakeholders to whom it must be accountable. As one of the most progressive institutions in the society, the corporation is expected to provide balanced prosperity in all fields. Two generations ago, the idea of a business being a party to a contract with society would have provoked an indignant snort from most businesspeople. Even 10 years ago a business's contract with society was more likely material for a corporate president's speech to the stockholders than a basis for policy. It is a measure of how much the attitudes of middle-of-the-road businesspeople have changed that the notion of a social contract is now the basic assumption for their statements on the social responsibilities of a business. This new outlook extends the mission of the business beyond its primary obligation to owners.[8]

In today's environment, corporate strategy must be developed, not simply to enhance financial performance, but to maximize performance across the board, delivering the highest gains to all stakeholders, or corporate publics. And companies are responding to changing times. As former chairman Waldron of Avon Products noted, "We have 40,000 employees and 1.3 million representatives. . . . They have much deeper and more important stakes in our company than shareholders."[9]

The "concept of stakeholders" is really an extension of the marketing concept, the central doctrine in marketing.

> Marketing concept and stakeholder concept are strongly related with a common root or core. Clearly, one commonality is that the stakeholder concept recognizes the consumer as a public with concerns central to the organization's purpose. Perhaps a further element of this common core is a realization of the importance of cooperative exchange with the consumer. In fact, all publics of an organization can be viewed in a cooperative vs. adversarial perspective. Cooperative strategies with labor, marketing channel members, etc., may result in eventual but not mutual symbiosis. For example, if a manufacturer cooperates with wholesalers then these wholesalers may be more likely to cooperate with retailers. Similarly, retailers may then be more likely to treat the customer well. Consequently, the customer will be more loyal to certain brands and this catalyzes the manufacturer to continue to be cooperative with channel members. This eventual, but not necessarily mutual symbiosis, may result in more long run stability and evolutionary potential within the business system.[10]

One company that systematically and continuously examines and serves the interests of its stakeholders is Corning. It cooperates with labor, promotes diversity, and goes out of its way to improve the community. For example, the company's partnership with the glass workers' union promotes joint decision making. Worker teams determine job schedules and even factory design. All U.S. workers share a bonus based on point performance. All managers and salaried workers attend seminars to build sensitivity and support for women and African-American coworkers. A network of mentors helps African-Americans and women with career planning, and Asians and Hispanics are planned to be targeted, too. Corning acquires and rehabilitates commercial properties, then finds tenants (some minority-owned) at market rates to locate their business there. It works to attract new business to the region and has invested in the local infrastructure by building a Hilton hotel, a museum, and a city library.

> More than the biggest employer in town, Corning plays benefactor, landlord, and social engineer. The company is half-owner of a racetrack and sponsors a professional golf tournament. Affordable housing, day care, new business development—it's doing all that, too. Corning is more directly involved in its community than most big U.S. corporations. . . . When a flood in 1972 put the town under 10 feet of water, the company paid area teenagers to rehabilitate damaged homes and appliances, then spent millions to build a new library and skating rink. But Corning's recent efforts have been more focused: They aim to turn a remote, insular town into a place that will appeal to the smart professionals Corning wants to attract—a place that offers social options for young singles, support for new families, and cultural diversity for minorities.
>
> It's a strategy that often borders on corporate socialism. Corning bought the rundown bars—which "didn't fit with our objective," says one executive—as part of a block-long redevelopment of Market Street, the town's main commercial strip.
>
> More important, Corning is working to create a region less dependent on its headquarters and 15 factories. . . . To help support the flagging local economy, Corning bought the Watkins Glen auto-racing track, which had slipped into bankruptcy. It rebuilt the facility, took in a managing partner, and last summer, saw the track host 200,000 visitors. Similarly, the company lobbied a supermarket chain to build an enormous new store. It persuaded United Parcel Service to locate a regional hub nearby.
>
> In all, Corning expects its Corning Enterprises subsidiary, which spearheads community investments, to bring 200 new jobs to the Chemung River valley each year. It also wants to boost the number of tourists by 2% annually and attract four new businesses to town. Corning Enterprises funds its activities largely with rental income from real estate that it has purchased and rehabilitated.[11]

Corporate Publics—Analysis of Expectations

Although the expectations of different groups vary, in our society growth and improvement are the common expectations of many institutions. But this broad view does not take into account the stakes of different groups within a business. For planning purposes, a clearer definition of each group's hopes is needed.

Exhibit 3-2 summarizes the factors against which the expectations of different groups can be measured. The broad categories shown here should be broken down into subcategories as far as possible. For example, in a community where juvenile delinquency is rampant, youth programs become an important area of corporate concern. One must be careful, however, not to make unrealistic or false assumptions about the expectations of different groups. Take owners, for example. Typically, 50 percent of earnings after taxes must be reinvested in the business to sustain normal growth, but the payout desired by the owners may render it difficult to finance growth. Thus, a balance must be struck between the payment of dividends and the plowing back of earnings. A

EXHIBIT 3-2
Corporate Publics and Their Concerns

Publics	*Area of Concern*
Owners	Payout Equity Stock price Nonmonetary desires
Customers	Business reliability Product reliability Product improvement Product price Product service Continuity Marketing efficiency
Employees of all ranks	Monetary reward Reward of recognition Reward of pride Environment Challenge Continuity Advancement
Suppliers	Price Stability Continuity Growth
Banking community and other lenders	Sound risk Interest payment Repayment of principal
Government (federal, state, and local)	Taxes Security and law enforcement Management expertise Democratic government Capitalistic system Implementation of programs
Immediate community	Economic growth and efficiency Education Employment and training
Society at large	Civil rights Urban renewal and development Pollution abatement Conservation and recreation Culture and arts Medical care

vice president of finance for a chemical company with yearly sales over $100 million said in a conversation with the author:

> While we do recognize the significance of retaining more money, we must consider the desires of our stockholders. They happen to be people who actually live on dividend payments. Thus, a part of long-term growth must be given up in order to maintain their short-term needs for regular dividend payments.

Apparently this company would not be correct in assuming that growth alone is the objective of stockholders. Thus it behooves the marketing strategist to gain clear insight into the demands of different corporate publics.

Who in the company should study stakeholders' expectations? This task constitutes a project in itself and should be assigned either to someone inside the company (such as a strategic planner, an assistant to the president, a director of public affairs, or a marketing researcher) or to a consultant hired for this purpose. When this analysis is first undertaken, it will be fairly difficult to specify stakeholders, designate their areas of concern, and make their expectations explicit. After the initial study is made, updating it from year to year should be fairly routine.

The groups that constitute the stakeholders of a business organization are usually the same from one business to another. Mainly they are the owners, employees, customers, suppliers, the banking community and other lenders, government, the immediate community, and society at large. The areas of concern of each group and their expectations, however, require surveying. As with any other survey, this amounts to seeking information from an appropriate sample within each group. A structured questionnaire is preferable for obtaining objective answers. Before surveying the sample, however, it is desirable to obtain in-depth interviews with a few members of each group. The information provided by these interviews is helpful in developing the questionnaire. While overall areas of concern may not vary from one period to another, expectations certainly do. For example, during a recession stockholders may desire a higher payout in dividends than at other times. Besides, in a given period, the public may not articulate expectations in all of its areas of concern. During inflationary periods, for example, customers may emphasize stable prices only, while product improvement and marketing efficiency may figure prominently in times of prosperity.

Corporate Publics and Corporate Strategy

The expectations of different publics provide the corporation with a focus for working out its objectives and goals. However, a company may not be able to satisfy the expectations of all stakeholders for two reasons: limited resources and conflicting expectations among stakeholders.[12] For example, customers may want low prices and simultaneously ask for product improvements. Likewise, to meet exactly the expectations of the community, the company may be obliged to reduce dividends. Thus, a balance must be struck between the expectations of different stakeholders and the company's ability to honor them.

The corporate response to stakeholders' expectations emerges in the form of its objectives and goals, which in turn determine corporate strategy. While objectives and goals are discussed in detail in chapter 8, a sample of corporate objectives with reference to customers is given here.

Assume the following customer expectations for a food-processing company:

1. The company should provide wholesome products.
2. The company should clearly state the ingredients of different products in words that are easily comprehensible to an ordinary consumer.
3. The company should make all efforts to keep prices down.

The company, based on these expectations, may set the following goals:

Wholesome Products

1. Create a new position—vice president, product quality. No new products will be introduced into the market until they are approved for wholesomeness by this vice president. The vice president's decision will be upheld no matter how bright a picture of consumer acceptance of a product is painted by marketing research and marketing planning.
2. Create a panel of nutrient testers to analyze and judge different products for their wholesomeness.
3. Communicate with consumers about the wholesomeness of the company's products, suggesting that they deal directly with the vice president of product quality should there be any questions. (Incidentally, a position similar to vice president of product quality was created at Gillette a few years ago. This executive's decisions overruled the market introduction of products despite numerous other reasons for early introduction.)

Information on Ingredients

1. Create a new position—director, consumer information. The person in this position will decide what information about product ingredients, nutritive value, etc., should be included on each package.
2. Seek feedback every other year from a sample of consumers concerning the effectiveness and clarity of the information provided.
3. Encourage customers, through various forms of promotions, to communicate with the director of consumer information on a toll-free phone line to clarify information that may be unclear.
4. Revise information contents based on numbers 2 and 3.

Keeping Prices Low

1. Communicate with customers on what leads the company to raise different prices (e.g., cost of labor is up, cost of ingredients is up, etc.).
2. Design various ways to reduce price pressure on consumers. For example, develop family packs.
3. Let customers know how much they can save by buying family packs. Assure them that the quality of the product will remain intact for a specified period.
4. Work on new ways to reduce costs. For example, a substitute may be found for a product ingredient whose cost has gone up tremendously.

By using this illustration, the expectations of each group of stakeholders can be translated into specific goals. Some firms, NCR Corporation, for example, define their commitment to stakeholders more broadly (see Exhibit 3-3). However, NCR is not alone in articulating its concern for stakeholders. A whole corporate culture has sprung up that argues for the essential commonality of labor-management community-shareholder interests.

FACTORS IN APPRAISAL: VALUE ORIENTATION OF TOP MANAGEMENT

The ideologies and philosophies of top management as a team and of the CEO as the leader of the team have a profound effect on managerial policy and the strategic development process. According to Steiner:

> [The CEO's] aspirations about his personal life, the life of his company as an institution, and the lives of those involved in his business are major determinants of choice of strategy. His mores, habits, and ways of doing things determine how he behaves and decides. His sense of obligation to his company will decide his devotion and choice of subject matter to think about.[13]

Rene McPherson, former CEO of Dana Corporation, incessantly emphasized cost reduction and productivity improvement: the company doubled its productivity in seven years. IBM chairmen have always preached the importance

EXHIBIT 3-3
NCR's Commitment to its Stakeholders

NCR's mission is to create value for its stakeholders. We believe in building mutually beneficial and enduring relationships with all of our stakeholders, based on conducting business activities with integrity and respect.

Customers
We take customer satisfaction personally. We are committed to providing superior value in our products and services on a continuing basis.

Employees
We respect the individuality of each employee and foster an environment in which employees' creativity and productivity are encouraged, recognized, valued and rewarded.

Shareholders
We are dedicated to creating value for our shareholders and financial communities by performing in a manner that will enhance returns on investments.

Suppliers
We think of our suppliers as partners who share our goal of achieving the highest quality standards and the most consistent level of service.

Communities
We are committed to being caring and supportive corporate citizens within the worldwide communities in which we operate.

Source: Company records.

of calling on customers—to the point of stressing the proper dress for a call. Over time a certain way of dressing became an accepted norm of behavior for the entire corporation. Texas Instruments' ex-chairman Patrick Haggerty made it a point to drop in at a development laboratory on his way home each night when he was in Dallas to emphasize his view of the importance of new products for the company. Such single-minded focus on a value becomes an integral part of a company's culture. As employees steeped in the corporate culture move up the ladder, they become role models for newcomers, and the process continues.[14]

How companies in essentially the same business move in different strategic directions because of different top management values can be illustrated with an example from American Can Company and Continental Group. Throughout the 1970s, both Robert S. Hatfield, then Continental's chairman, and William F. May, his counterpart at American Can, made deep changes in their companies' product portfolios. Both closed numerous aged can-making plants. Both divested tangential businesses they deemed to have lackluster growth prospects. And both sought either to hire or promote executives who would steer their companies in profitable directions.

But similar as their overall strategies might seem, their concepts of their companies diverged markedly. May envisioned American Can as a corporate think tank, serving as both a trendspotter and a trendsetter. He put his trust in the advice of financial experts who, although lean on operating experience, were knowledgeable about business theory. They took American Can into such diverse fields as aluminum recycling, record distribution, and mail-order consumer products. By contrast, Hatfield sought executives with proven records in spotting new potential in old areas. The company acquired Richmond Corporation, an insurance holding company, and Florida Gas Company.[15]

Importance of Value Orientation in the Corporate Environment

It would be wrong to assume that every firm wants to grow. There are companies that probably could grow faster than their current rates indicate. But when top management is averse to expansion, sluggishness prevails throughout the organization, inhibiting growth. A large number of companies start small, perhaps with a family managing the organization. Some entrepreneurs at the helm of such companies are quite satisfied with what they are able to achieve. They would rather not grow than give up complete control of the organization. Obviously, if managerial values promote stability rather than growth, strategy will form accordingly. Of course, if the owners find that their expectations are in conflict with the value system of top management, they may seek to replace the company's management with a more philosophically compatible team. As an example, a flamboyant CEO who emphasizes growth and introduces changes in the organization to the extent of creating suspicion among owners, board members, and colleagues may lead to the CEO's exit from the organization. An unconventionally high debt-to-equity ratio can be sufficient cause for a CEO to be dismissed.

In brief, the value systems of the individual members of the top management serve as important inputs in strategy development.[16] If people at the top hold conflicting values, the chosen strategy will lack the willing cooperation and commitment of all executives. Generally, differing values are reflected in conflicts over policies, objectives, strategies, and structure.[17]

This point may be illustrated with reference to Johnson & Johnson,[18] a solidly profitable company. Its core businesses are entering market maturity and offer limited long-term growth potential. In the mid-1980s, therefore, the company embarked on a program to manufacture sophisticated technology products. But the development and marketing of high-tech products require a markedly different culture than that needed for Johnson & Johnson's traditional products. High-tech products require greater cooperation among corporate units, which is sometimes hard to obtain. Traditionally, Johnson & Johnson's various businesses have been run as completely decentralized units with total autonomy. To successfully achieve the shift to technology products, the CEO of the company, James E. Burke, is tinkering in subtle but important ways with a management style and corporate culture that have long been central to the company's success. Similar efforts are at work at Procter and Gamble: "Pressed by competitors and aided by new technology, P&G is, in fact, remodeling its corporate culture—a process bringing pain to some, relief to others and wonderment to most."[19]

Top Management Values and Corporate Culture

Over time, top management values come to characterize the culture of the entire organization. Corporate culture affects the entire perspective of the organization. It influences its product and service quality, advertising content, pricing policies, treatment of employees, and relationships with customers, suppliers, and the community.[20]

Corporate culture gives employees a sense of direction, a sense of how to behave and what they ought to be doing.[21] Employees who fail to live up to the cultural norms of the organization find the going tough. This point may be illustrated with reference to PepsiCo and J.C. Penney Company. At PepsiCo, beating the competition is the surest path to success. In its soft drink operation, Pepsi takes on Coke directly, asking consumers to compare the taste of the two colas. This kind of direct confrontation is reflected inside the company as well. Managers are pitted against each other to grab more market share, to work harder, and to wring more profits out of their businesses. Because winning is the key value at PepsiCo, losing has its penalties. Consistent runners-up find their jobs gone. Employees know they must win merely to stay in place and must devastate the competition to get ahead.[22]

But the aggressive manager who succeeds at Pepsi would be sorely out of place at J.C. Penney Company, where a quick victory is far less important than building long-term loyalty.

> Indeed, a Penney store manager once was severely rebuked by the company's president for making too much profit. That was considered unfair to customers, whose trust Penney seeks to win. The business style set by the company's founder—which one competitor describes as avoiding "taking unfair advantage of anyone the company did business with"—still prevails today. Customers know they can return

merchandise with no questions asked; suppliers know that Penney will not haggle over terms; and employees are comfortable in their jobs, knowing that Penney will avoid layoffs at all costs and will find easier jobs for those who cannot handle more demanding ones. Not surprisingly, Penney's average executive tenure is 33 years while Pepsi's is ten.[23]

These vastly different methods of doing business are just two examples of corporate culture. People who work at PepsiCo and at Penney sense that corporate values constitute the yardstick by which they will be measured. Just as tribal cultures have totems and taboos that dictate how each member should act toward fellow members and outsiders, a corporation's culture influences employees' actions toward customers, competitors, suppliers, and one another. Sometimes the rules are written, but more often they are tacit. Most often they are laid down by a strong founder and hardened by success into custom.

One authority describes four categories of corporate culture—academies, clubs, baseball teams, and fortresses.[24] Each category attracts certain personalities. The following are some of the traits among managers who gravitate to a particular corporate culture.

Academies

- Have parents who value self-reliance but put less emphasis on honesty and consideration
- Tend to be less religious
- Graduate from business school with high grades
- Have more problems with subordinates in their first ten years of work

Clubs

- Have parents who emphasize honesty and consideration
- Have a lower regard for hard work and self-reliance
- Tend to be more religious
- Care more about health, family, and security and less about future income and autonomy
- Are less likely to have substantial equity in their companies

Baseball Teams

- Describe their fathers as unpredictable
- Generally have more problems planning their careers in the first ten years after business school and work for more companies during that period than classmates do
- Include personal growth and future income among their priorities
- Value security less than others

Fortresses

- Have parents who value curiosity
- Were helped strongly by mentors in the first year out of school
- Are less concerned than others with feelings of belonging, professional growth, and future income
- Experience problems in career planning, on-the-job decisions, and job implementation

An example of an academy is IBM, where managers spend at least 40 hours each year in training being carefully groomed to become experts in a particular function. United Parcel Service represents a club culture, which emphasizes grooming managers as generalists, with initiation beginning at the entry level. Generally speaking, accounting firms, law firms, and consulting, advertising, and software development companies exhibit baseball team cultures. Entrepreneurial in style, they seek out talent of all ages and experience and value inventiveness. Fortress companies are concerned with survival and are usually best represented by companies in a perpetual boom-and-bust cycle (e.g., retailers and natural resource companies).

Many companies cannot be neatly categorized in any one way. Many exhibit a blend of corporate cultures. For example, within GE, the NBC unit has baseball team qualities, whereas the aerospace division operates like a club, the electronics division like an academy, and the home appliance unit like a fortress. Companies may move from one category to another as they mature or as forced by the environment. For example, Apple started out as a baseball team but now appears to be emerging as an academy. Banks have traditionally exhibited a club culture, but with deregulation, they are evolving into baseball teams.

In the current environment, the changes that businesses are being forced to make merely to stay competitive—improving quality, increasing speed, becoming customer oriented—are so fundamental that they must take root in a company's very essence; that is, its culture.[25] Cultural change, while difficult and time-consuming to achieve, is nevertheless feasible if approached properly. The CEO must direct change to make sure that it happens coherently. He or she must live the new culture, become the walking embodiment of it, and spot and celebrate subordinates who exemplify the values that are to be inculcated. The following are keys to cultural change:

—**Understand your old culture** first. You can't chart a course until you know where you are.
—**Encourage those employees** who are bucking the old culture and have ideas for a better one.
—**Find the best subculture** in your organization, and hold it up as an example from which others can learn.
—**Don't attack culture head on.** Help employees find their own new ways to accomplish their tasks, and a better culture will follow.
—**Don't count on a vision** to work miracles. At best it acts as a guiding principle for change.
—**Figure on five to ten years** for significant, organization-wide improvement.
—**Live the culture you want.** As always, actions speak louder than words.[26]

Trying to change an institution's culture is certain to be frustrating. Most people resist change, and when the change goes to the basic character of the place where they earn a living, many people get upset. A company trying to improve its culture is like a person trying to improve his or her character. The process is long, difficult, often agonizing. The only reason that people put themselves through such ardor is that it is correspondingly satisfying and valuable.

Measurement of Values

In emphasizing the significance of the value system in strategic planning, several questions become pertinent. Should the corporation attempt to formally establish values for important members of management? If so, who should do it? What measures or techniques should be used? If the values of senior executives are in conflict, what should be done? Can values be changed?

It is desirable that the values of top management should be measured. If nothing else, such measurement will familiarize the CEO with the orientation of top executives and will help the CEO to better appreciate their viewpoints. Opinions differ, however, on who should do the measuring. Although a good case can be made for giving the assignment to a staff person, a strategic planner or a human resources planner, for example, hiring an outside consultant is probably the most effective way to gain an objective perspective on management values. If a consultant's findings appear to create conflict in the organization, they can be scrapped. With help from the consultant, the human resources planner in the company, working closely with the strategic planner, can design a system for the measurement of values once the initial effort is made.

Values can be measured in various ways. A popular technique is the self-evaluating scale developed by Allport, Vernon, and Lindzey.[27] This scale divides values into six classes: religious, political, theoretical, economic, aesthetic, and social. A manual is available that lists the average scores of different groups. Executives can complete the test in about 30 minutes and determine the structure of their values individually. Difficulties with using this scale lie in relating the executives' values to their jobs and in figuring out the impact of these values on corporate strategy.

A more specific way is to pinpoint those aspects of human values likely to affect strategy development and to measure one's score in relation to these values on a simple five- or seven-point scale. For example, we can measure an executive's orientation toward leadership image, performance standards and evaluation, decision-making techniques, use of authority, attitude about change, and nature of involvement. Exhibit 3-4 shows a sample scale for measuring these values.

As a matter of fact, a formal value orientation profile of each executive may not be entirely necessary. By raising questions such as the following about each top executive, one can gather insight into value orientations. Does the executive:

- Seem efficiency-minded?
- Like repetition?
- Like to be first in a new field instead of second?
- Revel in detail work?
- Seem willing to pay the price of keeping in personal touch with the customer, etc.?[28]

Can the value system of an individual be changed? Traditionally, it has been held that a person's behavior is determined mainly by the inner self reacting within a given environment. In line with this thinking, major shifts in values

EXHIBIT 3-4
Measuring Value Orientation

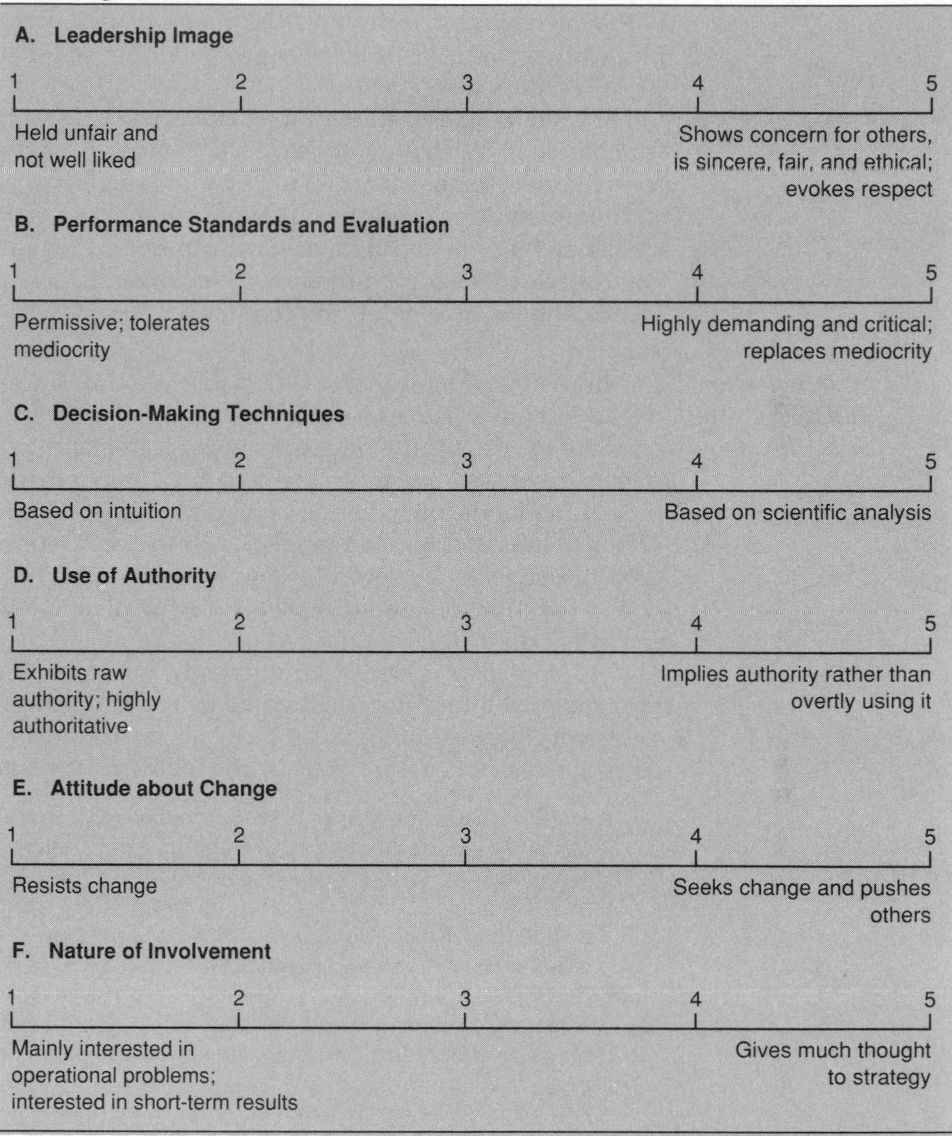

A. Leadership Image

1	2	3	4	5
Held unfair and not well liked				Shows concern for others, is sincere, fair, and ethical; evokes respect

B. Performance Standards and Evaluation

1	2	3	4	5
Permissive; tolerates mediocrity				Highly demanding and critical; replaces mediocrity

C. Decision-Making Techniques

1	2	3	4	5
Based on intuition				Based on scientific analysis

D. Use of Authority

1	2	3	4	5
Exhibits raw authority; highly authoritative				Implies authority rather than overtly using it

E. Attitude about Change

1	2	3	4	5
Resists change				Seeks change and pushes others

F. Nature of Involvement

1	2	3	4	5
Mainly interested in operational problems; interested in short-term results				Gives much thought to strategy

should be difficult to achieve. In recent years, a new school of behaviorists has emerged that assigns a more significant role to the environment. These new behaviorists challenge the concept of "self" as the underlying force in determining behavior.[29] If their "environmental" thesis is accepted, it should be possible to bring about a change in individual values so that senior executives can become more unified. However, the science of human behavior has yet to discover the tools that can be used to change values. Thus it would be appropriate to say that minor changes in personal values can be produced through manipulation of the environment; but where the values of an individual executive differ significantly from those of a colleague, an attempt to alter an individual's values would be difficult.

Several years ago, differing values caused a key executive at Procter and Gamble, John W. Hanley, to leave the company for the CEO position at Monsanto. Other members of the Procter and Gamble management team found him too aggressive, too eager to experiment and change practices, and too quick to challenge his superior. Because he could not be brought around to the conservative style of the company's other executives, he was passed over for the presidency and eventually left the company.[30]

Value Orientation and Corporate Strategy

The influence of the value orientation of top management on the perspectives of the business has already been emphasized. This section examines how a particular type of value orientation may lead to certain objectives and strategy perspectives. Two examples of this influence are presented in Exhibit 3-5. In the first example, the president is rated high on social and aesthetic values, which seems to indicate a greater emphasis on the quality of a single product than on growth per se. In the second example, again, the theoretical and social orientation of top management appears to stress truth and honesty rather than strictly growth. If the strategic plans of these two companies were to emphasize growth as a major goal, they would undoubtedly fail. Planned perspectives may not be implemented if they are constrained by top management's value system.

A corporation's culture can be its major strength when it is consistent with its strategies, as demonstrated by the following examples:

- At IBM, marketing drives a service philosophy that is almost unparalleled. The company keeps a hot line open 24 hours a day, seven days a week, to service IBM products.
- At International Telephone and Telegraph Corporation, financial discipline demands total dedication. To beat out the competition in a merger, an executive once called former chairman Harold S. Geneen at 3 A.M. to get his approval.
- At Digital Equipment Corporation, an emphasis on innovation creates freedom with responsibility. Employees can set their own hours and working style, but they are expected to articulate and support their activities with evidence of progress.
- At Delta Air Lines Inc., a focus on customer service produces a high degree of teamwork. Employees switch jobs to keep planes flying and baggage moving.
- At Atlantic Richfield Company, an emphasis on entrepreneurship encourages action. Managers have the autonomy to bid on promising fields without hierarchical approval.[31]

In summary, an organization in the process of strategy formulation must study the values of its executives. While exact measurement of values may not be possible, some awareness of the values held by top management is helpful to planners. Care should be taken not to threaten or alienate executives by

EXHIBIT 3-5
Influence of Personal Values on Objectives and Strategies

Example A

Values

The president of a small manufacturer of office duplicating equipment ranked relatively high on social values, giving particular attention to the security, welfare, and happiness of the employees. Second in order of importance to the president were aesthetic values.

Objectives and Strategies

1. Slow-to-moderate company growth
2. Emphasis on a single product
3. An independent-agent form of sales organization
4. Very high-quality products with aesthetic appeal
5. Refusal to compete on a price basis.

Example B

Values

The top-management team members of a high-fidelity loudspeaker systems manufacturer placed greater emphasis on theoretical and social values than on other values.

Objectives and Strategies

1. Scientific truth and integrity in advertising
2. Lower margins to dealers than competitors were paying
3. Maintenance of "truth and honesty" in relationships with suppliers, dealers, and employees.

Source: Reprinted by permission of the *Harvard Business Review*. Excerpt from "Personal Values and Corporate Strategies" by William D. Guth and Renato Tagiuri (September–October, 1965), pp. 137–138.

challenging their beliefs, traits, or outlooks. The strategy considering the value package of the management team should be duly formulated even if it means compromising on growth and profitability. Where no such compromise is feasible, it is better to transfer or change the assignment of a dissenting executive.

The experience of William Hartman, chairman of Interpace Corporation, is relevant here. After moving from International Telephone and Telegraph Corporation (ITT) in 1974, he drew on his ITT background to manage Interpace, a miniconglomerate with interests in such diverse products as teacups and concrete pipes. He used a formula that had worked well at ITT, which consisted of viewing assets primarily as financial pawns to be shifted around at the CEO's will, of compelling managers to abide by financial dicta, and of focusing on financial results. The approach seemed reasonable, but its implementation at Interpace was fraught with problems. ITT's management style did not fit the Interpace culture, despite the fact that Hartman replaced 35 members of a 51-person team.[32] Culture that prevents a company from meeting competitive threats or from adapting to changing economic or social environments can lead to stagnation and the company's ultimate demise unless the company makes a conscious effort to change.

FACTORS IN APPRAISAL: CORPORATE RESOURCES

The resources of a firm are its distinctive capabilities and strengths. Resources are relative in nature and must always be measured with reference to the competition. Resources can be categorized as financial strength, human resources, raw material reserve, engineering and production, overall management, and marketing strength. The marketing strategist needs to consider not only marketing resources but also resources of the company across the board. For example, price setting is a part of marketing strategy, yet it must be considered in the context of the financial strength of the company if the firm is to grow as rapidly as it should. It is obvious that profit margins on sales, combined with dividend policy, determine the amount of funds that a firm can generate internally. It is less well understood, but equally true, that if a firm uses more debt than its competitors or pays lower dividends, it can generate more funds for growth by decreasing profit margins. Thus it is important in strategy development that all of the firm's resources are fully utilized in a truly integrated way. The firm that does not use its resources fully is a target for the firm that will—even if the latter has fewer resources. Full and skillful utilization of resources can give a firm a distinct competitive edge.

Resources and Marketing Strategy

Consider the following resources of a company:

1. Has ample cash on hand (financial strength)
2. Average age of key management personnel is 42 years (human resources)
3. Has a superior raw material ingredient in reserve (raw material reserve)
4. Manufactures parts and components that go into the final product using the company's own facilities (plant and equipment)
5. The products of the company, if properly installed and serviced regularly, never stop while being used (technical competence)
6. Has knowledge of, a close relationship with, and expertise in doing business with grocery chains (marketing strength)

How do these resources affect marketing strategy? The cash-rich company, unlike the cash-tight company, is in a position to provide liberal credit accommodation to customers. GE, for example, established the General Electric Credit Corporation to help its dealers and ultimate customers to obtain credit. In the case of a manufacturer of durable goods whose products are usually bought on credit, the availability of easy credit can itself be the difference between success and failure in the marketplace.

If a company has a raw material reserve, it does not have to depend on outside suppliers when there are shortages. In the mid-1980s there was a shortage of high-grade paper. A magazine publisher with its own forests and paper manufacturing facilities did not have to depend on paper companies to acquire paper. Thus, even when a shortage forced its competitors to reduce the sizes of their magazines, the company not dependent on outsiders was able to provide the same preshortage product to its customers.

In the initial stages of the development of color television, RCA was the only company that manufactured color picture tubes. In addition to using these tubes in its own television sets, RCA also sold them to other manufacturers/competitors such as GE. When the market for color television began to grow, RCA was in a strong position to obtain a larger share of the growth partly because of its easy access to picture tubes. GE, on the other hand, was weaker in this respect.[33]

IBM's technical capabilities, among other things, helped it to be an innovator in developing data processing equipment and in introducing it to the market. IBM's excellent after-sale service facilities in themselves promoted the company's products. After-sale servicing put a promotional tool in the hands of salespeople to push the company's products.

Procter and Gamble is noted for its superior strength in dealing with grocery channels. The fact that this strength has served Procter and Gamble well hardly needs to be mentioned. More than anything else, marketing strength has helped Procter and Gamble to compete successfully with established companies, such as Coca-Cola and Seagram, in the frozen orange juice market. In brief, the resources of a company help it to establish and maintain itself in the marketplace. It is, of course, necessary for resources to be appraised objectively.

Measurement of Resources

A firm is a conglomerate of different entities, each having a number of variables that affects performance. How far should a strategist probe into these variables to designate the resources of the firm? Exhibit 3-6 is a list of possible strategic factors. Not all of these factors are important for every business; attention should be focused on those that could play a critical role in the success or failure of the particular firm. Therefore, the first step in designating resources is to have executives in different areas of the business go through the list and identify those variables that they deem strategic. Then each strategic factor may be evaluated either qualitatively or quantitatively. One way of conducting the evaluation is to frame relevant questions around each strategic factor, which may be rated on either a dichotomous or a continuous scale. As an example, the paragraphs that follow discuss questions relevant to a men's sportswear manufacturer.

Top Management. Which executives form the top management? Which manager can be held responsible for the firm's performance during the past few years? Is each manager capable of undertaking future challenges as well as past challenges were undertaken? Is something needed to boost the morale of top management? What are the distinguishing characteristics of each top executive? Are there any conflicts, such as personality conflicts, among them? If so, between whom and for what reasons? What has been done and is being done for organizational development? What are the reasons for the company's performance during the past few years? Are the old ways of managing obsolete? What more can be done to enhance the company's capabilities?

EXHIBIT 3-6
Strategic Factors in Business

A. General Managerial

1. Ability to attract and maintain high-quality top management
2. Ability to develop future managers for overseas operations
3. Ability to develop future managers for domestic operations
4. Ability to develop a better organizational structure
5. Ability to develop a better strategic planning program
6. Ability to achieve better overall control of company operations
7. Ability to use more new quantitative tools and techniques in decision making at
   a. Top management levels
   b. Lower management levels
8. Ability to assure better judgment, creativity, and imagination in decision making at
   a. Top management levels
   b. Lower management levels
9. Ability to use computers for problem solving and planning
10. Ability to use computers for information handling and financial control
11. Ability to divest nonprofitable enterprises
12. Ability to perceive new needs and opportunities for products
13. Ability to motivate sufficient managerial drive for profits

B. Financial

1. Ability to raise long-term capital at low cost
   a. Debt
   b. Equity
2. Ability to raise short-term capital
3. Ability to maximize value of stockholder investment
4. Ability to provide a competitive return to stockholders
5. Willingness to take risks with commensurate returns in what appear to be excellent new business opportunities in order to achieve growth objectives
6. Ability to apply return on investment criteria to research and development investments
7. Ability to finance diversification by means of
   a. Acquisitions
   b. In-house research and development

C. Marketing

1. Ability to accumulate better knowledge about markets
2. Ability to establish a wide customer base
3. Ability to establish a selective consumer base
4. Ability to establish an efficient product distribution system
5. Ability to get good business contracts (government and others)
6. Ability to assure imaginative advertising and sales promotion campaigns
7. Ability to use pricing more effectively (including discounts, customer credit, product service, guarantees, delivery, etc.)
8. Ability to develop better relationships between marketing and new product engineering and production
9. Ability to produce vigor in sales organization

EXHIBIT 3-6
continued

D. Engineering and Production

1. Ability to develop effective machinery and equipment replacement policies
2. Ability to provide more efficient plant layout
3. Ability to develop sufficient capacity for expansion
4. Ability to develop better materials and inventory control
5. Ability to improve product quality control
6. Ability to improve in-house product engineering
7. Ability to improve in-house basic product research capabilities
8. Ability to develop more effective profit improvement (cost reduction) programs
9. Ability to develop better ability to mass produce at low per-unit cost
10. Ability to relocate present production facilities
11. Ability to automate production facilities
12. Ability to inspire better management of and better results from research and development expenditures
13. Ability to establish foreign production facilities
14. Ability to develop more flexibility in using facilities for different products
15. Ability to be in the forefront of technology and be extremely scientifically creative

E. Products

1. Ability to improve present products
2. Ability to develop more efficient and effective product line selection
3. Ability to develop new products to replace old ones
4. Ability to develop new products in new markets
5. Ability to develop sales for present products in new markets
6. Ability to Diversify products by acquisition
7. Ability to attract more subcontracting
8. Ability to get bigger share of product market

F. Personnel

1. Ability to attract scientists and highly qualified technical employees
2. Ability to establish better relationships with employees
3. Ability to get along with labor unions
4. Ability to better utilize the skills of employees
5. Ability to motivate more employees to remain abreast of developments in their fields
6. Ability to level peaks and valleys of employment requirements
7. Ability to stimulate creativity in employees
8. Ability to optimize employee turnover (not too much and not too little)

G. Materials

1. Ability to get geographically closer to raw material sources
2. Ability to assure continuity of raw material supplies
3. Ability to find new sources of raw materials
4. Ability to own and control sources of raw materials
5. Ability to bring in house presently purchased materials and components
6. Ability to reduce raw material costs

Marketing. What are the major products/services of the company? What are the basic facts about each product (e.g., market share, profitability, position in the life cycle, major competitors and their strengths and weaknesses, etc.)? In which field can the firm be considered a leader? Why? What can be said about the firm's pricing policies (i.e., compared with value and with the prices of competitors)? What is the nature of new product development efforts, the coordination between research and development and manufacturing? How does the market look in the future for the planning period? What steps are being taken or proposed to meet future challenges? What can be said about the company's channel arrangements, physical distribution, and promotional efforts? What is the behavior of marketing costs? What new products are expected to be launched, when, and with what expectations? What has been done about consumer satisfaction?

Production. Are people capable of working on new machines, new processes, new designs, etc., which may be developed in the future? What new plant, equipment, and facilities are needed? What are the basic facts about each product (e.g., cost structure, quality control, work stoppages)? What is the nature of labor relations? Are any problems anticipated? What steps have been proposed or taken to avert strikes, work stoppages, and so forth? Does production perform its part effectively in the manufacturing of new products? How flexible are operations? Can they be made suitable for future competition and new products well on the way to being produced and marketed commercially? What steps have been proposed or taken to control pollution? What are the important raw materials being used or likely to be used? What are the important sources for each raw material? How reliable are these sources?

Finance. What is the financial standing of the company as a whole and of its different products/divisions in terms of earnings, sales, tangible net worth, working capital, earnings per share, liquidity, inventory, cash flow position, and capital structure? What is the cost of capital? Can money be used more productively? What is the reputation of the company in the financial community? How does the company's performance compare with that of competitors and other similarly sized corporations? What steps have been proposed or taken to line up new sources of capital, to increase return on investment through more productive use of resources, and to lower break-even points? Has the company managed tax matters aggressively? What contingency steps are proposed to avert threats of capital shortage or a takeover?

Research and Development. What is the research and development reputation of the company? What percentage of sales and profits in the past can be directly attributed to research and development efforts? Are there any conflicts or personality clashes in the department? If so, what has been proposed and what is being done? What is the status of current major projects? When are they expected to be completed? In what way will they help the company's performance? What kind of relationships does research and development have with marketing and manufacturing? What steps have been proposed and are being taken to cut overhead and improve quality? Are all scientists/researchers adequately used? If not, why not? Can we expect any breakthroughs from research and development? Are there any resentments? If so, what are they and for what reason do they exist?

Miscellaneous. What has been proposed or done to serve minorities, the community, the cause of education, and other such concerns? What is the nature of productivity gains for the company as a whole and for each part of the company? How does the company stand in comparison to industry trends and national goals? How well does the company compete in the world market? Which countries/companies constitute tough competitors? What are their strengths and weaknesses? What is the nature and scope of the company's public relations function? Is it adequate? How does it compare with that of competitors and other companies of similar size and character? Which government agencies—federal, state, or local—does the company deal with most often? Are the company's relationships with various levels of government satisfactory? Who are our stockholders? Do a few individuals/institutions hold majority stock? What are their corporate expectations? Do they prefer capital gains or dividend income?

Ratings on these questions may be added up to compute the total resource score in each area. It must be understood that not all questions can be evaluated using the same scale. In many cases quantitative measurement may be difficult and subjective evaluation has to be accepted. Further, measurement of resources should be done for current effectiveness and for future perspectives. Exhibit 3-7 shows two nine-point scales: one for current effectiveness and one for future perspectives. These scales can be simplified and/or altered to meet specific needs.

Strategic factors for success lie in different functional areas, the distribution network, for example, and they vary by industry. As shown in Exhibit 3-8, the

EXHIBIT 3-7
Scales for Measuring Resources

Current Effectiveness	*Future Perspectives*
9. Completely effective	9. Completely sound
8. Almost completely effective	8. Almost completely sound
7. Quite effective	7. Quite sound
6. Moderately effective	6. Moderately sound
5. As effective as ineffective	5. As sound as unsound
4. Moderately ineffective	4. Moderately unsound
3. Quite ineffective	3. Quite unsound
2. Almost completely ineffective	2. Almost completely unsound
1. Completely ineffective	1. Completely unsound

success factors for different industries fall at different points along a continuum of functional activities that begins with raw materials sourcing and ends with servicing. In the uranium industry, raw material sourcing is the key to success because low-quality ore requires much more complicated and costly processing. Inasmuch as the price of uranium does not vary among producers, the choice of the source of uranium supply is the crucial determinant of profitability. In contrast, the critical factor in the soda industry is production technology.[34] Because the mercury process is more than twice as efficient as the semipermeable membrane method of obtaining soda of similar quality, a company using the latter process is at a disadvantage no matter what else it might do to reduce extra cost. In other words, the use of mercury technology is a strategic resource for a soda company if its competitors have chosen not to go to the expense and difficulty of changing over from the semipermeable membrane method.

PAST PERFORMANCE OF BUSINESS UNITS

The past performance of business units serves as an important input in formulating corporatewide strategy. It helps in the assessment of the current situation and possible developments in the future. For example, if the profitability of

EXHIBIT 3-8
Sources of Competitive Information

	Specimen Industries	
Key Factor or Function	*To Increase Profit*	*To Gain Share*
Raw materials sourcing	Uranium	Petroleum
Product facilities (economies of scale)	Shipbuilding, steelmaking	Shipbuilding, steelmaking
Design	Aircraft	Aircraft, hi-fi
Production technology	Soda, semiconductors	Semiconductors
Product range/variety	Department stores	Components
Application engineering/engineers	Minicomputers	Large-scale integration (LSI), microprocessors
Sales force (quality × quantity)	Electronic code recorders (ECR)	Automobiles
Distribution network	Beer	Films, home appliances
Servicing	Elevators	Commercial vehicles (e.g., taxis)

Source: Kenichi Ohmae, *The Mind of the Strategist* (New York: McGraw-Hill Book Co., 1982), 47.

an SBU has been declining over the past five years, an appraisal of current performance as satisfactory cannot be justified, assuming the trend continues. In addition, any projected rise in profitability must be thoroughly justified in the light of this trend. The perspectives of different SBUs over time, vis-à-vis other factors (top management values, concerns of stakeholders, corporate resources, and the socioeconomic-political-technological environment), show which have the potential for profitable growth.

SBU performance is based on such measures as financial strength (sales—dollar or volume—operating profit before taxes, cash flow, depreciation, sales per employee, profits per employee, investment per employee, return on investment/sales/assets, and asset turnover); human resources (use of employee skills, productivity, turnover, and ethnic and racial composition); facilities (rated capacity, capacity utilization, and modernization); inventories (raw materials, finished products, and obsolete inventory); marketing (research and development expenditures, new product introductions, number of salespersons, sales per salesperson, independent distributors, exclusive distributors, and promotion expenditures); international business (growth rate and geographic coverage); and managerial performance (leadership capabilities, planning, development of personnel, and delegation).

Usually the volume of data that the above information would generate is much greater than required. It is desirable, therefore, for management to specify what measures it considers important in appraising the performance of SBUs. From the viewpoint of corporate management, the following three measures are frequently the principal measures of performance:

1. **Effectiveness** measures the success of a business's products and programs in relation to those of its competitors in the market. Effectiveness commonly is measured by such items as sales growth in comparison with that of competitors or by changes in market share.
2. **Efficiency** is the outcome of a business's programs in relation to the resources employed in implementing them. Common measures of efficiency are profitability as a percentage of sales and return on investment.
3. **Adaptability** is the business's success in responding over time to changing conditions and opportunities in the environment. Adaptability can be measured in a variety of ways, but common measures are the number of successful new product introductions in relation to those of competitors and the percentage of sales accounted for by products introduced within some recent time period.[35]

To ensure consistency in information received from different SBUs, it is worthwhile to develop a pro forma sheet listing the categories of information that corporate management desires. The general profile produced from the evaluation of information obtained through pro forma sheets provides a quick picture of how well things are going.

SUMMARY

Corporate appraisal constitutes an important ingredient in the strategy development process because it lays the foundation for the company to interact with the future environment. Corporate publics, value orientation of top management, and corporate resources were the three principal factors in appraisal discussed in this chapter. Appraisal of the past performance of business units, which also affects formulation of corporate strategy for the future, was covered briefly.

Corporate publics are all those groups having a stake in the organization; that is, owners, employees, customers, suppliers, the banking community and other lenders, government, the community in which the company does business, and society at large. Expetiations of all stakeholders should be considered in formulating corporate strategy. Corporate strategy is also deeply influenced by the value orientation of the corporation's top management. Thus, the values of top management should be studied and duly assessed in setting objectives. Finally, the company's resources in different areas should be carefully evaluated. They serve as major criteria for the formulation of future perspectives.

DISCUSSION QUESTIONS

1. How often should a company undertake corporate appraisal? What are the arguments for and against yearly corporate appraisal?
2. Discuss the pros and cons of having a consultant conduct the appraisal.
3. Identify five companies that in your opinion have failed to change with time and have either pulled out of the marketplace or continue in it as laggards.
4. Identify five companies that in your opinion have kept pace with time as evidenced by their performance.
5. What expectations does a community have of (a) a bank, (b) a medical group, and (c) a manufacturer of cyclical goods?
6. What top management values are most likely to lead to a growth orientation?
7. Is growth orientation necessarily good? Discuss.
8. In your opinion what marketing resources are the most critical for success in the cosmetics industry?
9. How should a company go about identifying the critical factors for success in its business?

NOTES

[1]*Perspectives on Corporate Strategy* (Boston: Boston Consulting Group, 1968), 93.

[2]John C. Boland, "Shareholders vs. Stakeholders," *Wall Street Journal*, 10 February 1988, p. 20. Also see George Mellon, "NCR's Exley Manages for His 'Stakeholders,' " *Wall Street Journal*, 16 June 1987, p. 31.

[3]Donald P. Robin and R. Eric Reidenback, "Social Responsibility Ethics and Marketing Strategy: Closing the Gap between Concept and Application," *Journal of Marketing* (January 1987): 55.

[4]Robin and Reidenbach, "Social Responsibility," 52.

[5]Thornton Bradshaw and David Vogel, eds., *Corporations and Their Critics* (New York: McGraw-Hill Book Co., 1981), 106.

[6]See Peter F. Drucker, "A New Look at Corporate Social Responsibility," in *Public-Private Partnership*, ed. H. Brooks, L. Liebman, and C. Schelling (Lexington, MA: Ballinger Publishing Co., 1984).

[7]Frederick D. Sturdivant, *Business and Society—A Managerial Approach* (Homewood, IL: Richard D. Irwin, Inc., 1977), chapter 4.

[8]See Mark Dowie, "Mother Jones Goes Searching for Excellence," *Wall Street Journal,* 6 May 1985, p. 34.

[9]"The Battle for Corporate Control," *Business Week* (18 May 1987): 102.

[10]Robert F. Lusch and Gene R. Laczniak, "The Evolving Marketing Concept, Competitive Intensity and Organizational Performance," *Journal of the Academy of Marketing Science* (Fall 1987): 10.

[11]"Corning's Class Act," *Business Week* (13 May 1991): 76.

[12]See William Rothje, "A Clash of Good Intentions," *Atlantic Monthly* (June 1986).

[13] George A. Steiner, *Top Management Planning* (New York: Macmillan Co., 1969), 241.

[14]Thomas J. Peters, "Putting Excellence into Management," *McKinsey Quarterly* (Autumn 1980): 37.

[15]"Where Different Styles Have Led Two Canmakers," *Business Week* (27 July 1981): 81–82. See also Bernard Wysocki, Jr., "The Chief's Personality Can Have a Big Impact—For Better or Worse," *Wall Street Journal,* 11 September 1984, p. 1.

[16]Rohit Deshpande and Frederick E. Webster, Jr., "Organizational Culture and Marketing: Defining the Research Agenda," *Journal of Marketing* (January 1989): 3–15.

[17]Terrence E. Deal and Allen A. Kennedy, *Corporate Cultures* (Reading, MA: Addison-Wesley Publishing Co., 1982).

[18]"Changing a Corporate Culture," *Business Week* (14 May 1984): 130. Also see Bala Chakravarthy, Worth Loomis, and John Vrabel, "Dexter Corporation's Value-Based Strategic Planning System," *Planning Review* (January–February 1988): 34–41.

[19]Brian Dumaine, "P&G Rewrites the Marketing Rules," *Fortune* (6 November 1989): 34.

[20]Shelby D. Hunt, Van R. Wood, and Lawrence B. Chonko, "Corporate Ethical Values and Organizational Commitment in Marketing," *Journal of Marketing* (July 1989): 79–90. See also Henry Mintzberg, "Who Should Control the Corporation?" *California Management Review* (Fall 1984): 90–115.

[21]See Robert M. Donnelly, "The Interrelationship of Planning with Corporate Culture in the Creation of Shared Values," *Managerial Planning* (May–June 1984): 8–13. Also see "Executives Need to Fit Corporate 'Marketing Culture,' " *Marketing News* (20 October 1984): 4.

[22]"Corporate Culture," *Business Week* (27 October 1980): 148. See also Geoffrey Colvin, "The De-Geneening of ITT," *Fortune* (11 January 1982): 34.

[23]"Corporate Culture," 34. See also Bro Uttal, "The Corporate Culture Vultures," *Fortune* (17 October 1983): 66–73; Trish Hall, "Demanding Pepsi Company Is Attempting to Make Work Nicer for Managers," *Wall Street Journal,* 23 October 1984, p. 31.

[24]Carol Hymowitz, "Which Corporate Culture Fits You?" *Wall Street Journal,* 17 July 1989, p. B1.

[25]Andrew Kupfer, "Bob Allen Rattles the Cages at AT&T," *Fortune* (19 June 1989): 58.

[26]Brian Dumaine, "Creating a New Company Culture," *Fortune* (15 January 1990): 128.

[27]Gordon W. Allport, Philip E. Vernon, and Gardner Lindzey, *Study of Values and the Manual of Study of Values* (Boston: Houghton Mifflin Co., 1960).

[28]See Charles Margerison, *How to Assess Your Managerial Style* (New York: AMACOM, 1979).

[29]B. F. Skinner, *Beyond Freedom and Dignity* (New York: Alfred A. Knopf, 1971).

[30]Aimee L. Horner, "Jack Hanley Got There by Selling Harder," *Fortune* (November 1976): 162.

[31]"Corporate Culture," 34.

[32]"How a Winning Formula Can Fail," *Business Week* (25 May 1981): 119–20.

[33]"General Electric Radio and Television Division," a case copyrighted by the President and Fellows of Harvard College, 1967.

[34]Kenichi Ohmae, *The Mind of the Strategist* (New York: McGraw-Hill Book Co., 1982), 46–47.

[35]Orville C. Walker, Jr., and Robert W. Ruekert, "Marketing's Role in the Implementation of Business Strategies: A Critical Review and Conceptual Framework," *Journal of Marketing* (July 1987): 19.

CHAPTER 4
Understanding Competition

The most complete and happy victory is this: to compel one's enemy to give up his purpose, while suffering no harm oneself.

BELISARIUS

In a free market economy, each company tries to outperform its competitors. A competitor is a rival. A company must know, therefore, how it stands up against each competitor with regard to "arms and ammunition"—skill in maneuvering opportunities, preparedness in reacting to threats, and so on. To obtain adequate knowledge about the competition, a company needs an excellent intelligence network.

Typically, whenever one talks about competition, emphasis is placed on price, quality of product, delivery time, and other marketing variables. For the purposes of strategy development, however, one needs to go far beyond these marketing tactics. Simply knowing that a competitor has been lowering prices, for example, is not sufficient. Over and above that, one must know how much flexibility the competitor has in further reducing the price. Implicit here is the need for information about the competitor's cost structure.

This chapter begins by examining the meaning of competition. The theory of competition is reviewed, and a scheme for classifying competitors is advanced. Various sources of competitive intelligence are mentioned, and models for understanding competitive behavior are discussed. Finally, the impact of competition in formulating marketing strategy is analyzed.

MEANING OF COMPETITION

The term *competition* defies definition because the view of competition held by different groups (e.g., lawyers, economists, government officials, and businesspeople) varies. Most firms define competition in crude, simplistic, and unrealistic terms. Some firms fail to identify the true sources of competition; others underestimate the capabilities and reactions of their competitors. When the business climate is stable, a shallow outlook toward the competition might work, but in the current environment, business strategies must be competitively oriented.

Natural and Strategic Competition

A useful way to define competition is to differentiate between natural and strategic competition. **Natural competition** refers to the survival of the fittest in a given environment. It is an evolutionary process that weeds out the weaker of two rivals. Applied to the business world, it means that no two firms doing business across the board the same way in the same market can coexist forever. To survive, each firm must have something uniquely superior to the other.

Natural competition is an extension of the biological phenomenon of Darwinian natural selection. Characteristically, this type of competition—evolution by adaptation—occurs by trial and error; is wildly opportunistic day to day; pursues growth for its own sake; and is very conservative, because growth from successful trials must prevail over death (i.e., bankruptcy) by random mistake.

Strategic competition, on the other hand, tries to leave nothing to chance. In Bruce Henderson's definition, **strategic competition** is the studied deployment of resources based on a high degree of insight into the systematic cause and effect in the business ecological system. Strategic competition is a new phenomenon in the business world that may well have the same impact upon business productivity that the industrial revolution had upon individual productivity. Strategic competition requires (a) an adequate amount of information about the situation, (b) development of a framework to understand the dynamic interactive system, (c) postponement of current consumption to provide investment capital, (d) commitment to invest major resources to an irreversible outcome, and (e) an ability to predict the output consequences even with incomplete knowledge of inputs. Henderson identifies the basic elements of strategic competition as follows:

- The ability to understand competitive interaction as a complete dynamic system that includes the interaction of competitors, customers, money, people, and resources
- The ability to use this understanding to predict the consequences of a given intervention in the system and how that intervention will result in new patterns of equilibrium
- The availability of uncommitted resources that can be dedicated to different uses and purposes in the present even though the dedication is permanent and the benefits will be deferred
- The ability to predict risk and return with sufficient accuracy and confidence to justify the commitment of such resources
- The willingness to deliberately act to make the commitment[1]

Japan's emergence as a major industrial power over a short span of time illustrates the practical application of strategic competition.

> The differences between Japan and the U.S. deserve some comparative analysis. There are lessons to be learned. These two leading industrial powers came from different directions, developed different methods, and followed different strategies.
>
> Japan is a small group of islands whose total land area is smaller than a number of our 50 states. The U.S. by comparison is a vast land.
>
> Japan is mountainous with very little arable land. The U.S. is the world's largest and most fertile agricultural area in a single country.

Japan has virtually no energy or natural resources. The U.S. is richly endowed with energy, minerals and other vital resources.

Japan has one of the oldest, most homogenous, most stable cultures. For 2,000 years or more, there was virtually no immigration, no dilution of culture or any foreign invasion. The U.S. has been a melting pot of immigrants from many cultures and many languages over one-tenth the time span. For most of our history, the U.S. has been an agrarian society and a frontier society.

The Japanese developed a high order of skill in living together in cooperation over many centuries. We Americans developed a frontier mentality of self-reliance and every man for himself.

The evolution of the U.S. into a vast industrial society was a classic example of natural competition in a rich environment with no constraints or artificial barriers.

This option was not open to Japan. It had been in self-imposed isolation from the rest of the world for several hundred years until Commodore Perry sailed into Tokyo harbor and forced the signing of a navigation and trade treaty. Japan had been unaware of the industrial revolution already well underway in the West. It decided to compete in that world. But it had no resources.

To rise above a medieval economy, Japan had to obtain foreign materials. To obtain foreign materials, it had to buy them. To buy abroad required foreign exchange. To obtain foreign exchange exports were required. Exports became Japan's lifeline. But effective exports meant the maximum value added, first with minimum material and then with minimum direct labor. Eventually this led Japan from labor intensive to capital intensive and then to technology intensive businesses. Japan was forced to develop strategic business competition as part of national policy.[2]

THEORY OF COMPETITION

Competition is basic to the free enterprise system. It is involved in all observable phenomena of the market—the prices at which products are exchanged, the kinds and qualities of products produced, the quantities exchanged, the methods of distribution employed, and the emphasis placed on promotion. Over many decades economists have contributed to the theory of competition. A well-recognized body of theoretical knowledge about competition has emerged and can be grouped broadly into two categories: (a) economic theory and (b) industrial organization perspective. These and certain other hypotheses on competition from the viewpoint of businesspeople will now be introduced.

Economic Theory of Competition

Economists have worked with many different models of competition. Still central to much of their work is the model of *perfect competition,* which is based on the premise that, when a large number of buyers and sellers in the market are dealing in homogeneous products, there is complete freedom to enter or exit the market and everyone has complete and accurate knowledge about everyone else.

Industrial Organization Perspective

The essence of the industrial organization (IO) perspective is that a firm's position in the marketplace depends critically on the characteristics of the industry environment in which it competes. The industry environment comprises structure, conduct, and performance. This structure refers to the economic and technical perspectives of the industry in the context in which firms compete. It includes (a) concentration in the industry (i.e., the number and size distribution of firms), (b) barriers to entry in the industry, and (c) product differentiation among the offerings of different firms that make up the industry. Conduct, which is essentially strategy, refers to firm's behavior in such matters as pricing, advertising, and distribution. Performance includes social performance, measured in terms of allocative efficiency (profitability), technical efficiency (cost minimization), and innovativeness.

Following the IO thesis, the structure of each industry vis-à-vis concentration, product differentiation, and entry barriers varies. Structure plays an important role in the competitive behavior of different firms in the market.

> Businessmen must be continually aware of the structure of the markets they are presently in or of those they seek to enter. Their appraisal of their present and future competitive posture will be influenced substantially by the size and concentration of existing firms as well as by the extent of product differentiation and the presence or absence of significant barriers to entry.
>
> If a manager has already introduced his firm's products into a market, the existence of certain structural features may provide him with a degree of insulation from the intrusion of firms not presently in that market. The absence, or relative unimportance, of one or more entry barriers, for example, supplies the manager with insights into the direction from which potential competition might come. Conversely, the presence or absence of entry barriers indicates the relative degree of effort required and the success that might be enjoyed if he attempted to enter a specific market. In short, a fundamental purpose of marketing strategy involves the building of entry barriers to protect present markets and the overcoming of existing entry barriers around markets that have an attractive potential.[3]

Business Viewpoint

From the businessperson's perspective, **competition** refers to rivalry among firms operating in a market to fill the same customer need. The businessperson's major interest is to keep the market to himself or herself by adopting appropriate strategies. How and why competition occurs, its intensity, and what escape routes are feasible have not been conceptualized.[4] In other words, no formulation of a theory of competition from the business viewpoint exists.

In recent years, however, Henderson has developed the theory of strategic competition discussed above. Some of the hypotheses on which his theory rests derive from military warfare:[5]

- Competitors who persist and survive have a unique advantage over all others. If they did not have this advantage, then others would crowd them out of the market.
- If competitors are different and coexist, then each must have a distinct advantage over the other. Such an advantage can only exist if differences in a competitor's characteristics match differences in the environment that give those characteristics their relative value.
- Any change in the environment changes the factor weighting of environmental characteristics and, therefore, shifts the boundaries of competitive equilibrium and "competitive segments." Competitors who adapt best or fastest gain an advantage from change in the environment.[6]

Henderson presents an interesting new way of looking at the marketplace: as a battleground where opposing forces (competitors) devise ways (strategies) to outperform each other. According to Henderson, some of his hypotheses can be readily observed, tested, and validated and could lead to a general theory of business competition. However, many of his interlocking hypotheses must still be revised and tested, with the science of sociobiology playing a big role. As Henderson observes:

> To understand competition and its homeostasis, we must be able to integrate its entire system. The quantification of sociobiology has demonstrated the power of analysis when competition is viewed as a dynamic, ever-changing system.
>
> If competition is fully understood as a system, the benefits in rationalization of public policy with respect to antitrust regulation and international trade can be far-reaching.
>
> I believe that insight into strategic competition has the promise of quantum increase in our productivity and our ability to both control and expand the potential of our own future.[7]

CLASSIFYING COMPETITORS

A business may face competition from various sources either within or outside its industry. Competition may come from essentially similar products or from substitutes. The competitor may be a small firm or a large multinational corporation. To gain an adequate perspective on the competition, a firm needs to identify all current and potential sources of competition.

Competition is triggered when different industries try to serve the same customer needs and demands. For example, a customer's entertainment needs may be filled by television, sports, publishing, or travel. New industries may also enter the arena to satisfy entertainment needs. In the early 1980s, for example, the computer industry entered the entertainment field with video games.

Different industries position themselves to serve different customer demands—existing, latent, and incipient. **Existing demand** occurs when a product is bought to satisfy a recognized need. **Latent demand** refers to a situation where a particular need has been recognized, but no products have yet been offered to satisfy the need. **Incipient demand** occurs when certain trends lead to the emergence of a need of which the customer is not yet aware.

A competitor may be an existing firm or a new entrant. The new entrant may enter the market with a product developed through research and development or through acquisition. For example, Texas Instruments entered the educational toy business through research and development that led to the manufacture of their Speak and Spell product. Philip Morris entered the beer market by acquiring Miller Brewery Company.

Often an industry competes by producing different product lines. General Foods Corporation, for example, offers ground, regular instant, freeze-dried, decaffeinated, and "international" coffee to the coffee market. Product lines can be grouped into three categories: a me-too product, an improved product, or a breakthrough product. A **me-too product** is similar to current offerings. One of many brands currently available in the market, it offers no special advantage over competing products. An **improved product** is one that, while not unique, is generally superior to many existing brands. A **breakthrough product** is an innovation and is usually technical in nature. The digital watch and the color television set were once breakthrough products.

In the watch business, companies have traditionally competed by offering me-too products. Occasionally, a competitor comes out with an improved product, as Bulova did in the early 1960s by introducing the Caravelle line of watches. Caravelle watches were a little fancier and supposedly more accurate than other watches. Texas Instruments, however, entered the watch business via a breakthrough product, the digital watch.

Finally, the scope of a competing firm's activities may be limited or extensive. For example, PepsiCo may not worry if a regional chain of pizza parlors is established to compete against its Pizza Hut subsidiary. However, if Procter and Gamble were to enter the pizza restaurant business, PepsiCo would be concerned at the entry of such a strong and seasoned competitor.

Exhibit 4-1 illustrates various sources of competition available to fulfill the liquid requirements of the human body. Let us analyze the competition here for a company that maintains an interest in this field. Currently the thrust of the market is to satisfy existing demand. An example of a product to satisfy latent demand would be a liquid that promises weight loss; a liquid to prevent aging would be an example of a product to satisfy incipient demand.

The industries that currently offer products to quench customer thirst are the liquor, beer, wine, soft drink, milk, coffee, tea, drinking water, and fruit juice industries. A relatively new entrant is mineral and sparkling water. Looking just at the soft drink industry, assuming that this is the field that most interests our company, we see that the majority of competitors offer me-too products (e.g., regular cola, diet cola, lemonade, and other fruit-based drinks). However, caffeine-free cola has been introduced by two major competitors, Coca-Cola Company and PepsiCo. There has been a breakthrough in the form of low-calorie, caffeine-free drinks. A beverage containing a day's nutritional requirements is feasible in the future.

The companies that currently compete in the regular cola market are Coca-Cola, PepsiCo, Seven-Up, Dr. Pepper, and a few others. Among these, however, the first two have a major share of the cola market. Among new industry entrants, General Foods Corporation and Nestle Company are likely candidates (an assumption). The two principal competitors, Coca-Cola Company and PepsiCo, are large multinational, multibusiness firms. This is the competitive arena where our company will have to fight if it enters the soft drink business.

INTENSITY, OR DEGREE, OF COMPETITION

The degree of competition in a market depends on the moves and countermoves of various firms active in the market. Usually it starts with one firm

EXHIBIT 4-1
Sources of Competition

Customer Need: Liquid for the Body	
Existing need	Thirst
Latent need	Liquid to reduce weight
Incipient need	Liquid to prevent aging
Industry Competition (How Can I Quench My Thirst?)	
Existing industries	Hard liquor Beer Wine Soft drink Milk Coffee Tea Water
New industry	Mineral water
Product Line Competition (What Form of Product Do I Want?)	
Me-too products	Regular cola Diet cola Lemonade Fruit-based drink
Improved product	Caffeine-free cola
Breakthrough product	Diet and caffeine-free cola providing full nutrition
Organizational Competition (What Brand Do I Want?)	
Type of Firm	
Existing firms	Coca-Cola PepsiCo Seven-Up Dr. Pepper
New entrants	General Foods Nestle
Scope of Business	
Geographic	Regional, national, multinational
Product/market	Single versus multiproduct industry

trying to achieve a favorable position by pursuing appropriate strategies. Because what is good for one firm may be harmful to rival firms, rival firms respond with counterstrategies to protect their interests.

Intense competitive activity may or may not be injurious to the industry as a whole. For example, while a price war may result in lower profits for all members of an industry, an advertising battle may increase demand and actually be mutually beneficial. Exhibit 4-2 lists the factors that affect the intensity of competition in the marketplace. In a given situation, a combination of factors determines the degree of competition.

Opportunity Potential

A promising market is likely to attract firms seeking to capitalize on an available opportunity. As the number of firms interested in sharing the pie increases, the degree of rivalry increases. Take, for example, the home computer market. In the early 1980s, everyone from mighty IBM to such unknowns in the field as Timex Watch Company wanted a piece of the personal computer pie. As firms started jockeying for position, the intensity of competition increased manifold. Texas Instruments, for example, drastically reduced the price of its home computers, leaving such firms as Apple and Atari no choice but to slash their own prices.[8]

Ease of Entry

When entry into an industry is relatively easy, many firms, including some marginal ones, are attracted to it. The long-standing, committed members of the industry, however, do not want "outsiders" to break into their territory. Therefore existing firms discourage potential entrants by adopting strategies that enhance competition.

Nature of Product

When the products offered by different competitors are perceived by customers to be more or less similar, firms are forced into price and, to a lesser degree, service competition. In such situations, competition can be really severe.

Exit Barriers

For a variety of reasons, it may be difficult for a firm to get out of a particular business. Possible reasons include the relationship of the business to other businesses of the firm, high investment in assets for which there may not be an advantageous alternative use, high cost of discharging commitments (e.g., fixed

EXHIBIT 4-2
Factors Contributing to Competitive Rivalry

Opportunity potential
Ease of entry
Nature of product
Exit barriers
Homogeneity of market
Industry structure or competitive position of firms
Commitment to the industry
Feasibility of technological innovations
Scale economies
Economic climate
Diversity of firms

labor contracts and future purchasing agreements), top management's emotional attachment to the business, and government regulations prohibiting exit (e.g., the legal requirement that a utility must serve all customers).

Homogeneity of the Market When the entire market represents one large homogeneous unit, the intensity of competition is much greater than when the market is segmented. Even if the product sold is a commodity, segmentation of the market is possible. It is possible, for example, to identify frequent buyers of the commodity as one segment; occasional buyers as another. But if a market is not suited to segmentation, firms must compete to serve it homogeneously, thus intensifying competition.

Industry Structure When the number of firms active in a market is large, there is a good chance that one of the firms may aggressively seek an advantageous position. Such aggression leads to intense competitive activity as firms retaliate. On the other hand, if only a few firms constitute an industry, there is usually little doubt about industry leadership. In situations where there is a clear industry leader, care is often taken not to irritate the leader since a resulting fight could be very costly.

Commitment to the Industry When a firm has wholeheartedly committed itself to a business, it will do everything to hang on, even becoming a maverick that fearlessly makes moves without worrying about the impact on either the industry or its own resources. Polaroid Corporation, for example, with its strong commitment to instant photography, must maintain its position in the field at any cost. Such an attachment to an industry enhances competitive activity.

Feasibility of Technological Innovations In industries where technological innovations are frequent, each firm likes to do its best to cash in while the technology lasts, thus triggering greater competitive activity.

Scale Economies Where economies realizable through large-scale operations are substantial, a firm will do all it can to achieve scale economies. Attempts to capture scale economies may lead a firm to aggressively compete for market share, escalating pressures on other firms. A similar situation occurs when a business's fixed costs are high and the firm must spread them over a large volume. If capacity can only be added in large increments, the resulting excess capacity will also intensify competition.

Economic Climate During depressed economic conditions and otherwise slow growth, competition is much more volatile as each firm tries to make the best of a bad situation.

Diversity of Firms Firms active in a field over a long period come to acquire a kind of industry standard of behavior. But new participants invading an industry do not necessarily like to play the old game. Forsaking industry patterns, newcomers may have different strategic perspectives and may be willing to go to any lengths to achieve their goals. The Miller Brewery Company's unconventional marketing practices are a case in point. Miller, nurtured and guided by its parent, Philip Morris, segmented the market by introducing a light beer to an industry that had hitherto considered beer a commodity-type product. When different cultures meet in the marketplace, competition can be fierce.

COMPETITIVE INTELLIGENCE

Competitive intelligence is the publicly available information on competitors, current and potential, that serves as an important input in formulating marketing strategy. No general would order an army to march without first fully knowing the enemy's position and intentions. Likewise, before deciding which competitive moves to make, a firm must be aware of the perspectives of its competitors. Competitive intelligence includes information beyond industry statistics and trade gossip. It involves close observation of competitors to learn what they do best and why and where they are weak and why. No self-respecting business admits to not doing an adequate job of scanning the competitive environment, but what sets the outstanding companies apart from the merely self-respecting ones is that they watch their competition in such depth and with such dedication that, as a marketing executive once remarked to the author, "The information on competitive moves reaches them before even the management of the competing company learns about it."

Three types of competitive intelligence may be distinguished: defensive, passive, and offensive intelligence.[9] **Defensive intelligence**, as the name suggests, is gathered to avoid being caught off balance. A deliberate attempt is made to gather information on the competition in a structured fashion and to keep track of moves that are relevant to the firm's business. **Passive intelligence** is ad hoc information gathered for a specific decision. A company may, for example, seek information on a competitor's sales compensation plan when devising its own compensation plan. Finally, **offensive intelligence** is undertaken to identify new opportunities. From a strategic perspective, offensive intelligence is the most relevant.

Strategic Usefulness of Competitive Intelligence

Such information as how competitors make, test, distribute, price, and promote their products can go a long way in developing a viable marketing strategy. The Ford Motor Company, for example, has an ongoing program for tearing down competitors' products to learn about their cost structure. Exhibit 4-3 summarizes the process followed at Ford. This competitive knowledge has helped Ford in its strategic moves in Europe. For example, from regularly tearing down the Leyland Mini (a small truck), the company concluded that (a) Leyland was not making money on the Mini at its current price and (b) Ford should not enter the small truck market at current price levels. Based on these conclusions, Ford was able to arrive at a firm strategic decision not to assemble a "Mini."

The following example compares two companies that decided to enter the automatic dishwasher market at about the same time. One of the companies ignored the competition, floundered, and eventually abandoned the field; the

EXHIBIT 4-3
Ford Motor Company's Competitive Product Tear-Down Process

1. **Purchase the product.** The high cost of product teardown, particularly for a carmaker, gives some indication of the value successful competitors place on the knowledge they gain.
2. **Tear the product down—literally.** First, every removable component is unscrewed or unbolted; the rivets are undone; finally, individual spot welds are broken.
3. **Reverse-engineer the product.** While the competitor's car is being dismantled, detailed drawings of parts are made and parts lists are assembled, together with analyses of the production processes that were evidently involved.
4. **Build up costs.** Parts are costed out in terms of make-or-buy, the variety of parts used in a single product, and the extent of common assemblies across model ranges. Among the important facts to be established in a product teardown, obviously, are the number and variety of components and the number of assembly operations. The costs of the processes are then built up from both direct labor requirements and overheads (often vital to an understanding of competitor cost structures).
5. **Establish economies of scale.** Once individual cost elements are known, they can be put together with the volume of cars produced by the competitor and the total number of people employed to develop some fairly reliable guides to the competitor's economies of scale. Having done this, Ford can calculate model-run lengths and volumes needed to achieve, first, break even and then profit.

Source: Robin Leaf, "How to Pick Up Tips from Your Competitors," *Director* (February 1978): 60.

other did a superior job of learning from the competition and came out on top. When the CEO of the first company, a British company, learned from his marketing department about the market growth potential for dishwashers and about current competitors' shares, he lost no time setting out to develop a suitable machine.

Finding little useful information available on dishwasher design, the director of research and development decided to begin by investigating the basic mechanics of the dishwashing process. Accordingly, she set up a series of pilot projects to evaluate the cleaning performance of different jet configurations, the merits of alternative washing-arm designs, and the varying results obtained with different types and quantities of detergent on different washing loads. At the end of a year she had amassed a great deal of useful knowledge. She also had a pilot machine running that cleansed dishes well and a design concept for a production version. But considerable development work was still needed before the prototype could be declared a satisfactory basis for manufacture.

To complicate matters, management had neglected to establish effective linkages among the company's three main functions—marketing, technology and production. So it was not until the technologists had produced the prototype and design concepts that marketing and production began asking for revisions and suggesting new ideas, further delaying the development of a marketable product.

So much for the first company, with its fairly typical traditional response to market opportunities. The second company, which happened to be Japanese, started with the same marketing intelligence but responded in very different fashion.

First, it bought three units of every available competitive dishwasher. Next, management formed four special teams: (a) a product test group of marketing and technical staff, (b) a design team of technologists and production people, (c) a distribution team of marketing and production staff, and (d) a field team of production staff.

The product test group was given one of each competitive model and asked to evaluate performance: dishwashing effectiveness, ease of use, and reliability (frequency and cause of breakdown). The remaining two units of each competitive model were given to the design team, who stripped down one of each pair to determine the number and variety of parts, the cost of each part, and the ease of assembly. The remaining units were stripped down to "life-test" each component, to identify design improvements and potential sources of supply, and to develop a comprehensive picture of each competitor's technology. Meanwhile the distribution team was evaluating each competitor's sales and distribution system (numbers of outlets, product availability, and service offered), and the field team was investigating competitors' factories and evaluating their production facilities in terms of cost of labor, cost of supplies, and plant productivity.

All this investigating took a little less than a year. At the end of that time, the Japanese still knew a lot less about the physics and chemistry of dishwashing than their British rivals, but the knowledge developed by their business teams had put them far ahead. In two more months they had designed a product that outperformed the best of the competition, yet would cost 30 percent less to build, based on a preproduction prototype and production process design. They also had a marketing plan for introducing the new dishwasher to the Japanese domestic market before taking it overseas. This plan positioned the product relative to the competition and defined distribution system requirements in terms of stocking and service levels needed to meet the expected production rate. Finally, the Japanese had prepared detailed plans for building a new factory, establishing supply contracts, and training the labor force.

The denouement of this story is what one might expect: the competitive Japanese manufacturer brought its new product to market two years ahead of the more traditionally minded British manufacturer and achieved its planned market share 10 weeks later. The traditional company steadily lost money and eventually dropped out of the market.[10]

As the above anecdote shows, competitive analysis has three major objectives:

1. It allows you to understand your position of comparative advantage and your competitors' positions of comparative advantage.
2. It allows you to understand your competitors' strategies—past, present, and as they are likely to be in the future.

3. It is a key criterion of strategy selection, the element that makes your strategies come alive in the real world.

Knowing the Competition

Knowledge about the competition may be gained by raising the following questions. To answer each question requires systematic probing and data gathering on different aspects of competition.

- Who is the competition? now? five years from now?
- What are the strategies, objectives, and goals of each major competitor?
- How important is a specific market to each competitor and what is the level of its commitment?
- What are the relative strengths and limitations of each competitor?
- What weaknesses make competitors vulnerable?
- What changes are competitors likely to make in their future strategies?
- So what? What will be the effects of all competitors' strategies, on the industry, the market, and our strategy?[11]

The following procedure may be adopted to review competition:

1. **Recognize key competitors in market segments in which the company is active.** Presumably a product will be positioned to serve one or more market segments. In each segment there may be different competitors to reckon with; an attempt should be made to recognize all important competitors in each segment. If the number of competitors is excessive, it is sufficient to limit consideration to the first three competitors. Each competitor should be briefly profiled to indicate total corporate proportion.
2. **Analyze the performance record of each competitor.** The performance of a competitor can be measured with reference to a number of criteria. As far as marketing is concerned, sales growth, market share, and profitability are the important measures of success. Thus, a review of each competitor's sales growth, market share, and profitability for the past several years is desirable. In addition, any ad hoc reasons that bear upon a competitor's performance should be noted. For example, a competitor may have lined up some business, in the nature of a windfall from Kuwait without making any strategic moves to secure the business. Similar missteps that may limit performance should be duly pointed out. Occasionally a competitor may intentionally pad results to reflect good performance at year end. Such tactics should be noted, too. Rothschild advises the following:

   > To make it really useful, you must probe how each participant keeps its books and records its profits. Some companies stress earnings; others report their condition in such a way as to delay the payment of taxes; still other bookkeep to increase cash availability.
   >
   > These measurements are important because they may affect the company's ability to procure financing and attract people as well as influence stockholders' and investors' satisfaction with current management.[12]

3. **Study how satisfied each competitor appears to be with its performance.** Refer to each competitor's objective(s) for the product. If results are in concert with the expectations of the firm's management and stakeholders, the competitor will be satisfied. A satisfied competitor is most likely to follow its current

successful strategy. On the other hand, if results are at odds with management expectations, the competitor is most likely to come out with a new strategy.

4. **Probe each competitor's marketing strategy.** The strategy of each competitor can be inferred from game plans (i.e., different moves in the area of product, price, promotion, and distribution) that are pursued to achieve objectives. Information on game plans is available partly from published stories on the competitor and partly from the salespeople in contact with the competitor's customers and salespeople.

   To clarify the point, consider a competitor in the small appliances business who spends heavily for consumer advertising and sells products mainly through discount stores. From this brief description, it is safe to conclude that, as a matter of strategy, the competitor wants to establish the brand in the mass market through discounters. In other words, the competitor is trying to reach customers who want to buy a reputable brand at discount prices and hopes to make money by creating a large sales base.
5. **Analyze current and future resources and competencies of each competitor.** In order to study a competitor's resources and competencies, first designate broad areas of concern: facilities and equipment, personnel skills, organizational capabilities, and management capabilities, for example. Refer to the checklist in Exhibit 4-4. Each category may then be examined generally with reference to different functional areas (general management, finance, research and development, operations, and especially marketing). In the area of finance, the availability of a large credit line would be listed as a strength under management capabilities. Owning a warehouse and refrigerated trucks is a marketing strength listed under facilities and equipment. A checklist should an attempt to specifically pinpoint those strengths that a competitor can use to pursue goals against your firm as well as other firms in the market. Simultaneously, areas in which competitors look particularly vulnerable should also be noted. The purpose here is not to get involved in a ritualistic, detailed account of each competitor but to demarcate those aspects of a competitor's resources and competencies that may account for substantial difference in performance.
6. **Predict the future marketing strategy of each competitor.** The above competitive analysis provides enough information to make predictions about future strategic directions that each competitor may pursue. Predictions, however, must be made qualitatively, using management consensus. The use of management consensus as the basic means for developing forecasts is based on the presumption that, by virtue of their experience in gauging market trends, executives should be able to make some credible predictions about each competitor's behavior in the future. A senior member of the marketing research staff may be assigned the task of soliciting executive opinions and consolidating the information into specific predictions on the moves competitors are likely to make. Management consensus may, however, by systematized to a certain extent by using the *delphi technique* (described in chapter 12). To summarize the technique briefly, the executive in charge of the product develops perspectives on the future strategy of each competitor. Then the marketing researcher presents these predictions to a panel of marketing executives who are familiar with the industrywide marketing of the product. Their opinions are then used to refine the predictions made by the product executive.

EXHIBIT 4-4
Sources of Economic Leverage in the Business System

	Facilities and Equipment	*Personnel Skills*	*Organizational Capabilities*	*Management Capabilities*
1. General Mgmt.				
2. Finance				Large credit line
3. R&D				
4. Operations				
5. Marketing	Warehousing	Door-to-door selling	Direct sales	Industrial marketing
	Retail outlets	Retail selling	Distributor chain	Consumer purchasing
	Sales offices	Wholesale selling	Retail chain	Department of Defense marketing
	Service offices	Direct industry selling	Consumer service organization	State and municipality marketing
	Transportation equipment	Department of Defense selling	Industrial service organization	Well-informed and receptive management
	Training facilities for sales staff	Cross-industry selling	Department of Defense product support	Large customer base
	Data processing equipment	Applications engineering	Inventory distribution and control	Decentralized control
		Advertising	Ability to make quick response to customer requirements	Favorable public image
		Sales promotion	Ability to adapt to sociopolitical upheavals in the marketplace	Future orientation
		Servicing	Loyal set of customers	Ethical standards
		Contract administration	Cordial relations with media and channels	
		Sales analysis	Flexibility in all phases of corporate life	
		Data analysis	Consumer financing	
		Forecasting	Discount policy	
		Computer modeling	Treamwork	
		Product planning	Product quality	
		Background of people		
		Corporate culture		

7. **Assess the impact of competitive strategy on the company's product/market.** The delphi technique can also be used to specify the impact of competitive strategy. Here, again, the product executive must first analyze the impact, using competitive information and personal experiences on the job as a basis. Thereafter, the consensus of a larger group of executives can be obtained on the impact analysis performed by the product executive.

   Needless to say, an analysis of the impact of various competitive strategies using the delphi technique is expensive and time-consuming. The amount of money and time that can be devoted to analyze such matters depends on the strategic importance of the product.

Sources of Competitive Information

Essentially, three sources of competitive information can be distinguished: (a) what competitors say about themselves, (b) what others say about them, and (c) what employees of the firm engaged in competitive analysis have observed and learned about competitors. Information from the first two sources, as shown in Exhibit 4-5, is available through public documents, trade associations, govern-

EXHIBIT 4-5
Sources of Competitive Information

	Public	*Trade Professionals*	*Government*	*Investors*
What competitors say about themselves	• Advertising • Promotional materials • Press releases • Speeches • Books • Articles • Personnel changes • Want ads	• Manuals • Technical papers • Licenses • Patents • Courses • Seminars	• SEC reports • FIC • Testimony • Lawsuits • Antitrust	• Annual meetings • Annual reports • Prospectors • Stock/bond issues
What others say about them	• Books • Articles • Case studies • Consultants • Newspaper reporters • Environmental groups • Consumer groups • Unions • "Who's Who" • Recruiting firms	• Suppliers/vendors • Trade press • Industry study • Customers • Subcontractors	• Lawsuits • Antitrust • State/federal agencies • National plans • Government programs	• Security analyst reports • Industry studies • Credit reports

Source: Adapted, by permission of the publisher, from "Competitor Analysis: The Missing Link in Strategy," by William E. Rothschild, *Management Review,* July, 1979, p. 27.

ment, and investors. Take, for example, information from government sources. Under the Freedom of Information Act, a great amount of information can be obtained at low cost.

As far as information from its own sources is concerned, the company should develop a structured program to gather competitive information. First, a tear-down program like Ford's (Exhibit 4-3) may be undertaken. Second, salespeople may be trained to carefully gather and provide information on the competition, using such sources as customers, distributors, dealers, and former salespeople. Third, senior marketing people should be encouraged to call on customers and speak to them in depth. These contacts should provide valuable information on competitors' products and services. Fourth, other people in the company who happen to have some knowledge of competitors should be encouraged to channel this information to an appropriate office.

Information gathering on the competition has grown dramatically in recent years. Almost all large companies designate someone specially to seek competitive intelligence. A *Fortune* article has identified more than 20 techniques to keep tabs on the competition.[13] These techniques, summarized below, fall in seven groups. Virtually all of them can be legally used to gain competitive insights, although some may involve questionable ethics. A responsible company should carefully review each technique before using it to avoid practices that might be considered illegal or unethical.

1. **Gathering information from recruits and employees of competing companies.** Firms can collect data about their competitors through interviews with new recruits or by speaking with employees of competing companies. According to the *Fortune* article:

    > When they interview students for jobs, some companies pay special attention to those who have worked for competitors, even temporarily. Job seekers are eager to impress and often have not been warned about divulging what is proprietary. They sometimes volunteer valuable information. . . . Several companies now send teams of highly trained technicians instead of personnel executives to recruit on campus.
    >
    > Companies send engineers to conferences and trade shows to question competitors' technical people. Often conversations start innocently—just a few fellow technicians discussing processes and problems . . . [yet competitors'] engineers and scientists often brag about surmounting technical challenges, in the process divulging sensitive information.
    >
    > Companies sometimes advertise and hold interviews for jobs that don't exist in order to entice competitors' employees to spill the beans. . . . Often applicants have toiled in obscurity or feel that their careers have stalled. They're dying to impress somebody.
    >
    > In probably the hoariest tactic in corporate intelligence gathering, companies hire key executives from competitors to find out what they know.

2. **Gathering information from competitors' customers.** Some customers may give out information on competitors' products. For example, a while back Gillette told a large Canadian account the date on which it planned to begin selling its new Good News disposable razor in the United States. The Canadian distributor promptly called Bic about Gillette's impending product launch. Bic put on a crash program and was able to start selling its razor shortly after Gillette introduced its own.

3. **Gathering information by infiltrating customers' business operations.** Companies may provide their engineers free of charge to customers. The close, cooperative relationship that engineers on loan cultivate with the customer's staff often enables them to learn what new products competitors are pitching.
4. **Gathering information from published materials and public documents.** What may seem insignificant, a help wanted ad, for example, may provide information about a competitor's intentions or planned strategies. The types of people sought in help wanted ads can indicate something about a competitor's technological thrusts and new product development. Government agencies are another good source of information.
5. **Gathering information from government agencies under the Freedom of Information Act.** Some companies hire others to get this information more discreetly.
6. **Gathering information by observing competitors or by analyzing physical evidence.** Companies can get to know competitors better by buying their products or by examining other physical evidence. Companies increasingly buy competitors' products and take them apart to determine costs of production and even manufacturing methods.

   In the absence of better information on market share and the volume of product being shipped, companies have measured the rust on the rails of railroad sidings to their competitors' plants and have counted tractor-trailers leaving loading bays.
7. **Gathering information from competitors' garbage.** Some firms actually purchase such garbage. Once it has left a competitor's premises, refuse is legally considered abandoned property. Although some companies shred paper generated by their design labs, they often neglect to shred almost-as-revealing refuse from marketing and public relations departments.

Organization for Competitive Intelligence

Competitive, or business, intelligence is a powerful new management tool that enhances a corporation's ability to succeed in today's highly competitive global markets. It provides early warning intelligence and a framework for better understanding and coutering competitors' initiatives. Competitive activities can be monitored in-house or assigned to an outside firm. A recent survey indicates that over 300 U.S. firms are involved or interested in running their own competitive intelligence activities.[14] Usually companies depend partly on their own people and partly on external help to scan the competitive environment.

Within the organization, competitive information should be acquired both at the corporate level and at the SBU level. At the corporate level, competitive intelligence is concerned with competitors' investment strengths and priorities. At the SBU level, the major interest is in marketing strategy, that is, product, pricing, distribution, and promotion strategies that a competitor is likely to pursue. The true payoff of competitive intelligence comes from the SBU review.

Organizationally, the competitive intelligence task can be assigned to an SBU strategic planner, to a marketing person within the SBU who may be a marketing research or a product/market manager, or to a staff person. Whoever is given the task of gathering competitive intelligence should be allowed adequate time and money to do a thorough job.

As far as outside help is concerned, three main types of organizations may be hired to gather competitive information. First, many marketing research firms (e.g., A.C. Nielsen, Frost and Sullivan, SRI International, Predicasts) provide different types of competitive information, some on a regular basis and others on an ad hoc arrangement. Second, clipping services scan newspapers, financial journals, trade journals, and business publications for articles concerning designated competitors and make copies of relevant clippings for their clients. Third, different brokerage firms specialize in gathering information on various industries. Arrangements may be made with brokerage firms to have regular access to their information on a particular industry.

SEEKING COMPETITIVE ADVANTAGE

To outperform competitors and to grow despite them, a company must understand why competition prevails, why firms attack, and how firms respond. Insights into competitors' perspectives can be gained by undertaking two types of analysis: industry and competitive. **Industry analysis** assesses the attractiveness of a market based on its economic structure. **Competitive analysis** indicates how every firm in a particular market is likely to perform, given the structure of the industry.

Industry Analysis

Every industry has a few peculiar characteristics. These characteristics are bound by time and thus are subject to change. We may call them the dynamics of the industry. No matter how hard a company tries, if it fails to fit into the dynamics of the industry, ultimate success may be difficult to achieve.

An example of how the perspectives of an entire industry may change over time is provided by the cosmetics industry. The cosmetics business was traditionally run according to personal experience and judgment, by the seat-of-the-pants, so to speak, with ultimate dependence on the marketing genius of inventors. In the 1970s a variety of pressures began to engulf the industry. The regulatory climate is now tougher. Consumers have become more demanding and are fewer in number. Although the number of working women is expected to continue rising until 1995, this increase will not offset another more significant demographic change. The population of teenagers—traditionally the heaviest and most experimental makeup users—has been declining. In 1990 there were 15 percent fewer 18- to 24-year-olds than in 1980. As a result, sales of cosmetics are projected to increase only about 2.5 percent per year until the mid-1990s. These shifts, along with unstable economic conditions and rising costs, have made profits smaller. In the 1970s several pharmaceutical and packaged-goods companies, including Colgate-Palmolive Co., Eli Lilly and Co., Pfizer, and Schering Plough, acquired cosmetics companies. Among these, only Schering Plough, which makes the mass market Maybelline, has maintained a meaningful business. Colgate, which acquired Helena Rubenstein in 1973, sold the brand seven years later after it languished. In 1989 the industry began to change again. New mass marketers Procter and Gamble and Unilever entered the arena, bringing with them their great experience producing mundane products like soap and toilet paper, sparking disdain in the glamorous cosmetics trade. The mammoth marketing clout of these giant packaged-goods companies also sparked fear. Proctor and Gamble bought Noxell Corporation, producer of Cover Girl and Clarion makeup, making it the top marketer of cosmetics in mass market outlets. Unilever acquired Faberge and Elizabeth Arden.[15]

These changes made competition in the industry fierce. Although capital investment in the industry is small, inventory and distribution costs are extremely high, partly because of the number of shades and textures required in each product line. For example, nail polish and lipstick have to be available in more than 50 different shades.[16]

The cosmetics industry has gone through a tremendous change since the 1970s. In those days, success in the industry depended on having a glamorous product. As has been observed, Revlon was manufacturing lipstick in its factories, but it was selling beautiful lips. Today, however, success rests on such nuts-and-bolts matters as sharp positioning to serve a neatly defined segment and securing distribution to achieve specific objectives in sales, profit, and market share. Basic inventory and financial controls, budgeting, and planning are now utilized to the fullest extent to cut costs and waste: "In contrast to the glitzy, intuitive world of cosmetics, Unilever and P&G are the habitats of organization men in grey-flannel suits. Both companies rely on extensive market research."[17] This type of shift in direction and style in an industry have important ramifications for marketing strategy.

The dynamics of an industry may be understood by considering the following factors:

1. Scope of competitors' businesses (i.e., location and number of industries)
2. New entrants in the industry
3. Other current and potential offerings that appear to serve similar functions or satisfy the same need
4. Industry's ability to raise capital, attract people, avoid government probing, and compete effectively for consumer dollars
5. Industry's current practices (price setting, warranties, distribution structure, after-sales service, etc.)
6. Trends in volume, costs, prices, and return on investment, compared with other industries
7. Industry profit economics (the key factors determining profits: volume, materials, labor, capital investment, market penetration, and dealer strength)
8. Ease of entry into the industry, including capital investment
9. Relationship between current and future demand and manufacturing capacity and its probable effects on prices and profits
10. Effect of integration, both forward and backward
11. Effect of cyclical swings in the relationship between supply and demand

To formulate marketing strategy, a company should determine the relevance of each of these factors in its industry and the position it occupies with respect to competitors. An attempt should be made to highlight the dynamics of the company in the industry environment. It should be said here that the study of dynamics does not mean making projections of industry growth rates and assessing the likelihood that the company will match the industry's growth pattern: the fortunes of a particular company may not necessarily be related to the overall growth of its industry.

Porter's Model of Industry Structure Analysis

An alternative way to analyze an industry is to apply the Porter model. While the procedure for industry analysis described above is adequate, a more structured method for this proposc has been provided by Porter. He developed a five-factor model for industry analysis, as shown in Exhibit 4-6.[18] The model identifies five key structural features that determine the strength of the competitive forces within an industry and hence industry profitability.

EXHIBIT 4-6
Porter's Model of Industry Competition

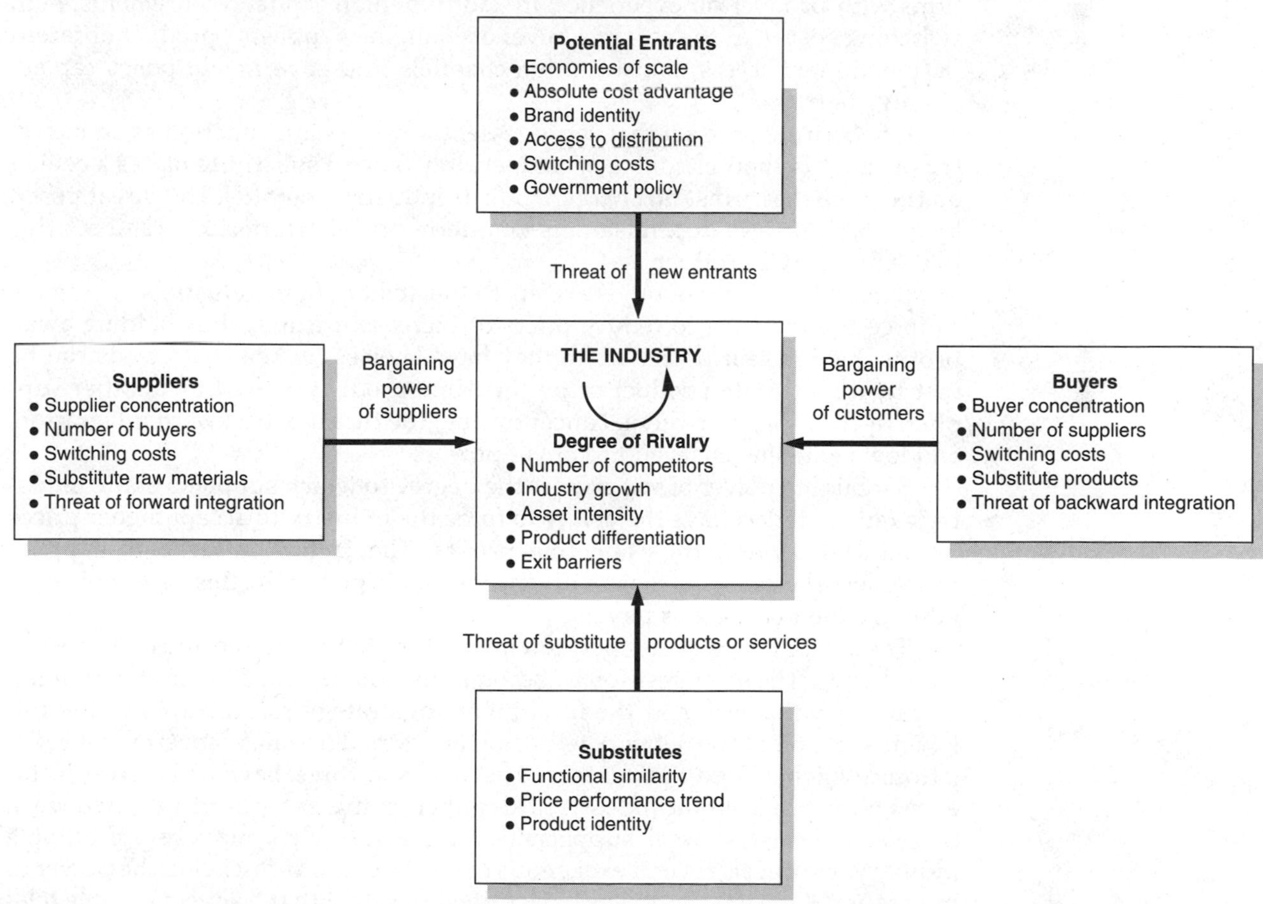

Source: Michael E. Porter, "Industry Structure and Competitive Strategy: Keys to Profitability," *Financial Analysis Journal,* July–August 1980, p. 33.

As shown in this model, the degree of rivalry among different firms is a function of the number of competitors, industry growth, asset intensity, product differentiation, and exit barriers. Among these variables, the number of competitors and industry growth are the most influential. Further, industries with high fixed costs tend to be more competitive because competing firms are forced to cut price to enable them to operate at capacity. Differentiation, both real and perceived, among competing offerings, however, lessens rivalry. Finally, difficulty of exit from an industry intensifies competition.

Threat of entry into the industry by new firms is likely to enhance competition. Several barriers, however, make it difficult to enter an industry. Two cost-related entry barriers are economies of scale and absolute cost advantage. Economies of scale require potential entrants either to establish high levels of production or to accept a cost disadvantage. Absolute cost advantage is enjoyed by firms with proprietary technology or favorable access to raw materials and by firms with production experience. In addition, high capital requirements, high switching costs (i.e., the cost to a buyer of changing suppliers), product differentiation, limited access to distribution channels, and government policy can act as entry barriers.[19]

A substitute product that serves essentially the same function as an industry product is another source of competition. Since a substitute places a ceiling on the price that firms can charge, it affects industry potential. The threat posed by a substitute also depends on its long-term price/performance trend relative to the industry's product.

Bargaining power of buyers refers to the ability of the industry's customers to force the industry to reduce prices or increase features, thus bidding away profits. Buyers gain power when they have choices—when their needs can be met by a substitute product or by the same product offered by another supplier. In addition, high buyer concentration, the threat of backward integration, and low switching costs add to buyer power.

Bargaining power of suppliers is the degree to which suppliers of the industry's raw materials have the ability to force the industry to accept higher prices or reduced service, thus affecting profits. The factors influencing supplier power are the same as those influencing buyer power. In this case, however, industry members act as buyers.

These five forces of competition interact to determine the attractiveness of an industry. The strongest forces become the dominant factors in determining industry profitability and the focal points of strategy formulation, as the following example of the network television industry illustrates. Government regulations, which limited the number of networks to three, have had a great influence on the profile of the industry. This impenetrable entry barrier created weak buyers (advertisers), weak suppliers (writers, actors, etc.), and a very profitable industry. However, several exogenous events are now influencing the power of buyers and suppliers. Suppliers have gained power with the advent of cable television because the number of customers to whom artists can offer their services has increased rapidly. In addition, as cable television firms reduce the size of the network market, advertisers may find substitute advertising media more cost-effective. In conclusion, while the industry is still very attractive and profitable, the changes in its structure imply that future profitability may be reduced.[20]

A firm should first diagnose the forces affecting competition in its industry and their underlying causes and then identify its own strengths and weaknesses relative to the industry. Only then should a firm formulate its strategy, which amounts to taking offensive or defensive action in order to achieve a secure position against each of the five competitive forces. According to Porter this involves

- Positioning the firm so that its capabilities provide the best defense against the existing array of competitive forces
- Influencing the balance of forces through strategic moves, thereby improving the firm's relative position
- Anticipating shifts in the factors underlying the forces and responding to them, hopefully exploiting change by choosing a strategy appropriate to the new competitive balance before rivals recognize it[21]

Take, for example, the U.S. blue jeans industry.[22] In the 1970s most firms except for Levi Strauss and Blue Bell, maker of Wrangler Jeans, took low profits. The situation can be explained with reference to industry structure (see Exhibit 4-7).

EXHIBIT 4-7
Structure of Blue Jeans Industry

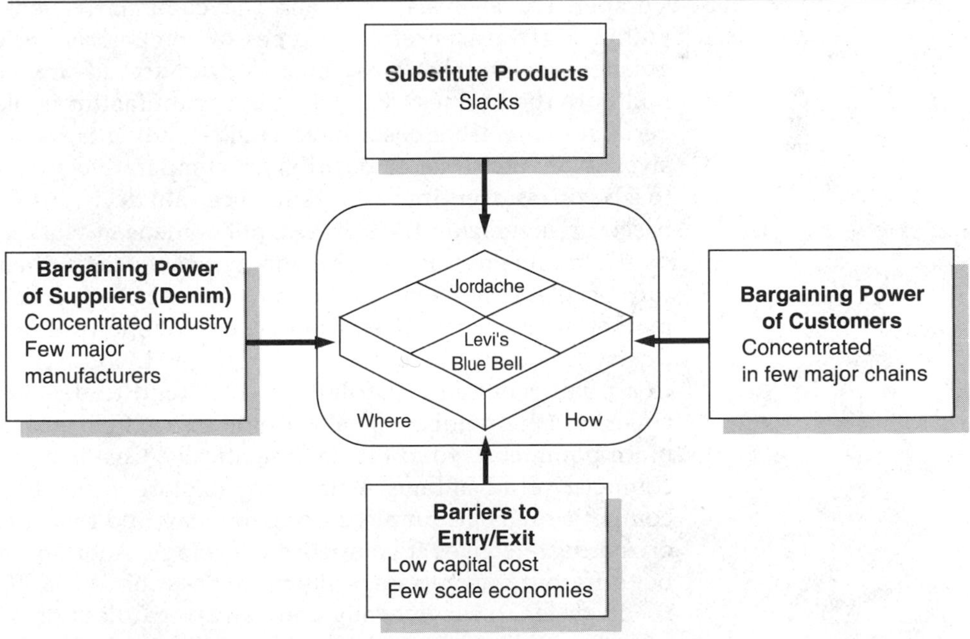

Source: Ennlus E. Bergsma, "In Strategic Phase, Line Management Needs 'Business' Research, Not Market Research," *Marketing News* (21 January 1983): 22.

The extremely low entry barriers allowed almost 100 small jeans manufacturers to join the competitive ranks; all that was needed to enter the industry was some equipment, an empty warehouse, and some relatively low-skilled labor. All such firms competed on price.

Further, these small firms had little control over raw materials pricing. The production of denim is in the hands of about four major textile companies. No one small blue jeans manufacturer was important enough to affect supplier prices or output; consquently, jeans makers had to take the price of denim or leave it. Suppliers (of denim) had strong bargaining power. Store buyers also were in a strong bargaining position. Most of the jeans sold in the United States were handled by relatively few buyers in major store chains. As a result, a small manufacturer basically had to sell at the price the buyers wanted to pay, or they could easily find someone else who would sell at their price.

But then along came Jordache. Creating designer jeans with heavy up-front advertising, Jordache designed a new way to compete that changed industry forces. First, it significantly lowered the bargaining power of its customers (i.e., store buyers) by creating strong consumer preference. The buyer had to meet Jordache's price rather than the other way around. Second, emphasis on the designer's name created significant entry barriers. In summary, Jordache formulated a strategy that neutralized many of the structural forces surrounding the industry and gave itself a competitive advantage.

Competitive Analysis

Competitive analysis examines the comparative advantage of competitors within a given market. Two types of comparative advantage may be distinguished: structural and response.[23] **Structural advantages** are those advantages built into the business. For example, a manufacturing plant in South Korea may, because of low labor costs, have a built-in advantage over another firm. **Responsive advantages** refer to positions of comparative advantage that have accrued to a business over time as a result of certain decisions. This type of advantage is based on leveraging the strategic phenomena at work in the business.

Every business is a unique mixture of strategic phenomena. For example, in the soft drink industry a unit of investment in advertising may lead to a unit of market share. In contrast, the highest-volume producer in the electronics industry is usually the lowest-cost producer. In industrial product businesses, up to a point, sales and distribution costs tend to decline as the density of sales coverage (the number of salespeople in the field) increases. Beyond this optimum point, costs tend to rise dramatically. Cost is only one way of achieving a competitive advantage. A firm may explore issues beyond cost to score over competition. For example, a company may find that distribution through authorized dealers gives it competitive leverage. Another company may find product differentiation strategically more desirable.

In order to survive, any company, regardless of size, must be different in one of two dimensions. It must have lower costs than its direct head-to-head competitors, or it must have unique values for which its customers will pay more. Competitive distinctiveness is essential to survival. Competitive distinctiveness can be achieved in different ways: (a) by concentrating on particular market segments, (b) by offering products that differ from rather than mirror competing products, (c) by using alternative distribution channels and manufacturing processes, and (d) by employing selective pricing and fundamentally different cost structures. Two analytical tools that may be used by a company seeking a position of competitive advantage/distinction are (a) the business-system framework and (b) the customer value/utility curve.

Business-System Framework. Examination of the business system operating in an industry is useful in analyzing competitors and in searching out innovative options for gaining a sustainable competitive advantage. The business-system framework enables a firm to discover the sources of greatest economic leverage, that is, stages in the system where it may build cost or investment barriers against competitors. The framework may also be used to analyze a competitor's costs and to gain insights into the sources of a competitor's current advantage in either cost or economic value to the customer.

Exhibit 4-8 depicts the business system of a manufacturing company. At each stage of the system—technology, product design, manufacturing, and so on—a company may have several options. These options are often interdependent. For example, product design will partially constrain the choice of raw materials. Likewise, the perspectives of physical distribution will affect manufacturing capacity and location and vice versa. At each stage a variety of ques-

EXHIBIT 4-8
Business System of a Manufacturing Company

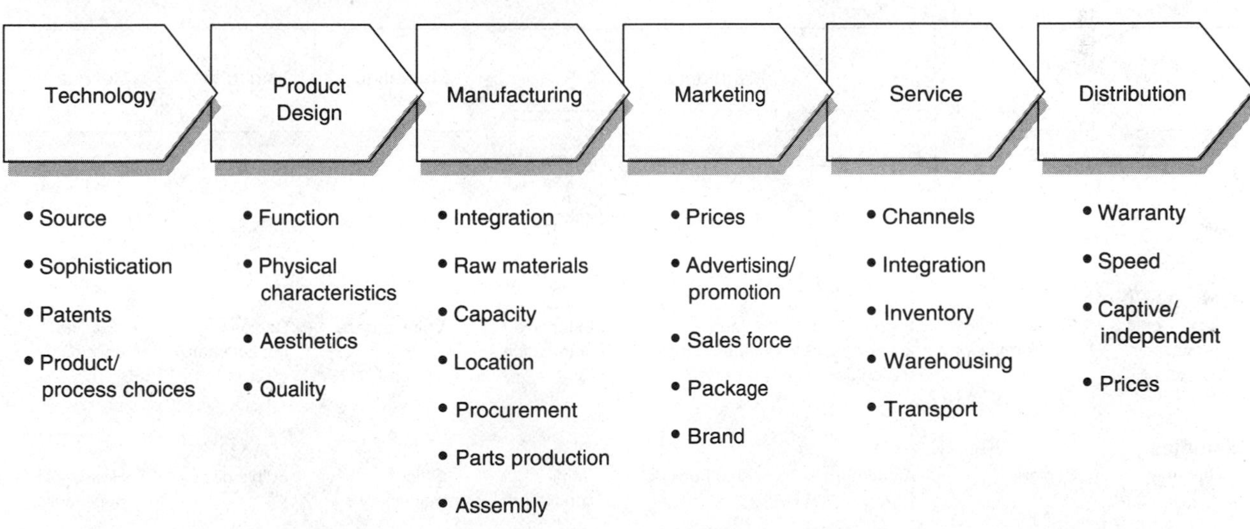

Source: Roberto Buaron, "New-Game Strategies," The *McKinsey Quarterly* (Spring 1981): 34. Reprinted by permission of the publisher. Also, "How to Win the Market-Share Game? Try Changing the Rules." Reprinted by permission of publisher, from *MANAGEMENT REVIEW*, January/1981

tions may by raised, the answers to which provide insights into strategic alternatives a company may consider: How are we doing this now? How are our competitors doing it? What is better about their way? About ours? How else might it be done? How would these options affect our competitive position? If we change what we are doing at this stage, how would other stages be affected? Answers to these questions reveal the sources of leverage a business may employ to gain competitive advantage (see Exhibit 4-9).

The use of the business-system framework can be illustrated with reference to Savin Business Machines Corporation. In 1975 this company with revenues of $63 million was a minor factor in the U.S. office copier market. The market was obviously dominated by Xerox, whose domestic copier revenues were approaching $2 billion. Xerox at that time accounted for almost 80 percent of plain-paper copiers in the United States. In November 1975, Savin introduced a plain-paper copier to serve customers who wanted low- and medium-speed machines (i.e., those producing fewer than 40 copies per minute). Two years later Savin's annual revenues passed $200 million; the company had captured 40 percent of all new units installed in the low-end plain-paper copier market in the United States. Savin managed to earn a 64 percent return on equity while maintaining a conservative 27 percent debt ratio. Meanwhile Xerox, which in 1974 had accounted for more than half of the low-end market, saw its share shrink to 10 percent in 1978. What reasons may be ascribed to Savin's success against mighty Xerox? Through careful analysis of the plain-paper copier busi-

EXHIBIT 4-9
Sources of Economic Leverage in the Business System

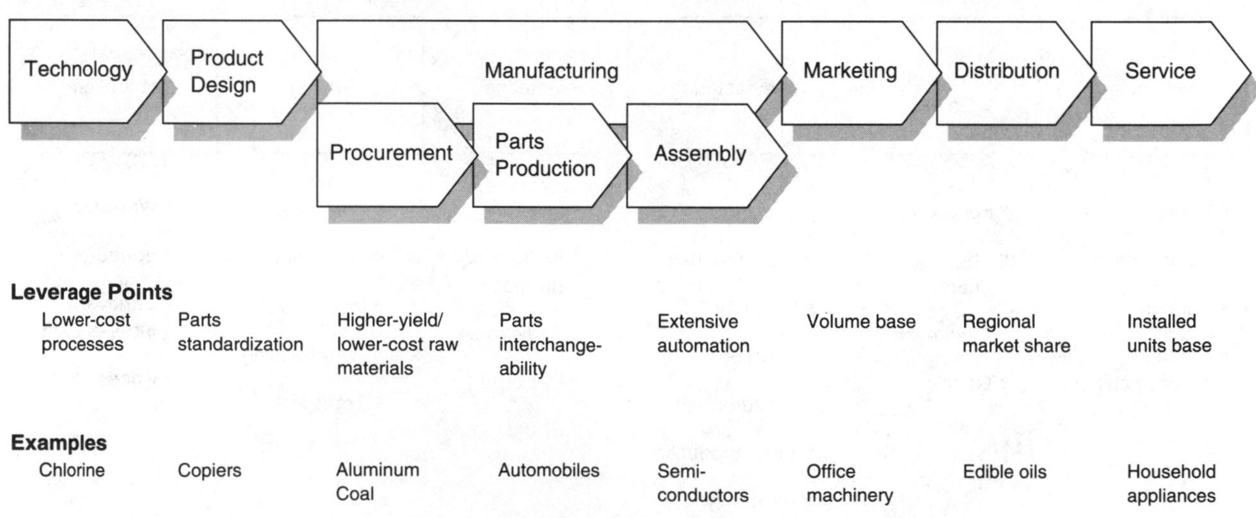

Source: Roberto Buaron, "New-Game Strategies," The *McKinsey Quarterly* (Spring 1981): 35. Reprinted by permission of the publisher. Also, "How to Win the Market-Share Game? Try Changing the Rules." Reprinted by permission of publisher, from *MANAGEMENT REVIEW*, January/1981 © 1981. American Management Association, New York. All rights reserved.

ness system, Savin combined various options at different stages of the system to develop a competitive advantage to successfully confront Xerox. As shown in Exhibit 4-10, by combining a different technology with different manufacturing, distribution, and service approaches, Savin was able to offer business customers, at some sacrifice in copy quality, a much cheaper machine. The option of installing several cheaper machines in key office locations in lieu of a single large, costly, centrally located unit proved attractive to many large customers.

At virtually every stage of the business system, Savin took a radically different approach. First, it used a low-cost technology that had been avoided by the industry because it produced a lower quality copy. Next, its product design was based on low-cost standardized parts available in volume from Japanese suppliers. Further, the company opted for low-cost assembly in Japan. These business-system innovations permitted Savin to offer a copier of comparable reliability and acceptable quality for half the price of Xerox's equivalent model.[24]

Customer Value / Utility Curve. The customer value/utility curve was developed to compare the maximum number of different product features various customer segments would be willing to pay for. The curve may be used to examine the perspectives of product/service offerings of different firms in the market. A firm may gain competitive advantage by aligning its product as close

EXHIBIT 4-10
Plain-Paper Copier Strategy: Xerox versus Savin

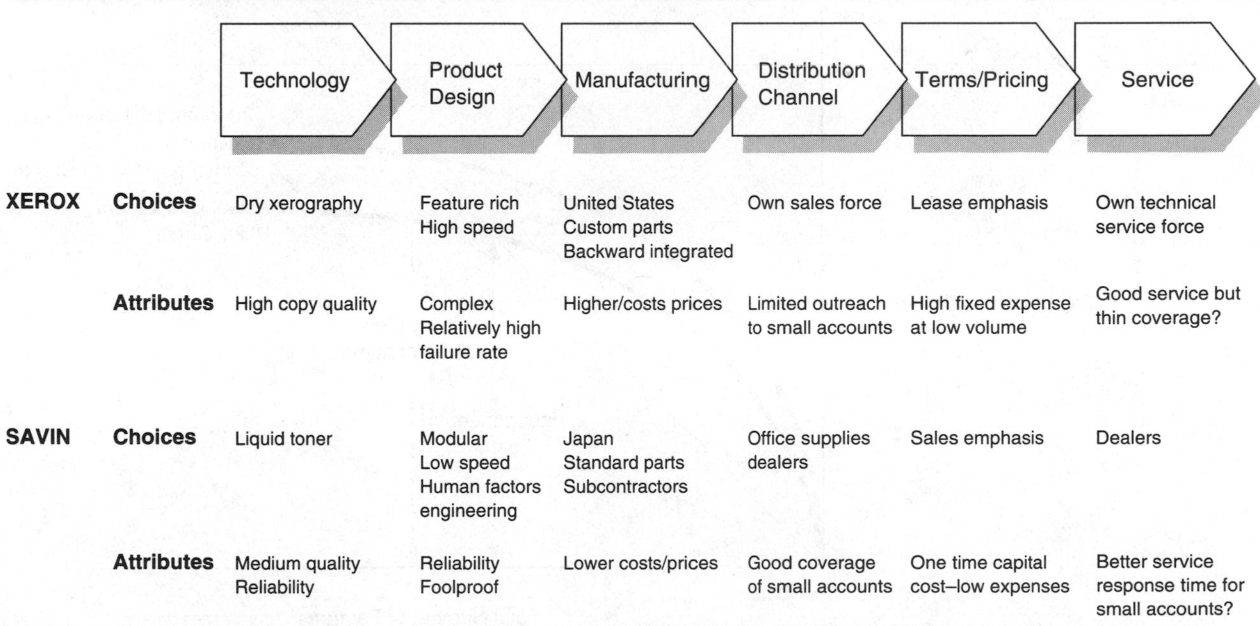

		Technology	Product Design	Manufacturing	Distribution Channel	Terms/Pricing	Service
XEROX	**Choices**	Dry xerography	Feature rich High speed	United States Custom parts Backward integrated	Own sales force	Lease emphasis	Own technical service force
	Attributes	High copy quality	Complex Relatively high failure rate	Higher/costs prices	Limited outreach to small accounts	High fixed expense at low volume	Good service but thin coverage?
SAVIN	**Choices**	Liquid toner	Modular Low speed Human factors engineering	Japan Standard parts Subcontractors	Office supplies dealers	Sales emphasis	Dealers
	Attributes	Medium quality Reliability	Reliability Foolproof	Lower costs/prices	Good coverage of small accounts	One time capital cost–low expenses	Better service response time for small accounts?

Source: Peter R. Sawers, "How to Apply Competitive Analysis to Strategic Planning," *Marketing News* (18 March 1983): 11. Reprinted by permission of the American Marketing Association.

to the actual customer utility curve as is feasible. This point may be illustrated with reference to gasoline retailers. In 1960 integrated oil companies believed that customers would be willing to pay a premium price for gasoline if their service stations offered additional features, including credit cards, windshield washes, and oil checks. Independent gasoline retailers, on the other hand, felt that the majority of customers wanted inexpensive gasoline. As it turned out, the latter group had more accurately positioned the customer utility curve than had integrated firms (see Exhibit 4-11). This forced the integrated firms to cut their prices to meet the challenge of smaller gasoline vendors.

A utility curve may be generated by plotting the total number of product features against the cost/value of all features. The manufacturer's total cost rises linearly with each additional feature; the marginal cost of each feature is assumed to remain constant. However, the marginal value to the customer of each additional feature does not remain constant. Conceptually, the value of the first few features added to the basic product may be high, but thereafter the value of each additional feature begins to diminish. Eventually a point is reached at which it costs a producer more to add a feature than that feature is worth to the customer. The intersection of the two curves defines the point at which the producer should cease adding features. A firm's deviation from the optimum point provides an opportunity for a competitive firm.

EXHIBIT 4-11
Customer Value / Utility Curve

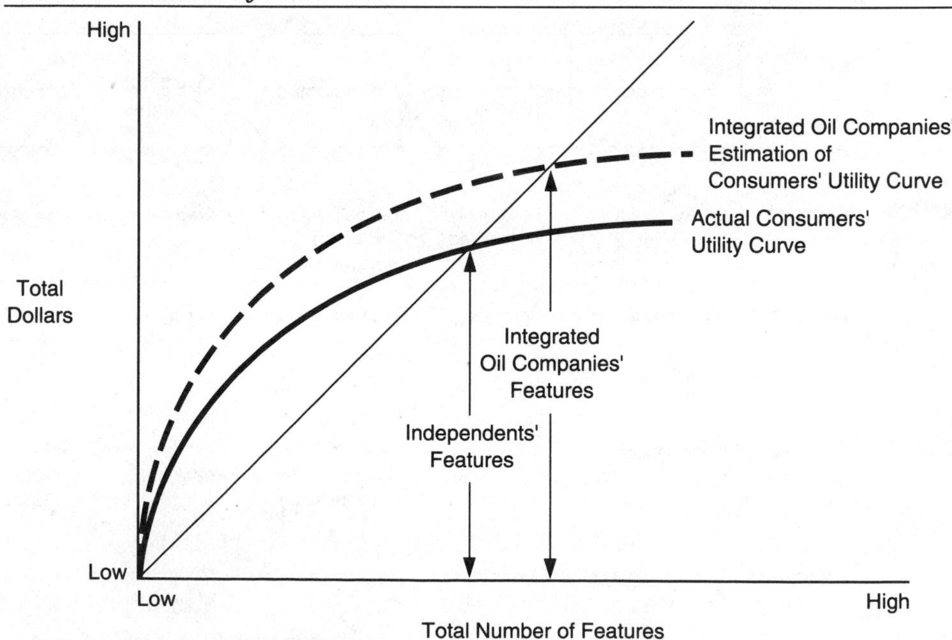

Source: Understanding the Competition: A Practical Guide to Competitive Analysis (Arlington, VA: Michael M. Daiser Associates, Inc., n.d.), 85. Reprinted by permission.

SUSTAINING COMPETITIVE ADVANTAGE

A good strategist seeks not only to "win the hill, but hold on to it." In other words, a business should not only seek competitive advantage but also sustain it over the long haul. Sustaining competitive advantage requires erecting barriers against the competition.

A barrier may be erected based on size in the targeted market, superior access to resources or customers, and restrictions on competitors' options.[25] Scale economies, for example, may equip a firm with an unbeatable cost advantage that competitors cannot match. Preferred access to resources or to customers enables a company to secure a sustainable advantage if (a) the access is secured under better terms than competitors have and (b) the access can be maintained over the long run. Finally, a sustainable advantage can be gained if, for various reasons, competitors are restricted in their moves (e.g., pending antitrust action or given past investments or existing commitments).

In financial terms barriers are based on competitive cost differentials or on price or service differentials. In all cases a successful barrier returns higher margins than the competition earns. Further, a successful barrier must be sustainable and, in a practical sense, unbreachable by the competition; that is, it must cost the competition more to surmount than it costs the protected competitor to defend.

The nature of the feasible barrier depends on the competitive economics of the business. A heavily advertised consumer product with a leading market share enjoys a significant cost barrier and perhaps a price-realization barrier against its competition. If a consumer product has, for example, twice the market share of its competition, it need spend only one-half the advertising dollar per unit to produce the same impact in the marketplace. It will always cost the competition more, per unit, to attack than it costs the leader to defend.

On the other hand, barriers cost money to erect and defend. The expense of the barrier may become an umbrella under which new forms of competition can grow. For example, while advertising is a barrier that protects a leading consumer brand from other branded competitors, the cost of maintaining the barrier is an umbrella under which a private-label product may hide and grow.

A wide product line, large sales and service forces, and systems capabilities are all examples of major barriers. Each of these has a cost to erect and maintain. Each is effective against smaller competitors who are attempting to copy the leader but have less volume over which to amortize barrier costs.

Each barrier, however, holds a protective umbrella over focused competitors. The competitor with a narrow product line faces fewer costs than the wide-line leader. The mail-order house may live under the umbrella of costs associated with the large sales and service force of the leader. The "cherry picker" may produce components compatible with the systems of the leader without bearing the systems engineering costs.

Exhibit 4-12 shows the relationship between barrier and umbrella strategies in sustaining competitive advantage. The best position in the system

EXHIBIT 4-12
Strategies for Sustaining Competitive Advantage

		Umbrella: Low	Umbrella: High
Barrier	High	Protected	Specialty at Risk
	Low	Commodity	Dying

Source: Sandra O. Moose, "Barriers and Umbrellas," *Perspectives* (Boston: Boston Consulting Group, 1980). Reprinted by permission.

is high barrier and low umbrella. A product or business with a position strong enough that the costs of maintaining the barrier are, on a per unit basis, insignificant is in a high-barrier, low-umbrella position. The low-barrier, low-umbrella quadrant is, by definition, a commodity without high profitability.

Most interesting is the high-barrier, high-umbrella quadrant. The business is protected by the existence of the barrier. At the same time, it is at risk because the cost of supporting the barrier is high. Profitability may be high, but the risk of competitive erosion, too, may be substantial. The marketplace issue is the trade-off between consumer preferences for more service, quality, choice, or "image" and lower prices from more narrowly focused competitors.

These businesses face profound decisions. Making no change in direction means continual threats from focused competition. Yet any change in spending to lower the umbrella means changing the nature of the competitive protection, that is, eroding the barrier.

Successful marketing strategy requires being aware of the size of the umbrella and continually testing whether to maintain investment to preserve or heighten the barrier or to withdraw investment to "cash out" as the barrier erodes.

A sustainable advantage is meaningful in marketing strategy only when the following conditions are met: (a) customers perceive a consistent difference in important attributes between the firm's product or service and those of its competitors, (b) the difference is the direct result of a capability gap between the firm and its competitors, and (c) both the difference in important attributes and the capability gap can be expected to endure over time.

SUMMARY

Competition is a strategic factor that affects marketing strategy formulation. Traditionally, marketers have considered competition as one of the uncontrollable variables to be reckoned with in developing the marketing mix. It is only in the last few years that the focus of business strategy has shifted to the competition. It is becoming more and more evident that a chosen marketing strategy should be based on competitive advantage to achieve sustained business success. To implement such a perspective, resources should be concentrated in those areas of competitive activity that offer the best opportunity for continuing profitability and sound investment returns.

There are two very different forms of competition: natural and strategic. Natural competition implies survival of the fittest in a given environment. In business terms, it means firms compete from very similar strategic positions, relying on operating differences to separate the successful from the unsuccessful. With strategic competition, on the other hand, underlying strategy differences vis-à-vis market segments, product offerings, distribution channels, and manufacturing process become paramount considerations.

Conceptually, competition may be examined from the viewpoint of economists, industrial organization theorists, and businesspeople. The major thrust of economic theories has centered on the model of perfect competition. Industrial organization emphasizes the industry environment (i.e., industry structure, conduct, and performance) as the key determinant of a firm's performance. A theoretical framework of competition from the viewpoint of the businessperson, other than the pioneering efforts of Bruce Henderson, hardly exists.

Firms compete to satisfy customer needs, which may be classified as existing, latent, or incipient. A firm may face competition from different sources, which may be categorized as industry competition, product line competition, or organizational competition. The intensity of competition is determined by a combination of factors.

A firm needs a competitive intelligence system to keep track of various facets of its rivals' businesses. The system should include proper data gathering and analysis of each major competitor's current and future perspectives. This chapter identified various sources of competitive information, including what competitors say about themselves, what others say about them, and what a firm's own people have observed. To gain competitive advantage, that is, to choose those product/market positions where victories are clearly attainable, two forms of analysis may be undertaken: industry analysis and competitive analysis. Porter's five-factor model is useful in industry analysis. Tools useful in competitive analysis are the business-system framework and the customer value/utility curve.

DISCUSSION QUESTIONS

1. Differentiate between natural and strategic competition. Give examples.
2. What are the basic elements of strategic competition? Are there any prerequisites to pursuing strategic competition?
3. How do economists approach competition? Does this approach suffice for businesspeople?

4. What is the industrial organization viewpoint of competition?
5. What is the underlying thesis supporting Henderson's hypotheses on competition?
6. Identify, with examples, different sources of competition.
7. How does industry structure affect intensity of competition?
8. What are the major sources of competitive intelligence?
9. Briefly explain Porter's five-factor model of industry structure analysis.

NOTES

[1]Bruce D. Henderson, "Understanding the Forces of Strategic and Natural Competition," *Journal of Business Strategy* (Winter 1981): 11.

[2]Bruce D. Henderson, "New Strategies for the Global Competition," A Special Commentary (Boston: Boston Consulting Group, 1981), 5-6.

[3]Louis W. Stern and John R. Grabner, Jr., *Competition in the Marketplace* (Glenview, IL: Scott, Foresman and Company, 1970), 29.

[4]See Michael E. Porter, *Competitive Strategy* (New York: The Free Press, 1980), chapter 1. See also E. T. Grether, *Marketing and Public Policy* (Englewood Cliffs, NJ: Prentice-Hall, 1960), 25; and George Fisk, *Marketing Systems: An Introductory Analysis* (New York: Harper & Row, 1967), 622.

[5]Bruce D. Henderson, "The Anatomy of Competition," *Journal of Marketing* (Spring 1983): 8–9.

[6]Henderson, "Anatomy," 8–9.

[7]Henderson, "Understanding the Forces of Strategic and Natural Competition," 15.

[8]Bro Uttal, "Sudden Shake-Up in Home Computers," *Fortune* (11 July 1983): 105.

[9]David Montgomery and Charles Weinberg, "Toward Strategic Intelligence Systems," *Journal of Marketing* (Fall 1979): 41–52.

[10]Robin Leaf, "How to Pick Up Tips from Your Competitors," *Director* (February 1980): 61–62.

[11]Michael G. Allen, "Strategic Planning with a Competitive Focus," *McKinsey Quarterly* (Autumn 1978): 6.

[12]William E. Rothschild, *Putting It All Together* (New York: AMACOM, 1976), 85.

[13]Steven Flax, "How to Snoop on Your Competitors," *Fortune* (14 May 1984): 29–33.

[14]Fahri Karakaya and Michael J. Stahl, "Barriers to Entry and Market Entry Decisions in Consumer and Industrial Goods Market," *Journal of Marketing* (April 1989): 80–91.

[15]"Unilever is All Made Up with Everywhere to Go," *Business Week* (31 July 1989): 33–34.

[16]"How Cosmetics Makers Are Touching Up Their Strategies," *Business Week* (23 September 1985): 63.

[17]Kathleen Deveny and Alecia Swasy, "In Cosmetics, Marketing Cultures Clash," *Wall Street Journal*, 31 October 1989, p. B1.

[18]See Michael E. Porter, "How Competitive Forces Shape Strategy," *Harvard Business Review* (March–April 1979): 137–45.

[19]Jan P. Herring, "Building a Business Intelligence System," *Journal of Business Strategy* (May–June 1988).

[20]*Understanding the Competition: A Practical Guide to Competitive Analysis* (Arlington, VA: Michael M. Kaiser Associates, Inc., n.d.), 96.

[21]Michael E. Porter, "Note on the Structural Analysis of Industries," Harvard Business School Case Service (1975), 22.

[22]Ennlus E. Bergsma, "In Strategic Phase, Line Management Needs 'Business' Research, Not Market Research," *Marketing News* (21 January 1983): 21–22.

[23]Peter R. Sawers, "How to Apply Competitive Analysis to Strategic Planning," *Marketing News* (18 March 1983): 11.

[24]Roberto Buaron, "New-Game Strategies," *McKinsey Quarterly* (Spring 1981): 24–40.

[25]Pankaj Ghemawat, "Sustainable Advantage," *Harvard Business Review* (September–October 1986): 53–58. See also Kevin P. Coyne, "The Anatomy of Sustainable Competitive Advantage," *Business Horizons* (January–February 1986): 16–17.

CHAPTER 5

Focusing on the Customer

Consumption is the sole end and purpose of production; and the interest of the producer ought to be attended to only so far as it may be necessary for promoting that of the consumer.

ADAM SMITH

Businesses compete to serve customer needs. Not only are there different types of customers, but their needs vary, too. Thus most markets are not homogeneous. Further, the markets that are homogeneous today may not remain so in the future. In brief, a market represents a dynamic phenomenon that, influenced by customer needs, evolves over time.

In a free economy, each customer group tends to want a slightly different service or product. But a business unit cannot reach out to all customers with equal effectiveness; it must distinguish easily accessible customer groups from hard-to-reach ones. Moreover, a business unit faces competitors whose ability to respond to customer needs and cover customer groups differs from its own. To establish a strategic edge over its competition with a viable marketing strategy, it is important for the business unit to clearly define the market it intends to serve. It must segment the market, identifying one or more subsets of customers within the total market, and concentrate its efforts on meeting their needs. Fine targeting of the customer group to serve offers the opportunity to establish competitive leverage.

This chapter introduces a framework for identifying markets to serve. Various underlying concepts of market definition are examined. The chapter ends with a discussion of alternative ways of segmenting a market.

IDENTIFYING MARKETS

Contemporary approaches to strategic planning require proper definition of the market; however, questions about how to properly characterize a market make it difficult to arrive at an acceptable definition. Depending on how the market is defined, the relative market positions of two companies and their two products can be reversed, as shown on the opposite page.[1]

Brands	Percentage Market Share: Unsegmented (Mass)	Segmented
S	32	40
T	24	30
U	16	20
V	8	10
X	12	60
Y	6	30
Z	2	10

Though brand X has a low share in the unsegmented, or mass, market (12 percent), it has a much higher share within its own segment of the mass market (60 percent) than does brand S (40 percent). Which of the two shares shown is better for the business: the total mass market for the product category or some segmented portion of that market? The arguments go both ways, some pointing out the merits of having a larger share of industry volume and others noting the favorable profit consequences of holding a larger share within a smaller market niche. Does Sanka compete in the total mass market for coffee with Maxwell House and Folgers or in a decaffeinated market segment against Brim and Nescafé? Does the market for personal computers include intelligent and dumb terminals as well as word processors, desktop and laptop computers, and intelligent telephones? Grape Nuts has 100 percent of the Grape Nuts market, a smaller percentage of the breakfast cereal market, an even smaller percentage of the packaged-foods market, a still smaller percentage of the packaged-goods market, a tiny percentage of the U.S. food market, a miniscule percentage of the world food market, and a microscopic percentage of total consumer expenditures. All descriptions of market share are meaningless, however, unless a company defines the market in terms of the boundaries separating it from its rivals.

Considering the importance of adequately defining the market, it is desirable to systematically develop a conceptual framework for that purpose. Exhibit 5-1 presents such a framework. The first logical step in defining the market is to determine customer need. Based on need, the market emerges. Because customer need provides a broad perspective of the market, it is desirable to establish market boundaries. Traditionally, market boundaries have been defined in terms of product/market scope, but recent work suggests that markets should be defined multidimensionally.

The market boundary delineates the total limits of the market. An individual business must select and serve those parts, or segments, of the total market in which it is best equipped to compete over the long run.

CUSTOMER NEED

Satisfaction of customer need is the ultimate test of a business unit's success. Thus, an effective marketing strategy should aim at serving customer needs and wants better than competitors do. Focus on customers is the essence of marketing strategy. As Robertson and Wind have said:

EXHIBIT 5-1
Identifying Markets to Serve

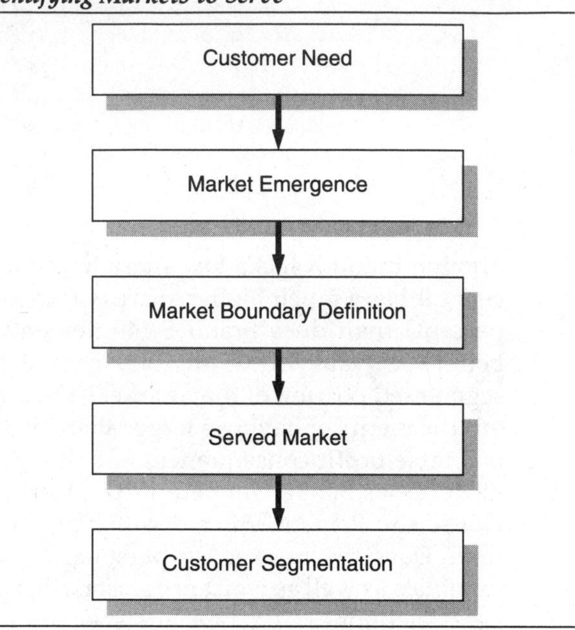

Marketing performs a boundary role function between the company and its markets. It guides the allocation of resources to product and service offerings designed to satisfy market needs while achieving corporate objectives. This boundary role function of marketing is critical to strategy development. Before marshalling a company's resources to acquire a new business, or to introduce a new product, or to reposition an existing product, management must use marketing research to cross the company-consumer boundary and to assess the likely market response.

The logic and value of consumer needs assessment is generally beyond dispute, yet frequently ignored. It is estimated, for example, that a majority of new products fail. Yet, there is most often nothing wrong with the product itself; that is, it works. The problem is simply that consumers do not want the product.

AT&T's Picture Phone is a classic example of a technology-driven product which works; but people do not want to see each other on a telephone. It transforms a comfortable, low involvement communication transaction into a demanding, high involvement one. The benefit is not obvious to consumers. Of course, the benefit could become obvious if transportation costs continue to outpace communication costs, and if consumers could be "taught" the benefits of using a Picture Phone.

Marketing's boundary role function is similarly important in maintaining a viable competitive positioning in the marketplace. The passing of Korvette from the American retail scene, for example, can be attributed to consumer confusion as to what Korvette represented—how it was positioned relative to competition. Korvette's strength was as a discount chain—high turnover and low margin. This basic mission of the business was violated, however, as Korvette traded-up in soft goods and fashion items and even opened a store on Manhattan's Fifth Avenue. The result was that Korvette became neither a discount store nor a department store and lost its previous customer base. Sears has encountered a similar phenomenon as it opted for higher margins in the 1970s and lost its reputation for "value" in the marketplace. The penalty has been declining sales and profitability for its retail store operation, which it is now trying valiantly to arrest by reestablishing its "middle America" value orientation. Nevertheless, consumer research could have indicated the beginning of the problem long before the crisis in sales and profits occurred.[2]

Concept of Need

Customer need has always formed the basis of sound marketing. Yet, as Ohmae points out, it is often neglected or ignored:

> Think for a moment about aching heads. Is my headache the same as yours? My cold? My shoulder pain? My stomach discomfort? Of course not. Yet when a pharmaceutical company asked for help . . . [it] asked 50 employees in the company to fill out a questionnaire—throughout a full year—about how they felt physically at all times of the day every day of the year. Then [it] pulled together a list of the symptoms described, sat down with the company's scientists, and asked them, item by item: Do you know why people feel this way? Do you have a drug for this kind of symptom? It turned out that there were no drugs for about 80% of the symptoms, these physical awarenesses of discomfort. For many of them, some combination of existing drugs worked just fine. For others, no one had ever thought to seek a particular remedy. The scientists were ignoring tons of profit.
>
> Without understanding customers' needs—the specific types of discomfort they were feeling—the company found it all too easy to say, "Headache? Fine, here's a medicine, an aspirin, for headache. Case closed." It was easy not to take the next step and ask, "What does the headache feel like? Where does it come from? What is the underlying cause? How can we treat the cause, not just the symptom?" Many of these symptoms, for example, are psychological and culture-specific. Just look at television commercials. In the United States, the most common complaint is headache; in the United Kingdom, backache; in Japan, stomachache. In the United States, people say that they have a splitting headache; in Japan it is an ulcer. How can we truly understand what these people are feeling and why?[3]

Looking closely at needs is the first step in delivering value to customers. Traditionally, needs have been classified according to Maslow's hierarchy of human needs. From lowest to highest, Maslow's hierarchy identifies five levels of needs: physiological, safety, belongingness, self-esteem, and self-actualization. Needs at each level of the hierarchy can be satisfied only after needs at the levels below it have been satisfied. A need unsatisfied becomes a source of frustration. When the frustration is sufficiently intense, it motivates a relief action—the purchase of a product, for example. Once a need is satisfied, it is forgotten, creating space for the awareness of other needs. In a marketing context, this suggests that customers need periodic reminders of their association with a product, particularly when satisfied.

Business strategy can be based on the certainty that needs exist. As we move up Maslow's hierarchy, needs become less and less obvious. The challenge in marketing is to expose nonobvious needs, to fill needs at all levels of the hierarchy.

Maslow's first two levels can be called survival levels. Most businesses operate at level 2 (safety), with occasional spikes into higher levels. Satisfying a safety need is what a business must do to have a viable operation. The customer must feel both physically and economically safe in buying the product. The next higher levels—belongingness and self-esteem—are customer reward levels, where benefits of consuming a product accrue to the customer personally, enhancing his or her sense of worth. At the highest level, self-actualization, the customer feels a close identification with the product. Of course, not all needs can be filled, nor would it be economically feasible to attempt to do so. But a business can move further toward satisfaction of customer needs by utilizing the insights of the Maslow hierarchy.

MARKET EMERGENCE

Customer need gives rise to a market opportunity, and a market emerges. To judge the worth of this market, an estimate of market potential is important. If the market appears attractive, the strategist takes the next step of delineating the market boundary. This section examines the potential of the market.

Simply stated, **market potential** is the total demand for a product in a given environment. While theoretically this definition appears adequate, its meaning in practice creates problems. Two aspects of the definition—demand and environment—are dynamic concepts, and their meanings vary from one situation to another. Realizing this difficulty, Kotler defines market potential as "the set of consumers who profess some level of interest in a defined market offer."[4] But such an abstract definition still leaves the meaning of market potential open to interpretation.

It is clear that market potential defies precise definition. We know, however, that it can be approached by estimating maximum reasonable limits of a saturation point in a given environment for a given product at a given time. Within these constraints, market potential for any product or service can be extrapolated using the following procedure: (a) define the market broadly enough to include all potential end users, thus identifing the appropriate drivers of demand and reducing the risk of surprise product substitutions; (b) divide total industry demand into its main components for separate analysis, making each category small and homogeneous enough so that the drivers of demand apply consistently across its various elements and, at the same time, making it large enough so that the analysis is worth the effort; (c) forecast the drivers of demand in each segment and project how they are likely to change using appropriate statistical techniques; (d) conduct sensitivity analysis to understand the most critical assumptions and to gauge risks to a baseline forecast. For further insights on the subject, a marketing management text may be consulted.

Market potential is measured to gain insights into five elements: market size, market growth, profitability, type of buying decision, and customer market structure. Exhibit 5-2 summarizes these elements and shows a pro forma scheme for measuring market potential.

The first element, *market size,* is best expressed in both units and dollars. Dollar expression in isolation is inadequate because of distortion by inflation and international currency fluctuations. Also, because of inflationary distortion, the screening criteria for new product concepts and product line extensions should separately specify both units and dollars. Market size can be expressed as total market sales potential or company market share, although most companies through custom utilize market share figures.

The second element, *market growth,* is meant to reflect the secular trend of the industry. Again, the screening criteria should be specified for new product

EXHIBIT 5-2
Measurement of Market Potential

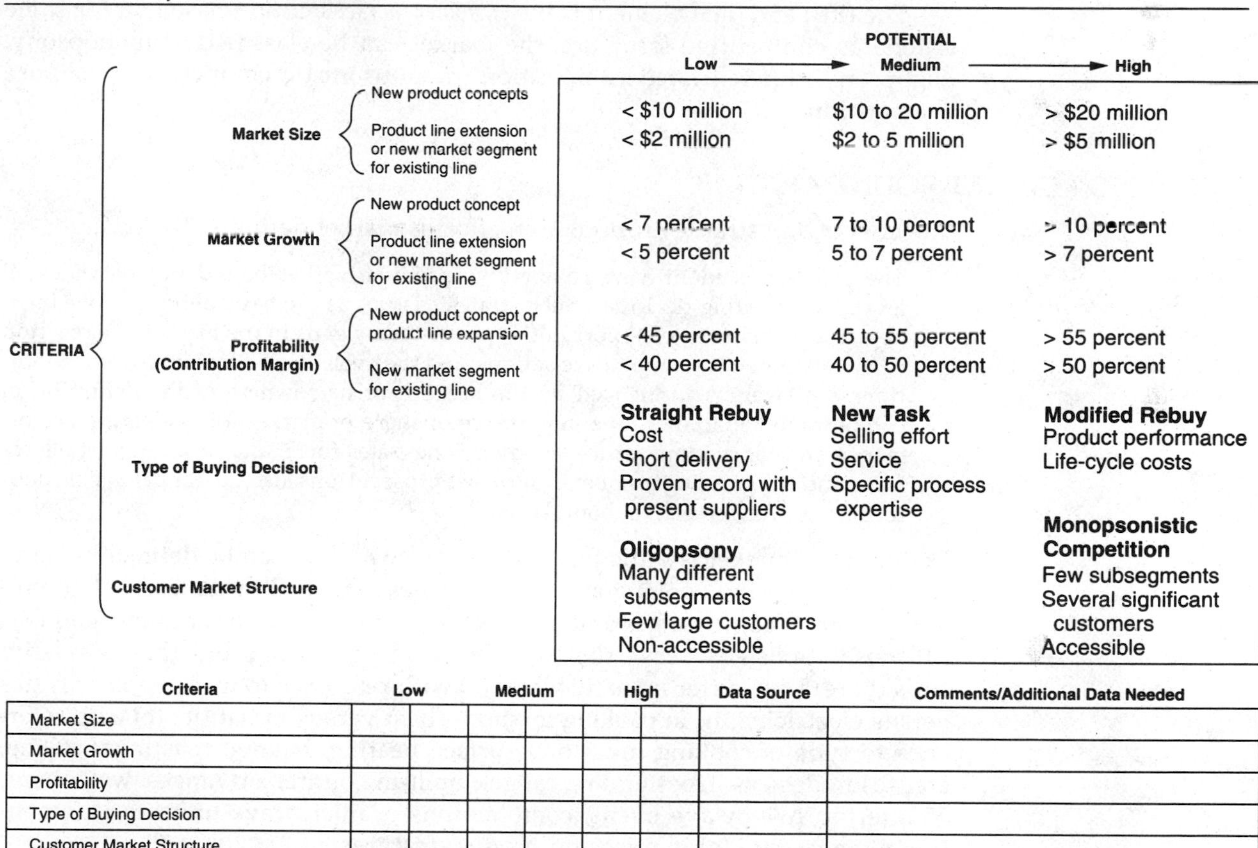

Criteria	Low	Medium	High	Data Source	Comments/Additional Data Needed
Market Size					
Market Growth					
Profitability					
Type of Buying Decision					
Customer Market Structure					
Overall Rating					

Source: Reprinted by permission of Terry C. Wilson, West Virginia University.

concepts and product line extensions. The criteria and projections should be based on percentage growth in units. Projections in industrial settings often are heavily dependent on retrofit possibilities and plans for equipment replacement.

The third element in this evaluation of strategic potential is *profitability*. It usually is expressed in terms of contribution margin or in one of the family of return calculations. Most U.S. companies view profitability in terms of return on investment (ROI), return on sales (ROS), or return on net assets (RONA). Return on capital employed (ROCE) is often calculated in multinational companies. For measuring market potential, no one of these calculations appears to function better than another.

The fourth element is the *type of buying decision*. The basis for a buying decision must be predicated on whether the decision is a straight rebuy, a modified rebuy, or a new task.

The fifth and final element is the *customer market structure*. Based on the same criteria as competitive structure, the market can be classified as monopsony, oligopsony, differentiated competition (monopsonistic competition), or pure competition.[5]

DEFINING MARKET BOUNDARIES

The crux of any strategy formulation effort is market definition:

> The problem of identifying competitive product-market boundaries pervades all levels of marketing decisions. Such strategic issues as the basic definition of a business, the assessment of opportunities presented by gaps in the market, the reaction to threats posed by competitive actions, and the decisions on major resource allocations are strongly influenced by the breadth or narrowness of the definition of competitive boundaries. The importance of share of market for evaluating performance and for guiding territorial advertising, sales force, and other budget allocations and the growing number of antitrust prosecutions also call for defensible definitions of product-market boundaries.[6]

Defining the market is difficult, however, since market can be defined in many ways. Consider the cooking appliance business.[7] Overall in 1990 about 14 million gas and electric ranges and microwave ovens were sold for household use. All these appliances serve the basic function of cooking, but their similarity ends there. They differ in many ways: (a) with reference to fuels—primarily gas versus electricity; (b) in cooking method—heat versus radiation; (c) with reference to type of cooking function—surface heating, baking, roasting, broiling, etc.; (d) in design—freestanding ranges, built-in countertop ranges, wall ovens, countertop microwave ovens, combinations of microwave units and conventional ranges etc.; (e) in price and product features.

These differences raise an important question: Should all household cooking appliances be considered a single market or do they represent several distinct markets? If they represent several distinct markets, how should these markets be defined? There are different possibilities for defining the market:

(a) with reference to product characteristics; (b) in terms of private brand sales versus manufacturers' brand sales; (c) with reference to sales in specific regions; (d) in terms of sales target, for example, sales to building contractors for installation in new houses versus replacement sales for existing homes.

Depending on the criteria adopted to define the market, the size of a market varies considerably. The strategic question of how the marketer of home cooking appliances should define the market is explored below.

Dimensions of Market Boundaries

Traditionally, market boundaries have been defined in terms of product/market space. Consider the following:

> A market is sometimes defined as a group of firms producing identical or closely related products. . . . A preferable approach is to define the markets in terms of products. . . . [What is meant by] a close relationship among products? Goods and services may be closely related in the sense that they are regarded as substitutes by consumers, or they may be close in that the factors of production used in each are similar.[8]

A market usually is identified with a generic class of products. One hears of the beer market, the cake mix market, or the cigarette market, product markets that refer to individuals who have purchased a given class of products.[9]

These two definitions of the market—the market as a class of closely related products versus the market as a class of people who purchases a certain kind of product—view it from one of two perspectives: who are the buyers and what are the products. In the first definition, buyers are implicitly assumed to be homogeneous in their behavior. The second definition suggests that the products and brands within a category are easily identified and interchangeable and that the problem is to search for market segments.

In recent years it has been considered inadequate to perceive market definition as simply a choice of products for chosen markets. Instead, the product may be considered a physical manifestation of a particular technology to a particular customer function for a particular customer group. Market boundaries should then be determined by choices along these three dimensions.[10]

Technology. A particular customer function can be performed by different technologies. In other words, alternative technologies can be applied to satisfy a particular customer need. To illustrate, consider home cooking appliances again. In terms of fuel, the traditional alternative technologies have been gas and electricity. In recent years, a new form of technology, microwave radiation, has also been used. In another industry alternative technologies may be based on the use of different materials. For example, containers may be made from metal, glass, or plastic. In defining market boundaries, a decision must be made whether the products of all relevant technologies or only those of a particular technology are to be included.

Customer Function. Products can be considered in terms of the functions they serve or in terms of the ways in which they are used. Some cooking appliances bake and roast, others fry and boil; some perform all these functions and perhaps more. Different functions provide varying customer benefits. In establishing market boundaries, customer benefits to be served should be spelled out.

Customer Group. A group refers to a homogeneous set of customers with similar needs and characteristics. The market for cooking appliances, for example, can be split into different groups: building contractors, individual households buying through retail stores, and so on. The retail stores segment can be further broken down into traditional appliance specialty stores, mass merchandisers, and so on. Decisions about market boundaries should indicate which types of customers are to be served.

In addition to these three dimensions for determining market boundaries, Buzzell recommends a fourth—level of production/distribution.[11] A business has the option of operating at one or more levels of the production/distribution process. For example, producers of raw materials (e.g., aluminum) or component products (e.g., semiconductors, motors, compressors) may limit their business to selling only to other producers, or they may produce finished products themselves, or they may do both. Decisions about production/distribution levels have a direct impact on the market boundary definition. This point may be illustrated with reference to Texas Instruments:

> The impact that a business unit's vertical integration strategy can have on competition in a market is dramatically illustrated by Texas Instruments' decision, in 1972, to enter the calculator business. At the time, it was a principal supplier of calculator components (integrated circuits) to the earlier entrants into the market, including the initial market leader, Bowmar Instruments. As most readers undoubtedly know, TI quickly took over a leadership position in calculators through a combination of "pricing down the experience curve" and aggressive promotion. For purposes of this discussion, the important point is one of a finished product. Some other component suppliers also entered the calculator business, while others continued to supply OEMs. In light of these varying strategies, is there a "calculator component market" and "calculator market," or do these constitute a single market?[12]

Exhibit 5-3 depicts the three dimensions of the market boundary definition from the viewpoint of the personal financial transactions industry. Market boundaries are defined in terms of customer groups, customer functions, and technologies. The fourth dimension, level of production/distribution, is not included in the diagram because it is not possible to show four dimensions in a single chart. The exhibit shows a matrix developed around customer groups on the vertical axis, customer functions on the right axis, and technologies on the left axis. Any three-dimensional cell in the matrix constitutes an elementary "building block" of market definition. Automatic teller machines (ATMs) for cash withdrawals at commercial banks is an example of such a cell.

Redefining Market Boundaries

As markets evolve, boundaries may need to be restated. George Day and Allan Shocker point to five sets of "environmental influences" that affect product/

EXHIBIT 5-3
Dimensions of Market Boundary Definition for Personal Financial Transactions

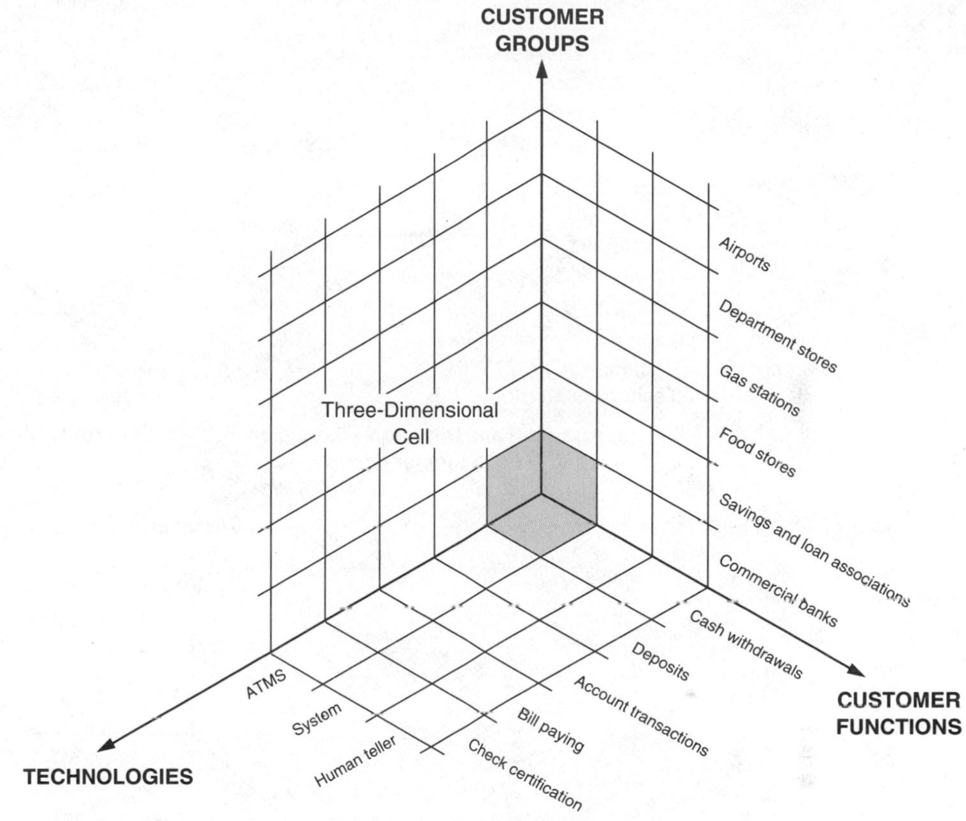

market boundaries. These influences are technological change (displacement by a new technology); market-oriented product development (e.g., combining the features of several products into one multipurpose offering); price changes and supply constraints (which influence the perceived set of substitutes); social, legal, or government trends (which influence patterns of competition); and international trade competition (which changes geographic boundaries).[13] For example, when management introduces a new product, markets an existing product to new customers, diversifies the business through acquisition, or liquidates a part of the business, the market undergoes a process of evolution. Redefinition of market boundaries may be based on any one or a combination of the three basic dimensions. The market may be extended through the penetration of new customer groups, the addition of products serving related customer functions, or the development of products based on new technologies. As shown in Exhibit 5-4, these changes are caused by three fundamentally different phenomena: "The adoption and diffusion process underlies the penetration

EXHIBIT 5-4
Market Evolution in Three Dimensions

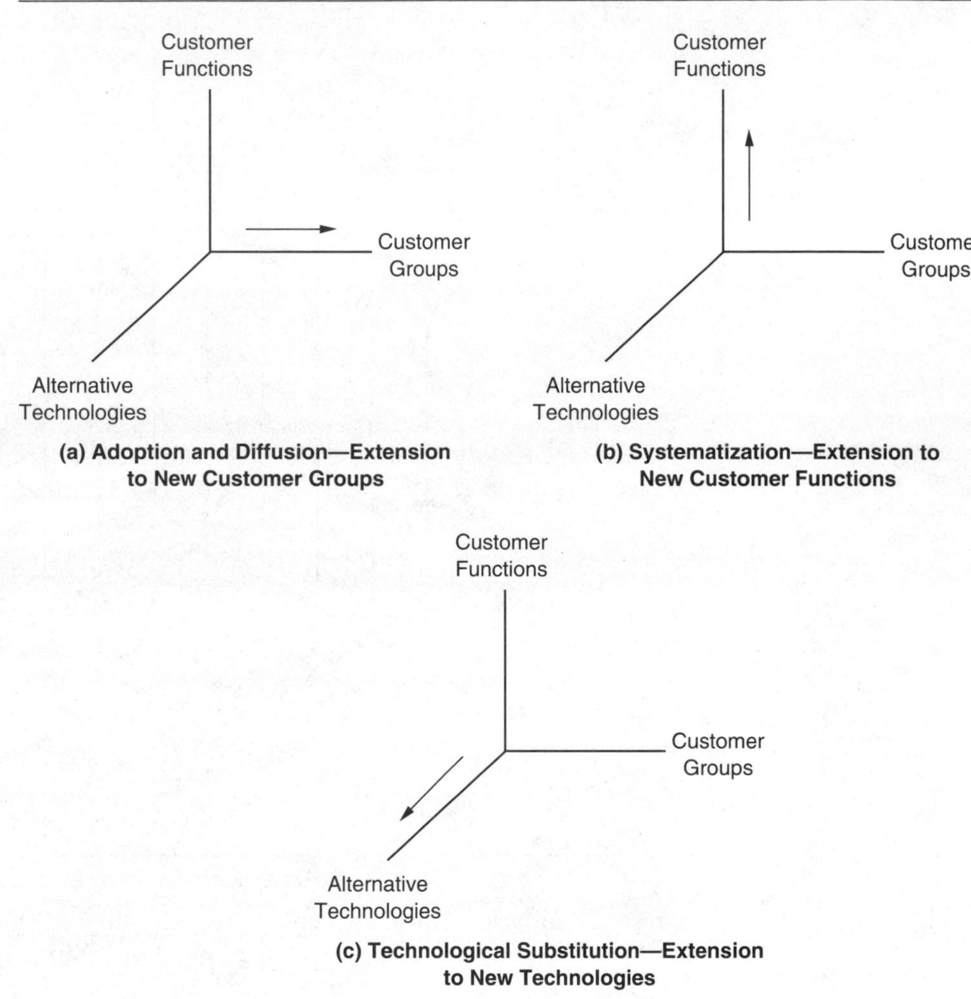

(a) Adoption and Diffusion—Extension to New Customer Groups

(b) Systematization—Extension to New Customer Functions

(c) Technological Substitution—Extension to New Technologies

Source: Derek F. Abell, *DEFINING THE BUSINESS: The Starting Point of Strategic Planning,* © 1980, p. 207. Reprinted by permission of Prentice-Hall, Inc., Englewood Cliffs, N.J.

of new customer groups, a process of systemization results in the operation of products to serve combinations of functions, and the technology substitution process underlies change on a technology dimension."[14]

SERVED MARKET

Earlier in this chapter, it was concluded that the task of market boundary definition amounts to grouping together a set of market cells (see Exhibit 5-3), each defined in terms of three dimensions: customer groups, customer functions, and technologies. In other words, a market may comprise any combination of these cells. An additional question must now be answered. Should a business unit serve the entire market or limit itself to serving just a part of it? While it is conceivable that a business unit may decide to serve the total market, usually the served market is considerably narrower in scope and smaller in size than the total market. The decision about what market to serve is based on such factors as the following:

1. Perceptions of which product function and technology groupings can best be protected and dominated
2. Internal resource limitations that force a narrow focus
3. Cumulative trial-and-error experience in reacting to threats and opportunities
4. Unusual competencies stemming from access to scarce resources or protected markets.[15]

In practice, the choice of served market is not based on conscious, deliberate effort. Rather, circumstances and perceptions surrounding the business unit dictate the decision. For some businesses, lack of adequate resources limits the range of possibilities. Apple Computer, for example, would be naive to consider competing against IBM across the board. Further, as a business unit gains experience through trial and error, it may extend the scope of its served market. For example, the U.S. Post Office entered the overnight package delivery market to participate in an opportunity established by the Federal Express Company. The task of delineating the served market, however, is full of complications. As Day has noted:

> In practice, the task of grouping market cells to define a market is complicated. First, there is usually no one defensible criterion for grouping cells. There may be many ways to achieve the same function. Thus, boxed chocolates compete to some degree with flowers, records, and books as semicasual gifts. Do all of these products belong in the total market? To confound this problem, the available statistical and accounting data are often aggregated to a level where important distinctions between cells are completely obscured. Second, there are many products which evolve by adding new combinations of functions and technologies. Thus, radios are multifunctional products which include clocks, alarms, appearance options. To what extent do these variants dictate new market cells? Third, different competitors may choose different combinations of market cells to serve or to include in their total market definitions. In these situations there will be few direct competitors; instead, businesses will encounter each other in different but overlapping markets, and, as a result, may employ different strategies.[16]

Strategically, the choice of a business unit's served market may be based on the following approaches:

I. Breadth of Product Line

   A. Specialized in terms of technology, broad range of product uses
   B. Specialized in terms of product uses, multiple technologies
   C. Specialized in a single technology, narrow range of product uses

   D. Broad range of (related) technologies and uses
   E. Broad versus narrow range of quality/price levels

II. Types of Customers

   A. Single customer segment
   B. Multiple customer segments

      1. Undifferentiated treatment
      2. Differentiated treatment

III. Geographic Scope

   A. Local or regional
   B. National
   C. Multinational

IV. Level of Production/Distribution

   A. Raw or semifinished materials or components
   B. Finished products
   C. Wholesale or retail distribution

An Example of a Served Market

The choice of served market may be illustrated with reference to one company's entry into the snowmobile business.[17] The management of this company found snowmobiles an attractive market in terms of sales potential. The boundaries of this market are extensive. For example, in terms of technology, a snowmobile may be powered by gas, diesel fuel, or electricity. A snowmobile may fulfill such customer functions as delivery, recreation, and emergency transportation. Customer groups include household consumers, industrial buyers, and the military.

Since the company could not cover the total market, it had to define the market it would serve. To accomplish this task, the company developed a product/market matrix (see Exhibit 5-5a). The company could use any technology—gasoline, diesel, or electric—and it could design a snowmobile for any one of three customer groups: consumer, industrial, or military. The matrix in Exhibit 5-5a furnished nine possibilities for the company. Considering market potential and its competencies to compete, the part of the market that looked best was the diesel-powered snowmobile for the industrial market segment, the shaded area in Exhibit 5-5a.

But further narrowing of the market to be served was necessary. A second matrix (see Exhibit 5-5b) laid out the dimensions of customer use (function) and customer size. Thus, as shown in Exhibit 5-5b, snowmobiles could be designed for use as delivery vehicles (e.g., used by business firms and the post office), as recreation vehicles (e.g., rented at resort hotel sites), or as emergency vehicles (e.g., used by hospitals and police forces). Further, the design of the snowmobile would be affected by whether the company would sell to large, medium, or small customers. After evaluating the nine alternatives in Exhibit 5-5b, the com-

EXHIBIT 5-5
Defining the Served Market

		Market		
		Consumer	Industrial	Military
Technology	Gas-driven snowmobiles			
	Diesel-driven snowmobiles			
	Electric-driven snowmobiles			

(a) Technology/Market Matrix

		Customer Use		
		Delivery	Recreation	Emergency
Customer Use	Large			
	Medium			
	Small			

(b) Customer Use/Customer Size Matrix

Source: Philip Kotler, "Strategic Planning and the Marketing Process," *Business* (May–June 1980): 6–7. Reprinted by permission of the author.

pany found the large customer, delivery use market attractive, defining its served market as diesel-driven snowmobiles for use as delivery vehicles by large industrial customers.

Served Market Alternatives

In the preceding example, the company settled on a rather narrow definition of the served market. It could, however, expand the scope of the served market as it gains experience and as opportunities elsewhere in the market appear attractive. The following is a summary of the served market alternatives available to a business similar to this one.

1. Product/market concentration consists of the company's niching itself in only one part of the market. In the above example, the company's niche was making only diesel-driven snowmobiles for industrial buyers.
2. Product specialization consists of the company's deciding to produce only diesel-driven snowmobiles for all customer groups.
3. Market specialization consists of the company's deciding to make a variety of snowmobiles that serve the varied needs of a particular customer group, such as industrial buyers.
4. Selective specialization consists of the company's entering several product markets that have no relation to each other except that each provides an individually attractive opportunity.
5. Full coverage consists of the company's making a full range of snowmobiles to serve all market segments.

CUSTOMER SEGMENTATION

In the snowmobile example, the served market consisted of one segment. But conceivably, the served market could be much broader in scope. For example, the company could decide to serve all industrial customers (large, medium, small) by offering diesel-driven snowmobiles for delivery use. The "broader" served market, however, must be segmented because the market is not homogeneous; that is, it cannot be served by one type of product/service offering.

Currently, the United States represents the largest market in the world for most products; it is not a homogeneous market, however. Not all customers want the same thing. Particularly in well-supplied markets, customers generally prefer products or services that are tailored to their needs. Differences can be expressed in terms of product or service features, service levels, quality levels, or something else. In other words, the large market has a variety of submarkets, or segments, that vary substantially. One of the crucial elements of marketing strategy is to choose the segment or segments that are to be served. This, however, is not always easy because different methods for dissecting a market may be employed and deciding which method to use may pose a problem.[18]

Virtually all strategists segment their markets. Typically, they use SIC codes, annual purchase volume, age, and income as differentiating variables. Categories based on these variables, however, may not suffice as far as the development of strategy is concerned.

RCA, for example, initially classified potential customers for color television sets according to age, income, and social class. The company soon realized that these segments were not crucial for continued growth because potential buyers were not confined to those groups. Later analysis discovered that there were "innovators" and "followers" in each of the above groups. This finding led the company to tailor its marketing strategy to various segments according to their "innovativeness." Mass acceptance of color television might have been delayed substantially if RCA had followed a more traditional approach.[19]

An American food processor achieved rapid success in the French market after discovering that "modern" Frenchwomen liked processed foods while "traditional" French housewives looked upon them as a threat.

A leading industrial manufacturer discovered that its critical variable was the amount of annual usage per item, not per order or per any other conventional variable. This proved to be critical since heavy users can be expected to be more sensitive to price and may be more aware of and responsive to promotional perspectives.

Segmentation aims at increasing the scope of business by closely aligning a product or brand with an identifiable customer group. Take, for example, cigarettes. Thirty years ago, most cigarette smokers chose from among three brands: Camel, Chesterfield, and Lucky Strike. Today more than 160 brands adorn retail shelves. In order to sell more cigarettes, tobacco companies have been dividing the smoking public into relatively tiny sociological groups and then aiming one or more brands at each group. Vantage and Merit, for example, are aimed at young women; Camel and Winston are aimed mostly at rural smokers.[20] Cigarette marketing success hinges on how effectively a company can design a brand to appeal to a particular type of smoker and then on how well it can reach that smoker with sharply focused packaging, product design, and advertising.

What is true of cigarettes applies to many, many products; it applies even to services. Banks, for example, have been vying with one another for important customers by offering innovative services that set each bank apart from its competition.

These illustrations underscore not only the significance of segmenting the market but also the importance of carefully choosing segmentation criteria.

Segmentation Criteria

Segmentation criteria vary depending on the nature of the market. In consumer-goods marketing, one may use simple demographic and socioeconomic variables, personality and lifestyle variables, or situation-specific events (such as use intensity, brand loyalty, and attitudes) as the bases of segmentation. In industrial marketing, segmentation is achieved by forming end use segments, product segments, geographic segments, common buying factor segments, and customer size segments. Exhibit 5-6 provides an inventory of different bases for segmentation. Most of these bases are self-explanatory. For a detailed account, however, reference may be made to a textbook on marketing management.

In addition to these criteria, creative analysts may well identify others. For example, a shipbuilding company dissects its tanker market into large, medium, and small markets; similarly, its cargo ship market is classified into high-, medium-, and low-grade markets. A forklift manufacturer divides its market on the basis of product performance requirements. Many consumer-goods

EXHIBIT 5-6
Bases for Customer Segmentation

A. Consumer Markets

1. Demographic factors (age, income, sex, etc.)
2. Socioeconomic factors (social class, stage in the family life cycle)
3. Geographic factors
4. Psychological factors (liefstyle, personality traits)
5. Consumption patterns (heavy, moderate, and light users)
6. Perceptual factors (benefit segmentation, perceptual mapping)
7. Brand loyalty patterns

B. Industrial Markets

1. End use segments (identified by SIC code)
2. Product segments (based on technological differences or production economics)
3. Geographic segments (defined by boundaries between countries or by regional differences within them)
4. Common buying factor segments (cut across product/market and geographic segments)
5. Customer size segments

companies, General Foods, Procter and Gamble, and Coca-Cola among them, base their segments on lifestyle analysis.[21]

Data for forming customer segments may be analyzed with the use of simple statistical techniques (e.g., averages) or multivariate methods. Conceptually, the following procedure may be adopted to choose a criterion for segmentation:

1. Identify potential customers and the nature of their needs.
2. Segment all customers into groups having
   a. Common requirements.
   b. The same value system with respect to the importance of these requirements.
3. Determine the theoretically most efficient means of serving each market segment, making sure that the distribution system selected differentiates each segment with respect to cost and price.
4. Adjust this ideal system to the constraints of the real world: existing commitments, legal restrictions, practicality, and so forth.

A market can also be segmented by level of customer service, stage of production, price/performance characteristics, credit arrangements with customers, location of plants, characteristics of manufacturing equipment, channels of distribution, and financial policies. The key is to choose a variable or variables that so divide the market that customers in a segment respond similarly to some aspect of the marketer's strategy. The variable should be measurable; that is, it should represent an objective value, such as income, rate of consumption, or frequency of buying, not simply a qualitative viewpoint, such as the degree of customer happiness. Also, the variable should create segments that may be accessible through promotion. Even if it is feasible to measure happiness, segments based on the happiness variable cannot be reached by a specific promotional medium. Finally, segments should be substantial in size; that is, they should be sufficiently large to warrant a separate marketing effort.

Once segments have been formed, the next strategic issue is deciding which segment should be selected. The selected segment should comply with the following conditions:

1. It should be one in which the maximum differential in competitive strategy can be developed.
2. It must be capable of being isolated so that competitive advantage can be preserved.
3. It must be valid even though imitated.

The success of Volkswagen in the United States in 1960 can be attributed to its fit into a market segment that had two unique characteristics. First, the segment served by VW could not be adequately served by a modification to conventional U.S. cars. Second, U.S. manufacturers' economies of scale could not be brought to bear to the disadvantage of VW. In contrast, American Motors was equally successful in identifying a special segment to serve with its compact car, the Rambler. The critical difference was that American Motors could not protect that segment from the superior scale of manufacturing volume of the other three U.S. automobile producers.

The choice of strategically critical segments is not straightforward. It requires careful evaluation of business strengths as compared with the competition. It also requires analytical marketing research to uncover market segments in which these competitive strengths can be significant.

In consumer markets, rarely do market segments conveniently coincide with such obvious categories as religion, age, profession, or family income; in the industrial sector, with the size of company. For this reason, market segmentation is emphatically not a job for statisticians. Rather, it is a task that can be mastered only by the creative strategist.

Micromarketing, or Segment-Of-One Marketing

An interesting development in the past few years has been the emergence of a new segmentation concept called **micromarketing**, or **segment-of-one marketing**. Forced by competitive pressures, mass marketers have discovered that a segment can be trimmed down to smaller subsegments, even to an individual. Micromarketing combines two independent concepts: information retrieval and service delivery. On one side is a proprietary database of customers' preferences and purchase behaviors; on the other is a disciplined, tightly engineered approach to service delivery that uses the database to tailor a service package for individual customers or a group of customers. Of course, such custom-designed service is nothing new, but until recently, only the very wealthy could afford it. Information technology has brought the level of service associated with the old carriage trade within reach of the middle class.

Micromarketing requires

1. **Knowing the customers**—Using high-tech techniques, find out who the customers are—and aren't. By linking that knowledge with data about ads and coupons, fine-tune marketing strategy.
2. **Making what they want**—Tailor products to individual tastes. Where once there were just Oreos, now there are Fudge Covered Oreos, Oreo Double Stufs, and Oreo Big Stufs.
3. **Using targeted and new media**—Advertising on cable television and in magazines can be used to reach special audiences. In addition, develop new ways to reach customers. For example, messages on walls in high-school lunchrooms, on videocassettes, and even on blood pressure monitors may be considered.
4. **Using nonmedia**—Sponsor sports, festivals, and other events to reach local or ethnic markets.
5. **Reaching customers in the store**—Consumers make most buying decisions while they are shopping, so put ads on supermarket loudspeakers, shopping carts, and in-store monitors.
6. **Sharpening promotions**—Couponing and price promotions are expensive and often harmful to a brand's image. Thanks to better data, some companies are using fewer, more effective promotions. One promising approach: aiming coupons at a competitor's customers.
7. **Working with retailers**—Consumer-goods manufacturers must learn to "micro market" to the retail trade, too. Some are linking their computers to retailers' computers, and some are tailoring their marketing and promotions to an individual retailer's needs.

An example of micromarketing is provided by a North Carolina bank, First Wachovia.[22] The bank's staff serves all customers the way it used to serve its best customer. The staff greets each customer by name and provides personalized information about her or his finances and how they relate to long-term objectives. Based on this knowledge, the staff suggests new products. In this way, the commodity retail banking has been turned into a customized, personalized service. This marketing strategy has resulted in more sales at lower marketing costs and powerful switching barriers relative to the competition. Three major investments are behind this seemingly effortless new level of service: a comprehensive customer database, accessible wherever the customer makes contact with the bank; an extensive training program that teaches a personalized service approach; and an ongoing personal communications program with each customer. Similarly, Noxell's Clarion line illustrates how micromarketing can be implemented. When the company introduced this line of mass market cosmetics in drugstores, it looked for a way to differentiate it in a crowded market. The answer was the Clarion computer. Customers type in the characteristics of their skin and receive a regimen selected from the Clarion line, thus providing department store–type personal advice without sales pressure in the much more convenient drug channel.

SUMMARY

This chapter examined the role of the third strategic C—the customer—in formulating marketing strategy. One strategic consideration in determining marketing strategy is the definition of the market. A conceptual framework for defining the market was outlined.

The underlying factor in the formation of a market is customer need. The concept of need was discussed with reference to Maslow's hierarchy of needs. Once a market emerges, its worth must be determined through examining its potential. Different methods may be employed to study market potential.

Based on its potential, if a market appears worth tapping, its boundaries must be identified. Traditionally, market boundaries have been defined on the basis of product/market scope. Recent work on the subject recommends that market boundaries be established around the following dimensions: technology, customer function, and customer group. Level of production/distribution was suggested as a fourth dimension. The task of market boundary definition amounts to grouping together a set of market cells, each defined in terms of these dimensions.

Market boundaries set the limits of the market. Should a business unit serve a total market or just a part of it? Although it is conceivable to serve an entire market, usually the served market is considerably narrower in scope and smaller in size than the total market. Factors that influence the choice of served market were examined.

The served market may be too broad to be served by a single marketing program. If so, then the served market must be segmented. The rationale for segmentation was given, and a procedure for segmenting the market was outlined.

DISCUSSION QUESTIONS

1. Elaborate on marketing's boundary role function. How is it related to customer needs?
2. Identify the elements determined by market potential.
3. What dimensions may be used to define market boundaries?
4. Illustrate the use of these dimensions with a practical example.
5. What is meant by served market? What factors determine the served market?
6. How may a business unit choose the criteria for segmenting the market?
7. Describe the concept of micromarketing. How may a durable goods company adopt it to its business?

NOTES

[1]See Bruce D. Henderson, "The Origin of Strategy," *Harvard Business Review* (November–December 1989): 141.

[2]Thomas S. Robertson and Yoram Wind, "Marketing Strategy," in *Handbook of Business Strategy* (New York: McGraw-Hill Book Co., 1982). See also Yoram Wind and Thomas S. Robertson, "Marketing Strategy: New Directions for Theory and Research," *Journal of Marketing* (Spring 1983): 12–25.

[3]Kenichi Ohmae, "Getting Back to Strategy," *Harvard Business Review* (November–December 1988): 155–56.

[4]Philip Kotler, *Marketing Management*, 5th ed. (Englewood Cliffs, NJ: Prentice-Hall, 1984), 230.

[5]Terry C. Wilson, "An Opportunity Screening Model," in *1983 AMA Educators' Proceedings* (Chicago: American Marketing Association, 1983), 324–25.

[6]George S. Day and Allan D. Shocker, *Identifying Competitive Product-Market Boundaries: Strategic and Analytical Issues* (Cambridge, MA: Marketing Science Institute, 1976), 1.

[7]Adapted from Robert D. Buzzell, "Note on Market Definition and Segmentation," a Harvard Business School Note, 1978, distributed by HBS Case Services.

[8]Peter Asch, *Economic Theory and the Antitrust Dilemma* (New York: John Wiley & Sons, 1970), 168. See also George S. Day, Allan D. Shocker, and Rajendra K. Srivastava, "Customer-oriented Approaches to Identifying Product Markets," *Journal of Marketing* (Fall 1979): 8–19; and Rajendra K. Srivastava, Robert P. Leone, and Allan D. Shocker, "Market Structure Analysis: Hierarchical Clustering of Products Based on Substitution-in-Use," *Journal of Marketing* (Summer 1981): 38–48.

[9]Jack Z. Sissors, "What Is a Market?" *Journal of Marketing* (July 1968): 17.

[10]Derek F. Abell, *Defining the Business: The Starting Point of Strategic Planning* (Englewood Cliffs, NJ: Prentice-Hall, 1980).

[11]Buzzell, "Note on Market Definition and Segmentation."

[12]Buzzell, "Note on Market Definition and Segmentation," 6.

[13]Day and Shocker, *Identifying Competitive Product-Market Boundaries.*

[14]Abell, *Defining the Business*, 207.

[15]George S. Day, "Strategic Market Analysis and Definition: An Integrated Approach," *Strategic Management Journal* 2 (1981): 284.

[16]Day, "Strategic Market Analysis and Definition," 288.

[17]See Philip Kotler, "Strategic Planning and the Marketing Process," *Business* (May–June 1980): 2–9.

[18]Peter R. Dickson and James L. Ginter, "Market Segmentation, Product Differentiation, and Marketing Strategy," *Journal of Marketing* (April 1987): 1–10

[19]"Strategy and Market Segment Research," an informal statement issued by the Boston Consulting Group, 1968.

[20]John Koten, "Tobacco Marketer's Success Formula: Make Cigarettes in Smoker's Own Image," *Wall Street Journal*, 29 February 1980, p. 22. See also "Banking Squeeze: The Search for Special Niches," *Business Week* (12 April 1982): 70.

[21]See Jack A. Lesser and Marie Adele Hughes, "The Generalizability of Psychographic Market Segments across Geographic Locations," *Journal of Marketing* (January 1986): 18–27. See also "Stalking the New Consumer," *Business Week* (28 August 1989).

[22]Kathleen Deveny, "Segments of One," *Wall Street Journal*, 22 March 1991, p. B4. See also "Segment-of-One Marketing," *Perspectives* (Boston: Boston Consulting Group, 1989).

CHAPTER 6

Scanning the Environment

I hold that man is in the right who is most in league with the future.
HENRIK IBSEN

An organization is a creature of its environment. Its very survival and all of its perspectives, resources, problems, and opportunities are generated and conditioned by the environment. Thus, it is important for an organization to monitor the relevant changes taking place in its environment and formulate strategies to adapt to these changes. In other words, for an organization to survive and prosper, the strategist must master the challenges of the profoundly changing political, economic, technological, social, and regulatory environment. To achieve this broad perspective, the strategist needs to develop and implement a systematic approach to environmental scanning. As the rate and magnitude of change increase, this scanning activity must be intensified and directed by explicit definitions of purpose, scope, and focus. The efforts of businesses to cope with these problems are contributing to the development of systems for exploring alternatives with greater sensitivity to long-run implications. This emerging science has the promise of providing a better framework for maximizing opportunities and allocating resources in anticipation of environmental changes.

This chapter reviews the state of the art of environmental scanning and suggests a general approach that may be used by a marketing strategist. Specifically, the chapter discusses the criteria for determining the scope and focus of scanning, the procedure for examining the relevance of environmental trends, the techniques for evaluating the impact of an environmental trend on a particular product/market, and the linking of environmental trends and other "early warning signals" to strategic planning processes.

IMPORTANCE OF ENVIRONMENTAL SCANNING

Without taking into account relevant environmental influences, a company cannot expect to develop its strategy. It was the environmental influences emerging out of the energy crisis that were responsible for the popularity of smaller, more fuel-efficient automobiles and that brought about the demise of less efficient rotary engines. It was the environmental influence of a coffee bean shortage and geometric price increases that spawned the "coffee-saver" modification in Mr. Coffee automatic drip coffee makers. Shopper and merchant complaints from an earlier era contributed to the virtual elimination of deposit bottles; recent pressures from environmental groups, however, have forced their return and have prompted companies to develop low-cost recyclable plastic bottles.

Another environmental trend, Americans' insatiable appetite for eating out (in 1990 restaurant sales accounted for $0.44 of every $1 spent on food; this number is expected to reach $0.63 by the year 2000), worries food companies like Kraft. In response, Kraft is trying to make cooking as convenient as eating out (e.g., by providing high-quality convenience foods) to win back food dollars.[1]

The sad tales of companies that seemingly did everything right and yet lost competitive leadership as a result of technological change abound. Du Pont was beaten by Celanese when bias-ply tire cords changed from nylon to polyester. B.F. Goodrich was beaten by Michelin when the radial overtook the bias-ply tire. NCR wrote off $139 million in electromechanical inventory and the equipment to make it when solid-state point-of-sale terminals entered the market. Indeed, none of the leading vacuum tube manufacturers in 1957 remained as competitive forces after 1977. These companies lost even though they were low-cost producers. They lost even though they were close to their customers. They lost even though they were market leaders. They lost because they failed to make an effective transition from old to new technology.[2]

In brief, business derives its existence from the environment. Thus, it should monitor its environment constructively. Business should scan the environment and incorporate the impact of environmental trends on the organization by continually reviewing the corporate strategy. According to Glover:

> Perceiving in the environment needs and opportunities for adaptation—even before they actually materialize—and designing and seeing through a continuous procession of actions to carry out adaptive innovation, these are the essence of business strategy. More—these are the distinguishing functions of the top management. It is the job of corporate top management to direct and to manage the transformation of every aspect of the corporation in response to developments of the dynamic environment. A corporation gets left behind whose management lacks these capacities. The environment represents an ever-changing sum total of the "facts of life" with which the corporation has to come to terms. Willy-nilly the environment is the unyielding, unforgiving frame of reference for everything top management does as it guides the corporation.[3]

The underlying importance of environmental scanning is captured in Darwinian laws: (a) the environment is ever-changing, (b) organisms have the ability to adapt to a changing environment, and (c) organisms that do not adapt do not survive. The Naisbitt Group has identified 10 megatrends that will deeply affect individuals and businesses for the rest of this century (see Exhibit 6-1). We are indeed living in a rapidly changing world. Many things that we take for granted today were not even imagined in the 1960s. Before the end of this century, many more "wonders" will come to exist.

EXHIBIT 6-1
10 Trends for the Twenty-First Century

1. **From Fixed to Responsive Systems.** Businesses and government agencies are responding to changing consumer and employee needs by showing a new flexible attitude toward a fast-paced and convenience-oriented society. In many offices, workers now share jobs or even arrange their own hours. At some schools, children arrive earlier and leave later to accommodate working parents' busy schedules. But the shift is most apparent in the retail sector where a number of stores, including beauty salons and walk-in medical clinics, stay open around the clock.
2. **From Nation State to Business State.** Business leaders are the politicians of the future. Worldwide, corporations deal with domestic and international issues once considered the sole purview of government. The future also will bring a new breed of politician, who runs his or her government like a corporation, heavily promoting advantages for business. In the future, the international ties between business leaders and politicians will grow stronger. This trend bodes well for world peace and stability.
3. **From Technological Complexity to Technological "Transparency."**—Tomorrow's technology will be so efficient that we won't even notice it's there. This is the trend toward transparency—invisible technology that's so simple to use, it's taken for granted. Spurning confusing gadgetry, consumers want products that use technology effortlessly.
4. **From the Mass Middle to the Extremes.** Manufacturers, hospitals, shopping malls and magazines—all are profiteers (and victims) of the shift from the mass middle to the extreme. In both business and society, the nation is moving away from middle size, middle quality, and middle price.

   The results of this shift are shakeouts and new niches at the same time. One example: In health care, hospitals must either cater to specialized markets or be part of large health networks. In the retail segment, the thriving retailers are either high-volume discounters or specialty boutiques. In most cases, the "in-between" is disappearing.

   In the future, watch for more superstores that steer clear of midsize and midprice. Just as middle managers were the corporate casualties of the early 1980s, the ranks of middlemen in many industries will diminish during the rest of the decade.
5. **From a National Lifestyle to a Global Lifestyle.** Deep-dish pizza in New Delhi, coffee and bagels in Tokyo and "les shakes" along the Champs-Elysees: All are part of the globalization of lifestyles, an international crisscross of work and leisure trends. Characteristic of this movement is the rapid growth of multinational corporations, which now can sell almost anything anywhere. More and more, people from vastly different cultures and climates are eating the same foods, wearing similar clothes, living in the same kinds of housing, sharing music and movies, magazines and television shows. Satellite technology, international travel and the gradual loosening of previously closed borders play a large role. But at the same time that countries are welcoming foreign technology and conveniences, they also are trying harder to preserve old traditions. So while we may watch more internationally broadcast TV shows, more of us will celebrate our "roots," embracing products and events that represent our special heritage. It's the best of all cultures.
6. **From a Permissive to an "Open Square" Society.** If you think society is sending you mixed signals, you're right. Today's society is both "square" and open at the same

continued

EXHIBIT 6-1
continued

time. Call it the age of social paradox, a time when seemingly contradictory events and attitudes occur simultaneously. Just look at how some retailers have banned the sale of certain obscene material, while television talk shows openly examine once-taboo subjects such as sex, drug addiction, and mental illness. It's as if our moral foundation is sturdier, yet the door is always ajar to allow new ideas to enter. For corporate America, this trend means operating in a milieu that emphasizes business ethics but remains unschockable and nonjudgmental. Expect businesses to establish both stricter ethical codes and, at the same time, more sympathetic policies toward employees' problems.

7. **From Competition to Cooperation.** No company is an island. At least that's what today's businesses are discovering as more and more of them join forces to save operating and advertising costs. Take Montgomery Ward and Toys R Us, for example, two separate companies that jointly own a store in Gaithersburg, Maryland. Financial institutions have begun to share electronic banking systems. The cooperation trend is sweeping through almost every industry, from communications to food to health care. The good news for corporations: cooperation will lead to a better competitive stance. But don't think for one minute that the business environment will be any less competitive in the future. Cooperation will be just another tool savvy businesses use to compete more successfully.
8. **From Responsibility by Institution to Responsibility by Function.** Once upon a time, we took for granted that governments would provide public services, mothers would raise children, religious institutions would set moral values and schools would educate. But massive social and economic changes over the last two decades have altered these expectations. Private institutions and businesses are stepping in to shoulder the burden by providing day care, housing, crime prevention and transportation, as well as setting and teaching values. Service providers no longer are determined by traditional lines of responsibility, but instead by ability. This relentless restructuring of societal responsibility will call for a more responsive and flexible style of leadership in all institutions.
9. **From Central City to Polynucleic Metropolis.** If you suggested a rendezvous in "downtown" Orlando, you'd garner a few snickers. That's because Orlando has at least four downtown areas. It's part of the demographic shift away from the central city to sprawling "urban villages" sprouting up in the suburbs outside major metropolitan areas. In scores of places nationwide, bedroom communities and farmland are being transformed into megacenters, providing less expensive housing but choking transportation and educational systems. It's a shift that directly affects the quality of life: while it grants residents more open space and more aesthetic surroundings, it has also made commuting a nightmare. Our work habits are being transformed, giving rise to alternative arrangements such as office/residential parks and the use of home computers to "telecommute."
10. **From Complacency to Accountability.** It's nearly impossible to get away with anything these days. While we've grown more tolerant of people's foibles, we also demand that individuals and businesses be held accountable for their actions. Accountability transcends criminal or insurance liabilities; it affects manufacturers,

EXHIBIT 6-1
continued

politicians, Wall Street brokers, teachers, and others. Even grandparents of children born to unmarried minors in Wisconsin can be held liable for child support.

The trend is clear: it's no longer safe to be "nonneligent." Complacency—often the norm of the past—will be a risky stance to take in the future.

Source: John Elkins, "Ten Trends for the 21st Century," *Old Oregon*, no date, pp. 25–28.

To survive and prosper in the midst of a changing environment, companies must stay at the forefront of changes affecting their industries. First, it must be recognized that all products and processes have performance limits and that the closer one comes to these limits the more expensive it becomes to squeeze out the next generation of performance improvements. Second, one must take all competition seriously. Normally competitor analyses seem to implicitly assume that the most serious competitors are the ones with the largest resources. But in the context of taking advantage of environmental shifts, this assumption is frequently not adequate. Texas Instruments was a $5- to $10-million company in 1955 when it took on the mighty vacuum tube manufacturers—RCA, GE, Sylvania, and Westinghouse—and beat them with its semiconductor technology. Boeing was nearly bankrupt when it successfully introduced the commercial jet plane, vanquishing larger and more financially secure Lockheed, McDonnell, and Douglas corporations.

Third, if the environmental change promises potential advantage, one has to attack to win and attack even to play the game. Attack means gaining access to new technology, training people in its use, investing in capacity to use it, devising strategies to protect the position, and holding off on investments in mature lines. For example, IBM capitalized on the emerging personal computer market created by its competitor, Apple Computer. By becoming the low-cost producer, distributor, seller, and servicer of personal computers for business use, IBM took command of the marketplace in less than two years.

Fourth, the attack has to begin early. The substitution of one product or process for another proceeds slowly and then rarely predictably explodes. One cannot wait for the explosion to occur to react. There is simply not enough time. B.F. Goodrich lost 25 percentage points of market share to Michelin in four years. Texas Instruments passed RCA in sales of active electronic devices in five to six years.

Fifth, a close tie is needed between the CEO and the operating managers. Facing change means incorporating the environmental shifts in all aspects of the company's strategy.[4]

WHAT SCANNING CAN ACCOMPLISH

Scanning improves an organization's abilities to deal with a rapidly changing environment in a number of ways:

1. It helps an organization capitalize on early opportunities rather than lose these to competitors.
2. It provides an early signal of impending problems, which can be defused if recognized well in advance.
3. It sensitizes an organization to the changing needs and wishes of its customers.
4. It provides a base of objective qualitative information about the environment that strategists can utilize.
5. It provides intellectual stimulation to strategists in their decision making.
6. It improves the image of the organization with its publics by showing that it is sensitive to its environment and responsive to it.
7. It is a means of continuing broad-based education for executives, especially for strategy developers.

THE CONCEPT OF ENVIRONMENT

Operationally, five different types of environments may be identified—technological, political, economic, regulatory, and social—and the environment may be scanned at three different levels in the organization—corporate, SBU, and product/market level (see Exhibit 6-2). Perspectives of environmental scanning vary from level to level. Corporate scanning broadly examines happenings in different environments and focuses on trends with corporatewide implications. For example, IBM, at the corporate level, may review the impact of competition

EXHIBIT 6-2
Constituents of Environment

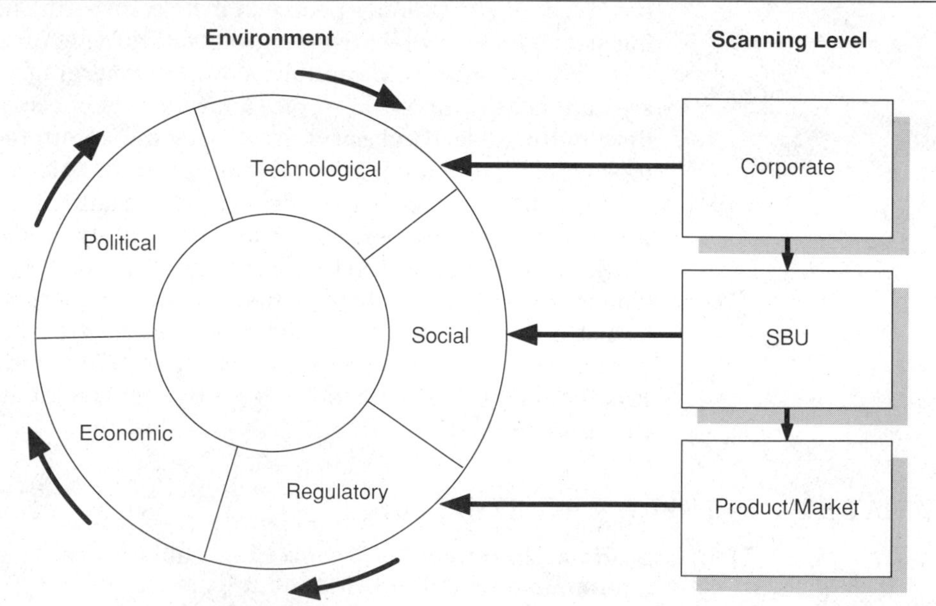

in the telephone industry on the availability and rates of long-distance telephone lines to its customers. Emphasis at the SBU level focuses on those changes in the environment that may influence the future direction of the business. At IBM the SBU concerned with personal computers may study such environmental perspectives as diffusion rate of personal computers, new developments in integrated circuit technology, and the political debates in progress on the registration (similar to automobile registration) of personal computers. At the product/market level, scanning is limited to day-to-day aspects. For example, an IBM personal computer marketing manager may review the significance of rebates, a popular practice among IBM's competitors.

The emphasis in this chapter is on environmental scanning from the viewpoint of the SBU. The primary purpose is to gain a comprehensive view of the future business world as a foundation on which to base major strategic decisions.

STATE OF THE ART

Scanning serves as an early warning system for the environmental forces that may impact a company's products and markets in the future. Environmental scanning is a comparatively new development. Traditionally, corporations evaluated themselves mainly on the basis of financial performance. In general, the environment was studied only for the purpose of making economic forecasts. Other environmental factors were brought in haphazardly, if at all, and intuitively. In recent years, however, most large corporations have started doing systematic work in this area.[5]

The slow progress made in relating the environment to one's business can be explained by the difficulty involved in undertaking such an analysis. It is only during the past decade that management science has concerned itself with environmental analysis. The work done or sponsored by such institutions as the Hudson Institute, the Rand Corporation, SRI International, and the World Future Society has made it easier for corporations to undertake scientific analysis of the environment.

A pioneering study on environmental scanning was done by Francis Aguilar. In his investigation of selected chemical companies in the United States and Europe, he found no systematic approach to environmental scanning. Aguilar's 16 types of information (see Exhibit 6-3) about the environment that the companies found interesting have been consolidated into five groups: market tidings, acquisition leads, technical tidings, broad issues, and other tidings. Among these groups, market tidings was found to be the dominant category and was of most interest to managers across the board.

Aguilar also identified four patterns for viewing information: undirected viewing (exposure without a specific purpose), conditioned viewing (directed exposure but without undertaking an active search), informal search (collection of purpose-oriented information in an informal manner), and formal search (a structured process for collection of specific information for a designated pur-

EXHIBIT 6-3
What External Information Do Managers Obtain?

Category	*General Concept*
Market Tidings	
Market potential	Supply and demand consideration for market areas of current or potential interest: e.g., capacity, consumption, imports, exports
Structural change	Mergers, acquisitions, and joint ventures involving competitors, new entries into the industry
Competitors and industry	General information about a competitor, industry policy, concerted actions in the industry, and so forth
Pricing	Effective and proposed prices for products of current and potential interest
Sales negotiations	Information relating to a specific current or near-potential sale or contract for the firm
Customers	General information about current or near-potential customers, their markets, their problems
Acquisition Leads	
Leads for mergers, joint ventures	Information concerning possibilities for the manager's own company
Technical Tidings	
New products, processes, and technology	Technical information relatively new and unknown to the company
Product problems	Problems involving existing products
Costs	Costs for processing, operations, and so forth for current and potential competitors, suppliers, and customers, and for proposed company activities
Licensing and patents	Products and processes
Broad Issues	
General Conditions	Events of a general nature: political, demographic, national, and so forth
Government actions and policies	Governmental decisions affecting the industry

EXHIBIT 6-3
continued

Other Tidings	
Suppliers and raw materials	Purchasing considerations for products of current or potential interest
Resources available	Persons, land, and other resources possibly available for the company
Miscellaneous	Items not elsewhere classified

Source: Francis Joseph Aguilar, *Scanning the Business Environment* (New York: Macmillan Co., 1967), p. 40.

pose). Both internal and external sources were used in seeking this information. The external comprised both personal sources (customers, suppliers, bankers, consultants, and other knowledgeable individuals) and impersonal sources (various publications, conferences, trade shows, exhibitions, and so on). The internal personal sources included peers, superiors, and subordinates. The internal impersonal sources included regular and general reports and scheduled meetings. Aguilar's study concluded that while the process is not simple, a company can systematize its environmental scanning activities for strategy development.[6]

Aguilar's framework may be illustrated with reference to the Coca-Cola Company. The company looks at its environment through a series of analyses. At the corporate level, considerable information is gathered on economic, social, and political factors affecting the business and on competition both in the United States and overseas. The corporate office also becomes involved in special studies when it feels that some aspect of the environment requires special attention. For example, in 1982, to address itself to a top management concern about Pepsi's claim that the taste of its cola was superior to Coke's, the company undertook a study to understand what was going on in the minds of their consumers and what they were looking for. How was the consumption of Coca-Cola related to their lifestyle, to their set of values, to their needs? This study spearheaded the work toward the introduction of New Coke.

In the mid-1980s, the corporate office also made a study of the impact of antipollution trends on government regulations concerning packaging. At the corporate level, environment was scanned rather broadly. Mostly market tidings, technical tidings, and broad issues were dealt with. Whenever necessary, in-depth studies were done on a particular area of concern, and corporate information was made available to different divisions of the company.

At the division level (e.g., Coca-Cola, USA), considerable attention is given to the market situation, acquisition leads, and new business ventures. The division also studies general economic conditions (trends in GNP, consumption, income), government regulation (especially antitrust actions), social factors, and even the political situation. Part of this division-level scanning duplicates the efforts of the corporate office, but the divisional planning staff felt that it was in a position to do a better job for its own purpose than could the corporate office, which had to serve the needs of other divisions as well. The division also undertakes special studies. For example, in the early 1980s, it wondered whether a caffeine-free drink should be introduced and, if so, when.

The information received from the corporate office and that which the division had collected itself was analyzed for events and happenings that could affect the company's current and potential business. Analysis was done mostly through meetings and discussions rather than through the use of any statistical model. At the Coca-Cola Company, environmental analysis is a sort of forum. There is relatively little cohesion among managers; the meetings, therefore, respond to a need for exchange of information between people.

A recent study of environmental scanning identifies four evolutionary phases of activity, from primitive to proactive (see Exhibit 6-4). The scanning activities in most corporations can be characterized by one of these four phases.[7]

In phase 1, the primitive phase, the environment is taken as something inevitable and random about which nothing can be done other than to accept each impact as it occurs. Management is exposed to information, both strategic and nonstrategic, without making any effort to distinguish the difference. No dis-

EXHIBIT 6-4
Four Phases in the Evolution of Environmental Scanning

PHASE 1	PHASE 2	PHASE 3	PHASE 4
Primitive	**Ad Hoc**	**Reactive**	**Proactive**
Face the environment as it appears	*Watch out for a likely impact on the environment*	*Deal with the environment to protect the future*	*Predict the environment for a desired future*
• Exposure to information without purpose and effort	• No active search • Be sensitive to information on specific issues	• Unstructured and random effort • Less specific information collection	• Structured and deliberate effort • Specific information collection • Preestablished methodology
Scanning without an Impetus	Scanning to Enhance Understanding of a Specific Event	Scanning to Make an Appropriate Response to Markets and Competition	Strategic Scanning to Be on the Lookout for Competitive Advantage

crimination is used to discern strategic information, and the information is rarely related to strategic decision making. As a matter of fact, scanning takes place without management devoting any effort to it.

Phase 2, the ad hoc phase, is an improvement over phase 1 in that management identifies a few areas that need to be watched carefully; however, there is no formal system for scanning and no initiative is taken to scan the environment. In addition, that management is sensitive to information about specific areas does not imply that this information is subsequently related to strategy formulation. This phase is characterized by such statements as this: All reports seem to indicate that rates of interest will not increase substantially in the 1990s, but our management will never sit down to seriously consider what we might do or not do as a company to capitalize on this trend in the pursuit of our goals. Typically, the ad hoc phase characterizes companies that have traditionally done well and whose management, which is intimately tied to day-to-day operations, recently happened to hire a young M.B.A. to do strategic planning.

In phase 3, the reactive phase, environmental scanning begins to be viewed as important, and efforts are made to monitor the environment to seek information in different areas. In other words, management fully recognizes the significance of the environment and dabbles in scanning but in an unplanned, unstructured fashion. Everything in the environment appears to be important, and the company is swamped with information. Some of the scanned information may never be looked into; some is analyzed, understood, and stored. As soon as the leading firm in the industry makes a strategic move in a particular matter, presumably in response to an environmental shift, the company in phase 3 is quick to react, following the footsteps of the leader. For example, if the use of glass bottles for soft drinks appears uncertain, the phase 3 company will understand the problem on the horizon but hesitate to take a strategic lead. If the leading firm decides to experiment with plastic bottles, the phase 3 firm will quickly respond in kind. In other words, the phase 3 firm understands the problems and opportunities that the future holds, but its management is unwilling to be the first to take steps to avoid problems or to capitalize on opportunities. A phase 3 company waits for a leading competitor to pave the way.

The firm in phase 4, the proactive phase, practices environmental scanning with vigor and zeal, employing a structured effort. Careful screening focuses the scanning effort on specified areas considered crucial. Time is taken to establish proper methodology, disseminate scanned information, and incorporate it into strategy. A hallmark of scanning in phase 4 is the distinction between macro and micro scanning. **Macro scanning** refers to scanning of interest to the entire corporation and is undertaken at the corporate level. **Micro scanning** is often practiced at the product/market or SBU level. A corporatewide scanning system is created to ensure that macro and micro scanning complement each other. The system is designed to provide open communication between different micro scanners to avoid duplication of effort and information.

A multinational study of the subject concluded that environmental scanning is on its way to becoming a full-fledged formalized step in the strategic planning process. This commitment to environmental scanning has been triggered in part by the recognition of environmental turbulence and a willingness to confront relevant changes within the planning process. Commitment aside, there is yet no accepted, effective methodology for environmental scanning.[8]

TYPES OF ENVIRONMENT

Corporations today, more than ever before, are profoundly sensitive to technological, political, economic, social, and regulatory changes. Although environmental changes may be felt throughout an organization, the impact most affects strategic perspectives. To cope with a changing and shifting environment, the marketing strategist must find new ways to forecast the shape of things to come and to analyze strategic alternatives and, at the same time, develop greater sensitivity to long-term implications. Various techniques that are especially relevant for projecting long-range trends are discussed in the appendix at the end of this chapter. Suffice it to say here that environmental scanning necessarily implies a forecasting perspective.

Technological Environment

Technological developments come out of the research effort. Two types of research can be distinguished: basic and applied. A company may engage in applied research only or may undertake both basic and applied research. In either case, a start has to be made at the basic level, and from there the specific effect on a company's product or process has to be derived. A company may choose not to undertake any research on its own, accepting a secondary role as an imitator. The research efforts of imitators will be limited mainly to the adaptation of a particular technological change to its business.

Three different aspects of technology are category, process, and impetus. Technology itself can be grouped into five categories: energy, materials, transportation, communications and information, and genetic (includes agronomic and biomedical). The original impetus for technological breakthroughs can come from any or all of three sources: meeting defense needs, seeking the welfare of the masses, and making a mark commercially. The three stages in the process of technological development are invention, the creation of a new product or process; innovation, the introduction of that product or process into use; and diffusion, the spread of the product or process beyond first use.

The category of technology a company prefers is dictated, of course, by the company's interests. Impetus points to the market for technological development, and the process of development shows the state of technological development and whether the company is in a position to interface with the technology in any stage. For example, the invention and innovation stages may call for basic research beyond the resources of a company. Diffusion, however, may require adaptation, which may not be as difficult as the other two stages.

To illustrate the point, let us look at personal computers. In the 1960s, as computers made inroads in the business world, a number of data processing bureaus were born to service small companies that could not afford computers.

Over the years, these bureaus have rendered a very useful service by processing such information as payroll, accounts receivable, and accounts payable. Developments in the field of computer technology made it feasible in the late 1970s to build and market small computers at a price within the reach of small businesses. While a typical computer in the 1960s sold for more than $100,000, in 1991 a personal computer could be purchased for as little as $500. The personal computer has become a threat to the data processing service bureaus because small businesses can now choose between buying their own computers and hiring the services of a data processing bureau.

Let us also consider technology's impact on the consumer-goods industry. Before long, technology will enable a music fan to pull out a small sheet of plastic, about the size of a slice of toast, and put this "record" containing millions of bits of computer data on a machine that reads the computer code with a low-power laser beam. Such computerized, or digital, records will be capable of playing uninterruptedly for $2\frac{1}{2}$ hours, long enough to encompass a full-length opera on one side alone.

Prototypes of this technological breakthrough already exist, and more than 20 manufacturers in Japan, the United States, and Europe are racing to bring this new technology to a stage suitable for the mass market. This technological development has been likened to such breakthroughs as the introduction of electrically made commercial records in 1925 and the switch from 78 rpm shellac records to vinyl LP disks in the 1950s. Needless to say, this new technological leap poses a great threat to the $4-billion-a-year record and tape industry. Many members of the industry may join the race to embrace the new development and themselves offer computerized records. Others may be obliged to leave the industry. A changeover to the new technology cannot be accomplished overnight. Those record companies that have scanned their technological environment and followed the trend will be able to make a positive response. Those who do not keep up with the changing technology will have a hard time coping with the technological breakthrough.[9]

Startling things have been happening to the television set in the last few years. For example, Panasonic now offers a color-projection system with a 60-inch screen. Toshiba Corp. of Japan has developed large, flat screen television sets that are so slim that they can hang on the wall like paintings. Even traditional 19-inch sets aren't just for looking at anymore; they are basic equipment on which to play video games, to learn how to spell, or to practice math. Videodisc players produce television images from discs; videocassette recorders tape television shows and play prerecorded videotapes. With two-way television, the viewer can respond to questions flashed on the screen. Teleprint enables the conversion of television sets into video-display tubes so that viewers can scan the contents of newspapers, magazines, catalogs, or whatever and call up any sections of interest. Finally, cable television permits the viewer to call on the system's library for a game, movie, or even a French lesson.

The 1990s are almost certain to be a period of technological change and true innovation. One of the areas of greatest impact is going to be communications.

Until now, electronic communication has largely been confined to the traditional definition of voice (telephone), pictures (television), and graphics (computer), distinct kinds of communication devices. From now on, electronics will increasingly produce total communications. In 1986, Trintex, a joint venture of IBM and Sears, came into operation in this country, making simultaneous and instantaneous electronic transmission of voice, pictures, and graphics possible. People scattered over the face of the globe can now talk to each other directly, see each other, and, if need be, share the same reports, documents, and graphs without leaving their own offices or homes. Consider the impact of this innovation on the airline industry. Business travel should diminish in importance, though its place may well be taken by travel for vacations and learning.

According to the Futures Group, perhaps the most important driver of technological change is the computer revolution. Computers will become more and more pervasive even though they will be less and less visible. Powerful computers will be embedded in appliances and machines, touching almost every part of life. Emerging computer applications include

- Digital television (computerized receivers using only three to five integrated circuits)
- Improved definition television (image processing to eliminate ghosts, snow, etc.)
- High-definition television (HDTV) that produces pictures that are nearly "photo" quality
- Low-cost pocketphones (digital "go-anywhere" phones at the price of a good pager)
- User-programmed radio, delivered via cable or phone, that allows you to hear what you want, when you want
- Mainframe computer power in your desktop computer
- Low-cost speech recognition systems that provide "instant dictation" capability to productive managers
- Electronic publishing that allows writers to self-publish (do-it-yourself publishing) (authors receive a fee for each article or book sold and pay a monthly storage charge to make the document available)
- Smart houses that cut energy bills for many by 40 percent, provide improved fire and theft security, reduce telephone costs, and provide improved monitoring of children (actually anticipating and preventing accidents)
- Medical advice available via phone using artificial intelligence systems that know your voice (in detail) and can ask questions and understand your answers about symptoms, then recommend treatment or tell you where to get help
- Small, automated stores that sell both unique and commodity products using entertaining (artificial intelligence) selling methods to close the sale
- Digital (computer-based) picturephones that make "being their" take on a new meaning
- Your credit card will be "smart" because it will know all about your finances, just as your medical card will "know" all about your health history
- Cars that are drive-by-wire (just as planes are fly-by-wire)[10]

To analyze technological changes and capitalize on them, marketing strategists may utilize the technology management matrix shown in Exhibit 6-5. It

EXHIBIT 6-5
Technology Management Matrix

	TECHNOLOGY POSITION		
		Different Technology	
Product Position	*Same Technology*	*Older Technology*	*Newer Technology*
Behind competitors	Take traditional strategic actions —Assess marketing strategy and target markets —Enhance product features —Improve operational efficiency	Evaluate viability of your technology —Implement newer technology —Divest products based on older technology	Evaluate availability of resources to sustain technology development and full market acceptance —Continue to define new applications and product enhancements —Scale back operations
Ahead of competitors	Define new applications for the technology and enhance products accordingly	Take advantage of all possible profit	Define new applications for the technology and enhance products accordingly

Source: Susan J. Levine, "Marketers Need to Adopt a Technological Focus to Safeguard Against Obsolescence," *Marketing News* (28 October 1938): 16. Reprinted by permission of the American Marketing Association.

should aid in choosing appropriate strategic options based on a business's technological position. The matrix has two dimensions: technology and product. The technology dimension describes technologies in terms of their relationships to one another; the product dimension establishes competitive position. The interaction of these two dimensions suggests desirable strategic action. For example, if a business's technology is superior to anything else on the market, the company should enhance its leadership by identifying and introducing new applications for the technology. On the other hand, if a business's technology lags behind the competition, it should either make a technological leap to the competitive process, abandon the market, or identify and pursue those elements that are laggards in terms of adopting new technologies.[11]

Clark recommends the following principles of action to link technology to customer requirements:

- **Know the technological core and link it to strategic intent**—Top managers must descend into the technological black box and teach technologists the imperatives of business.
- **Take a global view of business competence**—Multiple sources of technical skill are available through worldwide alliances and strategic partnerships.
- **Time is of the essence**—Evidence is mounting that the effort to reduce cycle time helps improve the technical self-consciousness of the whole organization.

- **Discipline functions around the science of production**—Integrate such functions as research and development, design, and manufacturing. The focus of integration should be a scientific understanding of the manufacturing process.
- **Integrate operations around the information system**—One cannot exploit the virtues of such systems without aiming for structural changes compatible with them: flattened hierarchies and value-added networks.[12]

Briefly, the rapid development and exploitation of new technologies are causing serious strategic headaches for companies in almost every type of industry. It has become vital for strategists to be able to recognize the limits of their core technologies, know which new technologies are emerging, and decide when to incorporate new technology in their products.

Political Environment

In stable governments, political trends may not be as important as in countries where governments are weak. Yet even in stable countries, political trends may have a significant impact on business. For example, in the United States one can typically expect greater emphasis on social programs and an increase in government spending when Democrats are in power in the White House. Therefore, companies in the business of providing social services may expect greater opportunities during Democratic administrations.

More important, however, are political trends overseas because the U.S. economy is intimately connected with the global economy. Therefore, what goes on in the political spheres of other countries may be significant for U.S. corporations, particularly multinational corporations.

The following are examples of political trends and events that could affect business planning and strategy:

1. An increase in geopolitical federations
   a. Economic interests: resource countries versus consumer countries
   b. Political interests: third world versus the rest
2. Rising nationalism versus world federalism
   a. Failure of the United Nations
   b. Trend toward world government or world law system
3. Limited wars: Middle East, Serbia-Croatia
4. Increase in political terrorism; revolutions
5. Third-party gains in the United States; rise of socialism
6. U.S. parliamentary government; cabinet becoming ad hoc leaders
7. Decline of the major powers; rise of emerging nations (e.g., India, Brazil)
8. Minority (female) president
9. Rise in senior citizen power in developed nations
10. Political turmoil in Saudi Arabia that threatens world oil supplies and peace in the Middle East
11. Revolutionary change in Indonesia, jeopardizing Japanese oil supplies
12. Revolutionary change in South Africa, limiting Western access to important minerals and threatening huge capital losses to the economies of Great Britain, the United States, and Germany

13. Instability in other places where the economic consequences could be important, including Mexico, Turkey, Zaire, Nigeria, South Korea, Brazil, Chile, and the People's Republic of China

Already in the 1980s we have seen the overwhelming impact that political shocks can have on the world economy. The value of the dollar is the perfect illustration: it is not just the product of an arbitrary monetary policy that is temporarily out of control but a rational response to problems that are fundamentally political. In the 1980s the problem of adjusting to new terms of trade created by the oil embargo of 1973 and, more recently, the problem of trading off the costs of higher unemployment in the short run against the longer-run benefits of lower inflation continue to be concerns.

Marketing strategy is deeply affected by political perspectives. For example, government decisions have significantly affected the U.S. automotive industry. Stringent requirements, such as fuel efficiency standards, have burdened the industry in several ways.[13] The marketing strategist needs to study both domestic and foreign political happenings, reviewing selected published information to keep in touch with political trends and interpret the information as it relates to the particular company.

Governments around the world help their domestic industries strengthen their competitiveness through various fiscal and monetary measures. Political support can play a key role in an industry's search for markets abroad. Without it, an industry may face a difficult situation. For instance, the U.S. auto industry would benefit from a U.S. government concession favoring U.S. automotive exports. European countries rely on value-added taxes to help their industries. Value-added taxes are applied to all levels of manufacturing transactions up to and including the final sale to the end user. However, if the final sale is for export, the value-added tax is rebated, thus effectively reducing the price of European goods in international commerce. Japan imposes a commodity tax on selected lines of products, including automobiles. In the event of export, the commodity tax is waived. The United States has no corresponding arrangement. Thus, when a new automobile is shipped from the United States to Japan, its U.S. taxes upon export are not rebated and the auto also must bear the cost of the Japanese commodity tax (15 or 20 percent, depending on the size of the vehicle) when it is sold in Japan. This illustrates how political decisions affect marketing strategy. Exhibit 6-6 shows a framework for analyzing the political environment.

Economic Environment

Economic trends and events affecting businesses include the following possibilities:

- Depression; worldwide economic collapse
- Increasing foreign ownership of the U.S. economy
- Increasing regulation and management of national economies
- Several developing nations become superpowers (e.g., Brazil, India, China)
- World food production: famine relief versus holistic management

EXHIBIT 6-6
A Framework for Analyzing the Political Environment

Sources of Political Risk	*Groups through Which Political Risk Can Be Generated*	*Effects on International Business Operations*
• Competing political philosophies (nationalism, socialism, communism) • Social unrest and disorder • Vested interests of local business groups • Recent and impending political independence • Armed conflicts and internal rebellions for political power • New international alliances	• Government in power and its operating agencies • Parliamentary opposition groups • Nonparliamentary opposition groups (Algerian "FLN," guerrilla movements working within or outside country) • Nonorganized common interest groups: students, workers, peasants, minorities, and so on • Foreign governments or intergovernmental agencies such as the EEC • Foreign governments willing to enter into armed conflict or to support internal rebellion	• Confiscation: loss of assets without compensation • Expropriation with compensation: loss of freedom to operate • Operational restrictions: market shares, product characteristics, employment policies, locally shared ownership, and so on • Loss of transfer freedom: financial (dividends, interest payments, goods, personnel, or ownership rights, for example) • Breaches or unilateral revisions in contracts and agreements • Discrimination such as taxes or compulsory subcontractings • Damage to property or personnel from riots, insurrections, revolutions, and wars

Source: Stefan H. Robock and Kenneth Simmonds, *International Business and Multinational Enterprises*, 4th ed. (Homewood, IL: Richard D. Irwin, Inc., 1989), 383.

- Decline in real world growth or stable growth
- Collapse of world monetary system
- High inflation
- Significant employee-union ownership of U.S. businesses
- Worldwide free trade

It is not unrealistic to say that all companies, small or large, engaged in strategic planning examine the economic environment. Relevant published information is usually gathered, analyzed, and interpreted for use in planning. In some corporations the entire process of dealing with economic information may be manual and intuitive. The large ones, however, not only buy specific and detailed economic information from private sources, over and above what may be available from government sources, but they analyze the information for meaningful conclusions by constructing econometric models. For example, one large corporation with nine divisions has developed 26 econometric models of its different businesses. The data used for these models are stored in a database and are regularly updated. The information is available on-line to all divisions for further analysis at any time. Other companies may occasionally buy information from outside and selectively undertake modeling.

Usually the economic environment is analyzed with reference to the following key economic indicators: employment, consumer price index, housing starts, auto sales, weekly unemployment claims, real GNP, industrial production, personal income, savings rate, capacity utilization, productivity, money supply (weekly M1: currency and checking accounts), retail sales, inventories, and durable goods orders. Information on these indicators is available from government sources. These indicators are adequate for short-run analysis and decision making because, by and large, they track developments over the business cycle reasonably well. However, companies that try to base strategic plans on these indicators alone can run into serious trouble. Deficiencies in the data prove most dangerous when the government moves to take a more interventionist role in the economy. Further, rapid changes in the structure of the economy when the ability of statistical agencies to respond has been hampered by unprecedented budget stringency cause a gradual deterioration in the quality of many of the economic statistics that the government publishes.

The problem of government-supplied data begins with a recondite document called the *Standard Industrial Classification (SIC) Manual,* which divides all economic activity into 12 divisions and 84 major groups of industries. The *SIC Manual* dictates the organization of and the amount of data available about production, income, employment, and other vital economic indicators. Each major group has a two-digit numerical code. The economy is then subdivided into hundreds of secondary groups, each with a three-digit code, and is further subdivided into thousands of industries, each with four-digit codes. But detail in most government statistical series is available only at the major group level; data at the three-digit level are scarce; at the four-digit level, almost nonexistent.

To illustrate the effect of economic climate on strategy consider the following trends. In the more elderly capitalist countries, it is expected that old markets will become saturated much faster than new markets will take their place. Staple consumer goods, such as cars, radios, and television sets, already outnumber households in North America and in much of Western Europe; other products are fast approaching the same fate. The slow growth of populations in most of these countries means that the number of households is likely to grow at only about 2 percent per year in the 1990s and that demand for consumer goods is unlikely to grow any faster. Furthermore, while demand in these markets decreases, supply will increase, leading to intensified price competition and pressure on profit margins.

For example, in the 1990s the auto industry is likely to suffer from overcapacity. It is expected that there will be three buyers for every four cars.[14] Already the market concentration in many consumer sectors has fallen significantly, mainly because of increased foreign competition. And the expansion of production capacity in such primary industries as metals and chemicals, especially in developing countries, threatens to bring some kind of increased competition to producer goods.[15]

In the early 1980s consumers embraced Japanese cars, Chrysler was on the brink of bankruptcy, Ford was furiously cutting costs, and General Motors was incurring huge losses. U.S. auto companies wanted an environment that eliminated Japanese advantages of cheap labor and a weak yen. Detroit companies got what they wanted. Seven years of informal restraints on Japanese imports let U.S. companies improve their product lines. The United Auto Workers has held down costs to preserve as many jobs as possible. The plunging dollar has wiped out the remaining gap between U.S. and Japanese production costs. Japanese automakers are even moving production facilities to the United States and using American auto workers to manufacture their cars. The marketplace has never been so level, yet U.S. automakers are still in trouble.

The problem is overcapacity. With flat demand for cars and no letup in imports, capacity is not shrinking fast enough to prevent a serious glut. By 1995 the Japanese may be building some 2.8 million vehicles a year in the United States—more than the current output of Chrysler. As the glut intensifies competition, all carmakers are going to have to hold the line on prices—or even reduce them. U.S. companies can wait until everyone cuts prices, thereby conceding over one-third of the U.S. market to imports, or it can take the offensive on prices now.

These trends indicate the kind of economic issues that marketing strategists must take into account to determine their strategies.

Social Environment

The ultimate test of a business is its social relevance. This is particularly true in a society where survival needs are already being met. It therefore behooves the strategic planner to be familiar with emerging social trends and concerns. The relevance of the social environment to a particular business will of course vary depending on the nature of the business. For a technology-oriented business, scanning of the social environment may be limited to aspects of pollution control and environmental safety. For a consumer-products company, however, the impact of the social environment may go much further.

An important aspect of the social environment concerns the values consumers hold. Observers have noted many value shifts that directly or indirectly influence business. Values mainly revolve around a number of fundamental concerns regarding time, quality, health, environment, home, personal finance, and diversity.[16]

Orientation toward Time. Given the scarcity of time and/or money to have products repaired or to buy new ones, consumers look for offerings that endure. Time will become the scarce resource of the 1990s as the result of the prevalence of dual income-earning households. Convenience will be a critical source of differential advantage, particularly in foods and services. In addition, youth will be making or influencing more household purchasing decisions than ever before. Moreover, as the population ages, time pressures will become more widespread and acute. Consumers are going to need innovative and, in some cases, almost customized solutions. With time generally scarcer than money, offerings that ease time pressures will garner higher margins.

Quality. Given the standards set by the influx of imported products, American consumers have developed a new set of expectations regarding quality; hence, they assign high priorities to those offerings that provide optimal price/quality. The 1990s will witness a move toward the adoption of a greater price/quality orientation in mass markets. There will also be a strong general desire for authenticity and lasting quality. Consumers will require fewer and more durable products rather than more ephemeral, novelty products. Heightened consumer expectations will translate into trying a manufacturer once. If the value, the quality, or the intrinsic characteristics that the consumer demands are not found, the consumer will not return to that manufacturer.

Health. A large and growing segment of the American population has become increasingly preoccupied with health. Health concerns are a function of both an aging population and changing predispositions. America is hungry for health and is impatient for its achievement. Industry experts are predicting that nutritional tags, such as low in fat, will probably be the newest food fad to sweep the United States. There is some consensus that a diet rich in soluble fiber and low in fat and a lifestyle that includes plenty of regular exercise reduce cholesterol. As an aging population strives to maintain its youth and vitality, alcohol and tobacco consumption and other nonhealthy dietary habits will continue to decline. In short, American consumers in the 1990s will be highly health conscious. The impact of this trend will not only be felt in the grocery store but in the travel and hospitality sectors of the economy as well as in an array of services that contribute to lifelong wellness.

Environment. Perhaps the 1990s will become known as the "earth decade." A growing number of Americans consider themselves "environmentalists." Outdoor activities, such as rock-climbing expeditions and white-water rafting, are superseding more vicarious, passive ways of spending time. This heightened appreciation of the outdoors is being translated in choice criteria in the marketplace. Hence, more and more marketers will be pressured into adopting "green" strategies; that is, offering products and services that are beneficial to the environment.

Home. In a more domesticated society, the many technological innovations of the 1990s will make staying at home more fun. Some of the most beneficial advances of this home-centered decade will be in the design and construction of houses that resemble self-contained entertainment/educational activity centers. The current slump in the housing market will rebound, and opportunities for marketers to provide creative, more personalized, high-value offerings in home furnishings will evolve.

Personal Finance. Most experts on consumer behavior expect that in the decade ahead, people will be more frugal than they were in the 1980s. The slow-and-steady consumer approach spawned by an attitude for upscale products that may outstrip finances makes every purchase especially important. The 1990s are projected to witness several important consumer finance trends. First, consumers will continue to seek out the best price/value before buying and will accordingly place downward pressure on seller profit margins. Second, American consumers may have the income to spend freely, but recent economic difficulties will nonetheless cause them to remain cautious. Finally, quality will be insisted upon, and a competitive premium price will be willingly paid for performance and durability.

Diversity of Lifestyles. The predominance of diverse lifestyles is reflected by the significant increase in the number and the stature of women in the labor market. The increased presence of women in the labor force has dramatically influenced how men and women relate to one another and the personal and professional roles assumed by each. There has also been a dramatic change in racial integration and improved race relations. The United States has also witnessed the development of openly gay and lesbian lifestyles as well as an increase in the number of unmarried, cohabitating relationships. Significant changes in attitudes toward work and careers have also resulted in a new sense of independence and individuality. Accordingly, there has been an upsurge in the number of people who are self-employed and greater interest in job and career changes. Experts hold that this pattern of social diversity will likely continue into the future. Social diversity creates opportunities for marketers to develop personalized offerings that allow individuals to derive satisfaction in the pursuit of different living alternatives.

In conclusion, underlying all these changes in the landscape of American consumer concerns and as important as all of them will be a markedly changed inner sense. More specifically, people will continue to search for basic values and will experience heightened ethical awareness. The 1990s are predicted to be a far less cynical decade that the 1980s. Consumers will still care about what things cost, but they will value only things that will endure—family, community, earth, faith. The discredited "yuppie" credo of the 1980s, that "you can have it all," will be replaced in the 1990s with more diverse yet simplified lifestyles and more saving.

Information on social trends may be derived from published sources. The impact of social trends on a particular business can be studied in-house or with the help of outside consultants. A number of consulting firms specialize in studying social trends.

Let us examine the strategic impact of two of the value shifts mentioned above: orientation toward time and concern for health. Take the retail industry. Little is being done to support consumers in their quest to reduce shopping stress, although stress is a major consumer concern. Fast service has been the basis for growth for a number of well-known firms, among them American Express, McDonald's, and Federal Express; however, only a small but significant number of businesses have recognized and responded to the consumer's lack of free time for shopping and service transactions:

- Dayton-Hudson has moved away from a mazelike floor design to a center aisle design, making it easier for customers to find their way through the store.

- At Childworld, toys are coordinated in learning centers so that buyers can examine and play with products. Management feels that this arrangement enables buyers to shop more quickly.
- A new firm, Shopper's Express, is assisting large chains like A&P and Safeway by taking telephone orders and delivering merchandise.
- Rather than forcing the consumer to sit at home for an entire day awaiting a service call, GE, for years, has been making specific service appointments
- Sears now offers a six-day-a-week and evening repair service. In addition, in specifying when a repair person will arrive, Sears assigns a two-hour window.
- Montgomery Ward authorizes 7700 sales clerks to approve sales checks and handle merchandise returns on their own, eliminating the time needed to get a floor manager's approval.
- Burger King uses television monitors that enable drive-up customers to see the waiter and the order.
- A&P, Shop Rite, and Publix are experimenting with automated grocery checkout systems that reduce waiting time in checkout lines.
- Wegman's, a supermarket chain in Rochester, New York, has a computer available for entering deli orders so that the customer does not have to wait to be served. The customer simply enters the order and picks it up on the way out of the store.[17]

More and more companies need to focus on developing shopping support systems and environments that help customers move through the buying process quickly. For firms that pride themselves for providing customers with a leisurely shopping environment, this will be a radical departure. Firms accepting this challenge will be able to support and stay closer to their customers through such changes. In addition, firms that help customers reduce shopping time will be able to differentiate themselves from competitors more easily.

For health reasons, salads and fish are replacing the traditional American dinner of meat and potatoes. Vegetarianism is on the rise. According to *Time,* about 8 million Americans call themselves vegetarians.[18] Increasing varieties of decaffeinated coffee and tea and substitutes for sugar and salt are crowding supermarket shelves. Shoppers are reading the small print to check for artificial ingredients in foods and beverages that they once bought without a thought. Smoking is finally declining. Manufacturers and retailers of natural foods are building a healthy "health industry." Even products that do not easily accommodate healthier choices are being redeveloped in response to consumer concerns. For example, Dunkin Donuts has yanked the egg yolks from all but four of its 52 varieties to make its donuts cholesterol-free.[19] Fast food firms—McDonald's Corporation and Hardee's Food Systems, for example—have introduced low-fat foods into their menus.[20]

The nation's dramatic new awareness of health is prompting these changes. The desire to feel better, look younger, and live longer exerts a powerful influence on what people put into their bodies. This strong force is now moving against a well-entrenched habit that affects millions and dates back to biblical times—the consumption of too much alcohol.[21]

Health substitutes for alcoholic beverages, labeled "dealcoholized" beverages, are now being offered to American consumers. For some time, gourmet food shops have stocked champagnelike bottles of carbonated grape juice and cans containing a not-fully-brewed mixture of water, malt, corn, yeast, and hops. Except for their packaging, these alcohol-free imitations failed to resemble wine and beer, especially in the crucial area of taste. New dealcoholized beverages, however, are fully fermented, or brewed, before their alcohol is separated out—either by pressure or heat—to below an unnoticeable 0.5 percent, the federal maximum before classifying a drink as alcoholic. The taste and body of the new beverages match that of their former alcoholized selves.

This 0.5 percent level is so low that a drinker would need to consume 24 glasses of dealcoholized wine or 8 cans of dealcoholized beer to obtain the amount of alcohol in one 4-ounce glass of regular wine or one 12-ounce can of regular beer. Thus the drinker avoids not only intoxication but also worthless calories. A regular glass of wine or beer has about 150 calories, while their dealcoholized copies contain about 40 to 60 calories, respectively. And their prices are the same.[22] Introduced in Europe about five years ago, dealcoholized wines are slowly making headway in the United States.

Regulatory Environment

Even in a capitalistic society like the United States, government influence on business appears to be increasing. It is estimated that businesses spend, on the average, twice as much time fulfilling government requirements today as they did 10 years ago.

> Few businesses, large or small, can operate without considering a myriad of government restrictions and regulations. Costs and profits can be affected as much by a regulation written by a government official as by their own management decisions or their customers' changing preferences. The types of management decisions which increasingly are subject to governmental influence, review, or control are fundamental to the business system:
>
> - What lines of business to go into?
> - What products can be produced?
> - Which investments can be financed?
> - Under what conditions can products be produced?
> - Where can they be made?
> - How can they be marketed?
> - What prices can be charged?
> - What profit can be kept?
>
> Virtually every major department of the typical corporation in the United States has one or more counterparts in a federal agency that controls, or strongly influences, its internal decision making.[23]

Even a cautious company like Procter and Gamble can get into problems for not heeding the regulatory environment. The Food and Drug Administration (FDA) has been complaining that Procter and Gamble has been misleading consumers through its advertising claims. Although initially the company denied any improprieties, ultimately it had to reform a number of products:

Ultra Protection Crest—Halted national launch after FDA said new toothpaste with antibacterial agent required new drug approval.

Citrus Hill Fresh Choice—Agreed to drop "fresh" from product name after FDA seized some of the orange juice and said the labeling was false and misleading.

Crisco Corn Oil—Dropped "no cholesterol" labels from all food products after FDA told vegetable oil marketers to stop using the claim.

Metamucil—Increased clinical research to support cholesterol-reduction claims for this fiber laxative after FDA asked for more data.

Didronel—Sought FDA approval to market this prescription drug as an osteoporosis treatment, but an advisory panel has questioned some of the company's data. Still awaiting approval.

Olestra—Has not won FDA's go-ahead four years after its initial petition to sell this fat substitute.[24]

Interestingly, government in recent years has changed its emphasis from regulating specific industries to focusing on problem areas of national interest, including environmental cleanup, elimination of job discrimination, establishment of safe working conditions, and reduction of product hazards. A number of steps have been taken toward deregulation of various industries. Listed below are the measures that the government has taken to deregulate the telecommunications and broadcasting industries:[25]

Telecommunications

- **Telephone equipment**—Broke telephone company monopoly by permitting other companies to sell devices that connect with AT&T's network; permitted consumers to buy their own telephones (1968–82).
- **Long distance**— Promoted competition in long-distance phone service by permitting independent companies to resell AT&T service (1980).
- **Tariff regulations**—Freed smaller nonmonopoly communications companies to change prices or add services without approval (1982).
- **Licensing**—Abandoned lengthy comparative hearings in favor of lotteries in awarding licenses for some new services, cellular mobile telephones, for example (1983–84).
- **Pricing**—Moved toward market pricing of telephone service by shifting costs from long-distance to local users (1985).

Broadcasting

- **Children's programming**—Relaxed rules requiring broadcasters to air "informative" children's programming; rejected restrictions on cartoon shows based on toys (1983).
- **Public service**—Loosened guidelines requiring nonentertainment programming and coverage of community issues (1984).
- **Commercials**—Eliminated time and frequency limits on television commercials, allowing more commercials per hour and program-length ads (1984).
- **Station ownership**—Raised limit on group ownership of television and AM and FM stations from seven each to twelve each (1984).
- **Station transfer**—Rescinded rule prohibiting buyer from reselling a station for three years after purchase; speeded consideration of license transfers (1982–85).

This shift in focus in the regulatory environment deeply affects the internal operations of business. To win or even survive in the competitive free-for-all environment that follows deregulation, companies in once-regulated industries have to make some hard choices. Astute management can avoid some of the trauma by developing an explicit strategy to operate in a deregulated environment well in advance of the event, rethinking relationships with customers, considering new roles to play in the market, and realigning their organizations accordingly.

To study the impact of the regulatory environment, that is, of laws already on the books and of pending legislation, legal assistance is required. Small firms may seek legal assistance on an ad hoc basis. Large firms may maintain offices in Washington staffed by people with legal backgrounds who are well versed in the company's business, who know important government agencies from the point of view of their companies, who maintain a close liaison with them, and who pass on relevant information to planners in different departments of their companies. For example, a company that did a substantial amount of business in less-developed countries had a person in Washington who closely followed developments in the Agency for International Development. As soon as foreign aid to a country was approved, this legal expert signaled company headquarters, which in turn alerted its office in that developing nation to begin seeking business.

ENVIRONMENTAL SCANNING AND MARKETING STRATEGY

The impact of environmental scanning on marketing strategy can be illustrated with reference to videotex technology.[26] Videotex technology—the merging of computer and communications technologies—delivers information directly to the consumer. The consumer may instantly view desired textual and visual information from on-line databases on television screens or other video receivers by pushing the appropriate buttons or typing in the proper commands.

Possibilities for business and personal use of videotex are as endless as the imagination. Consumers are already utilizing videotex for shopping, travel, personal protection, financial transactions, and entertainment, in greater privacy and autonomy than ever before.

With the mechanism for getting things done most efficiently and cost effectively, marketing strategists have begun to explore the implications of videotex on marketing decisions. Videotex will alter the demand for certain kinds of goods and services and the ways in which consumers interact with marketing activities. For the first time, the average consumer, not just the affluent consumer, can interact directly with the production process, dictating final product specifications as the product is being manufactured. As small-batch production becomes more cost-effective, this type of consumer-producer interaction will become more common.

Product selection might also be enhanced by videotex, as sellers stock a more complete inventory at fewer, more central locations rather than dealing with many retail outlets. Because packages will no longer serve as the communications vehicle for selling the product, less money will be spent on packaging. Product changes can also be kept up-to-date. Information on videotex will be current, synthesized, and comprehensive. The user will have the power to access only desired information at the time it is desired. Advertising messages and articles will be available in index form.

Direct consumer interaction with manufacturers will eliminate distribution channels. Reduced or zero-based inventory will reduce obsolescence and turnover costs. Centrally located warehouses and new delivery routes will become increasingly cost-effective. The remaining retail stores will be transformed into showrooms with direct-order possibilities via viewdatalike terminals.

For example, Sears offers 11,000 types and sizes of curtains, blinds, and shutters, but each store can stock only a few. So Sears is testing an interactive video system in Atlanta, Chicago, and Los Angeles, where customers can browse through the entire range, receive optional decorating tips, and get a printout of any items they decide to order.[27]

Promotional material will become more educational and information-based, including the provision of product specifications and independent product evaluations. Interactive video channels will provide advertisers and interested shoppers with prepackaged commercials and live shopping programs.

With more accurate price and product information, more perfect competition will result. Price discrepancies will be reduced. Consumers will engage in more preshopping planning, price-comparison shopping, and in-home shopping.

The market segment concept will be more important than ever before. The individualizing possibilities of videotex will enable the seller to measure and reach segments with unparalleled accuracy and will also enable consumers to effectively self-segment. Advertisers and consumers will benefit from 24-hour, 7-day-a-week salespeople. Everyone will be better prepared through videotex to satisfy customers. For yet another example, Exhibit 6-7 examines the emerging trends in the field of dentistry and their impact on marketing strategy.

ENVIRONMENTAL SCANNING PROCEDURE

Like any other new program, the scanning activity in a corporation evolves over time. There is no way to introduce a foolproof system from the beginning. If conditions are favorable—if there is an established system of strategic planning in place and the CEO is interested in a structured effort at scanning—the evolutionary period shortens, of course, but the state of the art may not permit the introduction of a fully developed system at the outset. Besides, behavioral and organizational constraints require that things be done over a period of time. The level and type of scanning that a corporation undertakes should be custom designed, and a customized system takes time to emerge into a viable system.

EXHIBIT 6-7
Dentistry in the Twenty-First Century

In 2020 we expect the dental office to be more automated, with computer and robot-assisted diagnostic procedures. New imaging technology services, such as subtraction radiography and magnetic resonance imaging (MRI), could be in each office, or provided by a centralized facility. Advances in immunochemistry have opened the potential for new diagnostic and monitoring systems that will be suitable for in-office use. We expect dental office instrumentation and procedures to be reorganized to include these emerging technologies.

Because of these advances, the dental practice of the 21st century will have time and resources allocated for the collecting, recording, and processing of biotechnical data, just as time is now allocated for procedures such as X-rays. And while we expect the dentist and other office personnel to perform some of these procedures, it is very likely that a good deal of the chairside data collection will be robot assisted. In addition, the majority of those procedures performed in the dental laboratory will be robot assisted as well.

We expect the diagnostic information collected during each patient visit to be "input" to a data base for processing and evaluation. This data base may be located within the dental office, but the information could easily be transmitted (via modem) to a data base at some centralized location, such as the office of the patient's insurance carrier. After processing and evaluation of the diagnostic information, therapeutic options will be returned to the dentist for evaluation, selection, and presentation to the patient. It is already apparent that the dentist no longer is the only decisionmaker in choosing between therapeutic alternatives. Because of the increased role of insurance carriers, we expect the selection of appropriate therapeutic alternatives to be guided by national norms, based on parameters that include evaluations of quality assurance, cost/effectiveness ratios, and risk/benefit ratios. We believe all organizations involved with the management of data, including the development of software for its processing, and hardware for its transmission, should become aware of the needs and opportunities available in the dental market.

The advances in biotechnology that have taken place, having finally made their way out of the research laboratory and passed through the first phase of clinical trials, have led to the development of a wide range of new products. However, because these new products are based on recent advances in areas such as immunology, biochemistry, and molecular biology, the rate of their development has outpaced their understanding by both the dentist and the public. Thus, special educational/advertising programs may be required to facilitate public acceptance and successful utilization by the dentist of these new products.

Recent changes in political configurations worldwide will also have a major impact on marketing dental products. The effect, however, will vary, depending on which part of the world is being considered. For example, economic unification in Western Europe will require strategies different from those to be used in countries in Eastern Europe and the Far East. Clearly, the size of these populations and the lack of emphasis on preventive dental care in Eastern Europe and the Far East suggest these areas are available for expansion by corporations already established in sales of dental products.

The rapid rate of growth in information will present a unique opportunity. For example, training and communications will include not only print, but also self-instruc-

EXHIBIT 6-7
continued

tional videos and on-line computer update services. These scientific advances also have implications for other special types of businesses. Venture capitalists and financial planners need to be aware that developments in biotechnology will provide unique opportunities for investors in the dental market.

Source: Reprinted with the permission of Dr. Edward F. Rossomando, School of Dental Medicine, University of Connecticut.

Exhibit 6-8 shows the process by which environmental scanning is linked to marketing strategy. Listed on the next page are the procedural steps that explain this relationship.

EXHIBIT 6-8
Linking Environmental Scanning to Corporate Strategy

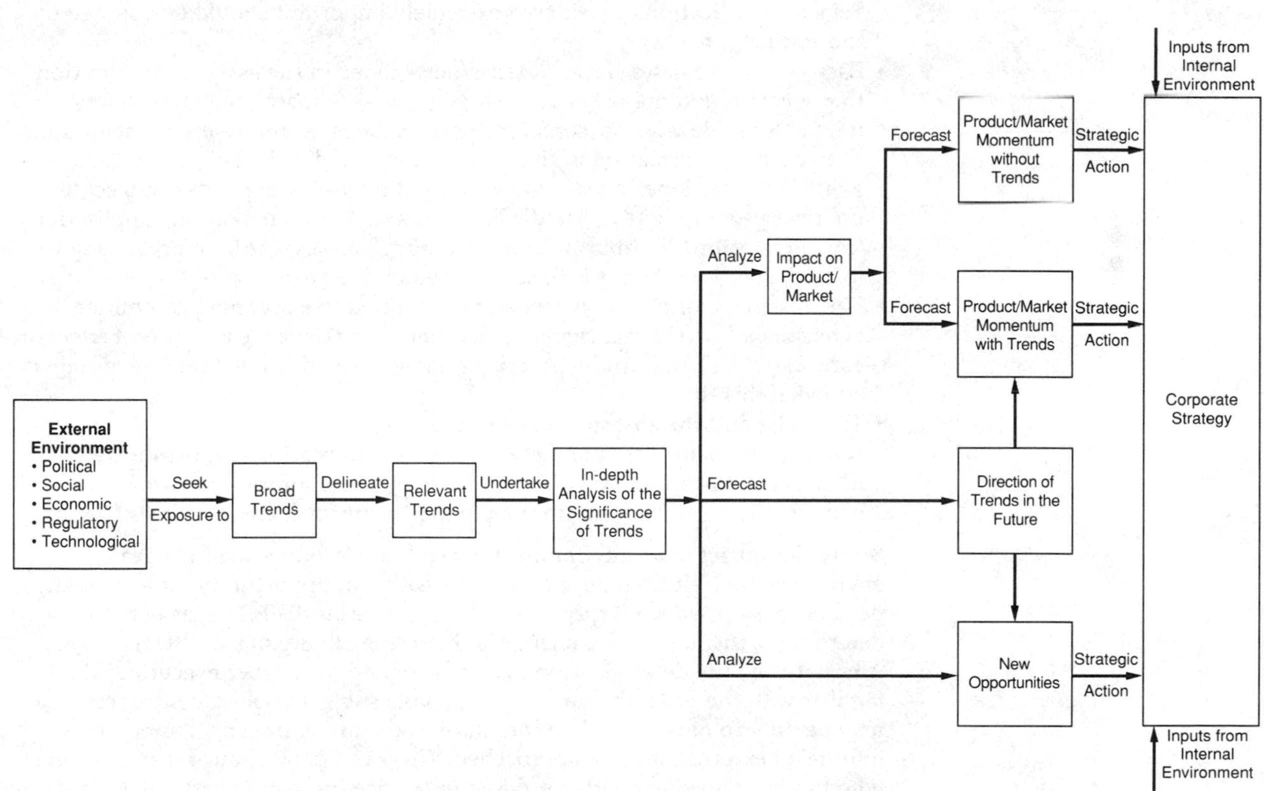

1. **Keep a tab on broad trends appearing in the environment**—Once the scope of environmental scanning is determined, broad trends in chosen areas may be reviewed from time to time. For example, in the area of technology, trends in energy utilization, material science, transportation capability, mechanization and automation, communications and information processing, and control over natural life may be studied.
2. **Determine the relevance of an environmental trend**—Not everything happening in the environment may be relevant for a company. Therefore, attempts must be made to select those trends that have significance for the company. There cannot be any hard-and-fast rules for making a distinction between relevant and irrelevant. Consider, for example, the demise of the steam locomotive industry. Perhaps its constituencies would have been more receptive to changes had they come from within the industry itself. Management's creativity and farsightedness would play an important role in a company's ability to pinpoint relevant areas of concern. Described below is one way (for a large corporation) of identifying relevant trends in the environment:
   - Place a senior person in charge of scanning.
   - Identify a core list of about 100 relevant publications worldwide.
   - Assign these publications to volunteers within the company, one per person. Selected publications considered extremely important should be scanned by the scanning manager.
   - Each scanner reviews stories/articles/news items in the assigned publication that meet predetermined criteria based on the company's aims. Scanners might also review books, conference proceedings, lectures, and presentations.
   - The scanned information is given a predetermined code. For example, a worldwide consumer-goods company used the following codes: subject (e.g., politics); geography (e.g., Middle East); function (e.g., marketing); application (e.g., promotion, distribution); and "uniterm," or keyword, for organizing the information. An abstract is then prepared on the story.
   - The abstract, along with the codes, is submitted to a scanning committee, consisting of several managers, to determine its relevance in terms of effect on corporate, SBU, and product/market strategy. An additional relevance code is added at this time.
   - The codes and the abstract are computerized.
   - A newsletter is prepared to disseminate the information companywide. Managers whose areas are directly affected by the information are encouraged to contact the scanning department for further analysis.
3. **Study the impact of an environmental trend on a product/market**—An environmental trend can pose either a threat or an opportunity for a company's product/market; which it turns out to be must be studied. The task of determining the impact of a change is the responsibility of the SBU manager. Alternatively, the determination may be assigned to another executive who is familiar with the product/market. If the whole subject appears controversial, it may be safer to have an ad hoc committee look into it, or consultants, either internal or external, may be approached. There is a good chance that a manager who has been involved with a product or service for many years will look at any change as a threat. That manager may, therefore, avoid the issue by declaring

the impact to be irrelevant at the outset. If such nearsightedness is feared, perhaps it would be better to rely on a committee or a consultant.

4. **Forecast the direction of an environmental trend into the future**—If an environmental trend does appear to have significance for a product/market, it is desirable to determine the course that the trend is likely to adopt. In other words, attempts must be made at environmental forecasting.
5. **Analyze the momentum of the product/market business in the face of the environmental trend**—Assuming that the company takes no action, what will be the shape of the product/market performance in the midst of the environmental trend and its future direction? The impact of an environmental trend is usually gradual. While it is helpful to be the "first" to recognize a trend and take action, all is not lost if a company waits to see which way the trend proceeds. But how long one waits depends on the diffusion process, the rate at which the change necessitated by the trend is adopted. People did not jump to replace their black-and-white television sets overnight. Similar examples abound. A variety of reasons may prohibit an overnight shift in markets due to an environmental trend that may deliver a new product or process. High prices, religious taboos, legal restrictions, and unfamiliarity with the product or service would restrict changeover. In brief, the diffusion process should be predicted before arriving at a conclusion.
6. **Study the new opportunities that an environmental trend appears to provide**—An environmental trend may not be relevant for a company's current product/market, but it may indicate promising new business opportunities. For example, the energy crisis provided an easy entry point for fuel-efficient Hondas into the United States. Such opportunities should be duly pinpointed and analyzed for action.
7. **Relate the outcome of an environmental trend to corporate strategy**—Based on environmental trends and their impacts, a company needs to review its strategy on two counts: changes that may be introduced in current products/markets and feasible opportunities that the company may embrace for action. Even if an environmental trend poses a threat to a company's product/market, it is not necessary for the company to come out with a new product to replace an existing one. Neither is it necessary for every competitor to embrace the "change." Even without developing a new product, a company may find a niche in the market to which it could cater despite the introduction of a new product by a competitor. The electric razor did not make safety razor blades obsolete. Automatic transmissions did not throw the standard shift out of vogue. New markets and new uses can be found to give an existing product an advantage despite the overall popularity of a new product.

Although procedural steps for scanning the environment exist, scanning is nevertheless an art in which creativity plays an important role. Thus, to adequately study the changing environment and relate it to corporate strategy, companies should inculcate a habit of creative thinking on the part of its managers. The experience of one insurance company illustrates the point: in order to "open up" line managers to new ideas and to encourage innovation in their plans, they are, for a while, withdrawn from the line organization to serve as staff people. In staff positions, they are granted considerable freedom of action, which enhances their ability to manage creatively when they return to their management positions.

CONDUCTING ENVIRONMENTAL SCANNING—AN EXAMPLE

Following the steps in Exhibit 6-9, an attempt is made here to illustrate how specific trends in the environment may be systematically scanned.

A search of the literature in the area of politics shows that the following federal laws were considered during the 1990s:

1. Requiring that all ad claims be substantiated
2. Publishing corporate actions that endanger workers or the environment
3. Disclosing lobbying efforts in detail
4. Reducing a company's right to fire workers at will
5. Eliminating inside directors

The marketing strategist of a consumer-goods company may want to determine if any of these trends has any relevance for the company. To do so the strategist may undertake trend-impact analysis. Trend-impact analysis requires the formation of a delphi panel (see chapter 17) to determine the desirability (0–1), technical feasibility (0–1), probability of occurrence (0–1), and probable time of occurrence (1995, 2000, and beyond 2000) of each event listed. The panel may also be asked to suggest the area(s) that may be affected by each event (i.e., production, labor, markets [household, business, government, foreign], finance, or research and development).

EXHIBIT 6-9
Systematic Approach to Environmental Scanning

1. Pick up events in different environments (via literature search).
2. Delineate events of interest to the SBU in one or more of the following areas: production, labor, markets (household, business, government, foreign), finance, or research and development. This could be achieved via trend-impact analysis of the events.
3. Undertake cross-impact analysis of the events of interest.
4. Relate the trends of the noted events to current SBU strategies in different areas.
5. Select the trends that appear either to provide new opportunities or to pose threats.
6. Undertake forecasts of each trend
   —wild card prediction
   —most probable occurrence
   —conservative estimate
7. Develop three scenarios for each trend based on three types of forecasts.
8. Pass on the information to strategists.
9. Repeat steps 4 to 7 and develop more specific scenarios vis-à-vis different products/markets. Incorporate these scenarios in the SBU strategy.

Information about an event may be studied by managers in areas that, according to the delphi panel, are likely to be affected by the event. If their consensus is that the event is indeed important, scanning may continue (see Exhibit 6-10).

Next, cross-impact analysis may be undertaken. This type of analysis studies the impact of an event on other events. Where events are mutually exclusive, such analysis may not be necessary. But where an event seems to reinforce or inhibit other events, cross-impact analysis is highly desirable for uncovering the true strength of an event.

Cross-impact analysis amounts to studying the impact of an event (given its probability of occurrence) upon other events. The impact may be delineated either in qualitative terms (such as critical, major, significant, slight, or none) or in quantitative terms in the form of probabilities.

Exhibit 6-11 shows how cross-impact analysis may be undertaken. Cross-impact ratings, or probabilities, can best be determined with the help of another delphi panel. To further sharpen the analysis, whether the impact of an event on other events will be felt immediately or after a certain number of years may also be determined.

Cross-impact analysis provides the "time" probability of the occurrence of an event and indicates other key events that may be monitored to keep track of

EXHIBIT 6-10
Trend-Impact Analysis: An Example

Event	*Requiring That All Ad Claims Be Substantiated*	*Reducing a Company's Right to Fire Workers at Will*
Desirability	0.8	0.5
Feasibility	0.6	0.3
Probability of occurrence	0.5	0.1
Probable time of occurrence	1995	Beyond 2000
Area(s) impacted	Household markets Business markets Government markets Finance Research and development Production	Labor Finance
Decision	Carry on scanning	Drop from further consideration

Note: Two to three rounds of delphi would be needed to arrive at the above probabilities.

EXHIBIT 6-11
Cross-Impact Analysis: An Example

Event	*Probability of Occurrence*	Impact *a*	*b*	*c*	*d*	*e*
a. Requiring that all ad claims be substantiated	0.5				0.1*	
b. Publishing corporate actions that endanger workers or environment	0.4	0.7**				
c. Disclosing lobbying efforts in detail	0.4					
d. Reducing a company's right to fire workers at will	0.1					
e. Eliminating inside directors	0.6					

*This means that requiring that all claims be substantiated has no effect on the probability of event d.

**This means that if publishing corporate actions that endanger workers or the environment occurs (probability 0.4), the probability of requiring that all ad claims be substantiated increases from 0.5 to 0.7.

the first event. Cross-impact analysis is more useful for project-level scanning than for general scanning.

To relate environmental trends to strategy, consider the following environmental trends and strategies of a cigarette manufacturer:

Trends

T1: Requiring that all ad claims be substantiated
T2: Publishing corporate actions that endanger workers or the environment
T3: Disclosing lobbying efforts in detail
T4: Reducing a company's right to fire workers at will
T5: Eliminating inside directors

Strategies

S1: Heavy emphasis on advertising, using emotional appeals
S2: Seasonal adjustments in labor force for agricultural operations of the company
S3: Regular lobbying effort in Washington against further legislation imposing restrictions on the cigarette industry
S4: Minimum number of outside directors on the board

The analysis in Exhibit 6-12 shows that strategy S1, heavy emphasis on advertising, is most susceptible and requires immediate management action. Among the trends, trend T5, eliminating inside directors, will have the most positive overall impact. Trends T1 and T2, requiring that all ad claims be substantiated and publishing corporate actions that endanger workers or the environment, will have a devastating impact. This type of analysis indicates where management concern and action should be directed. Thus, it will be desirable to

EXHIBIT 6-12
Matrix to Determine the Impact of Selected Trends on Different Corporate Strategies

	Strategies				Impact (I_1)	
Trends	S_1	S_2	S_3	S_4	+	−
T_1	−8	0	+2	−2		8
T_2	−4	−2	−6	0		12
T_3	0	+4	−4	+2	2	
T_4	0	−4	0	+6	2	
T_5	−2	+6	+4	+2	10	
+	—	4	—	8		
−	14	—	4	—		

Scale

+8	*Enhance the implementation of strategy*	Critical
+6		Major
+4		Significant
+2		Slight
0		No effect
−2	*Inhibit the implementation of strategy*	Slight
−4		Significant
−6		Major
−8		Critical

undertake forecasts of trends T1 and T2. The forecasts may predict when the legislation will be passed, what will be the major provisions of the legislation, and so on. Three different forecasts may be obtained:

1. Extremely unfavorable legislation
2. Most probable legislation
3. Most favorable legislation

Three different scenarios (using three types of forecasts) may be developed to indicate the impact of each trend. This information may then be passed on to product/market managers for action. Product/market managers may repeat steps 4 through 7 (see Exhibit 6-9), studying selected trend(s) in depth.

ORGANIZATIONAL ARRANGEMENTS AND PROBLEMS

Corporations organize scanning activity in three different ways: (a) line managers undertake environmental scanning in addition to their other work, (b) scanning is made a part of the strategic planner's job, (c) scanning responsibility is instituted in a new office of environmental scanning.

Structuring Responsibility for Scanning

Most companies use a combination of the first two types of arrangements. The strategic planner may scan the corporatewide environment while line managers concentrate on the product/market environment. In some companies, a new office of environmental scanning has been established with a responsibility for all types of scanning.[28] The scanning office undertakes scanning both regularly and on an ad hoc basis (at the request of one of the groups in the company). Information scanned on a regular basis is passed on to all in the organization for whom it may have relevance. For example, GE is organized into sectors, groups, and SBUs. The SBU is the level at which product/market planning takes place. Thus, scanned information is channeled to those SBUs, groups, and sectors for which it has relevance. Ad hoc scanning may be undertaken at the request of one or more SBUs. These SBUs then share the cost of scanning and are the principal recipients of the information.

The environmental scanner serves to split the work of the planner. If the planner already has many responsibilities and if the environment of a corporation is complex, it is desirable to have a person specifically responsible for scanning. Further, it is desirable that both planners (and/or scanners) and line managers undertake scanning because managers usually limit their scanning perceptions to their own industry; that is, they may limit their scanning to the environment with which they are most familiar. At the corporate level, scanning should go beyond the industry. Morrison H. Beach, former chairman of the board and CEO, Travelers Insurance Companies, advises:

> Traditional planning seeks to identify the environment in which we will be operating and then lays out the alternative strategies for accomplishing our objectives within that environment. It generally assumes that a vast number of organizational, regulatory and economic factors are beyond our control. I encourage you to challenge such traditional assumptions. In fact, some of these factors may be at least partially within our ability to control, and modifying our environment may be part of the answer to accomplishing our objectives.[29]

Whoever is assigned to scan the environment should undertake the following six tasks:

1. **Trend monitoring**—Systematically and continuously monitoring trends in the external environments of the company and studying their impact upon the firm and its various constituencies
2. **Forecast preparation**—Periodically developing alternative scenarios, forecasts, and other analyses that serve as inputs to various types of planning and issue management functions in the organization
3. **Internal consulting**—Providing a consulting resource on long-term environmental matters and conducting special futures research studies as needed to support decision-making and planning activities
4. **Information center**—Providing a center to which intelligence and forecasts about the external environment from all over the organization can be sent for interpretation, analysis, and storage in a basic library on long-range environmental matters

5. **Communications**—Communicating information on the external environment to interested decision makers through a variety of media, including newsletters, special reports, internal lectures, and periodic analyses of the environment
6. **Process improvement**—Continually improving the process of environmental analysis by developing new tools and techniques, designing forecasting systems, applying methodologies developed elsewhere, and engaging in a continuing process of self-evaluation and self-correction.

Successful implementation of these tasks should provide increased awareness and understanding of long-term environments and improve the strategic planning capabilities of the firm. More specifically, environmental inputs are helpful in product design, formulation of marketing strategies, determination of marketing mix, and research and development strategies.

In addition, the scanner should train and motivate line managers to become sensitive to environmental trends, encouraging them to identify strategic versus tactical information and to understand the strategic problems of the firm as opposed to short-term sales policy and tactics.

Time Horizon of Scanning

Scanning may be for a short term or a long term. Short-term scanning is useful for programming various operations, and the term may last up to two years. Long-term scanning is needed for strategic planning, and the term may vary from three to twenty-five years. Rarely does the term of scanning go beyond twenty-five years. The actual time horizon is determined by the nature of the product. Forest products, for example, require a longer time horizon because the company must make decisions about tree planting almost twenty-five years ahead of harvesting those trees for lumber. Fashion designers, however, may not extend scanning beyond four years. As a rule of thumb, the appropriate time horizon for environmental scanning is twice as long as the duration of the company's strategic plan. For example, if a company's strategic plan extends eight years into the future, the environmental scanning time horizon should be sixteen years. Likewise, a company with a five-year planning horizon should scan the environment for ten years. Presumably, then, a multiproduct, multimarket company should have different time horizons for environmental scanning. Using this rule of thumb, a company can be sure not only of discovering relevant trends and their impact on its products/markets but also of implementing necessary changes in its strategy to marshal opportunities provided by the environment and to avert environmental threats.

Problems Faced

Discussed below are the major problems companies face in the context of environmental scanning. Many of these problems are, in fact, dilemmas that may be attributed to a lack of theoretical frameworks on the subject.

1. The environment per se is too broad to be tracked by an organization; thus, it is necessary to separate the relevant from the irrelevant environment. Separating the relevant from the irrelevant may not be easy since, in terms of perceptible realities, the environment of all large corporations is as broad as the world itself.

For example, the steam locomotive industry, presumably, would have been more receptive to changes had they emerged within the industry itself rather than outside it (via General Motors). Therefore, a company needs to determine what criteria to develop to select information on a practical basis.

2. Another problem is concerned with determining the impact of an environmental trend, that is, with determining its meaning for business. For example, what does the feminist movement mean for a company's sales and new business opportunities?
3. Even if the relevance of a trend and its impact are determined, making forecasts of the trend poses another problem. For example, how many women will be in managerial positions ten years from now?
4. A variety of organizational problems hinder environmental scanning. Presumably managers are the company's ears and eyes and therefore should be good sources for perceiving, studying, and channeling pertinent information within the organization. But managers are usually so tied up mentally and physically within their specific roles that they simply ignore happenings in the environment. The structuring of organizations by specialized functions can be blamed for this problem to a certain extent. In addition, organizations often lack a formal system for receiving, analyzing, and finally disseminating environmental information to decision points.
5. Environmental scanning requires "blue sky" thinking and "ivory tower" working patterns to encourage creativity, but such work perspectives are often not justifiable in the midst of corporate culture.
6. Frequently top managers, because of their own values, consider dabbling in the future a waste of resources; therefore, they adopt unkind attitudes toward such projects.
7. Many companies, as a matter of corporate strategy, like to wait and see; therefore, they let industry leaders, the ones who want to be first in the field, act on their behalf.
8. Lack of normative approaches on environmental scanning is another problem.
9. Often a change is too out of the way. It may be perceived, but its relationship to the company is not conceivable.
10. It is also problematic to decide what department of the organization should be responsible for environmental scanning. Should marketing research undertake environmental scanning? How about the strategic planning office? Who else should participate? Is it possible to divide the work? For example, the SBUs may concentrate on their products, product lines, markets, and industry. The corporate level may deal with the rest of the information.
11. Often information is gathered that is overlapping, leading to a waste of resources. Frequently there are informational gaps that require duplication of effort.

SUMMARY

The environment is ever-changing and complex; thus firms must constantly scan and monitor it. Environmental scanning may be undertaken at three levels in the organization: corporate level, SBU level, and product/market level. This chapter approached scanning primarily from the SBU viewpoint. The environments discussed were technological, political, economic, social, and regulatory.

Environmental scanning evolves over a long haul. It is sufficient, therefore, to make a humble beginning rather than designing a fully structured system.

The impact of different environments on marketing strategy was illustrated by numerous examples. A step-by-step procedure for scanning the environment was outlined. A systematic approach to environmental scanning, using such techniques as trend-impact analysis, cross-impact analysis, and the delphi method, was illustrated. Feasible organizational arrangements for environmental scanning were examined, and problems that companies face in their scanning endeavors were discussed.

DISCUSSION QUESTIONS

1. Explain the meaning of environmental scanning. Which constituents of the environment, from the viewpoint of a corporation, require scanning?
2. Illustrate with examples the relevance of technological, political, economic, social, and regulatory environments in the context of marketing strategy.
3. Who in the organization should be responsible for scanning the environment? What role may consultants play in helping corporations in their environmental scanning activity?
4. Explain the use of trend-impact analysis and cross-impact analysis with reference to environmental scanning.
5. How may the delphi technique be useful in the context of environmental scanning? Give an example.
6. What types of responsibilities should be assigned to the person in charge of environmental scanning?
7. How may managers be involved in environmental scanning?

NOTES

[1]Richard Gibson, "Super-Cheap and Midpriced Eateries Bite Fast-Food Chains from Both Sides," *Wall Street Journal,* 22 June 1990, p. B1.

[2]Richard N. Foster, "To Exploit New Technology, Know When to Junk the Old," *Wall Street Journal,* 2 May 1983, p. 30. See also John Diebold, "Where We Are Heading in the Age of Automation," *Management Review* (March 1983): 9–15.

[3]J. D. Glover, *The Revolutionary Corporations: Engines of Plenty, Engines of Growth, Engines of Change* (Homewood, IL: Dow Jones-Irwin, 1980), 370.

[4]Yezdi M. Godiwalla, Wayne A. Meinhart, and William D. Warde, "Environmental Scanning—Does It Help the Chief Executive?" *Long Range Planning* (October 1980): 87–99.

[5]See Philip S. Thomas, "Environmental Scanning—The State of the Art," *Long Range Planning* (February 1980): 20–28. See also Liam Fahey, William R. King, and Vadake K. Narayanan, "Environmental Scanning and Forecasting in Strategic Planning—The State of the Art," *Long Range Planning* (February 1981): 32–39.

[6]Francis Joseph Aguilar, *Scanning the Business Environment* (New York: Macmillan Co., 1967), 40.

[7]Subhash C. Jain, "Environmental Scanning—How the Best Companies Do It," *Long Range Planning* (April 1984): 117–28.

[8]Harold E. Klein and Robert E. Linneman, "Environmental Assessment: An International Study of Corporate Practice," *Journal of Business Strategy* (Summer 1984): 66–92.

[9]See "Record Executives Are on Pins and Needles," *Business Week* (16 February 1987): 112. See also Stephen K. Yoder, "Sony to Market Digital Tape Decks in the U.S., *Wall Street Journal*, 5 June 1990, p. B4.

[10]"The Ubiquitous 'Disappearing' Computer," *TFG Reports* (February 1989).

[11]Richard N. Foster, *Innovation: The Attacker's Advantage* (New York: Summit Books, 1986).

[12]Kim B. Clark, "Strategy Can Do for Technology," *Harvard Business Review* (November–December 1989): 94–98.

[13]"Electric Cars in California," *Business Week* (1 October 1990): 40.

[14]"Will the Auto Glut Choke Detroit?" *Business Week* (7 March 1988): 54.

[15]Lester C. Thurow, "A Time to Dismantle the World Economy," *The Economist* (9 November 1985): 16.

[16]Anne B. Fisher, "What Consumers Want in the 1990s," *Fortune* (29 January 1990): 108. See also Christopher Knowlton, "Consumers: A Tougher Sell," *Fortune* (26 September 1988): 64.

[17]"The Time Compressed Shopper," *Marketing Insights* (Summer 1991): 36.

[18]*Time* (7 March 1988): 84.

[19]"Yolkless Dunkin Donuts," *Business Week* (8 April 1991): 70.

[20]Richard Gibson, "Lean and Mean: Hardee's Joins Low-Fat Fray," *Wall Street Journal*, 15 July 1991, p. B1.

[21]John B. Hinge, "Some Companies Serve Up Lighter Liquor," *Wall Street Journal*, 25 April 1991, p. B1. See also "Changing the Game," *Marketing Insights* (Summer 1990): 68–81.

[22]Trish Hall, "Americans Drink Less, and Makers of Alcohol Feel a Little Woozy," *Wall Street Journal*, 14 March 1984, p. 1; and Allan Luks, "Dealcoholized Beverages: Changing the Way Americans Drink," *The Futurist* (October 1982): 44–49. See also "The Spirited Battle for Those Who Want to Drink Light," *Business Week* (16 June 1986): 84; and Michael Rogers, "A Sales Kick from Beer without the Buzz," *Fortune* (23 June 1986): 89.

[23]Murray L. Weidenbaum, "The Future of Business/Government Relations in the United States," in *The Future of Business*, ed. Max Ways (New York: Pergamon Press, 1978), 50. See also Robert Reich, "The Fourth Wave of Regulation," *Across the Board* (May 1982).

[24]"Procter & Gamble: On a Short Leash," *Business Week* (22 July 1991): 76.

[25]"Has the FCC Gone Too Far?" *Business Week* (5 August 1985): 48.

[26]Paul B. Carroll, "Computer-Ordering Method Helps Newcomer Blossom," *Wall Street Journal*, 22 January 1991, p. B2. See also Bill Saportio, "Are IBM and Sears Crazy? or Canny?" *Fortune* (28 September 1987): 74.

[27]"Birth of a Salesman: How Video Is Revving Up Retailing," *Business Week* (7 September 1987): 109.

[28]See R. T. Lenz and Jack L. Engledow, "Environmental Analysis Units and Strategic Decision-Making: A Field Study of Selected Leading-Edge Corporations," *Strategic Management Journal* 7 (1986): 69–89. See also *TFG Reports* (November 1990).

[29]Morrison H. Beach, "Corporate Planning" (Remarks delivered at the 1985 Conference Board Meeting, New York).

APPENDIX | *Scanning Techniques*

Traditionally, environmental scanning has been implemented mainly with the use of conventional methods, including marketing research, economic indicators, demand forecasting, and industry studies. But the use of such conventional techniques for environmental scanning is not without pitfalls. These techniques have failed to provide reliable insights into the future. Discussed below are a variety of new techniques that have been adapted for use in environmental scanning.

Extrapolation Procedures These procedures require the use of information from the past to explore the future. Obviously their use assumes that the future is some function of the past. There are a variety of extrapolation procedures that range from a simple estimate of the future (based on past information) to regression analysis.

Historical Analogy Where past data cannot be used to scan an environmental phenomenon, the phenomenon may be studied by establishing historical parallels with other phenomena. Assumed here is the availability of sufficient information on other phenomena. Turning points in the progression of these phenomena become guideposts for predicting the behavior of the phenomenon under study.

Intuitive Reasoning This technique bases the future on the "rational feel" of the scanner. Intuitive reasoning requires free thinking unconstrained by past experience and personal biases. This technique, therefore, may provide better results when used by freelance think tanks than when used by managers on the job.

Scenario Building This technique calls for developing a time-ordered sequence of events bearing a logical cause-and-effect relationship to one another. The ultimate forecast is based on multiple contingencies, each with its respective probability of occurrence.

Cross-Impact Matrices When two different trends in the environment point toward conflicting futures, this technique may be used to study these trends simultaneously for their effect. As the name implies, this technique uses a two-dimensional matrix, arraying one trend along the rows and the other along the columns.

Some of the features of cross-impact analyses that make them attractive for strategic planning are (a) they can accommodate all types of eventualities (social or technological, quantitative or qualitative, and binary events or continuous functions), (b) they rapidly discriminate important from unimportant sequences of developments, and (c) their underlying rationale is fully retraceable from the analysis.

Morphological Analysis This technique requires identification of all possible ways to achieve an objective. For example, the technique can be employed to anticipate innovations and to develop optimum configurations for a particular mission or task.

Network Methods There are two types of network methods: contingency trees and relevance trees. A contingency tree is simply a graphical display of logical relationships among environmental trends that focuses on branch-points where several alternative outcomes are possible. A relevance tree is a logical network similar to a contingency tree but is drawn in a way that assigns degrees of importance to various environmental trends with reference to an outcome.

Missing-Link Approach The missing-link approach combines morphological analysis and the network method. Many developments and innovations that appear promising and marketable may be held back because something is missing. Under these circumstances, this technique may be used to scan new trends to see if they provide answers to any missing links.

Model Building This technique emphasizes the construction of models following deductive or inductive procedures. Two types of models may be constructed: phenomenological models and analytic models. Phenomenological models identify trends as a basis for prediction but make no attempt to explain underlying causes. Analytic models seek to identify underlying causes of change so that future developments may be forecast on the basis of a knowledge of their causes.

Delphi Technique The delphi technique is the systematic solicitation of expert opinion. Based on reiteration and feedback, this technique gathers opinions of a panel of experts on happenings in the environment.

PART THREE

Strategic Capabilities and Direction

CHAPTER 7
Measuring Strengths and Weaknesses

CHAPTER 8
Developing Marketing Objectives and Goals

CHAPTER 7

Measuring Strengths and Weaknesses

To measure is the first step to improve.
SIR WILLIAM PETTY

A business does not perform well by accident. Good performances occur because the people directing the affairs of the business interact well with the environment, capitalizing on its strengths and eliminating underlying weaknesses. In other words, to operate successfully in a changing environment, the business should plan its future objectives and strategies around its strengths and downplay moves that bear on its weaknesses. Thus, assessment of strengths and weaknesses becomes an essential task in the strategic process.

In this chapter, a framework will be presented for identifying and describing a business's strengths and weaknesses. This framework provides a systematic scheme for an objective appraisal of the performance and strategic moves of the marketing side of business. It can also be used for identifying those corporatewide perspectives that can be considered strengths and those that constitute weaknesses.

The appraisal of the marketing function has traditionally been pursued in the form of a marketing audit that stresses the review of current problems. From the strategic point of view, the review should go further to include the future as well. The importance of the measurement of strengths and weaknesses in the context of marketing strategy is well described by Alderson:

> The marketing executive may be visualized as operating on the basis of a sort of map. There are boundaries or limits marking off the class of customers he is trying to reach or the trade channels through which he is willing to sell. There are routes over which he can move in attaining his objectives which experience or investigation has indicated are better than other routes. This map may have to be brought up to date by a validation or a revision of operating assumptions.[1]

Strengths and weaknesses in the context of marketing are relative phenomena. Strengths today may become weaknesses tomorrow and vice versa. This is why a penetrating look at the different aspects of a business's marketing program is essential. This chapter is directed toward these ends—searching for opportunities and the means for exploiting them and identifying weaknesses and the ways in which they may be eliminated.

MEANING OF STRENGTHS AND WEAKNESSES

Strengths refer to the competitive advantages and other distinctive competencies that a company can exert in the marketplace. Andrews notes that "the distinctive competence of an organization is more than what it can do; it is what it can do particularly well."[2] **Weaknesses** are constraints that hinder movements in certain directions. For example, a business short of cash cannot afford to undertake a large-scale promotional offensive. In developing marketing strategy, the business should, among other things, dig deeply into its skills and competencies and chart its future in accordance with these competencies.

As an example, in many businesses, service—speed, efficiency, personal attention—makes a crucial difference in gaining leverage in the marketplace. Companies that score higher than their rivals in the category of service have a real competitive strength. McDonald's may not be everyone's idea of the best place in town to dine, but at its level, McDonald's provides a quality of service that is the envy of the industry. Whether at a McDonald's in a rural community or in the downtown area of a large city, the customer gets exactly the same service. Every McDonald's employee is supposed to strictly follow the rules. Cooks must turn, never flip, hamburgers one, never two, at a time. If they haven't been purchased, Big Macs must be discarded ten minutes after being cooked; french fries after seven minutes. Cashiers must make eye contact with and smile at every customer.

Similarly, visitors to Disney World come home impressed with its cleanliness and with the courtesy and competence of the staff. The Disney World management works hard to make sure that the 14,200 employees are, as described in a *Fortune* article, "people who fulfill an expectation of wholesomeness, always smiling, always warm, forever positive in their approach."[3]

STUDYING STRENGTHS AND WEAKNESSES: STATE OF THE ART

A systematic scheme for analyzing strengths and weaknesses is still in embryonic form.[4] One finds few scholarly works on the subject of strengths and weaknesses. An interesting study on the subject was done by Stevenson, who examined six companies.[5] He was interested in the process of defining strengths and weaknesses in the context of strategic planning. He was concerned with the company attributes examined, the organizational scope of the strengths and weaknesses identified, the measurement employed in the process of definition, the criteria used for distinguishing a strength from a weakness, and the sources of information used. Exhibit 7-1 illustrates the process in detail.

Companies should make targeted efforts to identify their competitive strengths and weaknesses. This is a far from easy process, however. Many companies, especially the large ones, have only the vaguest notion of the nature and degree of the competencies that they may possess. The sheer multiplicity of production stages and the overlapping among product lines hinder clear-cut assessment of the competitive strength of a single product line. Despite such

EXHIBIT 7-1
Steps in the Process of Assessing Strengths and Weaknesses

Which Attributes Can Be Examined?	*With What Organizational Entity Is the Manager Concerned?*	*What Types of Measurements Can the Manager Make?*	*What Criteria Are Applicable to Judge a Strength or a Weakness?*	*How Can the Manager Get the Information to Make These Assessments?*
Organizational structure	The corporation	Measure the existence of an attribute	Historical experience of the company	Personal observation
Major policies	Groups	Measure an attribute's efficiency	Intracompany competition	Customer contacts
Top manager's skills	Divisions	Measure an attribute's effectiveness	Direct competitors	Experience
Information system	Departments		Other companies	Control system documents
Operation procedures	Individual employees		Consultant's opinions	Meetings
Planning system			Normative judgments based on management's understanding of literature	Planning system documents
Employee attitudes			Personal opinions	Employees
Manager's attitudes			Specific targets of accomplishment, such as budgets, etc.	Subordinate managers
Union agreements				Superordinate managers
Technical skills				Peers
Research skills				Published documents
New product ideas				Competitive Intelligence
Production facilities				Board members
Demographic characteristics of personnel				Consultants
Distribution network				Journals
Sales force's skill				Books
Breadth of product line				Magazines
Quality control procedures				Professional meetings
Stock market reputation				Government economic indicators
Knowledge of consumer's needs				
Market domination				

Source: Reprinted from "Defining Corporate Strengths and Weaknesses," by Howard H. Stevenson, *Sloan Management Review,* Vol. 17, No. 3 (Spring, 1976), p. 54, by permission of the publisher.

problems, development of competitive strategy depends on having a complete perspective on strengths and weaknesses. Success requires putting the best foot forward.

Unique strengths may lie in different areas of the business and may impact the entire company. Stevenson found a general lack of agreement on suitable definitions, criteria, and information used to measure strengths and weaknesses. In addition to the procedural difficulties faced by managers in their attempts to measure strengths and weaknesses, the need for situational analysis, the need for self-protection, the desire to preserve the status quo, and the problems of definition and computational capacity complicated the process. Stevenson makes the following suggestions for improvement of the process of defining strengths and weaknesses. The manager should

- Recognize that the process of defining strengths and weaknesses is primarily an aid to the individual manager in the accomplishment of his or her task.
- Develop lists of critical areas for examination that are tailored to the responsibility and authority of each individual manager.
- Make the measures and the criteria to be used in evaluation of strengths and weaknesses explicit so that managers can make their evaluations against a common framework.
- Recognize the important strategic role of defining attributes as opposed to efficiency or effectiveness.
- Understand the difference in the use of identified strengths and identified weaknesses.[6]

Despite the primitive state of the art, today many more companies review their strengths and weaknesses in the process of developing strategic plans than did 10 years ago. Strengths and weaknesses may be found in the functional areas of the business, or they may result from some unusual interaction of functions. The following example illustrates how a study of strengths and weaknesses may uncover opportunities that might otherwise have not been conceived. A national distiller and marketer of whiskeys may possess such strengths as sophistication in natural commodity trading associated with its grain purchasing procedures; knowledge of complex warehousing procedures and inventory control; ability and connections associated with dealing in state political structures (i.e., state liquor stores, licensing agencies, and so on); marketing experience associated with diverse wholesale and retail outlets; advertising experience in creating brand images.[7] If these strengths are properly analyzed with a view to seeking diversification opportunities, it appears that the distiller has unique abilities for successfully entering the business of selling building products, wood flooring or siding and composition board. Its experience in commodity trading can be transferred to trading in lumber; experience in dealing with political groups can be used to gain building code acceptances; and experience in marketing can apply to wholesalers (e.g., hardware stores and do-it-yourself centers) of building products.

The case of XYZ Corporation illustrates how a company can get into trouble if it does not carefully consider its strengths and weaknesses. XYZ was a Northfield, Illinois, company with a penchant for diversifying into businesses that were in vogue in the stock market. Until it was reorganized as the Lori Corporation in 1985, it had been in the following businesses: office copying machines, mobile homes, jewelry, speedboats and cabin cruisers, computers, video recording systems, and small buses. Despite entry into some glamorous fields, XYZ did not share the growth and profits that other companies in some of these fields achieved. This is because XYZ entered new and diverse businesses without relating its moves to its basic skills and competencies. For example, despite the fact that it was the first company to develop a photocopy process, developing its process even before Xerox, its total market share for all types of copier machines and supplies in 1984 was well under 3 percent. XYZ Corporation could not keep pace with technological improvements nor with service on installed machines, an essential competency in the copier business. In addition, it overextended itself so much so that managerial controls were rendered inadequate. The company finally got out of all its *trendy* businesses and was reorganized in 1985 to design, manufacture, and distribute costume jewelry, fashion jewelry, and fashion accessories.[8]

SYSTEMATIC MEASUREMENT OF STRENGTHS AND WEAKNESSES

The strengths and weaknesses of a business can be measured at different levels in the organization: corporate, SBU, and product/market level. The thrust of this chapter is on the measurement of strengths and weaknesses at the SBU level. Inasmuch as the strengths and weaknesses of the SBU are a composite of the strengths and weaknesses of different products/markets, the major portion of the discussion will be devoted to the measurement of the marketing strengths and weaknesses of a product/market.

Exhibit 7-2 illustrates the factors that require examination in order to delineate the strengths and weaknesses of a product/market. These factors, along with competitive perspectives, describe the strengths and weaknesses of the product.

Current Strategic Posture

Current strategic posture constitutes a very important variable in developing future strategy. Although it is difficult and painful to try to understand current strategy if formal planning has not been done in the past, it is worth the effort to probe current strategy to achieve a good beginning in strategic planning.

The emphasis here is on the study of the current strategy of a product/market. Before undertaking such a study, however, it is desirable to assess companywide perspectives by raising such questions as

1. What underlies our company's success, given competitor's patterns of doing business?
2. Are there any characteristics and traits that have been followed regularly?
3. To what strategic posture do these characteristics and traits lead?
4. What are the critical factors that could make a difference in the success of the strategy?

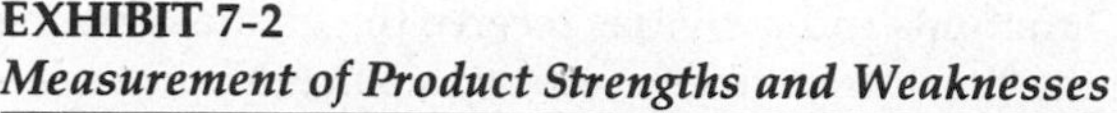

EXHIBIT 7-2
Measurement of Product Strengths and Weaknesses

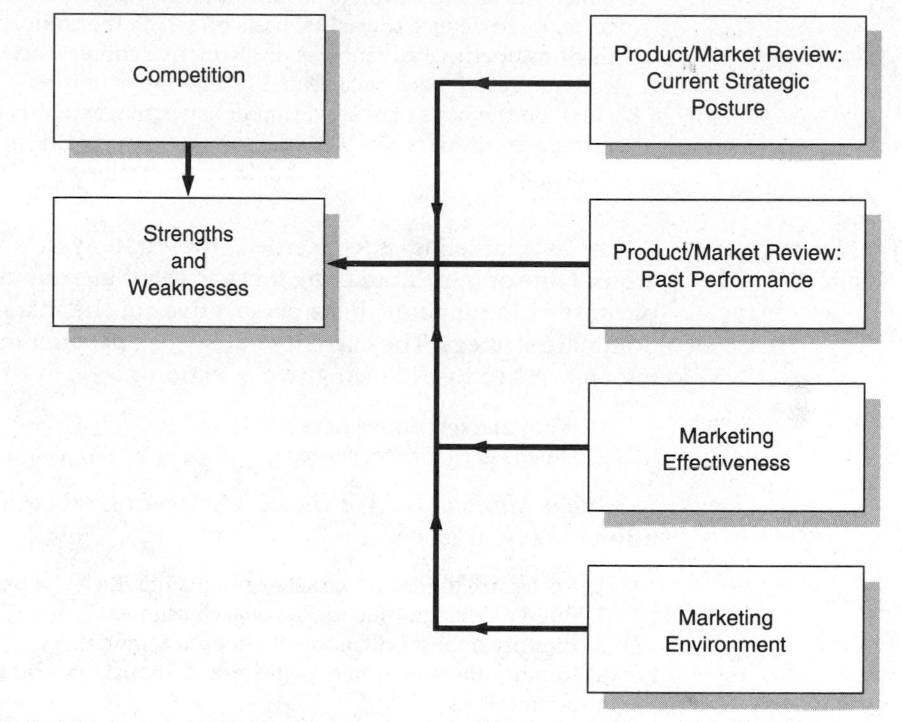

5. To what extent are critical factors likely to undergo a change? What may be the direction of change?

These questions cannot be answered entirely objectively; they call for creative responses. Often managers disagree on various issues. For example, the vice president of marketing of a company that had recently made a heavy investment in sales training considered this investment to be a critical success factor. He thought a well-trained sales staff was crucial for developing new business. On the other hand, the vice president of finance saw only that the investment in training had increased overhead. Though disagreements of this sort are inevitable, a review of current strategy is very important. The operational scheme for studying current strategy from the point of view of the entire corporation outlined below has been found useful.

1. Begin with an identification of the actual current scope of the company's activities. The delineation of customer/product/market emphasis and concentration will give an indication of what kind of a company the company is currently.
2. An analysis of current scope should be followed by identification of the pattern of actual past and existing resource deployments. This description will show

which functions and activities receive the greatest management emphasis and where the greatest sources of strength currently lie.

3. Given the identification of scope and deployment patterns, an attempt should be made to deduce the actual basis on which the company has been competing. Such competitive advantages or distinctive competencies represent the central core of present performance and future opportunities.
4. Next, on the basis of observation of key management personnel, the actual performance criteria (specifications), emphasis, and priorities which have governed strategic choices in the past should be determined.

Current Strategy of a Product/Market

As far as marketing is concerned, the strategy for a product is formulated around one or more marketing mix variables. In examining present strategy, the purpose is to pinpoint those perspectives of the marketing mix that currently dominate strategy. The current strategy of a product may be examined by seeking answers to the following two questions:

1. What markets do we have?
2. How is each market served?

What Markets Do We Have? Answering this question involves consideration of several aspects of the market:

1. Recognize different market segments in which the product is sold.
2. Build a demographic profile of each segment.
3. Identify important customers in each segment.
4. Identify those customers who, while important, also do business with competitors.
5. Identify reasons each important customer may have for buying the product from us. These reasons may be economic (e.g., lower prices), functional (e.g., product features not available in competing products), and psychological (e.g., "this perfume matches my individual chemistry").
6. Analyze the strategic perspective of each important customer as it concerns the purchase of our product. This analysis is relevant primarily for business customers. For example, an aluminum company should attempt to study the strategy of a can manufacturer as far as its aluminum can business is concerned. Suppose that the price of aluminum is consistently rising and more and more can manufacturers are replacing all-aluminum cans with cans of a new alloy of plastic and paper. Such strategic perspectives of an important customer should be examined.
7. Consider changes in each customer's perspectives that may occur in the next few years. These changes may become necessary because of shifts in the customer's environment (both internal and external), abilities, and resources.

Information concerning what markets a company has should, if properly analyzed, provide insight into why customers buy our products and what is their likelihood of doing business with us in the future. For example, a paper manufacturer discovered that most of his customers did business with him because, in their opinion, his delivery schedules were more flexible than those of other suppliers. The quality of his paper might have been superior, too, but this was not strategically important to his customers.

How Is Each Market Served? The means the company employs to serve different customers may be studied by analyzing the information contained in Exhibit 7-3. A careful examination of this information will reveal the current strategy the company utilizes to serve its main markets. For example, analysis of the information in Exhibit 7-3 may reveal the following facts pertaining to a breakfast cereal: Of the seven different segments in the market, the product is extremely popular in two segments. Customers buy the product mainly for health reasons or because of a desire to consume "natural" foods. This desire is strong enough for customers to pay a premium price for the product. Further, customers are willing to make a trip to another store (other than their regular grocery store) to buy this product. Different promotional devices keep customers conscious of the "natural" ingredients in the product. This analysis may point toward the following strategy for the product:

1. Concentrate on limited segments.
2. Emphasize the naturalness of the product as its unique attribute.
3. Keep the price high.
4. Pull the product through with heavy doses of consumer advertising.

Where strategy in the past has not been systematically formulated, recognition of current strategy will be more difficult. In this case, strategy must be inferred from the perspectives of different marketing decisions.

This discussion on present strategy of a product has been approached from two angles: which strategic aspects of the product are indeed valued by the customer and what constitutes marketing strategy in the eyes of the company.

Past Performance

Evaluation of past performance is invaluable in measuring strengths and weaknesses because it provides historical insights into a company's marketing strategy and its success. Historical examination should not be limited to simply noting the directions that the company adopted and the results it achieved but should also include a search for reasons for these results. Exhibit 7-4 shows the type of information that is helpful in measuring past performance.

Strategically, the following three types of analysis should be undertaken to measure past performance: product performance profile, market performance profile, and financial performance profile. Information used for developing a product performance profile is shown in Exhibit 7-5. A product may contribute to company performance in six different ways: through profitability, image of product leadership, furnishing a base for further technological growth, support of total product line, utilization of company resources (e.g., utilization of excess plant capacity), and provision of customer benefits (vis-à-vis the price paid). An example of this last type of contribution is a product that is a small but indispensable part of another product or process with low cost relative to the value of the finished product. Tektronics, a manufacturer of oscilloscopes, is an example. An oscilloscope is sold along with a computer. It is used to help install the

EXHIBIT 7-3
Information for Recognizing Present Marketing Strategy

1. Basis for segmenting the market
2. Definition of the markets for the product
3. Profile of customers in each segments: age, income level, occupation, geographical location, etc.
4. Scope and dimensions of each market: size, profitability, etc.
5. Expected rate of growth of each segment
6. Requirements for success in each market
7. Market standing with established customers in each segment: market share, pattern of repeat business, expansion of customer's product use.
8. Benefits that customers in different segments derive from the product: economics, better performance, displaceable costs, etc.
9. Reasons for buying the product in different segments: product features, awareness, price, advertising, promotion, packaging, display, sales assistance, etc.
10. Customer attitudes in different segments: brand awareness, brand image (mapping), etc.
11. Overall reputation of the product in each segment
12. Purchase or use habits that contribute to these attitudes
13. Reasons that reinforce customer's faith in the company and product
14. Reasons that force customers to turn elsewhere for help in using the product
15. Life-cycle status of the product
16. Story of the product line: quality development, delivery, service
17. Product research and improvements planned
18. Market share: overall and in different segments
19. Deficiencies in serving or assisting customers in using the product
20. Possibility of reducing services in areas where customers are becoming more self-sufficient
21. Resource base: nature of emerging and developing resources—technical, marketing, financial—that could expand or open new markets for the product
22. Geographic coverage of the product market
23. Identification of principal channels: dealer or class of trade
24. Buying habits and attitudes of these channels
25. Sales history through each type of channel
26. Industry sales by type of outlet: retail, wholesale, institutional; and by major types of outlets within each area: department store, chain store, specialty store, etc.
27. Overall price structure for the product
28. Trade discount policy
29. Variations in price in different segments
30. Frequency of price changes
31. Promotional deals offered for the product
32. Emphasis on different advertising media
33. Major thrust of advertising copy
34. Sales tips or promotional devices used by salespeople

EXHIBIT 7-4
Information for Measuring Past Performance

The Consumer

Identify if possible the current "light," "moderate," and "heavy" users of the product in terms of

1. Recent trends in percentage of brand's volume accounted for by each group
2. The characteristics of each group as to sex, age, income, occupation, income group, and geographical location
3. Attitudes toward the product and category and copy appeals most persuasive to each group

The Product

Identify the current consumer preference of the brand versus primary competition (and secondary competition, if available), according to

1. Light, moderate, heavy usage (if available)
2. The characteristics of each group as to sex, age, income, occupation, income group, geographical location, size of family, etc.

Shipment History

Identify the recent shipment trends of the brand by total units and units/M population (brand development), according to districts, regions, and nation.

Spending History

Identify the recent spending trends on the brand by total dollars, dollar/M population, and per unit sold for advertising, for promotion, and for total advertising and promotion by districts, regions, and nation.

Profitability History

Identify the recent trends of list price, average retail price (by sales areas), gross profit margins, and profit before taxes (PBT), *in addition* to trends in

1. Gross profit as a percentage of net sales
2. Total marketing as percentage of gross profit and per unit sold
3. PBT as a percentage of net sales and per unit sold
4. ROFE (Return of Funds Employed) for each recent fiscal year

Share of Market History

Identify recent trends of

1. The brand's share of market nationally, regionally, and district wide
2. Consumption by total units and percentage gain/loss versus year ago nationally, regionally, and district wide
3. Distribution by pack size nationally, regionally, districtwide

Where applicable, trends in all of the above data should also be identified by store classification: chain versus independent (large, medium, and small).

Total Market History

Identify recent trends of the total market in terms of units and percentage gain/loss versus year ago nationally, regionally, and districtwide per M population, store type, county size, type of user (exclusive versus partial user), retail price trends, and by user characteristics (age, income, etc.).

continued

EXHIBIT 7-4
continued

Competitive History (Major Brands), Where Available
Identify significant competitive trends in share; consumption levels by sales areas and store types; media and promotion expenditures; types of media and promotion; retail price differentials; etc.

computer, to test it, and to monitor its performance. The cost of the oscilloscope is small when one considers the essential role it plays in the use of the much more expensive computer.

A market performance profile is illustrated in Exhibit 7-6. In analyzing how well a company is doing in the segments it serves, a good place to begin is with the marginal profit contribution of each customer or customer group. Other measures used are market share, growth of end user markets, size of customer base, distribution strength, and degree of customer loyalty. Of all these, only distribution strength requires some explanation. Distribution and dealer networks can greatly influence a company's performance because it takes an enormous effort to cultivate dealers' loyalty and get repeat business from them. Distribution strength, therefore, can make a significant difference in overall performance.

The real value of a strategy must be reflected in financial gains and market achievements. To measure financial performance, four standards may be employed for comparison: (a) the company's performance, (b) competitor's performance, (c) management expectations, and (d) performance in terms of resources committed. With these standards, for the purposes of marketing strategy, financial performance can be measured with respect to the following variables:

1. Growth rate (percentage)
2. Profitability (percentage), that is, rate of return on investment
3. Market share (percentage as compared with that of principal competitors)
4. Cash flow

It is desirable to analyze financial performance for a number of years to determine the historical trend of performance. To show how financial performance

EXHIBIT 7-5
Product Performance Profile Contribution to Company Performance

Product Line	*Profitability*	*Product Leadership*	*Technological Growth*	*Support of Total Product Line*	*Utilization of Company Resources*	*Provision of Customer Benefits*

EXHIBIT 7-6
Market Performance Profile Contribution to Company Performance

Market Segments	*Profit-ability*	*Market Share*	*Growth of End User Markets*	*Size of Customer Base*	*Distribu-tion Strength*	*Degree of Customer Loyalty*

----						

analysis may figure in formulating marketing strategy, consider the following excerpt from a study on the subject:

> A maker of confectioneries that offers more than one hundred brands, flavors and packagings, prunes its lines—regularly and routinely—of those items having the lowest profit contribution, sales volume, and vitality for future growth. . . .
>
> Each individual product has been ranked on these three factors, and an "index of gross profitability" has been prepared for each in conjunction with annual marketing plans. These plans take into account longer-term objectives for the business, trends in consumer wants and expectations, competitive factors in the marketplace and, lastly, a deliberately ordered "prioritization" of the company's resources. Sales and profit performance are then checked against projected targets at regular intervals through the year, and the indexes of gross profitability are adjusted when necessary.
>
> The firm's chief executive emphasizes that even individual items whose indexes of profitability are ranked at the very bottom are nonetheless profitable and paying their way by any customary standard of return on sales and investment. But the very lowest-ranking items are regularly reviewed; and, on a judgmental basis, some are marked for pruning at the next convenient opportunity. This opportunity is most likely to arrive when stocks of special ingredients and packaging labels for the items have been exhausted.
>
> In a recent year, the company dropped 16 items that were judged to be too low on its index of gross profitability. Calculated and selective pruning is regarded within the company as a healthy means of working toward the best possible mix of products at all times. It has the reported advantages of increasing efficiencies in manufacturing as a result of cutting the "down time" between small runs, reducing inventories, and freeing resources for the expansion of the most promising items—or the development of new ones—without having to expand productive capacity. Another important benefit is that the sales force concentrates on a smaller line containing only the most profitable products with the largest volumes. On the negative side, however, it is acknowledged that pruning, as the company practices it, may result in near-term loss of sales for a line until growth of the rest of the items can compensate.[9]

Appraising Marketing Excellence

Marketing is concerned with the activities required to facilitate the exchange process toward managing demand. The perspectives of these activities are founded on marketing strategy. To develop a strategy, a company needs a philosophical orientation. Four different types of orientation may be considered: manufacturing, sales, technology, and marketing. Manufacturing orientation emphasizes a physical product or a service and assumes that the customer will be pleased with it if it has been well conceived and developed. Sales orientation focuses on promoting the product to make the customer want it. The thrust of technology orientation is on reaching the customer through new and varied products made feasible through technological innovations. Under marketing orientation, first the customer group that the firm wishes to serve is designated. Then the requirements of the target group are carefully examined. These requirements become the basis of product or service conception and development, pricing, promotion, and distribution. Exhibit 7-7 contrasts marketing-oriented companies with manufacturing-, sales-, and technology-oriented firms.

EXHIBIT 7-7
Comparison of Four Kinds of Companies

	Orientation			
	Manufacturing	*Sales*	*Technology*	*Marketing*
Typical strategy	Lower cost	Increase	Push research	Build share profitability
Normal structure	Functional	Functional or profit centers	Profit centers	Market or product or brand; decentralized profit responsibility
Key systems	Plant P&L's Budgets	Sales forecasts Results vs. plan	Performance tests R&D plans	Marketing plans
Traditional skills	Engineering	Sales	Science and engineering	Analysis
Normal focus	Internal efficiencies	Distribution channels; short-term sales results	Product performance	Consumers Market share
Typical response to competitive pressure	Cut costs	Cut price Sell harder	Improve product	Consumer research, planning, resting, refining
Overall mental set	"What we need to do in this company is get our costs down and our quality up."	"Where can I sell what we make?"	"The best product wins the day."	"What will the consumer buy that we profitably make?"

Source: Edward G. Michaels, "Marketing Muscle: Who Needs It?" *Business Horizons,* May–June, 1982, p. 72. Copyright, 1982, by the Foundation for the School of Business at Indiana University. Reprinted by permission.

An examination of Exhibit 7-7 shows that good marketers should think like general managers. Their approach should be unconstrained by functional boundaries. Without neglecting either near- or medium-term profitability, they should concentrate on building a position for tomorrow.[10]

Despite the lip service that has been paid to marketing for more than 30 years, it remains one of the most misunderstood functions of a business. According to Canning, only a few corporations, Procter and Gamble, Citibank, Avon, McDonald's, Emerson Electric, and Merck, for example, really understand and practice true marketing.[11] Inasmuch as marketing orientation is a prerequisite for developing a successful marketing strategy, it behooves a company to thoroughly examine its marketing orientation. The following checklist of 10 questions provides a quick self-test for a company that wants a rough measure of its marketing capabilities.

- Has your company carefully segmented the various segments of the consumer market that it serves?
- Do you routinely measure the profitability of your key products or services in each of these consumer market segments?
- Do you use market research to keep abreast of the needs, preferences, and buying habits of consumers in each segment?
- Have you identified the key buying factors in each segment, and do you know how your company compares with its competitors on these factors?
- Is the impact of environmental trends (demographic, competitive, lifestyle, governmental) on your business carefully gauged?
- Does your company prepare and use an annual marketing plan?
- Is the concept of "marketing investment" understood—and practiced—in your company?
- Is profit responsibility for a product line pushed below the senior management level?
- Does your organization "talk" marketing?
- Did one of the top five executives in your company come up through marketing?

The number of yes answers to these questions determines the marketing orientation of a company. For example, a score of nine or ten yes answers would mean that the company has a strong marketing capability; six to eight would indicate that the firm is on the way; and fewer than six yes answers would stress that the firm is vulnerable to marketing-minded competitors. Essentially, truly marketing-oriented firms are consumer oriented, take an integrated approach to planning, look further ahead, and have highly developed marketing systems. In such firms, marketing dominates the corporate culture.

This analysis reveals the overall marketing effectiveness of the company and highlights the areas that are weak and require management action. Management may take appropriate action—management training, reorganization, or installation of measures designed to yield improvements with or without the help of consultants. If weaknesses cannot be addressed, the company must live with them, and the marketing strategist should take note of them in the process of outlining the business's future direction. A marketing orientation perspective of a firm largely reflects its marketing excellence.

A word of caution is in order here. Although marketing must affect all elements of the business, it is important to avoid building a marketing function that dominates the company. Doing so could be fatal, especially in technological fields. Rather, the company should use marketing to define the benefits of its products more effectively. To achieve this goal, it is necessary that

- Measurement systems routinely provide data on customer satisfaction.
- Managers at all levels and in all functions have routine customer contact.
- Checks and balances are in place to subject any one individual's view of the marketplace to challenges and input by others.
- Compensation and advancement are unambiguously linked to customer satisfaction.

Marketing Environment

Chapter 6 was devoted to scanning the environment at the macro level. This section looks at the environment from the product/market perspective. Environmental scanning at the macro level is the job of a staff person positioned at the corporate, division, group, or business unit level. The person concerned may go by any of these titles: corporate planner, environmental analyst, environmental scanner, strategy planner, or marketing researcher.

Monitoring the environment from the viewpoint of products/markets is a line function that should be carried out by those involved in making marketing decisions because product/market managers, being in close touch with various marketing aspects of the product/market, are in a better position to read between the lines and make meaningful interpretations of the environment. The constituents of the product/market environment are social and cultural effects, political influences, ethical considerations, legal requirements, competition, economic climate, technological changes, institutional evolution, consumerism, population, location of consumers, income, expenditure patterns, and education. Not all aspects of the environment are relevant for every product/market. The scanner, therefore, should first choose which parts of the environment influence the product/market before attempting to monitor them.

The strategic significance of the product/market environment is well illustrated by the experience of Fanny Farmer Candy Shops, a familiar name in the candy industry. Review of the environment in the mid-1980s showed that Americans were watching their waistlines but that they were also indulging in chocolate. In 1983 the average American ate nearly 18 pounds of confections—up from a low of 16 pounds in 1975. Since the mid-1980s, the market for upscale chocolates has been growing fast. Chocolates are again popular gifts for dinner parties, providing a new opportunity for candy makers, who traditionally relied on Valentine's Day, Easter, and Christmas for over half of their annual sales.

Equipped with this analysis of the environment, Fanny Farmer decided to become a dominant competitor in the upscale segment. It introduced rich new specialty chocolates at $8 to $15 per pound, just below $20-per-pound designer chocolates (a market dominated by Godiva, a subsidiary of Campbell Soup Co., and imports such as Perugina of Italy) and above Russell Stover and Fannie May candies, whose chocolates averaged $6 per pound. The company thinks that its new strategic thrust will advance its position in the candy market, though implementing this strategy will require overcoming a variety of problems.[12]

ANALYZING STRENGTHS AND WEAKNESSES

The study of competition, current strategic perspectives, past performance, marketing effectiveness, and marketing environment provides insights into information necessary for designating strengths and weaknesses. Exhibit 7-8 provides a rundown of areas of strength as far as marketing is concerned. Where feasible, strengths should be stated in objective terms. Exhibit 7-8 is not an all-inclusive list, but it indicates the kind of strength a company may have over its competitors. It should be noted that most areas of strength relate to the excellence of personnel or are resource based. Not all factors have the same significance for every product/market; therefore, it is desirable to first recognize the critical factors that could directly or indirectly bear on a product's performance. For example, the development of an improved product may be strategic for drug companies. On the other hand, in the case of cosmetics, where image building is usually important, advertising may be a critical factor. After-sale

EXHIBIT 7-8
Areas of Strength

1. Excellence in product design and/or performance (engineering ingenuity)
2. Low-cost, high-efficiency operating skill in manufacturing and/or in distribution
3. Leadership in product innovation
4. Efficiency in customer service
5. Personal relationships with customers
6. Efficiency in transportation and logistics
7. Effectiveness in sales promotion
8. Merchandising efficiency—high turnover of inventories and/or of capital
9. Skillful trading in volatile price movement commodities
10. Ability to influence legislation
11. Highly efficient, low-cost facilities
12. Ownership or control of low-cost or scarce raw materials
13. Control of intermediate distribution or processing units
14. Massive availability of capital
15. Widespread customer acceptance of company brand name (reputation)
16. Product availability, convenience
17. Customer loyalty
18. Dominant market share position, deal from a position of strength
19. Effectiveness of advertising
20. Quality sales force
21. Make and sell products of highest quality
22. High integrity as a company

service may have significance for products such as copying machines, computers, and elevators. Critical factors may be chosen with reference to Exhibit 3-6. From among the critical factors, an attempt should be made to sort out strengths. It is also desirable to rate different strengths for a more objective analysis.

An example from the personal computer business illustrates the measurement of strengths and weaknesses. In 1982 Apple Computer, Atari (Warner Bros.), Commodore International, Digital Equipment, Fortune Systems, IBM, various Japanese firms, Radio Shack (Tandy Company), and Texas Instruments were active in the field. Of these, Tandy, IBM, and Commodore were the leading competitors. In 1987 Apple, IBM, Tandy, and imports from Taiwan and South Korea were the major competitors. In 1990 the major firms in the industry included Apple, IBM, Tandy, Compaq Computers, Zenith Electronics, and imports from Taiwan and South Korea. Exhibit 7-9 lists the relative strengths of these firms in 1990.

Success in the personal computer business depends on mastery of the following three critical areas:

EXHIBIT 7-9
Relative Strengths of Personal Computer Firms in 1990

Curent Strengths

Companies	Applications software	Brand image	Depth of management	Financial muscle	Low-cost production	National sales force	Retail distribution	Service and support
Apple Computer	●	●	●				●	●
Compaq Computer			●		●		●	
Zenith Electronics	●			●				●
IBM	●	●	●	●	●	●	●	●
Taiwan/S. Korea*	●		●	●	●		●	
Radio Shack (Tandy)*	●			●			●	●

*IBM clones

- **Low-cost production**—As personal computer hardware becomes increasingly standardized, the ability to provide the most value for the dollar greatly influences sales. The most vertically integrated companies have the edge.
- **Distribution**—Retailers have shelf space for just two or three brands; only those makers that are able to keep their products in the customer's line of sight are likely to survive.
- **Software**—Computer sales suffer unless a wide choice of software packages is offered to increase the number of applications.

Without these three strengths in place, a company cannot make it in the personal computer business.[13] Thus, Texas Instruments withdrew from the field in 1983 because they did not have enough applications software. Fortune Systems dropped out in 1984. Both Apple Computer and Atari appeared to be in trouble in 1984 because they were high-cost manufacturers. To overcome its weaknesses, Apple had been working to produce a computer for which users would need no training. The company believed that pursuing this goal would differentiate Apple computers from its competitors, thus compensating for its high costs. The company's efforts paid off. The introduction of the Macintosh line of personal computers, easy-to-use computers with desktop publishing capabilities, changed Apple's fortunes. Apple's example illustrates the importance of analyzing strengths and weaknesses to define objectives and strategies for the future.

Strengths should be further examined to undertake what may be called opportunity analysis (matching strengths, or competencies, to opportunity). Opportunity analysis serves as an input in establishing a company's economic mission. Opportunity analysis is also useful in developing an individual product's objectives. In Exhibit 7-10 the objectives for a food product are shown as they emerged from a study of its strengths. The objectives were to produce a premium product for an unscored segment and to develop a new channel outlet. In other words, at the product level, the opportunity analysis seeks to answer such questions as What opportunity does the company have to capitalize on a competitor's weaknesses? Modify or improve the product line or add new products? Serve the needs of more customers in existing markets or develop new markets? Improve the efficiency of current marketing operations?

Opportunities emerge from the changing environment. Thus, environmental analysis is an important factor in identifying opportunities. Exhibit 7-11 suggests a simple format for analyzing the impact of the environment.

The concept of opportunity analysis may be illustrated with Procter and Gamble's moves in the over-the-counter (OTC) drug business. There is an increasing sense in the drug industry that the OTC side of the drug business will grow faster than prescription sales will grow. Consumers and insurers are becoming more interested in OTC medications, partly because of the steep cost of prescription drugs. Further, with the patents of many major medicines expiring, generic drugs will pose an even greater threat to prescription products. Consequently, drugmakers are taking another look at the OTC business, where a well-marketed brand can keep a franchise alive long after exclusive

EXHIBIT 7-10
Matching Strengths with Opportunities

Strength	*Likely Impact*	*Opportunity Furnished by the Environment*	*Objectives and Goals*
Customer loyalty	Incremental product volume increases Price increases for premium quality/service New product introductions	A trend of changing taste An identified geographic shift of part of the market A market segment neglected by the industry	Develop a premium product Introduce the existing product in a segment hitherto not served Develop a new channel for the product, etc.
Cordial relationships with channels	New product introductions Point-of-purchase advertising Reduction of delivered costs through distribution innovations Tied-in products Merchandising differentiation	A product-related subconscious need not solicited by the competition A product weakness of the competition A distribution weakness of the competition Technical feasibility for improving existing package design A discovered new use for the product or container	

rights have expired. A case in point is the success of Advil, an ibuprofen-based painkiller.

To participate in the growing OTC market, Procter and Gamble has been making inroads into the industry. As a matter of fact, Procter and Gamble is already one of the largest marketers of OTC drugs. But to expand its position in the field, Procter and Gamble decided to speed things up by entering into partnerships with drugmakers and technology companies. By linking its formidable marketing strength with emerging technological advances in medicine, Procter and Gamble hopes to propel itself to the forefront of the health market.

Thus, the company is working on new formulations for minoxidil, a baldness remedy, and other new products promoting hair growth with UpJohn. It joined with Syntex to market anti-inflammatory analgesics, including a nonprescription version of Naprosyn, Syntex's antiarthritis drug. It hopes to sell De-Nol, a gastrointestinal medicine made by Dutch drugmaker Gist-Brocades, as an ulcer treatment. It may use technology from Alcide, a Connecticut maker

EXHIBIT 7-11
Impact of Environmental Trends

Trends	*Impact*	*Timing of Impact*	*Response Time*	*Urgency*	*Threats*	*Opportunities*

of disinfectants, in its toothpaste or mouthwash business. Finally, Procter and Gamble has an agreement with Triton Biosciences and Cetus to use Betaseron, a synthetic interferon, that it hopes will fight the common cold.[14]

In this case, it was Procter and Gamble's marketing strength that led it to enter the OTC drug industry. The opportunity was furnished by the environment—a concern for increasing health care costs—and many drug companies were glad to form alliances with this established OTC marketer.

An interesting observation with regard to opportunity analysis, made by Andrews, is relevant here:

> The match is designed to minimize organizational weakness and to maximize strength. In any case, risk attends it. And when opportunity seems to outrun present distinctive competence, the willingness to gamble that the latter can be built up to the required level is almost indispensable to a strategy that challenges the organization and the people in it. It appears to be true, in any case, that the potential capability of a company tends to be underestimated. Organizations, like individuals, rise to occasions, particularly when the latter provide attractive reward for the effort required.[15]

In the process of analyzing strengths, underlying weaknesses should also be noted. Exhibit 7-12 is a list of typical marketing weaknesses. Appropriate action must be taken to correct weaknesses. Some weaknesses have SBU-wide bearing; others may be weaknesses of a specific product. SBU weaknesses must be examined, and necessary corrective action must be incorporated into the

EXHIBIT 7-12
Typical Marketing Weaknesses

1. Inadequate definition of customer for product/market development
2. Ambiguous service policies
3. Too many levels of reporting in the organizational setup
4. Overlapping channels
5. Lack of top management involvement in new product development
6. Lack of quantitative goals

overall marketing strategy. For example, weaknesses 3, 5, and 6 in Exhibit 7-12 could have SBU-wide ramifications. These must be addressed by the chief marketing strategist. The remaining three weaknesses can be corrected by the person in charge of the product/market with which these weaknesses are associated.

CONCEPT OF SYNERGY

Before concluding the discussion of strengths and weaknesses, it will be desirable to briefly introduce the concept of synergy. **Synergy**, simply stated, is the concept that the combined effect of certain parts is greater than the sum of their individual effects. Let us say, for example, that product 1 contributes X and product 2 contributes Y. If they are produced together, they may contribute $X + Y + Z$. We can say that Z is the synergistic effect of X and Y being brought together and that Z represents positive synergy. There can be negative synergy as well. The study of synergy helps in analyzing new growth opportunities. A new product, for instance, may have such a high synergistic effect on a company's existing product(s) that it may be an extremely desirable addition.

Quantitative analysis of synergy is far from easy. Conceptually, however, synergy may be evaluated following the framework illustrated in Exhibit 7-13. This framework refers to a new product/market entry.

A new product/market entry contribution could take place at three levels: contribution to the parent company (from the entry), contribution to the new entry (from the parent), and joint opportunities (benefits that accrue to both as a result of consolidation). As far as it is feasible, entries in Exhibit 7-13 should be assigned a numerical value, such as increase in unit sales by 20 percent, time saving by two months, reduction in investment requirements by 10 percent, and so on. Finally, various numerical values may be given a common value in the form of return on investment or cash flow.

EXHIBIT 7-13
Measurement of the Synergy of a New Product/Market Entry

	SYNERGY MEASURES							
	Startup Economies			Operating Economies				
Synergistic Contribution to:	*Investment*	*Operating*	*Timing*	*Investment*	*Operating*	*Expansion of Present Sales*	*New Product and Market Areas*	*Overall Synergy*
Parent								
New entry								
Joint opportunities								

SUMMARY

This chapter outlined a scheme for the objective measurement of strengths and weaknesses of a product/market, which then become the basis of identifying SBU strengths and weaknesses. Strengths and weaknesses are tangible and intangible resources that may be utilized for seeking growth of the product. Factors that need to be studied in order to designate strengths and weaknesses are competition, current strategic perspectives, past performance, marketing effectiveness, and marketing environment. Present strategy may be examined with reference to the markets being served and the means used to serve these markets.

Past performance was considered in the form of financial analysis, ranging from simple measurements, such as market share and profitability, to developing product and market performance profiles. Marketing effectiveness was related to marketing orientation, which may be determined with reference to questions raised in the chapter. Finally, various aspects of the product/market marketing environment were analyzed.

These five factors were brought together to delineate strengths and weaknesses. An operational framework was introduced to conduct opportunity analysis. Also discussed was the concept of synergy. The analysis of strengths and weaknesses sets the stage for developing marketing objectives and goals, which will be discussed in the next chapter.

DISCUSSION QUESTIONS

1. Why is it necessary to measure strengths and weaknesses?
2. Because it is natural for managers and other employees to want to justify their actions and decisions, is it possible for a company to make a truly objective appraisal of its strengths and weaknesses?
3. Evaluate the current strategy of IBM related to personal computers and compare it with the strategy being pursued by Apple Computer.
4. Develop a conceptual scheme to evaluate the current strategy of a bank.
5. Is it necessary for a firm to be marketing oriented to succeed? What may a firm do to overcome its lack of marketing orientation?
6. Making necessary assumptions, perform an opportunity analysis for a packaged-goods manufacturer.
7. Explain the meaning of synergy. Examine what sort of synergy Procter and Gamble achieved by going into the frozen orange juice business.

NOTES

[1]Wroe Alderson, *Marketing Behavior and Executive Action* (Homewood, IL: Richard D. Irwin, 1957), 419. See also Philip Kotler, William Gregor, and William Rodgers, "The Marketing Audit Comes of Age," *Sloan Management Review* (Winter 1977): 25–44.

[2]Kenneth R. Andrews, *The Concept of Corporate Strategy* (Homewood, IL: Dow Jones-Irwin, 1971), 97.

[3]Jeremy Main, "Toward Service without a Snare," *Fortune* (23 March 1981): 64–66.

[4]Philip Kotler, William T. Gregor, and William H. Rodgers III, "The Marketing Audit Comes of Age," *Sloan Management Review* (Winter 1989): 49–62.

[5]Howard H. Stevenson, "Defining Corporate Strengths and Weaknesses: An Exploratory Study," (Ph.D. diss., Harvard Business School, 1969).

[6]Howard H. Stevenson, "Defining Corporate Strengths and Weaknesses," *Sloan Management Review* (Spring 1976): 66.

[7]Gordon R. Conrad, "Unexplored Assets for Diversification," *Harvard Business Review* (September–October 1963): 71.

[8]*Moody's Industrial Manual* (1991), 5872–73.

[9]David S. Hopkins, *Business Strategies for Problem Products* (New York: Conference Board, 1977), 29.

[10]Benson P. Shapiro, "What the Hell Is 'Market Oriented'?" *Harvard Business Review* (November–December 1988): 119–25.

[11]Gordon Canning, Jr., "Is Your Company Marketing Oriented?" *Journal of Business Strategy* (May–June 1988): 34–36.

[12]"Up from $4.95 Fudge: Fanny Farmer Tries to Be a Chocolatier," *Business Week* (10 December 1984): 102. See also David Tuller, "Repackaging Chocolates," *Working Women* (January 1987): 45–46.

[13]Thomas C. Hayes, "Compaq Rolls with the Punches," *New York Times*, 25 May 1991, pp. 35–36; and Alan Radding, "Big Blue Takes Aim at Toshiba, Compaq," *Advertising Age* (25 March 1991): 1, 48.

[14]"Can Procter & Gamble Commandeer More Shelves in the Medicine Chest?" *Business Week* (10 April 1989): 64.

[15]Andrews, *The Concept of Corporate Strategy*, 100.

CHAPTER 8

Developing Marketing Objectives and Goals

"Would you tell me, please, which way I ought to go from here?" said Alice. "That depends a good deal on where you want to get to," said the Cheshire Cat.

LEWIS CARROLL
(*ALICE IN WONDERLAND*)

An organization must have an objective to guide its destiny. Although the objective in itself cannot guarantee the success of a business, its presence will certainly mean more efficient and financially less wasteful management of operations.

Objectives form a specific expression of purpose, thus helping to remove any uncertainty about the company's policy or about the intended purpose of any effort. To be effective, objectives must present startling challenges to managers, jolting them away from traditional in-a-rut thinking. If properly designed, objectives permit the measurement of progress. Without some form of progress measurement, it may not be possible to know whether adequate resources are being applied or whether these resources are being managed effectively. Finally, objectives facilitate relationships between units, especially in a diversified corporation where the separate goals of different units may not be consistent with some higher corporate purpose.

Despite its overriding importance, defining objectives is far from easy: there is no mechanical or expert instant answer method. Rather, defining goals as the future becomes the present is a long, time-consuming, and continuous process. In practice, many businesses run either without any commonly accepted objectives and goals or with conflicting objectives and goals. In some cases, objectives may be understood in different ways by different executives. At times objectives may be defined in such general terms that their significance for the job is not understood. For example, a product manager of a large company once observed that "our objective is to satisfy the customer and increase sales." After cross-checking with the vice president of sales, however, she found that the company's goal was making a minimum 6 percent after-tax profit even when it meant losing market share. "Our objective, or whatever you choose to call it, is to grow," the vice president of finance of another company said. "This is a profit-oriented company, and thus we must earn a minimum profit of 10 percent on everything we do. You may call this our objective." Different companies define their objectives differently. It is the task of the CEO to set the company's objectives and goals and to obtain for them the support of his or her senior colleagues, thus paving the way for other parts of the organization to do the same.

The purpose of this chapter is to provide a framework for goal setting in a large, complex organization. A first step in planning is usually to state objectives so that, knowing where you are trying to go, you can figure out how to get there. However, objectives cannot be stated in isolation; that is, objectives cannot be formed without the perspectives of the company's current business, its past performance, resources, and environment. Thus, the subject matter discussed in previous chapters becomes the background material for defining objectives and goals.

FRAMEWORK FOR DEFINING OBJECTIVES

This chapter deals with defining objectives and goals at the SBU level. Because SBU objectives should bear a close relationship to corporate strategic direction, this chapter will start with a discussion of corporate direction and will then examine SBU objectives and goals. Product/market objectives will also be discussed, as they are usually defined at the SBU level and derived from SBU objectives.

The framework discussed here assumes the perspectives of a large corporation. In a small company that manufactures a limited line of related products, corporate and SBU objectives may be identical. Likewise, in a company with a few unrelated products, an SBU's objectives may be no different from those of the product/market.

It is desirable to define a few terms one often confronts in the context of goal setting: mission, policy, objective, goal, and strategic direction. A **mission** (also referred to as corporate concept, vision, or aim) is the CEO's conception of the organization's raison d'être, or what it should work toward, in the light of long-range opportunity. A **policy** is a written definition of general intent or company position designed to guide and regulate certain actions and decisions, especially those of major significance or of a recurring nature. An **objective** is a long-range purpose that is not quantified or limited to a time period (e.g., increasing the return on stockholders' equity). A **goal** is a measurable objective of the business, judged by management to be attainable at some specific future date through planned actions. An example of a goal is to achieve 10 percent growth in sales within the next two years. **Strategic direction** is an all-inclusive term that refers to the network of mission, objectives, and goals. Although we recognize the distinction between an objective and a goal, we will consider these terms simultaneously in order to give the discussion more depth.

The following are frequently cited types of frustrations, disappointments, or troubling uncertainties that should be avoided when dealing with objectives:

1. Lack of credibility, motivation, or practicality
2. Poor information inputs
3. Defining objectives without considering different options
4. Lack of consensus regarding corporate values
5. Disappointing committee effort to define objectives
6. Sterility (lack of uniqueness and competitive advantage)

Briefly, if objectives and goals are to serve their purpose well, they should represent a careful weighing of the balance between the performance desired and the probability of its being accomplished:

> Strategic objectives which are too ambitious result in the dissipation of assets and the destruction of morale, and create the risk of losing past gains as well as future opportunities. Strategic objectives which are not ambitious enough represent lost opportunity and open the door to complacency.[1]

CORPORATE STRATEGIC DIRECTION

Corporate strategic direction is defined in different ways. In some corporations it takes the form of a corporate creed, or code of conduct, that defines perspectives from the viewpoint of different stakeholders. At other corporations, policy statements provide guidelines for implementing strategy. In still others, corporate direction is outlined in terms of objective statements. However expressed, corporate direction consists of broad statements that represent a company's position on various matters and serve as an input in defining objectives and in formulating strategy at lower echelons in the organization.

A company can reasonably expect to achieve a leadership position or superior financial results only when it has purposefully laid out its strategic direction. Every outstanding corporate success is based on a direction that differentiates the firm's approach from that of others. Specifically, strategic direction helps in

1. Identifying what "fits" and what needs the company is well suited to meet
2. Analyzing potential synergies
3. Undertaking risks that simply cannot be justified on a project basis (e.g., willingness to pay for what might appear, on a purely financial basis, to be a premium for acquisition)
4. Providing the ability to act fast (presence of strategic direction not only helps in adequately and quickly scanning opportunities in the environment but capitalizing on them without waiting)
5. Focusing the search for opportunities and options more clearly[2]

Corporate Strategic Direction—An Example

To illustrate the point, consider the corporate direction of Dow Chemical Company, which has persisted for more than 60 years.[3] Herbert Dow founded and built Dow Chemical on one fundamental and energizing idea: start with a cheap and basic raw material; then develop the soundest, lowest-cost process possible.

This idea, or direction, defined certain imperatives Dow has pursued consistently over time:

1. First, don't copy or license anyone else's process. In other words, as Dow himself put it, "Don't make a product unless you can find a better way to do it."
2. Second, build large vertically integrated complexes to achieve maximum economies of scale; that is, maintain cost leadership by building the most technologically advanced facilities in the industry.
3. Third, locate near and tie up abundant sources of cheap raw materials.
4. Fourth, build in bad times as well as good. In other words, become the large-volume supplier for the long pull and preempt competitors from coming in. Be there, in place, when the demand develops.
5. Fifth, maintain a strong cash flow so that the corporation can pursue its vision.

Over the years, Dow has consistently acted in concert with this direction, or vision. It has built enormous vertically integrated complexes at Midland, Michigan; Freeport, Texas; Rotterdam, Holland; and the Louisiana Gulf Coast. And it has pursued with almost fanatical consistency the obtaining of secure, low-cost sources of raw materials.

Strategic Direction and Organizational Perspectives. Pursuing this direction has, in turn, mandated certain human and organizational characteristics of the company and its leadership. For example, Dow has been characterized as a company whose management shows "exceptional willingness to take sweeping but carefully thought out gambles."[4] The company has had to make leaps of faith about the pace and direction of future market and technological developments. Sometimes, as in the case of shale oil, these have taken a very long time to materialize. Other times these leaps of faith have resulted in failure. But as Ben Branch, a top Dow executive for many years, was fond of saying, "Dow encourages well-intentioned failure."

To balance this willingness to take large risks, the company has had to maintain an extraordinary degree of organizational flexibility to give it the ability to respond quickly to unexpected changes. For example, "Dow places little emphasis on, and does not publish, organization charts, preferring to define areas of broad responsibility without rigid compartments. Its informal style has given the company the flexibility to react quickly to change."[5]

Changing the Strategic Direction. Over the years, Dow's direction has had to expand to accommodate a changing world, its own growth, and expanding horizons of opportunity. The expansion of its direction, or vision, has included, for example:

1. Recognition of the opportunities and the need to diversify downstream into higher-value-added, technologically more sophisticated intermediate and end use products, with the concomitant requirement for greater technical selling capability after World War II.

2. The opportunity and the imperative to expand abroad. In fact, Herbert Dow's core vision may have initially been retarded expansion abroad, since raw material availability was not as good in Europe or in Japan as it was in the United States and since it was harder to achieve comparable economies of scale.
3. The need to reorganize and decentralize foreign operations, setting them up on a semiautonomous basis in the mid-1960s to give them room for growth and flexibility.

But throughout its history, Dow's leadership has consistently held to a guiding concept that perhaps has been best articulated as this: "In this business, it's who's there with the vision, the money, and the guts to seize an opportunity."[6]

Corporate Strategic Direction and Strategy Development. What can be concluded from this brief history of Dow Chemical's corporate direction? First, it seems clear that, for more than 50 years, all of Dow's major strategic and operating decisions have been amazingly consistent. They have been consistent because they have been firmly grounded in some basic beliefs about where and how to compete. The direction has evidently made it easier to make the always difficult and risky long-term/short-term decisions, such as investing in research for the long haul or aggressively tying up sources of raw materials.

This direction, or vision, has also driven Dow to be aggressive in generating the cash required to make risky investments possible. Most important, top management seems never to have eschewed its leadership role in favor of becoming merely stewards of a highly successful enterprise. They have been constantly aware of the need to question and reshape Dow's direction, while maintaining those elements that have been instrumental in achieving the company's long-term competitive success. Dow illustrates that corporate direction gives coherence to a wide range of apparently unrelated decisions, serving as the crucial link among them.

Corporate Strategic Direction and Marketing Strategy

The corporate direction of all successful companies without exception is based not only on a clear notion of the markets in which they compete but also on specific concepts of how they can sustain an economically attractive position in those markets. Their direction is grounded in deep understanding of industry and competitive dynamics and company capabilities and potential. Corporate direction should focus in general on continually strengthening the company's economic or market position, or both, in some substantial way. For example, Dow was not immobilized by existing industry relationships, current market shares, or its past shortcomings. It sought—and found—new ways to influence industry dynamics in its favor. Corporate direction should foster creative thinking about realistic and achievable options. In other words, in addition to having thought through the questions of where and how to compete, top management should also make realistic judgments about (a) the capital and human resources that are required to compete and where they should come from,

(b) the changes in the corporation's functional and cultural biases that have to be accomplished, (c) the unique contributions that are required of the corporation (top management and staff) to support pursuit of the new direction by the SBUs, and (d) a guiding notion of the timing or pace of change within which the corporation should realistically move toward the new vision.

In summary, strategic direction is not an abstruse construct based on the inspiration of a solitary genius. It is a hard-nosed, practical concept based on thorough understanding of the dynamics of industries, markets, and competition and of the potential of the corporation for influencing and exploiting these dynamics. It is only rarely the result of a flash of insight; much more often it is the product of deep and disciplined analysis.

Formulating Corporate Strategic Direction

Strategic direction frequently starts out fuzzy and is refined through a messy process of trial and error. It generally emerges in its full clarity only when it is well on its way to being realized. Likewise, changes in corporate direction occur by a long process and in stages.

Changing an established direction is much more difficult than starting from scratch, because one must overcome inherited biases and set norms of behavior. According to Quinn, change is effected through a sequence of steps.[7] First, a need for change is recognized. Second, awareness of the need for change is built throughout the organization by commissioning study groups, staff, or consultants to examine problems, options, contingencies, or opportunities posed by the sensed need. Third, broad support for the change is sought through unstructured discussions, probing of positions, definition of differences of opinion, and so on, among executives. Fourth, pockets of commitment are created by building necessary skills or technologies within the organization, testing options, and taking opportunities to make decisions to build support. Fifth, a clear focus is established either by creating an ad hoc committee to formulate a position or by expressing in written form the specific direction that the CEO desires. Sixth, a definite commitment to change is obtained by designating someone to champion the goal and be accountable for its accomplishment. Finally, after the organization arrives at the new direction, efforts are made to be sensitive to the need for further change in direction, if necessary.

Specific Statements about Corporate Strategic Direction

Many companies make specific statements to designate their direction. Usually these statements are made around such aspects as target customers and markets, principal products or services, geographic domain, core technologies, concern for survival, growth and profitability, company philosophy, company self-concept, and desired public image. Some companies make only brief statements of strategic direction (sometimes labeled corporate objectives); others elaborate on each aspect in detail. Texas Instruments expressed its strategic direction rather briefly: "[it] exists to create, make and market useful products and services to satisfy the needs of its customers throughout the world."[8] NCR defines its objectives, which it calls policies, separately for each functional area in a long report. Apple Computer states its objectives five years into the future with detailed statements under the following headings: corporate concept, internal growth, external growth, sales goal, financial, planning for growth and performance, management and personnel, corporate citizenship, and stockholders and financial community. Exhibit 8-1 shows the strategic direction of the Hewlett-Packard Corporation. As can be noted, this company defines its strategic perspective through brief statements.

No matter how corporate strategic direction is defined, it should meet the following criteria. First, it should present the firm's objectives in a way that enables progress toward them to be measured. Second, the strategic direction should differentiate the company from others. Third, strategic direction should define the business that the company wants to be in, not necessarily the business that it is in. Fourth, it should be relevant to all the firm's stakeholders. Finally, strategic direction should be exciting and inspiring, motivating people at the helm.

EXHIBIT 8-1
Hewlett-Packard's Corporate Direction

Profit
To achieve sufficient profit to finance our company growth and to provide the resources we need to achieve our other corporate objectives.

Customers
To provide products and services of the greatest possible value to our customers, thereby gaining and holding their respect and loyalty.

Field of Interest
To enter new fields only when the ideas we have, together with our technical, manufacturing and marketing skills, assure that we can make a needed and profitable contribution in the field.

Growth
To let our growth be limited only by our profits and our ability to develop and produce technical products that satisfy real customer needs.

People
To help our own people share in the company's success, which they make possible: to provide job security based on their performance, to recognize their individual achievements, and to help them gain a sense of satisfaction and accomplishment from their work.

Management
To foster initiative and creativity by allowing the individual great freedom of action in attaining well-defined objectives.

Citizenship
To honor our obligations to society by being an economic, intellectual and social asset to each nation and each community in which we operate.

Source: Company records.

SBU OBJECTIVES

An SBU was defined in chapter 1 as a unit comprising one or more products having a common market base whose manager has complete responsibility for integrating all functions into a strategy against an identifiable external competitor. We will examine the development and meaning of SBUs again in this chapter to make it clear why objectives must be defined at this level. Abell's explanation is as follows:

> The development of marketing planning has paralleled the growing complexity of business organizations themselves. The first change to take place was the shift from functionally organized companies with relatively narrow product lines and served-market focus to large diversified firms serving multiple markets with multiple product lines. Such firms are usually divided into product or market divisions, divisions may be divided into departments, and these in turn are often further divided into product lines or market segments. As this change gradually took place over the last two decades, "sales planning" was gradually replaced by "marketing planning" in most of these organizations. Each product manager or market manager drew up a marketing plan for his product line or market segment. These were aggregated together into an overall divisional "marketing plan." Divisional plans in turn were aggregated into the overall corporate plan.
>
> But a further important change is now taking place. There has been over the last decade a growing acceptance of the fact that individual units or subunits within a corporation, e.g., divisions, product departments, or even product lines or market segments, may play different roles in achieving overall corporate objectives. Not all units and subunits need to produce the same level of profitability; not all units and subunits have to contribute equally to cash flow objectives.
>
> This concept of the organization as a "portfolio" of units and subunits having different objectives is at the very root of contemporary approaches to strategic marketing planning. It is commonplace today to hear businesses defined as "cash cows," "stars," "question marks," "dogs," etc.* It is in sharp contrast to practice in the 1960s and earlier which emphasized primarily sales and earnings (or return on investment) as a major measure of performance. Although different divisions or departments were intuitively believed to have different capabilities to meet sales and earning goals, these differences were seldom made explicit. Instead, each unit was expected to "pull its weight" in the overall quest for growth and profits.
>
> With the recognition that organizational entities may differ in their objectives and roles, a new organizational concept has also emerged. This is the concept of a "business unit." A business unit may be a division, a product department, or even a product line or major market, depending on the circumstances. It is, however, usually regarded by corporate management as a reasonably autonomous profit center. Usually it has its own "general manager" (even though he may not have that title, he has general managerial responsibilities). Often it has its own manufacturing, sales, research and development, and procurement functions although in some cases some of these may be shared with other businesses (e.g., pooled sales). A business unit usually has a clear market focus. In particular it usually has an identifiable

---

*These terms are defined in chapter 10.

> strategy and an identifiable set of competitors. In some organizations (the General Electric Company, for example), business units are clearly identified and defined. In other organizations, divisions or product departments are treated as relatively autonomous business units although they are not explicitly defined as such.
>
> A business unit will usually comprise several "program" units. These may be product lines, geographic market segments, end-user industries to which the company sells, or units defined on the basis of any other relevant segmentation dimension. Program units may also sometimes differ in their objectives. In such cases, the concept of a portfolio exists both in terms of business units within a corporate structure (or substructure, such as a group) or in terms of programs within a business unit. Usually, however, the business unit is a major focus of strategic attention, and strategic market plans are of prime importance at this level.[9]

As Abell notes, a large, complex organization may have a number of SBUs, each playing its unique role in the organization. Obviously, then, at the corporate level, objectives can be defined only in generalities. It is only at each SBU level that more specific statements of objectives can be made. Actually it is the SBU mission and its objectives and goals that product/market managers need to consider in their strategic plans.

BUSINESS MISSION

Chapter 5 discussed the topic of market boundary. The definition of the business mission has an intimate chicken-and-egg relationship to the definition of market boundary. On the one hand, business mission must be defined, at least in part, in terms of market scope. On the other hand, the market scope should emerge from the business mission. To resolve the problem, Abell suggests:

> One useful distinction is between "served market" and "total market." When describing the way an individual business is defined, the market referred to in the term "product/market scope" is the served market—that portion of the total market which the firm specifically selects to serve. When describing the market arena in which the business competes, the term "market" usually means the total market.[10]

To continue the discussion, it is necessary to make a working assumption here that market boundary definition determines the individual business definition, whereas the business mission refers to the total market. Such a view is commonly accepted by marketing scholars. George Day and Allan Shocker state, for example, that "such issues as the basic definition of the business . . . are strongly influenced by the breadth or narrowness of the definition of competitive boundaries."[11] The above assumption helps to bring in the customer perspective in defining the business.

Defining the Business Mission—The Traditional Viewpoint

Mission is a broad term that refers to the total perspectives or purpose of a business. The mission of a corporation was traditionally framed around its product line and expressed in mottoes: "Our business is textiles," "We manufacture cameras," and so on. With the advent of marketing orientation and technological innovations, this method of defining the business mission has been decried. It has been held that building the perspectives of a business around its product limits the scope of management to enter new fields and thus to make use of growth opportunities. In a key article published in 1960, Levitt observed:

> The railroads did not stop growing because the need for passengers and freight transportation declined. That grew. The railroads are in trouble today not because the need was filled by others (cars, trucks, airplanes, even telephones), but because it was not filled by the railroads themselves. They let others take customers away from them because they assumed themselves to be in the railroad business rather than in the transportation business. The reason they defined their industry wrong was because they were railroad-oriented instead of transportation-oriented; they were product-oriented instead of customer-oriented.[12]

According to Levitt's thesis, the mission of a business should be defined broadly: an airline might consider itself in the vacation business, a publisher in the education industry, an appliance manufacturer in the business of preparing nourishment.

Recently Levitt's proposition has been criticized, and the question of whether simply extending the scope of a business leads far enough has been asked. The Boston Consulting Group, for example, has pointed out that the railroads could not have protected themselves by defining their business as transportation:

> Unfortunately, there is a prevalent notion that if one merely defines one's business in increasingly general terms—such as transportation rather than railroading—the road to successful competitive strategy will be clear. Actually, that is hardly ever the case. More often, the opposite is true. For example, in the case of the railroads, passengers and freight represent very different problems, and short haul vs. longer haul are completely different strategic issues. Indeed, as the unit train demonstrates, just coal handling is a meaningful strategic issue.[13]

In the early 1980s, Coca-Cola extended its business mission from being a soft drink marketer to a beverage company. Subsequently, the company bought three wine companies. A few years later the company decided to leave the wine business. What happened is simply this: although soft drinks and wine both are parts of the beverage industry, the management skills required to run a soft drink business are quite different from those required for the wine business. Coca-Cola overlooked some basics. For example, because wine has to be aged, inventory costs run a lot higher than for soft drinks. Further, grapes must be bought ahead of time. Coke added to its work by vastly overestimating the amount of grapes it needed. Another key characteristic of the wine business is a requirement for heavy capital investment; Coke did not want to make that investment.[14]

As the Coca-Cola example illustrates, the problem with Levitt's thesis is that it is too broad and does not provide what those in finance call a common thread: a relationship between a firm's past and future that indicates where the firm is headed and that helps management to institute directional perspectives. The common thread may be found in marketing, production technology, finance, or management. ITT took advantage of its managerial abilities when it ventured into such diverse businesses as hotels and bakeries. Merrill Lynch found a common thread via finance in entering the real estate business. Bic Pen Company used its marketing strength to involve itself in the razor blade business. Thus, the mission cannot be defined by making abstract statements that one hopes will pave the way for entry into new fields.

It would appear that the mission of a business is neither a statement of current business nor a random extension of current involvements. It signifies the scope and nature of business, not as it is today, but as it could be in the future. The mission plays an important role in designating opportunities for diversification either through research and development or through acquisitions. To be meaningful, the mission should be based on a comprehensive analysis of the business's technology and customer mission. Examples of technology-based definitions are computer companies and aerospace companies. Customer mission refers to the fulfillment of a particular type of customer need, such as the need for basic nutrition, household maintenance, or entertainment.

Whether the company has a written business mission statement or not is immaterial. What is important, however, is that due consideration is given to technological and marketing factors (as related to particular segments and their needs) in defining the mission. Ideally, business definitions should be based on a combination of technology and market mission variables, but some companies venture into new fields on the basis of one variable only. For example, Texas Instruments entered the digital watch market on the basis of its lead in integrated circuits technology. Procter and Gamble added Folgers coffee to its business out of its experience in fulfilling the ordinary daily needs of customers.

To sum up, the mission deals with these questions: What type of business do we want to be in at some future time? What do we want to become? At any given point, most of the resources of a business are frozen or locked into current uses, and the outputs in services or products are for the most part defined by current operations. Over an interval of a few years, however, environmental changes place demands on the business for new types of resources. Further, because of personnel attrition and depreciation of capital resources, management has the option of choosing the environment in which the company will operate and acquiring commensurate new resources rather than replacing the old ones in kind. This explains the importance of defining the business's mission. The mission should be so defined that it has a bearing on the business's strengths and weaknesses.

Defining the Business Mission—A New Approach

In his pioneering work on the subject, Abell has argued against defining a business as simply a choice of products or markets.[15] He proposes that a business be defined in terms of three measures: (a) scope; (b) differentiation of the company's offerings, one from another, across segments; and (c) differentiation of the company's offerings from those of competitors. The scope pertains to the breadth of a business. For example, do life insurance companies consider themselves to be in the business of underwriting insurance only or do they provide complete family financial planning services? Likewise, should a manufacturer of toothpaste define the scope of its business as preventing tooth decay or as providing complete oral hygiene? There are two separate contexts in which differentiation can occur: differentiation across segments and across competitors. Differentiation across segments measures the degree to which business segments are treated differently. An example is personal computers marketed to young children as educational aids and to older people as financial planning aids. Differentiation across competitors measures the degree to which competitors' offerings differ.

These three measures, according to Abell, should be viewed in three dimensions: (a) customer groups served; (b) customer functions served; (c) technologies used. These three dimensions (and a fourth one, level of production/distribution) were examined at length in chapter 5 in the context of defining market boundaries and will not be elaborated further here. An example will illustrate how a business may be defined using Abell's thesis.

Customer groups describe who is being satisfied; customer functions describe what needs are being satisfied; technologies describe how needs are being satisfied. Consider a thermometer manufacturer. Depending on which measure is used, the business can be defined as follows:

Customer Groups	*Customer Functions*	*Technologies Used*
Households	Body temperature	Mercury-base
Restaurants	Cooking temperature	Alcohol-base
Health care facilities	Atmospheric temperature	Electronic-digital

The manufacturer can confine the business to just health care facilities or broaden the scope to include restaurants and households. Thermometers can be provided only for measurement of body temperature or the line can be extended to offer cooking or atmospheric thermometers. The manufacturer could decide to produce only mercury-base thermometers or could also produce alcohol-base or electronic-digital thermometers. The decisions that the manufacturer makes about customer groups, customer functions, and technologies ultimately affects the definition of the business in terms of both scope and differentiation. Exhibits 8-2 and 8-3 graphically show how business can be defined narrowly or broadly around these three dimensions. In Exhibit 8-2, the manufacturer limits the business to service health care facilities only, offering just mercury-base thermometers for measuring body temperatures. In Exhibit 8-3, however, the definition has been broadened to serve three customer groups: households, restaurants, and health care facilities; two types of thermometers: mercury-base and alcohol-base; and three customer functions. The manufacturer could further expand the definition of the business in all three directions. Physicians could be added as a customer group. A line of electronic-digital thermometers could be offered. Finally, thermometers could be produced to measure temperatures of industrial processes.

EXHIBIT 8-2
Defining Business Mission—Narrow Scope

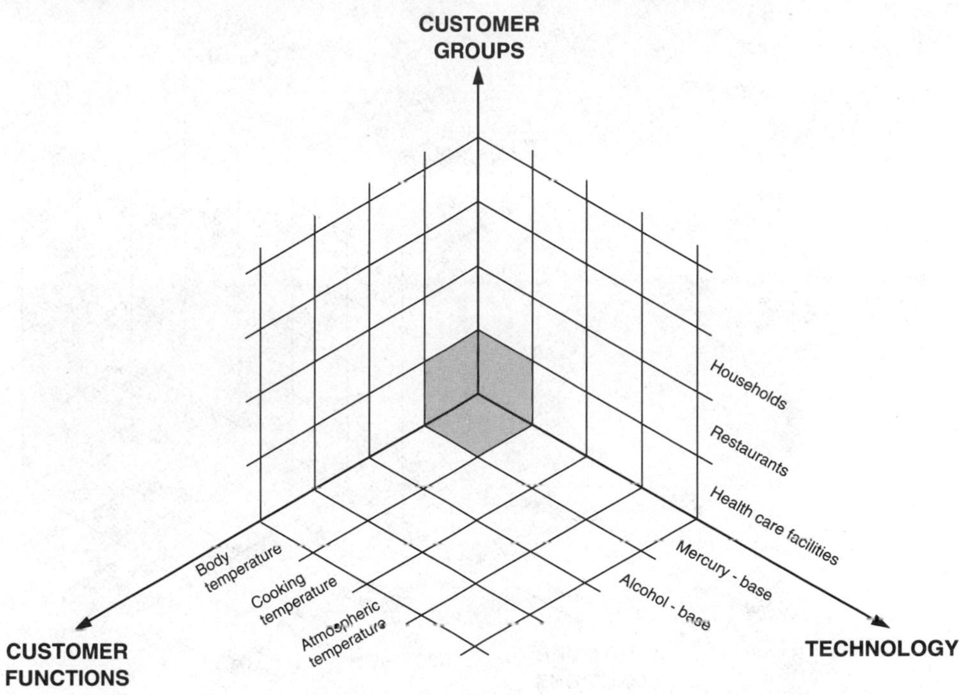

An adequate business definition requires proper consideration of the strategic three Cs: customer (e.g., buying behavior), competition (e.g., competitive definitions of the business), and company (e.g., cost behavior, such as efficiencies via economies of scale; resources/skills, such as financial strength, managerial talent, engineering/manufacturing capability, physical distribution system, etc.; and differences in marketing, manufacturing, and research and development requirements and so on, resulting from market segmentation).

Typology of Business Definitions

Abell proposed defining business in terms of three measures: scope, differentiation across segments, and differentiation across competitors. According to Abell, scope and both kinds of differentiation are related to one another in complex ways. One way to conceptualize these interrelationships is in terms of a typology of business definitions. Three alternative strategies for defining a business are recommended: (a) a focused strategy, (b) a differentiated strategy, and (c) an undifferentiated strategy.

Focused strategy. A business may choose to focus on a particular customer group, customer function, or technology segment. Focus implies a certain basis for segmentation along one or more of these dimensions, narrow scope involving only one or a

EXHIBIT 8-3
Defining Business Mission—Broader Scope

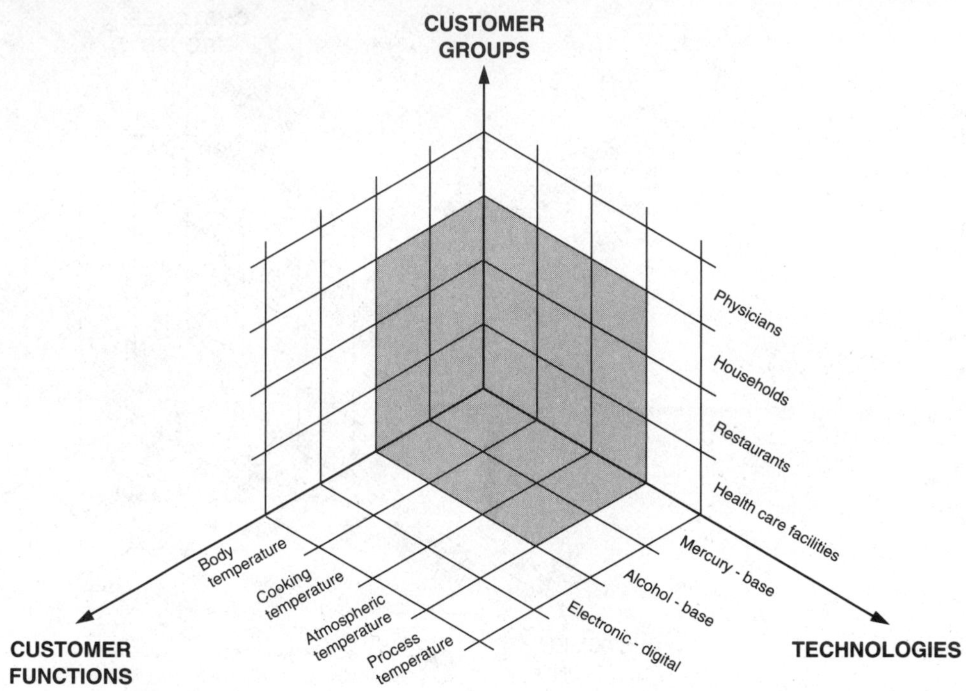

few chosen segments, and differentiation from competitors through careful tailoring of the offering to the specific need of the segment(s) targeted.

Differentiated strategy. When a business combines broad scope with differentiation across any or all of the three dimensions, it may be said to follow a differentiated strategy. Differentiation across segments may also be related to competitive differentiation. By tailoring the offering to the specific needs of each segment, a company automatically increases the chance for competitive superiority. Whether or not competitive differentiation also results is purely a function of the extent to which competitors have also tailored their offerings to the same specific segments. If they have, segment differentiation may be substantial, yet competitive differentiation may be small.

Undifferentiated strategy. When a company combines broad scope across any or all of the three dimensions with an undifferentiated approach to customer group, customer function, or technology segments, it is said to follow an undifferentiated strategy.[16]

Each of these strategies can be applied to the three dimensions (customer groups, customer functions, and technologies) separately. In other words, 27 different combinations are possible: (a) focused, differentiated, or undifferentiated across customer groups; (b) focused, differentiated, or undifferentiated across customer functions; (c) focused, differentiated, or undifferentiated across technologies, and so on.

A focused strategy serves a specific customer group, customer function, or technology segment. It has a narrow scope. Docutel Corporation's strategy in the late 1960s exemplified a focused strategy relative to customer function. When Docutel first pioneered the development of the automated teller machine (ATM), it defined customer function very narrowly, concentrating on one function only—cash dispensing.

A differentiated strategy combines broad scope with differentiation across one or more of the three dimensions. A differentiated strategy serves several customer groups, functions, or technologies while tailoring the product offered to each segment's specific needs. An example of a differentiated strategy applied to customer groups is athletic footwear. Athletic footwear serves a broad range of customer groups and is differentiated across those groups. Tennis shoes are tailored to meet the needs of one specific customer group; basketball shoes, another.

An undifferentiated strategy combines a broad scope across one or more of the three dimensions. This strategy is applied to customer groups in a business that serves a wide range of customer groups but does not differentiate its offerings among those groups. Docutel's strategy was focused with respect to customer function but not with respect to customer groups: they offered exactly the same product to commercial banks, savings and loans, mutual savings banks, and credit unions. To sum up, the strategy that a business chooses to follow, based on the amount of scope and differentiation applied to the three dimensions, determines the definition of the business.

SBU OBJECTIVES AND GOALS

The objectives and goals of the SBU may be stated in terms of activities (manufacturing a specific product, selling in a particular market); financial indicators (achieving targeted return on investment); desired positions (market share, quality leadership); and combinations of these factors. Generally an SBU has a series of objectives to cater to the interests of different stakeholders. One way of organizing objectives is to split them into the following classes: measurement objectives, growth/survival objectives, and constraint objectives. It must be emphasized that objectives and goals should not be based just on facts but on values and feelings as well. What facts should one look at? How should they be weighed and related to one another? It is in seeking answers to such questions that value judgments become crucial.

The perspectives of an SBU determine how far an objective can be broken down into minute details. If the objective applies to a number of products, only broad statements of objectives that specify the role of each product/market from the vantage point of the SBU are feasible. On the other hand, when an SBU is created around one or two products, objectives may be stated in detail.

Exhibit 8-4 illustrates how SBU objectives and goals can be identified and split into three groups: measurement, growth/survival, and constraint. Measurement objectives and goals define an SBU's aims from the point of view of

EXHIBIT 8-4
Illustration of an SBU's Objectives

I. SBU
   Cooking Appliances
II. Mission
   To market to *individual homes* cooking appliances that perform such *functions* as baking, boiling, and roasting, using electric fuel *technology*.
III. Objectives (general statements in the following areas):
   A. Measurement
      1. Profitability
      2. Cash flow
   B. Growth/Survival
      1. Market standing
      2. Productivity
      3. Innovation
   C. Constraint
      1. Capitalize on our research in certain technologies
      2. Avoid style businesses with seasonal obsolescence
      3. Avoid antitrust problems
      4. Assume responsibility to public
IV. Goals
   Specific targets and time frame for achievement of each objective listed above.

the stockholders. The word *profit* has been traditionally used instead of measurement. But, as is widely recognized today, a corporation has several corporate publics besides stockholders; therefore, it is erroneous to use the word profit. On the other hand, the company's very existence and its ability to serve different stakeholders depend on financial viability. Thus, profit constitutes an important measurement objective. To emphasize the real significance of profit, it is more appropriate to label it as a measurement tool.

It will be useful here to draw a distinction between corporate objectives and measurement objectives and goals at the level of an SBU. Corporate objectives define the company's outlook for various stakeholders as a general concept, but the SBU's objectives and goals are specific statements. For example, keeping the environment clean may be a corporate objective. Using this corporate objective as a basis, in a particular time frame an SBU may define prevention of water pollution as one of its objectives. In other words, it is not necessary to repeat the company's obligation to various stakeholders in defining an SBU's objectives as this is already covered in the corporate objectives. Objectives and goals should underline the areas that need to be covered during the time horizon of planning.

Growth objectives and goals, with their implicit references to getting ahead, are accepted as normal goals in a capitalistic society. Thus, companies often aim at growth. Although measurements are usually stated in financial terms, growth is described with reference to the market. Constraint objectives and goals depend on the internal environment of the company and how it wishes to interact with the outside world.

An orderly description of objectives may not always work out, and the three types of objectives and goals may overlap. It is important, however, that the final draft of objectives be based on investigation, analysis, and contemplation. The SBU's objectives and goals, as outlined in Exhibit 8-4, comprise all functional areas of a business; the objectives mainly concerned with marketing are the growth/survival objectives. However, as far as strategy development is concerned, at the SBU level the functional breakdown of a business may not be desirable.

PRODUCT/MARKET OBJECTIVES

Product/market objectives may be defined in terms of profitability, market share, or growth. Most businesses state their product/market purpose through a combination of these terms. Some companies, especially very small ones, may use just one of these terms to communicate product/market objectives. Usually product/market objectives are stated at the SBU level.

Profitability

Profits in one form or another constitute a desirable goal for a product/market venture. As objectives, they may be expressed either in absolute monetary terms or as a percentage of capital employed or of total assets.

At the corporate level, emphasis on profit in a statement of objectives is sometimes avoided because it seems to convey a limited perspective of the corporate purpose. But at the product/market level, an objective stated in terms of profitability provides a measurable criterion with which management can evaluate performance. Because product/market objectives are an internal matter, the corporation is not constrained by any ethical questions in its emphasis on profits.

An ardent user of the profitability objective is Georgia-Pacific Company. The company aims at achieving a return of 20 percent on stockholders' equity. The orthodox view has been that, in an industry where product differentiation is not feasible, the goal of profitability is irrelevant. But Georgia-Pacific's CEO, Marshall Hahn, insists on the profit goal, and the outcome has been very satisfactory. Georgia-Pacific's overall performance has been twice as good as any other competitor in the industry.[17]

How can the profitability goal be realized in practice? First, the corporate management determines the desired profitability, that is, the desired rate of return on investment. There may be a single goal set for the entire corporation, or goals may vary for different businesses. Using the given rate of return, the SBU may compute the percentage of markup on cost for its product(s). To do so, the normal rate of production, averaged over the business cycle, is computed. The total cost of normal production then becomes the standard cost. Next, the ratio of invested capital (in the SBU) to a year's standard cost (i.e., capital turnover) is computed. The capital turnover multiplied by the rate of return gives the markup percentage to be applied to standard cost. This markup is an average figure that may be adjusted both among products and over time.

Market Share

In many industries, the cigarette industry, for example, gaining a few percentage points in market share has a positive effect on profits. Thus, market share has traditionally been considered a desirable goal to pursue. In recent years extensive research on the subject has uncovered new evidence on the positive impact of market share on profitability.[18]

The importance of market share is explainable by the fact that it is related to cost. Cost is a function of scale or experience. Thus the market leader may have a lower cost than other competitors because superior market share permits the accumulation of more experience. Prices, however, are determined by the cost structure of the least effective competitor. The high-cost competitor must generate enough cash to hold market share and meet expenses. If this is not accomplished, the high-cost competitor drops out and is replaced by a more effective, lower-cost competitor. The profitability of the market leader is ascertained by the same price level that determines the profit of even the least effective competitor. Thus, higher market share may give a competitive edge to a firm. As a matter of fact, the effect of market share goes much further. As Henderson has stated:

> Ability to have a basic cost differential in a market sector provides the opportunity to gain a differential growth rate and a differential market share in that sector. This leads to an even greater differential advantage in cost. This advantage can be compounded until it becomes an advantage of such proportions that quite adequate profits can be earned even though competitors can barely finance the maintenance of their own shares.[19]

One strong proponent of market share goal is Eastman Kodak Co. The company takes a long-term view and commits itself to obtaining a big share of growth markets. It keeps building new plants even though its first plant for a product has yet to run at full capacity. It does so hoping large-scale operations will provide a cost advantage that it can utilize in the form of lower prices to customers. Lower prices in turn lead to a higher market share.

Kodak has 80 percent of the U.S. consumer film market and 50 percent of the global business. Yet even with such a high share, the company does not believe in simply maintaining market share. For Kodak, there are only two alternatives: grow the share or it will decline. After all, in the film business, one point of global market share amounts to $40 million in revenues.[20]

While market share is a viable goal, tremendous foresight and effort are needed to achieve and maintain market share positions. A company aspiring toward a large share of the market should carefully consider two aspects: (1) its ability to finance the market share and (2) its ability to effectively defend itself against antitrust action that may be instigated by large increases in market share. For example, when GE considered entering the computer business, it found that to meet its corporate profitability objective it had to achieve a specific market share position. To realize its targeted market share position required huge investment. The question, then, was whether GE should gamble in an industry dominated by one large competitor (IBM) or invest its monies in fields where there was the probability of earning a return equal to or higher than returns in the computer field. GE decided to get out of the computer field.

Fear of antitrust suits also prohibits the seeking of higher market shares. A number of corporations—Kodak, Gillette, Xerox, and IBM, for example—have been the target of such action.

These above reasons have led Bloom and Kotler to suggest that, although market share should be pursued as a desirable goal, companies should opt not for share maximization but for an optimal market share. They suggest the following procedure for figuring out optimal market share:

1. Estimate the relationship between market share and profitability.
2. Estimate the amount of risk associated with each share level.
3. Determine the point at which an increase in market share can no longer be expected to earn enough profit to compensate the company for the added risks to which it would expose itself.[21]

The advantages of higher market share do not mean that a company with a lower share may not have a chance in the industry. There are companies that earn a respectable return on equity despite low market shares. Examples of such corporations are Burroughs, Crown Cork and Seal, Union Camp, and Inland Steel. The following characteristics explain the success of low-share companies: they compete only in those market segments where their strengths have the greatest impact, they make efficient use of their modest research and development budgets, they shun growth for growth's sake, and they have innovative leaders.[22]

In brief, market share goals should not be taken lightly. Rather, a firm should aim at a market share after careful examination.

The following example illustrates the importance of market share. Exhibit 8-5 shows the experience of the industry leader in an industrial product. With an initially high share of a growing and competitive market, management shifted its emphasis from market share to high earnings. A manager with proven skills was put in charge of the business. Earnings increased for six years at the expense of some slow erosion in market share. In the seventh year, however, market share fell so rapidly that, though efforts to hold profits were redoubled, they dropped sharply. Share was never regained. The manager had been highly praised and richly rewarded for his profit results up to 1990. These results, however, were achieved in exchange for a certain unreported damage to the firm's long-term competitiveness. Only by knowing both and by weighing the gain in current income against the degree of market share liquidation that entailed could the true value of performance be judged. In other words, reported earnings do not tell the true story unless market share is constant. Loss of market share is liquidation of an unbooked asset upon which the value of all other assets depends. Gain in market share is like an addition to cost potential, just as

EXHIBIT 8-5
Relationship between Market Share and After-Tax Profit

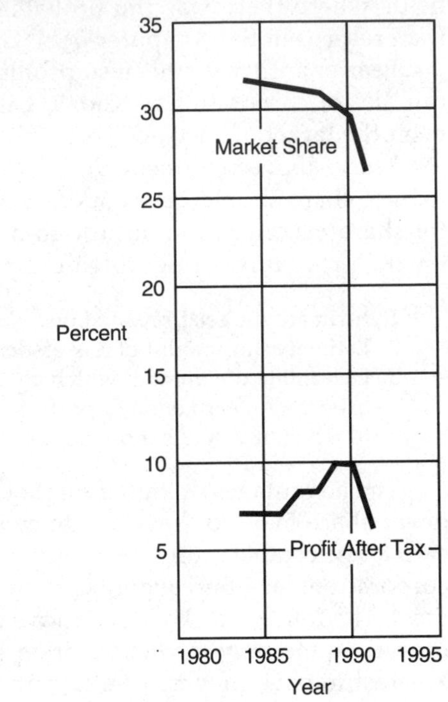

real an asset as credit rating, brand image, organization resources, or technology. In brief, market share guarantees the long-term survival of the business. Liquidation of market share to realize short-term earnings should be avoided. High earnings make sense only when market share is stable.

Growth Growth is an accepted phenomenon of a modern corporation. All institutions should progress and grow. Those which do not grow invite extinction. Static corporations are often subject to proxy fights.

There are a variety of reasons that make growth a viable objective: growth expectations of the stockholders, growth orientation of top management, employees' enthusiasm, growth opportunities furnished by the environment, corporate need to compete effectively in the marketplace, and corporate strengths and competencies that make it easy to grow. Exhibit 8-6 amplifies these reasons under the following categories: customer reasons; competitive reasons; company reasons; and distributor, dealer, and agent reasons.

An example of growth encouraged by corporate strength is provided by R.J. Reynolds Industries. In the early 1980s, the company was in an extremely

EXHIBIT 8-6
Reasons for Growth

Customer Reasons
The product line or sizes too limited for customer convenience
Related products needed to serve a specific market
Purchasing economies: one source, one order, one bill
Service economies: one receiving and processing; one source of parts, service, and other assistance
Ability to give more and better services
Production capacity not enough to fill needs of important customers who may themselves be growing

Competitive Reasons
To maintain or better industry position; growth is necessary in any but a declining industry
To counter or better chief competitors on new offerings
To maintain or better position in specific product or market areas where competition is making strong moves
To permit more competitive pricing ability through greater volume
To possess greater survival strength in price wars, product competition, and economic slumps by greater size

Company Reasons
To fulfill the growth expectations of stockholders, directors, executives, and employees
To utilize available management, selling, distribution, research, or production capacity
To supplement existing products and services that are not growth markets or are on downgrade of the profit cycle
To stabilize seasonal or cyclical fluctuations
To add flexibility by broadening the market and product base of opportunities
To attain greater borrowing and financial influence with size
To be able to attract and pay for better management personnel
To attain the stability of size and move to management by planning

Distributor, Dealer, and Agent Reasons
To add products, sizes, and ranges necessary to attract interest of better distributors, dealers, and agents
To make additions necessary to obtain needed attention and selling effort from existing distributors, dealers and agents

strong cash position, which helped it to acquire Heublein, Del Monte Corp., and Nabisco. H. S. Geneen's passion for growth led ITT into different industries (bakeries, car rental agencies, hotels, insurance firms, parking lots) in addition to its traditional communications business. Any field that promised growth was acceptable to him. Thus, the CEO's growth orientation is the most valuable prerequisite for growth. Similarly, growth ambitions led Procter and Gamble to venture into cosmetics and over-the-counter health remedies.

Other Objectives

In addition to the commonly held objectives of profitability, market share, and growth (discussed above), a company may sometimes pursue a unique objective. Such an objective might be technological leadership, social contribution, the strengthening of national security, or international economic development.

Technological Leadership. A company may consider technological leadership a worthwhile goal. In order to accomplish this, it may develop new products or processes or adopt innovations ahead of the competition, even when economics may not justify doing so. The underlying purpose in seeking this objective is to keep the name of the company in the forefront as a technological leader among security analysts, customers, distributors, and other stakeholders. To continue to be in the forefront of computer technology, in 1987 IBM entered the field of supercomputers, an area that it had previously shunned because the market was limited.[23]

Social Contribution. A company may pursue as an objective something that will make a social contribution. Ultimately that something may lead to higher profitability, but initially it is intended to provide a solution to a social problem. A beverage company, for example, may attack the problem of litter by not offering its product in throwaway bottles. As another example, a pharmaceutical company may set its objective to develop and market an AIDS-preventive medicine.

Strengthening of National Security. In the interest of strengthening national defense, a company may undertake activities not otherwise justifiable. For example, concern for national security may lead a company to deploy resources to develop a new fighter plane. The company may do so despite little encouragement from the air force, if only because the company sincerely feels that the country will need the plane in the coming years.

International Economic Development. Improvement in human welfare, the economic progress of less-developed countries, or the promotion of a worldwide free enterprise system may also serve as objectives. For example, a company may undertake the development of a foolproof method of birth control that can be easily afforded and conveniently used.

PROCESS OF SETTING OBJECTIVES

At the very beginning of the process of setting objectives, an SBU should attempt to take an inventory of objectives as they are currently understood. For example, the SBU head and senior executives may state the current objectives of the SBU and the type of SBU they want it to be in the future. Various executives perceive current objectives differently; and, of course, they will have varying ambitions for the SBU's future. It will take several top-level meetings and a good deal of effort on the part of the SBU head to settle on final objectives.

Each executive may be asked to make a presentation on the objectives and goals he or she would like the SBU to adopt for the future. Executives should be asked to justify the significance of each objective in terms of measuring performance, satisfying environmental conditions, and achieving growth. It is foreseeable that executives will have different objectives; they may express the same objectives in terms that make them appear different, but there should emerge, on analysis, a desire for a common destiny for the SBU. Sometimes disharmony of objectives may be based on diverse perceptions of a business's resource potential and corporate strategy. Thus, before embarking on setting SBU objectives, it is helpful if information on resource potential and corporate strategy is circulated.

Before finalizing the objectives, it is necessary that the executive team show a consensus; that is, each one should believe in the viability of the set objectives and willingly agree to work toward their achievement. A way must be found to persuade a dissenting executive to cooperate. For example, if a very ambitious executive works with stability-oriented people, in the absence of an opportunity to be creative, the executive may fail to perform routine matters adequately, thus becoming a liability to the organization. In such a situation, it may be better to encourage the executive to look around for another job. This option is useful for the organization as well as for the dissenting executive. This type of situation occurs when most of the executives have risen through the ranks and an "outsider" joins them. The dynamism of the latter is perceived as a threat, which may result in conflict. The author is familiar with a $100-million company where the vice president of finance, an "outsider," in his insistence on strategic planning came to be perceived as such a danger by the old-timers that they made it necessary for him to quit.

To sum up, objectives should be set through a series of executive meetings. The organizational head plays the role of mediator in the process of screening varying viewpoints and perceptions and developing consensus from them.

Once broad objectives have been worked out, they should be translated into specific goals, an equally challenging task. Should goals be set so high that only an outstanding manager can achieve them, or should they be set so that they are attainable by the average manager? At what level does frustration inhibit a manager's best efforts? Does an attainable budget lead to complacency? Presumably a company should start with three levels of goals: (a) easily attainable, (b) most desirable, and (c) optimistic. Thereafter, the company may choose a position somewhere between the most desirable goals and the optimistic goals, depending on the organization's resources and the value orientation of management. In no case, however, should performance fall below easily attainable levels, even if everything goes wrong. Attempts should be made to make the goals realistic and achievable. Overly elusive goals can discourage and affect motivation.

There are no universally accepted standards, procedures, or measures for defining objectives. Each organization must work out its own definitions of objectives and goals—what constitutes growth, what measures to adopt for their evaluation, and so on. For example, consider the concept of return on investment, which for decades has been considered a good measure of corporate performance. A large number of corporations consider a specified return on investment as the most sacrosanct of goals. But ponder its limitations. In a large, complex organization, ROI tends to optimize divisional performance at the cost of total corporate performance. Further, its orientation is short-term. Investment refers to assets. Different projects require a varying amount of assets before beginning to yield results, and the return may be slow or fast, depending on the nature of the project. Thus, the value of assets may lose significance as an element in performance measurement. As the president of a large company remarked, "Profits are often the result of expenses incurred several years previously." The president suggested that the current amount of net cash flow serves as a better measure of performance than the potential amount of net cash flow: "The net cash contribution budget is a precise measure of expectations with given resources."

Authors have suggested different procedures for developing objectives and goals. According to Boyd and Levy, the following six sources may be used to generate objectives and goals:

1. Focus on material resources (e.g., oil, minerals, forest)
2. Concern with fabricated objects (e.g., paper, nylon)
3. Major interest in events and activities requiring certain products or services, such as golfing and handling emergencies (Emery Air Freight)
4. Emphasis on the kind of person whose needs are to be met: "Babies Are Our Business" (Gerber).
5. Catering to specific parts of the body: eyes (Maybelline), teeth (Dr. West), feet (Florsheim), skin (Noxzema), hair (Clairol), beard (Gillette), and legs (Hanes).
6. Examination of wants and needs and seeking to adapt to them: generic use to be satisfied (nutrition, comfort, energy, self-expression, development, conformity, etc.) and consumption systems (for satisfying nutritional needs, e.g.).[24]

These categories are especially useful for defining growth/survival objectives, particularly at the SBU or product/market level.

Whichever procedure is utilized for finally coming out with a set of objectives and goals, the following serve as basic inputs in the process. At the corporate level, objectives are influenced by corporate publics, the value system of top management, corporate resources, the performance of business units, and the external environment. SBU objectives are based on the strategic three Cs of customer, competition, and corporation. Product/market objectives are dictated by product/market strengths and weaknesses and by momentum. Strengths and weaknesses are determined on the basis of current strategy, past performance, marketing excellence, and marketing environment. Momentum refers to future trends—extrapolation of past performance with the assumption that no major changes will occur either in the product/market environment or in its marketing mix.

Identified above are the conceptual framework and underlying information useful in defining objectives at different levels. Unfortunately there is no computer model to neatly relate all available information to produce a set of acceptable objectives. Thus, whichever conceptual scheme is followed and no matter how much information is available, in the final analysis objective setting remains a creative exercise.

Internal and external forces may require a business to redefine its objectives, shifting emphasis from one aspect to another. Control Data Corporation has traditionally been concerned more with building volume than with bolstering profit margins. This was necessary for survival. Unlike other computer firms, CDC had no established business machines sales to lean on, so year after year it had to be satisfied with slim profits. But in the mid-1980s, CDC's core businesses (i.e., large computer systems, data processing services, and peripheral equipment) matured, making it feasible for the company to stress profits over volume.[25] This change to a bottom-line orientation could be attributed in part to the new CEO of the company.

Once an objective has been set, it may be tested for validity using the following criteria:

1. Is it, generally speaking, a guide to action? Does it facilitate decision making by helping management select the most desirable alternative courses of action?
2. Is it explicit enough to suggest certain types of action? In this sense, "to make profits" does not represent a particularly meaningful guide to action, but "to carry on a profitable business in electrical goods" does.
3. Is it suggestive of tools to measure and control effectiveness? "To be a leader in the insurance business" and "to be a innovator in child care services" are suggestive of measuring tools in a helpful way; but statements of desires merely to participate in the insurance field or child care field are not.
4. Is it ambitious enough to be challenging? The action called for should in most cases be something in addition to resting on one's laurels. Unless the enterprise sets objectives that involve reaching, there is the threat that the end of the road may be at hand.

> Canon illustrates this point clearly. In 1975, Canon was a mediocre Japanese camera company. It was scarcely growing and had recently turned unprofitable for the first time since 1949. It set a few enormously aggressive goals, most of them quantitative. Its key goals were to increase sales *fivefold* over the next decade, to achieve 3 percent productivity improvement per *month*, to cut in half the time required to develop new products, and to build the premier manufacturing organization.
>
> To achieve these goals, Canon established policies that focused on continuous improvement through the elimination of waste, broadly defined. Among other new policies, Canon put in place a number of organizational measures to promote active employee cooperation. A prime objective was to increase the number of suggestions per employee to 30 per year by 1982, up from one in 1975. This goal was achieved and then surpassed: by 1986 each employee was contributing, on average, 50 suggestions annually.
>
> Planning within the company was refocused on methods to reach targets and, more importantly, on identifying internal capabilities required to achieve targets. Another policy was to make every performance measure visual, so employees could

see at a glance where they were in relation to goals. In each factory, for example, there are visual representations of ongoing improvement activity in relation to goals.

By 1982 Canon had achieved each of its goals. It is now a significant and vigorous competitor in cameras, copiers, and computers.[26]

5. Does it suggest cognizance of external and internal constraints? Most enterprises operate within a framework of external constraints (e.g., legal and competitive restrictions) and internal constraints (e.g., limitations in financial resources).

   In the late 1970s Toyota set as its goal to defeat General Motors. It realized that to do so, it needed scale. To achieve scale, it needed first to defeat Nissan. Toyota initiated a battle against Nissan in which it rapidly introduced a vast array of new autos, capturing market share from Nissan. That battle won, Toyota could turn its attention to its long-term goal—besting General Motors. Targeting the leader is a great way to build momentum and create and organizational challenge.
6. Can it be related to both the broader and the more specific objectives at higher and lower levels in the organization? For example, can SBU objectives be related to corporate objectives, and in turn, do they also relate to the objectives of one of its products/markets?

SUMMARY

The thrust of this chapter was on defining objectives and goals at the SBU level. Objectives may be defined as general statements of the long-term purpose the business wants to pursue. Goals are specific targets the corporation would like to achieve within a given time frame. Because SBU objectives should bear a close relationship to overall corporate direction, the chapter first examines the networks of mission, objectives, and goals that make up a company's corporate direction. The example of the Dow Chemical Company was given.

The discussion of SBU objectives begins with the business mission, which defines the total perspectives or purpose of a business. In addition to presenting the traditional viewpoint on business mission, a new framework for defining the business was introduced. SBU objectives and goals were defined in terms of either financial indicators or desired positions or combinations of these factors. Also considered were product/market objectives. Usually set at the SBU level, product/market objectives were defined in terms of profitability, market share, growth, and several other aspects. Finally, the process of setting objectives was outlined.

DISCUSSION QUESTIONS

1. Define the terms *policy, objective,* and *goal.*
2. What is meant by corporate direction? Why is it necessary to set corporate direction?
3. Does corporate direction undergo change? Discuss.
4. How does the traditional view of the business mission differ from the new approach?

5. Examine the perspectives of the new approach to defining the business mission.
6. Using the new approach, how may an airline define its business mission?
7. In what way is the market share objective viable?
8. Give examples of product/market objectives in terms of technological leadership, social contribution, and strengthening of national security.

NOTES

[1]*Perspectives on Corporate Strategy* (Boston: Boston Consulting Group, 1970), 44.

[2]Frederick W. Gluck, "Vision and Leadership in Corporate Strategy," *McKinsey Quarterly* (Winter 1981): 22–23. See also Tsun-Yan Hsieh, "Leadership Actions," *McKinsey Quarterly*, no. 4 (1990): 42–58.

[3]The discussion on Dow Chemical Company draws heavily on information provided by the company.

[4]"The Right Move Early," *Forbes* (8 January 1990): 130–31.

[5]Lee Smith, "Dow vs. Du Pont: Rival Formulas for Leadership," *Fortune* (10 September 1979): 74.

[6]"Dow Chemical's Drive to Change Its Market and Its Image," *Business Week* (9 June 1986): 92.

[7]James Brian Quinn, "Strategic Goals: Process and Politics," *Sloan Management Review* (Fall 1977): 34–36.

[8]Patrick E. Haggerty, "The Corporation and Innovation," *Strategic Management Journal* (1981): 101.

[9]Derek F. Abell, "Metamorphosis in Marketing Planning," in *Research Frontiers in Marketing: Dialogues and Directions*, ed. Subhash C. Jain (Chicago: American Marketing Association, 1978), 257.

[10]Derek F. Abell, *Defining the Business—The Starting Point of Strategic Planning* (Englewood Cliffs, NJ: Prentice-Hall, 1980), 23.

[11]George S. Day and Allan D. Shocker, *Identifying Competitive Product-Market Boundaries: Strategic and Analytical Issues* (Cambridge, MA: Marketing Science Institute, 1976), 1.

[12]Theodore Levitt, "Marketing Myopia," *Harvard Business Review* (July–August 1960): 46.

[13]*Perspectives on Corporate Strategy*, 42.

[14]"Coca-Cola: A Sobering Lesson from Its Journey into Wine," *Business Week* (3 June 1985): 96.

[15]This section relies heavily on Abell, *Defining the Business*.

[16]Abell, *Defining the Business*, 174–75.

[17]Erik Calonius, "America's Toughest Papermaker," *Fortune* (26 February 1990): 80.

[18]See Robert D. Buzzell and Bradley T. Gale, *The PIMS Principles* (New York: The Free Press, 1987).

[19]Bruce D. Henderson, "Market Share," an informal statement by the Boston Consulting Group, 1978.

[20]Bill Saporito, "Companies That Compete Best," *Fortune* (22 May 1989): 36.

[21]Paul N. Bloom and Philip Kotler, "Strategies for High Market Share Companies," *Harvard Business Review* (November–December 1975): 63.

[22]R. G. Hamermesh, M. J. Anderson, Jr., and J. E. Harris, "Strategies for Low Market Share Businesses," *Harvard Business Review* (May–June 1978): 95. See also Carolyn Y. Woo and Arnold C. Cooper, "The Surprising Case for Low Market Share," *Harvard Business Review* (November–December 1982): 106–13.

[23]*Time* (28 March 1988): 36.

[24]Harper W. Boyd, Jr., and Sidney J. Levy, "What Kind of Corporate Objectives," *Journal of Marketing* (October 1966): 53–58.

[25]"Profits Up 2.9% at Control Data," *New York Times*, 30 April 1991, p. D4. See also Control Data Corporation's annual report for 1990.

[26]Robert Reiner, "Goal Setting," in *Perspectives* (Boston: Boston Consulting Group, Inc., 1988).

PART FOUR

Strategy Formulation

CHAPTER 9

Strategy Selection

All men can see the tactics whereby I conquer, but what none can see is the strategy out of which victory is achieved.

SUN-TZU

Two things were achieved in the previous chapters. First, the internal and external information required for formulating marketing strategy was identified, and the methods for analyzing information were examined. Second, using the available information, the formulation of objectives was covered. This chapter takes us to the next step toward strategy formulation by establishing a framework for it.

Our principal concern in this chapter is with business unit strategy. Among several inputs required to formulate business unit strategy, one basic input is the strategic perspective of different products/markets that constitute the business unit. Therefore, as a first step toward formulating business unit strategy, a scheme for developing product/market strategies is introduced.

Bringing product/market strategies within a framework of business unit strategy formulation emphasizes the importance of inputs from both the top down and the bottom up. As a matter of fact, it can be said that strategic decisions in a diversified company are best made at three different levels: jointly by product/market managers and the SBU manager when questions of implementation are involved, jointly by the CEO and the SBU manager when formulation of strategy is the concern, and by the CEO when the mission of the business is at issue.

CONCEPTUAL SCHEME

Exhibit 9-1 depicts the framework for developing marketing strategy. As delineated earlier, marketing strategy is based on three key factors: corporation, customer, and competition. The interaction between these three factors is rather complex. For example, the corporation factor impacts marketing strategy formulation through (a) the business unit mission and its goals and objectives, (b) perspectives of strengths and weaknesses in different functional areas of the business at different levels, and (c) perspectives of the different products/markets that constitute the business unit. Competition affects the business unit mission as well as the measurement of strengths and weaknesses. The customer

EXHIBIT 9-1
Framework for Formulating Marketing Strategy

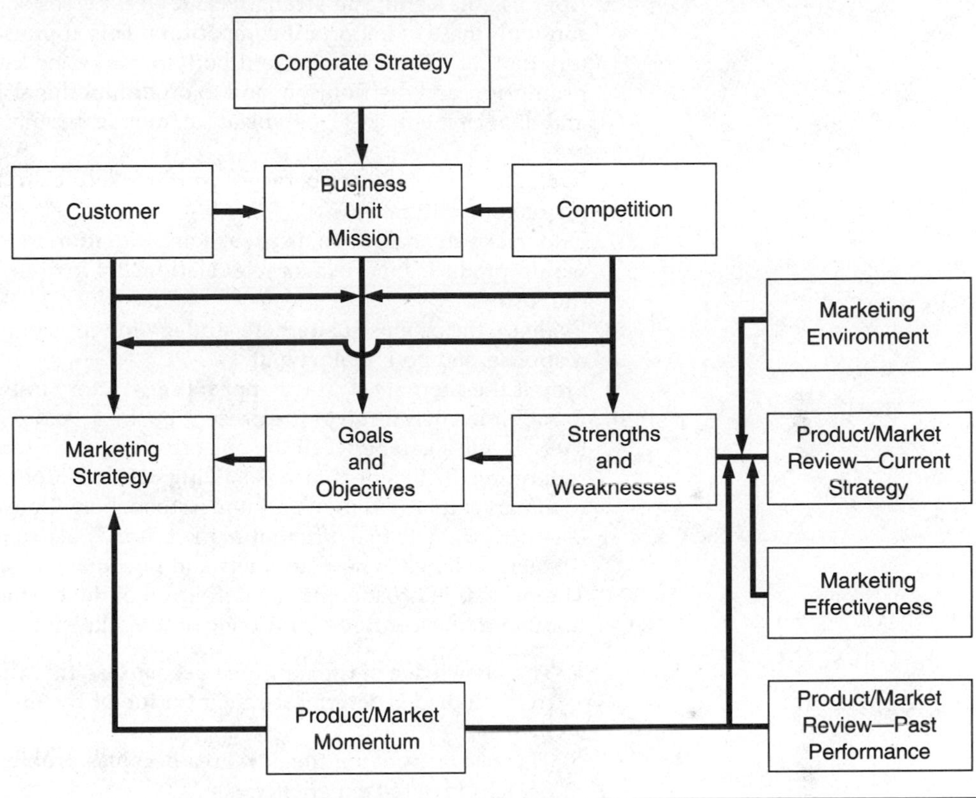

factor is omnipresent, affecting the formation of goals and objectives to support the business unit mission and directly affecting marketing strategy.

PRODUCT/MARKET STRATEGY

The following step-by-step procedure is used for formulating product/market strategy:

1. Start with the present business. Predict what the momentum of the business will be over the planning period if no significant changes are made in the policies or methods of operation. The prediction should be based on historical performance.
2. Forecast what will happen to the environment over the planning period. This forecast will include overall marketing environment and product/market environment.
3. Modify the prediction in step 1 in light of forecasted shifts in the environment in step 2.

4. Stop if predicted performance is fully satisfactory vis-à-vis objectives. Continue if the prediction is not fully satisfying.
5. Appraise the significant strengths and weaknesses of the business in comparison with those of important competitors. This appraisal should include any factors that may become important both in marketing (market, product, price, promotion, and distribution) and in other functional areas (finance, research and development, costs, organization, morale, reputation, management depth, etc.).
6. Evaluate the differences between your marketing strategies and those of your major competitors.
7. Undertake an analysis to discover some variation in marketing strategy that would produce a more favorable relationship in your competitive posture in the future.
8. Evaluate the proposed alternate strategy in terms of possible risks, competitive response, and potential payout.
9. Stop if the alternate strategy appears satisfactory in terms of objectives.
10. Broaden the definition of the present business and repeat steps 7, 8, and 9 if there is still a gap between the objective and the alternative strategy. Here, redefining the business means looking at other products that can be supplied to a market that is known and understood. Sometimes this means supplying existing products to a different market. It may also mean applying technical or financial abilities to new products and new markets simultaneously.
11. The process of broadening the definition of the business to provide a wider horizon can be continued until one of the following occurs:

    a. The knowledge of the new area becomes so thin that a choice of the sector to be studied is determined by intuition or by obviously inadequate judgment.
    b. The cost of studying the new area becomes prohibitively expensive because of lack of related experience.
    c. It becomes clear that the prospects of finding a competitive opportunity are remote.

12. Lower the objectives if the existing business is not satisfactory and if broadening of the business offers unsatisfactory prospects.

There are three tasks involved in this strategy procedure: information analysis, strategy formulation, and implementation. At the product/market level, these tasks are performed by either the product/market manager or an SBU executive. In practice, analysis and implementation are usually handled entirely by the product/market manager; strategy formulation is done jointly by the product/market manager and the SBU executive.

Essentially, all firms have some kind of strategy and plans to carry on their operations. In the past, both plans and strategy were made intuitively. However, the increasing pace of change is forcing businesses to make their strategies explicit and often to change them. Strategy per se is getting more and more attention.

Any approach to strategy formulation leads to a conflict between objectives and capabilities. Attempting the impossible is not a good strategy; it is just a waste of resources. On the other hand, setting inadequate objectives is obviously self-defeating. Setting the proper objectives depends upon prejudgment of the potential success of the strategy; however, you cannot determine the strategy until you know the objectives. Strategy development is a reiterative process requiring art as well as science. This dilemma may explain why many strategies are intuitively made rather than logically and tightly reasoned. But there are concepts that can be usefully applied in approximating opportunities and in speeding up the process of strategy development. The above procedure is designed not only to analyze information systematically but also to formulate or change strategy in an explicit fashion and implement it.

Measuring the Momentum

The first phase in developing product/market plans is to predict the future state of affairs, assuming that the environment and the strategy remain the same. This future state of affairs may be called momentum. If the momentum projects a desirable future, little planning is needed. More often, however, the future implied by the momentum may not be the desired future.

The momentum may be predicted using modeling, forecasting, and simulation techniques. Let us describe how these techniques were applied at a bank. This bank grew by opening two to three new branches per year in the trading area defined by state law. The measurement of momentum consisted of projecting income statement and balance sheet figures for new branches and merging them with the projected income statement and balance sheet of the original bank. A model was constructed to project the bank's future performance. The first step in construction of the model was the prediction of B_{ijt}, that is, balances for an account of type i in area j and in time period t. Account types included checking, savings, and certificates of deposit; areas were chosen to coincide with counties in the state. County areas were desirable because most data at the state level were available by county and because current branching areas were defined by counties. Balances were projected using multiple linear regression. County per capita income and rate of population growth were found to be important variables for predicting total checking account balances, and these variables, along with the last period's savings balance, were shown to be important in describing savings account balances.

The next step was to predict M_{jt} (i.e., the market share of the bank being considered in area j and time period t). This was done using a combination of data of past performances and managerial judgment. The total expected deposit level for the branch being considered, D_{it}, was then calculated as:

$$D_{it} = \sum_{jb} (B_{ijt}M_{jt})$$

For the existing operations of the bank, past data were utilized to produce a 10-year set of deposit balances. These deposit projections were added to those of new branches. Turning to other figures, certain line items on the income statement could be attributed directly to checking accounts, others to savings accounts. The remaining figures were related to the total of account balances.

For this model, ratios of income and expense items to appropriate deposit balances were predicted by a least-squares regression on historical data. This was not considered the most satisfactory method because some changing patterns of incurring income and expenses were not taken into account. However, more sophisticated forecasting techniques, such as exponential smoothing and Box-Jenkins, were rejected because of the potential management misunderstanding they could generate.

Once the ratio matrix was developed, income statements could be generated by simply multiplying the ratios by the proper account balance projection to arrive at the 10-year projection for income statement line items. These income statements, in conjunction with the bank's policy on dividends and capitalization, were then used to generate a 10-year balance sheet projection. The net results were presented to the bank's senior executive committee to be reviewed and modified. After incorporating executive judgment, final 10-year income statements and balance sheets were obtained, indicating the bank's momentum into the future.

Gap Analysis

In the banking example, momentum was extrapolated from historical data. Little attention was given to either internal or external environmental considerations in developing the momentum. However, for a realistic projection of future outcomes, careful analysis of the overall marketing environment as well as the product/market environment is necessary.

As a part of gap analysis, therefore, the momentum should be examined and adjusted with reference to environmental assumptions. The industry, the market, and the competitive environment should be analyzed to identify important threats and opportunities. This analysis should be combined with a careful evaluation of product/market competitive strengths and weaknesses. On the basis of this information, the momentum should be evaluated and refined.

For example, in the midst of continued concern about a recession in 1991, the chairman of the Federal Reserve System, Alan Greenspan, decided to increase the money supply. To do so, he significantly decreased the prime and short-term interest rates. For instance, the rate of interest on many 30-month certificates of deposit went from 7.5 percent in 1990 to 5.5 percent in 1991. This decrease led many depositors to choose other forms of investment over certificates of deposit. In the illustration discussed in the last section, the impact of such a decrease in interest rates was not considered in arriving at the momentum (i.e., in making forecasts of deposit balances). As a part of gap analysis, this shift in the environment would be duly taken into account and the momentum would be adequately adjusted.

The "new" momentum should then be measured against objectives to see if there is a gap between expectation and potential realization. More often than not, there will be a gap between desired objectives and what the projected momentum, as revised with reference to environmental assumptions, can deliver. How this gap may be filled is discussed next.

Filling the Gap

The gap must be filled to bring planned results as close to objectives as possible. Essentially, gap filling amounts to reformulating product/market strategy. A three-step procedure may be used for examining current strategy and coming up with a new one to fill the gap. These steps are issue assessment, identification of key variables, and strategy selection. The experience of some companies suggests that gap filling should be assigned to a multifunctional team. Nonmarketing people often provide fresh inputs; their objectivity and healthy skepticism are generally of great help in sharpening focus and in maintaining businesswide perspectives. The process the team follows should be carefully structured and the analytical work punctuated with regular review meetings to synthesize findings, check progress, and refocus work when desirable. The SBU staff should be deeply involved in the evaluation and approval of the strategies.

Issue Assessment. The primary purpose of this step is to raise issues about the status quo to evaluate the business's competitive standing in view of present and expected market conditions. To begin a team would typically work through a series of general questions about the industry to identify those few issues that will most crucially affect the future of the business. The following questions might be included: How mature is the product/market segment under review? What new avenues of market growth are conceivable? Is the industry becoming more cyclical? Are competitive factors changing (e.g., Is product line elaboration declining and cost control gaining in importance?)? Is our industry as a whole likely to be hurt by continuing inflation? Are new regulatory restrictions pending?

Next, the company should evaluate its own competitive position, for which the following questions may be raised: How mature is our product line? How do our products perform compared with those of leading competitors? How does our marketing capability compare? What about our cost position? What are our customers' most common criticisms? Where are we most vulnerable to competitors? How strong are we in our distribution channels? How productive is our technology? How good is our record in new product introduction?

Some critical issues are immediately apparent in many companies. For example, a company in a highly concentrated industry might find it difficult to hold on to its market share if a stronger, larger competitor were to launch a new low-priced product with intensive promotional support. Also, in a capital-intensive industry, the cyclical pattern and possible pressures on pricing are usually critical. If a product's transport costs are high, preemptive investments in regional manufacturing facilities may be desirable. Other important issues may be concerned with threats of backward integration by customers or forward integration by suppliers, technological upset, new regulatory action, or the entry of foreign competition into the home market. Most strategy teams supplement this brainstorming exercise with certain basic analyses that often lead to fresh insights and a more focused list of critical business issues.[1] Three such issues that may be mentioned here are profit economics analysis, market segmentation analysis, and competitor profiling.

Profit Economics Analysis. Profit economics analysis indicates how product costs are physically generated and where economic leverage lies. The contribution of the product to fixed costs and profits may be calculated by classifying the elements of cost as fixed, variable, or semivariable and by subtracting variable cost from product price to yield contribution per item sold. It is then possible to test the sensitivity of profits to possible variations in volume, price, and cost elements. Similar computations may be made for manufacturing facilities, distribution channels, and customers.

Market Segmentation Analysis. Market segmentation analysis shows alternate methods of segmentation and whether there are any segments not being properly cultivated. Once the appropriate segment is determined, efforts should be made to project the determinants of demand (including cyclical factors and any constraints on market size or growth rate) and to explain pricing patterns, relative market shares, and other determinants of profitability.

Competitor Profiling. Profiling competitors may involve examining their sales literature, talking with experts or representatives of industry associations, and interviewing shared customers and any known former employees of competitors. If more information is needed, the team may acquire and analyze competing products and perhaps even arrange to have competitors interviewed by a third party. With these data, competitors may be compared in terms of product features and performance, pricing, likely product costs and profitability, marketing and service efforts, manufacturing facilities and efficiency, and technology and product development capabilities. Finally, each competitor's basic strategy may be inferred from these comparisons.

Identification of Key Variables. The information on issues described above should be analyzed to isolate the critical factors on which success in the industry depends. In any business there are usually about five to ten factors with a decisive effect on performance. As a matter of fact, in some industries one single factor may be the key to success. For example, in the airline industry, with its high fixed costs, a high load factor is critical to success. In the automobile industry, a strong dealer network is a key success factor because the manufacturer's sales crucially depend on the dealer's ability to finance a wide range of model choices and offer competitive prices to the customer. In a commodity component market, such as switches, timers, and relays, both market share and profitability are heavily influenced by product range. An engineer who is designing circuitry normally reaches for the thickest catalog with the richest product selection. In this industry, therefore, the manufacturer with a wide selection can collect more share points with only a meager sales force.

Key factors may vary from industry to industry. Even within a single company they may vary according to shifts in industry position, product superiority, distribution methods, economic conditions, availability of raw materials, and the like.[2] Therefore, suggested here is a set of questions that may be raised to identify the key success factors in any given situation:

1. What things have to be done exceptionally well to win in this industry? In particular, what must we do well today to lead the industry in profit results and competitive vitality in the years ahead?
2. What factors have caused or could cause companies in this industry to fail?
3. What are the unique strengths of our principal competitors?
4. What are the risks of product or process obsolescence? How likely are they to occur and how critical could they be?
5. What things have to be done to increase sales volume? How does a company in this industry go about increasing its share of the market? How could each of these ways of growing affect profits?
6. What are our major elements of cost? In what ways might each of them be reduced?
7. What are the big profit leverage points in this industry (i.e., What would be the comparative impact on profits of equal management efforts expended on each of a whole series of possible improvement opportunities?)?
8. What key recurring decisions have to be made in each major functional segment of the business? What impact on profits could a good or bad decision in each of these categories have?
9. How, if at all, could the performance of this function give the company a competitive advantage?

Once these key factors have been identified, they should be examined with reference to the current status of the product/market to define alternative strategies that may be pursued to gain competitive advantage over the long term. Each alternative strategy should be evaluated for profit payoff, investment costs, feasibility, and risk.

It is important that strategy alternatives be described as specifically as possible. Simply stating "maintain product quality," "provide high-quality service," or "expand market overseas" is not enough. Precise and concrete descriptions, such as "extend the warranty period from one year to two years," "enter U.K., French, and German markets by appointing agents in these countries," and "provide a $100 cash rebate to every buyer to be handed over by the company directly," are essential before alternatives can be adequately evaluated.

Initially the strategy group may generate a long list of alternatives, but informal discussion with management can soon pare these down to a handful. Each surviving alternative should be weighted in terms of projected financial consequences (sales, fixed and variable costs, profitability, investment, and cash flow) and relevant nonfinancial measures (market shares, product quality and reliability indices, channel efficiency, and so on) over the planning period.

At this time due attention should be paid to examining any contingencies and to making appropriate responses to them. For example, if market share increases by only half of what was planned, what pricing and promotional actions might be undertaken? If customer demand instantly shoots up, how can orders be filled? What ought to be done if the Consumer Product Safety Commission should promulgate new product usage controls? In addition, if the business is in a cyclical industry, each alternative should also be tested against several market-size scenarios, simultaneously incorporating varying assumptions about competitive pricing pressures. In industries dominated by a few competitors, an evaluation should be made of the ability of the business to adapt each strategy to competitive actions—pricing moves, shifts in advertising strategy, or attempts to dominate a distribution channel, for example.

Strategy Selection. After information on trade-offs between alternative strategies has been gathered as discussed above, a preferred strategy should be chosen for recommendation to management. Usually the chosen strategy has a focus on one of the areas of the marketing mix.[3] For example, the preferred strategy may be to reduce prices to maintain market share. Here the emphasis of the strategy is on pricing. Thus, pricing may be labeled as the core strategy, that is, the area of primary concern. However, in order to make an integrated marketing decision, appropriate changes may have to be made in product, promotion, and distribution areas.[4] The strategic perspectives in these areas may be called supporting strategies. Thus, once strategy selection has been undertaken, core and supporting strategy areas should be delineated. Core and supporting strategies should fit the needs of the marketplace, the skills of the company, and the vagaries of the competition.

Occasionally more than one decision area may constitute a core strategy. For example, in holding prices and in introducing a new, improved version of the product, both product and price are core strategies, whereas promotion and distribution are supporting ones. Exhibit 9-2 shows core and supporting strategies for a personal computer and a camcorder. Note that in the case of the personal computer, product constitutes the only core strategy. For the camcorder, however, both price and promotion are core strategies.

The concept of core and supporting strategies may be examined with reference to the Ikea furniture chain.[5] Ikea, the giant Swedish home-furnishings business, has done well in the U.S. market by pursuing price as its core strategy. Where other Scandinavian furniture stores have faltered in the United States, Ikea keeps growing. Despite its poor service, customers keep coming to buy trendy furniture at bargain basement prices. The company has well aligned its supporting strategies of product, promotion, and distribution with its core strategy. For example, it selects highly visible sites easily accessible from major highways to generate traffic. Few competitors can match the selection offered by its cavernous 200,000-square-foot branches, which on average are five times larger than full-line competitors. The products are stylish and durable as well as functional; the quality is good. Advertising attempts to mold Ikea's image as hip and appealing. Ikea's enticing in-store models, easy-to-find price tags, and attractive displays create instant interest in the merchandise. But all these supporting strategies are fully price relevant. The company is so price conscious that it has used components from as many as four different manufacturers to

EXHIBIT 9-2
Core and Supporting Strategies

Product/Market	*Core Strategy*	*Supporting Strategy*
1. Personal computer for household use	*Product:* Develop a new product within three years for household use	*Price:* Keep the price low to encourage customer interest *Promotion:* Hire and train a new sales force to call on distribution channels; advertise in print media to create consumer awareness *Distribution:* Seek intensive distribution through mass merchandisers
2. Camcorder for middle-class families	*Promotion:* Promote heavily by mail among families with annual income over $40,000; follow through with telephone calls *Price:* Keep prices down; make up for reduced prices by selling a package deal for blank cartridges, stand, and servicing	*Product:* Develop instructions in a very lucid fashion (i.e., a step-by-step procedure in easy-to-comprehend language); develop appropriate packaging for mail delivery *Distribution:* Arrange with a mail delivery organization, such as UPS, for fast and dependable delivery

make a single chair. Briefly, Ikea follows a strategy to satisfy the desire for contemporary furniture at moderate prices.

It is rather common for firms competing in the same industry to choose different core and supporting strategies through which to compete. The chosen strategy reflects the particular strength of the firm, the specific demands of the market, and the competitive thrust. As has been noted:

> Coca-Cola was born a winner, but Pepsi had to fight to survive by distinguishing itself from the leader. For most of its history, Pepsi differentiated itself purely on price: "Twice as much for a nickel, too." Only in the early 1970s did Pepsi start to believe that its product actually may be as good as if not better than Coke's. The resulting strategy was: "The Pepsi challenge."
>
> The first belief of Coca-Cola was that its product was sacred. The resulting strategy was simple: "Don't touch the recipe" and "don't put lesser products under the same brand name" (call them "Tab"). Coca-Cola's second belief was that anyone should be able to buy Coke within a few steps of anywhere on earth. This belief drove the company to make its product available in every conceivable outlet and required a distribution strategy that allowed all outlets a reasonable profit at competitive prices.
>
> While Coca-Cola was driven by a product focus, Pepsi developed a more market-oriented perspective. Pepsi was the first to offer new sizes and packages. When consumer trends toward health, fitness and sweeter taste emerged, Pepsi again was the innovator: It was the first to market diet and light varieties and it quickly sweetened its formula. Unencumbered by reverence for its base brand, it introduced the new varieties as extensions of the Pepsi signature. Where Coca-Cola feared a dilu-

tion of its brand name, Pepsi saw an opportunity to exploit the cost advantages and advertising of an umbrella brand.[6]

It is important to remember that the core strategy is formulated around the critical variable(s) that may differ from one segment to another for the same product. This is well supported by the following quotation taken from a case study of the petroloids business. Petroloids, a family of such unique materials as oils, petro-rubbers, foams, adhesives, and sealants, are manufactured substances based on the synthesis of organic hydrocarbons:

> Major producers competed with one another on a variety of dimensions. Among the most important were price, technical assistance, advertising and promotion, and product availability. Price was used as a competitive weapon primarily in those segments of the market where products and applications had become standardized. However, where products had been developed for highly specialized purposes and represented only a small fraction of a customer's total material cost, the market was often less price sensitive. Here customers were chiefly concerned with the physical properties of the product and operating performance.
>
> Technical assistance was an important means of obtaining business. A sizable percentage of total petroloid sales were accounted for by products developed to meet the unique needs of particular customers. Products for the aerospace industry were a primary example. Research engineers of petroloid producers were expected to work closely with customers to define performance requirements and to insure the development of acceptable products.
>
> Advertising and promotional activities were important marketing tools in those segments which utilized distribution channels and/or which reached end users as opposed to OEM's. This was particularly true of foams, adhesives, and sealants which were sold both to industrial and consumer markets. A variety of packaged consumer products were sold to hardware, supermarkets, and "do-it-yourself" outlets by our company as well as other competitors. Advertising increased awareness and stimulated interest among the general public while promotional activities improved the effectiveness of distribution networks. Since speciality petroloid products accounted for only a small percentage of a distributor's total sales, product promotion insured that specific products received adequate attention.
>
> Product availability was a fourth dimension on which producers competed. With manufacturing cycles from 2–16 weeks in length and thousands of different products, no supplier could afford to keep all his items in stock. In periods of heavy demand, many products were often in short supply. Those competitors with adequate supplies and quick deliveries could readily attract new business.[7]

Apparently, strategy development is difficult because different emphases may be needed in different product/market situations. Emphasis is built around critical variables that may themselves be difficult to identify. Luck plays a part in making the right move; occasionally sheer intuition suffices. Despite all this, a careful review of past performance, current perspectives, and environmental changes should go a long way in choosing the right areas on which to concentrate. Appendix A at the end of this chapter provides a framework of business strategy concepts and an interesting review for strategy selection. This framework is not meant to introduce a new scheme for strategy development. Rather, it provides an opportunity to reflect on business strategy formulation as an aid in articulating a system for one's own use.

Reformulation of current strategy may range from making slight modifications in existing perspectives to coming out with an entirely different strategy. For example, in the area of pricing, one alternative for an automobile manufacturer may be to keep prices stable from year to year (i.e., no yearly price increases). A different alternative is to lease cars directly to consumers instead of selling them. The decision on the first alternative may be made by the SBU executive. But the second alternative, being far-reaching in nature, may require the review and approval of top management. In other words, how much examination and review a product/market strategy requires depends on the nature of the strategy (in terms of the change it seeks from existing perspectives) and the resource commitment required.

Another point to remember in developing core strategy is that the emphasis should always be placed on searching for new ways to compete. The marketing strategist should develop strategy around those key factors in which the business has more freedom than its competitors have. The point may be illustrated with reference to Body Shop International, a cosmetic company that spends nothing on advertising, even though it is in one of the most image-conscious industries in the business world.[8] Based in England, this company operates in 37 nations. Unlike typical cosmetic manufacturers, which sell through drugstores and department stores, Body Shop sells its own franchise stores. Further, in a business in which packaging costs often outstrip product costs, the Body Shop offers its products in plain, identical rows of bottles and gives discounts to customers who bring Body Shop bottles in for refills. The company has succeeded because it is so different from its rivals. Instead of assailing its customers with promotions and ads, it educates them. A great deal of Body Shop's budget is spent on training store personnel on the detailed nature of how its products are made and how they ought to be used. Training, which is accomplished through newsletters, videotapes, and classroom study, enables salesclerks to educate consumers on hair care, problem skin treatments, and the ecological benefits of such exotic products as rhassoul and mud shampoo, white grape skin tonic, and peppermint foot lotion. Consumers have also responded to Body Shop's environmental policies: the company uses only natural ingredients in its products, doesn't use animals for lab testing, and publicly supports saving whales and Brazilian rain forest preservation.

In the final analysis, companies with the following characteristics are most likely to develop successful strategies:[9]

1. **Informed opportunism**—Information is the main strategic advantage, and flexibility is the main strategic weapon. Management assumes that opportunity will keep knocking but that it will knock softly and in unpredictable ways.
2. **Direction and empowerment**—Managers at renewing companies define the boundaries, and their subordinates figure out the best way to do the job within them. Managers give up some control to gain results.

3. **Friendly facts, congenial controls**—Renewing companies love information that provides context and removes decision making from the realm of mere opinion. Managers regard financial controls as the benign checks and balances that allow them to be creative and free.
4. **A different mirror**—Leaders are open and inquisitive. They get ideas from almost anyone in and out of the hierarchy—customers, competitors, even next-door neighbors.
5. **Teamwork, trust, politics, and power**—Renewers stress the value of teamwork and trust their employees to do the job. Relentless at fighting office politics, they acknowledge that politics are inevitable in the workplace.
6. **Stability in motion**—Renewing companies are constantly changing but have a base of underlying stability. They understand the need for consistency and norms, but they also realize that the only way to respond to change is to deliberately break the rules.
7. **Attitudes and attention**—Visible management attention, rather than exhortation, gets things done. Action may start with words, but it has to be backed by symbolic behavior that makes those words come alive.
8. **Causes and commitment**—Commitment results from management's ability to turn grand causes into small actions so that everyone can contribute to the central purpose.

DETERMINING SBU STRATEGY

SBU strategy concerns how to create competitive advantage in each of the products/markets it competes with. The business unit-level strategy is determined by the three Cs (customer, competition, and company). The experience of different companies shows that, for the purposes of strategy formulation, the strategic three Cs can be articulated by placing SBUs on a two-by-two matrix with industry maturity or attractiveness as one dimension and strategic competitive position as the other.

Industry attractiveness may be studied with reference to the life-cycle stage of the industry (i.e., embryonic, growth, mature, or aging). Such factors as growth rate, industry potential, breadth of product line, number of competitors, market share perspectives, purchasing patterns of customers, ease of entry, and technology development determine the maturity of the industry. As illustrated in Exhibit 9-3, these factors behave in different ways according to the stage of industry maturity. For example, in the embryonic stage, the product line is generally narrow, and frequent changes to tailor the line to customer needs are common. In the growth stage, product lines undergo rapid proliferation. In the mature stage, attempts are made to orient products to specific segments. During the aging stage, the product line begins to shrink.

Going through the four stages of the industry life cycle can take decades or a few years. The different stages are generally of unequal duration. To cite a few examples, personal computers and solar energy devices are in the embryonic category. Home smoke alarms and sporting goods in general fall into the growth category. Golf equipment and steel represent mature industries. Men's

EXHIBIT 9-3
Industry Maturity Guide

	Stages of Industry Maturity			
Descriptors	*Embryonic*	*Growth*	*Mature*	*Aging*
Growth rate	Accelerating; meaningful rate cannot be calculated because base is too small	Substantially faster than GNP; industry sales expanding significantly	Growing at rate equal to or slower than GNP; more subject to cyclicality	Industry volume declining
Industry potential	Usually difficult to determine	Demand exceeds current industry volume but is subject to unforeseen developments	Well known; primary markets approach saturation	Saturation is reached; supply capability exceeds long-term demand
Product line	Line generally narrow; frequent changes tailored to customer needs	Product lines undergo rapid proliferation; some evidence of products oriented toward multiple industry segments	Product line turnover but little or no change in breadth; products frequently oriented toward narrow industry segments	Product line shrinking but tailored to major customer needs
Number of competitors	Few competing at first but number increasing rapidly	Number and types are unstable; increase to peak followed by shakeout and consolidation	Generally stable or declining slightly	Declines or industry may break up into many small regional suppliers
Market share stability	Volatile; share difficult to measure; share frequently concentrated	Rankings can change; a few firms have major shares	Little share volatility; firms with major shares are entrenched; significant niche competition; firms with minor shares are unlikely to gain major shares	Some change as marginal firms drop out; as market volume declines, market share generally becomes more concentrated
Purchasing patterns	Varies; some customers have strong loyalties; others have none	Some customer loyalty; buyers are aggressive but show evidence of repeat or add-on purchases; some price sensitivity	Suppliers are well known; buying patterns are established; customers generally loyal to limited number of acceptable suppliers; increasing price sensitivity	Strong customer loyalty as number of alternatives decreases; customers and suppliers may be tied to each other
Ease of entry (exclusive of capital considerations)	Usually easy; opportunity may not be apparent	Usually easy; presence of competitors is offset by vigorous growth	Difficult; competitors are entrenched; growth is slowing	Little incentive
Technology	Important to match performance to market needs; industries started on technological breakthrough or application; multiple competing technologies	Fewer competing technologies; significant product line refinements or extensions likely; performance enhancement is important	Process and materials refinement; technologies developed outside this industry are used in seeking efficiencies	Minimal role in ongoing products; new technology may be sought to renew growth

hats and rail cars are in the aging category. It is important to remember that industries can experience reversals in the aging processes. For example, roller skates have experienced a tremendous resurgence (i.e., moving from the aging stage back to the growth stage) because of the introduction of polyurethane wheels. It should also be emphasized that there is no "good" or "bad" life-cycle position. A particular stage of maturity becomes "bad" only if the expectations or strategies adopted by an industry participant are inappropriate for its stage of maturity. The particular characteristics of the four different stages in the life cycle are discussed in the following paragraphs.

Embryonic industries usually experience rapid sales growth, frequent changes in technology, and fragmented, shifting market shares. The cash deployment to these businesses is often high relative to sales as investment is made in market development, facilities, and technology. Embryonic businesses are generally not profitable, but investment is usually warranted in anticipation of gaining position in a developing market.

The growth stage is generally characterized by a rapid expansion of sales as the market develops. Customers, shares, and technology are better known than in the embryonic stage, and entry into the industry can be more difficult. Growth businesses are usually capital borrowers from the corporation, producing low-to-good earnings.

In mature industries, competitors, technology, and customers are all known and there is little volatility in market shares. The growth rate of these industries is usually about equal to GNP. Businesses in mature industries tend to provide cash for the corporation through high earnings.

The aging stage of maturity is characterized by

1. Falling demand for the product and limited growth potential
2. A shrinking number of competitors (survivors gain market share through attrition)
3. Little product line variety
4. Little, if any, investment in research and development or plant and equipment

The competitive position of an SBU should depend not only on market share but also on such factors as capacity utilization, current profitability, degree of integration (forward or backward), distinctive product advantages (e.g., patent protection), and management strength (e.g., willingness to take risks). These factors may be studied for classifying a given SBU in one of the following competitive positions: dominant, strong, favorable, tenable, or weak.

Exhibit 9-4 summarizes the typical characteristics of firms in different competitive positions. An example of a dominant firm is IBM in the computer field; its competitors pattern their behavior and strategies on what IBM does. In the beer industry, Anheuser-Busch exemplifies a strong firm, a firm able to make an independent move without being punished by the major competitor.

Determining strategic competitive position is one of the most complex elements of business analysis and one of the least researched. With little state-of-the-art guidance available, the temptation is to fall back on the single criterion

EXHIBIT 9-4
Classification of Competitive Strategic Positions

Dominant	• Controls behavior and/or strategies of other competitors • Can choose from widest range of strategic options, independent of competitor's actions
Strong	• Can take independent stance or action without endangering long-term position • Can generally maintain long-term position in the face of competitor's actions
Favorable	• Has strengths that are exploitable with certain strategies if industry conditions are favorable • Has more than average ability to improve position • If in a niche, holds a commanding position relatively secure from attack
Tenable	• Has sufficient potential and/or strengths to warrant continuation in business • May maintain position with tacit consent of dominant company or of the industry in general but is unlikely to significantly improve position • Tends to be only marginally profitable • If in a niche, is profitable but clearly vulnerable to competitors' actions
Weak	• Has currently unsatisfactory performance but has strengths that may lead to improvement • Has many characteristics of a better position but suffers from past mistakes or current weaknesses • Inherently short-term position; must change (up or out)
Nonviable	• Has currently unsatisfactory performance and few, if any, strengths that may lead to improvement (may take years to die)

of market share, but the experiences of successful companies makes it clear that determining competitive position is a multifaceted problem embracing, for example, technology, breadth of product line, market share, share movement, and special market relationships. Such factors change in relative importance as industry maturity changes.

Choice of Strategy

Once the position of an SBU is located on the industry maturity/competitive position matrix, the guide shown in Exhibit 9-5 may be used to determine what strategy the SBU should pursue. Actually the strategies shown in the exhibit are guides to strategic thrust rather than strategies per se. They show the normal strategic path a business unit may adopt, given its industry maturity and competitive position. Appendix B at the end of this chapter further examines the strategic thrusts identified in Exhibit 9-5. Each strategic thrust is defined, and its objective, requirements, and expected results are noted.

EXHIBIT 9-5
Guide to Strategic Thrust Options

	Stages of Industry Maturity			
Competitive Position	*Embryonic*	*Growth*	*Mature*	*Aging*
Dominant	Grow fast Start up	Grow fast Attain cost leadership Renew Defend position	Defend position Focus Renew Grow fast	Defend position Renew Grow into maturity
Strong	Start up Differentiate Grow fast	Grow fast Catch up Attain cost leadership Differentiate	Attain cost leadership Renew, focus Differentiate Grow with industry	Find niche Hold niche Hang in Grow with industry Harvest
Differentiate Favorable	Start up Catch up Focus Grow fast	Differentiate, focus Find niche, hold niche Grow with industry	Harvest, hang in Turn around Renew, turn around Differentiate, focus Grow with industry	Retrench
Tenable	Start up Grow with industry Focus	Harvest, catch up Hold niche, hang in Find niche Turn around Focus Grow with industry	Harvest Turn around Find niche Retrench	Divest Retrench
Weak	Find niche Catch up Grow with industry	Turn around Retrench	Withdraw Divest	Withdraw

To bridge the gap between broad guidelines and specific strategies for implementation, further analysis is required. A three-stage process is suggested here. First, using broad guidelines, the SBU management may be asked to state strategies pursued during previous years. Second, these strategies may be reviewed by using selected performance ratios to analyze the extent to which strategies were successfully implemented. Similarly, current strategies may be identified and their link to past strategies established. Third, having identified and analyzed past and current strategy with the help of strategic guidelines, the management, using the same guidelines, selects the strategy it proposes to pursue in the future. The future perspective may call for the continuation of current strategies or the development of new ones. Before accepting the future strategic course, however, it is desirable to measure its cash consequences or internal deployment (i.e., percentage of funds generated that are reinvested). Exhibit 9-6 illustrates an SBU earning 22 percent on assets with an internal deployment of 80 percent. Such an SBU would normally be considered in the mature stage. However, if the previous analysis showed that the SBU was in fact operating in a growth industry, the corporation would need to rethink its investment policy. All quantitative information pertaining to an SBU may be summarized on one form, as shown in Exhibit 9-7.

Different product/market plans are reviewed at the SBU level. The purpose of this review is twofold: (a) to consider product/market strategies in finalizing SBU strategies and (b) to approve product/market strategies. The underlying criterion for evaluation is a balanced achievement of SBU goals, which may be specified in terms of profitability and cash consequences. If there is a conflict of interest between two product/market groups in the way the strategy is either articulated or implemented, the conflict should be resolved so that SBU goals are maximized. Assume that both product/market groups seek additional investments during the next two years. Of these, the first product/market will start delivering positive cash flow in the third year. The second one is not likely to generate positive cash flow until the fourth year, but it will provide a higher overall return on capital. If the SBU's need for cash is urgent and if it desires

EXHIBIT 9-6
Profitability and Cash Position of a Business

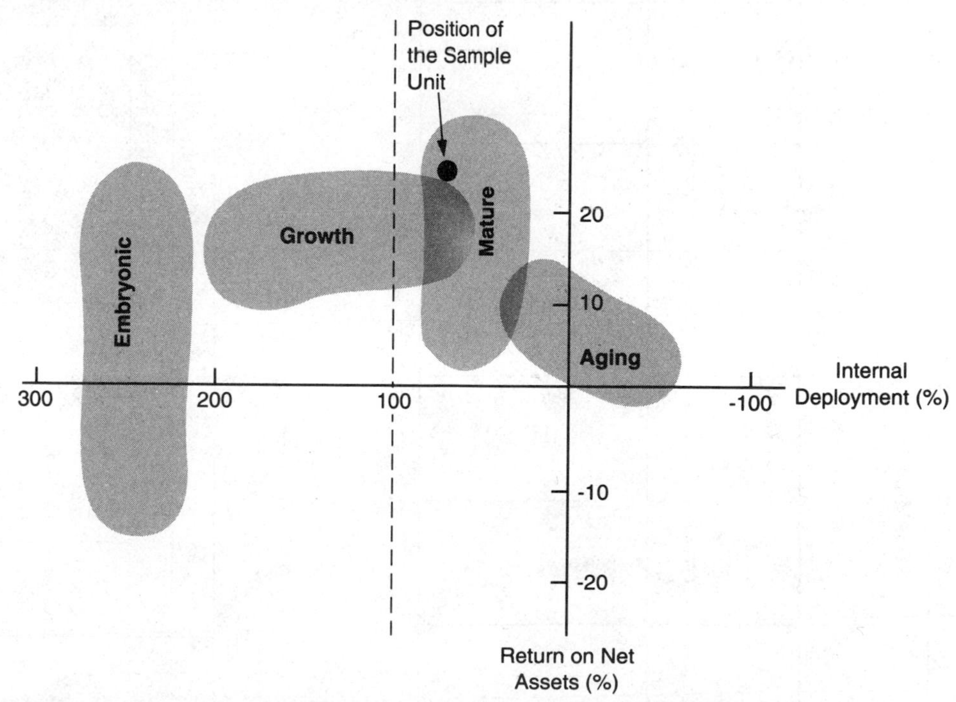

EXHIBIT 9-7
Sources of Competitive Information

PERFORMANCE

	Indices of:					Return					
						Investment (per $ sales)					
Year	*Industry Capacity (A)*	*Business Unit's Product Capacity (B)*	*Business Unit's Sales (C)*	*Profits after Taxes (D)*	*Net Assets (E)*	*Receivables (F)*	*Inventories (G)*	*New Current Liabilities (H)*	*Working Capital (I)*	*Other Assets (J)*	*Total Net Assets (K)*

INVESTMENT

	Return (continued)								Funds Generation and Deployment			
	Cost and Earnings (per $ sales)								(per $ sales)			(%)
Year	*Cost of Goods Sold (L)*	*Research and Develop-ment (M)*	*Sales and Marketing (N)*	*General and Administrative (O)*	*Other Income and Expenses (P)*	*Profit before Taxes (Q)*	*Profit after Taxes (R)*	*Return on Net Assets (S)*	*Operating Funds Flow (T)*	*Changes in Assets (U)*	*Net Cash Flow to Corporation (V)*	*Internal Deployment (U ÷ T) (W)*

Source: Arthur D. Little, Inc. Reprinted by permission.

additional cash for its goals during the third year, the first product/market group will appear more attractive. Thus, despite higher profit expectations from the second product/market group, the SBU may approve investment in the first product/market group with a view to maximizing the realization of its own goals.

At times the SBU may require a product/market group to make additional changes in its strategic perspective before giving its final approval. On the other hand, a product/market plan may be totally rejected and the group instructed to pursue its current perspective.

Industry maturity and competitive position analysis may also be used in further refining the SBU itself. In other words, after an SBU has been created and is analyzed for industry maturity and competitive position, it may be found that it has not been properly constituted. This would require redefining the SBU and undertaking the analysis again. Drawing an example from the car radio industry, considerable differences in industry maturity may become apparent between car radios with built-in cassette players and traditional car radios. Differences in industry maturity or competitive position may also exist with regard to regional markets, consumer groups, and distribution channels. For example, the market for cheap car radios sold by discount stores to end users doing their own installations may be growing faster than the market served by specialty retail stores providing installation services. Such revelations may require further refinement in formulating SBUs. This may continue until the SBUs represent the highest possible level of aggregation consistent with the need for clear-cut analyses of industry maturity and competitive position.

STRATEGY EVALUATION

"The time required to develop resources is so extended, and the timescale of opportunities is so brief and fleeting, that a company which has not carefully delineated and appraised its strategy is adrift in white water." This quotation from an article by Seymour Tilles underlines the importance of strategy evaluation.[10]

The adequacy of a strategy may be evaluated using the following criteria:[11]

1. **Suitability**—Is there a sustainable advantage?
2. **Validity**—Are the assumptions realistic?
3. **Feasibility**—Do we have the skills, resources, and commitments?
4. **Internal consistency**—Does the strategy hang together?
5. **Vulnerability**—What are the risks and contingencies?
6. **Workability**—Can we retain our flexibility?
7. **Appropriate time horizon**

Suitability

Strategy should offer some sort of competitive advantage. In other words, strategy should lead to a future advantage or an adaptation to forces eroding current competitive advantage. The following steps may be followed to judge the competitive advantage a strategy may provide: (a) review the potential threats and opportunities to the business, (b) assess each option in light of the capabilities of the business, (c) anticipate the likely competitive response to each option, and (d) modify or eliminate unsuitable options.

Validity (Consistency with the Environment) Strategy should be consistent with the assumptions about the external product/market environment. After the fall of the Shah of Iran in 1979, gasoline prices shot up, and a nationwide gas shortage for the coming years became imminent. In that environment, an automobile company that introduced new features in its middle-of-the-line car that substantially increased gas consumption might not be doing the right thing. At a time when more and more women are seeking jobs, a strategy assuming traditional roles for women (i.e., raising children and staying home) would be inconsistent with the environment.

Feasibility (Appropriateness in Light of Available Resources) Money, competence, and physical facilities are the critical resources a manager should be aware of in finalizing strategy. A resource may be examined in two different ways: as a constraint limiting the achievement of goals and as an opportunity to be exploited as the basis for strategy. It is desirable for a strategist to make correct estimates of resources available without being excessively optimistic about them. Further, even if resources are available in the corporation, a particular product/market group may not be able to lay claim to them. Alternatively, resources currently available to a product/market group may be transferred to another group if the SBU strategy deems it necessary.

Internal Consistency Strategy should be in tune with the different policies of the corporation, the SBU, and the product/market arena.[12] For example, if the corporation decided to limit the government business of any unit to 40 percent of total sales, a product/market strategy emphasizing greater than 40 percent reliance on the government market would be internally inconsistent.

Vulnerability (Satisfactory Degree of Risk) The degree of risk may be determined on the basis of the perspectives of the strategy and available resources. A pertinent question here is Will the resources be available as planned in appropriate quantities and for as long as it is necessary to implement the strategy? The overall proportion of resources committed to a venture becomes a factor to be reckoned with: the greater these quantities, the greater the degree of risk.

Workability The workability of a strategy should be realistically evaluated with quantitative data. Sometimes, however, it may be difficult to undertake such objective analysis. In that case, other indications may be used to assess the contributions of a strategy. One such indication could be the degree of consensus among key executives about the viability of the strategy. Identifying ahead of time alternate strategies for achieving the goal is another indication of the workability of a strategy. Finally, establishing resource requirements in advance, which eliminates the need to institute crash programs of cost reduction or to seek reduction in planned programs, also substantiates the workability of the strategy.

Appropriate Time Horizon

A viable strategy has a time frame for its realization. The time horizon of a strategy should allow implementation without creating havoc in the organization or missing market availability. For example, in introducing a new product to the market, enough time should be allotted for market testing, training of salespeople, and so on. But the time frame should not be so long that a competitor can enter the market first and skim the cream off the top.

SUMMARY

This chapter was devoted to strategy formulation for the SBU. A conceptual framework for developing SBU strategy was outlined. Strategy formulation at the SBU level requires, among different inputs, the perspectives of product/market strategies. For this reason, a procedure for developing product/market strategy was discussed first.

Product/market strategy development requires predicting the momentum of current operations into the future (assuming constant conditions), modifying the momentum in the light of environmental changes, and reviewing the adjusted momentum against goals. If there is no gap between the set goal and the prediction, the present strategy may well be continued. Usually, however, there is a gap between the goal and expectations from current operations. Thus, the gap must be filled.

The following three-step process was suggested for filling the gap: (a) issue assessment (i.e., raising issues with the status quo vis-à-vis the future), (b) identification of key variables (i.e., isolating the key variables on which success in the industry depends) and development of alternative strategies, and (c) strategy selection (i.e., choosing the preferred strategy). The thrust of the preferred strategy is on one or more of the four variables in the marketing mix—product, price, promotion, or distribution. The major emphasis of marketing strategy, the core strategy, is on this chosen variable. Strategies for the remaining variables are supporting strategies.

The SBU strategy is based on the three Cs (customer, competition, and company). SBUs were placed on a two-by-two matrix with industry maturity or attractiveness as one dimension and strategic competitive position as the other. Stages of industry maturity—embryonic, growth, mature, and aging—were identified. Competitive position can be classified as dominant, strong, favorable, tenable, or weak. Classification by industry maturity and competitive position generates 20 different quadrants in the matrix. In each quadrant an SBU requires a different strategic perspective. A compendium of strategies was provided to figure out the appropriate strategy in a particular case.

The chapter concluded with a procedure for evaluating the selected strategy. This procedure consists of examining the following aspects of the strategy: suitability, validity, feasibility, internal consistency, vulnerability, workability, and appropriateness of time horizon.

DISCUSSION QUESTIONS

1. Describe how a manufacturer of washing machines may measure the momentum of the business for the next five years.
2. List five issues Sears may raise to review its strategy for large appliances.
3. List five key variables on which success in the home construction industry depends.
4. In what industry state would you position (a) light beer and (b) color television?
5. Based on your knowledge of the company, what would you consider to be Miller's competitive position in the light beer business and GE's position in the appliance business?
6. Discuss how strategy evaluation criteria may be employed to review the strategy of an industrial goods manufacturer.

NOTES

[1]See Francis Buttle, "The Marketing Strategy Worksheet—A Practical Planning Tool," *Long Range Planning* (August 1985): 80–88.

[2]See George S. Day and Robin Wensley, "Assessing Advantage: A Framework for Diagnosing Competitive Superiority," *Journal of Marketing* (April 1988): 1-20.

[3]Peter R. Dickson and James L. Ginter, "Market Segmentation, Product Differentiation, and Marketing Strategy," *Journal of Marketing* 51 (April 1987): 1–10.

[4]Benson P. Shapiro, "Rejuvenating the Marketing Mix," *Harvard Business Review* (September-October 1985): 28–34.

[5] Jeffrey A. Trachtenberg, "Ikea Furniture Chain Pleases with Its Prices, Not with Its Service," *Wall Street Journal*, 17 September 1991, p. 1.

[6]Michael Norkus, "Soft Drink Wars: A Lot More Than Just Good Taste," *Wall Street Journal*, 8 July 1985, p. 12.

[7]"Tex-Fiber Industries—Petroloid Products Division (A)," a case developed by John Craig under the supervision of Derek F. Abell, copyrighted by the President and Fellows of Harvard College, 1970, 7.

[8]Allan J. Magrath, "Contrarian Marketing," *Across the Board* (October 1990): 46–50.

[9]Adapted from Robert H. Waterman, Jr., *The Renewal Factor: How the Best Get and Keep the Competitive Edge* (New York: Bantam Books, 1987).

[10]Seymour Tilles, "How to Evaluate Corporate Strategy," *Harvard Business Review* (July-August 1963): 111-21.

[11]Discussion in this section was adapted from George S. Day, "Tough Questions for Developing Strategies," *Journal of Business* (Winter 1986): 60–68.

[12]See Roderick E. White, "Generic Business Strategies, Organizational Context and Performance: An Empirical Investigation," *Strategic Management Journal* 7 (1986): 217-31.

APPENDIX A *Business Strategy Concepts*

Spectacular business successes usually involve new ways of doing business in familiar markets with familiar products. These are the true strategic victories,

---

Source: Bruce D. Henderson, "Business Strategy Concepts" (Boston: The Boston Consulting Group, Inc., 1969), Perspectives No. 61. Reprinted by permission.

won by using corporate resources to substantially outperform a competitor with superior strength.

The concept of superior performance without superior resources is usually identified with trying harder. Yet most companies seem to work very hard to produce only minor differentials in performance.

The underlying principle of a good strategy is simple: "Concentrate your strength against your competitor's relative weakness." This principle has a major corollary in a dynamic competitive environment—concentration of effort will inevitably produce a counter-concentration by competition; therefore, timing and sequence are critical. A major attack should never be launched against a competent well-entrenched competitor without first eliminating his ability or willingness to respond in kind.

There are many prerequisites to a successful strategy:

1. The characteristics of the competition must be known in detail, including characteristic attitudes and behaviors.
2. The environment in which competition will take place must be equally well understood.
3. Your own relative strengths must be accurately and objectively appraised.
4. The strategic concept must not be based on the obvious exercise of known strengths. If it is, you don't need a strategy, just a plan.
5. It must be possible to achieve stability if the strategy succeeds.
6. Your own organization must not be misled by your efforts to outmaneuver competition. Strategic goals must be very explicit.

Once the strategic framework has been designed, the tactics of attack must be selected. Concentration of resources can be achieved in several ways:

1. Choose the most vulnerable market segment.
2. Choose products or markets that require response rates beyond a competitor's ability.
3. Choose products or markets that require capital that a competitor is unwilling to commit.
4. Recognize the commercial potentials of new technology early.
5. Exploit managerial differences in style, method, or system such as overhead rate, distribution channels, market image, or flexibility.

The value of the initiative depends on when and how the competition responds. Therefore, an effective strategy must choose the best initiative and also dissuade competition from responding. This is a fundamental strategic concept that is often neglected. Most strategic success depends upon the competition's decision not to compete. Therefore, strategic success almost always depends upon the ability to influence competitors' decisions. It is necessary to win in the mind of the competition.

Diversion and dissuasion fall into classic categories:

1. Appear to be unworthy of attention. Quickly cut off a part of the market that is too small to justify a major response. Repeat, and repeat, and so on.

2. Appear to be unbeatable. Convince competition that if they follow your lead and practices, they will gain nothing because you will equal or better any market actions they take.
3. Avoid attention. Be secretive. Do not let competition know about new products, new policies, or capabilities until it is too late to respond effectively.
4. Redirect attention. Focus competitive attention on the major volume areas of company sales, not the high potential areas.
5. Attract attention but discredit significance. Overstate and overpublicize the potentials of new products or policies.
6. Be apparently irrational. Take actions that seem emotional or impulsive but that make competitive investment unattractive.

These and other patterns have exact counterparts in military behavior. In business as in war, the lessons of experience teach the same thing.

> We can at least crystallize the lessons into two simple maxims—one negative, the other positive. The first is that, in the face of the overwhelming evidence of history, no general is justified in launching his troops in a direct attack upon an enemy firmly in position. The second, that instead of seeking to upset the enemy's equilibrium by one's attack, it must be upset before a real attack is, or can be, successfully launched.
> (Liddell Hart, *Strategy*, Praeger)

APPENDIX B | *Perspectives on Strategic Thrusts*

A. Start Up

Definition: Introduction of new product or service with clear, significant technology breakthrough.

Objective: To develop a totally new industry to create and satisfy new demand where none existed before.

Requirements: Risk-taking attitude of management; capital expenditures; expense.

Expected Results: Negative cash flow; low-to-negative returns; a leadership position in new industry.

B. Grow with Industry

Definition: To limit efforts to those necessary to maintain market share.

Objective: To free resources to correct market, product, management, or production weaknesses.

Requirements: Management restraint; market intelligence; some capital and expense investments; time-limited strategy.

Expected Results: Stable market share; profit, cash flow, and RONA not significantly worse than recent history, fluctuating only as do industry averages.

C. Grow Fast

Definition: To pursue aggressively larger share and/or stronger position relative to competition.

Objective: To grow volume and share faster than competition and faster than general industry growth rate.

Requirements: Available resources for investment and follow-up; risk-taking management attitude; and appropriate investment strategy.

Expected Results: Higher market share; in the short term, perhaps lower returns; above average returns in the longer term; competitive retaliation.

D. Attain Cost Leadership

Definition: To achieve lowest delivered costs relative to competition with acceptable quality levels.

Objective: To increase freedom to defend against powerful entries, strong customer blocks, vigorous competitors, or potential substitute products.

Requirements: Relatively high market share; disciplined, persistent management efforts; favorable access to raw materials; substantial capital expenditures; aggressive pricing.

Expected Results: In early stages may result in start-up losses to build share; ultimately, high margins; relatively low capital turnover rates.

E. Differentiate

Definition: To achieve the highest degree of product/quality/service difference (as perceived by customers) in the industry with acceptable costs.

Objective: To insulate the company from switching, substitution, price competition, and strong blocks of customers or suppliers.

Requirements: Willingness to sacrifice high market share; careful target marketing; focused technological and market research; strong brand loyalty.

Expected Results: Possibly lowered market share; high margins; above-average earnings; highly defensible position.

F. Focus

Definition: To select a particular segment of the market/product line more narrow in scope than competing firms.

Objective: To serve the strategic target area (geographic, product, or market) more efficiently, more fully, and more profitably than it can be served by broad line competitors.

Requirements: Disciplined management; persistent pursuit of well-defined scope and mission; premium pricing; careful target selection.

Expected Results: Above-average earnings; may be low-cost producer in its area; may attain high differentiation.

G. Renew

Definition: To restore the competitiveness of a product line in anticipation of future industry sales.

Objective: To overcome weakness in product/market mix in order to improve share or to prepare for a new generation of demand, competition, or substitute products.

Requirements: Strong enough competitive position to generate necessary resources for renewal efforts; capital and expense investments; management capable of taking risk; recognition of potential threats to existing line.

Expected Results: Short-term decline in sales, then sudden or gradual breakout of old volume/profit patterns.

H. Defend Position

Definition: To ensure that relative competitive position is stable or improved.

Objective: To create barriers that make it difficult, costly, and risky for competitors, suppliers, customer blocks, or new entries to erode your firm's market share, profitability, and growth.

Requirements: Establishment of one or more of the following: proprietary technology, strong brand, protected sourcing, favorable locations, economies of scale, government protection, exclusive distribution, or customer loyalty.

Expected Results: Stable or increasing market share.

I. Harvest

Definition: To convert market share or competitive position into higher returns.

Objective: To bring returns up to industry averages by trading, leasing, or selling technology, distribution rights, patents, brands, production capacity, locations, or exclusive sources to competitors.

Requirements: A better-than-average market share; rights to entry or mobility barriers that the industry values; alternative investment opportunities.

Expected Results: Sudden surge in profitability and return; a gradual decline of position, perhaps leading to withdrawal strategy.

J. Find Niche

Definition: To opt for retaining a small, defensible portion of the available market rather than withdraw.

Objective: To define the opportunity so narrowly that large competitors with broad lines do not find it attractive enough to dislodge you.

Requirements: "Think small" management style; alternative uses for excess production capacity; reliable sources for supplies and materials; superior quality and/or service with selected sector.

Expected Results: Pronounced decline in volume and share; improved return in medium to longer term.

K. Hold Niche

Definition: To protect a narrow position in the larger product/market arena from larger competitors.

Objective: To create barriers (real or imagined) that make it unattractive for competitors, suppliers, or customer blocks to enter your segment or switch to alternative products.

Requirements: Designing, building, and promoting "switching costs" into your product.

Expected Results: Lower-than-industry average but steady and acceptable returns.

L. Catch Up

Definition: To make up for poor or late entry into an industry by aggressive product/market activities.

Objective: To overcome early gains made by first entrants into the market by careful choice of optimum product, production, distribution, promotion, and marketing tactics.

Requirements: Management capable of taking risk in flexible environment; resources to make high investments of capital and expense; corporate understanding of short-term low returns; probably necessary to dislodge weak competitors.

Expected Results: Low-to-negative returns in near term; should result in favorable to strong position by late growth stage of industry.

M. Hang In *Definition:* To prolong existence of the unit in anticipation of some specific favorable change in the environment.

Objective: To continue funding a tenable (or better) unit only long enough to take advantage of unusual opportunity known to be at hand; this might take the form of patent expiration, management change, government action, technology breakthrough, or socioeconomic shift.

Requirements: Clear view of expected environmental shift; a management willing and able to sustain poor performance; opportunity and resources to capitalize on new environment; a time limit.

Expected Results: Poorer-than-average performance, perhaps losses; later, substantial growth and high returns.

N. Turn Around *Definition:* To overcome inherent, severe weaknesses in performance in a limited time.

Objective: To halt further declines in share and/or volume; to bring about at least stability or, preferably, a small improvement in position; to protect the line from competitive and substitute products.

Requirements: Fast action to prevent disaster; reductions or redirection to reduce losses; change in morale.

Expected Results: Stable condition and average performance.

O. Retrench *Definition:* To cut back investment in the business and reduce level of risk and exposure to losses.

Objective: To stop unacceptable losses or risks; to prepare the business for divestment or withdrawal; to strip away loss operations in hopes of exposing a "little jewel."

Requirements: Highly disciplined management system; good communication with employees to prevent wholesale departures; clear strategic objective and timetable.

Expected Results: Reduced losses or modestly improved performance.

P. Divest *Definition:* To strip the business of some or all of its assets through sale of the product line, brands, distribution facilities, or production capacity.

Objective: To recover losses sustained through earlier strategic errors; to free up funds for alternative corporate investments; to abandon part or all of a business to competition.

Requirements: Assets desirable to others competing or desiring to compete in the industry; a recognition of the futility of further investments.

Expected Results: Increase in cash flow; reduction of asset base; probable reduction in performance levels and/or losses.

Q. Withdraw | *Definition:* To remove the business from competition.

Objective: To take back from the business whatever corporate assets or expenses can be recovered through shutdown, sale, auction, or scrapping of operations.

Requirements: A decision to abandon; a caretaker management; a phased timetable; a public relations plan.

Expected Results: Losses and write-offs.

CHAPTER 10

Portfolio Analysis

Induce your competitors not to invest in those products, markets, and services where you expect to invest the most. That is the most fundamental rule of strategy.

BRUCE D. HENDERSON

The previous chapters dealt with strategy development for individual SBUs. Different SBU strategies must ultimately be judged from the viewpoint of the total organization before being implemented. In today's environment most companies operate with a variety of businesses. Even if a company is primarily involved in a single broad business area, it may actually be operating in multiple product/market segments. From a strategy angle, different products/markets may constitute different businesses of a company because they have different roles to play. This chapter is devoted to the analysis of the different businesses of an organization so that each may be assigned the unique role for which it is suited, thus maximizing long-term growth and earnings of the company.

Years ago Peter Drucker suggested classifying products into six categories that reveal the potential for future sales growth: tomorrow's breadwinners, today's breadwinners, products capable of becoming net contributors if something drastic is done, yesterday's breadwinners, the "also rans," and the failures. Drucker's classification provides an interesting scheme for determining whether a company is developing enough new products to ensure future growth and profits.

In the past few years, the emphasis has shifted from product to business. Usually a company discovers that some of its business units are competitively well placed, whereas others are not. Because resources, particularly cash resources, are limited, not all SBUs can be treated alike. In this chapter three different frameworks are presented to enable management to select the optimum combination of individual SBU strategies from a spectrum of possible alternatives and opportunities open to the company, still satisfying the resource limitations within which the company must operate. The frameworks may also be used at the SBU level to review the strategic perspective of its different product/market segments.

The first framework to be discussed, the **product life cycle**, is a tool many marketers have traditionally used to formulate marketing strategies for different products. The second framework was developed by the Boston Consulting Group and is commonly called the product portfolio approach. The third, the multifactor portfolio approach, owes its development to the General Electric Company and McKinsey & Co.

PRODUCT LIFE CYCLE

Products tend to go through different stages, each stage being affected by different competitive conditions.[1] These stages require different marketing strategies at different times if sales and profits are to be efficiently realized. The length of a product's life cycle is in no way a fixed period of time. It can last from weeks to years, depending on the type of product. The discussion of the product life cycle in most texts portrays the sales history of a typical product as following an S-shaped curve. The curve is divided into four stages: introduction, growth, maturity, and decline. (Some authors include a fifth stage, saturation.)

Not all products follow an S-shaped curve. Marketing scholars have identified varying product life cycle patterns. For example, Tellis and Crawford[2] identify 17 product life cycle patterns, while Swan and Rink name 10.[3] Exhibit 10-1 conceptualizes a typical product life cycle curve, which shows the relationship between profits and corresponding sales throughout a product's life.

Introduction is the period during which initial market acceptance is in doubt; thus, it is a period of slow growth. Profits are almost nonexistent because of high marketing and other expenses. Setbacks in the product's development, manufacture, and market introduction exact a heavy toll. Marketing strategy

EXHIBIT 10-1
Product Life Cycle

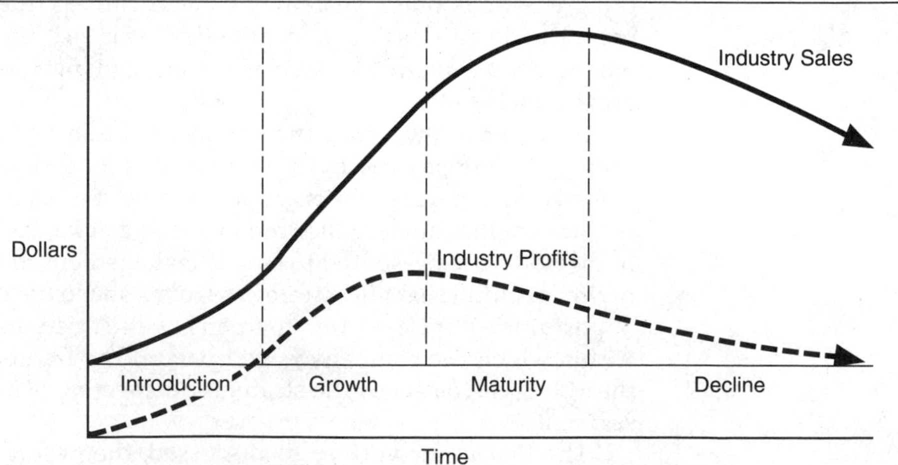

during this stage is based on different combinations of product, price, promotion, and distribution. For example, price and promotion variables may be combined to generate the following strategy alternatives: (a) high price/high promotion, (b) high price/low promotion, (c) low price/heavy promotion, and (d) low price/low promotion.

Survivors of the introduction stage enjoy a period of rapid growth. During this **growth** period, there is substantial profit improvement. Strategy in this stage takes the following shape: (a) product improvement, addition of new features and models; (b) development of new market segments; (c) addition of new channels; (d) selective demand stimulation; and (e) price reductions to vie for new customers.

During the next stage, **maturity**, there is intense rivalry for a mature market. Efforts may be limited to attracting a new population, leading to a proliferation of sizes, colors, attachments, and other product variants. Battling to retain the company's share, each marketer steps up persuasive advertising, opens new channels of distribution, and grants price concessions. Unless new competitors are obstructed by patents or other barriers, entry is easy. Thus, maturity is a period when sales growth slows down and profits peak and then start to decline.

Strategy in the maturity stage comprises the following steps: (a) search for new markets and new and varied uses for the product, (b) improvement of product quality through changes in features and style, and (c) new marketing mix perspectives. For the leader firm, (c) may mean introducing an innovative product, fortifying the market through multibrand strategy, or engaging in a price-promotion war against the weaker members of the industry; the non-leader may seek a differential advantage, finding a niche in the market through either product or promotional variables.

Finally, there is the **decline** period. Though sales and profits continue their downward trend, the declining product is not necessarily unprofitable. Some of the competition may have left the market by this stage. Customers who remain committed to the product may be willing to use standard models, pay higher prices, and buy at selected outlets. Promotional expenses can also be reduced.

An important consideration in strategy determination in the decline stage is exit barrier. Even when it appears appropriate to leave the industry, there may be one or more barriers to prevent easy exit. For example, there may be durable and specialized assets peculiar to the business that have little value outside the business; the cost of exit may be prohibitive because of labor settlement costs or contingent liabilities for land use; there may be managerial resistance; the business may be important in gaining access to financial markets; quitting the business may have a negative impact on other businesses in the company; or there may be government pressure to continue in the business, a situation that a multinational corporation may face, particularly in developing countries.[4]

Overall, in the decline stage, the choice of a specific alternative strategy is based on the business's strengths and weaknesses and the attractiveness of the industry to the company. The following alternative strategies appear appropriate:

1. Increasing the firm's investment (to dominate or get a good competitive position)
2. Holding the firm's investment level until the uncertainties about the industry are resolved
3. Decreasing the firm's investment posture selectively by sloughing off unpromising customer groups, while simultaneously strengthening the firm's investment posture within the lucrative niches of enduring customer demand
4. Harvesting (or milking) the firm's investment to recover cash quickly, regardless of the resulting investment posture.
5. Divesting the business quickly by disposing of its assets as advantageously as possible.[5]

In summary, in the introduction stage, the choices are primarily with what force to enter the market and whether to target a relatively narrow segment of customers or a broader customer group. In the growth stage, the choices appear to be to fortify and consolidate previously established market positions or to develop new primary demand. Developing new primary demand may be accomplished by a variety of means, including developing new applications, extending geographic coverage, trading down to previously untapped consumer groups, or adding related products. In the late growth and early maturity stages, the choices lie among various alternatives for achieving a larger share of the existing market. This may involve product improvement, product line extension, finer positioning of the product line, a shift from breadth of offering to in-depth focus, invading the market of a competitor that has invaded one's own market, or cutting out some of the "frills" associated with the product to appeal better to certain classes of customers. In the maturity stage, market positions have become established and the primary emphasis is on nose-to-nose competition in various segments of the market. This type of close competition may take the form of price competition, minor feature competition, or promotional competition. In the decline stage the choices are to continue current product/market perspectives as is, to continue selectively, or to divest.

Exhibit 10-2 identifies the characteristics, marketing objectives, and marketing strategies of each stage of the S-shaped product life cycle. The characteristics help locate products on the curve. The objectives and strategies indicate what marketing perspective is relevant in each stage. Actual choice of strategies rests on the objective set for the product, the nature of the product, and environmental influences operating at the time. For example, in the introductory stage, if a new product is launched without any competition and the firm has spent huge amounts of money on research and development, the firm may pursue a high price/low promotion strategy (i.e., skim the cream off the top of the market). As the product gets established and enters the growth stage, the price may be cut to bring new segments into the fold—the strategic perspective Texas Instruments used for its digital watches.

EXHIBIT 10-2
Perspectives of the Product Life Cycle

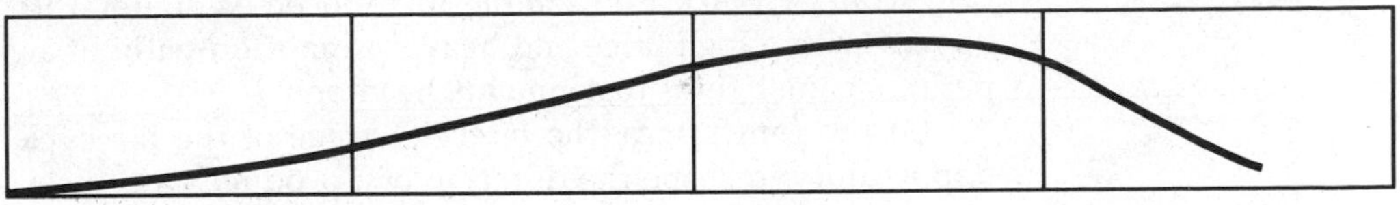

	Introduction	*Growth*	*Maturity*	*Decline*
Characteristics				
Sales	Low sales	Rapidly rising sales	Peak sales	Declining sales
Costs	High cost per customer	Average cost per customer	Low cost per customer	Low cost per customer
Profits	Negative	Rising profits	High profits	Declining profits
Customers	Innovators	Early adopters	Middle majority	Laggards
Competitors	Few	Growing number	Stable number beginning to decline	Declining number
Marketing Objectives				
	Create product awareness and trial	Maximize market share	Maximize profit while defending market share	Reduce expenditure and milk the brand
Strategies				
Product	Offer a basic product	Offer product extensions, service, warranty	Diversify brands and models	Phase out weak items
Price	Use cost-plus	Price to penetrate market	Price to match or beat competitors	Cut price
Distribution	Build selective distribution	Build intensive distribution	Build more intensive distribution	Go selective phase out unprofitable outlets
Advertising	Build product awareness among early adopters and dealers	Build awareness and interest in the mass market	Stress brand differences and benefits	Reduce to level needed to retain hardcore loyals
Sales Promotion	Use heavy sales promotion to entice trial	Reduce to take advantage of heavy consumer demand	Increase to encourage brand switching	Reduce to minimal level

Source: Philip Kotler, *Marketing Management: Analysis, Planning and Control*, 7th Ed., © 1991, p. 365. Reprinted by permission of Prentice-Hall, Inc., Englewood Cliffs, N.J.

On the other hand, if a product is introduced into a market where there is already a well-established brand, the firm may follow a high price/high promotion strategy. Seiko, for example, introduced its digital watch among well-to-do buyers with a high price and heavy promotion without any intention of competing against Texas Instruments head on.

Of the four stages, the maturity stage of the life cycle offers the greatest opportunity to shape the duration of a product's life cycle. These critical questions must be answered: Why have sales tapered off? Has the product approached obsolescence because of a superior substitute or because of a fundamental change in consumer needs? Can obsolescence be attributed to management's failure to identify and reach the right consumer needs or has a competitor done a better marketing job? Answers to these questions are crucial if an appropriate strategy is to be employed to strengthen the product's position. For example, the product may be redirected on a growth path through repackaging, physical modification, repricing, appeals to new users, the addition of new distribution channels, or the use of some combination of marketing strategy changes. The choice of a right strategy at the maturity stage can be extremely beneficial, since a successfully revitalized product offers a higher return on management time and funds invested than does a new product.

This point may be illustrated with reference to a Du Pont product, Lycra, a superstretching polymer invented in its labs in 1959. A little more than 30 years after its humble start as an ingredient for girdles, demand for Lycra is exploding so fast that the company has to allocate sales of the fiber. The product's success may be directly attributed to a shrewd marketing strategy, initiated during the maturity stage, that allowed Lycra's use to expand steadily, from bathing suits in the 1970s to cycling pants and aerobic outfits in the 1980s. Teenagers were lured to it and use it in their everyday fashion wardrobes. Avant-garde designers picked up on the trend, using Lycra in new, body-hugging designs. Now, this distinctly unnatural fiber is part of the fashion mainstream. Du Pont's marketing strategy has paid off well. A recent study showed that consumers would pay 20 percent more for a wool-Lycra skirt than for an all-wool version.[6]

Product Life Cycle Controversy

The product life cycle is a useful concept that may be an important aid in marketing planning and strategy. A concept familiar to most marketers, it is given a prominent place in every marketing textbook. Its use in practice remains limited, however, partly because of the lack of normative models available for its application and partly because of the vast amount of data needed for and the level of subjectivity involved in its use. As a matter of fact, the product life cycle concept has many times been criticized for its lack of relevance to businesspeople. Years ago Buzzell remarked: "There is very little empirical evidence to show how the life cycles operate and how they are related to competition and marketing strategy."[7] A few years ago, Dhalla and Yuspeh challenged the whole concept of the product life cycle. They contend that the product life cycle has led many companies to make costly mistakes and pass up promising opportunities.[8] Such criticism of the product life cycle may be attributed to the lack of a research base on the subject. As Levitt has observed:

> Most alert and thoughtful senior marketing executives are by now familiar with the concept of the product life cycle. Even a handful of uniquely cosmopolitan and up-to-date corporate presidents have familiarized themselves with this tantalizing concept. Yet a recent survey I took of such executives found none who used the concept in any strategic way whatever and pitifully few who used it in any kind of tactical way. It has remained—as have so many fascinating theories in economics, physics, and sex—a remarkably durable but almost totally unemployed and seemingly unemployable piece of professional baggage whose presence in the rhetoric of professional discussions adds a much-coveted but apparently unattainable legitimacy to the idea that marketing management is somehow a profession. The concept of the product life cycle is today at about the stage that the Copernican view of the universe was 300 years ago: A lot of people know about it, but hardly anybody seems to use it in any effective or productive way.[9]

While Levitt's criticism is very penetrating, many academicians and practitioners feel that, even in its present stage of development, the product life cycle has proved to be remarkably durable because it has been valuable to those who know how to use it. Smallwood claims that

> the product life cycle is a useful concept. It is the equivalent of the periodic table of the elements in the physical sciences. The maturation of production technology and product configuration along with marketing programs proceeds in an orderly, somewhat predictable course over time with the merchandising nature and marketing environment noticeably similar between products that are in the same stage of their life cycle. Its use as a concept in forecasting, pricing, advertising, product planning, and other aspects of marketing management can make it a valuable concept, although considerable amounts of judgment must be used in its application.[10]

One caution that is in order when using the product life cycle is to keep in mind that not all products follow the typical life cycle pattern. According to Kotler, the same product may be viewed in different ways: as a brand (Pepsi Light), as a product form (diet cola), and as a product category (cola drink), for example. Among these, the product life cycle concept is most relevant for product forms.[11] Further, in recent years, research on the subject has provided new and interesting insights that should help in its continued refinement.[12] For example, Tellis and Crawford suggest that products, influenced by market dynamics, managerial creativity, and government intervention, are in a state of constant evolution in the direction of greater efficiency, greater complexity, and greater diversity. The five stages in this evolutionary process, which the authors call the **product evolutionary cycle (PEC)**, are as follows:

> 1. Divergence . . . is the start of a new product type (e.g., TV). This term is suggested because most often a product is not an entirely new concept but a modification or combination of existing products and technologies. It is a divergence from a line of product evolution. Thus TV may be considered an evolutionary divergence from the radio and the motion picture.

2. Development . . . is the pattern where a new product's sales increase rapidly and the product is increasingly adapted to suit consumer needs best. Thus in the '50s, TV sales increased rapidly accompanied by frequent product improvements.
3. Differentiation . . . is the pattern that occurs when a highly successful product is differentiated to suit varying consumer interests. More recently TV's are available as black and white, color, portable, and console sets, and variation has extended to CRTs, rear-projection screens, home computers, and videodiscs.
4. Stabilization . . . is a pattern characterized by few and minor changes in the product category, but numerous changes in packaging, service deals, product accessories, and stable or fluctuating sales. Black and white television was in stabilization for years prior to differentiation into portable sets and the other uses mentioned above.
5. Demise . . . occurs when a product fails to meet consumer expectations or can no longer satisfy changes in consumer demand. Sales decline and the product is ultimately discontinued.[13]

Following this framework, the growth of a product is to some extent a function of the strategy being pursued. Thus, a product is not necessarily predestined to mature, as propounded by the traditional concept of product life cycle, but can be kept profitable by proper adaptation to the evolving market environment.

Locating Products in Their Life Cycles

The easiest way to locate a product in its life cycle is to study its past performance, competitive history, and current position and to match this information with the characteristics of a particular stage of the life cycle. Analysis of past performance of the product includes examination of the following:

1. Sales growth progression since introduction
2. Any design problems and technical bugs that need to be sorted out
3. Sales and profit history of allied products (those similar in general character or function as well as directly competitive products)
4. Number of years the product has been on the market
5. Casualty history of similar products in the past

The review of competition focuses on

1. Profit history
2. Ease with which other firms can get into the business
3. Extent of initial investment needed to enter the business
4. Number of competitors and their strength
5. Number of competitors that have left the industry
6. Life cycle of the industry
7. Critical factors for success in the business

In addition, current perspectives may be reviewed to gauge whether sales are on the upswing, have leveled out for the last couple of years, or are heading down; whether any competitive products are moving up to replace the product under consideration; whether customers are becoming more demanding vis-à-vis price, service, or special features; whether additional sales efforts are necessary to keep the sales going up; and whether it is becoming harder to sign up dealers and distributors.

This information on the product may be related to the characteristics of different stages of the product life cycle as discussed above; the product perspectives that match the product life cycle indicate the position of the product in its life cycle. Needless to say, the whole process is highly qualitative in nature, and managerial intuition and judgment bear heavily on the final placement of the product in its life cycle. As a matter of fact, making the appropriate assumptions about the types of information described here can be used to construct a model to predict the industry volume of a newly introduced product through each stage of the product life cycle.[14]

A slightly different approach for locating a product in its life is to use past accounting information for the purpose. Listed below are the steps that may be followed to position a product in its life cycle:

1. Develop historical trend information for a period of three to five years (longer for some products). Data included should be unit and dollar sales, profit margins, total profit contribution, return on invested capital, market share, and prices.
2. Check recent trends in the number and nature of competitors, number and market share rankings of competing products and their quality and performance advantages, shifts in distribution channels, and relative advantages enjoyed by products in each channel.
3. Analyze developments in short-term competitive tactics, such as competitors' recent announcements of new products or plans for expanding production capacity.
4. Obtain (or update) historical information on the life cycle of similar or related products.
5. Project sales for the product over the next three to five years, based on all information gathered, and estimate an incremental profit ratio for the product during each of these years (the ratio of total direct costs—manufacturing, advertising, product development, sales, distribution, etc.—to pretax profits). Expressed as a ratio (e.g., 4.8 to 1 or 6.3 to 1), this measure indicates the number of dollars required to generate each additional dollar of profit. The ratio typically improves (becomes lower) as the product enters its growth period, begins to deteriorate (rise) as the product approaches maturity, and climbs more sharply as it reaches obsolescence.
6. Estimate the number of profitable years remaining in the product's life cycle and, based on all information at hand, fix the product's position on its life cycle curve: (a) introduction, (b) early or late growth, (c) early or late maturity, or (d) early or late decline.

Developing a Product Life Cycle Portfolio

The current positions of different products in the product life cycle may be determined by following the procedure described above, and the net results (i.e., the cash flow and profitability) of these positions may be computed. Similar analyses may be performed for a future period. The difference between current and future positions indicates what results management may expect if no strategic changes are made. These results may be compared with corporate expectations to determine the gap. The gap can be filled either by making strategic changes to extend the life cycle of a product or by bringing in new products through research and development or acquisition. This procedure may be put into operation by following these steps:

1. Determine what percentage of the company's sales and profits fall within each phase of the product life cycle. These percentages indicate the present life cycle (sales) profile and the present profit profile of the company's current line.
2. Calculate changes in life cycle and profit profiles over the past five years and project these profiles over the next five years.
3. Develop a target life cycle profile for the company and measure the company's present life cycle profile against it. The target profile, established by marketing management, specifies the desirable share of company sales that should fall within each phase of the product life cycle. It can be determined by industry obsolescence trends, the pace of new product introductions in the field, the average length of product life cycles in the company's line, and top management's objectives for growth and profitability. As a rule, the target profile for growth-minded companies whose life cycles tend to be short call for a high proportion of sales in introductory and growth phases.

With these steps completed, management can assign priorities to such functions as new product development, acquisition, and product line pruning, based on the discrepancies between the company's target profile and its present life cycle profile. Once corporate effort has been broadly allocated in this way among products at various stages of their life cycles, marketing plans can be detailed for individual product lines.

PORTFOLIO MATRIX

A good planning system must guide the development of strategic alternatives for each of the company's current businesses and new business possibilities. It must also provide for management's review of these strategic alternatives and for corresponding resource allocation decisions. The result is a set of approved business plans that, taken as a whole, represent the direction of the firm. This process starts with, and its success is largely determined by, the creation of sound strategic alternatives.

The top management of a multibusiness firm cannot generate these strategic alternatives. It must rely on the managers of its business ventures and on its corporate development personnel. However, top management can and should establish a conceptual framework within which these alternatives can be developed. One such framework is the portfolio matrix associated with the Boston Consulting Group (BCG). Briefly, the **portfolio matrix** is used to establish the best mix of businesses in order to maximize the long-term earnings growth of the firm. The portfolio matrix represents a real advance in strategic planning in several ways:

- It encourages top management to evaluate the prospects of each of the company's businesses individually and to set tailored objectives for each business based on the contribution it can realistically make to corporate goals.
- It stimulates the use of externally focused empirical data to supplement managerial judgment in evaluating the potential of a particular business.
- It explicitly raises the issue of cash flow balancing as management plans for expansion and growth.
- It gives managers a potent new tool for analyzing competitors and for predicting competitive responses to strategic moves.
- It provides not just a financial but a strategic context for evaluating acquisitions and divestitures.[15]

As a consequence of these benefits, the widespread application of the portfolio matrix approach to corporate planning has sounded the death knell for planning by exhortation, the kind of strategic planning that sets uniform financial performance goals across an entire company—15 percent growth in earnings or 15 percent return on equity—and then expects each business to meet those goals year in and year out. The portfolio matrix approach has given top management the tools to evaluate each business in the context of both its environment and its unique contribution to the goals of the company as a whole and to weigh the entire array of business opportunities available to the company against the financial resources required to support them.

The portfolio matrix concept addresses the issue of the potential value of a particular business for the firm. This value has two variables: first, the potential for generating attractive earnings levels now; second, the potential for growth or, in other words, for significantly increased earnings levels in the future. The portfolio matrix concept holds that these two variables can be quantified. Current earnings potential is measured by comparing the market position of the business to that of its competitors. Empirical studies have shown that profitability is directly determined by relative market share. There are some types of businesses, however, in which the economies do not respond significantly to scale and other factors are important determinants of return. In such cases, the terminology for the earnings potential yardstick may be changed from market share to market leadership.

Growth potential is measured by the growth rate of the market segment in which the business competes. Clearly, if the segment is in the decline stage of its life cycle, the only way the business can increase its market share is by taking volume away from competitors. Although this is sometimes possible and economically desirable, it is usually expensive, leads to destructive pricing and erosion of profitability for all competitors, and ultimately results in a market that is ill served. On the other hand, if a market is in its rapid growth stage, the business can gain share by preempting the incremental growth in the market. So if these two dimensions of value are arrayed in matrix form, we have the basis for a business classification scheme. This is essentially what the Boston Consulting Group portfolio matrix is. Each of the four business categories tends to have specific characteristics associated with it. The two quadrants corresponding to high market leadership have current earnings potential, and the two corresponding to high market growth have growth potential.

Exhibit 10-3 shows a matrix with its two sides labeled product sales growth rate and relative market share. The area of each circle represents dollar sales. The market share position of each circle is determined by its horizontal position. Each circle's product sales growth rate (corrected for inflation) in the market in which it competes is shown by its vertical position.

With regard to the two axes of the matrix, relative market share is plotted on a logarithmic scale in order to be consistent with the experience curve effect, which implies that profit margin or rate of cash generation differences between two competitors tends to be proportionate to the ratio of their competitive positions. A linear axis is used for growth, for which the most generally useful measure is volume growth of the business concerned; in general, rates of cash use should be directly proportional to growth.

EXHIBIT 10-3
Product Portfolio Matrix

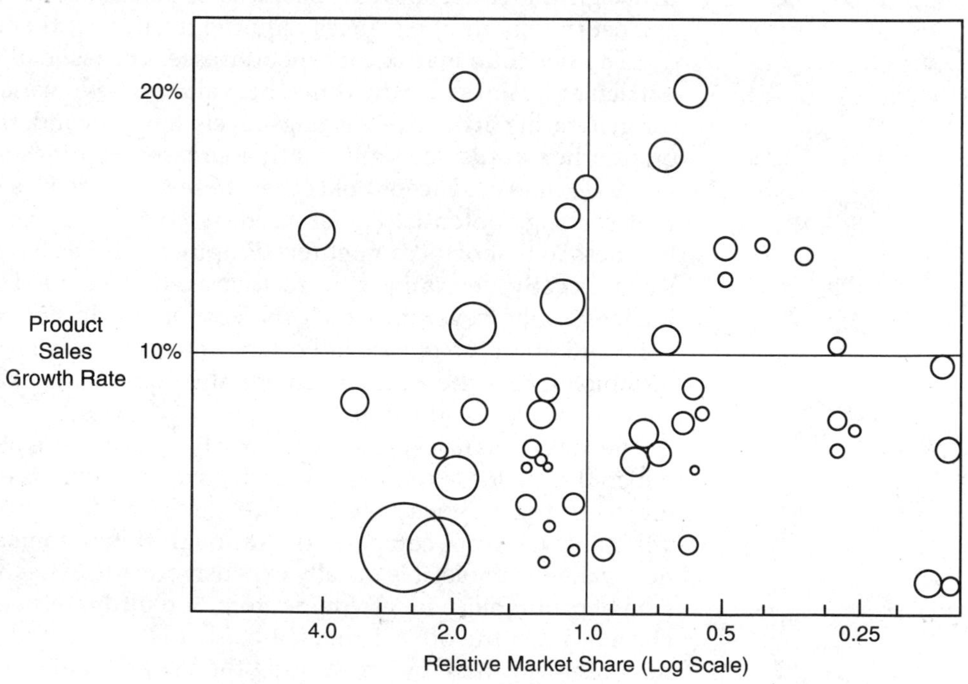

The lines dividing the matrix into four quadrants are arbitrary. Usually high growth is taken to include all businesses growing in excess of 10 percent annually in volume. The line separating areas of high and low relative competitive position is set at 1.0.

The importance of growth variables for strategy development is based on two factors. First, growth is a major influence in reducing cost because it is easier to gain experience or build market share in a growth market than in a low-growth situation. Second, growth provides opportunity for investment. The relative market share affects the rate at which a business will generate cash. The stronger the relative market share position of a product, the higher the margins it will have because of the scale effect.

Classification of Businesses

Using the two dimensions discussed here one can classify businesses and products into four categories (see Exhibit 10-4). Businesses in each category exhibit different financial characteristics and offer different strategic choices.

Stars. High-growth market leaders are called stars. They generate large amounts of cash, but the cash they generate from earnings and depreciation is more than offset by the cash that must be put back in the form of capital expenditures and increased working capital. Such heavy reinvestment is necessary to fund the capacity increases and inventory and receivable investment that go along with market share gains. Thus, star products represent probably the best profit opportunity available to a company, and their competitive position must be maintained. If a star's share is allowed to slip because the star has been used to provide large amounts of cash in the short run or because of cutbacks in

EXHIBIT 10-4
Matrix Quadrants

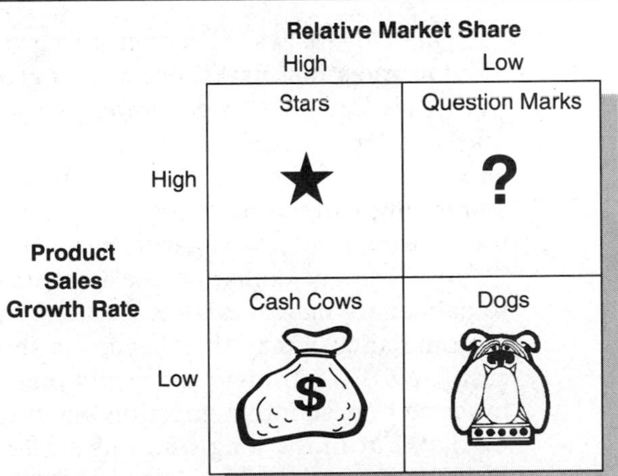

investment and rising prices (creating an umbrella for competitors), the star will ultimately become a dog.

The ultimate value of any product or service is reflected in the stream of cash it generates net of its own reinvestment. For a star, this stream of cash lies in the future, sometimes in the distant future. To obtain real value, the stream of cash must be discounted back to the present at a rate equal to the return on alternative opportunities. It is the future payoff of the star that counts, not the present reported profit. For GE, the plastics business is a star in which it keeps investing. As a matter of fact, the company even acquired Thomson's plastics operations (a French company) to further strengthen its position in the business.

Cash Cows. Cash cows are characterized by low growth and high market share. They are net providers of cash. Their high earnings, coupled with their depreciation, represent high cash inflows, and they need very little in the way of reinvestment. Thus, these businesses generate large cash surpluses that help to pay dividends and interest, provide debt capacity, supply funds for research and development, meet overheads, and also make cash available for investment in other products. Thus, cash cows are the foundation on which everything else depends. These products must be protected. Technically speaking, a cash cow has a return on assets that exceeds its growth rate. Only if this is true will the cash cow generate more cash than it uses. For NCR Company, the mechanical cash register business is a cash cow. The company still maintains a dominant share of this business even though growth since the introduction of electronic cash registers has slowed down. The company uses the surplus cash from its mechanical cash registers to develop electronic machines with a view to creating a new star. Likewise, the tire business can be categorized as a cash cow for Goodyear Tire and Rubber Company. The tire industry is characterized by slow market growth, and Goodyear has a major share of the market.

Question Marks. Products in a growth market with a low share are categorized as question marks. Because of growth, these products require more cash than they are able to generate on their own. If nothing is done to increase market share, a question mark will simply absorb large amounts of cash in the short run and later, as the growth slows down, become a dog. Thus, unless something is done to change its perspective, a question mark remains a cash loser throughout its existence and ultimately becomes a cash trap.

What can be done to make a question mark more viable? One alternative is to gain share increases for it. Because the business is growing, it can be funded to dominance. It may then become a star and later, when growth slows down, a cash cow. This strategy is a costly one in the short run. An abundance of cash must be poured into a question mark in order for it to win a major share of the market, but in the long run, this strategy is the only way to develop a sound business from the question mark stage. Another strategy is to divest the business. Outright sale is the most desirable alternative. But if this does not work out, a firm decision must be made not to invest further in the business. The business must simply be allowed to generate whatever cash it can while non-reinvested.

When Joseph E. Seagram and Sons bought Tropicana from Beatrice Co. in 1988, it was a question mark. The product had been trailing behind Coke's Minute Maid and was losing ground to Procter and Gamble's new entry in the field, Citrus Hill. Since then, Seagram has invested heavily in Tropicana to develop it into a star product. After just two years, Tropicana has emerged as a leader in the not-from-concentrate orange juice market, far ahead of Minute Maid, and has been trying to make inroads in other segments.[16]

Dogs. Products with low market share positioned in low-growth situations are called dogs. Their poor competitive position condemns them to poor profits. Because growth is low, dogs have little potential for gaining sufficient share to achieve viable cost positions. Usually they are net users of cash. Their earnings are low, and the reinvestment required just to keep the business together eats cash inflow. The business, therefore, becomes a cash trap that is likely to regularly absorb cash unless further investment is rigorously avoided. An alternative is to convert dogs into cash, if there is an opportunity to do so. GE's consumer electronics business had been in the dog category, maintaining only a small percentage of the available market in a period of slow growth, when the company decided to unload the business (including the RCA brand acquired in late 1985) to Thomson, France's state-owned leading electronics manufacturer.

Exhibit 10-5 summarizes the investment, earning, and cash flow characteristics of stars, cash cows, question marks, and dogs. Also shown are viable strategy alternatives for products in each category.

Strategy Implications

In a typical company, products could be scattered in all four quadrants of the portfolio matrix. The appropriate strategy for products in each cell is given briefly in Exhibit 10-5. The first goal of a company should be to secure a position with cash cows but to guard against the frequent temptation to reinvest in them excessively. The cash generated from cash cows should first be used to support those stars that are not self-sustaining. Surplus cash may then be used to finance selected question marks to dominance. Any question mark that cannot be funded should be divested. A dog may be restored to a position of viability by shrewdly segmenting the market; that is, by rationalizing and specializing the business into a small niche that the product may dominate. If this is not practical, a firm should manage the dog for cash; it should cut off all investment in the business and liquidate it when an opportunity develops.

Exhibit 10-6 shows the consequences of an incorrect strategic move. If a question mark is given adequate support, it may become a star and ultimately a cash cow (success sequence). On the other hand, if a star is not appropriately funded, it may become a question mark and finally a dog (disaster sequence).

EXHIBIT 10-5
Characteristics and Strategy Implications of Products in the Strategy Quadrants

Quadrant	*Investment Characteristics*	*Earning Characteristics*	*Cash Flow Characteristics*	*Strategy Implication*
Stars	—Continual expenditures for capacity expansion —Pipeline filing with cash	Low to high	Negative cash flow (net cash user)	Continue to increase market share, if necessary at the expense of short-term earnings
Cash cows	—Capacity maintenance expenditures	High	Positive cash flow (net cash contributor)	Maintain share and leadership until further investment becomes marginal
Question marks	—Heavy initial capacity expenditures —High research and development costs	Negative to low	Negative cash flow (net cash user)	Assess chances of dominating segment: if good, go after share; if bad, redefine business or withdraw
Dogs	—Gradually deplete capacity	High to low	Positive cash flow (net cash contributor)	Plan an orderly withdrawal so as to maximize cash flow

Top management needs to answer two strategic questions: (a) How promising is the current set of businesses with respect to long-term return and growth? (b) Which businesses should be developed? maintained as is? liquidated? Following the portfolio matrix approach, a company needs a cash-balanced portfolio of businesses; that is, it needs cash cows and dogs to throw off sufficient cash to fund stars and question marks. It needs an ample supply of question marks to ensure long-term growth and businesses with return levels appropriate to their matrix position. In response to the second question, capital budgeting theory requires the lining up of capital project proposals, assessment of incremental cash flows attributable to each project, computation of discounted rate of return on each, and approval of the project with the highest rate of return until available funds are exhausted. But the capital budgeting approach misses the strategic content; that is, it ignores questions of how to validate assumptions about volume, price, cost, and investment and how to eliminate natural biases. This problem is solved by the portfolio matrix approach.

Portfolio Matrix and Product Life Cycle

The product portfolio matrix approach propounded by the Boston Consulting Group may be related to the product life cycle by letting the introduction stage begin in the question mark quadrant; growth starts toward the end of this quadrant and continues well into the star quadrant. Going down from the star to the cash cow quadrant, the maturity stage begins. Decline is positioned between the cash cow and the dog quadrants (see Exhibit 10-7). Ideally a company should enter the product/market segment in its introduction stage, gain market share in the growth stage, attain a position of dominance when the product/

EXHIBIT 10-6
Product Portfolio Matrix: Strategic Consequences

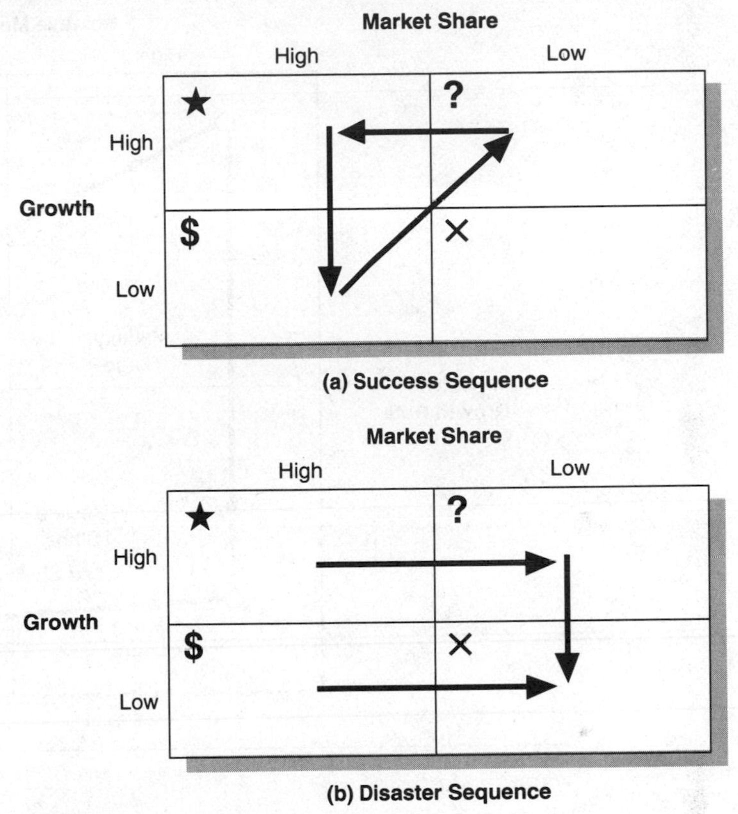

Source: Bruce D. Henderson, "The Product Portfolio" (Boston: The Boston Consulting Group, Inc., 1970). *Perspectives* No. 66. Reprinted by permission.

market segment enters its maturity stage, maintain this dominant position until the product/market segment enters its decline stage, and then determine the optimum point for liquidation.[17]

Balanced and Unbalanced Portfolios

Exhibit 10-8 is an example of a balanced portfolio. With three cash cows, this company is well positioned with stars to provide growth and to yield high cash returns in the future when they mature. The company has four question marks, two of which present good opportunities to emerge as stars at an investment level that the cash cows should be able to support (based on the area of the circles). The company does have dogs, but they can be managed to avoid drain on cash resources.

EXHIBIT 10-7
Relationship between Product Portfolio Matrix and Product Life Cycle

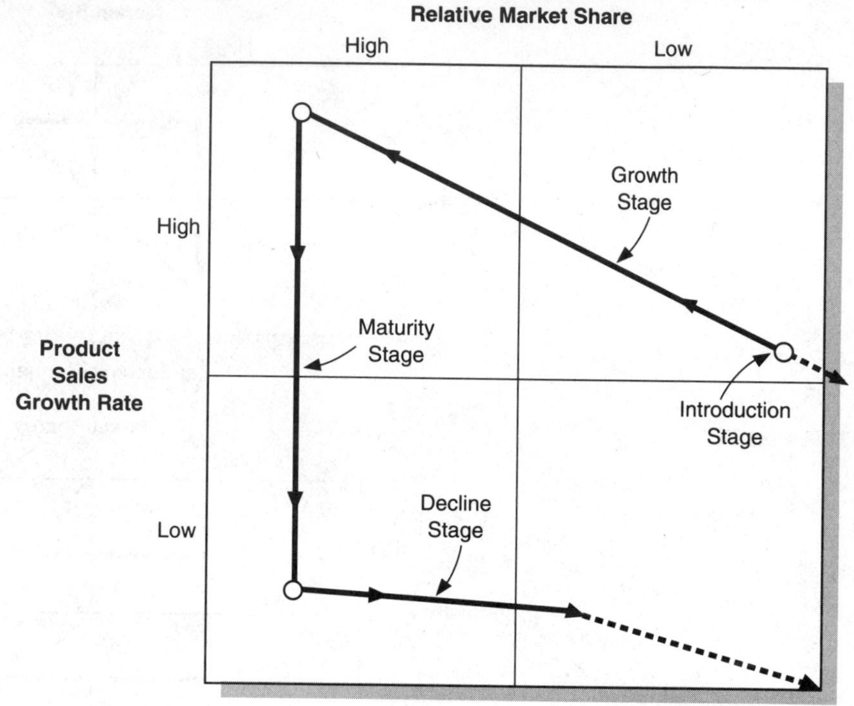

Unbalanced portfolios may be classified into four types:

1. Too many losers (due to inadequate cash flow, inadequate profits, and inadequate growth)
2. Too many question marks (due to inadequate cash flow and inadequate profits)
3. Too many profit producers (due to inadequate growth and excessive cash flow)
4. Too many developing winners (due to excessive cash demands, excessive demands on management, and unstable growth and profits)

Exhibit 10-9 illustrates an unbalanced portfolio. The company has just one cash cow, three question marks, and no stars. Thus, the cash base of the company is inadequate and cannot support the question marks. The company may allocate available cash among all question marks in equal proportion. Dogs may also be given occasional cash nourishment. If the company continues its current strategy, it may find itself in a dangerous position in five years, particularly when the cash cow moves closer to becoming a dog. To take corrective action, the company must face the fact that it cannot support all its question marks. It must choose one or maybe two of its three question marks and fund them adequately to make them stars. In addition, disbursement of cash in dogs should be totally

EXHIBIT 10-8
Illustration of a Balanced Portfolio

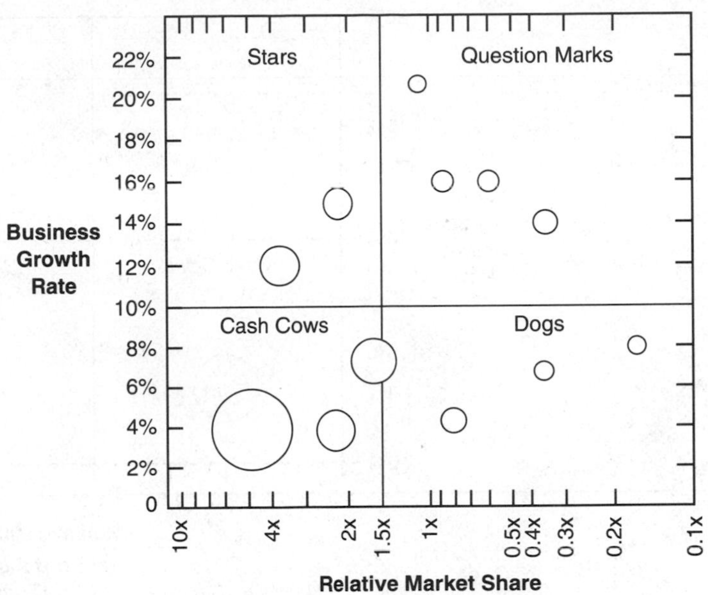

prohibited. In brief, the strategic choice for the company, considered in portfolio terms, is obvious. It cannot fund all question marks and dogs equally.

The portfolio matrix focuses on the real fundamentals of businesses and their relationships to each other within the portfolio. It is not possible to develop effective strategy in a multiproduct, multimarket company without considering the mutual relationships of different businesses.

Conclusion

The portfolio matrix approach provides for the simultaneous comparison of different products. It also underlines the importance of cash flow as a strategic variable. Thus, when continuous long-term growth in earnings is the objective, it is necessary to identify high-growth product/market segments early, develop businesses, and preempt the growth in these segments. If necessary, short-term profitability in these segments may be forgone to ensure achievement of the dominant share. Costs must be managed to meet scale-effect standards. The appropriate point at which to shift from an earnings focus to a cash flow focus must be determined and a liquidation plan for cash flow maximization established. A cash-balanced mix of businesses should be maintained.

Many companies worldwide have used the portfolio matrix approach in their strategic planning. The first company to use this approach was the Norton Company, which began employing the concept in the late 1960s. Since then, many large corporations have reported following it, among them Mead, Borg-Warner, Eaton, and Monsanto.

EXHIBIT 10-9
Illustration of an Unbalanced Portfolio

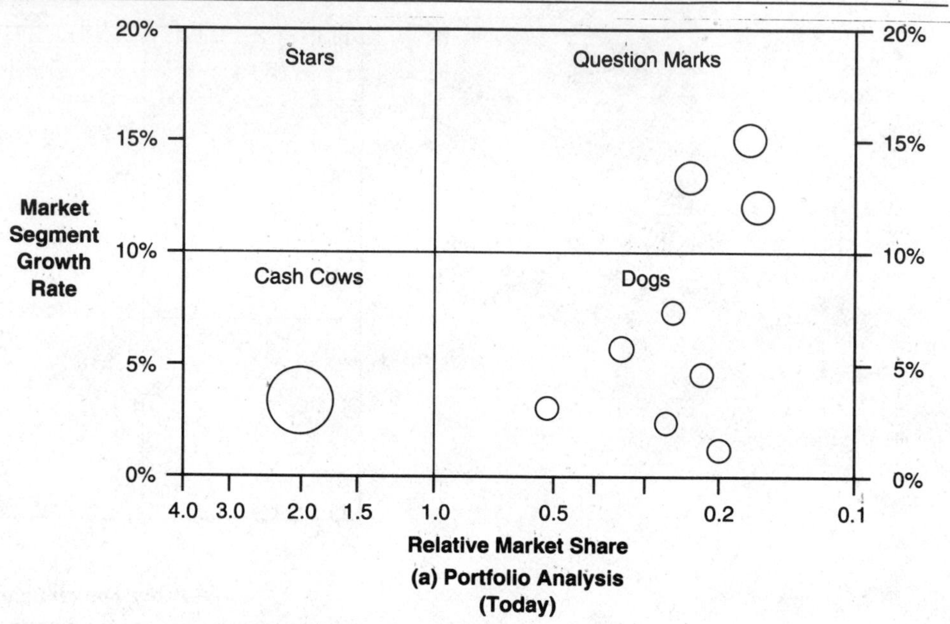

(a) Portfolio Analysis (Today)

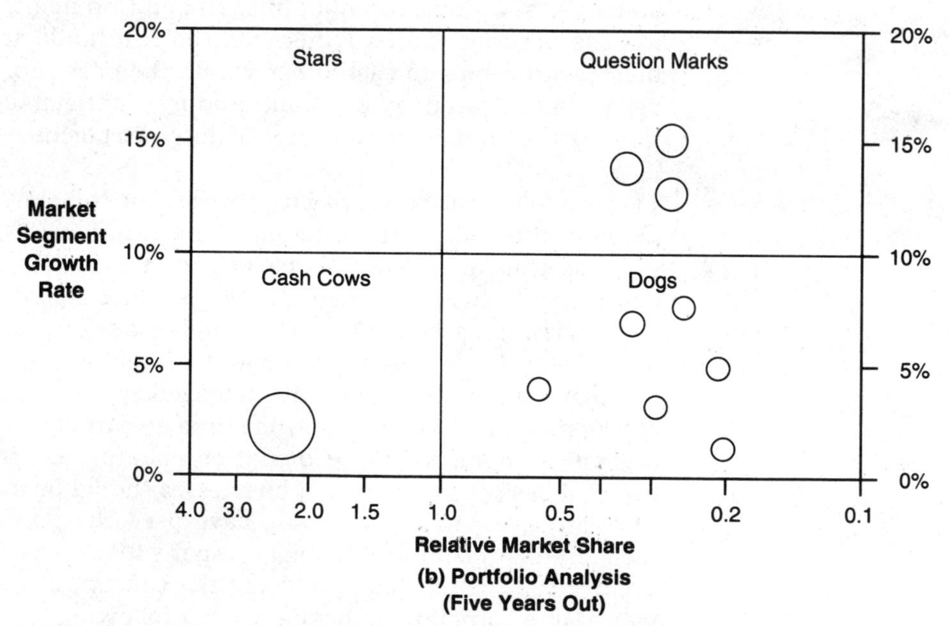

(b) Portfolio Analysis (Five Years Out)

The portfolio matrix approach, however, is not a panacea for strategy development. In reality, many difficulties limit the workability of this approach. Some potential mistakes associated with the portfolio matrix concept are

1. Overinvesting in low-growth segments (lack of objectivity and "hard" analysis)
2. Underinvesting in high-growth segments (lack of guts)
3. Misjudging the segment growth rate (poor market research)
4. Not achieving market share (because of improper market strategy, sales capabilities, or promotion)
5. Losing cost effectiveness (lack of operating talent and control system)
6. Not uncovering emerging high-growth segments (lack of corporate development effort)
7. Unbalanced business mix (lack of planning and financial resources)

Thus, the portfolio matrix approach should be used with great care.

MULTIFACTOR PORTFOLIO MATRIX

The two-factor portfolio matrix discussed above provides a useful approach for reviewing the roles of different products in a company. Generally, however, the growth rate–relative market share matrix approach leads to many difficulties. At times, factors other than market share and growth rate bear heavily on cash flow, the mainstay of this approach. Some managers may consider return on investment a more suitable criterion than cash flow for making investment decisions. Further, the two-factor portfolio matrix approach does not address major investment decisions between dissimilar businesses. These difficulties can lead a company into too many traps and errors. For this reason many companies (such as GE and the Shell Group) have developed the multifactor portfolio approach.

Exhibit 10-10 illustrates the GE matrix. Its two dimensions, industry attractiveness and business strengths, are based on a variety of factors. It is this multifactor characteristic that differentiates this approach from the one discussed in the previous section. In its early attempts with the portfolio matrix, GE used the criteria and measures shown in Exhibit 10-11 to determine industry attractiveness and business strengths.[18] These criteria and measures are only suggestions; another company may adopt a different list. For example, GE later added cyclicality as a criterion under industry attractiveness. The measure of relative profitability, as shown in the exhibit, was used for the first time in 1985.

Rothschild recommends considering the following factors in measuring both "industry environment" (industry attractiveness) and "our position" (business strengths): market, competition, financial and economic factors, technological factors, sociopolitical factors, and overall factors. Each factor may be treated equally or assigned a different weight.[19] Exhibits 10-12 and 10-13 illustrate how factors may be weighed and how a final industry attractiveness and business strengths score may be computed. Management may establish cutoff points for high, medium, and low industry attractiveness and competitive position scores.

EXHIBIT 10-10
Multifactor Portfolio Matrix

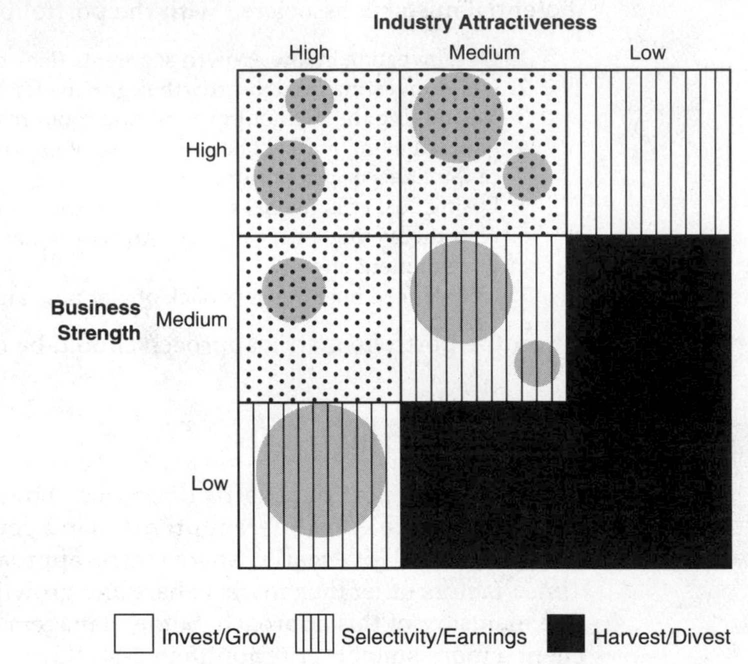

It is worthwhile to mention that the development of a multifactor matrix may not be as easy as it appears. The actual analysis required may take considerable amount of foresight and experience and many, many days of work. The major difficulties lie in identifying relevant factors, relating factors to industry attractiveness and business strengths, and weighing factors.

Strategy Development

The overall strategy for a business in a particular position is illustrated in Exhibit 10-10. The area of the circle refers to the business's sales. Investment priority is given to products in the high area (upper left), where a stronger position is supported by the attractiveness of an industry. Along the diagonal, selectivity is desired to achieve a balanced earnings performance. The businesses in the low area (lower right) are the candidates for harvesting and divestment.

A company may position its products or businesses on the matrix to study its present standing. Forecasts may be made to examine the directions different businesses may go in the future, assuming no changes are made in strategy. Future perspectives may be compared to the corporate mission to identify gaps between what is desired and what may be expected if no measures are taken now. Filling the gap requires making strategic moves for different businesses. Once strategic alternatives for an individual business have been identified, the final choice of a strategy should be based on the scope of the overall corporation

EXHIBIT 10-11
Portfolio Considerations and Measures Used by GE in 1980

Industry Attractiveness		Business Strengths	
Criterion	*Measure*	*Criterion*	
1. Market size	• Three-year average served industry market dollars	1. Market position	• Three-year average market share (total dollars) • Three-year average international market share • Two-year average relative market share (SBU/Big Three competitors)
2. Market growth	• Ten-year constant dollar average market growth rate		
3. Industry profitability	• Three-year average ROS, SBU and Big Three competitors: • Nominal • Inflation adjusted	2. Competitive position	Superior, equal, or inferior to competition in 1980: • Product quality • Technological leadership • Manufacturing/cost leadership • Distribution/marketing leadership
4. Cyclicality	• Average annual percent variation of sales from trend		
5. Inflation recovery	• Five-year average ratio of combined selling price and productivity change to change in cost due to inflation	3. Relative profitability	Three-year average SBU ROS less average ROS, Big Three competitors: • Nominal • Inflation adjusted
6. Importance of non-U.S. markets	• Ten-year average ratio of international to total market		

[ ] Indicates measure used for first time in 1980

Source: General Electric Co. Reprinted by permission. The measurements do not reflect current GE practice.

vis-à-vis the matrix. For example, the prospects for a business along the diagonal may appear good, but this business cannot be funded in preference to a business in the high-high cell. In devising future strategy, a company generally likes to have a few businesses on the left to provide growth and to furnish potential for investment and a few on the right to generate cash for investment in the former. The businesses along the diagonal may be selectively supported (based on resources) for relocation on the left. If this is not feasible, they may be slowly harvested or divested. Exhibit 10-14 summarizes desired strategic perspective in different cell positions.

For an individual business, there can be four strategy options: investing to maintain, investing to grow, investing to regain, and investing to exit. The choice of a strategy depends on the current position of the business in the matrix (i.e., toward the high side, along the diagonal, or toward the low side) and its future direction, assuming the current strategic perspective continues to be followed. If the future appears unpromising, a new strategy for the business is called for.

Analysis of present position on the matrix may not pose any problem. At GE, for example, there was little disagreement on the position of the business.[20]

EXHIBIT 10-12
Assessing Industry Attractiveness

Criteria	*Weights**	× *Ratings***	= *Values*
Market size	.15	4	.60
Growth rate	.12	3	36
Profit margin	.05	3	.15
Market diversity	.05	2	.10
Demand cyclicality	.05	2	.10
Expert opportunities	.05	5	.25
Competitive structure	.05	3	.15
Industry profitability	.20	3	.60
Inflation vulnerability	.05	2	.10
Value added	.10	5	.50
Capital intensity	GO	4	—
Raw material availability	GO	4	—
Technological role	.05	4	.20
Energy impact	.08	4	.32
Social	GO	4	—
Environmental impact	GO	4	—
Legal	GO	4	—
Human	GO	4	—
	1.00	1 to 5	3.43

*Some criteria may be of a GO/NO GO type. For example, many *Fortune* 500 firms would probably not invest in industries viewed negatively by society even if it were legal and profitable to do so.
**"1" deontes very unattractive; "5" denotes very attractive.

The mapping of future direction, however, may not be easy. A rigorous analysis has to be performed, taking into account environmental shifts, competitors' perspectives, and internal strengths and weaknesses.

The four strategy options are shown in Exhibit 10-15. Strategy to maintain the current position (strategy 1 in the exhibit) may be adopted if, in the absence of a new strategy, erosion is expected in the future. Investment will be sought to hold the position; hence, the name invest-to-maintain strategy. The second option is the invest-to-grow strategy. Here, the product's current position is perceived as less than optimum vis-à-vis industry attractiveness and business strengths. In other words, considering the opportunities furnished by the industry and the strengths exhibited by the business, the current position is considered inadequate. A growth strategy is adopted with the aim of shifting the product position upward or toward the left. Movement in both directions is an expensive option with high risk.

The invest-to-regain strategy (strategy 3 in Exhibit 10-15) is an attempt to rebuild the product or business to its previous position. Usually, when the en-

EXHIBIT 10-13
Assessing Business Strengths

Criteria	*Weights**	× *Ratings***	= *Values*
Market share	.10	5	.50
SBU growth rate	X	3	—
Breadth of product line	.05	4	.20
Sales/distribution effectiveness	.20	4	.80
Proprietary and key account effectiveness	X	3	—
Price competitiveness	X	4	—
Advertising and promotion effectiveness	.05	4	.20
Facilities location and newness	.05	5	.25
Capacity and productivity	X	3	—
Experience curve effects	.15	4	.60
Value added	X	4	—
Investment utilization	.05	5	.25
Raw materials cost	.05	4	.20
Relative product quality	.15	4	.60
R&D advantage/position	.05	4	.20
Cash throwoff	.10	5	.50
Organizational synergies	X	4	—
General image	X	5	—
	1.00	1 to 5	4.30

*For any particular industry, there will be some factors that, while important in general, will have little or no effect on the relative competitive position of firms within that industry.

**"1" denotes very weak competitive position; "5" denotes a very strong competitive position.

vironment (i.e., industry) continues to be relatively attractive but the business position has slipped because of some strategic past mistake (e.g., premature harvesting), the company may decide to revitalize the business through new investments. The fourth and final option, the invest-to-exit strategy, is directed toward leaving the market through harvesting or divesting. Harvesting amounts to making very low investments in the business so that in the short run the business will secure positive cash flow and in a few years die out. (With no new investments, the position will continue to deteriorate.) Alternatively, the whole business may be divested, that is, sold to another party in a one-time deal. Sometimes small investments may be made to maintain the viability of business if divestment is desired but there is no immediate suitor. In this way the business can eventually be sold at a higher price than would have been possible right away.

EXHIBIT 10-14
Prescriptive Strategies for Businesses in Different Cells

Market Attractiveness \ Competitive Position	Strong	Medium	Weak
High	**Protect Position** • Invest to grow at maximum digestible rate • Concentrate effort on maintaining strength	**Invest to Build** • Challenge for leadership • Build selectively on strengths • Reinforce vulnerable areas	**Build Selectively** • Specialize around limited strengths • Seek ways to overcome weaknesses • Withdraw if indications of sustainable growth are lacking
Medium	**Build Selectively** • Invest heavily in most attractive segments • Build up ability to counter competition • Emphasize profitability by raising productivity	**Selectivity/Manage for Earnings** • Protect existing program • Concentrate investments in segments where profitability is good and risk is relatively low	**Limited Expansion or Harvest** • Look for ways to expand without high risk; otherwise, minimize investment and rationalize investment
Low	**Protect and Refocus** • Manage for current earnings • Concentrate on attractive strengths • Defend strengths	**Manage for Earnings** • Protect position in most profitable segments • Upgrade product line • Minimize investment	**Divest** • Sell at time that will maximize cash value • Cut fixed costs and avoid investment meanwhile

Source: Reprinted by permission from *Analysis for Strategic Market Decisions* by George S. Day, copyright 1986 by West Publishing Company. All rights reserved. Page 204.

Unit of Analysis The framework discussed here may be applied to either a product/market or an SBU. As a matter of act, it may be equally applicable to a much higher level of aggregation in the organization, such as a division or a group. Of course, at the group or division level, it may be very difficult to measure industry attractiveness and business strengths unless the group or division happens to be in one business.

In the scheme followed in this book, the analysis may be performed first at the SBU level to determine the strategic perspective of different products/

EXHIBIT 10-15
Strategy Options

Industry Attractiveness

Business Strength

	Current Position Strategy (to maintain this position	

(a) Invest to Maintain

Industry Attractiveness

Business Strength

Strategy	Current Position	
Current Position		

(b) Invest to Grow

Industry Attractiveness

Business Strength

Strategy		
Current Position		

(c) Invest to Regain

Industry Attractiveness

Business Strength

	Current Position	Strategy

(d) Invest to Exit

markets. Finally, all SBUs may be simultaneously positioned on the matrix to determine a corporatewide portfolio.

Directional Policy Matrix

A slightly different technique, the directional policy matrix, is popularly used in Europe. It was initially worked out at the Shell Group but later caught the fancy of many businesses across the Atlantic. Exhibit 10-16 illustrates a directional policy matrix. The two sides of the matrix are labeled business sector prospects

EXHIBIT 10-16
Directional Policy Matrix

Company's Competitive Capabilities	Business Sector Prospects: Unattractive	Average	Attractive
Weak	Disinvest	Phased withdrawal Proceed with care	Double or quit
Average	Phased withdrawal	Proceed with care	Try harder
Strong	Cash generator	Growth Leader	Leader

(industry attractiveness) and company's competitive capabilities (business strengths). Business sector prospects are categorized as unattractive, average, and attractive; and the company's competitive capabilities are categorized as weak, average, and strong. Within each cell is the overall strategy direction for a business depicted by the cell. The consideration of factors used to measure business sector prospects and a company's competitive capabilities follows the same logic and analyses discussed above.

PORTFOLIO MATRIX—CRITICAL ANALYSIS

In recent years, a variety of criticisms have been leveled at the portfolio framework. Most of the criticism has centered on the Boston Consulting Group matrix.

1. A question has been raised about the use of market share as the most important influence on marketing strategy.[21] The BCG matrix is derived from an application of the learning experience curve to manufacturing and other costs. It was observed that, as a firm's product output (and thus market share) increases, total cost declines by a fixed percentage. This may be true for commodities; however, in most product/market situations, products are differentiated, new products and brands are continually introduced, and the

pace of technological changes keeps increasing. As a result, one may move from learning curve to learning curve or encounter a discontinuity. More concrete evidence is needed before the validity of market share as a dimension in strategy formulation is established or rejected.

2. Another criticism, closely related to the first, is how product/market boundaries are defined. Market share varies depending on the definition of the corresponding product/market. Hence, a product may be classified in different cells, depending on the market boundaries used.[22]
3. The stability of product life cycles is implicitly assumed in some portfolio models. However, as in the case of the learning curve, it is possible for the product life cycle to change during the life of the product. For example, recycling can extend the life cycle of a product, sparking a second growth stage after maturity.[23] A related subissue concerns the assumption that investment is more desirable in high-growth markets than in low-growth ones. There is insufficient evidence to support this proposition.[24] This overall issue becomes more problematic for international firms because a given product may be in different stages of its life cycle in different countries.
4. The BCG portfolio framework was developed for balancing cash flows. It ignores the existence of capital markets. Cash balancing is not always an important consideration.
5. The portfolio framework assumes that investments in all products/markets are equally risky, but this is not the case. In fact, financial portfolio management theory does take risk into account. The more risky an investment, the higher the return expected of it. The portfolio matrix does not consider the risk factor.
6. The BCG portfolio model assumes that there is no interdependency between products/markets. This assumption can be questioned on various grounds. For instance, different products/markets might share technology or costs.[25] These interdependencies should be accounted for in a portfolio framework.
7. There is no consensus on the level at which portfolio models are appropriately used. Five levels can be identified: product, product line, market segment, SBU, and business sector. The most frequent application has been at the SBU level; however, it has been suggested that the framework is equally applicable at other levels. Because it is unlikely that any one model could have such wide application, the suggestion that it does casts doubt on the model itself.
8. Most portfolio approaches are retrospective and overly dependent on conventional wisdom in the way in which they treat both market attractiveness and competitive position.[26] For example, despite evidence to the contrary, conventional wisdom suggests the following:

    a. Dominant market share endows companies with sufficient power to maintain price above a competitive level or to obtain massive cost advantages through economies of scale and the experience curve. However, the returns for such companies as Goodyear and Maytag show that this is not always the case.

Market Situation	Conventional Wisdom	Examples	Return on Total Capital Employed 1975–79
Dominant market share	Market leader gains: —Premium prices —Cost advantages due to scale and experience curve	Goodyear: 40% of U.S. tire market; market leader	7.0%
		Maytag: 5% of U.S. appliance industry; niche competitor	26.7%

b. High market growth means that rivals can expand output and show profits without having to take demand out of each other's plants and provoking price warfare. But the experience of industries as different as the European tungsten carbide industry and the U.S. airline industry suggest that it is not always true.

Market Situation	Conventional Wisdom	Examples	Return on Total Capital Employed 1975–79
High market growth	High market growth allows companies to expand output without provoking price competition and leads to higher profits	European tungsten carbide industry: 1% annual growth	15.0%
		U.S. airline industry: 13.6% annual growth	5.7%

c. High barriers to entry allow existing competitors to keep prices high and earn high profits. But the experience of the U.S. brewing industry seems to refute conventional wisdom.

Market Situation	Conventional Wisdom	Examples	Return on Total Capital Employed 1975–79
High barriers to entry	High barriers prevent new entrants from competing away previously excess profits	U.S. brewing industry is highly concentrated with very high barriers to entry	8.6%

9. There are also issues of measurement and weighting. Different measures have been proposed and used for the dimensions of portfolio models; however, a product's position on a matrix may vary depending on the measures used.[27] In addition, the weights used for models having composite dimensions may impact the results, and the position of a business on the matrix may change with the weighting scheme used.
10. Portfolio models ignore the impact of both the external and internal environments of a company. Because a firm's strategic decisions are made within its environments, their potential impact must be taken into account. Day highlights a few situational factors that might affect a firm's strategic plan. As examples of internal factors, he cites rate of capacity utilization, union

pressures, barriers to entry, and extent of captive business. GNP, interest rates, and social, legal, and regulatory environment are cited as examples of external factors.[28] No systematic treatment has been accorded to such environmental influences in the portfolio models. These influences are always unique to a company, so the importance of customizing a portfolio approach becomes clear.

11. The relevance of a particular strategy for a business depends on its correct categorization on the matrix. If a mistake is made in locating a business in a particular cell of the matrix, the failure of the prescribed strategy cannot be blamed on the framework.[29] In other words, superficial and uncritical application of the portfolio framework can misdirect a business's strategy. As Gluck has observed:

    > Portfolio approaches have their limitations, of course. First, it's just not all that easy to define the businesses or product/market units appropriately before you begin to analyze them. Second, some attractive strategic opportunities can be overlooked if management treats its businesses as independent entities when there may be real advantages in their sharing resources at the research or manufacturing or distribution level. And third, like more sophisticated models, when it's used uncritically the portfolio can give its users the illusion that they're being rigorous and scientific when in fact they've fallen prey to the old garbage-in, garbage-out syndrome.[30]

12. Most portfolio approaches suggest standard or generic strategies based on the portfolio position of individual SBUs. But these kinds of responses can often result in lost opportunities, turn out to be impractical or unrealistic, and stifle creativity. For example, the standard strategy for managing dogs (SBUs that have a low share of a mature market) is to treat them as candidates for divestment or liquidation. New evidence demonstrates, however, that, with proper management, dogs can be assets to a diversified corporation. One recent study of the performance of more than a thousand industrial-product businesses slotted into the four cells of the BCG matrix found that the average dog had a positive cash flow even greater than the cash needs of the average question mark. Moreover, in a slow-growth economy, more than half of a company's businesses might qualify as dogs. Disposing of them all would be neither feasible nor desirable. Yet the portfolio approach provides no help in suggesting how to improve the performance of such businesses.[31]
13. Portfolio models fail to answer such questions as (a) how a company may determine whether its strategic goals are consistent with its financial objectives, (b) how a company may relate strategic goals to its affordable growth, and (c) how relevant the designated strategies are vis-à-vis competition from overseas companies. In addition, many marketers have raised other questions about the viability of portfolio approaches as a strategy development tool. For example, it has been claimed that the BCG matrix approach is relevant only for positioning existing businesses and fails to prescribe how a question mark may be reared to emerge as a star, how new stars can be located, and so on.

In response to these criticisms, it should be pointed out that the BCG portfolio framework was developed as an aid in formulating business strategies in complex environments. Its aim was not to prescribe strategy, though many executives and academicians have misused it in this way. As one writer has noted:

> No simple, monolithic set of rules or strategy imperatives will point automatically to the right course. No planning system guarantees the development of successful strategies. Nor does any technique. The Business Portfolio (the growth/share matrix) made a major contribution to strategic thought. Today it is misused and overexposed. It can be a helpful tool, but it can also be misleading or, worse, a straightjacket.[32]

NEW PRODUCT PORTFOLIO APPROACHES

In spite of its shortcomings, the portfolio approach appears to be an attractive strategy formulation tool. An empirical study estimates that as many as 75 percent of diversified companies widely use portfolio frameworks.[33] This statistic may be explained by the fact that a two-variable approach condenses a considerable amount of information into a simple framework for decision making. The framework also facilitates communication. Examined in this section are three new portfolio approaches: (a) the Boston Consulting Group's new framework, (b) Porter's generic strategies framework, and (c) the commodity/specialty matrix.

Boston Consulting Group's New Approach

According to the Boston Consulting Group, the requirements for strategic success vary depending on the economic environment and competitive dynamics. In the 1970s most successful companies achieved their success by anticipating market evolution and by creating a unique and defensible advantage over their competitors in the new environment. In the 1980s the focus of strategy development shifted to the competitive environment and the potential for change in that environment. To articulate this focus, Boston Consulting Group developed a new portfolio matrix around two factors: (a) the size of the advantage that can be created over other competitors and (b) the number of unique ways in which that advantage can be created. The combination of these two factors provides long-term value for the business and dictates strategy requirements.[34]

There is a fundamental difference between businesses in which the size of the potential advantage that a single competitor can create over all other competitors is large and those in which it is small. The reward potential for a successful strategy is only large when the size of the advantage that can be created is also large. There is also a fundamental difference between businesses that have only one way or only a few ways to achieve advantage and those that have several ways. When product differentiation is costly and not valued by customers, only low price and relative cost position determine success. When a variety of approaches are possible, however, a variety of strategies are also possible. Competitors can succeed by tuning their offering and costs exactly to meet a specific segment's demand. If advantage can be created by doing this, a small competitor can thrive as an industry specialist.

These two factors—the size of the advantage and the number of ways it can be achieved—can be combined into a simple matrix to help guide creative strategy development (see Exhibit 10-17). The specific requirements for success are different in each quadrant. Corporate success depends on retaining advantaged positions in volume and specialization businesses. Even high market share or relatively low-cost positions in stalemated and fragmented industries may not be exceptionally valuable. In fact, the value of success in businesses that best fit on the right side of the matrix is always higher than in those that fit best on the left.

Following this framework, too many companies pursue strategies that are inappropriate to their specific competitive environments. Market share, for example, often lacks value in stalemated and fragmented businesses. In specialization businesses, focus and superior brand image may be more rewarding than mere size.

Over time, the nature of the competitive environment can change. Businesses that start out as fragmented industries can evolve toward specialization and even toward the volume category. McDonald's did this in away-from-home eating. Businesses that start out as volume businesses can migrate toward stalemate. This has happened to much of the world's paper industry. Other businesses that were clearly volume businesses have moved toward specialization, as both the Japanese auto producers and a few European companies have proved to the large U.S. auto companies. Some businesses have remained volume businesses by moving toward world-scale economies, as Caterpillar has shown in construction equipment. The challenge for companies is to anticipate, or even cause, these major evolutions toward a new basis of competition.

EXHIBIT 10-17
Boston Consulting Group's New Portfolio Matrix

Number of Approaches to Achieve Advantage	Size of Advantage: Small	Size of Advantage: Large
Many	Fragmented	Specialization
Few	Stalemate	Volume

Source: "Strategy in the 1980s," in *Perspectives* (Boston: The Boston Consulting Group, 1981). Reprinted by permission.

In a diversified company, the challenge is immense. A portfolio of businesses that is disadvantaged in specialization and volume and weighed down by assets tied up in stalemated and fragmented industries spells failure. Successful companies are those with advantaged positions in volume and specialization. Extraordinary success will accrue to those few strategists willing and able to create sustainable advantage but will accrue especially to those able to change the basis of competition.

Porter's Generic Strategies Framework

Porter has identified three generic strategies: **(a)** overall cost leadership (i.e., making units of a fairly standardized product and underpricing everybody else); **(b)** differentiation (i.e., turning out something customers perceive as unique—an item whose quality, design, brand name, or reputation for service commands higher-than-average prices); and **(c)** focus (i.e., concentrating on a particular group of customers, geographic market, channel of distribution, or distinct segment of the product line).[35]

Porter's choice of strategy is based on two factors: the **strategic target** at which the business aims and the **strategic advantage** that the business has in aiming at that target. According to Porter, forging successful strategy begins with understanding what is happening in one's industry and deciding which of the available competitive niches one should attempt to dominate. For example, a firm may discover that the largest competitor in an industry is aggressively pursuing cost leadership, that others are trying the differentiation route, and that no one is attempting to focus on some small speciality market. On the basis of this information, the firm might sharpen its efforts to distinguish its product from others or switch to a focus game plan. As Porter says, the idea is to position the firm "so it won't be slugging it out with everybody else in the industry; if it does it right, it won't be directly toe-to-toe with anyone." The objective is to mark out a defensible competitive position—defensible not just against rival companies but also against the forces driving industry competition (discussed in chapter 4). What it means is that the give-and-take between firms already in the business represents only one such force. Others are the bargaining power of suppliers, the bargaining power of buyers, the threat of substitute products or services, and the threat of new entrants. In conclusion, Porter's framework emphasizes not only that certain characteristics of the industry must be considered in choosing a generic strategy, but that they in fact dictate the proper choice.

Commodity/ Specialty Matrix

The commodity/specialty matrix uses two concepts—product differentiation and price sensitivity—to categorize an industry and the customer segments served by that industry. The positioning of a product on the matrix requires a qualitative assessment of the level of product differentiation in the industry and the degree of price sensitivity exercised by consumers.[36]

The degree of product differentiation can be determined by analysis of the product quality, the number of features, the functional use, and the impact of advertising. For example, Rolls-Royces, Calvin Klein jeans, and specialty plastics are all differentiated; sugar, gasoline, and lumber are not. The level of price sensitivity exercised by buyers depends on several factors. If the cost of the product is high relative to that of other purchases, buyers tend to be more price sensitive. If the product does not have a great impact on the buyers' budget, buyers tend to be less price sensitive. Finally, unprofitable businesses tend to be more price sensitive than successful businesses.

To illustrate the point, personal computers, from the perspective of home buyers, are a relatively undifferentiated product; they all perform similar functions and are of similar quality. Because business buyers place greater demands on the machines, they are likely to perceive greater differences between competitors' offerings. The degree of price sensitivity also differs between these two buyer segments. Home buyers are more price sensitive because the purchase accounts for a large part of their total discretionary expenditures; they are more concerned with cost than quality. For business buyers, on the other hand, the product's cost is small relative to total purchases. As a result, this segment is less price sensitive and more feature sensitive because the purchase can have a major impact on their operations.

The commodity/specialty matrix explains the impact of industry evolution on a product (see Exhibit 10-18). When a product is introduced, it tends to be a specialty, unless it is a relatively minor substitute for an existing product. New products are usually expensive. Sales depend upon the goodwill of a limited number of customers who are less price sensitive and care more about the novelty of the product than others. For example, superstrong engineered plastics, a potential replacement for other more expensive raw materials, currently earn high margins for the few firms that manufacture them.

As more firms enter the industry, however, the market becomes more competitive. Buyers begin to understand how the product works and which features are important. As competitors start to make similar products, customers get more choice and are able to exercise their natural price sensitivity. Products that still have differentiated characteristics but sell to price sensitive buyers are termed "transitional." The stock brokerage industry is currently in transition as customers are switching from full-service to discount brokers. Most industries do not remain in the transitional mode. As the industry matures and the growth slows, competitors fight harder to increase sales. Firms that want large market shares are in a race to appeal to the largest segment of customers. Since all firms are receiving the same signals from customers, products start to look alike. This lack of differentiation, in combination with the price sensitivity of buyers, implies a commodity product; it would be difficult to differentiate Exxon's gasoline from the gasoline pumped by Shell Oil.

EXHIBIT 10-18
The Commodity/Specialty Matrix

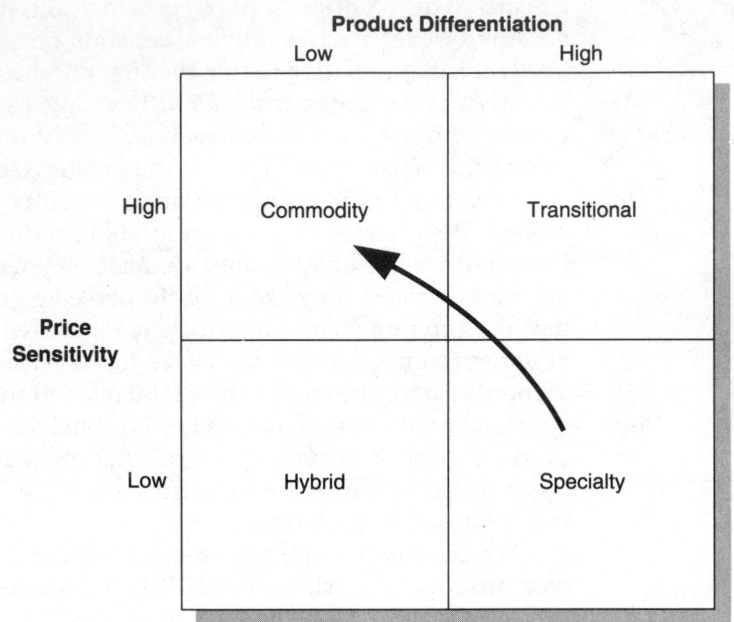

Source: Understanding the Competition: A Practical Guide to Competitive Analysis (Arlington, VA: Michael M. Kaiser Associates, Inc., no date). Reprinted by permission.

Although most products tend to become commodities, as in the auto industry, there are usually segments that retain the characteristics of specialties. Only a few products fall in the "hybrid" category, that is, undifferentiated products that sell to non-price-sensitive buyers. An example is the fine abrasives sold to eyeglass manufacturers. These abrasives usually represent a very small percentage of the manufacturer's purchases. The manufacturer has little reason to exercise price sensitivity and remains loyal to its supplier, regardless of the price.

The commodity/specialty framework implies that there are two basic strategies businesses can employ. A business unit can either attempt to make a product at a lower cost than the competition and sell it at a comparable price, or it can attempt to make a product that meets the needs of a particular customer segment and therefore that earns a higher price than competitors' offerings. These basic strategies can be used to serve either an entire market or a particular segment of the market, but the basic functional requirements do not change.

A firm that chooses to serve commodity markets must be the low-cost producer. The cost-effective firm will price low enough to gain sales and still earn a required return. Higher-cost competitors will have to meet the market price. Specialty manufacturers are less concerned with cost; they must isolate the customer segments they wish to serve and develop a superior product at an appropriate price. Businesses that do not pursue either strategy may "fall in the middle"; by not focusing their efforts on either product development or cost reduction, they may succeed at neither.

The ability to pursue one of these two strategies successfully depends on the environment and the strengths of the business. An examination of the environment in which the business operates determines whether or not there are external constraints placed on the firm's actions or chances of success. The ability of the firm to develop and market a specialty product or to be a low-cost producer depends on its ability to overcome environmental constraints.

To sum up, following the commodity/specialty matrix approach, a business, in the majority of cases, has two strategic options depending on its position on the matrix. In the case of commodity products, the emphasis should be on low cost and large customer segments. Specialty products call for differentiated product focus and small customer segments. The other two matrix positions, hybrid and transitional, are either temporary in nature or only infrequently faced.

Conclusion

Portfolio approaches provide a useful tool for strategists. Granted, these approaches have limitations, but all these limitations can be overcome with a little imagination and foresight. The real concern about the portfolio approach is that its elegant simplicity often tempts managers to believe that it can solve all problems of corporate choices and resource allocation. The truth is that it addresses only half the problem: the back half. The portfolio approach is a powerful tool for helping the strategist select from a menu of available opportunities, but it does not put the menu into his or her hands. That is the front half of the problem. The other critical dimension in making strategic choices is the need to generate a rich array of business options from which to choose. No simple tool is available that can provide this option-generating capability. Here only creative thinking about one's environment, one's business, one's customers, and one's competitors can help.

For a successful introduction of the portfolio framework, the strategist should heed the following advice:

1. Once introduced, move quickly to establish the legitimacy of portfolio analysis.
2. Educate line managers in its relevance and use.
3. Redefine SBUs explicitly because their definition is the "genesis—and nemesis"—of adequately using the portfolio framework.
4. Use the portfolio framework to seek the strategic direction for different businesses without haggling over the fancy labels by which to call them.

5. Make top management acknowledge SBUs as portfolios to be managed.
6. Seek top management time for reviewing different businesses using the portfolio framework.
7. Rely on a flexible, informal management process to differentiate influence patterns at the SBU level.
8. Tie resource allocation to the business plan.
9. Consider strategic expenses and human resources as explicitly as capital investment.
10. Plan explicitly for new business development.
11. Make a clear strategic commitment to a few selected technologies or markets early.[37]

SUMMARY

A diversified organization needs to examine its widely different businesses at the corporate level to see how each business fits within the overall corporate purpose and to come to grips with the resource allocation problem. The portfolio approaches described in this chapter help management determine the role that each business plays in the corporation and allocate resources accordingly.

Three portfolio approaches were introduced: product life cycle, growth rate–relative market share matrix, and multifactor portfolio matrix. The product life cycle approach determines the life status of different products and whether the company has enough viable products to provide desired growth in the future. If the company lacks new products with which to generate growth in coming years, investments may be made in new products. If growth is hurt by the early maturity of promising products, the strategic effort may be directed toward extension of their life cycles.

The second approach, the growth rate–relative market share matrix, suggests locating products or businesses on a matrix with relative market share and growth rate as its dimensions. The four cells in the matrix, whose positions are based on whether growth is high or low and whether relative market share is high or low, are labeled stars, cash cows, question marks, and dogs. The strategy for a product or business in each cell, which is primarily based on the business's cash flow implications, was outlined.

The third approach, the multifactor portfolio matrix, again uses two variables (industry attractiveness and business strengths), but these two variables are based on a variety of factors. Here, again, a desired strategy for a product/business in each cell was recommended. The focus of the multifactor matrix approach is on the return-on-investment implications of strategy alternatives rather than on cash flow, as in the growth rate–relative market share matrix approach.

Various portfolio approaches were critically examined. The criticisms relate mainly to operational definitions of dimensions used, weighting of variables, and product/market boundary determination. The chapter concluded with a discussion of three new portfolio approaches: the Boston Consulting Group's new framework, Porter's generic strategies, and the commodity/specialty matrix.

DISCUSSION QUESTIONS

1. What purpose may a product portfolio serve in the context of marketing strategy?
2. How can the position of a product in its life cycle be located?
3. What is the strategic significance of products in the maturity stage of the product life cycle?
4. What is the meaning of relative market share?
5. What sequence should products follow for success? What may management do to ensure this sequence?
6. What factors may a company consider when measuring industry attractiveness and business strengths? Should these factors vary from one business to another in a company?
7. What is the basic difference between the growth rate–relative market share matrix approach and the multifactor portfolio matrix approach?
8. What major problems with portfolio approaches have critics identified?
9. What generic strategies does Porter recommend? Discuss.

NOTES

[1]Philip Kotler, *Marketing Management*, 7th ed. (Englewood Cliffs, NJ: Prentice-Hall, 1991), 348–70. See also David R. Rink and John E. Swan, "Product Life Cycle Research: A Literature Review," *Journal of Business Research* (September 1979): 219–42.

[2]Gerald J. Tellis and C. Merle Crawford, "An Evolutionary Approach to Product Growth Theory," *Journal of Marketing* (Fall 1981): 125–34.

[3]John E. Swan and David R. Rink, "Fitting Market Strategy to Varying Product Life Cycles," *Business Horizons* (January–February 1982): 72–76; and Yoram J. Wind, *Product Policy: Concepts, Methods, and Strategy* (Reading, MA: Addison-Wesley Publishing Co., 1982).

[4]Kathryn Rudie Harrigan, "The Effect of Exit Barriers upon Strategic Flexibility," *Strategic Management Journal* 1 (1980): 165–76; and Kathryn Rudie Harrigan and Michael E. Porter, "End-Game Strategies for Declining Industries," *Harvard Business Review* (July–August 1983): 111–20.

[5]Kathryn Rudie Harrigan, "Strategies for Declining Industries," *Journal of Business Strategy* (Fall 1980): 27.

[6]How Du Pont Keeps Them Coming Back for More, *Business Week* (20 August 1990): 80.

[7]Robert D. Buzzell, "Competitive Behavior and Product Life Cycles," in *New Ideas for Successful Marketing*, ed. John S. Wright and Jac L. Goldstrucker (Chicago: American Marketing Association, 1966), 47.

[8]Nariman K. Dhalla and Sonia Yuspeh, "Forget the Product Life Cycle Concept," *Harvard Business Review* (January-February 1976): 102–09.

[9]Theodore Levitt, "Exploit the Product Life Cycle," *Harvard Business Review* (November-December 1965): 81.

[10]John E. Smallwood, "The Product Life Cycle: A Key to Strategic Market Planning," *MSU Business Topics* (Winter 1973): 35. See also George S. Day, "The Product Life Cycle: Analysis and Applications Issues," *Journal of Marketing* (Fall 1981): 60–67.

[11]Kotler, *Marketing Management*, 350.

[12]See Mary Lambkin and George S. Day, "Evolutionary Processes in Competitive Markets: Beyond the Product Life Cycle," *Journal of Marketing* (July 1989): 4–20.

[13]Tellis and Crawford, "An Evolutionary Approach."

[14]Stephen G. Harrell and Elmer D. Taylor, "Modeling the Product Life Cycle for Consumer Durables," *Journal of Marketing* (Fall 1981): 68–75.

[15]See Philippe Haspeslagh, "Portfolio Planning: Uses and Limits," *Harvard Business Review* (January-February 1982): 60, 73.

[16]"They're All Juiced Up at Tropicana," *Business Week* (13 May 1991).

[17]See Hiram C. Barksdale and Clyde E. Harris, Jr., "Portfolio Analysis and the Product Life Cycle," *Long Range Planning* (December 1982): 74–83.

[18]Francis J. Aguilar and Richard Hamermesh, "General Electric: Strategic Position: 1981," 25. Harvard Business School Case 9-381-174.

[19]William E. Rothschild, *Putting It All Together* (New York: AMACOM, 1976), 141–62.

[20]*Organizing and Managing the Planning Function* (Fairfield, CT: GE Company, n.d.).

[21]Yoram Wind and Vijay Mahajan, "Designing Product and Business Portfolios," *Harvard Business Review* (January-February 1981): 155–65.

[22]Rajendra K. Srivastava, Robert P. Leone, and Allan D. Shocker, "Market Structure Analysis: Hierarchical Clustering of Products Based on Substitution-in-Use," *Journal of Marketing* (Summer 1981): 38–48.

[23]George Day, "Diagnosing the Product Portfolio," *Journal of Marketing* (April 1977): 29–38.

[24]Robin Wensley, "Strategic Marketing: Betas, Boxes, or Basics," *Journal of Marketing* (Summer 1981): 173–82.

[25]Michael E. Porter, *Competitive Strategy* (New York: The Free Press, 1981).

[26]Fred Gluck, "A Fresh Look at Strategic Management," *Journal of Business Strategy* (Fall 1985): 23.

[27]Yoram Wind, Vijay Mahajan, and Donald J. Swire, "An Empirical Comparison of Standardized Portfolio Models," *Journal of Marketing* (Spring 1983): 89–99.

[28]Day, "Diagnosing the Product Portfolio," 29–38.

[29]D. E. Hussey, "The Brief Case—A Portfolio of Commentary and Opinion," *Long Range Planning* (February 1981): 100–03.

[30]Frederick W. Gluck, "Strategic Choice and Resource Allocation," *McKinsey Quarterly* (Winter 1980): 24.

[31]Donald Hambrick and Ian MacMillan, "The Product Portfolio and Man's Best Friend," *California Management Review* (Fall 1982): 16–23.

[32]*The Boston Consulting Group Annual Perspective* (Boston: Boston Consulting Group, 1981).

[33]Haspeslagh, "Portfolio Planning," 63.

[34]See "Strategy in the 1980s," in *Perspectives* (Boston: Boston Consulting Group, 1981).

[35]Michael Porter, *Competitive Strategy*.

[36]See *Understanding the Competition: A Practical Guide to Competitive Analysis* (Arlington, VA: Michael M. Kaiser Associates, Inc., n.d.).

[37]Haspeslagh, "Portfolio Planning," 70–71.

PART FIVE

Strategy Implementation and Control

CHAPTER 11

Organizational Structure

Whatever action is performed by a great man, common men follow in his footsteps, and whatever standards he sets by exemplary acts, all the world pursues.

BHAGAVAD GITA

A strategic planning system should provide answers to two basic questions: what to do and how to do it. The first question refers to selection of a strategy; the second, to organizational arrangements. An organization must have not only a winning strategy to pursue but also a matching structure to facilitate its implementation. The emphasis in the preceding chapters has been on strategy formulation. This chapter is devoted to building a viable organizational structure to administer the strategy.

As we move further into the 1990s, principles of strategic analysis and planning have been fully integrated into corporate decision making at all levels. Yet, although these precepts now enjoy global acceptance, the need to translate strategic guidelines into long-term results—and adapt them to rapidly changing market conditions—continues to rank among the major challenges confronting today's companies. Essentially, there are three aspects of implementation that, if properly organized, can lead to superior corporate performance and competitive advantage: organization planning, management systems, and executive reward programs.

Fitting these aspects to the underlying strategy requires strategic reorganization. There is no magic formula to ensure successful reorganization and, generally, no "perfect" prototype to follow. Reorganization is a delicate process that above all requires a finely tuned management sense.

The discussion in this chapter focuses on five dimensions: (a) the creation of market-responsive organizations, (b) the role of systems in implementing strategy, (c) executive reward systems, (d) leadership style (i.e., the establishment of an internal environment conducive to strategy implementation), and (e) the measurement of strategic performance (i.e., the development of a network of control and communication to monitor and evaluate progress in achieving strategic goals). In addition, the impact of strategic planning on marketing organization is studied.

THE TRADITIONAL ORGANIZATION

Corporations have traditionally been organized with a strong emphasis on pursuing and achieving established objectives. Such organizations adapt well to growing internal complexities and provide adequate incentive mechanisms and systems of accountability to support objectives. However, they fail to provide a congenial environment for strategic planning. For example, one of the organizational capabilities needed for strategic planning is that of modifying, or redefining, the objectives themselves so that the corporation is prepared to meet future competition. The traditional organizational structure, based on "command and control" principles, resists change, which is why a new type of structure is needed for strategic planning:

> The forces shaping organization today are dramatically different from those facing Frederick Taylor and Alfred Sloan. End-use markets are fragmenting, requiring faster and more targeted responses. Advances in the ability to capture, manipulate, and transmit information electronically make it possible to distribute decision making ("command") without losing "control." Gone is the abundant, primarily male, blue-collar workforce. Workers today are better educated, in short supply, and demanding greater participation and variety in their jobs.
>
> Individually all these changes are dramatic; collectively they shape a new era in organization and strategy. Strategies are increasingly shifting from cost- and volume-based sources of competitive advantage to those focusing on increased value to the customer. Competitive strength is derived from the skills, speed, specificity, and service levels provided to customers. The Command and Control organization is under strain. Indeed, many businesses are finding that C&C principles now result in competitive disadvantage.[1]

Exhibit 11-1 differentiates the characteristics of command and control structure (i.e., traditional organization with emphasis on the achievement of established objectives) and strategic planning. By and large, command and control structure works in known territory and is concerned with immediate issues. Strategic planning stresses unfamiliar perspectives and is oriented toward the future.

CREATING MARKET-RESPONSIVE ORGANIZATIONS

As markets and technologies change more and more rapidly, organizations must respond quickly and frequently to strategic moves if they are to sustain competitive advantage. Although corporations have learned to make changes in strategy quickly, their organizations may lack parallel market responsiveness. One major reason for this failure is the conflict between scale economics, which is geared to the expansion and aggregation of resources, and the economics of vertical integration, which links differentiated functions and resources for maximum efficiency.

The opposing pressures fueling this conflict are both subtle and complex. On one side of the equation are all the forces contributing to the need to reap

EXHIBIT 11-1
Organizational Characteristics

Command and Control Structure	*Strategic Planning*
1. Concerned with goals derived from established objectives.	1. Concerned with the identification and evaluation of new objectives and strategies.
2. Goals usually have been validated through extensive experience.	2. New objectives and strategies can be highly debatable; experience within the organization or in other companies may be minimal.
3. Goals are reduced to specific subgoals for functional units.	3. Objectives usually are evaluated primarily for corporate significance.
4. Managers tend to identify with functions or professions and to be preoccupied with means.	4. Managers need a corporate point of view oriented to the environment.
5. Managers obtain relatively prompt evidence of their performance against goals.	5. Evidence of the merit of new objectives or strategies is often available only after several years.
6. Incentives, formal and social, are tied to operating goals.	6. Incentives are at best only loosely associated with planning.
7. The "rules of the game" become well understood. Experienced individuals feel competent and secure.	7. New fields of endeavor may be considered. Past experience may not provide competence in a "new game."
8. The issues are immediate, concrete, and familiar.	8. Issues are abstract, deferrable (to some extent), and may be unfamiliar.

maximum scale advantage. On the other side of the equation, the accelerated pace of change—environmental, competitive, and technological—drives corporations toward increased flexibility, high levels of internal integration, and smaller operating units.

Although scale advantage has traditionally held high ground, evidence is mounting that highly integrated organizations can increase productive capacity through the efficient coordination of functions and resources while remaining highly adaptive and market sensitive. Such organizations respond to the strategic need for change more quickly, smoothly, and successfully than centralized, large-unit organizations oriented toward scale aggregation.[2]

Management has basically three options for resolving the conflict between scale and integration. First, a company can choose to centralize its functions in order to achieve scale at the expense of market responsiveness. Second, it can opt for market responsiveness over scale; that is, it can emphasize small, independent units. Third, it can adopt another, more difficult approach, exploiting the strengths associated with both large and small organizational units to achieve benefits of scale and market responsiveness simultaneously. The key to sustainable competitive advantage lies in successful pursuit of the third alternative.

Exploiting the benefits of both large and small organizational structures involves creating market-responsive units within a framework of shared resources. Such units can combine the strengths of a small company (lean, entrepreneurial management; sharp focus on the business; immediacy of the relationship with the customer; dedication to growth; and action-oriented viewpoint) with those of the large company (extensive financial information and resources; availability of multiple technologies; recognition as an established business; people with diverse skills to draw on; and an intimate knowledge of markets and functions).

The creation of such units demands that planners determine, as precisely as possible, in what form and to what degree resources must be integrated to ensure the level of market responsiveness dictated by their business strategy. This process can be successful only when it is undertaken in the context of a rigorous analytical framework that links strategy to organization.[3]

A Procedure for Creating a Market-Responsive Organization

To create a market-responsive organization, management can use a three-phase process: (a) determine corporate strategic boundaries, (b) balance the demands of scale and market responsiveness, and (c) organize for strategic effectiveness.

Determine Corporate Strategic Boundaries. How successfully a corporation aligns its structure with its strategic objectives depends on its success in making a number of key decisions: determining the stage of the value-added process at which it will compete, identifying those activities in which it has a competitive edge, selecting the functions it should execute internally, and developing a plan of action for integrating those functions most productively. These decisions determine how resources should be allocated and how external and internal boundaries should be drawn. They define the company's business—its products, services, customers, and markets—and determine both long- and short-term strategic potential. How well the company exploits its assets and the degree to which each division's performance supports strategic objectives determine how close it will come to achieving that potential.[4]

How strategic boundary setting reflects the trade-offs between scale and integration becomes clearer when one considers the case of an assembler facing a typical make-or-buy decision for components. As long as the components manufacturer is able to produce common components for several customers, the assembler among them, it enjoys scale advantage. As the products ordered by the assembler become more specialized in response to market demands or increased competitive pressures, however, the benefits the components manufacturer gains from scale begin to decline. At the same time, the cost of integrating operations with those of the assembler increases as technical specifications become more complex and as manufacturing operations become more interdependent. To continue their relationship and sustain their respective advantages, the components manufacturer and the assembler are required to make additional investments: the components manufacturer in capital equipment outlays and product design; the assembler in negotiating terms, research and development planning, quality control, and related areas. As a result, a substantial "disruption cost" is incurred if the components manufacturer and the assembler decide to end their business relationship. Both parties attempt to guard against this potential loss through longer-term contracts, whether explicit or implicit. As interdependence increases, prices and contract negotiations become cumbersome and unresponsive. At some point, the economies of scale may decline enough and the integration costs climb high enough that the assembler finds it more cost effective to produce components internally—to bring that particular function inside its corporate boundaries.

In this classic make-or-buy example, economic trade-offs between scale and integration costs are direct and relatively clear-cut. As we move from simple make-or-buy decisions to issues of full-scale vertical integration, the economic impact can be far more subtle and far-reaching. Scale advantage is not expressed solely in terms of lower unit manufacturing costs but may also flow from the critical mass of skills gained or from the transferability of new product or process technologies. Valuable integration benefits, on the other hand, may be gained from the willingness to undertake more profitable research and development investments because vertical integration ensures a "market" in downstream operations.

Balance the Demands of Scale and Market Responsiveness. The balancing of scale and market responsiveness demands may be illustrated with reference to a large insurance company. The company faced a complex set of internal and market-based organizational trade-offs in its core business—property and casualty insurance. Lagging market growth, increased price sensitivity, new forms of product distribution, new information technology, and escalating competition were all placing enormous pressures on the company's traditional mode of operation. Top management realized that fundamental changes in organization were needed in both its home office and in its field network if the company was to remain competitive and meet aggressive new growth and profit goals.

In responding to these pressures, the company found itself facing a familiar dilemma. On the one hand, it was vital that its organizational structure become more responsive to local market demand, particularly in terms of regional product pricing and agent deployment. This need pointed to decentralization as the logical method for restructuring operations, with the field divided into smaller sales and marketing regions and more responsibility assigned to local management. On the other hand, however, management was determined to reduce the costs of transaction processing. Meeting this need for administrative streamlining appeared to require that field offices around the country be reorganized into larger regional centers to exploit fully the scale economies offered by improvements in automated processing capacity.

Initially, these strategic requirements seemed to set large centers against locally responsive marketing and sales units. Yet, by carefully analyzing and "rewiring" its structure, the company was able to resolve the apparent conflict cost-effectively and efficiently. Here is the approach it pursued. The company's field operations consisted of essentially self-sufficient regional centers; each center included all functional departments under its umbrella, ranging from sales, claims, and underwriting to operations and personnel. Two of these functions dominated field operations: customer interaction through sales and marketing and transaction processing. Originally the field organization was designed around exploiting administrative scale in the processing function and balancing the need to locate sales and marketing functions to serve the customer base effectively. The underlying basis for the organizational design was the need to coordinate sales and processing functions because of the high volume of transactions and interactions between them. A layer of management between the home office and the regional centers coordinated programs and enforced company policies.

In line with its new strategic objectives (greater market responsiveness and increased productivity), the company instituted major organizational changes. First, the layer of management between the home office and regional centers was eliminated to improve communications and to facilitate more market-responsive decision making. Second, to achieve scale economies and contain costs, the reporting relationships of the processing centers were shifted from the regional level directly to the home office. New information technology allowed the company to "unhook" processing centers from sales functions and still remain adequately integrated. As a result, the number of regions of independent sale organizations was no longer tied to the number of processing centers. The number of processing centers was reduced as information-technology innovations allowed additional processing capacity, whereas the number of marketing and sales regions was increased as market requirements demanded, allowing the entire sales organization to move closer to its local client base. The needs for both market responsiveness and scale economies in processing was fully satisfied.

Organize for Strategic Effectiveness. To organize for strategic effectiveness, it is important to recognize that the ultimate goal of a business organization is competitive advantage, and the drive for competitive advantage must be expressed in economic terms and pursued through the use of economic tools.[5] Only by placing organizational decisions in an economic context can the value of alternative forms of structure, incentive, and management process be determined. It is only in the light of these assessments that the steps needed to strike the proper balance between scale and market responsiveness can be taken. Needless complexity, excessive layers of management, and nonessential integration of channels must all be eliminated. The design phase is easy when compared to the difficulties of execution (i.e., implementing organizational change). It requires strong leadership, consistent signals and actions, and strategically driven incentive programs.

Managing a Market-Responsive Organization

Designing and managing a market-responsive organization requires overturning old assumptions. First, the *linearity* from strategy to structure and on to systems, staff, etc., cannot be reasoned. The process is instead *iterative*: a team is formed to meet a strategic need; it sizes up the situation, develops a specific strategy, and reorganizes itself as necessary. What's more, the structure is temporary. The organization needs to be ready to change its configuration quickly to respond to new needs and circumstances. Second, the organization's purpose is not to control from the top; it is to *empower* a group of people to get a job done. Management occurs through training, incentives, and strongly articulated goals, strategies, and standards.

Market-responsive organizations are found most often in businesses that are driven by product development and customer service—electronics and software companies, for example—and are often smaller, younger organizations where traditional boundaries are weaker. Some large-scale models include parts of Honda and Panasonic, 3M, and also, in some ways, GE, which has developed extraordinary flexibility in recent years in reshaping its organization and pushing authority down to front-line managers.

Market-responsive organizations have obvious drawbacks: they lack tight controls, they are ill-suited to exploit scale or to accomplish massive tasks, and they depend on capable and motivated people at the working level. However, companies that cannot use the full market-responsive model can appropriate aspects of it, new product development teams, for instance.

Some large companies, such as IBM, Digital Equipment, and Dow Chemical, with the need for both innovation and coordination of resources among markets, product lines, and technologies, often use the concept in modified form. They frequently change the focus of resources and control by reshuffling product groups—shifting power among parts of the organization—or by using ad hoc teams.[6]

Experience suggests that people are quite willing and able to change as long as they have a clear understanding of what's expected of them, know why it is important to change, and have latitude in designing the new organization. Five key elements that companies should carefully consider in seeking strategic effectiveness are discussed below:[7]

1. **Forge a clear link between strategy and skills**—A company's strategy, which should embody the value it proposes to deliver to its customers, determines the skills it needs. Many companies, however, are not sufficiently clear or rigorous about this linkage. Because Frank Perdue promises to deliver more tender chickens, his organization has to excel at the breeding and logistics skills necessary to deliver them. Because Volvo promises to deliver more reliable, tougher, and safer station wagons, it must be skilled in designing and manufacturing them. Because Domino's Pizza says it will deliver fresh pizza hot to your door within 30 minutes, each of its 5000 outlets needs to be skilled at making a good pizza quickly and at customer order processing and delivery. Strategy drives skills, but if this linkage is missed, a company may end up doing some things right but not the *right* things right.
2. **Be specific—and selective—about core skills**—Managers often describe the core skills their companies need in terms that are too general. Saying that you need to be first rate at customer service or marketing is not good enough. For example, the employees of a department store committed to being better at customer service will not know what to do differently because the term *customer service* doesn't paint a specific enough picture of the behavior desired of them. In fact, a department store needs to be good in at least three different types of

customer services: with hard goods like refrigerators or furniture, customer service must have a high component of product and technical knowledge; with fine apparel, what counts is expertise in fashion counseling; with basics and sundries, the need is for friendly, efficient self-service. Each of these service goals translates into a different set of day-to-day behaviors expected of employees. Unless these behaviors are precisely defined, even willing employees won't change their behavior very much because they won't know how.

3. **Clarify the implications for pivotal jobs**—Consider the department store again. The definition of different types of customer services drives through to the identification of several specific jobs whose performance determines whether customers think the store is good at customer service: the product salesperson for refrigerators, the fashion counselor for fine apparel, and the cashier for sundries. Pushing the skill definition to these specific jobs, which may be called *pivotal jobs*, allows the company to describe in specific terms what the holders of these jobs should do or not do, which kind of people to hire, which kind of training and coaching to give them, which rewards motivate them, and which kind of information they need. For example, at Nordstrom, the excellent Seattle-based fashion specialty retailer, the pivotal job is the front-line sales associate. Because Nordstrom is clear about the type of person they want for this job—someone interested in a career, not just a summer position—they look more for a service orientation than prior experience. They pay better than the industry average and offer incentives that allow top sales associates to make over $80,000 a year. Nordstrom stresses customer service above all else. The company philosophy is to offer the customer, in this order, "the best service, selection, quality, and value."

   This clarity about priorities helps sales associates determine appropriate service behavior. So does the excellent product and service training they receive. And so does the customer information system that provides them with up-to-date sales and service records on their customers. Nordstrom recognizes that their business success depends on the success of pivotal jobholders in delivering value to customers, and they have geared their entire organization to support these front-line associates.

4. **Provide leadership from the top**—The key ingredients that have been found workable in this task include

   - Appeal to the pride of the organization. Most people want to do a superior job, especially for a company that expresses its mission with an idea bigger than just making money. Providing them with a single noble purpose—be it "quality, service, cleanliness, value" or "innovation"—will unleash energy but keep it focused.
   - Clarify the importance and value of building core skills. Provide the organization with a good economic understanding of the value as well as a clear picture of the consequences of *not* paying attention to core skills.
   - Be willing to do the tough things that break bottlenecks and establish credibility for the belief that "this change is for real." Usually the toughest things involve replacing people who are change blockers, committing key managers to the skill-building effort, and spending money on it.
   - Treat the program to build skills as something special, not as business as usual. Reflect this in the leader's own time allocation, in the questions he or she asks

subordinates, in the special assignments he or she gives people, in the choice of the special measurements he or she looks at, and so on.

- Over communicate to superiors, subordinates, customers, and especially to pivotal jobholders. Talk and write incessantly about the skill-building program—about the skills the company is trying to build and about why they are critical; about early wins, heroes, and lessons learned from failures; about milestones achieved.

5. **Empower the organization to learn**—Organizations, like individuals, learn best by doing. Building new core skills is preeminently a learning process. Sketch out for employees the boundaries of their playing field by defining the strategy, the skills the company is trying to build, the pivotal job behaviors required, and the convictions they must hold about what is right. But within these boundaries, give them a lot of room to run—to try things, succeed, fail—and to learn for themselves exactly what works and what doesn't. They will figure out for themselves details that could never be prescribed from above.

   To illustration the point, take, for example, the 10,000 route salespeople of Frito-Lay. Michael Jordan, the company's president, says that these people with their "store to door service" control the destiny of Frito-Lay. Wayne Calloway, PepsiCo president and past CEO of Frito-Lay, describes this pivotal job as follows: "Our sales people are entrepreneurs of the first order. Over 100,000 times a day they encounter customers who are making buying decisions on the spot. How in the world could an old-fashioned sort of management deal with those kinds of conditions? Our approach is to find good people and to give them as much responsibility as possible because they're closest to the customer, they know what's going on.[8]

ROLE OF SYSTEMS IN IMPLEMENTING STRATEGY

The term *systems* refers to management systems, which include any of the formally organized procedures that pervade a business. Three types of systems may be distinguished: execution systems, monitoring systems, and control systems.

1. **Execution systems** focus directly on the basic processes for conducting the firm's business. They include systems that enable products to be designed, supplies to be ordered, production to be scheduled, goods to be shipped, cash to be applied, and employees to be paid.
2. **Monitoring systems** are any procedures that measure and assess basic processes. They can be designed to gather information in different ways to serve a number of internal or external reporting purposes: to meet SEC or other regulatory requirements, to control budgets, to pay taxes, and to serve the strategic and organizational intent of the company.
3. **Control systems** are the means through which processes are made to conform or are kept within tolerable limits. At the broadest level, they include separation of duties, authority limits, product inspection, and plan submittals.

As can be seen from this brief description, systems pervade the conduct of business. For that very reason, systems provide ample opportunity for strategies to fail. In most companies, the major emphasis is on execution systems. But creating systems that support strategies and organizational intent requires top management to include monitoring and control systems in addition to executing systems in strategic thinking and to focus on systems in strategy implementation. It means, as part of the strategic planning, answering such key questions as What are the critical success factors? How do they translate into operational performance? How should that operational performance be measured and motivated? How should information about financial performance be derived? What business cycles are important? How should systems support them? What is the role of financial controls and measures? Where should control of information reside? How should strategic objectives and organizational performance be monitored and modified? How should internal and external information be linked?[9]

In short, integrating all systems with strategy requires great vision—the ability to see the firm as an organic whole. Unfortunately, too many systems managers lack vision or clout and too many executives lack the understanding or the inclination to make this integration happen.

Techniques for Systems Design

To create systems that support strategic and organizational intent, top management must include systems in strategic thinking and focus on systems in strategy implementation. Once critical success factors have been identified and translated into operational measurements, good systems design techniques are needed to ensure that those factors and measurements are appropriately accommodated by all systems. Following are some guidelines for good systems design:

1. **Design an effective information-capturing procedure**—Data should be captured close to the source, and source documents should be linked. For example, at one company, data processing personnel collected information on raw materials from receiving reports two days after delivery and entered that information into purchasing control and inventory management systems. Two days later, accounting gathered information on the same delivery from invoices, this time entering it into accounting systems. The failure to link source documents led to apparent inventory discrepancies. Purchasing and inventory processes focused on inventory codes and quantities; accounting process dealt with accounting codes and monetary amounts, which were available only at the end of the month.[10]

   These problems required a three-part solution: placing terminals at the receiving dock, where receiving clerks could enter operating information; using internal links to accounting codes; and creating a reconciliation proof on which quantities and amounts were entered as invoices were received.
2. **Manage commonly used data elements for firmwide accessibility and control**—If a multidivisional firm allows each unit to code inventory discretely, stock that is commonly used cannot be traded and rebalanced. Traditionally, auto dealers maintained independent inventory controls. By contrast, Ford Motor Company has worked to keep its inventory records consistent and thus accessible to dealers so that imbalances at one lead to opportunities for another.

3. **Decide which applications are common and which tolerate distributed processing**—Typical considerations here include pinpointing the need to share data, determining the availability of hardware and software offerings that make a distributed approach feasible, and investigating the effect of geographical distance. Once a particular application or function is judged appropriate for a distributed approach, it must be integrated into an information network.
4. **Manage information, not reports**—Often systems are developed with end reports in mind, focusing on output, not content. If needs change or if developers and users misunderstand each other, the results can lead to frustration at best or the inability to modify output at worst. When the development focus is on content, on information that has been strategically identified as critical to success, users can tailor the presentation of output to their purposes. For example, in one company with a well-constructed receivables database, one manager chose to compare cash collections to target amounts, another used days outstanding, a third used turnover ratios.
5. **Examine cost-effectiveness**—Questioning the value of a system and of the work required to support it is healthy. But such questioning must be handled properly. As an example, to escape merely chipping away at existing processes through cost reduction, Procter and Gamble developed its elimination approach, which is based on the key "if" question: If it were not for this [reason], this [cost] would be eliminated.[11]

Designing and maintaining systems that focus on strategic intent and that assess performance in terms of that intent is crucial to the success of a strategy. In fact, a lack of integration between systems and strategy is an important reason why sound strategic and organizational concepts get bogged down in implementation and do not achieve the results their creators intended. Soundly designed and managed systems do not happen casually: they emerge only with top management involvement and with a clear vision of the importance of systems to strategic outcomes.

EXECUTIVE REWARD SYSTEMS

Executive compensation and strategy are mutually dependent and reinforcing. A good reward system should have three characteristics:[12] (a) it should optimize value to all key stakeholders, including both shareholders and management alike (the so-called agency problem); (b) it should properly measure and recapture value; and (c) it should integrate compensation signals with those implicit in strategy and structure. Although these issues are generally addressed from the perspective of plan implementation, they also have an important but rarely noted strategic dimension. And that strategic dimension actually has a make-or-break impact on plan effectiveness.

The Agency Problem

The agency problem refers to the potential conflict of interest between shareholders and their agents, the executives charged with implementing corporate strategy. The executives of a corporation serve as agents of the corporation's shareholders. Yet, though both executives and shareholders are stakeholders in a corporation, their interests do not coincide. In fact, they naturally diverge on three counts: risk position (e.g., shareholders stand last in line among claimants to the resources of the corporation, whereas executives have the right to payment of salaries and benefits before the claims of shareholders are met); ability to redeploy (e.g., shareholders can freely redeploy their investments; the executives' human capital invested in the course of a career may not be easily redeployable at full value); time horizon (e.g., shareholders embrace long time horizons to earn competitive returns; time horizons of executives are usually shorter). These differences lead to differences in the ways each group measures the risks and rewards of any corporate action. In general, the differences in risk evaluation make a company's executives more averse to risk than are its shareholders.

Resolving the agency problem requires bridging the gap between the inherently divergent interests of shareholders and the executives entrusted with the responsibility of safeguarding and increasing shareholder investments. Though executive compensation plans can and should help resolve this problem, they often compound it. Most incentive plans, for example, are based on improvements in short-term earnings; therefore, they actually inhibit the very risk decisions required to provide highly competitive returns to shareholders.

New and creative ways of compensating executives must be developed to synchronize their interests with those of shareholders. One suggested scheme, an "exploding options" scheme, constantly induces executives to assume risk, irrespective of changes in stock price. This scheme simultaneously grants executives several layers of options at successively higher exercise prices, with the lowest price being the current market price. If the stock price rises to the next highest exercise price, the plan immediately cashes out the lowest-level options and introduce a new option layer at an exercise price one level above the previous exercise price (but always at or above the current market price). Consequently, achieving an option exercise price would always be a realistic goal for an executive.[13] This is an example of the kind of creative thinking required to solve compensation problems.

The Value Problem

From the company's viewpoint, the value issue is twofold. One aspect revolves around the need to reward executive performance in a way that is systematically related to the market value of the corporation. The other is the need to create incentive plans for managers of individual business units.

To determine executive value, most companies use one of two approaches: the earnings-per-share (EPS) model or the cash-flow model. The EPS model assumes that a company can directly control its stock price by careful management of earnings-per-share and price-earnings ratios. The cash-flow model postulates that expected cash flows to an asset determine its present worth.[14] Unfortunately, both approaches have shortcomings that render them inappropriate for developing adequate compensation plans. As an alternative, the market-to-book model is recommended. This model is based on three variables. The first variable is the ratio of stock market price to the per-share book value of the corporation (market-to-book, or M/B). This ratio indicates the value of the firm for each dollar of shareholder investment. The second variable is expected return on equity (ROE). The third variable is expected growth in the corporation's returns as measured by analysts' projections. In reality an adjustment factor is employed to account for corporations whose market-to-book ratios are high or low (given their ROE) because the market anticipates growth or shrinkage in investment opportunities.

The application of the market-to-book model, however, is limited to the determination of compensation for the CEO and a few other top executives with overall corporate responsibilities. In this book, however, our major concern is with creating incentive plans for managers of individual business units. Compensation planning for individual business units is illustrated with reference to a hypothetical company, Hellenic Corporation.[15]

Hellenic Corporation consists of four businesses: Alpha, Beta, Gamma, and Delta. Alpha operates in a promising market but needs to increase market share rapidly. Beta is an efficient, well-run business that already has the largest share of a mature market. Gamma, once a top performer, has suffered recently from serious management mistakes; nevertheless, it has the potential to be a winner again. Delta is a mediocre performer in a mediocre market; moreover, its business is largely unrelated to the other businesses of the corporation.

Hellenic's strategic plan calls for Alpha to grow rapidly, for Beta to capitalize on its well-established position, for Gamma to turn itself around, and for Delta to be divested. This plan maximizes the value of the corporation as a whole. Each division is vital to the corporation's success; however, the management objectives of the chiefs at Alpha, Beta, Gamma, and Delta differ from one another and influence the market value of the firm in distinct ways. This conflict, however, does not mean that shareholder value is an impractical standard for determining executive reward. Even when a manager's performance is related only indirectly to shareholder value, increasing shareholder value need not be abandoned as the aim of executive compensation planning. The challenge is to craft a plan that links performance to value in a way that is consistent with the corporation's long-term strategy. To do this requires tailoring a specific compensation package for the manager of each business unit. The determinants of compensation at Alpha must be different from those at Beta, which again must be different from those at Gamma and at Delta.

This overall plan can be created by analyzing how risk and time horizons in executive pay plans suit the strategic objectives of each business unit. For example, the top manager at Alpha is engaged in a very long-term project. Exceptional growth and profitability are planned, and the risks incurred in executing the plan are considerable. These circumstances call for a pay package geared to the entrepreneurial challenges facing Alpha. Accordingly, the time horizon is very long and the risk posture is high. At Beta, where the prime objective is to maximize returns from a well-established market position, the time horizon and risk posture are moderate. At Gamma, the turnaround candidate, the time horizon is short and the risk posture is very high. At Delta, being managed for window dressing, the time horizon is short and the risk posture is low. In addition, other special sell-off compensation arrangements (e.g., a percentage of the sale price) may be needed.

The Signaling Problem

A signal is simply an inducement to action. Because pay is clearly a powerful inducement to action, compensation systems are powerful signaling devices. Other signaling devices include financial controls, the planning process, and the top management succession plan. All these factors convey messages about what a corporation expects and what it values. Collectively, these signals shape the corporation's culture and determine the actions it takes in given situations.

When management sends consistent signals through all channels, it adheres to a clear strategic track. Unfortunately, conflicting internal signals are common, and compensation is frequently the area of greatest dissonance. Companies must tackle the signaling problem directly. Winners should be paid like winners, and poor performers must not be rewarded. Briefly, executive compensation plans require more risk taking based on real value.

Incentive plans should be designed to induce risk taking. They should make executives think like owners. That is, the plan must bring the interests of executives in line with the interests of shareholders.[16] By resolving the problems of agency and value, by ensuring that high levels of risk taking reap commensurate rewards, and by eliminating conflicting signals, companies can put in place the kinds of incentives required to create exceptional value for owners and agents alike.

LEADERSHIP STYLE

However strategic plans are arrived at, only one person, the CEO, can ensure that energies and efforts throughout the organization are orchestrated to attain desired objectives. What the Chinese general and philosopher Sun-tzu said in 514 B.C. is still true today: "Weak leadership can wreck the soundest strategy; forceful execution of even a poor plan can often bring victory." This section examines the key role of the CEO in shaping the organization for strategy implementation. Also discussed is the role of the strategic planner, whose activities also have a major impact on the organization and its attitude toward strategic change.

Role of the CEO

The CEO of a company is the chief strategist. He or she communicates the importance of strategic planning to the organization. Personal commitment on the part of the CEO to the significance of planning must not only be highly visible it must also be consistent with all other decisions that the CEO makes to influence the work of the organization. To be accepted within the organization, the strategic planning process needs the CEO's support. People accustomed to a short-term orientation may resist the strategic planning process, which requires different methods. But the CEO can set an example for them by adhering to the planning process. Essentially, the CEO is responsible for creating a corporate climate conducive to strategic planning. The CEO can also set a future perspective for the organization. One CEO remarked:

> My people cannot plan or work beyond the distance of my own vision. If I focus on next year, I'll force them to become preoccupied with next year. If I can try to look five to ten years ahead, at least I'll make it possible for the rest of the organization to raise their eyes off the ground immediately in front of them.[17]

The CEO should focus attention on the corporate purpose and approve strategic decisions accordingly. To perform these tasks well, the CEO should support the staff work and analysis upon which his or her decisions are based. Along the same lines, the CEO should ensure the establishment of a noise-free communications network in the organization. Communications should flow downward from the CEO with respect to organizational goals and aspirations and the values of top management. Similarly, information about risks, results, plans, concepts, capabilities, competition, and the environment should flow upward. The CEO should avoid seeking false uniformity, trying to eliminate risk, trusting tradition, dominating discussion, and delegating strategy development.[18] A CEO who does these things could inadvertently discourage strategy implementation.

Concern for the future may require a change in organizational perspectives, as discussed above. The CEO should not only perceive the need for a change but should also be instrumental in making it happen.[19] Change is not easy, however, because past success provides a strong motive for preserving the status quo. As long as the environment and competitive behavior do not change, past perspectives are fine. However, as the environment shifts, changes in policies and attitudes become essential. The CEO must rise to the occasion and not only initiate change but encourage others to accept it and adapt to it. The timing of a change may be more important than the change itself. The need for change must be realized before the optimum time for it has passed so that competitive advantage and flexibility are not lost.[20]

Zaleznink makes a distinction between the CEO who is a manager and the CEO who is a leader. Managers keep things running smoothly; leaders provide longer-term direction and thrust.[21] Successful strategic planning requires that the CEO be a good leader. In this capacity the CEO should

1. Gain complete and willing acceptance of his or her leadership.
2. Determine those business goals, objectives, and standards of behavior that are as ambitious as the potential abilities of the organization will permit.
3. Introduce these objectives and motivate the organization to accept them as their own. The rate of introduction should be the maximum that is consistent with continued acceptance of the CEO's leadership. Because of this need for acceptance, the new manager must always go slowly, except in emergencies. In emergencies the boss must not go slowly if he or she is to maintain leadership.
4. Change the organizational relationships internally as necessary to facilitate both the acceptance and attainment of the new objectives.[22]

A coordinated program of change in pursuit of a sound and relevant strategy under the active direction of the chief executive and the chief planner can lead to significant progress. Although this may only begin a long-term program, it should yield benefits far beyond the time and effort invested. Although pace and effectiveness of strategic change cannot be judged in quantitative terms, there are useful criteria by which they may be assessed.[23] Some of the more important hallmarks of progress are listed here:

- Strategies are principally developed by line managers, with direct, constructive support by the staff.
- Real strategic alternatives are openly discussed at all levels within the corporation.
- Corporate priorities are relatively clear to senior management, but they permit flexible response to new opportunities and threats.
- Corporate resources are allocated based on these priorities and in view of future potential as well as historical performance.
- The strategic roles of business units are clearly differentiated as are the performance measures applied to their managers.
- Realistic responses to likely future events are worked out well in advance.
- The corporate staff adds real value to the consideration of strategic issues and receives cooperation from most divisions.[24]

Role of the Strategic Planner

A strategic planner is a staff person who helps line executives in their planning efforts. Thus, there may be a corporate strategic planner working closely with the CEO. A strategic planner may also be attached to an SBU. This section examines the role of a strategic planner at the SBU level.

The planner conceptualizes the planning process and helps translate it for line executives who actually do the planning. As part of this function, the planner works out a planning schedule and may develop a planning manual. He or she may also design a variety of forms, charts, and tables that may be used to collect, analyze, and communicate planning-oriented information. The planner may also serve as a trainer in orienting line managers to strategic planning.

The planner generates innovative ways of performing difficult tasks and educates line managers in new techniques and tools needed for an efficient job of strategic planning. The planner also coordinates the efforts of other specialists (i.e., marketing researchers, systems persons, econometricians, environmental monitors, and management scientists) with those of line management. In this role the planner exposes managers to the newest and most sophisticated concepts and techniques in planning.

The planner serves as an adviser to the head of the SBU. In matters of concern, the SBU head may ask the planner to undertake a study. For example, the SBU head may seek the advice of the SBU strategic planner in deciding whether private branding should be accepted so as to increase market share or whether it should be rejected for eroding the quality image of the brand.

Another key role the planner plays is that of evaluator of strategic plans. For example, strategic plans relative to various products/markets are submitted to the SBU head. The latter may ask the planner to develop an evaluation system for products/markets. In addition, the planner may also be asked to express an opinion on strategic issues.

The planner may be involved in integrating different plans. For example, the planner may integrate different product/market plans into an SBU strategic plan. Similarly, an SBU's plans may be integrated by the corporate strategic planner from the perspectives of the entire corporation. For example, if a company uses the growth rate–relative market share matrix (see Exhibit 10-4) to judge plans submitted by different businesses, the planner may be asked not only to establish the position of these businesses on the matrix but also to furnish a recommendation on such matters as which of two question marks (businesses in the high-growth-rate, low-market-share quadrant of the matrix) should be selected for additional funding. The planner's recommendation on such strategic issues helps crystallize executive thinking.

Matter of a nonroutine nature may be assigned to the planner for study and recommendation. For example, the planner may head a committee to recommend structural changes in the organization.

Obviously the job of strategic planner is not an easy one. The strategic planner must

1. Be well versed in theoretical frameworks relevant to planning and, at the same time, realize their limitations as far as practical applications are concerned.
2. Be capable of making a point with conviction and firmness and, at the same time, be a practical politician who can avoid creating conflict in the organization.
3. Maintain a working alliance with other units in the organization.
4. Command the respect of other executives and managers.
5. Be a salesperson who can help managers accept new and difficult tools and techniques.

In short, a planner needs to be a jack-of-all-trades.

MEASURING STRATEGIC PERFORMANCE

Tracking strategy, or evaluating progress toward established objectives, is an important task in strategy implementation. There are three basic considerations in putting together a performance measurement system: (a) selecting performance measures, (b) setting performance standards, and (c) designing reports. A strategic performance measurement system requires reporting not by profit center or cost center but by SBU. It may require allocation or restatement of financial results based on the new type of reporting center. Most management reporting is geared to SEC and FASB requirements and focuses on the bottom line. For many business units, however, profit is not the pertinent measure of a unit's strategic performance.

In selecting performance measures, only those measures that are relevant to the strategies adopted by each SBU should be chosen. Further, when setting performance standards, the targets, or expected values, should be established so that they are consistent with both the strategic position of business units and the strategies selected. Finally, reports should focus management attention on key performance measures. Exhibit 11-2 summarizes significant issues in measuring strategic performance.

ACHIEVING STRATEGIC PLANNING EFFECTIVENESS

As mentioned above, most companies have made significant progress in the last 10 to 15 years in improving their strategic planning capabilities. Clear, concise methods have been developed for analyzing and evaluating market segments,

EXHIBIT 11-2
Strategic Performance Measurements

1. To be effective, strategic performance measures must be tailored to the particular strategy of each individual business unit. While there is a basket of generic strategic measurement tools, selection and application is highly dependent on detailed understanding of the particular business strategy and situation.
2. Strategic performance measurements have two dimensions:
   - **Monitoring key program implementation** to ensure that the necessary elements of strategy are being provided.
   - **Monitoring results** to ensure that the programs are having the desired effects.
3. Strategy performance necessarily involves trade-offs—costs and benefits. Both must be recognized in any useful strategic performance measurement system:
   - **Objectives** assessing progress toward primary goals.
   - **Constraints** monitoring other dimensions of performance which may be sacrificed, to some degree and for some period, in order to achieve strategic objectives.
4. Strategic performance measurements do not replace, but rather supplement, short-term financial measurements. They do provide management with a view of long-term progress in contrast to short-term performance. They may indicate that fundamental objectives are being met in spite of short-term problems, and that strategic programs should be sustained despite adversity. They may also show that fundamentals are *not* being met although short-term performance is satisfactory, and, therefore, strategy needs to be changed.
5. Strategic-performance measurement is linked to competitive analysis. Performance measurements should be stated in competitive terms (share, relative profitability, relative growth). While quantitative goals must be established, evaluating performance against them should include an assessment of what competition has been able to attain.
6. Strategic-performance measurement is linked to environmental monitoring. Reasonable goals cannot always be met by dint of effort if the external world turns against us. Strategic-performance measurement systems must attempt to filter uncontrollable from controllable performance, and provide signals when the measures themselves may be the problem, rather than performance against them.

Source: Rochelle O'Connor, *Tracking the Strategic Plan* (New York: The Conference Board, Inc., 1983), p. 11. Reprinted by permission of the publisher.

business performance, and pricing and cost structures. Creative, even elegant, methods have been devised for displaying the results of these strategic analyses to top management.

Few today would argue the value—in theory at least—of the strategic approach to business planning. RJR Nabisco's CEO, Lou Gerstner, describes that value in the following words: "It is my absolute conviction that you can outmanage your competition by having brilliant strategies."[25] Unfortunately, RJR Nabisco's successful experience appears to be more the exception than the rule. Much more typical are reports of dissatisfaction with the results of strategic planning.

Why the achievement gap between strategic planning and strategic performance? Reasons undoubtedly will vary from corporation to corporation, but certain ones appear to be critical. First, many companies have found that top-down strategic planning produces resistance on the part of operating managers. Second, strategic planning efforts have failed to encourage innovative ideas, techniques, and products and to create an innovative business strategy to implement them.[26] Third, even in companies known for excellence in strategic planning, lack of adequate emphasis on marketing has led to poor implementation of strategic plans.

Strategy Implementation and Management Behavior

Strategic planning as currently practiced has produced resistance on the part of operating managers. One observer has identified three types of resistance: measurement myopia (i.e., managers behave in ways that show good short-term performance), measurement invalidation (i.e., managers supply top management with distorted or selected biased data), and measurement justification (i.e., managers justify their behavior excessively and become excessively cautious about specific factors identified as critical cash flow or ROI determinants).[27]

To solve this resistance problem, it is important to remember that, although sophisticated management tools and the up-to-the-minute techniques of business schools may help identify a desirable strategic course, implementation of a strategy requires time-honored simple and straightforward approaches. As a matter of fact, the latter are still vital prerequisites for success. The following are the eight basic attributes common to the management of companies generally regarded as successful:[28]

1. **A bias toward action**—Avoid analyzing and questioning products to death and avoid complicated procedures for developing new ideas; rather, perpetuate a do-it, fix-it, try-it attitude.
2. **Simple form and lean staff**—Keep staffs small to avoid bureaucracies.
3. **Continued contact with customers**—Maintain constant contact with the customer to seek insights that direct the company; in other words, view the customer as an integral element of the business.
4. **Productivity improvement via people**—Motivate and stimulate employees by giving them autonomy and use effective means to reward them.
5. **Operational autonomy to encourage entrepreneurship**—Authorize and encourage managers to act like entrepreneurs.

6. **Stress on one key business value**—Identify and pursue a key value with religious zeal. An example is IBM's emphasis on solving the problems of individual customers.
7. **Emphasis on doing what they know best**—Define and build on strengths, such as product innovation or low-cost manufacturing.
8. **Simultaneous loose-tight controls**—Control a few variables tightly but allow flexibility and looseness in others.

These above attributes should help to put excellence into management. As Peters has observed:

> By sticking to these eight basics, successful companies have achieved better-than-average growth. Their managements are able not only to change but to change quickly. They keep their sights aimed externally at their customers and competitors and not at their own financial reports.
>
> Excellence in management takes brute perseverance—time, repetition and simplicity. The tools include plant visits, internal memos and focused systems. Ignoring these rules may mean that the company slowly loses its vitality, its growth flattens and its competitiveness is lost.[29]

Effective Innovative Planning

Effective strategic planning should eliminate organizational restraints, not multiply them; it should contribute to innovation, not inhibit it. In the coming years, strategic planners face a unique challenge because innovation and new product development must be stimulated within the structure of large, multinational corporate enterprises. A number of companies have proved that innovation and entrepreneurial drive can be institutionalized and fostered by a responsive organizational structure. Celanese and IBM, for example, have established technology review boards to ensure that promising product ideas and new technologies receive adequate start-up support. Adopting another approach, Dow Chemical has instituted an "innovation department" to streamline technology commercialization.

To encourage perpetuation of new ideas and innovation, management should:[30]

1. Focus attention on the goals of strategic planning rather than on process; that is, concentrate on substance, not form.
2. Integrate into its business strategy the analysis of emerging technologies and technology management, consumer trends and demographic shifts, regulatory impact and global economics.
3. Design totally new planning processes and review standards and acceptance criteria for technological advances and new business "thrusts" that may not conform completely to the current corporate base.
4. Adopt a longer planning horizon to ensure that a promising business or technological development will not be cut off prematurely.
5. Ensure that overly stringent financial requirements aren't imposed during the start-up phase of a promising project.
6. Create special organizational "satellites," such as new venture groups, whose mission is to pursue new ideas free from the pressures of day-to-day operations.

7. Institute financial and career reward systems that encourage bold, innovative development programs.

STRATEGIC PLANNING AND MARKETING ORGANIZATION

Strategic planning deals with the relationship of the organization to its environment and thus relates to all areas of a business. Among all these areas, however, marketing is the most susceptible to outside influences. Thus, marketing concerns are pivotal to strategic planning. Initially, however, the role of marketing in the organization declined with the advent of strategic planning. As Kotler noted in 1978:

> Strategic planning threatens to demote marketing from a strategic to an operational function. Instead of marketing being in the driver's seat, strategic planning has moved into the driver's seat. Marketing has moved into the passenger seat and in some companies into the back seat.[31]

It has generally been believed that the only marketing decision that has strategic content is the one concerned with product/market perspectives. As far as other marketing decisions are concerned, they are mainly operational in nature; that is, they deal with short-term performance, although they may occasionally have strategic marketing significance. Product/market decisions, however, being the most far-reaching in nature as far as strategy is concerned, are frequently made by top management; the marketing organization is relegated to making operating decisions. In brief, the inroads of strategic planning have tended to lower marketing's status in the organization.

Empirical evidence on the role of marketing vis-à-vis strategic planning is provided by Rich. In his 1979 study of 20 forest products companies, he found that not one had a marketing executive with the title of vice president at the corporate level. According to Rich, this was not true in the 1960s, when in every company except one a vice president of marketing reported directly to the president.[32] A recent Conference Board survey on the subject supports Rich's findings:

> Seventy percent of the multibusiness manufacturing companies surveyed do not have a senior executive at the corporate level who is generally regarded as being the chief marketing executive. The other 30 percent of these companies have a corporate chief marketing executive. This is, without question, a substantially lower proportion than in former times.[33]

Many marketers have opined that marketing should continue to be important but mainly for day-to-day operations. For example, Kotler predicted that

1. The marketer's job would be harder than ever in the 1980s because of the tough environment.
2. The strategic planner would provide the directive force to the company's growth, not the marketer.

3. The marketer would be relied on to contribute a great deal of data and appraisal of corporate purposes, objectives and goals, growth decisions, and portfolio decisions.
4. The marketer would assume more of an operational and less of a strategic role in the company.
5. The marketer would still have to champion the customer concept because companies tend to forget it.[34]

Experience has shown, however, that marketing definitely has an important strategic role to play. How neglect of marketing can affect strategy implementation and performance can be illustrated by Atari's problems. This company had been a pioneer in developing video games. Because of negligence in marketing, however, Atari failed to realize how quickly the market for video games would mature. Atari based earnings projections on the assumption that demand would grow at the same rate as in the past and that the company would hold its share of the market. But its assumption proved to be wrong. The market for video games grew at a much lower rate than anticipated.

Continuous close contact with the marketplace is an important prerequisite to excellent performance that no firm can ignore:

> Stay close to the customer. No company, high tech or low, can afford to ignore it. Successful companies always ask what the customer needs. Even if they have strong technology, they do their marketing homework.[35]

More businesses today than during the establishment years of strategic planning are making organizational arrangements to bring in marketing perspectives—an understandable development because, with the emergence of strategic planning (particularly in organizations that have adopted the SBU concept), marketing has become a more pervasive function. Thus, although marketing positions at the corporate level may have vanished, the marketing function still plays a key strategic role at the SBU level.[36]

Businesses, by and large, have recognized that an important link is missing in their strategic planning processes: inadequate attention to marketing. Without properly relating the strategic planning effort to marketing, the whole process tends to become static. Business exists in a dynamic setting. It is only through marketing inputs that perspectives of changing social, economic, political, and technological environments can be brought into the strategic planning process.

Overall, marketing is once again assuming prominence. Businesses are finding that marketing is not just an operations function relevant to day-to-day decision making. It has strategic content as well.

As has been mentioned before, strategic planning emerged largely as an outgrowth of the budgeting and financial planning process, which demoted marketing to a secondary role. However, things are different now. In some companies, of course, concern with broad strategy considerations has long forced routine, high-level attention to issues closely related to markets and marketing.

There is abundant evidence, however, of renewed emphasis on such issues on the part of senior management—and hence of staff planners—in a growing number of other companies as well. Moreover, both marketers and planners are drawing increasingly from the same growing body of analytical techniques for futurist studies, market forecasts, competitive appraisals, and the like. Such overlapping in orientation, resources, and methods no doubt helps to reinstate the crucial importance of marketing in the strategic planning effort.

Accumulating forces have caused most firms to reassess their marketing perspectives at both the corporate and the SBU level. Although initially marketing got lost in the midst of the emphasis on strategic planning, now the role of marketing is better understood and is reemerging in the form of strategic marketing.[37] The 1990s will indeed be considered as a period of marketing renaissance.

SUMMARY

The chapter examined five dimensions of strategy implementation and control: creation of a market-responsive organization, the role of systems in implementing strategy, executive reward systems, leadership style, and measurement of strategic performance. It is not enough for an organization to develop a sound strategy. It must, at the same time, structure the organization in a manner that ensures the implementation of the strategy. This chapter examined how to accomplish this task, that is, to match organizational structure to strategy.

Inasmuch as strategic planning is a recent activity in most corporations, no basic principles have been developed on the subject. As a matter of fact, little academic research has been reported in this area. However, it is clear that one fundamental aspect that deeply impacts strategy implementation is the proper linking of organization, systems, and compensation. This chapter examined how to ensure maximum market responsiveness, how to fully exploit management systems as a strategic tool, and how to tie the reward system to the strategic mission.

Strategy implementation requires establishing an appropriate climate in the organization. The CEO plays a key role in adapting the organization for strategic planning. Also examined was the role of the strategic planner in the context of strategic planning and its implementation.

Many companies have not been satisfied with their strategic planning experiences. Three reasons were given for the gap between strategic planning and strategic performance: (a) resistance on the part of operating managers, (b) lack of emphasis on innovations, and (c) neglect of marketing. Suggestions were made for eliminating dysfunctional behavior among managers and for improving innovation planning.

As far as the strategic role of marketing is concerned, with the advent of strategic planning, marketing appears to have lost ground. Lately, however, marketing is reemerging as an important force in strategy formulation and implementation.

DISCUSSION QUESTIONS

1. What is the meaning of scale integration in the context of creating a market-responsive organization?
2. Discuss the three broad principles of establishing a market-responsive organization.
3. Define the term *systems*. Discuss the three categories of systems examined in this chapter.
4. Discuss the three problems that affect the establishment of a sound executive reward system.
5. What is the significance of the office of the CEO in strategic planning?
6. How does the role of a strategic planner at the corporate level differ from the role of a planner within the SBU?

NOTES

[1]Steven F. Dichter, "The Organization of the '90s," *McKinsey Quarterly* (1 November 1991): 146–47.

[2]Annabel Beerel, "Strategic Financial Control Can Provide Light and Guidance," *Accountancy* (June 1986): 70–74.

[3]Alex Taylor III, "Kodak Scrambles to Refocus," *Fortune* (3 March 1986): 34. Also see Andrell E. Pearson, "Tough-Minded Ways to Get Innovative," *Harvard Business Review* (May–June 1988): 99–106.

[4]H. Igor Ansoff, "Competitive Strategy: Analysis on the Personal Computer," *Journal of Business Strategy* (Winter 1986): 28–36.

[5]John D. C. Roach, "From Strategic Planning to Strategic Management: Closing the Achievement Gap," *Strategic Management* (1981): 5–12.

[6]Robert H. Waterman, Jr., *The Renewal Factor: How the Best Get and Keep the Competitive Edge* (New York: Bantam Books, 1987).

[7]This section draws heavily on Robert A. Irwin and Edward G. Michaels III, "Core Skills: Doing the Right Things Right," *McKinsey Quarterly* (Summer 1989): 4–19.

[8]Ron Zemke and Dick Schaaf, *The Service Edge* (New York: New American Library, 1989), 342.

[9]Ian C. MacMillan and Patricia E. Jones, "Designing Organizations to Compete," *Journal of Business Strategy* (Spring 1984): 11–26.

[10]Raymond G. Ernst, "How to Streamline Operations," *Journal of Business Strategy* (Fall 1987): 32–36.

[11]"The New Breed of Strategic Planner," *Business Week* (17 September 1984): 62.

[12]Paul F. Anderson, "Integrating Strategy and Executive Rewards: Solving the Agency, Value and Signaling Problems" (Speech delivered at the Strategic Financial Planning Seminar at Northwestern University, Evanston, IL, March 1985).

[13]Paul F. Anderson, "Rewarding the Corporate Entrepreneur," (Address to the First Annual Fall Conference, Human Resources Management Association of Chicago, October 1985).

[14]See Paul J. Stonich, "Using Rewards in Implementing Strategy," *Strategic Management Journal* 2 (1981): 345–52.

[15]Louis J. Brindisi, Jr., "Paying for Strategic Performance: A New Executive Compensation Imperative," *Strategic Management* (1981): 31–39. See also Joel A. Bleeke, "Peak Strategies," *McKinsey Quarterly* (Spring 1989): 19–27.

[16]"Wanted: A Manager to Fit Each Strategy," *Business Week* (25 February 1980): 166.

[17]Frederick G. Hilmer, "Real Jobs for Real Managers," *McKinsey Quarterly* (Summer 1989): 24.

[18]Thomas A. Stewart, "New Ways to Exercise Power," *Fortune* (6 November 1989): 52.

[19]Robert Howard, "Values Make the Company: An Interview with Robert Haas," *Harvard Business Review* (September–October 1990): 132–44.

[20]Stratford P. Sherman, "The Mind of Jack Welch," *Fortune* (27 March 1991): 39.

[21]See Abraham Zaleznink, "Managers and Leaders: Are They Different?" *Harvard Business Review* (May–June 1977): 67–68.

[22]Bruce D. Henderson, *Henderson on Corporate Strategy* (Cambridge, MA: Abt Associates, 1979), 54. See also Thomas J. Peters, "A Style for All Seasons," *Best of Business* (Spring 1981): 23–27.

[23]Thomas A. Stewart, "CEOs See Clout Shifting," *Fortune* (6 November 1989): 66.

[24]Robert D. Paulson, "Making It Happen: The Real Strategic Challenge," *McKinsey Quarterly* (Winter 1982): 65.

[25]Irwin and Michaels, "Core Skills," 5.

[26]Ronald Henkoff, "How to Plan for 1995," *Fortune* (31 December 1990): 70.

[27]Thomas V. Bonoma and Victoria L. Crittenden, "Managing Marketing Implementation," *Sloan Management Review* (Winter 1988): 7–14.

[28]Thomas J. Peters, "Putting Excellence into Management," *Business Week* (21 July 1980): 196. See also Walter Kiechel III, "Corporate Strategists under Fire," *Fortune* (27 December 1982): 34.

[29]Peters, "Putting Excellence into Management," 205.

[30]See Ray Stata, "Organizational Learning—The Key to Management Innovation," *Sloan Management Review* (Spring 1989): 63–74.

[31]Philip Kotler, "The Future Marketing Manager," in *Marketing Expansion in a Shrinking World: 1978 Business Proceedings*, ed. Betsy D. Gelb (Chicago: American Marketing Association, 1978), 3.

[32]Stuart U. Rich, "Organization Structure and the Marketing Function in Forest Products Companies" (Paper presented at the AMA Western Marketing Educator's Conference, San Jose, CA, 20 April 1979).

[33]David S. Hopkins and Earl L. Bailey, *Organizing Corporate Marketing* (New York: Conference Board, Inc., 1984), 5.

[34]Kotler, "The Future Marketing Manager," 5.

[35]Susan Fraker, "High-Speed Management for the High-Tech Age," *Fortune* (5 March 1984): 62.

[36]See Stewart, "New Ways to Exercise Power," 52.

[37]Ravi S. Achrol, "Evolution of the Marketing Organization: New Forms for Turbulent Environments," *Journal of Marketing* (October 1991): 77–93.

CHAPTER 12
Strategic Tools

The Red Queen said:
"Now, here, it takes all the running you can do to keep in the same place. If you want to get somewhere else, you must run at least twice as fast as that."
LEWIS CARROLL
ALICE IN WONDERLAND

Strategy development is by no means an easy job. Not only must decision makers review a variety of inside factors, they must also incorporate the impact of environmental changes in order to design viable strategies. Strategists have become increasingly aware that the old way of "muddling through" is not adequate when confronted by the complexities involved in designing a future for a corporation.

Economic uncertainty, leveling off of productivity, international competition, and environmental problems pose new challenges with which corporations have to cope when planning their strategies. There is, therefore, a need for systematic procedures for formulating strategy. This chapter discusses selected tools and models that serve as aids in strategy development.

A **model** may be defined as an instrument that serves as an aid in searching, screening, analyzing, selecting, and implementing a course of action. Because marketing strategy interfaces with and affects the perspectives of an entire corporation, the tools and models of the entire science of management can be considered relevant here. In this chapter, however, we deal with seven models that exhibit direct application to marketing strategies: the experience curve concept, the PIMS model, value-based planning, the delphi technique, trend-impact analysis, cross-impact analysis, and scenario building.

EXPERIENCE CURVE CONCEPT

Experience shows that practice makes perfect. It is common knowledge that beginners are slow and clumsy and that with practice they generally improve to the point where they reach their own permanent level of skill. Anyone with business experience knows that the initial period of a new venture or expansion into a new area is frequently not immediately profitable. Many factors, such as making a product name known to potential customers, are often cited as reasons for this nonprofitability. In brief, even the most unsophisticated businessperson acknowledges that experience and learning lead to improvement. Unfortunately the significance of experience is realized only in abstract terms. For example, managers in a new and unprofitable situation tend to think of experience in vague terms without ever analyzing it in terms of cost. This statement applies to all functions of a business where cost improvements are commonly sought except for production management.

As growth continues, we anticipate greater efficiency and more productive output. But how much improvement can one reasonably expect? Generally, management makes an arbitrary decision to ascertain what level of output reflects the optimum level. Obviously, in the great majority of situations, this decision is primarily based on pure conjecture. Ideally, however, one should be able to use historical data to predict cost/volume relationships and learning patterns. Many companies have, in fact, developed their own learning curves but only in the area of production or manufacturing where tangible data are readily available and most variables can be quantified.

Several years ago the Boston Consulting Group observed that the concept of experience is not limited to production alone. The experience curve concept embraces almost all cost areas of business.

> Unlike the well-known "learning curve" and "progress function," the experience curve effect is observed to encompass all costs—capital, administrative, research and marketing—and to have transferred impact from technological displacements and product evolution.[1]

In the rest of this section, the application of the experience curve concept to marketing is examined.

Historical Perspective

The experience effect was first observed in the aircraft industry. Because the expense incurred in building the first unit is exceptionally high in this industry, any reduction in the cost of manufacturing succeeding units is readily apparent and becomes extremely pertinent in any management decision regarding future production. For example, it has been observed that an "80 percent air frame curve" could be developed for the manufacture of airplanes. This curve depicts a 20 percent improvement every time production doubles (i.e., to produce the fourth unit requires 80 percent of the time needed to produce the second unit, and so on).[2] Studies of the aircraft industry suggest that this rate of improvement seems to prevail consistently over the range of production under study; hence, the label *experience* is applied to the curve.

Implications

Although the significance of the experience curve concept is corporatewide, it bears most heavily on the setting of marketing objectives and the pricing decision. As already mentioned, according to the experience curve concept, all costs go down as experience increases. Thus, if a company acquired a higher market share, its costs would decline, enabling it to reduce prices. The lowering of prices would enable the company to acquire a still higher market share. This process is unending as long as the market continues to grow. But as a matter of strategy, while aiming at a dominant position in the industry, the company may be wise to stop short of raising the eyebrows of the Antitrust Division of the U.S. Department of Justice.

During the growth phase, a company keeps making the desired level of profit, but in order to provide for its growth, a company needs to reinvest profits. In fact, further resources might need to be diverted from elsewhere to support such growth. Once the growth comes to an end, the product makes available huge cash throw-offs that can be invested in a new product.

The Boston Consulting Group claims that, in the case of a second product, the accumulated experience of the first product should provide an extra advantage to the firm in reducing costs. However, experience is transferable only imperfectly. There is a transfer effect between identical products in different locations, but the transfer effect between different products occurs only if the products are somewhat the same (i.e., in the same family). This is true, for instance, in the case of the marketing cost component of two products distributed through the same trade channel. Even in this case, however, the loss of buyer "franchise" can result in some lack of experience transferability. Exhibit 12-1 is a diagram of the implications of the experience curve concept.

Some of the Boston Consulting Group's claims about the experience effect are hard to substantiate. In fact, until enough empirical studies have been done on the subject, many claims may even be disputed.[3] But even in its simplest form, the concept adds new importance to the market share strategy.

To summarize, the experience curve concept leads to the conclusion that all producers must achieve and maintain the full cost-reduction potential of their experience gains if they hope to survive.[4] Furthermore, the experience framework has implications for strategy development, as shown in Exhibit 12-2. The appendix at the end of this chapter describes construction of experience curves, showing how the relationship between costs and accumulated experience can be empirically developed.

Application to Marketing

The application of the experience curve concept to marketing requires sorting out various marketing costs and projecting their behavior for different sales volumes. It is hoped that the analyses will show a close relationship between increases in cumulative sales volume and declines in costs. The widening gap between volume and costs establishes the company's flexibility in cutting prices in order to gain higher market share.[5]

Declines in costs are logical and occur for reasons such as the following:

1. Economies of scale (e.g., lower advertising media costs)
2. Increase in efficiency across the board (e.g., ability of salespersons to reduce time per call)
3. Technological advances

Conceivably, four different techniques could be used to project costs at different levels of volume: regression, simulation, analogy, and intuition. Because

EXHIBIT 12-1
Schematic Presentation of Implications of the Experience Concept

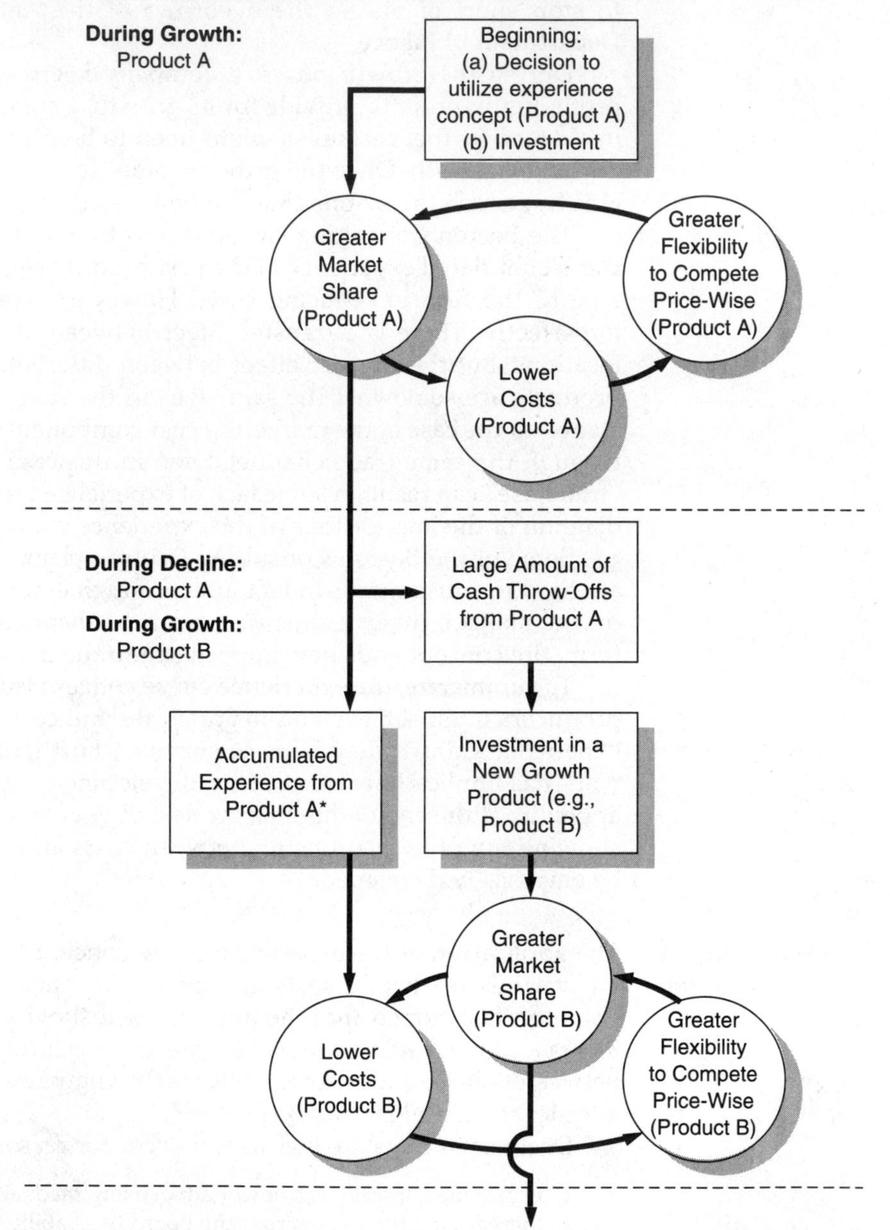

*An assumption is made here that Product B is closely related to Product A.

EXHIBIT 12-2
Experience Curves: Strategy Implications

Industry Growth Rate	Market Power: High	Market Power: Low
High	Continue to invest increased market share up to "target" level	Assess competition; then either invest heavily in increased share, segment market, or withdraw
Low	Obtain highest possible earnings consistent with maintaining market share	Assess competition; then either challenge, segment market, or withdraw

historical information on growing products may be lacking, the regression technique may not go very far toward the projection of costs. Simulation is a possibility, but it continues to be rarely practiced because it is strenuous. Drawing an analogy between the subject product and the one that has matured perhaps provides the most feasible means of projecting various marketing costs as a function of cumulative sales. But analogy alone may not suffice. As with any other managerial decision, analogy may have to be combined with intuition.

The cost characteristics of experience curves can be observed in all types of costs: labor costs, advertising costs, overhead costs, distribution costs, development costs, or manufacturing costs. Thus, marketing costs as well as those for production, research and development, accounting, service, etc., should be combined to see how total cost varies with volume. Further, total costs over different ranges of volume should be projected while considering the company's ability to finance an increased volume of business, to undertake an increased level of risk, and to maintain cordial relations with the Antitrust Division.

Each element of cost included in total cost may have a different slope on a graph. The aggregation of these elements does not necessarily produce a straight line on logarithmic coordinates. Thus, the relationship between cost and volume is necessarily an approximation of a trend line. Also, the cost derivatives of the curve are not based on accounting costs but on accumulated cash input divided by accumulated end product output. The cost decline of the experience curve is the rate of change in that ratio.

Management should establish a market share objective that projects well into the future. Estimates should be made of the timing of price cuts in order to achieve designated market share. If at any time a competitor happens to challenge a firm's market share position, the firm should go all out to protect its market share and never surrender it without an awareness of its value. Needless to say, the perspective of the entire corporation has to change if the gains expected from a particular market share strategy are to become reality. Thus, proper coordination among different functions becomes essential for the timely implementation of related tasks.

Although the experience effect is independent of the life cycle, of growth rate, and of initial market share, as a matter of strategy it is safer to base one's actions on experience when the following conditions are operating: (a) the product is in the early stages of growth in its life cycle, (b) no one competitor holds a dominant position in the market, and (c) the product is not amenable to nonprice competition (e.g., emotional appeals, packaging). Because the concept demands undertaking a big offensive in a battle that might last many years, a well-drawn long-range plan should be in existence. Top management should be capable of undertaking risks and going through the initial period of fast activity involved in sudden moves to enlarge the company's operations; the company should also have enough resources to support the enlargement of operations.

The experience effect has been widely accepted as a basis for strategy in a number of industries, the aircraft, petroleum, consumer electronics, and a variety of durable and maintenance-related industries among them. The application of this concept to marketing has been minimal for the following reasons:

1. Skepticism that improvement can continue
2. Difficulty with the exact quantification of different relationships in marketing
3. Inability to recognize experience patterns even though they are already occurring
4. Lack of awareness that the improvement pattern can be subjectively approximated and that the concept can apply to groups of employees as well as to individual performance across the board in different functions of the business
5. Inability to predict the effect of future technological advances, which can badly distort any historical data
6. Accounting practices that may make it difficult to segregate costs adequately

Despite these obstacles, the concept is too exciting for one to give up striving for its smooth application to marketing.

PROFIT IMPACT OF MARKET STRATEGY (PIMS)

In 1960 the vice president of marketing services at GE authorized a large-scale project (called PROM, for profitability optimization model) to examine the profit impact of marketing strategies. Several years of effort produced a computer-based model that identified the major factors responsible for a great deal of the variation in return on investment. Because the data used to support the model came from diverse markets and industries, the PROM model is often referred to as a cross-sectional model. Even today cross-sectional models are popularly used at GE.

In 1972, the PROM program, henceforth called PIMS, was moved to the Marketing Science Institute, a nonprofit organization associated with the Harvard Business School. The scope of the PIMS program has increased so much and its popularity has gained such momentum that a few years ago its administration moved to the Strategic Planning Institute, a new organization established for PIMS.

The PIMS program is based on the experience of more than 500 companies in nearly 3800 "businesses" for periods that range from two to twelve years. "Business" is synonymous with "SBU" and is defined as an operative unit that sells a distinct set of products to an identifiable group of customers in competition with a well-defined set of competitors. Essentially, PIMS is a cross-sectional study of the strategic experience of profit organizations. The information gathered from participating businesses is supplied to the PIMS program in a standardized format in the form of about 200 pieces of data. The PIMS database covers large and small companies; markets in North America, Europe, and elsewhere; and a wide variety of products and services, ranging from candy to heavy capital goods to financial services. The information deals with such items as[6]

- A description of the market conditions in which the business operates, including such things as the distribution channels used by the SBU, the number and size of its customers, and rates of market growth and inflation
- The business unit's competitive position in its marketplace, including market share, relative quality, prices and costs relative to the competition, and degree of vertical integration relative to the competition
- Annual measures of the SBU's financial and operating performance over periods ranging from two to twelve years

Overall Results

The PIMS project indicated that the profitability of a business is affected by 37 basic factors, explaining the more than 80 percent profitability variation among businesses studied. Of the 37 basic factors, seven proved to be of primary importance (see Exhibit 12-3).

Based on analysis of information available in the PIMS database, Buzzell and Gale have hypothesized the following strategy principles, or links between strategy and performance

1. In the long run, the most important single factor affecting a business unit's performance is the quality of its products and services relative to those of competitors. A quality edge boosts performance in two ways. In the short run, superior quality yields increased profits via premium prices. In the longer term, superior or improving relative quality is the more effective way for a business to grow, leading to both market expansion and gains in market share.
2. Market share and profitability are strongly related. Business units with very large shares—over 50 percent of their served markets—enjoy rates of return more than three times greater than small-share SBUs (those that serve under 10 percent of their markets). The primary reason for the market share–profitability

EXHIBIT 12-3
Return on Investment and Key Profit Issues

Return on Investment (ROI):
The ratio of net pretax operating income to average investment. Operating income is what is available after deduction of allocated corporate overhead expenses but before deduction of any financial charges on assets employed. "Investment" equals equity plus long-term debt, or, equivalently, total assets employed minus current liabilities attributed to the business.

Market Share:
The ratio of dollar sales by a business, in a given time period, to total sales by all competitors in the same market. The "market" includes all of the products or services, customer types, and geographic areas that are directly related to the activities of the business. For example, it includes all products and services that are competitive with those sold by the business.

Product (Service) Quality:
The quality of each participating company's offerings, appraised in the following terms: What was the percentage of sales of products or services from each business in each year which were superior to those of competitors? What was the percentage of equivalent products? Inferior products?

Marketing Expenditures:
Total costs for sales force, advertising, sales promotion, marketing research, and marketing administration. The figures do not include costs of physical distribution.

R&D Expenditures:
Total costs of product development and process improvement, including those costs incurred by corporate-level units which can be directly attributed to the individual business.

Investment Intensity:
Ratio of total investment to sales.

Corporate Diversity:
An index which reflects (1) the number of different 4-digit Standard Industrial Classification industries in which a corporation operates, (2) the percentage of total corporate employment in each industry, and (3) the degree of similarity or difference among the industries in which it participates.

Source: Reprinted by permission of the *Harvard Business Review*. Exhibit from "Impact of Strategic Planning on Profit Performance" by Sidney Schoeffler, Robert D. Buzzell, and Donald F. Heany (March–April 1974): 140.

link, apart from the connection with relative quality, is that large-share businesses benefit from scale economies. They simply have lower per-unit costs than their smaller competitors.

3. High-investment intensity acts as a powerful drag on profitability. Investment-intensive businesses are those that employ a great deal of capital per dollar of sales, per dollar of value added, or per employee.

4. Many so-called "dog" and "question mark" businesses generate cash, while many "cash cows" are dry. The guiding principle of the growth-share matrix approach [see chapter 10] to planning is that cash flows largely depend on market growth and competitive position (your share relative to that of your largest competitor). However, the PIMS-based research shows that, while market growth and relative share are linked to cash flows, many other factors also influence this dimension of performance. As a result, forecasts of cash flow based solely on the growth-share matrix are often misleading.
5. Vertical integration is a profitable strategy for some kinds of businesses, but not for others. Whether increased vertical integration helps or hurts depends on the situation, quite apart from the question of the cost of achieving it.
6. Most of the strategic factors that boost ROI also contribute to long-term value.[7]

These principles are derived from the premise that business performance depends on three major kinds of factors: the characteristics of the market (i.e., market differentiation, market growth rate, entry conditions, unionization, capital intensity, and purchase amount), the business's competitive position in that market (i.e., relative perceived quality, relative market share, relative capital intensity, and relative cost), and the strategy it follows (i.e., pricing, research and development spending, new product introductions, change in relative quality, variety of products/services, marketing expenses, distribution channels, and relative vertical integration). Performance refers to such measures as profitability (ROS, ROI, etc.), growth, cash flow, value enhancement, and stock prices.

Managerial Applications

The PIMS approach is to gather data on as many actual business experiences as possible and to search for relationships that appear to have the most significant effect on performance. A model of these relationships is then developed so that an estimate of a business's return on investment can be made from the structural competitive/strategy factors associated with the business. Obviously the PIMS conceptual framework must be modified on occasion. For example, repositioning structural factors may be impossible and the costs of doing so prohibitive. Besides, actual performance may reflect some element of luck or some unusual event.[8] In addition, results may be influenced by the transitional effect of a conscious change in strategic direction. Despite these reservations, the PIMS framework can be beneficial in the following ways:

1. It provides a realistic and consistent method for establishing potential return levels for individual businesses.
2. It stimulates managerial thinking on the reasons for deviations from par performance.
3. It provides insight into strategic moves that will improve the par return on investment.
4. It encourages a more discerning appraisal of business unit performance.

Since the mid-1970s, the PIMS database has been used by managers and planning specialists in many ways. Applications include developing business plans, evaluating forecasts submitted by divisional managers, and appraising possible strategies. To illustrate the kind of information that the PIMS program generates, consider Exhibit 12-4. The data in the exhibit suggest that[9]

- For followers, current profitability is adversely affected by a high level of product innovation, measured either by the ratio of new product sales to total sales or by research and development spending. The penalty paid for innovation is especially heavy for businesses ranked fourth or lower in their served markets. The market leader's profitability, on the other hand, is not hurt by new product activity or research and development spending.
- High rates of marketing expenditure depress return on investment for followers, not for leaders.
- Low-ranking market followers benefit from high inflation. For businesses ranked first, second, and third, inflation has no relation to return on investment.

MEASURING THE VALUE OF MARKETING STRATEGIES

In the last few years, a new yardstick for measuring the worth of marketing strategies has been suggested. This new approach, called **value-based**

EXHIBIT 12-4
How Some Profit-influencing Factors Affect Return on Investment for Market Leaders versus Followers

	AVERAGE ROI		
	Market Leaders	Market Followers	
Profit Influences	*(No. 1)*	*No. 2 or 3*	*No. 4 or Lower*
New Products, % of Sales:			
Under 1%	31	20	13
1%–5%	31	21	17
Over 5%	32	17	9
R&D Expense, % of Sales:			
Under 1%	29	21	13
1%–5%	34	19	14
Over 5%	28	14	1
Marketing Costs, % of Sales:			
Under 5%	29	20	15
5%–12%	33	20	14
Over 12%	32	17	7
Rate of Inflation:			
Under 5%	33	20	11
5%–10%	31	19	11
Over 10%	30	20	16

Source: Reprinted with permission of The Free Press, a Division of Macmillan, Inc., from *THE PIMS PRINCIPLES: Strategy to Performance* by Robert D. Buzzell and Bradley T. Gale. Copyright © 1987 by The Free Press.

planning, judges marketing strategies by their ability to enhance shareholders' value. It emphasizes the impact a strategic move has on the *value* investors place on the equity portion of a firm's assets.[10] The principal feature of value-based planning is that managers should be evaluated on their ability to make strategic investments that produce returns greater than their cost of capital.

Value-based planning draws ideas from contemporary financial theory. For example, a company's primary obligation is to maximize returns from capital appreciation. Similarly, the market value of a stock depends on investors' expectations of the ability of each business unit in the firm to generate cash.

Value is created when the financial benefits of a strategic activity exceed costs. To account for differences in the timing and riskiness of the costs and benefits, value-based planning estimates overall value by discounting all relevant cash flows.

A company that has been using the value-based approach for sometime is the Connecticut-based Dexter Corporation. Its value-based planning uses four subsystems:[11]

- The Dexter financial decision support system (DSS), which provides strategic business segments (SBS) with financial data. The DSS provides a monthly profit and loss and balance sheet statement of each strategic business segment. All divisional expenses, assets, and current liabilities are allocated to the SBSs.
- A microcomputer-based system, which transforms this data for use in the two following subsystems: corporate financial reports system and value planner system. The financial data generated by DSS must be transformed to fit the input specifications of these two subsystems.
- The corporate financial reports system, which estimates the cost of capital of an SBS. For estimating cost of capital, Dexter uses two models. The first is the bond-rating simulation model. This model is used to estimate the capital structure appropriate to each of its SBSs, given its six-year financial history. Each SBS is assigned the highest debt-to-total capital ratio that would allow it to receive an A bond rating. The second model used to compute cost of capital is the business risk index estimation model. This model allows cost of equity to be estimated for business segments that are not publicly traded.
- The value planner system for estimating a business's future cash flows. The basic premise of the value planner system is that business decisions should be based on a rigorous consideration of expected future cash flows. Dexter uses the 12 most recent quarters of SBS data to produce a first-cut projection of future cash flows. As information on a new quarter becomes available, the oldest quarter in the model is deleted. These historical trends are used for projecting financial ratios into the future. The following assumptions are made to compute future cash flows:

  Sales growth—Based on the expectation that each SBS will maintain market share
  Net plant investment—Based on the growth rate in unit volume deemed necessary to maintain Dexter's market share
  Unallocated divisional expenses—Projected for each SBS using the same percentage of sales used for the division as a whole
  The appropriate time horizon for cash flow projections—Based on the expected number of years that a business can reinvest at an expected rate of return

These assumptions are controversial because they do not allow cash flow projections to be tailored to each SBS. Dexter management terms its historical forecast a *naive* projection and uses it to challenge its managers to explain why the future will be different from the recent past.

The next step in the value-based planning process is to compute the value of projected future cash flows and to discount them by the cost of capital for an SBS. If the estimated value of an SBS is in excess of its book value, the SBS contributes positively to the wealth of Dexter's stockholders, which means it makes sense to reinvest in it.

The major strengths of Dexter's SBS value planner system have been articulated as follows:

- **Its emphasis on being intelligible to line managers**—A value-based planning model can indicate which SBSs are not creating value for the firm's stockholders. However, it is the SBS manager who must initiate action to rectify problems that the analysis uncovers.
- **Its degree of accuracy**—The real dilemma in designing models for value-based planning is to make them easy to use while improving the accuracy with which they reflect or predict the firm's market value.
- **Its integration with existing systems and databases**—By developing a system that works with existing systems, costs are reduced and upgrades are easier to implement. Also, it is easier to gain the acceptance of line managers if the value-based planning system is presented as an extension of the decision support system they are currently using.

In the four years that Dexter has used the value-based approach, it has made important contributions to the decision-making process. Using this approach, Dexter managers made the following decisions:

- Not to invest further in an SBS with high-growth prospects until its valuation, based on actual performance, increases significantly
- To harvest and downsize an SBS with a negative value
- To sell an SBS with negative value to its employees for book value
- To sell an SBS with a value higher than book value but for which an offer was received that was significantly greater than any valuation that could be reasonably modeled in Dexter's hands

The interesting characteristic of these decisions is that they can run somewhat counter to the prescriptions that flow out of a typical portfolio-planning approach. The first decision, for example, refers to a star business, presumably worthy of further investment. Unlike portfolio planning, in which growth is desirable in and of itself, under value-based planning, growth is healthy only if the business is creating value.

Dexter uses value-based planning as a guideline for decision making, not as an absolute rule. The approach is, in general, understood and accepted, but many managers question its relevance. They now know whether their divisions create value for the company, but they do not understand how they can use that information to make or change important business decisions. Top management understands that value-added planning needs more time before it is completely accepted.

DELPHI TECHNIQUE

The **delphi technique**, named after Apollo's oracle at Delphi, is a method of making forecasts based on expert opinion. Traditionally, expert opinions were pooled in committee. The delphi technique was developed to overcome the weaknesses of the committee method. Wedgewood lists some of the problems that occur when issues are discussed in committee:[12]

1. The influence of a dominant individual
2. The introduction of a lot of redundant or irrelevant material into committee workings
3. Group pressure that places a premium on compromise
4. Reaching decisions is slow, expensive, and sometimes painful
5. Holding members accountable for the actions of a group

All of these factors provide certain psychological drawbacks to people in face-to-face communication. Because people often feel pressure to conform, the most popular solution, instead of the best one, prevails. With the delphi technique, a staff coordinator questions selected individuals on various issues. The following is a sample of questions asked:

1. What is the probability of a future event occurring? (E.g., By what year do you think there will be widespread use of robot services for refuse collection, as household slaves, as sewer inspectors, etc.?)

   a. 1995
   b. 2000
   c. 2010
   d. 2020
   e. 2030

2. How desirable is the event in question 1?

   a. needed desperately
   b. desirable
   c. undesirable but possible

3. What is the feasibility of the event in question 1?

   a. highly feasible
   b. likely
   c. unlikely but possible

4. What is your familiarity with the material in question 1?

   a. fair
   b. good
   c. excellent

The coordinator compiles the responses, splitting them into three groups: lower, upper, and inner. The division into groups may vary from one investigation to another. Frequently, however, the lower and upper groups each represent 10 percent, whereas the inner group takes the remaining 80 percent. When a person makes a response in either the upper or lower group, it is customary to ask about the reasons for his or her extreme opinion.

In the next round the respondents are given the same questionnaire, along with a summary of the results from the first round. The data feedback includes the consensus and the minority opinion. During the second round, the respondents are asked to specify by what year the particular product or service will come to exist with 50 percent probability and with 90 percent probability. Results are once again compiled and fed back. This process of repeating rounds can be continued indefinitely; however, rarely has any research been conducted past the sixth round. In recent years, the delphi technique has been refined by the use of interactive computer programs to obtain inputs from experts, to present summary estimates, and to store revised judgments in data files that are retrievable at user terminals.

The delphi technique is gradually becoming important for predicting future events objectively. Most large corporations use this technique for long-range forecasting. Some of the advantages of the delphi technique are listed below:

1. It is a rapid and efficient way to gain objective information from a group of experts.
2. It involves less effort for a respondent to answer a well-designed questionnaire than to participate in a conference or write a paper.
3. It can be highly motivating for a group of experts to see the responses of knowledgeable persons.
4. The use of systematic procedures applies an air of objectivity to the outcomes.
5. The results of delphi exercises are subject to greater acceptance on the part of the group than are the consequences arrived at by more direct forms of interaction.

Delphi Application

Change is an accepted phenomenon in the modern world. Change coupled with competition makes it necessary for a corporation to pick up the trends in the environment and to determine their significance for company operations. In light of the changing environment, the corporation must evaluate and define strategic posture to be able to face the future boldly. Two types of changes can be distinguished: cyclical and developmental. A **cyclical change** is repetitive in nature; managers usually develop routine procedures to meet cyclical changes. A **developmental change** is innovative and irregular; having no use for the "good" old ways, it abandons them. Developmental change appears on the horizon so slowly that it may go unrecognized or ignored until it becomes an accomplished fact with drastic consequences. It is this latter category of change that assumes importance in the context of strategy development. The delphi technique can be fruitfully used to analyze developmental changes. Functionally, a change may fall into one of the following categories: social, economic, political, regulatory, or technological. The delphi technique has been used by organizations to study emerging perspectives in all these areas.

The Delphi Technique—An Illustration

The use of the delphi technique can be illustrated with reference to a proprietary study that was conducted to assess the impact of emerging socioeconomic/political trends on the department store industry. A list of areas of particular concern to department store executives was first prepared (see Exhibit 12-5).

The panel for this study, conducted in the early 1980s, consisted of 11 executives from a Connecticut metropolitan area. Before the panel was approached, however, a sample run was conducted using 28 students from a marketing class of a local university. Exhibit 12-6 presents instructions for using the questionnaire. Each prediction had to be rated for its desirability, feasibility, and probability of occurrence in a scale ranging from 0 to 1. Responses on each round were sorted into lower, inner, and upper groups, as shown in Exhibit 12-6.

The percentage of respondents falling into each category on every variable (i.e., desirability, feasibility, probability of occurrence, and probable time of occurrence) for each prediction was fed back to the panel members on the completion of the first round. The respondents were asked to complete the same questionnaire in the second round after they had had a chance to digest findings from the first round. This process continued for four rounds.

EXHIBIT 12-5
Aspects of the Department Store Industry That Are of Special Interest

A. Products
   1. Women's better dresses
   2. Housedresses and undergarments
   3. Children's clothing
   4. Men's socks and shirts
   5. Furniture
   6. Large appliances
   7. Towels, sheets, blankets, and spreads
   8. Kitchen utensils and small electric appliances
B. Telephone shopping
C. Downtown versus suburban (shopping center) shopping
D. Competition, such as from discount stores
E. Shopping motivations: convenience, fun, etc.
F. Nature and scope of services, such as charge accounts, delivery, gift wrapping, salesclerks, etc.
G. Mail-order/electronic shopping
H. Fashion
I. Store decor
J. Advertisements and other aspects of promotion
K. Time preferences
L. Significance of comparison shopping, bargain hunting, impulse buying, browsing, etc.

EXHIBIT 12-6
Delphi Study Questionnaire: Future Perspective of Retailing

1. A well-known consulting organization has recognized 31 socioeconomic trends that it claims will have far-reaching impact on people's lifestyles. These trends are personalization, physical self-enhancement, physical fitness and well-being, social/cultural self-expression, conspicuous cultivation, personal creativity, meaningful work, introspection, hedonism, liberal sex attitudes, female careerism, concern about privacy, mysticism, sensuousness, new romanticism, novelty and change, beauty in the home, return to nature, scientism and technocracy, concern about environment, search for community, simplification, antibigness, antihypocrisy, the new cynicism, antimaterialism, away from posessions, living for today, blurring of the sexes, rejection of authority, tolerance for chaos and disorder. Our purpose here is to study the significance of these trends on the department store industry (especially the aspects listed here, but not necessarily limited to them).
2. Please read and ponder the trends and indicate below in column 1 all anticipated changes expected in the sphere of the department store industry. For each change, indicate the source, the particular trend(s) leading you to such an anticipation. Then evaluate each projected change with respect to the four factors at the right in view of the total environment as you see it.

	Desirability	Feasibility	Probability of Occurrence	Probable Time of Occurrence				
Description of Change	*0 — 1*	*0 — 1*	*0 — 1*	*1995*	*2000*	*2010*	*2020*	*2020+*
Example: Popularity of women's hosiery products among men	0.3	0.9	0.4		2000			

Desirability:
Lower Group: Not Needed
Inner Group: Desirable
Upper Group: Needed Desperately

Feasibility:
Lower Group: Unlikely
Inner Group: Likely
Upper Group: Highly Feasible

Probability:
Lower Group: Improbable
Inner Group: Possible
Upper Group: Highly Probable

Probable Time of Occurrence:
Upper Group: Imperceptible Future
Inner Group: Distant Future
Lower Group: Immediate Future

The process could have continued beyond round 4, but results of a comparison of round 3 with round 4 were statistically insignificant (results were significant between rounds 1 and 2 and rounds 2 and 3). Thus, there was no point in carrying the study to the next round. Exhibit 12-7 shows a sample of the results obtained in each of the three rounds.

Tabulation of data obtained in the first round provided a list of 37 changes in the area of concern in this study. After attrition and the screening out of irrelevant, trivial, and duplicate changes, 23 meaningful retailing predictions were considered in the final round. They are listed in Exhibit 12-8. The panel predicted that the most prominent trends (i.e., those most desirable, most highly feasible, and most likely to occur in the immediate future) would consist of the following:

1. Checkless shopping
2. Market for natural products

EXHIBIT 12-7
Sample Results of the Delphi Technique (Three Rounds)—Percentage Responses

	Desirability			Feasibility			Probability of Occurrence			Probable Time of Occurrence		
Round	*Not Needed*	*Desirable*	*Needed Desperately*	*Unlikely*	*Likely*	*Highly Feasible*	*Improbable*	*Possible*	*Highly Probable*	*Imperceptible Future*	*Distant Future*	*Immediate Future*
Prediction: Twenty-Four Hour Shopping												
1	75	20	5	38	40	22	59	28	15	55	30	15
2	58	35	7	49	38	23	44	47	9	62	27	11
3	43	46	11	54	35	11	29	62	9	69	21	10
Prediction: New Role of a Salesclerk: "A Doctor-in-Waiting"												
1	27	45	28	40	33	27	32	56	12	38	44	18
2	31	58	11	45	39	16	28	62	10	26	52	22
3	28	63	9	48	42	10	21	70	9	3	68	29

3. Electronic shopping
4. Cooperative stores
5. International shopping
6. Store guarantee
7. Common products for men and women

Needless to say, these trends have great significance for the department store industry.

Other Uses of the Delphi Technique

The delphi technique has great potential. It has so far been used mainly for predicting distant and abstract changes. Occasionally it has been used for forecasting short-term sales and for determining optimum bid price. As work with the technique continues, perhaps many more applications will be developed. It is safe to say that the delphi technique can be used to determine the value of any uncertain event. Even if the event happens to be completely unknown, at least initial insights (what statisticians call *prior distribution*) can be gained. As more information becomes available, then original predictions can be revised with the use of statistical techniques, such as the Bayes theorem.

Comments

The following points are relevant when using the delphi technique:

1. Choice of panel members
2. Number of people on a panel
3. Number of rounds
4. Impact of interactive variables

The choice of panel members should be related to the purpose for which the delphi technique is employed. If the purpose is to make broad predictions, an interdisciplinary team of experts would be most appropriate. On the other hand, if the forecast deals with a specific industry, persons knowledgeable about the industry would be preferred. But if the forecast is concerned with the company's perspective, in-house experts should make up the panel. Exhibit 12-9 suggests an appropriate mix of experts for different types of forecasts.

EXHIBIT 12-8
Prediction: Retailing

1. Twenty-four-hour shopping
2. New role of salesclerk
3. Shops for different moods
4. Declining market for "artificial" products
5. Checkless shopping
6. Growth through vertical integration
7. Increased emphasis on electronic shopping
8. Computerized shopping
9. High-rise shopping centers
10. Recyclable clothes
11. Personal wear adjustable with physical growth
12. Universal merchandise standards
13. Rise of holding companies
14. Shopping across national boundaries
15. Frequent changes in store decor
16. Intellectual advertising
17. Customers' cooperative stores
18. Store's guarantee on merchandise
19. Trade-ins for unconventional merchandise
20. New forms of common products for men and women
21. Matching brands to moods and occasions
22. Temperature-proof clothes
23. Computerized service: what outfit to wear

As far as the size of the panel is concerned, experiments at Rand Corporation have shown a positive correlation between the reliability of results and the size of the panel. In other words, error goes down with every increase in the size of the panel. For example, the error factor decreases from 1.2 to 0.6 as panel size increases from one to nine. In fact, errors continue to decline even when the size of the panel stretches to 29. The Rand study does not pinpoint exactly a desirable size for a given panel; however, certain generalizations can be made. The minimum size should be somewhere between 9 and 11; it is helpful for the sake of reliability to go as high as 30. There are organizations, however, that have used panels of 140 people.[13]

The question of the number of rounds that should be tried has already been discussed. In brief, an additional round should be tried as long as the variance between the results of the previous two rounds is statistically significant.

One drawback of the delphi technique is that each trend is given unilateral consideration on its own merits. Thus, one may end up with conflicting forecasts; that is, one trend may suggest that something will happen, whereas another may lead in the opposite direction. To resolve this problem, another forecasting technique, the cross-impact matrix (discussed later) has been used by some researchers. With this technique, the effect of potential interactions

EXHIBIT 12-9

Important Factors in the Selection of a Panel of Experts

		Judgment			Diversity of Participants		Imagination	
Specific Corporate Orientation to the Future	*Empirical Data*	*Specialized Expertise*	*Less-Specialized Expertise*	*Informal Generalists*	*Close to Specialized Fields and Interests*	*Widely Diversified and Inter-Disciplinary*	*Extrapolative*	*Creative Conjecture*
1. Broadened applications of existing technologies	high	high	high	low	high	low	high	medium
2. New alternatives evolving from existing	medium	medium to high	high	medium	medium	medium	medium	medium
3. New alternatives evolving from new knowledge derived from trends of research, analysis, and social developments	low	medium	high	high	medium to low	high	medium to low	high
4. New alternatives evolving from new knowledge derived from responsible, educated conjecture	low	medium low	high	high	low	high	low	high
5. New alternatives evolving from creative conjecture not discernable from any existing knowledge	low	low	high	high	low	high	low	high

among items in a forecasted set of occurrences can be investigated. If the behavior of an individual item is predictable (i.e., if it varies positively or negatively with the occurrence or nonoccurrence of other items), the cross-impact effect is present. It is thus possible to determine whether a predicted event will have an enhancing or inhibiting influence upon each of the other events under study by using a cross-impact matrix.

Recent research shows that the use of the delphi technique has undergone quite a change. The salient features of the revised delphi technique are (a) identifying recognized experts in the field of interest; (b) seeking their cooperation and sending them a summary paper on the topic being examined (based on a literature search); and (c) conducting personal interviews with each expert based on a structured questionnaire, usually by two interviewers. Feedback and repeated rounds of responding to written questionnaires are no longer considered necessary.

TREND-IMPACT ANALYSIS

Trend-impact analysis is a technique for projecting future trends from information gathered on past behavior. The uniqueness of this method, which was developed by the Futures Group, a consulting firm, lies in its combination of statistical method and human judgment. If predictions are based on quantitative data alone, they will fail to reflect the impact of unprecedented future events. On the other hand, human judgment provides only subjective insights into the future. Therefore, because both human judgment and statistical extrapolation have their shortcomings, both should be taken into consideration when predicting future trends.

In trend-impact analysis (TIA), past history is first extrapolated with the help of a computer. Then the judgment of experts is sought (usually by means of the delphi technique) to specify a set of unique future events that may have a bearing on the phenomenon under study and to indicate how the trend extrapolation may be affected by the occurrence of each of these events. The computer then uses these judgments to modify its trend extrapolation. Finally, the experts review the adjusted extrapolation and modify the inputs in those cases in which an input appears unreasonable.[14]

To illustrate TIA methods, let us consider the case of the average price of a new prescription drug in the 1990s. As shown in Exhibit 12-10, statistical extrapolation of historical data shows that price will rise to $13 by 1995 and to $14.23 by the year 2000. The events considered relevant are listed in Exhibit 12-11. The first forecast, that generic dispensing will increase to 20 percent of all prescriptions filled, is shown to have a 75 percent chance of occurring by 1992. If this event does occur, it is expected that its first impact on the average price of a new prescription will begin right away. The maximum impact, a 3 percent reduction in the average price, will occur after five years.

The combination of these events, probabilities, and impacts with the baseline extrapolation leads to a forecast markedly different from the baseline ex-

EXHIBIT 12-10
Average Retail Price of a New Prescription

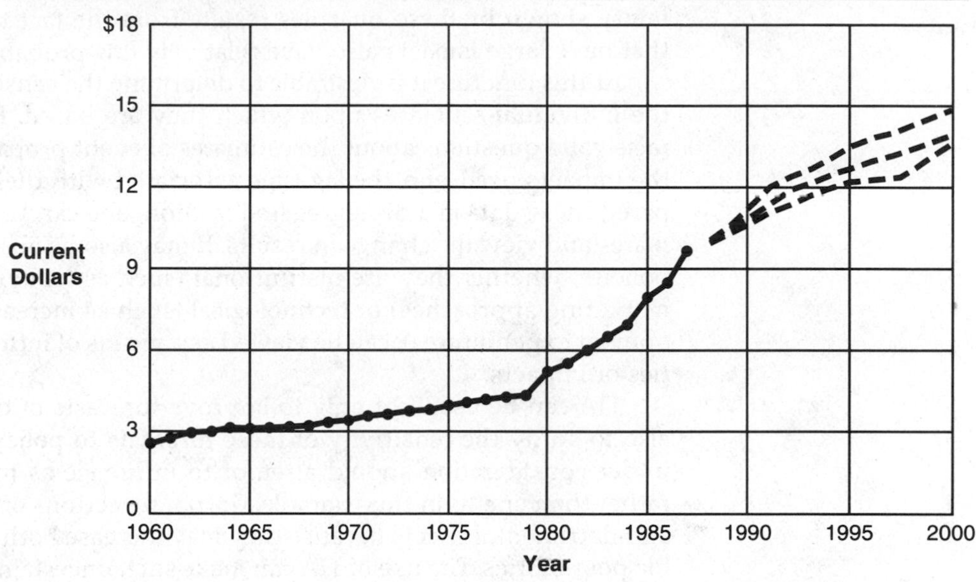

Historical Data					Forecast		
					Lower Quartile	*Mean*	*Upper Quartile*
1957	2.17	1974	3.86	1988	10.65	10.70	10.75
1959	2.41	1975	4.02	1989	10.92	11.03	11.14
1961	2.78	1976	4.19	1990	11.21	11.40	11.61
1962	2.92	1977	4.32	1991	11.54	11.79	12.10
1963	2.99	1978	4.45	1992	11.83	12.15	12.54
1964	3.15	1979	4.70	1993	12.08	12.45	12.92
1965	3.22	1980	5.20	1994	12.30	12.74	13.25
1966	3.27	1981	5.60	1995	12.52	13.00	13.55
1967	3.26	1982	5.98	1996	12.74	13.25	13.83
1968	3.35	1983	6.44	1997	12.95	13.50	14.10
1969	3.42	1984	7.03	1998	13.17	13.75	14.38
1970	3.48	1985	7.66	1999	13.39	13.99	14.64
1971	3.56	1986	8.63	2000	13.60	14.23	14.90
1972	3.63	1987	10.37				
1973	3.70						

trapolation (see Exhibit 12-10). The curve even begins to taper off in the year 2000. The level of uncertainty is indicated by quartiles above and below the mean forecast. (The quartiles indicate the middle 50 percent of future values of the curve, with 25 percent lying on each side of the forecast curve.) The uncertainty shown by these quartiles results from the fact that many of the events that have large impacts also have relatively low probabilities.

At this juncture it is desirable to determine the sensitivity of these results to the individual estimates upon which they are based. For example, one might raise valid questions about the estimates of event probability, the magnitude of the impacts used, and the lag time associated with these impacts. Having prepared these data in a disaggregated fashion, one can very easily vary such estimates and view the change in results. It may also be observed that intervention policies, whether they are institutional (such as lobbying, advertising, or new marketing approaches) or technological (such as increased research and development expenditures), can be viewed as a means of influencing event probabilities or impacts.

TIA can be used not only to improve forecasts of time series variables but also to study the sensitivity of these forecasts to policy. Of course, any policy under consideration should attempt to influence as many events as possible rather than one, as in this example. Corporate actions often have both beneficial and detrimental effects because they may increase both desirable and undesirable possibilities. The use of TIA can make such uncertainties more clearly visible than can traditional methods.

CROSS-IMPACT ANALYSIS

Cross-impact analysis, as mentioned earlier, is a technique used for examining the impacts of potential future events upon each other. It indicates the relative importance of specific events, identifies groups of reinforcing or inhibiting events, and reveals relationships between events that appear unrelated. In brief, cross-impact analysis provides a future forecast, making due allowance for the effect of interacting forces on the shape of things to come.

Essentially, this technique consists of selecting a group of five to ten project participants who are asked to specify critical events having any relationship with the subject of the analysis. For example, in an analysis of a marketing project, events may fall into any of the following categories:

1. Corporate objectives and goals
2. Corporate strategy
3. Markets or customers (potential volume, market share, possible strategies of key customers, etc.)
4. Competitors (product, price, promotion, and distribution strategies)
5. Overall competitive strategic posture, whether aggressive or defensive
6. Internally or externally developed strategies that might affect the project
7. Legal or regulatory activities having favorable or unfavorable effects
8. Other social, demographic, or economic events

The initial attempt at specifying critical events presumably will generate a long list of alternatives that should be consolidated into a manageable size (e.g., 25 to

EXHIBIT 12-11

Events Used in Trend-Impact Analysis

Event Number	*Forecast*	*Estimated Probability by Year Shown*	*Years to First Impact*	*Years to Maximum Impact*	*Maximum Impact (Percent)*	*Forecast Source Number(s)*
496	Generic dispensing increases 20 percent of all prescriptions filled (1979 = 11 percent).	0.75 / 1992	0	5	−3	6900
1346	Medicaid and Medicare prescription reimbursement is based on a fixed monthly fee per covered patient ("capitation plan").	0.50 / 1989	0	2	−2.5	6226, 6227, 6228, 6229, 7071
766	Private third-party insurance carriers institute cost containment programs for prescription drugs: MAC-type limits on generics, negotiated prices for single-source products, fixed fee per patient covered, etc.	0.40 / 1995	0	5	−5	6900
207	Fifty percent decrease in the average rate of growth in prescription size.	0.90 / 1988	0	5	−1	5557
492	Medicaid state funding replaced by block grants	0.50 / 1988	1	5	−1	5568, 5569, 5570, 5571, 5572, 5573, 5574, 5575, 5576
995	Prices of single-source or co-marketed drugs negotiated by state or federal government as major purchaser.	0.35 / 2000	0	5	−3	6625, 6230, 7016, 7020
500	All outpatient drugs for persons over age 65 are covered by national health insurance or Medicare with some deductible or co-pay.	0.40 / 1994	0	3	1	4479, 5329, 5330, 5331, 7021
483	Unit of use dispensing for at least one-fourth of all prescriptions: units prepared and packaged by manufacturer.	0.35 / 1995	1	5	2	3908, 4397, 4496, 6030, 6031, 6032
497	Nearly all drugs are covered under national health insurance with a maximum price schedule.	0.30 / 2000	0	5	4	6900
478	Pharmacist dispensing fees and mark-ups for Medicaid and Medicare prescriptions increase at least 5 percent annually.	0.40 / 1990	0	5	2	5559, 5560, 6231, 7018, 7019
499	Manufacturers increase prices of single-source drugs in response to government regulation of multi-source pharmaceuticals and the diminishing patent protection period.	0.80 / 1995	0	2	2	6900
481	Drugs covered by expiring patents are displaced by new, single-source products at an accelerated rate.	0.35 / 1990	0	5	5	6900
715	Government regulations increase manufacturers' cost of doing business for at least 5 percent above inflation for a three-year period.	0.50 / 1990	1	3	4	6900

30 events) by means of group discussion, concentrated thinking, elimination of duplications, and refinement of the problem. It is desirable for each event to contain one and only one variable, thus avoiding double counting. Selected events are represented in an $n \times n$ matrix for developing the estimated impact of each event on every other event. This is done by assuming that each specific event has already occurred and that it will have an enhancing, an inhibiting, or no effect on other events. If desired, impacts may be weighted. The project coordinator seeks impact estimates from each project participant individually and consolidates the estimates in the matrix form. Individual results, in summary form, are presented to the group. Project participants vote on the impact of each event. If the spread of votes is too wide, the coordinator asks those persons voting at the extremes to justify their positions. The participants are encouraged to discuss differences in the hope of clarifying problems. Another round of voting takes place. During this second round, opinions usually converge, and the median value of the votes is entered in the appropriate cell in the matrix. This procedure is repeated until the entire matrix is complete.

In the process of completing the matrix, a review of occurrences and interactions identifies events that are strong actors and significant reactors and provides a subjective opinion of their relative strengths. This information then serves as an important input in formulating strategy.

The use of cross-impact analysis may be illustrated with reference to a study concerning the future of U.S. automobile component suppliers. The following events were set forth in the study:

1. Motor vehicle safety standards that come into effect between 1989 and 1993 will result in an additional 150 pounds of weight for the average-sized U.S. car.
2. The 1990 NO_X emissions regulations will be relaxed by the EPA.
3. The retail price of gasoline (regular grade) will be $2 per gallon.
4. U.S. automakers will introduce passenger cars that will achieve at least 40 mpg under average summer driving conditions.

These events are arranged in matrix form in Exhibit 12-12. The arrows show the direction of the analysis. For example, the occurrence of event A would be likely to bring more pressure to bear upon regulatory officials; consequently, event B would be more likely to occur. An enhancing arrow is therefore placed in the cell where row A and column B intersect. Moving to column C, it is not expected that the occurrence of event A will have any effect on event C, so a horizontal line is placed in this cell. It is judged that the occurrence of event A would make event D less likely to occur, and an inhibiting arrow is placed in this cell. If event B were to occur, the consensus is that event A would be more likely; hence the enhancing arrow. Event B is not expected to affect event C but would make event D more likely. Cells are completed in accordance with these judgments. Similar analyses for events C and D complete the matrix.

The completed matrix shows the direction of the impact of rows (actors) upon columns (reactors). An analysis of the matrix at this point reveals that reactor C has only one actor (event D) because there is only one reaction in

EXHIBIT 12-12
Basic Format for Cross-Impact Matrix

If This Event Were to Occur	Then the Impact upon This Event Would Be: A	B	C	D
A MVSS (1989 through 1990) requires 150 pounds additional weight for average-sized U.S. autos		↑	—	↓
B 1990 NO_x emissions requirements are relaxed by EPA	↑		—	↑
C Retail price of gasoline is $2/gallon	↓	↑		↑
D U.S. automakers introduce cars capable of 40 mpg in average summer driving	↑	↓	↓	

↑ = enhancing
— = no effect
↓ = inhibiting

column C. If interest is primarily focused on event D, column D should be studied for actor events. Then each actor should be examined to determine what degree of influence, if any, it is likely to have on other actors in order to bring about event D.

Next, impacts should be quantified to show linkage strengths (i.e., to determine how strongly the occurrence or nonoccurrence of one event would influence the occurrence of every other event). To assist in quantifying interactions, a subjective rating scale, such as the one shown here, may be used.

Voting Scale	*Subjective Scale*	
+8	Critical: essential for success	**Enhancing**
+6	Major: major item for success	
+4	Significant: positive and helpful but not essential	
+2	Slight: noticeable enhancing effect	
0	**No effect**	
−2	Slight: noticeable inhibiting effect	**Inhibiting**
−4	Significant: retarding effect	
−6	Major: major obstacle to success	
−8	Critical: almost insurmountable hurdle	

Consider the impact of event A upon event B. It is felt that the occurrence of event A would significantly improve the likelihood of the occurrence of event B. Both the direction and the degree of enhancing impact are shown in Exhibit 12-13 by the +4 rating in the appropriate cell. Event A's occurrence would make

EXHIBIT 12-13
Cross-Impact Matrix Showing Degrees of Impact

If This Event Were to Occur	Then the Impact upon This Event Would Be: A	B	C	D
A MVSS (1989 through 1990) requires 150 pounds additional weight for average-sized U.S. autos		+4	0	-4
B 1990 NO_x emissions requirements are relaxed by EPA	+2		0	+4
C Retail price of gasoline is $2/gallon	-4	+4		+2
D U.S. automakers introduce cars capable of 40 mpg in average summer driving	+2	-2	-2	

event D less likely; therefore, the consensus rating is −4. This process continues until all interactions have been evaluated and the matrix is complete.

There are a number of variations for quantifying interactions. For example, the subjective scale could be 0 to 10 rather than −8 to +8, as shown in the example on the previous page.

Another technique for quantifying interactions involves the use of probabilities. If the probability of the occurrence of each event is assessed before the construction of the matrix, then the change in that probability can be assessed for each interaction. As shown in Exhibit 12-14, the probabilities of occurrence can be entered in a column preceding the matrix, and the matrix is constructed in the conventional manner. Consider the impact of event A on the probable occurrence of event B. It is judged to be an enhancing effect, and the consensus is that the probability of event B occurring will change from 0.8 to 0.9. The new probability is therefore entered in the appropriate cell. Event A is judged to have no effect upon event C; therefore, the original probability, 0.5, is unchanged. Event D is inhibited by the occurrence of event A, and the resulting probability of occurrence is lowered from 0.5 to 0.4. The occurrence of event B increases the probability of event A occurring from 0.7 to 0.8. Event B has no impact upon event C (0.5, unchanged) and increases the probability of event D to 0.7. This procedure is followed until all cells are completed.

An examination of the matrix at this stage reveals several important relationships. For example, if we wanted event D to occur, then the most likely actors are events B and C. We would then examine columns B and C to determine what actors might be influenced. Often influences that bring about desired results at a critical moment are secondary, tertiary, or beyond. In many instances, the degree of impact is not the only important information to be

EXHIBIT 12-14
Cross-Impact Matrix Showing Interactive Probabilities of Occurrence

If This Event Were to Occur	Probability of Occurrence	Then the Impact upon This Event Would Be: A	B	C	D
A MVSS (1989 through 1993) requires 150 pounds additional weight for average-sized U.S. autos	0.7		0.9 (immed.)	0.5	0.4 (immed.)
B 1990 NO_x emissions requirements are relaxed by EPA	0.8	0.8 (immed.)		0.5	0.7 (+2 yrs.)
C Retail price of gasoline is $2/gallon	0.5	0.6 (+1 yr.)	0.9 (+1 yr.)		0.7 (+2 yrs.)
D U.S. automakers introduce cars capable of 40 mpg in average summer driving	0.5	0.8 (immed.)	0.6 (immed.)	0.4 (+ 1 yr.)	

gathered from a consideration of interactions. Time relationships are often very important and can be shown in a number of ways. For example, in Exhibit 12-14, information about time has been added in parentheses. It shows that if event A were to occur, it would have an enhancing effect upon event B, raising B's probability of occurrence from 0.8 to 0.9, and that this enhancement would occur immediately. If event B were to occur, it would raise the probability of the occurrence of event D from 0.5 to 0.7. It would also take two years to reach the probable time of occurrence of event D.[15]

SCENARIO BUILDING

Plans for the future were traditionally developed on a single set of assumptions. Restricting one's assumptions may have been all right during times of relative stability, but in the 1990s and beyond, as experience has shown, it may not be desirable to commit an organization to the most probable future alone. It is equally important to make allowances for unexpected or less probable future trends that may seriously jeopardize strategy. One way to focus on different future outcomes within the planning process is to develop scenarios and to design strategy so that it has enough flexibility to accommodate whatever outcome occurs. In other words, by developing multiple scenarios of the shape of things to come, a company can make a better strategic response to the future environment. **Scenario building** in this sense is a synopsis that depicts potential actions and events in a likely order of development, beginning with a set of conditions that describe a current situation or set of circumstances. In addition, scenarios depict a possible course of evolution in a given field. Identification of changes and evolution of programs are two stages in scenario building.

Changes in the environment can be grouped into two classes: (a) scientific and technological changes and (b) socioeconomic-political changes. Chapter 6 dealt with environmental scanning and the identification of these changes. Identification should take into consideration the total environment and its possibilities: What changes are taking place? What shape will change take in the future? How are other areas related to environmental change? What effect will change have on other related fields? What opportunities and threats are likely?[16]

A scenario should be developed without any intention of predicting the future. It should be a time-ordered sequence of events that reflects logical cause-and-effect relationships among events. The objective of a scenario building should be to clarify certain phenomena or to study the key points in a series of developments in order to evolve new programs. One can follow an inductive or a deductive approach in building a scenario. The deductive approach, which is predictive in nature, studies broad changes, analyzes the impact of each change on a company's existing lines, and at the same time, generates ideas about new areas of potential exploitation. Under the inductive approach, the future of each product line is simulated by exposing its current environment to various foreseen changes. Through a process of elimination, those changes that have relevance for one's business can be studied more deeply for possible action. Both approaches have their merits and limitations. The deductive approach is much more demanding, however, because it calls for proceeding from the unknown to the specific.

Exhibit 12-15 describes how step-by-step scenarios may be constructed. Scenarios are not a set of random thoughts: they are logical conclusions based on past behaviors, future expectations, and the likely interactions of the two. As a matter of fact, a variety of analytical techniques (e.g., the delphi technique, trend-impact analysis, and cross-impact analysis) may be used to formulate scenarios.

Scenarios may be analyzed following Linneman and Kennell's 10-step approach:[17]

1. Identify and make explicit your company's mission, basic objective, and policies.
2. Determine how far into the future you wish to plan.
3. Develop a good understanding of your company's points of leverage and vulnerability.
4. Determine factors that you think will definitely occur within your planning time frame.
5. Make a list of key variables that will have make-or-break consequences for your company.
6. Assign reasonable values to each key variable.
7. Build scenarios in which your company may operate.
8. Develop a strategy for each scenario that will most likely achieve your company's objectives.
9. Check the flexibility of each strategy in each scenario by testing its effectiveness in the other scenarios.
10. Select—or develop—an "optimum response" strategy.

EXHIBIT 12-15
Scenario-building Method at GE

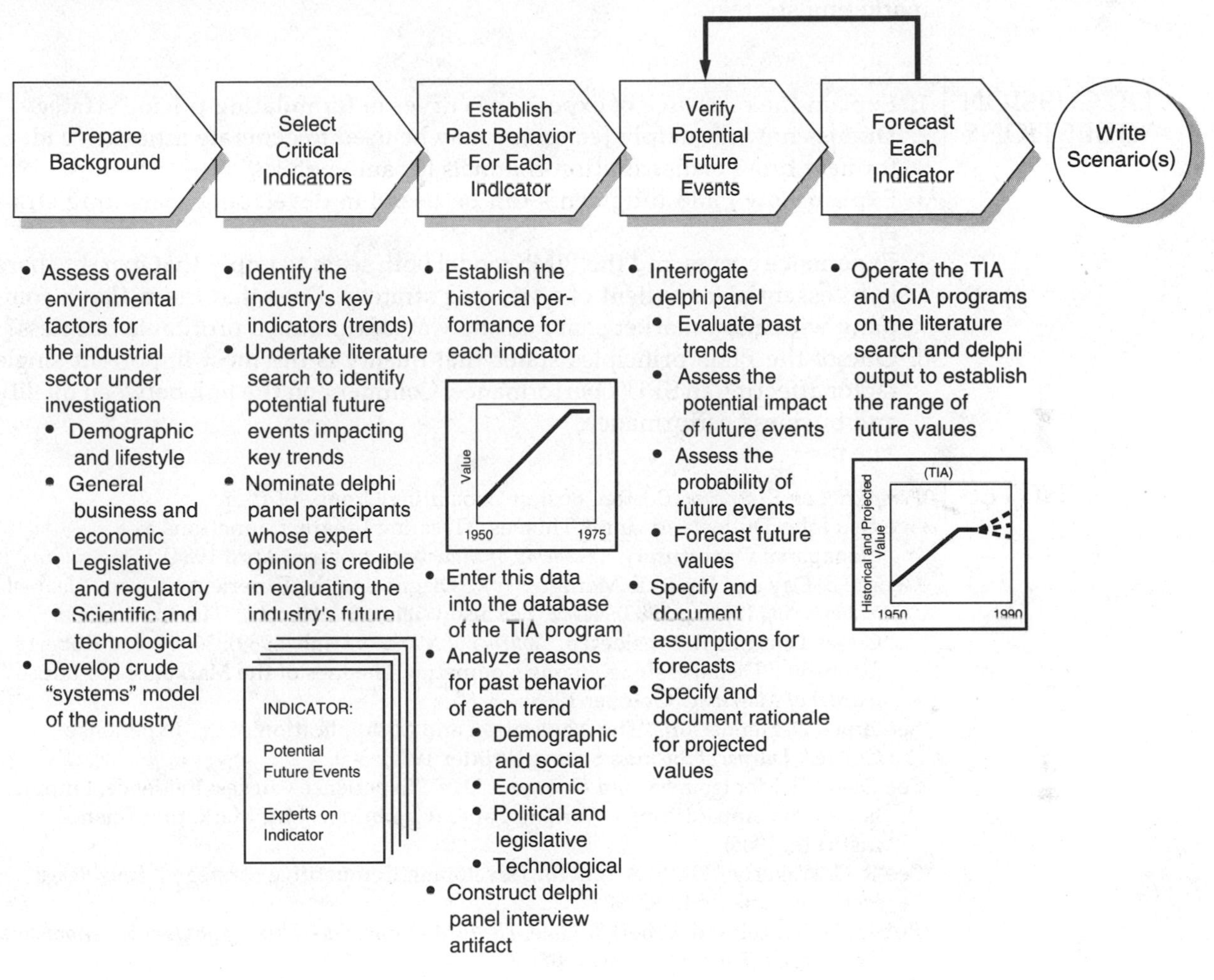

Note: TIA = trend-impact analysis.

SUMMARY

This chapter presented a variety of tools and techniques that are helpful in different aspects of strategy formulation and implementation. These tools and techniques include experience curves, the PIMS model, a model for measuring the value of marketing strategies, the delphi technique, trend-impact analysis, cross-impact analysis, and scenario building. Most of these techniques require data inputs both from within the organization and from outside. Each tool or technique was examined for its application and usefulness. In some cases, procedural details for using a technique were illustrated with examples from the field. Of the many techniques discussed in this chapter, the experience curve concept and the PIMS model are the most far-reaching from the viewpoint of marketing strategy.

DISCUSSION QUESTIONS

1. Explain the relevance of experience curves in formulating pricing strategy.
2. Discuss how the delphi technique may be used to generate innovative ideas for new types of distribution channels for automobiles.
3. Explain how PIMS judgments can be useful in developing marketing strategy.
4. Experience curves and the PIMS model both seem to imply that market share is an essential ingredient of a winning strategy. Does that mean that a company with a low market share has no way of running a profitable business?
5. One of the PIMS principles states that quality is the most important single factor affecting an SBU's performance. Comment on the link between quality and business performance.

NOTES

[1]*Perspective on Experience* (Boston: Boston Consulting Group, 1970), 1.

[2]See also John Dutton and Annie Thomas, "Treating Progress Functions as a Managerial Opportunity," *Academy of Management Review* (April 1984).

[3]George S. Day and David B. Montgomery, "Diagnosing the Experience Curve," *Journal of Marketing* (Spring 1983): 44–58. See also William W. Alberts, "The Experience Curve Doctrine Reconsidered," *Journal of Marketing* (July 1989): 36–49; and Robert Jacobson, "Distinguishing among Competing Theories of the Market Share Effect," *Journal of Marketing* (October 1988): 68–80.

[4]See Bruce D. Henderson, "The Application and Misapplication of the Experience Curve," *Journal of Business Strategy* (Winter 1984): 3–9.

[5]See David B. Montgomery and George S. Day, "Experience Curves: Evidence, Empirical Issues and Applications," Working Paper (Cambridge, MA: Marketing Science Institute, 1985).

[6]See R. G. Wakerly, "PIMS: A Tool for Developing Competitive Strategy," *Long Range Planning* (June 1984): 92–97.

[7]Robert D. Buzzell and Robert T. Gale, *The PIMS Principles—Linking Strategy to Performance* (New York: The Free Press, 1987), 2.

[8]Robert Jacobson and David A. Aaker, "Is Market Share All It's Cracked Up to Be?" *Journal of Marketing* (Fall 1985): 11–22. See also John E. Prescott, Ajay K. Kohli, and N. Venkatraman, "The Market Share-Profitability Relationship: An Empirical Assessment of Major Assertions and Contradictions," *Strategic Management Journal* 7 (1986): 377–94.

[9]Buzzell and Gale, *PIMS Principles*, 192–93. Also see V. Ramanujan and N. Venkatraman, "An Inventory and Critique of Strategy Research Using the PIMS Data Base," *Academy of Management Review* (January 1984): 138–51.

[10]George S. Day and Liam Fahey, "Valuing Market Strategies," *Journal of Marketing* (July 1988): 45–57.

[11]The following discussion draws heavily on Bala Chakravarthy and Worth Loomis, "Dexter Corporation's Value-Based Strategic Planning System," *Planning Review* (January–February 1988): 34–41.

[12]H. C. Wedgewood, "Fewer Camels, More Horses: Where Committees Go Wrong," *Personnel* (July-August 1967): 64.

[13]Harper Q. North and Donald L. Pyke, "Probes of the Technological Future," *Harvard Business Review* (May-June 1969): 68.

[14]See "Trend Impact Analysis," a reference paper of the Futures Group, Glastonbury, CT, 1978.

[15]See *A Guide to Cross-Impact Analysis* (Cleveland: Eaton Corp., n.d.).

[16]See Harold E. Klein and Robert E. Linneman, "The Use of Scenarios in Corporate Planning—Eight Case Histories," *Long Range Planning* (October 1981): 69-77.

[17]Robert E. Linneman and John D. Kennell, "Shirt-Sleeve Approach to Long-Range Plans," *Harvard Business Review* (March-April 1977): 141-51.

APPENDIX | *Experience Curve Construction*

The experience curve concept can be used as an aid in developing marketing strategy. The procedure for constructing curves discussed below describes how the relationship between costs and accumulated experience can be empirically developed.

The first step in the process of constructing the experience curve is to compute experience and accumulated cost information. Experience for a particular year is the accumulation of all volume up to and including that year. It is computed by adding the year's volume to the experience of previous years. Accumulated cost (constant dollars) is the total of all constant costs incurred for the product up to and including that year. It is computed by adding the year's constant dollar cost to the accumulated costs of previous years. A year's constant dollar cost is the real dollar cost for that year, corrected by inflation. It is computed by dividing cost (actual dollars) by the appropriate deflator.

The second step is to plot the initial and annual experience/accumulated cost (constant dollars) data on log-log graph paper (see Exhibit 12-A). It is important that the experience axis of this graph be calibrated so that its point of intersection with the accumulated cost axis is at 1 unit of experience. The accumulated cost axis may be calibrated in any convenient manner.

The next step is to fit a straight line to the points on the graph, which may be accomplished by using the least-squares method (Exhibit 12-A). It is useful at this point to stop and analyze the accumulated cost diagram. In general, the closer the data points are to the accumulated cost curve, the stronger the evidence that the experience effect is present. Deviations of the data points from the curve, however, do not necessarily disprove the presence of the experience effect. If the deviations can be attributed to heavy investment in plant, equipment, etc. (as is common to very capital-intensive industries), the experience effect still holds but only in the long run because, in the long run, the fluctuations are averaged out. If, on the other hand, significant deviations from the line cannot be explained as necessary periodic changes in the rate of investment, then the presence of the experience effect, or at least its consistency, is open to

EXHIBIT 12-A
Accumulated Cost Diagram

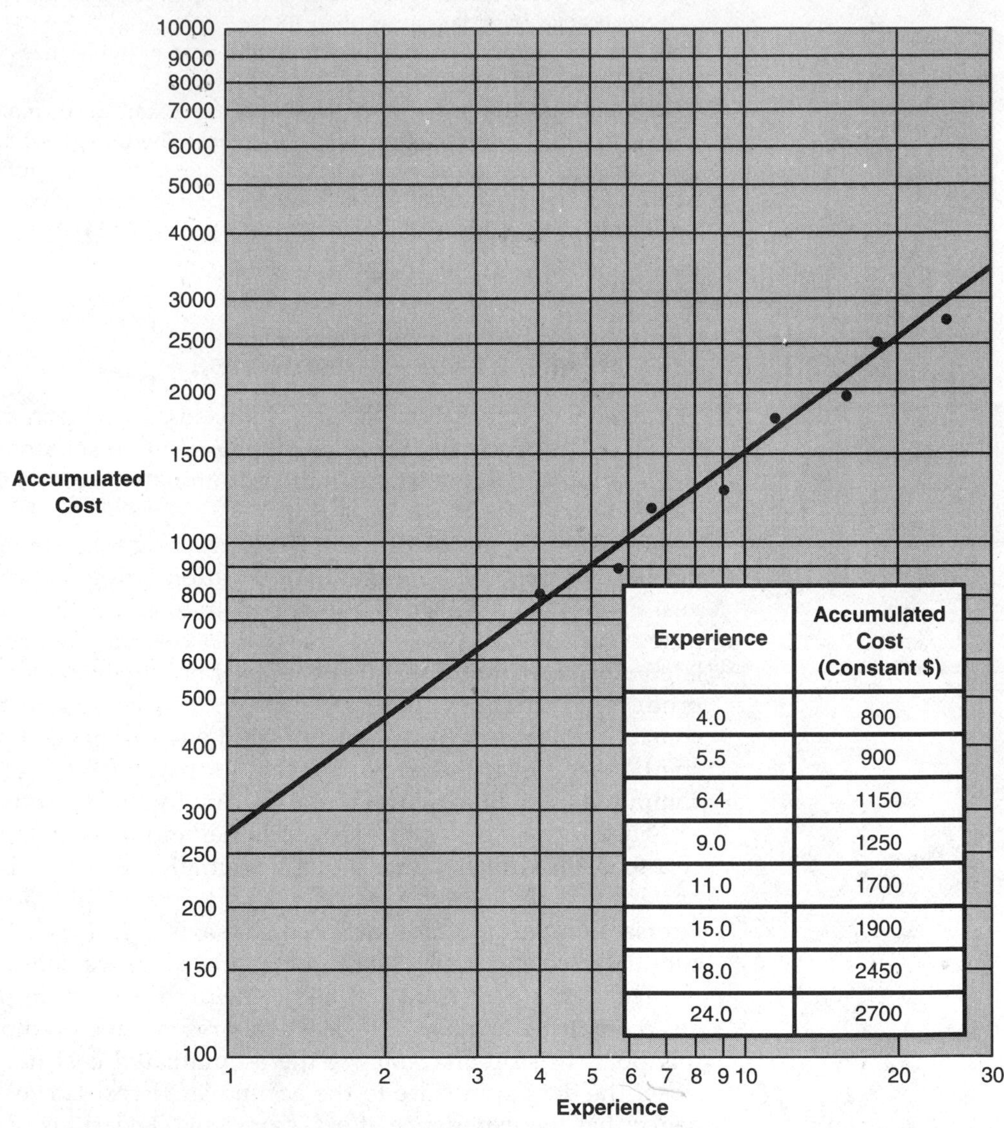

Experience	Accumulated Cost (Constant $)
4.0	800
5.5	900
6.4	1150
9.0	1250
11.0	1700
15.0	1900
18.0	2450
24.0	2700

question. In Exhibit 12-B there is one deviation (see point *X*) that stands out as significant. If this can be ascribed to heavy investment (in plant, equipment, etc.), the experience effect is still viable here.

The next step in the process of constructing the experience curve is to calculate the intensity of the product's experience effect. Intensity is the percent-

EXHIBIT 12-B
Interpretation of Deviations from Accumulated Cost Curve

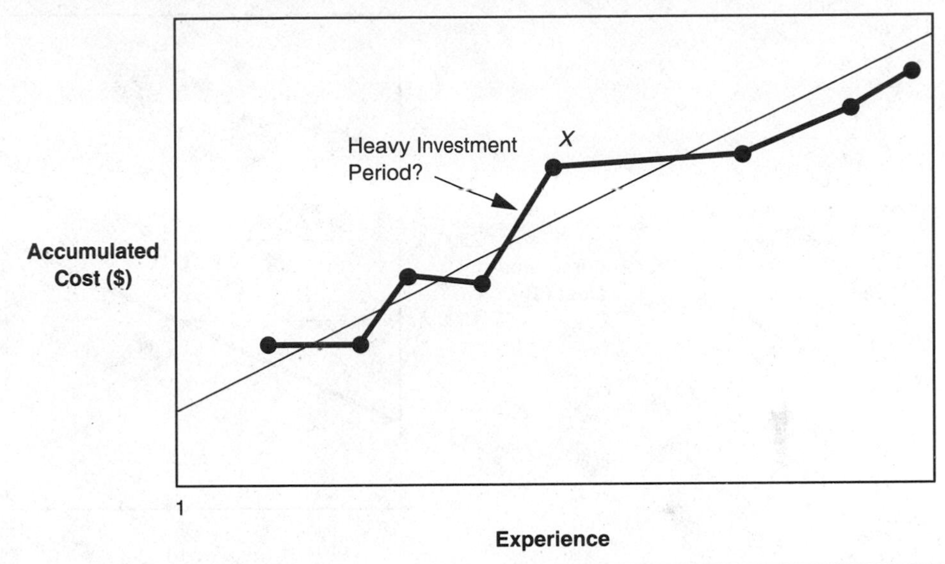

age in unit cost reduction achieved each time the product's experience is doubled. As such, it determines the slope of the experience curve. To compute the intensity from the accumulated cost curve, arbitrarily select an experience level on the experience axis (e.g., point E_1 in Exhibit 17-C). Draw a line vertically up from E_1 until it intersects the accumulated cost curve. From that point on the curve, draw a horizontal line left until it intersects the accumulated cost axis. Read the corresponding accumulated cost (A_1) from the scale. Follow the same procedure for experience level E_2, where E_2 equals $E_1 \times 2$, to obtain A_2. Divide A_2 by A_1, divide the result by 2, and subtract the second result from the number 1. The final answer is the product's intensity. With the information given in Exhibit 12-C, the intensity equals 16.7 percent:

$$1 - \frac{2500}{1500} \times \frac{1}{2} = 0.167 = 16.7\%$$

When the intensity has been computed, the slope of the experience curve is determined. However, as shown in Exhibit 12-D, this information in itself is not sufficient for constructing the curve. Because all of the lines in Exhibit 12-D are parallel, they have the same slope and represent the same intensity. To construct the experience curve, it is necessary to find a point (C_1) on the unit cost axis. This can be achieved in the following manner. Find the *intensity multiplier* corresponding to the product's intensity from the table specially prepared for the purpose (Exhibit 12-E). If the intensity falls between two values in Exhibit 12-E, the appropriate intensity multiplier should be determined by

EXHIBIT 12-C
Product Intensity Computation

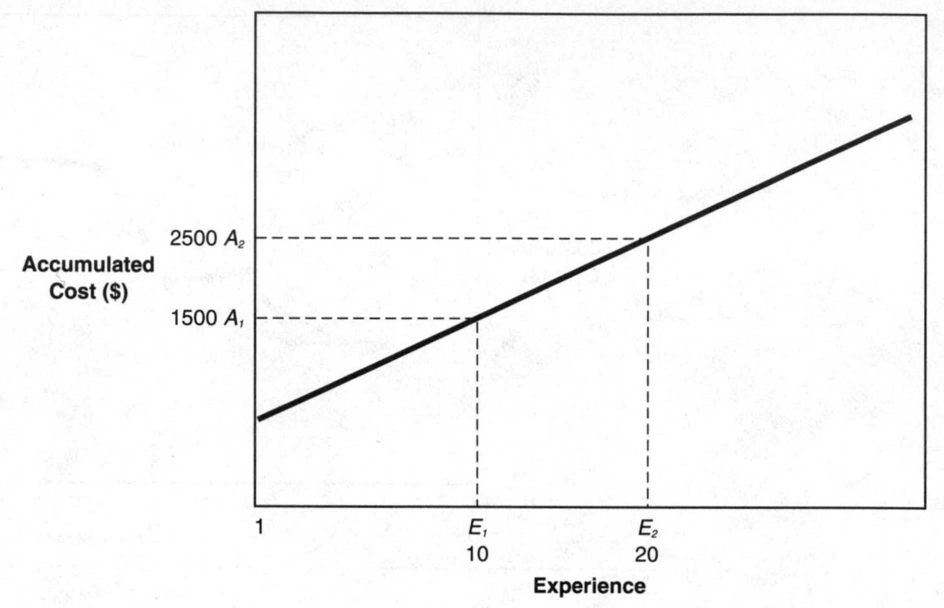

EXHIBIT 12-D
Slopes of Parallel Lines

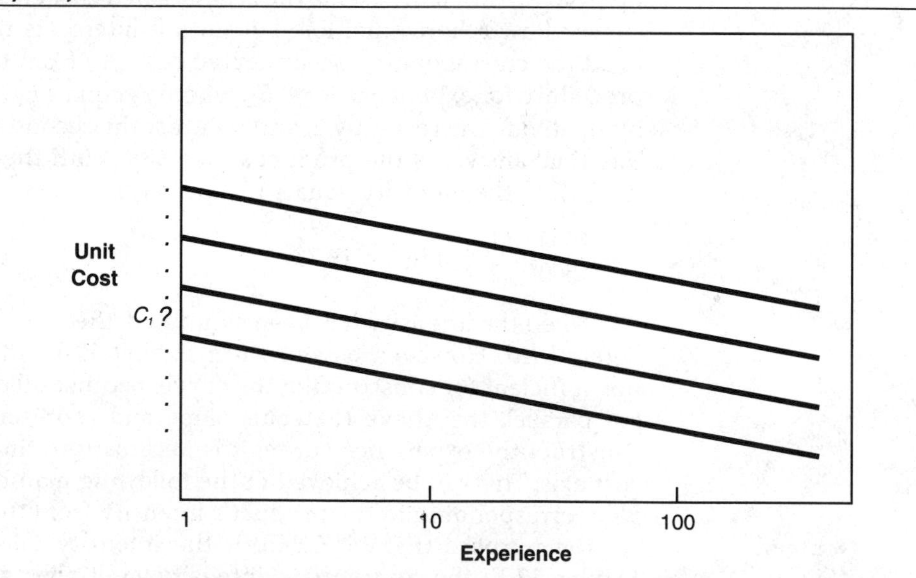

EXHIBIT 12-E
Intensity Multipliers

Intensity	*Intensity Multiplier*	*Intensity*	*Intensity Multiplier*
5.0%	.926	20.5%	.669
5.5	.918	21.0	.660
6.0	.911	21.5	.651
6.5	.903	22.0	.642
7.0	.895	22.5	.632
7.5	.888	23.0	.623
8.0	.880	23.5	.614
8.5	.872	24.0	.604
9.0	.864	24.5	.595
9.5	.856	25.0	.585
10.0	.848	25.5	.575
10.5	.840	26.0	.566
11.0	.832	26.5	.556
11.5	.824	27.0	.546
12.0	.816	27.5	.536
12.5	.807	28.0	.526
13.0	.799	28.5	.516
13.5	.791	29.0	.506
14.0	.782	29.5	.496
14.5	.774	30.0	.485
15.0	.766	30.5	.475
15.5	.757	31.0	.465
16.0	.748	31.5	.454
16.5	.740	32.0	.444
17.0	.731	32.5	.433
17.5	.722	33.0	.422
18.0	.714	33.5	.411
18.5	.705	34.0	.401
19.0	.696	34.5	.390
19.5	.687	35.0	.379
20.0	.678	35.5	.367

interpolation. Read the value on the accumulated cost axis where the curve intersects that axis. Multiply this value by the intensity multiplier. The result is C_1.

The intensity was calculated above as 16.7 percent. By using Exhibit 12-E, the corresponding intensity multiplier can be interpolated as approximately 0.736. As shown in Exhibit 12-A, the accumulated cost at the point of intersection can be read as approximately \$260. Multiplying \$260 by 0.736 yields a C_1 of \$191. The experience curve can now be plotted on log-log graph paper. Position C_1 on the unit cost axis. Multiply C_1 by the quantity (1 − intensity) to obtain C_2:

$$\$191 \times (1 - 0.167) = \$159$$

Locate C_2 on the unit cost axis. Find the point of intersection (y) of a line drawn vertically up from 2 on the experience axis and a line drawn horizontally right from C_2 on the unit cost axis. Draw a straight line through the points C_1 and y. The result is the product's experience curve (Exhibit 12-F).

The application of the experience curve concept to marketing strategy requires the forecasting of costs. This can be achieved by using the curve. Determine the current cumulative experience of the product. Add to this value the planned cumulative volume from the present to the future time point. The result is the planned experience level at that point. Locate the planned experience level on the experience axis of the graph. Move vertically up from that point until the line extension of the experience curve is reached. Move horizontally left from the line to the unit cost axis. Read the estimated unit cost value from the scale. The unit cost obtained is expressed in constant dollars, but it can be converted to an actual dollar cost by multiplying it by the projected inflator for the future year.

Cost forecasts can also be used to determine the minimum rate of volume growth necessary to offset an assumed rate of inflation. For example, with an assumed inflation rate of 3.8 percent, a producer having an intensity of 20 percent must realize a volume growth of approximately 13 percent per year just to maintain unit cost in real dollars. Should growth be slower or should full cost-reduction potential not be realized, the producer's unit cost would rise.

Competitor cost is one of the most fundamental yet elusive information needs of the producer attempting to develop marketing strategy. The experience curve concept provides a sound basis for estimating the cost positions of competitors as well. With certain assumptions, competitors' curves can be estimated.

EXHIBIT 12-F
Experience Curve Estimation

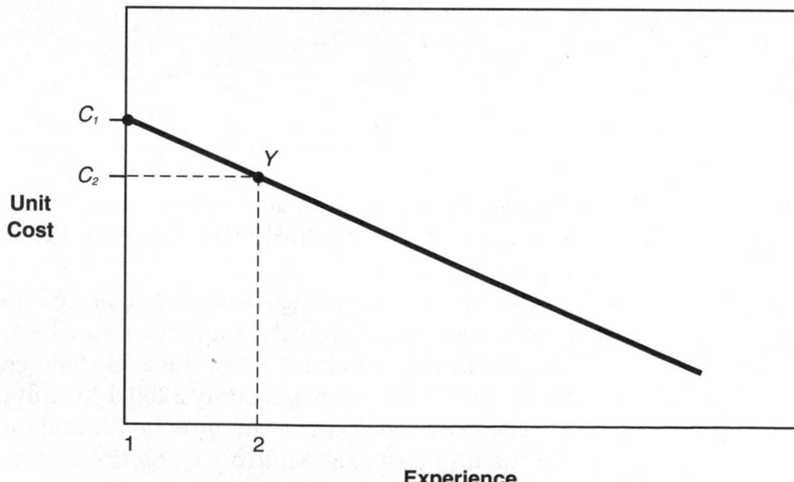

PART SIX

Marketing Strategies

CHAPTER 13

Market Strategies

Three women and a goose make a marketplace.
ITALIAN PROVERB

In the final analysis, all business strategies must be justified by the availability of a viable market. When there is no viable market, even the best strategy will flop. In addition, the development of marketing strategies for each business should be realistically tied to the target market. Because the market should be the focus of successful marketing, strategies aligned to the market point the way for each present business, serve as underpinnings for overall corporate-wide strategy, and provide direction for programming key activities and projects in all functional areas.

When corporate resources are scarce and corporate strengths are limited, it is fatal to spread them across too many markets. Rather, these critical resources should be concentrated on those key markets (key in terms of type of market, geographic location, time of entry, and commitment) that are decisive for the business's success. Merely allocating resources in the same way that other firms do yields no competitive differential. If, however, it can be discovered which markets really hold potential, the business will be able to lever itself into a position of relative competitive superiority.

This chapter will identify different aspects of market strategies that companies commonly pursue and will analyze their impact on performance vis-à-vis SBU objectives. The use of these strategies will be illustrated with examples from the marketing literature. The appendix at the end of this chapter will summarize each strategy in terms of definition, objectives, requirements, and expected results.

DIMENSIONS OF MARKET STRATEGIES

Market strategies deal with the perspectives of markets to be served. These perspectives can be determined in different ways. For example, a company may serve an entire market or dissect it into key segments on which to concentrate its major effort. Thus, market scope is one aspect of market strategy. The geographic dimensions of a market constitute another aspect: a company may focus on a local, regional, national, or international market. Another strategic variable is the time of entry into a market. A company may be the first, among the first few, or among the last to enter a market. Commitment to a market is still another aspect of market strategy. This commitment can be to achieve market dominance, to become a major factor in the market, or merely to play a minor le in it. Finally, a company may intentionally decide to dilute a part of its rket as a matter of strategy. Briefly, then, the following constitute the major market strategies that a company may pursue:

Market-scope strategy
Market-geography strategy
Market-entry strategy
Market-commitment strategy
Market-dilution strategy

MARKET-SCOPE STRATEGY

Market-scope strategy deals with the coverage of the market. A business unit may serve an entire market or concentrate on one or more parts of it. Three major alternatives in market-scope strategy are single-market strategy, multimarket strategy, and total-market strategy.

Single-Market Strategy

A variety of reasons may lead a company to concentrate its efforts on a single segment of a market. For example, in order to avoid confrontation with large competitors, a small company may find a unique niche in a market and devote its energies to serving this niche. Design and Manufacturing Corporation (D&M) is a classic example of a successful single-market strategy. In the late 1950s, Samuel Regenstrief studied the dishwasher market and found (a) high growth potential; (b) market domination by GE; and (c) absence of a manufacturer to supply large retailers, such as Sears, with their own private brand. These conclusions led him to enter the dishwasher market and to concentrate his efforts on a single segment: national retailers. The company has emerged as the largest producer of dishwashers in the world with over 25 percent of the U.S. market. A D&M executive states the company's strategy in the following words: "Sam knew precisely what segment of the market he was going after; he hit it at exactly the right time; and he has set up a tightly run organization to take full advantage of these opportunities."[1]

The story of Tampax also illustrates the success of the single-market strategy. Tampax had a minimal share of a market dominated by Kimberly-Clark's Kotex and Personal Product's Modess. Tampax could not afford to compete head-on with these major brands. To sell its different concept of sanitary protection—internal protection—the company found that newer, younger users were more open-minded and very brand loyal. Starting from a premise that had great appeal for the young user, that internal protection offers greater freedom of action, Tampax concentrated on reaching young women. Its single-market strategy has proved to be highly beneficial.[2] Even today the company's advertising is scarcely distinguishable from the firm's first efforts.

In the competitive field of cosmetics, Noxell Corporation (a division of Procter and Gamble), marketer of the popular Noxzema and Cover Girl brands of makeup and skin cream, found success in a single segment of the $12-billion cosmetics industry that its rivals disdain: the mass market. Noxell's products are aimed primarily at teenagers and evoke the image of fresh-faced natural beauty. Widely distributed and heavily advertised, Noxell's brands are easily recognizable by their low price. Content to sell its products in chains such as K-Mart and F.W. Woolworth, the company avoids more prestigious, but cutthroat, department and specialty store businesses. The determination to sell exclusively through mass merchandisers is based on Noxell's belief that distribution through department stores is unattractive: it requires leasing counter space, keeping large inventories on hand, and paying commissions to salespeople. Noxell's continued sales growth and healthy profit performance attest to the viability of concentrating on a single segment of the market.[3]

There is no magic formula for choosing a segment. A business should analyze the market carefully to find a segment that is currently being ignored or served inadequately. Then it should concentrate on the chosen segment wholeheartedly, despite initial difficulties, and avoid competition from the established firms.[4]

Often new market segments emerge as a result of changes in the environment. For example, the women's movement motivated Smith and Wesson Corp. to launch Lady Smith in 1989, a line of guns specifically designed for women. The result: sales to women jumped from 5 percent of the company's total to nearly 18 percent.[5]

The single-market strategy consists of seeking out a market segment that larger competitors consider too small, too risky, or just plain unappealing. The strategy will not work in areas where the market power of big companies is important in realizing economies of scale, the extractive and process industries, for example. Companies concentrating on a single market have the advantage of being able to make quick responses to market opportunities and threats through appropriate changes in policies. The single-market, or niche, strategy is often born of necessity. Lacking the resources to fight head-to-head battles across the board with larger entrenched competitors, winners typically seek out niches that are too small to interest the giants or that can be captured and protected by sheer perseverance and by serving customers surpassingly well.

As far as the impact of the single-market strategy is concerned, it affects profitability in a positive direction. When effort is concentrated on a single market, particularly when competition is minimal, it is feasible to keep costs down while prices are kept high, thus earning substantially higher profits. Although its growth objective may not be achieved when this strategy is followed, a company may be able to increase its market share if the chosen segment is large enough vis-à-vis the overall market.

Multimarket Strategy

Instead of limiting business to one segment and thus putting all its eggs in one basket, a company may opt to serve several distinct segments. To implement a multimarket strategy successfully, it is necessary to choose those segments with which the company feels most comfortable and in which the company is able to avoid confronting companies that serve the entire market. This point may be illustrated with reference to Crown Cork and Seal Company. The company is a major producer of metal cans, crowns (bottle caps), closures (screw caps and bottle lids), and filling machinery for beer and soft drink cans. The industry is characterized by a really dynamic environment: technological breakthroughs, new concepts of packaging, new materials, and threats of self-manufacture by large users are common. Crown Cork and Seal, as a matter of strategy, decided to concentrate on two segments: (a) cans for such "hard-to-hold" products as beer and soft drinks and (b) aerosol containers. Its new strategy paid off. The company outperformed its competitors both in sales growth and in return on sales in the 1980s. As it should with any strategic choice, the company fully committed itself to its strategy despite the lure of serving other segments. For example, in spite of its 50 percent share in the motor oil can business, Crown Cork decided not to continue to compete aggressively in that market.[6]

The multimarket strategy can be executed in one of two ways: either by selling different products in different segments or by distributing the same product in a number of segments. Toyota Motor Corporation, for example, introduced its Lexus line of cars in 1989. The car was directed toward luxury car buyers who traditionally had looked to BMW and Mercedes-Benz. Toyota entered a different segment with a different product. In contrast, the Green Giant Company expanded into another segment by distributing an existing product more widely; that is, by supplying its frozen vegetables, corn on the cob, for example, to all Church's Fried Chicken and Kentucky Fried Chicken fast-food outlets.[7]

Total-Market Strategy

A company using the total-market strategy serves an entire spectrum of a market by selling different products directed toward different segments of the market. The strategy evolves over a great number of years of operation. A company may start with a single product. As the market grows and as different segments emerge, leading competitors may attempt to compete in all segments by employing different combinations of product, price, promotion, and distribution strategies. These dominant companies may also attempt to enter new segments as they emerge. As a matter of fact, the leading companies may themselves create new segments and try to control them from the outset.

A number of companies in different industries have followed this strategy. General Motors, for one, has traditionally directed its effort to securing an entire market: "A car for every pocket and taste." With its five auto lines (Chevrolet, Pontiac, Oldsmobile, Buick, and Cadillac), along with a variety of small trucks, the company attempts to compete in all conceivable segments.

IBM now also follows an across-the-board strategy. It has a system for meeting the requirements of all types of customers. In the middle 1980s, as the personal computer segment emerged, IBM was somewhat slow to respond but finally developed a personal computer of its own. Similarly, in the consumer products area, Coca-Cola has Coca-Cola, Diet Coke, Tab, Sprite, Fresca, and Fanta to satisfy different drinking tastes. The company even has a brand of orange juice, Minute Maid, for the segment of consumers who drink juice rather than carbonated beverages.

The total-market strategy is highly risky. For this reason only a very small number of companies in an industry may follow it. Embracing an entire market requires top management commitment. In addition, a company needs ample resources to implement it. Finally, only companies in a strong financial position may find this strategy attractive. As a matter of fact, a deteriorating financial position may force a company to move backward from an across-the-board market strategy. Chrysler Corporation's financial woes in the 1990s led it to reduce the scope of its markets overseas at a time when experts were anticipating the emergence of a single global market. The total-market strategy can be highly rewarding in terms of achieving growth and market share, but it may or may not lead to increased profitability.

Seeking Changes in Market Scope

There are only limited periods during which the fit between the key requirements of a market and the particular competencies of a firm competing in that market is at an optimum. Companies should not, therefore, tie themselves to a particular market strategy permanently. Environmental shifts may necessitate a change in perspective from one period to another. Consider the Household Finance Corporation (HFC). It gave such short shrift to its traditional business in the 1970s that the company appeared to be a prime candidate for a name change; in 1977 only 46 percent of its net income came from consumer lending, compared with 78 percent in 1965. In the 1970s, the big banks were beginning to promote their new national credit cards aggressively, mass merchandisers were touting their own credit cards more actively, and credit unions were capitalizing on their tax-exempt status to attract more borrowers with low-interest loans. In response to these trends, HFC had to take it easy in the household finance business as a defensive measure. Thus, HFC reduced the scope of its market. In 1978, as new opportunities emerged for expanding its financial services, the company decided to revitalize its position in the household finance market.[8] In the 1990s, the company continued its thrust in household finance. Similarly, Gerber Products long dominated the U.S. baby food market, but declining birth rates forced it to seek growth elsewhere. The company has been planning to introduce foods for older people.[9]

The J.C. Penney Company, after 75 years of being identified as a retailer of private-label soft goods to price-conscious customers, decided around 1978 to change the scope of its market. The company transformed itself so that it occupied a position between a traditional department store and a discount store (something along the lines of a moderately priced department store with emphasis on higher-priced fashion) in hard goods, housewares, and especially apparel. The company continued to upgrade throughout the 1980s and has successfully been able to attract more upscale customers.[10]

Disney's emphasis on the 5- to 13-year-old age market has been a phenomenon in itself. During the 1960s, this segment continued to grow, providing the company with opportunities for expansion. In the 1970s, however, this segment shrank; it declined further in the 1980s, leading the company to change its strategic perspectives. It began serving the over-25 age group by making changes in its current offerings and by undertaking new projects: Epcot Center, Disney MGM Studios theme park, and Typhoon Lagoon are all attached to Disney World in Florida.[11]

Briefly, then, markets are moving targets, and a company's strategic perspectives must change accordingly.

MARKET-GEOGRAPHY STRATEGY

Geography has long been used as a strategic variable in shaping market strategy. History provides many examples of how businesses started locally and gradually expanded nationally, even internationally. Automobiles, telephones, televisions, and jet aircraft have brought all parts of the country together so that distance ceases to be important, thus making geographic expansion an attractive choice when seeking growth.

Take the case of Ponderosa System, a fast-food chain of steak houses (a division of Metromedia Steak Houses, Inc.). The company started in 1969 with four restaurants in Indiana. By 1970 it had added 10 more restaurants in Indiana and southern Ohio. At the end of 1991, there were almost 800 Ponderosa Steak Houses all over the country. The company continues to expand geographically; by 1993 Ponderosa Steak Houses are expected to be found coast to coast.

There are a variety of reasons for seeking geographic expansion: to achieve growth, reduce dependence on a small geographic base, use national advertising media, realize experience (i.e., economies of scale), utilize excess capacity, and guard against competitive inroads by moving into more distant regional markets. This section examines various alternatives of market-geography strategy. The purpose here is to highlight strategic issues that may dictate the choice of a geographic dimension in the context of market strategy.

Local-Market Strategy

In modern days the relevance of local-market strategy may be limited to (a) retailers and (b) service organizations, such as airlines, banks, and medical centers. In many cases, geographic dimensions of doing business are decided by law. For example, until recently, an airline needed permission from the Civil Aeronautics Board (which was dissolved in 1983 after the airline industry deregulation) to change the areas it could cover. By the same token, banks traditionally could only operate locally.

Of the 2 million retailers in the United States, about half have annual sales of less than $100,000. Presumably, these are all local operations. Even manufacturers may initially limit the distribution of new products to a local market. Local-market strategy enables a firm to prosper by serving customers in a narrow geographic area well. The strategy emphasizes personal service, which bigger rivals may shun.

Regional-Market Strategy

The regional scope of a business may vary from operations in two or three states to those spread over larger sections of the country: New England, the Southwest, the Midwest, or the West, for example. Regional expansion provides a good compromise between doing business locally and going national.

Regional expansion ensures that, if business in one city is depressed, favorable conditions prevailing in other regions allow the overall business to remain satisfactory. In the 1980s, Marshall Field, the Chicago-based department store (now a division of Dayton-Hudson Company), found itself pummeled by recent demographic and competitive trends in that city. Therefore, it decided to expand into new regions in the South and West. This way it could lessen its concentration in the Midwest and expand into areas where growth was expected.

Further, it is culturally easier to handle a region than an entire country. The logistics of conducting business regionally are also much simpler. As a matter of fact, many companies prefer to limit themselves to a region in order to avoid competition and to keep control centralized. Regional-market strategy allows companies to address America's diversity by dividing the country into well-defined geographic areas, choosing one or more areas to serve, and formulating a unique marketing mix to serve each region.

Many businesses continue to operate successfully on a regional scale. The following large grocery chains, for example, are regional in character: Safeway in the West, Kroger's in the Midwest, and Stop & Shop in the East. Regional expansion of a business helps achieve growth and, to an extent, to gain market share. Simply expanding a business regionally, however, may or may not affect profitability.

Geographic expansion of a business to a region may become necessary either to achieve growth or to keep up with a competitor. For example, a small pizza chain with about 30 restaurants in an Ohio metropolitan area had to expand its territory when Pizza Hut started to compete aggressively with it.

At times, a regional strategy is much more desirable than going national. A company operating nationally may do a major portion of its business in one region, with the remainder spread over the rest of the country, or it may find it much more profitable to concentrate its effort in a region where it is most successful and divest itself of its business elsewhere. Although with the acquisition of Stroh Brewery Company in 1989 Coors now has a national presence, traditionally it has only been distributed in about 50 percent of the U.S. market.[12]

National-Market Strategy

Going from a regional to a national market presumably opens up opportunities for growth. This may be illustrated with reference to Borden, Inc. A dairy business by tradition, in the 1980s Borden decided to become a major player in the snack food arena. It acquired seven regional companies, among them Snacktime, Jays, and Laura Scudder's, to compete nationally, to grow, and to provide stiffer competition for PepsiCo's Frito-Lay division.[13]

It was the prospect of growth that influenced the Radisson Hotel Corporation of Minneapolis to go national and become a major competitor in the hotel business. Radisson decided to move into prime "gateway" markets—New York,

Los Angeles, Boston, Chicago, and San Francisco—where it could compete against such giants as Marriott and Hyatt.

In some cases, the profit economics of an industry requires going national. For example, success in the beer industry today demands huge advertising outlays, new product introductions (e.g., light beer), production efficiencies, and wide distribution. These characteristics forced Adolph Coors to go national.

Going national, however, is far from easy. Each year a number of products enters the market, hoping eventually to become national brands. Ultimately, however, only a small percentage of them hits the national market; a still smaller percentage succeeds.

A national-market strategy requires top management commitment because a large initial investment is needed for promotion and distribution. This requirement makes it easier for large companies to introduce new brands nationally, partly because they have the resources and are in the position to take the risk and partly because a new brand can be sheltered under the umbrella of a successful brand. For example, a new product introduced under GE's name has a better chance of succeeding than one introduced by an unknown company.

To implement a national-market strategy successfully, a company needs to institute proper controls to make sure that things are satisfactory in different regions. Where controls are lacking, competitors, especially regional ones, may find it easy to break in. If that situation comes about, the company may find itself losing business in region after region. Still a national-market strategy, if implemented properly, can go a long way in providing growth, market share, and profitability.

International-Market Strategy

A number of corporations have adopted international-market postures. The Singer Company, for example, has been operating overseas for a long time. The international-market strategy became a popular method for achieving growth objectives among large corporations in the post–World War II period.

In its attempts to reconstruct war-torn economies, the U.S. government provided financial assistance to European countries through the Marshall Plan. Because the postwar American economy emerged as the strongest in the world, its economic assistance programs, in the absence of competition, stimulated extensive corporate development of international strategies.

At the end of 1990, according to a U.S. Department of Commerce report, U.S. direct investment abroad was estimated at $410 billion, up from $262 billion in 1986. About 75 percent of U.S. investment overseas has traditionally been in developed countries. However, as many less-developed countries (LDCs) gained political freedom after World War II, their governments also sought U.S. help to modernize their economies and to improve their living standards. Thus, LDCs have provided additional investment opportunities for U.S. corporations, especially in more politically stable countries. It is interesting, however, that although for cultural, political, and economic reasons more viable opportunities were found in Western Europe, Canada, and, to a lesser extent, Japan, LDCs provided a better return on direct U.S. investment. For example, in 1988 LDCs accounted for about 30 percent of income but less than 23 percent of investment.[14]

In recent years, overseas business has become a matter of necessity from the viewpoint of both U.S. corporations and the U.S. government. The increased competition facing many industries, resulting from the saturation of markets and competitive threats from overseas corporations doing business domestically, has forced U.S. corporations to look to overseas markets. At the same time, the unfavorable balance of trade, partly due to increasing energy imports, has made the need to expand exports a matter of vital national interest. Thus, although in the 1950s and 1960s international business was considered a means of capitalizing on a new opportunity, in today's changing economic environment it has become a matter of survival.

Generally speaking, international markets provide additional opportunities over and above domestic markets. In some cases, however, a company may find the international market an alternative to the domestic market. Massey-Ferguson decided long ago to concentrate on sales outside of North America rather than compete with powerful U.S. farm equipment producers. Massey's entire organization, including engineering, research, and production, is geared to market changes overseas. It has learned to live with the instability of foreign markets and to put millions of dollars into building its worldwide manufacturing and marketing networks. The payoff for the company from its emphasis on the international market has been encouraging. In the 1980s, the company outperformed both Deere and International Harvester.

With the world's biggest private inventory of commercial softwood, Weyerhaeuser has been able to build an enviable export business—a market its competitors have virtually ignored until recently. This focus has given Weyerhaeuser a unique advantage in a rapidly changing world market. Consumption of forest products overseas in the 1990s is projected to increase at double the domestic rate of 2 to 3 percent annually. Particularly dramatic growth is expected in the Pacific Basin, which Weyerhaeuser is ideally located to serve. Moreover, dwindling timber supplies and high oil costs are putting European and Japanese producers at an increasing disadvantage even in their own markets, creating a vacuum that North American producers are now rushing to fill. With a product mix already heavily weighted toward export commodities and with unmatched access to deep-water ports, Weyerhaeuser is way ahead of its competitors in what is shaping up to be an export boom in U.S. forest products. Exports, which in 1988 accounted for 25 percent of Weyerhaeuser's sales and an even higher percentage of its profits, could account for fully half of the company's total revenues by the year 2000.[15]

Other Dimensions of Market-Geography Strategy

A company may be regional or national in character, yet it may not cover its entire trading area. These gaps in the market provide another opportunity for growth. For example, the Southland Corporation has traditionally avoided putting its 7-Eleven stores (now a division of the Yokado Group of Japan) in downtown areas. About 6500 of these stores in suburban areas provide it with more than $2 billion in sales. A few years ago, the company opened a store at 34th and Lexington in New York City, signaling the beginning of a major drive into the last of the U.S. markets that 7-Eleven had not yet tapped. Similarly, Hyatt Corp. has hotels in all major cities but not in all resort and suburban areas. To continue to grow, this is the gap the company plans to fill in the 1990s.[16] Bloom and Kotler label this type of strategic posture "market fortification." The advantage of this strategy is to prevent the competition from moving in.[17]

Gaps in the market are left unfilled either because certain markets do not initially promise sufficient potential or because local competition appears too strong to confront. However, a corporation may later find that these markets are easy to tap if it consolidates its position in other markets or if changes in the environment create favorable conditions.

MARKET-ENTRY STRATEGY

Market-entry strategy refers to the timing of market entry. Basically, there are three market-entry options from which a company can choose: (a) be first in the market, (b) be among the early entrants, or (c) be a laggard. The importance of the time of entry can be illustrated with reference to computers. Experience has shown that if new product lines are acceptable to users and if their impact is properly controlled through pricing and contractual arrangements, sales of an older line can be stimulated. Customers are more content to upgrade within the current product line if they know that a more advanced machine is available whenever they need it. A successful introduction, therefore, requires that the right product is announced at the right time. If it is announced too early, the manufacturer will suffer a drop in revenues and will lose customers to the competition.

First-In Strategy

To be the first in the market with a product provides definite advantages. The company can create a lead for itself that others will find difficult to match. Following the experience curve concept, if the first entrant gains a respectable share of the market, across-the-board costs should go down by a fixed percentage every time experience doubles. This cost advantage can be passed on to customers in the form of lower prices. Thus, competitors will find it difficult to challenge the first entrant in a market because, in the absence of experience, their costs and hence their prices for a similar product will be higher. If the new introduction is protected by a patent, the first entrant has an additional advantage because it will have a virtual monopoly for the life of the patent.

The success story of Kinder-Care Learning Centers illustrates the significance of being first in the market. In 1968 a real estate developer, Perry Mendel, had an idea that many people thought was outrageous, impractical, and probably immoral. He wanted to create a chain of child care centers, and he wanted to use the same techniques of standardization that he had seen work for motels and fast-food chains.

Convinced that the number of women working outside the home would continue to increase, Mendel started Kinder-Care Learning Centers. In its brief history, the company has become a dominant force in the commercial child care industry.

The strategy to be the first, however, is not without risks. The first entrant must stay ahead of technology or risk being dethroned by competitors. Docutel Corporation provides an interesting case. This Dallas-based company was the first to introduce automated teller machines (ATMs) in the late 1960s. These machines made it possible for customers to withdraw cash from and make deposits to their savings and checking accounts at any time by pushing a few buttons. Docutel had virtually no competition until 1975, and as recently as 1976, the company had a 60 percent share of the market for ATMs. Then the downfall began. Market share fell to 20 percent in 1977 and to 8 percent in 1978. Docutel's fortunes changed because the company failed to maintain its technological lead. Its second-generation ATM failed miserably and thus made room for competitors. Diebold was the major beneficiary of Docutel's troubles: its share of the market jumped to 70 percent in 1978 from barely 15 percent in 1976. Although Docutel's comeback efforts have been encouraging, the company may never again occupy a dominant position in the ATM industry.

A company whose strategy is to be the first in the market must stay ahead no matter what happens because the costs of yielding the first position to someone else later can be very high. Through heavy investment in promotion, the first entrant must create a primary demand for a product where none exists. Competitors will find it convenient to piggyback because by the time they enter the market, primary demand is already established. Thus, even if a company has been able to develop a new product for an entirely new need, it should carefully evaluate whether it has sufficient technological and marketing strength to command the market for a long time. Competitors will make every effort to break in, and if the first company is unsure of itself, it should wait. Apple Computer, for example, was the first company in the personal computer field. Despite its best efforts, it could not compete against IBM. The upstart company that always talked confrontation with IBM finally decided to play second fiddle. The strategy to be first, however, if properly implemented, can be highly rewarding in terms of growth, market share, and profitability.

Early-Entry Strategy

Several firms may be working on the same track to develop a new product. When one introduces the product first, the remaining firms are forced into an early-entry strategy, whether they had planned to be first or had purposely waited for someone else to take the lead. If the early entry takes place on the heels of the first entry, there is usually a dogfight between the firms involved. By and large, the fight is between two firms, the leader and a strong follower (even though there may be several other followers). The reason for the fight is that both firms have worked hard on the new product, both aspire to be the first in the market, both have made a strong commitment to the product in terms of resources. In the final phases of their new-product development, if one of the firms introduces the product first, the other one must rush to the market right away to prevent the first company from creating a stronghold. Ultimately, the competitor with a superior marketing strategy in terms of positioning, product, price, promotion, and distribution comes out ahead.

After the first two firms find their natural positions in the market and the market launches itself on a growth course, other entrants may follow. These firms exist on the growth wave of the market and exit as the market matures.

Back in the 1960s, General Foods Corporation was working on the development of a new type of coffee product by freeze-drying it. The company already had a strong position in the regular and instant coffee markets. As General Foods was finalizing various aspects of the marketing strategy for its new coffee, later to be called Maxim, Nestlè introduced its own brand of freeze-dried coffee (Taster's Choice). General Foods immediately followed suit, and the two firms aggressively fought for market share. Nestlè carried the ball, however, because General Foods rushed to the market when it was not quite ready.

Early entry on the heels of a leader is desirable if a company has an across-the-board superior marketing strategy and the resources to fight the leader. As a matter of fact, the later entrant may get an additional boost from the groundwork laid by the leader (in the form of creation of primary demand). A weak early entrant, however, will be conveniently swallowed by the leader. The Docutel case discussed above illustrates the point. Docutel was the leader in the ATM market. However, being a weak leader, it paved the way for a later entrant, Diebold, to take over the market it had developed.

As the market reaches the growth phase, a number of other firms may enter it. Depending on the length of the growth phase and the point at which firms enter the market, some could be labeled as early entrants. Most of these early entrants prefer to operate in specific market niches rather than compete against major firms. For example, a firm may concentrate on doing private branding for a major retailer. Many of these firms, particularly marginal operations, may be forced out of the market as growth slows down. In summary, an early-entry strategy is justifiable in the following circumstances:[18]

1. When the firm can develop strong customer loyalty based upon perceived product quality and retain this loyalty as the market evolves
2. When the firm can develop a broad product line to help discourage entries and combat competitors who choose a single market niche
3. When either current investment is not substantial or when technological change is not anticipated to be so rapid and abrupt as to create obsolescence problems
4. When an early entrant can initiate the experience curve and when the amount of learning is closely associated with accumulated experience that cannot readily be acquired by later entrants
5. When absolute cost advantages can be achieved by early commitment to raw materials, component manufacture, distribution channels, and so forth

6. When the initial price structure is likely to be high because the product offers superior value to products being displaced
7. When prospective competitors can be discouraged as the market is not strategically crucial to them and existing competitors are willing to see their market shares erode

Early entry, therefore, can be a rewarding experience if the entry is made with a really strong thrust directed against the leader's market or if it is carefully planned to serve an untapped market. Early entry can contribute significantly to profitability and growth. For the firm that takes on the leader, the early entry may also help in gaining market share.

Laggard Entry Strategy

The laggard entry strategy refers to entering the market toward the tail end of the growth phase or in the maturity phase of the market. There are two principal alternatives to choose from in making an entry in the market as a laggard: to enter as imitator or as initiator. An **imitator** enters the market as a me-too competitor; that is, imitators develop a product that, for all intents and purposes, is similar to one already on the market. An **initiator**, on the other hand, questions the status quo and, after doing some innovative thinking, enters the market with a new product. Between these two extremes are companies that enter stagnant markets with modified products.

Entry into a market as an imitator is short-lived. A company may be able to tap a portion of a market initially by capitalizing on the customer base of the major competitor(s). In the long run, however, as the leader discards the product in favor of a new or improved one, the imitator is left with nowhere to go. In the early 1970s Honeywell was faced with a decision: Which type of advanced computer system should it develop, an imitation of the IBM 360 or its own new version? The company favored the second alternative:

> [Although] the copy might make it easier to tap IBM's huge customer base, it was rejected on several counts. First, it relegated Honeywell to the status of a "me too" company. Secondly, even if a high performance/low cost system were developed, there was no assurance that customers would want an imitation. "After all, if you are looking for a Ford, you go to a Ford dealer." It was agreed that the Task Force would develop its own state-of-the-art system.[19]

This strategy worked well for Honeywell. The company developed a new series of computers especially suited to manufacturing operations and made strong inroads into European markets.

Imitators have many inherent advantages that make it possible to run a profitable business. These advantages include availability of the latest technological improvements; feasibility of achieving greater economies of scale; ability to obtain better terms from suppliers, employees, or customers; and ability to offer lower prices. Thus, even without superior skills and resources, an imitator may perform well.[20]

The initiator starts by seeking ways to dislodge the established competitor(s) in some way. Consider the following examples:

> The blankets produced by an electrical appliance manufacturer carried the warning: "Do not fold or lie on this blanket." One of the company's engineers wondered why no one had designed a blanket that was safe to sleep on while in operation. His questioning resulted in the production of an electric underblanket that was not only safe to sleep on while in operation, but was much more efficient: being insulated by the other bed clothes, it wasted far less energy than conventional electric blankets, which dissipate most of their heat directly into the air.
>
> A camera manufacturer wondered why a camera couldn't have a built-in flash that would spare users the trouble of finding and fixing an attachment. To ask the question was to answer it. The company proceeded to design a 35 mm camera with built-in flash, which has met with enormous success and swept the Japanese medium-priced single-lens market.[21]

These two examples illustrate how a latecomer may be able to make a mark in the market through creativity and initiative. In other words, by exploiting technological change, avoiding direct competition, or changing the accepted business structure (e.g., a new form of distribution), the initiator has an opportunity to establish itself in the market successfully.[22]

The Wilmington Corporation adopted the middle course when entering the pressed glass-ceramic cookware market in 1977. Until that time, Corning Glass Works was the sole producer of this product. Corning held a patent that expired in January 1977. The Wilmington Corporation opted not to enter the market with a me-too product. It sought entry into the market with a modified product line: round containers in solid colors. Corning's product was square-shaped and white and had a cornflower design. The company felt that its product would enlarge the market by appealing to a broader range of consumer tastes.[23]

Whatever course a company may pursue to enter the market, as a laggard, it cannot expect much in terms of profitability, growth, or market share. When laggards enter the market, it is already saturated; only established firms can operate profitably. As a matter of fact, their built-in experience affords the established competitors an even greater advantage. An initiator, however, may be able to make a profitable entry, at least until an established firm adds innovation to its own line.

MARKET-COMMITMENT STRATEGY

The **market-commitment strategy** refers to the degree of involvement a company seeks in a particular market. It is widely held that not all customers are equally important to a company. Often such statements as "17 percent of our customers account for 60 percent of our sales" and "56 percent of our customers provide 11 percent of our sales" are made, which indicate that a company should make varying commitments to different customer groups. The commitment can be in the form of financial or managerial resources or both. Presumably, the results from any venture are commensurate with the commitment made, which explains the importance of the commitment strategy.

Commitment to a market may be categorized as strong, average, or light. Whatever the nature of the commitment, it must be honored: a company that fails to regard its commitment can get into trouble. In 1946 the Liggett and Myers Tobacco Company had a 22 percent share of the U.S. cigarette market. In 1978 its share of the market was less than 3.5 percent; in 1989, slightly less than 3 percent. A variety of reasons has been given for the company's declining fortunes, all amounting to a lack of commitment to a market that at one time it had commanded with an imposing market share. These reasons include responding too slowly to changing market conditions, using poor judgment in positioning brands, and failing to attract new and younger customers. The company lagged behind when filters were introduced. It also missed industry moves to both king-size and extra-long cigarettes. It missed the market move toward low-tar cigarettes. Its major entry in that category, Decade, was not introduced until 1977, well after competitors had established similar brands.[24] Liggett and Myers illustrates that a company can lose a comfortable position in any market if it fails to commit itself adequately to it.

Strong-Commitment Strategy

The strong-commitment strategy requires a company to operate in a market optimally by realizing economies of scale in promotion, distribution, manufacturing, and so on. If a competitor challenges a company's position in the market, the latter must fight back aggressively by employing different forms of product, price, promotion, and distribution strategies. In other words, because the company has a high stake in the market, it should do all it can do to defend its position.

A company with a strong commitment to a market should refuse to be content with the status quo. It should foresee its own obsolescence by developing new products, improving product quality, and increasing expenditures for sales force, advertising, and sales promotion relative to the market's growth rate.[25]

This point may be illustrated with reference to the Polaroid Corporation. The company continues to do research and development to stay ahead of the field. The original Land camera, introduced in 1948, produced brown-and-white pictures. Thereafter, the company developed film that took truly black-and-white pictures with different ASA speeds. Also, the time involved in the development of film was reduced from the original 60 seconds to 10 seconds. In 1963 the company introduced color-print film with a development time of 60 seconds; in the early 1970s, the company introduced the SX-70 camera, which made earlier Polaroid cameras obsolete. Since its introduction, a variety of changes and improvements have been made both in the SX-70 camera and in the film that goes into it. A few years later, the company introduced yet another much-improved camera, Spectra. In 1976 Kodak introduced its own version of the instant camera. Polaroid charged Kodak with violating seven Polaroid patents and legally forced Kodak out of the instant photography business.[26] The result:

Polaroid has retained its supremacy in the instant photography field, a field to which it has been solely committed.

The nature of a company's commitment to a market may, of course, change with time. Until 1971 Procter and Gamble had a weak commitment to the coffee market, especially in the East. Its Folgers coffee was almost unknown east of the Mississippi. In the early 1970s, the company made a strong commitment to the coffee market in the East, city by city. At that time a small company called Breakfast Cheer Coffee Company made $12 million a year in sales and had an 18 percent share of the coffee market in Pittsburgh. By 1974, because of Procter and Gamble's strength, Breakfast Cheer's sales had plummeted to $2.3 million and its market share had dwindled to under 1 percent. Procter and Gamble had become a major factor in coffee in the Pittsburgh market.[27]

Strong commitment to a market can be highly rewarding in terms of achieving growth, market share, and profitability. A warning is in order, however. The commitment made to a market should be based on a company's resources, its strengths, and its willingness to take risks to live up to its commitment. For example, Procter and Gamble could afford to implement its commitment to the Pittsburgh market because it had a good rapport with distributors and dealers and the resources to launch an effective promotional campaign. A small company could not have afforded to do all that.

Average-Commitment Strategy

When a company has a stable interest in a market, it must stress the maintenance of the status quo, leading to an only average commitment to the market. Adoption of the average-commitment strategy may be triggered by the fact that a strong-commitment strategy is not feasible. The company may lack the resources to make a strong commitment; a strong commitment may be in conflict with top management's value orientation; or the market in question may not constitute a major thrust of the business in, for example, a diversified company.

In April 1976, when the Eastman Kodak Company announced its entry into the instant photography field, the company most worried was Polaroid. Because Polaroid had a strong commitment to the instant photography market, it did not like Kodak being there just for the sake of competition. As Polaroid's president commented, "This is our very soul that we are involved with. This is our whole life. For them it's just another field."[28] Similarly, when Frito-Lay (a division of PepsiCo) entered the cookie business in 1982, the industry leader, Nabisco, had to adopt a new strategy to defend its title in the business. As an executive of the company noted, "We aren't going to sit on our haunches and let 82 years of business go down the drain."[29]

A company with an average commitment to a market can afford to make occasional mistakes because it has other businesses to compensate for them. Essentially, the average-commitment strategy requires keeping customers happy by providing them with what they are accustomed to. This can be accomplished by making appropriate changes in a marketing program as required by environmental shifts, thus making it difficult for competitors to lure customers away. Where commitment is average, however, the company becomes vulnerable to the lead company as well as the underdog. The leader may wipe out the average-commitment company by price cutting, a feasible strategy because of the experience effect. The underdog may challenge the average-commitment company by introducing new products, focusing on new segments within the market, trying out new forms of distribution, or launching new types of promotional thrusts. The best defense for a company with an average commitment to a market is to keep customers satisfied by being vigilant about developments in its market.

An average commitment may be adequate, as far as profitability is concerned, if the market is growing. In a slow-growth market, an average commitment is not conducive to achieving either growth or profitability.

Light-Commitment Strategy

A company may have only a passing interest in a market; consequently, it may make only a light commitment to it. The passing interest may be explained by the fact that the market is stagnant, its potential is limited, it is overcrowded with many large companies, and so on. In addition, a company may opt for light commitment to a market to avoid antitrust difficulties. GE maintained a light commitment in the color television market because the field was overcrowded, particularly by Japanese companies. (In 1988 GE sold its television business to Thomson, a French company.) In the early 1970s, Procter and Gamble adopted the light-commitment strategy in the shampoo market, presumably to avoid antitrust difficulties like those it had encountered with Clorox several years previously; Procter and Gamble let its share of the shampoo market slip from around 50 percent to a little over 20 percent, delayed reformulating its established brands (Prell and Head and Shoulders), introduced only one new brand in many years, and substantially cut its promotional efforts.[30]

A company with a light commitment to a market operates passively and does not make any new moves. It is satisfied as long as the business continues to be in the black and thus seeks very few changes in its marketing perspectives. Overall, this strategy is not of much significance for a company pursuing increasing profitability, greater market share, or growth.

MARKET-DILUTION STRATEGY

In many situations, a company may find reducing a part of its business strategically more useful than expanding it. The **market-dilution strategy** works out well when the overall benefit that a company derives from a market, either currently or potentially, is less than it could achieve elsewhere. Unsatisfactory profit performance, desire for concentration in fewer markets, lack of top management knowledge of the market, negative synergy vis-à-vis other markets that the company serves, and lack of resources to develop the market fully are other reasons for diluting market position.

There was a time when dilution of a market was considered an admission of failure. In the 1970s, dilution came to be accepted purely as a matter of strategy.

Different ways of diluting a market include demarketing, pruning marginal markets, key account strategy, and harvesting strategy.

Demarketing Strategy

Demarketing, in a nutshell, is the reverse of marketing. This term became popular in the early 1970s when, as a result of the Arab oil embargo, the supply of a variety of products became short. **Demarketing** is the attempt to discourage customers in general or a certain class of customers in particular on either a temporary or permanent basis.

The demarketing strategy may be implemented in different ways. One way involves keeping close track of time requirements of different customers. Thus, if one customer needs the product in July and another in September, the former's order is filled first even though the latter confirmed the order first. A second way of demarketing is rationing supplies to different customers on an equitable basis. Shell Oil followed this route toward the end of 1978 when a gasoline shortage occurred. Each customer was sold a maximum of 10 gallons of gasoline at each filling. Third, recommending that customers use a substitute product temporarily is a form of demarketing. The fourth demarketing method is to divert a customer with an immediate need for a product to another customer to whom the product was recently supplied and who is unlikely to use it immediately. The company becomes an intermediary between two customers, providing supplies of the product to one customer whenever they are needed if present supplies are transferred to the customer in need.

The demarketing strategy is directed toward maintaining customer goodwill during times when customer demands cannot be adequately met. By helping customers in the different ways discussed above, the company hopes that the situation requiring demarketing is temporary and that, when conditions are normal again, customers will be inclined favorably toward the company. In the long run, the demarketing strategy should lead to increased profitability.

Pruning-of-Marginal-Markets Strategy

A company must undertake a conscious search for those markets that do not provide rates of return comparable to those rates that could be attained if it were to shift its resources to other markets. These markets potentially become candidates for pruning. The pruning of marginal markets may result in a much higher growth rate for the company as a whole. Consider two markets, one providing 10 percent and the other 20 percent on original investments of $1 million. After 15 years, the first market will show an equity value of $4 million, as opposed to $16 million for the second one. Pruning can improve return on investment and growth rate by ridding the company of markets that are growing more slowly than the rest of its markets and by providing cash for investment in faster-growing, higher-return markets. Several years ago, A&P closed more than 100 stores in markets where its competitive position was weak. This pruning effort helped the company to fortify its position and to concentrate on markets where it felt strong.

Pruning also helps to restore balance. A company may be out of balance when it has too many diverse and difficult markets to serve. By pruning, the company may limit its operations to growth markets only. Because growth markets require heavy doses of investment (in the form of price reductions, promotion, and market development) and because the company may have limited resources, the pruning strategy can be very beneficial. Chrysler Corporation, for example, decided in 1978 to quit the European market so that it could use its limited resources to restore its position in the U.S. market. The pruning strategy is especially helpful in achieving market share and profitability.

Key-Markets Strategy

In most industries, a few customers account for a major portion of volume. This characteristic may be extended to markets. If the breakdown of markets is properly done, a company may find that a few markets account for a very large share of its revenues. Strategically, these key markets may call for extra emphasis in terms of selling effort, after-sales service, product availability, and so on. As a matter of fact, the company may decide to limit its business to these key markets alone.

The key-markets strategy requires

1. A strong focus tailored to environmental differences (i.e., don't try to do everything; rather compete in carefully selected ways with the competitive emphasis differing according to the market environment)
2. A reputation for high quality (i.e., turn out high-quality products with superior performance potential and reliability)
3. Medium to low relative prices complimenting high quality
4. Low total cost to permit offering high-quality products at low prices and still show high profits[31]

Harvesting Strategy

The harvesting strategy refers to a situation where a company may decide to let its market share slide deliberately. The harvesting strategy may be pursued for a variety of reasons: to increase badly needed cash flow, to increase short-term earnings, or to avoid antitrust action. Usually only companies with high market share can expect to harvest successfully.

If a product reaches the stage where continued support can no longer be justified, it may be desirable to realize a short-term gain by raising the price or by lowering quality and cutting advertising to turn an active brand into a passive one. In any event, the momentum of the product may continue for years with sales declining but with useful revenues still coming in.

Because they reduce a firm's strategic flexibility, exit barriers may prevent a company from implementing a harvesting strategy. **Exit barriers** refer to circumstances within an industry that discourage the exit of competitors whose performance in that particular business may be marginal. Three types of exit barriers are (a) a thin resale market for the business's assets, (b) intangible strategic barriers as deterrents to timely exit (e.g., value of distribution networks, customer goodwill for the other products of the company, or strong corporate identification with the product), and (c) management's reluctance to terminate a sick line.[32] When exit barriers disappear or when their effect ceases to be of concern, a harvesting strategy may be pursued.

SUMMARY

This chapter illustrated various types of market strategies that a company may pursue. Market strategies rest on a company's perspective of the customer. Customer focus is a very important factor in market strategy. By diligently delineating the markets to be served, a company can effectively compete in an industry even with established firms.

The five different types of market strategies and the various alternatives under each strategy that were examined in this chapter are outlined below:

1. Market-scope strategy
   a. Single-market strategy
   b. Multimarket strategy
   c. Total-market strategy
2. Market-geography strategy
   a. Local-market strategy
   b. Regional-market strategy
   c. National-market strategy
   d. International-market strategy
3. Market-entry strategy
   a. First-in strategy
   b. Early-entry strategy
   c. Laggard-entry strategy
4. Market-commitment strategy
   a. Strong-commitment strategy
   b. Average-commitment strategy
   c. Light-commitment strategy
5. Market-dilution strategy
   a. Demarketing strategy
   b. Pruning-of-marginal-markets strategy
   c. Key-markets strategy
   d. Harvesting strategy

Application of each strategy was illustrated with examples from marketing literature. The impact of each strategy was considered in terms of its effect on marketing objectives (i.e., profitability, growth, and market share).

DISCUSSION QUESTIONS

1. What circumstances may lead a business unit to change the scope of its market?
2. Under what conditions may a company adopt across-the-board market strategy?
3. Can a company operating only locally go international? Discuss and give examples.
4. Examine the pros and cons of being the first in a market.

5. What underlying conditions must be present before a company can make a strong commitment to a market?
6. Define the term *demarketing*. What circumstances dictate the choice of demarketing strategy?
7. List exit barriers that may prevent a company from implementing a harvesting strategy.

NOTES

[1]"Design and Manufacturing Corporation," a case copyrighted in 1972 by the President and Fellows of Harvard College, p. 4.

[2]"They're More Single-Minded at Tambrands," *Business Week* (28 August 1989): 28.

[3]"Why Noxell Is Touching Up Its Latest Creation," *Business Week* (11 July 1988): 92.

[4]Peter R. Dickson and James L. Ginter, "Market Segmentation, Product Differentiation and Marketing Strategy," *Journal of Marketing* (April 1987): 1-10. See also "Can Pete and Jeff Coors Brew Up a Comeback," *Business Week* (16 December 1985): 86.

[5]"This Bud's For You, No Not You—Her," *Business Week* (4 November 1991): 86.

[6]"Crowning Achievement," *Forbes* (29 October 1990): 178.

[7]"Green Giants Growth Ho-Ho-Hopes," *Advertising Age* (28 May 1990): 20.

[8]"Household Finance: Revitalizing the Business That Got It Started," *Business Week* (25 September 1978): 129. Also see the company's 1987 annual report.

[9]"Gerber's New Chief Doesn't Take Baby Steps," *Business Week* (7 November 1988): 30. See also *Fortune* (13 March 1989): 140.

[10]"The Newly Minted Penney: Where Fashion Rules," *Business Week* (17 April 1989): 88.

[11]Christopher Knowlton, "How Disney Keeps the Magic Going," *Fortune* (4 December 1989): 111.

[12]*Time* (9 October 1989): 80. See also Adolph Coors Company's annual report for 1990.

[13]Bill Saporito, "How Borden Milks Packaged Goods," *Fortune* (21 December 1987): 139.

[14]*Statistical Abstract of the United States*, 1988.

[15]Marc Beauchamp, "Lost in the Woods," *Forbes* (16 October 1989): 22; see also Weyerhaeuser Company's annual report for 1990.

[16]"Glitzy Resorts and Suburban Hotels: Hyatt Breaks New Ground," *Business Week* (4 May 1987): 100.

[17]Paul N. Bloom and Philip Kotler, "Strategies for High Market-Share Companies," *Harvard Business Review* (November-December 1975): 63.

[18]David A. Aaker and George S. Day, "The Perils of High-Growth Markets," *Strategic Management Journal* 7 (1986): 419.

[19]"Honeywell Inc.—EDP Division," a case copyrighted in 1975 by the President and Fellows of Harvard College, p. 10.

[20]George S. Yip, "Gateways to Entry," *Harvard Business Review* (September-October 1982): 85-92.

[21]Kenichi Ohmae, "Effective Strategies for Competitive Success," *McKinsey Quarterly* (Winter 1978): 55.

[22]Yip, "Gateways to Entry."

[23]"Wilmington Corporation," a case copyrighted in 1976 by the President and Fellows of Harvard College.

[24]John Koten, "Liggett's Cigarette Unit Lags, and Some Believe It May Be Snuffed Out," *Wall Street Journal*, 27 November 1978, p. 1.

[25]Robert D. Buzzell and Frederik D. Wiersema, "Successful Share-Building Strategies," *Harvard Business Review* (January–February 1981): 135–44.
[26]Alex Taylor III, "Kodak Scrambles to Refocus," *Fortune* (3 March 1986): 34.
[27]Bill Henderickson, "Tiny Firms Are Losers in Coffee War Fought by Two Big Marketers," *Wall Street Journal,* 3 November 1977, p. 1.
[28]*New York Times,* 28 April 1976, p. 23.
[29]Ann M. Morrison, "Cookies Are Frito-Lay's New Bag," *Fortune* (9 August 1982): 64.
[30]Nancy Giges, "Shampoo Rivals Wonder When P&G Will Seek Old Dominance," *Advertising Age* (23 September 1974): 3.
[31]Carolyn Y. Woo and Arnold C. Cooper, "The Surprising Case for Low Market Share," *Harvard Business Review* (November–December 1982): 106–13. See also Edward P. DiMingo, "Marketing Strategies for Small-Share Players," *Journal of Business Strategy* (January–February, 1990): 26–30.
[32]Kathryn Rudie Harrigan and Michael E. Porter, "End-Game Strategies for Declining Industries," *Harvard Business Review* (July–August 1983): 111–20.

APPENDIX | *Perspectives of Market Strategies*

I Market-Scope Strategy

A. Single-Market Strategy

Definition: Concentration of efforts in a single segment.

Objective: To find a segment currently being ignored or served inadequately and meet its needs.

Requirements: (a) Serve the market wholeheartedly despite initial difficulties. (b) Avoid competition with established firms.

Expected Results: (a) Low costs. (b) Higher profits.

B. Multimarket Strategy

Definition: Serving several distinct markets.

Objective: To diversify the risk of serving only one market.

Requirements: (a) Careful selection of segments to serve. (b) Avoid confrontation with companies serving entire market.

Expected Results: (a) Higher sales. (b) Higher market share.

C. Total-Market Strategy

Definition: Serving the entire spectrum of the market by selling differentiated products to different segments in the market.

Objective: To compete across the board in the entire market.

Requirements: (a) Employ different combinations of price, product, promotion, and distribution strategies in different segments. (b) Top management commitment to embrace entire market. (c) Strong financial position.

Expected Results: (a) Increased growth. (b) Higher market share.

II Market-Geography Strategy

A. Local-Market Strategy

Definition: Concentration of efforts in the immediate vicinity.

Objective: To maintain control of the business.

Requirements: (a) Good reputation in the geographic area. (b) Good hold on requirements of the market.

Expected Results: Short-term success; ultimately must expand to other areas.

B. Regional-Market Strategy

Definition: Operating in two or three states or over a region of the country (e.g., New England).

Objectives: (a) To diversify risk of dependence on one part of a region. (b) To keep control centralized.

Requirements: (a) Management commitment to expansion. (b) Adequate resources. (c) Logistical ability to serve regional area.

Expected Results: (a) Increased growth. (b) Increased market share. (c) Keep up with competitors.

C. National-Market Strategy

Definition: Operating nationally.

Objective: To seek growth.

Requirements: (a) Top management commitment. (b) Capital resources. (c) Willingness to take risks.

Expected Results: (a) Increased growth. (b) Increased market share. (c) Increased profitability.

D. International-Market Strategy

Definition: Operating outside national boundaries.

Objective: To seek opportunities beyond domestic business.

Requirements: (a) Top management commitment. (b) Capital resources. (c) Understanding of international markets.

Expected Results: (a) Increased growth. (b) Increased market share. (c) Increased profits

III Market-Entry Strategy

A. First-In Strategy

Definition: Entering the market before all others.

Objective: To create a lead over competition that will be difficult for them to match.

Requirements: (a) Willingness and ability to take risks. (b) Technological competence. (c) Strive to stay ahead. (d) Heavy promotion. (e) Create primary demand. (f) Carefully evaluate strengths.

Expected Results: (a) Reduced costs via experience. (b) Increased growth. (c) Increased market share. (d) Increased profits.

B. Early-Entry Strategy

Definition: Entering the market in quick succession after the leader.

Objective: To prevent the first entrant from creating a stronghold in the market.

Requirements: (a) Superior marketing strategy. (b) Ample resources. (c) Strong commitment to challenge market leader.

Expected Results: (a) Increased profits. (b) Increased growth. (c) Increased market share.

C. Laggard Entry Strategy

Definition: Entering the market toward tail end of growth phase or during maturity phase. Two modes of entry are feasible: (a) Imitator—Entering market with me-too product; (b) Initiator—Entering market with unconventional marketing strategies.

Objectives: Imitator—To capture that part of the market that is not brand loyal. Initiator—To serve the needs of the market better than present firms.

Requirements: Imitator—(a) Market research ability. (b) Production capability. Initiator—(a) Market research ability. (b) Ability to generate creative marketing strategies.

Expected Results: Imitator—Increased short-term profits. Initiator—(a) Put market on a new growth path. (b) Increased profits. (c) Some growth opportunities.

IV Market-Commitment Strategy

A. Strong-Commitment Strategy

Definition: Fighting off challenges aggressively by employing different forms of product, price, promotion, and distribution strategies.

Objective: To defend position at all costs.

Requirements: (a) Operate optimally by realizing economies of scale in promotion, distribution, manufacturing, etc. (b) Refuse to be content with present situation or position. (c) Ample resources. (d) Willingness and ability to take risks.

Expected Results: (a) Increased growth. (b) Increased profits. (c) Increased market share.

B. Average-Commitment Strategy

Definition: Maintaining stable interest in the market.

Objective: To maintain the status quo.

Requirements: Keep customers satisfied and happy.

Expected Results: Acceptable profitability.

C. Light-Commitment Strategy

Definition: Having only a passing interest in the market.

Objective: To operate in the black.

Requirements: Avoid investing for any long-run benefit.

Expected Results: Maintenance of status quo (no increase in growth, profits, or market share).

V Market-Dilution Strategy

A. Demarketing Strategy

Definition: Discouraging customers in general or a certain class of customers in particular, either temporarily or permanently, from seeking the product.

Objective: To maintain customer goodwill during periods of shortages.

Requirements: (a) Monitor customer time requirements. (b) Ration product supplies. (c) Divert customers with immediate needs to customers who have a supply of the product but no immediate need for it. (d) Find out and suggest alternative products for meeting customer needs.

Expected Results: (a) Increased profits. (b) Strong customer goodwill and loyalty.

B. Pruning-of-Marginal-Markets Strategy

Definition: Weeding out markets that do not provide acceptable rates of return.

Objective: To divert investments in growth markets.

Requirements: (a) Gain good knowledge of the chosen markets. (b) Concentrate all energies on these markets. (c) Develop unique strategies to serve the chosen markets.

Expected Results: (a) Long-term growth. (b) Improved return on investment. (c) Decrease in market share.

C. Key-Markets Strategy

Definition: Focusing efforts on selected markets.

Objective: To serve the selected markets extremely well.

Requirements: (a) Gain good knowledge of the chosen markets. (b) Concentrate all energies on these markets. (c) Develop unique strategies to serve the chosen markets.

Expected Results: (a) Increased profits. (b) Increased market share in the selected markets.

D. Harvesting Strategy

Definition: Deliberate effort to let market share slide.

Objectives: (a) To generate additional cash flow. (b) To increase short-term earnings. (c) To avoid antitrust action.

Requirements: High market share.

Expected Results: Sales decline but useful revenues still come in.

CHAPTER 14

Product Strategies

How many things there are here that I do not want.
SOCRATES

Product strategies specify market needs that may be served by different product offerings. It is a company's product strategies, duly related to market strategies, that eventually come to dominate both overall strategy and the spirit of the company. Product strategies deal with such matters as number and diversity of products, product innovations, product scope, and product design. In this chapter different dimensions of product strategies are examined for their essence, their significance, their limitations, if any, and their contributions to objectives and goals. Each strategy will be exemplified with illustrations from marketing literature.

DIMENSIONS OF PRODUCT STRATEGIES

The implementation of product strategies requires cooperation among different groups: finance, research and development, the corporate staff, and marketing. This level of integration makes product strategies difficult to develop and implement. In many companies, to achieve proper coordination among diverse business units, product strategy decisions are made by top management. At Gould, for example, the top management decides what kind of business Gould is and what type it wants to be. The company pursues products in the areas of electromechanics, electrochemistry, metallurgy, and electronics. The company works to dispose of products that do not fall strictly into its areas of interest.[1]

In some companies, the overall scope of product strategy is laid out at the corporate level, whereas actual design is left to business units. These companies contend that this alternative is more desirable than other arrangements because it is difficult for top management to deal with the details of product strategy in a diverse company. In this chapter the following product strategies are recognized:

- Product-positioning strategy
- Product-repositioning strategy
- Product-overlap strategy
- Product-scope strategy
- Product-design strategy
- Product-elimination strategy

New-product strategy
Diversification strategy

Each strategy is examined from the point of view of an SBU. The appendix at the end of this chapter summarizes each strategy, giving its definition, objectives, requirements, and expected results.

PRODUCT-POSITIONING STRATEGY

The term *positioning* refers to placing a brand in that part of the market where it will receive a favorable reception compared to competing products. Because the market is heterogeneous, one brand cannot make an impact on the entire market. As a matter of strategy, therefore, a product should be matched with that segment of the market in which it is most likely to succeed. The product should be positioned so that it stands apart from competing brands. **Positioning** tells what the product stands for, what it is, and how customers should evaluate it.[2]

Positioning is achieved by using marketing mix variables, especially design and communication. Although differentiation through positioning is more visible in consumer goods, it is equally true of industrial goods. With some products, positioning can be achieved on the basis of tangible differences (e.g., product features); with many others, intangibles are used to differentiate and position products. As Levitt has observed:

> Fabricators of consumer and industrial goods seek competitive distinction via product features—some visually or measurably identifiable, some cosmetically implied, and some rhetorically claimed by reference to real or suggested hidden attributes that promise results or values different from those of competitors' products.
>
> So too with consumer and industrial services—what I call, to be accurate, "intangibles." On the commodities exchanges, for example, dealers in metals, grains, and pork bellies trade in totally undifferentiated generic products. But what they "sell" is the claimed distinction of their execution—the efficiency of their transactions in their client's behalf, their responsiveness to inquiries, the clarity and speed of their confirmations, and the like. In short, the offered product is differentiated, though the generic product is identical.[3]

The desired position for a product may be determined using the following procedure:

1. Analyze product attributes that are salient to customers.
2. Examine the distribution of these attributes among different market segments.
3. Determine the optimal position for the product in regard to each attribute, taking into consideration the positions occupied by existing brands.
4. Choose an overall position for the product (based on the overall match between product attributes and their distribution in the population and the positions of existing brands).

For example, cosmetics for the career woman may be positioned as "natural," cosmetics that supposedly make the user appear as if she were wearing no makeup at all. An alternate position could be "fast" cosmetics, cosmetics to give the user a mysterious aura in the evenings. A third position might be "light" cosmetics, cosmetics to be worn for tennis and other leisure activities.

Consider the positioning of beer. Two positioning decisions for beer are light versus heavy and bitter versus mild. The desired position for a new brand of beer can be determined by discovering its rating on these attributes and by considering the size of the beer market. The beer market is divided into segments according to these attributes and the positions of other brands. It may be found that the heavy and mild beer market is large and that Schlitz and Budweiser compete in it. In the light and mild beer market, another big segment, Miller may be the dominant competitor. Management may decide to position a new brand in competition with Miller.

Disney stores demonstrate how adequate positioning can lead to instant success.[4] Disney stores earn more than three times what other specialty stores earn for every square foot of floor space. Disney has created retail environments with entertainment as their chief motif. As a customer enters the store, he/she sees the Magic Kingdom, a land of bright lights and merry sounds packed full of Mickey Mouse merchandise. From a phone at the front of each store, a customer can get the Disney channel or book a room in a Disney World hotel. Disney designers got down on their hands and knees when they laid out the stores to be sure that their sight lines would work for a three-year-old. The back wall, normally a prime display area, is given over to a large video screen that continuously plays clips from Disney's animated movies and cartoons. Below the screen, at kid level, sit tiers of stuffed animals that toddlers are encouraged to play with. Adult apparel hangs at the front of the stores to announce that they are for shoppers of all ages. Floor fixtures that hold the merchandise angle inward to steer shoppers deeper into this flashy money trap. Managers spend six weeks in intensive preparatory classes and in training before being assigned to a store. Garnished with theatrical lighting and elaborate ceiling displays, the stores have relatively high start-up and fixed costs, but once up and running, they earn high margins.

Six different approaches to positioning may be distinguished:

1. Positioning by attribute (i.e., associating a product with an attribute, feature, or customer benefit)
2. Positioning by price/quality (i.e., the price/quality attribute is so pervasive that it can be considered a separate approach to promotion)
3. Positioning with respect to use or application (i.e., associating the product with a use or application)
4. Positioning by the product user (i.e., associating a product with a user or a class of users)
5. Positioning with respect to a product class (e.g., positioning Caress soap as a bath oil product rather than as soap)
6. Positioning with respect to a competitor (i.e., making a reference to competition as in Avis's now-famous campaign: "We're number two, so we try harder."[5]

Two types of positioning strategy are discussed here: single-brand strategy and multiple-brand strategy. A company may have just one brand that it may place in one or more chosen market segments, or, alternatively, it may have several brands positioned in different segments.

Positioning a Single Brand

To maximize its benefits with a single brand, a company must try to associate itself with a core segment in a market where it can play a dominant role. In addition, it may attract customers from other segments outside its core as a fringe benefit. BMW does very well, for example, positioning its cars mainly in a limited segment to high-income young professionals.

An alternative single-brand strategy is to consider the market undifferentiated and to cover it with a single brand. Several years ago, for example, the Coca-Cola Company followed a strategy that proclaimed that Coke quenched the thirst of the total market. Such a policy, however, can work only in the short run. To seek entry into a market, competitors segment and challenge the dominance of the single brands by positioning themselves in small, viable niches. Even the Coca-Cola Company now has a number of brands to serve different segments: Classic Coke, New Coke, Diet Coke, Fanta, Sprite, Tab, Fresca, and even orange juice.

Take the case of beer. Traditionally brewers operated as if there were one homogeneous market for beer that could be served by one product in one package. Miller, in order to seek growth, took the initiative to segment the market and positioned its High Life brand to younger customers. Thereafter, it introduced a seven-ounce pony bottle that turned out to be a favorite among women and older people who thought that the standard twelve-ounce size was simply too much beer to drink. But Miller's big success came in 1975 with the introduction of another brand, low-calorie Lite. Lite now stands to become the most successful new beer introduced in the United States in this century.

To protect the position of a single brand, sometimes a company may be forced to introduce other brands. Kotler reports that Heublein's Smirnoff brand had a 23 percent share of the vodka market when its position was challenged by Wolfschmidt, priced at $1 less a bottle. Instead of cutting the price of its Smirnoff brand to meet the competition, Heublein raised the price by one dollar and used the increased revenues for advertising. At the same time, it introduced a new brand, Relska, positioning it against Wolfschmidt, and also marketed Popov, a low-price vodka. This strategy effectively met Wolfschmidt's challenge and gave Smirnoff an even higher status. Heublein resorted to multiple brands to protect a single brand that had been challenged by a competitor.[6]

Anheuser-Busch has been dependent on Bud and Bud Light for more than 75 percent of its brewery volume and for 56 percent of its $8.3 billion in sales. It was this dependence on a single brand that led the company to introduce Michelob. This brand, however, is not doing as well as expected, and at the same time, rivals are showing signs of fresh energy and determination, making it urgent for the company to diversify.[7]

Whether a single brand should be positioned in direct competition with a dominant brand already on the market or be placed in a secondary position is another strategic issue. The head-on route is usually risky, but some variation of this type of strategy is quite common. Avis seemingly accepted a number-two position in the market next to Hertz. Gillette, on the other hand, positioned Silkience shampoo directly against Johnson's Baby Shampoo and Procter and Gamble's Prell. Generally, a single-brand strategy is a desirable choice in the short run, particularly when the task of managing multiple brands is beyond the managerial and financial capability of a company. Supposedly, this strategy is more conducive to achieving higher profitability because a single brand permits better control of operations than do multiple brands.

There are two requisites to managing a single brand successfully: a single brand must be so positioned that it can stand competition from the toughest rival, and its unique position should be maintained by creating an aura of a distinctive product. Take the case of Cover Girl. The cosmetics field is a crowded and highly competitive industry. The segment Cover Girl picked out—sales in supermarkets and discount stores—is one that large companies, such as Revlon, Avon, and Max Factor, have not tapped. Cover Girl products are sold at a freestanding display without sales help or demonstration. As far as the second requisite is concerned, creating an aura of a distinctive product, an example is VW's success in protecting its position in the small car market until the 1970s, when Japanese cars entered the market. Another example is Perrier. Perrier continues to protect its position through the mystique attached to its name. In other words, a single brand must have some advantage to protect it from competitive inroads.

Positioning Multiple Brands

Business units introduce multiple brands to a market for two major reasons: (a) to seek growth by offering varied products in different segments of the market and (b) to avoid competitive threats to a single brand. General Motors has a car to sell in all conceivable segments of the market. Coca-Cola has a soft drink for each different taste. IBM sells computers for different customer needs. Procter and Gamble offers a laundry detergent for each laundering need. Offering multiple brands to different segments of the same market is an accepted route to growth.

To realize desired growth, multiple brands should be diligently positioned in the market so that they do not compete with each other and create cannibalism. For example, 20 to 25 percent of sales of Anheuser-Busch's Michelob Light are to customers who previously bought regular Michelob but switched because of the Light brand's low-calorie appeal.[8] The introduction of Maxim by General Foods took sales away from its established Maxwell House brand. Ford's introduction of the Falcon in 1960 as a "new-sized Ford" at a lower price led consumers to substitute Falcons for existing Ford models.[9] About 20 percent of sales of Miller's Genuine Draft beer come from Miller High Life.[10] Thus, it is necessary to be careful in segmenting the market and to position the product, through design and promotion, as uniquely suited to a particular segment.

Of course, some cannibalism is unavoidable. But the question is how much cannibalism is acceptable when introducing another brand. It has been said that 70 percent of Mustang sales in its introductory year were to buyers who would have purchased another Ford had the Mustang not been introduced; the remaining 30 percent of its sales came from new customers. Cadbury's experience with the introduction of a chocolate bar in England indicates that more than 50 percent of its volume came from market expansion, with the remaining volume coming from the company's existing products. Both the Mustang and the chocolate bar were rated as successful introductions by their companies. The apparent difference in cannibalism rates shows that cost structure, degree of market maturity, and the competitive appeal of alternative offerings affect cannibalism sales and their importance to the sales and profitability of a product line and to individual items.[11]

An additional factor to consider in figuring out actual cannibalism is the vulnerability of an existing brand to a competitor's entry into a presumably open spot in the market. For example, suppose that a company's new brand derives 50 percent of its sales from customers who would have bought its existing brand. However, if 20 percent of the sales of this existing brand were susceptible to a competitor's entry (assuming a fairly high probability that the competitor would have indeed positioned its new brand in that open spot), the actual level of cannibalism should be set at 30 percent. This is because 20 percent of the revenue from sales of the existing brand would have been lost to a competitive brand had there been no new brand.

Multiple brands can be positioned in the market either head-on with the leading brand or with an idea. The relative strengths of the new entry and the established brand dictate which of the two positioning routes is more desirable. Although head-on positioning usually appears risky, some companies have successfully carried it out. IBM's copier was positioned in head-on competition with Xerox. Datril, a Bristol-Myers painkiller, was introduced to compete directly with Tylenol.

Positioning with an idea, however, can prove to be a better alternative, especially when the leading brand is well established. Positioning with an idea was attempted by Kraft when it positioned three brands (Breyers and Sealtest ice cream and Light 'n' Lively ice milk) as complements rather than as competitors. Vick Chemical positioned Nyquil, a cold remedy, with the idea that Nyquil assured a good night's sleep. Seagram successfully introduced its line of cocktail mixes, Party Tyme, against heavy odds in favor of Holland House, a National Distillers brand, by promoting it with the Snowbird winter drink.[12]

Positioning of multiple brands and their management in a dynamic environment call for ample managerial and financial resources. When these resources are lacking, a company is better off with a single brand. In addition, if a company already has a dominant position, its attempt to increase its share of the market by introducing an additional brand may invite antitrust action. Such an eventuality should be guarded against. On the other hand, there is also a defensive, or share-maintenance, issue to be considered here even if one has the dominant entry. A product with high market share may not remain in this position forever if competitors are permitted to chip away at its lead with unchallenged positions.

As a strategy, the positioning of multiple brands, if properly implemented, can lead to increases in growth, market share, and profitability.

PRODUCT-REPOSITIONING STRATEGY

Often a product may require repositioning. This can happen if (a) a competitive entry is positioned next to the brand, creating an adverse effect on its share of the market; (b) consumer preferences change; (c) new customer preference clusters with promising opportunities are discovered; or (d) a mistake is made in the original positioning.

Citations from the marketing literature serve to illustrate how repositioning becomes desirable under different circumstances. Simmons Company introduced its Hide-A-Bed (convertible sofa) in 1940. Soon after its introduction, hundreds of competitors followed suit and affected Simmons's business. At the same time, consumer preferences shifted in favor of living room sofas, which plateaued industry sales. Also, consumers were becoming more quality conscious. These conditions led Simmons to reposition its product by reversing emphasis, stressing that their product was not essentially a bed that converted to a sofa but a sofa that converted to a bed. Repositioning was implemented by making appropriate changes in product design (i.e., using high-quality upholstery and elegant style) and by advertising (i.e., stressing utilitarian demand for living room sofas, quality, and fashion consciousness). Following the repositioning in 1960, Simmons's sales increased rapidly.[13]

Over the years, Coca-Cola's position has shifted to keep up with the changing mood of the market. In recent years, the theme of Coca-Cola's advertising has evolved from "Things go better with Coke" to "It's the real thing," to "Coke is it," to "Can't beat the feeling." The current perspective of Coca-Cola's positioning is to reach a generation of young people and those young at heart.

The risks involved in positioning or repositioning a product or service are high. The technique of *perceptual mapping* may be used gainfully to substantially reduce those risks. Perceptual mapping helps in examining the position of a product relative to competing products. It helps marketing strategists

— Understand how competing products or services are perceived by various consumer groups in terms of strengths and weaknesses.
— Understand the similarities and dissimilarities between competing products and services.
— Understand how to reposition a current product in the perceptual space of consumer segments.
— Position a new product or service in an established marketplace.
— Track the progress of a promotional or marketing campaign on the perceptions of targeted consumer segments.[14]

The use of perceptual mapping may be illustrated with reference to the automobile industry. Exhibit 14-1 shows how different cars are positioned on a perceptual map. The map helps the marketing strategist in calculating whether a company's cars are on target. The concentration of dots, which represent competing models, shows how much opposition there is likely to be in a specific territory on the map. Presumably, cars higher up on the graph fetch a higher price than models ranked toward the bottom where the stress is on economy

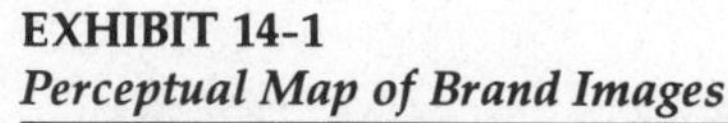

EXHIBIT 14-1
Perceptual Map of Brand Images

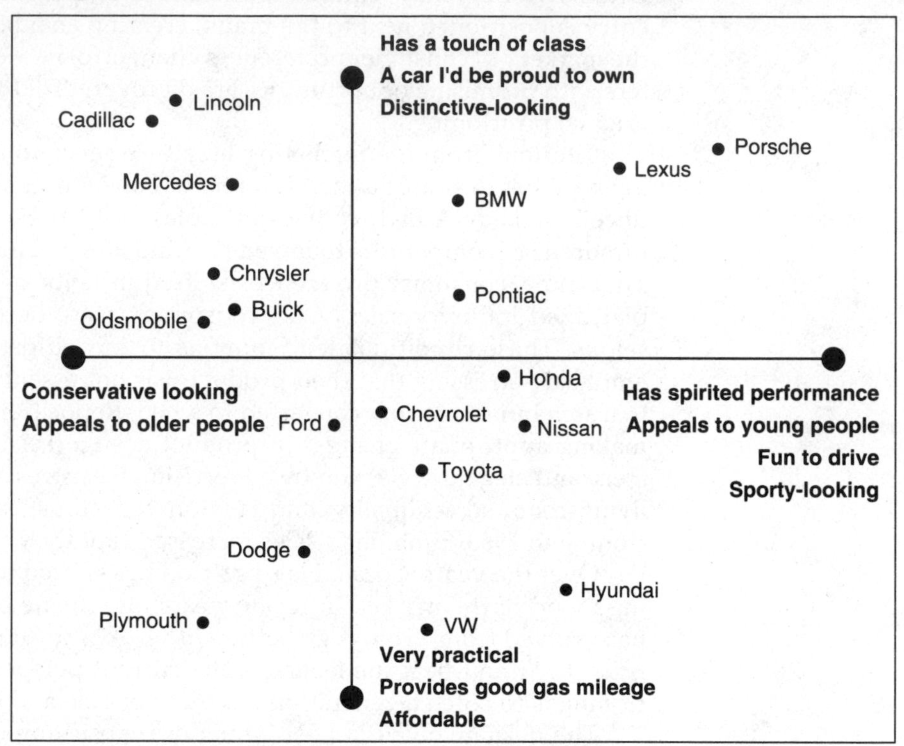

and practicality. After looking at the map, General Motors might find that its Chevrolet division, traditionally geared to entry-level buyers, ought to move down in practicality and more to the right in youthfulness. Another problem for General Motors, which the map so clearly demonstrates, is the close proximity of its Buick and Oldsmobile divisions. This close proximity suggests that the two divisions are waging a marketing war more against each other than against the competition.

Basically, there are three ways to reposition a product: among existing users, among new users, and for new uses. The discussion that follows will elaborate on these repositioning alternatives.

Repositioning among Existing Customers

Repositioning a product among existing customers can be accomplished by promoting alternative uses for it. To revitalize its stocking business, Du Pont adopted a repositioning strategy by promoting the "fashion smartness" of tinted hose. Efforts were directed toward expanding women's collections of hosiery by creating a new fashion image for hosiery: hosiery was not simply a neutral accessory; rather, a suitable tint and pattern could complement each garment in a woman's wardrobe.

General Foods Corporation repositioned Jell-O to boost its sales by promoting it as a base for salads. To encourage this usage, the company introduced a variety of vegetable-flavored Jell-Os. A similar strategy was adopted by 3M Company, which introduced a line of colored, patterned, waterproof, invisible, and write-on Scotch tapes for different types of gift wrapping.

The purpose of repositioning among current users is to revitalize a product's life by giving it a new character as something needed not merely as a staple product but as a product able to keep up with new trends and new ideas. Repositioning among users should help the brand in its sales growth as well as increasing its profitability.

Repositioning among New Users

Repositioning among new users requires that the product be presented with a different twist to people who have not hitherto been favorably inclined toward it. In so doing, care must be taken to see that, in the process of enticing new customers, current customers are not alienated. Miller's attempts to win over new customers for Miller High Life beer are noteworthy. Approximately 15 percent of the population consumes 85 percent of all the beer sold in the United States. Miller's slogan "the champagne of bottled beer" had more appeal for light users than for heavy users. Also, the image projected too much elegance for a product like beer. Miller decided to reposition the product slightly to appeal to a wider range of beer drinkers without weakening its current franchise: "Put another way, the need was to take Miller High Life out of the champagne bucket, but not to put it in the bathtub." After conducting a variety of studies, Miller came up with a new promotional campaign built around this slogan: "If you've got the time, we've got the beer." The campaign proved to be highly successful. Through its new slogan, the brand communicated three things: that it was a quality product worth taking time out for; that it was friendly, low-key, and informal; and that it offered relaxation and reward after the pressures of the workday.[15]

At Du Pont new users of stockings were created by legitimizing the wearing of hosiery among early teenagers and subteenagers. This was achieved by working out a new ad campaign with an emphasis on the merchandising of youthful products and styles to tempt young consumers. Jell-O attempted to develop new users among consumers who did not perceive Jell-O as a dessert or salad product. Jell-O was advertised with a new concept—a fashion-oriented, weight-control appeal.

The addition of new users to a product's customer base helps enlarge the overall market and thus puts the product on a growth route. Repositioning among new users also helps increase profitability because very few new investments, except for promotional costs, have to be made.

Repositioning for New Uses

Repositioning for new uses requires searching for latent uses of the product. The case of Arm and Hammer's baking soda is a classic example of an unexplored use of a product. Today this product is popular as a deodorizer, yet deodorizing was not the use originally conceived for the product. Although new uses for a product can be discovered in a variety of ways, the best way to discover them is to gain insights into the customer's way of using a product. If it is found that a large number of customers are using the product for a purpose other than the one originally intended, this other use could be developed with whatever modifications are necessary.

Repositioning for new uses may be illustrated with reference to a United States Borax and Chemical Corporation's product named Borateem. Initially it was positioned primarily as a laundry deodorant. The company stressed deodorizing and freshening as benefits of the product. After nine years in the market, the company found that a large number of women who had negative feelings about bleaches considered a modified version of this company's product, Borateem Plus, a good substitute for bleach. This led the United States Borax and Chemical Corporation to seek a new position for Borateem—that of a bleach substitute. The repositioning provided consecutive month-to-month sales gains for the product.[16]

At Du Pont, new uses for nylon sprang up in varied types of hosiery (stretch stockings and stretch socks), tires, bearings, etc. Its new uses have kept nylon on the growth path: wrap knits in 1945, tire cord in 1948, textured yarns in 1955, carpet yarns in 1959, and so on. Without these new uses, nylon would have hit the saturation level as far back as 1962.

General Foods found that women used powdered gelatin dissolved in liquid to strengthen their fingernails. Working on this clue, General Foods introduced a flavorless Jell-O as a nail-building agent.

The new-use strategy is directed toward revamping the sales of a product whose growth, based on its original conceived use, has slowed down. This strategy has the potential to increase sales growth, market share, and profitability.

PRODUCT-OVERLAP STRATEGY

The product-overlap strategy refers to a situation where a company decides to compete against its own brand. Many factors lead companies to adopt such a strategic posture. For example, alone A&P stores cannot keep the company's 42 manufacturing operations working at full capacity. Therefore, A&P decided to distribute many of its products through independent food retailers. A&P's Eight O'Clock coffee, for example, is sold through 7-Eleven stores.[17] Procter and Gamble has different brands of detergents virtually competing in the same market. Each brand has its own organization for marketing research, product development, merchandising, and promotion. Although sharing the same sales force, each brand behaves aggressively to outdo others in the marketplace. Sears, Roebuck's large appliance brands are actually manufactured by the Whirlpool Corporation. Thus, Whirlpool's branded appliances compete against those that it sells to Sears.

There are alternative ways in which the product-overlap strategy may be operationalized. Principal among them are having competing lines, doing private labeling, and dealing with original-equipment manufacturers.

Competing Brands

In order to gain a larger share of the total market, many companies introduce competing products to the market. When a market is not neatly delineated, a single brand of a product may not be able to make an adequate impact. If a second brand is placed to compete with the first one, overall sales of the two brands should increase substantially, although there will be some cannibalism. In other words, two competing brands provide a more aggressive front against competitors.

Often the competing-brands strategy works out to be a short-term phenomenon. When a new version of a product is introduced, the previous version is allowed to continue until the new one has fully established itself. In this way, the competition is prevented from stealing sales during the time that the new product is coming into its own. In 1989 Gillette introduced the Sensor razor, a revolutionary new product that featured flexible blades that adjusted to follow the unique contours of the face. At the same time, its previous razor, Atra, continued to be promoted as before. It is claimed that together the two brands were very effective in the market. It is estimated that 36 percent of Sensor users converted from Atra. If Atra had not been promoted, this figure would have been much more, and Sensor would have been more vulnerable to the Schick Tracer and other rigid Atra lookalikes.[18]

To expand its overall coffee market, Procter and Gamble introduced a more economical form of ground coffee under the Folgers label in 1977. A more efficient milling process that refines coffee into flakes allows hot water to come into contact with more of each coffee particle when brewing, resulting in savings of up to 15 percent per cup. The new product, packaged in 13-, 26-, and 32-ounce cans, yielded the same number of cups of coffee as standard 16-, 32-, and 48-ounce cans, respectively. Both the new and the old formulations were promoted aggressively, competing with each other and, at the same time, providing a strong front against brands belonging to other manufacturers.

Reebok International products under the Reebok brand name directly compete with its subsidiary's brand, Avia. As noted earlier, the competing-brands strategy is useful in the short run only. Ultimately, each brand, Avia and Reebok, should find its special niche in the market. If that does not happen, they will create confusion among customers and sales will be hurt. Alternatively, in the long run, one of the brands may be withdrawn, thereby yielding its position to the other brand. This strategy is a useful device for achieving growth and for increasing market share.

Private Labeling

Private labeling refers to manufacturing a product under another company's brand name. In the case of goods whose intermediaries have significant control of the distribution sector, private labeling, or branding, has become quite common. For large food chains, items produced with their label by an outside manufacturer contribute significantly to sales. Sears, J.C. Penney, and other such companies merchandise many different types of goods—textile goods, electronic goods, large appliances, sporting goods, etc.—each carrying the company's brand name.

The private-label strategy may be discussed from two viewpoints, that of the manufacturer and that of the intermediary. A manufacturer offers a private brand if it will help increase total revenues. Of course, the manufacturer's first effort will be to push its own brand, but if the choice is between producing a private brand or having no business, the manufacturer will seriously consider labeling for others. Many companies manufacture solely for others. For example, the Design and Manufacturing Corporation was established to manufacture exclusively privately branded dishwashers for large distributors. This can be a risky position, however, because the manufacturer is at the mercy of customers with whom it may be difficult to negotiate. They know that the manufacturer is not known in the market and will be forced to come to terms. The situation becomes critical if the manufacturer deals mainly with one customer, Sears, for example. There have been many cases where a small manufacturer gave up and sold its business to a distributor with whom it did a major part of its dealings because it just could not operate profitably and still meet the distributor's demand for price reductions.

Many large manufacturers deal in private brands while simultaneously offering their own brands. In this situation, they are competing against themselves. They do so, however, hoping that overall revenues will be higher with the offering of the private brand than without it. Coca-Cola, for example, supplies to A&P stores both its own brand of orange juice, Minute Maid, and the brand it produces with the A&P label. At one time, many companies equated supplying private brands with lowering their brands' images. But the business swings of the 1970s changed attitudes on this issue. Frigidaire appliances at one time were not offered under a private label. However, in 1975 Frigidaire started offering them under Montgomery Ward's name.

A retailer's interest in selling goods under its own brand name is also motivated by economic considerations. The retailer buys goods with its brand name at low cost, then offers the goods to customers at a slightly lower price than the price of a manufacturer's brand (also referred to as a national brand). The assumption is that the customer, motivated by the lower price, will buy a private brand, assuming that its quality is on a par with that of the national brand. This assumption is, of course, based on the premise that a reputable retailer will not offer something under its name if it is not high quality.

Dealing with Original-Equipment Manufacturers (OEMs)

Following the strategy of dealing with an OEM, a company may sell to competitors the components used in its own product. This enables competitors to compete with the company in the market. For example, in the initial stages of color television, RCA was the only company that manufactured picture tubes. It sold these picture tubes to GE and to other competitors, enabling them to compete with RCA color television sets in the market.

The relevance of this strategy may be discussed from the viewpoint of both the seller and the OEM. The motivation for the seller comes from two sources: the desire to work at near-capacity level and the desire to have help in promoting primary demand. Working at full capacity is essential for capitalizing on the experience effect (see chapter 12). Thus, by selling a component to competitors, a company may reduce the across-the-board costs of the component for itself, it will have the price leverage to compete with those manufacturers to whom it sold the component. Besides, the company will always have the option of refusing to do business with a competitor who becomes a problem.

The second source of motivation is the support competitors can provide in stimulating primary demand for a new product. Many companies may be working on a new-product idea. When one of them successfully introduces the product, the others may be unable to do so because they lack an essential component or the technology that the former has. Since the product is new, the innovator may find the task of developing primary demand by itself tedious. It may make a strategic decision to share the essential-component technology with other competitors, thus encouraging them to enter the market and share the burden of stimulating primary demand.

A number of companies follow the OEM strategy. Auto manufacturers sell parts to each other. Texas Instruments sold electronic chips to its competitors during the initial stages of the calculator's development. In the 1950s, Polaroid bought certain essential ingredients from Kodak to manufacture film. IBM has shared a variety of technological components with other computer producers. In many situations, however, the OEM strategy may be forced upon companies by the Justice Department in its efforts to promote competition in an industry. Both Kodak and IBM shared the products of their technology with competitors at the behest of the government. Thus, as a matter of strategy, when government interference may be expected, a company will gain more by sharing its components with others and assuming industry leadership. From the standpoint of results, this strategy is useful in seeking increased profitability, though it may not have much effect on market share or growth.

As far as the OEMs are concerned, the strategy of depending upon a competitor for an essential component only works in the short run because the supplier may at some point refuse entirely to sell the component or may make it difficult for the buyer to purchase it by delaying deliveries or by increasing prices enormously.

PRODUCT-SCOPE STRATEGY

The product-scope strategy deals with the perspective of the product mix of a company (i.e., the number of product lines and items in each line that the company may offer). The product-scope strategy is determined by making reference to the business unit mission. Presumably, the mission defines what sort of business it is going to be, which helps in selecting the products and services that are to become a part of the product mix.

The product-scope strategy must be finalized after a careful review of all facets of the business because it involves long-term commitment. In addition, the strategy must be reviewed from time to time to make any changes called for because of shifts in the environment. The point may be elaborated with reference to Eastman Kodak Company's decision to enter the instant photography market in the early 1970s. Traditionally, Polaroid bought negatives for its films, worth $50 million, from Kodak. In 1969 Polaroid built its own negative plant. This meant Kodak would lose some $50 million of Polaroid's business and be left with idle machinery that had been dedicated to filling Polaroid's needs. Further, by producing its own film, Polaroid could lower its costs; if it then cut prices, instant photography might become more competitive with Kodak's business. Alternatively, if Polaroid held prices high, it would realize high margins and would soon be very rich indeed. Encouraged by such achievements, Polaroid could even develop a marketing organization rivaling Kodak's and threaten it in every sphere. In brief, Kodak was convinced that it would be shut out of the instant photography market forever if it delayed its entry any longer. Subsequently, however, a variety of reasons led Kodak to change its decision to go ahead with instant photography. Its pocket instamatic cameras turned out to be highly successful, and some of the machinery and equipment allocated to instant photography had to be switched over to pocket instamatics. A capital shortage also occurred, and Kodak, as a matter of financial policy, did not want to borrow to support the instant photography project. In 1976 Kodak again revised its position and did enter the field of instant photography.[19]

In brief, commitment to the product-scope strategy requires a thorough review of a large number of factors both inside and outside the organization. The three variants of product-scope strategy that will be discussed in this section are single-product strategy, multiple-products strategy, and system-of-products strategy. It will be recalled that in the previous chapter three alternatives were discussed under market-scope strategy: single-market strategy, multimarket strategy, and total-market strategy. These market strategies may be related to the three variants of product-scope strategy, providing nine different product/market-scope alternatives.

Single Product

A business unit may have just one product in its line and must try to live on the success of this one product. There are several advantages to this strategy. First, concentration on a single product leads to specialization, which helps achieve scale and productivity gains. Second, management of operations is much more efficient when a single product is the focus. Third, in today's environment, where growth leads most companies to offer multiple products, a single-product company may become so specialized in its field that it can stand any competition.

A narrow product focus, for example, cancer insurance, has given American Family Life Assurance Company of Columbus, Georgia, a fast track record. Cancer is probably more feared than any other disease in the United States today. Although it kills fewer people than heart ailments, suffering is often lingering and severe. Cashing in on this fear, American Family Life became the nation's first marketer of insurance policies that cover the expenses of treating cancer. Today 60 percent of all cancer policies in force have been written by American Family. The company ranked 74th in 1986 among North American life, accident, and health insurance companies as measured by premiums; in 1976 its rank had been 135. In 1987 it ranked 63rd.[20]

Despite its obvious advantages, the single-product company has one drawback: if changes in the environment make the product obsolete, the single-product company can be in deep trouble. American history is full of instances where entire industries were wiped out. The disposable diaper, initially introduced by Procter and Gamble via its brand Pampers, pushed the cloth diaper business out of the market. The Baldwin Locomotive Company's steam locomotives were made obsolete by General Motor's diesel locomotives.

The single-product strategy has an additional drawback. It is not conducive to growth or market share. Its main advantage is profitability. If a company with a single-product focus is not able to earn high margins, it is better to seek a new posture. Companies interested in growth or market share will find the single-product strategy of limited value.

Multiple Products

The multiple-products strategy amounts to offering two or more products. A variety of factors lead companies to choose this strategic posture. A company with a single product has nowhere to go if that product gets into trouble; with multiple products, however, poor performance by one product can be balanced out. In addition, it is essential for a company seeking growth to have multiple product offerings.

In 1970, when Philip Morris bought the Miller Brewing Company, it was a one-product business ranking seventh in beer sales. Growth prospects led the company to offer a number of other products. By 1978 Miller had acquired the number two position in the industry with 15 percent of the market. Miller continues to maintain its position (market share in 1990 was 16.5 percent), although Anheuser-Busch, the industry leader, has taken many steps to dislodge it.[21] As another example, consider Chicago-based Dean Foods Company, which traditionally has been a dairy concern. Over the years, diet-conscious and aging consumers have increasingly shunned high-fat dairy products in favor of low-calorie foods, and competition for the business that remains is increasingly fierce. In the early 1980s, to successfully operate in such an environment, the company decided to add other faster-growing, higher-margin refrigerated foods, such as party dips and cranberry drink, to the company's traditional dairy business. Dean's moves have been so successful that, although many milk processors were looking to sell out, it was concerned that it might be bought out.

Multiple products can be either related or unrelated. Unrelated products will be discussed later in the section on diversification. Related products consist of different product lines and items. A food company may have a frozen vegetable line, a yogurt line, a cheese line, and a pizza line. In each line, the company may produce different items (e.g., strawberry, pineapple, apricot, peach, plain, and blueberry yogurt). Note, in this example, the consistency among the different food lines: (a) they are sold through grocery stores, (b) they must be refrigerated, and (c) they are meant for the same target market. These underpinnings make them related products.

Although not all products may be fast moving, they must complement each other in a portfolio of products. The subject of product portfolios was examined in chapter 10. Suffice it to say here that the multiple-products strategy is directed toward achieving growth, market share, and profitability. Not all companies get rich simply by having multiple products: growth, market share, and profitability are functions of a large number of variables, only one of which is having multiple products.

System of Products The word *system*, as applied to products, is a post–World War II phenomenon. Two related forces were responsible for the emergence of this phenomenon: (a) the popularity of the marketing concept that businesses sell satisfaction, not products; and (b) the complexities of products themselves often call for the use of complementary products and after-sale services. A cosmetics company does not sell lipstick, it sells the hope of looking pretty; an airline should not sell plane tickets, it should sell pleasurable vacations. However, vacationers need more than an airline ticket. Vacationers also need hotel accommodations, ground transportation, and sightseeing arrangements. Following the systems concept, an airline may define itself as a vacation packager that sells air transportation, hotel reservations, meals, sightseeing, and so on. IBM is a single source for hardware, operating systems, packaged software, maintenance, emergency repairs, and consulting services. Thus, IBM offers its customers a system of different products and services to solve data processing problems.

Offering a system of products rather than a single product is a viable strategy for a number of reasons. It makes the customer fully dependent, thus allowing the company to gain monopolistic control over the market. The system-of-products strategy also blocks the way for the competition to move in. With such benefits, this strategy is extremely useful in meeting growth, profitability, and market share objectives. If this strategy is stretched beyond its limits, however, a company can get into legal problems. Several years ago, IBM was charged by the Justice Department with monopolizing the computer market. In the aftermath of this charge, IBM has had to make changes in its strategy.

The successful implementation of the system-of-products strategy requires a thorough understanding of customer requirements, including the processes and functions the consumer must perform when using the product. Effective implementation of this strategy broadens both the company's concept of its product and market opportunities for it, which in turn support product/market objectives of growth, profitability, and market share.

PRODUCT-DESIGN STRATEGY

A business unit may offer a standard or a custom-designed product to each individual customer. The decision about whether to offer a standard or a customized product can be simplified by asking these questions, among others:

What are our capabilities? What business are we in? With respect to the first question, there is a danger of overidentification of capabilities for a specific product. If capabilities are overidentified, the business unit may be in trouble. When the need for the product declines, the business unit will have difficulty in relating its product's capabilities to other products. It is, therefore, desirable for a business unit to have a clear perspective about its capabilities. The answer to the second question determines the limits within which customizing may be pursued.

Between the two extremes of standard and custom products, a business unit may also offer standard products with modifications. These three strategic alternatives, which come under the product-design strategy, are discussed below.

Standard Products

Offering standard products leads to two benefits. First, standard products are more amenable to the experience effect than are customized products; consequently, they yield cost benefits. Second, standard products can be merchandised nationally much more efficiently. Ford's Model T is a classic example of a successful standard product. The standard product has one major problem, however. It orients management thinking toward the realization of per-unit cost savings to such an extent that even the need for small changes in product design may be ignored.

There is considerable evidence to suggest that larger firms derive greater profits from standardization by taking advantage of economies of scale and long production runs to produce at a low price.[22] Small companies, on the other hand, must use the major advantage they have over the giants, that is, flexibility. Hence, the standard-product strategy is generally more suitable for large companies. Small companies are better off as job shops, doing customized work at a higher margin.

A standard product is usually offered in different grades and styles with varying prices. In this manner, even though a product is standard, customers have broader choices. Likewise, distribution channels get the product in different price ranges. The result: standard-product strategy helps achieve the product/market objectives for growth, market share, and profitability.

Customized Products

Customized products are sold on the basis of the quality of the finished product, that is, on the extent to which the product meets the customer's specifications. The producer usually works closely with the customer, reviewing the progress of the product until completion. Unlike standard products, price is not a factor for customized products. A customer expects to pay a premium for a customized product. As mentioned above, a customized product is more suitable for small companies to offer. This broad statement should not be interpreted to mean that large companies cannot successfully offer customized products. The ability to sell customized products successfully actually depends on the nature of the product. A small men's clothing outlet is in a better position to offer custom suits than a large men's suit manufacturer. On the other hand, GE is better suited to manufacture a custom-designed engine for military aircraft than a smaller business.

Over and above price flexibility, dealing in customized products provides a company with useful experience in developing new standard products. A number of companies have been able to develop mass market products out of their custom work for NASA projects. The microwave oven, for example, is an offshoot of the experience gained from government contracts. Customized products also provide opportunities for inventing new products to meet other specific needs. In terms of results, this strategy is directed more toward realizing higher profitability than are other product-design strategies.

Standard Products with Modifications

The strategy of modifying standard products represents a compromise between the two strategies already discussed. With this strategy, a customer may be given the option to specify a limited number of desired modifications to a standard product. A familiar example of this strategy derives from the auto industry. The buyer of a new car can choose type of shift (standard or automatic), air conditioning, power brakes, power steering, size of engine, type of tires, and color. Although some modifications may be free, for the most part the customer is expected to pay extra for modifications.

This strategy is directed toward realizing the benefits of both a standard and a customized product. By manufacturing a standard product, the business unit seeks economies of scale; at the same time, by offering modifications, the product is individualized to meet the specific requirements of the customer. The experience of a small water pump manufacturer that sold its products nationally through distributors provides some insights into this phenomenon. The company manufactured the basic pump in its facilities in Ohio and then shipped it to its four branches in different parts of the country. At each branch the pumps were finished according to specifications requested by distributors. Following this strategy, the company lowered its transportation costs (because the standard pump could be shipped in quantity) even while it provided customized pumps to its distributors.

Among other benefits, this strategy permits the business unit to keep in close contact with market needs that may be satisfied through product improvements and modifications. It also enhances the organization's reputation for flexibility in meeting customer requirements. It may also encourage new uses of existing products. Other things being equal, this strategy can be useful in achieving growth, market share, and profitability.

PRODUCT-ELIMINATION STRATEGY

Marketers have believed for a long time that sick products should be eliminated. It is only in recent years that this belief has become a matter of strategy. A business unit's various products represent a portfolio, with each product playing a unique role in making the business viable. If a product's role diminishes or if it does not fit into the portfolio, it ceases to be important.

When a product reaches the stage where continued support is no longer justified because performance is falling short of expectations, it is desirable to pull the product out of the marketplace. Poor performance is easy to spot. It may be characterized by any of the following:

1. Low profitability
2. Stagnant or declining sales volume or market share that is too costly to rebuild
3. Risk of technological obsolescence
4. Entry into a mature or declining phase of the product life cycle
5. Poor fit with the business unit's strengths or declared mission

Products that are not able to limp along must be eliminated. They drain a business unit's financial and managerial resources, resources that could be used more profitably elsewhere. Hise, Parasuraman, and Viswanathan cite examples of a number of companies, among them Hunt Foods, Standard Brands, and Crown Zellerbach, that have reported substantial positive results from eliminating products.[23] The three alternatives in the product-elimination strategy are harvesting, line simplification, and total-line divestment.

Harvesting

Harvesting refers to getting the most from a product while it lasts. It is a controlled divestment whereby the business unit seeks to get the most cash flow it can from the product. The harvesting strategy is usually applied to a product or business whose sales volume or market share is slowly declining. An effort is made to cut the costs associated with the business to improve cash flow. Alternatively, price is increased without simultaneous increase in costs. Harvesting leads to a slow decline in sales. When the business ceases to provide a positive cash flow, it is divested.

Du Pont followed the harvesting strategy in the case of its rayon business. Similarly, BASF Wyandotte applied harvesting to soda ash. As another example, GE harvested its artillery business a few years ago. Even without making any investments or raising prices, the business continued to provide GE with positive cash flow and substantial profits. Lever Brothers applied this strategy to its Lifebuoy soap. The company continued to distribute this product for a long time because, despite higher price and virtually no promotional support, it continued to be in popular demand.

Implementation of the harvesting strategy requires severely curtailing new investment, reducing maintenance of facilities, slicing advertising and research budgets, reducing the number of models produced, curtailing the number of distribution channels, eliminating small customers, and cutting service in terms of delivery time, speed of repair, and sales assistance. Ideally, harvesting strategy should be pursued when the following conditions are present:

1. The business entity is in a stable or declining market.
2. The business entity has a small market share, but building it up would be too costly; or it has a respectable market share that is becoming increasingly costly to defend or maintain.

3. The business entity is not producing especially good profits or may even be producing losses.
4. Sales would not decline too rapidly as a result of reduced investment.
5. The company has better uses for the freed-up resources.
6. The business entity is not a major component of the company's business portfolio.
7. The business entity does not contribute other desired features to the business portfolio, such as sales stability or prestige.[24]

Line Simplification

Line-simplification strategy refers to a situation where a product line is trimmed to a manageable size by pruning the number and variety of products or services offered. This is a defensive strategy that is adopted to keep a falling line stable. It is hoped that the simplification effort will restore the health of the line. This strategy becomes especially relevant during times of rising costs and resource shortages.

The application of this strategy in practice may be illustrated with an example from GE's housewares business. In the early 1970s, the housewares industry faced soaring costs and stiff competition from Japan. GE took a hard look at its housewares business and raised such questions as Is this product segment mature? Is it one we should be harvesting? Is it one we should be investing money in and expanding? Analysis showed that there was a demand for housewares, but demand was just not attractive enough for GE at that time. The company ended production of blenders, fans, heaters, and vacuum cleaners because they were found to be on the downside of the growth curve and did not fit in with GE's strategy for growth.

The implementation of a line-simplification strategy can lead to a variety of benefits: potential cost savings from longer production runs; reduced inventories; and a more forceful concentration of marketing, research and development, and other efforts behind a shorter list of products. According to one point of view, a business unit with an extensive line can trim costs and add to revenues by cutting just 10 percent of the varieties being offered.[25]

Despite obvious merits, simplification efforts may sometimes be sabotaged. Those who have been closely involved with a product may sincerely feel either that the line as it is will revive when appropriate changes are made in the marketing mix or that sales and profits will turn up once temporary conditions in the marketplace turn around. Thus, careful maneuvering is needed on the part of management to simplify a line unhindered by corporate rivalries and intergroup pressures.

The decision to drop a product is more difficult if it is a core product that has served as a foundation for the company. Such a product achieves the status of motherhood, and a company may like to keep it for nostalgic reasons. For example, the decision by General Motors to drop the Cadillac convertible was probably a difficult one to make in light of the prestige attached to the vehicle. Despite the emotional aspects of a product-deletion decision, the need to be objective in this matter cannot be overemphasized. Companies establish their own criteria to screen different products for elimination.

In finalizing the decision, attention should be given to honoring prior commitments. For example, replacement parts must be provided even though an item is dropped. A well-implemented program of product simplification can lead to both growth and profitability. It may, however, be done at the cost of market share.

Total-Line Divestment

Divestment is a situation of reverse acquisition. It may also be a dimension of market strategy. But to the extent that the decision is approached from the product's perspective (i.e., to get rid of a product that is not doing well even in a growing market), it is an aspect of product strategy. Traditionally, companies resisted divestment for the following reasons, which are principally either economic or psychological in nature:

1. Divestment means negative growth in sales and assets, which runs counter to the business ethic of expansion.
2. Divestment suggests defeat.
3. Divestment requires changes in personnel, which can be painful and can result in perceived or real changes in status or have an adverse effect on the entire organization.
4. Divestment may have to be effected at a price below book and thus may have an adverse effect on the year's earnings.
5. The candidate for divestment may be carrying overhead, buying from other business units of the company, or contributing to earnings.

With the advent of strategic planning in the 1970s, divestment became an accepted option for seeking faster growth. More and more companies are now willing to sell a business if the company will be better off strategically. These companies feel that divestment should not be regarded solely as a means of ridding the company of an unprofitable division or plan; rather, there are some persuasive reasons supporting the divestment of even a profitable and growing business. Businesses that no longer fit the corporate strategic plan can be divested for a number of reasons.

— There is no longer a strategic connection between the base business and the part to be divested.
— The business experiences a permanent downturn, resulting in excess capacity for which no profitable alternative use can be identified.
— There may be inadequate capital to support the natural growth and development of the business.
— It may be dictated in the estate planning of the owner that a business is not to remain in the family.
— Selling a part of the business may release assets for use in other parts of the business where opportunities are growing.
— Divestment can improve the return on investment and growth rate both by ridding the company of units growing more slowly than the basic business and by providing cash for investment in faster-growing, higher-return operations.

Whatever the reason, a business that may have once fit well into the overall corporate plan can suddenly find itself in an environment that causes it to become a drain on the corporation, either financially, managerially, or opportunistically. Such circumstances suggest divestment.

Divestment helps restore balance to a business portfolio. If the company has too many high-growth businesses, particularly those at an early stage of development, its resources may be inadequate to fund growth. On the other hand, if a company has too many low-growth businesses, it will often generate more cash than is required for investment and will build up redundant equity. For a business to grow evenly over time while showing regular increments in earnings, a portfolio of fast- and slow-growth businesses is necessary. Divestment can help achieve this kind of balance. Finally, divestment helps restore a business to a size that will not raise the eyebrows of the Justice Department nor lead to an antitrust action.

The use of this strategy is reflected in GE's decision to divest its consumer electronics business in the early 1980s. In order to realize a return that GE considered adequate, the company would have had to make additional heavy investments in this business. GE figured that it could use the money to greater advantage in an area other than consumer electronics. Hence, it divested the business by selling it to Thomson, a French company.

Essentially following the same reasoning, Olin Corporation divested its aluminum business on the grounds that maintaining its small 4 percent share required big capital expenditures that could be employed more usefully elsewhere in the company. Westinghouse sold its major appliance line because it needed at least an additional 3 percent beyond the 5 percent share it held before it could compete effectively against industry leaders GE and Whirlpool. GE and Whirlpool divided about half the total market between them. Between 1986 and 1988, Beatrice sold two-thirds of its business, including such well-known names as Playtex, Avis, Tropicana, and Meadow Gold. The company considered these divestments necessary to transform itself into a manageable organization.[26]

It is difficult to prescribe generalized criteria to determine whether to divest a business. However, the following questions may be raised, the answers to which should provide a starting point for considering divestment:

1. **What is the earnings pattern of the unit?** A key question is whether the unit is acting as a drag on corporate growth. If so, then management must determine whether there are any offsetting values. For example, are earnings stable compared to the fluctuation in other parts of the company? If so, is the low-growth unit a substantial contributor to the overall debt capacity of the business? Management should also ask a whole series of what if questions relating to earnings: What if we borrowed additional funds? What if we brought in new management? What if we made a change in location? etc.
2. **Does the business generate any cash?** In many situations, a part of a company may be showing a profit but may not be generating any discretionary cash. That is, every dime of cash flow must be pumped right back into the operation just to keep it going at existing levels. Does this operation make any real contribution

to the company? Will it eventually? What could the unit be sold for? What would be done with the cash from this sale?

3. **Is there any tie-in value—financial or operating—with existing business?** Are there any synergies in marketing, production, research and development? Is the business countercyclical? Does it represent a platform for growth—internally based or through acquisitions?
4. **Will selling the unit help or hurt the acquisitions effort?** What will be the immediate impact on earnings (write-offs, operating expenses)? What effect, if any, will the sale have on the company's image in the stock market? Will the sale have any effect on potential acquisitions (Will I, too, be sold down the river)? Will the divestment be functional in terms of the new size achieved? Will a smaller size facilitate acquisitions by broadening the "market" of acceptable candidates, or, by contrast, will the company become less credible because of the smaller size?

In conclusion, a company should undertake continual in-depth analysis of the market share, growth prospects, profitability, and cash-generating power of each business. As a result of such reviews, a business may have to be divested to maintain balance in the company's total business. This, however, is feasible only when the company develops enough self-discipline to avoid increasing sales volume beyond a desirable size and instead buys and sells businesses with the sole objective of enhancing overall corporate performance.

NEW-PRODUCT STRATEGY

New-product development is an essential activity for companies seeking growth. By adopting the new-product strategy as their posture, companies are better able to sustain competitive pressures on their existing products and make headway. The implementation of this strategy has become easier because of technological innovations and the willingness of customers to accept new ways of doing things.

In a survey of 700 companies, Booz, Allen, and Hamilton reported that these companies were likely to derive 31 percent of their profits over the next five years from new products.[27] Consumers are being bombarded with new products as manufacturers learn how to make new things more quickly. In the last half of 1988, Sony introduced more than a hundred new audio, television, and video products. Apple Computer makes, on average, one new product announcement every week.[28]

The Booz, Allen, and Hamilton survey shows the importance that companies attach to new products. Despite their importance in strategy determination, implementation of new-product programs is far from easy. Too many products never make it in the marketplace. The risks and penalties of product failure require that companies move judiciously in adopting new-product strategies.

Interestingly, however, the mortality rate of new product ideas has declined considerably since the 1960s. In 1968, on average, 58 new product ideas were considered for every successful new product. In 1981, only seven ideas were required to generate one successful new product. However, these statistics vary by industry. Consumer nondurable companies consider more than twice as many new product ideas in order to generate one successful new product as industrial or consumer durable manufacturers.[29]

Top management can affect the implementation of new-product strategy; first, by establishing policies and broad strategic directions for the kinds of new products the company should seek; second, by providing the kind of leadership that creates the environmental climate needed to stimulate innovation in the organization; and third, by instituting review and monitoring procedures so that managers are involved at the right decision points and can know whether or not work schedules are being met in ways that are consistent with broad policy directions.[30]

The term *new product* is used in different senses. For our purposes, the new-product strategy will be split into three alternatives: (a) product improvement/modification, (b) product imitation, and (c) product innovation.

Product improvement/modification is the introduction of a new version or an improved model of an existing product, such as "new, improved Crest." Usually improvements and modifications are achieved by adding new features or styles, changing processing requirements, or altering product ingredients. When a company introduces a product that is already on the market but new to the company, it is following a product-imitation strategy. For example, Schick was imitating when it introduced its Tracer razor to compete with Gillette's Sensor. For our purposes, a product innovation will be defined as a strategy with a completely new approach in fulfilling customer desires (e.g., Polaroid camera, television, typewriter) or one that replaces existing ways of satisfying customer desires (e.g., the replacement of slide rules by pocket calculators).

New-product development follows the experience curve concept; that is, the more you do something, the more efficient you become at doing it (for additional details, see chapter 12). Experience in introducing products enables companies to improve new-product performance. Specifically, with increased new-product experience, companies improve new-product profitability by reducing the cost per introduction. More precisely, with each doubling of the number of new-product introductions, the cost of each introduction declines at a predictable and constant rate. For example, among the 13,000 new products introduced by 700 companies surveyed by Booz, Allen, and Hamilton between 1976 and 1981, the experience effect yielded a 71 percent cost curve. At each doubling of the number of new products introduced, the cost of each introduction declined by 29 percent.[31]

Product Improvement/Modification

An existing product may reach a stage that requires that something be done to keep it viable. The product may have reached the maturity stage of the product life cycle because of shifts in the environment and thus has ceased to provide an adequate return. Or product, pricing, distribution, and promotion strategies employed by competitors may have reduced the product to the me-too category. At this stage, management has two options: either eliminate the product or revitalize it by making improvements or modifications. Improvements or modifications are achieved by redesigning, remodeling, or reformulating the product so that it satisfies customer needs more fully. This strategy seeks not only to restore the health of the product but sometimes seeks to help distinguish it from competitors' products as well. For example, it has become fashionable these days to target an upscale, or premium, version of a product at the upper end of the price performance pyramid.[32] *Fortune*'s description of Kodak's strategy is relevant here:

> On the one hand, the longer a particular generation of cameras can be sold, the more profitable it will become. On the other hand, amateur photographers tend to use less film as their cameras age and lose their novelty; hence, it is critical that Kodak keep the camera population eternally young by bringing on new generations from time to time. In each successive generation, Kodak tries to increase convenience and reliability in order to encourage even greater film consumption per camera—a high "burn rate," as the company calls it. In general, the idea is to introduce as few major new models as possible while ringing in frequent minor changes powerful enough to stimulate new purchases.
>
> Kodak has become a master of this marketing strategy. Amateur film sales took off with a rush after 1963. That year the company brought out the first cartridge-loading, easy-to-use instamatic, which converted many people to photography and doubled film usage per camera. A succession of new features and variously priced models followed to help stimulate film consumption for a decade. Then Kodak introduced the pocket instamatic, which once again boosted film use—both because of its novelty and because of its convenience. Seven models of that generation have since appeared.[33]

Kodak's strategy points out that it is never enough just to introduce a new product. The real payoff comes if the product is managed in such a way that it continues to flourish year after year in a changing and competitive marketplace.

There is no magic formula for restoring the health of a product. Occasionally it is the ingenuity of the manager that may bring to light a desired cure. Generally, however, a complete review of the product from marketing perspectives is needed to analyze underlying causes and to come up with the modifications and improvements necessary to restore the product to health. For example, General Mills continues to realize greater profits by rejuvenating its old products—cake mixes, Cheerios, and Hamburger Helper. The company successfully builds excitement for old products better than anyone else in the food business by periodically improving them. Compared with Kellogg, which tends not to fiddle with its core products, General Mills takes much greater risks with established brands. For instance, the company introduced two varieties of Cheerios—Honey Nut in 1979 and Apple Cinnamon in 1988—and successfully created a megabrand.[34]

To identify options for restoring a damaged product to health, it may be necessary to tear down competing products and make detailed comparative analyses of quality and price.[35] One framework for such an analysis is illustrated in Exhibit 14-2.

The basic premise of Exhibit 14-2 is that by comparing its product with that of its competitors, a company is able to identify unique product strengths on which to pursue modifications and improvements. The use of the analysis suggested by Exhibit 14-2 may be illustrated with reference to a Japanese manufacturer. In 1978 Japan's amateur color film market was dominated by Kodak, Fuji, and Sakura, the last two being Japanese companies. For the previous 15 years,

EXHIBIT 14-2
Product-Change Options after Competitive Teardown

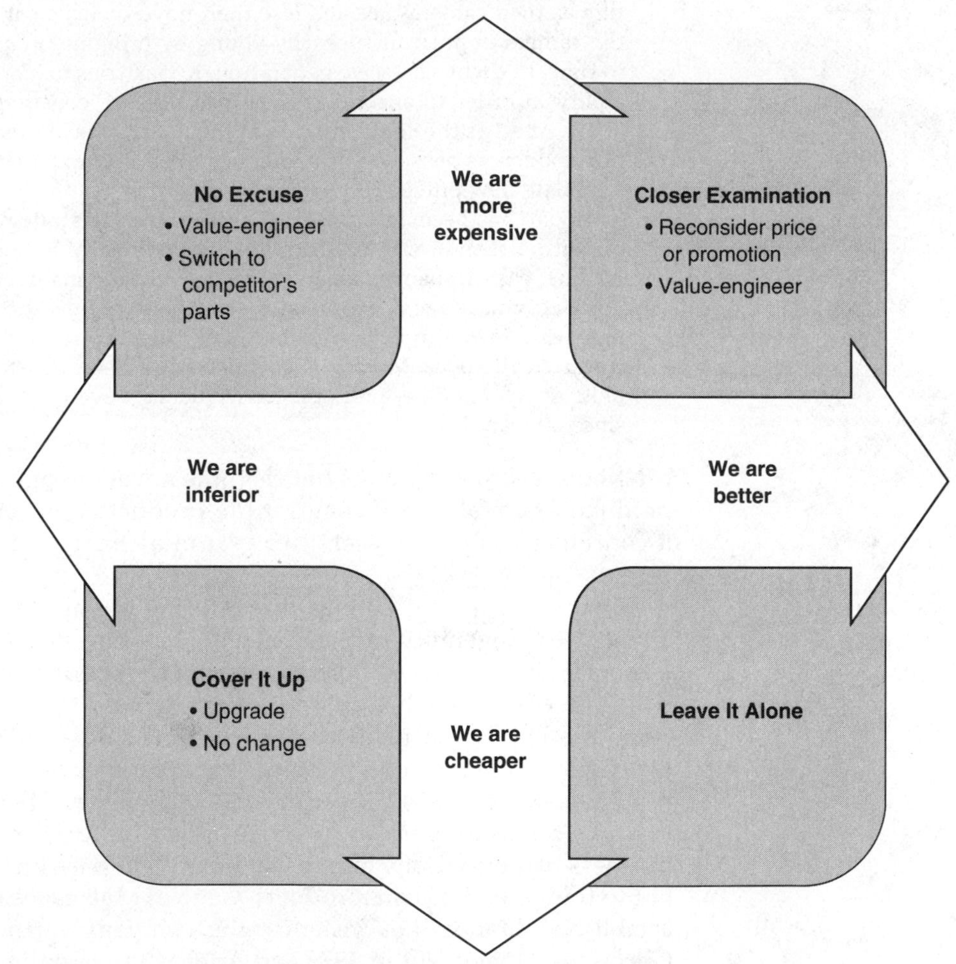

Source: Kenichi Ohmae, "Effective Strategies for Competitive Success," *McKinsey Quarterly*, (Winter 1978): 57. Reprinted by permission of the publisher.

Fuji had been gaining market share, whereas Sakura, the market leader in the early 1950s with over half the market, was losing ground to both its competitors. By 1976 Sakura had only about a 16 percent market share. Marketing research showed that, more than anything else, Sakura was the victim of an unfortunate word association. Its name in Japanese means "cherry blossom," suggesting a soft, blurry, pinkish image. The name Fuji, however, was associated with the blue skies and white snow of Japan's sacred mountain. Being in no position to change perceptions, the company decided to analyze the market from structural, economic, and customer points of view. Sakura found a growing cost consciousness among film customers: to wit, amateur photographers commonly left one or two frames unexposed in a 36-exposure roll, but they almost invariably tried to squeeze extra exposures onto 20-exposure rolls. Here Sakura saw an opportunity. It decided to introduce a 24-exposure film. Its marginal costs would be trivial, but its big competitors would face significant penalties in following suit. Sakura was prepared to cut its price if the competition lowered the price of their 20-frame rolls. Its aim was twofold. First, it would exploit the growing number of cost-minded users. Second, and more important, it would be drawing attention to the issue of economics, where it had a relative advantage, and away from the image issue, where it could not win. Sakura's strategy paid off. Its market share increased from 16 percent to more than 30 percent.[36] Overall, the product-improvement strategy is conducive to achieving growth, market share, and profitability alike.

Product Imitation

Not all companies like to be first in the market with a new product. Some let others take the initiative. If the innovation is successful, they ride the bandwagon of the successful innovation by imitating it. In the case of innovations protected by patents, imitators must wait until patents expire. In the absence of a patent, however, the imitators work diligently to design and produce products not very different from the innovator's product to compete vigorously with the innovator.

The imitation strategy can be justified in that it transfers the risk of introducing an unproven idea/product to someone else. It also saves investment in research and development. This strategy particularly suits companies with limited resources. Many companies, as a matter of fact, develop such talent that they can imitate any product, no matter how complicated. With a limited investment in research and development, the imitator may sometimes have a lower cost, giving it a price advantage in the market over the leader.

Another important reason for pursuing an imitation strategy may be to gainfully transfer the special talent a company may have for one product to other similar products. For example, the Bic Pen Corporation decided to enter the razor business because it thought it could successfully use its aggressive marketing posture in that market. In the early 1970s, Hanes Corporation gained resounding success with L'eggs, an inexpensive pantyhose that it sold from freestanding racks in food and drugstore outlets.

The imitation strategy may also be adopted on defensive grounds. Being sure of its existing product(s), a company may initially ignore new developments in the field. If new developments become overbearing, however, they may cut into the share held by an existing product. In this situation, a company may be forced to imitate the new development as a matter of survival. Colorado's Adolph Coors Company conveniently ignored the introduction of light beer and dismissed Miller Lite as a fad. Many years later, however, the company was getting bludgeoned by Miller Lite. Also, Anheuser-Busch began to challenge the supremacy of Coors in the California market with its light beer. The matter became so serious that Coors decided to abandon its one-product tradition and introduced a low-calorie light beer.[37]

Imitation also works well for companies that want to enter new markets without resorting to expensive acquisitions or special new-product development programs. For example, Owens-Illinois adapted heavy-duty laboratory glassware into novelty drinking glasses for home use.

Although imitation does avoid the risks involved in innovation, it is wrong to assume that every imitation of a successful product will succeed. The marketing program of an imitation should be as carefully chalked out and implemented as that of an innovation. Imitation strategy is most useful for achieving increases in market share and growth.

Product Innovation

Product-innovation strategy includes introducing a new product to replace an existing product in order to satisfy a need in an entirely different way or to provide a new approach to satisfy an existing or latent need. This strategy suggests that the entrant is the first firm to develop and introduce the product. The ballpoint pen is an example of a new product; it replaced the fountain pen. The VCR was a new product introduced to answer home entertainment needs.

Product innovation is an important characteristic of U.S. industry. Year after year companies spend billions of dollars on research and development to innovate. In 1988, for example, American industry spent about $120 billion on research and development over and above the research and development supported by the federal government. Research and development expenditures are expected to continue rising at an average of 10 percent annually throughout the 1990s.[38] These data show that industry takes a purposeful attitude toward new-product and new-process development.

Product innovation, however, does not come easy. Besides involving major financial commitments, it requires heavy doses of managerial time to cut across organizational lines.[39] And still the innovation may fail to make a mark in the market. A number of companies have discovered the risks of this game. Among them is Texas Instruments, which lost $660 million before withdrawing from the home computer market. RCA lost $575 million on ill-fated videodisc players. RCA, GE, and Sylvania, leaders in vacuum-tube technology, lost out when transistor technology revolutionized the radio business. RJR Nabisco abandoned the "smokeless" cigarette, Premier, after a 10-year struggle and after spending over $500 million.[40]

Most innovative products are produced by large organizations. Initially, an individual or a group of individuals may be behind it, but a stage is eventually reached where individual efforts require corporate support to finally develop and launch the product. To encourage innovation and creativity, many large companies are spinning off companies. For example, Colgate-Palmolive Co. launched Colgate Venture Co. to support entrepreneurship and risk taking. In this way, a congenial environment within the large corporation is maintained for generating and following creative pursuits.[41]

In essence, innovation flourishes where *divisions are kept small* (permitting better interaction among managers and staffers), where there is *willingness to tolerate failure* (encouraging plenty of experimentation and risk taking), where *champions are motivated* (through encouragement, salaries, and promotions), where *close liaison is maintained with the customer* (visiting customers routinely; inviting them to brainstorm product ideas), where *technology is shared corporate-wide* (technology, wherever it is developed, belongs to everyone), and where *projects are sustained,* even if initial results are discouraging.

The development of a product innovation typically passes through various stages: idea generation, screening, business analysis, development of a prototype, test market, and commercialization. The idea may emerge from different sources: customers, private researchers, university researchers, employees, or research labs. An idea may be generated by recognizing a consumer need or just by pursuing a scientific endeavor, hoping that it may lead to a viable product. Companies follow different procedures to screen ideas and to choose a few for further study. If an idea appears promising, it may be carried to the stage of business analysis, which may consist of investment requirements, revenue and expenditure projections, and financial analysis of return on investment, payback period, and cash flow. Thereafter, a few prototype products may be produced to examine engineering and manufacturing aspects of the product. A few sample products based on the prototype may be produced for market testing. After changes suggested in market testing have been incorporated, the innovation may be commercially launched.[42]

Exhibit 14-3 is a self-administered questionnaire for measuring the new-product management perspectives of a business unit. This questionnaire may be completed to determine what changes, if any, the business unit should make to revamp its new-product development effort.

Procter and Gamble's development of Pringles is a classic case of recognizing a need in a consumer market and then painstakingly hammering away to meet it.[43] Americans consume about one billion dollars' worth of potato chips annually, but manufacturers of potato chips face a variety of problems. Chips made in the traditional way are so fragile that they can rarely be shipped for more than 200 miles; even then, a quarter of the chips get broken. They also spoil quickly; their shelf life is barely two months. These characteristics have

EXHIBIT 14-3
New-Product Management Scorecard

To determine how well your business unit manages new products, rate your business from 1-10 points for each question: 10 = "Fully Meets"; 5 = "Partially Meets"; and 1 = "Does Not Meet."

	SCORE
1. Our corporate growth plan includes an explicit strategic description on the role of internally developed new products over the next five years.	____
2. We have a well-defined new product strategy which identifies the financial gap and strategic roles which new products must satisfy.	____
3. We establish different hurdle rates, based on associated risk.	____
4. We have had a systematic, yet adaptive, new products process in place for at least five years.	____
5. Idea generation for us begins **after** we have identified external market niches and assessed our internal competitive strengths.	____
6. We have a formalized monitoring and tracking system in place to measure cost per introduction and new product performance against established objectives.	____
7. We have compensation programs that encourage entrepreneurship, reward risk-takers, and reinforce innovative management.	____
8. We have a clear understanding of who is responsible for new product development.	____
9. Top management provides consistent commitment to new products in terms of funds and requisite managerial know-how.	____
10. We adapt our new products organization to match the requirements of our new products portfolio.	____
TOTAL	____

SCORE	
90–100	We are one of the best!
80–89	Improvement areas exist, but we're in good shape.
70–79	We should consider making changes to our new products program.
<70	We better get some assistance in managing new products.

Source: New Products Management for the 1980s (New York: Booz, Allen & Hamilton, 1982). Reprinted by permission.

kept potato chip manufacturers split into many small regional operations. Nobody, before Procter and Gamble, had applied much technology to the product since it was invented in 1853.

Procter and Gamble knew these problems because it sold edible oils to the potato chip industry, and it set out to solve them. Instead of slicing potatoes and frying them in the traditional way, Procter and Gamble's engineers developed a process somewhat akin to papermaking. They dehydrated and mashed potatoes and pressed them for frying into a precise shape, which permitted the chips to be stacked neatly on top of each other in hermetically sealed containers that resemble tennis ball cans. Pringles potato chips stay whole and have a shelf life of at least a year.

After a new product is screened through the lab, the division that will manufacture it takes over and finances all further development and testing. In some companies, division managers show little interest in taking on new products because the costs of introduction are heavy and hold down short-term profits. At Procter and Gamble, executives ensure that a manager's short-term record is not marred by the cost of a new introduction.

Before a new Procter and Gamble product is actually introduced to the market, it must prove that it has a demonstrable margin of superiority over its prospective competitors. A development team begins refining the product by trying variations of the basic formula, testing its performance under almost any conceivable condition, and altering its appearance. Eventually, a few alternative versions of the product are produced and tested among a large number of Procter and Gamble employees. If the product gets the approval of employees, the company presents it to panels of consumers for further testing. Procter and Gamble feels satisfied if a proposed product is chosen by fifty-five out of a hundred consumers tested. Though Pringles potato chips passed all these tests, they only recently started showing any profits for Procter and Gamble.

There is hardly any doubt that, if an innovation is successful, it pays off lavishly. For example, nylon still makes so much money for Du Pont that the company would qualify for the *Fortune* 500 list even if it made nothing else.[44] However, developing a new product is a highly risky strategy requiring heavy commitment and having a low probability of achieving a breakthrough. Thus, the choice of this strategy should be dictated by a company's financial and managerial strengths and by its willingness to take risks. Take the case of Kevlar, a super-tough fiber (lightweight but five times stronger than steel) invented by Du Pont. It took the company 25 years and $900 million to come out with this product, more time and money than the company had ever spent on a single product. Starting in 1985, however, the payoff began: annual sales reached $300 million. Du Pont forecasts Kevlar's annual sales growth at 10 percent during the 1990s. Meanwhile, the company continues its quest for new applications that it hopes will make Kevlar a blockbuster.[45]

Suggested below is an approach that may be used to manage innovations successfully. As a company grows more complex and decentralized, its new-product development efforts may fail to keep pace with change, weakening vital lines between marketing and technical people and leaving key decisions to be made by default. The possible result is the ultimate loss of competitive edge. To solve the problem, as shown in Exhibit 14-4a, both technical and market opportunity may be plotted on a grid. From this grid, innovations may be grouped into three classes: heavy emphasis (deserving full support, including basic research and development); selective opportunistic development (i.e.,

EXHIBIT 14-4
Managing Innovations

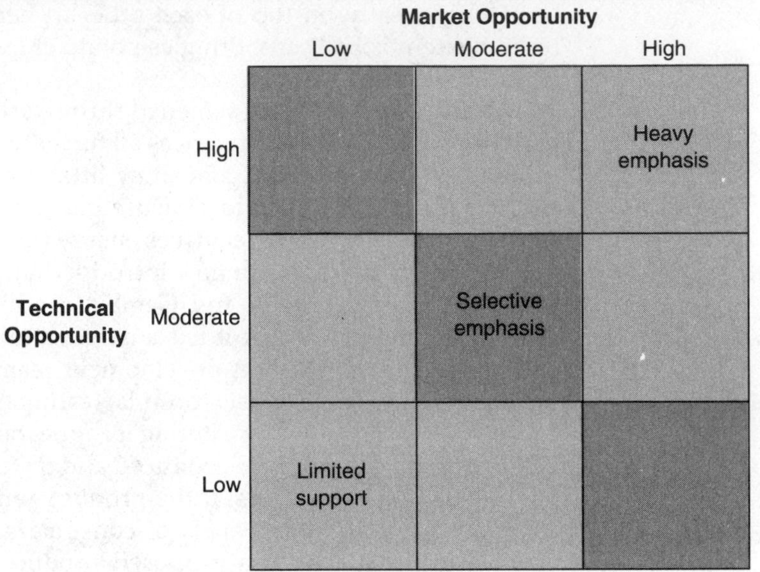

(a) The R&D Effort Portfolio

R&D Program Elements						
R&D Emphasis	***Level of Funding***	***Primary Focus of Work***	***Level of Basic Research***	***Technical Risk***	***Acceptable Time for Payoff***	***Projects to Exceed or Maintain Competitive Parity***
Heavy	High	Balance between new and existing products	High	High	Long	Many
Selective	Medium	Mainly existing products	Low	Medium	Medium	Few
Limited	Low	Existing processes	Very low	Low	Short	Very few

(b) Implied Nature of R&D Effort

Source: Richard N. Foster, "Linking R&D to Strategy," *Business Horizons*, December, 1980. Copyright, 1980, by the Foundation for the School of Business at Indiana University. Reprinted by permission.

may be good or may be bad; may require a careful approach and top management attention); and limited defense support (i.e., merits only minimum support). Exhibit 14-4b lists the relevant kinds of programs for each area. This approach helps gear research efforts to priority strategic projects.

DIVERSIFICATION STRATEGY

Diversification refers to seeking unfamiliar products or markets or both in the pursuit of growth. Every company is best at certain products; diversification requires substantially different knowledge, thinking, skills, and processes. Thus, diversification is at best a risky strategy, and a company should choose this path only when current product/market orientation does not seem to provide further opportunities for growth. A few examples will illustrate the point that diversification does not automatically bring success. CNA Financial Corporation faced catastrophe when it expanded the scope of its business from insurance to real estate and mutual funds: it ended up being acquired by Loews Corporation. Schrafft's restaurants did little for Pet Incorporated. Pacific Southwest Airlines acquired rental cars and hotels, only to see its stock decline fast. Diversification into the wine business (by acquiring Taylor Wines) did not work for the Coca-Cola Company.[46]

The diversification decision is a major step that must be taken carefully. On the basis of a sample from 200 *Fortune* 500 firms and the PIMS database (see chapter 12), Biggadike notes that it takes an average of 10 to 12 years before the return on investment from diversification equals that of mature businesses.[47]

The term *diversification* must be distinguished from integration and merger. **Integration** refers to the accumulation of additional business in a field through participation in more of the stages between raw materials and the ultimate market or through more intensive coverage of a single stage. **Merger** implies a combination of corporate entities that may or may not result in integration. Diversification is a strategic alternative that implies deriving revenues and profits from different products and markets. The following factors usually lead companies to seek diversification:

1. Firms diversify when their objectives can no longer be met within the product/market scope defined by expansion.
2. A firm may diversify because retained cash exceeds total expansion needs.
3. A firm may diversify when diversification opportunities promise greater profitability than expansion opportunities.
4. Firms may continue to explore diversification when the available information is not reliable enough to permit a conclusive comparison between expansion and diversification.

Diversification can take place at either the corporate or the business unit level. At the corporate level, it typically entails entering a promising business outside the scope of existing business units. At the business unit level, it is most likely to involve expanding into a new segment of the industry in which the business presently participates. The problems encountered at both levels are similar and may differ only in magnitude.

Diversification strategies include internal development of new products or markets (including development of international markets for current products), acquisition of an appropriate firm or firms, a strategic alliance with a complementary organization, licensing of new product technologies, and importing or distributing a line of products manufactured by another company. The final choice of an entry strategy involves a combination of these alternatives in most cases. This combination is determined on the basis of available opportunities and of consistency with the company's objectives and available resources.

Caterpillar Tractor Company's entry into the field of diesel engines is a case of internal diversification. Since 1972 the company has poured more than $1 billion into developing new diesel engines "in what must rank as one of the largest internal diversifications by a U.S. corporation."[48] Hershey Foods ventured into the restaurant business by buying the Friendly Ice Cream Corporation, illustrating diversification by acquisition. Hershey adopted the diversification strategy for growth because its traditional business, chocolate and candy, was stagnant because of a decline in candy consumption, sharp increases in cocoa prices, and changes in customer habits. Hershey subsequently sold Friendly in 1988 to a private company, Tennessee Restaurant Co.[49]

An empirical study of entry strategy shows that higher barriers are more likely to be associated with acquisition than with entry through internal development. Thus, in choosing between these two entry modes, business unit managers should take into account, among other factors, the entry barriers surrounding the market and the cost of breaching them. Despite high apparent barriers, the entrant's relatedness to the new entry may make entry financially more desirable.[50]

Essentially, there are three different forms of diversification a company may pursue: concentric diversification, horizontal diversification, and conglomerate diversification. No matter what kind of diversification a company seeks, the three essential tests of success are

1. **The attractiveness test**—The industries chosen for diversification must be structurally attractive or capable of being made attractive.
2. **The cost-of-entry test**—The cost of entry must not capitalize all future profits.
3. **The better-off test**—The new unit must either gain competitive advantage from its link with the corporation or vice versa.[51]

Concentric Diversification

Concentric diversification bears a close synergistic relationship to either the company's marketing or its technology. Thus, new products that are introduced share a common thread with the firm's existing products either through marketing or production. Usually the new products are directed to a new group of customers. Texas Instrument's venture into pocket calculators illustrates this type of diversification. Using its expertise in integrated circuits, the company developed a new product that appealed to a new set of customers. On the other hand, PepsiCo's venture into the fast-food business through the acquisition of Pizza Hut is a case of concentric diversification in which the new product bears a synergistic relationship to the company's existing marketing experience.

Although a diversification move per se is risky, concentric diversification does not lead a company into an entirely new world because in one of two major fields (technology or marketing), the company will operate in familiar territory. The relationship of the new product to the firm's existing product(s), however, may or may not mean much. All that the realization of synergy does is make the task easier; it does not necessarily make it successful. For example, Gillette entered the market for pocket calculators in 1974 and for digital watches in 1976. Later it abandoned both businesses. Both pocket calculators and digital watches were sold to mass markets where Gillette had expertise and experience. Despite this marketing synergy, it failed to sell either calculators or digital watches successfully. Gillette found that these lines of business called for strategies totally different from those it followed in selling its existing products.[52] Two lessons can be drawn from Gillette's experience. One, there may be other strategic reasons for successfully launching a new product in the market besides commonality of markets or technology. Two, the commonality should be analyzed in breadth and depth before drawing conclusions about the transferability of current strengths to the new product.

Philip Morris's acquisition of Miller Brewing Company illustrates how a company may achieve marketing synergies through concentric diversification. Cigarettes and beer are distributed through many of the same retail outlets, and Philip Morris had been dealing with them for years. In addition, both products serve hedonistic consumer markets. Small wonder, therefore, that the marketing research techniques and emotional promotion appeals of cigarette merchandising worked equally well for beer. Miller moved from seventh to second place in the beer industry in the short span of six years.

Horizontal Diversification

Horizontal diversification refers to new products that technologically are unrelated to a company's existing products but that can be sold to the same group of customers to whom existing products are sold. A classic case of this form of diversification is Procter and Gamble's entry into potato chips (Pringles), toothpaste (Crest and Gleem), coffee (Folgers), and orange juice (Citrus Hill). Traditionally a soap company, Procter and Gamble diversified into these products, which were aimed at the same customers who bought soap. Similarly, Maytag's entry into the medium-priced mass market to sell refrigerators and ranges, in addition to selling its traditional line of premium-priced dishwashers, washers, and dryers, is a form of horizontal diversification.[53]

Note that in the case of concentric diversification, the new product may have certain common ties with the marketing of a company's existing product except that it is sold to a new set of customers. In horizontal diversification the customers for the new product are drawn from the same ranks as those for an existing product.

Other things being equal, in a competitive environment horizontal diversification is more desirable if present customers are favorably disposed toward the company and if one can expect this loyalty to carry over to the new product; in the long run, however, a new product must stand on its own. For example, if product quality is lacking, if promotion is not effective, or if the price is not right, a new product will flop despite customer loyalty to the company's other products. Thus, while Crest and Folgers made it for Procter and Gamble, Citrus Hill has been struggling, and Pringles has been disappointing, even though all these products are sold to the same "loyal" customers. In other words, horizontal diversification should not be regarded as a route to success in all cases. An important limitation of horizontal diversification is that the new product is introduced and marketed in the same economic environment as the existing products, which can lead to rigidity and instability. Stated differently, horizontal diversification tends to increase the company's dependence on a few market segments.

Conglomerate Diversification

In conglomerate diversification, the new product bears no relationship to either the marketing or the technology of the existing product(s). In other words, through conglomerate diversification, a company launches itself into an entirely new product/market arena. ITT's ventures into bakery products (Continental Baking Company), insurance (Hartford Insurance Group), car rentals (Avis Rent-A-Car System, Inc.), and the hotel business (Sheraton Corporation) illustrate the implementation of conglomerate diversification. (ITT divested its car rental business a few years ago.)

It is necessary to remember here that companies do not flirt with unknown products in unknown markets without having some hidden strengths to handle conglomerate diversification. For example, the managerial style required for a new product to prosper may be just the same as the style the company already has. Thus, managerial style becomes the basis of synergy between the new product and an existing product. By the same token, another single element may serve as a dominant factor in making a business attractive for diversification.

Inasmuch as conglomerate diversification does not bear an obvious relationship to a company's existing business, there is some question as to why companies adopt it. There are two major advantages of conglomerate diversification. One, it can improve the profitability and flexibility of a firm by venturing into businesses that have better economic prospects than the firm's existing businesses have. Two, a conglomerate firm, because of its size, gets a better reception in capital markets.

Overall, this type of diversification, if successful, has the potential of providing increased growth and profitability.

VALUE MARKETING STRATEGY

Value is becoming the marketer's watchword for the 1990s. Today, customers are demanding something different than they did in the 1980s. They want the right combination of product quality, good service, and timely delivery. These are the keys to performing well in the next decade. It is for this reason that we examine this new strategic focus.

Value marketing strategy stresses real product performance and delivering on promises. Value marketing doesn't mean high quality if it is only available at ever-higher prices. It doesn't necessarily mean cheap, if cheap means bare bones or low-grade. It doesn't mean high prestige, if the prestige is viewed as snobbish or self-indulgent. At the same time, value is not about positioning and image mongering.[54] It simply means providing a product that works as claimed, is accompanied by decent service, and is delivered on time.

The emphasis on value is part atmospherics, part economics, and part demographics. Consumers are repudiating the wretched excesses of the 1980s and are searching for more traditional rewards of home and family. They are concerned about the seemingly nonending recession. The growing focus on value also stems from profound changes in the American consumer marketplace.[55]

For example, real income growth for families got a boost when women entered the work force. But now, with many women already working and many baby boomers assuming new family responsibilities, the growth in disposable income is scarily slow. Aging baby boomers whose debt burden is already high realize that they have to worry about college tuitions and retirement. At the same time, the new generation of consumers is both savvier and more cynical than were its predecessors. Briefly, consumers want products that perform, sold by advertising that informs. They are concerned about intrinsic value, not simply buying to impress others.

Quality Strategy

Traditionally, quality has been viewed as a manufacturing concern. Strategically, however, the idea of total quality is perceived in the market; that is, quality must exude from the offering itself and from all the services that come with it. The important point is that quality perspectives should be based on customer preferences, not on internal evaluations. The ultimate objective of quality should be to delight the customer in every way possible, providing levels of service, product quality, product performance, and support that are beyond his/her expectations. Ultimately, quality may mean striving for excellence throughout the entire organization.[56] For assessing perceived quality, the step-by-step procedure used by the Strategic Planning Institute may be followed:

1. A meeting is held, in which a multifunctional team of managers and staff specialists identify the non-price product and service attributes that affect customer buying decisions. For an office equipment product, these might include durability, maintenance costs, flexibility, credit terms, and appearance.
2. The team is then asked to assign "importance weights" for each attribute representing their relative decisions. These relative importance weights sum to 100. (For markets in which there are important segments with different importance weights, separate weights are assigned to each segment.)
3. The management team creates its business unit's product line, and those of leading competitors, on each of the performance dimensions identified in Step 1. From these attribute-by-attribute ratings, each weighted by its respective importance weight, an overall relative quality score is constructed.
4. The overall relative quality score and other measures of competitive position (relative price, and market share) and financial performance (ROI, ROS, and IRR) are validated against benchmarks based on the experience of "look-alike" businesses in similar strategic positions in order to:
   - Check the internal consistency of strategic and financial data.
   - Confirm the business and market definition.

5. Finally, the management team tests their plans and budgets for reality, develops a blueprint for improving market perceived quality, relative to competitors', and calibrates the financial payoff.

   In many cases, the judgmental ratings assigned by the management team are tested (and, when appropriate, modified) by collecting ratings from customers via field interviews.[57]

This approach to assessing relative quality is similar to the multiattribute methods used in marketing research. These research methods are, however, employed primarily for evaluating or comparing individual products (actual or prospective), whereas the scores here apply to a business unit's entire product line.

Attaining adequate levels of excellence and customer satisfaction often requires significant cultural change; that is, change in decision-making processes, interfunctional relationships, and the attitudes of each member of the company.[58] In other words, achieving total quality objectives requires teamwork and cooperation. People are encouraged and rewarded for doing their jobs right the first time rather than for their success in resolving crises. People are empowered to make decisions and instilled with the feeling that quality is everyone's responsibility.

The following are the keys to success in achieving world-class total quality. First, the program requires unequivocal support of top management. The second key to success is understanding customer need. The third key is to fix the business process, if there are gaps in meeting customer needs. The fourth key is to compress cycle time to avoid bureaucratic hassles and delays. The next is empowering people so that they are able to exert their best talents. Further, measurement and reward systems must be reassessed and revamped to recognize people. Finally, the total quality program should be a continuous concern, a constant focus on identifying and eliminating waste and inefficiency throughout the organization.

Organizationally, the single most important aspect of implementing a quality strategy is to maintain a close liaison with the customer. Honda's experience in this matter in designing the new Accord is noteworthy:

> When Honda's engineers began to design the third-generation (or 1986) Accord in the early 1980s, they did not start with a sketch of a car. The engineers started with a concept—"man maximum, machine minimum"—that captured in a short, evocative phrase the way they wanted customers to feel about the car. The concept and the car have been remarkably successful: since 1982, the Accord has been one of the best-selling cars in the United States; in 1989, it was the top-selling car. Yet when it was time to design the 1990 Accord, Honda listened to the market, not to its own success. Market trends were indicating a shift away from sporty sedans toward family models. To satisfy future customers' expectations—and to reposition the Accord, moving it up-market just a bit—the 1990 model would have to send a new set of product messages—"an adult sense of reliability." The ideal family car would allow the driver to transport family and friends with confidence, whatever the weather or road conditions; passengers would always feel safe and secure.

This message was still too abstract to guide the engineers who would later be making concrete choices about the new Accord's specifications, parts, and manufacturing processes. So the next step was finding an image that would personify the car's message to consumers. The image that managers emerged with was "a rugby player in a business suit." It evoked rugged, physical contact, sportsmanship, and gentlemanly behavior—disparate qualities the new car would have to convey. The image was also concrete enough to translate clearly into design details. The decision to replace the old Accord's retractable headlamps with headlights made with a pioneering technology developed by Honda's supplier, Stanley, is a good example. To the designers and engineers, the new lights' totally transparent cover glass symbolized the will of a rugby player looking into the future calmly, with clear eyes.

The next and last step in creating the Accord's product concept was to break down the rugby player image into specific attributes the new car would have to possess. Five sets of key words captured what the product leader envisioned: "open-minded," "friendly communication," "tough spirit," "stress-free," and "love forever." Individually and as a whole, these key words reinforced the car's message to consumers. "Tough spirit" in the car, for example, meant maneuverability, power, and sure handling in extreme driving conditions, while "love forever" translated into long-term reliability and customer satisfaction. Throughout the course of the project, these phrases provided a kind of shorthand to help people make coherent design and hardware choices in the face of competing demands.[59]

There are three generic approaches to improving quality performance: catching up, pulling ahead, and leapfrogging.[60] **Catching up** involves restoring those aspects about which the firm has been behind to standard. Catching up is a defensive strategy where the emphasis is either to be as good as the competition or to barely meet market requirements. **Pulling ahead**, going further than the customer asks or achieving superiority over the competition, provides a firm competitive advantage that may lead to greater profitability. Thus, it makes sense to resist the temptation to focus on just catching up and to find a way to make a sustainable move to pull ahead. Finally, **leapfrogging** involves negating competitive disadvantage, that is, creating a sustainable competitive advantage through differentiation. In other words, leapfrogging comprises coming from behind and getting ahead of the competition through providing a quality product in keeping with customer demands. For example, by leapfrogging Detroit on several key attributes, Japanese companies rolled farther up the "quality-for-price curve"; that is, they shifted into better value positions.

Several benefits accrue to businesses that offer superior perceived quality, including stronger customer loyalty, more repeat purchases, less vulnerability to price wars, ability to command higher relative price without affecting share, lower marketing costs, and share improvements.[61]

Customer Service Strategy

Customer service has come to occupy an important place in today's competitive market. Invariably, customers want personal service, the kind of service delivered by live bodies behind a sales counter, a human voice at the other end of a telephone, or people in the teller's cage at the bank. Paying attention to the customer is not a new concept. In the 1950s, General Motors went all the way toward consumer satisfaction by designing cars for every lifestyle and pocketbook, a breakthrough for an industry that had been largely driven by production needs ever since Henry Ford promised to deliver any color car as long as it was black. General Motors rode its insights into customers' needs to a 52 percent share of the U.S. car market in 1962.[62] But with a booming economy, a rising population, and virtually no foreign competition, many U.S. companies had it too easy. Through the 1960s and into the 1970s, many U.S. carmakers could sell just about anything they could produce. With customers seemingly satisfied, management concentrated on cutting production costs and making splashy acquisitions. To manage these growing behemoths, CEOs turned to strategic planning, which focused on winning market share, not on getting in touch with remote customers. Markets came to be defined as aggregations of competitors, not as customers.

In recent times, Japanese companies were the first to recognize a problem. They started to rescue customers from the limbo of so-so merchandise and take-it-or-leave-it service. They built loyalty among U.S. car buyers by assiduously uncovering and accommodating customer needs. The growing influence of Japanese firms as well as demographics and hard economic times have forced American companies to realize the need to listen to customers.

Creative changes in service can make the difference. For example, companies offering better service can charge 10 percent more for their products than competitors.[63] Even smaller companies with fewer management layers are finding that personal relationships between senior executives and customers can help in various ways.[64] Many companies attach so much importance to service that they require their senior managers to put in time at the front lines. For example, Xerox requires that its executives spend one day a month taking complaints from customers about machines, bills, and service. Similarly, at Hyatt Hotels, senior executives put in time as bellhops.[65]

Briefly, a company must decide who it wants to serve, discover what those customers want, and set a strategy that single-mindedly provides that service to those customers. With such clearly articulated goals, top management can give front line employees responsibility for responding instantly to customer needs in those crucial moments that determine the company's success or failure. The following episode, which underlines Scandinavian Airlines' emphasis on service, shows how far a company can go to stand by the customer.

> Rudy Peterson was an American businessman staying at the Grand Hotel in Stockholm. Arriving at Stockholm's Arlanda airport for an important day trip with a colleague to Copenhagen on a Scandinavian Airlines (SAS) flight, he realized he'd left his ticket in his hotel room.
>
> Everyone knows you can't board an airplane without a ticket, so Rudy Peterson resigned himself to missing the flight and his business meeting in Copenhagen. But when he explained his dilemma to the ticket agent, he got a pleasant surprise. "Don't worry, Mr. Peterson," she said with a smile. "Here's your boarding card. I'll insert a temporary ticket in here. If you just tell me your room number at the Grand Hotel and your destination in Copenhagen, I'll take care of the rest."

While Rudy and his colleague waited in the passenger lounge, the ticket agent dialed the hotel. A bellhop checked the room and found the ticket. The ticket agent then sent an SAS limo to retrieve it from the hotel and bring it directly to her. They moved so quickly that the ticket arrived before the Copenhagen flight departed. No one was more surprised than Rudy Peterson when the flight attendant approached him and said calmly, "Mr. Peterson? Here's your ticket."

What would have happened at a more traditional airline? Most airline manuals are clear: "No ticket, no flight." At best, the ticket agent would have informed her supervisor of the problem, but Rudy Peterson almost certainly would have missed his flight. Instead, because of the way SAS handled his situation, he was both impressed and on time for his meeting.[66]

The SAS experience shows how far a business must be willing to go to become a truly customer-driven company—a company that recognizes that its only true assets are satisfied customers, all of whom expect to be treated as individuals.

Many firms argue that service by definition is difficult to guarantee. Services are generally delivered by human beings, who are less predictable than machines. Services are also usually produced at the same time that they are consumed. Although there can be exceptions to the rule, service can be guaranteed in any field. Consider the guarantee offered by "Bugs" Burger Bug Killers (BBBK), a Miami-based pest extermination company, a division of S.C. Johnson and Sons:

Most of BBBK's competitors claim that they will reduce pests to "acceptable levels"; BBBK promises to eliminate them entirely. Its service guarantee to hotel and restaurant clients promises:

- You don't owe one penny until all pests on your premises have been eradicated.
- If you are ever dissatisfied with BBBK's service, you will receive a refund for up to 12 months of the company's services—plus fees for another exterminator of your choice for the next year.
- If a guest spots a pest on your premises, BBBK will pay for the guest's meal or room, send a letter of apology, and pay for a future meal or stay.
- If your facility is closed down due to the presence of roaches or rodents, BBBK will pay any fines, as well as all lost profits, *plus* $5,000.

In short, BBBK says, "If we don't satisfy you 100%, we don't take your money."[67]

The company's service program has been extremely successful. It charges up to 10 times more than its competitors and yet has a disproportionately high market share in its operating areas.

In designing a good service program, a company should be conversant with a number of important trends.[68] First, customers don't read (e.g., customers don't read assembly and operation instructions). Second, customers don't understand ownership responsibilities (e.g., some hotels require customers to program their own wake-up calls into a confusing computerized system). Third, high technology and product complexity make product differentiation difficult (i.e., with like products, better service can become an important differentiating factor). Fourth, consumers have lower confidence and expectations for products and services (i.e., customer service can have an enormous impact on consumer confidence). Fifth, high-quality service has become a product attribute (i.e., consumers rate qualitative service factors as more important than product cost and features). Sixth, consumer attention is drawn to negative publicity (i.e., negative word of mouth is extremely detrimental). Seventh, consumers believe they are not getting their money's worth.

Improved customer service can play a major role in changing customer perceptions about a product and its value and can directly affect a company's success and profitability. The quality of service a company provides depends largely on people, not only those with direct customer responsibility but also with managers, supervisors, and support staff. Thus, success in providing adequate service largely depends on preparing employees for it.

Time-Based Strategy

When a product market changes quickly, companies must respond fast if they want to preserve their positions. In today's changing markets, time-based strategy that aims to beat the competition has assumed new dimensions.

GE has cut the time to deliver a custom-made industrial circuit breaker box from three weeks to *three days*. In the past, AT&T needed two years to design a new phone. Now it can do it in *one*. Motorola used to take three weeks to turn out electronic pagers after the factory received the order. Now it takes *two hours*.[69]

Time-based strategy brings about important competitive benefits. Market share grows because customers love getting their orders now. Inventories of finished goods shrink because they are not necessary to ensure quick delivery; the fastest manufacturers can make and ship an order the day it is received. For this and other reasons, costs fall. Many employees become satisfied because they are working for a more responsive, more successful company and because speeding operations requires giving them more flexibility and responsibility. Quality also improves. Briefly, doing it fast forces a firm to do it right the first time.

Speed can also pay off in product development—even if it means going over budget by as much as 50 percent. For example, a model developed by McKinsey and Co. shows that high-tech products that come to market on budget but six months late earn 33 percent *less* profit over five years. In contrast, coming out 50 percent over budget but on time cuts profits only by 4 percent.[70]

To implement a time-based strategy, the entire production process must be redesigned for speed. GE's experience is relevant here. Its circuit breaker business was old and stagnant. Market growth was slow and Siemens and Westinghouse were strong competitors. GE assembled a team of manufacturing, design, and marketing experts to focus on overhauling the entire process. The goal was to cut the time between order and delivery from three weeks to three days. Six plants around the United States were producing circuit breaker boxes. The team consolidated production into one plant and automated its facilities. But the team did not automate operations as they were. In the old system, engineers custom-designed each box, a task that took about a week. Engineers chose from

28,000 unique parts to create a box. To set up an automated system to handle that many parts would have been a nightmare. The design team reduced the number of parts to 1275, making most parts interchangeable. Even with this drastic reduction in parts, customers were still given 40,000 different sizes, shapes, and configurations from which to choose.

The team also devised a way to phase out the engineers, by replacing them with computers. Now a salesperson enters the specifications for a circuit breaker into a computer at GE's main office and the order flows to a computer at the plant, which automatically programs factory machines to custom make the order with minimum waste.

Although these advances are indeed impressive, the team still had to conquer another source of delay—solving problems and making decisions on the factory floor. The solution was to eliminate all line supervisors and quality inspectors, reducing the organizational layers between worker and plant manager from three to one. Everything middle managers used to handle—vacation scheduling, quality, work rules—became the responsibility of the 129 workers on the floor, who were divided into teams of 15 to 20. It worked. The more responsibility GE gave the workers, the faster problems were solved and decisions were made.

The results: the plant that used to have a two-month backlog of orders now works with a *two-day* backlog. Productivity has increased 20 percent over the past year. Manufacturing costs have dropped 30 percent, or $5.5 million a year, and return on investment is running at over 20 percent. The speed of delivery for a higher-quality product with more features has shrunk from three weeks to three days. *And* GE is gaining share in a flat market.[71]

Another area ripe for time-based strategy is the administrative/approval area. According to the Thomas Group, a Dallas-based consulting firm specializing in speed, manufacturing typically takes only 5 to 20 percent of the total time that is needed to get an order for a given product to market; the rest is administrative.[72] For example, at Adca Bank, a subsidiary of West Germany's Reebobank (with assets of $90 billion), an application for a loan used to go through numerous layers of bureaucracy. A branch would send a loan application to a loan officer at headquarters who would look at it and change it. Then the loan officer's manager would look at the application and change it, and so on. The bank eventually got rid of five layers of management and gave officers in all branches more authority to make loans. It used to take 24 managers to approve a loan. Now it takes 12.

Teamwork seems to be the key ingredient among the fastest companies. Nearly all of them form multidepartment teams. AT&T formed teams of six to twelve members, including engineers, manufacturers, and marketers, with complete authority to make every decision about how a product would look, work, be made, and cost. At AT&T the key was setting rigid speed requirements, such as six weeks, and leaving the rest to the team. Teams could meet these strict deadlines because they did not need to send each decision up the line for approval. With this new approach, AT&T cut development time for its new 4200 phone from two years to just a year while lowering costs and increasing quality.

Application of time-based strategy to distribution is equally important. Even the world's fastest factory cannot provide much of a competitive advantage if everything it produces gets snagged in the distribution chain. For example, Benetton takes its distribution very seriously and has created an electronic loop that links sales agent, factory, and warehouse. If a saleswoman in one of Benetton's Los Angeles shops finds that she is starting to run out of a best-selling sweater, she calls one of Benetton's 80 sales agents, who enters the order in a personal computer, which sends it to a mainframe in Italy. The mainframe computer, which has all of the measurements for the sweater, sets the knitting machines in motion. Once the sweaters are finished, workers box them up and label the box with a bar code containing the Los Angeles address. The box then goes into the warehouse. The computer next sends a robot flying. The robot finds the box and any others going to Los Angeles, picks them up, and loads them onto a truck. Including manufacturing time, Benetton can get an order to Los Angeles in four weeks.

Implementation of time-based strategy requires a number of steps. First, **start from scratch** (set a time goal and revamp entire operations to meet this goal rather than simply improving efficiency in current operations). Second, **wipe out approvals** (i.e., cut down bureaucratic layers of control and let people make decisions on the spot). Third, **emphasize teamwork** (i.e., establish multidepartment teams to handle the work). Fourth, **worship the schedule** (i.e., nothing short of disaster should be a valid excuse for delay). Fifth, **develop time-effective distribution** (i.e., snags in distribution must be simultaneously worked out). Sixth, **put speed in the culture** (i.e., train people in the company at all levels to understand and appreciate the significance of speed).

The advantages of speed are undeniably impressive. Although it is a common precept that time is money, in practice, companies have paid only lip service to it. The time it took to do a job, whatever the amount, was considered a necessity to meet organizational requirements, systems, procedures, and hierarchical relationships. Now, however, there is a new realization that time saved is a strategic factor for gaining competitive advantage. Companies that grasp and appreciate the unprecedented advantages of getting new products to market sooner and orders to customers faster hold the key for achieving competitive preeminence in the 1990s.

SUMMARY

Product strategies reflect the mission of the business unit and the business it is in. Following the marketing concept, the choice of product strategy should bear a close relationship to the market strategy of the company. The various product strategies and the alternatives under each strategy that were discussed in this chapter are

1. Product-positioning strategy
   a. Positioning a single brand
   b. Positioning multiple brands

2. Product-repositioning strategy
   a. Repositioning among existing customers
   b. Repositioning among new users
   c. Repositioning for new uses
3. Product-overlap strategy
   a. Competing brands
   b. Private labeling
   c. Dealing with original-equipment manufacturers (OEMs)
4. Product-scope strategy
   a. Single product
   b. Multiple products
   c. System of products
5. Product-design strategy
   a. Standard products
   b. Customized products
   c. Standard product with modifications
6. Product-elimination strategy
   a. Harvesting
   b. Line simplification
   c. Total-line divestment
7. New-product strategy
   a. Product improvement/modification
   b. Product imitation
   c. Product innovation
8. Diversification strategy
   a. Concentric diversification
   b. Horizontal diversification
   c. Conglomerate diversification
9. Value marketing strategy
   a. Quality strategy
   b. Customer service strategy
   c. Time-based strategy

The nature of different strategies was discussed, and their relevance for different types of companies was examined. Adaptations of different strategies in practice were illustrated with citations from published sources.

DISCUSSION QUESTIONS

1. Discuss how a business unit may avoid problems of cannibalism among competing brands.
2. Conceptualize how a lagging brand (assume a grocery product) may be repositioned for new uses.
3. What criteria may be employed to determine the viable position for a brand in the market?

4. What conditions justify a company's dealing in multiple products?
5. Are there reasons other than profitability for eliminating a product? Discuss.
6. What factors must be weighed to determine the viability of divesting an entire product line?
7. Under what circumstances is it desirable to adopt a product-imitation strategy?

NOTES

[1]"Gould Is So Thin, You Can Hardly See It," *Business Week* (29 August 1988): 74. See also Edward H. Kolcum, "Gould Will Use Same Market Strategy under Encore Ownership," *Aviation Week and Space Technology* (17 April 1989): 53.

[2]Peter R. Dickson and James L. Ginter, "Market Segmentation, Product Differentiation and Marketing Strategy," *Journal of Marketing* (April 1987): 1-10.

[3]Theodore Levitt, "Marketing Success through Differentiation—of Anything," *Harvard Business Review* (January-February 1980): 82. See also Theodore Levitt, "Marketing Intangible Products and Product Intangibles," *Harvard Business Review* (May-June 1981): 94-102.

[4]Christopher Knowlton, "How Disney Keeps the Magic Going," *Fortune* (4 December 1989): 11.

[5]David A. Aaker and J. Gary Shansby, "Positioning Your Product," *Business Horizons* (May-June 1982): 56-62.

[6]Philip Kotler, *Marketing Management*, 5th ed. (Englewood Cliffs, NJ: Prentice-Hall, 1984), 392.

[7]"How Do You Follow an Act Like Bud?" *Business Week* (2 May 1988): 118. See also Anheuser-Busch Companies, Inc., annual report for 1990.

[8]"Anheuser-Busch, Inc., Has Another Entry in 'Light Beer' Field," *Wall Street Journal*, 13 February 1978, p. 4.

[9]William Copulsky, "Cannibalism in the Marketplace," *Journal of Marketing* (October 1976): 103-05.

[10]Ira Teinowitz, "Beer Battle Heats Up: New Brands Score," *Advertising Age* (13 August 1990): 21.

[11]Roger A. Kerin, Michael G. Harvey, and James T. Rothe, "Cannibalism and New Product Development," *Business Horizons* (October 1978): 31.

[12]John P. Maggard, "Positioning Revisited," *Journal of Marketing* (January 1976): 63-66.

[13]Carl Spielvogel, "Brand Positioning and Repositioning," in *Marketing Strategies*, ed. Earl L. Bailey (New York: The Conference Board, 1974), 10.

[14]William D. Neal, "Strategic Product Positioning: A Step-by-Step Guide," *Business* (May-June 1980): 40.

[15]Spielvogel, "Brand Positioning and Repositioning," 13-16.

[16]Spielvogel, "Brand Positioning and Repositioning," 11-12.

[17]Robert E. Weigand, "Fit Products and Channels to Your Markets," *Harvard Business Review* (January-February 1977): 97.

[18]Based on an interview with a Gillette executive. See also Lawrence Ingrassia, "Schick Razor to Try for Edge against Gillette," *Wall Street Journal*, 9 October 1990, p. B1.

[19]Alex Taylor III, "Kodak Scrambles to Reforms," *Fortune* (3 March 1986): 34.

[20]"American Family Life: Expanding beyond Its Cancer Insurance Market," *Business Week* (15 January 1979): 100. See also A.M. Best Company, annual reports for 1986 and 1987.

[21]Alix M. Freedman, "Upstart Miller Brew Stirs Up Beer Market," *Wall Street Journal*, 5 October 1988, p. B1. Also see Patricia Sellers, "Busch Fights to Have It All," *Fortune* (15 January 1990): 87.

[22]See Lynn W. Phillips, Dae R. Chang, and Robert D. Buzzell, "Product Quality, Cost Position and Business Performance: A Test of Some Key Hypotheses," *Journal of Marketing* (Spring 1983): 26–43. Also see Robert Jacobson and David A. Aaker, "The Strategic Role of Product Quality," *Journal of Marketing* (October 1987): 31–44.

[23]Richard T. Hise, A. Parasuraman, and Ramaswamy Viswanathan, "Product Elimination: The Neglected Management Responsibility," *Journal of Business Strategy* (Spring 1984): 56–63.

[24]Philip Kotler, "Harvesting Strategies for Weak Products," *Business Horizons* (August 1978): 17–18.

[25]David S. Hopkins, "New Emphasis in Marketing Strategies," *Conference Board Record* (August 1976): 35.

[26]"How Sweet It Is to Be out from under Beatrice's Thumb," *Business Week* (9 May 1988): 98.

[27]*New Products Management for the 1980s* (New York: Booz, Allen, & Hamilton Inc., 1982).

[28]"Another Day, Another Bright Idea," *The Economist* (16 April 1988): 82.

[29]*New Products Management for the 1980s*, 14.

[30]See Hirotaka Takeuchi and Ikujiro Nonaka, "The New Product Development Game," *Harvard Business Review* (January–February 1986): 137–46.

[31]*New Products Management for the 1980s*, 18.

[32]John A. Quelch, "Marketing the Premium Product," *Business Horizons* (May–June 1987): 38–45. See also David A. Garvin, "Competing on the Eight Dimensions of Quality," *Harvard Business Review* (November–December 1987): 101–09.

[33]Bro Uttal, "Eastman Kodak's Orderly Two-Front War," *Fortune* (September 1976): 123.

[34]Patricia Sellers, "A Boring Brand Can Be Beautiful," *Fortune* (18 November 1991): 48.

[35]See "G.E. Refrigerator Woes Illustrate the Hazards in Changing a Product," *Wall Street Journal*, 7 May 1990, p. 2.

[36]Kenichi Ohmae, "Effective Strategies for Competitive Success," *McKinsey Quarterly* (Winter 1978): 56–57.

[37]John Huey, "Men at Coors Beer Find the Old Ways Don't Work Anymore," *Wall Street Journal*, 19 January 1979, p. 1.

[38]See "Masters of Innovation," *Business Week* (10 April 1989): 58.

[39]See Robert W. Ruekert and Orville C. Walker, Jr., "Interactions Between Marketing and Research and Development Departments in Implementing Different Business Strategies," *Strategic Management Journal* 8 (1987): 233–48.

[40]Peter Waldman and Betsy Morris, "RJR Nabisco Abandons 'Smokeless' Cigarette," *Wall Street Journal*, 16 March 1989, p. B1.

[41]Ronald Alsop, "Consumer-Product Giants Relying on 'Intrapreneurs' in New Ventures," *Wall Street Journal*, 22 April 1988, p. 35. See also John Bussey and Douglas R. Sease, "Manufacturers Strive to Slice Time Needed to Develop Products," *Wall Street Journal*, 23 February 1988, p. 1; and Peter F. Drucker, "Best Research and Development Is Business Driven," *Wall Street Journal*, 10 February 1988, p. 24.

[42]T. Michael Nevens, Georges L. Summe, and Bro Uttal, "Commercializing Technology: What the Best Companies Do," *Harvard Business Review* (May–June 1990): 154–63.

[43]Peter Vanderwicken, "P&G's Secret Ingredient," *Fortune* (July 1974): 75. See also "The Miracle Company," *Business Week* (19 October 1987): 84.

[44]*The Economist* (23 January 1988): 75.

[45]Laurie Hays, "Du Pont's Difficulties in Selling Kevlar Show Hurdles of Innovation," *Wall Street Journal*, 29 September 1987, p. 1. See also E. I. du Pont de Nemours and Company, annual report for 1990.

[46]"Coke's Man on the Spot," *Business Week* (25 July 1985): 56.

[47]E. Ralph Biggadike, "The Risky Business of Diversification," *Harvard Business Review* (May-June 1979): 103-11. See also E. Ralph Biggadike, Corporate Diversification: Entry Strategy and Performance (Boston: Division of Research, Harvard Business School, 1979).

[48]"A Revved-up Market for Diesel Engine Makers," *Business Week* (5 February 1979): 76.

[49]Richard Gibson, "Restaurant Rescuer Don Smith Hopes for More Than Potluck at Friendly's," *Wall Street Journal*, 11 August 1988, p. 34.

[50]George S. Yip, "Diversification Entry: Internal Development Versus Acquisition," *Strategic Management Journal* (October-December 1982): 331-46. See also Malcolm S. Salter and Wolf A. Weinhold, "Choosing Compatible Acquisitions," *Harvard Business Review* (January-February 1981): 117-27.

[51]Michael E. Porter, "From Competitive Advantage to Corporate Strategy," *McKinsey Quarterly* (Spring 1988): 43.

[52]"Gillette: After Diversification That Failed," *Business Week* (28 February 1977): 58-62.

[53]"Maytag's New Girth Will Test Its Marketing Muscle," *Business Week* (16 February 1987): 68.

[54]"Value Marketing," *Business Week* (11 November 1991): 132.

[55]Patricia Sellers, "What Customers Really Want," *Fortune* (4 June 1990): 58.

[56]Robert Jacobson and David A. Aaker, "The Strategic Role of Product Quality," *Journal of Marketing* (October 1987): 31-44.

[57]Bradley T. Grale and Robert D. Buzzell, "Market Perceived Quality: Key Strategic Concept," *Planning Review* (March-April 1989): 11.

[58]"King Customer," *Business Week* (12 March 1990): 88.

[59]Kim B. Clark and Takahiro Fujimoto, "The Power of Product Integrity," *Harvard Business Review* (November-December 1990): 110.

[60]Grale and Buzzell, "Market Perceived Quality," 14-16.

[61]Grale and Buzzell, "Market Perceived Quality," 7-8.

[62]Frank Rose, "Now Quality Means Service Too," *Fortune* (22 April 1991): 98.

[63]"King Customer," 90.

[64]Michael Siverstein, "World-Class Customer Service Builds Consumer Loyalty," *Marketing News* (19 August 1991): 11.

[65]Rose, "Now Quality Means Service Too," 100.

[66]Jan Carlzon, "Putting the Customer First: The Key to Service Strategy," *McKinsey Quarterly* (Summer 1987): 38-39.

[67]Christopher W. L. Hart, "The Power of Unconditional Service Guarantees," *Harvard Business Review* (July-August 1988): 54.

[68]*A Checklist of Key Factors in Customer Service Today* (Stamford, CT: Learning International, n.d.). Also see Daniel P. Finkelman and Anthony R. Goland, "How *Not* to Satisfy Your Customers," *McKinsey Quarterly* (Winter 1990): 2-12.

[69]Brian Dumaine, "How Managers Can Succeed through Speed," *Fortune* (13 February 1989): 54.

[70]Edward G. Krubasik, "Customize Your Product Development," *Harvard Business Review* (November-December 1988): 46–52.

[71]Dumaine, "How Managers Can Succeed through Speed," 57–58.

[72]This example and the ones that follow are based on Dumaine, "How Managers Can Succeed through Speed."

APPENDIX | *Perspectives on Product Strategies*

I Product-Positioning Strategy

Definition: Placing a brand in that part of the market where it will have a favorable reception compared with competing brands.

Objectives: (a) To position the product in the market so that it stands apart from competing brands. (b) To position the product so that it tells customers what you stand for, what you are, and how you would like customers to evaluate you. In the case of positioning multiple brands: (a) To seek growth by offering varied products in differing segments of the market. (b) To avoid competitive threats to a single brand.

Requirements: Use of marketing mix variables, especially design and communication efforts. (a) Successful management of a single brand requires positioning the brand in the market so that it can stand competition from the toughest rival and maintaining its unique position by creating the aura of a distinctive product. (b) Successful management of multiple brands requires careful positioning in the market so that multiple brands do not compete with nor cannibalize each other. Thus it is important to be careful in segmenting the market and to position an individual product as uniquely suited to a particular segment through design and promotion.

Expected Results: (a) Meet as much as possible the needs of specific segments of the market. (b) Limit sudden changes in sales. (c) Make customers faithful to the brands.

II Product-Repositioning Strategy

Definition: Reviewing the current positioning of the product and its marketing mix and seeking a new position for it that seems more appropriate.

Objectives: (a) To increase the life of the product. (b) To correct an original positioning mistake.

Requirements: (a) If this strategy is directed toward existing customers, repositioning is sought through promotion of more varied uses of the product. (b) If the business unit wants to reach new users, this strategy requires that the product be presented with a different twist to the people who have not been favorably inclined toward it. In doing so, care should be taken to see that, in the process of enticing new customers, current ones are not alienated. (c) If this strategy aims at presenting new uses of the product, it requires searching for latent uses of the product, if any. Although all products may not have latent uses, there are products that may be used for purposes not originally intended.

Expected Results: (a) Among existing customers: increase in sales growth and profitability. (b) Among new users: enlargement of the overall market, thus putting the product on a growth route, and increased profitability. (c) New product uses: increased sales, market share, and profitability.

III
Product-Overlap Strategy

Definition: Competing against one's own brand through introduction of competing products, use of private labeling, and selling to original-equipment manufacturers.

Objectives: (a) To attract more customers to the product and thereby increase the overall market. (b) To work at full capacity and spread overhead. (c) To sell to competitors; to realize economies of scale and cost reduction.

Requirements: (a) Each competing product must have its own marketing organization to compete in the market. (b) Private brands should not become profit drains. (c) Each brand should find its special niche in the market. If that doesn't happen, it will create confusion among customers and sales will be hurt. (d) In the long run, one of the brands may be withdrawn, yielding its position to the other brand.

Expected Results: (a) Increased market share. (b) Increased growth.

IV
Product-Scope Strategy

Definition: The product-scope strategy deals with the perspectives of the product mix of a company. The product-scope strategy is determined by taking into account the overall mission of the business unit. The company may adopt a single-product strategy, a multiple-product strategy, or a system-of-products strategy.

Objectives: (a) Single product: to increase economies of scale by developing specialization. (b) Multiple products: to cover the risk of potential obsolescence of the single product by adding additional products. (c) System of products: to increase the dependence of the customer on the company's products as well as to prevent competitors from moving into the market.

Requirements: (a) Single product: company must stay up-to-date on the product and even become the technology leader to avoid obsolescence. (b) Multiple products: products must complement one another in a portfolio of products. (c) System of products: company must have a close understanding of customer needs and uses of the products.

Expected Results: Increased growth, market share, and profits with all three strategies. With system-of-products strategy, the company achieves monopolistic control over the market, which may lead to some problems with the Justice Department, and enlarges the concept of its product/market opportunities.

V
Product-Design Strategy

Definition: The product-design strategy deals with the degree of standardization of a product. The company has a choice among the following strategic options: standard product, customized product, and standard product with modifications.

Objectives: (a) Standard product: to increase economies of scale of the company. (b) Customized product: to compete against mass producers of standardized products through product-design flexibility. (c) Standard product with modifications: to combine the benefits of the two previous strategies.

Requirements: Close analysis of product/market perspectives and environmental changes, especially technological changes.

Expected Results: Increase in growth, market share, and profits. In addition, the third strategy allows the company to keep close contacts with the market and gain experience in developing new standard products.

VI
Product-Elimination Strategy

Definition: Cuts in the composition of a company's business unit product portfolio by pruning the number of products within a line or by totally divesting a division or business.

Objectives: To eliminate undesirable products because their contribution to fixed cost and profit is too low, because their future performance looks grim, or because they do not fit in the business's overall strategy. The product-elimination strategy aims at shaping the best possible mix of products and balancing the total business.

Requirements: No special resources are required to eliminate a product or a division. However, because it is impossible to reverse the decision once the elimination has been achieved, an in-depth analysis must be done to determine (a) the causes of current problems; (b) the possible alternatives, other than elimination, that may solve problems (e.g., Are any improvements in the marketing mix possible?); and (c) the repercussions that elimination may have on remaining products or units (e.g., Is the product being considered for elimination complementary to another product in the portfolio? What are the side effects on the company's image? What are the social costs of an elimination?).

Expected Results: In the short run, cost savings from production runs, reduced inventories, and in some cases an improved return on investment can be expected. In the long run, the sales of the remaining products may increase because more efforts are now concentrated on them.

VII
New-Product Strategy

Definition: A set of operations that introduces (a) within the business, a product new to its previous line of products; (b) on the market, a product that provides a new type of satisfaction. Three alternatives emerge from the above: product improvement/modification, product imitation, and product innovation.

Objectives: To meet new needs and to sustain competitive pressures on existing products. In the first case, the new-product strategy is an offensive one; in the second case, it is a defensive one.

Requirements: A new-product strategy is difficult to implement if a "new product development system" does not exist within a company. Five components of this system should be assessed: (a) corporate aspirations toward new products, (b) organizational openness to creativity, (c) environmental favor toward creativity, (d) screening method for new ideas, and (e) evaluation process.

Expected Results: Increased market share and profitability.

VIII
Diversification Strategy

Definition: Developing unfamiliar products and markets through (a) concentric diversification (products introduced are related to existing ones in terms of marketing or technology), (b) horizontal diversification (new products are unrelated to existing ones but are sold to the same customers), and (c) conglomerate diversification (products are entirely new).

Objectives: Diversification strategies respond to the desire for (a) growth when current products/markets have reached maturity, (b) stability by spreading the risks of fluctuations in earnings, (c) security when the company may fear backward integration from one of its major customers, and (d) credibility to have more weight in capital markets.

Requirements: In order to reduce the risks inherent in a diversification strategy a business unit should (a) diversify its activities only if current product/market opportunities are limited, (b) have good knowledge of the area in which it diversifies, (c) provide the products introduced with adequate support, and (d) forecast the effects of diversification on existing lines of products.

Expected Results: (a) Increase in sales. (b) Greater profitability and flexibility.

IX Value Marketing Strategy

Definition: The value marketing strategy concerns delivering on promises made for the product or service. These promises involve product quality, customer service, and meeting time commitments.

Objectives: Value marketing strategies are directed toward seeking total customer satisfaction. It means striving for excellence to meet customer expectations.

Requirements: (a) Examine customer value perspectives; (b) design programs to meet customer quality, service, and time requirements; and (c) train employees and distributors to deliver on promises.

Expected Results: This strategy enhances customer satisfaction, which leads to customer loyalty and, hence, to higher market share. This strategy makes the firm less vulnerable to price wars, permitting the firm to charge higher prices and, thus, earn higher profits.

CHAPTER 15

Pricing Strategies

The real price of everything is the toil and trouble of acquiring it.

ADAM SMITH

Pricing has traditionally been considered a me-too variable in marketing strategy. The stable economic conditions that prevailed during the 1960s may be particularly responsible for the low status now ascribed to the pricing variable. Strategically, the function of pricing has been to provide adequate return on investment. Thus, the timeworn cost-plus method of pricing and its sophisticated version, return-on-investment pricing, have historically been the basis for arriving at price.

In the 1970s, however, a variety of events gave a new twist to the task of making pricing decisions. Double-digit inflation, material shortages, the high cost of money, consumerism, and post-price controls behavior all contributed to making pricing an important part of marketing strategy.

Despite the importance attached to it, effective pricing is not an easy task, even under the most favorable conditions. A large number of internal and external variables must be studied systematically before price can be set. For example, the reactions of a competitor often stand out as an important consideration in developing pricing strategy. Simply knowing that a competitor has a lower price is insufficient; a price strategist must know how much flexibility a competitor has in further lowering price. This presupposes a knowledge of the competitor's cost structure. In the dynamics of today's environment, however, where unexpected economic changes can render cost and revenue projections obsolete as soon as they are developed, pricing strategy is much more difficult to formulate.

This chapter provides a composite of pricing strategies. Each strategy is examined for its underlying assumptions and relevance in specific situations. The application of different strategies is illustrated with examples from pricing literature. The appendix at the end of this chapter summarizes each strategy by giving its definition, objectives, requirements, and expected results.

REVIEW OF PRICING FACTORS

Basically, a pricer needs to review four factors to arrive at a price: pricing objectives, cost, competition, and demand. This section briefly reviews these factors, which underlie every pricing strategy alternative.

Pricing Objectives

Broadly speaking, pricing objectives can be either profit oriented or volume oriented. The profit-oriented objective may be defined either in terms of desired net profit percentage or as a target return on investment. The latter objective has been more popular among large corporations. The volume-oriented objective may be stated as the percentage of market share that the firm would like to achieve. Alternatively, it may simply be stated as the desired sales growth rate. Many firms also consider the maintenance of a stable price as a pricing goal. Particularly in cyclical industries, price stability helps to sustain the confidence of customers and thus keeps operations running smoothly through peaks and valleys.

For many firms, there can be pricing objectives other than those of profitability and volume, as shown in Exhibit 15-1. Each firm should evaluate different objectives and choose its own priorities in the context of the pricing problems that it may be facing. The following list contains illustrations of typical pricing problems:

1. Decline in sales
2. Higher or lower prices than competitors
3. Excessive pressure on middlemen to generate sales
4. Imbalance in product line prices
5. Distortion vis-à-vis the offering in the customer's perceptions of the firm's price
6. Frequent changes in price without any relationship to environmental realities

EXHIBIT 15-1
Potential Pricing Objectives

1. Maximum long-run profits
2. Maximum short-run profits
3. Growth
4. Stabilize market
5. Desensitize customers to price
6. Maintain price-leadership arrangement
7. Discourage entrants
8. Speed exit of marginal firms
9. Avoid government investigation and control
10. Maintain loyalty of middlemen and get their sales support
11. Avoid demands for "more" from suppliers—labor in particular
12. Enhance image of firm and its offerings
13. Be regarded as "fair" by customers (ultimate)
14. Create interest and excitement about the item
15. Be considered trustworthy and reliable by rivals
16. Help in the sale of weak items in the line
17. Discourage others from cutting prices
18. Make a product "visible"
19. "Spoil market" to obtain high price for sale of business
20. Build traffic

Source: Alfred R. Oxenfeldt, "A Decision-Making Structure for Price Decisions," *Journal of Marketing* (January 1973): 50. Reprinted by permission of the American Marketing Association.

These problems suggest that a firm may have more than one pricing objective, even though these objectives may not be articulated as such. Essentially, pricing objectives deal directly or indirectly with three areas: profit (setting a high enough price to enable the company to earn an adequate margin for profit and reinvestment), competition (setting a low enough price to discourage competitors from adding capacity), and market share (setting a price below competition to gain market share).

As an example of pricing objectives, consider the goals that Apple Computer set for Macintosh:[1]

1. To make the product affordable and a good value for most college students
2. To get certain target market segments to see the Macintosh as a better value than the IBM PC
3. To encourage at least 90 percent of all Apple retailers to carry the Macintosh while providing a strong selling effort
4. To accomplish all this within 18 months

Cost

Fixed and variable costs are the major concerns of a pricer. In addition, the pricer may sometimes have to consider other types of costs, such as out-of-pocket costs, incremental costs, opportunity costs, controllable costs, and replacement costs.

To study the impact of costs on pricing strategy, the following three relationships may be considered: (a) the ratio of fixed costs to variable costs, (b) the economies of scale available to a firm, and (c) the cost structure of a firm vis-à-vis competitors. If the fixed costs of a company in comparison to its variable costs form a high proportion of its total costs, adding sales volume will be a great help in increasing earnings. Consider, for example, the case of the airlines, whose fixed costs are as high as 60 to 70 percent of total costs. Once fixed costs are recovered, any additional tickets sold add greatly to earnings. Such an industry is called *volume sensitive.* There are some industries, such as the paper industry, where variable costs constitute a higher proportion of total costs than do fixed costs. Such industries are *price sensitive* because even a small increase in price adds much to earnings.

If the economies of scale obtainable from a company's operations are substantial, the firm should plan to expand market share and, with respect to long-term prices, take expected declines in costs into account. Alternatively, if operations are expected to produce a decline in costs, then prices may be lowered in the long run to gain higher market share.

If a manufacturer is a low-cost producer relative to its competitors, it will earn additional profits by maintaining prices at competitive levels. The additional profits can be used to promote the product aggressively and increase the overall market share of the business. If, however, the costs of a manufacturer are high compared to those of its competitors, the manufacturer is in no position to reduce prices because that tactic may lead to a price war that it would most likely lose.

Different elements of cost must be differently related in setting price. Exhibit 15-2 shows, for example, how computations of full cost, incremental cost, and conversion cost may vary and how these costs affect product line prices. Exhibit 15-3 shows the procedure followed for setting target-return pricing.

Competition

Exhibit 15-4 shows the competitive information needed to formulate pricing strategy. The information may be analyzed with reference to these competitive characteristics: number of firms in the industry, relative size of different members of the industry, product differentiation, and ease of entry.

In an industry where there is only one firm, there is no competitive activity. The firm is free to set any price, subject to constraints imposed by law. As an Illinois Bell executive said about pricing (before the AT&T split): "All we had to do was determine our costs, and then we would go to the commission—the Illinois Commerce Commission, and they would give us the allowable rate of return."[2] Conversely, in an industry comprising a large number of active firms, competition is fierce. Fierce competition limits the discretion of a firm in setting price. Where there are a few firms manufacturing an undifferentiated product (such as in the steel industry), only the industry leader may have the discretion to change prices. Other industry members will tend to follow the leader in setting price.

The firm with a large market share is in a position to initiate price changes without worrying about competitor's reactions. Presumably, a competitor with

EXHIBIT 15-2
Effect of Costs on Pricing

Cost Pricing

Costs	*Product A*	*Product B*
Labor (*L*)	$ 80	$120
Material (*M*)	160	80
Overhead (*O*)	40	80
Full cost ($L + M + O$)	280	280
Incremental cost ($L + M$)	240	200
Conversion cost ($L + O$)	120	200

Production Line Pricing

	Markup (M′)	*Product A*	*Product B*
Full-Cost Pricing			
$P = FC + (M')FC$	20%	$336	$336
Incremental-Cost Pricing			
$P = (L + M) + M'(L + M)$	40%	336	280
Conversion-Cost Pricing			
$P = (L + O) + M'(L + O)$	180%	336	560

EXHIBIT 15-3
Computation of Target-Return Pricing

Manufacturing capacity	200,000
Standard volume (80%)	160,000
Standard full cost before profit	$100/unit
Target profit	
Investment	$20,000,000
ROI target	20%
ROI target	$4,000,000
Profit per unit at standard ($4,000,000 ÷ 160,000)	$25/unit
Price	$125/unit

a large market share has the lowest costs. The firm can, therefore, keep its prices low, thus discouraging other members of the industry from adding capacity, and further its cost advantage in a growing market.

If a firm operates in an industry that has opportunities for product differentiation, it can exert some control over pricing even if the firm is small and competitors are many. This latitude concerning price may occur if customers perceive one brand to be different from competing brands: whether the difference is real or imaginary, customers do not object to paying a higher price for preferred brands. To establish product differentiation of a brand in the minds of consumers, companies spend heavily for promotion. Product differentiation, however, offers an opportunity to control prices only within a certain range.

In an industry that is easy to enter, the price setter has less discretion in establishing prices; if there are barriers to market entry, however, a firm already

EXHIBIT 15-4
Competitive Information Needed for Pricing Strategy

1. Published competitive price lists and advertising
2. Competitive reaction to price moves in the past
3. Timing of competitors' price changes and inititing factors
4. Information on competitors' special campaigns
5. Competitive product line comparison
6. Assumptions about competitors' pricing/marketing objectives
7. Competitors' reported financial performance
8. Estimates of competitors' costs—fixed and variable
9. Expected pricing retaliation
10. Analysis of competitors' capacity to retaliate
11. Financial viability of engaging in price war
12. Strategic posture of competitors
13. Overall competitive aggressiveness

in the industry has greater control over prices. Barriers to entry may take any of the following forms:

1. Capital investment
2. Technological requirements
3. Nonavailability of essential materials
4. Economies of scale that existing firms enjoy and that would be difficult for a newcomer to achieve
5. Control over natural resources by existing firms
6. Marketing expertise

In an industry where barriers to entry are relatively easy to surmount, a new entrant will follow what can be called *keep-away pricing*. This pricing strategy is necessarily on the lower side of the pricing spectrum.

Demand

Exhibit 15-5 contains the information required for analyzing demand. Demand is based on a variety of considerations, of which price is just one. Some of these considerations are

1. Ability of customers to buy
2. Willingness of customers to buy
3. Place of the product in the customer's lifestyle (whether a status symbol or a product used daily)
4. Benefits that the product provides to customers
5. Prices of substitute products
6. Potential market for the product (is demand unfulfilled or is the market saturated)
7. Nature of nonprice competition
8. Customer behavior in general
9. Segments in the market

All these factors are interdependent, and it may not be easy to estimate their relationship to each other precisely.

Demand analysis involves predicting the relationship between price level and demand while considering the effects of other variables on demand. The relationship between price and demand is called elasticity of demand or sensitivity of price. **Elasticity of demand** refers to the number of units of a product that would be demanded at different prices. Price sensitivity should be considered at two different levels: total industry price sensitivity and price sensitivity for a particular firm.

Industry demand for a product is considered to be elastic if, by lowering prices, demand can be substantially increased. If lowering price has little effect on demand, demand is considered inelastic. The environmental factors previously mentioned have a definite influence on demand elasticity. Let us illustrate with a few examples. During the energy crisis, the price of gasoline went up, leading consumers to reduce gasoline usage. By the same token, since gasoline prices have gone down, people have again started using gas more freely. Thus, demand for gasoline can be considered somewhat elastic.

EXHIBIT 15-5
Customer Information Needed for Pricing Strategy

1. The customer's value analysis of the product: performance, utility, profit-rendering potential, quality, etc.
2. Market acceptance level: the price level of acceptance in each major market, including the influence of substitutes
3. The price the market expects and the differences in different markets
4. Price stability
5. The product's *S* curve and its present position on it
6. Seasonal and cyclical characteristics of the industry
7. The economic conditions now and during the next few periods
8. The anticipated effect of recessions; the effect of price change on demand in a declining market (e.g., very little with luxury items)
9. Customer relations
10. Channel relations and channel costs to figure in calculations
11. The markup at each channel level (company versus intermediary costs)
12. Advertising and promotion requirements and costs
13. Trade-in, replacement parts, service, delivery, installation, maintenance, preorder and postorder engineering, inventory, obsolescence, and spoilage problems and costs
14. The product differentiation that is necessary
15. Existing industry customs and reaction of the industry
16. Stockholder, government, labor, employee, and community relations

A case of inelastic demand is provided by salt. No matter how much the price fluctuates, people are not going to change the amount of salt that they consume. Similarly, the demand for luxury goods, yachts, for example, is inelastic because only a small proportion of the total population can afford to buy yachts.

Sometimes the market for a product is segmented so that demand elasticity in each segment must be studied. The demand for certain types of beverages by senior citizens might be inelastic, though demand for the same products among a younger audience may be especially elastic. If the price of a product goes up, customers have the option of switching to another product. Thus, availability of substitute products is another factor that should be considered.

When the total demand of an industry is highly elastic, the industry leader may take the initiative to lower prices. The loss in revenue due to decreased prices will be more than compensated for by the additional demand expected to be generated; therefore, the total dollar market expands. Such a strategy is highly attractive in an industry where economies of scale are achievable. Where demand is inelastic and there are no conceivable substitutes, price may be increased, at least in the short run. In the long run, however, the government may impose controls, or substitutes may be developed.

The demand for the products of an individual firm derives from total industry demand. An individual firm is interested in finding out how much market share it can command by changing its own prices. In the case of undifferentiated standardized products, lower prices should help a firm increase its market share as long as competitors do not retaliate by matching the firm's prices. Similarly, when business is sought through bidding prices, lower prices should help achieve the firm's objectives. In the case of differentiated products, however, market share can be improved even when higher prices are maintained (within a certain range). Products may be differentiated in various real and imaginary ways. For example, by providing adequate guarantees and after-sale service, an appliance manufacturer may maintain higher prices and still increase market share. Brand name, an image of sophistication, and the perception of high quality are other factors that may help to differentiate a product in the marketplace and thus create an opportunity for the firm to increase prices and not lose market share. Of course, other elements of the marketing mix should reinforce the product's image suggested by its price. In brief, a firm's best opportunity lies in differentiating the product and then communicating this fact to the customer. A differentiated product offers more opportunity for increasing earnings through price increases.

The sensitivity of price can be measured by taking into account historical data, consumer surveys, and experimentation. Historical data can either be studied intuitively or analyzed through quantitative tools, such as regression, to see how demand goes up or down based on price. A consumer survey to study the sensitivity of prices is no different from any other market research study. Experiments to judge what level of price generates what level of demand can be conducted either in a laboratory situation or in the real world. For example, a company interested in studying the sensitivity of prices may introduce a newly developed grocery product in a few selected markets for a short period at different prices. Information obtained from this experiment should provide insights into the elasticity of demand for the product. In one study, the prices of 17 food products were varied in 30 food stores. It was found that the product sales generally followed the law of demand: when prices were raised 10 percent, sales decreased about 25 percent; a price increase of 5 percent led to a decrease in sales of about 13 percent; a lowering of prices by 5 percent increased sales by 12 percent; and a 10 percent decrease in price improved sales by 26 percent. In another study, a new deodorant that was priced at 63 cents and at 85 cents in different markets resulted in the same volume of sales. Thus, price elasticity was found to be absent, and the manufacturer set the product price at 85 cents.[3]

To conclude this discussion on pricing factors, it would not be out of place to say that, while everybody thinks businesses go about setting prices scientifically, very often the process is incredibly arbitrary. Although businesses of all types devote a great deal of time and study to determine the prices to put on their products, pricing is often more art than science. In some cases, setting prices does involve the use of a straightforward equation: material and labor costs + overhead and other expenses + profit = price. But in many other cases, the equation includes psychological and other such subtle subjective factors that the pricing decision may essentially rest on gut feeling.[4] Exhibit 15-6 suggests one way of combining information on different pricing factors to make an objective pricing decision in industrial marketing. For example, price sensitivity, visibility to competition, and strength of supplier relationships are used to rank various customers, allowing a different pricing strategy to be adopted for each customer to effectively achieve profit, share, and communication objectives.

PRICING STRATEGIES FOR NEW PRODUCTS

The pricing strategy for a new product should be developed so that the desired impact on the market is achieved while the emergence of competition is discouraged. Two basic strategies that may be used in pricing a new product are skimming pricing and penetration pricing.

Skimming Pricing

Skimming pricing is the strategy of establishing a high initial price for a product with a view to "skimming the cream off the market" at the upper end of the demand curve. It is accompanied by heavy expenditure on promotion. A skimming strategy may be recommended when the nature of demand is uncertain, when a company has expended large sums of money on research and development for a new product, when the competition is expected to develop and market a similar product in the near future, or when the product is so innovative that the market is expected to mature very slowly. Under these circumstances, a skimming strategy has several advantages.[5] At the top of the demand curve, price elasticity is low. Besides, in the absence of any close substitute, cross-elasticity is also low. These factors, along with heavy emphasis on promotion, tend to help the product make significant inroads into the market. The

EXHIBIT 15-6
Pricing Guide

Company Relationship with Customer (Leverage)	*Visibility of Price to Competition (Knowledge)*	Customer's Price Sensitivity	
		Low	*High*
Strong	High	To gain profit and communicate high price	To maintain share and communicate willingness to fight
	Low	To gain profit	
Weak	High	To communicate high price	
	Low	To gain share	
Price high	**Price low**	**Price to match competition**	

Source: Robert A. Garda, "Industrial Pricing: Strategy vs. Tactics." Reprinted by permission of publisher, from *MANAGEMENT REVIEW*, November 1983, © 1983. American Management Association, New York. All rights reserved.

high price also helps segment the market. Only nonprice-conscious customers will buy a new product during its initial stage. Later on, the mass market can be tapped by lowering the price.

If there are doubts about the shape of the demand curve for a given product and the initial price is found to be too high, price may be slashed. However, it is very difficult to start low and then raise the price. Raising a low price may annoy potential customers, and anticipated drops in price may retard demand at a particular price. For a financially weak company, a skimming strategy may provide immediate relief. This model depends on selling enough units at the higher price to cover promotion and development costs. If price elasticity is higher than anticipated, a lower price will be more profitable and "relief giving."

Modern patented drugs provide a good example of skimming pricing. At the time of its introduction in 1942, penicillin was priced as high as $20 for a 100,000-unit vial. By 1944 the price was down to $2; it decreased to a few cents in 1949. Many new products are priced following this policy. Videocassette recorders (VCRs), frozen foods, and instant coffee were all priced very high at the time of their initial appearance in the market. But different versions of these products are now available at prices ranging from very high to very low. No conclusive research has yet been done to indicate how high an initial price should be in relation to cost. As a rule of thumb, the final price to the consumer should be at least three or four times the factory door cost.

The decision about how high a skimming price should be depends on two factors: (a) the probability of competitors entering the market and (b) price elasticity at the upper end of the demand curve. If competitors are expected to introduce their own brands quickly, it may be safe to price rather high. On the other hand, if competitors are years behind in product development and a low rate of return to the firm would slow the pace of research at competing firms, a low skimming price can be useful. However, price skimming in the face of impending competition may not be wise if a larger market share makes entry more difficult. If limiting the sale of a new product to a few selected individuals produces sufficient sales, a very high price may be desirable.

Determining the duration of time for keeping prices high depends entirely on the competition's activities. In the absence of patent protection, skimming prices may be forced down as soon as competitors join the race. However, in the case of products that are protected through patents (e.g., drugs), the manufacturer slowly brings down the price as the patent period draws near an end; then, a year or so before the expiration of the patent period, the manufacturer saturates the market with a very low price. This strategy establishes a foothold for the manufacturer in the mass market before competitors enter it, thereby frustrating their expectations.

So far, skimming prices have been discussed as high prices in the initial stage of a product's life. Premium and umbrella prices are two other forms of price skimming. Some products carry premium prices (high prices) permanently and build an image of superiority for themselves. When a mass market cannot be developed and upper-end demand seems adequate, manufacturers will not risk tarnishing the prestigious image of their products by lowering prices, thereby offering the product to everybody. Estee Lauder cosmetics, Olga intimate apparel, Brooks Brothers clothes, and Johnston and Murphy shoes are products that fall into this category.

Sometimes higher prices are maintained in order to provide an umbrella for small high-cost competitors. Umbrella prices have been aided by limitation laws that specify minimum prices for a variety of products, such as milk.

Du Pont provides an interesting example of skimming pricing. The company tends to focus on high-margin specialty products. Initially it prices its products high; it then gradually lowers price as the market builds and as competition grows.[6] Polaroid also pursues a skimming pricing strategy. The company introduces an expensive model of a new camera and follows up the introduction with simpler lower-priced versions to attract new segments.[7]

Penetration Pricing

Penetration pricing is the strategy of entering the market with a low initial price so that a greater share of the market can be captured. The penetration strategy is used when an elite market does not exist and demand seems to be elastic over the entire demand curve, even during early stages of product introduction. High price elasticity of demand is probably the most important reason for adopting a penetration strategy. The penetration strategy is also used to discourage competitors from entering the market.[8] When competitors seem to be encroaching on a market, an attempt is made to lure them away by means of penetration pricing, which yields lower margins. A competitor's costs play a decisive role in this pricing strategy because a cost advantage over the existing manufacturer might persuade another firm to enter the market, regardless of how low the margin of the former may be.

One may also turn to a penetration strategy with a view to achieving economies of scale. Savings in production costs alone may not be an important factor in setting low prices because, in the absence of price elasticity, it is difficult to generate sufficient sales. Finally, before adopting penetration pricing, one must make sure that the product fits the lifestyles of the mass market. For example, although it might not be difficult for people to accept imitation milk, cereals made from petroleum products would probably have difficulty in becoming popular.

How low the penetration price should be differs from case to case. There are several different types of prices used in penetration strategies: restrained prices, elimination prices, promotional prices, and keep-out prices. Restraint is applied so that prices can be maintained at a certain point during inflationary periods. In this case, environmental circumstances serve as a guide to what the price level should be. Elimination prices are fixed at a point that threatens the survival of a competitor. A large, multiproduct company can lower prices to a level where a smaller competitor might be wiped out of the market. The pricing of suits at factory outlets illustrates promotional prices. Factory outlets constantly stress low prices for comparable department store–quality suits. Keep-out prices are fixed at a level that prevents competitors from entering the market. Here the objective is to keep the market to oneself at the highest chargeable price.

A low price acts as the sole selling point under penetration strategy, but the market should be broad enough to justify low prices. Thus, price elasticity of demand is probably the most important factor in determining how low prices can go. This point can be easily illustrated.[9] Convinced that shoppers would willingly sacrifice convenience for price savings, an entrepreneur in 1981 introduced a concentrated cleaner called 4 + 1. Unlike such higher-priced cleaners as Windex, Fantastik, and Formula 409, this product did not come in a spray bottle. It also needed to be diluted with water before use. The entrepreneur hoped for 10 percent of the $160-million market. But the product did not sell well. The product was not as price elastic as the entrepreneur had assumed. Though the consumer tends to talk a lot about economy, the lure of convenience is apparently stronger than the desire to save a few cents. Ultimately, 4 + 1 had to be withdrawn from most markets.

Unlike Du Pont, Dow Chemical Company stresses penetration pricing. It concentrates on lower-margin commodity products and low prices, builds a dominant market share, and holds on for the long haul. Texas Instruments also practices penetration pricing. Texas Instruments starts by building a large plant capacity. By setting the price as low as possible, it hopes to penetrate the market fast and gain a large market share.

Penetration pricing reflects a long-term perspective in which short-term profits are sacrificed in order to establish sustainable competitive advantage. Penetration policy usually leads to above-average long-run returns that fall in a relatively narrow range. Price skimming, on the other hand, yields a wider range of lower average returns.[10]

PRICING STRATEGIES FOR ESTABLISHED PRODUCTS

Changes in the marketing environment may require a review of the prices of products already on the market. For example, an announcement by a large firm that it is going to lower its prices makes it necessary for other firms in the industry to examine their prices. In 1976 Texas Instruments announced that it would soon sell a digital watch for about $20. The announcement jolted the entire industry because only 15 months earlier the lowest-priced digital was selling for $125. It forced a change in everyone's strategy and gave some producers real problems. Fairchild Camera and Instrument Corporation reacted with its own version of a $20 plastic-cased digital watch. So did National Semiconductor Corporation. American Microsystems, however, decided to get completely out of the finished watch business.[11]

A review of pricing strategy may also become necessary because of shifts in demand. In the late 1960s, for example, it seemed that, with the popularity of miniskirts, the pantyhose market would continue to boom. But its growth slowed when the fashion emphasis shifted from skirts to pants. Pants hid runs, or tears, making it unnecessary to buy as many pairs. The popularity of pants also led to a preference for knee-high hose over pantyhose. Knee-high hose, which cost less, meant lower profits for manufacturers. Although the pantyhose market was dwindling, two new entrants, Bic Pen Corporation and Playtex Corporation, were readying their brands for introduction. Their participation made it necessary for the big three hosiery manufacturers—Hanes, Burlington, and Kayser-Roth—to review their prices and protect their market shares.

Exhibit 15-7 lists questions to raise to determine if a given pricing strategy is desirable. An examination of existing prices may lead to one of three strategic alternatives: maintaining the price, reducing the price, or increasing the price.

Maintaining the Price

If the market segment from which the company derives a big portion of its sales is not affected by changes in the environment, the company may decide not to initiate any change in its pricing strategy. The gasoline shortage in the aftermath of the fall of the Shah of Iran did not affect the luxury car market because buyers of Cadillac, Mercedes-Benz, and Rolls-Royce were not concerned about higher gas prices. Thus, General Motors did not need to redesign the Cadillac to reduce its gas consumption or lower its price to make it attractive to the average customer.

The strategy of maintaining price is appropriate in circumstances where a price change may be desirable, but the magnitude of change is indeterminable. If the reaction of customers and competitors to a price change cannot be predicted, maintaining the present price level may be appropriate. Alternatively, a price change may have an impact on product image or sales of other products in a company's line that it is not practical to assess. Several years ago, when Magnavox and Sylvania cut the prices of their color television sets, Zenith maintained prices at current levels. Because the industry appeared to be in good shape, Zenith could not determine why its competitors adopted such a strategic posture. Zenith continued to maintain prices and earned higher profits.

Politics may be another reason for maintaining prices. During the year from 1978 to 1979, President Carter urged voluntary control of wages and prices. Many companies restrained themselves from seeking price changes in order to align themselves behind the government's efforts to control inflation.

Concern for the welfare of society may be another reason for maintaining prices at current levels. Even when supply is temporarily short of demand, some businesses may adopt a socially responsible posture and continue to charge current prices. For example, taxi drivers may choose not to hike fares when subway and bus service operators are on strike.

Reducing the Price

There are three main reasons for lowering prices. First, as a defensive strategy, prices may be cut in response to competition. For example, in October 1978, Congress authorized the deregulation of the airline industry. Deregulation gave airlines almost total freedom to set ticket prices. Thus, in 1991, in response to Continental Airline's $198 round-trip fare on its New York–Los Angeles route, United Airlines acted to meet this competitive fare. United's regular round-trip coach fare at the time was about $680. Similarly, other carriers were forced to

EXHIBIT 15-7
Are You a Proactive Pricer?

The 20 questions below provide a simple diagnostic test of your pricing strategy and tactics. If you can answer no to the first 10 and yes to the second 10, you are a shrewd pricer. If the results are otherwise, it may be rewarding to reconsider how you set prices.

1. Is your market share constant or declining while prices are falling in real terms?
2. Do you have a nagging suspicion—but no real evidence—that you are regularly bidding too high for contracts?
3. Do your salespeople keep complaining that your prices are several percentage points too high, although your share is holding steady?
4. Do your contribution margins for the same product vary widely from customer to customer?
5. Are you unsure who is the industry price leader?
6. Do your pricing approval levels seem to be functioning more as a volume discount device than as a control mechanism?
7. Would you have trouble describing your competitors' pricing strategies?
8. Do you find that too many pricing decisions seem aimed at gaining volume, despite an overall non-volume strategy?
9. Are most of your prices set at minimum approval levels?
10. Do your competitors seem to anticipate your pricing actions with ease, while theirs often take you by surprise?
11. Do you have a planned method of communicating price changes to customers and distributors?
12. Do you know how long to wait before following a competitor's price change?
13. Are your prices set to reflect such customer-specific costs as transportation, set-up charges, design costs, warranty, sales commissions, and inventory?
14. Do you know how long it takes each of your major competitors to follow one of your price moves?
15. Do you know the economic value of your product to your customers?
16. Do you use the industry's price/volume curve as an analytical aid to price setting?
17. Do you know whether you would be better off making a single large price change or several small changes?
18. Do you know how to go about establishing price leadership in your industry?
19. Are your prices based strictly on your own costs?
20. Do you have a consistent and effective policy for intracompany pricing?

Source: Elliot B. Ross, "Making Money with Proactive Pricing." Reprinted by permission of *Harvard Business Review*. An exhibit from "Making Money with Proactive Pricing," by Elliot B. Ross, November–December, 1984.

reduce their fares on different routes to match these prices. In addition, to successfully compete in mature industries, many companies reduce prices, following a strategy that is often called value pricing. For example, in light of slipping profit margins and lower customer counts, McDonald's cut prices under pressure from major rivals Taco Bell and Wendy's.[12]

A second reason for lowering prices is offensive in nature. Following the experience curve concept (see chapter 12), costs across the board go down by a fixed percentage every time experience doubles. Consequently, a company with greater experience has lower costs than one whose experience is limited. Lower costs have a favorable impact on profits. Thus, as a matter of strategy, it behooves a company to shoot for higher market share and to secure as much experience as possible in order to gain a cost and, hence, a profit advantage. A company that successfully follows this strategy is Home Depot, the largest home repair chain in the country. The policy of everyday low prices has enabled the company to grow into a $2.8-billion chain of 118 stores, mostly in the sunbelt. Home Depot's goal is to go national with $10 billion in sales at more than 350 locations by 1995.[13]

Technological advances have made possible the low-cost production of high-quality electronics gear. Many companies have translated these advances into low retail prices to gain competitive leverage.[14] For example, in 1978 a Sony clock radio, with no power backup and a face that showed nothing more than the current time, sold for $80. In 1985, a Sony clock radio priced at about $40 had auxiliary power and showed the time at which the alarm was set as well as the current time. In 1991 the same radio was available for less than $25.

Texas Instruments has followed the experience curve concept in achieving cost reductions in the manufacture of integrated circuits. This achievement is duly reflected in its strategy to slowly lower prices of such products as electronic calculators. Even in other businesses where technological advances have a less critical role to play in the success of the business, a price reduction strategy may work out. Take the case of Metpath, a clinical laboratory. In the late 1960s, at about the time Metpath was formed, the industry leader, Damon Corporation, was acquiring local labs all around the country; by the early 1970s, other large corporations in the business, Revlon, Bristol-Myers, Diamond Shamrock, and W.R. Grace, began doing the same. Metpath, however, adopted a price-cutting strategy. In order to implement this strategy, it took a variety of measures to achieve economies of scale. Figuring that there were not many economies of scale involved in simply putting together a chain of local labs that operated mostly as separate entities, to reduce costs, Metpath focused on centralizing its testing. A super lab that did have those economies of scale was created, along with a nationwide network to collect specimens and distribute test results. Metpath's strategy paid off well. It emerged as the industry leader in the clinical lab-testing field. Heavy price competition, much of it attributed to Metpath, led some of the big diversified companies, including W.R. Grace and Diamond Shamrock, to pull out of the business.[15]

The recent recession has caused consumers to tighten belts and to be more sensitive to prices. Sears, therefore, adopted a new pricing policy whereby prices on practically all products were permanently lowered. The company closed its 824 stores for two days to remark price tags and to implements its "everyday low pricing" strategy. A number of other companies, Wal-Mart, Toys "R" Us, and Circuit City, also pursue this strategy by keeping prices low year-round, avoiding the practice of marking them up and down. Consumers like year-round low prices because constantly changing sale prices makes it hard to recognize a fair deal.[16]

The third and final reason for price cutting may be a response to customer need. If low prices are a prerequisite for inducing the market to grow, customer need may then become the pivot of a marketing strategy, all other aspects of the marketing mix being developed accordingly.

In adopting a low-price strategy for an existing product, a variety of considerations must be taken into account. The long-term impact of a price cut against a major competitor is a factor to be reckoned with. For example, a regional pizza chain can cut prices to prevent Pizza Hut from gaining a foothold in its market only in the short run. Eventually Pizza Hut (a division of PepsiCo) will prevail over the local chain through price competition. Pizza Hut may lower prices to such an extent that the local chain may find it difficult even to recover its costs. Thus, competitive strength should be duly evaluated in opting for low-price strategy.

In a highly competitive situation, a product may command a higher price than other brands if it is marketed as a "different" product, for example, as one of deluxe quality. If the price of a deluxe product is reduced, the likely impact on its position should be looked into. Sony television sets have traditionally sold at premium prices because they have been promoted as quality products. Sony's higher-price strategy paid off: the Sony television rose to prominence as a quality product and captured a respectable share of the market . A few years later, however, consumer pressures led Sony dealers to reduce prices. This action not only hurt Sony's overall prestige, it made some retailers stop selling Sony because it had now become just one of the many brands they carried. In other words, the price cut, though partly initiated by its dealers, cost Sony its distinction. Even if its sales increased in the short run, in the long run, the price cut did not prove to be a viable strategy because it went against the perception consumers had of Sony's being a distinctive brand. Ultimately, consumers may perceive Sony as just another brand, which will affect both sales and profits.

It is also necessary to examine thoroughly the impact of a price cut of one product on other products in the line. Price is often considered an indication of product quality.[17] Thus, the same product with a different price tag may be perceived differently. The impact of lowering prices can be illustrated with reference to the Bulova Watch Company. In 1972 the company was considering reducing the prices of its tuning-fork Accutron watches for men. Before finalizing its decision, the company had to consider the following effects of reducing price:

1. The pricing decision extended beyond Bulova's Accutron watches for men. In 1972 Bulova had, for the first time, started to market Accutron watches for women. This new line could more than double the market for Accutron watches. Also, in 1972 Bulova had started to market Accuquartz watches for men, Bulova's entry into the new market for quartz watches. If the prices for men's Accutron watches were reduced, the prices for the other two lines would have to be adjusted downward as well.

2. A reduced-price Accutron line might affect Bulova's long-established conventional watch line. In 1972 the sale of "Bulova" brand watches—jeweled-lever watches retailing at prices across the entire mid-price segment of the market—continued a major piece of Bulova's business. In the past, a price gap separated most Bulova brand watches from those in the more expensive Accutron line. If the gap were closed, the company might find that it was trading sales of its most expensive Bulova brand watches for sales of its least expensive Accutron watches.
3. The price reduction, if approved, could not be limited strictly to Bulova's domestic business. Bulova's watch prices overseas, though not identical with those in the United States, were related to its watch prices at home. Eventually, to maintain some sort of order on a worldwide basis, Bulova's foreign prices would have to ease down, too.
4. Related to point 3, Bulova's operations, particularly its manufacturing activities, were highly international in nature. Most of what the firm sold in the United States came from its overseas plants. But, with recurring monetary crises and currency realignments, the pricing decision had to be made against a backdrop of confused international economic conditions.
5. Finally, Bulova's financial performance in the preceding two years was nothing to cheer about. Declining defense orders since 1970 had, by 1972, cut $26 million out of Bulova's sales, and even though increases in Bulova's consumer business had picked up some of the slack, profits had suffered badly. Bulova's net income for its fiscal year ending March 31, 1972, was $3.9 million, down 40% from its record 1970 net income of $6.8 million. While fiscal 1973 looked more promising, the company clearly had some distance to go to get back to its previous performance level.[18]

Finally, the impact of a price cut on a product's financial performance must be reviewed before the strategy is implemented. If a company is financially so positioned that a price cut will weaken its profitability, it may decide not to lower the price even if lowering price may be in all other ways the best course to follow.

Increasing the Price

An increase in price may be implemented for various reasons. First, in an inflationary economy, prices may have to be adjusted upward in order to maintain profitability. During periods of inflation, all types of costs go up, and to maintain adequate profits, an increase in price becomes necessary. How much the price should be increased is a matter of strategy that varies from case to case. Conceptually, however, price should be increased to such a level that the profits before and after inflation are approximately equal. An increase in price should also take into account any decline in revenue caused by shifts in demand due to price increases. Strategically, the decision to minimize the effects of inflationary pressures on the company through price increases should be based on the long-term implications of achieving a short-run vantage.[19]

Mention must be made that it is not always necessary for a company to increase prices to offset inflationary pressures. A company can take nonprice measures as well to reduce the effects of inflation. For example, many fast-food chains expanded menus and seating capacity to partially offset rising costs. Similarly, a firm may substantially increase prices, much more than justified by inflation alone, by improving product quality or by raising the level of accompanying services. High quality should help keep prices and profits up because inflation-weary customers search for value in the marketplace. Improved product quality and additional services should provide such value.[20]

Price may also be increased by downsizing (i.e., decreasing) package size while maintaining price. In a recession, downsizing helps hold the line on prices despite rising costs. Under inflationary conditions, downsizing provides a way of keeping prices from rising beyond psychological barriers. Downsizing is commonly practiced by packaged-goods companies. For example, recently Procter and Gamble cut the number of diapers in a package from 88 to 80 while leaving the price the same. In this example, downsizing effectively resulted in a price increase of 9.1 percent. Similarly, H. J. Heinz reduced the contents of its 6.5-ounce StarKist Seafood (tuna) can by three-eighths of an ounce. By keeping exactly the same price as before, the company gained an invisible 5.8 percent price increase.[21]

Prices may also be increased when a brand has a monopolistic control over the market segments it serves. In other words, when a brand has a differential advantage over competing brands in the market, it may take advantage of its unique position, increasing its price to maximize its benefits. Such a differential advantage may be real or may exist just in the mind of the consumer. In seeking a price increase in a monopolistic situation, the increase should be such that customers will absorb it and still remain loyal to the brand. If the price increase is abnormal, differential advantage may be lost, and the customer will choose a brand based on price.

The downside of increasing price may be illustrated with reference to coffee. Let us say that there is a segment of customers who ardently drink Maxwell House coffee. In their minds, Maxwell House has something special. If the price of Maxwell House goes up (assuming that the prices of other brands remain unchanged), these coffee drinkers may continue to purchase it because the brand has a virtual monopoly over their coffee-drinking behavior. There is a limit, however, to what these Maxwell House loyalists will pay for their favorite brand of coffee. Thus, if the price of Maxwell House is increased too much, these customers may shift their preference.

From the perspective of strategy, this example indicates that, in monopolistic situations, the price of a brand may be set high to increase revenues and profits. The extent of the increase, however, depends on many factors. Each competitor has a different optimum price level for a given end product for a given customer group. It is rare that such optimum prices are the same for any two competitors. Each competitor has different options based on different cost components, capacity constraints, financial structure, product mix, customer mix, logistics, culture, and growth rate. The competitor with the lowest optimum price has the option of setting the common price; all others must follow or retreat. However, the continued existence of competitors depends on each firm retreating from competition when it is at a disadvantage until each competes primarily in a "competitive segment," a monopolistic situation where it has an advantage compared to all others. This unique combination of characteristics, matched with differentials in the competitive environment, enables each firm to coexist and prosper in its chosen area (i.e., where it has monopolistic control).

Sometimes prices must be increased to adhere to an industry situation. Of the few firms in an industry, one (usually the largest) emerges as a leader. If the leader raises its price, other members of the industry must follow suit, if only to maintain the balance of strength in the industry. If they refuse to do so, they are liable to be challenged by the leader. Usually no firm likes to fight the industry leader because it has more at stake than the leader.

In the U.S. auto industry, there are three domestic firms: General Motors, Ford, and Chrysler. General Motors is the industry leader in terms of market share. If General Motors increases its prices, all other members of the industry all increase prices. Thus, a firm may be compelled to increase price in response to a similar increase by the industry leader. The leader also sets a limit on price increases, with followers frequently setting their prices very close to those of the leader. Although an increase is forced on a firm in this situation, it is a good strategic move to set a price that, without being obviously different, is higher than the leader's price.

Prices may also be increased to segment the market. For example, a soft drink company may come out with a new brand and direct it toward busy executives/professionals. This brand may be differentiated as one that provides stamina and invigoration without adding calories. To substantiate the brand's worth and make it appear different, the price may be set at double the price of existing soft drinks. Similarly, the market may be segmented by geography, with varying prices serving different segments. For example, in New York City, a 6.4-ounce tube of Crest toothpaste may sell for $3.29 on Park Avenue, for $2.79 on the Upper East Side, and for $1.79 on the Lower East Side.[22]

Hewlett-Packard Company operates in the highly competitive pocket calculator industry, where the practice of price cutting is quite common. Nonetheless, Hewlett-Packard thrives by offering high-priced products to a select segment of the market. It seems to appeal to a market segment that is highly inelastic with respect to price but highly elastic with respect to quality. The company equips its calculators with special features and then offers them at a price that is much higher than the industry average. In other words, rather than running the business on the basis of overall volume, Hewlett-Packard realizes high prices by being a specialist that serves a narrow segment. In cosmetics or automobiles, for example, there may be a tenfold cost difference between mass market products and those designed, produced, packaged, distributed, and promoted for small high-quality niches. Up-market products are often produced by specialists, companies like Daimler-Benz or BMW, that can compete successfully around far-larger producers of standard products.

Many airlines have successfully used price structure to differentiate market segments and objectives based on customer price sensitivity. Business travelers are relatively price insensitive; whereas tourists are very sensitive to the price of tickets. In order to increase the volume of tourist traffic without forgoing bread-and-butter revenues from business customers, airlines have developed price structures based on characteristics that differentiate these two customer segments.

For example, tourists generally spend a weekend at their destination, business travelers do not. By changing the structure from pricing flights to pricing itineraries, the airlines can discount itineraries that include a Saturday night. Most business customers cannot take advantage of such discounts without incurring substantial inconvenience. This enables the airline to increase tourist volume while maintaining high prices among the business customer segment. Such pricing policies have led to as much as 10 times the difference in fares paid for the same seat. Thus, a flexible pricing strategy permits a company to realize high prices from customers who are willing to pay them without sacrificing volume from customers who are not.[23]

Increase in price should be considered for its effect on long-term profitability, demand elasticity, and competitive moves. Although a higher price may mean higher profits in the short run, the long-run effect of a price increase may be disastrous. The increase may encourage new entrants to flock to the industry and competition from substitutes. Thus, before a price increase strategy is implemented, its long-term effect should be thoroughly examined. Further, an increase in price may lead to shifts in demand that could be detrimental. Likewise, the increase may negatively affect market share if the competition decides not to seek similar increases in price. Thus, competitive posture must be studied and predicted. In addition, a company should review its own ability to live with higher prices. A price increase may mean a decline in revenues but an increase in profits. Whether such a situation will create any problem needs to be looked into. Will laying off people or reassigning sales territories be problematic? Is a limit to price increases called for as a matter of social responsibility? In 1979 President Carter asked businesses to adhere to 7 percent increases in prices and wages voluntarily. In a similar situation, should a company that otherwise finds a 10 percent increase in price strategically sound go ahead with it? Finally, the price increase should be duly reinforced by other factors in the marketing mix. A Chevy cannot be sold at a Cadillac price. A man's suit bearing a K-Mart label cannot be sold on a par with one manufactured by Brooks Brothers. Chanel No. 5 cannot be promoted by placing an ad in *TV Guide.* The increased price must be evaluated before being finalized to see whether the posture of other market mix variables will substantiate it.

PRICE-FLEXIBILITY STRATEGY

A price-flexibility strategy usually consists of two alternatives: a one-price policy and a flexible-pricing policy. Influenced by a variety of changes in the environment, such as saturation of markets, slow growth, global competition, and the consumer movement, more and more companies have been adhering in recent years to flexibility in pricing of different forms. Pricing flexibility may consist of setting different prices in different markets based on geographic location, varying prices depending on the time of delivery, or customizing prices based on the complexity of the product desired.

One-Price Strategy

A one-price strategy means that the same price is set for all customers who purchase goods under essentially the same conditions and in the same quantities. The one-price strategy is fairly typical in situations where mass distribution and mass selling are employed. There are several advantages and disadvantages that may be attributed to a one-price strategy. One advantage of this pricing strategy is administrative convenience. It also makes the pricing process easier and contributes to the maintenance of goodwill among customers because no one customer receives special pricing favors over another.

A general disadvantage of a one-price strategy is that the firm usually ends up broadcasting its prices to competitors who may be capable of undercutting the price. Total inflexibility in pricing may undermine the product in the marketplace. Total inflexibility in pricing may also have highly adverse effects on corporate growth and profits in certain situations. It is very important that a company remain responsive to general trends in economic, social, technological, political/legal, and competitive environments. Realistically, then, a pricing strategy should be periodically reviewed to incorporate environmental changes as they become pronounced. Any review of this type would have to include a close look at a company's position relative to the actions of other firms operating within its industry. As an example, it is generally believed that one reason for the success of discount houses is that conventional retailers have rigidly held to traditional prices and margins.

Flexible-Pricing Strategy

A flexible-pricing strategy refers to situations where the same products or quantities are offered to different customers at different prices. A flexible-pricing strategy is more common in industrial markets than in consumer markets. An advantage of a flexible-pricing strategy is the freedom allowed to sales representatives to make adjustments for competitive conditions rather than refuse an order. Also, a firm is able to charge a higher price to customers who are willing to pay it and a lower price to those who are unwilling, although legal difficulties may be encountered if price discrimination becomes an issue. Besides, other customers may become upset upon learning that they have been charged more than their competitors. In addition, bargaining tends to increase the cost of selling, and some sales representatives may let price cutting become a habit.

Recently, many large U.S. companies have added new dimensions of flexibility to their pricing strategies. Although companies have always shown some willingness to adjust prices or profit margins on specific products when market conditions have varied, this kind of flexibility is now being carried to the state of high art. The concept of price flexibility can be implemented in four different ways: by market, by product, by timing, and by technology.

Price flexibility with reference to the market can be achieved either from one geographic area to another or from one segment to another. Both Ford and General Motors charge less for their compact cars marketed on the West Coast than for those marketed anywhere else in the country. Different segments make different uses of a product: many companies, therefore, consider customer usage in setting price. For example, a plastic sold to industry might command only 30 cents a pound; sold to a dentist, it might bring $25 a pound. Here again, the flexible-pricing strategy calls for different prices in the two segments.[24]

Price flexibility with reference to the product is implemented by considering the value that a product provides to the customer. Careful analysis may show that some products are underpriced and can stand an upgrading in the marketplace. Others, competitively priced to begin with, may not support any additional margin because the matchup between value and cost would be lost.[25]

Costs of all transactions from raw material to delivery may be analyzed, and if some costs are unnecessary in a particular case, adjustments may be made in pricing a product to sell to a particular customer. Such cost optimization is very effective from the customer's point of view because he or she does not pay for those costs for which no value is received.

Price flexibility can also be practiced by adding to the price an escalation clause based on cost fluctuations. Escalation clauses are especially relevant in situations where there is a substantial time gap between confirmation of an order and delivery of the finished product. In the case of products susceptible to technological obsolescence, price is set to recover all sunken costs within a reasonable period.

The flexible-pricing strategy has two main characteristics: an emphasis on profit or margins rather than simply on volume and a willingness to change price with reference to the existing climate. Caution is in order here. In many instances, building market share may be essential to cutting costs and, hence, to increasing profits. Thus, where the experience curve concept makes sense, companies may find it advantageous to reduce prices to hold or increase market share. However, a reduction in price simply as a reactionary measure to win a contract is discounted. Implementation of this strategy requires that the pricing decision be instituted by someone high up in the organization away from salespeople in the field. In some companies the pricing executive may report directly to the CEO.

In addition, a systematic procedure for reviewing price at quarterly or semiannual intervals must be established. Finally, an adequate information system is required to help the pricing executive examine different pricing factors.

PRODUCT LINE-PRICING STRATEGY

A modern business enterprise manufactures and markets a number of product items in a line with differences in quality, design, size, and style. Products in a line may be complementary to or competitive with each other. The relationships among products in a given product line influence the cross-elasticities of demand between competing products and the package-deal buying of products complementary to each other. For example, instant coffee prices must bear some relationship to the prices of a company's regular coffee because these items are substitutes for one another; therefore, this represents a case of cross-elasticity. Similarly, the price of a pesticide must be related to that of a fertilizer if customers are to use both. In other words, a multiproduct company cannot afford to price one product without giving due consideration to the effect its price produces on other products in its line.[26]

The pricing strategy of a multiproduct firm should be developed to maximize the profits of the entire organization rather than the profitability of a single product. For products already in the line, pricing strategy may be formulated by classifying them according to their contribution as follows:

1. Products that contribute more than their pro rata share toward overhead after direct costs are covered
2. Products that just cover their pro rata share
3. Products that contribute more than incremental costs but do not cover their pro rata share
4. Products that fail to cover the costs savable by their elimination

With such a classification in mind, management is in a better position to study ways of strengthening the performance of its total product line. Pricing decisions on individual products in the four categories listed here are made in the light of demand and competitive conditions facing each product in the line. Consequently, some products (new products) may be priced to yield a very high margin of profit; others (highly competitive standard products) may have to show an actual loss. By retaining these marginal products to "keep the machines running" and to help absorb fixed overhead costs, management may be able to maximize total profit from all of its lines combined. A few items that make no contribution may have to be kept to round out the line offered.

General Motors' pricing structure provides a good illustration of this procedure. To offset lower profit margins on lower-priced small cars, the company raises the prices of its large cars. The prices of its luxury cars are raised much more than those of its standard cars. For example, in 1991 a Cadillac Seville sold for more than $50,000, four times the price of the company's lowest-priced car. Ten years ago, the top of the line was three times as costly as the lowest-priced car. The gap is widening, however, because the growing market for small cars with low markups makes it necessary for the company to generate high profits on luxury cars to meet its profit goals. Thus, it is expected that toward the end of the 1990s, General Motors will be selling a Cadillac for $80,000.

For a new product being considered for addition to the line, strategy development proceeds with an evaluation of the role assigned to it. The following questions could be asked:

1. What would the effect be on the company's competing products at different prices?

2. What would be the best new-product price (or range), considering its impact on the total company offering as a whole? Should other prices be adjusted? What, therefore, would be the incremental gain or loss (volumes and profits of existing lines plus volumes and profits of the new line at different prices)?
3. Is the new product necessary for staying ahead of or catching up with the competition?
4. Can it enhance the corporate image, and if so, how much is the enhancement worth?

If product/market strategy has been adequately worked out, it will be obvious whether the new product can profitably cater to a particular segment. If so, the pricing decision will be considerably easier to make; costs, profit goals, marketing goals, experience, and external competition will be the factors around which price will be determined.

Where there is no specific product/market match, pricing strategy for a new product considered for the line will vary depending on whether the product is complementary or competitive vis-à-vis other products in the line. For the complementary product, examination of the industry price schedule, which is the primary guide for the bottom price, top price, and conventional spread between product prices in a given industry, may be necessary. There are three particularly significant factors in product line–pricing strategy. The lowest price in the market is always the most remembered and unquestionably generates the most interest, if not the most traffic; the top market price implies the ability to manufacture quality products; and a well-planned schedule structure (one that optimizes profit and, at the same time, is logical to customers) is usually carefully studied and eventually followed by the competition regardless of who initiated it. In addition, however, there can be a product in the line with the objective of pricing to obtain the principal profit from a product's supplies or supplementary components.

If the anticipated product is competitive, a start will have to be made with the following market analysis:

1. Knowledge of the industry's pricing history and characteristics regarding the line
2. Comparison of company and competitor products and volumes, showing gaps and areas of popularity
3. Volume and profit potentials of the company line as is
4. Volume and profit potentials with the new internally competitive product
5. Effect on company volume and profit if competition introduced the proposed product and the company did not
6. Impact of a possible introduction delay or speedup

With this information on hand, computations for cost-plus markup should be undertaken. Thereafter, the pricer has three alternatives to set price: (a) add a uniform or individual markup rate to the total cost of the product, (b) add a markup rate that covers all the constant costs of the line, and (c) add the rate necessary for achieving the profit goal. These three alternatives have different characteristics. The first one hides the contribution margin opportunities. The second alternative, although revealing the minimum feasible price, tends to spread constant-cost coverage in such a manner that the product absorbing the most overhead is made the most price attractive. The third alternative assigns the burden to the product with the highest material cost, an action that may be competitively necessary. No matter which alternative is pursued, the final price should be arrived at only after it has been duly examined with reference to the market and the competition.

LEASING STRATEGY

The major emphasis of a pricing strategy is on buying a product outright rather than leasing it. Except in housing, leasing is more common in the marketing of industrial goods than among consumer goods, though in recent years there has been a growing trend toward the leasing of consumer goods. For example, some people lease cars. Usually, by paying a specified sum of money every month, similar to a rental on an apartment, one can lease a new car. Again, as in the case of housing, a lease is binding for a minimum period, such as two years. Thus, the consumer can lease a new car every other year. Because repairs in the first two years of a car's life may not amount to much, one is saved the bother of such problems.

Although there may be different alternatives for setting the lease price, the lessor usually likes to recover the investment within a few years. Thereafter, a very large portion of the lease price (or rent) is profit. A lessor may set the monthly rental on a car so that within a few months, say 30, the entire cost of the car can be recovered. For example, the monthly rental on a Ford Escort, based on its 1991 price (assuming no extras), may be about $250 a month. With the term set at 30 months, the dealer gets all his or her money back in about 27 months. (It should be noted that a dealer gets a car at the wholesale price, not the sticker price, which is the suggested retail price.) The important thing is to set the monthly lease rate and the minimum period for which the lease is binding in such proportions that the total amount that the lessee pays for the duration of the lease is less than what he or she would pay in monthly installments on a new car. As a matter of fact, the lease rate has to be substantially less than that in order for the buyer to opt to lease.

Furniture renting may be attractive to young adults, people of high mobility (e.g., executives, airline stewards), and senior citizens who may need appropriate furnishings only temporarily when their children's families come to visit. In addition, apartment owners may rent furniture to provide furnished units to tenants. The following excerpts from a case published by Richard D. Irwin describe the pricing mechanics of furniture renting:

> Custom Furniture Rental Corporation (CFRC) leased home furnishings for one month or longer. On direct-to-tenant business the firm realized a nine-month payback (i.e., 11% per month of the purchase price) but 20 months, 5%, on commercial.

CFRC's customers had the option of buying part or all of the rented furniture. The purchase price amounted to 25 times the monthly rental fee. A selection of furniture carrying a monthly rental of $30 would bear, therefore, a total purchase price of $750. The purchase option offered provided that credit toward the total purchase price be given as follows:

100% of the first year's rent;

75% of the second year's rent;

50% of the third year's rent; or

80% of this credit could be applied to the purchase of a similar piece of new furniture

Using the example of a $30-per-month rental and a $750 purchase price, the customer, having paid the first year's rental fees, would be given a credit of $360 and would pay the balance of $390 to complete the purchase. The customer who had completed making rental payments for two years would be given credit of $630 (100% of $360 plus 75% of $360) toward the $750 purchase price, leaving a balance of $120.

Persons opting to buy their rented furniture generally did so after the first year and certainly not beyond the second year. In 1971 there were 1,400 customers who decided to purchase one or more pieces of rented furniture. Gross receipts from those sales were $330,000. However, less than 8% of the total customer base exercised their buying option.

Used furniture was sent out for rental "like new," but the company openly invited all of its customers to return any piece that failed to meet the "like new" test.

A deposit of $35 was required for each account and was returned if the lease was in effect at least 12 months. This fee covered the cost of delivery and installation. Customers could make additions, deletions, or changes of items, but there was a $15 charge for each such order. The rate was in effect a delivery charge and applied to any and all pieces of furniture involved in the service call.

If the lessee moved, there was a $20 charge to shift the furniture. If a customer transferred to another geographical area serviced by CFRC, the lessee could return the furniture and ask for delivery at the new location.[27]

In industrial markets the leasing strategy is employed by essentially all capital goods and equipment manufacturers. Traditionally, shoe machinery, postage meters, packaging machinery, textile machinery, and other heavy equipment have been leased. Recent applications of the strategy include the leasing of computers, copiers, cars, and trucks. As a matter of fact, just about any item of capital machinery and equipment can be leased. From the customer's point of view, the leasing strategy makes sense for a variety of reasons. First, it reduces the capital required to enter a business. Second, it protects the customer against technological obsolescence. Third, the entire lease price, or rental, may be written off as an expense for income tax purposes. This advantage, of course, may or may not be relevant depending on the source of funds the customer would have used for the outright purchase (i.e., his or her own money or borrowed funds). Finally, leasing gives the customer the freedom not to get stuck with a product that may later prove not to be useful.

From the viewpoint of the manufacturer, the leasing strategy is advantageous in many ways. First, income is smoothed out over a period of years, which is very helpful in the case of equipment of high unit value in a cyclical business. Second, market growth can be boosted because more customers can afford to lease a product than can afford to buy. Third, revenues are usually higher when a product is leased than when it is sold.

BUNDLING-PRICING STRATEGY

Bundling, also called **iceberg pricing**, refers to the inclusion of an extra margin (for support services) in the price over and above the price of the product as such. This type of pricing strategy has been popular with companies that lease rather than sell their products. Thus, the rental price, when using a bundling strategy, includes an extra charge to cover a variety of support functions and services needed to maintain the product throughout its useful life. Because unit profit increases sharply after a product completes its planned amortization, it is desirable for firms that lease their products to keep the product in good condition, thus enhancing its working life for high resale or re-leasing value. The bundling strategy permits a company to do so because a charge for upkeep, or iceberg, services is included in the price.

IBM once followed a bundling strategy, whereby it charged one fee for hardware, service, software, and consultancy. In 1969, however, the Justice Department charged IBM with monopolizing the computer market. Subsequently, the company unbundled its price and started selling computers, software, service, and technical input separately.

Under the bundling strategy, not only are costs of hardware and profits covered, anticipated expenses for extra technical sales assistance, design and engineering of the system concept, software and applications to be used on the system, training of personnel, and maintenance are also included. Although the bundling strategy can be criticized for tending to discourage competition, one has to consider the complexities involved in delivering and maintaining a fault-free sophisticated system. Without the manufacturer taking the lead in adequately keeping the system in working condition, customers would have to deal with a variety of people to make use of such products as computers.[28] At least in the initial stages of a technologically oriented product, a bundling strategy is highly useful from the customer's point of view.

For the company, this strategy (a) covers the anticipated expenses of providing services and maintaining the product, (b) provides revenues for supporting after-sales service personnel, (c) provides contingency funds to meet unanticipated happenings, and (d) ensures the proper care and maintenance of the leased products. The bundling strategy also permits an ongoing relationship with the customer. In this way the company gains firsthand knowledge of the customer's needs that may help to shift the customer to a new generation of the product. Needless to say, the very nature of the bundling strategy makes it most relevant to technologically sophisticated products, particularly those marked by rapid technological obsolescence.

On the negative side, the bundling strategy tends to inflate costs and distort prices and profitability. For this reason, during unfavorable economic conditions, it may not be an appropriate strategy to pursue. Grocery wholesalers, for instance, may pass through a straight invoice cost and then charge for delivery, packaging, and so on, separately. A growing number of department stores now charge extra for home delivery, gift wrapping, and shopping bags. Thus, people who don't want a service need not pay for it.

PRICE-LEADERSHIP STRATEGY

The price-leadership strategy prevails in oligopolistic situations. One member of an industry, because of its size or command over the market, emerges as the leader of an entire industry. The leading firm then makes pricing moves that are duly acknowledged by other members of the industry. Thus, this strategy places the burden of making critical pricing decisions on the leading firm; others simply follow the leader. The leader is expected to be careful in making pricing decisions. A faulty decision could cost the firm its leadership because other members of the industry would then stop following in its footsteps. For example, if, in increasing prices, the leader is motivated only by self-interest, its price leadership will not be emulated. Ultimately the leader will be forced to withdraw the increase in price.

The price-leadership strategy is a static concept. In an environment where growth opportunities are adequate, companies would rather maintain stability than fight each other by means of price wars. Thus, the leadership concept works out well in this case. In the auto industry, General Motors is the leader, based on market share. The other two domestic members of the industry adjust their prices to come very close to any price increase by General Motors.

Usually the leader is the company with the largest market share. The leadership strategy is designed to stave off price wars and "predatory" competition that tend to force down prices and hurt all parties. Companies that deviate from this form are chastised through discounting or shaving by the leaders. Price deviation is quickly disciplined.

Successful price leaders are characterized by the following:

1. Large share of the industry's production capacity
2. Large market share
3. Commitment to a particular product class or grade
4. New cost-efficient plants
5. Strong distribution system, perhaps including captive wholesale outlets
6. Good customer relations, such as technical assistance for industrial buyers, programs directed at end users, and special attention to important customers during shortages
7. An effective market information system that provides analysis of the realities of supply and demand
8. Sensitivity to the price and profit needs of the rest of the industry
9. A sense of timing to know when price changes should be made

10. Sound management organization for pricing
11. Effective product line financial controls, which are needed to make sound price-leadership decisions
12. Attention to legal issues[29]

In an unfavorable business environment, it may not be feasible to implement a leadership strategy because firms may be differently placed to interact with the environment. Thus, the leader hesitates to make decisions on behalf of an entire industry because other firms may not always find its decisions to their advantage. For this reason, the price leader/follower pattern may be violated.

In order to survive during unfavorable conditions, even smaller firms may take the initiative to undercut the price leader. For example, during 1988 when the list prices of steel were similar, companies freely discounted their prices. In the chemical industry, with increasing competition from overseas, the price-leadership strategy does not work. Companies thus plan a variety of temporary allowances to generate business. The following quote highlights the erosion of the leadership strategy in the glass container industry:

> Traditional patterns of price leadership also are breaking down in the glass container industry, with smaller companies moving to the fore in pricing. Last year, for example, Owens-Illinois, Inc.—which is larger than its next five competitors combined—increased its list prices by $4\frac{1}{2}$%. Fearing that the increase would hurt sales to brewing companies that were just beginning to switch to glass bottles, the smaller companies broke ranks and offered huge discounts. The action not only negated O-I's increase but served notice that the smaller companies were after O-I's market share.[30]

An automatic response to a leader's price adjustment assumes that all firms are more or less similarly positioned vis-à-vis different price variables (i.e., cost, competition, and demand) and that different firms have common pricing objectives. Such an assumption, however, is far from being justified. The leadership strategy is an artificial way to enforce similar pricing responses throughout an industry. Strategically, it is a mistake for a company to price in a manner identical to that of its competitors. It should price either above or below the competition to set itself apart.

PRICING STRATEGY TO BUILD MARKET SHARE

Recent work in the area of marketing strategy has delineated the importance of market share as a key variable in strategy formulation.[31] Although market share has been discussed earlier with reference to other matters, this section examines the impact of market share on pricing strategy.

Time and again it has been noted that higher market share and experience lead to lower costs. Thus, a new product should be priced to improve experience and market share. The combination of enhanced market share and experience gives a company such a cost advantage that it cannot ever profitably be overcome by any competitor of normal performance. Competitors are prevented from entering the market and have to learn to live in a subordinate position.

Assuming the market is price sensitive, it is desirable to develop the market as early as possible. One way of achieving this is to reduce price. Unit costs are necessarily very high in the early stages of any product; if price is set to recover all costs, there may be no market for the product at its initial price in competition with existing alternatives. Following the impact of market share and experience on prices, it may be worthwhile to set price at a level that will move the product. During the early stages of a product introduction, operations may have to be conducted even at a loss. As volume is gained, costs go down, and even at an initial low price the company makes money, implying that future competitive cost differentials should be of greater concern than current profitability. Of course, such a strategic posture makes sense only in a competitive situation. In the absence of competition there is every reason to set prices as high as possible, to be lowered only when total revenue will not be affected by such an action.

The lower the initial price set by the first producer, the more rapidly that producer builds up volume and a differential cost advantage over succeeding competitors and the faster the market develops. In a sense, employing a pricing strategy that builds market share is a purchase of time advantage. However, the lower the initial price, the greater the investment required before the progressive reduction of cost results in a profit. This in turn means that the comparative investment resources of competitors can become a significant or even the critical determinant of competitive survival.

Two limitations, however, make the implementation of this type of strategy difficult. First, the resources required to institute this strategy are more than those normally available to a firm. Second, the price, once set, must not be raised and should be maintained until costs fall below price; therefore, the lower the price, the longer the time needed to realize any returns and the larger the investment required. When a future return is discounted to present value, there is obviously a limit.

It is these difficulties that lead many firms to set initial price to cover all costs. This policy is particularly likely to be adopted when there is no clear competitive threat. As volume builds and costs decline, visible profitability results, which in turn induces new competitors to enter the field. As competitors make their moves, the innovating firm has the problem of choosing between current profitability and market share. Strategically, however, pricing of a new product, following the relationship between market share and cost, should be dictated by a product's projected future growth.

SUMMARY

Pricing strategy is of interest to the very highest management levels of a company. Yet few management decisions are more subject to intuition than pricing. There is a reason for this. Pricing decisions are primarily affected by factors, such as pricing objectives, cost, competition, and demand, that are difficult to articulate and analyze. For example, assumptions must be made about what a competitor will do under certain hypothetical circumstances. There is no way to know that for certain; hence the characteristic reliance on intuition.

This chapter reviewed the pricing factors mentioned above and examines important strategies that a pricer may pursue. The following strategies were discussed:

1. Pricing strategies for new products
2. Pricing strategies for established products
3. Price-flexibility strategy
4. Product line-pricing strategy
5. Leasing strategy
6. Bundling-pricing strategy
7. Price-leadership strategy
8. Pricing strategy to build market share

There are two principal pricing strategies for new products, skimming and penetration. Skimming is a high-price strategy; penetration strategy sets a low initial price to generate volume. Three strategies for established products were discussed: maintaining the price, reducing the price, and increasing the price. A flexible-pricing strategy provides leverage to the pricer in terms of duration of commitment both from market to market and from product to product. Product line-pricing strategy is directed toward maintaining a balance among different products offered by a company. The leasing strategy constitutes an alternative to outright sale of the product. The bundling strategy is concerned with packaging products and associated services together for the purposes of pricing. Price-leadership strategy is a characteristic of an oligopoly, where one firm in an industry emerges as a leader and sets the pricing strategy to build market share. Setting price to build market share emphasizes the strategic significance of setting an initially low price to gain volume and market share, thereby enabling the firm to achieve additional cost reductions in the future.

DISCUSSION QUESTIONS

1. Is the maintenance of a stable price a viable objective? Why?
2. Is there a conflict between profit and volume objectives? Doesn't one lead to the other? Discuss.
3. What are the advantages of using incremental costs instead of full costs for pricing? Are there any negative implications of using incremental costs that a pricing strategist needs to be aware of?
4. What assumptions need to be made about competitive behavior for formulating pricing strategy?
5. "Short-term price increases tend to depress industry profits in the long run by accelerating the introduction of new capacity and depressing market demand." Discuss.
6. Following the experience curve concept, the initial price of a new product should be set rather low; as a matter of fact, it may be set below cost. Taking

into account the popularity of this thesis, discuss the relevance of the skimming strategy.

7. What factors are ascribed to the decline in popularity of the price-leadership strategy?

NOTES

[1]Thomas T. Nagle, *The Strategy and Tactics of Pricing* (Englewood Cliffs, NJ: Prentice-Hall, 1987), 8.

[2]Heywood Klein, "Illinois Bell Faces New Environment as Era of Competitive Pricing Nears," *Wall Street Journal*, 31 December 1981, p. 9.

[3]Mark I. Alpert, *Pricing Decisions* (Glenview, IL: Scott, Foresman, 1971), 96.

[4]See Jeffrey H. Birnbaum, "Pricing of Products Is Still an Art, Often Having Link to Costs," *Wall Street Journal*, 25 November 1981, p. 29.

[5]See William Robinson and Claes Fornell, "Sources of Market Pioneer Advantages in Consumer Goods Industries," *Journal of Marketing Research* (August 1985): 305.

[6]"Pricing Strategy in an Inflation Economy," *Business Week* (6 April 1974): 43.

[7]Philip Kotler, *Marketing Management*, 7th ed. (Englewood Cliffs, NJ: Prentice-Hall, 1991), 478.

[8]See Frank Barr and A. Bultez, "A Note on Optimal Strategic Pricing of Technological Innovations," *Marketing Science* (Fall 1982): 371–78.

[9]*Wall Street Journal*, 31 December 1981, p. 9.

[10]William H. Redmond, "Innovation, Price Strategy and Long Term Performance," Working Paper (Waltham, MA: Bentley College, 1987).

[11]"How T.I. Beat the Clock on Its $20 Digital Watch," *Business Week* (31 May 1976): 62–63. (For different reasons TI, a few years later, quit the digital watch business itself. But the point made here with reference to pricing is still relevant.)

[12] Richard Gibson, "Discount Menu Is Coming to McDonald's as Chain Tries to Win Back Customers," *Wall Street Journal*, 30 November 1990, p. B1. See also "Grocery Price Wars Squeeze Marketers" *Wall Steet Journal*, 7 November 1991, p. B1.

[13]"Will Home Depot Be the 'Wal-Mart of the '90s?" *Business Week* (19 March 1990): 124.

[14]See David J. Curry and Peter C. Riesz, "Prices and Price/Quality Relationships: A Longitudinal Analysis," *Journal of Marketing* (January 1988): 36–51.

[15]Ignatics Chitbebhen, "Clinical Case," *Forbes* (20 May 1989): 178.

[16]Francine Schwadel, "The 'Sale' Is Fading as a Retailing Tactic," *Wall Street Journal*, 11 March 1989, p. B1. See also "Looking Downscale—Without Looking Down," *Business Week* (8 October 1990): 62.

[17]Valarie A. Zeithaml, "Consumer Perceptives of Price, Quality, and Value: A Means-End Model and Synthesis of Evidence," *Journal of Marketing* (July 1988): 2–22.

[18]"Bulova Watch Company, Inc. (A)," a case copyrighted by the President and Fellows of Harvard College, 1973, 1-2.

[19]See Joseph A. Pechman, ed., *Economics for Policymaking, Selected Essays of Arthur M. Okun* (Cambridge, MA: MIT Press, 1983), 12-13. See also Arthur A. Thompson, Jr., "Strategies for Staying Cost Competitive," *Harvard Business Review* (January-February 1984): 110-17; and R. Dolan, "Pricing Strategies That Adjust to Inflation," *Industrial Marketing Management* (October 1981): 151–56.

[20]Mary Louise Hatten, "Don't Get Caught with Your Prices Down: Pricing in Inflationary Times," *Business Horizons* (March-April 1982): 23–28. See also David R. Lambert, "Price as a Quality Cue in Industrial Buying," *Journal of the Academy of Marketing Science* (Summer 1981): 227–38.

[21]John B. Hinge, "Critics Call Cuts in Package Size Deceptive Move," *Wall Street Journal*, 5 February 1991, p. B1.

[22]Jeffrey H. Birnbaum, "Location, Volume, Marketing Make Prices Vary Widely in New York City," *Wall Street Journal*, 3 December 1981, p. 31.

[23]Andrew A. Stern, "Pricing and Differentiation Strategies," *Planning Review* (September-October 1989): 30-34.

[24]Thomas Nagle, "Pricing as Creative Marketing," *Business Horizons* (July-August 1983): 14-19.

[25]Xavier Gilbert and Paul Strebel, "Strategies to Outpace the Competition," *Journal of Business Strategy* (Summer 1987): 28-36. See also David J. Curry, "Measuring Price and Quality Competition," *Journal of Marketing* (Spring 1985): 106-17.

[26]See Andrew A. Stern, "The Strategic Value of Price Structure," *Journal of Business Strategy* (Fall 1986): 22-31. See also Gerard J. Tellis, "Beyond the Many Faces of Price: An Integration of Pricing Strategies," *Journal of Marketing* (October 1986): 146-60.

[27]"Grantree Furniture Rental (A)," a case in Robert T. Davis, Harper W. Boyd, Jr., and Frederick E. Webster, Jr., *Marketing Management Casebook* (Homewood, IL: Richard D. Irwin, 1980), 10-11.

[28]Tellis, "Beyond the Many Faces of Price," 146-60.

[29]Stuart U. Rich, "Price Leaders: Large, Strong, but Cautious about Conspiracy," *Marketing News* (25 June 1982): 11.

[30]"Flexible Pricing," *Business Week* (12 December 1981): 81.

[31]J. K. Newton, "Market Share—Key to Higher Profitability," *Long Range Planning* (February 1983): 37-41.

APPENDIX | *Perspectives on Pricing Strategies*

I Pricing Strategies for New Products

A. Skimming Pricing

Definition: Setting a relatively high price during the initial stage of a product's life.

Objectives: (a) To serve customers who are not price conscious while the market is at the upper end of the demand curve and competition has not yet entered the market. (b) To recover a significant portion of promotional and research and development costs through a high margin.

Requirements: (a) Heavy promotional expenditure to introduce product, educate consumers, and induce early buying. (b) Relatively inelastic demand at the upper end of the demand curve. (c) Lack of direct competition and substitutes.

Expected Results: (a) Market segmented by price-conscious and not so price-conscious customers. (b) High margin on sales that will cover promotion and research and development costs. (c) Opportunity for the firm to lower its price and sell to the mass market before competition enters.

B. Penetration Pricing

Definition: Setting a relatively low price during the initial stages of a product's life.

Objective: To discourage competition from entering the market by quickly taking a large market share and by gaining a cost advantage through realizing economies of scale.

Requirements: (a) Product must appeal to a market large enough to support the cost advantage. (b) Demand must be highly elastic in order for the firm to guard its cost advantage.

Expected Results: (a) High sales volume and large market share. (b) Low margin on sales. (c) Lower unit costs relative to competition due to economies of scale.

II Pricing Strategies for Established Products

A. Maintaining the Price

Objectives: (a) To maintain position in the marketplace (i.e., market share, profitability, etc.). (b) To enhance public image.

Requirements: (a) Firm's served market is not significantly affected by changes in the environment. (b) Uncertainty exists concerning the need for or result of a price change. (c) Firm's public image could be enhanced by responding to government requests or public opinion to maintain price.

Expected Results: (a) Status quo for the firm's market position. (b) Enhancement of the firm's public image.

B. Reducing the Price

Objectives: (a) To act defensively and cut price to meet the competition. (b) To act offensively and attempt to beat the competition. (c) To respond to a customer need created by a change in the environment.

Requirements: (a) Firm must be financially and competitively strong to fight in a price war if that becomes necessary. (b) Must have a good understanding of the demand function of its product.

Expected Results: Lower profit margins (assuming costs are held constant). Higher market share might be expected, but this will depend upon the price change relative to competitive prices and upon price elasticity.

C. Increasing the Price

Objectives: (a) To maintain profitability during an inflationary period. (b) To take advantage of product differences, real or perceived. (c) To segment the current served market.

Requirements: (a) Relatively low price elasticity but relatively high elasticity with respect to some other factor such as quality or distribution. (b) Reinforcement from other ingredients of the marketing mix; for example, if a firm decides to increase price and differentiate its product by quality, then promotion and distribution must address product quality.

Expected Results: (a) Higher sales margin. (b) Segmented market (price conscious, quality conscious, etc.). (c) Possibly higher unit sales, if differentiation is effective.

III Price-Flexibility Strategy

A. One-Price Strategy

Definition: Charging the same price to all customers under similar conditions and for the same quantities.

Objectives: (a) To simplify pricing decisions. (b) To maintain goodwill among customers.

Requirements: (a) Detailed analysis of the firm's position and cost structure as compared with the rest of the industry. (b) Information concerning the cost variability of offering the same price to everyone. (c) Knowledge of the economies of scale available to the firm. (d) Information on competitive prices; information on the price that customers are ready to pay.

Expected Results: (a) Decreased administrative and selling costs. (b) Constant profit margins. (c) Favorable and fair image among customers. (d) Stable market.

B. Flexible-Pricing Strategy

Definition: Charging different prices to different customers for the same product and quantity.

Objective: To maximize short-term profits and build traffic by allowing upward and downward adjustments in price depending on competitive conditions and how much the customer is willing to pay for the product.

Requirements: Have the information needed to implement the strategy. Usually this strategy is implemented in one of four ways: (a) by market, (b) by product, (c) by timing, (d) by technology. Other requirements include (a) a customer-value analysis of the product, (b) an emphasis on profit margin rather than just volume, and (c) a record of competitive reactions to price moves in the past.

Expected Results: (a) Increased sales, leading to greater market share. (b) Increased short-term profits. (c) Increased selling and administrative costs. (d) Legal difficulties stemming from price discrimination.

IV Product Line-Pricing Strategy

Definition: Pricing a product line according to each product's effect on and relationship with other products in that line, whether competitive or complementary.

Objective: To maximize profits from the whole line, not just certain members of it.

Requirements: (a) For a product already in the line, strategy is developed according to the product's contributions to its pro rata share of overhead and direct costs. (b) For a new product, a product/market analysis determines whether the product will be profitable. Pricing is then a function of costs, profit goals, experience, and external competition.

Expected Results: (a) Well-balanced and consistent pricing schedule across the product line. (b) Greater profits in the long term. (c) Better performance of the line as a whole.

V Leasing Strategy

Definition: An agreement by which an owner (lessor) of an asset rents that asset to a second party (lessee). The lessee pays a specified sum of money, which includes principal and interest, each month as a rental payment.

Objectives: (a) To enhance market growth by attracting customers who cannot buy outright. (b) To realize greater long-term profits; once the production costs are fully amortized, the rental fee is mainly profit. (c) To increase cash flow. (d) To have a stable flow of earnings. (e) To have protection against losing revenue because of technological obsolescence.

Requirements: (a) Necessary financial resources to continue production of subsequent products for future sales or leases. (b) Adequate computation of lease rate and minimum period for which lease is binding such that the total amount the lessee pays for the duration of the lease is less than would be paid in monthly installments on an outright purchase. (c) Customers who are restrained by large capital requirements necessary for outright purchase or need write-offs for income tax purposes. (d) The capability to match competitors' product improvements that may make the lessor's product obsolete.

Expected Results: (a) Increased market share because customers include those who would have forgone purchase of product. (b) Consistent earnings over a period of years. (c) Greater cash flow due to lower income tax expense from depreciation write-offs. (d) Increased sales as customers exercise their purchase options.

VI Bundling-Pricing Strategy

Definition: Inclusion of an extra margin in the price to cover a variety of support functions and services needed to sell and maintain the product throughout its useful life.

Objectives: (a) In a leasing arrangement, to have assurance that the asset will be properly maintained and kept in good working condition so that it can be resold or re-leased. (b) To generate extra revenues to cover the anticipated expenses of providing services and maintaining the product. (c) To generate revenues for supporting after-sales service personnel. (d) To establish a contingency fund for unanticipated happenings. (e) To develop an ongoing relationship with the customer. (f) To discourage competition with "free" after-sales support and service.

Requirements: This strategy is ideally suited for technologically sophisticated products that are susceptible to rapid technological obsolescence because these products are generally sold in systems and usually require the following: (a) extra technical sales assistance, (b) custom design and engineering concept for the customer, (c) peripheral equipment and applications, (d) training of the customer's personnel, and (e) a strong service/maintenance department offering prompt responses and solutions to customer problems.

Expected Results: (a) Asset is kept in an acceptable condition for resale or release. (b) Positive cash flow. (c) Instant information on changing customer needs. (d) Increased sales due to "total package" concept of selling because customers feel they are getting their money's worth.

VII Price-Leadership Strategy

Definition: This strategy is used by the leading firm in an industry in making major pricing moves, which are followed by other firms in the industry.

Objective: To gain control of pricing decisions within an industry in order to support the leading firm's own marketing strategy (i.e., create barriers to entry, increase profit margin, etc.).

Requirements: (a) An oligopolistic situation. (b) An industry in which all firms are affected by the same price variables (i.e., cost, competition, demand). (c) An industry in which all firms have common pricing objectives. (d) Perfect knowledge of industry conditions; an error in pricing means losing control.

Expected Results: (a) Prevention of price wars, which are liable to hurt all parties involved. (b) Stable pricing moves. (c) Stable market share.

VIII
Pricing Strategy to Build Market Share

Definition: Setting the lowest price possible for a new product.

Objective: To seek such a cost advantage that it cannot ever be profitably overcome by any competitor.

Requirements: (a) Enough resources to withstand initial operating losses that will be recovered later through economies of scale. (b) Price-sensitive market. (c) Large market. (d) High elasticity of demand.

Expected Results: (a) Start-up losses to build market share. (b) Creation of a barrier to entry to the industry. (c) Ultimately, cost leadership within the industry.

CHAPTER 16
Distribution Strategies

The art of getting rich consists not in industry, much less in saving, but in a better order, in timeliness, in being at the right spot.

RALPH WALDO EMERSON

Distribution strategies are concerned with the channels a firm may employ to make its goods and services available to customers. **Channels** are organized structures of buyers and sellers that bridge the gap of time and space between the manufacturer and the customer.

Marketing is defined as an exchange process. In relation to distribution, exchange poses two problems. First, goods must be moved to a central location from the warehouses of producers who make heterogeneous goods and who are geographically widespread. Second, the goods that are accumulated from diversified sources should represent a desired assortment from the viewpoint of customers. These two problems can be solved by the process of sorting, which combines concentration (i.e., bringing the goods from different sources to a central location) and dispersion (i.e., picking an assortment of goods from different points of concentration). Two basic questions need to be answered here. Who should perform the concentration and dispersion tasks—the manufacturer or intermediaries? Which intermediary should the manufacturer select to bring goods close to the customer? These questions are central to distribution strategies.

Other strategy-related matters discussed in this chapter include scope of distribution (i.e., how widespread distribution may be), use of multiple channels to serve different segments, modification of channels to accommodate environmental shifts, resolution of conflict among channels, and use of vertical systems to institute control over channels. Each strategic issue is examined for its relevance in different circumstances. The application of each strategy is illustrated with examples from marketing literature.

CHANNEL-STRUCTURE STRATEGY

The **channel-structure strategy** refers to the number of intermediaries that may be employed in moving goods from manufacturers to customers. A company may undertake to distribute its goods to customers or retailers without involving any intermediary. This strategy constitutes the shortest channel and may be labeled a *direct distribution strategy*. Alternatively, goods may pass through one or more intermediaries, such as wholesalers or agents. This is an *indirect distribution strategy*. Exhibit 16-1 shows alternative channel structures for consumer and industrial products.

Decisions about channel structure are based on a variety of factors. To a significant extent, channel structure is determined by where inventories should be maintained to offer adequate customer service, fulfill required sorting processes, and still deliver a satisfactory return to channel members.

An underlying factor in determining channel-structure strategy is the use of intermediaries. The importance of using intermediaries is illustrated with reference to an example of a primitive economy used by Alderson.[1] In a primitive economy, five producers produce one type of item each: hats, hoes, knives, baskets, or pots. Because each producer needs all the other producers' products, a total of 10 exchanges are required to accomplish trade. However, with a market (or middlemen), once the economy reaches equilibrium (i.e., each producer-consumer has visited the market once), only five exchanges need to take place to meet everyone's needs. Let n denote the number of producer-consumers. Then the total number of transactions (T) without a market is given by

$$T_{\text{without}} = \frac{n(n-1)}{2}$$

and the total number of transactions with a market is given by

$$T_{\text{with}} = n$$

The efficiency created in distribution by using an intermediary may be viewed using this equation:

$$\text{Efficiency} = \frac{T_{\text{without}}}{T_{\text{with}}} = \frac{n(n-1)}{2} \times \frac{1}{n} = \frac{n-1}{2}$$

In the example of five producer-consumers, the efficiency of having a middleman is 2. The efficiency increases as n increases. Thus, in many cases, intermediaries may perform the task of distribution more efficiently than manufacturers alone.

Postponement-Speculation Theory

Conceptually, the selection of channel structure may be explained with reference to Bucklin's postponement-speculation framework.[2] The framework is based on risk, uncertainty, and costs involved in facilitating exchanges. Postponement seeks to eliminate risk by matching production/distribution with actual customer demand. Presumably, postponement should produce efficiency in marketing channels. For example, the manufacturer may produce and ship goods only on confirmed orders. Speculation, on the other hand, requires undertaking risk through changes in form and movement of goods within chan-

EXHIBIT 16-1
Typical Channel Structures

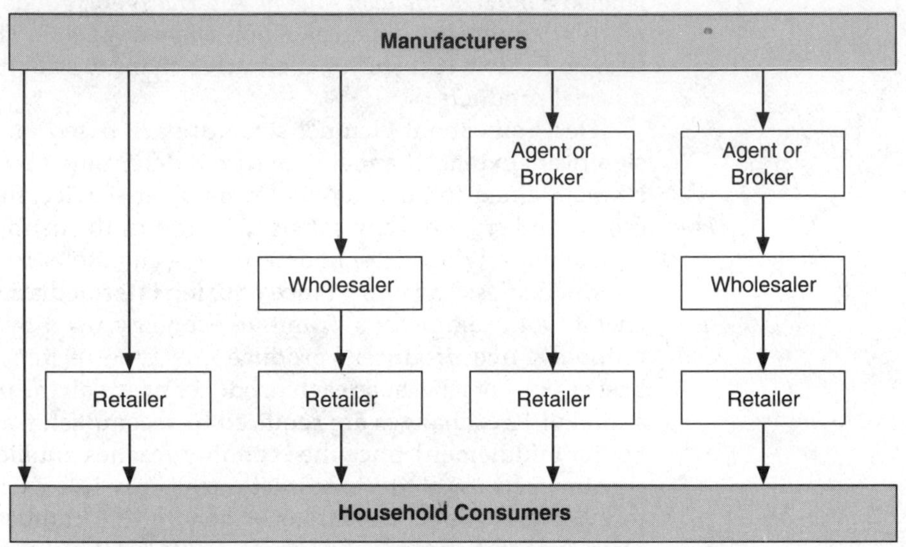

(a) Consumer Products

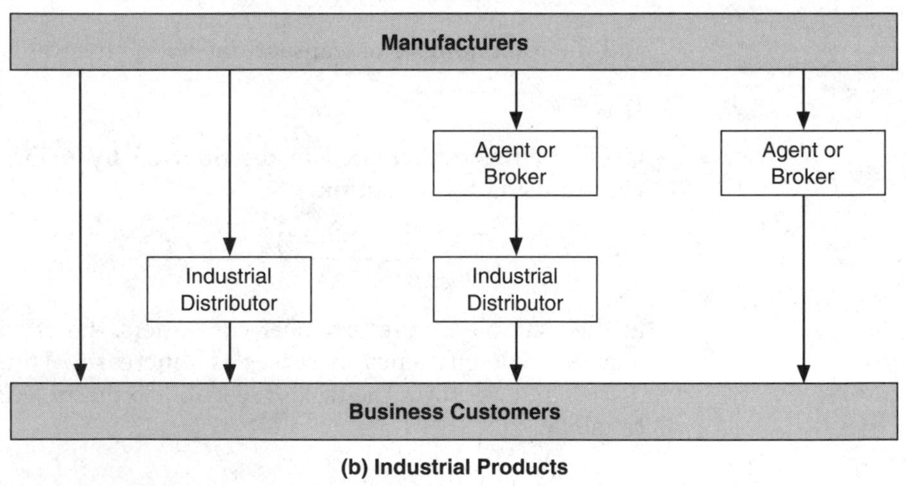

(b) Industrial Products

nels. Speculation leads to economies of scale in manufacturing, reduces costs of frequent ordering, and eliminates opportunity cost.

Exhibit 16-2 shows the behavior of variables involved in the postponement-speculation framework. The vertical axis shows the average cost of undertaking a function for one unit of any given commodity; the horizontal axis shows the time involved in delivering a confirmed order. Together the average cost and

EXHIBIT 16-2
Using the Postponement-Speculation Concept to Determine Channel Structure

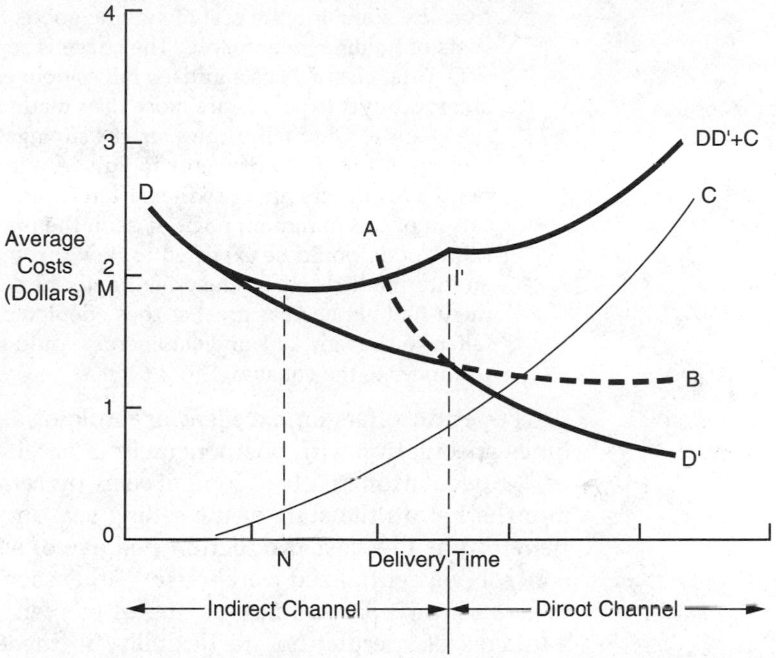

Source: Louis P. Bucklin and Leslie Halpert, "Exploring Channels of Distribution for Cement with the Principle of Postponement-Speculation," in *Marketing and Economic Development,* ed. Peter D. Bennett (Chicago: American Marketing Association, 1965), 698. Reprinted by permission of the American Marketing Association.

the delivery time measure the cost of marketing tasks performed in a channel with reference to delivery time. The nature of the three curves depicted in Exhibit 16-2 should be understood: *C* represents costs to the buyer for holding an inventory; *AD′*, costs involved in supplying goods directly from a manufacturer to a buyer; and *DB*, costs involved in shipping and maintaining speculative inventories (i.e., in anticipation of demand).

Following Bucklin's framework, one determines the channel structure by examining the behavior of the *C*, *AD′*, and *DB* curves:

1. The minimal cost of supplying the buyer for every possible delivery time is derived from curves *AD′* and *DB*. As may be seen in [Exhibit 16-2], especially fast delivery service can be provided only by the indirect channel (i.e., by using a stocking intermediary). However, at some delivery time, *I′*, the cost of serving the consumer directly from the producer will intersect and fall below the cost of indirect shipment. The minimal costs derived from both curves are designated *DD′*. From the perspective of channel cost, it will be cheaper to service the buyer from a speculative inventory if delivery times shorter than *I′* are

demanded. If the consumer is willing to accept delivery times longer than *I′*, then direct shipment will be the least expensive.

2. The minimal total cost curve for the channel with respect to delivery time is derived by summing the cost of moving goods to the buyer, *DD′*, and the buyer's costs of holding inventory, *C*. The curve is represented in [Exhibit 16-2] by *DD′* + *C*. Total channel costs initially fall as delivery time lengthens because increased buyer expenses are more than made up for by savings in other parts of the channel. Gradually, however, the savings from these sources diminish and buyer costs begin to rise more rapidly. A minimal cost point is reached, and expenses for the channel rise thereafter. Channel structure is controlled by the location of this minimum point. If, as in the present case, it falls to the left of *I′*, then goods would be expected to flow through the speculative inventory (i.e., an intermediary). If, on the other hand, the savings of the buyer from postponement had not been as great as those depicted, the minimum point would have fallen to the right of I′ and shipments would have been made directly from the producer to the consumer.[3]

Benetton offers an excellent example of a distribution strategy that combines speculation with postponement in an effort to optimize both service and cost. Speculation involves commitment by retailers to specific inventory items months before the start of the selling season. It leads to such advantages for Benetton as low-cost production (via use of subcontractors) and good quality control (via centralized warehousing and assembly of orders). Postponement of orders requires last-minute dyeing of woolen items at an added cost. The advantages of speculation are flexibility in meeting market needs and reduced inventory levels.[4]

Additional Considerations in Determining Channel Structure

The postponement-speculation theory provides an economic explanation of the way the channels are structured. Examined in this section are a variety of environmental influences on channel-structure strategy formulation. These influences may be technological, social and ethical, governmental, geographical, or cultural.

Many aspects of channel structure are affected by technological advances. For example, mass retailing in food has become feasible because of the development of automobiles, highways, refrigerated cars, cash registers, packaging improvements, and mass communications (television). In the coming years, television shopping with household computer terminals should have a far-reaching impact on distribution structures.[5] Technological advances permitted Sony to become dominant in the U.S. market for low-priced CD players. Sony developed prepackaged players that could be sold through mass retailers so that even sales clerks without technical know-how could handle customers.

How technology may be used to revamp the operations of a wholesaler, making it worthwhile to adopt indirect channels, is illustrated by the case of Foremost-McKesson, the nation's largest wholesale distributor. A few years ago, the company found itself in a precarious position. Distribution, though one of the company's most pervasive business functions, did not pay. Foremost-McKesson merely took manufacturers' goods and resold them to small retailers through a routine process of warehousing, transportation, and simple marketing that offered thin profits. As a matter of fact, at one time the company came close to selling off drug wholesaling, its biggest business. Instead, however, its new chief executive decided to add sophisticated technology to its operations in order to make the company so efficient at distribution that manufacturers could not possibly do as well on their own. It virtually redefined the function of the intermediary. Having used the computer to make its own operations efficient, it devised ways to make its data processing useful to suppliers and customers, in essence making Foremost part of their marketing teams. Since the company computerized its operations, Foremost has turned around dramatically. Here are the highlights of Foremost's steps in reshaping its role:

- Acting as middleman between drugstores and insurance offices by processing medical insurance claims.
- Creating a massive "rack jobbing" service by providing crews to set up racks of goods inside retail stores, offering what amounts to a temporary labor force that brings both marketing know-how and Foremost merchandise along with it.
- Taking waste products as well as finished goods from chemical manufacturers, and recycling the wastes through its own plants—its first entry into chemical waste management.
- Designing, as well as supplying, drugstores.
- Researching new uses for products it receives from manufacturers. Foremost found new customers, for example, for a Monsanto Co. food preservative from among its contacts in the cosmetics industry.[6]

Social taboos and ethical standards may also affect the channel-structure decision. For example, Mallen reports that *Viva,* a woman's magazine, had achieved a high circulation in supermarkets and drugstores in Canada. When *Viva* responded to readers' insistence and to competition from *Playgirl* by introducing nude male photos, most supermarkets banned the magazine. Because supermarkets accounted for more than half of *Viva*'s circulation, *Viva* dropped the photos so that it could continue to be sold through this channel.[7]

The channel-structure strategy can also be influenced by local, state, and federal laws in a variety of ways. For example, door-to-door selling of certain goods may be prohibited by local laws. In many states (e.g., California and Ohio) wine can be sold through supermarkets, but other states (e.g., Connecticut) do not permit this.

Geographic size, population patterns, and typology also influence the channel-structure strategy. In urban areas, direct distribution to large retailers may make sense. Rural areas, however, may be covered only by wholesalers.

With the inception of large grocery chains, it may often appear that independent grocery stores are dying. The truth is, however, that independent grocery stores as recently as 1988 accounted for 46 percent of all grocery sales in the country—over $148 billion. Thus, a manufacturer can ill afford not to deal with independents and to reach them it must go through wholesalers. Wetterau, for example, is a grocery wholesale firm in Hazelwood, Missouri, which did over $6 billion worth of business serving almost 3000 retail grocery stores. It does not do any business with chain stores. But because of Wetterau's determination to offer its customers relatively low prices, a wide selection of brands, service programs carefully designed to make brands more profitable, and a personal interest in their success, its customers are almost fanatically loyal. The company offers its customers—small independent retail stores—a variety of services, including lease arrangements, store design, financing packages, training, and computerized inventory systems. These services tend to enhance customers' competitiveness by reducing their operating costs and by simplifying their bookkeeping, which in turn helps Wetterau to earn profits.[8] The Wetterau example shows that to reach smaller retailers, particularly in areas far removed from large metropolises, the indirect distribution strategy is appropriate. The wholesaler provides services to small retailers that a large manufacturer can never match on its own.

Finally, cultural traits may require the adoption of a certain channel structure in a setting that otherwise might seem an odd place for it. For example, in many parts of Switzerland, fruits and vegetables are sold in a central marketplace in the morning by small vendors, even though there are modern supermarkets all over. This practice continues because it gives customers a chance to socialize while shopping. Similarly, changing lifestyles among average American consumers and their desire to have more discretionary income for life-fulfillment activities appear to be making warehouse retailing more popular.[9] This is so because prices at warehouse outlets—grocery warehouses, for example—are substantially lower than at traditional stores.

Channel Design Model

Presented below is a channel design model adapted from Frazier that can be used to make the direct/indirect distribution decision.[10] The model involves six basic steps.

1. List the factors that could potentially influence the direct/indirect decision. Each factor must be evaluated carefully in terms of the firm's industry position and competitive strategy.
2. Pick out the factors that will have the most impact on the channel design decision. No factor with a dominant impact should be left out. For example, assume that the following four factors have been identified as having particular significance: market concentration, customer service level, asset specificity, and availability of working capital.
3. Decide how each factor identified is related to the attractiveness of a direct or an indirect channel. For example, market concentration reflects the size distribution of the firm's customers as well as their geographical dispersion. Therefore, the more concentrated the market, the more desirable the direct channel because of the lower costs of serving that market (high = direct; low = indirect). Customer service level is made up of at least three factors: delivery time, lot size, and product availability. The more customer service required by customers, the less desirable is the direct channel (high = indirect; low = direct). The direct channel is more desirable, at least under conditions of high uncertainty in the environment, with a high level of asset specificity (high = direct; low = indirect). Finally, the greater the availability of working capital, the

more likely it is that a manufacturer can afford and consider a direct channel (high = direct; low = indirect). Note that a high level on a factor does not always correspond to a direct channel.

4. Create a matrix based on the key factors to consider the interactions among key factors. If only two factors are being considered, a two-by-two matrix of four cells would result. For three factors, a three-by-three matrix of nine cells would result. For four factors, a four-by-four matrix of sixteen cells would result, and so on. If more than five or six factors are involved, a series of smaller models could be constructed to make this fourth step more manageable. Exhibit 16-3 presents a four-by-four matrix developed for this example.
5. Decide (for each cell in the matrix) whether a direct channel, an indirect channel, or a combination of both a direct and an indirect channel is most appropriate, considering the factors involved. Combination channels are becoming more common in business practice, especially in industrial markets.

For some cells in the matrix, deciding which channel design is best is rather easy to do. For example, cell 1 in Exhibit 16-3 has all four factors in agreement that an indirect channel is best. This is also true for cell 16: a direct channel is the obvious choice. For other cells, choosing between a direct channel and an indirect channel is not as easy because factors conflict with each other to some extent. For example, in cell 14, asset specificity is low, suggesting that an indirect channel is best. The other three factors suggest otherwise, however; the market is concentrated, customer service requirements are low, and the availability of capital to the manufacturer is high. Taken together, the factors in cell

EXHIBIT 16-3
Designing a Distribution Channel Matrix

		Asset Specificity: Low		Asset Specificity: High	
		Capital Availability		**Capital Availability**	
Market Concentration	**Customer Service Level**	Low	High	Low	High
Low	High	*cell 1* indirect	*cell 3* indirect	*cell 2* indirect	*cell 4* combination
Low	Low	*cell 5* indirect	*cell 7* combination	*cell 6* combination	*cell 8* direct
High	High	*cell 9* indirect	*cell 11* combination	*cell 10* direct	*cell 12* direct
High	Low	*cell 13* combination	*cell 15* combination	*cell 14* direct	*cell 16* direct

Source: Gary L. Frazier, "Designing Channels of Distribution," *The Channel for Communication* (Seattle, Wash.; Center for Retail and Distribution Management, University of Washington, 1987): 3–7.

factors that conflict with one another, the strategist must make trade-offs among them to decide whether a direct channel, indirect channel, or combination of channels is best.

6. For each product or service in question, locate the corresponding cell in the box model. The prediction in this cell is the one that should be followed or at least the one that should be most seriously considered by the firm.

The accuracy of the model generated by this method depends totally on the expertise and skills of the person who builds and uses it. If carefully constructed, such a model can be invaluable in designing more efficient and effective channels of distribution.

DISTRIBUTION-SCOPE STRATEGY

For an efficient channel network, the manufacturer should clearly define the target customers it intends to reach. Implicit in the definition of target customers is a decision about the scope of distribution the manufacturer wants to pursue. The strategic alternatives here are exclusive distribution, selective distribution, and intensive distribution.

Exclusive Distribution

Exclusive distribution means that one particular retailer serving a given area is granted sole rights to carry a product. For example, Hart, Schaffner, and Marx suits are distributed exclusively through select stores in an area. Several advantages may be gained by the use of exclusive distribution. It promotes tremendous dealer loyalty, greater sales support, a higher degree of control over the retail market, better forecasting, and better inventory and merchandising control. The impact of dealer loyalty can be helpful when a manufacturer has seasonal or other kinds of fluctuating sales. An exclusive dealership is more willing to finance inventories and thus bear a higher degree of risk than a more extensive dealership. Having a smaller number of dealers gives a manufacturer or wholesaler greater opportunity to provide each dealer with promotional support. And with fewer outlets, it is easier to control such aspects as margin, price, and inventory. Dealers are also more willing to provide data that may be used for marketing research and forecasts. Exclusive distribution is especially relevant for products that customers seek out. Examples of such products include Rolex watches, Gucci bags, Regal shoes, Celine neckties, and Mark Cross wallets.

On the other hand, there are several obvious disadvantages to exclusive distribution. First, sales volume may be lost. Second, the manufacturer places all its fortunes in a geographic area in the hands of one dealer. Exclusive distribution brings with it the characteristics of high price, high margin, and low volume. If the product is highly price elastic in nature, this combination of characteristics can mean significantly less than optimal performance. Relying on one retailer can mean that if sales are depressed for any reason, the retailer is then likely to be in a position to dictate terms to other channel members (i.e., the retailer becomes the channel captain).

For example, assume that a company manufacturing traditional toys deals exclusively with J.C. Penney. For a variety of reasons, its line of toys may not do well. These reasons may be a continuing decline in the birthrate, an economic recession, the emerging popularity of electronic toys, higher prices of the company's toys compared to competitive brands, a poor promotional effort by Penney, and so on. Because it is the exclusive distributor, however, Penney may put the blame on the manufacturer's prices, and it may demand a reduction in prices from the manufacturer. Inasmuch as the manufacturer has no other reasons to give that could explain its poor performance, it must depend on Penney's analysis.

The last disadvantage of exclusive distribution is one that is easy to overlook. In certain circumstances, exclusive distribution has been found to be in violation of antitrust laws because of its restraint on trade. The legality of an exclusive contract varies from case to case. As long as an exclusive contract does not undermine competition and create a monopoly, it is acceptable. The courts appear to use the following criteria to determine if indeed an exclusive distribution lessens competition:

1. Whether the volume of the product in question is a substantial part of the total volume for that product type
2. Whether the exclusive dealership excludes competitive products from a substantial share of the market

Thus, a company considering an exclusive distribution strategy should review its decision in the light of these two ground rules.

Intensive Distribution

The inverse of exclusive distribution is intensive distribution. **Intensive distribution** makes a product available at all possible retail outlets. This may mean that the product is carried at a wide variety of different and also competing retail institutions in a given area. The distribution of convenience goods is most consistent with this strategy. If the nature of a product is such that a consumer generally does not bother to seek out the product but will buy it on sight if available, then it is to the seller's advantage to have the product visible in as many places as possible. The Bic Pen Corporation is an example of a firm that uses this type of strategy. Bic makes its products available in a wide variety of retail establishments, ranging from drugstores, to "the corner grocery store," to large supermarkets. In all, Bic sells through 250,000 retail outlets, which represent competing as well as noncompeting stores. The advantages to be gained from this strategy are increased sales, wider customer recognition, and impulse buying. All of these qualities are desirable for convenience goods.

There are two main disadvantages associated with intensive distribution. First, intensively distributed goods are characteristically low-priced and low-margin products that require a fast turnover. Second, it is difficult to provide any degree of control over a large number of retailers. In the short run, uncontrolled distribution may not pose any problem if the intensive distribution leads to increased sales. In the long run, however, it may have a variety of devastating effects. For example, if durable products such as Sony television sets were to be intensively distributed (i.e., through drugstores, discount stores, variety stores, etc.), Sony's sales would probably increase. But such intensive distribution could lead to the problems of price discounting, inadequate customer service, and noncooperation among traditional channels (e.g., department stores). Not only might these problems affect sales revenues in the long run, but the manufacturer might also lose some of its established channels. For example, a department store might decide to drop the Sony line for another brand of television sets. In addition, Sony's distinctive brand image could suffer. In other words, the advantages furnished by intensive distribution should be related carefully to product type to decide if this form of distribution is suitable. It is because of the problems outlined above that one finds intensive distribution limited to such products as candy, newspapers, cigarettes, aspirin, and soft drinks. For these types of products, turnover is usually high and channel control is usually not as strategic as it would be, say, for television sets.

Selective Distribution

Between exclusive and intensive distribution, there is selective distribution. **Selective distribution** is the strategy in which several but not all retail outlets in a given area distribute a product. **Shopping goods**—goods that consumers seek on the basis of the most attractive price or quality characteristics—are frequently distributed through selective distribution. Because of this, competition among retailers is far greater for shopping goods than for convenience goods. Naturally, retailers wish to reduce competition as much as possible. This causes them to pressure manufacturers to reduce the number of retail outlets in their area distributing a given product in order to reduce competition.

The number of retailers under a selective distribution strategy should be limited by criteria that allow the manufacturer to choose only those retailers who will make a contribution to the firm's overall distribution objectives. For example, some firms may choose retail outlets that can provide acceptable repair and maintenance service to consumers who purchase their products. In the automotive industry, selective criteria are used by manufacturers in granting dealerships. These criteria consist of such considerations as showroom space, service facilities, and inventory levels.

The point may be illustrated with reference to Pennsylvania House, a furniture company. The company used to have 800 retail accounts, but it cut this number to 500. This planned cut obviously limited the number of stores in which the company's product line was exposed. More limited distribution provided the company with much stronger support among surviving dealers. Among these 500 dealers, there was a higher average amount of floor space devoted to Pennsylvania House merchandise, better customer service, better supplier relations, and most important for the company, it increased sales per account by a factor of three.[11]

Selective distribution is best applied under circumstances in which high sales volume can be generated by a relatively small number of retailers or, in other words, in which the manufacturer would not appreciably increase its coverage by adding additional dealers. Selective distribution can also be used effectively in situations in which a manufacturer requires a high-caliber firm to carry a full product line and provide necessary services. A dealer in this position is likely to require promotional and technical assistance. The technical assistance is needed not only in conjunction with the sale but also after the sale in the form of repair and maintenance service. Again, by limiting the number of retail outlets to a select few capable of covering the market, the manufacturer can avoid unnecessary costs associated with signing on additional dealers.

Obviously, the greatest danger associated with a strategy of selective distribution is the risk of not adequately covering the market. The consequences of this error are greater than the consequences of initially having one or two extra dealers. Therefore, when in doubt, it is better to have too much coverage than not enough.

In selective distribution, it is extremely important for a manufacturer to choose dealers (retailers) who most closely match the marketing goals and image intended for the product. There can be segments within retail markets; therefore, identifying the right retailers can be the key to penetrating a chosen market. Every department store cannot be considered the same. Among them there can be price, age, and image segmentation. One does not have to be very accurate in distinguishing among stores of the same type in the case of products that have no special image (i.e., those that lend themselves to unsegmented market strategies and mass distribution). But for products with any degree of fashion or style content or with highly segmented customer groups, a selective distribution strategy requires a careful choice of outlets.

To appraise what type of product is suitable for what form of distribution, refer to Exhibit 16-4. This exhibit combines the traditional threefold classification of consumer goods (convenience, shopping, and specialty goods) with a threefold classification of retail stores (convenience, shopping, and specialty stores) to determine the appropriate form of distribution. This initial selection may then be examined in the light of other considerations to make a final decision on the scope of distribution.

MULTIPLE-CHANNEL STRATEGY

The **multiple-channel strategy** refers to a situation in which two or more different channels are employed to distribute goods and services. The market must be segmented so that each segment gets the services it needs and pays only for them, not for services it does not need. Usually this type of segmentation cannot be done effectively by direct selling alone or by exclusive reliance upon distributors. The Robinson-Patman Act makes the use of price for segmentation almost impossible when selling to the same kind of customer through the same distribution channel. Market segmentation, however, may be possible when selling directly to one class of customer and to another only through distributors, which usually requires different services, prices, and support. Thus, a multiple-channel strategy permits optimal access to each individual segment.

EXHIBIT 16-4
Selection of Suitable Distribution Policies Based on the Relationship between Type of Product and Type of Store

Classification	*Consumer Behavior*	*Most Likely Form of Distribution*
Convenience store/convenience good	The consumer prefers to buy the most readily available brand of a product at the most accessible store.	Intensive
Convenience store/shopping good	The consumer selects his or her purchase from among the assortment carried by the most accessible store.	Intensive
Convenience store/specialty good	The consumer purchase his or her favorite brand from the most accessible store carrying the item in stock.	Selective/exclusive
Shopping store/convenience good	The consumer is indifferent to the brand of product he or she buys but shops different stores to secure better retail service and/or retail price.	Intensive
Shopping store/shopping good	The consumer makes comparisons among both retail-controlled factors and factors associated with the product (brand).	Intensive
Shopping store/specialty good	The consumer has a strong preference as to product brand but shops a number of stores to secure the best retail service and/or price for this brand.	Selective/exclusive
Specialty store/convenience good	The consumer prefers to trade at a specific store but is indifferent to the brand of product purchased.	Selective/exclusive
Specialty store/shopping good	The consumer prefers to trade at a certain store but is uncertain as to which product he or she wishes to buy and examines the store's assortment for the best purchase.	Selective/exclusive
Specialty store/specialty good	The consumer has both a preference for a particular store and for a specific brand.	Selective/exclusive

Source: Louis P. Bucklin, "Retail Strategy and the Classification of Consumer Goods," *Journal of Marketing* (January 1963): 50–55; published by the American Marketing Association.

Basically, there are two types of multiple channels of distribution, complementary and competitive.

Complementary Channels

Complementary channels exist when each channel handles a different noncompeting product or noncompeting market segment. An important reason to promote complementary channels is to reach market segments that cannot otherwise be served. For example, Avon Products, which had sold directly to consumers for 100 years, broke the tradition in 1986 and began selling some perfumes (e.g., Deneuve fragrance, which sells for as much as $165 an ounce) through department stores. The rationale behind this move was to serve customer segments that the company could not reach through direct selling.[12] Samsonite Corporation sells the same type of luggage to discount stores that it distributes through department stores, with some cosmetic changes in design. In this way the company is able to reach middle- and low-income segments that may never shop for luggage in department stores. Similarly, magazines use newsstand distribution as a complementary channel to subscriptions. Catalogs serve as complementary channels for large retailers such as Sears and Penney.

The simplest way to create complementary channels is through private branding. This permits entry into markets that would otherwise be lost. The Coca-Cola Company sells its Minute Maid frozen orange juice to A&P to be sold under the A&P name. At the same time, the Minute Maid brand is available in A&P stores. Presumably, there are customers who perceive the private brand to be no different in quality from the manufacturer's brand. Inasmuch as the private brand is always a little less expensive than a manufacturer's brand, such customers prefer the lower-priced private brand. Thus private branding helps broaden the market base.

There is another reason that may lead a manufacturer to choose this strategy. In instances where other firms in an industry have saturated traditional distribution channels for a product, a new entry may be distributed through a different channel. This new channel may then in turn be different from the traditional channel used for the rest of the manufacturer's product line. Hanes, for example, decided to develop a new channel for L'eggs (supermarkets and drugstores) because traditional channels were already crowded with competing brands. Likewise, R. Dakin developed nontraditional complementary channels to distribute its toys. Although most toy manufacturers sell their wares through toy shops and department stores, Dakin distributes more than 60 percent of its products through a variety of previously ignored outlets such as airports, hospital gift shops, restaurants, amusement parks, stationery stores, and drugstores. This strategy lets Dakin avoid direct competition.[13] In recent years, many companies have developed new channels in the form of direct mail sales for such diverse products as men's suits, shoes, insurance, records, newly published books, and jewelry.

A company may also develop complementary channels to broaden the market when its traditional channel happens to be a large account. For example, Easco Corporation, the nation's second-largest maker of hand tools, had for years tied itself to Sears, Roebuck and Company, the world's largest retailer, supplying wrenches, sockets, and other tools for the retailer's Craftsman line. Sears accounted for about 47 percent of Easco's sales and about 62 percent of its pretax earnings as recently as 1980. But as Sears's growth slowed, Easco had a critical strategic dilemma: What do you do when one dominant customer stops growing and starts to slip? The company decided to lessen its dependence on Sears by adding some 500 new hardware and home-center stores for its hand tools.[14]

To broaden their markets in recent years, many clothing manufacturers, including Ralph Lauren, Liz Claiborne, Calvin Klein, Anne Klein, and Adrienne Vittadini, have opened their own stores to sell a full array of their clothes and accessories.[15]

Complementary channels may also be necessitated by geography. Many industrial companies undertake direct distribution of their products in such large metropolitan areas as New York, Chicago, Detroit, and Cleveland. Because the market is dense and because of the proximity of customers to each other, a salesperson can make more than 10 calls a day. The same company that sells directly to its customers in urban environments, however, may use manufacturer's representatives or some other type of intermediary in the hinterlands because the market there is too thin to support full-time salespeople.

Another reason to promote complementary channels is to enhance the distribution of noncompeting items. For example, many food processors package fruits and vegetables for institutional customers in giant cans that have little market among household customers. These products, therefore, are distributed through different channels. Procter and Gamble manufactures toiletries for hotels, motels, hospitals, airlines, and so on, which are distributed through different channel arrangements. The volume of business may also require the use of different channels. Many appliance manufacturers sell directly to builders but use distributors and dealers for selling to household consumers.

The basis for employing complementary channels is to enlist customers and segments that cannot be served when distribution is limited to a single channel. Thus, the addition of a complementary channel may be the result of simple cost-benefit analysis. If by employing an additional channel the overall business can be increased without jeopardizing quality or service and without any negative impact on long-term profitability, it may be worthwhile to do so. However, care is needed to ensure that the enhancement of the market through multiple channels does not lead to a charge of monopolizing the market by the Justice Department.

Competitive Channels

The second type of multiple-channel strategy is the competitive channel. **Competitive channels** exist when the same product is sold through two different and competing channels. This distribution posture may be illustrated with reference to a boat manufacturer, the Luhrs Company. Luhrs sells and ships boats directly to dealers, using one franchise to sell Ulrichsen wood boats and Alura fiberglass boats and another franchise to sell Luhrs wood and fiberglass/wood boats. The two franchises could be issued to the same dealer, but they are normally issued to separate dealers. Competition between dealers holding separate franchises is both possible and encouraged.[16] The two dealers compete against each other to the extent that their products satisfy similar consumer needs in the same segment.

The reason for choosing this competitive strategy is the hope that it will increase sales. It is thought that if dealers have to compete against themselves as well as against other manufacturers' dealers, the extra effort will benefit overall sales. The effectiveness of this strategy is debatable. It could be argued that a program using different incentives, such as special discounts for attaining certain levels of sales, could be just as effective as this type of competition. It could be even more effective because the company would eliminate costs associated with developing additional channels.

Sometimes a company may be forced into developing competing channels in response to changing environments. For example, nonprescription drugs were traditionally sold through drugstores. But as the merchandising perspectives of supermarkets underwent a change during the post–World War II period, grocery stores became a viable channel for such products because shoppers expected to find convenience drug products there. This made it necessary for drug companies to deal with grocery wholesalers and retail grocery stores along with drug wholesalers and drugstores. In the 1980s, Capital Holding Corp. (a life insurance company located in Louisville, Kentucky) adopted a variety of marketing innovations. For example, in 1985 it began selling life insurance in novel ways, notably through supermarkets. Impressed by Capital Holding's steady growth and strong financial performance, many other insurance companies were forced to develop new channels to sell their insurance products.[17]

The argument behind the competitive channel strategy is that, although two brands of the same manufacturer may be essentially the same, they may appeal to different sets of customers. Thus, General Motors engages different dealers for its Buick, Cadillac, Chevrolet, Oldsmobile, and Pontiac cars. These dealers vigorously compete with each other. A more interesting example of competing multiple channels adopted by automobile manufacturers is provided by their dealings with car rental companies. Carmakers sell cars directly to car rental agencies. Hertz, for example, buys from an assembly plant and regularly resells some of its slightly used cars in competition with new cars through its more than 100 offices across the United States. Many of these offices are located in close proximity to dealers of new cars. Despite such competition, a manufacturer undertakes distribution through multiple channels to come off, on the whole, with increased business.

In adopting multiple competing channels, a company needs to make sure that it does not overextend itself; otherwise it may spread itself too thin and face competition to such an extent that ultimate results are disastrous. McCammon cites the case of a wholesaler who adopted multiple channels and thus exposed itself to a grave situation:

> Consider, for example, the competitive milieu of Stratton & Terstegge, a large hardware wholesaler in Louisville. At the present time, the company sells to independent retailers, sponsors a voluntary group program, and operates its own stores. In these multiple capacities, it competes against conventional wholesalers (Belknap), cash and carry wholesalers (Atlas), specialty wholesalers (Garcia), corporate chains (Wiches), voluntary groups (Western Auto), cooperative groups (Colter), free-form corporations (Interco), and others. Given the complexity of its competitive environment, it is not surprising to observe that Stratton & Terstegge generates a relatively modest rate of return on net worth.[18]

One of the dangers involved in setting up multiple channels is dealer resentment. This is particularly true when competitive channels are established. When this happens, it obviously means that an otherwise exclusive retailer will now suffer a loss in sales. Such a policy can result in the retailer electing to carry a different manufacturer's product line, if a comparable product line is available. For example, if a major department store like R.H. Macy is upset with a manufacturer like the Arrow Shirt Company for doing business with discounters (i.e., for adopting competing channels), it can very easily give its business to another shirt manufacturer.

Multiple channels also create control problems. National Distillers and Chemical Corporation had a wholly owned New York distributor, Peel Richards, that strictly enforced manufacturer-stipulated retail prices and refused to do business with price cutters. Since R.H. Macy discounted National Distiller's products, Peel Richards stopped selling to them. R.H. Macy retaliated by placing an order with an upstate New York distributor of National Distillers.[19] National Distillers had no legal recourse against either R.H. Macy or the upstate New York distributor, who was an independent businessperson.

These problems do not diminish the importance of multiple distribution: they only suggest the difficulties that may arise with multiple channels and the difficulties with which management must contend. A manufacturer's failure to use multiple channels gives competitors an opportunity to segment the market by concentrating on one or the other end of the market spectrum. This is particularly disastrous for a leading manufacturer because it must automatically forgo access to a large portion of market potential for not being able to use the economies of multiple distribution.

CHANNEL-MODIFICATION STRATEGY

The **channel-modification strategy** is the introduction of a change in existing distribution arrangements based on evaluation and critical review. Channels should be evaluated on an ongoing basis so that appropriate modification may be made as necessary.[20] A shift in existing channels may become desirable for any of the following reasons:

1. Changes in consumer markets and buying habits
2. Development of new needs in relation to service, parts, or technical help
3. Changes in competitors' perspectives
4. Changes in relative importance of outlet types
5. Changes in a manufacturer's financial strength
6. Changes in the sales volume level of existing products
7. Changes in product (addition of new products), price (substantial reduction in price to gain dominant position), or promotion (greater emphasis on advertising) strategies

Channel Evaluation

Channels of distribution may be evaluated on such primary criteria as cost of distribution, coverage of market (penetration), customer service, communication with the market, and control of distribution networks. Occasionally such secondary factors as support of channels in the successful introduction of a new product and cooperation with the company's promotional effort also become evaluative criteria. To arrive at a distribution channel that satisfies all these criteria requires simultaneous optimization of every facet of distribution, something that is usually not operationally possible. Consequently, a piecemeal approach may be followed.

Cost of Distribution. A detailed cost analysis of distribution is the first step in evaluating various channel alternatives on a sales-cost basis. This requires classification of total distribution costs under various heads and subheads. Exhibit 16-5 illustrates such a cost classification based on general accounting practices; information about each item should be conveniently available from the controller's office.

The question of evaluation comes up only when the company has been following a particular channel strategy for a number of years. Presumably, the company has pertinent information to undertake distribution cost analysis by customer segment and product line. This sort of data allows the analyzer to find out how cost under each head varies with sales volume; for example, how warehousing expenses vary with sales volume, how packaging and delivery expenses are related to sales, and so on. In other words, the purpose here is to establish a relationship between annual sales and different types of cost. These relationships are useful in predicting the future cost behavior for established dollar-sales objectives, assuming present channel arrangements are continued.

To find out the cost of distribution for alternative channels, estimates should be made of all relevant costs under various sales estimates. Cost information can be obtained from published sources and interviews with selected informants. For example, assume that a company has been selling through wholesalers for a number of years and is now considering distribution through its own branches. To follow the latter course, the company needs to rent a number

EXHIBIT 16-5
Representative List of Distribution Costs by Function

1. Direct Selling

Salaries: administrative and supervisory
Clerical
Salespeople
Commission
Travel and entertainment
Training
Insurance: real and property; liability; workmen's comp
Taxes: personal property; social security; unemployment insurance
Returned-goods expense chargeable to salespeople
Pension
Rent
Utilities
Repair and maintenance
Depreciation
Postage and office supplies

2. Advertising and Sales Promotion

Salaries: administrative and supervisory; clerical; advertising production
Publication space: trade journals; newspapers
Product promotion: advertising supplier; advertising agency fees; direct-mail expenses; contests; catalogs and price list
Cooperative advertising: dealers; retail stores; billboards

3. Product and Package Design

Salaries: administrative and supervisory
Wages
Materials
Depreciation

4. Sales Discounts and Allowances

Cash discounts on sales
Quantity discounts
Sales allowances

5. Credit Extension

Salaries: administrative and supervisory; credit representatives; clerical
Bad debt losses
Forms and postage
Credit rating services
Legal fees: collection efforts
Travel
Financial cost of accounts receivable

6. Market Research

Salaries: administrative; clerical
Surveys: distributors; consumers
Industry trade data
Travel

7. Warehousing and Handling

Salaries: administrative
Wages: warehouse services
Depreciation: furniture; fixtures
Insurance
Taxes
Repair and maintenance
Unsalable merchandise
Warehouse responsibility
Supplies
Utilities

8. Inventory Levels

Obsolescence markdown
Financial cost of carrying inventories

9. Packing, Shipping, and Delivery

Salaries: administrative; clerical
Wages: truck drivers; truck maintenance persons; packers
Shipping clerks
Truck operators
Truck repairs
Depreciation: furniture; fixtures; trucks
Insurance
Taxes
Utilities
Packing supplies
Postage and forms
Freight: factory to warehouse; warehouse to customer; factory to customer
Outside trucking service

10. Order Processing

Order forms
Salaries: administrative

EXHIBIT 16-5
continued

Wages: order review clerks; order processing clerks; equipment operators
Depreciation: Order processing equipment

11. Customer Service

Salaries: administrative; customer service representatives; clerical
Stationery and supplies

12. Printing and Recording of Accounts Receivable

Sales invoice forms
Salaries: clerical; administrative; accounts receivable clerks; sales invoicing equipment operators
Depreciation: sales invoicing equipment

13. Returned Merchandise

Freight
Salaries: administrative; clerical; returned-goods clerical
Returned-goods processing: material labor
Forms and supplies

of offices in important markets. Estimates of the cost of renting or purchasing an office can be furnished by real estate agents. Similarly, the cost of recruiting and hiring additional help to staff the offices should be available through the personnel office. With the relevant information gathered, simple break-even analysis can be used to compute the attractiveness of the alternative channel.

Assume that a company has 20,000 potential customers and, on an average, that each of them must be contacted every two weeks. A salesperson who makes 10 calls a day and who works five days a week can contact 100 customers every two weeks. Thus, the company needs 20,000 ÷ 100 = 200 salespeople. If each salesperson receives $30,000 in salary and $20,000 in expenses, the annual cost of its salespeople is $10,000,000. Further, assume that 10 sales managers are required for control and supervision and that each one is paid, say, $50,000 a year. The cost of supervision would then be $500,000. Let $9,500,000 be the cost of other overhead, such as office and warehouse expenses. The total cost of direct distribution will then be $10,000,000 + $500,000 + $9,500,000, or $20 million. Assume that distribution through wholesalers (the arrangement currently being pursued) costs the company 25 percent of sales. Assuming sales to be $\$x$, we can set up an equation, $0.25x = \$20$ million, and solve for x ($x = \$80$ million). If the company decides to go to direct distribution, it must generate a sales volume of $80 million before it can break even on costs. Thus, if sales potential is well above the $80-million mark, direct distribution is worth considering.

One problem with break-even analysis is that distribution alternatives that are considered equally effective may not always be so. It is a pervasive belief that the choice of a distribution channel affects total sales revenue just as the selection of an advertising strategy does. For example, a retailer may receive the same number of calls under either of two channel alternatives: from the company's salesperson or from a wholesaler's salesperson. The question, however, is, whether the effect of these calls is the same. The best way to handle this problem is to calculate the changes that would be necessary in order to make channel alternatives equally effective. To an extent, this can be achieved either intuitively or by using one of the mathematical models reported in the marketing literature.[21]

Coverage of the Market. An important aspect of predicting future sales response is the penetration that will eventually be achieved in the market. For example, in the case of a drug company, customers can be divided into three groups: (a) drugstores, (b) doctors, and (c) hospitals.

One measure of the coverage of the market (or penetration of the market) is the number of customers in a group contacted or sold, divided by the total number of customers in that group. Another measure may be penetration in terms of geographical coverage of territory. But these measures are too general. Using just the ratio of customers contacted to the total number of customers does not give a proper indication of coverage because not all types of customers are equally important. Therefore, customers may be further classified, as shown in the accompanying display:

Customer Group	*Classification*	*Basis of Classification*
Drugstores	Large, medium, and small	Annual turnover
Hospitals	Large, medium, and small	Number of beds
Doctors	Large, medium, and small	Number of patients attended

Then the desired level of penetration for each subgroup should be specified (e.g., penetrate 90 percent of the large, 75 percent of the medium, and 50 percent of the small drugstores). These percentages can be used for examining the effectiveness of an alternative channel.

An advanced analysis is possible, however, by building a penetration model. The basis of the model is that increments in penetration for equal periods are proportional to the remaining distance to the aimed penetration. The increments in penetration in a period t will be: $t = rp(1 - r)t - 1$, where $p =$ targeted or aimed penetration and $r =$ penetration ratio. This ratio signifies how rapidly the cumulative penetration approaches aimed penetration. For example, if aimed penetration is 80 percent and if $r = 0.3$, then first-year penetration is $80 \times 0.3 = 24$ percent. Next year, the increment in penetration will be $80 \times 0.3 \times 0.7 = 16.8$ percent. Hence, cumulative penetration at the end of the second year will be $24 + 16.8 = 40.8$. The value of p for each subgroup is a matter of policy decision on the part of the company. The value of r depends on the period during which aimed penetration is to be achieved and on sales efforts in terms of the number of medical representatives/salespeople and their call pattern for each subgroup. For the existing channel (selling through the wholesalers), the value of r can be determined from past records. For the alternate channel (direct distribution), the approximate value of r can be computed in one of two ways:

1. Company executives should know how many salespeople would be kept on the rolls if the alternate channel were used. The executives can also estimate the average number of calls a day a salesperson can make and hence the average

number of customers in a subgroup he or she can contact. With this information, the value of r can be determined as follows:

$$\frac{\text{Number of customers in a subgroup contacted under existing channel}}{\text{Number of customers in a subgroup that would be contacted in alternate channel}} = \frac{\text{Value of } r \text{ for existing channel}}{\text{Value of } r \text{ for alternate channel}}$$

2. A second approach may be to find out (or estimate) the penetration that would be possible after one year if the alternate channel is used, then to substitute this in the penetration equation to find r when p and t are known.

The penetration model makes it easier to predict the exact coverage in each subgroup of customers over a planning period (say, five years hence). The marketing strategist should determine the ultimate desired penetration p and the time period in which it is to be achieved. Then the model would be able to predict which channel would take the penetration closer to the objective.

Customer Service. The level of customer service differs from customer to customer for each business. Generally speaking, the sales department, with feedback from the field force, should be able to designate the various services that the company should offer to different consumer segments. If this is not feasible, a sample survey may be planned to find out which services customers expect and which services are currently being offered by competitors. This information can be used to develop a viable service package. Then the capability and willingness of each channel alternative to provide these services may be matched to single out the most desirable channel. This can be done intuitively. A more scientific approach would be to list and assign weights to each type of service, then rate different channels according to their ability to handle these services. Cumulative scores can be used for the service ranking of channel alternatives. Conjoint measurement can be used to determine which services are most important to a particular segment of customers.

Communication and Control. **Control** may be defined as the process of taking steps to bring actual results and desired results closer together. **Communication** refers to the information flow between the company and its customers. To evaluate alternate channels on these two criteria, communication and control objectives should be defined. With reference to communication, for example, information may be desired on the activities of competitors, new products from competitors, the special promotional efforts of competitors, the attitudes of customers toward the company's and toward competitors' services, and the reasons for success of a particular product line of the company.[22] Each channel alternative may then be evaluated in terms of its willingness, capabilities, and interest in providing the required information. In the case of wholesalers, the communication perspective may also depend on the terms of the contract. But the mere fact that they are legally bound by a contract may not motivate wholesalers to cooperate willingly. Finally, the information should be judged for accuracy, timeliness, and relevance.

Channel Modification

Environmental shifts, internal or external, may require a company to modify existing channel arrangements. A shift in trade practice, for instance, may render distribution through a manufacturer's representative obsolete. Similarly, technological changes in product design may require frequent service calls on customers that wholesalers may not be able to make, thus leading the company to opt for direct distribution.

To illustrate the point, consider jewelry distribution. For centuries jewelry was distributed through jewelry shops that relied on uniqueness, craftsmanship, and mystique to reap fat margins on very small volumes. Traditionally, big retailers shunned jewelry as a highly specialized, slow-moving business that tied up too much money in inventory. But this attitude has changed in the last few years. For example, between 1978 and 1982, jewelry stores' share of the jewelry market declined from 65 percent to less than 50 percent. On the other hand, relying on hefty advertising and deep discounting, mass merchandisers (e.g., Penney, Sears, Montgomery Ward, Target, and others) have been making fast inroads into the jewelry business. For example, in 1983 J.C. Penney became the fourth-largest retail jewelry merchant in the United States behind Zale, Gordon Jewelry, and Best Products, the catalog showroom chain. Such a shift in trade practice requires that jewelry manufacturers modify their distribution arrangements.[23]

Similarly, as computer makers try to reach ever-broadening audiences with lower-priced machines, they need new distribution channels. Many of them, IBM and Xerox, for example, are turning to retail stores. In the 1970s people would have laughed at the idea of selling computers over the counter; now it is a preferred way of doing business. The tantalizing opportunity to sell computers to consumers has also given birth to specialty chains such as Computerland, CompuShop, MicroAge, and Computer Store.

Generally speaking, a new company in the market starts distribution through intermediaries. This is necessary because, during the initial period, technical and manufacturing problems are big enough to keep management busy. Besides, at this stage, the company has neither the insight nor the capabilities needed to deal successfully with the vagaries of the market. Therefore, intermediaries are used. With their knowledge of the market, they play an important role in establishing a demand for a company's product. But once the company establishes a foothold in the market, it may discover that it does not have the control of distribution it needs to make further headway. At this time, channel modification becomes necessary.

Managerial astuteness requires that the company do a thorough study before deciding to change existing channel arrangements. Taking a few half-hearted measures could create insurmountable problems resulting in loose control and poor communication.[24] Further, the intermediaries affected should be duly taken into confidence about a company's plans and compensated for any breach of terms. Any modification of channels should match the perspectives of the total marketing strategy. This means that the effect of a modified plan on other ingredients of the marketing mix (such as product, price, and promotion) should be considered. The managers of different departments (as well as the customers) should be informed so that the change does not come as a surprise. In other words, care needs to be taken to ensure that a modification in channel arrangements does not cause any distortion in the overall distribution system.

CHANNEL-CONTROL STRATEGY

Channel arrangements traditionally consisted of loosely aligned manufacturers, wholesalers, and retailers, all of whom were trying to serve their own ends regardless of what went on elsewhere in the channel structure. In such arrangements, channel control was generally missing. Each member of the channel negotiated aggressively with others and performed a conventionally defined set of marketing functions.

Importance of Channel Control

For a variety of reasons, control is a necessary ingredient in running a successful system. Having control is likely to have a positive impact on profits because inefficiencies are caught and corrected in time. This is evidenced by the success of voluntary and cooperative chains, corporate chains, franchise alignments, manufacturers' dealer organizations, and sales branches and offices. Control also helps to realize cost effectiveness vis-à-vis experience curves. For example, centralized organization of warehousing, data processing, and other facilities provide scale efficiencies. Through a planned perspective of the total system, effort is directed to achieving common goals in an integrated fashion.

Channel Controller

The focus of channel control may be on any member of a channel system: the manufacturer, wholesaler, or retailer. Unfortunately, there is no established theory to indicate whether any one of them makes a better channel controller than the others.[25] For example, one appliance retailer in Philadelphia with a 10 percent market share, Silo Incorporated, served as the channel controller there. This firm had no special relationship with any manufacturer, but if a supplier's line did not do well, Silo immediately contacted the supplier to ask that something be done about it.[26] Sears (in addition to J.C. Penney and K-Mart) can be expected to be the channel controller for a variety of products. Among manufacturers, Kraft ought to be the channel controller for refrigerated goods in supermarkets. Likewise, Procter and Gamble is a channel controller for detergents and related items. Ethan Allen decided to control the distribution channels for its line of Early American furniture by establishing a network of 200 dealer outlets. Sherwin-Williams decided to take over channel control to guide its own destiny because traditional channels were not showing enough aggressiveness. The company established its own chain of 2000 retail outlets.

These examples underscore the importance of someone taking over channel leadership in order to establish control. Conventionally, market leadership and the size of a firm determine its suitability for channel control. Strategically, a firm should attempt to control the channel for a product if it can make a commitment to fulfill its leadership obligations and if such a move is likely to be economically beneficial in the long run for the entire channel system.

Vertical Marketing Systems

Vertical marketing systems may be defined as

> professionally managed and centrally programmed networks [that] are pre-engineered to achieve operating economies and maximum market impact. Stated alternatively, vertical marketing systems are rationalized and capital-intensive networks designed to achieve technological, managerial, and promotional economies through the integration, coordination, and synchronization of marketing flows from points of production to points of ultimate use.[27]

The vertical marketing system is an emerging trend in the American economy. It seems to be replacing all conventional marketing channels as the mainstay of distribution. As a matter of fact, according to one estimate, vertical marketing systems in the consumer-goods sector account for about 70 to 80 percent of the available market.[28] In brief, vertical marketing systems (sometimes also referred to as centrally coordinated systems) have emerged as the dominant ingredient in the competitive process and thus play a strategic role in the formulation of distribution strategy.

Vertical marketing systems may be classified into three types: corporate, administered, and contractual. Under the **corporate vertical marketing system**, successive stages of production and distribution are owned by a single entity. This is achieved through forward and backward integration. Sherwin-Williams owns and operates its 2000 retail outlets in a corporate vertical marketing system (a case of forward integration). Other examples of such systems are Hart, Schaffner, and Marx (operating more than 275 stores), International Harvester, Goodyear, and Sohio. Not only a manufacturer but also a corporate vertical system might be owned and operated by a retailer (a case of backward integration). Sears, like many other large retailers, has financial interests in many of its suppliers' businesses. For example, about one-third of DeSoto (a furniture and home furnishings manufacturer) stock is owned by Sears. Finally, W. W. Grainger provides an example of a wholesaler-run vertical marketing system. This firm, an electrical distributor with 1987 sales of $590 million, has seven manufacturing facilities.

Another outstanding example of a vertical marketing system is provided by Gallo, the wine company.

> The [Gallo] brothers own Fairbanks Trucking company, one of the largest intrastate truckers in California. Its 200 semis and 500 trailors are constantly hauling wine out of Modesto and raw materials back in—including . . . lime from Gallo's quarry east of Sacramento. Alone among wine producers, Gallo makes bottles—two million a day—and its Midcal Aluminum Co. spews out screw tops as fast as the bottles are

> filled. Most of the country's 1,300 or so wineries concentrate on production to the neglect of marketing. Gallo, by contrast, participates in every aspect of selling short of whispering in the ear of each imbiber. The company owns its distributors in about a dozen markets and probably would buy many . . . more . . . if the laws in most states did not prohibit doing so.[29]

In an **administered vertical marketing system**, a dominant firm within the channel system, such as the manufacturer, wholesaler, or retailer, coordinates the flow of goods by virtue of its market power. For example, the firm may exert influence to achieve economies in transportation, order processing, warehousing, advertising, or merchandising. As can be expected, it is large organizations like Sears, Safeway, Penney, General Motors, Kraft, GE, Procter and Gamble, Lever Brothers, Nabisco, and General Foods that emerge as channel captains to guide their channel networks, while not actually owning them, to achieve economies and efficiencies.

In a **contractual vertical marketing system**, independent firms within the channel structure integrate their programs on a contractual basis to realize economies and market impact. Primarily, there are three types of contractual vertical marketing systems: wholesaler-sponsored voluntary groups, retailer-sponsored cooperative groups, and franchise systems. Independent Grocers Alliance (IGA) is an example of a wholesaler-sponsored voluntary group. At the initiative of the wholesaler, small grocery stores agree to form a chain to achieve economies with which to compete against corporate chains. The joining members agree to adhere to a variety of contractual terms, such as the use of a common name, to help realize economies on large order. Except for these terms, each store continues to operate independently. A retailer-sponsored cooperative group is essentially the same. Retailers form their own association (cooperative) to compete against corporate chains by undertaking wholesaler functions (and possibly even a limited amount of production); that is, they operate their own wholesale companies to serve member retailers. This type of contractual vertical marketing system is operated primarily, though not exclusively, in the food line. Associated Grocers Co-op and Certified Grocers are examples of retailer-sponsored food cooperative groups. Value-Rite, a group of 2298 stores, is a drugstore cooperative.[30]

A **franchise system** is an arrangement whereby a firm licenses others to market a product or service using its trade name in a defined geographic area under specified terms and conditions. In 1984 there were more than 2000 franchisers in the United States, twice as many as in 1973. Practically any business that can be taught to someone is being franchised. In 1985 sales of goods and services by all franchising companies (manufacturing, wholesaling, and retailing) exceeded $500 billion. Approximately one-third of all U.S. retail sales flow through franchise and company-owned units in franchise chains.[31]

In addition to traditional franchising businesses (e.g., fast food), banks are doing it, as are accountants, dating services, skin care centers, tub and tile refinishers, tutors, funeral homes, bookkeepers, dentists, nurses, bird seed shops, gift wrappers, wedding consultants, cookie bakers, popcorn poppers, beauty shops, babysitters, and suppliers of maid service, lawn care, and solar greenhouses.[32] The Commerce Department forecasts that by the year 2000 franchising will account for half of all retail sales. Four different types of franchise systems can be distinguished:

1. The *manufacturer-retailer franchise* is exemplified by franchised automobile dealers and franchised service stations.
2. The *manufacturer-wholesaler franchise* is exemplified by Coca-Cola, Pepsi-Cola, Royal Crown Cola, and Seven-Up, who sell the soft drink syrups they manufacture to franchised wholesalers who, in turn, bottle and distribute soft drinks to retailers.
3. The *wholesaler-retailer franchise* is exemplified by Rexall Drug Stores, Sentry Drug Centers, and ComputerLand.
4. The *service sponsor-retailer franchise* is exemplified by Avis, Hertz, and National in the car rental business; McDonald's, Chicken Delight, Kentucky Fried Chicken, and Taco-Tico in the prepared foods industry; Howard Johnson's and Holiday Inn in the lodging and food industry; Midas and AAMCO in the auto repair business; and Kelly Girl and Manpower in the employment service business.[33]

Vertical marketing systems help achieve economies that cannot be realized through the use of conventional marketing channels. In strategic terms, vertical marketing systems provide opportunities for building experience, thus allowing even small firms to derive the benefits of market power. If present trends are any indication, in the 1990s vertical marketing systems should account for almost 90 percent of total retail sales. Considering their growing importance, conventional channels will need to adopt new distribution strategies to compete against vertical marketing systems. For example, they may

1. Develop programs to strengthen customers' competitive capabilities. This alternative involves manufacturers and wholesalers in such activities as sponsoring centralized accounting and management reporting services, formulating cooperative promotional programs, and cosigning shopping center leases.
2. Enter new markets. For example, building supply distributors have initiated cash-and-carry outlets. Steel warehouses have added glass and plastic product lines to their traditional product lines. Industrial distributors have initiated stockless buying plans and blanket order contracts so that they may compete effectively for customers who buy on a direct basis.
3. Effect economies of operation by developing management information systems. For example, some middlemen in conventional channels have installed the IBM IMPACT program to improve their control over inventory.
4. Determine through research the focus of power in the channel and urge the channel member designated to undertake a reorganization of marketing flows.[34]

Despite the growing trend toward vertical integration, it would be naive to consider it an unmixed blessing. Vertical integration has both pluses and minuses—more of the latter, according to one empirical study on the subject.[35] For example, vertical integration requires a huge commitment of resources: in mid-1981, Du Pont acquired Conoco in a $7.3-billion transaction. The strategy may not be worth it unless the company gains needed insurance as well as cost savings. As a matter of fact, some observers have blamed the U.S. automobile industry's woes, in part, on excessive vertical integration: "In deciding to integrate backward because of apparent short-term rewards, managers often restrict their ability to strike out in innovative directions in the future."[36]

CONFLICT-MANAGEMENT STRATEGY

It is quite conceivable that the independent firms that constitute a channel of distribution (i.e., manufacturer, wholesaler, retailer) may sometimes find themselves in conflict with each other. The underlying causes of conflict are the divergent goals that different firms may pursue.[37] If the goals of one firm are being challenged because of the strategies followed by another channel member, conflict is the natural outcome. Thus, **channel conflict** may be defined as a situation in which one channel member perceives another channel member or members to be engaged in behavior that is preventing or impeding it from achieving its goals.

Disagreement between channel members may arise from incompatible desires and needs. Weigand and Wasson give four examples of the kinds of conflict that may arise:

> A manufacturer promises an exclusive territory to a retailer in return for the retailer's "majority effort" to generate business in the area. Sales increase nicely, but the manufacturer believes it is due more to population growth in the area than to the effort of the store owner, who is spending too much time on the golf course.
>
> A fast-food franchisor promises "expert promotional assistance" to his retailers as partial explanation for the franchise fee. One of the retailers believes that the help he is getting is anything but expert and that the benefits do not correspond with what he was promised.
>
> Another franchisor agrees to furnish accounting services and financial analysis as a regular part of his service. The franchisee believes that the accountant is nothing more than a "glorified bookkeeper" and that the financial analysis consists of several pages of ratios that are incomprehensible.
>
> A third franchisor insists that his franchisees should maintain a minimum stock of certain items that are regularly promoted throughout the area. Arguments arise as to whether the franchisor's recommendations constitute a threat, while the franchisee is particularly concerned about protecting his trade name.[38]

The four strategic alternatives available for resolving conflicts between channel members are bargaining, boundary, interpenetration, and superorganizational strategies.[39] Under the **bargaining strategy**, one member of the channel takes the lead in activating the bargaining process by being willing to concede something, with the expectation that the other party will reciprocate. For example, a manufacturer may agree to provide interest-free loans for up to 90 days to a distributor if the distributor will carry twice the level of inventory that it previously did and will furnish warehousing for the purpose. Or a retailer may propose to continue to carry the television line of a manufacturer if the manufacturer will supply television sets under the retailer's own name (i.e., the retailer's private brand). The bargaining strategy works out only if both parties are willing to adopt the attitude of give-and-take and if bottom-line results for both are favorable enough to induce them to accept the terms of the bargain.[40]

The **boundary strategy** handles the conflict through diplomacy; that is, by nominating the employee most familiar with the perspectives of the other party to take up the matter with his or her counterpart. For example, a manufacturer may nominate a veteran salesperson to communicate with the purchasing agent of the customer to see if some basis can be established to resolve the conflict. A department store manager may be upset with a manufacturer's decision to start supplying the product to a mass retailer, such as J.C. Penney. To resolve such a conflict, the manufacturer's salesperson may meet with the purchasing agent to talk over business in general, and in between the talks, the salesperson may indicate in a subtle way that the company's decision to supply the product to J.C. Penney for sale through catalogs is motivated by its desire to help the department store: in the long run, the department store will reap the benefits of the brand name popularity triggered by the deal with J.C. Penney. Besides, the salesperson may be authorized to propose that his or her company will agree not to sell the top of the line to Penney, thus ensuring that it will continue to be available only through major department stores. In order for this strategy to succeed, it is necessary that the diplomat (the salesperson in the example) be fully briefed on the situation and provided leverage with which to negotiate.

The **interpenetration strategy** is directed toward resolving conflict through frequent informal interactions with the other party to gain a proper appreciation of each other's perspectives. One of the easiest ways to develop interaction is for one party to invite the other to join its trade association. For example, several years ago television dealers were concerned because they felt that the manufacturers of television sets did not understand their problems. To help correct the situation, the dealers invited the manufacturers to become members of the National Appliance and Radio-TV Dealers Association (NARDA). Currently, manufacturers take an active interest in NARDA conventions and seminars. According to industry sources, the channel relationships in the television industry have improved a great deal.[41]

Finally, the focus of **superorganizational strategy** is to employ conciliation, mediation, and arbitration to resolve conflict. Essentially, a neutral third party is brought into the conflict to resolve the matter. **Conciliation** is an informal attempt by a third party to bring two conflicting organizations together and make them come to an agreement amicably. For example, an independent wholesaler may serve as a conciliator between a manufacturer and its customers. Under **mediation**, the third party plays a more active role. If the parties in conflict fail to come to an agreement, they may be willing to consider the procedural or substantive recommendations of the mediator.

Arbitration may also be applied to resolve channel conflict. Arbitration may be compulsory or voluntary. Under compulsory arbitration, the dispute must by law be submitted to a third party, the decision being final and binding on both conflicting parties. For example, the courts may arbitrate between two parties in dispute. Years ago, when automobile manufacturers and their dealers had problems relative to distribution policies, the court arbitrated. Voluntary arbitration is a process whereby the parties in conflict submit their disputes for resolution to a third party on their own. For example, in 1955 the Federal Trade Commission arbitrated between television set manufacturers, distributors, and dealers by setting up 32 industry rules to protect the consumer and to reduce conflicts over distribution. The conflict areas involved were tie-in sales; price fixing; mass shipments used to clog outlets and foreclose competitors; discriminatory billing; and special rebates, bribes, refunds, and discounts.[42]

Of all the methods of resolving conflict, arbitration is the fastest. In addition, under arbitration, secrecy is preserved and less expense is incurred. Inasmuch as industry experts serve as arbitrators, one can expect a fairer decision. Thus, as a matter of strategy, arbitration may be more desirable than other methods for managing conflict.

SUMMARY

Distribution strategies are concerned with the flow of goods and services from manufacturers to customers. The discussion in this chapter was conducted from the manufacturer's viewpoint. Six major distribution strategies were distinguished: channel-structure strategy, distribution-scope strategy, multiple-channel strategy, channel-modification strategy, channel-control strategy, and conflict-management strategy.

Channel-structure strategy determines whether the goods should be distributed directly from manufacturer to customer or indirectly through one or more intermediaries. Formulation of this strategy was discussed with reference to Bucklin's postponement-speculation theory. Distribution-scope strategy specifies whether exclusive, selective, or intensive distribution should be pursued. The question of simultaneously employing more than one channel was discussed under multiple-channel strategy. Channel-modification strategy involves evaluating current channels and making necessary changes in distribution perspectives to accommodate environmental shifts. Channel-control strategy focuses on vertical marketing systems to institute control. Finally, resolution of conflict among channel members was examined under conflict-management strategy.

The merits and drawbacks of each strategy were discussed. Examples from marketing literature were given to illustrate the practical applications of different strategies.

DISCUSSION QUESTIONS

1. What factors may a manufacturer consider to determine whether to distribute products directly to customers? Can automobiles be distributed directly to customers?
2. Is intensive distribution a prerequisite for gaining experience? Discuss.
3. What precautions are necessary to ensure that exclusive distribution is not liable to challenge as a restraint of trade?

4. What strategic factor makes the multiple-channel strategy a necessity for a multiproduct company?
5. What criteria may a food processor adopt to evaluate its channels of distribution?
6. What kinds of environmental shifts require a change in channel arrangements?
7. What reasons may be ascribed to the emergence of vertical marketing systems?
8. What strategies may conventional channels adopt to meet the threat of vertical marketing systems?
9. What are the underlying sources of conflict in distribution channel relations? Give examples.
10. What is the most appropriate strategy for resolving a channel conflict?

NOTES

[1]Wroe Alderson, "Factors Governing the Development of Marketing Channels," in *Marketing Channels for Manufactured Products,* ed. Richard M. Clewett (Homewood, IL: Richard D. Irwin, 1964), 7.

[2]Louis P. Bucklin, *A Theory of Distribution Channel Structure* (Berkeley: IBER Special Publications, University of California, 1966); and "Postponement, Speculation and Structure of Distribution Channels," in *The Marketing Channel: A Conceptual Viewpoint,* ed. Bruce E. Mallen (New York: John Wiley & Sons, 1967), 67–74.

[3]Louis P. Bucklin and Leslie Halpert, "Exploring Channel of Distribution for Cement with the Principle of Postponement-Speculation," in *Marketing and Economic Development,* ed. Peter D. Bennett (Chicago: American Marketing Association, 1965), 699.

[4]See "Benetton," in Robert D. Buzzell and John A. Quelch, *Multinational Marketing Management* (Reading, MA: Addison-Wesley Publishing Co., 1988), 47–76.

[5]See Louis W. Stern and Patrick J. Kaufmann, "Electronic Data Interchange in Selected Consumer Goods Industries: An Interorganizational Perspective," in *Marketing in an Electronic Age,* ed. Robert D. Buzzell (Boston: Harvard Business School Press, 1985), 52–73.

[6]"Foremost-McKesson: The Computer Moves Distribution to Center Stage," *Business Week* (7 December 1981): 115. See also "Waldenbooks: Countering B. Dalton by Aping Its Computer Operations," *Business Week* (8 October 1979): 116. See also Leslie Easton, "Distributing Value: A Revamped McKesson Corporation Is Producing Surprises," *Barron's* (3 August 1987): 13, 41–42.

[7]Bruce Mallen, *Principles of Marketing Channel Management* (Lexington, MA: Lexington Books, 1977), 179.

[8]Wetterau, Inc., annual report for 1991.

[9]Frank E. James, "Big Warehouse Outlets Break Traditional Rules of Retailing," *Wall Street Journal,* 22 December 1983, p. 27.

[10]See Gary L. Frazier, "Designing Channels of Distribution."

[11]Ronald L. Ernst, "Distribution Channel Détente Benefits Suppliers, Retailers and Consumers," *Marketing News* (7 March 1980): 19.

[12]"Avon Will Offer Perfumes through Department Stores." *Wall Street Journal,* 21 August 1986, p. 16.

[13]"R. Dakin: Marketing Old-Style Toys through Offbeat Outlets," *Business Week* (24 December 1979): 94.

[14]"Easco: Turning to New Customers While Helping Sears Promote Tools," *Business Week* (6 October 1980): 62.

[15]Terry Agins, "Clothing Makers Don Retailers' Garb," *Wall Street Journal,* 13 July 1989, p. B1.

[16]"Bangor Punta Operations, Inc.," a case copyrighted by the President and Fellows of Harvard College, 1969, 28–29.

[17]"Even Star Insurers Are Feeling the Heat," *Business Week* (14 January 1985): 119.

[18]Bert C. McCammon, Jr., "Future Shock and the Practice of Management" (Paper presented at the Fifth Annual Research Conference of the American Marketing Association, Madrid, Spain, 1973), 9.

[19]Robert E. Weigand, "Fit Products and Channels to Your Market," *Harvard Business Review* (January–February 1977): 95–105.

[20]See Donald H. Light, "A Guide for New Distribution Channel Strategies for Service Firms," *Journal of Business Strategy* (Summer 1986): 56–64.

[21]Gary L. Lilien and Philip Kotler, *Marketing Decision Making* (New York: Harper & Row, 1983), chapter 13.

[22]See Jakki Mohr and John R. Nevin, "Communication Strategies in Marketing Channels: A Theoretical Perspective," *Journal of Marketing* (October 1990): 36–51.

[23]"Chain Stores Strike Gold in Jewelry Sales," *Business Week* (6 February 1984): 56.

[24]See Howard Sulton, *Rethinking the Company's Selling and Distribution Channels* (New York: Conference Board, 1986), Research Report 885.

[25]Gul Butaney and Lawrence H. Wortzell, "Distributor Power versus Manufacturer Power: The Customer Role," *Journal of Marketing* (January 1988): 52–63.

[26]"An Appliance Dealer with a Real Clout," *Business Week* (6 November 1971): 76.

[27]Bert C. McCammon, Jr., "Perspectives for Distribution Programming," in *Vertical Marketing Systems,* ed. Louis P. Bucklin (Glenview, IL: Scott, Foresman, 1970), 43.

[28]Philip Kotler, *Marketing Management,* 7th ed. (Englewood Cliffs, NJ: Prentice-Hall, 1991), 525.

[29]Jaclyn Fireman, "How Gallo Crushes the Competition," *Fortune* (1 September 1986): 27.

[30]*Wall Street Journal,* 2 October 1986, p. 1.

[31]*Franchising in the Economy: 1983–85* (Washington, DC: Department of Commerce, 1985).

[32]Faye Rice, "How to Succeed at Cloning a Small Business," *Fortune* (28 October 1985): 60.

[33]William P. Hall, "Franchising: New Scope for an Old Technique," *Harvard Business Review* (January–February 1964): 60–72.

[34]Louis W. Stern, Adel I. El-Ansary, and James R. Brown, *Management in Marketing Channels* (Englewood Cliffs, NJ: Prentice-Hall, 1989), 299.

[35]Robert D. Buzzell, "Is Vertical Integration Profitable?" *Harvard Business Review* (January–February 1983): 92–102.

[36]Robert H. Hayes and William J. Abernathy, "Managing Our Way to Economic Decline," *Harvard Business Review* (July–August 1980): 72.

[37]See J. F. Gaski, "The Theory of Power and Conflict in Channels of Distribution," *Journal of Marketing* (Summer 1984): 9–29.

[38]Robert Weigand and Hilda C. Wasson, "Arbitration in the Marketing Channel," *Business Horizons* (October 1974): 40.

[39]The discussion on resolving conflicts draws heavily on Louis W. Stern and Adel I. El-Ansary, *Marketing Channels,* 3rd ed. (Englewood Cliffs, NJ: Prentice-Hall, 1988), 290–98.

[40]See Alvin A. Achenbaum and F. Kent Mitchel, "Pulling Away from Push Marketing," *Harvard Business Review* (May–June 1987): 38.

[41]Henry Assall, "Constructive Role of Interorganizational Conflict," *Administrative Science Quarterly* 14 (1969): 287.

[42]Stern and El-Ansary, *Marketing Channels.*

APPENDIX | *Perspectives on Distribution Strategies*

I Channel-Structure Strategy

Definition: Using perspectives of intermediaries in the flow of goods from manufacturers to customers. Distribution may be either direct (from manufacturer to retailer or from manufacturer to customer) or indirect (involving the use of one or more intermediaries, such as wholesalers or agents, to reach the customer).

Objective: To reach the optimal number of customers in a timely manner at the lowest possible cost while maintaining the desired degree of control.

Requirements: Comparison of direct versus indirect distribution on the basis of (a) cost, (b) product characteristics, (c) degree of control, and (d) other factors.

Costs: (a) Distribution costs, (b) opportunity costs incurred because product not available, and (c) inventory holding and shipping costs.

Product Characteristics: (a) Replacement rate, (b) gross margin, (c) service requirements, and (d) search time.

Degree of Control: Greater when direct distribution used.

Other Factors: (a) Adaptability, (b) technological changes (e.g., computer technology), and (c) social/cultural values.

Expected Results: (a) Direct distribution: (i) high marketing costs, (ii) large degree of control, (iii) informed customers, and (iv) strong image. (b) Indirect distribution: (i) lower marketing costs, (ii) less control, and (iii) reduced channel management responsibilities.

II Distribution-Scope Strategy

Definition: Establishing the scope of distribution, that is, the target customers. Choices are exclusive distribution (one retailer is granted sole rights in serving a given area), intensive distribution (a product is made available at all possible retail outlets), and selective distribution (many but not all retail outlets in a given area distribute a product).

Objective: To serve chosen markets at a minimal cost while maintaining desired product image.

Requirements: Assessment of (a) customer buying habits, (b) gross margin/turnover rate, (c) capability of dealer to provide service, (d) capability of dealer to carry full product line, and (e) product styling.

Expected Results: (a) Exclusive distribution: (i) strong dealer loyalty, (ii) high degree of control, (iii) good forecasting capability, (iv) sales promotion assistance from manufacturer, (v) possible loss in sales volume, and (vi) possible antitrust violation. (b) Selective distribution: (i) extreme competition in marketplace, (ii) price discounting, and (iii) pressure from channel members to reduce number of outlets. (c) Intensive distribution: (i) low degree of control, (ii) higher sales volume, (iii) wide customer recognition, (iv) high turnover, and (v) price discounting.

III Multiple-Channel Strategy

Definition: Employing two or more different channels for distribution of goods and services. Multiple-channel distribution is of two basic types: complementary (each channel handles a different noncompeting product or market segment) and competitive (two different and competing channels sell the same product).

Objective: To achieve optimal access to each individual market segment to increase business. Complementary channels are used to reach market segments otherwise left unserved; competitive channels are used with the hope of increasing sales.

Requirements: (a) Market segmentation. (b) Cost/benefit analysis. Use of complementary channels prompted by (i) geographic considerations, (ii) volume of business, (iii) need to distribute noncompeting items, and (iv) saturation of traditional distribution channels. Use of competitive channels can be a response to environmental changes.

Expected Results: (a) Different services, prices, and support provided to different segments. (b) Broader market base. (c) Increased sales. (d) Possible dealer resentment. (e) Control problems. (f) Possible overextension. Overextension can result in (a) decrease in quality/service and (b) negative effects on long-run profitability.

IV Channel-Modification Strategy

Definition: Introducing a change in the existing distribution arrangements on the basis of evaluation and critical review.

Objective: To maintain an optimal distribution system given a changing environment.

Requirements: (a) Evaluation of internal/external environmental shifts: (i) changes in consumer markets and buying habits, (ii) changes in the retail life cycle, (iii) changes in the manufacturer's financial strength, and (iv) changes in the product life cycle. (b) Continuous evaluation of existing channels. (c) Cost/benefit analysis. (d) Consideration of the effect of the modified channels on other aspects of the marketing mix. (e) Ability of management to adapt to modified plan.

Expected Results: (a) Maintenance of an optimal distribution system given environmental changes. (b) Disgruntled dealers and customers (in the short run).

V Channel-Control Strategy

Definition: Takeover by a member of the channel structure in order to establish control of the channel and provide a centrally organized effort to achieve common goals.

Objectives: (a) To increase control. (b) To correct inefficiencies. (c) To realize cost-effectiveness through experience curves. (d) To gain efficiencies of scale.

Requirements: Commitment and resources to fulfill leadership obligations. Typically, though not always, the channel controller is a large firm with market leadership/influence.

Expected Results (Vertical Marketing System): (a) Increased control. (b) Professional management. (c) Central programming. (d) Achievement of operating economies. (e) Maximum market impact. (f) Increased profitability. (g) Elimination of inefficiencies.

VI Conflict-Management Strategy

Definition: Resolving conflict among channel members.

Objective: To devise a solution acceptable to the conflicting members so that they will cooperate to make it work.

Requirements: Choice of a strategy for solving the conflict. (a) Bargaining: (i) both parties adopt give-and-take attitude and (ii) bottom line is favorable enough to both parties to induce them to accept the terms of the bargain. (b) Boundary: (i) nomination of an employee to act as diplomat, (ii) diplomat is fully briefed on the situation and provided with leverages with which to negotiate, and (iii) both parties are willing to negotiate. (c) Interpenetration: (i) frequent formal interactions with the other party to develop an appreciation of each other's perspectives and (ii) willingness to interact to solve problems. (d) Superorganizational: A neutral third party is brought into the conflict to resolve the matter by means of (i) conciliation, (ii) mediation, or (iii) arbitration (compulsory or voluntary).

Expected Results: (a) Elimination of snags in the channel. (b) Results that are mutually beneficial to the parties involved. (c) Need for management time and effort. (d) Increased costs. (e) Costs incurred by both parties in the form of concessions.

CHAPTER 17

Promotion Strategies

Advertisements contain the only truths to be relied on in a newspaper.

THOMAS JEFFERSON

Promotion strategies are concerned with the planning, implementation, and control of persuasive communication with customers. These strategies may be designed around advertising, personal selling, sales promotion, or any combination of these. The first strategic issue involved here is how much money may be spent on the promotion of a specific product/market. The distribution of the total promotional budget among advertising, personal selling, and sales promotion is another strategic matter. The formulation of strategies dealing with these two issues determines the role that each type of promotion plays in a particular situation.

Clear-cut objectives and sharp focus on target customers are necessary for an effective promotional program. In other words, merely undertaking an advertising campaign or hiring a few salespeople to call on customers may not suffice. Rather, an integrated communication plan consisting of various promotion methods should be designed to ensure that customers in a product/market cluster get the right message and maintain a long-term cordial relationship with the company. Promotional perspectives must also be properly matched with product, price, and distribution perspectives.

In addition to the strategic issues mentioned above, this chapter discusses strategies in advertising and personal selling. The advertising strategies examined are media strategy and copy strategy. Strategic matters explored in the area of personal selling are those concerned with designing a selling program and supervising salespeople. The formulation of each strategy is illustrated with reference to examples from the literature.

STRATEGIES FOR DEVELOPING PROMOTIONAL PERSPECTIVES

The amount that a company may spend on its total promotional effort, which consists of advertising, personal selling, and sales promotion, is not easy to determine. There are no unvarying standards to indicate how much should be spent on promotion in a given product/market situation. This is so because decisions about promotion expenditure are influenced by a complex set of circumstances.

Promotion-Expenditure Strategy

Promotion expenditure makes up one part of the total marketing budget. Thus, the allocation of funds to one department, such as advertising, affects the level of expenditure elsewhere within the marketing function. For example, a company may have to choose between additional expenditures on advertising or a new package design. In addition, the perspectives of promotion expenditure must be examined in the context of pricing strategy. A higher price obviously provides more funds for promotion than does a lower price. The amount set aside for promotion is also affected by the sales response to the product, which is very difficult to estimate accurately. A related matter is the question of the cumulative effect of promotion. The major emphasis of research in this area, even where the issue is far from being resolved, has been on the duration of advertising effects. Although it is generally accepted that the effects of advertising and maybe the effects of other forms of promotion as well may last over a long period, there is no certainty about the duration of these benefits. The cumulative effect depends on the loyalty of customers, frequency of purchase, and competitive efforts, each of which may be influenced in turn by a different set of variables.

Promotion expenditures vary from one product/market situation to another. Consider the case of McDonald's. It spent $185.9 million on television advertising in 1983, over twice as much as its rival Burger King. Yet the research showed that viewers remembered and liked Burger King's ads better than McDonald's. There is no way to be sure if McDonald's advertising budget was more than optimum. Similarly, the best-known and best-liked television ad in 1983 was for Miller Lite, a commercial showing people arguing whether Miller tasted great or was less filling. This campaign performed better than all other beer commercials even though several companies spent more money on their campaigns than Miller did.[1] Again, despite the ad's success, it is difficult to say if Miller's budget was optimum.

Promotion, however, is the key to success in many businesses. To illustrate this point, take the case of Isordil, a brand of nitrate prescribed to heart patients to prevent severe chest pains. Made by the Ives Laboratories division of the American Home Products Corporation, it was introduced in 1959 and has since grown to claim almost 50 percent of a $200-million-a-year market. Ives claims that Isordil is longer acting and in certain ways more effective than other nitrate drugs on the market. No matter that the Food and Drug Administration has not yet approved all of the manufacturer's claims nor that some doctors think that Isordil differs little from competing drugs, Ives has promoted its nitrate so aggressively for so long that many doctors think only of Isordil when they think of nitrates. The success of Isordil illustrates the key importance of promotion: "Indeed, the very survival of a drug in today's highly competitive marketplace often depends as much on a company's promotion talents as it does on the quality of its medicine."[2]

Promotion induces competitors to react, but there is no way to anticipate competitive response accurately, thus, it is difficult to decide on a budget. For example, during the decade from 1980 to 1990, the promotional costs of Anheuser-Busch rose by $6 a barrel of beer (from $3 in 1980 to $9 in 1990).[3] Although the company has been able to prevent Miller's inroads into its markets, the question remains if continuing to increase ad budgets is the best strategy.

Despite the difficulties involved, practitioners have developed rules of thumb for determining promotion expenditures that are strategically sound. These rules of thumb are of two types: they either take the form of a breakdown method or they employ the buildup method.

Breakdown Methods. There are a number of breakdown methods that can be helpful in determining promotion expenditures. Under the percentage-of-sales approach, promotion expenditure is a specified percentage of the previous year's or predicted future sales. Initially this percentage is arrived at by hunch. Later historical information is used to decide what percentage of sales should be allocated for promotion expenditure. The rationale behind the use of this approach is that expenditure on promotion must be justified by sales. This approach is followed by many companies because it is simple, it is easy to understand, and it gives managers the flexibility to cut corners during periods of economic slowdown. Among its flaws is the fact that basing promotion appropriation on sales puts the cart before the horse. Further, the logic of this approach fails to consider the cumulative effect of promotion. In brief, this approach considers promotion a necessary expenditure that must be apportioned from sales revenue without considering the relationship of promotion to competitor's activities or its influence on sales revenues.

Another approach for allocating promotion expenditure is to spend as much as can be afforded. In this approach, the availability of funds or liquid resources is the main consideration in making a decision about promotion expenditure. In other words, even if a company's sales expectations are high, the level of promotion is kept low if its cash position is tight. This approach can be questioned on several grounds. It makes promotion expenditures dependent on a company's liquid resources when the best move for a cash-short company may be to spend more on promotion with the hope of improving sales. Further, this approach involves an element of risk. At a time when the market is tight and sales are slow, a company may spend more on promotion if it happens to have resources available. This approach does, however, consider the fact that promotion outlays have long-term value; that is, advertising has a cumulative effect. Also, under conditions of complete uncertainty, this approach is a cautious one.

Under the return-on-investment approach, promotion expenditures are considered as an investment, the benefits of which are derived over the years. Thus, as in the case of any other investment, the appropriate level of promotion expenditure is determined by comparing the expected return with the desired return. The expected return on promotion may be computed by using present values of future returns. Inasmuch as some promotion is likely to produce immediate results, the total promotion expenditure may be partitioned between current expense and investment. Alternatively, the entire promotion expenditure can be considered an investment, in which case the immediate effect of promotion can be conceived as a return in period zero. The basic validity and soundness of the return-on-investment approach cannot be disputed. But there are several problems in its application. First, it may be difficult to determine the outcomes of different forms of promotion over time. Second, what is the appropriate return to be expected from an advertising investment? These limitations put severe constraints on the practical use of this approach.

The competitive-parity approach assumes that promotion expenditure is directly related to market share. The promotion expenditure of a firm should, therefore, be in proportion to that of competitors in order to maintain its position in the market. Thus, if the leader in the industry allocates 2 percent of its sales revenue for advertising, other members of the industry should spend about the same percentage of their sales on advertising. Considering the competitive nature of our economy, this seems a reasonable approach. It has, however, a number of limitations. First, the approach requires a knowledge of competitors' perspectives on promotion, and this information may not always be available. For example, the market leader may have decided to put its emphasis not on promotion per se but on reducing prices. Following this firm's lead in advertising expenditures without reference to its prices would be an unreliable guide. Second, one firm may get more for its promotion dollar through judicious selection of media, timing of advertising, skillful preparation of ads, a good sales supervision program, and so on. Thus it could realize the same results as another firm that has twice as much to spend. Because promotion is just one of the variables affecting market performance, simply maintaining promotional parity with competitors may not be enough for a firm to preserve its market share.

Buildup Method. Many companies have advertising, sales, and sales promotion (merchandising) managers who report to the marketing manager. The marketing manager specifies the objectives of promotion separately for the advertising, personal selling, and sales promotion of each product line. Ideally the spadework of defining objectives should be done by a committee consisting of executives concerned with product development, pricing distribution, and promotion. Committee work helps incorporate inputs from different areas; thus, a decision about promotion expenditure is made in the context of the total marketing mix. For example, the committee may decide that promotion should be undertaken to expose at least 100,000 households to the product; institutional customers may be sought through reductions in price.

In practice it may not always be easy to pinpoint the separate roles of advertising, personal selling, and sales promotion because these three methods of promotion usually overlap to some degree. Each company must work out its own rules for a promotion mix. Once the tasks to be performed by each method of promotion have been designated, they may be defined formally as objectives and communicated to the respective managers. On the basis of these objectives, each promotion manager probably redefines his or her own goals in more operational terms. These redefined objectives then become the modus operandi of each department.

Once departmental objectives have been defined, each area works out a detailed budget, costing each item required to accomplish the objectives of the program. As each department prepares its own budget, the marketing manager may also prepare a summary budget for each of them, simply listing the major expenditures in light of the overall marketing strategy. A marketing manager's budget is primarily a control device.

When individual departments have arrived at their estimates of necessary allocation, the marketing manager meets with each of them to approve budgets. At that time, the marketing manager's own estimates help assess department budgets. Finally, an appropriation is made to each department. Needless to say, the emphasis on different tasks is revised and the total budget refigured several times before an acceptable program emerges. A committee instead of just the marketing manager may approve the final appropriation for each department.

The buildup method forces managers to analyze scientifically the role they expect promotion to play and the contribution it can make toward achieving marketing objectives. It also helps maintain control over promotion expenditure and avoid the frustrations often faced by promotion managers as a result of cuts in promotion appropriations due to economic slowdown. On the other hand, this approach can become overly scientific. Sometimes profit opportunities that require additional promotion expenditure may appear unannounced. Involvement with the objective and task exercise to decide how much more should be spent on promotion takes time, perhaps leading to the loss of an unexpected opportunity.

Promotion Mix Strategy

Another strategic decision in the area of promotion concerns the allocation of effort among the three different methods of promotion. **Advertising** refers to nonpersonal communication transmitted through the mass media (radio, television, print, outdoors, and mail). The communication is identified with a sponsor who compensates the media for the transmission. **Personal selling** refers to face-to-face interaction with the customer. Unlike advertising, personal selling involves communication in both directions, from the source to the destination and back. All other forms of communication with the customer other than those included in advertising and personal selling constitute **sales promotion**. Thus, coupons, samples, demonstrations, exhibits, premiums, sweepstakes, trade allowances, sales and dealer incentives, cents-off packs, rebates, and point-of-purchase material are all sales promotion devices.

A variety of new ways have been developed to communicate with customers. These include telemarketing (i.e., telephone selling) and demonstration centers (i.e., specially designed showrooms to allow customers to observe and try out complex industrial equipment).[4] The discussion in this chapter will be limited to the three traditional methods of promotion. In some cases, the three types of promotion may be largely interchangeable; however, they should be blended judiciously to complement each other for a balanced promotional perspective.[5] Illustrated below is the manner in which a chemical company mixed advertising with personal selling and sales promotion to achieve optimum promotional performance:

> An advertising campaign aimed at customer industries, employees, and plant communities carried the theme, "The little chemical giant." It appeared in *Adhesive Age, American Paint & Coating Journal, Chemical & Engineering News, Chemical Marketing Reporter, Chemical Purchasing, Chemical Week, Modern Plastics,* and *Plastics World.*
>
> Sales promotion and personal selling were supported by publicity. Editorial tours of the company's new plants, programs to develop employee understanding and involvement in the expansion, and briefings for local people in towns and cities where USIC [the company] had facilities provided a catalyst for publicity.
>
> Personal selling was aggressive and provided direct communication about the firm's continued service. USIC reassured producers of ethyl alcohol, vinyl acetate monomer, and polyethylene that "we will not lose personal touch with our customers."[6]

Development of an optimum promotion mix is by no means easy. Companies often use haphazard seat-of-the-pants procedures to determine the respective roles of advertising, personal selling, and sales promotion in a product/market situation.

Decisions about the promotional mix are often diffused among many decision makers, impeding the formation of a unified promotion strategy. Personal selling plans are sometimes divorced from the planning of advertising and sales promotion. Frequently decision makers are not adequately aware of the objectives and broad strategies of the overall product program that the promotion plan is designed to implement. Sales and market share goals tend to be constant, regardless of decreases or increases in promotional expenditures. Thus they are unrealistic as guides and directives for planning, as criteria for promotional effectiveness, or even as a fair basis for application of the judgment of decision makers. Briefly, the present state of the art in the administration of the promotion function is such that cause-and-effect relationships as well as other basic insights are not sufficiently understood to permit knowledgeable forecasts of what to expect from alternate courses of action. Even identifying feasible alternatives can prove difficult.

A variety of factors should be considered to determine the appropriate promotion mix in a particular product/market situation. These factors may be categorized as product factors, market factors, customer factors, budget factors, and marketing mix factors, as outlined in Exhibit 17-1.

Product Factors. Factors in this category relate principally to the way in which a product is bought, consumed, and perceived by the customer. For industrial goods, especially technical products, personal selling is more significant than advertising because these goods usually need to be inspected and compared before being bought. Salespeople can explain the workings of a product and provide on-the-spot answers to customer queries. For customer goods such as cosmetics and processed foods, advertising is of primary importance. In

EXHIBIT 17-1
Criteria for Determining Promotion Mix

Product Factors
1. Nature of product
2. Perceived risk
3. Durable versus nondurable
4. Typical purchase amount

Market Factors
1. Position in its life cycle
2. Market share
3. Industry concentration
4. Intensity of competition
5. Demand perspectives

Customer Factors
1. Household versus business customers
2. Number of customers
3. Concentration of customers

Budget Factors
1. Financial resources of the organization
2. Traditional promotional perspectives

Marketing Mix Factors
1. Relative price/relative quality
2. Distribution strategy
3. Brand life cycle
4. Geographic scope of market

addition, advertising plays a dominant role for products that provide an opportunity for differentiation and for those being purchased with emotional motives.

The perceived risk of a purchase decision is another variable here. Generally speaking, the more risk a buyer perceives to be associated with buying a particular product, the higher the importance of personal selling over advertising. A buyer generally desires specific information on a product when the perceived risk is high. This necessitates an emphasis on personal selling.[7] Durable goods are bought less frequently than nondurables and usually require a heavy commitment of resources. These characteristics make personal selling of greater significance for durable goods than advertising. However, because many durable goods are sold through franchised dealerships, the influence of each type of promotion should be determined in light of the additional push it would provide in moving the product. Finally, products purchased in small quantities are presumably purchased frequently and require routine decision making. For these products, advertising should be preferable to personal selling. Often such products are of low value; therefore, a profitable business in these products can only be conducted on volume. This underlines the importance of advertising in this case.

Market Factors. The first market factor is the position of a product in its life cycle. The creation of primary demand, hitherto nonexistent, is the primary task during the introductory stage; therefore, a great promotion effort is needed to explain a new product to potential customers. For consumer goods in the introductory stage, the major thrust is on heavy advertising supported by missionary selling to help distributors move the product. In addition, different devices of sales promotion (e.g., sampling, couponing, free demonstrations) are employed to entice the customer to try the product. In the case of industrial products, personal selling alone is useful during this period. During the growth phase, there is increasing demand, which means enough business for all competitors. In the case of consumer goods, however, the promotional effort shifts to reliance on advertising. Industrial goods, on the other hand, begin to be advertised as the market broadens. However, they continue to require a personal selling effort. In the maturity phase, competition becomes intense, and advertising, along with sales promotion, is required to differentiate the product (a consumer good) from competitive brands and to provide an incentive to the customer to buy a particular product. Industrial goods during maturity call for intensive personal selling. During the decline phase, the promotional effort does not vary much initially from that during the maturity phase except that the intensity of promotion declines. Later, as price competition becomes keen and demand continues to decline, overall promotional perspectives are reduced.

For a given product class, if market share is high, both advertising and personal selling are used. If the market share is low, the emphasis is placed on either personal selling or advertising. This is because high market share seems to indicate that the company does business in more than one segment and uses multiple channels of distribution. Thus, both personal selling and advertising are used to promote the product. Where market share is low, the perspectives of the business are limited, and either advertising or personal selling will suffice, depending on the nature of the product.

If the industry is concentrated among a few firms, advertising has additional significance for two reasons: (a) heavy advertising may help discourage other firms from entering the field, and (b) heavy advertising sustains a desired position for the product in the market. Heavy advertising constitutes an implied warranty of product performance and perhaps decreases the uncertainty consumers associate with new products. In this way new competition is discouraged and existing positions are reinforced.

Intensity of competition tends to affect promotional blending in the same way that market share does. When competition is keen, all three types of promotion are needed to sustain a product's position in the market. This is because promotion is needed to inform, remind, and persuade customers to buy the product. On the other hand, if competitive activity is limited, the major function of promotion is to inform and perhaps remind customers about the product. Thus, either advertising or personal selling is emphasized.

Hypothetically, advertising is more suited for products that have relatively latent demand. This is because advertising investment should open up new opportunities in the long run, and if the carryover effect is counted, expenditure per sales dollar would be more beneficial. If demand is limited and new demand is not expected to be created, advertising outlay would be uneconomical. Thus, future potential becomes a significant factor in determining the role of advertising.

Customer Factors. One of the major dimensions used to differentiate businesses is whether products are marketed for household consumption or for organizational use. There are several significant differences in the way products are marketed to these two customer groups, and these differences exert considerable influence on the type of promotion that should be used. In the case of household customers, it is relatively easy to identify the decision maker for a particular product; therefore, advertising is more desirable. Also, the self-service nature of many consumer-product sales makes personal selling relatively unimportant. Finally, household customers do not ordinarily go through a formal buying process using objective criteria as organizational customers do. This again makes advertising more useful for reaching household customers. Essentially the same reasons make personal selling more relevant in promoting a product among organizational customers.

The number of customers and their geographic concentration also influence promotional blending. For a small customer base, especially if it is geographically concentrated, advertising does not make as much sense as it does in cases where customers are widely scattered and represent a significant mass. Caution is needed here because some advertising may always be necessary for consumer goods, no matter what the market perspectives are. Thus, these statements provide only a conceptual framework and should not be interpreted as exact yes/no criteria.

Budget Factors. Ideally, the budget should be based on the promotional tasks to be performed. However, intuitively and traditionally, companies place an upper limit on the amount that they spend on promotion. Such limits may influence the type of promotion that may be undertaken in two ways. First, a financially weak company is constrained in undertaking certain types of promotion. For example, television advertising necessitates a heavy commitment of resources. Second, in many companies the advertising budget is, by tradition, linked to revenues as a percentage. This method of allocation continues to be used so that expected revenues indicate how much may be spent on advertising in the future. The allocated funds, then, automatically determine the role of advertising.

Marketing Mix Factors. The promotion decision should be made in the context of other aspects of the marketing mix. The price and quality of a product relative to competition affect the nature of its promotional perspectives. Higher prices must be justified to the consumer by actual or presumed product superiority. Thus, in the case of a product that is priced substantially higher than competing goods, advertising achieves significance in communicating and establishing the product's superior quality in the minds of customers.

The promotion mix is also influenced by the distribution structure employed for the product. If the product is distributed directly, the sales force can largely be counted on to promote the product. Indirect distribution, on the other hand, requires greater emphasis on advertising because the push of a sales force is limited. As a matter of fact, the further the manufacturer is from the ultimate user, the greater the need for the advertising effort to stimulate and maintain demand. The influence of the distribution strategy may be illustrated with reference to two cosmetics companies that deal in similar products, Revlon and Avon. Revlon distributes its products through different types of intermediaries and advertises them heavily. Avon, on the other hand, distributes primarily directly to end users in their homes and spends less on advertising relative to Revlon.

Earlier we examined the effect on the promotion mix of a product's position in its life cycle. The position of a brand in its life cycle also influences promotional perspectives. Positioning a new brand in the desired slot in the market during its introduction phase requires a higher degree of advertising. As a product enters the growth phase, advertising should be blended with personal selling. In the growth phase, the overall level of promotion declines in scope. When an existing brand reaches the maturity phase in its life cycle, the marketer has three options: to employ life-extension strategies, to harvest the brand for profits, and/or to introduce a new brand that may be targeted at a more specific segment of the market. The first two options were discussed in chapter 13. As far as the third option is concerned, for promotional purposes, the new brand will have to be treated like a new product.

Finally, the geographic scope of the market to be served is another consideration. Advertising, relatively speaking, is more significant for products marketed nationally than for those marketed locally or regionally. When the market is geographically limited, one study showed that even spot television advertising proved to be more expensive vis-à-vis the target group exposures gained.[8] Thus, because advertising is an expensive proposition, regional marketers should rely less on advertising and more on other forms of promotion, or they should substitute another element of the marketing mix for it. For example, a regional marketer may manufacture private label brands.

Conclusion

Although these factors are helpful in establishing roles for different methods of promotion, actual appropriation among them should take into consideration the effect of any changes in the environment. For example, in the 1970s soft drink companies frequently used sales promotion (mainly cents off) to vie for customers. In the 1980s, however, the markers of soft drinks changed their promotion mix strategy to concentrate more on advertising. This is evidenced by the fact that the five largest soft drink makers spent about $250 million on advertising in 1984, 40 percent more than they spent in 1979. One reason for this change in promotional perspective was the realization that price discounting hurt brand loyalties; because Coke and Pepsi had turned their colas into commodities by means of cents-off promotion, the consumer now shopped for price.[9]

In addition, the promotion mix may also be affected by a desire to be innovative. For example, Puritan Fashions Corporation, an apparel company, traditionally spent little on advertising. In the late 1970s the company was continually losing money. Then, in 1977, the company introduced a new product, body-hugging jeans, and employed an unconventional promotion strategy. It placed Calvin Klein's label on its jeans, sold them as a prestige trouser priced at $35 (double the price of nonlabeled styles), and advertised them heavily. This promotion mix provided the company with instant success. Although Puritan had no previous experience with jeans, the company's production soared to 125,000 pairs a week within one year, giving Puritan a 25 percent share of a $1-billion retail market.[10] Although promotional innovation may not last long because competitors may soon copy it, it does provide the innovator with a head start.

Promotional blending requires consideration of a large number of variables, as outlined above. Unfortunately, it is difficult to assign quantitative values to the effect that these variables have on promotion. Thus, decisions about promotional blending must necessarily be made subjectively. These factors, however, provide a checklist for reviewing the soundness and viability of subjective decisions.

Recent research conducted by the Strategic Planning Institute for Cahners Publishing Co. identified the following decision rules that can be used in formulating ad budgets. These rules may be helpful in finalizing promotion mix decisions.[11]

1. **Market share**—A company that has a higher market share generally has to spend more on advertising to maintain its share.
2. **Sales from new products**—If a company has a high percentage of its sales resulting from new products, it has to spend more on advertising compared to companies that have well-established products.
3. **Market growth**—Companies competing in fast-growing markets should spend comparatively more on advertising.
4. **Plant capacity**—If a company has a lot of unused plant capacity, it should spend more on advertising to stimulate sales and production.
5. **Unit price (per sales transaction)**—The lower the unit price of a company's products, the more it should spend on advertising because of the greater likelihood of brand switching.
6. **Importance of product to customers (in relation to their total purchases)**—Products that constitute a lower proportion of customers' purchases generally require higher advertising expenditures.
7. **Product price**—Both very high-priced (or premium) products and very low-priced (or discount) products require higher ad expenditures because, in both cases, price is an important factor in the buying decision and the buyer has to be convinced (through advertising) that the product is a good value.
8. **Product quality**—Higher-quality products require a greater advertising effort because of the need to convince the consumer that the product is unique.
9. **Breadth of product line**—Companies with a broad line of products have to spend more on advertising compared to companies with specialized product lines.

10. **Degree of standardization**—Standardized products produced in large quantities should be backed by higher advertising outlays because they are likely to have more competition in the market.

ADVERTISING STRATEGIES

Media may be defined as those channels through which messages concerning a product or service are transmitted to targets. The following media are available to advertisers: newspapers, magazines, television, radio, outdoor advertising, transit advertising, and direct mail.

Media-Selection Strategy

Selection of an advertising medium is influenced by such factors as the product or service itself, the target market, the extent and type of distribution, the type of message to be communicated, the budget, and competitors' advertising strategies. Except for the advertising perspectives employed by the competition, information on most of these factors is presumably available inside the company. It may be necessary to undertake a marketing research project to find out what sorts of advertising strategies competitors have used in the past and what might be expected of them in the future. In addition, selection of a medium also depends on the advertising objectives for the product/market concerned. With this information in place, different methods may be used to select a medium.

Advertising Objectives. To build a good advertising program, it is necessary first to pinpoint the objectives of the ad campaign. It would be wrong to assume that all advertising leads directly to sales. A sale is a multiphase phenomenon, and advertising can be used to transfer the customer from one phase to the next: from unawareness of a product or service, to awareness, to comprehension, to conviction, to action. Thus, the advertiser must specify at what stage or stages he or she wants advertising to work. The objectives of advertising may be defined by any one of the following approaches: inventory approach, hierarchy approach, or attitudinal approach.

Inventory Approach. A number of scholars have articulated inventories of functions performed by advertising. The objectives of an ad campaign may be defined from an inventory based on a firm's overall marketing perspective. For example, the following inventory may be used to develop a firm's advertising objectives:

A. Increase sales by

1. Encouraging potential purchasers to visit the company or its dealers
2. Obtaining leads for salespeople or dealers
3. Inducing professional people (e.g., doctors, architects) to recommend the product
4. Securing new distributors
5. Prompting immediate purchases through announcements of special sales and contests

B. Create an awareness about a company's product or service by

1. Informing potential customers about product features
2. Announcing new models
3. Highlighting the unique features of the product
4. Informing customers as to where the product may be bought
5. Announcing price changes
6. Demonstrating the product in use

The inventory approach is helpful in highlighting the fact that different objectives can be emphasized in advertising and that these objectives cannot be selected without reference to the overall marketing plan. Thus, this approach helps the advertiser avoid operating in a vacuum. However, inherent in this approach is the danger that the decision maker may choose nonfeasible and conflicting objectives if everything listed in an inventory seems worth pursuing.

Hierarchy Approach. Following this approach, the objectives of advertising should be stated in an action-oriented psychological form. Thus, the objectives of advertising may be defined as (a) gaining customers' initial attention, perception, continued favorable attention, and interest; or (b) affecting customers' comprehension, feeling, emotion, motivation, belief, intentions, decision, imagery, association, recall, and recognition. The thesis behind this approach is that customers move from one psychological state to another before actually buying a product. Thus, the purpose of advertising should be to move customers from state to state and ultimately toward purchasing the product. Although it makes sense to define the purpose of an individual ad in hierarchical terms, it may be difficult to relate the purpose so defined to marketing goals. Besides, measurement of psychological states that form the basis of this approach is difficult and subjective compared to the measurement of goals such as market share.

Attitudinal Approach. According to this approach, advertising is instrumental in producing changes in attitudes; therefore, advertising goals should be defined to influence attitudinal structures. Thus advertising may be undertaken to accomplish any of the following goals:

1. Affect those forces that influence strongly the choice of criteria used for evaluating brands belonging to the product class.
2. Add characteristic(s) to those considered salient for the product class.
3. Increase/decrease the rating for a salient product class characteristic.
4. Change the perception of the company's brand with regard to some particular salient product characteristic.
5. Change the perception of competitive brands with regard to some particular salient product characteristic.

The attitudinal approach is an improvement over the hierarchical approach because it attempts to relate advertising objectives to product/market objectives. This approach indicates not only the functions advertising performs, it also targets the specific results it can achieve.

Advertising objectives should be defined by a person completely familiar with all product/market perspectives. A good definition of objectives aids in the writing of appropriate ad copy and in selecting the right media. It should be recognized that different ad campaigns for the same product can have varied objectives. But all ad campaigns should be complementary to each other to maximize total advertising impact.

Product/market advertising objectives may be used to derive media objectives. Media objectives should be defined so as to answer such questions as Are we trying to reach everybody? Are we aiming to be selective? If housewives under 30 with children under 10 are really our target, what media objectives should we develop? Are we national or regional? Do we need to concentrate in selected counties? Do we need reach or frequency or both? Are there creative considerations to control our thinking? Do we need color or permanence (which might mean magazines and supplements), personalities and demonstration (which might mean television), the best reminder for the least money (which might mean radio or outdoor), superselectivity (which might mean direct mail), or going all the way up and down in the market (which could mean newspapers)? The following is a list of sample media objectives based on these questions:

1. We need a national audience of women.
2. We want them between 18 and 34.
3. Because the product is a considered purchase, we need room to explain it thoroughly.
4. We need color to show the product to best advantage.
5. We have to keep after these women more than once, so we need frequency.
6. There's no way to demonstrate the product except in a store.

Media-Selection Procedure. Media selection calls for two decisions: (a) which particular medium to use and (b), within a given medium, which specific vehicles to choose. For example, if magazines are to be used, in which particular magazines should ads be placed? The following two approaches can be used in media selection: cost-per-thousand-contacts comparison and matching of audience and medium characteristics.

Cost-per-Thousand-Contacts Comparison. The cost-per-thousand-contacts comparison has traditionally been the most popular method of media selection. Although simple to apply, the cost-per-thousand method leaves much to be desired. Basing media selection entirely on the number of contacts to be reached ignores the quality of contacts made. For example, an advertisement for a women's dress line appearing in *Vogue* would make a greater impact on those exposed to it than would the same ad appearing in *True Confessions*. Similarly, *Esquire* would perhaps be more appropriate than many less-specialized magazines for introducing men's fashions.

Further, the cost-per-thousand method can be highly misleading if one considers the way in which advertisers define the term *exposure*. According to the media definition, exposure occurs as soon as an ad is inserted in the magazine. Whether the exposure actually occurs is never considered. This method also fails to consider editorial images and the impact power of different channels of a medium.

Matching of Audience and Media Characteristics. An alternative approach to media selection is to specify the target audience and match its characteristics to a particular medium. A step-by-step procedure for using this method is described below:

1. Build a profile of customers, detailing who they are, where they are located, when they can be reached, and what their demographic characteristics are. Setting media objectives (discussed earlier) is helpful in building customer profiles.
2. Study media profiles in terms of audience coverage. Implicit in this step is the study of the audience's media habits (i.e., an examination of who constitutes a particular medium's audience).
3. Match customer profiles to media profiles. The customer characteristics for a product should be matched to the audience characteristics of different media. This comparison should lead to the preliminary selection of a medium, based primarily on the grounds of coverage.
4. The preliminary selection should be examined further in regard to product and cost considerations. For some products, other things being equal, one medium is superior to another. For example, in the case of beauty aids, a product demonstration is helpful; hence, television would be a better choice than radio. Cost is another concern in media selection; information on cost is available from the media themselves. Cost should be balanced against the benefit expected from the campaign under consideration.
5. Finally, the total budget should be allocated to different media and to various media vehicles. The final selection of a medium should maximize the achievement of media objectives. For example, if the objective is to make people aware of a product, then the medium selected should be the one that reaches a wide audience.

Basically, two types of information are required for media selection: customer profile and audience characteristics. The advertiser should build a customer profile for his or her product/market. Information about various media is usually available from media owners. Practically all media owners have complete information available to them concerning their audiences (demographics and circulation figures). Each medium, however, presents the information in a way that makes it look best. It is desirable, therefore, to validate the audience information supplied by media owners with data from bureaus that audit various media. The Audit Bureau of Circulations, the Traffic Audit Bureau, and the Business Publications Audit of Circulation are examples of such audit bureaus.

Evaluation Criteria. Before money is committed to a selected medium, it is desirable to review the medium's viability against evaluation criteria. Is the decision maker being thorough, progressive (imaginative), measure-minded, practical, and optimistic? Thoroughness requires that all aspects of media selection be given full consideration. For maximum impact, the chosen medium should be progressive: it should have a unique way of doing the job. An example of progressiveness is putting a sample envelope of Sanka coffee in millions of copies of *TV Guide.* Because of postal regulations, this sampling could not be done in a magazine that is purchased primarily through subscriptions. But *TV Guide* is mainly a newsstand magazine. Measure-mindedness refers to more than just the number of exposures. It refers not only to frequency and timing in reaching the target audience but also to the quality of the audience; that is, to the proportion of heavy to light television viewers reached, proportion of men to women, working to nonworking women, and so on. Practicality requires choosing a medium on factual, not emotional, grounds. For example, it is not desirable to substitute a weak newspaper for a strong one just because the top management of the company does not agree with the editorial policy of the latter. Finally, the overall media plan should be optimistic in that it takes advantage of lessons learned from experience.

Advertising-Copy Strategy

Copy refers to the content of an advertisement. In the advertising industry, the term is sometimes used in a broad sense to include the words, pictures, symbols, colors, layout, and other ingredients of an ad. Copywriting is a creative job, and its quality depends to a large extent on the creative ability of writers in the advertising agency or in the company. However, creativity alone may not produce good ad copy. A marketing strategist needs to have his or her own perspectives incorporated in the copy (what to say, how to say it, and to whom to say it) and needs to furnish information on ad objectives, product, target customers, competitive activity, and ethical and legal considerations. The creative person carries on from there. In brief, although copywriting may be the outcome of a flash of inspiration on the part of an advertising genius, it must rest on a systematic, logical, step-by-step presentation of ideas.

This point may be illustrated with reference to Perrier, a brand of bottled water that comes from mineral springs located in southern France. In Europe this product has been quite popular for some years; in the United States, however, it used to be available in gourmet shops only. In 1977 the company introduced the product to the U.S. market as a soft drink by tapping the adult user market with heavy advertising. Perrier's major product distinction is that its water is naturally carbonated spring water. The product was aimed at the affluent adult population, particularly those concerned with diet and health, as a status symbol and a sign of maturity. Perrier faced competition from two sources: regular soft drink makers and potential makers of mineral water. The company took care of its soft drink competition by segmenting the market on the basis of price (Perrier was priced 50 percent above the average soft drink) and thus avoided direct confrontation. In regard to competition from new brands of mineral water, Perrier's association with France and the fact that it is constituted of naturally carbonated spring water were expected to continue as viable strengths. This information was used to develop ad copy for placement in high-fashion women's magazines and in television commercials narrated by Orson Welles. The results were astonishing. In less than five years, Perrier became a major liquid drink in the U.S. market.[12]

Essentially, ad copy constitutes an advertiser's message to the customer. To ensure that the proper message gets across, it is important that there is no distortion of the message because of what in communication theory is called *noise.* Noise may emerge from three sources: (a) dearth of facts (e.g., the company is unaware of the unique distinctions of its product), (b) competitors (e.g., competitors make changes in their marketing mix to counter the company's claims or position), and (c) behavior traits of the customers or audience. Failure to take into account the last source of noise is often the missing link in developing ad copy. It is not safe to assume that one's own perspectives on what appeals to the audience are accurate. It is desirable, therefore, to gain, through some sort of marketing research, insights into behavior patterns of the audience and to make this information available to the copywriter. For example, based on his research, Schiele provides the following clues for making an effective appeal to young customers:

1. Never talk down to a teenager. While "hip" phraseology and the generally flippant tone observed in the teenager's conversation may be coin of the realm from one youngster to another, it comes across as phony, foolish, and condescending when directed at him or her by an advertiser. Sincerity is infinitely more effective than cuteness. Entertainment and attention-getting approaches by themselves do little to attract a teenager to the merits of a product. In fact, they often dissuade the youngster from making a purchase decision.
2. Be totally, absolutely, and unswervingly straightforward. Teenagers may act cocky and confident in front of adults, but most of them are still rather unsure of themselves and are wary of being misled. They are not sure they know enough to avoid being taken advantage of, and they do not like to risk looking foolish by falling for a commercial gimmick. Moreover, teenagers as a group are far more suspicious of things commercial than adults are. Advertising must not only be noticed; it has to be believed.
3. Give the teenager credit for being motivated by rational values. When making a buying selection, adults like to think they are doing so on the basis of the benefits the product or service offers. Teenagers instinctively perceive what's "really there" in an offering. Advertising must clearly expose for their consideration the value a product or service claims to represent.
4. Be as personal as possible. Derived from the adult world of marketing, this rule has an exaggerated importance with teenagers. In this automated age, with so many complaining of being reduced en masse to anonymity, people are becoming progressively more aware of their own individuality. The desire to be personally known and recognized is particularly strong with young people, who are urgently searching for a clear sense of their own identity.[13]

Findings from communications research are helpful in further refining the attributes of ad copy that an advertising strategist needs to spell out for the copywriter.

Source Credibility. An ad may show a celebrity recommending the use of a product. It is hoped that this endorsement will help give the ad additional credibility, credibility that will be reflected in higher sales.

Research on the subject has shown that an initially credible source, such as Miss America claiming to use a certain brand of hair spray, is more effective in changing the opinion of an audience than if a similar claim is made by a lesser-known source, such as a unknown homemaker. However, as time passes, the audience tends to forget the source or to dissociate the source from the message.[14] Some consumers who might have been swayed in favor of a particular brand because it was recommended by Miss America may revert to their original choice, whereas those who did not initially accept the homemaker's word may later become favorably inclined toward the product she is recommending. The decreasing importance of the source behind a message over time has been called the **sleeper effect.**[15]

Several conclusions can be drawn from the sleeper effect. In some cases it may be helpful if the advertiser is disassociated as much as possible from the ad, particularly when the audience may perceive that a manufacturer is trying to push something.[16] On the other hand, when source credibility is important, advertisements should be scheduled so that the source may reappear to reinforce the message.

Balance of Argument. When preparing copy, there is a question of whether only the good and distinctive features of a brand should be highlighted or whether its demerits should be mentioned as well. Traditionally, the argument has been, "Put your best foot forward." In other words, messages should be designed to emphasize only the favorable aspects of a product. Recent research in the field of communication has questioned the validity of indiscriminately detailing the favorable side. It has been found that

1. Presenting both sides of an issue is more effective than giving only one side among individuals who are initially opposed to the point of view being presented.
2. Better-educated people are more favorably affected by presentation of both sides; poorly educated persons are more favorably affected by communication that gives only supporting arguments.
3. For those already convinced of the point of view presented, the presentation of both sides is less effective than a presentation featuring only those items favoring the general position being advanced.
4. Presentation of both sides is least effective among the poorly educated who are already convinced of the position advocated.
5. Leaving out a relevant argument is more noticeable and detracts more from effectiveness when both sides are presented than when only the side favorable to the proposition is being advanced.[17]

These findings have important implications for developing copy. If one is trying to reach executive customers through an ad in the *Harvard Business Review,* it probably is better to present both favorable and unfavorable qualities of a product. On the other hand, for such status products and services as Rolex diamond watches and Chanel No. 5 perfume, emphasis on both pros and cons can distort the image. Thus, when status is already established, a simple message is more desirable.

Message Repetition. Should the same message be repeated time and again? According to learning theory, reinforcement over time from different directions increases learning. It has been said that a good slogan never dies and that repetition is the surest way of getting the message across. However, some feel that, although the central theme should be maintained, a message should be presented with variations.

Communication research questions the value of wholesale repetition. Repetition, it has been found, leads to increased learning up to a certain point. Thereafter learning levels off and may, in fact, change to boredom and loss of attention. Continuous repetition may even counteract the good effect created earlier. Thus, advertisers must keep track of the shape of the learning curve and develop a new product theme when the curve appears to be flattening out. The Coca-Cola Company, for example, regularly changes its message to maintain audience interest.[18]

1886—Drink Coca-Cola
1905—Coca-Cola revives and sustains
1906—The Great National Temperance Beverage
1922—Thirst knows no season
1925—Six million a day
1927—Around the corner from everywhere
1929—The pause that refreshes
1938—The best friend thirst ever had
1948—Where there's Coke there's hospitality
1949—Along the highway to anywhere
1952—What you want is a Coke
1956—Makes good things taste better
1957—Sign of good taste
1958—The cold, crisp taste of Coke
1963—Things go better with Coke
1970—It's the real thing
1971—I'd like to buy the world a Coke
1975—Look up, America
1976—Coke adds life
1979—Have a Coke and a smile
1982—Coke is it
1985—We've got a taste for you
1986—Catch the wave
1987—When Coca-Cola is a part of your life, you can't beat the feeling
1988—Can't beat the feeling

Rational versus Emotional Appeals. Results of studies on the effect of rational and emotional appeals presented in advertisements are not conclusive. Some studies show that emotional appeals have definite positive results.[19] However, arousing emotions may not be sufficient unless the ad can rationally convince the subject that the product in question will fulfill a need. It appears that emphasis on one type of appeal—rational or emotional—is not enough. The advertiser must strike a balance between emotional and rational appeals. For example, Procter and Gamble's Crest toothpaste ad, "Crest has been recommended by the American Dental Association," has a rational content; but its reference to cavity prevention also excites emotions. Similarly, a Close-up toothpaste ad produced for Lever Brothers is primarily emotional in nature: "Put your money where your mouth is." However, it also has an economic aspect: "Use Close-up both as a toothpaste and mouthwash."

An example of how emotional appeal complemented by service created a market niche for an unknown company is provided by Singapore Airlines. Singapore is a Southeast Asian nation barely larger than Cleveland. Many airlines have tried to sell the notion that they have something unique to offer, but not many have succeeded. Singapore Airlines, however, thrives mainly on the charm of its cabin attendants, who serve passengers with warm smiles and copious attention. A gently persuasive advertising campaign glamorizes the attendants and tries to convey the idea of in-flight pleasure of a lyrical quality. Most of the airline's ads are essentially large soft-focus color photographs of various attendants. A commercial announces: "Singapore girl, you look so good I want to stay up here with you forever." Of course, its emotional appeals are duly supported by excellent service (rational appeals to complement emotional ones). The airline provides gifts, free cocktails, and free French wines and brandy even to economy-class passengers. Small wonder that it flies with an above-average load factor—higher than that of any other major international carrier. In brief, emotional appeal can go a long way in the development of an effective ad campaign, but it must have rational underpinnings to support it.

Comparison Advertising. Comparison advertising refers to the comparison of one brand with one or more competitive brands by explicitly naming them on a variety of specific product or service attributes. Comparison advertising became popular in the early 1970s; today one finds comparison ads for all forms of goods and services. Although it is debatable whether comparative ads are more or less effective than individual ads, limited research on the subject indicates that in some cases comparative ads are more useful.[20]

Many companies have successfully used comparison advertising. One that stands out is Helene Curtis Industries. The company used comparison ads on television for its Suave brand of shampoo. The ads said: "We do what theirs does for less than half the price." Competitors were either named or their labels were clearly shown. The message—that Suave is comparable to top-ranking shampoos—was designed to allay public suspicion that low-priced merchandise is somehow shoddy. The campaign was so successful that within a few years Suave's sales surpassed those of both Procter and Gamble's Head and Shoulders and Johnson & Johnson's Baby Shampoo in volume. The company continues to use the same approach in its advertising today. Comparison advertising clearly provides an underdog with the chance to catch up with the leader.

In using comparison advertising, a company should make sure that its claim of superiority will hold up in a court of law. More businesses today are counterattacking by suing when rivals mention their products in ads or promotions. For example, MCI has sought to stop an AT&T ad campaign (aimed at MCI) that claims that AT&T's long-distance and other services are better and cheaper.[21]

PERSONAL SELLING STRATEGIES

Selling Strategy There was a time when the problems of selling were simpler than they are today. Recent years have produced a variety of changes in the selling strategies of businesses. The complexities involved in selling in the 1990s are different than those in the 1980s. As an example, today a high-principled style of selling that favors a close, trusting, long-term relationship over a quick sell is recommended. The philosophy is to serve the customer as a consultant, not as a peddler.[22] Discussed below are objectives and strategic matters pertaining to selling strategies.

Objectives. Selling objectives should be derived from overall marketing objectives and should be properly linked with promotional objectives. For example, if the marketing goal is to raise the current 35 percent market share in a product line to 40 percent, the sales manager may stipulate the objective to increase sales of specific products by different percentage points in various sales regions under his or her control.

Selling objectives are usually defined in terms of sales volume. Objectives, however, may also be defined for (a) gross margin targets, (b) maximum expenditure levels, and (c) fulfillment of specific activities, such as converting a stated number of competitors' customers into company customers.

The sales strategist should also specify the role of selling in terms of personal selling push (vis à vis advertising pull). Selling strategies depend on the consumer decision process, the influence of different communication alternatives, and the cost of these alternatives. The flexibility associated with personal selling allows sales presentations to be tailored to individual customers. Further, personal selling offers an opportunity to develop a tangible personal rapport with customers that can go far toward building long-term relationships. Finally, personal selling is the only method that secures immediate feedback. Feedback helps in taking timely corrective action and in avoiding mistakes. The benefits of personal selling, however, must be considered in relation to its costs. For example, according to the research department of the McGraw-Hill Publications Company, per call personal selling expenditures for all types of personal selling in 1983 came to $205.40, up 15.4 percent from 1981.[23] Thus, the high impact of personal selling should be considered in light of its high cost.

Strategic Matters. As a part of selling strategy, several strategic matters should be resolved. A decision must be made on whether greater emphasis should be put on maintaining existing accounts or on converting customers. Retention and conversion of customers are related to the time salespeople spend with them. Thus, before salespeople can make the best use of their efforts, they must know how much importance is to be attached to each of these two functions.[24] The decision is influenced by such factors as the growth status of the industry, the company's strengths and weaknesses, competitors' strengths, and marketing goals. For example, a manufacturer of laundry detergent will think twice before attempting to convert customers from Tide (Procter and Gamble's brand) to its own brand. On the other hand, some factors may make a company challenge the leader. For example, Bic Pen Corporation is aggressively promoting its disposable razor to Gillette customers. The decision to maintain or convert customers cannot be made in isolation and must be considered in the context of total marketing strategy.

An important strategic concern is how to make productive use of the sales force. In recent years, high expenses (i.e., cost of keeping a salesperson on the road), affordable technological advances (e.g., prices of technology used in telemarketing, teleconferencing, and computerized sales have gone down substantially), and innovative sales techniques (e.g., video presentations) have made it feasible for marketers to turn to electronic marketing to make the most productive use of sales force resources. For example, Gould's medical products division in Oxnard, California, uses video to support sales efforts for one of its new products, a disposable transducer that translates blood pressure into readable electronic impulses. Gould produced two videotapes—a six-minute sales presentation and a nine-minute training film—costing $200,000. Salespeople were equipped with videorecorders—an additional $75,000 investment—to take on calls. According to Gould executives, video gives a concise, clear version of the intended communication and adds professionalism to their sales effort. Gould targeted its competitors' customers and maintains that it captured 45 percent of the $75-million transducer market in less than a year. At the end of nine months, the company had achieved sales of more than 25,000 units per month, achieving significant penetration in markets that it had not been able to get in before.[25]

Another aspect of selling strategy deals with the question of who should be contacted in the customer organization. The buying process may be divided into four phases: consideration, acceptance, selection, and evaluation. Different executives in the customer organization may exert influence on any of the four phases. The sales strategist may work out a plan specifying which salesperson should call upon various individuals in the customer organization and when. On occasion, a person other than the salesperson may be asked to call on a customer. Sometimes, as a matter of selling strategy, a team of people may visit the customer. For example, Northrop Corporation, an aerospace contractor, assigns aircraft designers and technicians—not salespeople—to call on potential customers. When Singapore indicated interest in Northrop's F-5 fighter, Northrop dispatched a team to Singapore that included an engineer, a lawyer, a pricing expert, a test pilot, and a maintenance specialist.

Van Leer cites this example from the literature: A manufacturer of vinyl acetate latex (used as a base for latex paint) built its sales volume by having its people call on the "right people" in the customer organization. The manufacturer recognized that its product was used by the customer to produce paint sold through its marketing department, not the purchasing agent or the manager of research. So the manufacturer planned for its people to meet with the customer's sales and marketing personnel to find out what their problems were, what kept them from selling more latex paint, and what role the manufacturer could play in helping the customer. It was only after the marketing personnel had been sold on the product that the purchasing department was contacted.[26] Thus, a good selling strategy requires a careful analysis of the situation to determine the key people to contact in the customer organization. A routine call on a purchasing agent may not suffice.

The selling strategy should also determine the size of the sales force needed to perform an effective job. This decision is usually made intuitively. A company starts with a few salespeople, adding more as it gains experience. Some companies may go a step beyond the intuitive approach to determine how many salespeople should be recruited. For instance, consideration may be given to factors such as the number of customers who must be visited, the amount of market potential in a territory, and so on. But all these factors are weighed subjectively. This work load approach requires the following steps:

1. Customers are grouped into size classes according to their annual sales volume.
2. Desirable call frequencies (number of sales calls on an account per year) are established for each class.
3. The number of accounts in each size class is multiplied by the corresponding call frequency to arrive at the total work load for the country in sales calls per year.
4. The average number of calls a sales representative can make per year is determined.
5. The number of sales representatives needed is determined by dividing the total annual calls required by the average annual calls made by a sales representative.[27]

Sales Motivation and Supervision Strategy

To ensure that salespersons perform to their utmost capacity, they must be motivated adequately and properly supervised. Often it has been found that salespeople fail to do well because management fails to carry out its part of the job, especially in the areas of motivation and supervision. Although motivation and supervision may appear to be mundane day-to-day matters, they have far-reaching implications for marketing strategy. The purpose of this section is to provide insights into the strategic aspects of motivation and supervision.

Motivation. Salespeople may be motivated through financial and nonfinancial means. Financial motivation is provided by monetary compensation. Nonfinancial motivation is usually tied in with evaluation programs.

Compensation. Most people work to earn a living; their motivation to work is deeply affected by the remuneration they receive. A well-designed compensation plan keeps turnover low and helps to increase an employee's productivity. A compensation plan should be simple, understandable, flexible (cognizant of the differences between individuals), and economically equitable. It should also provide incentive and build morale. It should not penalize salespeople for conditions beyond their control, and it should help develop new business, provide stable income, and meet the objectives of the corporation. Above all, compensation should be in line with the market price for salespeople. Because some of these requisites may conflict with each other, there can be no one perfect plan. All that can be done is to try to balance each variable properly and design a custom-made plan for each sales force.

Different methods of compensating salespeople are the salary plan, the commission plan, and the combination plan. Exhibit 17-2 shows the relative advantages and disadvantages of each plan.

The greatest virtue of the straight-salary method is the guaranteed income and security that it provides. However, it fails to provide any incentive for the ambitious salesperson and therefore may adversely affect productivity. Most companies work on a combination plan, which means that salespeople receive a percentage of sales as a commission for exceeding periodic quotas. Conceptually, the first step in designing a compensation plan is to define the objective. Objectives may focus on rewarding extraordinary performance, providing security, and so on. Every company probably prefers to grant some security to its people and, at the same time, distinguish top employees through incentive schemes. In designing such a plan, the company may first determine the going salary rate for the type of sales staff it is interested in hiring. The company should match the market rate to retain people of caliber. The total wage should be fixed somewhere near the market rate after making adjustments for the company's overall wage policy, environment, and fringe benefits. A study of the spending habits of those in the salary range of salespeople should be made. Based on this study, the percentage of nondiscretionary spending may be linked to an incentive income scheme whereby extra income could be paid as a commission on sales, as a bonus, or both. Care must be taken in constructing a compensation plan. In addition to being equitable, the plan should be simple enough to be comprehensible to the salespeople.

Once compensation has been established for an individual, it is difficult to reduce it. It is desirable, therefore, for management to consider all the pros and cons of fixed compensation for a salesperson before finalizing a salary agreement.

Evaluation. Evaluation is the measurement of a salesperson's contribution to corporate goals. For any evaluation, one needs standards. Establishment of standards, however, is a difficult task, particularly when salespeople are asked to perform different types of jobs. In pure selling jobs, quotas can be set for minimal performance, and salespeople achieving these quotas can be considered as doing satisfactory work. Achievement of quotas can be classified as follows: salespeople exceeding quotas between 1 to 15 percent may be designated as average; those between 16 and 30 percent as well-performing; finally, those over 30 percent can be considered extraordinary salespeople. Sales contests and awards, both financial and nonfinancial, may be instituted to give recognition to salespeople in various categories.

Supervision. Despite the best efforts in selecting, training, and compensating salespeople, they may not perform as expected. Supervision is important to ensure that salespeople provide the services expected of them. Supervision of

EXHIBIT 17-2
Advantages and Disadvantages of Various Sales Compensation Alternatives

Salary Plan

Advantages

1. Assures a regular income
2. Develops a high degree of loyalty
3. Makes it simple to switch territories or quotas or to reassign salesmen
4. Ensures that nonselling activities will be performed
5. Facilitates administration
6. Provides relatively fixed sales costs

Disadvantages

1. Fails to give balanced sales mix because salesmen would concentrate on products with greatest customer appeal
2. Provides little, if any, financial incentive for the salesman
3. Offers few reasons for putting forth extra effort
4. Favors salesmen or saleswomen who are the least productive
5. Tends to increase direct selling costs over other types of plans
6. Creates the possibility of salary compression where new trainees may earn almost as much as experienced salesmen

Commission Plan

Advantages

1. Pay relates directly to performance and results achieved
2. System is easy to understand and compute
3. Salesmen have the greatest possible incentive
4. Unit sales costs are proportional to net sales
5. Company's selling investment is reduced

Disadvantages

1. Emphasis is more likely to be on volume than on profits
2. Little or no loyalty to the company is generated
3. Wide variances in income between salesmen may occur
4. Salesmen are encouraged to neglect nonselling duties
5. Some salesmen may be tempted to "skim" their territories
6. Service aspect of selling may be slighted
7. Problems arise in cutting territories or shifting men or accounts
8. Pay is often excessive in boom times and very low in recession periods
9. Salesmen may sell themselves rather than the company and stress short-term rather than long-term relationships
10. Highly paid salesmen may be reluctant to move into supervisory or managerial positions
11. Excessive turnover of sales personnel occurs when business turns bad

continued

EXHIBIT 17-2
continued

Combination Plan

Advantages

1. Offers participants the advantage of both salary and commission
2. Provides greater range of earnings possibilities
3. Gives salesmen greater security because of steady base income
4. Makes possible a favorable ratio of selling expense to sales
5. Compensates salesmen for all activities
6. Allows a greater latitude of motivation possibilities so that goals and objectives can be achieved on schedule

Disadvantages

1. Is often complex and difficult to understand
2. Can, where low salary and high bonus or commission exist, develop a bonus that is too high a percentage of earnings; when sales fall, salary is too low to retain salesmen
3. Is sometimes costly to administer
4. Can, unless a decreasing commission rate for increasing sales volume exists, result in a "windfall" of new accounts and a runaway of earnings
5. Has a tendency to offer too many objectives at one time so that really important ones can be neglected, forgotten, or overlooked

Source: Reprinted by permission of the *Harvard Business Review.* Excerpt from "How to Pay Your Sales Force" by John P. Steinbrink (July–August, 1978), 111–22.

salespeople is defined in a broader sense to include the assignment of a territory to a salesperson, control over his or her activities, and communication with the salesperson in the field.

Assignment. Salespeople are assigned to different geographic territories. An assignment requires solving two problems: (a) forming territories so that they are as much alike as possible in business potential and (b) assigning territories so that each salesperson is able to realize his or her full potential. Territories may be formed by analyzing customers' locations and the potential business they represent. Customers can be categorized as having high, average, or low potential. Further, probabilities in terms of sales can be assigned to indicate how much potential is realizable. Thus, a territory with a large number of high-potential customers with a high probability of buying may be smaller in size (geographically) than a territory with a large number of low-potential customers with a low probability of buying.[28]

Matching salespeople to territories should not be difficult once the territories have been laid out. Regional preferences and the individual affiliations of salespeople require that employees be placed where they will be happiest. It may be difficult to attract salespeople to some territories; whereas other places may be in great demand. Living in big metropolitan areas is expensive and not always comfortable. Similarly, people may avoid places with poor weather. It may become necessary to provide extra compensation to salespeople assigned to unpopular places.

Control. Although salespeople are their own bosses in the field, the manager must keep informed of their activities. To achieve an adequate level of control, a system must be created for maintaining communication with employees in the field, for guiding their work, and for employing remedial methods if performance slackens. Firms use different types of control devices. Some companies require salespeople to fill in a call form that gives all particulars about each visit to each customer. Some require salespeople to submit weekly reports on work performed during the previous week. Salespeople may be asked to complete several forms about sales generated, special problems they face, market information collected, and so on. Using a good reporting system to control the sales force should have a positive influence on performance. In recent years, more and more companies have begun to use computer-assisted techniques to maintain control of the activities of their sales forces.[29]

Communication. Management communicates with salespeople through periodic mailings, regional and national conferences, and telephone calls. Two areas of communication in which management needs to be extra careful to maintain the morale of good salespeople are (a) in representing the problems of the field force to people at headquarters and (b) in giving patient consideration to the salesperson's complaints. A sales manager serves as the link between the people in the field and the company and must try to bring their problems and difficulties to the attention of top management. Top management, not being fully aware of operations in the field, may fail to appreciate problems. It is, therefore, the duty of the sales manager to keep top management fully posted about field activities and to secure for salespeople its favor. For example, a salesperson in a mountainous area may not be able to maintain his or her work tempo during the winter because of weather conditions. Management must consider this factor in reviewing the salesperson's work. It is the manager's duty to stand by and help with occupational or personal problems bothering salespeople.

Close rapport with salespeople and patient listening can be very helpful in recognizing and solving sales force problems. More often than not, a salesperson's problem is something that the company can take care of with a little effort and expenditure if it is only willing to accept such responsibility.[30] The primary thing, however, is to know the salesperson's mind. This is where the role of the supervisor comes in. It is said that the sales manager should be as much a therapist in solving the problems of his or her salespeople as the latter should be in handling customers' problems.

SUMMARY

Promotion strategies are directed toward establishing communication with customers. Three types of promotion strategies may be distinguished. Advertising strategies are concerned with communication transmitted through the mass media. Personal selling strategies refer to face-to-face interactions with the customer. All other forms of communication, such as sampling, demonstration, cents off, contests, etc., are known as sales promotion strategies. Two main promotion strategies were examined in this chapter: promotion-expenditure strategy, which deals with the question of how much may be spent on overall promotion, and promotion mix strategy, which specifies the roles that the three ingredients of promotion (i.e., advertising, personal selling, and sales promotion) play in promoting a product.

Discussed also were two advertising strategies. The first, media-selection strategy, focuses on the choice of different media to launch an ad campaign. The second, advertising-copy strategy, deals with the development of appropriate ad copy to convey intended messages. Two personal selling strategies were examined: selling strategy and sales motivation and supervision strategy. Selling strategy emphasizes the approach that is adopted to interact with the customer (i.e., who may call on the customer, whom to call on in the customer organization, when, and how frequently). Sales motivation and supervision strategy is concerned with the management of the sales force and refers to such issues as sales compensation, nonfinancial incentives, territory formation, territory assignments, control, and communication.

DISCUSSION QUESTIONS

1. Outline promotion objectives for a packaged food product in an assumed market segment.
2. Develop a promotion-expenditure strategy for a household computer to be marketed through a large retail chain.
3. Will promotion-expenditure strategy for a product in the growth stage of the product life cycle be different from that for a product in the maturity stage? Discuss.
4. How may a promotion budget be allocated among advertising, personal selling, and sales promotion? Can a simulation model be developed to figure out an optimum promotion mix?
5. Is comparison advertising socially desirable? Comment.
6. Should the media decision be made before or after the copy is first developed?
7. Which is more effective, an emotional appeal or a rational appeal? Are emotional appeals relevant for all consumer products?

NOTES

[1]John Koten, "Creativity, Not Budget Size, Is Vital to TV-Ad Popularity," *Wall Street Journal,* 1 March 1984, p. 25.

[2]Michael Waldholz, "Marketing Is the Key to Success of Prescription Drugs," *Wall Street Journal,* 24 January 1982, p. 1.

[3]Richard Gibson, "Marketers' Mantra: Reap More with Less," *Wall Street Journal,* 22 March 1991, p. B1.

[4]See Benson P. Shapiro and John Wyman, "New Ways to Reach Your Customers," *Harvard Business Review* (July–August 1981): 103–10.

[5]See John A. Quelch, "It Is Time to Make Trade Promotion More Productive?" *Harvard Business Review* (May–June 1983): 130–36. See also John Quelch and Dae Chang, "Sales Promotion vs. Advertising in Consumer Goods Marketing," The PIMS Letter, Strategic Planning Institute (1985).

[6]"USIC Chem. Ads Start to Support Effort to Double Sales in 5 Years," *Industrial Marketing* (June 1976): 1–4.

[7]F. Stewart DeBruieker and Gregory L. Summe, "Customer Experience: A Key to Marketing Success," *Harvard Business Review* (January–February 1985): 88–92.

[8]Michael E. Porter, "Interbrand Choice: Media Mix and Market Performance," *American Economic Review* (6 May 1976): 190–203.

[9]Trish Hall, "In Soft-Drink Wars, Brand Loyalty Can Last as Long as a Few Minutes," *Wall Street Journal,* 13 May 1985, p. 25.

[10]"Puritan Fashions: Trying to Protect a Bonanza Built on Designer Jeans," *Business Week* (13 August 1979): 56.

[11]See *Workbook for Estimating Your Advertising Budget* (Boston: Cahners Publishing Co., 1984).

[12]E. S. Browning, "Perrier's Vincent Plans Wave of Change as a Fresh Regime Displaces the Old?" *Wall Street Journal,* 14 February 1991, p. B1.

[13]George W. Schiele, "How to Reach the Young Consumer," *Harvard Business Review* (March–April 1974): 85–86.

[14]See Stratford P. Sherman, "When You Wish upon a Star," *Fortune* (19 August 1985): 66.

[15]See Carl I. Hoveland, Irving L. Janis, and Harold H. Kelley, *Communication and Persuasion* (New Haven: Yale University Press, 1953), 225.

[16]Thomas R. King, "Credibility Gap: More Consumers Find Celebrity Ads Unpersuasive," *Wall Street Journal,* 5 July 1985, p. B5.

[17]Carl I. Hoveland, Arthur A. Lumsdaine, and Fred D. Sheffield, "The Effect of Presenting 'One Side' versus 'Both Sides' in Changing Opinions on a Controversial Subject," in *The Process and Effect of Mass Communication,* ed. Wilbur Schramm (Urbana: University of Illinois Press, 1960), 274.

[18]Based on information supplied by the Coca-Cola Company.

[19]Hoveland, Janis, and Kelley, *Communication and Persuasion,* 57.

[20]E. C. Hackleman and Subhash C. Jain, "An Experimental Analysis of Attitudes toward Comparison and Non-Comparison Advertising," in *Advances in Consumer Research,* ed. William L. Wilkie (Proceedings of the Association for Consumer Research Conference, Miami, 26–29 October 1978), 90–94.

[21]"A Comeback May Be Ahead for Brand X," *Business Week* (4 December 1989): 35.

[22]Jeremy Main, "How to Sell by Listening," *Fortune* (4 February 1985): 52.

[23]"Average Cost Shatters $200 Mark for Industrial Sales Calls, but Moderation Seen in 1984 Hikes," *Marketing News* (17 August 1987): 16. The study also showed that the larger the sales force, the lower the cost. For instance, companies with fewer than 10 salespeople spent more than $290.70 per call; companies with more than 100 spent $147.10. This underscores the significance of the experience effect (see chapter 12).

[24]See B. P. Shapiro and S. X. Doyle, "Make the Sales Task Clear," *Harvard Business Review* (November–December 1983): 72.

[25]"Rebirth of a Salesman: Willy Loman Goes Electronic," *Business Week* (27 February 1984): 103.

[26]R. Karl van Leer, "Industrial Marketing with a Flair," *Harvard Business Review* (November-December 1976): 117-24.

[27]Philip Kotler, *Marketing Management*, 7th Ed. (Englewood Cliffs, NJ: Prentice-Hall, 1991), 657-58.

[28]Robert J. Zimmer and James W. Taylor, "Matching Profiles for Your Industrial Sales Force," *Business* (March-April 1981): 2-13.

[29]Lad Kuzela, "Slicing Costs with Smarter Selling," *Industry Week* (22 February 1982): 59-61.

[30]Lynn G. Coleman, "Sales Force Turnover Has Managers Wondering Why," *Marketing News* (4 December 1989): 6.

APPENDIX *Perspectives on Promotion Strategies*

I Promotion-Expenditure Strategy

Definition: Determination of the amount that a company may spend on its total promotional effort, which includes advertising, personal selling, and sales promotion.

Objective: To allocate enough funds to each promotional task so that each is utilized to its fullest potential.

Requirements: (a) Adequate resources to finance the promotion expenditure. (b) Understanding of the products/services sales response. (c) Estimate of the duration of the advertising effect. (d) Understanding of each product/market situation relative to different forms of promotion. (e) Understanding of competitive response to promotion.

Expected Results: Allocation of sufficient funds to the promotional tasks to accomplish overall marketing objectives.

II Promotion Mix Strategy

Definition: Determination of a judicious mix of different types of promotion.

Objective: To adequately blend the three types of promotion to complement each other for a balanced promotional perspective.

Requirements: (a) Product factors: (i) nature of product, (ii) perceived risk, (iii) durable versus nondurable, and (iv) typical purchase amount. (b) Market factors: (i) position in the life cycle, (ii) market share, (iii) industry concentration, (iv) intensity of competition, and (v) demand perspectives. (c) Customers factors: (i) household versus business customers, (ii) number of customers, and (iii) concentration of customers. (d) Budget factors: (i) financial resources of the organization and (ii) traditional promotional perspectives. (e) Marketing mix factors: (i) relative price/relative quality, (ii) distribution strategy, (iii) brand life cycle, and (iv) geographic scope of the market. (f) Environmental factors.

Expected Results: The three types of promotion are assigned roles in a way that provides the best communication.

III Media-Selection Strategy

Definition: Choosing the channels (newspapers, magazines, television, radio, outdoor advertising, transit advertising, and direct mail) through which messages concerning a product/service are transmitted to the targets.

Objective: To move customers from unawareness of a product/service, to awareness, to comprehension, to conviction, to the buying action.

Requirements: (a) Relate media-selection objectives to product/market objectives. (b) Media chosen should have a unique way of promoting the business. (c) Media should be measure-minded not only in frequency, in timing, and in reaching the target audience but also in evaluating the quality of the audience. (d) Base media selection on factual not connotational grounds. (e) Media plan should be optimistic in that it takes advantage of the lessons learned from experience. (f) Seek information on customer profiles and audience characteristics.

Expected Results: Customers are moved along the desired path of the purchase process.

IV Advertising-Copy Strategy

Definition: Designing the content of an advertisement.

Objective: To transmit a particular product/service message to a particular target.

Requirements: (a) Eliminate "noise" for a clear transmission of message. (b) Consider importance of (i) source credibility, (ii) balance of argument, (iii) message repetition, (iv) rational versus emotional appeals, (v) humor appeals, (vi) presentation of model's eyes in pictorial ads, and (vii) comparison advertising.

Expected Results: The intended message is adequately transmitted to the target audience.

V Selling Strategy

Definition: Moving customers to the purchase phase of the decision-making process through the use of face-to-face contact.

Objective: Achievement of stated sales volume and gross margin targets and the fulfillment of specific activities.

Requirements: (a) The selling strategy should be derived from overall marketing objectives and properly linked with promotional objectives. (b) Decision on maintenance of existing accounts versus lining up new customers. (c) Decision on who should be contacted in customer's organization. (d) Determine optimal size of sales force.

Expected Results: (a) Sales and profit targets are met at minimum expense. (b) Overall marketing goals are achieved.

VI Sales Motivation and Supervision Strategy

Definition: Achieving superior sales force performance.

Objective: To ensure optimal performance of the sales force.

Requirements: (a) Motivation—financial and nonfinancial. (b) Adequate compensation package. (c) Evaluation standards. (d) Appropriate territory assignment, activity control, and communication.

Expected Results: Business objectives are met adequately at minimum expense.

CHAPTER 18

Global Market Strategies

Competition in the U.S. marketplace is no longer national, but international. American businesses that adapt to changing circumstances and recognize opportunities will prosper; those that do not will at best survive temporarily.

PRESIDENT'S TASK FORCE ON INTERNATIONAL PRIVATE ENTERPRISE

One of the most significant developments in recent years has been the emergence of global markets. Today's market provides not only a multiplicity of goods but good from many places. It would not be surprising to discover that your shirt comes from Taiwan, your jeans from Mexico, and your shoes from Italy. You may drive a Japanese car equipped with tires manufactured in France, with nuts and bolts produced in India, and with paint from a U.S. company. Gucci bags, Sony Walkmans, and McDonald's golden arches are seen on the streets of Tokyo, London, Paris, and New York. Thai goods wind up on U.S. grocery shelves as Dole canned pineapple and on French farms as livestock feed. Millions of consumers worldwide want all the things that they have heard about, seen, or experienced via new communication technologies. Firms today are enmeshed in world competition to serve these consumers, no matter where they live.

A number of broad forces have led to growing globalization of markets.[1] These include

1. **Growing similarity of countries**—Because of growing commonality of infrastructure, distribution channels, and marketing approaches, more and more products and brands are available everywhere. Similar buyer needs thus manifest themselves in different countries. Large retail chains, television advertising, and credit cards are just a few examples of once-isolated phenomena that are rapidly becoming universal.
2. **Falling tariff barriers**—Successive rounds of bilateral and multilateral agreements have lowered tariffs markedly since World War II. At the same time,

regional economic agreements, such as the European Community (EC), have facilitated trade relations.

3. **Strategic role of technology**—Technology is not only reshaping industries but contributing toward market homogenization. For example, electronic innovations have permitted the development of more compact, lighter products that are less costly to ship. Transportation costs themselves have fallen with the use of containerization and larger-capacity ships. Increasing ease of communication and data transfer make it feasible to link operations in different countries. At the same time, technology leads to an easy flow of information among buyers, making them aware of new and quality products and thus creating demand for them.

The impact of these forces on the globalization of markets may be illustrated with reference to a few examples. Kids everywhere are playing Nintendo and bounding along the streets to the sound of Sony Walkmans. The videocassette recorder market took off simultaneously in Japan, Europe, and the United States, but the most extensive use of videocassette recorders today is probably in places like Riyadh and Caracas. Shopping centers from Dusseldorf to Rio sell Gucci shoes, Yves St. Laurent suits, and Gloria Vanderbilt jeans. Siemens and ITT telephones can be found almost everywhere in the world. The Mercedes-Benz 190E and the Toyota Corolla are as much objects of passion in Manila as in California.

Just about every gas turbine sold in the world has some GE technology or component in it, and what country doesn't need gas turbines? How many airlines around the world could survive without Boeing or McDonnell Douglas? Third World markets for high-voltage transmission equipment and diesel-electric locomotives are bigger than those in developed countries. And today's new industries—robotics, videodisks, fiber optics, satellite networks, high-technology plastics, artificial diamonds—seem global from birth.

Briefly, these forces have homogenized worldwide markets, triggering opportunities for firms to seek business across national borders. For U.S. corporations, the real impetus to overseas expansion occurred after World War II. Attempting to reconstruct war-torn economies, the U.S. government, through the Marshall Plan, provided financial assistance to European countries. As the postwar American economy emerged as the strongest in the world, its economic assistance programs, in the absence of competition, stimulated extensive corporate development of international strategies. Since then, many new players, not only from Europe but from Southeast Asia as well, have entered the arena to serve global markets. Asian competitors have been particularly quick to exploit new international competitive conditions as well as cross-cutting technologies to leapfrog well-established rivals.

Global markets offer unlimited opportunities. But competition in these markets is intense. To be globally successful, companies must learn to operate and compete as if the world were one large market, ignoring superficial regional and national differences. Corporations geared to this new reality can benefit from enormous economies of scale in production, distribution, marketing, and management. By translating these benefits into reduced world prices, they can dislodge competitors who still operate under the perspectives of the 1970s and 1980s. Companies willing to change their perspectives and become global can attain sustainable competitive advantage.

IDENTIFYING TARGET MARKETS

The World Bank lists 160 countries. Different countries represent varying market potential due to economic, cultural, and political contrasts. These contrasts mean that a global marketer cannot select target customers randomly but must employ workable criteria to choose countries where the company's product/service has the best opportunity for success.

Major Markets

The most basic information needed to identify markets concerns population because people, of course, constitute a market. The population of the world reached an estimated 5.3 billion in 1990. According to the latest estimates from the United Nations, this total is expected to increase to 6.2 billion by the year 2000 and to almost 8.5 billion by 2025. Current world population is growing at about 1.7 percent per year. This is a slight decline from the peak rate of 1.9 percent, but the absolute number of people being added to the world's population each year is still increasing. This figure is expected to peak in the mid-1990s at about 90 million additional people per year.

Population growth rates vary significantly by region. Europe has the lowest rate of population growth at only about 0.3 percent per year. Several European countries, including Austria, Denmark, West Germany, Luxembourg and Sweden, are experiencing declining populations. Growth rates are also below 1 percent per year in North America.

The regions with the highest population growth rates are Africa (3 percent per year), Latin America (2 percent per year) and South Asia (1.9 percent per year). China, the world's most populous country, is growing at only about 1.2 percent per year. Even so, it means that China's population increases by over 12 million people each year. The world's second largest country, India, is growing at over 1.7 percent per year. India's population is expected to grow from 850 million today to 1 billion by about 2003.

One striking aspect of population growth in developing countries is the rapid rate of urbanization. The urban population is growing at less than 1 percent in Europe and in North America, but it is growing at almost 3.5 percent in the developing world. Today 13 of the 20 largest urban agglomerations are in the developing world. By the year 2000, 17 of the 20 will be in the developing world. The only cities in the top 20 located in developed countries will be Tokyo, New York, and Los Angeles. The world's largest cities will be Mexico City (26 million) and Sao Paulo (24 million).

The above information shows that the total market in Europe and North America will not be increasing; the population of these two continents will not add much to total market size. Of course, these populations are growing older, so certain segments will increase in number. For example, the total population of Europe will increase only 2.8 percent from 1990 to 2000, but the over-65 population in Europe will increase by 14 percent during the same period.

In the developing world, the increase in numbers does not necessarily mean increased markets for U.S. business. The fastest-growing region in the world, Africa, is also experiencing low or negative rates of economic growth per capita. Many Latin American countries are hampered by huge external debts that force them to try to limit imports while using their resources to generate foreign exchange for debt service. In most of these cases, the problem of foreign debt will have to be solved before the growing populations in the developing world will translate into large markets for U.S. business.

Obviously, population figures alone provide little information about market potential because people must have the means in terms of income to become viable customers. In Exhibit 18-1, population combined with per capita GNP provides an estimate of consuming capacity. An index of consuming capacity depicts absolute, or aggregate, consumption, both in the entire world and in individual economies. Consumption rates can be satisfied either domestically or through imports.

The information in Exhibit 18-1 should be interpreted cautiously because it makes no allowances for difference in the purchasing power among different countries. Two conclusions are obvious, however: (a) aggregate consuming capacity depends upon total population as well as per capital income and (b) advanced countries dominate as potential customers.

Although population and income variables provide a snapshot of the market opportunity in a given country, a variety of other factors must be considered to identify viable markets. These factors are urbanization, consumption patterns, infrastructure, and overall industrialization. Taking these factors into account, *Business International* has identified twelve countries as major global markets (see Exhibit 18-2).[2] Interestingly, three of these twelve countries—China, Brazil, and India—are Third World countries.

Although these twelve countries have been identified as the principal global markets by *Business International,* they may not all be viable markets from the viewpoint of U.S. firms. A variety of environmental factors (political, legal, cultural) affect market opportunity in a nation. For example, Brazil is burdened with debt, which limits the amount of export potential in that country; China's political control limits freedom of choice; India's regulations make it difficult for foreign corporations to conduct business there. Thus, many countries may not have large market potential, yet they may constitute important markets for U.S. business.

Exhibit 18-3 lists the top 25 U.S. export markets. Also shown is the dollar amount of exports to each country in 1990. It should be noted that, although, globally speaking, Canada ranks as the 12th largest market (see Exhibit 18-2) in the world, it represents the single largest market for the United States, accounting for over one-fifth of its trade.

EXHIBIT 18-1
Consuming Capacities of Selected Countries

Country	*Population**	*Per Capita GNP†*	*Index of Consuming Capacity‡*
United States	243.4	18,430.0	4,485.5
Japan	122.1	15,770.0	1,925.5
Germany	60.8	14.460.0	879.2
France	55.6	12,860.0	715.0
United Kingdom	56.8	10,430.0	592.4
Italy	57.3	10,420.0	597.1
Canada	25.8	15,080.0	389.1
India	797.1	300.0	239.1
Australia	16.2	10,900.0	176.6
Brazil	141.2	2,020.0	285.2
Mexico	81.9	1,820.0	149.1
Sudan	23.2	330.0	7.7
The Netherlands	14.6	11,860.0	173.2
Belgium	9.9	11,360.0	112.5
Argentina	31.4	2,370.0	74.4
Switzerland	6.5	21,250.0	138.1
South Africa	33.3	1,890.0	62.9
Denmark	5.1	15,010.0	76.6
Philippines	58.3	590.0	34.4
Turkey	52.8	1,200.0	63.4
New Zealand	3.3	8,230.0	27.2
Peru	20.7	1,430.0	29.6
Israel	4.4	6,810.0	30.0
Ecuador	9.9	1,040.0	10.3
Uganda	15.6	260.0	4.1
Honduras	4.7	780.0	3.7
Paraguay	3.9	1,000.0	3.9

**World Bank Report*, 1988. Figures in millions.
†*Statistical Abstract of the United States: 1988* (Washington, DC: U.S. Department of Commerce). Figures in U.S. dollars.
‡Per capita GDP (gross domestic product) multiplied by total population. Figures in billions.

Emerging Markets

Traditionally, a major proportion of international business activities of U.S. corporations has been limited to developed countries. For example, at the end of 1990, total U.S. direct investment was estimated to be $410 billion, of which almost 75 percent was in developed countries. Slowly, however, new markets are unfolding. Consider the newly industrializing countries. During the decade of the 1980s, South Korea, Singapore, Taiwan, and Hong Kong were the world's fastest-growing economies and consequently offered new opportunities for U.S. firms.

In recent years, even developing countries, at least the more politically stable ones, have begun to show viable market potential. A number of developing countries are achieving higher and higher growth rates every year. Although an

EXHIBIT 18-2
Size, Growth, and Intensity of World's 12 Largest Markets

	Market Size (% of World Market)			Market Intensity (World = 1.00)			Five-Year Market Growth (%)
	1978	*1983*	*1988*	*1978*	*1983*	*1988*	*1988*
United States	23.30	20.96	18.08	4.82	4.40	3.99	17.50
USSR	14.32	13.16	12.17	2.14	2.03	1.97	9.15
China	3.84	6.64	11.56	0.16	0.26	0.61	333.25
Japan	9.14	9.07	8.10	3.31	3.42	3.29	12.15
Germany	4.92	4.93	3.95	3.55	3.91	3.47	5.63
Italy	3.94	4.06	3.69	3.09	3.35	3.38	10.96
France	3.67	3.77	3.39	3.10	3.38	3.22	9.96
United Kingdom	3.47	3.38	2.85	2.75	2.87	2.70	19.79
Brazil	2.24	2.21	2.58	0.82	0.78	0.88	25.79
India	1.33	1.53	2.44	0.08	0.09	0.17	155.95
Spain	2.30	2.41	2.12	2.64	2.87	2.76	18.33
Canada	2.23	2.02	1.94	4.25	3.81	3.92	22.09

Source: Business International, 30 July 1990, p. 256.
Notes: **Market size** shows the relative dimensions of each national or regional market as a percentage of the total world market. The percentages for each market are derived by averaging the corresponding data on total population (double-weighted), urban population, private consumption expenditure, steel consumption, cement and electricity production, and ownership of telephones, passenger cars, and televisions.

Market intensity measures the richness of the market, or the degree of concentrated purchasing power it represents. Taking the world's market intensity as 1.00, *BI* has calculated the intensity of each country or region as it relates to this base. The intensity figure is derived from an average of per capita ownership, production, and consumption indicators. Specifically, it is calculated by averaging per capita figures for cars in use (double-weighted), telephones in use, televisions in use, steel consumption, cement and electricity production, private consumption expenditure (double-weighted), and the percentage of population that is urban (double-weighted).

Market growth is a five-year average of the growth rates for several indicators: population, steel consumption, cement and electricity production, and ownership of passenger cars, trucks, buses, and televisions.

individual country may not provide adequate potential for U.S. corporations, developing countries as a group constitute a major market. In 1988 over one-fourth of U.S. trade was with developing countries. In future years, the flow of U.S. trade with developing countries should increase. An Organization of Economic Cooperation and Development (OECD) study showed that, in 1970, OECD countries, with just 20 percent of the world's people, had 83 percent of the world's trade in manufactures; whereas developing countries, with 70 percent of the world's people, captured 11 percent of the trade. In the year 2000, however, it is estimated that OECD countries, with 15 percent of the population, will have 63 percent of the world's trade in manufactures; developing countries, with 78 percent of the population, will account for 28 percent of world trade.[3] Interestingly, although for cultural, political, and economic reasons, Western Europe, Canada, and to a lesser extent Japan have always been predominantly important for business, many developing countries provide a better return on U.S. investment.

EXHIBIT 18-3
Top 25 U.S. Markets: U.S. Domestic and Foreign Merchandise Exports, 1990 (f.a.s. value)

	Dollars (in billions)
1. Canada	83.9
2. Japan	48.6
3. Mexico	28.4
4. United Kingdom	23.5
5. Germany	18.8
6. South Korea	14.4
7. France	13.7
8. Netherlands	13.0
9. Taiwan	11.5
10. Belgium-Luxembourg	10.4
11. Australia	8.5
12. Singapore	8.0
13. Italy	8.0
14. Hong Kong	6.8
15. Spain	5.2
16. Brazil	5.1
17. Switzerland	4.9
18. China	4.8
19. Suadi Arabia	4.0
20. Malaysia	3.4
21. Sweden	3.4
22. Israel	3.2
23. Venezuela	3.1
24. USSR	3.1
25. Thailand	3.0
Total Exports	**393.9**

Source: Business America (22 April 1991): 5.

The relevance of emerging markets for the United States can be illustrated with reference to Pacific basin countries. Over the last quarter century, streams of food, fuels, textiles, cameras, cars, and videocassette recorders flowing from countries all across Asia exerted heavy pressure on Western economies. Since 1962 this outpouring of exports has increased the Asian/Pacific share of world trade from 11 percent to 21 percent and has pushed one Asian economy after another out of the Dark Ages and into the global marketplace.

For U.S. marketers, rising Pacific power holds both a threat and a promise. The threat is dramatically increased competition for sales and market share, both at home and abroad. In 1990 alone, Asian/Pacific countries supplied 38 percent of all U.S. merchandise imports and contributed some $60 billion to the U.S. trade deficit, 68 percent of the total. As for the promise, there is the emergence of a market of more than two billion potential consumers. In the last 25 years, as the Pacific region began its time-bending leap into the twentieth century, millions of Asians began an equally rapid transition from rural to urban, from agrarian to industrial, from feudal to contemporary society. With more of the Pacific region's rural population traveling to cities to shop every day, the demand for goods and services—from the most basic household commodities to sophisticated technical devices—is soaring. In coming years, as rising incomes continue to bolster the spending power of Asia's new consumer population, the opportunities for shrewd marketers will be unparalleled.

Barriers to conducting business in the region are beginning to fall, too. Increasingly, throughout the region English is the language of commerce, and an allegiance to free market economics is widespread. And, as companies such as McDonald's, General Foods, Unilever, and Coca-Cola have already discovered, from Penang to Taipei, this is a region where well-made and well-marketed products and services are witnessing increasing acceptance.

As modern influences exert greater pressure on traditional Asian cultures, two trends with important implications for marketers are starting to take shape:

- Although each Asian nation is culturally distinct, consumers throughout the Pacific region are gradually sharing more of the same wants and needs. As Asian homogenization progresses, sophisticated strategies and considerable economies of scale in regional and global marketing and advertising will become increasingly relevant.[4]
- Many Western marketers misinterpret the nature of current changes in the Pacific region. Despite the Big Macs, the Levi's, the Nikes, and all the other familiar trappings, Asia is not Westernizing—it's modernizing. Asian consumers are buying Western goods and services, not Western values and cultures.

Elsewhere in the East, India and China, two large markets, should provide unprecedented opportunities for U.S. corporations in the 1990s as their economies become market oriented. A growing number of U.S. consumer-goods companies have begun to make inroads in China. In November 1987 Kentucky Fried Chicken Corp. opened the first Western fast-food restaurant in China. Coca-Cola and PepsiCo are aggressively expanding distribution. Kodak and other foreign film suppliers have attained a 70 percent share of the color film market. Nescafé and Maxwell House are waging coffee combat in a land of tea.[5]

A number of U.S. companies—Pepsi, Timex, General Foods, Kellogg—have entered India to serve its emerging middle class.[6] Thus, the developing countries provide new opportunities for U.S. corporations to expand business overseas: as their wealth grows, U.S. marketing possibilities expand.

It has been observed that during the 1990s Latin American countries, too, will emerge as modern, Northern-styled marketplaces with improved transportation systems, subsidized credit to native businesses, and marketing education programs. All of these changes should result in more efficient channels of distribution, more local marketing support services, and fewer bottlenecks that hamper exchanges. All these indications point toward a variety of emerging opportunities for U.S. corporations in Latin America.

A few years ago, Gillette Co., for example, discovered that only 8 percent of Mexican men who shave used shaving cream. Sensing an opportunity, Gillette in 1975 introduced plastic tubes of shaving cream in Guadalajara, Mexico, that sold for half the price of its aerosol. In a year's time, 13 percent of Guadalajaran men began to use shaving cream. Gillette is planning to sell its new product, *Prestobarba* (Spanish for "quick shave"), in the rest of Mexico, in Colombia, and in Brazil.[7]

These emerging markets in less-developed countries can help many U.S. corporations to counter the results of demographic changes in Western nations examined above.[8] In most advanced nations of the world, birthrates are declining while population in the Third World is growing. The largest population growth rates in the 1990s will be in Africa and Latin America.

With the fall of the wall and the lifting of the curtain, new opportunities await Western managers in Eastern Europe, hitherto a forbidden region. In many ways, the opening of Eastern Europe could prove even more important than the drive for a single market in Western Europe. Take, for example, Poland, Hungary, and Czechoslovakia. Their combined GNP is larger than that of china. These three countries also have relatively well-trained and reliable workers who work for less than a quarter of what Western Europeans are paid.[9] Giving them access to their developed neighbors' markets and hefty injections of Western capital, they could become the tigers of Europe. As their economies grow, they should develop into viable markets for a variety of goods and services.

Developments in Eastern Europe will benefit American companies in two ways. First, as Eastern Europe's backward economies finally integrate into the global economy and take off, new market opportunities should emerge. Second, sales to Western Europe by U.S. firms, made even more dynamic by its expanding Eastern frontier, will increase. Just as markets in the 1980s were developed by Reaganomics and Thatcherism, markets in the 1990s will be developed by the shifting of the ideological plates that have separated the world's geopolitical landmasses. Companies that aim for global market and remain competitive will be the winners.

The Triad Market

From a global perspective, the United States, Canada, Japan, and Western Europe, often referred to as *triad countries,* constitute the major market. Although elsewhere opportunities are emerging, in the foreseeable future these countries continue to be the leading markets. They account for approximately 14 percent of the worlds' population, but they represent over 70 percent of world gross product. As such, these countries absorb a major proportion of capital and consumer products and, thus, are the most advanced consuming societies in the world. Not only do most product innovations take place in these countries, but they also serve as the opinion leaders and mold the purchasing and consumption behavior of the remaining 84 percent of the world's population.

For example, over 90 percent of the world's computers are used by triad countries. In the case of numerically controlled machine tools, almost 100 percent are distributed in the triad market. The same pattern follows in consumer products. The triad accounts for 92 percent of the demand for electronic consumer goods. What these statistics point to is that a company that ignores the market potential of the triad does so at its own peril.[10]

An interesting characteristic of the triad market is the universalization of needs. For example, not too long ago manufacturers of capital equipment produced machinery that reflected strong cultural distinctions. West German machines reflected that nation's penchant for craftsmanship; American equipment was often extravagant in its use of raw materials. But these distinctions have disappeared. The best-selling factory machines have lost the "art" element that once distinguished them and have become both in appearance and in the level of skill that they require much more similar. The current revolution in production engineering has brought about ever-increasing global standards of performance. In an era when productivity improvements can quickly determine life or death on a global scale, companies cannot afford to indulge in a metallic piece of art that will last 30 years.

At the same time, consumer markets have become fairly homogeneous. Ohmae notes that

> the Triad consumption patterns, which is both a cause and an effect of cultural patterns, has its roots to a large extent in the educational system. As educational systems enable more people to use technology, they tend to become more similar to each other. It follows, therefore, that education leading to higher levels of technological achievement also tends to eradicate differences in lifestyles. Penetration of television, which enables everyone possessing a television set to share sophisticated behavioral information instantaneously throughout the world, has also accelerated this trend. There are, for example, 750 million consumers in all three parts of the Triad (Japan, the United States and Canada, the nations of Western Europe) with strikingly similar needs and preferences. . . . A new generation worships the universal "now" gods—ABBA, Levi's and Arpege. . . . Youngsters in Denmark, West Germany, Japan, and California are all growing up with ketchup, jeans, and guitars. Their lifestyles, aspirations, and desires are so similar that you might call them "OECDites" or Triadians, rather than by names denoting their national identity.[11]

There are many reasons for the similarities and commonalities in the triad's consumer demand and lifestyle patterns. First, the purchasing power of triad residents, as expressed in discretionary income per individual, is more than 10 times greater than that of residents of developing countries. For example, television penetration in triad countries is greater than 94 percent, whereas in newly industrialized countries it is 25 percent; for the developing countries, it is less than 10 percent. Second, their technological infrastructure is more advanced. For example, over 70 percent of triadian households have a telephone. This makes it feasible to use such products as facsimile, teletext, and digital data transmission/processing equipment. Third, the educational level is much higher in triad nations than in other parts of the world. Fourth, the number of physicians per 10,000 in triad countries, which creates demand for pharmaceuticals and medical electronics, exceeds 30. Fifth, better infrastructure in the triad leads to opportunities not feasible in less-developed markets. For example, paved roads have made rapid penetration of radial tires and sports cars possible.

ENTRY STRATEGIES

Four different modes of business offer a company entry into foreign markets: (a) exporting, (b) contractual agreement, (c) joint venture, and (d) manufacturing.

Exporting

A company may minimize the risk of dealing internationally by exporting domestically manufactured products either by minimal response to inquiries or by systematic development of demand in foreign markets. Exporting requires minimal capital and is easy to initiate. Exporting is also a good way to gain international experience. A major part of overseas involvement among large U.S. firms is through export trade.

Contractual Agreements

There are several types of contractual agreements:

- **Patent licensing agreements**—These agreements are based on either a fixed-fee or a royalty basis and include managerial training.
- **Turnkey operations**—These operations are based on a fixed-fee or cost-plus arrangement and include plant construction, personnel training, and initial production runs.
- **Coproduction agreements**—These agreements are most common in socialist countries, where plants are built and then paid for with part of the output.
- **Management contracts**—Currently widely used in the Middle East, these contracts require that a multinational corporation provide key personnel to operate a foreign enterprise for a fee until local people acquire the ability to manage the business independently. For example, Whittaker Corp. of Los Angeles operates government-owned hospitals in several cities in Saudi Arabia.
- **Licensing**—Licensing works as a viable alternative in some contractual agreement situations where risk of expropriation and resistance to foreign investments create uncertainty. *Licensing* encompasses a variety of contractual agreements whereby a multinational marketer makes available intangible assets—such as patents, trade secrets, know-how, trademarks, and company name—to foreign companies in return for royalties or other forms of payment. Transfer of these assets usually is accompanied by technical services to ensure proper use. Licensing, however, has some advantages and disadvantages as summarized below.[12]

Advantages of Licensing

1. Licensing requires little capital and serves as a quick and easy entry to foreign markets.
2. In some countries, notably in developed Communist countries, licensing is the only way to tap the market.
3. Licensing provides life extension for products in the maturity stage of their life cycles.
4. Licensing is a good alternative to foreign production and marketing in an environment where there is worldwide inflation, shortages of skilled labor, in-

creasing domestic and foreign governmental regulation and restriction, and tough international competition.
5. Licensing royalties are guaranteed and periodic, whereas shared income from investment fluctuates and is risky.
6. Domestically based firms can benefit from product development abroad without incurring research expense through technical feedback arrangements.
7. When exports no longer are profitable because of intense competition, licensing provides an alternative.
8. Licensing can overcome high transportation costs, which make some exports noncompetitive in target markets.
9. Licensing is also immune to expropriation.
10. In some countries, manufacturers of military equipment or any product deemed critical to the national interest (including communications equipment) may be compelled to enter licensing agreements.

Disadvantages of Licensing

1. To attract licensees, a firm must possess distinctive technology, a trademark, and a company or brand name that is attractive to potential foreign users.
2. The licensor has no control over production and marketing by the licensee.
3. Licensing royalties are negligible compared with equity investment potential. Royalty rates seldom exceed 5 percent of gross sales because of government restrictions in the host country.
4. The licensee may lose interest in renewing the contract unless the licensor holds interest through innovation and new technology.
5. There is a danger of creating competition in third, or even home, markets if the licensee violates territorial agreements. Going to court in these situations is expensive and time-consuming, and no international adjudicatory body exists.

Joint Ventures

Joint venture represents a higher-risk alternative than exporting or contractual agreements because it requires various levels of direct investment. A joint venture between a U.S. firm and a native operation abroad involves sharing risks to accomplish mutual enterprise. Once a firm moves beyond the exporting stage, joint ventures, incidentally, are the next most common form of entry. One example of a joint venture is General Motors Corporation's partnership with Egypt's state-owned Nasar Car Company, a joint venture to establish a plant for the assembly of trucks and diesel engines. Another example of a joint venture is between Matsushita of Japan and IBM, a joint venture established to manufacture small computers.[13] Joint ventures normally are designed to take advantage of the strong functions of the partners and to supplement their weak functions, be they management, research, or marketing.[14]

Joint ventures provide a mutually beneficial arrangement for domestic and foreign businesses to join forces.[15] For both parties, the venture is a means to share capital and risk and make use of each other's technical strength.[16] Japanese companies, for example, prefer entering into joint ventures with U.S. firms because such arrangements help ensure against possible American trade barriers. American firms, on the other hand, like the opportunity to enter a previously forbidden market, to utilize established channels, to link American product innovation with low-cost Japanese manufacturing technology, and to curb a potentially tough competitor.

As a case in point, General Foods Corporation tried for more than a decade to succeed in Japan on its own but watched the market share of its instant coffee (Maxwell House) drop from 20 to 14 percent. Then, in 1975, the firm established a joint venture with Ajinomoto, a food manufacturer, to use the full power of Ajinomoto's product distribution system and personnel and managerial capabilities. Within two years, Maxwell House's share of the Japanese instant coffee market had recovered and, in 1982, was close to 25 percent.[17]

Joint ventures, however, are not an unmixed blessing.[18] The major problem in managing joint ventures stems from one cause: there is more than one partner and one of the partners must play a key dominant role to steer the business to success.[19]

Joint ventures should be designed to supplement each partner's shortcomings, not to exploit each other's strengths and weaknesses. It takes as much effort to make a joint venture a success as to start a grass roots operation and eventually bring it up to a successful level. In both cases, each partner must be fully prepared to expend the effort necessary to understand customers, competitors, and itself. A joint venture is a means of resource appropriation and of easing a foreign business's entry into a new terrain. It should not be viewed as a handy vehicle to reap money without effort, interest, and/or additional resources.

Joint ventures are a wave of the future. There is hardly a *Fortune* 500 company active overseas that does not have at least one joint venture. Widespread interest in joint ventures is related to the following:

1. **Seeing market opportunities**—Companies in mature industries in the United States find joint venture a desirable entry mode to enter attractive new markets overseas.
2. **Dealing with rising economic nationalism**—Often host governments are more receptive to or require joint ventures.
3. **Preempting raw materials**—Countries with raw materials, such as petroleum or extractable material, usually do not allow foreign firms to be active there other than through joint venture.
4. **Sharing risk**—Rather than taking the entire risk, a joint venture allows the risk to be shared with a partner, which can be especially important in politically sensitive areas.
5. **Developing an export base**—In areas where economic blocs play a significant role, joint venture with a local firm smooths the entry into the entire region, such as entry into the Common Market through a joint venture with an English company.
6. **Selling technology**—Selling technology to developing countries becomes easier through a joint venture.[20]

Even a joint venture with a well-qualified majority foreign partner may provide significant advantages:

1. **Participation in income and growth**—The minority partner shares in the earnings and growth of the venture even if its own technology becomes obsolete.

2. **Low cash requirements**—Know-how and patents or both can be considered as partial capital contribution.
3. **Preferred treatment**—Because it is locally controlled, the venture is treated with preference by government.
4. **Easier access to a market and to market information**—A locally controlled firm can seek market access and information much more easily than can a firm controlled by foreigners.
5. **Less drain on managerial resources**—The local partner takes care of most managerial responsibilities.
6. **U.S. income tax deferral**—Income to the U.S. minority partner is not subject to U.S. taxation until distribution.[21]

Manufacturing

A multinational corporation may also establish itself in an overseas market by direct investment in a manufacturing and/or assembly subsidiary. Because of the volatility of worldwide economic, social, and political conditions, this form of involvement is most risky. An example of a direct investment situation is Chesebrough-Pond's operation of overseas manufacturing plants in Japan, England, and Monte Carlo.

Manufacturing around the world is riskier, as illustrated by Union Carbide's disaster in Bhopal, India: in the worst industrial accident that has ever occurred, a poisonous gas leak killed over 2000 people and permanently disabled thousands. It is suggested that multinational corporations should not manufacture overseas where the risk of a mishap may jeopardize the survival of the whole company. As a matter of fact, in the wake of the Bhopal accident, many host countries tightened safety and environmental regulations. For example, Brazil, the world's fourth-largest user of agricultural chemicals, restricted the use of the deadly methyl isocyanate.[22]

Conclusion

A firm interested in entering the international market must evaluate the risk and commitment involved with each entry and choose the entry mode that best fits the company's objectives and resources.[23] Entry risk and commitment can be examined by considering five factors:

1. Characteristics of the product
2. The market's external macroenvironment, particularly economic and political factors, and the demand and buying patterns of potential customers
3. The firm's competitive position, especially the product's life cycle stage, as well as various corporate strengths and weaknesses
4. Dynamic capital budgeting considerations, including resource costs and availabilities
5. Internal corporate perceptions that affect corporate selection of information and the psychic distance between a firm's decision makers and its target customers as well as control and risk-taking preferences

These five factors combined indicate that risk should be reviewed vis-à-vis a company's resources before determining a mode of entry.

Computerized simulation models can be employed to determine the desired entry route by simultaneously evaluating such factors as environmental opportunity, risk index, competitive risk index, corporate strength index, product channel direction index, comparative cost index, and corporate policy and perception index.[24]

GLOBAL MARKET ENVIRONMENT

Not only are the risk factors underlying the mode of entry largely contingent on the nature of the foreign environment, but these environmental forces also influence the development of marketing strategies. Decision making for expansion into global markets is strategically similar to the decision-making process guiding domestic marketing endeavors. More specifically, four marketing strategy variables—product, price, distribution, and promotion—need to be as systematically addressed in the context of international marketing as they are in formulating domestic marketing strategies. What is different about international marketing, however, is the environment in which marketing decisions must be made and the influence that environment has in shaping marketing strategies. The principal components of the international marketing environment include cultural, political, legal, commercial, and economic forces. Each of these forces represents informational inputs that must enter into the strategy formulation process.

Culture

Culture refers to learned behavior over time, passed on from generation to generation. This behavior manifests itself in the form of social structure, habits, faith, customs, rituals, and religion, each of which tends to affect individual lifestyles, which in turn shape consumption patterns in the marketplace. Thus, what people of a particular country buy, why they buy, when they buy, where they buy, and how they buy are largely culturally determined. There are five elements of culture: material culture, social institutions, man and universe, aesthetics, and language. Each of these elements varies from country to country. The importance to marketers of understanding these often subtle variations has been illustrated by Dichter:

> In puritanical cultures it is customary to think of cleanliness as being next to godliness. The body and its functions are covered up as much as possible.
>
> But in Catholic and Latin countries, to fool too much with one's body, to overindulge in bathing or toiletries, has opposite meaning. Accordingly, an advertising approach based on puritanical principles, threatening Frenchmen that if they didn't brush their teeth regularly, they would develop cavities or would not find a lover, failed to impress. To fit the accepted concept of morality, the French advertising agency changed this approach to a permissive one.[25]

Similarly, language differences from one country to another could lead to problems because literal translations of words often connote different meanings. Several classic examples of marketing blunders include "Body by Fisher," which when literally translated into Flemish meant "Corpse by Fisher"; "Let

Hertz Put You in the Driver's Seat," when literally translated into Spanish meant "Let Hertz Make You a Chauffeur."[26] Even the choice of color for packaging and advertising may influence marketing decisions. For example, in the United States, white is equated with purity. In most Asian countries, however, white is associated with death in the same way that black is a symbol of mourning in American culture. In short, culture could have and has had far-reaching effects on the success of overseas marketing strategies.

Politics

The laissez-faire era when governments had little if anything to do with the conduct of business is past history. Today, even in democratic societies, governments exercise a pervasive influence on business decisions. In fact, it is not uncommon to find that the governments of many overseas countries actually own and operate certain businesses. One example of a government-owned and -operated business is Air France.

Although the degree of intervention varies across countries, developments in developing countries perhaps represent situations where government policies are most extreme. Therefore, to be successful overseas, a global marketer should determine the most favorable political climates and exploit those opportunities first. Robinson suggests that the degree of political vulnerability in a given overseas market can be ascertained by researching certain key issues. Positive answers to the following questions signal political troubles for a foreign marketer:

1. Is the supply of the product ever subject to important political debates? (sugar, salt, gasoline, public utilities, medicines, foodstuffs)
2. Do other industries depend upon the production of the product? (cement, power, machine tools, construction machinery, steel)
3. Is the product considered socially or economically essential? (key drugs, laboratory equipment, medicines)
4. Is the product essential to agricultural industries? (farm tools and machinery, crops, fertilizers, seed)
5. Does the product affect national defense capabilities? (transportation industry, communications)
6. Does the product require important components that would be available from local sources and that otherwise would not be used as effectively? (labor, skill, materials)
7. Is there competition or is it likely from local manufacturers in the near future? (small, low-investment manufacturing)
8. Does the product relate to channels of mass communication media? (newsprint, radio equipment)
9. Is the product primarily a service?
10. Does the use of the product, or its design, rest upon some legal requirements?
11. Is the product potentially dangerous to the user? (explosives, drugs)
12. Does the product induce a net drain on scarce foreign exchange?[27]

Legal Aspects

Despite the best intentions, differences may reasonably arise between parties doing business. What recourse exists for the resolution of differences and whose laws will apply are of vital concern to global marketers. Although there is no simple solution to such a complex problem, it is important that marketers anticipate areas where disputes are likely to arise and establish beforehand agreements on the means to use and which country will have jurisdiction in the resolution of differences. Legal difficulties in marketing are most prevalent regarding the following issues:

1. Rules of competition about
   a. collusion
   b. discrimination against certain buyers
   c. promotional methods
   d. variable pricing
   e. exclusive territory agreement
2. Retail price maintenance laws
3. Cancellation of distributor or wholesaler agreements
4. Product quality laws and controls
5. Packaging laws
6. Warranty and after-sales exposure
7. Price controls and limitations on markups or markdowns
8. Patents, trademarks, and copyright laws and practices[28]

Needless to say, the marketer in conjunction with legal counsel should probe these areas and establish with the buyer various contingencies prior to the making of commitments.

Commercial Practices

An international marketer must be thoroughly familiar with the business customs and practices in effect in overseas markets. Although some evidence suggests that business traditions in a country may undergo a change as a result of dealing with foreign corporations, such transformations are long-term processes. Thus, local customs and practices must be researched and adhered to in order to gain the confidence and support of local buyers, channel intermediaries, and other business operatives. The specific customs and practices of a country may be studied with reference to the following factors:

Business Structure

Size
Ownership
Various business publics
Sources and level of authority
  Top management decision making
  Decentralized decision making
  Committee decision making

Management Attitudes and Behavior

Personal background
Business status
Objectives and aspirations

Security and mobility
Personal life
Social acceptance
Advancement
Power

Patterns of Competition

Mode of Doing Business

Level of contact
Communications emphasis
Formality and tempo
Business ethics
Negotiation emphasis[29]

Economic Climate

Only a small percentage of people in the world approach the standard of living experienced in the United States and in other advanced industrialized countries. The level of economic development in various countries can be explained and described through a number of measures. One common measure used to rank nations economically is per capita GNP.

According to Rostow, the countries of the world can be grouped into the following stages of economic development: (a) the traditional, (b) the precondition for take-off, (c) the take-off, (d) the drive to maturity, and (e) mass consumption.[30] Most African, Asian, and Latin American countries would be categorized as underdeveloped, having lower living standards and limited discretionary income. The amount of work required to earn enough to purchase a product varies greatly among different countries. For example, to buy one kilogram of sugar, a person in the United States needs to work a little over five minutes; in Greece it takes 53 minutes of labor to earn an equivalent amount. In many African and Asian countries the effort needed to buy a kilogram of sugar and, for that matter, other similar products is even higher.

STRATEGY FOR GLOBAL MARKETING PROGRAMS

Two opposite viewpoints for developing global marketing strategy are commonly expounded. According to one school of thought, marketing is an inherently local problem. Due to cultural and other differences among countries, marketing programs should be tailor-made for each country. The opposing view treats marketing as know-how that can be transferred from country to country. It has been argued that the worldwide marketplace has become so homogenized that multinational corporations can market standardized products and services all over the world with identical strategies, thus lowering their costs and earning higher margins.

Localized Strategy

The proponents of localized marketing strategies support their viewpoint based on four differences across countries:[31] (a) buyer behavior characteristics, (b) socioeconomic condition, (c) marketing infrastructure, and (d) competitive environment. A review of the marketing literature shows how companies often experience difficulties in foreign markets because they did not fully understand differences in buyer behavior. For example, Campbell's canned soups—mostly vegetable and beef combinations packed in extra-large cans—did not catch on in soup-loving Brazil. A postmortem study showed that most Brazilian housewives felt they were not fulfilling their roles if they served soup that they could not call their own. Brazilian housewives had no problems using dehydrated competitive products, such as Knorr and Maggi, which they could use as soup starters and still add their own ingredients and flair.[32] Also, Johnson & Johnson's baby powder did not sell well in Japan until its original package was changed to a flat box with a powder puff. Japanese mothers feared that powder would fly around their small homes and enter their spotlessly clean kitchens when sprinkled from a plastic bottle. Powder puffs allowed them to apply powder sparingly.[33] Similarly, advertisers have encountered difficulty when using colors in certain foreign countries. For example, purple is a death color in Brazil, white is for funerals in Hong Kong, and yellow signifies jealousy in Thailand. In Egypt the use of green, which is the national color, is frowned upon for packaging.[34]

Socioeconomic differences (i.e., per capita income, level of education, level of unemployment) among countries also call for a localized approach toward international marketing. For example, limited economic means may prevent masses in developing countries from buying the variety of products that U.S. consumers consider essential. To bring such products as automobiles and appliances within the reach of the middle class in developing countries, for example, the products must be appropriately modified to cut costs without reducing functional quality.

Differences in the character of local marketing infrastructure across countries may suggest pursuing country-specific marketing strategies. The marketing infrastructure consists of the institutions and functions necessary to create, develop, and service demand, including retailers, wholesalers, sales agents, warehousing, transportation, credit, media, and more.[35] Take the case of media. Commercial television is not available in many countries. Sweden, for example, lacks this element of the marketing infrastructure. In many countries, for example, Switzerland, commercials on television are allowed on a limited scale. Suntory (a Japanese liquor company) considers the ban on advertising liquor on U.S. television as a main deterrent for not entering the U.S. market in a big way.[36] Similarly, the physical conditions of a country (i.e., climate, topography, and resources) may require localized strategies. In hot climates, as in the Middle East, such products as cars and air conditioners must have additional features. Differences in telephone systems, road networks, postal practices, and the like may require modifications in marketing practices. For example, mail-order retailing is popular in the United States but is virtually nonexistent in Italy because of differences in its mail system.[37]

Finally, differences in the competitive environment among countries may require following localized marketing strategies. Nestlé, for example, achieved more than a 60 percent market share in the instant coffee market in Japan but less than 30 percent in the United States. Nestlé had to contend with two strong domestic competitors in the United States, namely General Foods, which markets the Maxwell House, Yuban, and Brim brands, and more recently Procter and Gamble, which markets Folgers and High Point. Nestlé faced relatively weak domestic competitors in Japan. IBM, which is the leading computer company in the world, slipped to third place in the Japanese market in 1984 behind Fujitsu Ltd. and NEC Corporation in terms of total revenue. Nestlé and IBM must reflect differences in their competitive environments in such marketing choices as pricing, sales force behavior, and advertising.[38]

Standardized Strategy

In contrast to the view that marketing strategies must be localized, many scholars and practitioners argue that significant benefits can be achieved through standardization of marketing strategies on a global basis. As a matter of fact, some people recommend an extreme strategy: offering identical products at identical prices through identical distribution channels and supporting these identical products by identical sales and promotional programs throughout the world. Levitt asserts that "commercially, nothing confirms this as much as the success of McDonald's from the Champs Elysées to the Ginza, of Coca-Cola in Bahrain and Pepsi-Cola in Moscow, and of rock music, Greek salad, Hollywood movies, Revlon cosmetics, Sony televisions, and Levi's jeans everywhere."[39] Although across-the-board standardization, as proposed by Levitt, may be difficult, it is commonly accepted that the marketplace is becoming increasingly global, and indeed standardized strategies have been successfully pursued in many cases. Among consumer durable goods, the Mercedes-Benz sells its cars by following a universal marketing program. Among nondurable goods, Coca-Cola is ubiquitous. Among industrial goods, Boeing jets are sold worldwide based on common marketing perspectives.

Past research shows that, other things being equal, companies usually opt for standardization. A recent study on the subject lends support to the high propensity to standardize all or parts of marketing strategy in foreign markets. For example, an extremely high degree of standardization appears to exist in brand names, physical characteristics of products, and packaging.[40] More than half the products that multinational corporations sell in less-developed countries originate in the parent companies' home markets. Of the 2200 products sold by the 61 subsidiaries in the sample, 1200 had originated in the United States or the United Kingdom.[41]

The arguments in favor of standardization are realization of cost savings, development of worldwide products, and achievement of better marketing performance. Standardization of products across national borders eliminates duplication of such costs as research and development, product design, and packaging. Further, standardization permits realization of economies of scale. Also, standardization makes it feasible to achieve consistency in dealing with customers and in product design. Consistency in product style—features, design, brand name, packaging—should establish a common image of the product worldwide and help increase overall sales.[42] For example, a person accustomed to a particular brand is likely to buy the same brand overseas if it is available. The global exposure that brands receive these days as a result of extensive world travel and mass media requires the consistency that is feasible through standardization. Finally, standardization may be urged on the grounds that a product that has proved to be successful in one country should do equally well in other countries that present more or less similar markets and similar competitive conditions.

Conclusion

Although standardization offers benefits, too much attachment to standardization can be counterproductive. Marketing environments vary from country to country, and thus a standard product originally conceived and developed in the United States may not really match the conditions in each and every market. In other words, standardization can lead to substantial opportunity loss.

Pond's cold cream, Coca-Cola, and Colgate toothpaste have been cited as evidence that a universal product and marketing strategy for consumer goods can win worldwide success. However, the applicability of a universal approach for consumer goods appears to be limited to products that have certain characteristics, among them universal brand name recognition (generally earned by huge financial outlays), minimal product knowledge requirements for consumer use, and product advertisements that demand low information content. Clearly, Coca-Cola, Colgate toothpaste, McDonald's, Levi's jeans, and Pond's cold cream display these traits. Thus, whereas a universal strategy can be effective for some consumer products, it is clearly an exception rather than the general rule. Those who argue that consumer products no longer require market tailoring due to the globalization of markets brought about by today's advanced technology are not always correct.

A multinational corporation that intends to launch a new product into a foreign market should consider the nature of its products, its organizational capabilities, and the level of adaptation required to accommodate cultural differences between the home and the host country. A multinational corporation should also analyze such factors as market structures, competitors' strategic orientations, and host government demands.[43]

The international marketplace is far more competitive today than in the 1980s and most likely will remain so throughout the 1990s. Thus, to enhance competitive advantage some sort of adaptation might provide a better match between a product and local marketing conditions.[44] Ohmae's charges against American companies for not adapting their products to Japanese needs are revealing:

> Yet, American merchandisers push such products as oversize cars with left-wheel drive, devices measuring in inches, appliances not adapted to lower voltage and

frequencies, office equipment without kanji capabiliaties and clothes not cut to smaller dimensions. Most Japanese like sweet oranges and sour cherries, not visa versa. That is because they compare imported oranges with domestic mikans (very sweet tangerines) and cherries with plums (somewhat tangy and sour).[45]

There are several patterns and various degrees of differentiation that firms can adopt to do business on an international scale. The most common of these are obligatory and discretionary product adaptation. An **obligatory**, or **minimal**, **product adaptation** implies that a manufacturer is forced to introduce minor changes or modifications in product design for either of two reasons. First, adaptation is mandatory in order to seek entry into particular foreign markets. Second, adaptation is imposed on a firm by external environmental factors, including the special needs of a foreign market. In brief, obligatory adaptation is related to safety regulations, trademark registration, quality standards, and media standards. An obligatory adaptation requires mostly physical changes in a product. **Discretionary**, or **voluntary**, **product adaptation** reflects a sort of self-imposed discipline and a deliberate move on the part of an exporter to build stable foreign markets through a better alignment of product with market needs and/or cultural preferences.

Swiss-based pharmaceutical maker Ciba-Geigy's efforts in adapting its products to local conditions are noteworthy. Basic to the company's adaptation program are quality circles. These circles include local executives with line responsibilities for packaging, labeling, advertising, and manufacturing. They are responsible for determining (a) if Ciba-Geigy's products are appropriate for the cultures in which they are sold and meet users' needs, (b) if products are promoted in such a way that they can be used correctly for purposes intended, and (c) if, when used properly, products present no unresponsible hazards to human health and safety.[46]

MARKETING IN GLOBAL BUSINESS STRATEGY[47]

International marketing strategy is significant in formulating global business strategy in three different ways. First, what should be the global *configuration* of marketing activities? That is, where should such activities as new product development advertising, sales promotion, channel selection, marketing research, etc., be performed? Second, how should global marketing activities performed in different countries be *coordinated*? Third, how should marketing activities be *linked* with other activities of the firm? Each of these aspects is examined below.

Configuration of Marketing Activities

Marketing activities, unlike those in other functional areas of a business, must be dispersed in each host country to make an adequate response to local environments. Although this configuration is valuable in being customer oriented, not all marketing activities need to be performed on a dispersed basis. In many cases, competitive advantage is gained in the form of lower cost or enhanced differentiation if selected activities are performed centrally as a result of technological changes, buyer shifts, and evolution of marketing media. These activities comprise production of promotional materials, sales force, service support organization, training, and advertising.

The centralized production of advertisements, sales promotion materials and user manuals can lead to a variety of benefits. Economies of scale can be reaped in both development and production. For example, experienced art directors and producers can be hired to create better ads at a greater speed or lower cost. The use of centralized printing permits the latest technology to be adopted. On the other hand, excessive transportation costs and cultural differences among nations may make the production of some materials (e.g., user manuals) impractical.

Sales force, at least for some businesses, can be centralized in one location. Alternatively, highly skilled sales specialists can be stationed at the headquarters or in a regional office to provide sales support in different countries. Centralization of the sales force is most effective when the complexity of the selling task is very high, and the products being sold are high-ticket items purchased infrequently.

Like sales force, high-skilled service specialists can be located at world or regional headquarters. They can visit different subsidiaries to provide nonroutine service. Along the same lines, service facilities (service center, repair shop) can be regionalized at a few locations, especially for complex jobs. Such centralization should permit the use of state-of-the-art facilities and qualified service people, resulting in better service at lower cost.

Training of marketing personnel can be effectively centralized and lead to economies of scale in production and delivery of training programs, faster accumulated learning (which people with varied experiences assembled in one place bring), and increased uniformity around the world in implementing marketing programs. Training centralization, however, must be weighed against travel time and cost.

Although cultural differences between nations require advertising to be tailored to each country, in many ways global advertising is gaining acceptance. First, a company may select one ad agency to handle its global campaign, economizing in campaign development, seeking better coordination between the parent and subsidiaries, and facilitating a consistent advertising approach worldwide. For example, British Airways uses one agency, Saatchi and Saatchi, worldwide. Second, many companies advertise in the global media, for example, in *The Economist,* in certain trade magazines, or at international sports events seen by viewers around the world, such as at U.S. Open tennis matches. Finally, many media (e.g., airport billboards, airline and hotel magazines) have a decidedly international reach. For these reasons, centralization of advertising makes sense. Yet government rules and regulations relative to advertising, distinct national habits, language differences, and lack of media outlets may require dispersion of advertising to different countries.

International Marketing Coordination

International marketing activities dispersed in different countries should be properly coordinated to gain competitive advantage. Such coordination can be achieved in the following ways:

1. **Performing marketing activities using similar methods across countries**—This form of coordination implies standardizing activities across nations. Some strategies, including brand name, product positioning, service standards, warranties, and advertising theme, are easier to coordinate than are other marketing strategies. On the other hand, distribution, personal selling, sales training, pricing and media selection are difficult to coordinate across nations.
2. **Transferring marketing know-how and skills from country to country**—For example, a market entry strategy successfully tried in one country can be transferred and applied in another country. Likewise, customer and market information can be transferred for use by other subsidiaries. Such information may relate to shifts in buyer purchasing patterns, recent trends in technology, lifestyle changes, successful new product or feature introductions, new promotion ideas, and early market signals by competitors.
3. **Sequencing of marketing programs across countries**—For example, new products or new marketing practices may be introduced in various countries in a planned sequence. In this way, programs developed by one subsidiary can be shared by others to their mutual advantage and, thus, should result in substantial cost savings. To reap the benefits of sequencing, a company must create organizational mechanisms to manage the product line from a worldwide perspective and to overcome manager resistance to change in all participating countries.
4. **Integrating the efforts of various marketing groups in different countries**—Perhaps the most common form of such integration is managing relationships with important multinational customers, often called *international account management.* International account management systems are commonly used in service firms. For example, Citibank handles some accounts on a worldwide basis. It has account officers responsible for coordinating services to its large corporate customers anywhere in the world.

Competitive advantage can result from international account management systems in a variety of ways. They can lead to economies in the utilization of the sales force if duplication of selling effort is avoided. They can allow a company to differentiate itself from its competitors by offering a single contact for international buyers. They can also leverage the skills of top salespersons by giving them more influence over the entire relationship with major customers. Some of the potential impediments to using international account management include increased travel time, language barriers, and cultural differences in how business is conducted. Dealing with a major customer through a single coordinator may also heighten the customer's awareness of its bargaining power.

Integration of effort across countries can lead to competitive advantage in other areas as well; for example, after-sale service. Some international companies have come to realize that the availability of after-sale service is often as important as the product itself, especially when a multinational customer has operations in remote areas of the world or when the customer moves from country to country.

Marketing's Linkage to Nonmarketing Activities

A global view of international marketing permits linking marketing functions to upstream and support activities of the firm, which can lead to advantage in various ways. For example, marketing can unlock economies of scale and learning in production and/or research and development by (a) supporting the development of universal products by providing the information necessary to develop a physical product design that can be sold worldwide; (b) creating demand for more universal products even if historical demand has been for more varied products in different countries; (c) identifying and penetrating segments in many countries to allow the sale of universal products; and (d) providing services and/or local accessories that effectively tailor the standard physical product.

DEVELOPING GLOBAL MARKET STRATEGY—AN EXAMPLE

Decisions related to foreign market entry, expansion, and conversion as well as to phasing out of foreign markets call for systematic effort. Illustrated here is one method of developing a global market strategy. The method consists of three phases:[48]

1. Appropriate national markets are selected by quickly screening the full range of options without regard to any preconceived notions.
2. Specific strategic approaches are devised for each country or group of countries based on the company's specific product technologies.
3. Marketing plans for each country or group of countries are developed, reviewed, revised, and incorporated into the overall corporate concept without regard to conventional wisdom or stereotypes.

Phase 1: Selecting National Markets

There are over 160 countries in the world; of these the majority may appear to present entry opportunities. Many countries go out of their way to attract foreign investment by offering lures ranging from tax exemptions to low-paid, amply skilled labor. These inducements, valid as they may be in individual cases, have repeatedly led to hasty foreign market entry.

A good basis for selecting national markets is arrived at through a comparative analysis of different countries, with long-term economic environment having the greatest weight. First, certain countries, because of their political situations (e.g., Libya under Qaddafi), should be considered unsuitable for market entry. It might help to consult a political index that rates different countries for business attractiveness. The final choice should be based on the company's own assessment and risk preference. Further, markets that are either too small in terms of population and per capita income or that are economically too weak should be eliminated. For example, a number of countries with populations of less than 20 million and with annual per capita incomes below $2000 are of little interest to many companies because of limited demand potential.

The markets surviving this screening should then be assessed for strategic attractiveness. A battery of criteria should be developed to fit the specific requirements of the corporation. Basically, the criteria should focus on the following five factors (industry/product characteristics may require slight modification):

1. Future demand and economic potential
2. Distribution of purchasing power by population groups or market segments
3. Country-specific technical product standards
4. Spillover from the national market (e.g., the Andes Pact provides for low-duty exports from Colombia to Peru)
5. Access to vital resources (qualified labor force, raw materials sources, suppliers)

There is no reason to expand the list because additional criteria are rarely significant enough to result in useful new insights. Rather, management should concentrate on developing truly meaningful and practical parameters for each of the five criteria listed above so that the selection process does not become unnecessarily costly and the results are fully relevant to the company concerned. For example, a German flooring manufacturer, selling principally to the building industry, selected the following yardsticks:

1. **Economic potential**—New housing needs and GNP growth
2. **Wealth**—Per capita income, per capita market size for institutional building or private dwellings (the higher the per captia income, market volume, and share of institutional buildings, the more attractive the market)
3. **Technical product standards**—Price level of similar products, for example, price per square meter for floor coverings (the higher the price level, the more attractive the market tends to be for a technically advanced producer)
4. **Spillover**—Area in which the same building standards (especially fire safety standards) apply (e.g., the U.S. National Electrical Manufacturers' Association standards are widely applicable in Latin America; British standards apply in most Commonwealth countries)
5. **Resource availability**—Annual production volume of PVC (an important raw material for the company)

Through these criteria, the analysis of economic potential was based on two factors: housing needs and economic base (see Exhibit 18-4). In specifying these criteria, the company deliberately confined itself to measures that (a) could readily be developed from existing sources of macroeconomic data, (b) would show trends as well as current positions, and (c) matched the company's particular characteristics as closely as possible.

Since German producers of floor covering employ a highly sophisticated technology, it would have been senseless to give a high ranking to a country with only rudimentary production technology in this particular facet. Companies in other industries, of course, would consider other factors—auto registrations per 1000 population, percentage of households with telephones, density of household appliance installations, and the like.

The resulting values are rated for each criterion on a scale of one to five so that, by weighting the criteria on a percentage basis, each country can be

EXHIBIT 18-4

Assessing Country Economic Potential: The Case of a Building Industry Flooring Supplier

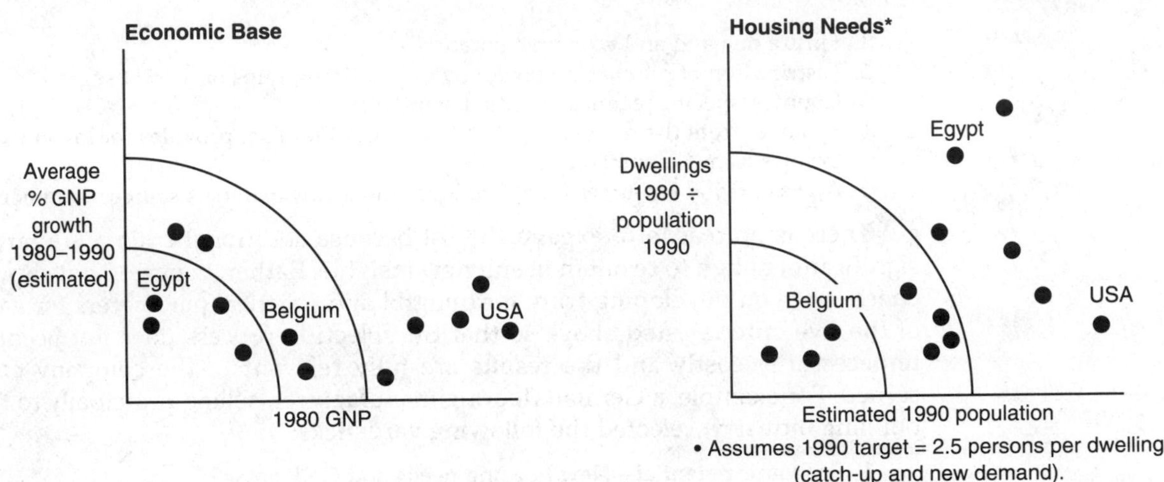

Economic Base

Housing Needs	Weak	Medium	Strong
High	Egypt Pakistan	Korea Nigeria	USA Japan
Medium	Yugoslavia	United Kingdom	West Germany France
Low	Denmark	Belgium	Sweden

Examples: Sweden—needs only in replacement sector; Pakistan—economically too weak to meet needs.

assigned an index number indicating its overall attractiveness. In this particular case, the result was that, out of the 49 countries surviving the initial screening, 16 were ultimately judged attractive enough on the basis of market potential, per capita market size, level of technical sophistication, prevailing regulations, and resource availability to warrant serious attention.

Interestingly, the traditionally German-favored markets of Austria and Belgium emerged with low rankings from this strategically based assessment because the level of potential demand was judged to be insufficient. Some new markets, Egypt and Pakistan, for example, were also downgraded because of inadequate economic base. Likewise, even such high-potential markets as Italy and Indonesia were eliminated for objective reasons (in the latter case, the low technical standard of most products).

Phase 2: Determining Marketing Strategy

After a short list of attractive foreign markets has been compiled, the next step is to group these countries according to their respective stages of economic development. Here the criterion of classification is not per capita income but the degree of market penetration by the generic product in question. For example, the floor covering manufacturer grouped countries into three categories, developing, takeoff, and mature, as defined by these factors (see Exhibit 18-5):

1. **Accessibility of markets**—Crucial for the choice between export and import production
2. **Local competitive situation**—Crucial for the choice between independent construction, joint venture, and acquisition
3. **Customer structure**—Crucial for sales and distribution strategy
4. **Re-import potential**—Crucial for international product/market strategy

The established development phases and their defining criteria must be very closely geared to the company situation because it is these factors, not the apparent attractiveness of markets, that will make or break the company's strategic thrust into a given country.

This being the case, for each country or group of countries on the short list, management should formulate a generic marketing strategy with respect to investment, risk, product, and pricing policies; that is, a unified strategic framework applicable to all the countries in each stage of development should be prepared. This step should yield a clear understanding of what the respective stages of economic development of each country entail for the company's marketing strategies (see Exhibit 18-6).

Companies are too often inclined to regard "overseas" as a single market or at least to differentiate very little among individual overseas markets. Another common error is the assumption that product or service concepts suited to a highly developed consumer economy work as well in any foreign market. This is rarely true: different markets demand different approaches.

Across-the-board strategic approaches typically result in ill-advised and inappropriate allocation of resources. In less-developed markets that could be perfectly well served by a few distributors, companies have in some cases established production facilities that are doomed to permanent unprofitability.

EXHIBIT 18-5
Grouping Countries by Phase of Development

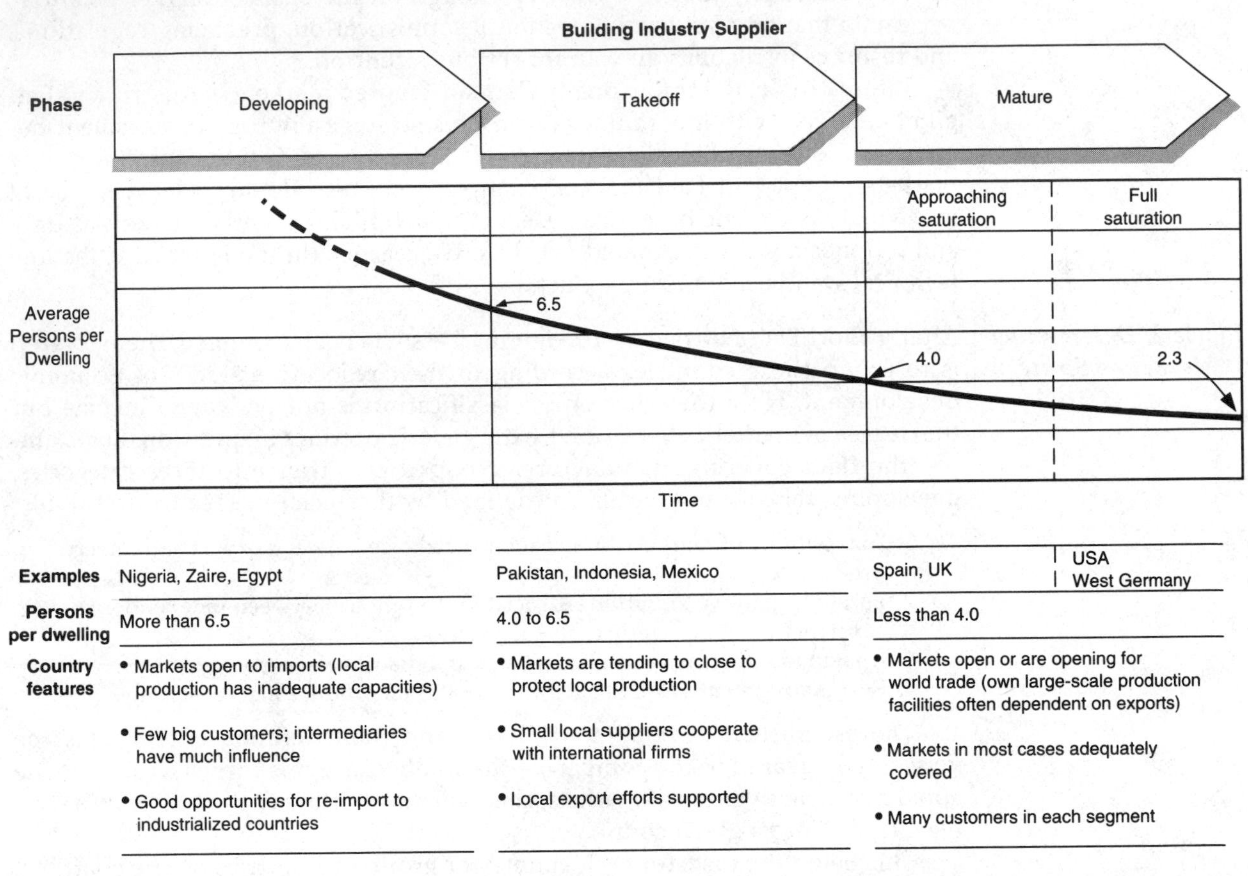

In markets already at the takeoff point, companies have failed to build the necessary local plants and instead have complained about declining exports only to finally abandon the field to competitors. In markets already approaching saturation, companies have often sought to impose domestic technical standards where adequate standards and knowledge already exist or have tried to operate like minireplicas of parent corporations, marketing too many product lines with too few salespeople. Again and again, product line offerings are weighted toward either cheaper- or higher-quality products than the local market will accept. Clearly, the best insurance against such errors is to select strategies appropriate to the country.

Phase 3: Developing Marketing Plans

In developing detailed marketing plans, it is first necessary to determine which product lines fit which local markets as well as the appropriate allocation of

EXHIBIT 18-6
Developing Standard Strategies

Phase	*Developing*	*Takeoff*	*Mature*
Basic Strategy	**Test Market** Pursue profitable individual projects and/or export activities	**Build Base** Allocate substantial resources to establish leading position in market	**Expand/Round Off Operations** Allocate resources selectively to develop market niches
Elements of Strategy			
Investment	Minimize (distribution and services)	Invest to expand capacity (relatively long payback)	Expand selectively in R&D, production, and distribution (relatively short payback)
Risk	Avoid	Accept	Limit
Know-how transfer (R&D)	Document know-how on reference projects	Use local know-how in • Product technology • Production engineering	Transfer know-how in special product lines; acquire local know-how to round off own base
Market share objective	Concentrate on key projects; possibly build position in profitable businesses with local support	Extend base with • New products • New outlets • New applications	Expand/defend
Cost leadership objective	Minimum acceptable (especially reduction of guarantee risks)	Economies of scale; reduction of fixed costs	Rationalize; optimize resources
Product	Standard technology; simple products	Aim for wide range; "innovator" role	Full product line in selected areas; products of high technical quality
Price	Price high	Aim for price leadership (at both ends)	Back stable market price level
Distribution	Use select local distributors (exclusive distribution)	Use a large number of small distributors (intensive distribution)	Use company sales force (selective distribution)
Promotion	Selective advertising • With typical high-prestige products • Aiming at decision makers	Active utilization of selective marketing resources	Selected product advertising

resources. A rough analysis of potential international business, global sales, and profit targets based on the estimates worked out in phase 1 help in assigning product lines. A framework for resource allocation can then be mapped according to rough comparative figures for investment quotas, management needs, and skilled labor requirements. This framework should be supplemented by company-specific examples of standard marketing strategies for each group of countries.

Exhibit 18-7 illustrates the resource allocation process. Different product lines are assigned to different country groups, and for each country category, different strategic approaches—for example, support on large-scale products, establishment of local production facilities, cooperation with local manufacturers—are specified.

EXHIBIT 18-7
A Specimen Framework for Resource Allocation

		Resource Allocation by Product Division					
Phase	*Specimen Countries*	*PVC Floor Coverings*	*Carpeting*	*Suspended Ceilings*	*Wall Paneling*	*PVC Tubes*	*Plastic-Coated Roof Insulation*
Developing "Test market"	Nigeria	Intensive	No operations	Moderate	No operations	Intensive	Intensive
(Share of total resources: 20%)	Specific plans • Develop own plastics-processing facilities • Acquire plastics processors						
Takeoff "Build base"	Indonesia	Moderate	No operations	No operations	No operations	Moderate	Moderate
(Share of total resources: 50%)	Specific plans • Give support in key projects • Cooperative with state-owned construction organization						
Mature "Expand/round off operations"	Spain	Moderate	Moderate	Intensive	Intensive	No operations	No operations
(Share of total resources: 30%)	Specific plans • Develop local facilities for tufting and paneling • Acquire/cooperate with suppliers using unique product and production technology • Develop own distribution channel • Extend range to provide complete interior equipment program (system concept)						

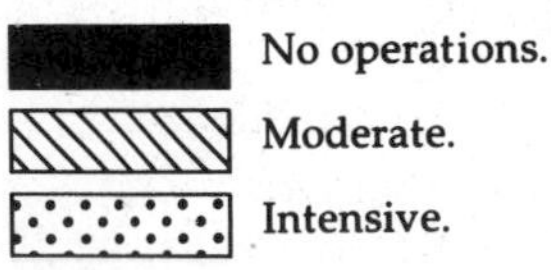

The level of detail in this resource allocation decision framework depends on a number of factors: company history and philosophy, business policy objectives, scope and variety of product lines, and the number of countries to be served. Working within this decision framework, each product division should analyze its own market in terms of size, growth, and competitive situations; assess its profitability prospects, opportunities, and risks; and identify its own current strategic position on the basis of market share, profit situation, and vulnerability to local risks. Each product division is then in a position to develop country-specific marketing alternatives for servicing each national market. Top management's role throughout is to coordinate marketing strategy development efforts of various divisions and continually to monitor the strategic decision framework.

The three-phase approach illustrated above exhibits a number of advantages:

- It allows management to set up, with a minimum of planning effort, a strategic framework that gives clear priority to market selection decisions, thus making it much easier for divisions to work out effective product line strategies unhampered by the usual chicken or egg problem.
- Division managers can foresee at a fairly early stage what reallocations of management, labor, and capital resources are needed and what adjustments may have to be imposed from the top due to inadequate resources.
- The company's future risk profile can be worked out in terms of resource commitment by country group and type of investment.
- The usual plethora of "exceptional" (and mostly opportunistic) product/market situations is sharply reduced. Only the really unique opportunities pass through the filter; exceptions are no longer the rule.
- The dazzling-in-theory but unrealistic-in-practice concept of establishing production bases in low-wage countries, buying from the world's lowest-cost sources, and selling products wherever best prices can be had is replaced by a realistic country-by-country market evaluation.
- Issues of organization, personnel assignment, and integration of overseas operations into corporate planning and control systems reach management's attention only after the fundamental strategic aspects of the company's overseas involvement have been thoroughly prepared.

In brief, the three-phase approach enables management to profitably concentrate resources and attention on a handful of really attractive countries instead of dissipating its efforts in vain attempts to serve the entire world.

SUMMARY

Internationalization of business has become a fact of life. Company after company finds that decisions made elsewhere in the world have a deep impact on its business. Although many firms have long been engaged in foreign business ventures, the real impetus to overseas expansion came after World War II. The globalization of business is accounted by such forces as (a) growing similarity of countries (e.g., commonality of infrastructure and channels of distribution); (b) falling tariff barriers; and (c) technological developments that, for example, permit the development of compact, easy-to-ship products.

Traditionally, major U.S. business activities overseas have been concentrated in developed countries. In recent years, developing countries have provided additional opportunities for U.S. corporations, especially in more politically stable countries. Yet although an individual developing country may not provide adequate potential for U.S. companies, developing countries as a group constitute a major market. The emerging markets in developing countries can help many U.S. corporations counter the results of matured markets in Western nations.

A firm aspiring to enter the international market may choose among various entry modes—exporting, contractual agreement, joint venture, or manufacturing. Each entry mode provides different opportunities and risks. The differentiation of global and domestic marketing largely revolves around the nature of environmental forces impinging on the formulation of strategy. International marketers must be sensitive to the environmental influences operating in overseas markets. The principal components of the international marketing environment include cultural, political, legal, commercial, and economic forces. Each of these forces represents informational inputs that must be factored into the decision-making process.

An important question that global marketers need to answer is whether the same product, price, distribution and promotion approach is adequate in foreign markets. In other words, a decision must be made about which is the more appropriate of two marketing strategies: localization or standardization. On the one hand, environmental differences between nations suggest using localization. On the other hand, there are potential gains to consider in standardizing market strategy. International marketers must examine all criteria in order to decide the extent to which marketing perspectives should vary from country to country.

International marketing plays three important roles in global business strategy. These are *configuration* of marketing activities (i.e., where different marketing activities should be performed), *coordination* (i.e., how international marketing activities dispersed in different countries should be coordinated), and the *linkage* of international marketing with other functions of the business.

The chapter ended with a framework for designing global market strategy. The framework consists of three steps: (a) selecting national markets, (b) determining marketing strategy, and (c) developing marketing plans.

DISCUSSION QUESTIONS

1. What forces are responsible for the globalization of markets?
2. How does culture affect international marketing decisions? Explain with examples.
3. Given their low per capita income, why should companies be interested in developing countries?

4. What are the different modes of entry into the international market? What are the relative advantages and disadvantages of each mode?
5. What are the advantages of international marketing strategy standardization?
6. Under what circumstances should marketing be adapted to local conditions?
7. What role does marketing play in global business strategy?

NOTES

[1]George S. Yip, "Global Strategy in a World of Nations?" *Sloan Management Review* (Fall 1991): 29–39; John Sharpe, "Making It in the Global Market," *Business Quarterly* (Winter 1990): 23–27; and Robert J. Allio, "Formulating Global Strategy," *Planning Review* (March–April 1989): 22–29.

[2]*Business International* (30 July 1990): 256.

[3]"Leap Forward or Sink Back," *Development Forum* (March 1982): 3.

[4]See Richard N. Farmer, "Would You Want Your Granddaughter to Marry a Taiwanese Marketing Man?" *Journal of Marketing* (October 1987): 111–16.

[5]"Laying Foundation for the Great Mall of China," *Business Week* (25 January 1988): 68.

[6]Subhash C. Jain, *Market Evolution in Developing Countries: Unfolding of the Indian Market,* in press.

[7]David Wessel, "Gillette Keys Sales to Third World Tastes," *Wall Street Journal,* 23 January 1986, p. 35.

[8]See Anthony J. O'Reilly, "Establishing Successful Joint Ventures in Developing Nations: A CEO's Perspective," *Columbia Journal of World Business* (Spring 1988): 3–9.

[9]Richard I. Kirkland, Jr., "Who Gains from the New Europe," *Fortune* (18 December 1989): 83.

[10]Kenichi Ohmae, *Triad Power* (New York: The Free Press, 1985), chapter 4.

[11]Ohmae, *Triad Power,* 23.

[12]Allan C. Reddy, "International Licensing May Be Best Bet for Companies Seeking Foreign Markets," *Marketing News* (12 November 1982): 6. Also see Farok J. Contractor, "Technology Licensing Practice in U.S. Companies: Corporate and Public Policy Implications," *Columbia Journal of World Business* (Fall 1983): 80–88.

[13]See O'Reilly, "Establishing Successful Joint Ventures," 9–13.

[14]Robert B. Reich and Eric D. Mankin, "Joint Ventures with Japan Give Away Our Future," *Harvard Business Review* (March–April 1978): 78.

[15]See Peter Lorange and Gilbert Probst, "Joint Ventures as Self-organizing Systems: A Key to Successful Join Venture Design and Implementation," *Columbia Journal of World Business* (Summer 1987): 71–78.

[16]See Allen R. Janger, *Organization of International Joint Ventures* (New York: Conference Board, Inc., 1980). Also see Ann Hughey and Masayoshi Kanabayashi, "More U.S. and Japanese Companies Decide to Operate Joint Ventures," *Wall Street Journal,* 10 May 1983, p. 37.

[17]Ohmae, *Triad Power,* 116.

[18]Marjorie A. Lyles, "Common Mistakes of Joint Venture Experienced Firms," *Columbia Journal of World Business* (Summer 1987): 79–85.

[19]J. Peter Killing, "How to Make a Global Joint Venture Work," *Harvard Business Review* (May–June 1982): 120. Also see Farok J. Contractor, "Strategies for Structuring Joint Ventures: A Negotiations Planning Paradigm," *Columbia Journal of World Business* (Summer 1984): 30–39.

[20]Janger, *Organization of International Joint Ventures,* 1–3. Also see Robert B. Reich, "Japan Inc., U.S.A.," *New Republic* (26 November 1984).

[21]F. Kingston Berlew, "The Joint Venture: A Way into Foreign Markets," *Harvard Business Review* (July–August 1984): 48. Also see Farok Contractor, "A Generalized Theorem of Joint-Venture and Licensing Negotiations," *Journal of International Business Studies* (Summer 1985): 23–49.

[22]"For Multinationals It Will Never Be the Same," *Business Week* (24 December 1984): 57.

[23]See M. Krishna Erramilli and C. P. Rao, "Choice of Foreign Market Entry Modes by Service Firms," *1988 Educators' Conference Proceedings* (Chicago: American Marketing Association, 1988), 20.

[24]James D. Goodnow, "Individual Product/Market Transnational Mode of Entry Strategies—Some Eclectic Decision-Making Formats," *Working Papers Series 1980,* no. 1 (Chicago: Roosevelt University, Walter E. Heller College of Business Administration, 1980), 6. Also see William H. Davidson, *Global Strategic Management* (New York: John Wiley & Sons, 1982); James D. Goodnow, "Development of Personal Computer Software for International Mode of Entry Decisions" (Paper presented at the 1985 Annual Meeting of the Academy of International Business, New York, October 1985); and C. K. Prahalad and Yves L. Doz, *The Multinational Mission* (New York: The Free Press, 1987), chapters 3–4.

[25]Ernest Dichter, "The World Customer," *Harvard Business Review* (July–August 1962): 116.

[26]David A. Ricks, *Big Business Blunders* (Homewood, IL: Dow Jones-Irwin, 1983): 83–85.

[27]Richard D. Robinson, "Background Concepts and Philosophy of International Business from World War II to the Present," *Journal of International Business Studies* (Spring–Summer 1981): 13–21. Also see Joseph S. Nye, Jr., "Multinational Corporations in World Politics," *Foreign Affairs* (October 1974): 153–75.

[28]Subhash C. Jain, *International Marketing Management* (Boston: Kent Publishing Co., 1984), chapter 9.

[29]Philip R. Cateora, *International Marketing,* 5th ed. (Homewood, IL: Richard D. Irwin, 1983), chapter 5.

[30]Walt W. Rostow, *The Stages of Economic Growth* (London: Cambridge University Press, 1960): 10.

[31]Subhash C. Jain, "Standardization of International Marketing Strategy," *Journal of Marketing* (January 1989): 70–79.

[32]"Brazil: Campbell Soup Fails to Make It to the Table," *Business Week* (21 October 1981): 66.

[33]Louis Kraar, "Inside Japan's 'Open' Market," *Fortune* (5 October 1981): 122.

[34]C. L. Lapp, "Marketing Goofs in International Trade," *The Diary of Alpha Kappa Psi* (February 1983): 4.

[35]Daniel C. Bello and Lee D. Dahringer, "The Influence of Country and Product on Retailer Operating Practices: A Cross National Comparison," *International Marketing Review* (Summer 1990): 42–52.

[36]Hirotaka Takeuchi and Michael E. Porter, "Three Roles of International Marketing in Global Strategy," in *Competition in Global Industries,* ed. Michael Porter (Boston: Harvard Business School Press, 1986): 113.

[37]Takeuchi and Porter, "Three Roles of International Marketing," 114.

[38]Ralph Z. Sorenson and Ulrich E. Wiechmann, "How Multinationals View Marketing Standardization," *Harvard Business Review* (May–June 1975): 38.

[39]Ted Levitt, "The Globalization of Markets," *Harvard Business Review* (May–June 1983): 92–102.

[40]Sorenson and Wiechmann, "How Multinationals View Marketing Standardization," 38-56.

[41]John S. Hill and Richard R. Still, "Adapting Products to LDC Tastes," *Harvard Business Review* (March-April 1984): 93-94.

[42]See "Brazil: U.S. Jeans Makers Find a Market Than Fits," *Business Week* (30 August 1982): 39.

[43]W. Chan Kim and R. A. Manborgue, "Cross-cultural Strategies," *Journal of Business Strategy* (Spring 1987): 31. See also M. P. Kacker, "Export-oriented Product Adaptation—Its Patterns and Problems," *Management International Review*, no. 6 (1976): 61-70.

[44]Warren J. Keegan, Richard R. Still, and John S. Hill, "Transferability and Adaptability of Products and Promotion Themes in Multinational Marketing—MNCs in LDCs," *Journal of Global Marketing* (Fall-Winter 1987): 85-101.

[45]Ohmae, *Triad Power*, 101-02.

[46]Kim and Manborgue, "Cross-cultural Strategies," 30.

[47]This section draws heavily on Takeuchi and Porter, "Three Roles of International Marketing," 111-46.

[48]Herbert Henzler, "Shaping an International Investment Strategy," *Manager Magazine* (April 1979): 69-81. Also see Marie E. Wicks Kelly and George C. Philippatos, "Comparative Analysis of the Foreign Investment Evaluation Practices by U.S. Based Manufacturing Multinational Companies," *Business Studies* (Winter 1982): 19-42; Robert Weigand, "International Investments: Weighing the Incentives," *Harvard Business Review* (July-August 1983): 146-53; and Philip Kotler and Liam Fahey, "The World's Champion Marketers: The Japanese," *Journal of Business Strategy* (Summer 1982): 3-13.

Cases

CASE 1 | *The Gillette Company*

In the spring of 1986, Joseph A. Marino, vice president of marketing in Gillette's shaving division, was concerned about the future prospects of his business. With sales of $2.4 billion, Gillette is the world's largest blade and razor manufacturer and claims a remarkable 62 percent share of the $700-million U.S. shaving market.

Growth in razors and blades has been slowing down, however, and competitors were putting a few nicks in Gillette's performance. Revenues increased just 3 percent over the past three years (i.e., 1982–85), and during 1985, profits rose only 1 percent to $160 million. Gillette had to produce a steady stream of new shaving products just to hold its ground in the United States.

More disturbing was that cheap disposable razors—unknown 12 years ago—now accounted for more than half of U.S. sales. That figure has been growing, and even though Gillette dominated the disposable market, cheaper razors meant lower profits. For a company that received one-third of its sales and two-thirds of its earnings from blades and razors, that was bad news. Foreign business, which accounted for about 57 percent of corporate sales and 61 percent of profits, was a sore spot, too. Although a weaker dollar was expected to boost Gillette's overseas earnings, a weaker dollar would help Gillette only in the short term. Foreign razor and blade markets were also mature.

RAZOR TECHNOLOGY

Ever since an ambitious inventor named King C. Gillette introduced the first safety razor in 1903, men have been accustomed to continual, extensively advertised advances from Gillette in the state of the art of shaving. The company spends more than $20 million a year on shaving research and development. With the aid of the latest scientific instruments, a staff of 200 explores the fringes of metallurgical technology and biochemical research. They subject the processes of beard growth and shaving to the most rigorous scrutiny.

Every day some 10,000 men carefully record the results of their shaves for Gillette on data processing cards, including the precise number of their nicks and cuts. Five hundred of those men shave in 32 special inplant cubicles under carefully controlled and monitored conditions, including observation by two-way mirrors and videotape cameras. In certain cases, sheared whiskers are collected, weighed, and measured. The results of the tests are fed into a computer and processed by sophisticated statistical programs.

Gillette scientists know, for instance, that a man's beard grows an average of 15/1000 of an inch a day, or $5\frac{1}{2}$ inches a year; that it covers about a third of a square foot of his face and contains 15,500 hairs; that shaving removes about 65 milligrams of whiskers daily, which amounts to a pound of hair every 16 years; that during an average lifetime a man will spend 3350 hours scraping $27\frac{1}{2}$ feet of whiskers from his face.

Occasionally other companies have obtained a technological jump on Gillette. In the early 1960s, a new longer-life stainless steel blade from Wilkinson Sword of Great Britain temporarily stole a big share of the market from Gillette's carbon steel Super Blue Blade. But Gillette, as it always does, soon introduced its own longer-life version and recaptured much of the lost market.

To fully comprehend Gillette's research and development inroads, one has to visit its research facilities in South Boston. Displayed there are pictures taken through a field emission scanning electron microscope that can magnify objects

This case was prepared as a basis for class discussion rather than to illustrate either effective or ineffective handling of an administrative situation.

50,000 times. The photographs showed tiny sections—1/10,000 of an inch—of the edges of razor blades made by Gillette and some of its competitors. The edges of the competitors' blades looked rough and jagged. Although not exactly Iowa farmland, the edges of the Gillette blade resembled softly rolling hills, like the Berkshires in Connecticut. The reason for Gillette's less formidable topography was the new "microsmooth" process invented by Gillette, whereby blades are given extra smooth edges by particles of aluminum oxide energized by ultrasonic waves.

COMPETITION

Probably no company in this country has so thoroughly dominated one consumer market as long as Gillette. A huge concern with $2.4 billion in annual sales (1985 figure), it controls over 62 percent of the shaving market. Electric razors in their initial years appeared to pose a big challenge to Gillette's wet-shaving products. But today, they are used by only a quarter of all shavers, and most owners shave with them only occasionally. As a matter of fact, due to continual advances in wet shaving and the inability of electrics to deliver a comparably close shave, their use is slowly declining. Gillette's few competitors, such as Schick (22 percent of the market), American Safety Razor, and Wilkinson, have been reduced mainly to manufacturing knockoff versions of and refill blades for Gillette razors.

Just when its competitors adjusted to one shaving system, Gillette unleashed yet another advance. In 1971 it was Trac II, a razor system that featured two parallel blades mounted in a cartridge 60/1000 of an inch apart. Gillette said the idea arose from a phenomenon called *hysteresis* discovered by its research and development people through slow motion microphotography. When a razor blade cuts through a whisker, the whisker is pulled slightly out of the follicle. A second blade, arranged in tandem, can thus take a second, closer slice off the whisker before it retracts and can thus provide a cleaner shave. In 1977, after research and development expenditures of over $8 million, Gillette made another "quantum leap forward," as the company termed it, with Atra, a razor featuring a twin-blade cartridge that swivels during shaving and thus follows the face's contours. Gillette said its tests showed that, whereas the twin Trac II blades are in contact with the face an average of only 77 percent of the time, the Atra can raise the figure to 89 percent.

The $7.95 Atra razor is the apotheosis of Gillette technology, engineering, and design. Weighing a hefty $1\frac{1}{2}$ ounces, it is a luxurious, elaborately crafted machine with a thick, beautifully tooled aluminum handle. Refill blades retail for 56 cents each. The Atra is available in expensive gift versions: one ($19.95) is goldplated with a rosewood handle; another ($49.95) features a sterling silver handle designed by Reed and Barton that resembles an antique table knife.

Recently the company rolled out a new version of Atra called Atra Plus, a razor with a lubricating strip above the blade for smoother shaves.

A relatively recent entrant into the shaving business is the Bic Pen Corporation, maker of the familiar ballpoint pen. The company, which has $200 million in annual sales, is located in modest quarters in Milford, Connecticut. It does not have anyone regularly assigned to explore the fringes of shaving technology. It does not have a field emission scanning electron microscope. It does not do any ultrasonic honing. It maintains only a small shave-testing panel of about a hundred people who do not fill out data processing cards. It does not know and does not care how many hairs are in the average man's beard or how fast they grow.

The apotheosis of Bic technology, engineering, and design is the Bic Shaver. Weighing only a quarter of an ounce, it is a diminutive, characterless object made of white plastic that looks like something used in hospitals. In fact, a version of it *is* used in hospitals. It has only one blade mounted on a short, hollow handle and sells for about 99 cents for four or for 25 cents each. When the blade wears out, you throw the whole thing away. The Bic Shaver is not available in gold or silver plate or aluminum or anything else but plastic. It does not come in gift versions.

Bic Pen Corporation, though, is selling 200 million shavers a year in the United States, nearly twice as many as the number of Atra blades that Gillette is selling. The Bic Shaver, in fact, is the most serious challenge Gillette has faced since the early days of King Gillette.

Though Bic and Gillette came to purvey disposability from different perspectives, it was inevitable that sooner or later they would clash. The first clash between Gillette and Bic was in pens. Beginning in the 1950s, the pen market rapidly became commoditized as inexpensive but high-quality ballpoints gained at the expense of high-priced, high-status pens. When Bic's throwaway "stick" pen began selling for 19 cents in the U.S. market in 1958, its major competitor was a 98-cent refillable pen made by Paper Mate, which Gillette had acquire in 1955. Paper Mate fought back with its low-priced Write Brothers line of stick pens. But Gillette's mass market advertising and promotion skills were no match for those of Baron Bich. Bic now has 60 percent of the ballpoint market versus Paper Mate's 20 percent.

The next clash involved butane cigarette lighters. Gillette initially went the cachet route with the 1971 purchase of S.T. Dupont, a prestigious French concern that produces luxury lighters selling for several hundred dollars. According to an ad, 500 separate steps and six months are required to manufacture Dupont lighters. Bic and Gillette, though, recognized that the lighter market was ripe for commoditization. By 1974 both were selling disposable lighters for $1.49, which were later reduced to 89 cents. These disposable lighters quickly stole market share from status brands.

"Dupont lighters are in a class by themselves, and people are willing to pay a premium for them." It was said that the click of a Dupont was so distinctive that, if you lit up in a restaurant, people knew you were using a Dupont. Now you can buy a disposable—a light at the end of a piece of plastic—for 89 cents. Why do people want a disposable lighter? They're utilitarian. They work. You can lose them and not care because you have no investment in them, no loyalty toward them.

Gillette has done only slightly better with disposable lighters than with disposable pens. Bic's lighter now has a 52 percent share of the market; Gillette's disposable Cricket has 30 percent. Bic's feel for the mass market, it should be noted, is not unerring. Its felt-tip Bic Banana pen, though lower priced, has solidly been bested by Gillette's Flair. "In all honesty, the Banana just wasn't a very good product," concedes a Bic marketing manager.

The shaving market is the most recent and most crucial clash. Bic introduced its disposable shaver to Europe in 1975 and moved into Canada the following year. Aware that the United States would be next, Gillette came out with its own blue plastic disposable called Good News!, which has a Trac II twin-blade head, in 1976. Gillette, which knows a lot more about selling shavers than lighters and pens, has been no pushover for Bic. Each company now has about half of the disposable market.

Good News!, though, is really bad news for Gillette. One must appreciate that the razor blade business is a fixed-sum game: sales in this country are relatively static at about two billion blades a year. Since Gillette is the dominant manufacturer, every new razor and blade it introduces in effect cannibalizes its older products. Atra takes business away from Trac II, which took business away from double-edge blades. But Gillette has never bothered much about this because its new products are invariably higher priced than its old products.

The problem is that Good News! sells for a lot less than any of Gillette's older products. Price is the key to commodity competition, and to stay competitive with the 25-cent Bic Shaver and with disposables from a few other producers, Gillette has had to sell Good News! for much less than the retail price of an Atra or Trac II cartridge. As many

Trac II and Atra users have figured out, although you have to pay as much as 56 cents for a twin-blade refill cartridge from Gillette, you can get precisely the same cartridge mounted on a plastic handle for as little as 25 cents. Good News! not only produces fewer revenues per blade sale for Gillette but creates higher costs because Gillette has to supply a handle as well as a cartridge. Every time Good News! gains a couple of points of market share, Gillette loses millions of dollars in sales and profits.

CORPORATE CULTURE

To fully grasp the intensity of Bic Pen Corporation's challenge, it is necessary to flash back briefly to the early days of Bic and Gillette. The founders of the two companies were strong-willed men who single-mindedly pursued powerful and remarkably similar visions. King Gillette's vision came one morning in 1895 when he started shaving with his old straight-edged razor. It was not only dull, he realized, but beyond the help of his leather strop. To reestablish its edge, it would have to be honed by the local barber or cutler. At the time, Gillette was working for a company that made a great deal of money manufacturing bottle caps. The inventor of the bottle cap had often regaled Gillette with the bountiful proceeds derived from putting out an inexpensive item that people repeatedly use and throw away. In a flash, as he looked at his spent straight-edged razor, Gillette conceived of the idea of a safety razor with a disposable blade.

Less is known of the early vision of Marcel L. Bich, the reclusive Italian-born businessman and yachtsman who founded Société Bic in Paris, which controls the U.S.-based Bic Pen Corporation. But it is said that, in the late 1940s, "Baron" Bich, as he calls himself, hit upon the idea of a low-priced, reliable, disposable ballpoint pen. Existing ballpoints, which not only were expensive and required refills, frequently malfunctioned.

Gillette and Bich went on to make fortunes from disposability. But over a period of time, the philosophies of their companies diverged. Particularly after the death of King Gillette in 1932, his company sought to give its blades, and especially its handsome razor handles, an aura of not only superior performance but class and cachet. Each new technological leap could thus be more easily accompanied by a liberal leap in price and profit margin. Gillette's chief marketing strategy became the promotion of new captive "systems," or blade-handle combinations. Just as Kodak makes most of its money not on its cameras but on its film, profits in shaving are not in razor handles but in blades. Yet if a man could become convinced to trade up to a new, more expensive handle, such as Atra, he would then have to buy new, more expensive blades designed to fit only that handle.

Gillette was never concerned about what its people call "the low end of the market," that is, cheap private label blades. If you put out a class product, Gillette believed, the major portion of the always-status-seeking masses would buy it. Shaving being serious business and the way one's face appears to other people all day being a matter of some importance, most men, Gillette knew, didn't want to skimp and settle for an ordinary shave when for a little more money they could feel secure that they were getting the "best" shave from Gillette.

In recent years, as the vision of its founder faded, Gillette conglomerated into nondisposability. It acquired other companies and began marketing such class durables as cameras and hi-fi equipment. Durables, though, have never been as profitable for Gillette as razors and blades. In 1985 although the company's shaving division produced only 33 percent of its sales, it yielded 67 percent of the year's profits.

Baron Bich, whose first business venture was making parts for pen makers in Paris, eschewed class and pursued mass with a vengeance. He was taken with the potential of what Bic people call "commoditization," the devolution in recent years of certain expensive, high-status durables, including watches and cigarette lighters, into inexpensive, nonstatus, more or less disposable items. Commoditization has several basic causes. One is a shift in taste: different eras accord cachet to different products. More important is the technology of mass production. Often an item has status because it is difficult and time-consuming to make and must sell at a high price. But if production techniques are developed that allow the item to be spewed out by automated assembly lines at a cost of pennies with little if any loss in functional quality, its status and allure will abate. People will not feel embarrassed to buy and to be seen using the new, cheap version of the item.

A final cause of commoditization is consumers' growing resistance to what is called market "segmentation," the proliferation of new brands, flavors, and other diverse variants of common consumer goods. Although 35 years ago, according to a *Los Angeles Times* article, a retailer could satisfy 88 percent of his or her customers by stocking only five brands of cigarettes, now, to supply the same percentage of smokers, 58 different cigarette brands with a bewildering variety of lengths, filters, packages, flavors, and tar and nicotine contents must be carried. Large conglomerate consumer goods firms compete, not on the basis of who can sell for the lowest price, but on the basis of who can churn out and most aggressively market the largest number of new products.

Though all of this adds heavily to cost, consumers have generally been willing to pay premium prices for cosmetic differentiation. This allows companies to recoup their extra costs and to earn extra profits. But now, according to a recent *Harvard Business Review* study, consumers have become more price- and value-conscious and are beginning to rebel. In growing numbers, they are refusing to pay extra for individualized frills. They are bypassing national brands in favor of heavily discounted brandless products.

Baron Bich put a brand on his products. But to sell them as cheaply as possible and make them appeal to as many people as possible, he stripped them of all traces of cachet, glamour, and nonfunctional frills. He reduced them to pure generic utility and simplicity. He made them commodities. His marketing strategy was just as simple: high value at a low price. It was a strategy that would have won the admiration of King C. Gillette.

PSYCHOLOGY OF SHAVING

The battle between Bic and Gillette is more than a conventional contest over which kind of razor people want to use. It is a battle over one of the most enduring male rituals of daily American life.

Those of us who are old enough remember how the ritual used to be conducted because many of us watched it every morning. Like a chemist with mortar and pestle, our fathers would whip up a rich lather by stirring their shaving brushes around in their large ceramic mugs. Like an orchestra conductor during a brisk allegro, they would strop their gleaming straight-edge razors on long strips of leather. Writer Richard Armour once recalled the scene: "I loved to watch him grimace and pull the skin taut with his fingers preparatory to a daring swipe from cheekbone to chin. I held my breath while he shaved his upper lip, coming perilously close to his nose, and when he started his hazardous course along his jawbone, risking an ear lobe. When he scraped around his Adam's apple, with a good chance of cutting his throat, I had to turn away until I thought the danger was past."

Armour lamented that safety razors and aerosol lathers had taken the "skill, fun, and danger" out of shaving. Though the audience, if there is an audience, may be less apt, the morning ritual continues to occupy a very special place in most men's lives. Face shaving is one of the few remaining exclusively male prerogatives. It is a daily affirmation of masculinity. One study indicated that beard growth is actually stimulated by the prospect of sexual relations. A survey by New York psychologists reported that, although men complain about the bother of shaving, 97 percent of the sample would not want to use a cream, were one to be developed, that would permanently rid them of all facial hair. Gillette once introduced a new razor that came in versions for heavy, regular and light beards. Almost nobody bought the light version because nobody wanted to acknowledge lackluster beard production. (Later Gillette brought out an adjustable razor that enabled men with sparse whiskers to cope with their insufficiency in private.)

The first shave remains a rite of passage into manhood that is often celebrated with the gift of a handsome new razor (or the handing down of a venerable old razor) and a demonstration of its use from the father. Though shaving may now require less skill and involve less danger than it once did, most men still want the razor they use to reflect their belief that shaving remains serious business. They regard their razor as an important personal tool, a kind of extension of self, like an expensive pen, cigarette lighter, attaché case, or golf club set. Gillette has labored hard, with success, to maintain the razor's masculine look, heft, and feel as well as its status as an item of personal identification worthy of, for instance, a Christmas gift.

For over 80 years, Gillette's perception of the shaving market and the psychology of shaving has been unerring. Though its products formally have only a 62 percent share, its technology and marketing philosophy have held sway over the entire market.

Now, however, millions of men—about 12 million, to be more precise—are scraping their faces with small, asexual, nondescript pieces of plastic costing 25 cents, an act that would seem to be the ultimate deromanticization, even negation, of the shaving ritual, thus relegating shaving to a pedestrian, trivial daily task.

NEW SEGMENTS

Good News! is a defensive product for Gillette. Though distributing it widely, the company is spending negligible money advertising it. Gillette knows, though, that it must do more than counter the Bic threat. It must keep the whole disposable market contained. That means, most immediately, luring from disposables two chief categories of users: teenagers and women.

According to Marino, shaving is just not a high-interest category to a lot of kids in high school: "They don't have to have a Gillette razor or their father's razor to prove they're old enough to shave. They don't need life-style reflection in a razor. They want a good shave, but they don't want to pay a lot of money." One might venture several explanations for kids' indifference to the traditional aura of shaving. According to some people, there has been a progressive emasculation of the American male. Given this hypothesis, the unisex plastic disposable is a predictable response. Another view is that boys today are more secure in their sexual identities than the previous generation and thus don't need the old symbols of masculinity.

Whatever the case, as far as Gillette is con cerned, use of disposables is an ephemeral adolescent affection. As kids grow up, Gillette expects that promotion, advertising, and sampling will convince them that captive systems, such as Atra and Trac II, are a better and more mature way to shave.

Women are a more complex problem. Despite the fact that as many adult women shave as men, though much less often, Gillette and the other U.S. razor manufacturers are so male oriented that until quite recently they never sold a razor designed for women. Women had no choice but to pay for such masculine features as hefty metal handles. One Gillette marketing man contends with a leer, that "women seem to like a longer handle for some unknown reason." Yet already nearly 40 percent of women who shave have switched to disposables. Bic is now selling the Bic Lady Shaver, a slightly modified version of its regular disposables. Gillette, Schick, and other producers are trying to find ways to entice women away from disposables with feminine versions of their male products.

So far, Gillette's contain-and-switch strategy has not been very successful. In 1976 Gillette said disposables would never get more than 7 percent of the market. Marino said at the time, "You know, we considered it for trips and locker rooms, for the guy who forgets his razor." The disposable market, though, soon soared past 7 percent, forcing Gillette into continual upward revisions of its estimates. In terms of units sold, disposables have now reached 50 percent of the market.

Bic is predicting that disposables will ultimately capture 60 percent of the market. Indeed, Bic has been investing so much money advertising its shaver—$15 million in 1985—that it lost $5 million on the product. Baron Bich is known for his willingness to run a deficit promoting a product as long as it keeps gaining market share. As evidence that gains will continue, Bic people point to the huge disposable market share in many European countries: 75 percent in Greece, 50 percent in Austria, 45 percent in Switzerland, 40 percent in France. According to Bic, mass products tend to follow the population curve. If 40 percent of one segment of the population uses disposables, eventually everybody will.

PRODUCT IMPROVEMENTS

When it got into a war in the old days, Gillette could always win by unleashing its ultimate weapon: superior technological strength. Shaving technology, though, has come a long way since 1903. Further innovations are not easy. It is awfully hard to make the next dramatic improvement.

One potential leap would be a blade so tough that you would not have to wash your face to soften your beard. But few experts see such a blade as technically feasible. Dry beard hair is extremely abrasive and about as strong as copper wire of the same thickness. Even though today's blades are made of very durable steel, their precision-honed edges are quickly destroyed by dry whiskers.

Another potential improvement is a much longer-lasting blade. Yet such an advance may not be worth the effort. The only technology that matters now is that of assembly lines, which can reduce manufacturing costs.

Whatever the likelihood of future quantum leaps, the fact remains: despite the topographical differences discernable by high-powered microscopes, today all brands of razor blades deliver an extremely good shave. Gillette studies show that over 93 percent of shavers rate the shaves they are receiving as very good or excellent. Asked about the quality of Schick's blades, a Gillette executive conceded that it is much the same as that of his company's blades. "They have the same steel, the same coatings. Schick has copied us very well and done a hell of a good job. I think our quality is more consistent, but as far as giving you a good shave, their blades are damn good."

Gillette's chief selling point against Bic is the alleged superiority of twin blades against a single blade. But to what degree this advantage can be capitalized on is debatable. As a Bic executive put it, "We don't really know what happens when two blades shave the skin, but our tests show that a large percentage of customers can't tell the difference. I give Gillette a lot of credit for coming up with the two-blade concept. It's a magnificent marketing idea. Two blades are better than one. It has a surface sense of logic to it. But on a perceptual level, which is the level most of us deal on, there isn't any difference."

OPPORTUNITIES IN THIRD WORLD MARKETS

Gillette discovered a while back that only 8 percent of Mexican men who shave use shaving cream. The rest soften their beards with soapy water or —ouch!—plain water, neither of which Gillette sells.

Sensing an opportunity, Gillette introduced plastic tubes of shaving cream that sold for half the price of its aerosol in Guadalajara (Mexico) in 1985. After a year, 13 percent of Guadalajaran men used shaving cream. Gillette is now planning to sell its new product, Prestobarba (Spanish for "quick shave"), in the rest of Mexico, Colombia, and Brazil.

Tailoring its marketing to third world budgets and tastes—from packaging blades so they can be sold one at a time to educating the unshaven about the joys of a smooth face—has become an important part of Gillette's growth strategy. The company sells its pens, toiletries, toothbrushes, and other products in developing countries. But despite Gillette's efforts to diversify, razor blades still produce one-third of the company's revenue and two-thirds of its pre-tax profit.

The market for blades in developed countries is stagnant. On the other hand, in the third world a very high proportion of the population is under 15 years old. All those young men are going to be in the shaving population in a very short time.

Few U.S. consumer-products companies that compete in the third world have devoted as much energy or made as many inroads as Gillette, which draws more than half its sales from abroad. Since the company targeted the developing world in 1969, the proportion of its sales that come from Latin America, Asia, Africa, and the Middle East has doubled to 20 percent; dollar volume has risen sevenfold.

Gillette has had a strong business in Latin America since it began building plants there in the 1940s. Fidel Castro once told television interviewer Barbara Walters that he grew a beard because he couldn't get Gillette blades while fighting in the mountains.

The company's push into Asia, Africa, and the Middle East dates to 1969 when Gillette dropped a policy of investing only where it could have 100 percent-owned subsidiaries. That year, it formed a joint venture in Malaysia, which was threatening to bar imports of Gillette products. The company has added one foreign plant nearly every year in such countries as China, Egypt, Thailand, and India and is now looking at Pakistan, Nigeria, and Turkey.

The company always starts with a factory that makes doubled-edged blades—still popular in the third world—and, if all goes well, expands later into production of pens, deodorants, shampoo, or toothbrushes. Only a few ventures have gone sour: a Yugoslav project never got off the ground and Gillette had to sell its interest in Iran to its local partners.

In a few markets, Gillette has developed products exclusively for the third world. Low-cost shaving cream is one. Another is Black Silk, a hair relaxer developed for sale to blacks in South Africa that is now being introduced in Kenya.

Gillette often sells familiar products in different packages or smaller sizes. Because many Latin American consumers cannot afford a seven-ounce bottle of Silkience shampoo, for instance, Gillette sells it in half-ounce plastic bubbles. In Brazil, Gillette sells Right Guard deodorant in plastic squeeze bottles instead of metal cans.

But the toughest task for Gillette is convincing third world men to shave. The company recently began dispatching portable theaters to remote villages—Gillette calls them "mobile propaganda units"—to show movies and commercials that teach daily shaving. In South African and Indonesian versions, a bewildered bearded man enters a locker room where clean-shaven friends show him how to shave. In the Mexican one, a handsome sheriff, tracking bandits who have kidnapped a woman, pauses on the trail to shave every morning. The camera lingers as he snaps a double-edged blade into his razor, lathers his face, and strokes it carefully. In the end, of course, the smooth-faced sheriff gets the woman.

In other commercials, Gillette agents with an oversized shaving brush and a mug of shaving cream lather up and shave a villager while others watch. Plastic razors are then distributed free and blades, which of course, must be bought, are left with the local storekeeper.

Such campaigns may not win immediate converts, but in the long run, they should establish the company's name in the market.

GILLETTE'S OTHER PRODUCTS

The outlook is even dimmer in toiletries, Gillette's second most important market. The company has lost market share in each of its major product categories since 1981. Consider Right Guard, Gillette's leading brand. In 1970 it claimed 30 percent of the $1.2-billion deodorant business; now its gets a mere 7 percent. Right Guard's positioning as a "family deodorant" was undercut when rivals successfully split the market into men's and women's products. Gillette's current $30-million advertising campaign, reasserting the brand as a man's deodorant, hasn't stopped the slide.

Because of the limited prospects in blades and toiletries, Gillette is searching for other opportunities in personal health care products. Given Gillette's track record and cautious nature, that won't be easy. Sales of writing and office products, such as Paper Mate and Flair pens, peaked at $304 million in 1981. In 1985 profits fell 12 percent, to $10 million. The writing and office products division now accounts for 11 percent of company revenues but just 2 percent of earnings. In another recent attempt to diversify, Gillette bought small stakes in a half-dozen tiny companies in such diverse fields as hearing aids, biotechnology, and personal computer software. But these "green house projects" have yet to bloom.

Why hasn't the company done better? Critics say Gillette has become risk-averse, partly because of a civil service mentality among employees. Middle management is considered weak because the company has a history of promoting people who've been there the longest. That tendency has kept Gillette from moving aggressively.

Gillette's plan for creating a new line of branded low-price personal care products is an example. For 18 months it has been testing a line of unisex toiletries under its Good News! label, which now appears only on disposable razors. Gillette plans to sell 12 products, from shaving cream to shampoo, all for the same price in nearly identical packages. It hopes these "branded generics" will rack up $100 million in sales when available nationally.

Unfortunately, that date keeps being postponed. Test marketing took six months longer than planned, and a national rollout is still more than a year off. Part of the delay resulted from a change in advertising. Initial ads, which had a patriotic theme, failed to emphasize quality and low price. Gillette has also cut the wholesale price on the generics from $1.25 to $1.09.

A second new venture also had problems. Gillette's West German subsidiary, Braun, introduced an electric shaver in the United States. Backed by a relatively small $7-million budget, it started running national advertising in the fall of 1985. But success is not easy. Braun has been entering a declining U.S. electric shaver market where rigid consumer loyalties have generated a phenomenal 90 percent repurchase rate for market leaders Norelco and Remington.

GILLETTE'S STRATEGY

In the final analysis, Gillette's strategy is to keep as much pressure as possible on Bic's profits with the hope that its rival will be forced out of the razor market. To increase that pressure, Gillette has been putting the squeeze on Bic's other businesses.

The competition between the Boston-based giant and the French-owned upstart has begun to take on the characteristics of a vicious street fight in which price slashing is the main weapon and market share the main prize. In terms of size, the match is uneven. Gillette weighs in at about $24 billion in sales; Bic tips the scales at around $750 million, some $225 million of which comes from its American offshoot, Bic Pen Company. Even so, the smaller company has managed to cut up its competitor first with disposable ballpoint pens, then disposable lighters, and most recently with disposable razors.

Take the seesaw battle over lighters. Gillette was the first of the two companies to go after the U.S. market. In 1972 it brought out its Cricket brand. By the time Bic introduced its own lighter the following year, Gillette had cornered 40 percent of the market. Demand was growing so rapidly, however, that at first Bic had no trouble gaining on Gillette. But when supply began to catch up with demand, Bic recognized it had a problem. Despite what it claimed was a better product and despite its flashy "Flick My Bic" ad campaign, sales of the two lighters ran neck and neck.

At the time Bic had to decide what it wanted to achieve. As a company executive recalls: "We had to decide whether we wanted to just sit back and enjoy substantial short-term profits or go after market share." Bic opted for market share and in mid-1977 slashed the wholesale price of its lighter by 32 percent.

Gillette did not follow suit immediately, largely because its per unit manufacturing costs were higher than Bic's and its management was reluctant to accept such a low return. When Gillette finally did retaliate with a price cut, Bic reduced its price still further and a ferocious price war ensued. By the end of 1978, it was apparent that Bic's "big play" was successful. Bic had taken over nearly 50 percent of the market; Gillette's share had slumped to 30 percent. Moreover, in 1978 Bic reported $9.2 million on pre-tax profits for its lighter division, while Gillette suffered an estimated loss of almost the same amount.

In 1981 despite continuing losses, Gillette turned the tables and stared selling its Cricket lighters at a 10 percent discount off the Bic price. The counterattack hasn't substantially hurt Bic's market share, but it has effectively limited profits and thus the amount of money Bic can keep pouring into razors.

The big question is whether such pressure on profits will force Bic to abandon the razor market before Gillette's own business is radically altered or even irreparably harmed. According to one observer, the competition between the rivals is no longer just a matter of one pen or one lighter or one razor against another. It is a war on all fronts.

CASE 2 | *Nissan Motor Co., Ltd.: Marketing Strategy for the European Market*

In February 1989, in anticipation of the European Community (EC) market integration in 1992, Kiyoshi Sekiguchi, general manager, and Shu Gomi, deputy general manager, European sales group of Nissan Motor Co., Ltd., were discussing how to expand Nissan's market penetration in three principal southern European countries: France, Italy, and Spain.

Japanese carmakers had voluntarily limited their total exports to Europe to a ceiling of about 10% of the EC market, which accounted for 90% of the total Western European market. In addic-

This case was prepared by Professor Kyoichi Ikeo of Keio University, Japan, in association with Professor John A. Quelch of Harvard Business School as the basis for class discussion rather than to illustrate either effective or ineffective handling of an administrative situation. Certain company data have been disguised. Reprinted by permission of the Harvard Business School.

tion, France, Italy, and Spain had imposed severe restrictions on Japanese imports, resulting in quite small sales of Nissan in these countries. However, because Nissan started to export the Bluebird (equivalent to its Stanza model in the United States), which was manufactured in its U.K. factory, to the European continent in late 1988 and because the restrictions by individual EC countries on Japanese car imports were likely to be relieved at the advent of EC integration, Nissan believed that full-scale penetration into these three European countries would become possible.

Although Sekiguchi and Gomi needed to develop a marketing strategy for the entire European market in light of the tougher competition expected after 1992, the more immediate decision was how much marketing effort to allocate to two models, the 1800-cc upper-medium-sized Bluebird and a supermini car like the Micra (hereafter New Micra). Nissan manufactured the Bluebird in its U.K. factory, but it planned to manufacture the New Micra there as well until 1992. Of course, to serve the markets adequately, it needed to market a complete product line of five or six models, including exports from Japan. Among them, the models that were especially important strategically were the Bluebird and the New Micra. Because resources—especially for advertising—that could be allocated to France, Italy, and Spain were limited, Sekiguchi and Gomi had to decide which model to emphasize and how to promote both of them in those countries and then recommend their decision to Yoshikazu Kawana, director of the European sales group.

COMPANY BACKGROUND

In 1935, Nissan Motor Co., Ltd., which had been established in 1933 by Gisuke Ayukawa, started the mass production of automobiles in Japan with a small 750-cc car. It eventually grew to include a full-sized 3670-cc car in its product line, expanding its production volume and becoming, along with Toyota and Isuzu, one of the leading companies in the Japanese automobile industry. However, due to shortage of material during World War II, Nissan was obliged to focus on truck production and to decrease its car output. The end of the war brought its production to a standstill.

Nissan's growth in truck and car production after World War II was due to the special procurement needs of the Korean War and the increased household penetration of cars in Japan beginning in the late 1950s. In particular, the enormous success of the new small-sized cars in the 1960s, when a major portion of vehicle demand moved from trucks and medium-sized cars for business use to small-sized cars for personal use, gave Nissan a firm footing in the Japanese automobile industry.

Exports of Nissan cars started in 1958 and increased from 10,000 units in 1960 to 400,000 in 1970. During the 1970s, partly because of the rise in gasoline prices, high-quality, fuel-efficient Japanese cars dramatically increased their share of the North American market. Nissan exported 1.46 million units in 1980.

By the 1988 fiscal year, Nissan sales totaled 3,400 billion yen. It manufactured 2.16 million units in domestic factories and 0.52 million units in foreign factories, and it exported 1.14 million units from Japan. Exhibit 1 presents Nissan income statements for 1984 to 1988, and Exhibit 2 summarizes total sales, in yen, of Japanese automobile manufacturers for 1983 to 1988.

PENETRATING THE EUROPEAN MARKET

Nissan's European market penetration began with exports to Finland in 1959. The company concentrated first on the northern European countries, not entering the EC countries until the late 1960s. Its exports to Europe increased from 3,600 vehicles in 1964 to 163,000 in 1973 and reached 240,000 in 1978.

However, protectionist sentiment against increased car exports from Japan began appearing in several countries in the late 1970s, resulting in the 1981 voluntary ceiling on exports to the United

EXHIBIT 1
Nissan Motor Co., Ltd.
Nonconsolidated Statements of Income: 1984–1988[a] (in Millions of Yen)

	1984	*1985*	*1986*	*1987*	*1988*
Net sales	3,460,124	3,618,076	3,754,172	3,429,317	3,418,671
Cost of sales	2,811,052	2,943,384	3,099,243	2,948,127	2,882,252
Gross profit	649,071	674,692	654,928	481,190	536,418
Selling, general, and administrative expenses	572,947	585,155	584,870	475,691	470,779
Operating income	76,124	89,537	70,057	5,499	65,639
Other Income (Expense)					
Interest income	67,559	72,325	70,494	58,989	50,548
Interest expense	(46,012)	(46,190)	(42,237)	(38,428)	(36,594)
Other, net[b]	30,377	43,385	10,084	83,652	59,971
	51,925	69,519	38,343	104,214	73,924
Income before income taxes	128,049	159,056	108,400	109.711	139,562
Income taxes	57,517	84,780	43,648	63,105	100,978
Net income	70,532	74,276	64,752	46,606	38,584

[a]Years ended March 31, 1984–1988.
[b]*Other, net* consists of dividend income, net realized gain on sales of securities, and other sources.

States and various restrictions and surveillances in European countries. Management expected this protectionist atmosphere to continue and decided in 1980 to begin to move local production overseas. In Europe, it acquired Motor Iberica, S.A. to make commercial vehicles in Spain and founded Nissan Motor Manufacturing U.K., Ltd. to make passenger cars in the United King-

EXHIBIT 2
Nissan Motor Co., Ltd.
Total Sales of Japanese Car Manufacturers: 1983–1988 (in Millions of Yen)

	1983	*1984*	*1985*	*1986*	*1987*	*1988*
Nissan	3,187,722	3,460,124	3,618,076	3,754,172	3,429,317	3,418,671
Toyota	4,892,663	5,472,681	6,064,420	6,304,858	6,024,909	6,691,299
Honda	1,746,919	1,846,028	1,929,519	2,245,743	2,334,597	2,650,077[a]
Mazda	1,364,229	1,431,815	1,569,553	1,626,187	1,602,293	1,844,300
Mitsubishi	1,061,375	1,173,631	1,408,307	1,578,823	1,558,670	1,752,697
Isuzu	684,624	769,071	1,016,250	1,013,434	909,915	1,023,300
Suzuki	542,319	524,259	580,841	722,336	744,854	759,550
Subaru	580,052	602,735	672,071	768,424	715,717	686,238
Daihatsu	425,909	469,950	515,911	535,645	557,627	445,665[b]

Source: Company records.
[a]Thirteen months, due to alteration of settlement term.
[b]Nine months, due to alteration of settlement term.

dom. These decisive steps were in stark contrast to Toyota's strategy, which placed much less emphasis on local production.

Nissan Motor Iberica, S.A. (NMISA)

In 1980 Nissan acquired a 35.85% equity stake in Motor Iberica, the largest commercial vehicle manufacturer in Spain, participated in its administration, and helped make it a more efficient manufacturer. In 1983, it started to manufacture vehicles under its own brand, gradually increasing its share holdings to 68% by 1989.

In 1988, NMISA manufactured 76,000 commercial vehicles, of which 66% were Nissan's and the rest Motor Iberica's. Of all the commercial vehicles NMISA manufactured, 32% were exported, mainly to other European countries. NMISA's performance was favorable, and its cumulative losses were covered by profits in fiscal year 1988.

Nissan Motor Manufacturing U.K. Ltd. (NMUK)

To manufacture passenger cars, Nissan founded NMUK as a local subsidiary in 1984 and began constructing a factory in Sunderland, near Newcastle, in northeast England. Completed in 1986, the factory produced an upper-medium-sized car called the Bluebird. Because Nissan volunteered to manufacture with 60% value-based local content rising to 80% by 1991, the British government in January 1988 authorized the Bluebird as a U.K.-made car.[1] The EC Commission supported the U.K. position. However, the French government insisted that local content had to reach 80% for EC approval and threatened to count U.K.-built Bluebirds against its 3% Japanese import ceiling until they reached 80% local content. The U.K.-made Bluebird began to be exported to other EC member countries in late 1988, when it had reached 70% local content. In 1988, the Sunderland factory purchased components from 113 European companies. The French government finally conceded that the Bluebird could be exported to France without any restriction or duty, though the possibility of reducing quotas on car imports from Japan to France remained.

Although it would be some time before NMUK would be operating in the black because of the huge initial investment,[2] production volume grew smoothly: 5,079 in 1986, 28,797 in 1987, and 56,744 in 1988. Nissan planned to expand production even further, to 100,000 a year in 1990, when it would introduce a new version of the Bluebird, and to 200,000 by 1992, when it would add the New Micra. By 1988, NMUK had invested 50 billion yen and planned to invest an additional 80 billion yen before full production was reached in 1992. Although Nissan's U.K. cost structure was not publicly available, Exhibit 3, which shows Nissan's cost structure for selling in the Netherlands, can be treated as an approximation.

MARKET INTEGRATION OF THE EC

A major impact on Nissan's European operations was the planned market integration of the EC in 1992. An integrated EC would liberate the movement of products, services, people, and capital within the Community and consolidate technical standards that hitherto had been determined by individual member countries. Much progress had already been achieved towards harmonization of technical standards for cars. By 1988, 41 of 44 voluntary technical directives proposed in 1970 had been adopted by all EC-member states. The re-

[1]Value-based local content was calculated by subtracting from the factory price of the car the value of components and materials imported from outside the EC. Some protectionists advocated the use of cost-based local content which took into account the full production cost including all overheads as well as design and engineering costs. However, this approach was much harder to moniter and police. Others demanded local manufacturing of specific components such as engines, transmissions, axles and electronic components. To achieve 80% local content, it was, however, necessary for either engines or transmissions to be locally sourced.

[2]£125 million of the investment was contributed by the U.K. government, motivated by the additional employment opportunities the plant would bring to the northeast.

EXHIBIT 3
Nissan Motor Co., Ltd.
Cost Structure of Nissan for Selling in the Netherlands (%)[a]

	Nissan's U.K.-Made Cars		
	Bluebird[b]	*New Micra[c]*	*Nissan's Japan-Made Cars (Average)*
Retail price	100	100	100
Dealer margin	18	18	18
Distributor selling price	82	82	82
Distributor margin	12	12	12
Nissan selling price	70	70	70
Transportation cost	3.5	4	8
Duty	0	0	10
Labor cost	8	10	12
Parts & material cost	39	40	32
overhead & selling cost	12	10	3

[a]Percent of retail price, exluding taxes other than duty.
[b]1988 figures.
[c]Estimated figures for the year production began.

maining three—on tires, windshields and towing weights—were expected to be tabled soon by the European Commission and all were expected to be made mandatory by 1990, permitting single-type approval for the entire EC market.

Thanks to a more efficient allocation of production facilities, and concentration and reduction of inventories, production and logistics costs were expected by industry analysts to decrease as a result of the 1992 program. According to the EC Commission, such cost reductions were valued at 853 billion yen. If all these cost savings were passed through as lower prices, average retail auto prices would be lowered by 5.7%, and consequently, the market would expand by more than 6%. Market expansion would be especially strong in countries such as Spain and the U.K., where harmonization of value-added taxes and excise taxes on cars would substantially reduce retail prices.

At the same time, market integration was expected by analysts to intensify competition in the automobile industry and, thereby, to magnify the differences among companies. Therefore, in preparing for 1992, European auto companies made great efforts to expand, modernize, or reallocate their production resources.

Market integration promised to affect import restrictions on Japanese automobiles. Although the voluntary EC-wide ceiling on all Japanese imports was expected to remain, the bilateral import quotas on Japanese cars imposed by France, Italy, and Spain had to cease. French officials, in particular, pressed for maintenance of the EC-wide ceiling on Japanese imports, for an 80% EC-wide local content requirement, and for higher exports of EC-made cars to Japan. They were also sensitive to the possibility of Japanese companies shipping U.S.-made cars to Europe to circumvent the EC-wide quota. Realistic observers foresaw a transition period whereby restrictions on Japanese automobile imports would be phased out gradually to give national producers such as Fiat and Renault time to improve the efficiency of their operations before they had to face open Japanese competition.

In addition, the possibility of cost reductions made local production more attractive for the

Japanese. In this respect, Nissan had an advantage over other Japanese companies: a proven record in Spain and the United Kingdom. However, the other Japanese automobile companies, such as Toyota and Mazda, were moving toward local production in Europe. Exhibit 4 summarizes these endeavors. Some executives of European automobile companies worried that Japanese local production would bring overcapacity and price erosion to the European market. But countries with no automotive industry, such as Greece and Ireland, welcomed the Japanese as a means of increasing price competition in their markets. In addition, certain EC countries, particularly the U.K., actively sought additional Japanese investment in car production following the decline of their domestic manufacturers.

MIDDLE-RANGE PLAN FOR THE EUROPEAN MARKET

Although Japanese automobile sales in Europe were small when compared with domestic or North American counterparts, there was large potential for growth if their plans for local production were put into practice and EC market integration was carried out. In particular, Nissan, which trailed Toyota and was closely followed by Honda in share of the domestic and North American markets, had capitalized on its competitive advantage in the European market where it had the largest market share among the Japanese companies, thanks in part to its early establishment of local production facilities. Exhibit 5 shows the overall market shares of Japanese and major European companies in the Western European car market.

Given the importance and rapid growth of the European market (car registrations increased 5% in 1988), Nissan management formulated a plan in the fall of 1988 to strengthen its competitive position until 1992. The main goals to be achieved by 1992 were as follows:

1. Raise Nissan's market share in the European car market to 4.5% by 1992 and increase car produc-

EXHIBIT 4
Nissan Motor Co., Ltd.
Movements of Major Japanese Automobile Companies toward Local Production in Europe[a]

Company's Name	*Country*	*Outline*
Nissan	Spain	Manufacturing 76,000 commercial vehicles a year (in 1988).
Nissan	U.K.	Manufacturing 57,000 upper-medium-sized cars a year (in 1988).
Toyota	West Germany	Planning to manufacture 15,000 small trucks a year (from 1989) in a Volkswagen factory in Hanover.
Toyota	U.K.	Planning to manufacture 200,000 upper-medium-sized cars a year (from 1992).
Honda	U.K.	Manufacturing 84,000 medium-sized cars a year (in 1987) jointly with the Rover Group.
Mazda	Spain	Considering the manufacture of 25,000 commercial vehicles a year.
Mazda	Undecided	Considering the manufacture of 200,000 upper-medium-sized cars a year (from 1992) in a Ford factory with which Mazda is affiliated.
Isuzu	U.K.	Manufacturing 5,400 commercial vehicles a year (in 1987) in a joint venture with General Motors.
Suzuki	Spain	Manufacturing 25,000 small four-wheel-drive off-road vehicles a year (in 1987) jointly with Land-Rover Santana.
Subaru	France	Considering the manufacture of 30,000 vehicles a year in northwestern France.

[a]Excluding knockdown productions.

EXHIBIT 5
Nissan Motor Co., Ltd.
Western Europe—Overall Market Share in Car Market (%) 1983–1988

	1983	*1984*	*1985*	*1986*	*1987*	*1988 (Estimated)*
VW group[a]	13.02	13.56	14.37	14.70	14.95	14.44
Ford Europe	12.47	12.80	11.90	11.67	11.93	11.45
Fiat group[b]	13.78	14.48	13.74	14.01	14.20	15.35
Peugeot group[c]	11.71	11.50	11.52	11.38	12.12	12.83
GM Europe[d]	11.07	11.04	11.36	10.95	10.55	10.29
Renault group	12.63	10.90	10.65	10.61	10.62	10.34
Total Japanese:	10.06	10.27	10.77	11.71	11.38	11.00
Nissan	2.79	2.83	2.89	3.00	2.93	2.84
Toyota	2.25	2.24	2.58	2.88	2.81	2.66
Honda	1.02	1.14	1.11	1.17	1.03	1.11
Mazada	2.01	1.97	1.91	2.05	1.90	1.88
Mitsubishi	0.98	1.09	1.10	1.21	1.22	1.10
Suzuki	0.42	0.43	0.47	0.58	0.65	0.66
Subaru	0.29	0.30	0.38	0.44	0.45	0.40
Daihatsu	0.27	0.24	0.28	0.32	0.30	0.25

Source: DRI World Automotive Forecase Report.

[a]VW group consisted of Volkswagen and Audi until 1985. In 1986, SEAT joined the VW group.

[b]Fiat group consisted of Fiat, Autobianchi, Lancia, and Ferrari until 1986. In 1987, Alfa Romeo joined the Fiat group.

[c]Peugeot group includes Peugeot, Citroen, and Talbot.

[d]GM Europe includes Opel and Vauxhall.

tion in the United Kingdom to 200,000 and truck production in Spain to 100,000.
2. Improve Nissan's brand image by reinforcing the quality of its sales and service organizations in Europe.
3. Further decentralize Nissan's responsibility for European operations, including product design, production, marketing, and sales.

According to the plan, Nissan's sales increase in Europe would be accomplished mainly through its U.K.-made cars, because exports from Japan had to contend with trade restrictions, political friction, and a decrease in per-unit contribution and price competitiveness due to appreciation of the yen. Reinforcing the sales and service organization and localizing overall European operations were measures to achieve the market penetration needed to justify increased production, achieve further scale economies, and increase productivity.

To coordinate European operations, Nissan established a European Technical Center (NETC) in the United Kingdom in 1988 and planned to start the operation of Nissan Europe N.V. in the Netherlands in 1990. Whereas Nissan had previously developed all of its products in Japan, NETC would through the combined efforts of Japanese and European staff produce new cars to meet European consumer needs. Moreover, because models for local production, which were designed in Japan, often required special orders from European parts suppliers, materials costs increased. NETC's objective was to design cars that incorporated standard parts available in Europe at lower costs, for example, a new Bluebird model to be launched in 1990, the New Micra to be launched by 1992, and any new commercial vehicles that would be manufactured in Spain.

Nissan Europe N.V. would be responsible for coordinating all development, production, logistics, and marketing in Europe, most of which had been done in Tokyo. And it would formulate overall marketing strategy for Europe, in place of the Europe Sales Group in Tokyo. Distributors in each country would continue to draft national marketing plans that were integrated with the regional plan.

Furthermore, Nissan Europe would play a key role in consolidating logistics under EC integration, which would facilitate the free flow of goods within the EC community and unify the technical standards. Nissan's plan was to gather orders from local distributors in each country and to relay them to the United Kingdom, Spain, and Tokyo. Also, Nissan Europe would totally oversee the transportation from each factory to each dealer via the large-scale collection and delivery center and predelivery inspection facility, which were under construction in Amsterdam. Therefore, transportation and inventory functions for cars and commercial vehicles, which had been shared by Nissan and local distributors, would be performed by Nissan Europe and its subsidiary logistics company. The only logistics function left to distributors would be that for parts.

TRENDS IN THE EUROPEAN MARKET

The European car market in 1987 comprised 12.4 million units, one-third of the total world market, and 10 million of these sales were accounted for by five countries: West Germany, the United Kingdom, France, Italy, and Spain. Exhibit 6 shows new car sales in European countries and

EXHIBIT 6
Nissan Motor Co., Ltd.
New Car Sales—Overall World Market: 1983–1983 (000s of units)

	1983	*1984*	*1985*	*1986*	*1987*	*1988 (est.)*	*1989 (est.)*
West Germany	2,427	2,394	2,379	2,829	2,916	2,730	2,660
France	2,018	1,758	1,766	1,912	2,105	2,217	2,146
United Kingdom	1,792	1,750	1,832	1,882	2,014	2,195	1,939
Italy	1,581	1,636	1,746	1,825	1,977	2,131	2,002
Spain	547	520	572	686	925	1,039	1,089
Netherlands	459	461	496	561	556	485	550
Belgium	339	352	360	395	406	435	426
Other EC countries	329	342	388	402	353	388	531
EC total	9,492	9,212	9,540	10,492	11,251	11,620	11,343
Sweden	217	231	263	270	316	331	352
Switzerland	274	267	265	300	303	322	327
Other Western European countries	486	450	540	572	509	505	599
Western European total	10,494	10,161	10,608	11,635	12,380	12,779	12,622
United States	9,181	10,393	11,043	11,452	10,227	10,699	10,623
Canada	842	964	1,137	1,089	1,057	1,013	1,196
North American total	10,023	11,357	12,180	12,541	11,284	11,711	11,819
Japan	3,136	3,096	3,104	3,146	3,275	3,609	3,497
World total	29,151	30,289	31,821	33,049	32,657	34,277	35,528

Source: DRI World Automotive Forecast Report.

other major markets. Exhibits 7 and 8 provide new car sales data for European countries in 1987 and 1988. Exhibits 9 and 10 provide market segmentation data for each major European country. Exhibit 11 shows profiles of European countries. Exhibit 12 profiles Nissan's distributors, and Exhibit 13 lists the car models Nissan marketed in Europe and their retail list price ranges.

To catch up to the Japanese, European car makers needed to improve productivity by one-third; it took Japanese workers 20 hours to assemble a car, whereas the European average was 36 hours and the U.S., 26½ hours. While local content restrictions were designed to make Japanese assembly in Europe more costly, industry analysts believed that, even with a 90% requirement, Japanese plants in Europe would be more efficient than those run by the European manufacturers.

West Germany

West Germany had the largest car market in Europe, with sales of about three million units a year and no restrictions imposed on imports; therefore, Japanese companies were able to achieve considerable car sales. However with highly competitive companies like Volkswagen, the West German market was regarded as having the stiffest competition in Europe. Generally, West German consumers, known as serious readers of car magazines, were knowledgeable about cars and apt to consider numerous data before purchasing.

EXHIBIT 7
Nissan Motor Co., Ltd.
New Car Sales in Major European Countries: 1987 (000s of units)

	West Germany	*France*	*United Kingdom*	*Italy*	*Spain*	*Netherlands*	*Belgium*	*Sweden*	*Switzerland*
Total	2,915.7	2,105.2	2,013.7	1,976.5	924.8	555.7	406.2	316.0	303.3
By Manufacturer									
VW group	872.2	159.3	116.2	225.8	161.2	63.0	65.6	37.7	50.0
Ford Europe	300.8	143.4	580.1	78.4	142.1	56.0	39.5	34.3	21.2
Fiat group	132.8	151.8	74.3	1,179.9	69.6	35.3	18.5	8.2	29.5
Peugeot group	123.3	703.5	147.3	148.8	154.2	65.0	57.3	11.0	25.1
GM Europe	453.3	96.8	270.8	57.3	130.1	88.6	46.8	31.1	37.6
Renault group	89.6	641.7	78.7	154.2	209.4	22.6	35.3	5.1	16.6
Total Japanese[a]	441.4	63.1	225.4	13.7	6.8	144.0	83.5	68.5	87.6
Nissan	84.5	17.8	114.2	0.0	2.1	31.3	19.4	18.1	13.7
Toyota	93.3	14.3	38.3	2.0	2.1	31.2	26.8	22.8	26.6
Honda	41.5	10.2	24.7	0.2	0.5	11.9	8.5	4.1	7.6
Mazda	91.0	16.6	18.8	0.0	0.5	24.5	10.6	13.9	8.1
Mitsubishi	68.6	3.3	11.8	0.7	1.0	15.3	9.6	3.6	11.1
Suzuki	27.1	0.9	5.6	9.9	0.4	18.0	3.3	2.4	4.1
Subaru	16.7	0.0	5.0	0.4	0.1	4.7	3.0	1.8	14.3
Daihatsu	13.0	0.0	4.6	0.5	0.0	7.1	2.3	1.7	1.4

Source: DRI World Automotive Forecast Report.

[a]Total Japanese in Italy and Spain exceed the quotas on car imports from Japan, because some parts of commercial vehicles, manufactured by Nissan and Suzuki in Spain and knocked down by Toyota and Mitsubishi in Portugal, are counted as passenger cars. Furthermore, in the case of Italy, indirect imports via other European countries boost the sales of Japanese cars. Total Japanese figures may exceed slightly the sum of units for the eight manufacturers listed.

EXHIBIT 8
Nissan Motor Co., Ltd.
Estimated New Car Sales in Major European Countries: 1988 (000s of units)

	West Germany	*France*	*United Kingdom*	*Italy*	*Spain*	*Netherlands*	*Belgium*	*Sweden*	*Switzerland*
Total	2,730.2	2,216.8	2,195.4	2,030.9	1,039.2	484.8	435.0	331.3	322.1
By Manufacturer									
VW group	797.0	168.8	125.4	220.3	196.5	54.7	70.7	36.8	50.9
Ford Europe	269.9	139.2	582.2	79.6	152.9	50.6	44.5	34.0	21.5
Fiat group	138.9	217.1	86.6	1,211.7	85.4	29.4	16.3	7.6	31.0
Peugeot group	108.4	740.2	187.1	165.1	197.4	60.6	65.6	14.7	23.9
GM Europe	418.4	104.1	302.2	71.6	136.6	69.0	50.4	28.7	38.4
Renault group	84.8	639.4	84.4	148.0	217.7	21.3	38.9	4.7	16.6
Total Japanese									
Nissan	71.9	18.7	132.6	0.2	2.8	23.9	20.5	19.8	13.5
Toyota	77.2	14.9	39.2	0.6	2.2	23.3	29.1	25.5	31.0
Honda	45.7	10.6	25.9	0.5	0.6	12.0	9.0	5.5	8.3
Mazda	82.6	17.2	20.4	0.1	0.6	24.5	9.8	18.3	12.3
Mitsubishi	55.0	3.0	12.4	0.8	1.0	13.1	9.4	6.0	13.1
Suzuki	26.7	0.6	5.9	7.8	1.0	18.2	3.8	3.3	4.7
Subaru	13.7	0.0	4.5	0.2	0.1	5.1	3.3	1.6	14.1
Daihatsu	10.7	0.0	3.4	0.5	0.0	7.3	3.2	1.2	1.7

Source: DRI World Automotive Forecast Report.

Table A shows the relative importance of product attributes in major European countries. Regarding vehicle size, models larger than the supermini had a large market share, especially when compared with their share in the southern European countries.

Among Japanese competitors, Mazda focused on West Germany, where it had a relatively high market share, followed by Toyota and then Nissan. Although Nissan hoped to increase its market share in West Germany as production volume in its U.K. factory increased, it was thought that the market could absorb only a limited quantity.

West Germany took the most liberal view toward Japanese competition in the automobile industry because its car companies dominated other EC car manufacturers in the Japanese market, holding a 2% market share (80,000 units) by 1988. In addition, an open EC car market with the French, Spanish and Italian bilateral quotas removed would mean that the bulk of imported Japanese cars would no longer be forced on the northern EC countries as was currently the case.

United Kingdom

A unique feature of the U.K. market was that fleet sales, purchases by companies for use by their employees, accounted for more than half of the total car sales. Because most of the fleet sales were of upper-medium-sized 1600-cc to 2000-cc cars, this class held about a 25% unit share of the total car market. The U.K.-made Bluebird was an upper-medium-sized car suitable for fleet sales.

In addition to the voluntary ceiling on all Japanese imports to EC countries, Japanese car imports in the United Kingdom were limited to 11% of the total market by a gentlemen's agreement

EXHIBIT 9
Nissan Motor Co., Ltd.
New Car Sales by Segment: 1987 (000s of units)

	West Germany	*France*	*United Kingdom*	*Italy*	*Spain*
Total Sales	2,915.7	2,105.2	2,013.7	1,976.6	924.8
By Segmentt (%)					
Utility	2.22	4.06	2.30	18.50	} 43.0[a]
Supermini	14.46	40.31	25.51	38.94	
Lower-medium	35.62	23.03	34.41	25.37	37.1
Upper-mediuim	22.92	22.25	25.48	8.06	13.9
Executive	24.76	10.35	12.31	9.14	6.0[b]

Source: DRI World Automotive Forecast Report and company records.
[a]Includes utility and Supermini.
[b]Includes sports cars such as the Nissan 300ZX. In other countries, sports cars are included in each segment according to vehicle size.
Note: Typical models included in each segement are the following:

Utility	Fiat 126, Renault R4, Suzuki Cervo
Supermini	Fiat Uno, Ford Fiesta, Nissan New Micra, Paugeot 104, Toyota Starlet, VW Polo
Lower-medium	Fiat Tipo, Ford Escort, Honda Civic, Nissan Sunny, Nissan Violet, Toyota Corolla, Toyota Tercel, VW Golf
Upper-medium	Audi 80/90, Ford Capri, Honda Accord, Nissan Bluebird, Nissan Prairie, Renault Fuego, Toyota Camry, Toyota Carina
Executive	Audi 100/200, BMW (all models), Honda Legend, Mazda RX7, Nissan Cedric/Laurel, Nissan 280/300ZX, Nissan Silvia, Toyota Celica, Toyota Crown, Toyota Supra

TABLE A
Relative Importance of Product Attributes by Country[a]

	West Germany	*United Kingdom*	*France*	*Italy*	*Spain*
Performance	*	*			
Fuel economy					*
Price		*	*	*	*
Styling			*		
Quality	*				
Accessories				*	
Maintenance	*				

Source: Estimate of Mr. Shu Gomi, deputy general manager.
[a]An asterisk (*) indicates a particularly important attribute. Its absence does not mean a lack of importance.

EXHIBIT 10
Nissan Motor Co., Ltd.
New Car Sales of Japanese Companies by Segment: 1987 (000s of units)

	West Germany	*France*	*United Kingdom*	*Italy*
Nissan				
Supermini	21.8	5.1	38.9	0.0
Lower-medium	31.6	6.2	36.7	0.0
Upper-medium	25.0	4.8	35.3	0.0
Executive	6.2	1.7	3.3	0.0
Toyota				
Supermini	16.6	0.0	1.2	0.0
Lower-medium	39.0	7.9	17.1	0.0
Upper-medium	28.7	3.1	9.8	0.0
Executive	9.0	3.3	10.1	2.0
Honda				
Supermini	0.1	0.0	0.0	0.0
Lower-medium	19.3	5.2	5.8	0.0
Upper-medium	21.9	4.8	18.2	0.2
Executive	0.2	0.2	0.8	0.0
Mazda				
Supermini	0.0	0.0	0.0	0.0
Lower-medium	47.9	9.7	11.9	0.0
Upper-medium	40.0	5.6	6.2	0.0
Executive	3.0	1.2	0.7	0.0

Source: DRI World Automotive Forecast Report.

between each country's associations of automobile manufacturers. But, because Nissan's sales were so high when this casual agreement was made, it obtained a very favorable import quota, gaining 6% of the market, the largest share of all the Japanese imports, and vying with Volkswagen for fourth position in the market, following Ford, GM, and Peugeot. Owing to the growth of the U.K. market, Nissan sales reached more than 100,000, representing 35% of its European unit sales. Also, the U.K.-made Bluebird was sold mostly in the U.K. market from 1986 to 1988, partly because until 1987 the EC had treated it as a Japanese import.

On January 27, 1989, Toyota announced that it would construct a factory in the United Kingdom to manufacture, beginning in 1992, 200,000 units a year of an upper-medium-sized 1800-cc car. The local content was set to start at 60% and reach 80% as soon as possible. Local production by Toyota would inevitably make competition more severe because a considerable portion of Toyota's U.K.-made cars had to be sold in the U.K. market. Therefore, the extent to which Nissan could depend on the U.K. market was more circumscribed; when it increased U.K. production, it needed to depend more heavily on exports to the European continent.

The local distributor was Nissan U.K., which was 100%-owned by a local businessman and had 450 dealers. Nissan U.K. was an excellent distributor, as shown by its market share in the United Kingdom, however, Nissan wished to increase its own influence over marketing in the United

EXHIBIT 11
Profiles of Major European Countries: 1987

	West Germany	France	United Kingdom	Italy	Spain	Netherlands	Belgium	Sweden	Switzerland
Car sales (000)	2,915.7	2,105.2	2,013.7	1,976.5	924.8	555.7	406.2	316.0	303.3
Commercial vehicle sales (000)	113.7	369.4	252.8	163.0	170.0	69.6	28.8	29.5	24.3
Nissan's commercial vehicle sales (000)	2.9	3.1	10.5	4.0	33.7	3.1	1.5	2.8	1.3
Total sales (000)	3.029.4	2,474.6	2,266.5	2,139.5	1,094.8	625.3	435.0	345.5	327.6
Car production (000)	4,374	3,052	1,143	1,713	1,403	125	277	432	0
Car export (000)	2,451	1,681	226	641	707	112	228	340	0
Car import (000)	1,012	760	1,041	780	188	535	NA	226	NA
Number of cars per 1,000 people	468	385	360	392	264	340	351	400	423
Car price index[a] (exclusive of tax)	128	128	144	129	151	122	121	NA	NA
Car price index[a] (inclusive of tax)	105	124	129	112	139	135	109	NA	NA

Source: DRI World Automotive Forecast Report, BEUC Car Report, company records.
[a]The EC market with the lowest price is indexed at 100 in both cases.

EXHIBIT 12
Nissan Motor Co., Ltd.
Profiles of Nissan's Distributors in Major European Countries

Country	*Name of Distributor*	*% of Shares Held by Nissan*	*No. of Dealers*	*No. of Nissan Employees*
West Germany	Nissan Motor Deutschland	100	734	4
France	Richard-Nissan	9.6	203	1
United Kingdom	Nissan U.K.	0	450	0
Italy	Nissan Italia	64.2	160	2
Spain	Nissan Motor Iberica	68	148	19
Netherlands	Nissan Motor Nederland	100	170	3
Belgium	N.V. Nissan Belgium	0	345	0
Sweden	Philipson Bil	0	50	0
Switzerland	Nissan Motor Schweiz	100	284	3

Source: Company records.

Kingdom and to coordinate it under a single strategy for Europe, and therefore planned to acquire the distributor. But negotiations between the two had not been successful so far, and it was somewhat uncertain that Nissan could control the marketing and logistics in the United Kingdom as they did in other countries.

France

Although France had a large car market, with about 2.2 million units a year, total imports of Japanese cars were limited to five manufacturers: Toyota, Nissan, Mitsubishi, Honda, and Mazda, which shared 3% of the market. The supermini class was the largest segment, followed by the lower- and upper-medium-sized cars. French consumers were thought to be price conscious and less sensitive to quality than consumers in West Germany and the Netherlands.

The French automobile companies, Peugeot and Renault, held more than a 60% market share, and the total share of imported cars was only one-third. Despite having the largest market share, Peugeot had not achieved productivity as high as had the Japanese manufacturers and, therefore, attempted to enlarge and modernize its production facilities in preparation for 1992. However, Renault was heavily in debt and lacked the capital to make substantial investments to raise productivity.

Nissan's marketing organization in France was weak because sales had been restricted. The exclusive distributor, Richard-Nissan S.A., of which Nissan owned 9.6%, was limited in management and marketing capability. Thus, Nissan was making efforts to strengthen the capability of Richard-Nissan. Richard-Nissan served 203 dealers in France, most of which sold only Japanese-made cars and Nissan's Spanish-made commercial vehicles. However, these dealers were relatively small in size, varying from family-run shops with 3 to 4 employees to companies with about 20 employees.

Italy

The Italian car market, highly restricted since 1957, represented about 2 million units a year; however, in 1988, Japanese car imports were restricted to only 3,300 units, of which 750 were off-road vehicles. Fiat, which was the largest automobile company in Italy, held the highest market share not only in Italy (60%) but in all of Europe

EXHIBIT 13

Nissan Motor Co., Ltd.

Marketed Car Models and Their Retail List Price Ranges in Major European Countries (¥ thousands)

Name in Europe *Name In U.S.* *Name in Japan*	*300ZX* *300ZX* *Fairlady*	*Laurel* *Laurel*	*Maxima* *Maxima* *Bluebird*	*Bluebird* *Stanza* *Auster*	*Silvia* *200SX* *Silvia*	*Sunny* *Sentra* *Sunny*	*New Micra* *New Micra* *March*	*Prairie* *Stanza-Wagon* *Prairie*	*Sunny-Wagon* *Sentra-Wagon* *Sunny-California*
West Germany	4,088	2,023– 2,138	2,861– 3,035	1,613– 1,873	2,791– 2,962	1,315– 1,912	962– 1,179	2,093 2,512	
France	4,386– 5,256			1,675– 2,360	2,670[a]	1,364 2,308	972– 1,262	2,027	
United Kingdom	4,533– 5,394	3,339	Undecided	2,110– 2,965	3,440[a]	1,721 2,645	1,246 1,588	2,369– 2,743[a]	1,453
Italy				Undecided	3,689		Undecided		
Spain	7,095			2,543– 2,917	Undecided	2,668	Undecided	Undecided	
Netherlands	5,493	2,872		1,788– 2,257		1,260– 2,347	1,086		1,046
Belgium	3,974– 5,072	2,110– 2,474		1,527– 1,764	2,722– 3,171	1,266– 1,752	825– 1,106	1,589	1,172
Sweden				2,056– 2,144	2,826	1,645– 2,215	1,373– 1,416	2,661	
Switzerland	4,323			1,643– 2,108	2,705– 2,870	1,346– 1,931	984– 1,206	1,890– 2,545	

Source: Company records.

[a]Old model is being marketed.

(15.5%), due in part to its dominance of the domestic market and the launch of a successful new lower-medium-sized car. However, 54% of its sales were in Italy. Expecting an end to the Italian market's restrictive quota on Japanese imports by 1992, Fiat aggressively increased its investment in production facilities and R&D, shortened the time to develop new products, and improved productivity.

A unique characteristic of the Italian car market was the large market share of the utility-class car. Italian consumers, like the French and Spanish, but unlike the other Europeans, tended to be price rather than quality sensitive.

Nissan sold through 160 dealerships organized under Nissan Italia S.p.A., a joint venture of Nissan (64.2%) and NMISA (35.8%). However, because the company's car imports had been so restricted, these dealers were experienced mainly in selling Spanish-manufactured commercial vehicles, which accounted for 6,200 units in 1988. Therefore, because the average dealership had fewer than ten employees and sold other companies' vehicles as well as Nissan's, sales performance was not strong. Nissan Italia planned to recruit or establish larger dealerships that were expected to stock Nissan vehicles only.

Spain

The car market in Spain expanded rapidly from a plateau of 500,000 units in 1985 to more than one million units in 1988. However, in 1988, the total Japanese quota was still only 3,200 units, including imports via other EC countries. This quota was slated to increase to about 7,000 in 1990 and, eventually, be integrated into the voluntary ceiling on total Japanese imports into EC countries.

Spanish market characteristics were similar to those in France and Italy; car demand concentrated on utility, supermini, and lower-medium classes, and price tended to be more important than quality.

Although Spain's car market was the fifth-largest in Europe in unit sales, it had outstripped the United Kingdom in production to become the fourth-largest since 1984, because of heavy investment by foreign companies attracted by lower labor costs and Spain's entry into the EC. However, all Spanish car manufacturers were controlled by foreign companies. Among them, SEAT, an affiliate of Volkswagen, was positioned as a base for manufacturing smaller cars for southern Europe and considered fairly competitive.

Japanese companies had little business presence in passenger cars. However, regarding commercial vehicles, Nissan carried out local production through NMISA and held about a 20% market share in 1987. Also, Suzuki bought 17% of a local commercial vehicle manufacturer, Land-Rover Santana S.A., which made a small four-wheel-drive off-road vehicle in Spain.

Although NMISA had 143 dealers for selling its commercial vehicles, it served also as a local distributor of Nissan's passenger cars. With 70 to 80 employees, the dealerships were on average relatively larger than those in other European countries. But, because they handled mostly commercial vehicles, they had very limited experience in selling passenger cars. Recognizing the need to alter the dealerships, Nissan asked them to meet appropriate standards as to space, appearance, capital, organization, and other qualities conducive to selling passenger cars.

Other Countries

In addition to the "Big Five," the Japanese held more than a 30% market share in countries such as Ireland, Denmark, Finland, Norway, and Austria, which had no automobile industry and no restrictions on car imports. Even in other European countries, such as the Netherlands, Belgium, Sweden, and Switzerland, the Japanese held more than a 20% market share, except in Portugal, where quotas were enforced. Consequently, room for raising market share was limited. Also, because individual market sizes were small, Nissan could not depend much on additional sales in these countries as it expanded production in the United Kingdom.

However, the three major southern European markets, France, Italy, and Spain, were large in size and underexploited due to import restrictions. And in Italy and Spain, the U.K.-made Bluebird was expected to be approved for import as an EC-made car. Even in France, importation was close to being conceded, though some uncertainties remained. Therefore, it was mostly agreed within Nissan that to increase sales in Europe on a large scale, exploiting these three markets would be critical.

PROMOTION STRATEGY

Sekiguchi and Gomi consulted with their colleagues on Nissan's marketing strategy for southern Europe. All agreed that the European market was important and that the three southern countries needed to be exploited in order to retain the competitive advantage in Europe. And they agreed to market five or six car models, including the Bluebird and the New Micra, in the three countries. The major issue was how to allocate marketing resources between the two U.K.-made models, because both the cars were strategically important yet available marketing funds for the three countries were limited.

The most significant constraint was on the advertising budget. Nissan advertising in Europe was placed by Nissan itself, by national distributors, and by local dealers. Nissan's advertising copy was created first in English, translated into the appropriate language, and exposed to all European countries at the same time with the same message. Consequently, it was not that easy to stress a particular model for a particular country.

Advertising by each local distributor was prepared separately, though guided by Nissan's total marketing strategy for Europe. Distributor advertisements were paid for mostly out of their 12% margins and placed mainly in print media. The importance of television advertising was increasing though its role was still relatively limited compared with that in North America or Japan. Recently, the West German distributor, planning to run a large-scale TV campaign, had asked Nissan to bear some part of the cost. In France, Italy, and Spain the distributors' small sales volumes restricted the level of their advertising budgets. Any mass medium advertising in these markets would therefore have to focus on either the Bluebird or the New Micra, even if Nissan or Nissan Europe provided supplemental funds.

Dealer advertisements, which were placed mostly in print media, were often funded by local distributors—so long as the advertising met certain content criteria—usually up to 50% of their cost. These allowances to dealers reduced correspondingly the size of distributor advertising budgets.

BLUEBIRD VS. NEW MICRA

Executives supporting the New Micra pointed to the relatively faster growth in sales of small cars and emphasized that a higher percentage of consumers in the southern European countries purchased smaller cars. They asserted that these markets where more potential demand existed should be targeted. And, to establish strong distribution channels, Nissan needed a rapid sales increase, which was more likely to be accomplished by the New Micra than the Bluebird.

That the New Micra would not face direct competition with other Japanese companies was another important factor in its favor. Nissan felt uneasy about competitors of similar background and image, though it would also have to compete with local European companies. But the only other Japanese car company currently engaged in local production was Honda, which jointly manufactured medium-sized cars with the Rover Group in the United Kingdom. Although Toyota decided to start local production in the United Kingdom in 1992 and needed to exploit the French, Italian, and Spanish markets for the same reasons as Nissan, the model to be manufactured in the Toyota U.K. factory was an upper-medium-sized car. Moreover, Nissan executives were confident that no other Japanese car company could manufacture in Europe a supermini-class car like the New Micra, at least not before 1992. Therefore, the New Micra would be insulated from direct Japanese competition for a while.

One of the major reasons for supporting the Bluebird was that its profit margin per unit was higher than that for the New Micra. Also emphasizing the Bluebird would generate further increases in unit profit contribution because of experience curve and scale economy effects in the U.K. factory. If the New Micra were emphasized, reaching break-even on Bluebird production in the U.K. factory would be delayed.

Another reason for supporting the Bluebird was the probability that the New Micra would attract more attention among Nissan's European competitors. Major southern European car companies like Fiat, Peugeot and Renault, which were very influential in automobile-related policy making in their respective countries, focused mainly on the small-sized-car market, especially in southern Europe. Accordingly, stressing the New Micra meant head-on competition with these companies and, in the long term, could cause further trade friction, which in turn might result in regulations detrimental to Japanese car companies.

Furthermore, Nissan's image in Europe had to be considered. Formerly, European countries had been in advance of Japan in developing the medium- or small-sized car; therefore, Japanese car designers had some yearning for the European car. Then, Japanese car companies became competitive in the North American and European markets by improving production technology and manufacturing efficiencies. However, differing from North America, where the Japanese had earlier faced no direct local competition for medium- or small-sized cars, Europe had had several competitive local manufacturers in those classes of car. Thus, in Europe, the Japanese car had long been regarded as low-priced, and higher-priced Japanese cars had tended to sell poorly. But the image of Japanese cars was improving and they were now regarded as superior in quality to French and Italian cars, though still inferior to the West German.

At the same time, each Japanese company tried to create its own unique image. For example, Toyota featured high performance, Honda emphasized upgraded value-added cars, and Mazda focused on building market share in sophisticated, performance-oriented West Germany, making special efforts to develop cars tailored to the European market. Among these competitors, Nissan was seen as an average Japanese car maker. Hence, it sometimes happened that Nissan perpetuated the low-priced car image of the Japanese car, and focusing on the New Micra would reinforce this view.

However, in the three southern European countries, Nissan was not a well-known name, except in Spain, thanks to its locally produced commercial vehicles. Because sales were currently low due to import restrictions, Nissan executives believed it would be important to raise awareness immediately upon the lifting of the restrictions in order to obtain a favorable competitive position in these countries. The New Micra, with its broader appeal and promise of higher unit sales volume, seemed to be the model to emphasize.

CASE 3 | *Northern Telecom, Inc.*

Hall Miller, Vice President of Marketing for the Central Office Switching Division of Northern Telecom, Inc., looked up from the magazine on his desk to a picture of a single, snow-covered log cabin with stately mountains rising in the background. The picture reminded him of his childhood in British Columbia.

His eyes moved from the picture to the window, where he could see traffic already starting to pile up on the portion of Interstate 40 which ran through Research Triangle Park, North Carolina, between Durham, Chapel Hill, and Raleigh. It was mid-afternoon in March 1988, and the traffic would be bumper-to-bumper in another hour.

Hall smiled as he realized that the picture on the wall represented his perception of Northern's performance in the U.S. while the impending traffic jam reminded him of the changing market conditions he felt the company would soon be facing.

Hall had been reviewing the results of a survey conducted by *Communications Week* in the fourth quarter of 1987. The purpose of the study was to identify purchase trends and priorities in the selection of central office telephone switching equipment. The survey respondents were primarily telephone company planners who were directly involved with selecting and purchasing central office switches.

Hall was interested in the results of the *Communications Week* survey since he wanted to use the information to prepare for the quarterly meeting of the Regional Marketing Managers, which would be held in early April. These managers were assigned to each of the seven regions into which Northern Telecom had divided the U.S. for marketing purposes. It was these managers' responsibility to work with the sales force in each region to develop overall marketing strategies. They also worked on quotations in response to bid requests and new business development in their regions.

Hall felt the time had come to get the group to step back and assess the overall market situation faced by the Central Office Switching Division and to identify potential changes in the Division's marketing strategy.

HISTORY

Northern Telecom, Inc. (NTI), the U.S. subsidiary of Canadian-based Northern Telecom, Ltd. (NTL), was originally part of the Bell System. Bell Canada, the parent company of NTL, was a subsidiary of AT&T until the late 1950s when AT&T was ordered to divest its foreign subsidiaries. Prior to that divestiture and for some time afterwards, Northern Telecom was known as Northern Electric, the Canadian counterpart of AT&T's U.S. manufacturing arm, Western Electric.

Despite the divestiture, Northern Telecom still had a captive customer in its parent, Bell Canada; and this relationship gave it roughly 80% of the Canadian market. However, Northern's management realized that if it were to survive it would have to design its own equipment. Previously, Northern had made copies of telephone equipment manufactured by Western Electric. To make its own equipment, Northern would have to be able to afford the massive research and development budgets required in the telecommunica-

---

This case was prepared by Professor Lew G. Brown, Joseph M. Bryan School of Business and Economics, Department of Management and Marketing, University of North Carolina at Greensboro, and Professor Richard Sharpe, University of Tennessee at Knoxville for classroom discussion and was not intended to illustrate either effective or ineffective handling of administrative situations. It is reproduced here by permission of the North American Case Research Association and the authors.

tions equipment industry. The Canadian market alone would not support the required level of investment. Therefore, Northern broadened its market by establishing its presence in the U.S. in the 1960s and 1970s as a supplier of telephone switches.

A telephone switch is a device that routes individual calls from the person making the call to and through the telephone network. Once in the network, the call is routed from switch to switch until reaching the person being called. Initially, Northern Telecom had sold switches known as "private branch exchanges." These private branch exchanges were switches which were owned by the customer, such as a manufacturing company or a university, and were housed in the customer's facilities. Northern also sold the telephone sets which went with its systems.

Manufacturing and support facilities were established in West Palm Beach, Florida; Atlanta, Georgia; Richardson, Texas; Minnetonka, Minnesota; San Ramon, California; and Nashville, Tennessee, the U.S. headquarters of NTI. Northern's first facility in North Carolina opened in the early 1970s in Creedmoor, a small community north of Durham. It still amazed Hall to think that Northern had grown from 300 people at Creedmoor to 10,000 employees in the Raleigh area in less than a decade.

DEVELOPMENT OF THE DIGITAL SWITCH

Throughout the 1970s, Northern Telecom, in conjunction with Bell-Northern Research (BNR), Northern's R&D equivalent to Bell Labs, developed a process known as *digital* switching. Unlike *analog* signals—a continuous wave of electrical signals varying in amplitude and frequency in response to changes in sound—*digital* signals involve sampling the human voice at a rate of 8,000 times per second and breaking it into a stream of thousands of bits of electrical pulses in a binary code. As the pulses are routed through the network, they are multiplexed, which involves coding each pulse and sending them together in streams. Because each pulse is coded, it can be sent immediately and followed by other pulses from other conversations. This allows transmission of multiple conversations simultaneously on the same line. At each telephone switch, the pulses are either routed to another switch or are multiplexed (put back together) into voice signals and sent to the appropriate terminating party for the call.

Digital technology offered a number of advantages over analog switching, including faster and "cleaner" transmission, lower costs per line, and decreased floor space requirements for switching equipment (a digital switch required less than 50% the space of an analog switch).

In 1970, Northern developed the SP-1, a hybrid electro-mechanical switch whose functions were digitally controlled. In 1975, it introduced the first completely computerized telephone switch, the SL-l. The SL-l was a significant technological advance over the analog and hybrid switches then in use and became a platform for a high-performance product line that allowed businesses to significantly reduce their telecommunications costs.

With its development of the digital switch, Northern entered the central office switch market. As opposed to private branch exchanges, central office switches are located in the telephone company's facilities. The customer's telephone sets are connected directly to the telephone company's switch rather than to its own switch located in its facilities. Thus, Northern's customer became the telephone company rather than individual businesses. Northern installed its first digital central office switch in 1979.

THE BREAKUP OF AT&T EQUAL ACCESS

Until the early 1980s, AT&T had a near monopoly in the U.S. telephone market, providing local and long-distance telephone service through the Bell System to more than 85% of the U.S. Western Electric was the only supplier of telecommunications equipment to AT&T. The remaining 15% of the telephone service market was served by 1200 "independent" telephone companies. Northern Telecom, along with other equipment vendors, sold its products to these independent telephone companies.

In 1982, through the provisions of the Modification of Final Judgment, which ordered the breakup of AT&T, AT&T divested the 22 local operating companies comprising the Bell System. Although the "new" AT&T retained the long-distance portion of the business (called AT&T Communications), the newly formed Bell operating companies provided local telephone service and became distinct entities which were no longer tied to AT&T. As such, the Bell operating companies were now free to buy telecommunications equipment from suppliers other than Western Electric (renamed AT&T Technologies). For Northern Telecom and other vendors, divestiture was the end of a monopoly and the beginning of a highly competitive marketplace. Exhibit 1 shows how the 22 Bell operating companies, such as Southern Bell and South Central Bell, were grouped to form seven Regional Holding Companies, such as Bell South.

The Modification of Final Judgment also included the provision that the local telephone companies must provide exchange access to all long-distance carriers (such as MCI and US Sprint) "equal in type, quality, and price to that provided to AT&T and its affiliates." In order to provide "equal access," many telephone exchanges (central office switches) had to be replaced with digital technology switches. Northern Telecom was well positioned at that time for success in the U.S. central office switching market, having a product lead in digital switching and being able to compete in an open market driven by equal access. Thus began an era for Northern which some industry observers called one of the great marketing successes of recent times. Northern's sales went from $2.7 billion (U.S. dollars) in 1983 to $4.2 billion in 1985, and it ranked second only to AT&T.

NORTHERN'S PRODUCTS

Hardware

Northern Telecom's digital central office switching components fell into four categories: systems, remotes, extensions, and lines. "Systems" equated to digital central office switches. Northern had three versions collectively known as the

EXHIBIT 1
Regional Bell Operating Companies (RBOCs)

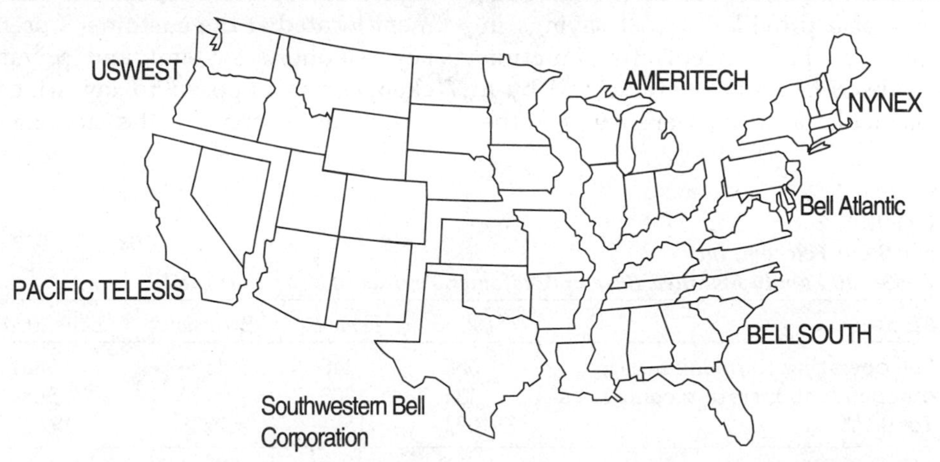

DMS Family (Digital Multiplex System)—the DMS-100, the DMS-100/200, and the DMS-200. The DMS-100 handled local lines only, the DMS-100/200 handled both local lines and toll trunks (trunks were lines between offices carrying long-distance traffic), and the DMS-200 handled toll trunks only. Each DMS system had a maximum capacity of 100,000 lines.

The DMS-100 switch contains numbers of line cards, one per subscriber line. The software resident in the switch and each line card allows the "programming" of each telephone served by the switch to determine which Centrex features that telephone will have.

Exhibits 2 and 3 show Northern Telecom's U.S. installed equipment base by customer type, by product category, and sales by year.

"Remotes" were digital switching units that extended central office features to remote areas. Northern's remotes ranged in size from 600 to 5,000 lines. Unlike central office systems which were housed in buildings, remotes were often constructed in environmentally controlled cabinets and placed outside on concrete platforms in areas away from central offices. In addition to extending central office features and services, most remotes had some "stand-alone" capability (i.e., if the host central office switch went out of service for some reason, calls could still be made between customers being served by the same remote). Remotes also provided a cost savings in lines by performing a line concentrating function since all the subscribers who were served by a remote in a particular location were wired to the remote rather than to the central office. Thus, all the customers on the remote were served by a single pair of wires extending from the remote to the central office. Remotes could be located up to 150 miles away from their hosts.

"Extensions" represented hardware additions and software upgrades to existing Northern switches.

"Lines" were reported in thousands; thus, as of year-end 1987, NTI had over 15.5 million lines in-service. A line represented the ability to serve one customer.

Software

In addition to hardware, an important portion of Northern Telecom's product line was software. Northern Telecom's DMS switches were driven by both operating software (similar to DOS in a PC environment) and applications software performing specific functions (such as an accounting program to log and bill long-distance calls). Centrex (originally an AT&T brand name) had become a generic term describing any central-office-based applications software package combining business-oriented voice, data networking, and control features bundled with intercom calling and offered to end users as a package. As a shared central-office-based service, Centrex was designed to replace applications served by equipment located at the customer's premises, such as key telephone systems and private branch exchanges. As opposed to investing in telephone switching equipment, the customer simply paid

EXHIBIT 2
Northern Telecom, Inc.
DMS-100 Family Installed Base by Customer Type as of Year-End 1987

Customer	*Systems*	*Remotes*	*Extensions*	*Lines (000's)*
Bell operating companies	658	248	1106	9841
Independent operating companies	434	1303	1120	5686
Total U.S.	1092	1551	2226	15,527

Source: Northern Telecom data.

EXHIBIT 3
DMS-100 Family U.S. Sales by Year

Year	*Systems*	*Remotes*	*Extensions*	*Lines (000's)*
1979	5			2
1980	13			75
1981	69	31	19	453
1982	51	86	41	492
1983	83	130	58	798
1984	116	210	152	1379
1985	266	304	332	3665
1986	235	359	604	3962
1987	254	431	1015	4701
Total	1092	1551	2226	15,527

Source: Northern Telecom data.

the telephone company a monthly fee per Centrex line for access to a multitude of sophisticated business voice and high-speed data features. Call Forwarding and Call Waiting were examples of Centrex basic voice features that had been offered to the residential market. Centrex (as an AT&T brand offering) was widespread throughout the 22 local Bell System telephone companies prior to divestiture. Centrex (as a generic product) was a major source of revenue for the telephone operating companies. The companies billed the customers each month for the features they had selected for use in their telephone systems.

AT&T's STRATEGY

In the late 1970s, AT&T began what was known as a "migration" strategy, urging business customers to a private branch exchange (on-site) solution for their telecommunications needs as opposed to a central-office-based solution. Implementation of this strategy, which was designed to "bypass" the local telephone companies, intensified during and following divestiture. Telephone companies were directly affected by this strategy, for end users began purchasing their own private branch exchanges directly from AT&T and other vendors, rather than paying the telephone company's monthly per-line fees for central-office-based business services. Telephone companies did not like this migration strategy since it threatened their revenues.

Northern Telecom introduced its digital Centrex applications software and was able to capitalize on the resentment telephone companies felt towards AT&T. Meridian Digital Centrex (MDC), Northern's Centrex software offering, was introduced in 1982, and sales grew significantly from 1985 to 1987. Exhibit 4 shows NTI's MDC statistics by customer type.

Telephone companies purchased Northern's MDC software for their DMS switches for the purpose of reselling to end users the business services features the applications software provided.

EXHIBIT 4
Meridian Digital Centrex Status—USA as of March 26, 1988

	In-Service		Shipped and In-Service		In-Service, Shipped and Firm Orders		
	Systems	*Lines*	*Systems*	*Lines*	*Systems*	*Lines*	*SRs*
Bell operating companies	594	1,610,166	696	1,956,973	757	2,087,921	44
Independent operating companies	265	292,633	280	387,810	288	401,299	6
Total U.S.	859	1,902.799	976	2,344,783	1,045	2,489,220	50

Source: Northern Telecom data.
Numbers are cumulative across the page.
"SRs"—schedule requests; jobs not yet firm orders.

EXHIBIT 5
Meridian Digital Centrex Major End Users

Vertical Markets	*# of Major MDC End Users*	*Example*
Universities	35	Indiana University
Government:		
Municipal	30	City of Las Vegas
State	20	Suncom (Florida)
Federal	11	Senate/White House
Major businesses	50	Ford Motor Company
Airports	15	Los Angeles Airport
Banks	27	Citicorp
Hospitals	16	Marquette Hospital
Telephone companies	11	NYNEX Headquarters

Source: Northern Telecom data.

The telephone companies often renamed the service for the purpose of developing brand identity and loyalty (much as in the same way Sears bought appliances made by Whirlpool and sold them under the Kenmore label). Bell South, for example, used John Naismith, the author of *Megatrends,* to advertise Centrex as ESSX service. Exhibit 5 provides a profile of some of the major MDC software end users by vertical markets served. Exhibit 6 provides a breakdown by line size of the Northern's DMS systems that had MDC software.

FINANCIAL PERFORMANCE

Exhibit 7 is a consolidated review of the financial performance of Northern Telecom Limited and its subsidiaries during the period 1979–1987. As indicated, revenues for 1987 were $4.8 billion, up 11% from 1986. Net earnings for 1987 rose 15% to $329 million, up from $287 million in 1986.

As noted in the bottom portion of Exhibit 7, Northern Telecom Limited had four principal business areas: Central Office Switching, Integrated Business Systems and Terminals, Transmission, Cable and Outside Plant, and Other. Central office switching, Hall's division, accounted for $2.6 billion or 53% of total revenues in 1987.

The Integrated Business Systems and Terminals group sold on-premises customer equipment such as private branch exchanges, local area networks, data terminals, electronic and key telephone systems, residential telephones, and special applications telephone systems. Many of the products sold by the Business Systems and Terminals group were offered under the Meridian product line name.

The Transmission group and Cable and Outside Plant group sold digital subscriber carrier systems, microwave radio transmission systems, fiber optic systems and cable, and network management systems.

Exhibit 8 presents a summary of Northern's income statements by geographic area for the 1985 to 1987 period. Although sales outside of the U.S.

EXHIBIT 6
Meridian Digital Centrex Line Size Distribution

Number of MDC Lines	*Number of Installed Systems of this Size*
1–1,999	658
2000–9,999	241
10,000+	71
MDC software, no lines	75
Total in-service, shipped, and on order through 1988	1,045

Source: Northern Telecom data.

EXHIBIT 7
Consolidated 11-Year Review

		1987	1986	1985	1984	1983	1981	1979	1977
Northern Telecom Ltd. and subsidiaries (millions of dollars)	***Earnings and Related Data***								
	Revenues	$4,853.5	$4,383.6	$4,262.9	$3,374.0	$2,680.2	$2,146.1	$1,625.5	$1,149.7
	Cost of revenues	2,895.8	2,730.5	2,078.9	2,074.1	1,713.3	1,542.5	1,117.0	821.4
	Selling, general, and administrative expense	917.8	764.6	701.9	603.2	454.8	300.1	234.9	149.1
	Research and development expense	587.5	474.5	430.0	333.1	263.2	151.8	117.6	64.2
	Depreciation on plant and equipment	264.1	247.3	203.3	162.8	126.6	100.8	77.9	29.1
	Provision for income taxes	141.5	127.9	132.8	120.3	79.3	29.8	30.3	45.5
	Earnings before extraordinary items	347.2	313.2	299.2	255.8	183.2	92.1	97.4	76.3
	Net earnings applicable to common shares	328.8	286.6	273.8	243.2	216.7	105.4	97.4	80.2
	Earnings per revenue dollar (cents)	6.8	6.5	6.4	7.2	8.1	4.9	6.0	7.0
	Earnings per common share (dollars)								
	before extraordinary items	1.39	1.23	1.18	1.06	0.83	0.45	0.53	0.48
	after extraordinary items	1.39	1.23	1.18	1.06	0.98	0.50	0.53	0.51
	Dividends per share (dollars)	0.23	0.20	0.18	0.16	0.16	0.14	0.12	0.11
	Financial Position at December 31								
	Working capital	570.7	1,188.7	933.9	859.0	563.4	421.6	477.4	307.3
	Plant and equipment (at cost)	2,345.6	1,975.2	1,737.5	1,458.0	1,152.2	829.8	602.4	356.9
	Accumulated depreciation	1,084.2	877.3	672.4	591.5	506.4	355.0	237.8	184.3
	Total assets	4,869.0	3,961.1	3,490.0	3,072.9	2,309.4	1,809.4	1,620.8	698.8
	Long-term debt	224.8	101.1	107.6	100.2	102.3	207.5	165.0	48.0
	Redeemable retractable preferred shares	153.9	281.0	277.5	293.6	—	—	—	—
	Redeemable preferred shares	73.3	73.3	73.3	—	—	—	—	—
	Common shareholders' equity	2,333.3	1,894.9	1,614.6	1,379.8	1,178.3	719.5	793.5	431.0
	Return on common shareholders' equity	15.6%	16.3%	18.3%	19.0%	21.7%	15.7%	14.6%	19.4%
	Capital expenditures	416.7	303.8	457.3	437.3	305.7	174.9	148.4	42.1
	Employees at December 31	48,778	46,202	46,549	46,993	39,318	35,444	33,301	24,962

		4th Qtr.		3rd Qtr.		2nd Qtr.		1st Qtr.	
		1987	1986	1987	1986	1987	1986	1987	1986
Quarterly financial data (unaudited) (millions of dollars except per share figures)	Revenues	$1,299.1	$1,314.4	$1,158.1	$1,032.2	$1,253.0	$1,067.4	$1,143.3	$969.6
	Gross profit	584.9	536.1	479.1	404.5	489.9	389.4	403.8	323.1
	Net earnings	140.0	132.2	69.5	66.0	77.6	64.9	60.1	50.1
	Net earnings applicable to common shares	136.0	125.9	66.2	59.4	72.9	58.0	53.7	43.3
	Earnings per common share	0.57	0.54	02.8	0.25	0.31	0.25	0.23	0.19
	Weighted average number of common shares outstanding (thousands)	236.444	234,767	236,024	234,199	235,573	223,650	235,237	233,154

		1987	1986	1985	1984	1983
Revenues by principal product lines (millions of dollars)	Central office switching	$2,577.2	$2,230.9	$2,141.3	$1,452.9	$981.9
	Integrated business systems and terminals	1,302.0	1,284.7	1,256.6	1,162.9	985.8
	Transmission	498.6	468.1	431.2	385.1	376.3
	Cable and outside plant	408.2	348.4	373.3	314.9	275.5
	Other telecommunications	67.5	51.5	60.4	58.9	60.7
	Total	$4,853.5	$4,383.6	$4,262.9	$3,374.0	$2,680.2

EXHIBIT 8
Northern Telecom, Limited
Income by Geographic Area, 1985–87 (Dollars in Millions)

	1987	*1986*	*1985*
Total Revenues			
United States	$3,103.0	$2,965.6	$2,967.3
Canada	2,140.3	1,771.1	1,792.8
Other	272.1	245.9	215.2
Less, inter-area transfers	(661.9)	(599.0)	(712.4)
Total revenues	$4,853.5	$4,383.6	$4,262.9
Operating Earnings			
United States	$787.0	$674.2	$699.6
Canada	491.6	383.8	319.8
Other	(11.1)	18.8	12.0
Total operating earnings	$1,267.5	$1,076.8	$1,031.4
Less, research and development	($587.5)	($474.5)	($430.0)
Less, general corporate expenses	($227.6)	($188.3)	($179.3)
Net operating earnings	$452.4	$414.0	$422.1
Plus, other income	36.3	27.1	9.9
Earnings before tax	$488.7	$441.1	$432.0
Identifiable Assets			
United States	$1,807.2	$1,749.6	$1,868.2
Canada	1,297.5	1,189.3	1,389.8
Other	181.1	210.1	264.2
Corporate assets*	332.4	460.3	204.6

Source: Northern Telecom, Limited. 1987 Annual Report.
*Corporate assets are principally cash and short-term investments and corporate plant and equipment.

and Canada represented only a small percentage of total sales, Northern had scored a major breakthrough in 1985 by landing a five-year, $250 million contract with Nippon Telegraph and Telephone (NTT) and becoming the first foreign company to sell switches to NTT.

NTL had 48,778 employees as of year-end 1987, and 1987 earnings per share were $1.39.

THE CHANGING MARKETPLACE

Hall felt that Northern's success through the 1980s had been driven by five major factors

- A sustained product development lead in digital central office switching technology (AT&T did not introduce a digital central office switch until 1983);

- Access to a huge market which had previously been restricted due to monopolistic constraints;
- A willingness in that new market to be served by a vendor other than AT&T (AT&T had moved from the position of supplier and parent organization to that of a competitor);
- Equal access legislation requiring product replacement of old technology exchanges with new digital switches; and
- The ability to dilute the effect of AT&T's migration strategy on the Bell operating companies by providing them with revenue-generating features in MDC applications software for the DMS.

Despite Northern's success, however, Hall realized that the marketplace was changing and that Northern needed to reconsider its strategy to respond to these changes.

AT&T'S 5ESS

Demand for digital switches had exceeded supply in the early 1980s, and AT&T had not entered the digital switching marketplace until 1983 with the 5ESS switch. As a result, Northern Telecom had a substantial competitive lead in both product/feature development and in marketing its products to the telephone companies. AT&T had found itself in the unusual position of being an industry technology "follower" rather than the industry leader. Moreover, because of its monopoly position, AT&T had not been concerned previously with having to market its products.

Exhibit 9 compares Northern's DMS and AT&T's 5ESS shipments in half-year increments starting in 1985. Although only 13 of AT&T's 5ESS units were in-service by the end of 1983, with an additional 72 being placed in-service in 1984, pent-up demand in the telephone companies for additional products to help satisfy equal access requirements and the desire to have multiple suppliers helped sales of the 5ESS grow rapidly. Moreover, Northern experienced delivery problems in 1985 with one of its remote switch products and performance problems with a particular release of operating system software. Combined with the strong market demand for digital technology, these events helped to assure that AT&T's 5ESS would be a successful product. The U.S. telephone digital switching market became a two-supplier arena.

EXHIBIT 9
Northern DMS and AT&T 5ESS System Shipments by Half Year

	Northern	*AT&T*
1H85	144	169
2H85	145	141
1H86	108	152
2H86	139	144
1H87	128	135
2H87	127	130

Source: Northern Telecom Data; AT&T Estimates.

AT&T claimed to have 800 5ESS systems, 660 remotes, and 15 million lines in-service as of September, 1987 (these figures included some switches located outside the U.S. and some within the AT&T system itself). Northern Telecom had 1,092 systems, 1,551 remotes, and 15.5 million lines in service as of the end of 1987.

PRICING

Due to equal access, demand for digital switches exceeded supply from 1982–1986. During this period, delivery was the primary determinant of which vendor would be chosen. Volume sales agreements negotiated with each regional or local telephone company for multiple change outs of old technology switches were the norm rather than the exception. Price was not a key selection criteria.

However, with supply exceeding the demand for digital switches from 1986 onward, the situation had become one of competitive bidding for each switch replacement, with bidding parties offering aggressive discounts. The objective was to win the initial system even at the sake of short-term profits, for winning the switch meant additional opportunities for revenue through software and hardware upgrades and extensions.

In 1987, the industry average price of a digital switch was estimated at $326 per line of capacity. However, discounts of up to 30% on this price were not uncommon. A switch with a 20,000 line capacity might be bid in the $4.5 million range. Switch prices ranged from $1 million to $10 million, with an average price of $2.5 million.

Hall had concerns that the discounts the vendors were offering often resulted in the winner leaving large sums of money on the table (e.g., coming in with a bid at $500,000 less than the next lowest competitor, when all that would have been necessary to win the switch was a $100,000 discount). Moreover, Hall did not want bids to be so low that the telephone companies would refuse to accept higher bids.

THE END OF EQUAL ACCESS

In addition to increased competition and pricing pressures from AT&T, other factors were affecting the market. With the completion of the equal access process, telephone company construction budgets were declining 3–4% annually. Along with the decline in capital budgets was a corresponding increase in the expense budgets. As a result of this shift, telephone companies were expected to allocate more budget dollars towards upgrading equipment and less towards the purchase of new switches.

THE ANALOG SWITCH REPLACEMENT MARKET

Following equal access, the next major determinant of growth in the U.S. telecommunications market was replacement of analog switches. These switches were analog stored program control (software driven) AT&T switches that were installed in the late 1960s and the 1970s. Exhibit 10 shows historical information and projections of the central office switch market by technology from 1988 through 1991. As indicated in Exhibit 10, analog switches accounted for 57 million lines of the total installed base in 1987, or 46% of the market, compared to a total of 36 million digital lines. The "Other" category represents olderanalog switches which were electro-mechanical switches (no software).

Numerous factors were involved in analog replacement, which was estimated to be a $30 billion market over the next 30 years. Unlike other switches that had to be replaced, analog switches had been upgraded to support equal access requirements since they were software driven. With depreciation service lives of 15–20 years, they would remain in the network until the early 1990s, assuming that the depreciation rates and regulatory positions did not change (switch replacement required approval from the appropriate state public utility commission). The latest versions of these switches offered a comprehensive set of Centrex features, and they were large in terms of line size (30,000–55,000 lines). As such, a digital replacement switch would require both sufficient capacity and an equivalent set of Centrex features.

These analog switches were usually housed in "wire centers," which were simply buildings that housed more than one type of central office switch and were typically located in high-growth metropolitan areas. Northern had a number of strategies to establish a presence in these wire centers in the hope that this initial presence would provide a competitive advantage when an analog switch became available for digital replacement. Other vendors were marketing adjuncts for the analog switches, which were enhancements designed to prolong their life, while these same vendors worked to develop competitive digital switches. As such, these adjuncts were basically "stopgap" measures designed to meet a particular need and to buy additional time for R&D switch development.

ISDN

Beyond the replacement of analog switches, the next phase of telecommunications technology was called ISDN (Integrated Services Digital Network). ISDN would allow the transmission of

EXHIBIT 10
Central Office Equipment Market by Technology (Thousands of Lines)
Total Market (Projected)

	86	*87*	*88*	*89*	*90*	*91*
Installed Base						
Digital	27,048	36,560	45,230	54,072	62,693	72.057
Analog	56,143	57,022	57,426	57,854	56,750	54,800
Other	38.175	31.322	25,613	19,826	15,933	12,293
Total	121,366	124,904	128,269	131,752	135,376	139,150
Percent						
Digital	22.3	29.3	35.3	41.0	46.3	51.8
Analog	46.3	45.6	44.8	43.9	41.9	39.4
Other	31.4	25.1	19.9	15.1	11.8	8.8
Demand						
Digital	10,066	9,508	8,670	8,844	8,620	9,365
Analog	1,591	881	417	429	36	0
Total	11,657	10,389	9,087	9,273	8,656	9,365
Total Bell Operating Companies						
Installed Base						
Digital	14,509	21,341	27,389	33,553	39,997	46,966
Analog	53,899	54,729	55,114	55,451	54,317	52,379
Other	25,246	20,114	15,998	11,891	9,077	6,648
Total	93,654	96,184	98,501	100,895	103,391	105.993
Percent						
Digital	15.5	22.2	27.8	33.3	38.7	44.3
Analog	57.6	56.9	56.0	55.0	52.5	49.4
Other	27.0	20.9	17.2	11.8	8.8	6.2
Demand						
Digital	6,904	6,832	6,048	6,165	6,443	6,969
Analog	1,530	830	385	338	0	0
Total	8,434	7,662	6,432	6,502	6,443	6,969
Total Independent Operating Companies						
Installed Base						
Digital	12,539	15,219	17,841	20,519	22,696	25,091
Analog	2,244	2,293	2,312	2,403	2,433	2,421
Other	12,929	11,208	9,615	7,935	6,856	5,645
Total	27,712	28,720	29,768	30,857	31,895	33,157
Percent						
Digital	45.2	53.0	59.9	66.5	71.0	75.7
Analog	8.1	7.9	7.8	7.8	7.6	7.3
Other	46.7	39.1	32.3	25.7	21.4	17.0
Demand						
Digital	3,162	2,676	2,622	2,679	2,177	2,396
Analog	61	51	32	91	36	0
Total	3,223	2,727	2,654	2,770	2,213	2,396

Source: Northern Business Information, *Central Office Equipment Market*, 1987 Edition.

voice, data, and video simultaneously over the same facilities. With existing technology, voice, high-speed data, and video had to be transmitted separately or over separate lines. While business telecommunications in 1988 were 90% voice and 10% data, this ration was predicted to move to 50%/50%. Cost, space, and time constraints would require that voice and data be integrated over one network.

ISDN would also allow standard interfaces between different pieces of equipment, such as computers; and it would free end users from concerns as to whether new equipment from one vendor would interface with equipment made by another vendor which an end user might already own.

Although universal standards for ISDN had yet to be resolved, useful applications were already apparent. Since ISDN phones were designed to display the calling number and the name assigned to the number on a small screen simultaneous with ringing, the party being called would be able to know where the call was coming from prior to answering. This call screening ability would provide opportunities to enhance 911 services (police, fire department, rescue squad, etc.) by immediately identifying the calling party's location and other useful information (such as a known medical condition or the location of the nearest fire hydrant) and by efficiently routing both the call and the information to all parties involved. A person served by ISDN could talk to her banker while looking at her account information on a computer terminal and send data instructions to move funds, simultaneously on the same line.

ISDN was flexible in that from any ISDN telephone jack, one could connect a computer terminal, personal computer, file server, printer, facsimile or telex machine, or video camera. Equipment could be moved to any location without having to worry if a specific kind of cable were available. The various pieces of equipment could share a common ISDN loop for data and voice transmission, reducing or eliminating the need for modems and multiplexers. Data on an ISDN network could be transmitted at a rate up to six times faster than standard analog networks but at a comparable cost.

Northern was positioning ISDN as its premier Meridian Digital Centrex software offering, since it offered both business voice features and high-speed data capabilities over a single line. Northern's strategy was to "migrate" end users from MDC to ISDN, stressing that existing MDC feature capabilities could serve customer needs today while ISDN standards and applications were being developed by industry regulatory organizations and other telecommunications equipment and computer vendors. In addition, MDC integrated with ISDN, with ISDN combining existing voice and data services while adding additional new features and sophisticated applications.

AT&T, on the other hand, had been advertising ISDN heavily to end users and was attempting to position it as a technologically superior *replacement* to Centrex, rather than as a Centrex enhancement. AT&T was pursuing this strategy since BRCS, its digital Centrex offering, was perceived as being much less "feature-rich" than its analog Centrex systems or Northern's Meridian Digital Centrex.

Northern Telecom placed the first successful ISDN phone call in the U.S. in November, 1987, and had a number of DMS sites in service offering ISDN capabilities. In addition, both Northern Telecom and AT&T had numerous ISDN field trials and commercial applications scheduled with telephone companies and business end users throughout the country at specific sites during the 1988–1990 time frame.

COMPETITION

In addition to the changing market and technological environments, Northern faced a number of strong competitors. Replacement of analog switches and ISDN were two potential markets attracting other equipment companies into the U.S. digital central office telecommunications market. Also, most of the telephone companies were interested in having a third equipment supplier in addition to AT&T and Northern Telecom to ensure that pricing and product development remained highly competitive.

Another potential opportunity/threat for Northern was that the seven Regional Holding Companies (RHCs) had petitioned Judge Green to lift the restrictions barring them from providing information services, going into the long-distance business, and manufacturing terminals and central office switches through direct subsidiaries and/or joint ventures.

Finally, although the level of competition was increasing, the number of competitors was actually decreasing. In 1979, there had been 30 major telecommunications equipment manufacturing companies in the developed world. Estimates were, however, that this number would decrease to 15 by 1989. Some experts estimated that a firm needed a 10% worldwide market share to survive. The worldwide telecommunications construction market was estimated to be $109 billion for 1988, up from $100 billion in 1987, with the U.S. accounting for 22% of this market

Following is a discussion of some of Northern's competitors and the inroads each had made into the Bell operating companies.

Siemens

Siemens, a West German conglomerate, had sales of 8 billion DMs for its telecommunications segment in 1987 (sales for the entire company in 1987 were $20 billion U.S.). Seventy-three percent of Siemens' total sales for the year were from Germany and Europe, with 10% from North America.

The headquarters for Siemens' U.S. telecommunications division was in Boca Raton, Florida. An R&D facility was also located at Boca Raton, while manufacturing sites were located at Cherry Hill, New Jersey, and Hauppauge, New York. Siemens had 25,000 employees in the U.S.

Siemens' digital central office offering was the EWSD. It was available in three versions: DE3, with a maximum capacity of 7,500 lines; DE4, with a maximum capacity of 30,000 lines; and DE5, with a maximum capacity of 100,000 lines.

Siemens had announced ambitious feature roll out plans for its offerings, promising both Centrex and ISDN feature parity with both AT&T and Northern Telecom. However, whether it could effectively leapfrog the software development intervals incurred by the industry leaders remained to be seen.

Siemens had made inroads with five of the seven RHCs: Ameritech, BellSouth, Bell Atlantic, NYNEX, and Southwestern Bell. Siemens' progress had been based primarily on both competitive pricing and the desire of the Bell operating companies to increase competition in the central office switch market.

In spite of its recent success, industry consultants cited operational/maintenance problems with the EWSD regarding system reliability, architecture, and compliance to Bellcore standards (Bell Communications Research, or "Bell core," was a standards organization jointly owned by the seven RHCs). However, heavy R&D efforts were underway to resolve these issues at Boca Raton, and Siemens was fully committed to adapting its products to U.S. market specifications.

Siemens had a $2.1 million contract with West Virginia University to develop computer-based training courses in the operation of EWSD central office equipment. In terms of joint ventures and acquisitions, the company purchased 80% of GTE's foreign transmissions operations in 1986.

Ericsson

Ericsson, a Swedish-based telecommunications company, had consolidated international sales of $5.5 billion U.S. in 1987. Europe and Sweden accounted for 84% of the geographic distribution of total sales for the year, with the U.S. and Canada contributing 7%. Like Siemens, Ericsson was attempting to crack the hold that Northern Telecom and AT&T shared on the U.S. central office switch market. Ericsson had targeted the Bell Operating Company market in BellSouth, NYNEX, Southwestern Bell, and US West.

Ericsson's digital central office offering was the AXE 10. Ericsson had already installed the AXE in 64 countries, had a worldwide installed base of over 11 million lines, and dominated markets in the developing world. Like Siemens, Ericsson had announced aggressive feature roll out plans (bypassing years of software development by AT&T Technologies and Bell-Northern Research) which it might not be able to deliver.

The AXE was manufactured in 16 countries and was being made available by Ericsson's Network Systems Division in Richardson, Texas. No plans were underway to construct manufacturing facilities for the AXE in the U.S., although Ericsson was considered to have superior skills in setting up manufacturing plants in foreign countries and training local workers for skilled jobs.

Ericsson had made a number of recent strategic moves intended to strengthen its position in the U.S. The company had reorganized by regions to serve more effectively the RHC markets; moreover, it had reorganized marketing for the division into the functional areas of Market Development, Marketing Communications, Systems Engineering, and Marketing Systems. Plans had been announced for a Technical Training Center at the company's U.S. headquarters in Richardson, Texas. In addition, Ericsson had announced that it would be working with IBM to develop private networking capabilities.

NEC

NEC had $13 billion in sales in US. dollars for 1987, $4 billion of which was from its "communications" segment. Geographic sales distribution percentages were classified as "domestic" (Japan) at 67% and "overseas" at 33%.

NEC's digital central office offering was the NEAX61E. The switch was primarily an ISDN adjunct that interfaced analog systems and grew into a full central office. As such, it was basically an interim offering that was designed to extend the life of analog switches while buying time to improve the product in the hopes of having a competitive offering ready when analog replacement began. NEC claimed that the NEAX61 was serving 4.8 million lines in over 250 sites in 40 countries.

NEC's U.S. headquarters was located in Irving, Texas, where production of the system was scheduled to begin by mid-1988. NEC had made inroads with four of the seven RHCs—Bell Atlantic, NYNEX, Pacific Telesis, and US West.

The company had recently announced plans for a Switching Technology Center in Irving, Texas, dedicated to developing software for central office switches and customer premises equipment. A second facility in San Jose, California, would develop software for intelligent transport networks, transmission systems, data communications, and network management systems. NEC claimed that it was moving its software development closer to its customers.

A major problem that NEC had to overcome was one of perception. NEC's first attempt to enter the U.S. market with the NEAX61 in the early 1980s met with little success. The product was highly touted, launched, and subsequently withdrawn due to numerous performance issues. Many industry experts felt that NEC was again entering the market prematurely with a product that was not powerful enough to meet U.S. requirements to support advanced business features or large capacities.

Stromberg-Carlson

Stromberg-Carlson was a division of Plessy, a British telecommunications corporation. Plessy had 1987 revenues of $2.45 billion from all product lines. Because Stromberg was a division, reliable data on its 1987 financial performance was not available. Stromberg-Carlson's product offering was the DCO (Digital Central Office). It was available in three versions: the DCO-CS, which was a toll version of the DCO (7,000 trunks maximum); the DCO-SE (a 1,080 line switch designed to serve as a rural central office); and the DCO (32,000 lines maximum). In addition, Stromberg-Carlson offered a full line of remotes, ranging in size from 90 lines to 10,000 lines.

Unlike Siemens, Ericsson, and NEC, Stromberg-Carlson had been a player in the U.S. telecommunications marketplace for a number of years Stromberg was a primary supplier to the independent operating companies and was committed to maintaining strong ties with them. Stromberg's strategy was to target small-to-midsize central offices (5,000–12,000 lines), focusing on rural applications. While Stromberg's lack of a large switch limited the market it could address, its niche strategy had served it well over the years in that it could economically provide digital central capabilities in small line sizes.

However, Stromberg was now trying to crack the Bell operating company market as well. The company had made inroads with BellSouth and Pacific Telesis and had recently signed a volume supply agreement with South Central Bell for the 1989–1990 time frame.

Stromberg-Carlson's U.S. headquarters and DCO manufacturing facility were located in Lake Mary, Florida (a suburb of Orlando). While Stromberg stated that it had a manufacturing capacity of 1 million lines per year at the Lake Mary facility, less than half of this capability was being used.

In response to its agreement with South Central Bell, Stromberg-Carlson had recently opened sales offices in Birmingham, Alabama. The company had a small installation force and was negotiating with AT&T to arrange to install some of its switches in South Central Bell.

Stromberg-Carlson shipped its 1000th remote in December, 1987, and placed its two millionth line in service in January, 1988. Two hundred switches, 400 remotes, and 400,000 lines were shipped by Stromberg-Carlson to the U.S. market in 1987.

Alcatel N.V.

Alcatel was established in France in 1985 as a subsidiary of Alcatel S.A. On December, 1986, the firm's present name was adopted with the transfer of assets from its parent, Compagnie General d'Electricite (CGE). At the same time, CGE and International Telephone and Telegraph (ITT) combined their telecommunications activities with ITT assuming 37% ownership of Alcatel. Alcatel offered digital switches, cable and fiber optic transmission networks, and radio and satellite transmission systems. 1986 sales were 10.6 million French francs.

The ITT deal allowed Alcatel to gain a position in West Germany, Italy, and Spain. While Alcatel had been insignificant in the world telecommunications market, the arrangement with ITT set the stage for it to become a major equipment manufacturer. Alcatel's strengths in transmission facilities offset ITT's weakness in this area. ITT contributed a dominant position in switching the European market. Although the acquisition introduced Alcatel to the U.S. market due to ITT's presence, it was not clear what effect this would have on the U.S. market. ITT had been working unsuccessfully for several years to develop a switch for the U.S. market.

CONCLUSION

Musing over the status of Northern's potential competitors, Hall Miller's gaze returned to the magazine on his desk. Overall, the *Communications Week* study had given Northern high marks relative to most of the competitors. However, there were shortcomings in particular areas he wanted to address (Exhibits 11 and 12 contain the results of the study, segmented by Bell and independent operating company respondents).

EXHIBIT 11
Summary of Vendor Performance Rankings by Bell Operating Company Respondents

	AT&T	*Ericsson*	*NEC*	*Northern Telecom*	*Siemens*	*Stromberg-Carlson*
Initial cost	3.12	3.37	3.42	3.83	3.51	3.76
Life cycle cost	3.55	3.26	3.29	3.53	3.48	3.26
Strength of financial backing	4.66	3.48	3.74	4.24	4.05	3.05
Availability	3.90	3.36	3.29	4.17	3.40	3.56
Service/support	4.07	3.21	2.97	3.39	3.22	3.50
Reliability	4.06	3.31	3.08	3.52	3.47	3.24
Delivery	3.76	3.18	2.80	3.71	3.21	3.39
Experience in industry	4.88	3.97	3.34	4.29	3.78	3.91
High-technology company	4.63	3.77	3.69	4.28	4.08	3.23
Sound technical documentation	4.32	3.24	2.67	3.50	3.37	3.10
Breadth of product line	4.07	3.24	3.14	3.90	3.33	2.80
International experience	3.19	4.08	3.83	3.58	4.20	2.64
Long-Term commitment to R&D	4.44	3.81	3.83	3.99	3.91	3.04

Source: Communitcations Week, April, 1988.
$N = 497$
Scale of 1–5: 5-Excellent; 1-Poor

EXHIBIT 12
Summary of Vendor Performance Rankings by Independent Operating Company Respondents

	AT&T	*Ericsson*	*NEC*	*Northern Telecom*	*Siemens*	*Stromberg-Carlson*
Initial cost	2.40	2.67	3.70	3.67	3.12	3.96
Life cycle cost	3.24	2.74	3.17	3.71	3.04	3.61
Strength of financial backing	4.65	3.31	3.69	4.34	3.65	3.50
Availability	3.56	2.61	3.22	4.06	2.93	4.03
Service/support	3.79	2.81	2.98	3.81	3.02	3.75
Reliability	4.23	2.80	3.41	4.08	3.25	3.63
Delivery	3.46	2.61	3.16	3.83	2.91	3.80
Experience in industry	4.74	3.27	3.55	4.58	3.62	4.19
High-technology company	4.72	3.35	3.93	4.45	3.84	3.72
Sound technical documentation	4.47	2.78	2.95	4.08	3.32	3.63
Breadth of product line	4.16	2.83	3.43	4.12	3.27	3.47
International experience	3.84	3.48	4.04	3.84	4.03	3.27
Long-Term commitment to R&D	4.67	3.21	3.80	4.29	3.69	3.57

Source: Communitcations Week, April, 1988.
$N = 1{,}047$
Scale of 1–5: 5-Excellent; 1-Poor

In terms of the changing market and increased competition, Hall felt Northern had a competitive advantage in that the company had the largest installed base of digital switches of any vendor. This would help generate revenue through hardware and software extensions and new features prior to the replacement of analog switches. However, Hall had seen AT&T's 5ESS shipments reach parity in a relatively short period of time, and it seemed that competitors were popping up everywhere. In addition, 1988 MDC sales had been sluggish. Hall felt this was largely due to customer confusion resulting from AT&T's hype of ISDN.

Hall glanced out the window towards the Raleigh-Durham Airport. It was 5:20 P.M., and the highway was packed with traffic. He decided that he would develop a presentation for the Regional Marketing Managers which outlined the Division's position and presented a number of possible changes in the marketing strategy that the Division could consider. This would generate discussion and help the group focus on the options that needed more in-depth study before a decision could be made.

Hall closed the magazine and placed it, along with several other pieces of information that had been gathered for him, in his briefcase. Despite the traffic and the work, he had to get home in time for his daughter's 6 P.M. soccer game. Perhaps he would be able to work on his analysis after supper.

CASE 4 | *Benetton*

Luciano Benetton leaned across his desk in an office decorated with frescoes carefully restored to their original beauty in the splendid eighteenth-century Villa Minelli in Ponzano Veneto near Treviso, the soft light of the early winter Italian sun providing a contrast to the forcefulness of his voice:

> When speaking of the "second generation" Benetton, I am thinking of a new business reality which is extra-European in scope. But we have to take into account the diverse requirements of the markets we are planning to enter.

In particular, decisions were being made in late 1982 about how the Benetton Group should best carry out its plans to enter the U.S. and Japanese markets for casual wear garments. In addition to questions as to how best to present its products to consumers in such markets, Benetton's management was reviewing alternative methods of providing production and logistical support for new markets. It was hoped that some or all of the unique features of the company's marketing and operating strategies could be preserved to provide it with the advantages it would need in these new, highly competitive markets.

This case was prepared by Professors James L. Heskett and Sergio Signorelli as the basis for class discussion rather than to illustrate either effective or ineffective handling of an administrative situation. Selected data in the case were based on estimates or are disguised. Reprinted by permission of the Harvard Business School.

COMPANY BACKGROUND

The Benetton[1] Group was one of several entities comprising the INVEP Group, an organization that encompassed all of the business activities controlled equally by three brothers, Luciano, Gilberto, and Carlo Benetton, and their sister, Giuliana. By specializing in the production and retailing of casual wear clothing items, particularly woolen sweaters, cotton T-shirts, and jeans, Benetton had, by 1982, become the world leader in the field of knitwear. In that year it had sold 26.9 million units of clothing, of which nearly half were for export from Italy. It supplied more than 1,900 shops, nearly all of which were operated with the understanding that the shops would stock only Benetton products. As a result, Benetton was thought to be the largest consumer of wool in the world, purchasing nearly nine million pounds in 1982. About 60% of all garments sold through Benetton stores were of wool.

The Benettons had developed their business from rather meager beginnings. Their father, a truck driver in Treviso, a town situated north of Venice, had died just after World War II when the eldest, Luciano, was 10 years old, requiring that he and his siblings find work at an early age. Nineteen years later, in 1965, they formed their company when Luciano and Giuliana decided that their complementary skills could provide the basis for a venture. At the time, Giuliana was sewing woolen sweaters of traditional somber colors and scratchy wool for one of the region's many textile artisans while developing much more colorful and fashionable designs in her own time. Luciano, a wholesaler who sold the output of a number of artisans to department stores, remarked: "I saw Giuliana's designs and I was sure I could sell them."[2]

Soon the pair had their first success with a violet pullover made of a soft blend of wool, angora, and cashmere. Other colorful sweaters achieved similar success, and the two youngest Benetton brothers joined the partnership. Gilberto, formerly employed by the Crafts Association of Treviso, was put in charge of administration, and Carlo, the youngest and a draftsman in a small local engineering company, assumed responsibility for production.

The Benettons initially sold their products through leading Italian department stores. But in 1968, as soon as their product line was sufficiently extensive to permit it, they opened their first shop in Belluno. It occupied only about 400 square feet, in part because of the limited Benetton product line at the time. But it set the pattern for the stores to follow. By 1975 they owned or franchised some 200 shops throughout Italy.

In 1978, the company realized $78 million in sales, 98% of it in Italy. The decision to launch a major export program to the rest of Europe at that time provided the basis for even more significant growth. By 1982, Benetton's sales had grown to roughly $311 million,[3] or about two-thirds of that for the INVEP Group. The latter included revenues from Benetton Cotone (cotton) (20%), as well as three manufacturing operations.

Financial statements for the Benetton Group are presented in Exhibits 1 and 2.

THE KNITWEAR INDUSTRY

The knitwear industry generally was considered to comprise basic categories of knitted underwear, hosiery, and knitted overwear. Its development in Italy and the United States had followed distinctly different paths.

In Italy, knitted overwear represented about two-thirds of the industry production. In general,

[1]Pronounced be-net-ón. Many people mistakenly pronounced the name as if it were spelled b-e-n-e-l-t-o-n. Names ending in consonants, while not typical of Italy in general, were quite common in the region of Treviso.

[2]Kenneth Labich, "Benetton Takes on the World," *Fortune*, June 13, 1983, p. 114.

[3]Actual sales figures for Benetton were 404 billion lire and for INVEP 624 billion lire. An approximate average exchange rate of $1 = 1,300 lire has been assumed throughout the case for 1982.

EXHIBIT 1
Income Statements for the Benetton Group, 1981 and 1982

	1981[a]		1982[a]	
	In Billions of Lire	*As % of Adjusted Billings*	*In Billions of Lire*	*As % of Adjusted Billings*
Net consolidated billings	373.7	92.9%	404.1	100.6%
= adjusted	+28.4	+7.1	−2.4	−.6
Adjusted billings	402.1	100.0	401.7	100.0
Expenses				
Purchases	(157.4)	(39.1)	(134.5)	(33.5)
Labor costs	(21.1)	(5.2)	(26.4)	(6.6)
Other costs[b]	148.0	(36.7)	(175.4)	(43.7)
Balance	75.9	19.0	65.5	16.3
Less financial charges	(15.1)	(3.8)	(20.7)	(5.2)
Plus interest income	2.4	.6	3.5	.9
Less miscellaneous charges	(5.2)	(1.3)	(6.3)	(1.6)
Plus miscellaneous income	6.5	1.6	7.4	1.8
Less depreciation of multiannual charges[c]	(9.1)	(2.3)	(6.3)	(1.6)
Less equipment and plant write-offs	(10.4)	(2.6)	(12.6)	(3.1)
Gross Profit Before Reserves and Transfers	45.1	11.2%	30.4	7.6%
Less various reserves	(9.8)[d]	(2.4)	(1.7)[e]	(.4)
Less losses on transfers of assets	(.1)	—	(.1)	—
Plus gains on transfers of assets	.7	.2	.3	.1
Plus capitalized financial charges	—	—	—	—
Gross Profit before Taxes	35.9	8.9%	29.0	7.2%
Less taxes	(16.3)	(4.1)	(12.6)	(3.1)
Net profit	19.6[f]	4.8%	16.4[f]	4.2%

[a]In evaluating 1981 data, please note that they cover 18 months for the main operating company (Benetton SpA).

[b]Of which royalties of 10.0 billion in 1981 and 13.0 billion lire in 1982 were paid to INVEP. Roughly 80% of these costs represented payments to Benetton's manufacturer-contractors.

[c]Including depreciation of start-up costs.

[d]Of which 4.0 billion lire was placed in reserves for future risks and 4. 0 billion lire was placed in reserves for reinvestment funds (according to Law No. 675-1977).

[e]Of which 1.4 billion lire of exchange fluctuation reserves were increased by Benetton and Benetton Lana.

[f]For purposes of rough calculations, the average exchange rate for the dollar against the lira was about \$1 = 1,150 lire in 1981 and \$1 = 1,300 lire in 1982.

knitted overwear production involved more steps, more labor, less expensive equipment, and lower levels of technology than either underwear or hosiery production.

Starting with low-level industrialization of knitting between 1870 and 1890, the industry extended from the Biella area across northern Italy. It was concentrated in areas in which small subcontractors, specializing in one or more of the several steps in production shown in Exhibit 3, were located. This "externally decentralized" system of production had evolved from the original

EXHIBIT 2
Consolidated Balance Sheets of the Benetton Group, December 31, 1981 and 1982 (in billions of lire)*

Account	*December 31, 1981*	*December 31, 1982*
Cash	12.8	3.4
Net commercial credits	85.5	140.1
Remainders of the period	52.0	49.6
Financial credits to the Holding Society	9.7	6.7
Other current active accounts	11.5	25.6
Gross current assets (1)	171.6	225.4
Suppliers (accounts payable)	65.3	72.6
Negative balances with banks	23.2	47.3
Financial debits to the Holding Society	1.7	—
Other current debits	18.8	16.9
Current debits (2)	109.0	136.8
Current net assets (1 − 2) = (3)	62.6	88.6
Gross technical investments	57.8	71.9
Less depreciation	(10.4)	(22.6)
Net technical investments	47.5	49.3
Preemptions for investments	.4	8.4
Financing for third parties	—	—
Net investments (4)	47.9	57.7
Multiannual charges (5)	1.2	2.5
Start-up charges (6)	16.3	10.5
Medium- and long-term passive funds:		
Guaranteed loans	5.1	4.6
Nonguaranteed loans	.1	47.7
Employees' pension fund	2.8	3.7
Tax fund	16.2	.3
Currency fluctuation fund	1.1	2.0
Total, medium- and long-term passive funds (7)	25.3	58.3
Net capital (3) + (4) + (5) + (6) − (7)	102.6	100.9

*Exchange rates were $1 = 1,212 lire, December 31, 1981, and $1 = 1,382 lire, December 31, 1982.

system based on homework that prevailed into the 1950s.

Reliance on homework offered significant labor cost savings, often involving low wages and no responsibility for fringe benefits. It limited investment in fixed assets to that required for relatively simple knitting machines. It allowed a company to smooth its workload while passing fluctuations on to individual home workers. And it provided surprisingly high productivity.

In the 1950s, institutions called "groupers" began to appear. They were owned by artisans who acted as intermediaries between a company and homeworkers, collecting orders and in some cases material from contracting companies, organizing work by distributing it to various individuals paid directly by the grouper, and guaranteeing the final product. Relationships between companies, groupers, and homeworkers seldom were exclusive.

By the 1970s, the small artisanal subcontractor companies had replaced many of the homeworkers. Among factors accounting for this were: growth in the sector requiring subcontractors with greater production capability; more complex products; the passage of a new law on homework introducing standards and making use of homework more expensive and less flexible; and the introduction of tax reform in 1973 to discourage the hiding of income. As a result, the importance of the grouper had declined.

Nevertheless, in 1981, according to an estimate by Databank, the knitted overwear sector of Italy consisted of approximately 17,500 companies (consisting in turn of 27,000 local units) employing a total of 130,000 people, other than home workers. There were thought to be only 17 companies with 250 employees or more. Among these, Benetton was dominant, with more than three times the sales volume of the next largest manufacturer in the industry.

As a nation, Italy had become the largest producer of knitted overwear in Europe, producing 60% of all European Economic Community output in 1977 followed by the U.K. with 16%. Of its pro-

EXHIBIT 3
Diagram Showing the Flow of Work through Benetton's Factories and Subcontractors

SUPPLIERS
Spun wool and cotton

SUPPLIERS
Woven cotton jeans velvet, other material

PONZANO VENETO
Raw material Warehouse → Knitting → Dyeing → Finishing Ironing Packaging

CUSIGNANA WAREHOUSE
Shipping

MONZAMBINO
Knitting
Finishing
Ironing
Packaging

REGGIO EMILIA
Knitting
Finishing
Ironing
Packaging

ROSANA
Chemical Treatment
Finishing
Ironing
Packaging

VILLORBA
Raw material
Warehouse
Cutting
Packaging

CUSIGNANA
Raw material
Warehouse
Cutting
Packaging

SUBCONTRACTORS
Knitting, Assembling, Finishing, Packaging

SUBCONTRACTORS
Cutting, Assembling, Finishing, Ironing

RAW MATERIAL FLOW
FINISHED PRODUCTS FLOW
SEMI-MANUFACTURED FLOW

duction, 47% was for export, with Germany (38.5% of Italian exports) representing by far the largest market, followed by France and the Benelux countries. In total, EEC countries took 80% of Italy's exports. In contrast to major exporters in the Far East, most Italian exports of knitted overwear were marketed abroad under the trademarks of the producing companies.

Imports of knitted overwear garments in the EEC had been restricted by a series of so-called Multifibre Agreements which imposed strict limits on the growth of imports of such items from non-EEC countries. The most recent agreement extended such controls to 1986. By 1982, only 19% of the 810 million items of knitted overwear sold in the EEC originated from outside the community. Twenty-seven percent originated from EEC countries other than Italy, with Italian firms commanding a 54% share of total sales.

In contrast, the knitwear industry in the United States had become concentrated in its early stages of development on the production of knitted underwear and hosiery. The need for high productivity in these sectors had resulted in relatively high investments, factories employing hundreds of persons, and vertically integrated companies engaged in many stages between the spinning of yarn to the production of finished garments. The largest of these firms was Burlington Industries, with 1982 sales of more than $2.5 billion. The strong promotion of, and preference for, garments of synthetic yarns had, if anything, accentuated the trend toward investment and industry consolidation. Manufacturers of knitted overwear, in contrast, had steadily declined in importance. The proportion of the total of nearly one billion knitted overwear garments sold in the U.S. in 1982 that were imported, primarily from the Far East, had climbed to roughly 40% in 1982 and was significantly higher in lower-priced categories.

MANUFACTURING

The basic process for the production of knitted overwear garments from wool and cotton is shown in Exhibit 3. Traditionally, it had involved the spinning or purchase and dyeing of yarn, the warehousing of spun material in finished or unfinished form, finishing operations such as mercerizing (immersion in caustic soda to produce a shinier material), waxing (to improve gliding properties and reduce friction during manufacturing and cleaning), and the removal of residual oil.

For women's garments, for example, first a prototype and sample collection was prepared. At Benetton, this generally was done four times per year under the direction of Giuliana Benetton, twice for the major spring/summer and fall/winter collections and twice for "integrative" collections for Christmas and for sport. Including woolen and other garments, a major collection contained typically 450 items, while the "integrative" collection following it featured perhaps 50 fashion-oriented items. The same line was created for all countries. It was estimated that about half of the items contained in the two main collections represented about 90% of sales.

Once designed, garments were then manufactured by machines producing parts of garments in their correct shapes or woven materials that had to be shaped. The next stage, assembly, involved joining the basic parts of each garment, such as front, back, and sleeves for sweaters. This could be accomplished in a visible manner with the edges of two parts sewn together, or a remeshing process associated with higher-quality garments that produced an invisible seam. The latter was used for most Benetton garments. Finishing operations included those of making buttonholes, sewing buttons, ironing, labeling, and final inspection prior to packaging for shipment.

In contrast to operations required for knitted products of natural materials, those made from synthetic fibers which dominated the U.S. market could be shaped and assembled with highly machine-intensive operations. This ranged from hosiery, which could be produced nearly totally by machine in several operations, to knitted underwear, for which finishing operations often were simple and performed in the least expensive manner.

Putting Fashion on an Industrial Level

Benetton had, over the years, been an innovator in the production of knitted overwear products. Ten years before the development of machinery for making hard and rough wool soft and pliable, for example, Luciano Benetton had improved on a crude process that he had observed in Scotland for achieving the effect produced by rudimentary machines with wooden arms that battered the raw knitwear in water. Similarly, in order to avoid the use of centrifugal dryers that shrank the wet knitwear, at Benetton a process was developed by which it was placed in a bag on a stick and rotated vertically in the air.

At a time when women's seamless stockings became popular, hosiery knitting machines that could only produce seamed stockings were made obsolete. One of Benetton's employees had recommended buying and converting the equipment for the production of overwear. Machines providing 90% of Benetton's knitting capacity in its early years were thus purchased for approximately $1,000 per machine, converted for an additional $4,000 each at the time, and performed the work of machines valued at much more. They since had been replaced by more modern knitting machines, some of them driven by magnetic tape programmed to provide intricate knitted designs.

But perhaps the most significant development in Benetton's operations occurred when the company began dyeing assembled garments rather than yarn in 1972. It required that garments first be treated in a strong chemical solution for about 20 minutes to soften them and increase their receptiveness to dye. Next, garments were "cooked" for 40 minutes and then stirred in dye-filled vats. Including time for softening, the vat time required for the entire process was about two hours.

The dyeing rooms at the Ponzano plant contained ten smaller vats in which batches with an average size of about 300 garments were processed. They required careful loading and checking of dyes to insure desired colors. The room also contained four newer dyeing machines with automatic dye control and water extracting capability with capacities of 530 garments each per batch.

Dyeing represented a bottleneck at the Ponzano factory. As a result, for much of the year the dyeing machines were operated on a three-shift basis. Even though the process was critical to product quality, Benetton was able to dye only about 35% of its total production at the Ponzano factory and an additional 20% at other company plants. The remaining 45% was dyed by contractors, with more than half of it dyed by two large contractors owned by the Benetton family.

It was estimated that labor and production overhead costs for garments dyed after manufacture were 10% higher than those for garments knitted from dyed thread. Benetton, it was thought, was the only manufacturer of woolen garments that dyed them from grey stock.

The garment-dyeing capability allowed more popular items in Benetton's line to be produced in response to requests for changes in preseason orders from agents serving retail outlets. As a result of this development, it was estimated that Benetton's inventory turnover for cotton and woolen items at the factory and warehouse was no more than the typical industry figure of 4.5 times per year in spite of the fact that its product line for knitted wear contained nearly 500 different color and style combinations.

As Luciano Benetton had remarked in an interview with an American business journalist:

> . . . we have kept the same strategy all along—to put fashion on an industrial level. Most of the rest of Italian fashion is still on an artisan level.[4]

Manufacturing Organization

The company relied heavily both on internally and externally decentralized operations in the language of the industry. Its internal decentralization involved nine Benetton facilities, seven in Italy, one in France, and one in Scotland, employing about 1,700 people. Operations performed at the seven Italian locations, along with the associated flow of material, are shown in Exhibit 3.

All thread was received at the Cusignana warehouse (about 12 miles from Ponzano) and subsequently shipped to various factories. Textile fabrics were shipped by suppliers directly to Benetton's plants, including those of two of its contractors. Each factory in the group differed in size and functions performed.

For example, some woolen knit wear was produced in Ponzano (all processes), some in Rosana (chemical treatment and finishing), and some in Reggio Emilia and Mozambino (knitting and finishing). Some manufactured items (those in "tintura d'al greggio" or undyed form) were then returned to Ponzano for dyeing and reshipment to the warehouse in Cusignana.

Ready-made material for cotton garments was shipped to the Cusignana factory, assembled there, and stocked in the central warehouse. Summer cotton shirts, however, were produced in Fontane, where only a part of the manufacturing was done internally.

Jeans were the only product category manufactured nearly totally outside Benetton's factories.

---

[4]Labich, "Benetton Takes on the World," p. 116.

However, final stages providing necessary controls were centralized in the Cusignana factory.

Functions performed and products made at Benetton's foreign factories differed as well. For example, the plant in Scotland manufactured only items knitted of cashmere for distribution through some twenty shops operated under the name Casa di Hogg, in Italy, with no association with Benetton's name. Another plant at Troyes, France, produced only woolen garments for distribution to a portion of the French retail stores. Constituting only about 5% of Benetton's total sales, none of these garments required dyeing.

Selected data on Benetton's factories is contained in Exhibit 4.

In addition, Benetton utilized a network of about 220 production units, either subcontractors or groupers, employing a total of about 10,000 people. These were located mostly near Benetton's production facilities in northeast Italy at Ponzano Veneto, Cusignana, and Fontane, but increasingly were being developed near other plants as well. Subcontractors and groupers performed about 40% of the company's knitting of wool, 60% of the work of assembling garments and 20% of the finishing operations. Typically, the more complex garments were produced internally in Benetton's factories. Cutting and dyeing of nearly all wool was performed in Benetton's plants.

The contracting network on which Benetton relied represented a kind of "parallel empire" to the company itself. Many of the contractors were owned in whole or in part by managers of Benetton. According to one trade article:

> The system is now established, and one can say that there is no head or manager from Benetton who is not at the same time owner, president, or director of a leading contracting company in the whole Lombardia-Veneto area (northern Italy).[5]

[5]Giuseppe Cosentino, "The Benetton Case—The Top of the Iceberg," *Panorama*, December 15, 1982.

EXHIBIT 4
Selected Data for Benetton's Facilities, December 1982

Company Name	*Location*	*Land and Building Surface in Square Meters*[a]		*Number of Employees*	*Product (Processes)*
Benetton Lana	Ponzano Veneto	39,720[b]	(19,901)[b]	346	Wool knitwear
Benetton Lana	Rosana	20,440	(3,233)	138	Wool knitwear
Benetton Lana	Mozambino	6,500	(4,751)	180	Wool knitwear
Benetton Lana	Quattro Castella	23,542	(3,523)	77	Wool knitwear
Benetton Cotone	Fontane	16,852	(5,794)	94	Cotton overwear
Benetton Cotone	Villorba	13,865	(14,100)	130	Cotton overwear
Benetton Jeans	Cusignana	65,665[c]	(40,417)[c]	274	Trousers, jeans
Benetton[d]	Castrette	—	—	—	
Benetton	Ponzano Veneto	—	—	247[f]	Control, mangement
Benetton	Cusignana	—	—	51	Control, management
Totals		186,584	(91,719)	1,537	

[a]One square meter = approximately 10 square feet.
[b]Includes the area of the technical offices in Ponzano Veneto rented by Benetton.
[c]Includes the area of the factory rented by Benetton.
[d]The company also owned the Villa Minelli located in Ponzano Veneto. This was an historical building used for management offices situated on 37,935 square meters of land with a floor space of 5,049 square meters.
[e]This was a piece of land on which the building of an industrial complex was started in 1982. Warehousing for finished products now located at Cusignana in the factory owned by Benetton Jeans was to be moved here.
[f]Including the employees at Villa Minelli.

According to the head of the textile section of the trade union, the production rates among contractors were superior to those of Benetton's factories for comparable jobs. There was a second tier to this system of external decentralization as well, consisting of subcontractors. It was alleged by one trade unionist that trade union minima and working hours were adhered to only at the first level of decentralization. There was no doubt that subcontractor costs included lower employment tax payments to the state than those incurred by Benetton. In addition to other benefits, the contracting network provided Benetton with a flexible production capacity that absorbed most of the fluctuations in demand. It provided work for many relatives of the company's full-time employees as well.

However, the production processes required a constant shuttling of work in process from one location to another, a function performed largely by subcontractors. While this reduced cost savings from external decentralization, it resulted in total production costs for woolen items that were perhaps 85% of those producers of garments of comparable quality in Europe and on a par with those in the Far East. More important, it reduced Benetton's risk from business fluctuations.

Still other functions were centralized at the company's headquarters. Technical research and planning, for example, were carried out at Ponzano Veneto. Under the supervision of Giuliana Benetton, product planning and design as well as the acquisition and exploitation of necessary patents and rights was managed.

All purchasing was done at Ponzano Veneto. Wool was purchased in spools from Italian producers. Material for newer items in the product line was purchased in more nearly finished form. Cotton was purchased already woven. Velvet arrived already dyed and ready for cutting. And the predyed cloth for jeans, introduced by the company first in 1972, was totally imported from the United States. Cutting was done on the basis of layouts produced by computer at Ponzano.

The Supply Cycle

The large volume of business done by the company required that production planning for woven cotton and woolen items be begun far in advance of shipment to the stores. For example, for the spring-summer major line to be introduced in the stores early in January, final designs were prepared in February and early March, as shown in Exhibit 5. Samples of each of the 600 items in the total collection were assembled. In April about a fourth of the items were eliminated in a "pre-presentation" meeting between Giuliana Benetton, Benetton's product and manufacturing managers, and several of the company's 70 agents. The remaining were then produced in small quantities for presentation by area managers to agents and by agents to their individual clients (store owners) in a process that extended from mid-May to mid-July. Within two weeks after the collection of the first orders from franchisees by agents in early June, a rough production plan for the season, by fabrics and styles, was "exploded" from the first 5% to 10% of total orders. This allowed time for the placement of final orders for purchased threads and garments as well as negotiations with subcontractors for necessary increases or decreases in subcontracted volumes prior to the start of production of "basic" retail stocks early in July in advance of the company's three- to four-week vacation in August.

As orders for basic stocks were received from agents, they were assigned reserved slots in the rough production plan by fabric, style, color, and individual store. These orders were produced for delivery to stores from early November through late May for a sales season beginning early in January in the stores. They were scheduled so that each store could present 80% to 90% of all items (fabrics, styles, and colors) in its basic collection to its customers at the outset of the selling season. Other items and remaining quantities ordered arrived at the stores during the selling season.

EXHIBIT 5
Operating Cycle, Benetton Group

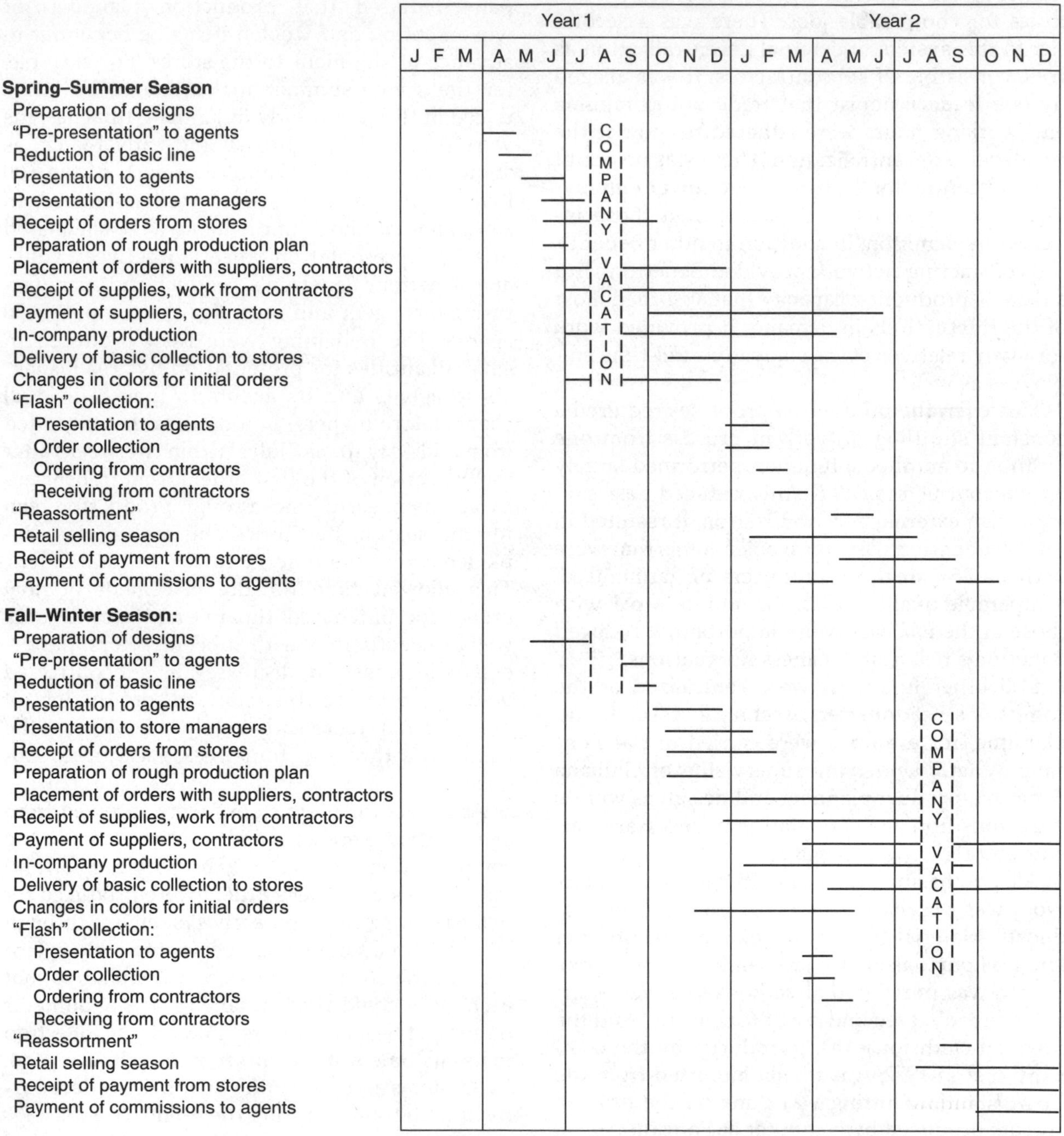

	Year 1	Year 2
	J F M A M J J A S O N D	J F M A M J J A S O N D

Spring–Summer Season
Preparation of designs
"Pre-presentation" to agents
Reduction of basic line
Presentation to agents
Presentation to store managers
Receipt of orders from stores
Preparation of rough production plan
Placement of orders with suppliers, contractors
Receipt of supplies, work from contractors
Payment of suppliers, contractors
In-company production
Delivery of basic collection to stores
Changes in colors for initial orders
"Flash" collection:
  Presentation to agents
  Order collection
  Ordering from contractors
  Receiving from contractors
"Reassortment"
Retail selling season
Receipt of payment from stores
Payment of commissions to agents

COMPANY VACATION

Fall–Winter Season:
Preparation of designs
"Pre-presentation" to agents
Reduction of basic line
Presentation to agents
Presentation to store managers
Receipt of orders from stores
Preparation of rough production plan
Placement of orders with suppliers, contractors
Receipt of supplies, work from contractors
Payment of suppliers, contractors
In-company production
Delivery of basic collection to stores
Changes in colors for initial orders
"Flash" collection:
  Presentation to agents
  Order collection
  Ordering from contractors
  Receiving from contractors
"Reassortment"
Retail selling season
Receipt of payment from stores
Payment of commissions to agents

COMPANY VACATION

Because Benetton required its clients to commit themselves to specific orders seven months in advance of the start of the selling season, it provided several opportunities to franchisees to adjust the actual items presented to their customers. From August through early December, as they gathered more information about color preferences, clients and agents were allowed to specify colors for woven items held in "greggio" up to that point, with a limit of 30% of the total orders for woolen items on such orders. During this period, Benetton's product managers negotiated with agents to encourage them to concentrate their orders on items achieving the highest order popularity.

A second process, called the "flash collection," involved the addition of about 50 items to each season's product line based on early customer requests for fabric-style-color combinations not found in the store. This occurred for the spring-summer collection in January, and required the analysis of requests by Benetton's product and manufacturing managers and a subset of agents prior to the presentation of the flash collection by agents to the stores.

A third process, "reassortment," involved the acceptance of additional orders for rapid delivery later in the selling season, approximately March for the spring-summer collection. Fill-in reassortment orders were processed for store delivery roughly five weeks from the date of their receipt at Benetton. It was made available only for a small number of items determined through a process of negotiation between Benetton's product managers and agents. Because of its process of dyeing "grey" garments, Benetton's plant at Ponzano had the capability to fill an order within seven days of its receipt from an agent. This practice, occasionally requested by agents through Luciano Benetton and product managers, was not encouraged, because it often resulted in dye batches smaller than vat capacity and interfered with long-standing production plans.

Major collections were planned so that about 80% of a season's total sales volume was represented by the basic collection, less than 10% by the flash collection, and less than 10% by reassortment. The remaining sales were realized from a small "cruise" collection presented in the spring and a small "Christmas" collection presented in the fall. In total, sales of the fall-winter collection approximated 60% of a typical year's sales volume.

Production of the basic spring-summer collection ended in late April for final deliveries to stores by late May, by which time production for the following season's fall-winter collection was well underway.

Payments to subcontractors, representing a major cash outflow, were made 70 days after the end of the month in which production occurred or, in the case of the spring-summer collection, in October. Collections from retail franchisees were based on a season-beginning date of March 30 for the spring-summer season, with one-third of payment due 30, 60, and 90 days after that date or the date of actual receipt of merchandise. This was designed to minimize retailers' investment in inventories.

The construction of a company-owned wool-spinning mill which could supply about 20% of Benetton's needs was in the planning stage.

MARKETING

From the beginning, Benetton's marketing strategy had been based on the development of fashionable, but casual, knitted garments featuring bright colors, in contrast to much of the available product in European stores at the time. Colors such as pink and turquoise were staples at the time only in Benetton's product line and continued to be popular items.

Product Development

The basic philosophy behind the design of products had varied little over the years. According to one recent report:

> The company has no plans to vary the design philosophy behind its product line. Though Giuliana has

hired designers from top firms all over the world and follows major fashion trends, she contends that she has merely enlarged on her original insight that young, free-spending customers will always be attracted to brilliant reds and greens and a variety of pastels. "You never discover a new design," she says. "You merely make small changes in the old ones."[6]

The number of product lines had, however, been expanded in conjunction with efforts to retail Benetton products under different labels and store names. Thus, a "012 Benetton" line of children's wear had been developed for presentation in shops decorated with stuffed animals and rainbows carrying the same name. "Jeans West" shops carried Benetton knitwear and trousers targeted to the youth market. Stores carrying Benetton knitwear and trousers with higher fashion content for men and women were named "My Market." A line of items was produced for the "Sisley" label, directed to sophisticated men and presented in stores carrying that name. Although there was no direct equivalent to Sisley for women, shops with the "Mercerie" name stocked some items aimed at a similar market segment, but bearing the Benetton label. Shops under all of these names were intended for center city locations in European cities. In addition, recently a number of shops named "Tomato" had been opened in outlying urban areas to carry knitwear and trousers aimed at the youth market. They featured flashing lights and rock music.

In fact, for each trade name, the appropriate style of furniture and equipment, color of lighting, type of music, and appropriate sex, age, and dress style for salespeople was studied and selected to attract the targeted clientele.

Overall, Benetton shops were identified by more than 10 different names, most of which were not known outside Italy. In spite of the multiplicity of names for stores, it was estimated that during 1982, 70% of total sales were made under the Benetton label and 25% under the 012 Benetton label. However, in total, the Benetton catalogue listed more than 2,000 different item-label combinations.

Pricing

The median retail price of Benetton garments in 1982 was about $20. Prices ranged from under $10 for a pair of socks to $120 for a high-fashion denim jacket. While opinions differed, prices generally were considered lower than competition for the quality of product, nearly always offered in natural wool or cotton. The price-quality combination, high-fashion content, and the multiplicity of bright colors were at the core of the company's retailing strategy.

Distribution

Concurrent with the development of their product line, Benetton began searching for ways of gaining control over their channels of distribution.

Benetton had achieved its retail distribution through an unusual arrangement with "agents" in Italy and other countries of Europe. According to one company marketing executive, the use of the term "franchising" in describing Benetton was a misnomer. Largely through verbal agreement, agents of the company were assigned large territories in which to encourage the development of Benetton retail outlets. They would in turn find smaller investors and store operators with the "Benetton mentality" (according to Benetton's director of communications) with whom they established individual partnerships at the level of the individual outlet. An individual agent might thus supervise and hold an interest in a number of stores. Late in 1982, Benetton conducted its business with 70 such agents. Agents were compensated by Benetton on the basis of a commission of about 4% of the factory sales of goods sold through their retail outlets, in addition to their share of the profits of the stores in which they held ownership.

[6]Labich, "Benetton Takes on the World," p. 115.

For their part, agents found and helped train individual store operators, displayed the Benetton collection to store operators in their regions, assembled orders for the initial stock and stock reordered during each season, and generally supervised the merchandising and pricing at the stores.

Store owners were required to pay Benetton neither a fee for use of its name nor a royalty based on a percentage of sales or profits. Among other things, they were required to carry only Benetton merchandise, maintain a minimum sales level (equivalent to orders for about 3,500 garments per year), adhere to suggested mark-ups of about 80% from cost, pay for their orders according to a preset schedule,[7] and, in the words of one Benetton manager, develop "an understanding of Benetton's way of doing business."

In a recent interview, Luciano Benetton had provided some insight into the company's strategy for developing shop owners:

> We have caused a (new) type of retailer to become important, who until the day before was perhaps a florist or a hairdresser. His prior career was of no importance, but he had to have the right spirit to work in a Benetton shop.

The ideal Benetton retailer was relatively young and thought to have good potential for "growing with Benetton."

All Benetton outlets were required to use Benetton fixtures and follow basic merchandising concepts, the most important among them being that all merchandise was to be displayed on open shelves accessible to customers who could touch it and try it on. The open displays in an otherwise undecorated space created an impression of great color and fashion to the window-shopping customer. This was thought to be especially effective with the 19-to-25 year-old market toward which Benetton had directed its European marketing efforts.

Benetton clients were expected to maintain storage facilities which, in combination with their store shelves, could accommodate 30% to 40% of a season's sales in addition to merchandise still being sold from the preceding season. Typically, such storage consisted of small basement rooms under the retail outlets. However, the company's written agreement with a client when it existed, typically was limited to the use and protection of Benetton's trademark.

Benetton's relationship with agents was managed largely on a verbal basis of trust. Agents rarely had to be replaced for failure to meet expectations.

Benetton had given a great deal of attention to store location, emphasizing areas of high traffic for young adults. Most important, European locations had been selected by Luciano Benetton and his assistants, according to a pattern of market development in which the first store in a given market often was sited in a high-prestige location. According to one legend in the company, it had taken Mr. Benetton six years to find the proper location for one shop in Turin. Once the site for a lead store had been selected and developed, an effort was made rapidly to blanket the area around it with shops offering Benetton's merchandise.

As many as six different shops, of which no more than two might be called Benetton, could be located within several city blocks of one another. The company had 46 shops in Milan, Italy, alone. While they were adapted in layout to fit desirable sites, all were much smaller and had several characteristics that set them apart from other young women's casual apparel shops, as suggested by the comparative profiles shown in Exhibit 6. The layout of a typical Benetton shop is shown in Exhibit 7.

By the end of 1982, shops were being opened in Europe at the rate of one every working day. Of

---

[7]Payment terms calling for one-third of payment within 30, 60, and 90 days each of the beginning date of the season (for goods received prior to that time) could result in payments on average being made to Benetton in about 80 days, depending on the relation between the date the merchandise actually was received and the date set for determining payment dates.

EXHIBIT 6

Comparative Profits for Typical Benetton Store, European Young Women's Apparel Store, and American Specialty Chain Store for Young Women's Apparel

Item	*Typical Benetton Store*[a]	*Store of European Competition*	*American Specialty Chain Store*[a]
Annual sales, in $	$305,000	$150,000	$400,000
Selling space, in sq. ft.	500	1,200	2,700
Storage space, in sq. ft.	200	300	300
Type of location	Downtown street	Downtown street	Suburban shopping mall
Initial margins, as % of sales price	44%	50%	57%
Realized margins, as % of sales price	37%	45%	45%
Median sales price per unit, in $	18	40	23[b]
Average size per transaction, in $	26	50	35[b]
Employee hours per week	90	200	230
Selling hours per week	45	45	76
Average store inventory, at cost[c]	$40,000	$30,000	$50,000
Expense Categories, as a % of Sales			
Cost of goods sold	61%	55%	55%
Labor	7	29	13
Occupancy (rent and utilities)	5	7	10
Other (including overhead)	8	6	10
Net profit before tax	19%	3%	12%

[a]Based on casewriters' estimates.

[b]These figures had risen with the introduction of designers' clothing for casual wear. Stores not carrying such clothing realized average prices of perhaps $18 per garment. Stores featuring such clothing averaged as much as $55 per item for lines of clothing comparable to those sold by Benetton.

[c]Estimated on the basis of a store capacity of 2,000 pieces plus a back-up stock varying between 500 pieces toward the end of one season and 2,500 pieces at the beginning of the next.

the more than 1,800 shops in operation at the time in Europe, 1,165 were located in Italy alone. (See Exhibit 8 for a tabulation of shops by type and by location.) According to one company executive, while many shops had been moved, "none had been closed."

While Benetton retail shops differed, depending on available real estate, they all had one thing in common. They carried only Benetton products, in spite of the fact that only 20 of Benetton's stores outside Italy were owned by the company.

Retailers were expected to follow guidelines for offering sale merchandise. These were established and managed by agents in each region, who also moved merchandise among shops as sales patterns developed. As a result, the typical level of mark-downs as a percentage of sales for a Benetton retail outlet was relatively low, approximating seven percentage points of a retailer's prescribed initial margin. The "model" for Benetton retail store operations was that a store would have no more or less than 15% of a season's merchandise as it entered the last two weeks of a season. This could then be sold at cost to allow the retailer to present a newly merchandised store to the customer at the outset of the new season. Be-

EXHIBIT 7
Typical Layout of a Benetton Retail Store*

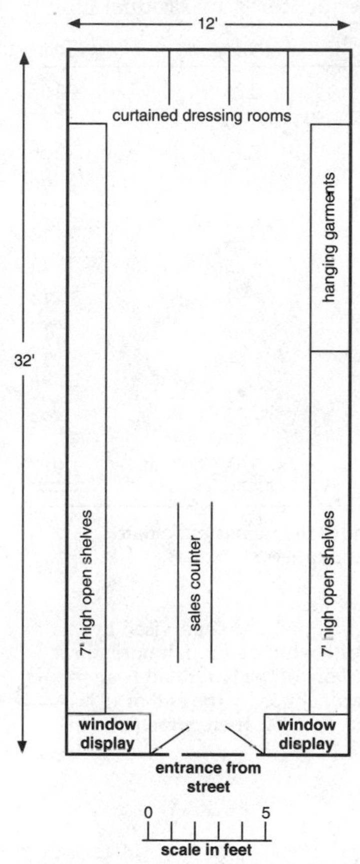

*In cases where a Benetton and Benetton 012 store were located next to one another, they might be connected by an interior doorway.

netton did not accept merchandise returns from its agents or retailers.

Promotion

Benetton relied on location and bright, inviting store appearance as a cornerstone for its promotional effort. Window displays often were spare and allowed a clear view of the open shelves of colorful merchandise from the street. In addition, it used mainly three media in Europe to advertise its name: television, press, and the sponsoring of sports events.

On television, spots were placed that concentrated on the "sport" and "youth" image of the Benetton name. Magazine advertising was used for institutional campaigns and emphasized color and the Benetton "lifestyle."

Benetton management had invested in the sponsoring of sports events throughout much of the company's existence, reflecting the interests of the Benettons themselves. Thus the company sponsored a rugby team which had moved into the top league in Italy, later adding the sponsorship of a handball team as well. It had already committed what was estimated to be well over $2 million for the sponsorship of a race car for the 1983 season of World F-1 auto racing.

All of these efforts were put forth on behalf of the Benetton name, the only Benetton trade name with enough volume and outlets to support a multinational campaign, and were intended to support the image of a product line aimed at the active, young adult or child. Benetton had spent over twice as much for advertising in Italy as its nearest European competitor, Maglificio Piave, manufacturer of the Stehnel brand of clothing. Over two-thirds of Benetton's 1981 advertising budget for Italy, 955 million lire, was spent for magazine advertising.

LOGISTICS

Logistics played an important role in the Benetton strategy. Starting at the retail level, stores carrying Benetton products were designed with limited storage space for back-up stocks. Upon arrival at the store direct from Benetton, merchandise often was checked and placed directly on the display shelves. This required that shipments to stores be planned and executed according to a carefully prepared schedule.

Agents managed the replenishment process by collecting and assembling orders from individual stores and relaying them electronically to Vil-

EXHIBIT 8
Location of Benetton Stores, by Country and Product Line, December 1982

	Number of Stores, by Product Line			
Country	*Benetton*[a]	*012*[b]	*Sisley*[c]	*Total*
Italy[d]	659	380	126	1,165
France	198	80	5	283
Germany	138	30	—	168
Switzerland	53	10	3	66
United Kingdom	35	8	1	44
Austria	28	8	—	36
Belgium	12	2	—	14
Ireland	8	5	1	14
Sweden	9	4	—	13
Holland	8	3	—	11
Spain	9	—	—	9
Other	79	15	—	94
	1,236	545	136	1,917

[a]Figures for Benetton in Italy only included stores operated under the names of Tomato, Mercerie, My Market, Fantomex, Jeans West, Pulloveria, and several others.
[b]The 012 stores carried children's clothing.
[c]The Sisley stores specialized in fashion-oriented casual wear for men.
[d]Figures for Italy included "franchised affiliates," store sites developed and supervised by agents in the manner described in the case, and "third party shops," which, although not bound by agreements, adopted the same sales formula as the affiliates. Many of the latter had been converted to franchised affiliates, leaving only about 400 third-party shops by the end of 1982. At its peak in 1978, the number of company-owned shops reached 58. By 1982, there were none in Italy.

lorba, where directions were given for orders to be manufactured to order. In principle, Benetton did not manufacture anything without an order in hand. From receipt of a replenishment order, the company could have merchandise at the retail site in Europe no more than five weeks from the transmission of an order from an agent. (This contrasted with the shipment of a season's initial assortment, for which production began six months and ended 40 days in advance of the display of merchandise in the stores.)

All merchandise was premarked in the currency of the country of destination with tickets coded to be processed electronically at the time of the sale. To facilitate replenishment, Benetton had under design two major improvements in the logistics system. An elaborate new information network, relying on automatic cash registers in clusters of 10 shops each hooked into Benetton's three large Siemen's 7865 computing units in Italy and an Olivetti 5330 unit in Paris, recently had been proposed by Elio Aluffi, managing director of internal operations. It would be capable of instantly recording individual sales in Benetton's European shops. Its cost was estimated to be roughly $7.5 million. Although proposed for possible implementation by the summer of 1983, there was some question about its acceptance by agents, several of whom had indicated that the new system was not needed.

In addition, Luciano Benetton had on his desk a proposal for the construction of a new 200,000 square-foot central warehousing facility at Castrette, about 12 miles from the Ponzano headquarters, at a cost of about $20 million. The core of this facility would be 10 robot stacker cranes capable of stowing and picking cartons from its stocking capacity of nearly 250,000 boxes of merchandise. Its daily total handling capacity was estimated to be 15,000 boxes (either in or out of the warehouse). With the new warehouse operating by the end of 1984, plans called for a reduction in minimum lead time required for the distribution of orders for each collection from 40 to 35 days.

The number of items per box to be handled at Castrette would vary, but it was thought to average 28. It depended on the size of the order directed to an individual factory where the items would be boxed and shipped to Castrette. No boxes would be opened while at the Castrette warehouse. All were labeled at the factory for use with optical scanners which routed the merchandise through the warehouse. Prices to retailers did not vary on the basis of the number of items shipped per box.

In addition to service improvements, the new warehouse offered the possibility of savings of perhaps 20% on transport costs for finished products. Not only could orders be consolidated for an individual store at Castrette but they could be loaded in sequence for store delivery by truck. (All orders were sold at a "store delivered" price. This price did not vary by destination.) While a detailed analysis of current transportation costs had not been completed, the casewriters estimated that they could be as high as 5% of sales.

With the opening of the Castrette facility, the current warehouse at Cusignana would be closed and all items produced in Italy moved through Castrette.

EUROPEAN COMPETITION

Benetton had experienced increasing competition in Italy and Europe, primarily from firms emulating elements of its strategy. For example, other Italian manufacturers recently had instituted programs of direct selling by franchising local retailers. Both had had to abandon gradually their wholesale customers and launch new trademarks.

One, Maglificio Torinese, had, since 1980, been opening shops for the exclusive sales of the Kappa Sport product line specializing in casual sportswear. It now had more than 100 outlets in Italy with plans to extend its sales network to other countries. Maglificio Piave, launching its "Stefanel" trademark in 1979 to replace the Sigma brand formerly sold to wholesalers, already sold through 150 exclusive outlets in Italy and some 30 others throughout Europe.

It was apparent to Benetton's management that its current product lines were reaching the saturation point in the Italian market. As a result of this as well as increasing competition from emulators, a growing amount of competitive imported merchandise, and a stagnant economy, Benetton's billings in Italy had leveled out in real terms.

There had been some debate about the importance of other European markets in Benetton's future strategy. As Elio Aluffi, a long-time Benetton employee recently moved to his new post as head of internal operations, had said: "We haven't completed our work yet in Europe. We have to consolidate that market."[8]

But while there still appeared to be significant potential for Benetton in the rest of Europe, with expected annual increases in sales of 15% resulting from expanded efforts in England, Belgium, and the Netherlands, it was generally concluded that potential margins to be obtained from incremental sales in Europe were lower than those that might be realized in totally new markets like Japan and the United States. As a result, the Benettons and their senior managers were studying alternatives for developing the U.S. market, where it was felt there might be a potential for 1,000 or more retail outlets.

---

[8]Labich, "Benetton Takes on the World," p. 118.

THE U.S. STRATEGY

Many issues had been raised at Benetton in the process of developing alternatives for serving the U.S. market. They reflected questions among managers whether the formula so successful in Italy could be applied in the U.S., and if it couldn't, whether Benetton would enjoy the competitive advantage that was responsible for its success in Europe.

Several elements of the U.S. market were particularly worrisome. First was its sheer size and the ability of Benetton to accommodate the volumes of potential sales it might enjoy. Second, the Benetton name and its associated labels were unknown except among those who had traveled in Europe. There was already formidable U.S. competition, primarily in the form of well-established manufacturers and retailers of casual wear. Several of these manufacturers carried on their own extensive consumer advertising program. Levi Strauss, with 1982 sales of about $2.3 billion, not only manufactured jeans and related items, but also operated retail stores, budgeting more than $100 million each year for advertising and promotion. In addition, several large retail chains carried a great deal of merchandise aimed at Benetton's prime markets, including The Limited (with approximately 750 retail stores), Charming Shops (260 stores), Petrie (nearly 800 stores), and Miller-Wohl (nearly 300 stores). While none of these competitors manufactured garments, many offered products produced with their labels. And several had engaged relatively heavily in media advertising to solidify their position; The Limited alone was thought to have an annual advertising budget of $20 million. All owned and controlled their own stores, mostly in modern shopping malls (largely nonexistent in many parts of Europe), with a size and sales volume per store considerably larger than Benetton's.

Nevertheless, it was thought that Benetton could capitalize on the strong image of Italian design and the upsurge of popularity of Italian fashion in the United States. And its nontraditional (for the U.S.) approach to retailing might provide advantages in finding good store locations that competitors couldn't utilize.

A debate had arisen concerning the product line and its presentation. Basic among the issues discussed was whether the product mix should be altered significantly. For example, there was some support for upgrading the target market, average sales points, and dollar margins per item for a U.S. strategy. This could be centered around the Sisley and Mercerie merchandise lines for men and women. Consistent with this long-term target, the INVEP Group recently had acquired a 50% interest in an Italian fashion house, Fiorucci. While the company was not highly profitable, the acquisition gave the Benettons entry into higher fashion markets, with potential benefits for the image of other of the group's labels.

On the other hand, it was argued that the company could gain maximum penetration by maintaining its European price points, adjusted only for U.S. import tariffs of 35% of manufactured cost. If this were done, however, little or no additional budget could be devoted to the development of designs especially for the U.S. market.

American preference for easy-to-care-for garments raised questions about the potential attraction of Benetton's natural fibers. Also, tastes seemed to be changing more rapidly than in the past. New products made of "plush" (velvet) and heavy knitted cotton had replaced wool among some consumers' preferences. As Luciano Benetton pointed out, however: "Heavy knitted cotton items have played an important part in all our recent collections. In cases such as this a company must be adaptable and ready to respond to the demands of the market."

In the process of developing an appropriate retailing strategy for the U.S., several questions had been raised. Should Benetton develop markets as they had in Europe, relying on agents to develop and control a retailing network? Twenty regions for U.S. development had been identified on the basis of population and per capita clothing purchase data. In addition, the question had been posed as to whether Benetton should rely on existing or new agents. Nearly all of its current agents were from Europe or the Middle East. But they knew the company and its policies and were trusted by Benetton's management. In addition, an opportunity to participate in the development of the U.S. market could increase their loyalty to the company. On the other hand, many of the existing agents did not know the U.S. market well. Several were thought already to be getting overloaded with work.

Whether agents were used or not, a decision had to be made whether "lead" stores displaying the Benetton name at prestigious addresses should be opened prior to blanketing a metropolitan area with numerous outlets. Or whether Benetton could rely on department stores to provide space for Benetton products until the name could become better known in the U.S. At least two leading U.S. department store organizations, Macy's and Associated Dry Goods, had approached Benetton with proposals to open small Benetton boutiques in their department stores, if necessary under the agent arrangement. However, both had desired an exclusive agreement with Benetton or its agents. Or should a new type of retailing outlet be designed altogether? In addressing this last question, Luciano Benetton commented:

> The idea we are looking for would represent a new era in the point-of-sale development. For instance, instead of small structures, we would have larger retail areas in which we would present more diverse merchandise. . . . Small shops like our conventional points of sale cannot serve as points of reference where people meet or listen to music. Today the necessity is felt, abroad as in Italy, for large spaces where consumers can meet.

Even Benetton's small shops required an investment estimated to average about $70,000 each for the U.S. This assumed pre-work to condition the space for Benetton's fixtures of $15,000 to $20,000, about $40,000 for the fixtures, and from $5,000 to $15,000 for transportation of the fixtures from Italy, depending on whether surface or air transport were used. It assumed no investment, for well-run stores, in inventory and the payment of no "key money" to obtain desirable retail locations.

It was clear to everyone concerned that it would be impossible to launch a full-scale advertising program for the Benetton name in the U.S. similar to that already existing in Europe. But it was thought that some promotional effort would be expected by Benetton's retailers. One estimate of the minimum annual advertising budget required just to achieve visibility and begin to build awareness for the name in the U.S. was $2 million. Questions remained, however, as to how a budget of that size should be allocated to various media.

How would a new U.S. market be supported operationally? Alternatives under consideration were: (1) the development of a new plant with dyeing facilities and a warehouse in the U.S.; (2) the opening only of a new warehouse to stock finished product shipped from the Ponzano factory; or (3) direct distribution to U.S. retail sites from Europe, either using conventional forms of communication or an extended computer linked up with product shipment by air.

The first of these would require a capital investment of perhaps $10 million and labor costs perhaps 50% higher than at the Ponzano plant. Of more importance would be the difficulty of managing the crucial dyeing operation at a foreign site. Regardless of whether a new dyeing facility were opened in the U.S., it was assumed that the company could not afford to source "grey" garments in the U.S. at anywhere near the cost it experienced in Italy. Thus, added costs of shipping such garments by surface or air would be incurred anyway, with the difference in total transit time for the two methods being about three weeks. It was estimated that delivery by air to the U.S. in semifinished or finished form would add perhaps 50% to the current average of transportation costs for garments shipped in Europe or by surface means across the Atlantic Ocean.

The second alternative would make an investment in U.S. plant capacity unnecessary for the time being. But Benetton would lose inventory savings of the kind enjoyed in Europe, and its new warehouse at Castrette already could provide sufficient capacity to serve both the U.S. and European markets.

The third alternative would allow Benetton to delay significant commitments of capital to either plant or inventory but would require increased transportation costs even if no computer link-up were attempted. The latter would, it was thought, pay for itself in perhaps three years by providing more timely information.

Nor was entry into the U.S. market the only new venture confronting Benetton's management. Plans were underway to develop the Japanese market as well. And in one move apparently aimed at enhancing Benetton's image further, the family was reported to be considering a joint venture with a French manufacturer of perfumes to produce a new line of Benetton perfumes and cosmetics.

Benetton was reported to be having difficulties with its recent acquisition of an Italian shoe manufacturer, Calza Turificio di Varese, manufacturing one Million pairs of shoes per year with 86 retail shops and 1982 sales of about $40 million. Benetton had bought a 70% interest in it for $12 million in June 1982. While this had not dimmed management's enthusiasm for adding Benetton shoes to its retail lines, Luciano Benetton commented that "as an experience, it has been quite interesting. But the factory is old and there have been many problems."[9]

In response to an interviewer who had questioned the acquisition of the shoe manufacturer, Luciano Benetton replied:

> I don't agree, because there are too many logical relationships. We are known for woolen knitwear. And when we started making trousers, we thought this already might be a different sector. Instead, it was coordinated exactly as we can coordinate the shoes. . . . If the common denominator is clothing, we will also have to produce evening dresses. But we don't because ours is the "casual" market segment comprising clothing without too much elegance for specific hours of the day.

By the end of 1982, action had been taken on a number of the issues concerning the development of the U.S. market. But others remained, several of which could greatly affect the company's U.S. strategy.

[9]Labich, "Benetton Takes on the World," p. 119.

CASE 5 | *Magna International, Inc.*

By mid-1986 annual sales of Magna International, Inc. were projected to top $1 billion for the first time. As Canada's largest manufacturer of automotive parts. Magna's corporate objectives of having an average of $100 of its auto parts built into every North American car was also in sight.

Although company founder Frank Stronach and his management team continuously espoused a "small is beautiful" philosophy, their dreams for Magna were by no means small. Stronach stated in 1985 that he was intent on creating "one of the largest corporations in North

America" and that he felt Magna could maintain 30 percent annual growth for many years. By 1986 it was also clear that Magna was committed to a strategy of increased internationalization of its operations. These goals clearly raised questions about the appropriateness of Magna's current operating philosophy and organization for the planned growth.

FRANK STRONACH AND MAGNA INTERNATIONAL

In 1985 Magna's flamboyant chairman and chief executive officer, Frank Stronach, was the highest-paid executive in Canada with a salary of $1.85 million. Many felt this was justified given Magna's almost unprecedented 30 percent annual growth in sales and profits over the last 15 years. Exhibit 1 provides financial statements from Magna's 1985 annual report detailing the company's financial performance.

The company in its original form was founded in 1957 by its controlling shareholder, chairman and CEO Frank Stronach. By 1986 it employed more than 7,500 people in approximately 65 Canadian and 5 American plants and in 1 additional plant in West Germany. In 1984 75 percent of sales were to U.S. customers. Magna's primary customers were the various operating divisions of Ford, General Motors, Chrysler, and AMC—the "Big Four" North American auto manufacturers. In fact, 95 percent of their products went into North American cars.

The history of Magna was really the entrepreneurial life story of Frank Stronach, who immigrated to Canada from Austria in 1954. Trained as a tool and die maker, Stronach invested what little savings he had and opened up his own tool and die shop in a rented Toronto garage while still in his mid-20s. Business was good in the first two years, and Stronach soon employed 30 people. When his foreman told him that he wanted to leave and start his own business, Stronach offered the man part ownership in the business in order to keep him. The foreman stayed and set up the company's second tool and die shop. This was the first glimmer of what was to be part of Magna's future strategy for corporate growth—decentralization with equity participation by its employees.

Stronach summed up his feelings and reasons behind the philosophy: "If I lose a good person, I'm losing somebody who could be a competitor. I want those people in my camp. That's what business is all about—people management."

By 1969 Stronach owned eight plants that were run autonomously. In order to implement a plan to facilitate employee share ownership, he merged with the publicly traded Magna Electronics Corporation, substituting *International* for the word *Electronics* to reflect the company's broad range of products and greater ambitions.

For the next 15 years Magna grew almost continually at an annual rate of 30 percent or more and by 1985 was opening one new factory every six to eight weeks to keep pace with demand. Its product lines had grown to over 4,000 different components and assemblies, encompassing parts for nearly every section of the automobile. Exhibit 2 provides a list of product families manufactured by each of Magna's operating groups in 1984. Some products were manufactured to customer specifications while others were designed by Magna's staff and sold as original equipment based on their innovative designs.

THE MAGNA "SUCCESS FORMULA"

Magna consistently performed well in the cyclical auto-parts industry whose performance followed the auto industry's traditional four-year up-and-down cycle. One investment analyst commented that Magna had "the best growth record and highest returns on equity in the business." Exhibit 3 provides a brief analysis of the auto-parts industry and shows Magna's financial performance in comparison with three other major auto-parts manufacturers.

Many explanations were offered to explain Magna's unequalled success. In the end, however,

EXHIBIT 1
Magna International Inc.
10-Year Financial Summary (Canadian Dollars in Thousands except per Share Figures)

	1985	*1984*	*1983*	*1982*	*1981*[1]	*1980*	*1979*	*1978*	*1977*	*1976*
Operations Data										
Sales	**$690,400**	$493,559	$302,451	$226,534	$232,114	$183,456	$165,738	$128,189	$80,953	$55,010
Income from operations	**69,430**	57,124	25,473	9,055	12,054	9,249	15,924	12,899	8,185	5,734
Net income[4]	**43,191**	31,480	14,647	5,265	6,911	5,640	8,455	6,595	4,093	2,786
Extraordinary items						(1,922)	272	795		
Basic earnings per Class A and Class B share[2,3]	**$2.00**	$1.93	$1.10	$0.49	$0.64	$0.34	$0.89	$0.80	$0.48	$0.36
Fully diluted earnings per Class A and Class B share	**$1.93**	$1.85	$1.07	$0.44	$0.57	$0.33	$0.78	$0.68	$0.47	$0.32
Depreciation	**24,322**	15,044	11,267	9,325	9,188	6,154	4,506	3,349	2,210	1,416
Cash flow from operations	**85,974**	55,945	32,522	14,604	14,672	12,052	15,275	13,160	7,542	5,171
Dividends declared per Class A and Class B share[2,3]	**$0.48**	$0.31	$0.13[5]	$0.13	$0.18	$0.18	$0.14	$0.10	$0.06	$0.03
Financial Position										
Working capital	**64,121**	79,804	48,291	31,792	30.792	28,223	19,174	15,351	7,412	4,925
Capital expenditures	**222,878**	110,239	29,806	17,434	21,052	23,630	23,085	16,231	8,584	3,456
Fixed assets (less accumulated depreciation)	**357,371**	179,817	87,388	70,553	74,074	62,629	47,089	30,269	19,387	8,940
Long-term debt	**103.997**	96,497	42,159	55,554	56,308	45,830	30,441	19,588	10,238	4,627
Equity related to Class A and Class B shares	**297,935**	143,566	81,590	41,071	39,631	33,792	32,086	23,270	15,226	9,646
Equity per Class A and Class B share[2,3]	**$12.44**	$8.43	$5.59	$4.13	$3.84	$3.35	$3.18	$2.41	$1.68	$1.25

[1]1981 and prior figures include sales and income from Aerospace/Defence operations sold effective August 1, 1981.
[2]Adjusted for years prior to 1979 to give effect to the capital reorganization during 1979.
[3]1983 and prior figures adjusted to give effect to the stock dividend issued June 1983.
[4]Before extraordinary items.
[5]In addition, stockholders received a special stock dividend issued June 1983.

EXHIBIT 2
Magna Product Directory

CMT Group
Seat track mechanisms
Window winding regulators
Hand brake assemblies
Hood hinges
Door hinges
Door latches
Hood latches
Trunk latches
Clutch and brake pedal assemblies

Decorative Products Group
Front bumper and grille fascia
Rear bumper fascia
Rocker panels
Wheel house opening mouldings
Window channels
Weather strip channels
Headlamp retainers
Centre hood mouldings
Windshield mouldings
Rear window mouldings
Drain trough mouldings
Exterior window mouldings
Tail light bezels
Rocker panel mouldings
Body side mouldings

MACI Group
Cooling fan motors
Heating fan motors
Windshield wiper motors
Immersible fuel pumps
Thermostatic air controllers
Magnetic capsule switches
Relay switches
Instrument clusters
Fuel control devices
Electronic tone and voice synthesized alarms
Electronic fluid level devices

Magna Manufacturing Group
Aluminum bumper reinforcements
Shock absorber towers
Rear cross members
Fuel tank straps
Sill plates
Scuff plates
Alternator fans
Motor mounts
Canister support brackets
Glove box doors
Seat belt anchors
Heat shields
Catalytic converters
Thermostat housings
Water pumps
Instrument panel supports
Headrests

Maple Group
Poly V crankshaft pulleys
Power steering pulleys
Alternator pulleys
Automatic Poly V belt tensioners
Water pump pulleys
Compressor pump pulleys
Two speed accessory drive system
Oil strainers
Oil pick-up tubes
Dip-stick tubes

it seemed to boil down to the company's ability to manufacture the highest quality product at the lowest possible cost.

Some observers, including Magna's management and especially Frank Stronach, attributed its success to Magna's unique "corporate culture," whose key elements were embodied in the company's "Corporate Constitution," published for the first time in Magna's 1984 annual report. The stated purpose of the constitution was to "define the rights of employees and investors to participate in the company's profits and growth and impose discipline on management." Stronach thought that Magna might be the only company in the Western world with a corporate constitution which guaranteed employee rights and imposed discipline on management. Exhibit 4 shows the Magna Corporate Constitution, and Exhibit 5 gives some excerpts from the 1985 annual report that demonstrate the constitution in practice at Magna.

Other critical components of the corporate culture included a commitment of keeping all Magna plants small with a maximum of 100 employees each, an emphasis on research and development, and rewards for both management and workers through an attractive profit-sharing plan and a range of social benefits from day care for employees' children to a recently opened company-owned conservation and recreation area.

ORGANIZATION AND OPERATING STRUCTURE

Exhibit 6 illustrates and describes Magna's unique operating structure, which consisted of three

EXHIBIT 3
Market Overview

The auto-parts market can be divided into eight sections. Passenger car, light truck, medium and heavy truck, and off-highway vehicles give the four major sections, and each of these can be broken into original equipment (O.E.) and aftermarket. A further subdivision could be made in aftermarket between the original equipment aftermarket and the third-party aftermarket. That subdivision is not considered here.

Most auto-parts companies cover more than one segment, so companies can be competitors with some products and not with others. Competitors also depend upon whether a company is in the original equipment market or aftermarket. Canadian aftermarket firms concentrate on the Canadian market because of the duty collectible in crossing the Canada-U.S. border. Original equipment, on the other hand, is duty free under the autopact, and therefore firms in both Canada and the United States compete for this business.

The business cycles for original equipment and the aftermarket tend to be countercyclical. When new vehicle sales are down, the sales of replacement parts tend to be up, thereby giving some protection to firms that are in both market segments.

The companies below have the following characteristics:

Budd Canada	Passenger	O.E. and aftermarket
	Light truck	O.E.
Hayes-Dana	Passenger car	O.E. and aftermarket
	Light truck	O.E. and aftermarket
	Medium and heavy truck	O.E. and aftermarket
	Off-highway vehicles	O.E. and aftermarket
Magna International	Passenger car	O.E. and aftermarket
	Light truck	O.E. and aftermarket
Long Manufacturing	Passenger car	O.E. and aftermarket
	Light truck	O.E. and aftermarket
	Medium and heavy truck	O.E. and aftermarket
	Off-highway vehicles	O.E.

Industry Overview for 1984

Sales of cars and light trucks again increased by 19 percent. The market for other trucks and off-highway vehicles did not improve.

Statistical process control and just-in-time delivery were taken up by the whole auto-parts industry. The new threat to the auto-parts industry was the statement from the manufacturers that the supplier base was to be cut 50 percent within three years to reduce their overhead in dealing with suppliers and to increase control.

Budd Canada in 1984

Budd had a good year in 1984. Sales increased by 36 percent, and net profits were $11.2 million compared to 1983's loss of $2.2 million. This was due to several factors:

- General administration expenses were kept under control and resulted in expenses as a percentage of sales of only 8 percent compared with their historical average of about 10 percent.
- Cost of goods sold was reduced even lower than the 1980 level (81.2 percent compared with 84.9 percent in 1980). This was the result of the fully utilized Kitchener plant which in turn was because of the increased sales and productivity gains made with the recent plant additions.

Budd not only showed a good profit in 1984, they also outperformed the market in terms of the net profits/net sales ratio. Their return on investment ratios compared favourably with the industry averages.

The working capital management ratios show that Budd compares favourably with other companies. Aggressive management of accounts receivable shows a decrease in days receivable from 78 to 58 days.

EXHIBIT 3
continued

Liquidity and solvency ratios show an excellent position.

Hayes-Dana in 1984

The year 1984 saw Hayes-Dana sales increase by 31 percent and profitability increase by 170 percent. The favourable picture comes from

- Improving the cost of goods sold percentage by 3.5 percent of sales, resulting in a favourable variance of $11.9 million.
- Depreciation expense was not at the 1983 levels, resulting in an additional favourable variance of $2.5 million. This plus the increase in investment income were offset by increased operating expenses of a full 1 percent of sales, resulting in an unfavourable variance of $3.9 million.

Days receivable again continued to increase in a year where all other manufacturers studied managed to reduce their collection period. Inventory turnover improved but still lagged the industry. These working capital items accounted for $24 million of the funds available. As well, plant additions of $9 million and an increase of investment in affiliates used the funds raised from increasing current loans and other liabilities and from increasing long-term debt.

The end-of-year inventory at Hayes-Dana was higher than in other companies. Cost of goods sold was improving but was not at the level Budd had achieved.

The $9 million plant addition in 1984 should improve their operating expense ration in upcoming years. It would be reasonable to assume that Hayes-Dana could achieve the 81 percent cost-of-goods-sold level that Budd and others have achieved.

Magna in 1984

Magna's sales increased 63 percent in 1984, and net profits more than doubled. Magna obtained more than its share of the improving market in 1984, when we see the other companies' sales increase somewhere from 30 to 40 percent. The very favourable net profit results can be explained by the management of operating expenses. Operating expenses as a percent of sales dropped from 85.3 percent to 74.9 percent; this level of operating expense reduction was not achieved by any of the other three companies.

Accounts receivable management was excellent, reducing the days receivable from 68.8 days to 63.9 days, the lowest it had been since 1980. It still remained significantly higher, however, than the other companies studied.

Inventory management resulted in a slight drop of inventory turns; the result was, however, well within the results obtained by the other companies studied.

Plant expenditures for the year totaled $107 million; this obviously had a good effect on the operating expense reduction discussed above. The plant expansion was funded by an increase in long-term debt of $54 million and a stock offering which raised an additional $35 million.

At year-end 1984, Magna is in a favourable liquidity and solvency position relative to the other companies studied.

Long Manufacturing in 1984

Long's sales increased to $49.5 million, up 39 percent from 1983. Return on equity at 41 percent was the best of the companies studied.

Long was driving down debt. The success was shown in the long-term debt to total assets ratio, dropping to the low of the group of companies studied, and the common stock equity to total assets ratio, rising to a more usual level of 26 percent. This was achieved by paying off $6 million of the $7 million of long-term debt and an additional $1.1 million of current debt.

The current ratio remained at 1.1, and the quick ratio dropped slightly to 0.5. Accounts receivable were brought down to 35 days, and inventory turns rose again, up to 9.3, both better than the other three companies.

EXHIBIT 4
Magna's Corporate Constitution

Board of Directors
Magna believes that outside directors provide independent counsel and discipline. A majority of Magna's Board of Directors will be outsiders.

Employee Equity and Profit Participation
Ten percent of Magna's profit before tax will be allocated to employees. These funds will be used for the purchase of Magna shares in trust for employees and for cash distributions to employees, recognizing both performance and length of service.

Shareholder Profit Participation
Magna will distribute, on average, 20 per cent of its annual net profit to its shareholders.

Management Profit Participation
In order to obtain a long term contractual commitment from management, the Company provides a compensation arrangement which, in addition to a base salary comparable to industry standards, allows for the distribution to corporate management of up to 6 per cent of Magna's profit before tax.

Research and Technology Development
Magna will allocate 7 per cent of its profit before tax for research and technology development to ensure the long term viability of the Company.

Social Responsibility
The Company will contribute a maximum of 2 per cent of its profit before tax to charitable, cultural, educational and political institutions to support the basic fabric of society.

Minimum Profit Performance
Management has an obligation to produce a profit. If Magna does not generate a minimum after-tax return of 4 percent on share capital for two consecutive years. Class A shareholders, voting as a Class, will have the right to elect additional directors.

Major Investments
In the event that more than 20 percent of Magna's equity is to be committed to a new unrelated business, Class A and Class B shareholders will have the right to approve such an investment with each class voting separately.

Constitutional Amendments
Any change to Magna's Corporate Constitution will require the approval of the Class A and Class B shareholders with each class voting separately.

(Copies of the complete Constitution can be obtained from the Corporate Secretary's office.)

levels of responsibility: the operating unit, group management (in charge of an operating group), and executive management.

At the operating unit or individual factory level, maximum employment was kept to no more than 100 workers because of Stronach's belief that management and employees should maintain close working relationships and that smaller units sparked individual initiative and a degree of entrepreneurship. Stronach felt that a "family relationship" should exist among coworkers and management with each person knowing the name of all his fellow employees.

"Communication is very important. If you have a few thousand people under one roof, you need a hundred thousand rules. You lose the human touch. You create a faceless kind of management," said Stronach, adding that Magna's environment simply created "a damned good atmosphere to work in!"

Every Magna factory was unique in its own right, with its own product mandate, R&D department, and production and profit objectives established by that unit's management team. Every employee had access to management, and since each earned shares in the company through a profit-sharing plan, they were likely to come forward with assembly-line suggestions to improve quality or cut costs—suggestions that could lead to promotion, more profits to share, and increased equity participation. The small scale of each unit's operations and Magna's emphasis on factory-floor technical skills (promoted by in-house technical education and upgrading programs) resulted in a high degree of flexibility and an ability to adapt quickly to changes in manufacturing operations.

EXHIBIT 5

Excerpts from 1985 Annual Report: Corporate Constitution in Practice

Magna's continued growth is based upon our unique corporate culture which allows the company to make a better product for a better price.

Our culture recognizes that it takes three ingredients to be successful in business, namely: management, employees, and capital. Furthermore, it requires that each of these ingredients has a right to share in the profits that it helps to generate. This foremost principle and other operating principles are enshrined in Magna's Corporate Constitution.

We in management continuously search for ways to stimulate employees to achieve greater productivity. In recent years this has been partially accomplished through the introduction of new technology. At Magna we continue to emphasize the human capital as we introduce technology in a manner that does not result in the displacement of employees. We are focusing on product productivity improvements through new technology as a means of continuing to upgrade wages for production employees in the years ahead while maintaining our competitive position in the marketplace.

Management's primary responsibility is to demonstrate to employees that we care for their well-being particularly with regard to wages, environment, safety in the workplace, fairness and equal opportunity for advancement. We are committed to these principles and intend to strengthen further our Human Resources department to make sure that our standards are maintained. A structure like this can only function through total openness. It is an education process. In our view the employees must fully understand the competitive factors facing the company as well as the facts surrounding our financial structure. I like to see employees reading the financial section of the papers in the morning, realizing that they are shareholders of Magna. In fact, at this stage, our manufacturing and office employees own more than $30 million of Magna stock.

Members of management are also large shareholders in the company. The value of their shares amounts to approximately $30 million, and accordingly, they have an interest in protecting the value of their investments. It is important for a healthy, growing company to have a strong equity base in relation to debt, but we are sensitive to the effect of equity dilution on our ability to maintain investor confidence. Accordingly, we try to balance issues of new equity with growth in earnings per share.

Sales growth translates into the need for new production facilities. As a result, Magna's investment in land and buildings continues to increase. Management utilizes Magna's job creation capability to obtain favourable terms when purchasing land. We also seek joint venture partners to assist in the development of those lands. Our objective is to minimize Magna's capital outlay for land so as not to divert capital from our automotive components manufacturing activities.

Quality Assurance

Quality is stressed throughout Magna—our success has been built on it—our future depends on it. We continue to train employees at all levels in matters relating to quality including the use of sophisticated measuring devices and statistical process control techniques. As a result of efforts in the area of quality, our operating units received many quality awards from our customers. Magna is dedicated to supplying automotive components and systems which are "world class" in quality and value.

Human Resources

Magna's greatest asset is its motivated work force. We continuously strive to provide a positive, safe, and fair environment for all employees.

With this in mind we continue to expand our Human Resources department at the group and corporate offices and sponsor seminars which stress the importance of good communications between management and employees. Wherever possible, productivity gains are recognized with improved wages and expenditures to improve the working environment.

continued

EXHIBIT 5
continued

During the year we introduced "Magna People," a bimonthly newsletter about Magna and its people. Simeon Park, which opened officially in June 1984, saw the introduction of many employee organized functions, both winter and summer. The allocation to our Employee Equity Participation and Profit Sharing Program amounted to $8.3 million in 1985 compared to $6.4 million last year.

Other Employee Programs

We provide a number of other programs for our employees including the following:

A. Simeon Park

Magna has developed a recreational park on 100 acres of natural countryside just north of Toronto. This park, available to all Magna employees and their families, features a 23-acre lake, sports and recreation facilities including children's playgrounds, tennis and volleyball courts, soccer fields, a baseball diamond, barbecue pits and picnic areas, nature trails, fishing docks, and a large swimming pool.

The park is readily accessible to the majority of Magna's employees. During 1985 it was used extensively for company picnics, competitive team sports, and casual family outings.

B. Industrial Campus Concept

To provide employees with an improved work environment, Magna is developing an industrial campus which will consist of a cluster of 10–20 small autonomous plants together with the related group office and product development centre supported by social and recreational facilities such as day care, a medical office, and educational and sporting facilities.

In 1985 three new plants went into production in our first campus being developed in Newmarket, Ontario. A new group administration office and product development centre associated with these plants also opened during the year. Two additional plants were under construction at year-end. Land for other campuses is being assembled in preparation for our future growth.

C. Technical Training Centre

Consistent with our commitment to high-quality in-house technical strength, Magna opened its first technical training centre in the fall of 1984. The school is equipped with modern classroom and shop facilities and the latest in machinery and equipment.

On completion of their training, apprentices will work in a Magna operating unit to complete the requirements for trade qualification.

The purpose of the centre is to help fulfill Magna's demand for skilled tool and die makers and other technical trades. These students will also receive training in management practices.

D. Continuing Education

Magna encourages all employees to improve continually their skills and education. For this reason, we offer in-house training and education in areas of communication, safety, quality control, microcomputer applications, and management skills.

Social Responsibility

Magna believes it has a responsibility to support the basic fabric of society. We fulfill this obligation by giving financial assistance and contributing our time to programs and projects in the areas of health and welfare, youth, the advancement of art and culture, education, and in support of the political process. Examples of the programs we support include:

A. University Teaching and Research Support

Magna currently provides financial support to four universities for teaching and research concerning entrepreneurship and fair enterprise.

continued

EXHIBIT 5
continued

B. Student Sponsorship
Each year Magna sponsors a number of outstanding students to attend the GMI Engineering and Management Institute in Michigan. GMI is a private university offering degrees in engineering and industrial administration.

Sponsorship guarantees students financial support and planned work assignments in Magna plants as well as the offer of a full-time position with Magna upon graduation.

Growth at the operating unit level, as for all levels of Magna, was somewhat "organic" in nature, rather than "planned" in the traditional sense. When a particular unit (factory) could no longer keep pace with demand and was running three shifts of 100 people on a 24-hour schedule, the unit's general manager would be allowed to build a second factory. If more factories had to be built for a common product line, these might eventually form the basis of a new management group with the former general manager as group vice president. As this suggests, Magna had a rather unusual and interesting method of delegating responsibility and controls between the executive management, group management, and the operating units. Magna's unit general managers were given 100 percent control, authority, and responsibility for their units, with the requirement that they clearly identify themselves as part of Magna International when communicating with suppliers or customers.

This high degree of decentralization did give rise to a number of trade-offs at the operating-unit level. Magna realized higher transportation costs in shipping from widely dispersed locations to the automotive assembly plants of the major manufacturers; however, significant quantities were still shipped such that discounts were not completely forgone.

Some diseconomies also arose from the lack of centralized purchasing of raw materials. Each unit dealt with its own suppliers, but frequently general managers in the same operating group would cooperate to secure volume discounts when available.

Administrative costs were duplicated in some cases since each operating unit had its own personnel, accounting, and other staff departments, but management felt that, in general, the benefits of decentralization outweighed its costs.

At Magna, financial control was maintained by accountants at each of the group offices and operating units. Each operating unit was required to submit a business plan for the year outlining the operating and capital budget to group management. These plans were assessed by the groups and submitted to corporate executive officers for final approval.

Once approved, the groups and operating units set out independently in pursuit of their defined business goals. Performance was monitored monthly using uniform financial reports comparing actual operating results to budget and measuring capital spending against plan.

Although organic, growth was not indiscriminate at the factory level and was monitored by group management which worked within the broad corporate policy set by executive management. Executive management consisted of Frank Stronach and a handful of senior executives. Corporate headquarters were housed in a two-storied office in a suburban Toronto business park and consisted of a 100-person staff.

Operating units were grouped geographically and by market under one of five group management teams which were destined to divide and form more groups as Magna expanded. Each group was responsible for specific technologies and product lines and had its own marketing, R&D, and planning responsibilities.

EXHIBIT 6
Operating Structure

Operating Unit
Each operating unit is directed by a general manager and an assistant general manager who have complete authority and responsibility for the operation of their unit within broad guidelines established by executive group management. These decentralized units generally employ approximately 100 people, thus giving the management teams close contact with staff and immediate control of all matters affecting personnel, product quality, efficiency, and profitability of the unit.

Group Management
The operating units are grouped—geographically and by markets—under the direction of a group management team which is accountable to executive management. A group vice president is responsible for all areas of activity in his group and is supported by marketing, financial, and human resources executives.

Each group has its own sales team which maintains the day-to-day contact with the customers, the group office, and the operating units.

The group financial staff monitors all financial activities including capital spending and operating results. Each group has its own quality control and human resources personnel which review the operating unit's performance and serve as a resource to the units.

Group management also oversees research and technology development conducted for their group.

Executive Management
Executive management is responsible for establishing policies consistent with the company's philosophy as developed by the board of directors.

Strategic planning is a priority of executive management. This involves the identification of specific products and technologies that Magna must develop in order to meet the challenges of an evolving marketplace. It also includes the establishment of management teams capable of implementing Magna's marketing, quality, human resources, and financial goals and objectives. As part of its responsibilities, executive management secures and allocates financial resources and, together with group management, monitors the performance of the operating units.

The corporate office serves as a resource to the groups and operating units in the acquisition of capital equipment, raw materials, and services.

This system allows the groups and operating units to benefit from Magna's corporate buying power when it is to their advantage. However, responsibility for product quality and delivery rests with each operating unit, and accordingly, the units make purchases from whatever source best meets their individual requirements.

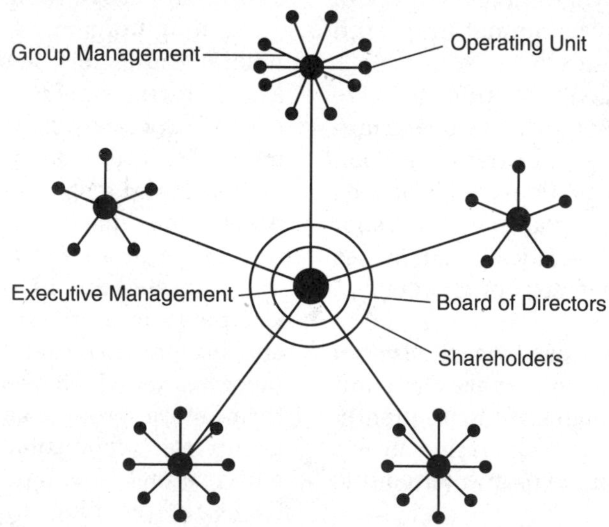

On average, each group management nucleus had 10 to 15 factories responsible to it. Magna's strategy was to keep these factories close together geographically, wherever possible, and as the company grew sufficiently, to develop its own industrial parks.

In 1985 Magna consisted or five management groups: the CMT Group (Creative Mechanical Technologies), the Decorative Products Group, the MACI Group, the Magna Manufacturing Group, and the Maple Group. The products manufactured by each group in 1984 are found in Exhibit 2.

EQUITY PARTICIPATION

Frank Stronach maintained that employees had "a moral right to some of the profits they help generate. . . . If they get profit and they put it into the company equity, there's a sort of discipline which helps the employee. We've got some people on machines who've got $30,000 sitting there. That's a lot of money for an average person."

In keeping with Stronach's belief, Magna had a type of deferred profit-sharing program for its employees to reward productivity and loyalty. Employees were awarded a point for every $1,000 they earned and a point for each year they stayed with the company. The more points they had accumulated, the greater their share in the fund. Each year 7 percent of profits before tax were transferred to an employee equity trust fund. Employees received quarterly statements of how many shares they owned and their value. If an employee left within two years, his shares reverted to other employees. After his third year with Magna, he owned a percentage which increased until the 10th year when it became completely his, even if he left. In Magna's earlier years, profit sharing was available only to middle management but was expanded to cover all employees in 1978.

Magna's senior management team of about 20 executives enjoyed a separate profit participation program for which 6 percent of before-tax profits were set aside. The result was some very generous bonuses in addition to their competitive salaries, but Frank Stronach had no qualms about this, stating, "Good management doesn't come cheap—I don't come cheap." In addition to Stronach, the compensation received by four other Magna executives placed them among the 15 most highly paid managers in Canada in 1985.

Exclusive of the top executive, Magna's approximately 250 managers owned about 12 1/2% of the company. The over 7,000 workers held about the same equity position.

Although Magna's workers enjoyed equity participation, their hourly salaries were low by industry standards—approximately $6 per hour in 1985. Some estimated that Magna, without a single union in any of its plants, therefore, had an hourly wage burden about half the size of its unionized competitors—a substantial competitive advantage in an industry where cost control was a key success factor. Stronach maintained that increases in productivity were resulting in rising wages at Magna and that Magna would soon be catching up in terms of hourly wage rates. But low hourly wages and the lack of a union in any of its plants made Magna a favourite target of attacks by the United Auto Workers (UAW) union.

MAGNA AND THE UAW

Magna seemed to be an impregnable target for union organizers—a fact which some industry followers felt was vital to Magna's success. Stronach himself did not appear to harbour anti-union sentiments, stating, "Unions can be part of free enterprise because society needs checks and balances," and, "If you run a lousy ship, you deserve a union."

Regardless of the sincerity of these views, Stronach had the grudging respect of his UAW adversaries. Buzz Hargrove, administrative assistant to Canadian UAW leader Bob White, knew Frank Stronach personally and said, "I didn't agree with his ideology or his philosophy, but I thought he was a well-motivated, decent human being."

In one instance, in 1978, the UAW was granted automatic certification at one of Magna's Toronto plants because of management interference in the organizing drive. However, some union cards were burned, the UAW failed to negotiate a contract, and it was then voted out by the Magna employees. The negotiations stalled on the single issue of the now mandatory Rand formula (where all employees in the bargaining unit must pay union dues regardless of whether they choose to become union members), but in the UAW's opinion, this issue was irrelevant because Magna had really just chosen to dig in its heels.

Buzz Hargrove said, "Frank Stronach and I had lunch together one day, and he told me that their strategy was essentially to find an issue that they knew we would not agree to that would force us to strike the plant in order to try to get an agreement, and they would just let the thing sit. They wouldn't try to run the plant or hire scabs, but to all intents and purposes, the plant would remain closed as long as there was a picket line. Whether it took a year, or two, or three, or forever, it didn't matter. They were not going to have a union in their shop." Hargrove continued, "We have no alternative but to continue . . . and probably even step up . . . our efforts to organize Magna. We can't have a major segment of the automotive parts industry unorganized."

It was possible that the UAW would be aided in subsequent attempts to organize Magna by the company's ongoing strategy to cluster its five management groups and their related plants into industrial campuses. Frank Stronach, in a 1985 interview, admitted that he was concerned by the threat of renewed UAW action because, "It's always a concern if someone would interfere with your environment, with your philosophies, with your basic framework." In an interview a year earlier, he had claimed:

> I don't believe the UAW would really get out to organize us. They would if they heard complaints, or if the employees were unhappy. . . . We try to provide a better alternative. We say that if we had unions, we would lose individually because everything is then divided into group one, group two, group three. Such groups stop a person from voicing his opinion. This is the danger when one body or one group gets too strong; it's too structured and the individual gets lost. . . . Three or four years ago we had two people in labour relations. Now we have a department with 10 people. We employ a labour lawyer whose function is to make our managers understand that we insist on certain principles and standards. His job is not to squeeze employees but to educate managers.

CORPORATE STRATEGY

Magna had a clear set of corporate objectives and a strategy for achieving them. As Magna's success became well-known, its senior executives, especially Frank Stronach, were increasingly sought out for interviews. Features appeared repeatedly in newspapers, popular magazines, on television, and even in books, which described Magna's objectives and plans for realizing them.

The company's primary objective was to become the most diversified supplier of parts, components, and assemblies to the North American automotive industry and to steadily increase its dollar share of total industry sales from its 1985 level of 1 percent. Magna intended to accomplish this by increasing its average "penetration level" or the average dollar value of Magna parts that went into every North American automobile.

Over the period 1979 to 1985 Magna's penetration level had risen from $8.95 to $49.00 with a goal of $100 per vehicle by 1988. The company exceeded the $100 goal in the middle of its 1986 fiscal year.

Management consistently referred to a three-pronged strategy that it felt would allow Magna to sustain its remarkable growth and achieve its objectives: (1) continued increases in market share for existing Magna products; (2) introduction of new products and technologies to the marketplace, driven by ongoing in-house research and development and through joint ventures with partners who were leaders in product design and manufacturing capabilities; and (3) manufacturing and marketing of modular assemblies using a variety of Magna parts and components. For example, instead of manufacturing cooling fans and radiators independently, Magna intended to market one complete unit that included a fan, radiator, and shrouds and could be bolted directly into a vehicle on an assembly line.

In addition to its diversification strategy of building ever-greater numbers of parts and components, Magna simultaneously pursued an ongoing strategy of vertical integration. This was mainly in the form of backward integration, described by many as a key reason for Magna's success as it allowed the company to reduce costs and respond quickly and flexibly to design changes by its customers. Magna integrated vertically by undertaking its own tool and die making—the company's original business—and by developing and applying its in-house expertise in robotics and computer-aided-design/computer-aided-manufacturing (CAD/CAM) to equip Magna for the so-called factory of the future. There was even speculation that a Magna company, which had designed and built its own robotics system, might market the system as another product in the future.

Magna's medium-term strategy was to geographically cluster its operating units and their plants into "industrial campuses," each with an infrastructure of company-supported social and recreational services, such as day care, medical, educational, and fitness centres. Each campus would consist of a cluster of 10 to 20 small autonomous plants, with the related operating group's office and product development centre located on the campus as well. The goal of this concept was to enhance the working environment for Magna employees. Stronach estimated, "Fifty cents spent on something like day care in our campuses will return $1.50 in increased productivity." Magna's first campus was begun in Newmarket, Ontario, in 1985, with three new plants and associated offices. Land for other campuses was quickly being assembled in anticipation of future growth. An announcement had also been made that Magna would begin construction of another 10 to 20 factory industrial campuses on a 26-acre parcel of land in Waterloo, Ontario, in 1986.

One strategy for dealing with the company's rapid growth was raised by Jim McAlpine, Magna's executive vice president and chief financial officer, who suggested in a 1985 interview that Magna intended to spin off at least one of its operating units by selling or distributing shares to the public in 1986. Magna would retain at least 52 percent of the unit's shares, 20 percent would be given to the unit's employees, 5 percent would go to management, and the remainder would probably be distributed to the public through an equity issue or divided plan. Such a strategy would reinforce Magna's corporate philosophy of decentralization. McAlpine added, "A spin-off allows our management teams to continue to grow as managers. We hope it reduces the buildup of bureaucracy." It seemed that Magna International's main role in the future might be that of a holding company or a birthplace for a number of new companies.

INTERNATIONAL ACTIVITIES

An increasingly important component of Magna's corporate strategy was the recognition of the emphasis on international activity within the automobile industry. By 1985 Magna's international activities, on a number of fronts, had been relatively modest but had resulted in the development of relationships that management felt would position the company to take advantage of a variety of opportunities. The 1985 annual report stated, "With patience and persistence, we will be able to build successfully upon these relationships and established Magna as a participant in the key automotive markets of the world."

Magna's international activities before 1986 had consisted primarily of joint ventures with foreign companies where Magna's goal was to acquire new technologies and knowledge of new products and processes. Magna sought joint ventures to build a technology base quickly. Frank

Stronach said, "It's too time-consuming to do it on our own. . . . We don't want to re-invent the wheel constantly." A list of some major joint ventures that Magna had been involved in up to 1986 is provided below. In 1985 Magna was in 13 active joint ventures.

Typical joint ventures entered into by Magna were those with two French auto-parts suppliers. With Veglia SA, a French producer of dashboard equipment, Magna set up Invotek Instruments of Toronto to manufacture instrument clusters for the Renault Alliance and Encore. In 1984 with Société Anonyme des Usines Chausson, a Renault subsidiary, Magna established Thermag Industries Inc. of Mississauga. The purpose was to produce aluminum radiators for Renaults built in North America by AMC, instead of shipping radiators from France. An $8 million plant was to be built with production to begin in 1986. Magna took a 60 percent interest in the venture in order to gain access to technology and markets, while Chausson took the minority 40 percent interest and supplied its technology.

In July 1984 Magna signed a joint venture agreement with the Japanese parts manufacturer Niles Buhin Co., at a time when Japanese manufacturers were beginning to try to increase their penetration of the lucrative North American market. Simultaneously, Magna began negotiating with four or five other Japanese companies for similar ventures that Frank Stronach felt could bring Magna hundreds of millions of dollars in revenues over the next few years.

Niles Buhin was an electronics components maker and, unlike many Japanese parts suppliers, did not belong to a particular car-making group, although most of its business was with Nissan and Mitsubishi. At the time, Niles Buhin had sales of $150 million while Magna's sales were $302 million.

Magna was again seeking access to advanced technology, primarily in electronics and lightweight materials while Niles Buhin saw the venture as a good way to gain entry to a large and growing market far from their domestic bases. They were being encouraged to do so by the large Japanese car makers who wanted the parts makers to follow them to North America; but because Japanese vehicle production would be insufficient to support them, the Japanese parts manufacturers required access to the big U.S. manufacturers as well. Some planned to try this on their own, but many saw joint ventures, like the one between Magna and Niles Buhin, as a better alternative.

Japanese manufacturers were extremely sensitive about labour problems, but Magna's main selling point to the Japanese was its record of good labour relations. Management was of the opinion that the Japanese felt "quite comfortable" with Magna.

According to its 1985 annual report, in seeking additional joint ventures with the Japanese, Magna's primary targets were the Japanese vehicle manufacturers who had, or were planning to locate, production facilities in North America as well as their suppliers who were exploring opportunities to do business in North America. Magna's strategy was to demonstrate to the manufacturers that it could provide "world class" products in

Typical Joint Ventures Undertaken by Magna International Inc.

Joint Venture Partner	*Partner's Nationality*	*Part Produced*
1. Philips Group	Dutch	Electronic components
2. Veglia SA	French	Instrument clusters for Renault
3. Chausson	French	Aluminum radiators for Renault
4. Webasto GmbH	West German	Sun roofs
5. Willibald Grammer	West German	Foam technology for seats
6. Brown, Boveri et Cie AG	Swiss	Power trains for electric vehicles

terms of quality and value. With Japanese part suppliers, Magna sought to develop forms of cooperation in North America where both parties could contribute and prosper.

By 1985 Magna had licensed one of its products to Japanese parts suppliers for production and sale in Japan and had acquired licenses to manufacture and sell certain Japanese products in North America. The company was also in the midst of establishing a trading company with a Japanese parts supplier to coordinate the supply of certain products manufactured by Magna to one of the Japanese automakers located in North America.

In 1985 a tooling and production facility had been established in West Germany to supply European OEMs. Contracts had also been signed to supply some North American produced components to two German automakers.

An agreement was signed late in the year to establish a joint venture in the People's Republic of China to manufacture components for the Chinese auto market.

As fiscal 1986 approached, it was increasingly clear that Magna International was stepping up the pace of its international activities with ambitious hopes for the future of these operations.

MAGNA'S FUTURE PROSPECTS

As fiscal 1986 came to a close, it was becoming evident that the company Frank Stronach had built up from a rented Toronto garage might be coming to a crossroads in its history. A number of questions and issues required resolution.

It appeared certain that the company's strong growth would continue unabated for at least the next few years. However, one could not help but wonder if Magna's traditional success formula would be adequate to accommodate further phenomenal growth. Would continued growth and the spinning-off of new companies make it easier for the UAW to finally unionize some of Magna's factories, and what repercussions would such an event have on Magna as a whole?

There had been a trend for the North American automakers to source 100 percent of their components in one place to ensure consistency. Certainly, no company in Canada was better positioned than Magna to make the most of the trend. Yet would this trend continue?

Magna's increasing international activities seemed to be the next logical step in the company's uninterrupted growth, but concern existed about how this would fit into Magna's current organizational structure which emphasized geographical clustering and a commonality of product lines among related operating units. Would modifications or exceptions to the Magna "formula" have to be made to accommodate these relatively new activities that were growing rapidly in relative importance?

Stronach's dynamic, entrepreneurial personality and vision undoubtedly accounted for a considerable measure of Magna's success. How would this role change as Magna continued to grow and Stronach became a smaller part of Magna's operations? One observer had noted that Stronach seemed to have all the pieces in place so that any of his chief executives could manage the company quite well. Yet others wondered what effect his retirement might have on the company.

Frank Stronach once called Magna International's Corporate Constitution "perhaps the most important chapter in western industrial society in many years. . . that I believe will have an enormous bearing in the future structure of corporations [and] law making." As the new fiscal year approached, one could not help wondering whether that document was well suited to guide Magna International and other corporations into the 1990s.

REFERENCES

Arnott, Sheila. "What Our Top Executives Are Earning." *The Financial Post,* May 1986.

Avery, Nick, and Alison Burkett. "Comparison of the Auto-Parts Market 1981–1984." Wilfrid Laurier University MBA Report, November 27, 1985.

Barnes, Kenneth, and Everett Banning. *Money-Makers! The Secrets of Canada's Most Successful Entrepreneurs.* Toronto: McClelland & Stewart, Ltd., 1985.

"Everybody's Business." Global television program. Various video excerpts re: Magna International, Inc.

Galt, Virginia. "Decentralizing, Worker Participation Plans Help Put Magna on the Road to Recovery." *The Globe and Mail,* July 6, 1981, B1, B5.

Harrison, Douglas. "Franco-Canadian Economic Bonds Are Increasing." *Kitchener-Waterloo Record,* February 17, 1985, B9.

Hart, Matthew. "Frank as He'll Ever Be." *The Financial Post Moneywise Magazine,* May 1986, pp. 64-7.

Koch, Henry. "Magna Spinoffs to Spur Waterloo Growth: Carroll." *Kitchener-Waterloo Record,* January 23, 1985, B9.

Lilley, Wayne. "Small is Beautiful." *Canadian Business* 57, no. 6 (1984), pp. 170–71.

"Magna Executive Optimistic about Firm's 1985 Showing." *The Globe and Mail,* August 3, 1985, B5.

Magna International Inc. *Annual Report 1984,* 1984.

Annual Report 1985. 1985.

"Magna International Inc."*Toronto Stock Exchange Review,* November 1984, pp. 1-4.

"Milner, Brian. "Magna, Japanese Firm Form Joint Venture." *The Globe and Mail,* July 30, 1984, B1.

Partridge, John, "Small Is Beautiful to Magna Chief but He Still Aims to Be the Biggest." *The Globe and Mail,* January 5, 1985, B1, B3.

Waddell, Christopher. "Magna Chairman Sells Shares but Remains Firmly in the Saddle." *The Globe and Mail,* December 7, 1984, B1, B2.

"Magna Hopes to Be Supplier for GM's Saturn." *The Globe and Mail,* April 19, 1985, B3.

Walker, Dean. "The Capitalist's Gospel According to Frank Stronach." *Executive,* May 1984, pp. 46–49.

Wilson, Sharon E. "The Best of Both Worlds: How Large Corporations Can Benefit from Decentralized Manufacturing." Wilfrid Laurier University Report, August 1985.

CASE 6 | *Muse Air Corporation*

En route to the Love Field airport in Dallas in one of the company's planes, Michael Muse had many things on his mind. He deeply wanted his company, Muse Air Corporation, to be profitable. There was more at stake here than money: it was a matter of pride. "How could anyone have the misfortune to start an airline just a few weeks before the air traffic controllers' strike?" Michael

---

This case was prepared by Professors Robert McGlashan and Tim Singleton of the University of Houston–Clear Lake as a basis for class discussion rather than to illustrate either effective or ineffective handling of an administrative situation. Research was prepared by Sheryl Dawson, Frederick Mullin, David Olson, and Margaret Parish, MBA students at the University of Houston–Clear Lake. It is reproduced here by permission of the North American Case Research Association and the authors.

asked his father, Lamar Muse, who was in the next seat. "It's just not possible to control everything at all times. You just have to make the best of things," Lamar responded. "Well it's time we took control again," Michael said firmly. "Let's map out our revised strategy for expansion." Lamar knew that he was going to have to review the major factors facing Muse Air to resolve things in Michael's mind.

THE AIRLINE INDUSTRY

Regulation

The major issues facing the airline industry today stem from its continuing struggle to adjust to the changing environment created by the Airline Deregulation Act of 1978. Under deregulation, the control of the Federal Aviation Administration (FAA) and the Civil Aeronautics Board (CAB) over airlines was drastically reduced. As controls over routes and fares were lifted, the industry faced rapidly changing market conditions in which competition increased significantly. The immediate result for the major established airlines was a dramatic drop in corporate earnings as new low-priced entrants forced price wars. The industry continues to be plagued by financial losses and excess passenger capacity. From thirty-six certified carriers prior to deregulation, the industry has mushroomed to about 125 airlines today. But the rate of failure has increased also as twenty-eight carriers have gone out of business since 1978.

The primary long-term result of deregulation and increased competition is a stronger and more efficient industry. Overall inflation-adjusted ticket prices, because of discount fares, are now 10–20% lower than in 1974. Departures at major hub cities in 1983 were up 15.7%, and at medium hubs were up 22.5% from 1978. The number of interstate carriers has risen from 36 to 98 with big airlines now controlling 79% of the market, versus 91% before deregulation. Although since 1978 the major carriers have reduced their work forces by 24,000 employees, nearly that many jobs have been created by the smaller airlines.

The FAA continues to exercise regulatory authority over airlines in regard to ground facilities, communication, training of pilots and other personnel, and aircraft safety. Airlines must obtain an operating certificate, subject to compliance with all regulations in these areas. Environmental regulation is also imposed to control noise and engine emissions. Local pressure groups may exert influence on airports to limit flights over certain areas in order to control noise pollution. One special regulation imposed by the International Air Transportation Competition Act of 1979 is the limitation on flights out of Love Field in Dallas. Destinations from Love Field may include locations only in the four states neighboring Texas—Arkansas, Oklahoma, New Mexico and Louisiana.

When the CAB is dissolved on January 1, 1985, the regulatory authority over mergers and interlocking relationships will be transferred to the Justice Department, under which the FAA operates. For other businesses, this regulatory authority is the jurisdiction of the Federal Trade Commission. Other responsibilities which the CAB handles, such as selection of carriers for international route operations, have been reassigned to the Department of Transportation. Since both of these departments are in the Executive Branch, there is congressional debate as to whether sufficient control over the airline industry can be retained without the CAB or another congressional agency. Re-regulation considerations will continue to surface as the CAB deadline approaches.

Air Traffic Control

Airlines are still dealing with the effects of the August 2, 1981, union strike of the Professional Air Traffic Controllers Organization (PATCO). The air controller's job is to keep airplanes moving at a safe distance from one another as they are passed from one tower to another. As planes taxi, take off, fly and land, they stay in touch with the pilots by radio and follow their progress on radar screens. These screens display each plane's location, altitude, speed and any problems, such as two planes moving too close together. The screens are all computer-generated.

When 12,000 of the 17,000 controllers walked out at the start of the strike, the traffic control system was thrown into confusion. Under FAA emergency controls, which reduced flight frequencies, nearly 75% of the 22,000 daily flights were kept flying. All the major airlines experienced a decrease in revenues and available slots, both airport and en-route, which reduced flexibility in route structuring despite deregulation. Once the initial pandemonium over the strike abated, the airlines began to tailor their operations to meet the new environment. Steps taken included grounding of the least fuel-efficient planes, concentration on the more important routes, reduction in the work force and restrictions placed on discount fares. A drop in revenue of 12% was reported by TWA and 15% by United Airlines. These figures were typical for the airline industry.

Only since October 30, 1983, has the FAA eliminated most slot restrictions, enabling airlines to determine destinations without having to negotiate and trade for landing slots. Because of continued air traffic control problems in Chicago, Los Angeles, New York and Denver airports, restrictions have not as yet been lifted in these high-density cities. The post-strike rules are slated to expire April 1, 1984, in Denver, but will remain in effect in Los Angeles until after the Olympics. Expiration of the rules in New York and Chicago has been delayed until January, 1985, however, based on the FAA's assessment of air control's inability to handle unrestricted air traffic at these airports. The temporary preferential route system requires that aircraft fly special mandatory routes to circumvent congested airspace, but the routes are often considerably longer in distance than airlines would normally fly. Costing time and fuel, these restrictions have affected airlines' cost reduction efforts, especially for the majors who serve longer hauls. It is expected that the FAA will finally eliminate the preferential route system early in 1984. The future of air traffic control is enhanced by the long awaited decision to modernize the system. The FAA has embarked on a ten-year ten-billion-dollar effort to upgrade air traffic control in order to cope with the projected 26.5% growth in aviation by the year 2000.

Cooperative Routing

The flexibility in routing brought about by deregulation has given rise to the hub and spoke system, with its central exchange point. This system enables airlines to carry passengers to their final destinations without having to share revenues, as is necessary in interlining agreements. This prederegulation system of interlining is beginning to fall apart as the majors re-evaluate their benefit. Under multi-lateral, open-ended agreements, which have created an integrated national air transportation system, the major airlines provide passengers with interchangeable ticketing and baggage service to final destination. United, American and Delta are now advising interlining partners that their agreements will be on a bilateral basis with periodic review. The change is contemplated by the majors because of Continental Airlines' action in seeking protection under bankruptcy regulations in 1983. Because Continental did not cease operations completely and resumed service within two days, the bankruptcy court judge ruled that Continental's partners should continue to honor the interline agreement and yet would not be able to collect money owed for services prior to the bankruptcy. At issue, too, is the industry's default protection plan, which protects ticket-holders in the event of airline bankruptcy. The end to either system would place new competitive pressures on financially weak airlines.

A new form of cooperative routing has developed in which airlines agree bilaterally to link their route systems in an effort to strengthen their individual hub and spoke networks. Muse Air has such an arrangement with Air Cal. Cooperative routing could be achieved by other means, such as arrangements similar to franchise service exchange agreements or outright acquisition of commuter carriers by larger airlines.

Economy

The airline industry is highly affected by the business cycle. The current upturn in the economy has brought increases in revenue passenger miles to help reduce the pressures of over-capacity which plagued the industry throughout the recession of 1981 and 1982. As disposable income grows and air travel increases during the favorable economy, airlines will experience increasing revenues. The temptation in an upturn is to be less vigilant regarding rising costs. Whether these increased revenues translate into increased profits or not depends on the ability of airlines to keep costs down.

In fact, cost control is the primary key to profitability in the airline industry. With labor cost representing 37% of the total expenses of the established major and national carriers, in contrast to the new entrants' 18%, there is a significant disequilibrium in the industry that market forces will inevitably eliminate. Entering into this equation is the labor relations dilemma facing the industry. Recognizing that a favorable employee attitude is essential to high-quality service, how airlines achieve labor cost control directly impacts effectiveness as well as efficiency. Two advantages that new entrants have in labor productivity are:

1. established airline employees and their unions have little understanding or sympathy for the effects of deregulation and
2. employees of new airlines have no allegiance to the preregulation structure and possess the enthusiasm of sharing in a new enterprise.

There have been several approaches to labor cost control, including employee ownership programs, establishment of new subsidiary carriers, revocation of labor contracts through declaration of bankruptcy and a two-tiered wage system for old and new employees.

The second major cost factor is fuel availability. The sporadic shortages, political instability in oil producing countries, and decontrol of oil prices are uncontrollable external conditions that directly impact profitability of airlines. When fuel costs rose dramatically in 1979–1980, competitive pressures prevented airlines from passing on those increases to passengers. Although fuel costs have declined for the past three years, they still represent 25% of total airline costs. Fuel efficient aircraft have become an important consideration as a result of high fuel costs.

Beyond operating expenses, the major cost of airlines is the aircraft itself. The high cost of new aircraft has made their acquisition economically prohibitive in spite of their greater fuel efficiency. At current fuel costs, the savings is not sufficient to cover the cost of buying expensive new aircraft. One of the reasons for the high price of aircraft is the fact that manufacturers produce aircraft on an individual job-order basis rather than by mass-production. This non-standardized production not only increases the original cost but reduces the residual value of aircraft.

Additionally, the fragmentation of the market has reduced opportunities to use larger aircraft. The per seat cost savings on a 150- vs. 100-seat aircraft, for instance, can only be realized if the extra capacity is utilized. This is difficult to achieve in a competitive market already facing over-capacity. Once again, the impact of deregulation seems to be responsible for setting a new trend. In an effort to reduce capacity, airlines are seeking smaller aircraft. The transition to the downsized transport will be costly to airlines and place new competitive pressures on aircraft manufacturers who have suffered decreased sales for five years. As airlines return to profitability, fleet acquisition will be a priority in order to gain competitive position.

Reservation System

The distribution of airline ticketing is dominated by travel agents utilizing computerized reservation systems. In fact, 65% of airline reservations are handled by travel agents. Airlines subscribe to one of the majors' computerized systems of which American's Sabre is dominant in Texas markets. There are two advantages to the owners or host carriers of the reservation systems. One is a computer bias in which the host is given priority listing among available flights with more information listed than for other airlines. This tends to encourage the choice of the host by travel agents in reserving flights resulting in increased market share for the host. Secondly, it is commonplace for travel agents to book (or plate) tickets to the servicing carrier, which is the computer host. Since there is a four- to ten-week ticket settlement period, in effect this gives the host utilization of the amounts "plated away" from airline subscribers who are denied cash settlement for that period. It is estimated that the float created by this plating process amounts to $3 billion and costs the airlines financing that float $360 million a year in new interest expense. The Justice Department has asked CAB to adopt rules to reduce competitive abuses of the computerized systems.

With agent commissions representing 6.7% of total airline operating expenses, the CAB's plan to abolish travel agent exclusivity at the end of 1984 will increase competitive initiatives in retail marketing. By breaking up the travel agent monopoly, new innovations in the distribution of airline ticketing are possible. For instance, direct reservations by individuals through cable television may be implemented, discount houses for airline ticket sales could develop, and business travel departments may gain access to direct reservation systems. New economies may also be realized if the practice of "plating away" from airlines, which attempts to reduce travel agent commissions, is eliminated.

COMPANY HISTORY

The Beginning

Muse Air Corporation was organized in early 1980 by two ex-Southwest Airlines employees, Lamar and Michael Muse. The airline was organized to provide high-frequency, single-class, low-cost air transportation for the general public. It was one of the many new regional airlines entering the market after deregulation of the airline industry.

Lamar Muse, one of Southwest Airlines' founders and former chief executive officers, left Southwest Airlines after a bitter policy dispute in 1978. His two-year no-competition agreement with Southwest ran out in October, 1980, when he joined his son, Michael, to operate Muse Air. Michael was former chief financial officer for Southwest Airlines.

Muse Air began service on July 15, 1981, with two DC-9 Super 80s flying between Dallas and Houston. The plans were to compete directly with Southwest on their most lucrative route. Muse had an aggressive expansion program laid out for the next several years, planning to become a major airline as quickly as possible. Fate had no intention of allowing Muse's plans to run smoothly.

Air Traffic Controllers' Strike

On August 2, 1981, just 18 days after Muse began service, PATCO went out on a nationwide strike, causing the FAA to place restrictions on landing slots.

With the delivery of two McDonnell Douglas DC-9 Super 80s, Muse Air planned to expand its routes to include Midland-Odessa and Tulsa by May, 1982. Even though the FAA planned to increase the air traffic system's capacity to 90% of normal (before strike) by September, 1982, no changes or increases in landing slots were authorized for Dallas or Houston. This was at a time when airline officials were expressing strong dissatisfaction with the FAA's continued use of emergency powers to allocate the additional capacity instead of switching to normal administrative procedures. Many airlines felt the allocation of additional slots and routes was not handled fairly.

Planned expansion by Muse into these two new markets in May, 1982, and two additional markets in July, 1982, was being delayed because of Federal Aviation Administration restrictions on operating slots at Love Field in Dallas and Hobby Airport in Houston. Muse Air had applied for permission to provide Houston-Dallas-Tulsa with seven daily round trips and six daily round trips from Dallas to Midland-Odessa. Refer to Exhibit 1.

The FAA approved Muse Air for operation for one evening off-peak round trip to Tulsa and denied all other requested slots. The FAA also denied a request for 13 flights daily between Love Field and Austin and 14 flights between Love Field and San Antonio. Muse Air officials argued that the slot restrictions were contrary to the meaning of the deregulation act, tending to favor established carriers over new entrants. Obtaining the slots was vital for Muse Air, not only to pre-

EXHIBIT 1
Muse Air Corporation
Aircraft Delivery Schedule

	Aircraft			
Delivery Date	*Type*	*Quantity*	*Seating*	*Cities Served*
July, 1981	DC9-80 (Super 80)	2	155	Dallas Houston
May, 1982	DC9-80	2	155	Midland-Odessa Tulsa
Oct., 1982	DC9-80	2	155	Los Angeles
Aug., 1983	DC9-51 (Super 50)	1	130	*Lubbock
Nov., 1983	DC9-51	2	130	Austin
Feb., 1984	DC9-51	1	130	Ontario, CA New Orleans
Projected Delivery Date				*New Cities*
Apr., 1984	DC9-51	1	130	**Little Rock Las Vegas
Mar., 1985	DC9-51	2	130	San Antonio Chicago
Mar., 1986	DC9-51	2	130	Atlanta Florida

Source: 1983 Muse Air Annual Report and Muse Air News Release.
*Service discontinued in February, 1984.
**Service start-up cancelled February, 1984.

vent grounding of the two DC-9s that were being received, but to boost the load factors system-wide as the result of traffic the new cities would give to its present operation.

The Collapse of Braniff

In May, 1982, Braniff Airlines ceased operations and filed for bankruptcy-court protection under Chapter 11 of the Federal Bankruptcy Code. Braniff needed protection from creditors' lawsuits as it tried to work out a plan to repay all debts. This opened up many slots for other airlines to pick up and expand service. Muse Air was one of the first to present its request to the FAA for some of the Braniff slots.

Of all the new slots received by Muse Air, they were able to finally begin service to Midland-Odessa and Tulsa in late May, 1982. Attention was then turned toward the next planned expansion, that of Austin and San Antonio. Muse Air felt they still had enough Dallas slots to accomplish this expansion on schedule.

The FAA gave Muse Air seven en-route slots and eight airport slots at Dallas on a temporary basis. These slots were former Braniff slots which the FAA later rescinded away and allocated to other airlines by lottery. This left Muse in a position of negotiating for needed slots at Dallas in exchange for slots it did not want, such as at New York LaGuardia. So, again in August, 1982, Muse Air was in a position of having to ground newly acquired aircraft for lack of available slots.

The West Coast

On October 1, 1982, as a way to keep from grounding aircraft, Muse Air began service to Los Angeles, California. This was a complete shift in original expansion plans. While the continuing restrictions on landing rights imposed by the FAA forestalled planned expansion to Austin and San Antonio, the new service to California achieved a break-even level of operations by December, 1982.

During the first part of 1983, Muse Air worked very hard at strengthening existing routes and increasing market share. For the first eight months of 1983, passenger traffic, as measured by revenue passenger miles, was up 195 percent. The fact that gains in traffic outpaced any increase in capacity was due to growing passenger load factors, the percent of seats filled. Growing identity with the traveling public, as much as anything else, was a major reason for these gains. This was accomplished by increasing the number of flights serving a particular market (the Dallas-Houston route was increased to 17 round trip flights daily) and attracting a larger portion of the business community as passengers, since these are the people who travel most frequently.

Continuing Expansion

In late 1983, Muse Air began the expansion again, with service to Lubbock in August and Austin in November, 1983. A major factor that made this possible was the elimination of most FAA slot restrictions on October 30, 1983. Muse's new \$3-million-dollar terminal at Hobby Airport was completed in November, 1983, thus adding another large upgrade to the system.

Muse Air continued with expansion in early 1984, with the opening of the New Orleans market in February. With the Mardi Gras festival in the Spring and the World's Fair opening in the Summer, this meant increased traffic to the New Orleans area. Muse Air fully expects to take advantage of this increased traffic flow and become very quickly established in the area.

Service was also begun to Ontario International in California in February, 1984, plus a selective joint marketing agreement was signed with Air Cal. Through these two "gateway" locations, Muse Air passengers can quickly connect to eight of Air Cal's markets. In essence, this agreement represents a doubling of marketing destinations available to Muse Air customers. All the conveniences of expanded service to eight new West Coast markets were achieved without the costly capital outlays required for opening individual on-site operations.

In late February of 1984, Muse Air discontinued service to Lubbock as it had proved to be unprofitable for the company. Plans for new service to Little Rock, Arkansas, were abandoned the following month. Southwest Airlines moved into Little Rock first and saturated the market with flights.

In response to this, Muse Air opened up nonstop service between Dallas and New Orleans, began service to Las Vegas from Houston in April of 1984 and began special discount fares and Olympic tour packages. At this time, all eleven of their planes were being fully utilized and earning a profit for Muse Air.

COMPANY MANAGEMENT

Management Organization

The organization of Muse Air's top management is a straightforward top-down style (see Exhibit 2). Lamar Muse is Chairman of the Board and Michael is President and Chief Executive Officer. There are nine vice presidents that report to Michael Muse, who cover all the major areas of company operation. These people are:

Vice President-Flight Operations—Mr. Ferguson served as a senior captain for Texas International Airlines and is now responsible for all operations and pilots.

Vice President-Maintenance & Engineering—Mr. Minter worked previously for Braniff in their maintenance department and as Staff Vice President.

Vice President-Purchasing & Stores—Mr. Lane came from Southwest Airlines as Director of Purchasing.

Vice President-Planning & Budgeting—Mr. Thomson is another former Southwest Airlines employee. He was Director of Treasury Operation.

Vice President-Finance & Treasurer—Mr. Coogan, a former Audit Manager for Price Waterhouse, has been with Muse Air two years.

Vice President-Airport Services—Mr. Savage has worked for Texas International, Air Couriers International and TWA, managing airports and airport facilities.

Vice President-In-Flight Services—Ms. Coffin has worked as a flight attendant and as Director of Training and Support for Eastern Airlines.

Vice President-Sales Advertising—Mr. Mumaugh worked for United Airlines previously in sales, marketing, inflight operations and customer service.

The Muse Air management team contains a great amount of experience and expertise concerning the airline industry from a wide variety of sources and companies.

Employee Benefits

Muse Air has no pension plan for their employees but does have a profit-sharing plan. When operating profits exceed a set amount for a quarter, 20% of these excess profits are distributed to the employees as cash. This is only for employees who have been with the company for a set period of time. Muse Air will also adopt a stock purchase plan for their employees and highly encourage participation in the program. With the employees having a portion of ownership in the company, they will be more inclined to keep productivity up and costs down.

At present, there is a stock option plan for employees as far down in the company as mid-management. The employee's position with the company determines how many shares he may purchase and at what price. An employee must have one year of service with Muse Air to participate and can only purchase one third of the option shares within a given year. The employee has five years to purchase all the stocks available to him under the option agreement.

A non-monetary benefit of Muse Air is the rotation of employees within different ground oper-

EXHIBIT 2
Muse Air Corporation
Corporate Organization Chart

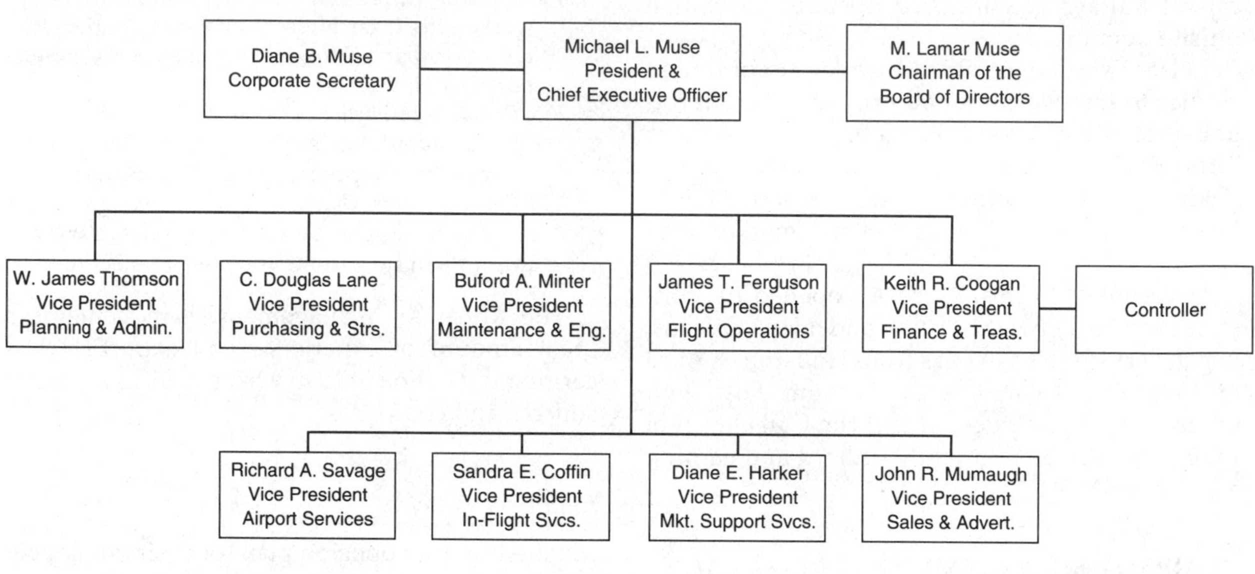

ation positions. This allows the employees to become well cross-trained in various jobs while keeping their interest rate at a high level. Cross-training helps keep productivity up while keeping costs down for Muse Air since they do not have to keep excess people on the payroll.

AIRCRAFT AND FACILITIES

Muse Air uses the McDonnell Douglas DC-9 Super 80 and DC-9 Super 50 aircraft. These planes both use the cost efficient two engine design and require only two pilots, instead of three, as needed by other aircraft. All planes are set up for single-class service with a distinguished, club style atmosphere. The exterior is white with the Muse Air signature in blue on the side of the plane.

The corporate signature of Muse Air, as analyzed by Ray Walker, handwriting expert, announces strength and character. The backstroke on the letter "M" shows an awareness of the past, complimented by a powerful forward sweep that indicates confidence in the future. The "A" is an indication of pride. The dot over the "I" is close to the stem, showing an appropriate caution with emphasis on the safety and well-being of others.

Muse Air has implemented a cost efficient work force. Employees are non-union, which helps keep wage levels moderate. Also, employees are cross-utilized between various jobs, eliminating the work restriction rules that plague many major carriers and raise their effective labor costs. Finally, because Muse Air is such a young company, there are no long-time employees, meaning lower overall wage levels.

Within the air terminals, Muse Air uses cash register type ticketing and standardized check-in and baggage handling procedures. Operating costs are substantially reduced and passenger arrival-departure time kept to a minimum.

Keeping the comfort and convenience of passengers in mind, all flights are non-smoking. The DC-9 Super 80 carries 155 passengers while the

Super 50 carries 130. This, plus the 3-2 style of seating that has been installed, means more room and comfort for the passengers. The DC-9 gives the passenger a very quiet and smooth ride.

COMPETITION

General

The airline industry is divided into three segments: the major airlines, the national airlines and the regionals, such as Muse Air. The market share of the majors has been declining since deregulation. At the same time, market share for the regionals has been increasing, picking up what the majors have lost. The load factors of the major airlines have stabilized over the past few years, neither growing nor decreasing. Muse Air's competition consists of three types. The first is Southwest Airlines, with whom Muse Air initiated head-on competition. Second are the regionals that have come into existence following deregulation. Last are the majors who are reestablishing on a much smaller scale, including Braniff and Continental Airlines.

Southwest Airlines

Southwest Airlines provides a single-class, high-frequency air service to cities in Texas and surrounding states. The company concentrates on short haul markets and stresses high level of aircraft utilization and employee productivity. The principal hubs of Southwest's systems are Dallas' Love Field and Houston's Hobby Airport, with a new hub established in Phoenix. These airports are located substantially closer to downtown business centers than the major airports.

Southwest is considered one of the best-run airlines in the country. Revenues and revenue passenger miles rose all during 1983. The airline has a load factor around 62%, well above its break-even point. Southwest will be expanding into the longer haul routes with the delivery of new Boeing 737-300 aircraft in 1984. With a young and efficient fleet, the company is well positioned to benefit from any improvement in the domestic economic activity.

Regional Airlines

People's Express began operating in April, 1981, and intends to triple its size by mid-1985 through the purchase of several Boeing 727s. It also began offering transatlantic service during the summer of 1983, with a leased 747-200. People's Express services 17 cities domestically, mostly in the Northeast. It flies from its base at Newark, New Jersey, as far as Houston's Hobby. It was one of the few airlines to report a profit in 1982.

New York Air initiated service in late 1980 in the New York, Boston, Washington, D.C., corridor, competing directly with Eastern's shuttle service. Since then it has added cities in the Southeast. The airline experienced an increase of profitability in 1983. New York Air pioneered the concept of business class service at coach class rates. Passengers have been lured with such items as two-by-two seating, more leg room, bagels and the *New York Times*.

In February, 1984, Air Atlanta began service between Atlanta, Memphis and New York. The airline is using fewer seats, bigger chairs, more leg room, shorter ticket lines and waiting areas with telephones and refreshments to lure full-fare business passengers. Air Atlanta plans to specialize totally for this market. The planes and waiting areas have been completely redesigned for the business passenger to move on and off the plane quickly. Air Atlanta intends to cater to business passengers.

St. Louis–based Air One began operations in April, 1983, with flights to Dallas, Kansas City, Washington, D.C., and Newark, N.J. Air One is another airline that caters to the business traveler, offering first-class service between St. Louis and Houston's Hobby, the first of 22 cities it eventually plans to include in its route system. Air One currently has seven Boeing 727s and will add five more in late 1984.

Rebirths

Like the "Phoenix" that rose from the ashes, Braniff Airlines began flying again on March 1, 1984. It plans to operate a premium service, low-cost airline, aimed strictly at the business travel market. From its Dallas hub, Braniff will serve 17 cities, including Houston, Austin, Los Angeles, New Orleans, San Antonio and Tulsa. Braniff is flying from Dallas-Fort Worth Regional Airport and Houston's Intercontinental. Estimates are that it will take several years for the airline to regain the market share it lost in the Houston market.

Braniff restructured itself with the financial backing of the Hyatt Corporation. It has reduced salaries, employees and operating costs to the bare minimum. Even at these low levels, Braniff needs a 47% load factor to break even. The first stock offering by Braniff indicated moderate public confidence in the reborn airline.

Continental Airlines filed to reorganize under Chapter 11 of the Federal Bankruptcy Code during the third quarter of 1983. In February, 1984, the airline reappeared with bare bones pay scales, unrestricted low air fares and employees with a stake in the airline's profitability. Like many of the new airlines, Continental is aiming for the single-class business market with competitive fares and many special services.

MARKETING STRATEGY

Muse Air endeavors to provide the highest-quality airline service to its target market, primarily business men and women. The marketing strategy is based on service, price, name recognition, and expansion of routes

Service

Quality service on Muse Air includes many features: a quiet, comfortable ride on a Super 80 or Super 50 aircraft, with comfortable, large leather seats in a clean, smoke-free environment; dependable service with convenient close-in airport locations and convenient departure times; the convenience of reserved seating to prevent the crush to board; the best service provided by motivated employees; easy booking for travel agents through American Airlines' computerized SABRE system.

Price

The air transportation market is growing, as the economy improves. Muse Air must gain its share of this market growth. To accomplish this goal, they use competitive prices to attract customers. In March, 1983, Muse Air offered the "lowest" discounted fare to Los Angeles of $88.

Off-peak pricing is used to attract more customers and keep more planes flying at higher occupancy. Muse Air primarily utilizes a two-tier fare structure: business class, providing low-cost, first-class air transportation during prime time; and leisure class, providing an economically competitive alternative to various forms of ground transportation.

Muse Air has always had to meet or beat the low fares of their major competitor, Southwest Airlines. The recent revival of Continental and Braniff Airlines in March, 1984, increased competition on most of the Muse Air routes. This competitive environment may spark another round of price slashing. Braniff has already announced reduced economy fares during March, 1984.

The reborn Continental Airlines precipitated fare discounting as a means to fill seats and gain the customers it lost after filing to reorganize under Chapter 11. Additionally, Delta Air Lines, Pan Am, American, Eastern and TWA have joined in with their own discounting in order to remain competitive. Of these majors, Delta began service on March 1, 1984, from Houston's Hobby Airport to seven cities including Dallas-Ft. Worth, the major market for Muse Air.

Because of deregulation and the Chapter 11 alternative, the airline industry is becoming more efficient. Everyone is trying to keep costs low, so their rates can be competitive. It is with Southwest that Muse Air must be competitive in order to gain the needed traffic. Muse Air has a lower average cost than Southwest (5.2 cents a seat mile against Southwest's six cents and the industry average of nearly eleven cents). Since overhead is almost identical, Muse Air must differentiate itself from Southwest in order to "break the Southwest habit" to which the frequent flier has become accustomed.

Name Recognition

Lamar Muse feels that name recognition is critical to success. Therefore, Muse Air devotes a lot of effort to promote a premium product with a reserved and sophisticated image.

To enhance the club car image, they provide many in-service extras, including drinks on afternoon flights and a complimentary copy of the *Wall Street Journal.*

To encourage repeat customers, Muse Air has developed several packages and clubs that provide benefits for frequent flyers. For example, the Muse Air Club is for travel coordinators, secretaries, and people in business and government who are responsible for travel arrangements. Club members can earn free trips, participate in monthly drawings for special prizes, receive the Muse Air magazine, and invitations to special receptions.

Muse Air continues to spend heavily for advertising. In 1982, expenditures were over $6 million, or 16% of all operating expenses, for marketing. The initial ad campaign, "Big Daddy is Back," emphasized their leader, Lamar Muse, and his experience in the airline industry. The next campaign was testimonials from customers.

The latest advertising effort on radio and television is intended to reach a wider group of potential passengers by using people of various ages and occupations. The campaign also attempts to entice the customer with a mystical, indescribable, beautiful experience. The themes are "You just gotta fly it," and "See how beautiful Muse Air can be." Initial response to this campaign has been very positive.

Route Expansion

The fourth component of the Muse Air marketing strategy is expansion of routes. Muse Air began service in July, 1981, between Dallas (Love Field) and Houston (Hobby Airport). As of February, 1984, Muse Air flies 17 round trips daily on the Dallas-Houston route, which is its most popular.

From 1982, Muse Air has expanded service to Midland-Odessa, Texas; Tulsa, Oklahoma; Los Angeles, California; Lubbock, Texas; Austin, Texas; Ontario, California; and New Orleans, Louisiana. As of April 29, 1984, Muse Air will be offering service to Las Vegas. See Exhibit 3 for a map of the expanded service area. Plans for future expansion include San Antonio, St. Louis, Chicago, New York, Atlanta, and Florida.

Originally, Muse Air expansion plans were to fly to the South and Mid-West. Exhibit 4 is a map of the initial strategic plan of Muse Air as formulated in 1980. There are indications that the westward air travel market is served to over-capacity. Muse may try to return to these original plans to increase profitability. Houston will become the center of operations.

At the end of February, 1984, Muse Air had to cancel plans for beginning service to Little Rock, Arkansas. Muse's service to Little Rock had been announced in January and was to begin April 19, 1984. After the announcement, Southwest Airlines flooded the Little Rock market with new flights forcing Muse Air out before service began.

Muse Air will face other competitors as it tries to expand. Delta has already started service to Atlanta from Houston's Hobby Airport, the same route proposed by Muse for service in March, 1986.

Not only is Muse Air being crowded out of expansion routes, but existing routes as well. After several months of service, Muse Air discontinued flights to Lubbock, Texas. Delta, American, and Southwest Airlines all service Lubbock. This is the

EXHIBIT 3
Proposed Expansion of Muse Air Routes (Effective April 29, 1984)

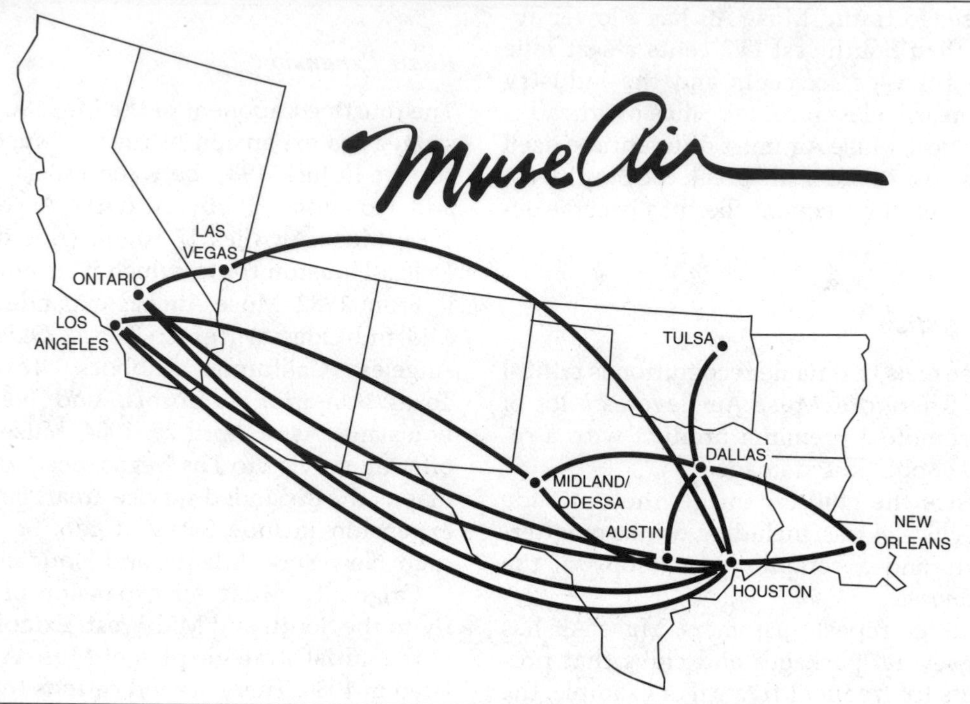

first route that Muse Air has ever had to discontinue.

Besides planned route expansion, an innovative joint marketing program with Air Cal should help Muse Air grow beyond its strictly regional status. The Muse Air/Air Cal joint marketing agreement began February 5, 1984. Muse Air passengers can connect quickly to eight of Air Cal's markets including: San Francisco, Sacramento, San Jose, Palm Springs, and Oakland, California; Seattle, Washington; Portland, Oregon; and Reno, Nevada. See Exhibit 5 for a map of Air Cal routes.

This selective joint marketing agreement represents a doubling of market destinations available to Muse Air customers virtually overnight. All the conveniences of expanded service to eight new West Coast markets were achieved without the costly capital outlays required for opening individual airline on-site operations. According to John Mumaugh, Vice President of Sales and Advertising, this joint marketing program illustrates clearly how deregulation has freed carriers to pursue creative marketing techniques in a cost-effective manner to ultimately benefit the traveling public.

FINANCES

Equity

The company was initially capitalized in February, 1980, through the issuance of 31,250 shares of common stock to Michael L. Muse for $25,000 in cash. In October, 1980, the company issued and sold an aggregate of 318,750 shares of common

EXHIBIT 4
Muse Air Strategic Route Plan (1980)

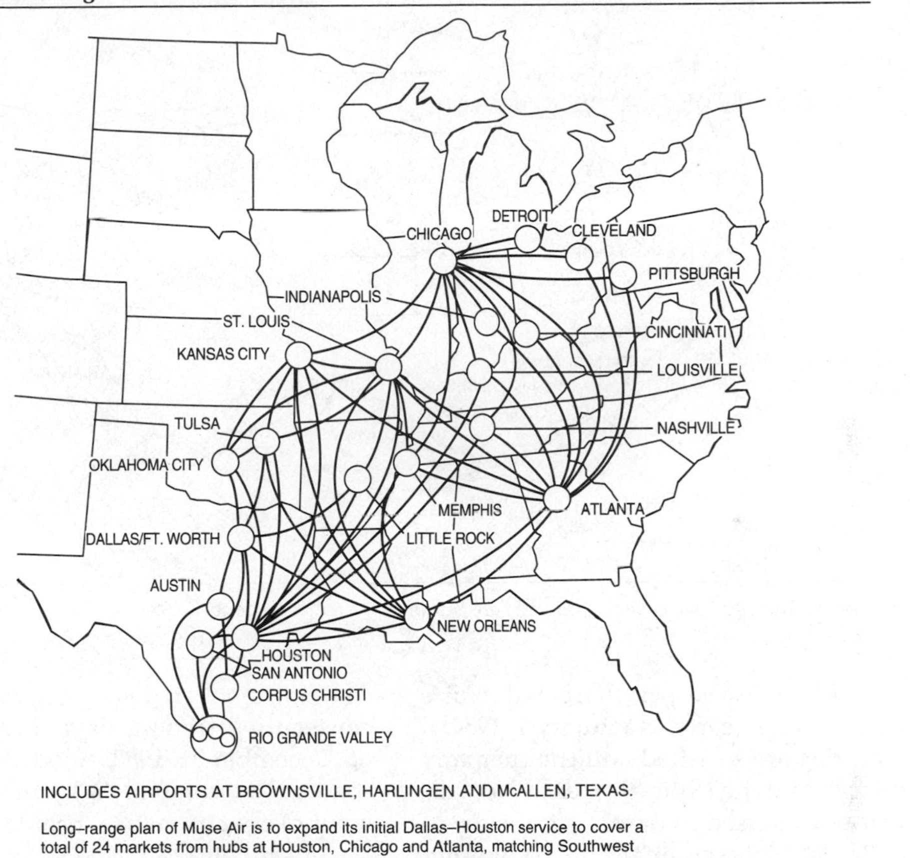

Long–range plan of Muse Air is to expand its initial Dallas–Houston service to cover a total of 24 markets from hubs at Houston, Chicago and Atlanta, matching Southwest Airlines' fares in its markets and undercutting any other competition.

stock to five members of the Muse family and Cole, Brumley & Eichner, Inc. for cash payment of $.80 per share. In October, 1980, the company also issued and sold to five members of the Muse family an aggregate of $190,000, principal amount of its 12% convertible subordinated debentures, at the face amount. In February, 1981, 237,500 shares of common stock were issued to the five members of the Muse family upon conversion of the debentures. On March 20, 1981, the company's stock was split five-for-four.

On April 30, 1981, the company made a public offering of 2,200,000 shares of common stock with warrants to purchase 1,100,000 shares of common stock priced at $17.50 per unit (one share of common stock and one-half warrant). The proceeds of this offering were used as a deposit and fee relating to the future acquisition of four new DC-9 Super 80 aircraft, the prepayment of a one-year lease on the two Super 80 aircraft that were in operation, the acquisition of aircraft spare parts and engines, the purchase of ground equipment and leasehold improvements, and the unrestricted addition to working capital. The stock was traded in the over-the-counter market under the symbol "MUSE." The warrants provide for the purchase

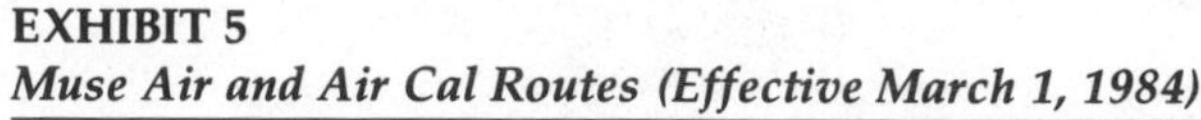

EXHIBIT 5
Muse Air and Air Cal Routes (Effective March 1, 1984)

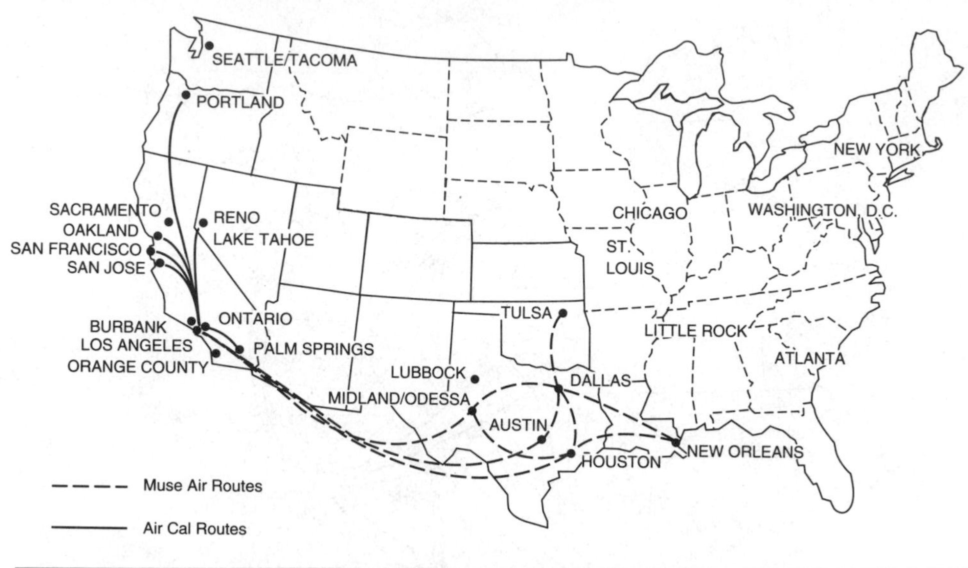

Source: Muse Air Flight Schedule and Fare Summary, effective March 1, 1984.

of common stock at $16.00 per share and expire on April 30, 1986, or as early as January 1, 1984, if certain conditions are satisfied and the company chooses to accelerate the expiration date. No warrants have been exercised to date.

On May 24, 1983, the company made another public offering of 1,540,000 shares of common stock at $16.25. The net proceeds of this offering were used to prepay a secured bank note due in July, 1984, and to increase the equity base and working capital position of the company to support future expansion. The common stock commenced trading on the American Stock Exchange under the symbol "MAC" on April 18, 1983, at which time it ceased trading in the over-the-counter market.

With this last equity offering, no further financing is expected in 1984. A cash flow of $12.5 million in 1983 and $25 million in 1984 should pose few difficulties requiring further equity. In addition, the company will likely force the conversion of the 1.1 million warrants at $16 per share if the common stock trades at or above $24 per share for consecutive trading days. Market capitalization on December 31, 1983, stood at 4,030,113 common shares. The company's balance sheet and statement of operations are included as Exhibits 6 and 7, respectively.

In 1982 Muse sold tax benefits of depreciation and investment tax credits on four of its DC-9 Super 80 aircraft producing net proceeds to the company of approximately $21.6 million. This item was treated as "other" income and accounted for the net earnings of $3.87 per share during fiscal 1982. Without these tax-related benefits, the company would have reported a 1982 full-year net loss of $3.17 per share.

Capital Stock Valuation

Because of the various crisis situations Muse has encountered, the stock's price has fluctuated widely from a high of $19\frac{3}{8}$ to a low of $3\frac{1}{2}$ during its short life (see Exhibit 8). While the stock price

EXHIBIT 6
Muse Air Corporation
Balance Sheet

Assets	December 31	
	1983	*1982*
Current Assets		
Cash and temporary investments of $16,931,000 in 1983 and $7,250,000 in 1982	$18,404,116	7,488,653
Accounts receivable	6,600,356	6,068,720
Inventories of parts and supplies	513,582	412,833
Prepaid expenses	1,001,455	555,246
Total current assets	26,519,509	11,525,452
Property and Equipment at Cost		
Flight equipment—aircraft	130,187,529	109,700,751
Aircraft purchase deposits	8,672,808	
Leasehold improvements	3,454,387	1,026,286
Other flight and ground equipment	14,100,401	9,325,544
	156,415,125	120,052,581
Less: Accumulated depreciation and amortization	(10,593,431)	(3,255,798)
	145,821,694	116,796,783
Other assets, net	445,502	2,470,381
	$172,786,705	$130,792,616

Liabilities and Stockholders' Equity	1983	1982
Current Liabilities		
Accounts payable	$4,352,121	$1,081,662
Unearned transportation revenues	1,637,359	681,535
Accrued liabilities	6,957,066	3,389,432
Current maturities of long-term debt	9,615,541	2,460,000
Total current liabilities	22,562,087	7,612,629
Long-term debt less current maturities	83,594,659	76,440,000
Deferred federal income taxes	263,501	715,740
Other long-term liabilities		1,013,790
Total liabilities	106,420,247	85,782,159
Stockholders' Equity		
Common stock, $1.00 par value: 20,000,000 shares authorized: issued and outstanding 4,636,750 shares in 1983 and 3,100,000 shares, $.10 par value, in 1982	4,636,750	310,000
Additional paid-in capital	56,183,993	37,196,245
Retained earnings	5,545,715	7,504,212
Total stockholders' equity	66,366,458	45,010,457
Commitments and contingencies	$172,786,705	$130,792,616

Source: Muse Air Corporation 1983 Annual Report.

EXHIBIT 7
Muse Air Corporation
Statement of Operations

	Year Ended December 31		
	1983	*1982*	*1981*
Operating Revenues			
Passenger	$68,976,808	$32,211,861	$6,217,593
Other	3,951,150	844,063	78,268
Total operating revenues	72,927,958	33,055,924	6,295,861
Operating Expenses			
Fuel and oil	20,940,064	12,182,590	3,201,335
Flight operations	8,360,307	6,130,036	2,871,844
Marketing	13,292,021	6,112,769	2,251,081
Maintenance	3,827,987	2,211,586	941,113
In-flight service	4,479,305	2,001,974	545,566
Terminal operations	5,109,215	2,889,318	832,069
Insurance and taxes	2,819,025	1,572,725	277,684
General and administrative	2,136,772	1,578,310	714,538
Depreciation and amortization	7,347,628	3,114,827	197,620
Total operating expenses	68,312,324	37,794,135	11,832,850
Operating income (loss)	4,615,634	(4,738,211)	(5,536,989)
Non-Operating Income (Expense)			
Interest income	1,647,481	897,928	1,569,469
Interest expense (less interest capitalized of $797,967 in 1983 and $1,353,943 in 1982)	(8,556,268)	(4,309,216)	
Other income	499,985	21,835,019	
Other expense	(617,568)	(1,502,186)	
Net non-operating income (expense)	(7,026,370)	16,921,545	1,569,469
Income (loss) before provision for federal income taxes and extraordinary item	(2,410,736)	12,183,334	(3,967,520)
Federal income tax profision (benefit)	(452,239)	2,540,800	
Income (loss) before extraordinary item	(1,958,497)	9,642,534	(3,967,520)
Extraordinary item—utilization of net operating loss carry forwards		1,825,060	
Net income (loss)	$(1,958,497)	$11,467,594	$(3,967,520)
Income (Loss) per Common Share			
Income (loss) before extraordinary item	$(.49)	$3.25	$(1.86)
Extraordinary item		.62	
Net income (loss)	$(.49)	$3.87	$(1.86)
Weighted average shares outstanding	4,030,113	2,963,151	2,136,781

Source: Muse Air Corporation 1983 Annual Report.

EXHIBIT 8
Muse Air Corporation
Summary of Book Value / Trading Price per Share

Year	Quarter	Book Value per Share Price	Trading Price per Share High	Low
1980	4th	$ .81	—	—
1981	1st	—	—	—
	2nd	12.19	15	11½
	3rd	11.26	15¼	7¼
	4th	10.83	12⅝	7⅜
1982	1st	10.35	8⅞	5½
	2nd	9.81	7⅜	3½
	3rd	11.05	9	4⅜
	4th	14.52	13⅝	6⅝
1983	1st	14.09	15	10⅜
	2nd	13.64	19⅜	14¼
	3rd	14.27	17¾	13½
	4th	14.31	16¾	14

Source: 1981, 1982, 1983 Muse Air Corporation Annual Report.

has changed with the outlook for the company's future, the book value has steadily increased. Currently, the stock is selling at a 25% discount from book value and about seven times estimated 1984 earnings. As a comparison, Southwest Airlines sells at three times book value and 20 times earnings; Midway and People's Express sell at comparable or higher multiples. Also, the earnings leverage is considerable because passenger traffic should increase more rapidly than growth in capacity and net loss carry forwards. Additionally, investment tax credits will be available to offset future income tax.

Based on estimates, Muse Air has the potential to earn $1.50 per share in fiscal year 1984 (see Exhibit 9). If these earnings estimates prove correct and based on a valuation of 12 times earnings, a value for Muse common of $18 per share is possible. The potential for substantial price appreciation is within reason. Since warrants move, percentage wise, to a greater extent than does the common, the excellent leverage provided by this vehicle would reward investors even more handsomely.

Muse Air reported its first operating profit of $780,000, or $.17 per share, in the third quarter of 1983. In the 1983 fourth quarter, the company again reported an operating profit of $202,000 or $.04 per share. Both quarters of operating profits helped reduce the 1983 operating net loss to $1,959,000, or $.49 per share. Mr. Michael L. Muse stated that the positive results of the third and fourth quarter ". . . provided Muse Air a solid launching pad for what should prove to be a very successful 1984."

Aircraft Acquisition

The company began service on July 15, 1981, with two Super 80 aircraft leased from McDonnell Douglas Corporation (MDC). The first equity offering in April, 1981, provided the funds for the lease of these aircraft as well as the purchase of four new aircraft. In August, 1982, the company repaid the subordinated debt of $4.1 million to MDC from proceeds received from the sale of tax benefits on one of these aircraft.

EXHIBIT 9
Muse Air Corporation
Statement of Operations ($ in Thousands except per Share Amounts)

	1984E	*1983*	*1982*	*1981*
REV	$135,000	$72,928	$33,056	$6,296
OP. EXP.	110,000	68,312	37,794	11,833
OP.I.	25,000	4,616	(4,748)	(5,537)
NON-OP.I.	(16,000)	(7,026)	16,922	1,569
E.B.T.	9,000	(2,410)	12,184	(3,968)
TAX	2,000	(452)	2,541	—
E.B.EXTRA	7,000	(1,958)	9,643	(3,968)
EXTRA	—	—	1,825	—
N.I.	$7,000	$(1,958)	$11,468	$(2,941)
SHARES	4,640	4,030	2,963	2,131
Earnings per Share				
E.B.T	$1.95	$(0.49)	$4.11	$(1.86)
E.B.EXTRA	—	—	$3.25	—
N.I.	$1.50	$(0.49)	$3.87	$(1.86)

Source: 1983 Muse Air Annual Report and Analyst Estimates.

REV	Revenues
OP. EXP	Operating expenses
OP.I.	Operating income
NON-OP.I.	Non-operating income
E.B.T.	Earnings before taxes
TAX	Tax liability
E.B.EXTRA	Earnings before extraordinary item
EXTRA	Extraordinary itemss
N.I.	Net income
SHARES	# Primary shares

The company purchased two additional Super 80 aircraft in September, 1982, and one in November, 1982, with $42 million provided from bank financing and with approximately $14 million of the proceeds from the sale of tax benefits associated with these aircraft. In December, 1982, the company leased a sixth Super 80 aircraft under a long-term operating lease agreement from the McDonnell Douglas Finance Corporation (MDFC). As of this date, Muse Air owns five of its Super 80 aircraft and holds a long-term lease for the sixth. Exhibit 1 shows the aircraft delivery schedule.

In August, 1983, Muse Air negotiated the purchase of ten used McDonnell Douglas DC-9-51 aircraft, five of those from SwissAir and the other five from Austrian Air. The total cost of this acquisition is approximately $100 million. The first two aircraft were delivered in October, 1983, the third in February, 1984. Two more are to be placed in service during late April or early May, 1984. Three additional aircraft are to be delivered in the first quarter of 1985 and the final two in the first quarter of 1986. Muse Air intends to use the smaller aircraft on its shorter hauls with less passenger demand while using the Super 80s on longer and more heavily traveled flights. Approximately $11 million from the second equity offering was used as a deposit on the aircraft with the balance to be financed with bank debt of $65 million as the planes are delivered through 1986.

THE PREDICAMENT

Lamar and Michael Muse were weary from reviewing all of the relevant information pertaining to their situation. The airline industry is going through a time of change. What is the best strategy for Muse Air Corporation to pursue in this rapidly changing environment? Is the time right to expand? Should expansion be regional or national? These were all important questions that Michael Muse felt required definite answers.

REFERENCES

Joan M. Feldman. "Deregulation Loose Ends Spark Debate About Regulation After 1984." *Air Transport World* 20 (May 1983): p. 23.

"FAA Nears Ruling on Preferential Routes." *Aviation Week & Space Technology* 119 (April 18, 1983): p. 34.

"Airline Cooperation Starts to Break Apart." *Business Week* (November 29, 1983): p. 45.

James Ott. "Airlines Gear for New Challenges." *Aviation Week & Space Technology* 118 (November 14, 1983): p. 48.

Michael Cieply. "Hardball." *Forbes* 132 (February 28, 1983): p. 33.

James Ott. "House Questions Agent Decision." *Aviation Week & Space Technology* 118 (May 30, 1983): p. 57–58.

John Mumaugh. "Executive Corner," *Muse Air Monthly* (October 1983): p. 7.

"Muse Air Reports Substantial Fourth Quarter Operating Profit; Finishes 1983 with Back-To-Back Quarterly Net Profits As Well," News Release, Muse Air, January 1984.

CASE 7 | *Leykam Mürztaler*

In February 1989, Dr. Gertrude Eder, Marketing Manager for Leykam Mürztaler AG, was reviewing a problem that had occupied her thoughts a great deal during the past few months. Although Leykam Mürztaler, like the paper industry in general, had been doing well in recent years, it was her opinion that it was time to think about ways to strengthen the company's ability to prosper as industry growth inevitably began slowing down. In particular, she was considering what recommendations to offer the Executive Board regarding the firm's branding strategy.

LEYKAM MÜRZTALER AG

The past few years had been good for the Leykam Mürztaler Group. Paralleling the industry's increased sales, the firm's total sales had risen from ASch4,842 million[1] in 1983 to ASch7,100 million in 1988, an increase of 47%. For Leykam Mürztaler AG, the principal operating component of the Group, 1988 revenues had reached ASch6,300 million, an increase over 1986 of 41%, enhanced by the successful start-up of a new production line and by above average growth in demand for high-grade coated woodfree printing papers, the firm's main sales segment.

Leykam Mürztaler AG, together with its predecessor companies, had been a producer of paper for over 400 years. Headquartered in Gratkorn, Austria, the firm produced coated woodfree printing paper and newsprint, with integrated pulp production. Principal mills and offices were located at Gratkorn and Bruck, Austria. Export sales offices for coated woodfree paper were headquartered in Vienna.

In 1988, woodfree papers represented approximately 80% of sales, newsprint 13% and pulp 7%. Twenty-two percent of revenues came from Austria, 56% from Western Europe and 22% from exports to the rest of the world (including Eastern Europe). The highest share of exports was for coated woodfree papers at approximately 90%.

(Production volumes in 1987 and 1988 are shown in Exhibit 1.) The large increase in production of printing and writing paper in 1988 (to 340,900 tonnes) reflected successful selling of the output of the new coated woodfree paper machine at Gratkorn, with a capacity of 138,000 tonnes per year. The decline in pulp production reflected a change in product mix. External sales of pulp were declining as the company's pulp production was further integrated into the company's own paper production.

With the addition of the new production line, the company had become the European market leader in coated woodfree papers, with a market share of 8–10%. In December 1987 the Supervisory Board approved a project to establish a new production line at Bruck to produce mechanical coated printing papers (LWC) for magazines, catalogues and printed advertising materials. Planned capacity was 135,000 tonnes, to be put into operation at the end of 1989.

Despite the increased level of investment, financial results were very good. In 1987, the last year for which complete financial details were available, profit was down slightly from the previous year (see Exhibit 2), reflecting the greatly increased depreciation charges associated with the new paper machine and the decision to use the reducing-balance method of depreciation for it and some other equipment. Cash flow, however, was close to an all-time record, results were "clearly better than originally forecast," and operating profits were near the top of the European woodfree paper producers, on a percent of sales basis. Preliminary indications were that financial results for 1988 would be still better.

The company marketed its coated products under its MAGNO series brand (e.g., MAGNOMATT, MAGNOPRINT, MAGNOMATT K) principally through wholly owned merchants in Austria and other merchants throughout Western Europe. In addition, it sold to other kinds of merchants in Austria as well as to some printers and publishers directly. Paper merchants were contacted by sales representatives in Vienna and Gratkorn, sales subsidiaries in Germany, Italy and France, and sales agents in other European countries. Some of its products were sold on a private brand basis to certain large merchants.

Although Leykam Mürztaler served paper markets on a worldwide basis, and planned to enter the LWC market, this case focuses on coated woodfree papers for printing applications in Western Europe.

[1] ASch12.48 = $1.00 in December 1988.

EXHIBIT 1
Highlights of the Development of the Leykam-Mürztaler Group

	1987	*1988*	*%*
Production (in tons)			
Printing and writing papers	272,900	340,900	+24.9
Newsprint (Bruck)	98,200	99,200	+1.0
Paper total	371,100	440,100	I 18.6
Chemical pulp	209,500	204,500	−2.4
Mechanical pulp	30,900	32,100	+3.9
Deink pulp	58,900	62,700	+6.4
Total sales (gross, in ASch mn)			
Leykam-Mürztaler AG	5,234	6,300	+20.4
Export share	4,056	5,100	+25.7
Exports in %	78	81	—
Leykam-Mürztaler Group	5,906	7,100	+20.2
Capital expenditure and prepayments for fixed assets (in ASch mn)	1,418	1,500	+5.8
Cash flow (in ASch mn)	1,020	1,500	+47.1
Employees (excluding apprentices) as of 31 December	2,825	2,865	+1.4

Source: Annual report.

THE PULP AND PAPER INDUSTRY IN WESTERN EUROPE[2]

Despite its maturity, the pulp and paper industry was undergoing major change. Characterized by high breakeven volumes, small fluctuations in demand could significantly impact profits, and there was some evidence that capacity was outgrowing demand. Despite the sophistication of paper-making technology, product differentiation was increasingly difficult to achieve. Some paper makers were integrating backwards to control the cost or assure the supply of pulp. Others were integrating forward, buying paper merchants in order to have better control of marketing. Still others were integrating horizontally to have a more complete product line.

Other changes were affecting the industry as well. Customers were being merged, acquired or reorganized, thus changing established purchasing patterns. Changes in advertising were impacting traditional usage patterns. Paper merchants were merging to gain economies of scale. Some were emphasizing private brands to reduce their dependence on paper makers. Markets were fragmenting as new, small businesses were forming at a record rate. Consumption patterns were changing. In Europe, consumption ranged from 233 kg per capita in Sweden to 60 in Portugal, but growth rates ranged from a high of 29.4% in Greece to a low of 2.4% in Denmark. There was some uncertainty about the implications of Eu-

[2]Western Eupore included the countries in the European Community plus Finland, Norway, Sweden, Austria and Switzerland.

EXHIBIT 2
Financial Results

	1983	*1984**	*1985***	*1986*	*1987*
Total sales (gross, in AS m)	4,842	5,367	5,420	5,187	5,906
Export sales (AS m)	2,973	3,413	3,537	3,331	4,062
Export share of Leykam-Mürztaler AG (%)	69	72	74	74	78
Capital investment (AS m)	313	253	444	2,461	1,518
Total depreciation (AS m) thereof: reducing-balance	374	344	337	476	1,064
Depreciation (AS m)	—	—	—	125	674
Cash flow (AS m)	373	1,025	959	871	1,020
Profit for the year (AS m)	1	422	81	101	67
Personnel expenditure (AS m)	1,096	993	1,046	1,076	1,231
Number of employees (excluding apprentices) as of 31 December	2,918	2,424	2,364	2,578	2,825
Dividend and bonus (AS m)	—	54	81	101	67
(%)	—	4+4	4+8	4+8	8

Source: Annual report.
*Excluding Niklasdorf Mill.
**Excluding Frohnierten Mill from 1 April 1985.

rope's move toward a true common market in 1992, although trade barriers were not a significant factor in the industry.

Printing and Writing Paper

In the pulp and paper industry, the major and high growth segment was printing and writing papers. Both coated and uncoated papers were produced from mechanically or chemically processed pulp to form four broad categories: coated woodfree, mechanical coated,[3] uncoated woodfree and mechanical uncoated. To be defined as coated, a paper had to have a surface coating of at least 5 grams per square meter (gsm).

Coated woodfree papers represented the highest quality category, in terms of printability, gloss, feel, ability to reproduce color and many other characteristics. Grades of coated woodfree papers were not precisely specified, but the industry had established further categories such as cast coated, art paper, standard and low coated. (See Exhibit 3 for categories and prices.) The standard grade represented the bulk of sales. Within this category, however, there were many gradations—the amount of whiteness, brightness, stiffness and other characteristics. Leykam Mürztaler competed principally at the high end of the standard grade, but was planning to enter the art paper segment also.

Coated woodfree was the smallest printing and writing paper segment (17.8% of total consumption), but it was also the most dynamic, with an average growth rate of 8.4% from 1980 to 1987. Expectations were that 1988 consumption would exceed three million tonnes.

Markets for Printing and Writing Paper

Principal markets for printing and writing paper were magazines (33%), direct mail (17%), brochures and general print advertising (15%), copy paper (11%), other office paper (9%) and books (5%). For coated woodfree papers, it was esti-

[3]Designated LWC or MWC, depending on the weight, although the dividing line was not precise.

EXHIBIT 3
Prices per Tonne (in $) of Woodfree Printing and Writing Papers in Western Europe (2nd Quarter 1987 Delivered)

Grade	*West Germany*	*UK*	*France*	*Netherlands*
Cast coated, sheets	2734	2324	2588	2480
Art paper, sheets	1897	1660	1837	1736
Standard, sheets	1283	1212	1235	1166
Standard, reels	1199	1145	1169	1091
Low coated, sheets	1172	1130	1136	1066

Source: EKONO Strategic Study, September 1988.
Note: Cast coated paper was estimated to represent 5% of the coated woodfree market, art paper 7–8%, standard coated 70% and low coated less than 20%. Within the standard coated category, actual transaction prices could vary as much as 25% as a function of quality and as much as 10% due to competitive or other factors.

mated that advertising, direct and indirect, accounted for 85–90% of consumption.[4]

On a country by country basis, there was significant variation in the mix of advertising expenditures, however. In the UK, for instance, the bulk of advertising expenditures went to newspapers and TV, whereas in Germany advertising expenditures were split somewhat evenly among newspapers, magazines, catalogues and direct mail.[5] Major uses for coated woodfree papers were direct mail, brochures, annual reports, etc. The dynamic growth of coated woodfree papers in recent years was largely fuelled by the rapid increases in "non-classical" advertising. Changes in this mix could significantly affect country consumption patterns for coated woodfree papers.

Despite cost pressures and shifts in individual markets and end uses, coated woodfree papers were benefitting from demand for more and better four-color printing as advertisers sought ways to improve the impact of their messages.

THE PRINTING INDUSTRY

The vast majority of orders for coated woodfree papers were placed by printers, either on the merchant or directly on the mill. In some instances, however, for very large orders, the order would be placed by either the printer or the publisher, depending on which seemed to have the strongest negotiating position with the supplier.

Selection of paper grade and manufacturer was a complex process that varied significantly according to end use, size of order, and sophistication of both the printer and the specifier or user. Almost without exception, the printer had the final say in the selection of paper make and could significantly influence the grade of paper as well. The specifier (ad agency) or user (advertiser, publisher, mail order house, etc.) influenced paper selection, particularly with respect to grade, and could also influence selection of make, subject to final agreement by the printer.

For the printer, key paper characteristics were printability and runability. Surface characteristics, whiteness and brightness were also important. Price was always important, especially when deciding between two suppliers with similar offerings or where paper costs represented a significant portion of the total cost of the printed product. Complaint handling, emergency assistance, speed and reliability of delivery were key service components. Sales representative knowledge was also important. Within limits, relative importance of decision criteria varied from one country to another. In Italy and the UK, for instance, price

[4]ECC International, Limited, 1987.
[5]Papis Limited.

and quality tended to be equally important, whereas quality and service factors tended to predominate importance rankings in Switzerland. There was some favoritism given producers for patriotic reasons, but seldom at the expense of quality or price.

The user or specifier considered many of the same characteristics as the printer. Printability and delivery were usually at the top of the list, but the major concern was the paper's suitability for the particular advertising message, within the constraints of the overall advertising budget.

Despite the apparent similarity of products offered by different mills, there was substantial variation in runability, which could only be determined by actual trial. According to one printer:

> The final test is how well the paper prints on our presses. This is a matter of "fit" between paper, ink and press characteristics. We find there are variations between papers that meet the same specifications, which can only be determined by actual trial. This is not cheap, as a trial involves printing 3,000 sheets. Because the paper characteristics cannot be completely specified, we like the idea of a mill brand. One time we tested two merchant brands that we thought were different. Then we found out that the paper came from the same mill, so we really wasted our time on the second test.
>
> The merchant's sales representative is important, but we don't need him to call all that frequently. We like to talk to him about trends or problems we're having, but when we need something quickly, we call the merchant.
>
> Once we have selected a paper, it is critically important that its quality be consistent. Most suppliers are pretty good. Except for obvious flaws, however, we find they tend to want to blame problems on the ink or the press.

Over the past several years, the number of printers remained relatively constant, at about 15,000–20,000, with decreases from mergers and acquisitions offset by a growth in instant print outlets. In the last 10 years, the number of commercial print customers doubled to over 500,000, half of whom used instant print outlets.

As the number of small businesses and the use of desktop publishing continued to grow, it was suggested that within ten years traditional printers would perhaps only handle longer-run full color work. Monochrome and spot color work would be produced in customers' offices, with the paper buying decision being made by people with little knowledge about paper or printing.[6] Inplant printing, however, was not expected to have a significant impact on the coated woodfree market.

PAPER MERCHANTS

Printers and publishers were reached in two principal ways: direct sales from the mill and sales from the mill through merchants, either independent or mill-owned. Direct sales were more common for high volume products sold in reels, such as newsprint and LWC magazine paper. The pattern of distribution was influenced by characteristics of the transaction (see Exhibit 4) and the pattern varied significantly from one country to another (see Exhibit 5). For coated woodfree papers it was estimated that 70–80% of sales went through merchants.

As with all wholesalers, stocking to provide quick delivery in small quantities was a principal merchant function. Fragmentation of the fastest growing market segments (business and small printers) had decreased the average order size and increased demand for a wide choice of paper grades, making it more difficult for mills to directly access these customers.

In warehousing, larger merchants had introduced expensive computer-controlled logistical systems, which reduced delivery times and the cost of preparing orders for delivery. Predictions were made that electronic interchange of information between merchants and their suppliers and larger customers would be the norm within the next few years. Merchants in the UK were

---

[6]By BIS Marketing Research Limited.

EXHIBIT 4
Transaction Characteristics: A Comparison of the Roles of Manufacturers and Merchants

Characteristics	*Manufacturer*	*Merchant*
Order size (kg)	>1,500	200–500
Items carried	Small	2,500–5,000
Fixed costs	High	Low
Stock level (kg)	>2,000/item	500–1,750
Delivery	Often slow	24 hours
Service	None	Possible
Cash flow	Low	Low

Source: The European Printing and Writing Paper Industry–1987.

spearheading an initiative to achieve industry standards for bar codes throughout Europe.

Changes in end user profiles and new customer needs had forced merchants to expand the scope of their activities and customer support functions. As a result, the merchants' role broadened to include a number of additional services, including technical advice on paper choice and broader printing problems.

Private branding, supported by advertising, had long been used by some merchants to differentiate their products and service. Some large merchants had also invested in testing apparatus, similar to that found in mills, to check conformance to specifications and to support their desire to become principals, with full responsibility for product performance.

Merchant margins varied with location, type of sale and nature of the transaction. For sales from stock, margins ranged from a low of 12% in Italy and 15% in Germany to 25% in France and Switzerland. Margins reduced to about 5%, or less, when a merchant acted as the intermediary solely for invoicing purposes.[7] (A typical income statement for a paper merchant is shown in Exhibit 6.)

Patterns of merchant ownership also varied from one country to another (see Exhibit 7). In the UK, for example, Wiggins Teape, a paper producer established in 1780, became a merchant in 1960 when existing merchants resisted introducing carbonless copy paper in the market. The company opened a network of offices to stimulate demand and provide technical support for the product. Between 1969 and 1984, the company acquired control of several major merchants operating in the UK, France, Belgium, Italy and Finland. In 1984, sales of $480 million made Wiggins Teape the largest merchant in Europe.

On the other hand, Paper Union, one of the two largest merchants in Germany (turnover of $142 million and market share of 12% in 1984), was an independent merchant. It was formed in the early 1960s, from three smaller merchants, in an attempt to reach the critical size of 100,000 tonnes per year. Due to low margins in Germany, Paper Union had emphasized reducing operating costs and consistently fast delivery. Plans were being made, however, to introduce further services and advertising in an attempt to add value and increase customer awareness.

[7]The European Printing and Writing Paper Industry–1987, IMEDE Case No. GM 375.

EXHIBIT 5
Market Shares per Distribution Channel (%)

	Country			
Form of Distribution	*UK*	*France*	*Germany*	*Italy*
Paper mills	48	50	59	80
Mill-owned merchants	52	50	—	20
Independent merchants		—	41	

Source: The European Printing and Writing Paper Industry–1987.

EXHIBIT 6
Typical Income Statement: Paper Merchant

Sales	100%
Cost of goods sold	75%
Contribution	25%
Other costs	23%
Net profit	2%
Depreciation	.5%
Cash flow	2.5%

Source: The European Printing and Writing Paper Industry-1987.

The move toward company-owned merchants was not without controversy. According to one independent merchant:

> We believe that independent merchants are very much in the best interest of paper mills. We're aware, of course, that many mills are integrating forward, buying merchants in order to maintain access to distribution. It is our view, however, that this will cause a number of problems. No one mill can supply all the products that a merchant must offer. Hence, even mill-owned merchants must maintain relations with a number of other mills, who will always want to supply their full range of products to the merchant, including those which compete with the parent mill. This will create serious tensions and frequently will put the merchant in the position of having to choose between corporate loyalty and offering the best package to the customer. The parent can, of course, impose restrictions on the merchant with respect to selling competing products, but the sales force would have serious problems with this.
>
> Our strong preference is for exclusive representation of a mill. This is particularly important where there are strong influencers, such as advertisers, to whom it is important for us to address considerable promotional effort. Also when we are an exclusive merchant, we provide the mill with extensive information on our sales, which allows the mill to do market analysis that both we and the mill find very valuable. We certainly would not provide this kind of information if the mill had intensive distribution. In a country like Switzerland, we can give the mill complete geographic and account coverage, so it's not clear to us why the mill needs more than one merchant. In our view, intensive distribution creates a situation where there is much more emphasis on price. While this first affects the merchant, it inevitably affects the mill as well.
>
> If we do sell for a mill that has intensive distribution, we prefer to sell it under our brand, although we identify the mill, in small print. This is somewhat an historical artifact, going back to the days when mills did not attempt to brand their products, but if we're going to compete for business with another merchant, selling for the same mill, we feel having our name on the product helps us differentiate ourselves from the competitor.

EXHIBIT 7
Paper Merchants: Ownership and Concentration per Country

Country	*Merchants Totaling 80% of Country Sales*	*Ownership*
Sweden	2	Mill-owned
Denmark	3	Mostly mill-owned
Netherlands	5	Mill-owned
Belgium	5	Mill-owned
Switzerland	5	Mostly mill-owned
Austria	2 (70%)	Mill-owned
France	6	Mill-owned
West Germany	7	All independent
UK	Few big and many small ones	Partly mill-owned Mostly independent

Source: Paper Merchanting, the Viewpoint of Independent Merchant.

> At the same time, we should point out that we don't sell competing brands. There are about five quality grades within standard coated woodfree, and we handle two to three brands.

One industry expert predicted significant changes in distribution patterns.[8]

> Looking to the future, it is predicted that there will be an increase in the number of paper grade classifications, moving from 4 just a few years ago to 20 or more. There will be an increasing number of different types of middlemen and distributors, and merchants will move into grades traditionally regarded as mill direct products (e.g., newsprint and mechanical grades) to bring these grades to the smaller customers.
>
> Just as we have seen a technological revolution hit the traditional printing industry, we must now see a marketing revolution hit the traditional paper industry. Selection of the correct channel of distribution and the development of an active working relationship with that channel will be vital.

COMPETITION IN COATED WOODFREE PAPERS

In varying degrees, Leykam Mürztaler encountered at least 10 major European firms in the markets it served in Europe. Some, like KNP and Zanders, competed principally in coated woodfree papers. Others, like Stora and Feldmühle, produced a wide range of products, from coated woodfree papers to tissue to newsprint.

There was considerable variation in competitive emphasis among producers. Zanders, for instance, generally regarded as the highest quality producer, mostly produced cast coated and premium art paper, competed only at the top end of the standard coated range and was relatively unusual in its extensive use of advertising. Hannover Papier was particularly strong in service, offering fast delivery. PWA Hallein, which had tended to emphasize price over quality, had recently improved its quality but was keeping prices low in an apparent effort to gain market share. Arjomari, the biggest French producer, owned the largest merchant chain in France and had recently purchased merchants in the UK and Southern Europe. It had recently entered the premium art paper segment, generally regarded as difficult to produce for. Burgo, a large Italian conglomerate, concentrated principally on the Italian market. (See Exhibit 8 for a report on the image of selected suppliers.)

Rapid growth in the coated woodfree market had stimulated capacity additions by existing producers and was also stimulating conversion of facilities from uncoated to coated. Nordland of Germany, for instance, switched 100,000 tonnes of capacity from uncoated to coated by adding a coater in October 1988. Excellent in service, there was, however, some question about its ability to produce high quality.

Branding was a relatively new aspect of the industry. All the major producers had established brand names for major products or grades. To date, however, only Zanders had actively promoted its brand to the trade or to advertisers.

MARKETING AT LEYKAM MÜRZTALER AG

Marketing activities at Leykam Mürztaler were divided between the Sales Director, Wolfgang Pfarl, and the Marketing Manager, Gertrude Eder. Pfarl, a member of the Executive Board, was responsible for pricing as well as all personal selling activities, both direct and through merchants. Eder was responsible for public relations, advertising and sales promotion, and marketing research. As a staff member, she reported to Dr. Siegfried Meysel, the Managing Director.

COATED WOODFREE PRODUCTS AND MARKETS

In coated woodfree papers, Leykam Mürztaler offered a comprehensive product line of standard coated papers under the MAGNO brand, for both sheet and web offset printing. These were produced in a wide variety of basis weights, ranging

[8]From a paper presented by BIS Marketing Research Limited.

EXHIBIT 8
Major Mill Reputation

Company	*Comments on Reputation*
Zanders (Germany)	—Mercedes-Benz in coated woodfrees —Excellent service —Strong promotion —Marketing activities have also been directed to advertising agencies, who can influence choice of brand
Leykam Mürztaler	—Reliable supplier —Good service
Arjomari (France)	—Strong positions in France due to its own merchants
Condat (France)	—Good and stable quality
Feldmühle (Germany)	—Stable quality —Rapid deliveries and good stocking arrangements
KNP (Netherlands)	—Flexible supplier, also accepts small orders —Good service
PWA Hallein (Germany)	—Competes with price
Scheufelen (Germany)	—Good and stable quality —Reliable deliveries
Stora Kopparberg (Sweden)	—Reliable deliveries —Quality and service OK

Source: EKONO Strategic Study, September 1988.

from 80–300 grams per square meter depending on the particular application. The firm targeted the high quality end of the standard coated category by offering higher coat weights, better gloss and print gloss, and better printability.

Using Austria as its home market, Leykam Mürztaler focused its principal efforts on countries in Europe. The majority of sales revenues came, in roughly similar amounts, from Austria, Italy, France and the UK, with somewhat higher sales in Germany. Belgium, Holland, Switzerland and Spain were important but smaller markets.

The firm also sold in a number of other countries, including the United States. Penetration of the US market by the European paper industry had been assisted by the favorable exchange rates during the early 1980s. The firm's policy, however, was to maintain its position in different countries despite currency fluctuations. As Gertrude Eder explained:

> We believe our customers expect us to participate in their markets on a long-term basis and to be competitive with local conditions. This may cost us some profits in the short term, as when we maintained our position in the UK despite the weak pound, but now that the pound is strong again, this investment is paying off. If we had reduced our presence when the exchange rate was unfavorable, it would have been very difficult to regain our position.

Channels of Distribution

Over the years, Leykam Mürztaler had sold most of its output through merchants. To some degree the method of distribution was influenced by the country served as the firm tended to follow the predominant trade practice in each country. In Switzerland, Germany and the UK, all its business was done through merchants. In France, Italy and Austria, there was a mixed pattern of distribution, but with a strong merchant orientation.

Merchants were carefully selected, and the firm did business only with stocking merchants who competed on service rather than price. In some countries (e.g., Holland) it used exclusive distribution, but this was not the normal pattern. Gertrude Eder explained:

> As a large producer, we have a volume problem. In the larger countries, one merchant simply can't sell enough product for us, plus we believe it is risky to commit completely to one merchant.

Similarly, Wolfgang Pfarl commented:

> In Germany, for instance, we could go to one merchant only, but to get the volume of business we need would require going into direct business with some non-stocking merchants, and that is something that neither we nor our stocking merchants want to happen.

To date, the trend toward mill ownership of merchants had not adversely affected the firm's ability to get good merchant representation. There was some concern, however, that with changing patterns of mill ownership, some merchants might be closed off to firms like Leykam Mürztaler in the future.

Service was also seen as a key to merchant relations. In this connection, the firm felt its computerized order system and new finishing facilities at the Gratkorn mill, highly automated, permitting flexibility in sheeting and packaging, and able to handle the total output of the new paper machine, provided great service capability and gave it a competitive advantage. As the mill superintendent put it:

> From a production standpoint, the ideal scenario is one in which we can run one grade of paper all year and ship it to customers in large reels. Reality is that meeting customer needs is critical, and I believe we have "state-of-the-art competence" in our ability to meet a tremendous variety of customer requirements efficiently.

Pricing

Pricing practices in the paper industry had a strong commodity orientation and, for coated woodfree papers, industry prices tended to serve as the basis for arriving at transaction prices. (See Exhibit 3 for information on industry prices and paper grades.) For sales to merchants, Leykam Mürztaler negotiated price lists, using the industry prices as a starting point, with final prices taking paper quality and other relevant factors into account. Price lists then remained in effect until there was a change in industry price levels. Routine orders were priced from the established price list. Large requirements, however, usually involved special negotiation.

According to one Leykam Mürztaler sales manager:

> We have some interesting discussions with our merchants about price. The customer knows we make a high quality product, so his principal interest is in getting it at the lowest possible price. In Europe there is no uniform classification of coated papers, as there is in the USA and Japan, so a standard approach is to try to get me to reclassify my product to a lower grade, and so a lower price. To some extent, though, my customer's preoccupation with price simply reflects price pressures he is experiencing from his customers. Still, it is frustrating because we believe we offer a lot more than just price and a good product. But I think we do a good job for the firm in getting the highest price possible.

Branding

In recent years, Leykam Mürztaler had followed the industry practice of branding its principal products. It did, however, supply products to certain merchants for private branding, a practice that was established when mill branding was not the norm. In 1988, some 30% of sales carried a merchant brand, largely reflecting the volume from

Germany and the UK, where private branding was customary. Recently, however, the firm had started to identify most of its products by using a typical Leykam Mürztaler packaging, even for private labels.

Brands had been promoted primarily by the sales force, in direct contact with customers, using brochures and samples and by packaging. More recently, a series of superb visual messages was commissioned, using the theme "Dimensions in Paper" to suggest ways that high quality paper combined with printing could produce more effective communication. The script accompanying the visual messages was designed to appeal to both the advertisers, with emphasis on communication, and printers, with emphasis on paper finish, touch, color, absorption, contrast and other key paper characteristics. On a limited basis, these messages had appeared in selected magazines and in brochures for customers.

There was general agreement within the firm that more emphasis needed to be placed on branding as a way to achieve product differentiation and convey the desired high quality image. There was less agreement on how much to spend promoting the brands or how to deal with merchants who were now buying Leykam Mürztaler products for sale under the merchants' labels. According to Gertrude Eder:

> Over the past few years we designed the corporate logo and corporate graphics and established blue, black and white as the colors for all corporate communication. We have worked hard to establish a consistent presentation of our corporate identity. Feedback from customers and the sales department indicates that this has helped improve our visibility and image. Nevertheless, we are currently spending considerably less than 1% of sales on advertising. Zanders, on the other hand, a firm of about our size, has been spending a lot of money on advertising for years and as a result has better visibility than we do, particularly with advertising agencies, as well as an enviable reputation for quality and service.
>
> I don't know what the right number is for us, but we will need to spend substantially more if we are to establish the kind of brand awareness and image we desire. I think that to have any significant impact would take a minimum of ASch3–4 million for classical advertising (i.e., advertising in trade publications, in various languages) and ASch8–10 million for promotions, including brochures, leaflets and trade fairs. In Western Europe we have to advertise in at least four to five languages, and sometimes more. In addition, the nature of the ads varies. In private brand countries, our ads emphasize the company name and focus on the Dimensions in Paper theme as well as the company's experience and modern production facilities. In other countries we emphasize the MAGNO brand.
>
> We are convinced that printers want to know what mill brand they are buying. Also, we believe that there is some subjectivity in selecting paper, particularly by the advertiser, and we want to convince the advertiser that his message will come across better on Leykam Mürztaler paper.

The decision on supplying Leykam Mürztaler products for private branding was even more complex. As Wolfgang Pfarl commented:

> I understand the position of the merchants who want to offer a private brand. The fact remains, however, that it is the mill that determines product characteristics and is responsible for meeting specifications. It is really a question of who is adding the value. In my view the merchant ought to emphasize those things which he controls, such as local stocks, good sales representation and service. Putting a merchant label on paper produced by Leykam Mürztaler misrepresents the value added picture. Don't get me wrong. Our firm strongly believes in merchants. In fact, we avoid direct business wherever there are strong stocking merchants. It's just that we think mills and merchants have distinct roles to play, and they should not be confused.
>
> Currently, we will still produce for a merchant's label, but we have started to insist that it also is identified as Leykam Mürztaler. The merchants aren't very happy about this, but we think it's the right thing to do.

Nevertheless, the situation with respect to existing merchants was difficult. As one of the senior sales managers said:

> We have been supplying some of our merchants with paper to be sold under a private label for a long

> time, and they have invested substantial sums of money in establishing their own brands. I completely support the company's position on this, but I don't know how we can get the practice to change. If we insist on supplying products only under our own brand, there are a lot of competitors who would, I think, be happy to step in and take over our position with some merchants. If we can't convince a merchant to switch over to our brand, we could lose a lot of business, in one or two instances as much as 6,000 tonnes. On the other hand, if we aren't uniform on this, we will not be able to really exploit the potential of developing our own brands.

In addition to questions about branding policy, it was not clear how to capitalize on increased brand preference, if indeed it were achieved. As Wolfgang Pfarl said:

> We might want to think in terms of higher prices or increased share, or some combination. Exactly what we would do could vary from market to market.

Personal Selling

Contact with merchants and with large, directly served accounts in Europe was mainly made by the company's own sales force headquartered in Vienna, by sales representatives in subsidiary companies in Germany, Italy and France, and by sales agents in other markets (e.g., the UK). Direct sales representatives numbered 20. Including clerical staff, Leykam had some 60 individuals in its sales department, most of whom had direct contact with customers.

The major activity of the sales force was making direct calls on large customers and on merchants. In addition, sales representatives made occasional calls on a merchant's customers, generally accompanied by the merchant's sales representative. Objectives usually included negotiating long-term contracts, "selling" the existing product line, new product introduction, and a review of customer requirements for products and service.

It was the firm's belief that its sales force was a major asset and that sales representatives could significantly influence relations with merchants. A major objective for all Leykam Mürztaler representatives was to do everything possible to develop close relations with assigned merchants. According to Wolfgang Pfarl:

> The average age of our sales force is between 35 and 40, and most of the individuals have spent their entire career in sales with Leykam Mürztaler. They are really committed to serve the customer, with on-time deliveries or any other aspect of our relationship, and the customer really respects their high level of service. In addition, they are good negotiators and represent Leykam effectively during contract negotiations. They do not need to be technical experts, but they make sure that our technical people provide technical information as required. Also, they monitor shipping performance, make presentations to merchants and may make joint customer calls with merchant sales representatives.

Mathias Radon, one of the Vienna based sales managers, made the following comments:

> In total we call on about 100 merchants in Europe. I work with our sales offices in Italy, France and Belgium and handle 5 merchants personally in the UK, in cooperation with our representative there. I call on the merchants two to three times a year and have extensive phone contact with our sales offices and representatives from Vienna.
>
> In general, the customer wants to talk about quantity, price and service. We have conversations about private labelling. The new merchants would like us to give them private labels, but I think they know they can't get it. On the other hand, the ones to whom we are currently providing private labels don't want to give it up. The problem varies from country to country. In France, for instance, it's not such a big problem.
>
> One of my objectives is to encourage more stock business versus indent (merchant orders for direct mill shipment to the customer). This means we have to give them better service and provide back-up stocks.
>
> Some merchants handle mill brands that compete directly with Leykam Mürztaler, but most tend to do this under a private label.
>
> From time to time we work to develop a new merchant, but generally we work on building long-

lasting relationships with existing merchants. We encourage trips by merchant personnel to the mill. I will make short presentations to merchant sales representatives when I call on the merchant, but generally they are pretty knowledgeable about paper. We've tried contests and other incentives with merchants and are still thinking about it, but I'm not sure if that's what we should do.

From a quality standpoint, I try to stress whiteness, opacity, printability/runability and consistency. Lots of customers ask for lab figures, but I don't think you can rely just on lab reports. We have trial print runs every week by an independent printer to check our consistency. I think most printers feel the same way.

We tend to have lots of small problems rather than any one large problem. Branding, for instance, pricing, friction when we appoint a new merchant and country variations with regard to ways of doing business. I think branding will be important in all countries, but how we capitalize on it may have to vary.

After Sales Service

Problems in printing could arise due to a number of circumstances. There might be variations or flaws in the paper or in the ink. Presses could develop mechanical problems. Even changes in temperature and humidity could negatively affect printing quality. Because of the complexity of the printing process, the cause of a problem was not always clear, and reaching an equitable settlement could be difficult.

When problems did arise, the printer turned to the merchant or mill for technical advice and frequently wanted financial compensation for lost production. According to Wolfgang Pfarl:

When the printer encounters a production problem, it is important for us to be able to give him technical advice and work with him to solve the problem. Sometimes the sales representative can do this. More often, we have to involve one of our technical people from the mill. All too often, however, the printer is just looking for someone to compensate him financially, and we have to be very tough or we're likely to find ourselves paying for a lot of other people's mistakes.

Future Issues

Looking to the future, the firm was focusing its attention on managing "through the business cycle." As Wolfgang Pfarl put it:

Our real challenge is to strengthen our market position in Western Europe. Most of our coated woodfree paper goes into advertising. We have seen extraordinary growth in this market in the last few years, but we have to expect there will be a significant downturn in one or two years and that advertisers will then look intensely at their costs. In many cases this means the printer will suggest a lower cost grade as a substitute for coated woodfree. Our task is to differentiate MAGNO from the generic category and position it as "a paper for all seasons," so to speak. In other words, we want our customers to think of MAGNO as the "right" paper for high quality advertising, separately from coated woodfree.

In general, this means strengthening our corporate identity, being partners of the strongest merchants and encouraging our merchants to support the MAGNO brand.

In a similar vein, Gertrude Eder commented:

This is a business where the impact of the business cycle is made worse by the tendency of merchants to overstock in good times and destock in bad times. Our objective, I think, should be to position Leykam as the last mill the merchant or printer would think of cancelling in a downturn.

CASE 8 | *Middlesex Mutual Assurance Company*

Middlesex Mutual Assurance Company (MMA) was a small 150-year-old property casualty insurer that did 95 percent of its business in Connecticut. It sold insurance strictly through the independent agency system. Currently about 25 percent of the agents in Connecticut represented MMA. MMA's forte was homeowners' insurance; it was the market leader in this line of insurance with approximately 10 percent of the market.

The key success factor for MMA had been excellent rapport with its independent agency force: agents enjoyed personalized service from company personnel who knew the Connecticut market quite well. MMA's main weakness was that it essentially offered only homeowners' insurance; it did not participate in any life or health insurance. However, these markets were of crucial importance to independent agents.

Recently, the coverage line for homeowners' insurance had been aggressively sought after by other insurance companies, and MMA was not confident that it could maintain market leadership in this line. Competition was becoming intense from sectors within and outside the independent agency system.

In the fall of 1985, Mr. Roger Smith, executive vice president of marketing at MMA, wondered what changes (if any) MMA could make in its distribution system to help ensure continued market leadership in the homeowners' insurance line.

INDUSTRY BACKGROUND

Financial

Property casualty insurance has characteristically been a good, healthy business to be in. Premium growth has been improving steadily since the 1950s, as shown in Exhibit 1.

The industry has been very profitable for most participants, particularly during the 1978–82 period. The average ROE for the property casualty insurance industry during this period was 18.5 percent versus 14 percent for Standard and Poor's Top 500. The tremendous profitability in the industry for this time period can be explained as follows. Operations for 1975 and 1976 produced an underwriting loss; that is, companies paid out more in claims and operating expenses than they received in premium dollars. Because of this underwriting loss, companies sought and received large rate increases, which greatly increased premium income. At about the same time, interest rates on investable funds rose dramatically as a result of the general economic conditions that prevailed at the time. Thus, insurers not only received a large increase in premiums but were able to earn very attractive rates of return on the premiums they collected. Insurers could earn investment dollars on premiums until the premiums were actually paid out in claims. Often claims were not paid until many years after premiums had been paid. This was particularly true in commercial lines where claims were not realized for many years (consider products liability where faulty parts cause an airplane to crash five years after they have been installed).

Naturally, the increase in premium levels and windfall investment income greatly increased insurers' profits. Increased profits led to increased capacity in the industry for two reasons:

1. Insurers, who were making high profits, wanted to provide more insurance coverage.
2. High profits attracted new entrants into the business.

This case was prepared as a basis for class discussion rather than to illustrate either effective or ineffective handling of an administrative situation.

EXHIBIT 1
Middlesex Mutual Assurance Company
Property Casualty Insurance Premium Growth, 1967 to 1983

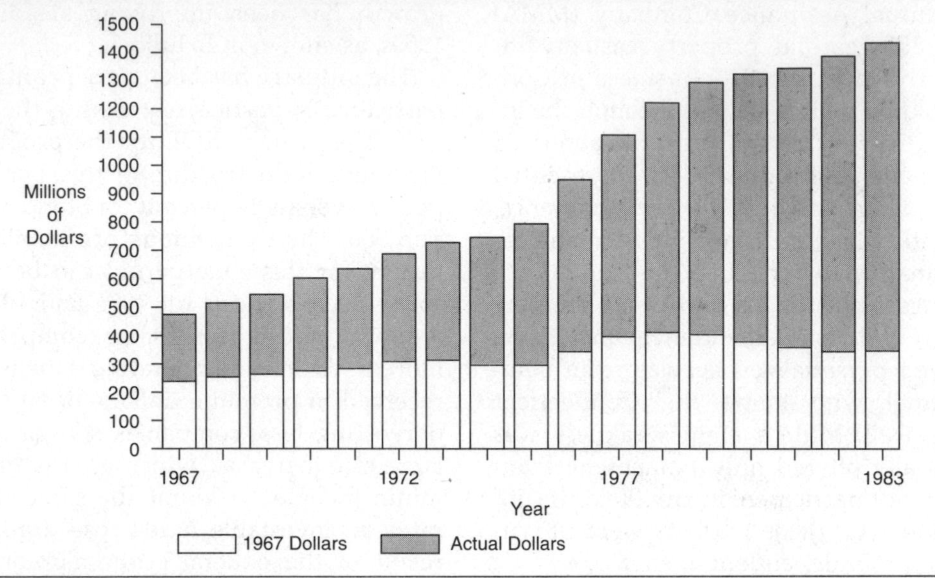

Source: Best's Aggregates and Averages.

Adequate insuring capacity to support society's needs was surpassed by an overcapacity, a "glut," in effect, of available insurance, as shown in Exhibit 2.

At first, companies could sustain an underwriting loss but still make a profit because of investment income on premium dollars. However, price cutting continued to a point where investment income could no longer offset huge underwriting losses and companies began to lose money. Worse, interest rates began to decline rapidly with the improving overall economy. By early 1985, many insurers were on the verge of becoming financially insolvent. In order to remain solvent, many insurers began to raise premium rates; others were forced to cancel many policies or provide more restrictive coverage.

In general, the commercial lines market was most subject to the volatility described above—commercial lines risks generated larger premiums and more investment income. Personal lines pricing, profitability, and availability were much more stable during this time.

DISTRIBUTION

The insurance industry employed two basic means of distribution: independent agents and direct writers. Independent agency companies essentially acted as wholesalers—their insurance was marketed by agents who represented their companies as well as competitors. Direct writers, on the other hand, employed their own sales forces, or marketed their products through print or television media. (Note: insurance for very large corporations is typically supplied by brokers who operate in much the same way as independent agents except that, unlike an agent, a broker represents the client rather than the insurer.)

Agency companies have been in business since before the turn of the century, whereas most direct writers gained prominence after World War

EXHIBIT 2
Middlesex Mutual Assurance Company
Growth in Policyholders Surplus, 1967 to 1983

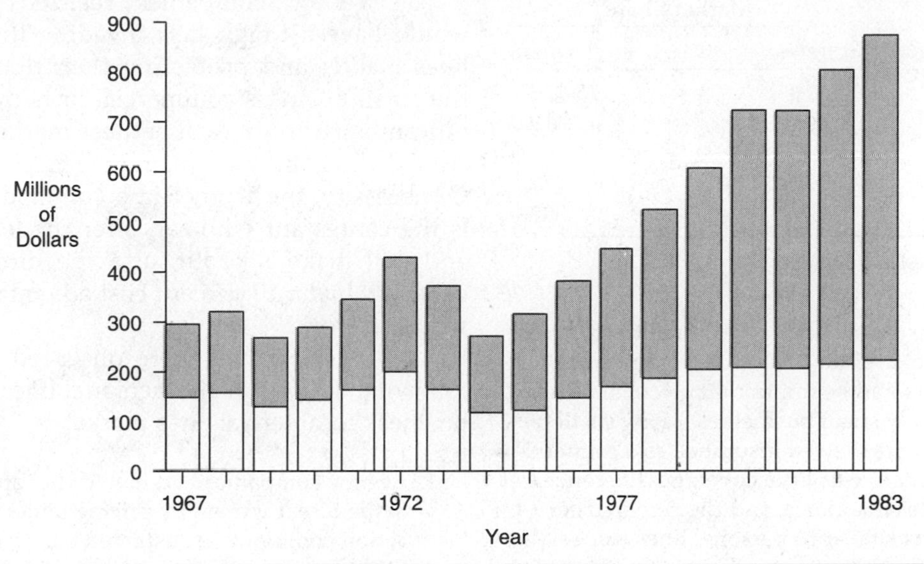

Source: Best's Aggregates and Averages.

II. In their traditional roles, agents, who were thought of as professionals similar to lawyers or accountants, would tailor a program of insurance to the needs of their clients. Direct writers approached insurance as more of a commodity; personal service was sacrificed for low price. Direct writing lent itself well to the personal lines business (i.e., auto and homeowners' insurance) because personal lines coverages are less complex and the personal lines customer generally does not require the degree of service that a commercial customer requires. During the past 20 years, agents tended toward commercial lines business—an area they continued to dominate. Direct writers had advanced dramatically in the personal lines. To illustrate the point, Exhibit 3 shows the direct writers' share in the homeowners' business.

Direct writers did not generally fare well in commercial lines. Their market shares remained low, and they were much less profitable in this area than agency companies. Most of their growth in commercial lines came from very small, unsophisticated accounts. However, the traditional roles of the direct writer and agency company had been somewhat changed, mainly for these reasons:

1. Agency companies were placing less emphasis on commercial lines. The chief factor was the terrible financial results they recently experienced in commercial lines. Their managements were under pressure to improve operating results, and emphasis on personal lines was the easiest way to accomplish the same. Further, as shown in Exhibit 4, the commercial lines market available to the independent agent was shrinking. On the other hand, the personal lines represented an area of potential growth.
2. Direct writers had come a long way in improving their level of service to the client. Direct writers had invested a great deal of time and effort in streamlining their operations. In some cases,

EXHIBIT 3
Middlesex Mutual Assurance Company
Market Share Trends in Homeowners' Insurance

	Market Share	
Year	*Agency*	*Direct*
1972	72%	28%
1978	59%	41%
1982	54%	46%
1983	53%	47%
1985	50%	50%

Source: Best Executive Data Service.

direct writers provided service equal to or better than the level provided by agency companies.

3. Direct writers had begun to pursue commercial lines, especially small businesses. Many small business owners viewed insurance as a commodity; indeed, there was little coverage difference in small business insurance, and the required service level was similar to personal lines (i.e., relatively low). Further, the small business was becoming highly important to the U.S. economy: over 600,000 new businesses were started each year. According to Naisbitt, author of *Megatrends*, the United States would be in an "entrepreneurial explosion" to the end of this decade. The implication was that there will be no shortage of small commercial lines prospects for some time to come. In order to preserve their dominance in the commercial lines, agency companies would have to become adept at handling small businesses that required commodity-oriented insurance.

It was generally conceded that the direct writers enjoyed a 10 percent distribution cost advantage over the agency companies. This advantage was due to the fact that the direct writers, owing to lack of a "middleman," were able to save on business distribution costs because their business systems were more streamlined. Further, they enjoyed a more efficient allocation of tasks: the producer spent time selling, while they company's wholesale function was to support the salesperson. With agency companies, the agent performed a great many activities (other than selling) that could be performed more efficiently at the company level, albeit at a less personalized level (e.g., claims handling, billing, etc.).

The agency companies realized that they would have a tough task invading the personal lines market and protecting their dominance in the small business commercial lines market. Significant portions of each of these markets demonstrated the belief that insurance is a commodity. Of necessity, the winner in a commodity market is the contestant who can offer the lowest price and still make a profit, and the direct writers generally had a 10 percent cost advantage to with which to work.

Agency companies were observed taking the following actions in the personal lines and small business commercial lines markets:

1. Agency companies had halted the rapid advance of the direct writers by pricing under costs. Such action could not be sustained indefinitely.
2. Efforts were made to improve efficiency of independent agency distribution channel by
    a. **Increasing emphasis on automation.** Many companies pursued electronic interface with their agencies; however, agents represent several companies, and they must interface with each one separately, which drastically decreases efficiency and increases agents' expenses. Lately, consulting firms have emerged, whose purpose is to standardize company/agency interface so that an agency can interface with all the companies it represents. This would substantially lower costs and enable companies to more effectively compete with direct writers. However, at the time of writing this case, the standardized system had not enjoyed widespread use.
    b. **Experimenting with alternative distribution systems.** Hartford Insurance Group began marketing auto insurance directly to the consumer; they directly solicited consumers who were members of the American Association of Retired Persons. Other companies actively pursued relationships or joint ventures with banks.
    c. **Beginning to pay agents lower commissions.** In return for accepting lower commissions,

EXHIBIT 4
Middlesex Mutual Assurance Company
Market Shares by Distribution Channel in the Commercial Lines Market

	Market Share				
Year	*Risk Retention*	*Captive*	*Brokers*	*Independent Agents*	*Direct Writers*
1975	10.2%	2.3%	26.4%	44.5%	16.6%
1977	12.1%	4.6%	21.9%	45.0%	16.1%
1980	13.9%	7.2%	23.0%	40.2%	15.7%
1990*	15.0%	11.0%	24.0%	35.0%	15.0%

Source: Best Executive Data Service.
*Data for 1990 are projections.

agents would have to perform fewer administrative and service tasks. The company would largely assume these tasks. Agents would spend more time selling rather than servicing.

d. **Dealing with fewer agents.** Economies of scale could be realized if companies could deal with fewer agencies, with each agency producing higher amounts of premium.
e. **Introducing product innovations.** Several insurers developed combination auto-homeowners' policies with broadened coverage. The slightly broadened coverage altered the commodity nature of the product. Further, an account with both auto and homeowners in one policy was less expensive to sell and service. Direct writers had yet to mimic this product. Other innovations included premium payment by credit cards.
f. **Using sophisticated marketing techniques.** Agency companies woke up and realized that consumers would not beat a path to their door to buy insurance. Companies started to mimic and improve some of the direct writers' effective promotion and pricing strategies.

As if the threat from existing direct writers wasn't enough, a significant threat was posed from new entrants, chiefly banks. Banks have intimate contact with all homeowners and automobile owners, not only because most people have checking and savings accounts, but because people utilize the bank for auto and homeowner mortgages and loans. Attitude surveys have shown that the average consumer places more credibility in a banker's advice than in an insurance agent's advice. Banks would possess an enormous competitive advantage because they see a large audience of insurance prospects on a daily basis. Further, as Exhibit 5 shows, the public as a whole would be predisposed to buy insurance from a banker if the purchase of insurance would enhance the likelihood of obtaining a loan.

Further trends affecting the industry were (a) the public's perception that it understood more about insurance than previously and (b) the increased level of information available to consumers.

According to the *Public Attitude Monitor,* people are more aware of what insurance is and does (see Exhibit 6). More-informed people might rely less on the advice of an agent, and be attracted to commoditylike pricing.

In regard to level of information, the day is not far off when people will have access to insurance pricing over personal computers at home.

To the extent that people are familiar with insurance and view it as a commodity, pricing will play a more important role in where insurance is purchased.

MMA PERSPECTIVES

MMA had been extremely profitable, although industry performance as a whole had deteriorated

EXHIBIT 5
Middlesex Mutual Assurance Company
Public Perceptions Regarding Relationships between Financial Transactions by Banks and Insurance Companies

	All Respondents						
Situation	*Strongly Agree*	*Agree*	*Probably Agree*	*Probably Disagree*	*Disagree*	*Strongly Disagree*	*No Answer*
If banks sold auto insurance people would be expected to buy auto insurance there in order to get an auto loan.	6%	25%	24%	14%	23%	6%	1%
If auto insurance companies owned banks people would be expected to finance cars there in order to get or keep auto insurance coverage.	5	28	26	15	20	5	1
If banks sold home insurance people would be expected to buy homeowners' insurance there in order to get a mortgage loan.	5	26	27	16	20	5	1
If home insurance companies offered mortgage loans people would be expected to get mortgages there in order to get a homeowner's policy.	5	24	29	16	20	5	1
Number = 1.516							

Source: Public Attitude Monitor, December, 1984.

markedly during the last few years. The homeowners' insurance business (MMA's forte) had been much more stable than commercial lines. Further, MMA had been operating in an unusually favorable competitive environment for these reasons:

1. Direct writers were not as strong in Connecticut (the main geographic area in which MMA operated) as they were on a countrywide basis (see Exhibit 7).

   Clearly, MMA's homeowners' insurance business had yet to be subjected to the degree of direct writer erosion exhibited in other areas of the country.
2. Despite the agency companies' dominance in the Connecticut personal lines market, most of their marketing thrust was directed toward commercial lines. Agency companies were not particularly aggressive in personal lines; they had really been asleep in regard to personal lines and were merely resting on their laurels.

Due to the relative weakness of direct writers in Connecticut and apathy on the part of agency companies, MMA had thrived and had become market leader in the homeowners' insurance business, with a 10 percent market share. However, the favorable competitive environment enjoyed by MMA would deteriorate for the following reasons:

1. **Increased competition**—In addition to the growing threat posed by direct writers and new en-

EXHIBIT 6
Middlesex Mutual Assurance Company
Percentage of Men and Women Saying They Consider Themselves Well Informed about Auto Insurance

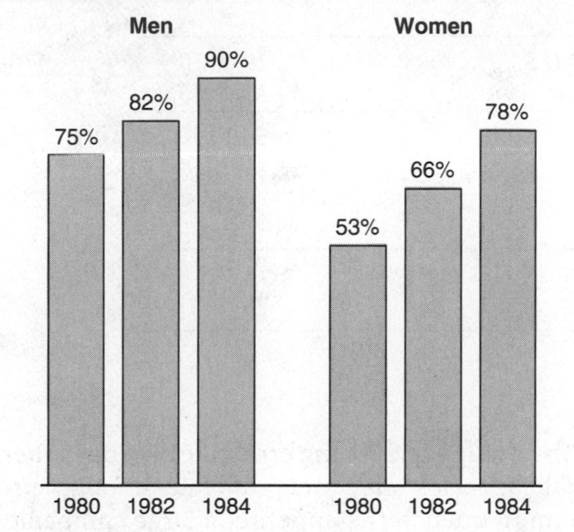

Source: Public Attitude Monitor, March 1985.

trants, agency companies would begin to emphasize personal lines coverage instead of commercial lines coverages. Agency companies were awakened from their slumber and were using sophisticated and aggressive marketing techniques to obtain homeowners' insurance. Profitability in the homeowners' insurance line was expected to deteriorate rapidly as competition intensified.

Of special concern to MMA was the degree of leverage that the large agency companies had over MMA agents (keep in mind that agents are independent and represent several companies). Large companies usually offer a full line of insurance services to their agents: personal lines (including personal auto), commercial lines, life and health insurance, and financial planning services. In order for an independent agent to survive, they needed to have all of these services available to their clients. Large agency companies realized how important they were to the agent, and they also realized that their agents were giving much homeowners' insurance business to MMA. Homeowners' insurance was now recognized as a profitable line, and companies became upset when agents were placing homeowners' insurance with MMA, only to place the less desirable lines of business with them. Many companies offered MMA agents lucrative deals for books of MMA homeowners' insurance business. Others threatened to terminate their relationship with MMA agents unless the companies targeted their agents who were also MMA agents with promotional policyholders (many of whom presumably had homeowners' insurance with MMA) indicating they would receive a 10 percent discount on both the auto and homeowners' policies if they would place both coverages with their company.

The "strong-arm tactics" referred to above were usually resisted by independent agents because they wished to retain their independence as to what company they placed their clients with. True to their name, most agents were highly independent in nature, and did not take kindly to insurance companies dictating business practice to them. However, agents were under a great deal of competitive pressure, and many had no choice but to submit to the demands of large full-service companies.

2. **Consumer trends**—There was increasing evidence that personal lines coverages were becoming viewed as more and more of a commodity, especially among the middle and lower socioeconomic classes. These people could be expected to seek out the lowest available price. As mentioned earlier, those persons wanting low price would be aided in the future by increasing access to information, probably by way of computer terminals.
3. **Distribution**—MMA did business exclusively through independent agents. The viability of the agency system, especially in personal lines, was being severely challenged by direct writers and new entrants. As previously mentioned, many companies weren't tying themselves directly to the fate of the independent agency system; many were beginning to develop alternative distribution mechanisms.

MMA corporate culture strongly opposed any experimentation with an alternative distribution

EXHIBIT 7
Middlesex Mutual Assurance Company
Competitive Position of Agency Companies versus Direct Writers

Personal Auto Insurance	*1983 U.S. Market Share*	*1983 CT Market Share*
Agency companies	38.2%	58.0%
Direct writers	61.8%	42.0%
Homeowners Insurance		
Agency companies	53.7%	74.3%
Direct writers	46.3%	25.7%

Source: A.M. Best Company, A7 reports, 1984.

system. The reasoning was simple. MMA was not a full-service company: it essentially offered only homeowners' insurance. MMA was viewed by agents as a nice company to represent but most often wasn't perceived as a bread-and-butter company. Other companies would be very happy to write an agent's homeowners' insurance book of business, albeit at a slightly lower service level. Because MMA was not an essential company to represent, agents could cease doing business with MMA without jeopardizing the viability of their own operations. Further, one of MMA's key success factors was its excellent rapport with agents. To damage this rapport was viewed as a serious mistake.

As previously mentioned, larger companies were actively reducing the number of agents through which they wrote business and were demanding that their remaining agents place higher amounts of premium with them. MMA executives believed that large companies, with their large overheads, could not economically service the small agent. MMA, on the other hand, had a strong local presence in Connecticut and could economically service smaller agents that larger companies could not. Industry data indicated that there were plenty of small agents in existence, with new agencies being created every day. These small agencies may not generate enough premium to quench the appetite of large companies, but MMA believed that enough small agents would survive and prosper to warrant consideration as a viable target market for MMA.

In short, Mr. Smith realized that the distribution of homeowners' insurance would change rapidly, and this was of great concern to him. After much deliberation, he felt that MMA should consider the following alternative courses of action:

1. Do nothing; just continue to sell homeowners' insurance through independent agents.
2. Continue selling just homeowners' insurance through agents but streamline the distribution system by using automation and more efficient allocation of tasks between company and agency.
3. Become a more important market to the agents by adding automobile insurance coverage. Otherwise, business as usual.
4. Become a more important market to the agent by adding automobile insurance, while adding the efficiency measures mentioned in step 2.
5. Develop direct writing capabilities that would bypass the agent.

EXHIBIT 8
Middlesex Mutual Assurance Company
Evaluation of Alternative Actions

Alternatives	Criteria				
	Action must benefit independent agent; alienation must be minimized or avoided	Action must complement and be compatible with MMA internal operations	Action must ensure short-term growth and viability of MMA homeowners' insurance product	Action must ensure long-term growth and viability of MMA homeowners' insurance product	Total
1 Do nothing; continue to sell just homeowners' insurance coverage through independent agents	3	2	2	0	7
2 Continue selling homeowners' insurance coverage through independent agents but streamline distribution process by use of automation and more efficient allocation of tasks between agent and company	2	2	3	2	12
3 Become a more important market to the agent by offering personal auto insurance; otherwise, business as usual	4	3	3	2	12
4 Become a more important market to the agent by offering personal auto insurance; also increase efficiency by taking actions outlined in alternative (2)	4	3	3	4	14
5 Develop direct writing capabilities that bypass the agents	0	2	0	3	5

Values
0—Very negative effect 1—Somewhat negative effect 2—Neutral effect 3—Somewhat beneficial effect 4—Very beneficial effect

Source: Company records.
MMA executives selected alternative 4; it had the highest score of 14.

Mr. Smith decided on the following criteria to evaluate potential alternative actions:

1. Action must be of benefit to independent agent; agent alienation must be avoided.
2. Action must be within reasonable current capabilities of MMA.
3. Action must ensure short-term growth and viability of MMA in the homeowners' insurance market.
4. Action must ensure long-term growth and viability of MMA in the homeowners' insurance market.

The alternative courses of action and the criteria by which they were evaluated are summarized in a decision matrix in Exhibit 8.

CASE 9 | *The North Face*

The North Face was a privately owned company which designed, manufactured, and sold high-quality outdoor equipment and clothing. It began as a specialty mountain shop in San Francisco in 1966 and started manufacturing in Berkeley in 1968. Since that time, the company had emphasized quality backpacking and mountaineering equipment featuring state-of-the-art design and functional detail. The North Face soon dominated this market and became the market leader in three of the four product categories it manufactured—tents, sleeping bags, backpacks and clothing. Sales in 1980 were in excess of $20 million (see Exhibits 1 and 2 for historical financial statements). All items were produced domestically at the company's manufacturing facility in Berkeley. In the early 1980s The North Face operated five well-located retail stores and two factory outlets in the San Francisco Bay area and Seattle. In addition, it employed fourteen independent sales representatives who covered ten sales territories in the U.S. Its dealer structure consisted of about 700 specialty shops throughout the U.S. as well as representation in 20 foreign countries.

The company's desire for continued growth in the face of a maturing backpacking market prompted Hap Klopp, President of The North Face and the driving force behind its success to date, to investigate expansion into new products related to the current backpacking business. One avenue of growth which appeared to have significant potential was that of Alpine (downhill) ski clothing. This opportunity was pursued, with the result that The North Face skiwear line was being readied for formal introduction in Fall 1981.

The uppermost question in management minds at this point was What was the most effective way to distribute the new skiwear line?

EARLY HISTORY

Hap Klopp, 39-year-old President of The North Face and a graduate of the Stanford MBA program, purchased the original company in 1968, following a brief period as manager of another backpacking retail outlet in the San Francisco Bay area. At that time the operation consisted of three retail stores and a small mail-order business. The

---

This case was prepared by Gary Mezzatesta and Valorie Cook, Stanford Graduate School of Business, under the supervision of Professor Robert T. Davis.

EXHIBIT 1
Profit and Loss Comparisons (in 000's)

	1977	1978	1979	1980
Sales				
Manufacturing	$11,437	$13,273	$15,153	$17,827
Retail	2,254	2,570	2,879	3,368
Total	$13,691	$15,843	$18,032	$21,195
Cost of sales	9,337	11,188	12,443	13,964
Gross margin	4,354	4,655	5,589	7,231
Selling and operating expense	2,186	2,320	2,646	3,306
Contributing to overhead	2,168	2,335	2,943	3,925
Corporate G&A expense	686	685	777	924
Interest expense	242	268	438	658
Incentive compensation and ESOP	235	204	253	330
Total	$1,163	$1,157	$1,468	$1,912
Total pre-tax profits	$1,005	$1,178	$1,475	$2,013
Total after-tax profits	$498	$609	$776	$1,019

firm sold a line of private-label backpacking and brand-name downhill ski equipment. Klopp closed two stores, brought in equity, and opened a small manufacturing facility for the production of down-filled sleeping bags in the back of the main store in Berkeley, California. Sales in 1969 were just under $500,000.

Prior to 1971, most of the retail sales were in Alpine (downhill) ski equipment, where competition had depressed the margins. To gain relief, management decided to concentrate on the backpacking and ski-touring (cross-country) markets, where margins were higher and such adverse influences as seasonality, fashion cycles, and weather conditions were less damaging.

THE NORTH FACE PRODUCTS

The North Face manufactured four key lines for the backpacking market: sleeping bags, packs, outdoor clothing, and tents. All products stressed quality, design, and durability and were priced for the high-end of the market. All products carried a full lifetime warranty.

Sleeping Bags

North Face sleeping bags ranged from "expeditionary" models (designed to provide protection to −40° F) to bags offering various combinations of lightness and warmth (aimed at satisfying the needs of the vacationing, leisure-oriented backpacker). The North Face bags were considered superior to competitive products in construction and durability and offered the optimal trade-off between warmth and weight. As the company grew, TNF expanded the variety of sleeping bags offered to meet virtually every environmental condition that a backpacker could expect in the U.S. The quality of down used, the nylon fabric thread count, the unique coil zippers, and the stitching were key points of differentiation. Goose down bags retailed from $162 to $400, with the price escalating as the warmth of the bag

EXHIBIT 2
Comparative Balance Sheets (Year Ended September 30—in 000's)

	1977	*1978*	*1979*	*1980*
Assets				
Current				
Cash	$110	$149	$201	$370
Accounts receivable	2,765	3,765	3,910	4,573
Inventories	4,496	4,494	4,452	5,947
Other	319	329	229	196
Long term	803	1,012	1,256	1,437
Other assets	65	68	100	104
Total assets	$8,558	$9,817	$10,148	$12,627
Liabilities				
Current				
Notes payable to bank	$2,624	$3,180	$ 2,563	$ 2,613
Accounts payable	2,019	2,186	2,109	2,231
Accrued liabilities	693	589	627	783
Income taxes payable	318	339	360	568
Current portion LT debt	141	159	222	316
Other				
Long term debt	351	302	360	1,103
Deferred income taxes	33	73	143	230
Stockholders' Equity				
Common stock—A	1,687	1,687	1,687	1,687
Common stock—B	0	2	2	2
Retained earnings	692	1,300	2,075	3,094
Total liabilities	$8,558	$9,817	$10,148	$12,627

increased. Initially, the bags were only down-filled, but in recent years, a complete line of synthetic-filled models were introduced. Synthetic fills were preferred by some for damp weather environments and where weight and compressibility were of lesser importance. Synthetic bags ranged in retail price from $75 to $205—also at the top end of the competitive market.

From the start, the company had manufactured only two sizes of sleeping bags instead of the usual three found in the industry. This policy not only simplified production but also reduced retailers' stocking needs and retail stock outs. When TNF began, sleeping bags had been the fastest-growing segment of the backpacking industry, but this growth had begun to slow during the early '70s.

Parkas and Other Outdoor Clothing

Parkas and functional outerwear were the growth leaders for The North Face in 1981. Their line included a range of parkas designed to appeal to the serious backpacker. Design stressed maximum comfort over a wide temperature range and contained convenient adjustments for ventilation control. Other features, such as pocket design, snap-closed flaps over zippers, and large overstuffed collars, further enhanced the line. As the industry grew and fashion became more of an element, a much wider range of colors and surface fabrics were incorporated into the line. Materials such as Gore-Tex (a breathable yet waterproof material) had been introduced which offered a functional advantage over existing products on the market. Two types of parkas were offered: those which afforded primary protection from cold, damp conditions (generally of synthetic material); and those which were intended to withstand cold, dry conditions (primarily of down). As in fabrics, a number of new, strongly promoted synthetics, such as Thinsulate, Polarguard, and Hollofill, had been incorporated into the line to meet expanding consumer base and desires. Parkas varied in price from approximately $50 for a synthetic-filled multipurpose vest to $265 for a deluxe expeditionary model. The company was in the process of trying to sell a system of clothing called "Layering," which utilized multiple layers of clothing confined in a variety of ways to meet climatic conditions.

Tents

In 1981, The North Face had revolutionized the world market for lightweight backpacking tents with its geodesic designs. With assistance from well-known design engineer R. Buckminster Fuller, the company's employees had created and patented geodesic tents. These tents provided the greatest volume of internal space with the least material and the highest strength-to-weight ratio of any tent design. They also had more headroom, better use of floor space, and better weather shedding. Because geodesics were freestanding, they also required less anchoring to the earth. Competitors throughout the world were beginning to copy the products; but to date, the company had not legally pursued its patent protection. Other special tent features included reinforced seams and polymer-coated waterproof fabric that management believed provided three times the tear strength and superior performance at subfreezing temperatures. The company had helped develop unique tent poles that were available nowhere else in the world. The North Face still carried two A-frame tents for the purpose of price and continuity of line at $200 and $240 price points, while the geodesic line had eight tents ranging from $220 to $600. As with the other North Face products, these were at the high end of the price spectrum; but management was convinced that consumers were getting very good value for their money.

The market for tents had accelerated recently with the introduction of the geodesics, which met new customers' needs better than did A-frame tents. Management felt that two to four years of rapid growth in geodesic tent sales would continue while A-frames were becoming obsolete, and then the market would return to its former modest levels of growth.

Backpacks

The North Face divided the pack market into three segments:

- Soft packs/day packs
- Internal frame packs
- External frame packs

The North Face introduced the first domestically made internal frame pack, which created a market niche and produced extremely good sales for the company. Retail price ranges from $45 to $115 were at the high end of the scale, but management was sure that the quality details (including extra-strength nylon, bartack stitching, extra loops and straps, high-strength aluminum, etc.) made these good values for the money.

In the soft-pack area, there were fewer features to distinguish the company's products from its competitors'. Price competition—with competitors' prices from $16 to $37—was much more noticeable.

In the external frame market, historically dominated by Kelty, the company had introduced a remarkably different patented product called the Back Magic. It was an articulated pack with independent shoulder and hip suspension which placed the weight of the pack closer to the backpacker's center of gravity than other packs had done. Although offering an expensive product ($150 to $160) and encountering some bothersome contractor delays, the company was significantly increasing its market share in this category.

Additionally, to expand this category of the company's sales and to open up a whole new market for its dealers, The North Face introduced a complete line of soft luggage in 1981. The company was attempting to capitalize upon the peripatetic nature of its customers and its belief that customers wanted the much higher quality traditionally found in luggage shops. Features such as binding in all seams, leather handles on nylon webbing, shoulder straps with leather handles, and numerous zippered internal pockets were incorporated. Prices ranged from $40 to $65.

MARKETING PHILOSOPHY

The North Face promoted more than just a product, it fostered a way of life. Throughout the ranks of management one found a cadre of outdoor enthusiasts.

It is important to note how Hap Klopp viewed his company's business:

> [The North Face] may be selling bags, tents, packs, boots, or parkas, but I suggest that people are buying better health, social contact, sunshine, adventure, self-confidence, youth, exercise, romance, a change of pace, or a chance to blow off steam and escape from the urban degeneration of pollution, economic collapse, and congestion.

One central theme served as the foundation for The North Face's corporate strategy. It was best summarized by Hap Klopp: "Make the best product possible, price it at the level needed to earn a fair return, and guarantee it forever." Hap contended that profits were not made from the first sale to a customer. After all, it took considerable effort and money to attract that purchase in the first place. Rather, the customer had to be treated well once he had been attracted. Repeat sales were the key to this business's profitability. Hence, there was the need to provide a product that would always satisfy.

A key conceptual tool that North Face used to analyze the backpacking market and similar specialty markets is what Klopp called "the pyramid of influence":

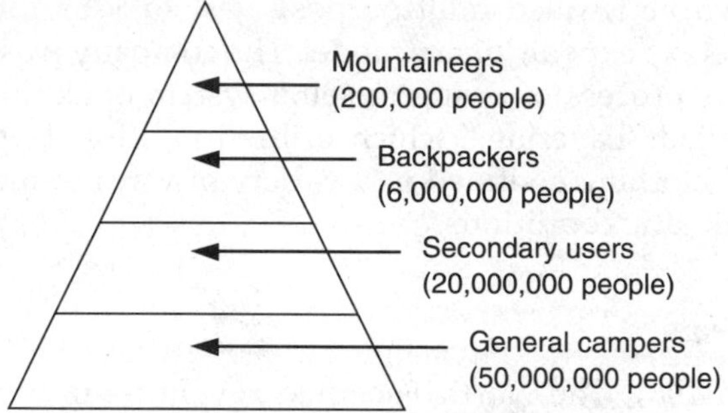

Within this hierarchy, management believed that word-of-mouth communication flowed down a chain of expertise from the mountaineer, to the backpacker, to the secondary user, and finally to the general camping public. Those at the high end of the chain, the "technocrats," tended to influence the buying decisions of the average outdoorsman who relied upon recommendations and brand image rather than his own research. The North Face characterized the market pyramid as follows:

Segment	*Use*	*Price*	*Preferred Product Characteristics*
Mountaineer	Frequent, hard	No object	Durable, functional, perfect workmanship
Backpacker	Frequent, careful	Value conscious	Lightweight, repairable, comfortable, brand more important
Secondary user	Inconsistent, careful	Value conscious	Durable, multipurpose, comfortable, brand name
General camper	Inconsistent, careless	Price sensitive	Simple, sturdy, multipurpose, brand name

The company believed that a number of its competitors had made serious marketing blunders in changing their distribution and products to meet the needs of the larger, lower strata, thereby ignoring the pattern of influence of the pyramid and the foundation of the business. This led to the erosion of their name and franchise in all of the strata. In contrast, The North Face's long-term strategy was to maintain an orientation toward the top of the pyramid and quietly broaden the line so that its existing dealers would be able to meet the needs of both the peak of the pyramid and the emerging customers.

The North Face adamantly declared that the pattern of influence in specialty markets only worked one way—downward. By designing and selling high-quality functional items focused at the top of the pyramid, a firm could systematically build a strong market image hinging on credibility. Klopp discounted the integrity and wisdom of the switch from a "top down" to a "bottom up" strategy. Many companies shortsightedly looked at the financials associated with each segment and changed their distribution network and products to meet the larger, lower strata. This process, he claimed, eventually led to failure, since ignoring the foundations of the business eventually caused a "franchise erosion" at all levels of the pyramid. In short, lowering the quality of product and service to maintain sales growth was a no-win game which would inevitably lead to erosion of market and image and to the advancement of someone who was at the top of the cone. If a company wanted to maintain its commitment to a market and customer group for the long term, it had to stick to the "top down" approach.

Because of its strict adherence to this philosophy, The North Face approached the marketplace with the following strategy: enter specialty markets; nurture them carefully; focus R&D at the top of the pyramid; use specialty shops to skim the market; target promo efforts for trendsetters. Once a dominant position in a market was established growth was sought via two paths:

1. finding new geographical or new use markets
2. introducing new quality products

The company led the backpacking industry with the following market shares (estimated from available data) in 1980:

	Market Share	*Industry Ranking*
Outerwear/clothing	47%	1
Sleeping bags	48%	1
Tents	28%	1
Packs	20%	3

The North Face accounted for 21.9% of the sales of backpacking products to specialty stores in 1980, while its closest competitor achieved a 13.5% market share. In summary, the company's distinctive competence, which distinguished it from its competition, was the manufacture of high-quality functional products of classic design, which sold at a premium price and carried a lifetime warranty. The key success factors were thought to be the company's reputation as a specialty supplier of quality products, its strong relationship with its distribution network, and its high-caliber management team. The North Face was generally recognized as having the best management team in the industry, due to its depth of industry knowledge and length of time in the business.

While the backpacking industry had enjoyed substantial growth over the past decade, from total U.S. industry specialty store sales of $15,400,000 in 1971 to $81,700,000 in 1980, the backpacking market appeared to be maturing, with total sales forecasted to grow to $95,100,000 by 1985. (See Exhibit 3 for historical and projected market size.) Klopp believed that the industry was out of the high-growth stage of the product life cycle, heading toward the maturity stages; the increasing difficulty the company reported in achieving product differentiation seemed to validate this observation.

Channels of Distribution

The North Face's reliance on the "pyramid of influence" also dictated its handling of distribution

EXHIBIT 3
U.S. Industry Specialty Store Sales* of Backpacking Products (Wholesale Prices in 000's)

	Total Sales
1971	$15,400
1972	$21,600
1973	$27,400
1974	$40,700
1975	$44,800
1976	$57,050
1977	$65,850
1978	$70,400
1979	$77,500
1980	$81,700
1981 (est.)	$84,300
1982 (est.)	$86,900
1983 (est.)	$90,100
1984 (est.)	$92,400
1985 (est.)	$95,100

*Domestic only.

channels. Since they were in specialized markets, The North Face preferred to build its brand name carefully by using specialty stores as a foundation. Once this foundation was established, The North Face attempted to nurture it carefully by providing the dealers with new products and techniques (via training classes) to attract new customers. The company only used the more general sporting goods stores (e.g., Herman's, EMS) when it needed geographic coverage in a particular area, and even then tried to limit distribution to certain outlets of the chain. The firm avoided mass merchandising stores as much as possible. TNF felt that specialty shops developed brand awareness and consumer franchise for their products, while the general shops exploited their brand name. Thus, it relied heavily upon the prosperity of these specialty outlets. Careful control of the channels lay at the cornerstone of The North Face's marketing strategy.

Wholesaling. Backpacking industry sales were distributed among retail stores in the following proportions:

	Dollar Value	*Number of Outlets*
Backpacking specialty stores	50%	40%
Sports specialty stores	25%	30%
General sporting goods stores	10%	5%
Ski shops, department stores, etc.	15%	25%

Sales were fairly evenly distributed among the Pacific, North Central, and Northeast regions of the U.S., with lesser proportions falling in the Mountain and Southern states.

The North Face sold primarily to approximately 700 retail stores, 75% of which specialize in backpacking and mountaineering equipment and the rest in general sporting goods. Wholesale distribution by The North Face was handled by fourteen independent sales representatives who carried hiking, mountaineering and cross-country skiing lines. These representatives covered ten sales territories in the U.S. and were paid on commission. The North Face products were their major source of income. Management felt that this network was especially valuable as a conduit for information about market conditions, product knowledge, retail management programs, and competition. It was estimated that 55–60% of all consumer purchases resulted from word-of-mouth endorsement from a satisfied friend or from a sales presentation in the store. Thus, the primary marketing thrust of The North Face was to

1. Sell dealers on the company's products and markets.
2. Provide information and point-of-sale aids to help floor salespeople.

The representatives were crucial to this effort and all were carefully chosen by the Sales and Marketing Vice-President and co-founder, Jack Gilbert. As a group, the reps had an average of seven to eight years' experience in the industry, were avid backpackers and lovers of the outdoors, and had been with The North Face since its inception. The reps were highly successful and had been well treated by the company through the years. Over that time, the nature of their responsibilities had evolved from pioneering or prospecting for new accounts to training existing accounts in industry and management techniques, having established The North Face as the authority in the backpacking field.

The company long pursued a policy of building stable, ongoing relationships with carefully selected dealers. It followed a limited distribution policy, seeking to maintain a balance of dealers and market demand in any geographic area. The company individually reviewed and approved all potential dealer locations, including new locations of existing accounts, and was committed to maintaining and strengthening its dealers. In seeking new product areas in which to expand, it was considered important for The North Face to evaluate the potential of its current dealers to sell the products under consideration.

Retailing. The North Face's retailing objective was to use its own retail stores to attain its desired market share and profit objectives only where wholesaling was unable to achieve satisfactory market penetration and where the policy had no adverse impact on wholesale distribution. To meet this objective, the strategy was to expand existing outlets and introduce new outlets in an orderly fashion, locating only where conflict with the wholesale division was minimized. This strategy was reinforced in the following policy statement:

> The Retail Division will continue to examine expansion possibilities on a local basis. The Retail Division will not expand into any domestic geographic area which will have a significant adverse effect on the wholesale sales of The North Face. The focus of expansion efforts will only be around those areas where The North Face presently has established stores.

The North Face currently owned and operated five well-located retail stores and two factory outlets in the San Francisco Bay area and Seattle. In 1980, the mail-order operation was closed down due both to its lack of profitability and its perceived conflict with the wholesaling operations. In recent years, the Retail Division had enjoyed considerable increases in sales and profits, significantly above the industry average:

	Company Stores (in 000's)			
	1977	*1978*	*1979*	*1980*
Sales	$2,189	$2,574	$2,884	$3,368
Gross margins	N/A	974	1,156	1,446
Profits/contribution	N/A	104	220	364
Inventory turns	1.6X	1.7X	2.1X	2.1X
Transfers to stores*	$918	$908	$770	$1,120

*Sales from company wholesale to company retail.

It should be noted that the "transfer" figures represent sales from company wholesale to company retail. Management felt that not all of these sales would have gone to independents if the company stores did not exist. This is important to consider in looking at The North Face's total profitability. The significance of these figures was underscored by the comparison that the average North Face store bought $200,000 from wholesaling, while the average wholesale account bought slightly over $30,000 annually. Additionally, the Retail Division test marketed some promotional programs and products and, through its factory outlets, took nearly $500,000 of seconds—which otherwise would have created image problems if sold through wholesale channels—as well as products which were made out of overstocked materials supplies. While the exact impact on corporate profit of these activities was hard, if not impossible, to calculate, it was thought to be considerable.

Conflict between Retailing and Wholesaling. A continual conflict existed between retail and wholesale because of the feeling that retail might expand into an area which was beyond its domain. In part to alleviate this problem, the Retail Division closed down its mail-order operation. The retail expansion into Seattle caused the loss of some wholesale business and was used as a lever by some competitive reps; but since The North Face did not terminate any existing dealers, the issue died. Although there were a number of good wholesale accounts left, The North Face did not sell to them because of the geographical protection it had granted its dealers. The company felt it received increased loyalty and purchases because of this protection and would lose them if its accounts were increased randomly.

Differing opinions on the subject of further retail expansion existed even at the highest levels of the company. At one point, at least, Klopp felt that retail expansion was the most effective means of generating market share and promoting brand-name allegiance, while Jack Gilbert, the Sales and Marketing Vice-President, had serious reservations in three areas:

1. *The impact on the dealers*—Gilbert felt that retailers in this industry were "very paranoid" that manufacturers would expand their retail operations. Indeed, competitive reps in the industry were known to advise dealers not to "give too much of your business to The North Face because they are out there gathering information about your market area in order to expand their retail operation." He believed that a North Face retail expansion would damage the company's excellent relationship with its dealers.

2. *The profit implications*—While the going margin at retail was 40% compared to a target margin at wholesale of 30%, entry into expanded retail operations was not a profitable strategy in the short run. The initial investment for a store was $40,000 in fixtures and capital improvements, plus $100,000 of inventory at retail prices. It took three years for an individual store to make the contribution management wanted—12% contribution to overhead and 8% to pretax profits.

3. *Growth*—Finally, Gilbert was concerned about whether The North Face could meet its growth objectives by going both the wholesale and retail routes, particularly given the company's limited financial resources.

Additional concerns regarding inventory control and the development of capable store managers via a training program were voiced by John McLaughlin, Financial Vice-President for The North Face.

Outlook toward Growth

Maintaining a healthy rate of growth was also a major goal of management. The style of the company was aggressive and entrepreneurial. Hap and his management team did not want to risk frustrating the young, energetic staff they had gathered. As mentioned earlier, the backpacking industry seemed to be entering the maturity phase of the product life cycle. Over the past few years, the total market was growing only at a 5% compound annual growth rate. The North Face had grown at a faster rate than the overall market, consistently gaining market share, but it was evident that this situation could not last forever, especially given the company's reliance on the "pyramid of influence" theory.

In evaluating potential new markets, management looked for opportunities that could fulfill the following objectives:

- An overlap with current customer base
- A product compatible with current machinery capabilities
- A line that would complement seasonal production peaks
- A market in which "top down" strategy would work
- A line which matched with the interests and expertise of the existing management team
- A line that would maintain and strengthen The North Face's current dealer network
- A line that would not threaten or cannibalize the base business

TNF's decision-making style added further complexity to the situation. The firm espoused a collaborative style of strategy formation and implementation. Employee input and consensus were essential. Hap fostered this environment by utilizing a paternalistic management style. In fact, each individual felt as if he or she had influence on the direction of TNF. In the context of the approaching decision, this meant that marketing needed to receive a general approval before entering a new business.

The Skiwear Line

The company's desire for continued growth in the face of this maturation of the backpacking market spurred management to investigate expansion into new products. In looking at manufacturing and marketing growth opportunities, the company analyzed its own sales, those of its dealers, and the markets highlighted to see what opportunities were not being completely exploited. Interestingly, the company found that, although it never manufactured or marketed its products specifically for skiing, it held nearly 2% of the skiwear market; in some categories, such as down vests, it had nearly 5%. It was also discovered that over two thirds of all dealers handling The North Face products also sold skiwear. Most appealing was the fact that the market appeared to be highly fragmented. As pointed out in an industry study published in May 1980: "Most skiwear categories have one or two market leaders, but in all areas no one brand dominates the market. In fact, in all categories studied, it required between 9 and 12 brands to make up 70% of the market share in dollars."

Market Size (1980—in 000's)	
Adult down parkas/vests	$30,000
Adult non-down parkas/vests	54,000
Adult bibs and pants	21,000
Shell pants	1,600
X-country ski clothing	2,600
	$109,200

Exhibits 4 and 5 contain details on the skiwear market.

EXHIBIT 4
Skiwear* Market Sales 1979–80 (in millions)

	Dollars	Market Share
1. White Stag	$27.0	12.5%
2. Roffee	19.0	8.8%
3. Skyr	13.5	6.3%
4. Head Ski & Sportswear	13.0	6.0%
5. Aspen	12.5	5.8%
6. Gerry	12.0	5.5%
7. Swing West (Raven)	10.0	4.6%
8. Alpine Designs	9.0	4.2%
9. Obermeyer	8.0	3.7%
10. Sportscaster	7.5	3.5%
11. Beconta	7.0	3.3%
12. Bogner America	7.0	3.3%
13. C.B. Sports	6.0	2.8%
14. Serac	5.0	2.3%
15. Profile	5.0	2.3%
16. Demetre	5.0	2.3%
17. Woolrich	4.5	2.0%
18. The North Face	4.0	1.9%
19. Other	41.0	18.9%
	$216.0	100.0%

*Excluding underwear.

These factors, coupled with an increasing number of requests for uniforms "which work" (i.e., functional, durable, and warm) from ski instructors, ski patrollers and other professional users thought to influence the market, led The North Face to introduce its skiwear line. The company's strategy in skiwear was predicated on the same strategy as its backpacking business—functionally designed, classically styled clothing. The skiwear was targeted to the "professional skier" (not the racer), since management felt that a Trendsetter and Uniform Program targeted to ski patrollers and lift operators would serve to trigger sales in the same manner that using mountaineers impacted the backpacking pyramid of influence.

Issues with Skiwear

The decision to introduce skiwear was also not without some problems. Although a majority of

EXHIBIT 5
Estimated Market Share by Segments of Skiwear Market

Down Parkas				Non-Down Parkas				Bibs			
Men's		*Women's*		*Men's*		*Women's*		*Men's*		*Women's*	
1. Gerry	21.7%	1. Gerry	15.0%	1. Roffee	14.6%	1. Roffee	12.4%	1. Skyr	13.7%	1. Roffee	15.0%
2. Roffee	8.6%	2. Slalom	9.8%	2. White Stag	8.7%	2. White Stag	12.3%	2. Roffee	12.4%	2. Skyr	14.6%
3. Alpine Designs	7.4%	3. Roffee	8.7%	3. Skyr	8.0%	3. Skyr	10.6%	3. White Stag	11.0%	3. White Stag	9.1%
4. Powder-horn	5.4%	4. Head	7.8%	4. Head	7.7%	4. Head	10.2%	4. Head	7.2%	4. Head	6.6%
5. Head	5.3%	5. Mountain Goat*	6.1%	5. C.B. Sports	7.2%	5. Slalom	6.2%	5. Beconta	5.2%	5. Slalom	6.5%
6. White Stag	4.7%	6. White Stag	4.7%	6. Serac	5.9%	6. Swing West	5.0%	6. Swing West	4.9%	6. Swing West	4.6%
7. Mountain Goat*	3.6%	7. Tempco	4.2%	7. Cevas	4.6%	7. Bogner	4.4%	7. Gerry	4.1%	7. No. 1 Sun**	4.6%
8. C.B. Sports	3.3%	8. Sports-caster	3.9%	8. Slalom	4.2%	8. Cevas	3.2%	8. Slalom	3.9%	8. Beconta	4.4%
9. Ober-meyer	3.1%	9. No. 1 Sun**	3.4%	9. Swing West	4.2%	9. No. 1 Sun**	3.0%	9. No. 1 Sun**	3.8%	9. Gerry	3.8%
10. Sports-caster	3.1%	10. C.B. Sports	2.8%	10. No. 1 Sun**	3.8%	10. C.B. Sports	2.6%	10. Alpine Designs	3.7%	10. Bogner	3.1%
11. All other	33.8%	11. All other	33.6%	11. All other	31.1%	11. All other	30.1%	11. All other	30.1%	11. All other	27.7%

*Second brand name of White Stag.
**Second brand name of Head.

the dealers carried skiwear, some did not. The latter might oppose "The North Face" trade name going into another local store, even if it was part of a product line they didn't carry. Further, the current dealers were not always the most influential top-end shops required to build a market, and their ski departments might not take The North Face's ski-oriented products as seriously as they did the company's backpacking offerings. Similarly, some of the best ski shops which influenced the entire market were not presently The North Face outlets. Out of a total market size of over 3,000 Alpine ski dealers, only about 475 were currently carrying The North Face products. Moreover, the sales reps already had a very extensive line and it was a concern of management that they might have difficulty pushing the ski items during the critical start-up phase. Further, this expansion into a new area in effect required the established sales reps to "start over" again with prospecting for new accounts, a task which might tax their capabilities and desires.

Different complications arose in each of TNF's markets. The following example from a metropolitan center in California highlights some critical issues.

At the time of the skiwear decision, TNF distributed its backpacking products primarily through one large specialty backpacking/skiing shop in the city. Suburban neighborhood stores were utilized for additional coverage. The city store ranked amongst the top 20% of TNF dealers. In the past, TNF had rewarded this supplier by witholding merchandise from direct competitors.

TNF serviced this account with regular visits of the local sales representative, frequent visits by sales managers, an annual dealer seminar, and periodic information-gathering visits by top man-

EXHIBIT 6
Partial Organization Chart

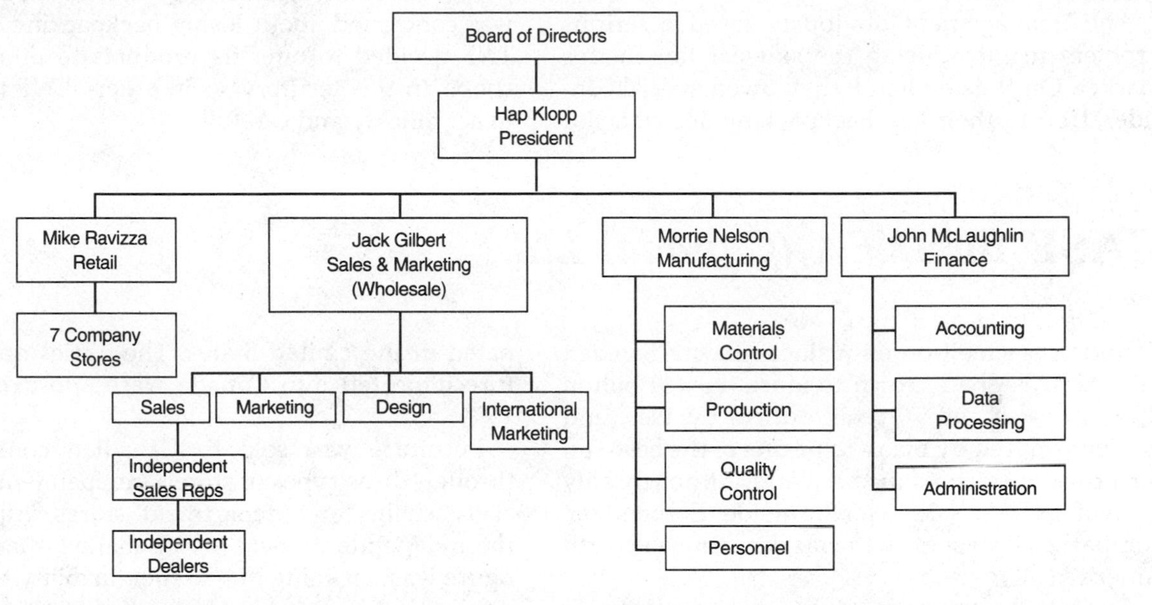

Backgrounds
Mike Ravizza, Retail—Joined The North Face in 1969; Stanford undergraduate.
Jack Gilbert, Sales & Marketing—Co-founder of The North Face in 1968; Stanford undergraduate.
Morrie Nelson, Manufacturing—Joined The North Face in 1975; University of Washington undergraduate, Santa Clara MBA.
John McLaughlin, Finance—Joined The North Face in 1970; Dartmouth undergraduate, Stanford MBA.

agement. The store's annual sales topped $1M, with 65–70% of this deriving from backpacking products. Sales of TNF items accounted for the majority of backpacking revenue. TNF management felt that this shop, as the largest specialty shop in the area, "made" the area backpacking market. TNF developed consumer awareness via close association with this outlet and by regular coop advertisements. In short, if a serious local backpacker needed equipment, he would most likely shop at this store.

In backpacking, this shop had little formidable competition. Some second-tier specialty shops existed but they offered less ease of access and a narrower product range. A wide variety of general sporting goods shops also competed in the territory. These stores each had backpacking sections but did not emphasize service. TNF did not associate with these stores.

Unfortunately, the skiing market was much more fragmented in this territory. Although TNF's key backpacking account also sold skiing products, it did not have a dominant position. The store was one of the handful of large dealers that handled skiwear. It did not "make the market." Instead, it often reacted to the environment in setting pricing, merchandising, and product selection policies. In addition, five comparably sized ski specialty shops (no backpacking gear at all) competed in this territory. Each shop carried roughly the same product line frequently featuring loss leadership on hardware (Rossignol,

Nodica, Lange, etc.). Soft goods were the primary profit maker. The offerings emphasized aesthetics and functionality.

TNF management obviously faced a serious problem in introducing the skiwear line in this market. On the one hand, they owed special consideration to their key backpacking account. But they also realized that this account alone would not develop sufficient brand awareness as a pioneer for the skiwear line. The key account's owner was concerned about losing backpacking sales if TNF decided to offer its products to other area shops. In this territory, as in others, TNF needed to act quickly and carefully.

CASE 10 | *IKEA (Canada) Ltd.*

Founded as a mail-order business in rural Sweden in 1943, IKEA had grown to more than $1 billion (U.S.) in sales and 70 retail outlets by 1985, and was considered by many to be one of the best-run furniture operations in the world. Although only 14% of IKEA's sales were outside Europe, the company's fastest growth was occurring in North America.

Success, however, brought imitators. In mid-1986, Bjorn Bayley and Anders Berglund, the senior managers of IKEA's North American operations, were examining a just published Sears Canada catalogue, which contained a new 20-page section called "Elements." This section bore a striking resemblance to the format of an IKEA Canada catalogue, and the furniture being offered was similar to IKEA's knocked-down, self-assembled line in which different "elements" could be ordered by the customer to create particular designs. Bayley and Berglund wondered how serious Sears was about its new initiative, and what, if anything, IKEA should do in response.

THE CANADIAN FURNITURE MARKET

Canadian consumption of furniture totalled more than $2 billion in 1985, an average of well over $600 per household. Imports accounted for approximately 18% of this total, half of which originated in the United States. The duties on furniture imported into Canada were approximately 15%.

Furniture was sold to Canadian consumers through three types of stores: independents, specialty chains and department stores. Although the independents held a 70% market share, this figure was declining due to their inability to compete with the chains in terms of advertising, purchasing power, management sophistication and sales support. The average sales per square metre in 1985 for furniture stores of all three types was $1666 (the figure was $2606 for stores which also sold appliances) and the average cost of goods sold was 64.5%.

While the major department stores such as Eaton's and Sears tended to carry traditional furniture lines close to the middle of the price/quality range, chains and independents operated from one end of the spectrum to the other. At the upper end of the market, specialty stores attempted to differentiate themselves by offering unique product lines, superior service and a specialized shopping atmosphere. The lower end of the market, on the other hand, was dominated by furniture warehouses which spent heavily on advertising, and offered lower price, less service, and less emphasis on a fancy image. The warehouses usually kept a larger inventory of furniture on

This case was written by Professor Paul W. Beamish as a basis for classroom discussion and condensed by Professor Peter Killing.

hand than the department stores, but expected customers to pick up their purchases. Over half the warehouse sales involved promotional financing arrangements, including delayed payments, extended terms, and so on.

The major firms in this group—both of whom sold furniture and appliances—were The Brick and Leon's. The Brick had annual sales of $240 million from 15 Canadian stores, and was rapidly expanding from its western Canada base. With 30 additional stores in California under the Furnishings 2000 name, The Brick intended to become the largest furniture retailing company in the world. Leon's had annual sales of $160 million from 14 stores, and was growing rapidly from its Ontario base. These 14 stores were operated under a variety of names. Leon's also franchised its name in smaller cities in Canada. For part of their merchandise requirements, The Brick and Leon's often negotiated with manufacturers for exclusive products, styles and fabrics and imported from the U.S., Europe and the Far East. Although both firms had had problems earlier with entry to the U.S. market, each intended on expanding there.

Most furniture retailers in Canada purchased their products from Canadian manufacturers after examining new designs and models at trade shows. There were approximately 1400 Canadian furniture manufacturers, most of which were located in Ontario and Quebec. Typically, these firms were small (78% of Canadian furniture plants employed less than 50 people), undercapitalized and minimally automated. One industry executive quipped that one of the most significant technological developments for the industry had been the advent of the staple gun.

Canadian-produced furniture typically followed American and European styling, which was generally of adequate to excellent quality but was often more costly to produce. The reason for high Canadian costs was believed to be a combination of short manufacturing runs and high raw material, labour and distribution costs. In an attempt to reduce costs, a few of the larger manufacturers such as Kroehler had vertically integrated—purchasing sawmills, fabric warehouses, fibreboard and wood frame plants—but such practices were very much the exception in the industry.

THE IKEA FORMULA

IKEA's approach to business was fundamentally different from that of the traditional Canadian retailers. The company focused exclusively on what it called "quick assembly" furniture, which consumers carried from the store in flat packages and assembled at home. This furniture was primarily pine, had a clean European design look to it, and was priced at 15% below the lowest prices for traditional furniture. Its major appeal appeared to be to young families, singles, and frequent movers, who were looking for well-designed items that were economically priced and created instant impact.

According to company executives, IKEA was successful because of its revolutionary approach to the most important aspects of the business: product design, procurement, store operations, marketing, and management philosophy, which stressed flexibility and market orientation rather than long-range strategy. Each of these items is discussed in turn.

Product Design

IKEA's European designers, not the company's suppliers, were responsible for the design of most of the furniture and accessories in IKEA's product line, which totalled 15,000 items. The heart of the company's design capability was a 50-person Swedish workshop which produced prototypes of new items of furniture and smaller components such as "an ingenious little snap lock for table legs, which makes a table stronger and cheaper at the same time," and a "clever little screw attachment, which allows for the assembly of a pin back chair in five minutes." IKEA's designers were very cost conscious, and were constantly working to lower costs in ways that were not critical to the consumer. The quality of a work top, for example, would be superior to that of the back of a bookshelf which would never be seen. "Low price with a meaning" was the theme.

Although it was not impossible to copyright a particular design or process, IKEA's philosophy was "if somebody steals a model from us we do not bring a lawsuit, because a lawsuit is always negative. We solve the problem by making a new model that is even better."

Procurement

IKEA's early success in Sweden had so threatened traditional European furniture retailers that they had promised to boycott any major supplier that shipped products to the upstart firm. As a result, IKEA had no choice but to go to the smaller suppliers. Since these suppliers had limited resources, IKEA began assuming responsibility for the purchase of raw materials, packaging materials, storage, specialized equipment and machinery, and engineering. What began as a necessity soon became a cornerstone of IKEA's competitive strategy, and by 1986 the firm had nearly 100 production engineers working as purchasers. Together with IKEA's designers, these engineers assisted suppliers in every way they could to help them lower costs, dealing with everything from the introduction of new technology to the alteration of the dimensions of a shipping carton.

Although IKEA sometimes leased equipment and made loans to its suppliers, the firm was adamant that it would not enter the furniture manufacturing business itself. In fact, to avoid control over—and responsibility for—its suppliers, the company had a policy of limiting its purchases to 50% of a supplier's capacity. Many products were obtained from multiple suppliers, and frequently suppliers produced only a single standardized component or input to the final product. Unfinished pine shelves, for example, were obtained directly from saw mills, cabinet doors were purchased from door factories, and cushions came from textile mills.

In total, IKEA purchased goods from 1500 suppliers located in 40 countries. About 52% of the company's purchases were from Scandinavia, 21% from other countries of western Europe, 20% from eastern Europe, and 7% elsewhere.

Store Operations

IKEA stores were usually large one- or two-storey buildings situated in relatively inexpensive standalone locations, neither in prime downtown sites nor as part of a shopping mall. Most stores were surrounded by a large parking lot, adorned with billboards explaining IKEA's delivery policy, product guarantee, and the existence of a coffee shop and/or restaurant.

On entering a store, the customer was immediately aware of the children's play area (a room filled with hollow multi-colored balls), a video room for older children, and a receptionist with copies of IKEA catalogues, a metric conversion guide, index cards for detailing purchase, and a store guide. The latter, supplemented by prominent signs, indicated that the store contained lockers and benches for shoppers, a first aid area, restrooms, strollers and a baby care area, an "As-Is" department (no returns permitted), numerous check outs, suggestion boxes and, in many cases, a restaurant. All major credit cards were accepted.

Traffic flow in most IKEA stores was guided so as to pass by almost all of the merchandise in the store, which was displayed as it would look in the home, complete with all accessories. Throughout a store, employees could be identified by their bright red IKEA shirts. Part-time employees wore yellow shirts which read "Temporary Help—Please Don't Ask Me Any Hard Questions." The use of sales floor staff was minimal. The IKEA view was that "salesmen are expensive, and can also be irritating. IKEA leaves you to shop in peace."

While IKEA stores were all characterized by their self-serve, self-wrapping, self-transport, and self-assembly operations, the company's philosophy was that each new store would incorporate the latest ideas in use in any of its existing stores. The most recent trend in some countries was in IKEA Contract Sales section, which provided a delivery, invoicing, and assembly service for commercial customers.

Marketing

IKEA's promotional activities were intended to educate the consumer public on the benefits of the IKEA concept and build traffic by attracting new buyers and encouraging repeat visits from existing customers. The primary promotional vehicle was the annual IKEA catalogue which was selectively mailed out to prime target customers which in the Toronto area, for instance, had the following characteristics:

- Income $35,000+
- Owned condominium or townhouse
- University degree
- White collar
- Primary age group 35-44
- Secondary age group 25-34
- Husband/wife both work
- 2 Children
- Movers

With minor variations, this "upscale" profile was typical of IKEA's target customers in Europe and North America. In Canada, IKEA management acknowledged the target market, but felt that in fact the IKEA concept appealed to a much wider group of consumers.

IKEA also spent heavily on magazine advertisements, which were noted for their humorous, slightly off-beat approach. In Canada, IKEA spent $2.5 million to print 3.6 million catalogues, $2 million on magazine advertising, and $1.5 million on other forms of promotion in 1984.

Management Philosophy

The philosophy of Ingvar Kamprad, the founder of IKEA , was "to create a better everyday life for the majority of people." In practice, this creed meant that IKEA was dedicated to offering, and continuing to offer, the lowest prices possible on good-quality furniture, so that IKEA products were available to as many people as possible. Fred Andersson, the head of IKEA's product range for the world stated, "Unlike other companies, we are not fascinated with what we produce—we make what our customers want." Generally, IKEA management felt that no other company could match IKEA's combination of quality and price across the full width of the product line.

IKEA also made a concerted effort to stay "close to its customers," and it was not unusual for the General Manager of IKEA Canada, for instance, to personally telephone customers who had made complaints or suggestions. Each week an employee newsletter detailed all customer comments, and indicated how management felt they should be dealt with.

Another guiding philosophy of the firm was that growth would be in "small bites." The growth objective in Canada, for instance, had been to increase sales and profits by 20% per year, but care was given to sequence store openings so that managerial and financial resources would not be strained.

Internally, the company's philosophy was stated as "freedom, with responsibility," which meant that IKEA's managers typically operated with a good deal of autonomy. The Canadian operation, for instance, received little in the way of explicit suggestions from head office, even in the one year when the budget was not met. The Canadian management team travelled to head office as a group only once every several years. As Bjorn Bayley explained, "We are a very informal management team, and try to have everyone who works for us believe that they have the freedom to do their job in the best way possible. It's almost impossible to push the philosophy down to the cashier level, but we try."

IKEA IN CANADA

IKEA's formula had worked well in Canada. Under the direction of a four-man management team, which included two Swedes, the company had grown from a single store in 1976 to nine stores totalling 800,000 square feet and, as shown in Exhibit 1, predicted 1986 sales of more than $140 million. The sales of IKEA Canada had exceeded budget in all but one of the past five years, and usually by a wide margin. Net profits were approximately 5% of sales. Profit and loss statements for 1983 and 1984, the only financial statements available, are presented in Exhibit 2.

IKEA Canada carried just less than half of the company's total product line. Individual items were chosen on the basis of what management thought would sell in Canada, and if IKEA could not beat a competitor's price by 10–15% on a particular item, it was dropped. Most of the goods sold in the Canadian stores were supplied from central warehouses in Sweden. To coordinate this process a five-person stock supply department in Vancouver provided Sweden with a three-year forecast of Canada's needs, and placed major orders twice a year. Actual volumes were expected to be within 10% of the forecast level. As Bayley noted, "You needed a gambler in the stock supply job."

Individual stores were expected to maintain 13.5 weeks of inventory on hand (10.5 weeks in the store and 3 weeks in transit), and could order from the central warehouse in Montreal, or, if a product was not in stock in Montreal, direct from Sweden. Shipments from Sweden took six to eight weeks to arrive, shipments from Montreal, two to three weeks. In practice about 50% of the product arriving at a store arrived via each route.

IKEA's success in Canada meant that the firm was often hard pressed to keep the best-selling items in stock. (Twenty percent of the firm's present line constituted 80% of sales volume.) At any given time in Canada IKEA stores might have 300 items out of stock, either because actual sales deviated significantly from forecasts or because suppliers could not meet their delivery promises. While management estimated that 75% of customers were willing to wait for IKEA products in a stockout situation, the company nevertheless began a deliberate policy of developing Canadian suppliers for high-demand items, even if this meant paying a slight premium. In 1984, the stock control group purchased $57 million worth of

EXHIBIT 1
IKEA Canada Sales by Store (Including Mail Order %)** (CDN. $000's)

	Actual						
	1981	*1982*	*1983*	*1984*	*1985*	*Forecast 1986*	Mail Order (%)
Vancouver	12122	11824	12885	19636	19240	25500	6.8
Calgary	7379	8550	7420	7848	9220	11500	8.6
Ottawa	5730	6914	8352	9015	10119	12500	1.8
Montreal			8617	12623	15109	22000*	2.2
Halifax	3634	4257	4474	6504	7351	9000	22.9
Toronto	11231	13191	16249	18318	22673	30500	1.8
Edmonton	6506	7474	8075	8743	9986	16000	15.4
Quebec City		5057	8284	9027	10037	12000	6.1
Victoria					2808	3500	—
Total	46611	57267	74176	91714	106543	142500	6.7

*Projected growth due to store size expansion.
**1984 most recent data available.

EXHIBIT 2
IKEA Limited
Statement of Earnings and Retained Earnings
Year Ended August 31, 1984
(With Comparative Figures for 1983)

	1984	*1983*
Sales	$92,185,188	74,185,691
Cost of merchandise sold	49,836,889	38,085,173
Gross profit	42,348,299	36,100,518
General, administrative and selling expenses	28,016,473	23,626,727
Operating profit before the undernoted	14,331,826	12,473,791
Depreciation and amortization	1,113,879	1,066,286
Franchise amortization	257,490	257,490
Franchise fee	2,765,558	2,225,571
	4,136,927	3,549,347
Earnings from operations	10,194,899	8,924,444
Rental income	769,719	815,683
Less rental expense	245,803	258,296
	523,916	557,387
Interest expense	2,453,116	3,042,471
Less other income	438,683	65,757
	2,014,433	2,976,714
Earnings before income taxes	8,704,382	6,505,117
Income Taxes		
Current	3,789,773	2,716,645
Deferred	(70,400)	175,500
	3,719,373	2,892,145
Net earnings for the year	4,985,009	3,612,972
Retained earnings, beginning of year	5,501,612	1,888,640
Retained earnings, end of year	$10,486,621	5,501,612

Source: Consumer and Corporate Affairs, Canada.

goods on IKEA's behalf, $12 million of which was from 30 Canadian suppliers, up from $7 million the previous year.

As indicated in Exhibit 1, IKEA Canada sold products, rather reluctantly, by mail order to customers who preferred not to visit the stores. A senior manager explained: "To date we have engaged in defensive mail order—only when the customer really wants it and the order is large enough. The separate handling, breaking down of orders, and repackaging required for mail orders would be too expensive and go against the economies-through-volume approach of IKEA. Profit margins of mail-order business tend to be half that of a store operation. There are more sales returns, particularly because of damages—maybe 4%—incurred in shipping. It is difficult to know where to draw the market boundaries for a mail-order business. We don't want to be substituting mail-order customers for store visitors."

In 1986, the management team which had brought success to IKEA's Canadian operations was breaking up. Bjorn Bayley, who had come to Canada in 1978, was slotted to move to Philadelphia to spearhead IKEA's entry into the U.S. market, which had begun in June 1985 with a single store. With early sales running at a level twice as high as the company had predicted, Bayley expected to be busy, and was taking Mike McDonald, the controller, and Mike McMullen, the personnel director, with him. Anders Berglund, who, like Bayley, was a long-time IKEA employee and had been in Canada since 1979, was scheduled to take over the Canadian operation. Berglund would report through Bayley to IKEA's North American Sales Director, who was located in Europe.

New Competition

IKEA's success in Canada had not gone unnoticed. IDOMO was a well-established Toronto-based competitor, and Sears Canada was a new entrant.

IDOMO

Like IKEA, IDOMO sold knocked-down furniture which customers were required to assemble at home. IDOMO offered a somewhat narrower selection than IKEA but emphasized teak furniture to a much greater extent. With stores in Hamilton, Mississauga (across from IKEA), Toronto and Montreal, IDOMO appeared to have capitalized on excess demand that IKEA had developed but was not able to service.

The products and prices offered in both the 96-page IDOMO and 144-page IKEA catalogues were similar, with IKEA's prices slightly lower. Prices in the IKEA catalogue were in effect for a year. IDOMO reserved the right to make adjustments to prices and specifications. A mail-order telephone number in Toronto was provided in the IDOMO catalogue. Of late, IDOMO had begun to employ an increased amount of television advertising. IDOMO purchased goods from around the world and operated a number of their own Canadian factories. Their primary source of goods was Denmark.

Sears

The newest entrant in the Canadian knocked-down furniture segment was Sears Canada, a wholly owned subsidiary of Sears, Roebuck of Chicago and, with $3.8 billion in annual revenues, one of Canada's largest merchandising operations. Sears operated 75 department stores in Canada, selling a wide range (700 merchandise lines comprising 100,000 stock keeping units) of medium price and quality goods. Sears Canada also ran a major catalogue operation which distributed 12 annual catalogues to approximately 4 million Canadian families. Customers could place catalogue orders by mail, by telephone, or in person through one of the company's 1500 catalogue sales units, which were spread throughout the country.

A quick check by Bayley and Berglund revealed that Sears' Elements line was being sold only in Canada and only through the major Sears catalogues. Elements products were not for sale, nor could they be viewed in Sears' stores. In the Fall–Winter catalogue that they examined, which was over 700 pages in length, the Elements line was given 20 pages. Although Sears appeared to offer the same "type" of products as IKEA , there was a narrower selection within each category. Prices for Elements' products seemed almost identical to IKEA prices. One distinct difference between the catalogues was the much greater emphasis IKEA placed on presenting a large number of coordinated settings and room designs.

Further checking indicated that at least some of the suppliers of the Elements line were Swedish, although it did not appear that IKEA and Sears had any suppliers in common. The IKEA executives knew that Sears was generally able to exert a great deal of influence over its suppliers, usually obtaining prices at least equal to and often below those of its competitors, because of the huge volumes purchased. Sears also worked closely with its suppliers in marketing, research, design and development, production standards and production planning. Many lines of merchandise were manufactured with features exclusive to Sears and were sold under its private brand names. There was a 75% buying overlap for the catalogue and store and about a 90% overlap between regions on store purchases.

Like any Sears product, Elements furniture could be charged to a Sears charge card. Delivery of catalogue items generally took about two weeks, and for a small extra charge catalogue orders would be delivered right to the consumer's home in a Sears truck. If a catalogue item were out of stock, Sears policy was either to tell the customer if and when the product would be available, or to substitute an item of equal or greater value. If goods proved defective (10% of Sears, Roebuck mail-order furniture purchasers had received damaged or broken furniture), Sears provided home pick up and replacement and was willing, for a fee, to install goods, provide parts, and do repairs as products aged. Sears emphasized that it serviced what it sold, and guaranteed everything that it sold—"satisfaction guaranteed or money refunded." In its advertising, which included all forms of media, Sears stressed its "hassle-free returns" and asked customers to "take a look at the services we offer . . . they'll bring you peace of mind, long after the bill is paid."

In their assessment of Sears Canada, Bayley and Berglund recognized that the company seemed to be going through something of a revival. Using the rallying cry that a "new" Sears was being created, Sears executives (the Canadian firm had ten vice presidents) had experimented with new store layouts, pruned the product line, and improved customer service for catalogue orders. Richard Sharpe, the Chairman of Sears Canada, personally addressed as many as 12,000 employees per year, and the company received 3000 suggestions from employees annually. Perhaps as a result of these initiatives, and a cut in workforce from 65,000 to 50,000 over a several year period, Sears Canada posted its best ever results in 1985.

CONCLUSION

With the limited data they had on Sears, IKEA management recognized their comparison of the two companies would be incomplete. Nonetheless, a decision regarding the Sears competitive threat was required. Any solution would have to reflect Kamprad's philosophy: **"Expensive solutions to problems are often signs of mediocrity. We have no interest in a solution until we know what it costs."**

CASE 11 | *Babbitt Brothers Trading Company*

Bill Galis stood at the window of his office and gazed out. It was late March 1986. At the moment, the sun shone in a cloudless, brilliant blue Arizona sky. The weather forecast was calling for precipitation however. Below, on the Flagstaff streets, a mix of early arriving tourists and local residents were on the move, some shopping for Native American rugs, jewelry or pottery, others just on their way to lunch. Bill was a relative newcomer to Flagstaff. Less than a year before, he had accepted the President and Chief Operating Officer position for the Babbitt Brothers Trading Company (BBTC), a diversified, multi-million dollar operation doing business throughout the vast, but sparsely populated, Northern Arizona trade region. Bill's office was located in Flagstaff's "Babbitt's Department Store" (BDS), one of the seven full-service stores which comprised the Department Store Division of BBTC. It was this division of the business which was on his mind now. During the past year, a majority of his time and energy had been consumed by the problems in this division. In two weeks, Bill would be making a recommendation to the BBTC Board of Directors on an issue that would determine the future of the Babbitt's Department Stores.

Bill began to reflect on the events which had transpired since he had first heard of BBTC. In January 1985, he had received a call from Kermit Halden, President of Halden and Associates (H&A), a consulting firm located in Minnetonka, Minnesota (a suburb of Minneapolis). Halden explained that he was trying to identify candidates who would be interviewed for the President and Chief Operating Officer position of a diversified business in Arizona. Halden further explained that he had gotten Bill's name from a common acquaintance, Jim Hamlin, Vice President of Retail Operations for Smitty's Inc. in Phoenix. Halden and Hamlin had been business associates years earlier when Halden was the Personnel Manager for Dayton-Hudson. Hamlin knew Bill Galis from their days together at Smitty's, where Galis had been the Vice President of Finance for almost three years (1979–1981). After determining that Galis was interested in learning more about the opening, Halden suggested that they meet for lunch. At the lunch meeting, Halden gave Galis a brief historical sketch of the Babbitt Brothers Trading Company.

BABBITT BROTHERS TRADING COMPANY

The story of BBTC is the story of five imaginative, energetic brothers from Cincinnati, Ohio, who came West in the late 1800s. These brothers had widely diverse interests, but with hard work and dreaming, parlayed a handful of cattle and a small lumber and hardware store into what was, in 1984, a $70 million a year mercantile and ranching empire. Between 1889 and the present, the Babbitts fed, clothed, equipped, transported, entertained and buried four generations of Arizonans. They also did it more profitably than anyone else.

The year was 1884. After listening to colorful tales of the Western United States from a close friend who had just returned from an extended tour, David, George, William, Charles and Ed Babbitt decided to investigate the West as a future home. Their family had been successful in business in Cincinnati. They were looking for the one best place in the West where they could settle and

This case was prepared by Professor Jon Ozmun, Northern Arizona University for classroom discussion and was not intended to illustrate either effective or ineffective handling of administrative situations. It is reproduced here by permission of the North American Case Research Association and the author.

invest the capital they could collectively realize from the sale of their grocery store, family home and farm. On April 2, 1884, David, the eldest, embarked on an "exploratory journey" to gather information about opportunities and places. After four months of travel, he had eliminated Kansas, Colorado and Wyoming and had begun to focus on the territories of New Mexico and Arizona. David ended his tour of the West in Tucson. He returned to Cincinnati and spent the next 14 months convincing the other four Babbitt brothers that their future lay in the American Southwest.

In early 1886, David and younger brother William arrived in New Mexico with $20,000. Their intention was to buy a herd of cattle, acquire water rights and grazing permits and locate near Springer, New Mexico. Conditions had become unfavorable since David's previous visit, so on a tip from a railroad clerk, the brothers set out to investigate Flagstaff and Northern Arizona. In Flagstaff, they were able to get the cattle, water and grazing rights they wanted for $17,640. Within a month, the cattle were branded with the "CO Bar" (for Cincinnati, Ohio) and the Babbitt empire had begun.

After the cattle business had become established, David returned to Cincinnati to marry his childhood sweetheart, Emma VerKamp. Emma's father, a wealthy Cincinnati mercantilist, thought ranching was too risky and that the life would be too harsh for his daughter. He agreed to finance David in a mercantile venture if one became available. Upon his return to Flagstaff with his bride, David encountered a range war and an Apache uprising and decided to look into his father-in-law's offer. The other brothers also believed that it made good business sense to diversify. David's expertise was in the grocery business, but this was crowded so he bought an existing lumber and hardware business. Babbitt's Department Store stands on this location toady.

The lumber and hardware business prospered. David expanded the business and in addition offered Flagstaff's only banking services. He eventually founded the Citizen's Bank of Flagstaff in December 1888. On December 31, 1889, David formed a partnership with his four brothers and BBTC was formed. Other significant events in the history of BBTC:

1891	The Babbitt store building was enlarged to house the "Babbitt Opera Hall," the cultural center of Flagstaff life.
1892–1922	Babbitt's Mercantile stores were opened in Winslow, Williams, Ashfork, Kingman, Oatman and Yucca. All but the Winslow store were later closed or sold.
1892	The Flagstaff Undertaking Parlor was opened for business.
1893–1905	Babbitt's ranching operations were expanded with the purchase of the "Circle S," "A-1," "Hashknife" and "Apache Maid" ranches. The Babbitts were shipping cattle eastward to Dodge City and at one time owned 100,000 acres in five Kansas counties which were used to fatten the cattle.
1904	Flagstaff Ice Plant was built.
1909	Flagstaff's first garage and automobile agency was built.
1918	The loosely organized partnership of 1889 was dissolved and BBTC was incorporated with a capitalization of $5 million.
1928	A new store was built at the Grand Canyon.
1931	A retail lumber yard was opened in Flagstaff.
1955	Thriftway Grocery Stores were opened in Flagstaff and Winslow.
1958–1983	Babbitt's Department Stores were introduced in Page (1958), Cottonwood (1975), Kingman (1978), Prescott (1981), and Yuma (1983).

From its beginnings in 1889 to 1984, BBTC had always had a "Babbitt" at the top. David Babbitt's two sons, Ray and Joseph, succeeded him in the top management position and this started the tradition. By 1984, Paul Babbitt, Jr., a great-grandson of Charles Babbitt, was CEO and Chairman of the Board of Directors of BBTC.

During the 1970s, BBTC was organized into six Divisions: Ranching, Real Estate, Grand Canyon Stores, Home Centers, Trading Posts, and Department Stores. The Grand Canyon Stores consisted of a grocery store, restaurant/cafeteria and a specialty (hiking, climbing and general outdoor supplies) store. The Home Centers sold a complete line of building materials from lumber to plumbing and electrical supplies to basic hardware items. The Trading Posts, located on the Indian Reservations, supplied the Indians with a variety of food, clothing, and miscellaneous other items.

By 1984, annual sales for the six divisions of BBTC had grown to over $70 million. Financial information is shown in Exhibits 1 and 2.

EXHIBIT 1
Babbitt Brothers Trading Company
Consolidated Statement of Income, Year Ended December 31, 1984

Revenues		
Department Stores	$14,628,637	
Trading Posts	3,571,169	
Home Centers	44,226,221	
Grand Canyon Stores	6,684,650	
Ranches	914,417	
Real estate	1,224,713	
		$71,249,807
Cost of Operations		
Department Stores	$16,106,369	
Trading Posts	3,305,392	
Home Centers	41,857,025	
Grand Canyon Stores	5,712,274	
Ranches	551,621	
Real estate	359,972	
		67,892,653
Income from operations		3,357,154
Other Expenses		
General and administrative	$3,772,831	
Net interest	721,506	
Income tax benefit	(773,000)	
		3,721,337
Income (loss) before extraordinary item and cumulative effect of change in accounting principles		(364,183)
Extraordinary item—recovery from termination of employee pension plan		216,000
Cumulative effect of prior years on changing depreciation method		201,215
Net Income		$53,032

EXHIBIT 2
Babbitt Brothers Trading Company
Consolidated Balance Sheet, December 31, 1984

Current Assets		
Cash	$84,611	
Receivables	7,317,213	
Other	2,928,310	
Prepaid expenses	124,595	
Inventories	7,494,791	
Total current assets		$17,979,520
Operating Property and Equipment		
Land	419,563	
Buildings and improvements	7,132,717	
Furniture and equipment	5,934,971	
Less: accumulated depr.	6,855,262	
Total		6,631,989
Investment and Rental Property		
Land and rental property	5,547,113	
Less: accumulated depr.	3,017,932	
Total		$2,529,181
Notes receivable		1,042,215
Total assets		$28,182,905
Current Liabilities		
Accounts payable	$2,102,578	
Short-term debt	5,400,000	
Accrued compensation	1,550,085	
Current portion of long-term debt	180,822	
Total current liabilities		9,233,485
Long-term debt		1,059,643
Deferred income		767,245
Stockholder's Equity		
Preferred and common stock	2,115,200	
Retained earnings	14,712,482	
Total stockholder's equity		16,827,682
Total liabilities and stockholder's equity		$28,182,905

WILLIAM R. (BILL) GALIS

Following the luncheon meeting with Kermit Halden, Bill sent his résumé to H&A and became a candidate for the position at BBTC. Within two weeks, he received a call from Halden, who had scheduled a formal interview session. During the four-hour interview, Halden went over Bill's résumé, gathering in-depth information on his education, professional experience, and personal life. H&A wrote up the content of the interview session and their appraisal of Bill. These comments and Bill's résumé were sent to BBTC along with those of several other candidates. In less than a month, Bill was informed that BBTC wanted to interview him in Flagstaff.

To prepare himself for the interview, Bill asked to be furnished with BBTC financial information for the past three years of operation. To his surprise, he was told that the information was not available. Bill was informed that Touche Ross & Co. was conducting a complete audit of BBTC for 1984 and the report was still in process. BBTC agreed to have Touche Ross & Co. furnish Bill with any information he needed to form an opinion about the operating and financial performance of BBTC. The information that Bill obtained from Touche Ross & Co. was essentially the same as what is shown in Exhibits 1 and 2.

Bill made two trips to Flagstaff in March and April. On the first, he spent a day interviewing with the BBTC CEO and a former Dillard's Department Store executive who was working as a consultant to BBTC. Bill's wife, Diana, accompanied him on his second trip to Flagstaff. This visit lasted three days and during that time, Bill and Diana met with other members of the extended Babbitt family and were generally "wined and dined." Bill was then offered the position and asked to make a decision within 30 days. While in Flagstaff for the second interview, Bill was asked to consult on the hiring of a person to fill the position of Company Controller. He interviewed three candidates and recommended one, who was subsequently hired. So, even before he had accepted a position with the company, Bill had made his first personnel decision. On May 1, 1985, Galis agreed to a two-year contract to serve as President and Chief Operating Officer for BBTC.

Bill had a BSC in Accounting from DePaul University and was a registered CPA. He had completed his MBA at the prestigious University of Chicago. After four years as an audit supervisor at Peat, Marwick, Mitchell & Company, he moved steadily to positions of higher responsibility in the consumer products industry, as is summarized in Exhibit 3.

The President and COO position at BBTC was interesting to Bill for a number of reasons. During his employment with Smitty's he had lived in Phoenix and had enjoyed the Arizona climate and lifestyle. But more important, Bill believed that running the diversified operations of this historic Arizona family business would be challenging and rewarding and that he had the training and experience to do the job. The Home Center and Cattle Ranching Divisions were the most interesting to Bill because these would be new and unique challenges.

During the interviews and negotiations that led up to his accepting the position, Bill became aware that his first priority would be to deal with the problems surrounding the ailing Department Store Division. He needed to either make the Div-

EXHIBIT 3
Employment History of William R. (Bill) Galis

Time Period	*Firm*	*Title*
1953–1956	Peat, Marwick, Mitchell & Company	Audit Supervisor
1956–1968	Helene Curtis Industries	Corporate Controller
1968–1977	Fingerhut Corporation	Senior VP, Corporate CFO
1977–1979	Council Laboratories, Inc.	President (Part Owner)
1979–1981	Smitty's Supervalu, Inc.	VP Finance & Operations
4/81–7/82	Hub Distributing, Inc. dba Miller's Outpost Stores	VP Finance & Operations
9/82–1/85	Team Central Inc.	Executive VP (Part Owner)

ision profitable within a short time horizon or develop an alternative course of action.

THE FIRST YEAR

Bill had learned enough during the interview process to determine an action agenda for his first few weeks on the job. Even before arriving in Flagstaff in mid May, he developed the following "must do" list:

1. Begin the process of developing an up-to-date management information system.
2. Familiarize himself with the management, operations, and facilities of the six Divisions of BBTC (Real Estate, Ranching, Department Stores, Grand Canyon Stores, Home Center Stores, and Trading Posts).
3. Develop an in-depth understanding of the Department Store Division by visiting each of the seven stores to determine strengths and weaknesses in terms of its market, personnel and facilities.

Based on what he found in agenda items 2. and 3. above, he would decide what immediate actions would be taken and what he would recommend to the Board of Directors regarding the Department Stores Division. Bill gave himself six weeks for his "must do" list and set July 1st as his deadline to have these activities accomplished.

Upgrading the Management Information System

During the interview process, Bill became aware that the quality and degree of detail coming from the management information system was totally inadequate to support rational objective decision making. For example, separate historical income statements were not available for each Division. As a result, it was not possible to accurately determine which of the Divisions was profitable, which was not, and why. Within the Department Store Division, detail was unavailable to determine which lines (e.g., furniture, ladies fashions, etc.) were generating profits and which were not. This lack of accurate, detailed financial information would be a severe handicap in making initial assessments as well as follow-up decisions. In an attempt to eliminate this severe weakness the following actions were taken:

1. The Corporate Controller (whom Bill had hired during his second on-site interview) and the MIS Director were assigned the task of generating separate income statements for each of the seven stores. Data for the first five months of the year would be estimated using corporate-level financial information. This would be combined with actual information on store revenues and expenditures for the remainder of 1985.
2. The "Retail Sales Analyst" (hired in April 1985) was assigned the task of building a computerized system for determining the sales volume and gross margin for each item in each product line for each location. This was done on a PC using sales tickets, manual reports and personal interviews. Bill knew that this information would be crude, but it would be a start and set the wheels in motion for the development of the system he would need for the future.

The target date for producing the separate income statements was January 1986. For the information on sales volume and gross margin by store and product line, the goal was to have 1985 information for one store (Flagstaff) compiled by early 1986.

The Divisions

During a three-week period in May, Bill held a series of meetings with each manager of the six Divisions and visited all of the facilities. He determined that some shifting of management responsibilities was in order for the Real Estate and Trading Post Stores Divisions. Ranching, Grand Canyon Stores, and Home Center Stores operations were operating in a satisfactory manner and could be allowed to continue in the short run without changes. Bill's first session with the "General Merchandise Manager" (Head of the Department Stores Division) confirmed his initial impressions made during the interview process. This division was badly managed and would require most of his attention and energy in the months to come.

The Department Store Division

The BBTC Board of Directors and Division Managers who were familiar with sketchy company financial information believed that the Department Store Division had been and was continuing to lose money. Lack of financial information made it impossible to determine which locations had been profitable, which had suffered losses, and the magnitude of profits and losses. Shortly after Bill arrived, an audited income statement for 1984 was made available. The quality of the accounting information was so poor that it took the accounting firm over 5 months to produce the audit. The results showed that the Department Stores Division lost almost $1.5 million during 1984 (See Exhibit 4). The losses could be traced to poor performance in gross margins and insufficient sales revenue. BDS gross margin for 1984 was just 27.5% compared to the industry average of 40% and sales revenue was $86 per sq. ft. of store space compared to the industry average of $140.

Bill suspected that a major reason for the poor performance of the Division was inadequate leadership by the General Merchandise Manager (GMM). The GMM was in his early 60s and had been with Babbitt's Department Stores for 17 years. He had retired in 1984, but a satisfactory replacement could not be found so he had been rehired just a few months before Bill arrived. Bill and the GMM both agreed that he did not have the energy and drive to oversee the reorganization ahead. With no hard feelings, the GMM reentered retirement.

On a structural level, Bill was concerned with the number of merchandise "buyers" employed. Based on his experience at Miller's Outpost, he was convinced that 18 buyers were excessive in a department store chain that annually sold less than $15 million. With the idea that he should try to understand why the sales to buyer ratio was so low and what he might do about it, Bill interviewed the entire staff. From these interviews, the following picture developed:

1. Buyers did not travel to "markets." Instead, they solicited information and advice from the sales representatives who called on them in their Flagstaff offices. Merchandise for all seven Department Stores was purchased in this manner.

EXHIBIT 4
Babbitt Brothers Trading Company
Department Stores Division Income Statements, 1984 and 1985

	1984	*1985*
Sales	$14,622,766	$10,204,589
Cost of goods	10,598,367	6,484,627
Gross margin	4,024,399	3,719,962
Other income	5,871	104,971
Total income	4,030,270	3,824,933
Total expenses	3,821,881	3,136,269
Store operations income	208,389	688,664
Cost of support operations	1,686,121	1,439,123
Income (loss)	($1,477,732)	($750,459)

2. Buyers did not regularly visit each of the individual stores to interact with managers and salespersons.
3. Buyers were not informed of customer complaints regarding items that were within their sphere of responsibility.
4. Buyers were generally unhappy with the way that their jobs were structured.
5. The General Merchandise Manager who developed this system and supervised the 18 buyers saw no reason for any changes.

Bill then visited the seven individual Department Stores in order to assess the strengths and weaknesses of the markets, facilities, and the personnel. Demographic information that was available for the seven markets is shown in Exhibit 5. A summary of information for individual store facilities is shown in Exhibit 6. In addition, Bill made the following determinations: Each store needed some degree of renovation, either general remodeling or replacement of fixtures. A building contractor who consulted for BBTC estimated the costs of the renovations at $800,000. Personnel was a mixed bag: several of the stores had good management and sales clerks; others did not. Two managers (Yuma and Winslow) would need to be replaced. Overall the stores were poorly merchandised primarily due to the lack of input from the buyers. The individual markets were dissimilar in demographics and climate.

With the number and magnitude of the problems, Bill gave strong consideration to making a proposal to the Board that the Department Store Division be sold or liquidated. There were several

EXHIBIT 5
Babbitt Brothers Trading Company
Demographic Information for Individual Markets

	1980	*1985*	*Est. 1990*	*Median Household Income*	*Population Characteristics*
Cottonwood	4550	5025	5975	$16,114	26% in 65 year over
Flagstaff	34743	38247	44610	16,867	47% in 20–44 years
Kingman	10249	10515	11041	16,413	24% in 35–54 years
Page	4907	6469	7665	10,812	
Prescott	20055	21336	24000	19,935	Median age is 55 yrs
Winslow	7921	8240	9295	14,592	29% in 20–39 years
Yuma	42481	49980	52795	15,770	36% in 20–44 years
United States				19,902	38% in 20–44 years

Other Information
Arizona population grew from 2,224,000 in 1974 to 3,135,000 in 1984.

Employment

Cottonwood	—Wholesale retain trade
Flagstaff	—Government (Northern Arizona University), Peabody Coal Co. (administrative offices), W. L. Gore (medical equipment manufacturer), tourism, wholesale retail trade
Kingman	—Tourism, wholesale retail trade
Page	—Navajo Generating Station (coal fired electricity), tourism
Prescott	—Government, tourism, wholesale retail trade
Winslow	—Sante Fe railroad, tourism, wholesale retail trade
Yuma	—Military (U.S. Marine Corps Air Station, U.S. Army Proving Ground), agriculture, wholesale retail trade

EXHIBIT 6
Information on Individual Stores

	Store Estab.	*Size Sq. Ft.*	*Store Cond.*	*Location/ Ownership*	*Department Store Competition*
Cottonwood	1975	15,000	Poor	Strip SC/BBTC	None
Flagstaff	1887	42,000	Good	Downtown/BBTC	Penney's, K-Mart Sears
Kingman	1978	18,000	Poor	Downtown/Leased	Penney's, Sears Catalog
Page	1958	13,000	Poor	Strip SC/BBTC	None
Prescott	1981	32,000	Fair	Downtown/Leased	Penney's, K-Mart, Sears
Winslow	1899	11,000	Poor	Strip SC/BBTC	None
Yuma	1983	40,000	Good	New Mall/Leased	Penney's Sears

factors mitigating against this however: First, three of the stores were located in facilities that were owned by other parties and had long-term lease obligations. Second, if the stores in company-owned strip shopping centers (Cottonwood, Page, and Winslow) were closed, there was the problem of subleasing the space to other businesses. The downtown Flagstaff store location, covering almost one-half of a city block, had no alternative use. In fact, businesses were migrating away from downtown in favor of the Flagstaff Mall. Third, there was strong support from the Board of Directors and Babbitt family stockholders for a continuation of the Department Store Division. For many, the department stores were the only part of the diversified business that they could identify with. Fourth, and most compelling, was that in every market served, Babbitt's Department Stores had virtually no direct competition. Bill knew from experience that there were few such opportunities in retailing.

After carefully considering all of the factors involved, Bill decided that a turnaround/reorganization strategy was appropriate for the Division. As a first step, he made several personnel changes in the Department Store Division. These changes were designed to improve operations while at the same time reducing administrative overhead. Bill first terminated 8 of the buyers. He then reorganized some of the responsibilities of the previous GMM into two new job categories:

Divisional Merchandise Manager #1	"Ready-to-Wear" Division Junior, Missy, Sportswear Dress Buyer
Divisional Merchandise Manager #2	"Mens & Homestore" Division Menswear and Furniture Buyer

The two new Divisional Merchandise Managers were promoted from within the organization, both having previously held positions as buyers. The remaining buyers' jobs were redefined. All buyers were to become actively involved with store managers and sales personnel and spend at least one day a week visiting stores. Finally, buyers were to attend the "market" which was appropriate to their product line.

Bill then assumed the remaining responsibilities of the GMM and began the process of finding a replacement. In his role as "acting" GMM, he set up a meeting schedule for store managers (once a month) and buyers (once a week). Bill used these meetings to discuss problems, exchange ideas, plan promotions, improve store merchandise offerings, plan markdowns and work on improving costs and cost controls. He also stressed the importance of developing and maintaining adequate gross margins as opposed to simply generating increased sales revenue. This partial reorganization was completed by the end of June 1985 and was expected to produce significant cost savings.

Bill contacted H&A and asked them to develop a candidate pool for the open GMM position. After a difficult search process that took almost a full year, the position was filled in March 1986. The new GMM was scheduled to begin employment on April 1. He would bring five years' experience managing a 12-unit Tulsa, Oklahoma, retail chain, which had gross sales of over $16 million annually.

During the search process, Bill interviewed six other well-qualified candidates only to be turned down by each. The basic reasons for the candidates' disinterest were the difficulty of the situation, the small size of the store chain, and the lack of alternative employment in the area. Candidates also expressed concern about being able to attract and retain the qualified middle-level managers and buyers who would be essential human resources for the revitalization of the division.

Unanticipated Developments

Early in September 1985, Bill got what was his biggest surprise in his first year at BBTC. A small group from the BBTC Board of Directors informed him that they intended to terminate the present CEO (a member of the Babbitt family) and asked for Bill's approval. Bill explained that he was too new to the company to have formed an opinion on a matter of this magnitude. Further, he explained that he had no problems with the CEO and was still accumulating operating information about BBTC from him. Bill asked that the Board members delay action on this issue for 3–6 months to allow him to develop a more substantial foundation regarding the operations of BBTC.

Approximately three months later, a majority of the Board voted to remove the CEO from his position. The major duties and decision-making responsibilities of the CEO were assumed by a sub-committee of the Board which included Bill. As the months went by, Bill began to make more and more decisions by himself. The ousted CEO, who retained his position on the Board, and another Babbitt family stockholder were quite unhappy with this situation. They expressed dissatisfaction with the new management structure and voiced a desire to liquidate their shares of stock in the family corporation. Since ownership of the corporation was "closed" to the Babbitt family and stock was not traded on any market, no easy solution was available to the Board for dealing with the situation. The two dissatisfied stockholders, in a maverick action not sanctioned by the Board, then began a campaign to interest outside buyers in purchasing the Company.

DEPARTMENT STORE OPERATIONS—1985

In January 1986, one of Bill's initial actions paid off. Financial information for the Department Store Division for the previous year became available. This was the first time that separate income statements were produced for each of the seven Department Stores (See Exhibit 7). Not surprisingly, the data showed that the Flagstaff store was the most profitable, followed by Prescott, Cottonwood and Kingman. The Page and Winslow operations were about "break-even," while the Yuma store showed a loss for the year. The major surprise was that the Prescott store had done so poorly. A comparison of the income statements for 1984 and 1985 showed that although sales revenues had declined sharply in 1985, losses had been cut by almost $750,000 (See Exhibit 4). The drop in sales volume between 1984

EXHIBIT 7
Babbitt's Department Stores
1985 Income Statements

	Cottonwood	*Flagstaff*	*Kingman*	*Page*	*Prescott*	*Winslow*	*Yuma*
Sales	$727,802	$3,349,307	$908,835	$853,305	$1,688,420	$608,611	$2,068,308
Cost of goods	461,932	2,130,602	568,313	584,012	1,049,768	402,861	1,286,639
Gross margin	265,870	1,218,705	340,522	269,012	638,652	205,750	781,669
Other operating income (exp.)	1,093	96,985	275	61	2,413	155	3,989
Total income	266,963	1,315,690	340,797	269,354	641,065	205,905	785,658
Variable expenses	149,295	630,760	223,406	166,504	399,221	119,335	499,025
Fixed expenses	67,530	193,408	89,392	102,792	114,347	84,820	296,434
Store income	$50,138	$491,522	$27,999	$58	$127,497	$1,750	$(9,801)

and 1985 was due primarily to a "liquidation" pricing policy assumed by the chain in late 1984. For example, gross margin in the 1984 holiday selling period was under 15%. In 1985, realistic sales prices were reintroduced. Sales revenues declined, but gross margins increased. The management reorganization and cost-cutting strategies implemented during 1985 had been in effect for only six months of the accounting period, so Bill could anticipate further improvement in 1986.

Since this was the first year that such financial information had been available, it was difficult to make objective assessments concerning individual store performance. The 1985 data became the benchmark for future years' comparison. A second goal for the management information system was to provide a breakdown of financial information (e.g., dollar value, gross margin) for individual departments and product lines for each store. With this level of detail, management could determine the optimal product mix for each location and evaluate buyer and sales performance. The MIS target objective was to have available 1985 financial information by department and product line for one store and this was accomplished. Data for 1985 for the Flagstaff Babbitt's Department Store are shown in Exhibit 8.

THE "MALL" DECISION

At about the same time as the Board terminated the CEO, another ominous event in the history of BBTC occurred. In late November 1985, Dillard's Department Stores, headquartered in Little Rock, Arkansas, announced that they would become an "anchor store" in the five-year-old Flagstaff Mall. Dillard's had decided to build a new 72,000 square foot addition to the present 284,000 square foot structure. Dillard's therefore would soon enter into competition in the Babbitt's Department Stores' largest market area. Dillard's Flagstaff Mall opening was scheduled for November 1986.

When the Flagstaff Mall was opened in 1980, the BBTC Board had considered moving their downtown Flagstaff operations into the Mall. They also considered opening a branch outlet in the Mall. The Board decided against both alternatives, opting instead to continue operations out of their downtown Flagstaff facility. Originally built in the early part of the century, it had not been remodeled since 1962. At the time the decision was made, the BBTC's Board believed that none of

EXHIBIT 8
Babbitt's Department Store—Flagstaff
1985 Performance by Department / Product Line

	Sales (000)	*Gross Margin (000)*	*Inventory at Cost (000)*
Men's casual dress	$253.0	$56.8	$114.2
Men's furnish. acc.	194.6	90.7	49.2
Women's casual dress	703.0	271.7	90.2
Women's furnishings	121.7	50.7	32.1
Women's accessories	53.4	24.7	7.6
Boy's clothing	70.9	23.0	19.8
Girl's clothing	83.5	32.6	17.7
Infant/toddlers	88.7	38.7	14.3
Shoes	385.6	154.7	120.4
Jewelry	145.9	57.9	37.7
Cosmetics	328.0	127.2	122.5
Toys	31.8	10.0	6.8
Electronics	117.3	−28.7	71.7
Furniture	347.5	162.9	67.3
Textiles	137.5	52.0	34.7
Luggage	25.2	10.2	9.4
Gifts	97.6	23.0	72.0
Stationery	76.8	30.7	22.2
China	19.8	4.2	25.1
Housewares	60.4	25.3	11.6
Total	$3342.2	$1218.3	$946.6

the large Phoenix-based chains would move into Babbitt's home territory. This position was based on the assumption that the market was simply too small to support still another major retailer. The Board knew that the Mall would bring a new Sears store into the competition and the downtown Penney's store was being relocated to the Mall. These were not considered significant threats to Babbitt's continued strong position in the Flagstaff market. Furthermore, the Board knew at the time (1980) that Babbitt's did not have the management expertise to compete in the Mall environment and the cost of a Mall store would be excessive.

The move by Dillard's took everyone by surprise. Bill now had to analyze a completely unanticipated situation and formulate a strategy to respond to the entry of Dillard's. It was apparent to Bill that several alternatives were worth considering. The major options were:

1. A "no location" strategy. This would mean closing down the Babbitt's store in downtown Flagstaff.
2. A "one location" strategy. Either maintain the present downtown location or develop a new Mall store, but not both.
3. A "two location" strategy. Maintain the downtown location and develop a new mall store with fixed space commitments.

To help sort out the complexities of the various alternatives, Bill hired the consulting firm, Management Horizons of Columbus, Ohio, to do a marketing study for Babbitt's. In particular, Bill wanted an assessment of how Dillard's entry into the Flagstaff market would affect Babbitt's downtown store.

In late March 1986, Bill received the consulting report from Management Horizons. (For an "Executive Summary" of the report, see Exhibit 9.) Of special interest to Bill was the conclusion that sales revenues at Babbitt's downtown Flagstaff store would decline by approximately $1–1.5 million annually as a result of the Dillard's entry.

While the consulting report was helpful, Bill felt that he should evaluate the alternatives from a financial perspective before making a recommendation to the Board. The monetary and logistical considerations for putting a store in the Mall were formidable. BBTC would have to quickly commit to a long-term lease to acquire a recently available 15,000 square foot space in the Mall. In order to enter the Mall at approximately the same time as the new Dillard's store opened, a decision would have to be made within the next month.

EXHIBIT 9
Management Horizons Report—"Executive Summary"

Research Findings

A considerable amount of research has been done, including an extensive secondary market analysis, an in-depth review of Babbitt's performance, and an on-site audit of Dillard's Farmington, New Mexico, store. Highlights of this research:

Regarding the Flagstaff market:

- Compared to the U.S., it is younger and less affluent.
- After adjusting for the influence of Northern Arizona University, the area still has a sizeable young family, household formation population of average means.
- Flagstaff is a small metro market, with some regional shopping attractiveness.
- Expenditures are skewed toward necessities, as well as reflective of transient tourist purchases (e.g., gas, meals, lodging).
- In terms of retail space, the area is clearly well above the average U.S. saturation index:

	Gross Leaseable Area Sq. Ft. per Capita
Flagstaff	27.0
Arizona average	21.3
U.S. average	14.3

- For department store merchandise, the market is growing but already well represented (not necessarily well served), with very little upscale potential.

With regard to Babbitt's performance:

- The company enjoys a 7% market share overall for its merchandise lines.
- There is an incredible degree of variation and inconsistency between departments; the essential point, however, is that in considering the combination of sales, market share, market size and market growth by category, space and inventory productivity and profit contribution, only a few categories are reasonably well situated as a base upon which to build at the Mall and against Dillard's.
- In general, the combination of market and performance analysis suggests that in the past, Babbitt's has taken sales from the market wherever a void existed. Market forces, rather than planning, have defined strategy. This may have been good enough. The result today, however, is an unfocused offer exacerbated by events such as the last year's sell-off of inventory.

EXHIBIT 9
continued

And with regard to Dillard's market entry:

- As is documented in the body of this report, Dillard's will present Flagstaff retailers with formidable challenges.
- Dillard's is, in brief, broadly assorted in moderate to better brands, competitively priced and aggressively promotional, an excellent marketer, very complete in apparel and related merchandise, attractive to a broad consumer segment, organized, strong in the financial and resource markets, and experienced in secondary city locations.
- Dillard's entry, while a challenge to Babbitt's in itself, can serve to highlight and motivate Babbitt's to deal with a broader set of challenges and focus on opportunities which in the end may strengthen the total Babbitt's retail operation.
- Over the past few years, Dillard's merchandising emphasis has shifted from a full-line moderate department store operation to a department store focusing on moderate to better soft lines.
- In 1985, Dillard's average square footage performance was estimated by the company at $125 and projected to be $140 for 1986.
- Dillard's assortment emphasizes apparel over other categories. While apparel represents 71.3% of Dillard's sales, Babbitt's performance in apparel categories represents 61.1% of Flagstaff volume and 66.4% of all locations volume (based on preliminary estimates of 1985 operations).
- Among apparel categories, Babbitt's junior/children category appears to be more developed than Dillard's.
- While Dillard's emphasizes the soft aspect of home over hard home, Babbitt's features a developed hard line area. Furthermore, it is expected that Dillard's Flagstaff volume will be even less dependent on home as the furniture category is not expected to be a part of the assortment.
- Dillard's projected sales volume for the Flagstaff Mall store in 1987 is approximately $7.2 million ($100 per sq. ft.). The volume will originate from three sources: the natural market expenditure growth; a portion of dollars currently spent outside of Flagstaff and especially in Phoenix at Diamond's; and thirdly, from dollars which until now were spent at Babbitt's and other Flagstaff retail outlets carrying similar types of merchandise.
- The impact from the Dillard's entry into the Flagstaff market is estimated to be a $1–1.5 million annual loss in sales revenues for Babbitt's downtown Flagstaff store.

The "up front" costs to put a store in the Mall would be approximately $1 million ($500,000 for inventory and the remainder for remodeling, fixtures and personnel).

In addition, to lease space in the Mall, BBTC would have to agree to an 8-year lease costing approximately $8,000 per month. Finally, personnel to staff the facility would have to be recruited and trained. After careful analysis, Bill estimated that the downtown Flagstaff store should generate sales of approximately $2 million during 1987. He made this estimate using the most recent annual level of sales ($3.35 million in 1985) adjusted for the impact of Dillard's entry into the market.

Bill sat down at his desk and turned his attention to a review of the events of his first eleven months as COO:

1. The essential first steps toward developing an effective management information system had been accomplished. Better financial information was available now than at any previous time in the history of BBTC.
2. The reorganization of the Department Stores Division had been accomplished. Early indications were that Division performance was improved.
3. A new GMM had been hired and would be on the job within a few days. This would free up Bill's time for other responsibilities. During the

past 11 months, he had spent about 40% of his time in various activities associated with the Department Stores Division.

4. Budgeting as a planning and control tool had been introduced starting in 1986. This was a milestone in proactive management for the company. For the first time, Division Managers were conscious of revenue forecasts, cost containment, gross margins and other performance criteria.

While Bill was pleased with the progress that he had made in his first year, he could not be sure about the Board of Directors' assessment. The episode involving the two dissatisfied stockholders had bothered him a great deal and he wondered how the Board evaluated the accomplishments of his first 12 months on the job.

Looking ahead to his second year, Bill could see that in addition to his responsibilities for the other BBTC Divisions, continuing attention would be required to keep the MIS improvements on track. Also, he would have to monitor the activities of the new GMM and the Department Stores Division. Of most immediate concern, however, was the Mall decision. Bill had to evaluate all of the information and make his recommendation to the Board within the next two weeks.

As he glanced up to the window, Bill noticed that a Spring snow had begun to fall. "This will please the skiers," he thought to himself.

CASE 12 | *Arctic Power*

"We've got some important decisions to make on Arctic Power for 1988," said Linda Barton, Senior Product Manager for the brand. "As I see it, we can continue to develop our strong markets in Quebec, the Maritimes, and British Columbia or we can try to build market share in the rest of Canada." Ms. Barton was discussing the future of Arctic Power, one of Colgate-Palmolive Canada's leading laundry detergents, with Gary Parsons, the Assistant Product Manager on the brand.

"Not only do we have to consider our strategic direction," replied Mr. Parsons, "but we also have to think about our positioning strategy for Arctic Power. I'm for running the Quebec approach in all our markets." Mr. Parsons was referring to the Quebec advertising campaign which positioned Arctic Power as the superior detergent for cold water cleaning.

"I'm not sure, given the mixed results achieved with our 1986 Western campaign," said Linda. "However, we are making great progress with our current advertising in British Columbia. It might be more effective outside of Quebec. Remember, cold water washing is a newer concept for the Western provinces. We have to overcome that obstacle before we can get people to buy Arctic Power. Let's go over the data again, then make our decisions."

This case was prepared by Professor Gordon McDougall, Wilfrid Laurier University and Professor Douglas Snetsinger, University of Toronto as the basis for classroom discussion rather than to illustrate either effective or ineffective handling of an administrative situation. Names and proprietary data have been disguised but all essential relationships have been preserved.

THE COMPANY

Colgate-Palmolive Canada is a wholly owned subsidiary of Colgate-Palmolive, a large, multinational with divisions in 58 countries. Worldwide company sales in 1986 were $4.9 billion with profits of $178 million. The Canadian subsidiary sales exceeded $250 million annually. Colgate-Palmolive Canada (CPC) manufactures a range of household, health, and personal care products. Among CPC's major brands are ABC, Arctic Power, and Fab (laundry detergents), Palmolive (dishwashing liquid), Ajax (cleanser), Irish Spring (bar soap), Ultra Brite and Colgate (toothpastes), Halo (shampoo), and Baggies (food wrap).

Under the product management system at CPC, product managers are assigned responsibility for specific brands, like Arctic Power. Their overall goals are to increase the sales and profitability of their brand. To meet these goals, the product manager supervises all marketing functions including planning, advertising, selling, promotion, and market research. In planning and executing programs for a brand the product manager usually is assigned an assistant product manager and they work closely together to accomplish the brand goals.

Prior to the late 1970's CPC essentially followed the strategy of nationally supporting most of its brands. The result was that CPC was spread too thin with too many brands. There were insufficient resources to properly promote and develop all of the CPC line and profits and market share were less than satisfactory. Beginning in the late 1970's and continuing to the early 1980's the Canadian division altered its strategy. An extensive review of the entire product line was conducted and CPC moved to what was referred to as a regional brand strategy. Where a brand had regional strength, resources were focused on that area with the objective of building a strong and profitable brand in that region. For example, Arctic Power had a relatively strong market share in Quebec and the Maritimes where the proportion of consumers using cold water to wash clothes was considerably higher than the national average. Promotional support was withdrawn from the rest of Canada and those resources were focused on Quebec and the Maritimes.[1] Arctic Power was still distributed nationally but by the end of 1981, national market share was 4%, consisting of an 11% share in Quebec, a 5% share in the Maritimes, and a 2% share in the rest of Canada. Over the next four years, marketing efforts were concentrated primarily on Quebec, and to a lesser extent in the Maritimes. This approach worked well for Arctic Power. By the end of 1985, Arctic Power's national share had increased to 6.4%; share in Quebec had risen to 18%, share in the Maritimes was 6%, and less than 2% in the rest of Canada. With the increase in sales and profitability, the decision was made to target Alberta and British Columbia for 1986. The results of these efforts exceeded expectations in British Columbia but were less than satisfactory in Alberta.

THE LAUNDRY DETERGENT MARKET

The laundry detergent market was mature with unit sales increasing by approximately 1% annually and dollar sales increasing by about 5% each year between 1983 and 1986 (Exhibit 1). Three large consumer packaged goods companies, Procter and Gamble, Lever Detergents, and CPC dominated the market. All three were subsidiaries of multinational firms and sold a wide range of household and personal care products in Canada. Procter and Gamble Canada had annual sales exceeding $1 billion and some of its major brands included Crest (toothpaste), Ivory and Zest (bar soaps), Secret (deodorant), Pampers and Luvs

[1]The Maritimes contained the four Eastern provinces: Newfoundland, Nova Scotia, Prince Edward Island, and New Brunswick. In 1988, the population of Canada was estimated at 25.8 million people: Maritimes (2.3 million), Quebec (6.6 million), Ontario (9.4 million), Manitoba and Saskatchewan (2.1 million) Alberta (2.4 million), and British Columbia (3.0 million).

EXHIBIT 1
Laundry Detergent Market

	1983	*1984*	*1985*	*1986*
Colgate				
ABC	6.0	9.8	11.8	13.9
Arctic Power	4.7	5.6	6.4	6.5
Fab	2.1	1.3	1.6	1.4
Punch	2.0	.7	.4	.3
Dynamo	1.0	.8	.6	.5
Total Colgate	15.8	18.2	20.8	22.6
Procter and Gamble				
Tide	34.1	35.1	32.6	34.1
Oxydol	4.9	4.2	4.0	3.3
Bold	4.8	4.2	3.2	2.3
Other P&G brands	4.7	4.8	4.4	4.3
Total P&G	48.5	48.3	44.2	44.0
Lever				
Sunlight	13.9	12.2	14.2	13.4
All	4.1	3.7	3.8	3.2
Surf	2.6	2.6	2.7	2.2
Wisk	3.8	4.1	4.1	4.4
Other Lever brands	.9	.8	.6	.4
Total Lever	25.3	23.4	25.4	23.6
All *other* brands	10.4	10.1	9.6	9.8
Grand total	100.0	100.0	100.0	100.0
Total Market				
• Metric Tonnes ('000)	171.9	171.9	173.6	175.3
(% change)	2.0	0.0	1.0	1.0
• Factory Sales ('000,000)	$265.8	$279.1	$288.5	$304.7
(% change)	6.2	5.0	3.0	6.0

Source: Company records.

(disposable diapers) and Head & Shoulders (shampoo). P&G held a 44% share of the laundry detergent market in 1986, due primarily to the large share (34%) held by Tide, the leading brand in Canada.

Lever Detergents with annual Canadian sales in excess of $400 million operated primarily in the detergent, soap, and toiletry categories. Major brands included Close-up (toothpaste) and Dove and Lux (bar soaps). Lever held a 24% share of the laundry detergent market and its leading brand was Sunlight with a 13% share.

CPC was the only one of the three companies to gain market share in the laundry detergent market between 1983 and 1986. In 1986, CPC's total share was 23%, up from 16, in 1983. ABC, a value brand, positioned to attract consumers interested in "value for less money," more than doubled its share between 1983 and 1986 and was the second leading brand with a 14% share.

COMPETITIVE RIVALRY

Intense competitive activity was a way of life in the laundry detergent business. Not only did the three major firms have talented and experienced marketers, but they competed in a low-growth market where increased sales could only be achieved by taking share from competitive brands. A difficult task facing any product manager in this business was to identify the marketing mix that would maximize share while maintaining or increasing brand profitability; a task that had both long- and short-term implications. In the long term, competitors strove for permanent share gains by building a solid franchise of loyal users based on a quality product and a strong brand image or position. These positioning strategies were primarily executed through product formulation and advertising campaigns. However, companies also competed through consumer and trade promotions (e.g., coupons, feature specials in newspaper ads), tactics that were more short-term in nature. Trade and consumer promotions were critical to maintain prominent shelf display and to attract competitors' customers. In virtually every week of the year, at least one brand of detergent would be "on special" in any given supermarket. The product manager's task was to find the best balance between these elements in making brand decisions.

Reformulating brands, the changing of the brand ingredients, was a frequent activity in the laundry detergent business. Reformulating a brand involved altering the amount and kind of active chemical ingredients in the detergents. These active ingredients cleaned the clothes. Each of these cleaning ingredients was efficacious for particular cleaning tasks. Some of these ingredients were good for cleaning clay and mud from cotton and other natural fibres, while others would clean oily soils from polyesters, and yet others were good for other cleaning problems. Most detergents were formulated with a variety of active ingredients to clean in a wide range of conditions. As well, bleaches, fabric softeners, and fragrances could be included.

Thus, laundry detergents contained different *levels* and *mixes* of active ingredients. The major decision was the *amount* of active ingredients that would be used in a particular brand. In simple terms, the greater the proportion of active ingredients, the better the detergent was at cleaning clothes. However, all detergents would get clothes clean. For example, in a recent test of 42 laundry detergents, *Consumer Reports* concluded: "Yes, some detergents get clothes whiter and brighter than others, but the scale is clean to cleanest, not dirty to clean."

The Canadian brands of laundry detergent contained various amounts of active ingredients. As shown in the following table, Tide and Arctic Power had more active ingredients than any other brand.

Level of Active Ingredients of Laundry Detergents

1	*2*	*3*	*4*	*5*
Some private labels	Bold III	ABC	—	Arctic Power
	Oxydol	Fab		Tide
	Surf	Cheer 2		
	All	Sunlight		

Source: Company records.
Note: The scale of active ingredients increases from (1) to (5).

In fact, Tide and Arctic Power were equivalent brands in terms of the level of active ingredients. These two brands, referred to as the "Cadillacs" of detergents, had considerably higher levels of active ingredients than all other detergents. While the actual mix of active ingredients differed between the two brands (with Arctic Power having a greater mix of ingredients that were more suited to cold water washing), the cleaning power of Tide and Arctic Power were equal.

As the amount of active ingredients in a brand increased, so did the cost. Manufacturers were constantly facing the trade-off between cost and level of active ingredients. At times they had the opportunity to reduce unit costs by switching one type of active ingredient (a basic chemical) for another, depending on the relative costs of the ingredients. In this way, the level of ingredients remained the same, only the mixture changed. Manufacturers changed the physical ingredients of a brand in order to achieve an efficient per unit cost, to provide a basis for the repositioning or restaging the brand, and to continue to deliver better consumer value.

Maintaining or increasing share through repositioning or other means was critical because of the profits involved. One share point was worth approximately $3 million in factory sales and the cost and profit structures of the leading brands were believed to be similar. While some economies of scale accrued to the largest brands, the average cost of goods sold was estimated at 54% of sales, leaving a gross profit of 46%. Marketing expenditures include trade promotions (16%), consumer promotions (5%), and advertising expenditures (7%), leaving a contribution margin of 18%. Not included in these estimates were management overheads and expenses (e.g., product management salaries, market research expenses, sales salaries, and factory overheads) which were primarily fixed. In some instances, lower share brands were likely to spend higher amounts on trade promotions to achieve their marketing objectives.

One indication of competitive activity was reflected in advertising expenditures between 1982 and 1986. Total category media advertising increased by 12% to $14.4 million (Exhibit 2). As well, substantial increases in trade promotions had occurred during that period. While actual expenditure data were not available, some managers felt that twice as much was being spent on trade promotions versus advertising. As one example in Montreal, in a nine-month period in 1986, Tide was featured in weekly supermarket advertisements 80 times and Arctic Power was featured 60 times. Typically, the advertisement cost for a feature was shared by the manufacturer and the retailer. At times during 1986, consumers could have purchased six litres of Arctic Power or Tide for $3.49 (regular price of $5.79). There was also a strong indication that the frequency and size of price specials on detergents was increasing. The average retail price of laundry detergents (based on the volume sold of all detergents at regular and special prices) had only increased by 4% in the last three years whereas cost of goods sold had increased by 15% during the same period.

One final observation was warranted. Between 1983 and 1986, the four leading brands—Tide, ABC, Sunlight, and Arctic Power—had increased their share from 58.7% to 67.9% of the total market. The three manufacturers appeared to be focusing their efforts primarily on their leading brands and letting the lesser brands decline in share.

POSITIONING STRATEGIES

While positioning strategies were executed through all aspects of the marketing mix, the strategy was most clearly seen in the advertising execution.

Tide was the dominant brand in terms of share of market and share of media expenditures. Tide's strategy was to sustain this dominance through positioning the brand as superior to any other brand on generic cleaning benefits. In 1986, four national and four regional commercials were aired to support this strategy. These commercials conveyed that Tide provided the benefits of being the most effective detergent for 'tough' situations such as for ground in dirt, stains and bad odours. Tide also aired copy in Quebec claiming effectiveness in all temperatures. Most of Tide's copy was usually developed around a 'slice of life' or testimonial format.

Other brands in the market faced the situation of going head-to-head with Tide's position or competing on a benefit Tide did not claim. Most had chosen the latter route. CPC's ABC brand had made strong gains in the past four years, moving from sixth to second place in market share based on its value position. ABC was positioned as the low-priced, good-quality, cleaning detergent. Re-

EXHIBIT 2
Share of National Media Expenditures (1982–1986)

	Percentages				
	1982	*1983*	*1984*	*1985*	*1986*
ABC	6.4	8.9	12.3	14.0	13.6
Arctic Power	6.1	6.1	6.7	7.2	9.3
Tide	21.0	17.8	19.1	16.4	29.77
Oxydol	5.1	4.5	5.9	6.6	6.4
Sunlight	14.1	10.8	10.5	9.1	11.3
All	10.3	5.5	6.9	7.7	4.0
Wisk	9.9	12.8	10.3	10.4	14.6
All *other* brands	27.1	33.6	28.3	28.6	12.1
Total	100.0	100.0	100.0	100.0	100.0
Total spending ('000)	$12,909	$13,338	$14,420	$13,718	$14,429
% Change	29.2	3.3	8.1	−4.9	5.2

Source: Company records.

cent copy for ABC utilized a demonstration format where the shirts for twins were as clean when washed in ABC versus a leading higher-priced detergent with the statement: "Why pay more, I can't see the difference." Sunlight, a Lever's brand, had for several years attempted to compete directly with Tide and build its consumer franchise based on efficacy and lemon-scent freshness. Advertising execution had been of the up-beat, up-scale lifestyle approach and less of the straightforward problem solution or straight talking approaches seen in other detergent advertising. More recently, Sunlight had been moving toward ABC's value position while retaining the lemon freshness heritage. Sunlight was positioned in 1986 as the detergent which gave a very clean fresh wash at a sensible price. The final brand which attempted to compete for the value position was All. The advertising for All also claimed that the brand particularly whitened white clothes and had a pleasant fragrance.

Arctic Power had been positioned as the superior cleaning laundry detergent especially formulated for cold water washing. For the Eastern market, Arctic Power advertising had utilized a humorous background to communicate brand superiority and its efficacy in cold water. For the Western market, a non-traditional, up-beat execution was used to develop the cold water market.

Wisk, which had received much attention for its 'ring around the collar' advertising, competed directly with Tide on generic cleaning qualities and provided the additional benefit of a liquid formulation. Tide Liquid was introduced in 1985 but received little advertising support in 1986.

Fab and Bold 3 competed for the 'softergents' market. Both products, which had fabric softeners in the formulation, were positioned to clean effectively while softening clothes and reducing static cling. Another detergent with laundry product additives was Oxydol, which was formulated with a mild bleach. Oxydol was positioned as the detergent which kept colours bright while whitening whites.

The other two nationally advertised brands were Cheer 2 and Ivory Snow. Cheer 2 was positioned as the detergent which got clothes clean and fresh. Ivory Snow, which was a soap and not a detergent, was positioned as the laundry cleaning product for infants' clothes which provided superior softness and comfort.

The positioning strategies of these brands reflected the benefit segmentation approach used to market laundry detergents. Most brands attempted to appeal to a wide target (primarily women in the 18 to 49 age group) based on benefits rather than specific demographic segments.

THE COLD WATER MARKET

Every February, CPC commissioned an extensive market research study to identify trends in the laundry detergent market. Referred to as the tracking study, approximately 1800 personal interviews were conducted with female heads-of-households across Canada each year. Among the wealth of data provided by the tracking study was information on cold water usage in Canada. Regular cold water usage was growing in Canada and, by 1986, 29% of households were classified as regular (five or more times out of ten) cold water users (Exhibit 3). Due to cultural and marketing differences, Quebec (55%) and the Maritimes (33%) had more cold water users than the national average.[2] A further 25% of all Canadian households occasionally (one to four times out of ten) used cold water for washing.

For households who washed regularly or occasionally with cold water, the most important benefits of using cold water fell into two broad categories (Exhibit 4). First, it was easier on or better for clothes in that; cold water stopped shrinkage, prevented colors from running, colors stayed bright, and it was easier on clothes. Second, it was more economical in that it saved energy, was cheaper, saved hot water, and saved on electricity. Households in Quebec, the Maritimes and British Columbia mentioned the "economy" benefit more frequently, whereas households in the rest of Canada mentioned the "easier/ better" benefit more often.

[2]Canada has two major cultural groups, the English (who emigrated primarily from the British Isles) and the French (who emigrated from France). Of the 6.2 million French-speaking Canadians, most reside in Quebec (5.3 million) and the Maritimes (264,000). Historically, many French-speaking Canadians had washed clothes in cold water.

ARCTIC POWER

Having achieved reasonable success in Eastern Canada and returned the brand to profitability, Linda Barton decided to increase the brand's share in Alberta and British Columbia for 1986. That brand plan is reported below.

The 1986 Brand Plan for Arctic Power

Objectives. Arctic Power's overall objective is to continue profit development by maintaining mod-

EXHIBIT 3
Proportion of Households Washing with Cold Water (1981–1986)

	Percentages					
	1981	*1982*	*1983*	*1984*	*1985*	*1986*
National	20[a]	22	26	26	26	29
Maritimes	23	25	32	40	32	33
Quebec	35	41	49	48	53	55
Ontario	14	13	18	16	11	17
Prairies	12	12	13	11	10	17
B.C.	13	19	20	17	22	21

Source: Tracking study.
[a]20% of respondents did 5 or more out of 10 washloads in cool or cold water.
$N = 1800$.

EXHIBIT 4
Most Important Benefit of Cold Water Washing, 1986

Reason	*National*	*Maritimes*	*Quebec*	*Ontario*	*Man/Sask*	*Alta.*	*B.C.*
• Stops shrinkage	22.7[a]	19.4	5.2	32.7	35.4	35.4	30.2
• Saves energy	16.5	12.5	32.1	8.2	2.1	9.9	12.9
• Prevents colors from running	11.6	17.4	0.0	21.8	21.3	9.9	2.9
• Cheaper	11.1	19.4	10.4	10.2	2.8	9.3	16.5
• Saves hot water	9.7	9.7	15.5	6.8	11.3	3.1	3.6
• Colors stay bright	8.8	4.2	7.8	11.6	9.2	6.8	7.9
• Saves on electricity	8.7	19.4	0.5	8.2	5.7	16.1	25.9
• Easier on clothes	8.5	11.1	6.7	8.8	10.6	13.7	5.0

Source: Tracking study.

[a]When asked what they felt was the most important benefit of cold water washing, 22.7% of all respondents said "stops shrinking."

Sample includes all households that washed one or more times out of last 10 washes in cold water.

$N = 956$.

Only the eight most frequent responses are reported.

est unit volume growth in Quebec and the Maritimes while developing the Alberta and B.C. regions.

Long Term (by 1996). The long-term objective is to become the number three brand in the category with market share of 12%. Arctic Power will continue to deliver a minimum 18% contribution margin. This will require (1) maintenance of effective creative/media support; (2) superior display prominence particularly in the key Quebec market; (3) continued investigation of development opportunities; and (4) cost of goods savings programs where possible.

Short Term. The short-term objective is to sustain unit growth while building cold water washing dominance. This will require current user reinforcement and continued conversion of warm water washing users. Specifically, in fiscal 1986, Arctic Power will achieve a market share of 6.5% on factory sales of $22.0 million and a contribution margin of 18%. Regional share objectives are Maritimes—6.3%; Quebec—17.2%; Alberta—5%; and B.C.—5%.

Marketing Strategy. Arctic Power will be positioned as the most effective laundry detergent especially formulated for cold water washing. The primary target for Arctic Power is women 18 to 49 and skewed towards the 25 to 34 segment. The secondary market is all adults.

Arctic Power will defend its franchise by allocating regional effort commensurate with brand development in order to maintain current users. In line with the Western expansion strategy, support will be directed to Alberta and B.C. to enhance the acceptance of cold water washing and thereby broaden the appeal among occasional and non-users of Arctic Power.

Media Strategy. The media strategy objective is to achieve high levels of message registration against the target group, through high message continuity and frequency/reach. Media spending behind regional television will be allocated 75% to brand maintenance and 25% to investment spending for brand and cold water market development. Arctic Power will have the number five share of media expenditure position nationally while being the number three detergent advertiser in Quebec.

	T.V. Spending	*GRP's Week*
1985 Plan	$1,010,000	92
Actual	$990,000	88
1986 Plan	$1,350,000	95

GRP (Gross Rating Points) is a measurement of advertising impact derived by multiplying the percentage of the target population exposed to an advertisement by the average number of exposures per person.

Arctic Power's 1986 media spending of $1.35 million is a 36% increase over 1985. This returns Arctic Power to its reach objective of 90% in Quebec, five points ahead of a year ago. In addition, two new television markets have been added with enhanced support in B.C. and Alberta. Reach objectives will be achieved by skewing more of Arctic Power's spending into efficient day time spots which cost less than night network, and is more flexible in light of regional reach objectives.

Scheduling will maintain continuous flighting established in 1985 with concentrations at peak dealing time representing 40 weeks on-air in the east and 32 weeks in the west.

Copy Strategy: Quebec / Maritimes. The creative objective is to convince consumers that Arctic Power is the superior detergent for cold water washing. The consumer benefit is that when they are washing in cold water, Arctic Power will clean clothes and remove stains more effectively than other detergents. The support for this claim is based on the special formulation of Arctic Power. The executional tone will be humorous but with a clear, rational explanation.

Copy Strategy: B.C. / Alberta. The creative objective is to convince consumers that cold water washing is better than hot and when washing in cold water to use Arctic Power. The consumer benefit is that cold water washing reduces shrinkage, colour run and energy costs. The executional tone needs to be distinct from other detergent advertising to break-through traditional washing attitudes and will be young-adult oriented, light, "cool" and up-beat.

Consumer Promotions. The objective of consumer promotions in Quebec/Maritimes is to increase the rate of usage by building frequency of purchase among existing users. The objective in B.C./Alberta is to increase the rate of trial of Arctic Power. In total $856,000 will be spent on consumer promotions.

1. **Jan.:** $.50 In-pack Coupon—To support trade inventory increases and retain current customers in the face of strong competitive activity 400,000 coupons will be placed in all sizes in the Quebec/Maritimes distribution region. The coupon is for 6L or 12L sizes and expected redemption is 18% at a cost of $50,000.
2. **April:** To generate a 17% recent trial of regular-sized boxes of Arctic Power in B.C. and Alberta a 500ml saleable sample pre-priced at $.49 will be distributed through food and drug stores. In addition, a $.50 coupon for the 6L or 12L size will be placed on the pack of all samples. The offer will penetrate 44% of households in the region at a total cost of $382,000.
3. **June:** $.40 Coupon through Free-Standing Insert—To sustain interest and foster trial a $.40 coupon will be delivered to 30% of homes in Alberta/B.C. The coupon is redeemable on the 3L size and expected redemption is 4.5% at a cost of $28,000.
4. **April/July:** Game (Cool-by-the-Pool)—Five in-ground pools and patio accessories will be given away through spelling POWER by letters dropped in boxes of Arctic Power. Two letters will be placed in each box through national distribution and will coincide with high trade activity and the period in which the desirability of the prizes is highest at a cost of $184,000.
5. **Sept.:** $.75 Direct Mail National Coupon Pack (excluding Ontario)—To maximize swing buyer volume (from competition) in Quebec and encourage trial in the west a $.75 coupon for the 6L or 12L size will be mailed to 70% of households in the primary market areas generating a 3% redemption rate at a cost of $212,000.

Trade Promotions. The objectives of the trade promotions is to maintain regular and feature pricing equal to Tide and encourage prominent shelf facing. An advertising feature is expected from each key account during every promotion event run in Quebec and the Maritimes. Distribution for any size is expected to increase to 95%. In the West, maximum effort will be directed at establishing display for the 6L size and four feature events will be expected from each key account. Distribution should be developed to 71% in B.C. and 56% in Alberta. Average deal size will be 14% off regular price or $5.00 per 6L case. In addition, most trade events will include a $1.00 per case allowance for co-op advertising and merchandising support. The total trade budget is $3.46 million which includes $1 million investment spending in the West. The promotion schedule is presented below.

Artic Power
1986 Promotional Schedule

Trade Promotions	*J*	*F*	*M*	*A*	*M*	*J*	*J*	*A*	*S*	*O*	*N*	*D*
Maritimes	X			X		X			X		X	
Quebec	X	X		X		X	X		X		X	X
Alberta/B.C.	X			X		X		X	X			
Consumer Promotions												
East $.50 coupon	X	X										
West sample/coupon				X								
West $.40 coupon						X						
National game				X	X	X	X					
National $.75 coupon									X			

Results of the Western Campaign

In August of 1986, during the middle of the Western campaign, a "minitracking" study was conducted in the two provinces to monitor the program. The results of the August study were compared with the February study and reported in Exhibit 5. Market share for Arctic Power was also measured on a bi-monthly basis and the figures are shown below.

Artic Power Market Share

				1986						Total
	1983	*1984*	*1985*	*D/J*	*F/M*	*A/M*	*J/J*	*A/S*	*O/N*	*1986*
Alberta	0.7	2.3	1.7	1.4	1.1	2.8	28	2.4	1.9	2.1
B.C.	3.2	4.0	3.9	4.0	4.0	6.1	61	7.3	5.4	5.5

The campaign clearly had an impact as brand and advertising awareness had increased, particularly in Alberta (Exhibit 5). Brand trial within the last six months had more than doubled in Alberta and was up over 25% in B.C. However, market share had peaked at 2.8% in Alberta and by the end of the year had declined to 1.9%. Market share in B.C. had reached a high of 7.3% and averaged 5.5% for the year.

In attempting to explain the different results in the two provinces, Linda Barton and Gary Parsons isolated two factors. First, B.C. had always been a "good" market for Arctic Power with share figures around 4%, whereas Alberta was less than half that amount. Second, there had been a considerable amount of competitive activity in Alberta during the year. Each of the three major firms had increased trade and consumer promotions to maintain existing brand shares.

ARCTIC POWER—1987

The 1987 brand plan for Arctic Power was similar in thrust and expenditure levels to the 1986 plan. Expenditure levels in Alberta were reduced until the full implications of the 1986 campaign could be examined. Market share in 1987 was expected to be 6.7%, up marginally from the 6.5% share achieved in 1986 (Exhibit 6).

Each year, every product manager at CPC conducted an extensive brand review. The review for Arctic Power included a detailed competitive analysis of the four leading brands on a regional basis and was based primarily on the tracking study. In July 1987, Linda Barton and Gary Parsons were examining the tracking information which summarized regional information on four critical aspects of the market—brand image (Exhibit 7), brand and advertising awareness (Exhibit 8), brand trial and usage in last six months (Exhibit 9), and market share and share of media expenditures (Exhibit 10). Future decisions for Arctic Power would be based, in large part, on this information.

EXHIBIT 5
Results of Western Campaign

	Prelaunch (February, 1986)		Postlaunch (August, 1986)	
	Alberta	*B.C.*	*Alberta*	*B.C.*
Unaided Brand Awareness[a]				
Brand mentioned total (%)	13.3	20.3	18.1	24.2
Advertising Awareness				
1. Advertising mentioned (unaided)[b] (%)	1.9	7.9	20.3	11.5
2. Advertising mentioned (aided)[c] (%)	18.5	27.9	31.4	34.6
Brand Trial				
1. Ever tried[d] (%)	25.0	43.0	36.3	48.0
2. Used (last six months)[e] (%)	6.8	15.1	17.1	19.4
Image Measure[f]				
• Cleaning and removing dirt	1.0	1.2	1.2	1.5
• Removing tough stains	.7	.9	0.9	1.4
• Being good value for the price	.5	.9	1.0	1.4
• Cleaning well in cold water	1.2	1.3	1.7	1.8
Conversion to Cold Water				
• Average number of loads out of 10 washed in cold water	1.8	2.2	2.0	2.3

Source: Tracking study.

[a]Question: When you think of laundry detergents, what three brands first come to mind? Can you name three more for me? *Brand mentioned total* is if the brand was mentioned at all. On average, respondents mentioned 4.5 brands.

[b]Question: What brand or brands of laundry detergent have you seen or heard advertised? *Advertising mentioned (unaided)* is any mention of brand advertising mentioned.

[c]Question: Have you recently seen or heard any advertising for *brand? Advertising mentioned (aided)* is if respondent said yes when asked.

[d]Question: Have you ever tried *brand*?

[e]Question: Have you used *brand* in the past six months?

[f]Respondents rated the brand on the four image measures. The rating scale ranged from −5 (doesn't perform well) to +5 (performs well).

THE DECISION

Prior to deciding on the strategic direction for Arctic Power, Ms. Barton and Mr. Parsons met to discuss the situation. It was a hot Toronto day in early July 1987. Ms. Barton began the discussion. "I've got some estimates on what our shares are likely to be for 1987. It looks like we'll have a national share of 6.7%, broken down as follows: Maritimes (6.3%), Quebec (18%), Ontario (1%), Manitoba/Saskatchewan (0.1%), Alberta (2%), B.C. (6%)."

Mr. Parsons responded, "I think our problem in Alberta was all the competitive activity. Under normal conditions we'd have achieved 5% of that market. But the Alberta objective is small when you think about what we could do in our other undeveloped markets. I've been giving it a lot of thought and we should go national with Arctic Power. We've got a brand that is equal to Tide and we've got to stop keeping it a secret from the rest of Canada. If we can duplicate the success we had in B.C., we'll turn this market on its ear."

EXHIBIT 6
Arctic Power
Market Share and Total Volume by Region (1983–1987E)

	Market Share					
Region	*1983*	*1984*	*1985*	*1986*	*1987E*	*1986 Total Volume[a] ('000 litres)*
National	4.7	5.6	6.4	6.5	6.7	406,512
Maritimes	5.3	5.7	6.3	6.3	6.3	32,616
Quebec	12.3	13.8	17.7	17.5	18.0	113,796
Ontario	.9	1.1	1.1	.8	1.0	158,508
Manitoba/Saskatchewan	.2	.2	.1	.1	.1	28,440
Alberta	.7	2.3	1.7	2.1	2.0	40,644
British Columbia	3.2	4.0	3.9	5.5	6.0	32,508

Source: Company records.
[a]All laundry detergent.
1987E = Estimated.

EXHIBIT 7
Brand Images by Region, 1986

Image Measure[a]	*National*	*Maritimes*	*Quebec*	*Ontario*	*Man/Sask*	*Alberta*	*B.C.*
Arctic Power							
• Cleaning and removing dirt	1.4	2.0	2.5	.8	.4	1.0	1.2
• Removing tough stains	1.1	1.6	1.9	.7	3.0	.7	.9
• Being good value for the price	1.1	1.4	2.6	.3	.2	.5	.9
• Cleaning well in cold water	1.6	2.1	2.8	1.0	.4	1.2	1.3
ABC							
• Cleaning—dirt	1.0	1.9	.5	.9	1.1	1.2	1.6
• Removing—stains	.5	1.1	.0	.6	.8	.7	.9
• Being—price	1.5	2.4	.8	1.5	1.3	1.7	2.1
• Cleaning—cold water	.6	1.0	.1	.7	.7	.7	.7
Sunlight							
• Cleaning—dirt	2.0	1.9	1.8	2.4	1.9	1.6	1.6
• Removing—stains	1.6	1.6	1.5	1.9	1.4	1.2	1.2
• Being—price	2.0	1.7	1.9	2.4	1.8	1.7	1.5
• Cleaning—cold water	1.4	1.1	1.5	1.7	1.2	1.1	.7

continued

EXHIBIT 7
continued

Image Measure[a]	*National*	*Maritimes*	*Quebec*	*Ontario*	*Man/Sask*	*Alberta*	*B.C.*
Tide							
• Cleaning—dirt	3.4	3.7	3.2	3.6	3.5	3.3	3.2
• Removing—stains	3.0	3.1	2.8	3.3	3.0	2.7	2.7
• Being—price	3.1	3.1	3.3	3.1	2.8	3.0	2.4
Cleaning—cold water	2.4	2.3	2.6	2.5	2.4	2.3	1.9

Source: Tracking study.

[a]Respondents rated each brand on the four image measures. The rating scale ranged from −5 (doesn't perform well) to +5 (performs well).

N = 1816.

A difference of .2 is likely to be significant in statistical terms.

EXHIBIT 8
Brand and Advertising Awareness by Region, 1986

	Percentages						
	National	*Maritimes*	*Quebec*	*Ontario*	*Man/Sask*	*Alberta*	*B.C.*
Unaided Brand Awareness[a]							
1. Brand Mentioned First							
Arctic Power	4.4	7.0	12.5	.0	0.0	1.0	2.6
ABC	8.1	18.4	4.6	7.3	4.7	8.4	12.8
Sunlight	9.3	8.4	9.6	9.3	12.0	9.1	7.9
Tide	57.9	55.5	41.9	69.7	63.1	59.7	54.4
2. Brand Mentioned Total							
Arctic Power	23.0	43.5	49.8	5.0	3.0	13.3	20.3
ABC	61.3	82.6	47.9	64.0	56.1	67.5	64.9
Sunlight	58.1	60.2	50.8	65.0	58.5	62.0	46.6
Tide	94.8	95.7	88.8	98.0	97.3	97.4	94.4
Advertising Awareness							
1. Advertising Mentioned (Unaided)[b]							
Arctic Power	7.0	10.7	17.5	.7	.0	1.9	7.9
ABC	25.2	32.8	20.8	27.0	17.3	30.5	24.9
Sunlight	8.6	4.7	5.9	13.0	5.0	6.8	8.2
Tide	44.0	40.1	32.7	55.0	46.2	48.4	35.4

EXHIBIT 8
continued

	Percentages						
	National	*Maritimes*	*Quebec*	*Ontario*	*Man/Sask*	*Alberta*	*B.C.*
2. Advertising Mentioned (Aided)[c]							
Arctic Power	*29.2*	*38.8*	*55.1*	*15.3*	*5.6*	*18.5*	*27.9*
ABC	*56.1*	*61.5*	*55.1*	*56.0*	*51.5*	*60.4*	*53.4*
Sunlight	*29.9*	*20.1*	*26.4*	*40.3*	*21.3*	*21.1*	*24.9*
Tide	*65.3*	*60.9*	*54.8*	*78.0*	*68.1*	*65.3*	*48.4*

Source: Tracking study.

[a]Question: When you think of laundry detergents, what three brands first come to mind? Can you name three more for me? *Brand mentioned first* is the first brand mentioned. *Brand mentioned total* is if the brand was mentioned at all. On average, respondents mentioned 4.5 brands.

[b]Question: What brand or brands of laundry detergent have you seen or heard advertised? *Advertising mentioned (unaided)* is any mention of brand advertising mentioned.

[c]Question: Have you recently seen or heard any advertising for *brand*? *Advertising mentioned (aided)* is if respondent said yes when asked.

N = 1816.

EXHIBIT 9
Brand Trial in Last Six Months by Region, 1986

Brand Trial	*National*	*Maritimes*	*Quebec*	*Ontario*	*Man/Sask*	*Alberta*	*B.C.*
1. Ever Tried[a]							
Arctic Power	42.4	67.9	75.6	19.7	20.3	25.0	43.0
ABC	60.4	83.9	50.8	60.0	53.5	62.7	67.9
Sunlight	66.3	65.6	59.4	75.0	67.1	58.1	58.7
Tide	93.6	91.0	90.1	97.3	95.0	91.9	92.1
2. Used (Last Six Months)[b]							
Arctic Power	19.4	29.8	46.5	4.3	2.3	6.8	15.1
ABC	37.2	56.2	34.7	32.3	29.2	39.3	47.5
Sunlight	38.3	29.8	38.0	44.3	36.2	36.7	28.5
Tide	68.1	66.6	66.0	73.3	67.8	69.5	54.8

Source: Tracking study.

[a]Question: Have you ever tried *brand*?

[b]Question: Have you used *brand* in the past six months?

Note: On average, respondents had 1.3 brands of laundry detergents in the home.

N = 1816.

EXHIBIT 10
Market Share and Share of Media Expenditures by Region, 1986

	Percentages						
	National	*Maritimes*	*Quebec*	*Ontario*	*Man/Sask*	*Alberta*	*B.C.*
Market Share							
Arctic Power	6.5	6.3	17.5	.8	.1	2.1	5.5
ABC	13.9	27.8	8.6	13.8	11.6	16.1	21.5
Sunlight	13.4	7.7	12.1	16.4	14.2	10.4	11.3
Tide	34.1	24.5	28.3	39.3	40.0	36.9	28.5
All other brands	32.1	33.7	33.5	29.7	34.1	34.5	33.2
Total	100.0	100.0	100.0	100.0	100.0	100.0	100.0
Share of Media Expenditures[a]							
Arctic Power	9.3	13.1	16.1	.5	1.4	16.0	13.1
ABC	13.6	14.7	9.1	18.4	17.3	12.1	12.1
Sunlight	11.3	11.1	11.1	12.6	10.2	10.1	9.8
Tide	29.7	27.8	25.1	33.1	38.1	30.2	28.7
All other brands	36.1	33.3	38.6	35.4	33.0	31.6	36.3
Total	100.0	100.0	100.0	100.0	100.0	100.0	100.0
Total $ ('000)	14,429	695	4,915	4,758	928	1,646	1,487

Source: Company records.
[a]The total amount of advertising spent by all brands was determined. The amount spent by each brand as a percentage of total spending was calculated.

"Wait a minute Gary," said Linda, "in 1986 we spent almost $2,000,000 on advertising, consumer and trade promotions in the West. Even though spending returned to normal levels, this year, that was a big investment to get the business going and it will be at least four years before we get that money back. If we go after the national market, you can well expect Tide to fight back with trade spending which will make your share or margin objectives even harder to achieve. On a per capita basis we'd have to spend at least as much in our underdeveloped markets as we spent in the West. We've got a real problem here. Our brand may be as good as Tide but I don't think we can change a lot of consumers' minds, particularly the loyal Tide users. I hate to say it but for many Canadians, when they think about washing clothes, Tide is the brand they think will clean their clothes better than any other brand. I agree that the size of the undeveloped market warrants another look. But remember, any decision will have to be backed up with a solid analysis and a plan that senior management will buy."

Gary replied, "I know that even if I am right it will be a tough sell. I haven't got it completed yet but I'm working out the share level we will need to break even if we expanded nationally."

Linda responded, "Well, when you get that done, we will talk about national expansion again. For the moment we have to resolve this positioning dilemma. I don't like a two country approach but it does seem to make sense in this case. I think we might still want to focus on the brand in the East and continue to develop the cold water washing market in the West."

Gary would have preferred to continue the discussion of national expansion but realized he would have to do some work and at least produce the share estimate before he raised the subject again and so replied, "I agree that Canada is not one homogeneous market but that perspective can be taken to extremes. I worry that all of this data we get on the regional markets is getting in the way of good marketing judgement. I prefer a unified strategy and the Quebec campaign has a proven track record."

Linda concluded, "Let's go over the data again, then start making our decisions. Remember, our goal is to develop a solid brand name for 1988 for Arctic Power."

CASE 13 | *Playboy Enterprises, Inc.*

In early 1986, Christie Hefner, president and chief operating officer, Playboy Enterprises, Inc., had been reviewing the company's strategies to face the changing world. Once considered a trendsetter for urban sophisticates, the adult leisure company in recent years has increasingly found its offerings out of step with the times.

As a writer on social issues put it, "The image of the playboy in a smoking jacket is obsolete. People today are more interested in their cars and their careers than they are in sex." Although that claim may be open to dispute, Playboy has reason to be alarmed. The circulation of its flagship magazine has dwindled to just over four million a month from more than seven million in 1972. The number of Playboy Club key holders has fallen steadily. The cable television Playboy Channel, once seen as crucial to the future, loses money and has yet to prove that it can survive in its highly competitive field.

Between 1983 and 1985, Playboy's revenue fell by nearly 50 percent. It earned a profit on operations in only one of four years between 1982 and 1985, when it was forced by old legal problems to give up its lucrative casinos. The company was in the black (by $6.7 million) in its 1985 fiscal year only because of returns on $60 million in investments. And its auditors qualified their opinion on the financial statement for that year because of uncertainty over whether Playboy can collect all it is owed on one casino sale.

COMPANY HISTORY

Initially Playboy Enterprises, Inc. was established as HMH Publishing Company in 1953 to publish *Playboy*. The present name was adopted in 1971.

Today the company's businesses, in addition to *Playboy* and *Games* magazines, include the development and production of programming principally for pay television and videocassettes and products for direct sale and licensing that feature the Playboy name and trademarks for worldwide distribution. In addition, the company owns and franchises Playboy Clubs. In the 1970s the company entered the resort hotel and casino business in different places, including London, Miami, the Bahamas, and Atlantic City. However, in 1982 the company discontinued its resort hotel and casino operations.

ENVIRONMENTAL CHANGES

Playboy is a victim of the social changes it helped promote. Attitudes toward sex have evolved rapidly since the days when the magazine could shock millions by publishing two photographs of an undraped Marilyn Monroe. Today Playboy has

This case was prepared as a basis for class discussion rather than to illustrate either effective or ineffective handling of an administrative situation.

to compete, not only with countless far more lurid "skin books," but also against the popular media. Rock songs may have X-rated lyrics and an episode of "Dynasty" may be nearly as titillating as a centerfold.

As Ms. Hefner puts it, "We no longer can contrast ourselves to a gray-flannel Eisenhower society. It's now a lot more difficult for us to offer something unique."

Yet Playboy also finds itself considerably vexed these days by those who consider its business immoral or sexist or both. Although its cable television fare isn't hard-core, for instance, it has repeatedly been challenged in court (so far unsuccessfully) by communities that want it banned.

After ABC recently broadcast a film based on Gloria Steinem's critical account of her 1963 stint as a bunny, Playboy President Christie Hefner fired off a memo asking her staff to "ponder what it is Playboy and all of its resources can and should be doing to counter the . . . misimpression out there that we are not good guys."

Perhaps a tougher problem for Hefner, though, is finding a clear mission for Playboy in the 1990s, one as potent as her father's former vision for the company. In an era of aggressive careerism among both sexes, the company no longer gets much mileage out of the so-called Playboy philosophy, Mr. Hefner's concept of the lifestyle of a man of leisure.

THE REAL PROBLEM

Some company officials believe that one of Playboy's biggest handicaps may be its association with the public image of its founder, now 59 years old. As a Playboy executive put it, "Pajamas just aren't as fashionable as they used to be."

Though still the best-selling magazine for men, *Playboy* has fallen far behind arch-rival *Penthouse* in lucrative newsstand sales. According to *Penthouse* publisher Bob Guccione, "*Playboy's* market is older and its readers are passing into oblivion." But Playboy executives say that the readership age difference is minimal. However, there are other worrisome signs. A Chicago newsstand operator who has sold a lot of copies of *Playboy* speaks of the typical buyer as "a guy who thinks he's up-to-date but isn't." One woman who posed for a pictorial was surprised when she saw the letters the feature generated: "a whole bunch of them were from guys in prison." A former public relations executive for Playboy contends that the company "doesn't want to face reality—that time has passed it by."

NEW STRATEGY

Against this background, Playboy Enterprises is undertaking what Hefner calls a "repositioning." The strategy, she says, is to go after a more upscale audience by being more in tune with current tastes and values. "I think we should be on the cutting edge of how people who have changed their behavior to reflect a more liberal lifestyle are going to live."

The October 1985 issue of *Playboy,* marked "Collector's Edition," began what the company calls the magazine's next generation. This included greater coverage of such 'life style' subjects as personal finance and home electronics. An ad in that issue asked, "What sort of man reads *Playboy*?" and offered as an example race car driver Danny Sullivan. Posing in a black silk evening jacket, he explained that he "grew with the magazine," learning, for instance, to care about clothes. Curiously, elsewhere in the issue was a piece satirizing the consumer society.

Sensitive to criticism that it portrays women as sex objects, *Playboy* intends to feature some who are more mature or more accomplished. The lead feature in the November 1985 issue was a nod in this direction, but it hardly seemed likely to defuse the moral issue. Picturing members of Mensa, the club people can join only if they have high IQs, the feature was entitled "America's Smartest Girls Pose Nude."

Nevertheless, Hefner says Playboy's effort to move upscale is working. As evidence, she notes that the October 1985 issue carried advertising for Campbell Soup's Le Menu frozen dinners.

Covers of the new generation *Playboy* are to have a glitzier look. They are planned in long meetings by a committee of fashion and art experts who try to base their designs as much on the latest fashions as on erotic content.

The graphics also are slicker and a different printing process binds pages with glue instead of staples, giving a more finished look. According to *Playboy's* art director, "The magazine is supposed to look a lot more like the kind of thing you'd put on a coffee table." That goal may be a bit optimistic, however; newsstands say that half of the buyers of Playboy still ask for a paper bag to carry it home in.

The new magazine retains many standard features, like the Playboy Advisor, which interperses advice about sex with answers to questions about stereos or turbochargers. Some editors complain about the uneven quality and occasionally questionable taste of color cartoons. Mr. Hefner himself is said to have rejected an editor's plea to eliminate the Party Jokes feature, which in the October 1985 issue regaled readers with one-liners like, "What's boffo box office among milkmaids? *Pail Rider.*"

The "repositioning" also applies to the Playboy Clubs, which haven't had a major updating since they were started a quarter-century ago. Even with a recent redecorating, the club in Chicago, with its plush red carpeting and black leather bar stools, looks a little like a museum for the jazz age. A gift shop upfront peddling Playboy T-shirts, cigarette lighters and golf putters lends a touristy atmosphere to the place.

Rather than confront the deteriorating image of its big-city clubs, Playboy several years ago headed for the hinterlands, franchising clubs in places like Lansing, Michigan, and Des Moines, Iowa, where they might still have novelty value. But without a strong big-city base, the whole chain lost its urban gleam. The Lansing club began resorting to such decidely unglamorous promotions as lip-sync contests and valet parking for farm tractors.

THE NEW YORK EXPERIMENT

In the fall of 1985, the company reopened its newly done New York club. It was a bold experiment. The cottontailed bunnies were replaced by hostesses greeting guests wearing long, glittering Jean Harlow-style gowns. Some of the waiters were men. Absent were the traditional pool table, party balloons, and Leroy Neiman paintings. Instead, video effects, stage acts, and music by a 10-piece house orchestra were offered.

The New York club's new look was sculpted by Richard Melman, who is noted for elaborate concept restaurants that are as much show-biz productions as eateries. He selected bunnies with talent as bodybuilders, astrologists, and jugglers. Costumes ranged from a sequined one called the Michael Jackson outfit, to sweaterdresses, to a takeoff of the current cottontail suit. The idea of male waiters (called rabbits) was to help women feel more comfortable in the club.

It remains to be seen if the company will convert other clubs to the New York style. The company has 12 other Playboy Clubs, ten of which are franchised rather than company owned. A section of the club called Cafe Playboy may be tested as a prototype for a chain of franchised bars open to the public. (A Playboy key still is needed for admittance to the clubs, though temporary memberships are readily available.)

STRATEGY FOR OTHER BUSINESSES

Playboy's products division, too, is working to bolster the company's image or at least to stop endangering it. The division has sold countless key chains, air fresheners, and the like, even though doing so risked cheapening the company's trademark. Now Playboy is moving away from novelty items and into fashion apparel and branded consumer products. One success is Playboy's men's underwear, the second-best-selling brand.

Playboy still has some hard thinking to do about its video operation. The division, which launched the first sex-oriented cable channel for a mass audience five years ago, had identity problems from the start. Unable to decide how racy to be, the channel wound up alienating viewers at both ends of the spectrum.

Earlier in 1985, for instance, the channel stopped offering erotic programming during prime time and switched to mainstream movies and quasi-journalistic specials such as "Omar Sharif Hosts the Prostitutes of Paris." Viewership dropped and Playboy soon reverted to prime-time prurience.

Partly because of its turnabouts, the Playboy Channel has had the highest disconnect rate in the industry, 13% of viewers each month. Its current level of about 762,000 subscribers isn't enough to pay for the quality programming that might attract a larger audience. At $20 million, the channel's yearly budget is less than a network might spend during a season on a single series.

As a result, Playboy is deemphasizing the channel as its main outlet for programming and will focus more on cassette sales and a recently launched pay-per-view service. It also is weighing a return to producing a late-night variety show or hour-long specials, either of which it would try to sell to one of the networks.

Still, Playboy's video operations, like the rest of its empire, is continuing to grope for the right formula for today's audience. As Ms. Hefner sums up, "We have to reflect a modern, sophisticated image."

CASE 14 | *Pizza Hut, Inc.*

In May 1986, Steve Reinemund, the newly appointed president of Pizza Hut, Inc., announced that he intended to pursue vigorously the "exciting opportunities afforded by our new segment, delivery." Seven months later, the home delivery units had produced mixed results, and Reinemund met with his senior managers to decide how to respond.

Entry into the home delivery market had been a major strategic decision at Pizza Hut, and Reinemund was well aware of the difficulties it presented. Half of the 5,025 Pizza Hut system restaurants were owned by large, powerful franchisees with exclusive rights to the territories they controlled. While some franchisees saw the benefits of home delivery in their markets, others were strongly opposed. Moreover, many franchisees did not agree with the manner in which Pizza Hut would implement delivery. Nevertheless, to be successful, the delivery strategy needed the franchisees' cooperation. Attaining this cooperation in the Pizza Hut franchise system would be, in the words of Jim Baxter, vice president of franchising, "a matter of *sell,* not *tell.*"

This case was prepared by Professor Patrick J. Kaufmann as the basis for class discussion rather than to illustrate either effective or ineffective handling of an administrative situation. Proprietary data have been disguised. Reprinted by permission of the Harvard Business School.

THE PIZZA MARKET

The rapid growth in home delivery in the mid-1980s revitalized the pizza market and was responsible for pizza's position as the fastest-growing part of the $53 billion fast food market. Three main segments comprised the pizza restaurant market: eat-in, carryout, and delivery. Below were the sales for each segment.

	Eat-in	*Carryout*	*Delivery*	*Total*
1982	$4.3 billion (57%)	$3.1 billion (41%)	$ .1 billion (1%)	$ 7.5 billion
1984	$4.7 billion (48%)	$4.0 billion (41%)	$1.0 billion (10%)	$ 9.7 billion
1986[a]	$5.1 billion (40%)	$5.0 billion (39%)	$2.6 billion (20%)	$12.7 billion
1990[a]	$5.9 billion (27%)	$9.0 billion (41%)	$7.0 billion (32%)	$21.9 billion

Source: GDR/Crest Enterprises, Inc.
[a]Projections based on limited Pizza Hut entry into delivery segment as of third-quarter 1986.

Many companies competed in more than one segment; for example, carryout was a significant percentage of most eat-in restaurants' business. At Pizza Hut, carryout accounted for 40% of the dollar volume in 1986, compared with 37% in 1982.

In 1986, while the overall pizza market expanded rapidly (because of home delivery), in-restaurant consumption of pizza was not increasing significantly. Industry observers believed that the restaurant industry was seriously overbuilt; pizza parlors seemed to be on every corner in some towns. They believed that the already intense local competition in the pizza eat-in and carryout segments would soon approach all-out warfare, as evidenced by increased use of couponing, deals, and price competition.

THE PIZZA CONSUMER

Pizza was a very popular restaurant food item, second only to hamburgers in frequency of purchase. Pizza was predominantly a dinner food, although many consumers also viewed it as an evening snack. Consumers did not react casually to pizza, unlike their feelings for hamburgers, chicken, and fish. Consumer research had shown that pizza was a personal, almost sensual experience for many people. Moreover, consumers generally did not believe that great pizza could be made by a fast food chain.

While pizza consumption was strongest in the northern and eastern parts of the United States, pizza's appeal was broad based with no areas exhibiting major rejection. However, tastes in pizza varied significantly by region. This presented a challenge for chains attempting to maintain product continuity while expanding into different regions.

By the early 1980s, convenience was crucial to many consumers. Two-career families often found cooking at home or eating in restaurants too time consuming, thereby increasing carryout and home delivery business. In both 1985 and 1986, consumer surveys undertaken by the *National Restaurant Association* identified pizza home delivery as the most important new fast food concept. Another study had shown that consumers generally viewed pizza as eat-at-home food. Many analysts believed that the rapid growth of the in-home video rental market, together with the increasing number of baby-boomers with small children, would further fuel the pizza delivery segment.

COMPETITION IN THE PIZZA MARKET

Although faced with intense competition from aggressive regional chains and single-unit owner-operated local competitors, Pizza Hut had dominated the eat-in pizza segment nationwide for years (Exhibit 1). Godfather's Pizza, another eat-in/carryout chain, which competed in many of the same local markets as Pizza Hut, traditionally was perceived as Pizza Hut's most significant national competitor.

EXHIBIT 1
Top Pizza Chains, 1986

	Systemwide Sales ($ millions)	*Units*	*Average Check/Person*	*Delivery*
Pizza Hut	1,934	5,025	$9.99	Separate delivery units plus franchisee add-on delivery out of restaurant
Domino's	1,550	3,696	$9.50	Delivery only
Little Caesar	520	1,308	$2.75	No delivery
Pizza Inn	278.7	748	$4.30	Separate delivery units
Godfather's	275	650	$9.75	Add-on delivery out of restaurant
Round Table Pizza	250	535	$5.00	Add-on delivery out of restaurant
Showbiz/Chuck E. Cheese	249	268	$5.20	No delivery
Shakey's	197	386	$4.25	Add-on delivery out of restaurant
Mr. Gatti's	139.2	319	$7.81	Add-on delivery out of restaurant

Adapted from *Nation's Restaurant News.*

Before 1984, neither Pizza Hut nor its franchisees thought that Domino's Pizza posed a serious competitive threat to Pizza Hut's leadership position in the overall pizza market. Domino's, however, had grown from sales of $626 million in 1984 to $1.085 billion in 1985, and to $1.55 billion by the end of 1986. In 1985 the chain opened 954 new outlets (bringing the total to 2,839)—the highest one-year total ever recorded by a food service company. Two-thirds of Domino's outlets were franchised; the company used its company-owned stores as sites for required franchisee training. Although there were several large franchisees operating many units all over the United States, most of the 600 franchisees in early 1986 owned only one or two stores. While some of its outlets had carryout windows, Domino's was essentially a delivery-only chain. Domino's management believed the large percentage of carryout business in the industry was especially vulnerable to Domino's delivery strategy.

Pizza Hut first experienced the effects of Domino's expansion in its company-owned stores. While Pizza Hut's franchisees had exclusive rights to most of the smaller markets, Pizza Hut's company-owned stores controlled most of the large, densely populated metropolitan markets. Domino's had initially focused its national expansion on those large metropolitan markets. By late 1985, Pizza Hut senior management was convinced that Domino's dominance of the fast-growing delivery segment was the major threat to Pizza Hut's continued leadership of the overall pizza market. By 1986, Domino's had begun to extend its expansion into the smaller towns generally controlled by Pizza Hut franchisees. Domino's clearly intended to gain total market leadership while maintaining its dominance of the delivery segment.

PIZZA HUT, INCORPORATED

On June 15, 1958, Dan and Frank Carney, two college students from Wichita, Kansas, opened the first Pizza Hut restaurant. It was a startling success. By the following February, the Carney brothers had opened two more restaurants and had begun to develop plans for the first franchised outlet. The chain grew rapidly, with 43 restaurants opened by 1963 and 296 by 1968. Pizza Hut went public in 1969, and in 1977 was acquired by PepsiCo, Inc. In 1971 Pizza Hut became the largest pizza restaurant chain in the world in both sales and number of restaurants. Sales reached $1 billion in 1981; by December 1986, Pizza Hut, still headquartered in Wichita, had a total of 5,025 domestic units and annual sales of almost $2 billion (Exhibit 2).

Since the 1960s, Pizza Hut restaurants were characterized by a distinctive freestanding design and familiar red roof. All Pizza Hut restaurants were full-service, eat-in/carryout family-style operations seating about 60 to 90 customers and normally open from 11 A.M. to midnight.

Although the menu had changed over the years, pizza was always the main product in Pizza Hut restaurants. The company paid careful attention to operational efficiency, and continued to offer a high-quality product at a premium price. A constant stream of new product introductions served to invigorate consumer interest, but many franchisees were concerned by the increased cost of operations caused by the expanding menu.

For more than 20 years, the Pizza Hut franchisees had taken the lead in marketing. In the early 1980s, however, the company further strength-

EXHIBIT 2
Pizza Hut Historical Data (U.S. Domestic Only)

	1979	*1980*	*1981*	*1982*	*1983*	*1984*	*1985*	*1986*
System net sales ($MM)	732	832	1,007	1,170	1,394	1,566	1,743	1,934
Market share[a]	14.9	15.7	17.0	17.2	18.0	17.3	16.0	15.4
Units[b]								
Company	1,940	1,888	1,843	1,845	1,911	2,051	2,224	2,534
Franchise	1,801	1,873	1,922	1,975	2,095	2,157	2,309	2,491
Total	**3,741**	**3,761**	**3,765**	**3,820**	**4,006**	**4,208**	**4,533**	**5,025**
Company								
PSA[c] sales ($M)	196	221	267	306	348	372		
(Traditional)							395	400
(Delivery)							282	289
PSA sales growth								
Real	(3.1)	4.7	11.8	8.0	9.8	1.8	2.0	(2.0)
Price	6.4	8.1	9.0	6.6	3.9	5.1	3.4	.8
Total	**3.7**	**12.8**	**20.8**	**14.6**	**13.7**	**6.9**	**5.4**	**(1.2)**
Net sales ($MM)	354	399	476	556	678	766	835	929
Net sales growth %	—	12.7	19.2	16.8	21.9	13.0	9.0	11.3
Total revenues ($MM)	495	556	489	569	699	795	867	967
ROAE %[d]	3.5	6.1	8.9	16.4	21.7	16.9	15.0	12.4
Franchisees								
PSA sales ($M)		237	280	314	350	386	400	415
Net sales ($MM)	378	433	531	613	715	799	908	1,005

[a]Based on data from GDR/Crest Enterprises, Inc.
[b]Total number of U.S. domestic units of all kinds: restaurant, delivery, and mobile open that year.
[c]PSA—Per Store Average: annual average computed by dividing total sales for each four-week store period by number of stores open during that period and then aggregating across all thirteen store periods.
[d]Return on Assets Employed: calculated as earnings divided by year's average net asset base.

ened its corporate marketing department and began developing comprehensive national and local market strategies. By 1986, the company was developing and implementing systemwide corporate marketing programs and realizing leverage from national TV advertising.

THE FRANCHISE SYSTEM AT PIZZA HUT

Franchising was an integral part of the Pizza Hut strategy since the corporation's founding. In 1968, there were 293 franchised restaurants and only seven company-owned restaurants. Over the next seven years, the company built new stores and acquired many more (including the acquisition of the 225 units of a large Pizza Hut franchisee). By the mid-1970s, there were almost as many company-owned as franchised units. In December 1986, 135 individuals, partnerships, and/or corporations operated 2,395 Pizza Hut system restaurants and 96 delivery-only units as franchisees. Meanwhile, the company itself operated 2,173 restaurants and 361 delivery-only units.

Many of the original franchisees, whose holdings had grown with the company, were still part of the system in 1986. Sixty percent of all franchised units were controlled by franchisees whose main offices were still in Wichita. In the Pizza Hut system, exclusive franchises were granted for specified market areas. Unlike franchise systems characterized by single-unit owner/operators, most Pizza Hut franchisees were large companies with diversified holdings, sometimes including other food service franchisor units like Kentucky Fried Chicken and Long John Silver. Of the 135 franchisees, almost two-thirds operated 10 or more Pizza Hut system restaurants in 1986. Except for minority opportunity programs, no new franchise areas had been offered to the public since 1971. When a franchisee chose to sell its holdings, they were purchased by the company or another franchise holder.

Franchisee rights and obligations were specified in formal franchise agreements. Under the agreements each franchisee was obligated to develop its exclusive market area in accordance with a five-year development schedule. Essentially, the agreement required the franchisee to open an agreed-upon number of new restaurants during the first year of the agreement, an agreed-upon number during the second year, and so on, up to year five. The development schedule represented franchisee commitment to significant continuing investment in the business. After the five-year period expired, the company could negotiate a secondary development schedule with the franchisee to open additional restaurants in the area, if the company deemed it practicable. Although franchisee failure to comply with either development schedule entitled the company to franchise others or to open company-owned restaurants in the previously exclusive area, this had never been necessary. In no case could there be a restaurant established within two miles of an existing franchisee restaurant.

Franchisees paid Pizza Hut an initial fee of $15,000 for each system restaurant they opened. Franchisees also paid the company an ongoing franchise fee of 4% of monthly gross sales. The company or franchisee invested about $466,000–$816,000 to open each eat-in/carryout restaurant. By contrast, delivery-only units required an estimated $128,500–$198,500 investment. However, by the time one included delivery vehicles, training, additional advertising, and the company's central order-taking computer system, the company's investment in a company-owned delivery unit was about equal to that of a traditional restaurant. Franchisees investing in delivery-only units typically did not buy vehicles and did not always adopt the company's computer-ordering system (see Exhibit 3 for expenses of company-owned delivery units).

THE INTERNATIONAL PIZZA HUT FRANCHISE HOLDERS ASSOCIATION

The International Pizza Hut Franchise Holders Association (IPHFHA) was formed in 1967 to "solidify the national image of Pizza Hut and to

EXHIBIT 3
Pro Forma Profit and Loss Statement (Based on $8,000 / Week Sales)[a]

	Company-owned Traditional Restaurant	*Company-owned Delivery Unit*
Gross sales	100.0%	100.0%
Advertising, discounts, promotions, and allowances	16.5%	18.5%
Cost of sales[b] & labor	48.5%	46.2%
Semivariables & premiums[c]	8.7%	5.2%
Vehicles[d]	—	6.1%
Occupancy costs	6.0%	2.1%
General and administrative	7.2%	7.2%
Customer service center costs	—	5.9%
Net field contribution	13.1%	8.8%

[a]Percentages reflect an assumed $8,000/week store. As weekly sales decreased below $8,000, expenses as percent of sales increased significantly. At approximately $7,000/week. Delivery Unit net field contribution was 0.

[b]Cost of sales tended to be lower in the Delivery Units due to a combination of upsizing and higher prices per order. Labor costs for Delivery Units did not include order-taking expenses that were reflected in the Customer Service Center costs.

[c]Semivariables refers to utilities, uniforms, and other operating supplies. Premiums refers to items such as special glassware or toys that were given away or sold below cost to promote the sale of a particular menu item.

[d]Vehicle expenses reflect a mix of driver- and company-owned vehicles. Eighty percent of the delivery vehicles were owned by the drivers, who were reimbursed for their use per trip.

further product loyalty," and to "devise the most appropriate use of the funds available for national advertising." By 1986, its role had been extended to render many other services to franchisees (e.g., accounting services, group life insurance, workman's compensation insurance, credit union).

Franchisees were required to become members of the IPHFHA. The IPHFHA communicated with the company regularly through the IPHFHA board of directors. The IPHFHA employed a professional staff headed by Gerald Aaron, president, who acted as intermediary between the board and the company. He directed for the association the broad policy areas of marketing, finance, and administration. Joint advisory committees (with franchisee and company members) were formed in 1985 to further enhance communication between the company and the franchisees on the issues of human resources, delivery, products, and buildings and equipment.

The IPHFHA was reorganized in 1975, and the Advertising Committee was formed to "determine and control the amount, kind, and quality of national advertising and sales promotion to be provided . . . for Pizza Hut and its franchisees." (In 1981 the role of the Advertising Committee was continued under the new franchise agreement.) Four marketing professionals made up the Advertising Committee, two representing the company and two representing the franchisees. IPHFHA members voted on funding for national advertising and other IPHFHA programs. The company, although not a member of IPHFHA, was contractually bound by the franchise agreement to contribute at the same rate as the franchisees. In 1986, the current assessment was 2% of the first $28,000 of monthly sales for each restaurant and 1% of all monthly sales above $28,000. The Advertising Committee controlled the entire advertising budget, and was also responsible for hiring and firing the national advertising agency.

Market area advertising was managed by local co-ops comprising all of those franchisees (and the company if applicable) operating restaurants within a particular market area. All co-op members, franchisees and company alike, were required to make contributions to the co-op for advertising in their area in the amount of 2% of monthly gross sales (in addition to the contributions to the national advertising fund). All disputes arising within co-ops were arbitrated by the Advertising Committee.

In addition to ad hoc interaction between the company and its franchisees at regional store manager meetings, there were two general systemwide meetings each year. Franchisees set the summer meeting agenda and the company set the winter meeting agenda. Company management also regularly met with the board of IPHFHA and with the franchisees on the advisory committees.

DELIVERY AT PIZZA HUT, INC.

For many years, the prospect of entering the delivery market worried Pizza Hut senior managers; delivery units might cannibalize the traditional restaurant business, causing reduced profit margins. In the summer of 1984, however, Pizza Hut began exploring the possibility of such an entry. Because it was believed that the addition of delivery service to traditional eat-in restaurants would create unmanageable operational bottlenecks, the solution for Pizza Hut management was to enter the delivery market with separate delivery-only units (i.e., with no eat-in or carryout facilities). These units would be considerably smaller than the traditional restaurant facilities and would not require parking space or highly visible locations; occupancy costs therefore would be about 2.1% of sales rather than 6% for the standard eat-in restaurants.

In 1985 a small delivery task group was formed at Pizza Hut and began opening company-owned delivery units in several markets. Their idea was to open a cluster of delivery-only units in each market and keep their costs as low as possible because of the small expected margins (Exhibit 3). There was considerable resistance to the delivery concept at all levels within the company, and company restaurant managers and supervisors in the markets where delivery units had been opened complained bitterly about the adverse effect on their sales. Nevertheless, Pizza Hut management was becoming increasingly concerned about Domino's rapid expansion, and deemed entry into the delivery segment necessary if the company was to maintain its market leadership position.

By August 1985, eight markets had been opened with a total of 51 company-owned delivery-only units. In the well-developed markets—Atlanta, Georgia, and Norfolk Virginia—customers called a single phone number. Orders were then sent by facsimile machine to the appropriate delivery unit. Although the system was relatively cheap, as the number of units grew, it became more and more unmanageable, and the "fax" machines presented a significant bottleneck. In late summer 1985, senior Pizza Hut managers visited the Norfolk market and became convinced that, with a number of operational adjustments, the delivery concept was workable, offered tremendous potential growth, and should be pursued. The company postponed further expansion into new markets while it contracted for the development of a computerized central ordering system and perfected other aspects of the delivery concept.

The computerized central ordering system, called the Customer Service Center (CSC), allowed customers in a particular market to call a single number to place an order. The caller first was asked his or her phone number and the system ascertained whether the caller had ordered before. If so, the operator would verify the caller's name and address and ask if the customer would like the same type of pizza previously ordered. The order would then be forwarded automatically to the appropriate delivery unit where a terminal would receive the order information.

The CSC system, although expensive to develop, was designed to be capable of handling the vast number of calls generated in a large market with a large number of delivery units. It was necessary, however, that the system work perfectly. Customers in an eat-in restaurant understood and tolerated waiting a few minutes to be seated. Delivery customers expected their phone call to be answered within seconds, even though 60% of the daily calls for an entire market area might come in during a one-hour period. While there were substantial marketing benefits to having only one phone number for an entire market, there were significant risks in operating such a complex system. In Norfolk, Virginia, initial problems with the installation of the CSC had created serious losses in a once profitable delivery market.

Although there had been some difficulties during its installation, Pizza Hut management was convinced that the CSC would be a significant competitive advantage. About 70% of Domino's franchisees owned only one store, and Pizza Hut believed that the costs of coordination and management of such a centralized ordering system at Domino's would be prohibitive. In the Pizza Hut system, the concentration of restaurant ownership in the hands of the company and relatively few franchisees would allow for much easier coordination and substantial cost savings. Under the company's delivery concept, the company would invest in the CSC for each market and manage it, coordinating the ordering process and providing service on a fee-per-call basis to participating franchisees and company stores (currently $.65 per call). Pizza Hut's investment in the CSCs was expected to be large, but management believed that such systems were essential to the delivery strategy. It was expected that eventually the franchisees would purchase the necessary equipment and manage the Customer Service Centers themselves in their own markets.

Another major issue presented in developing a profitable delivery concept was whether there would be a charge for service. Pizza Hut management was convinced that for competitive reasons the company could not charge for delivery (Domino's delivered free with a 30-minute guarantee). The additional cost of providing free delivery was the same, regardless of order size. This meant that, to the extent the average check price could be increased, margins would increase. To help maintain margins when offering free delivery, therefore, it was decided that the size and price of delivered pizzas would be slightly increased over pizza in traditional restaurants (i.e., delivery sizes would be 10-14-16" versus the 9-13-15" sizes in the traditional restaurants, and Domino's 12-16" sizes). Customers would pay approximately 10% more for a small, medium, or large pizza, but would get more as well. This "upsizing" would increase the average check price and gross margin, thereby helping to defray the cost of free delivery and the Customer Service Centers.

In early 1986, Pizza Hut was reorganized to reflect the increasing importance and autonomy of the delivery segment (Exhibit 4). A senior vice president of operations managed all traditional restaurant operations, while Senior Vice President Allan Huston was general manager of delivery. Still another senior vice president led the marketing function for the traditional restaurants. Delivery had its own separate marketing department that reported directly to Allan Huston. Even the regions into which the country was divided were different for delivery and the traditional restaurant business.

Although there was some experimentation with alternative delivery concepts (e.g., no upsizing in some markets) during the spring and summer of 1986, the marketing function for the delivery group was not fully operational until July. Huston concentrated primarily on the operational details surrounding the opening of new delivery units rather than on refining the Pizza Hut delivery concept. In the first half of 1986, Pizza Hut doubled the number of markets where it operated delivery units and had almost quadrupled the total number of units (Exhibit 5). Those delivery units were predominately in metropolitan areas—where most of the company's markets

EXHIBIT 4
Organization Chart

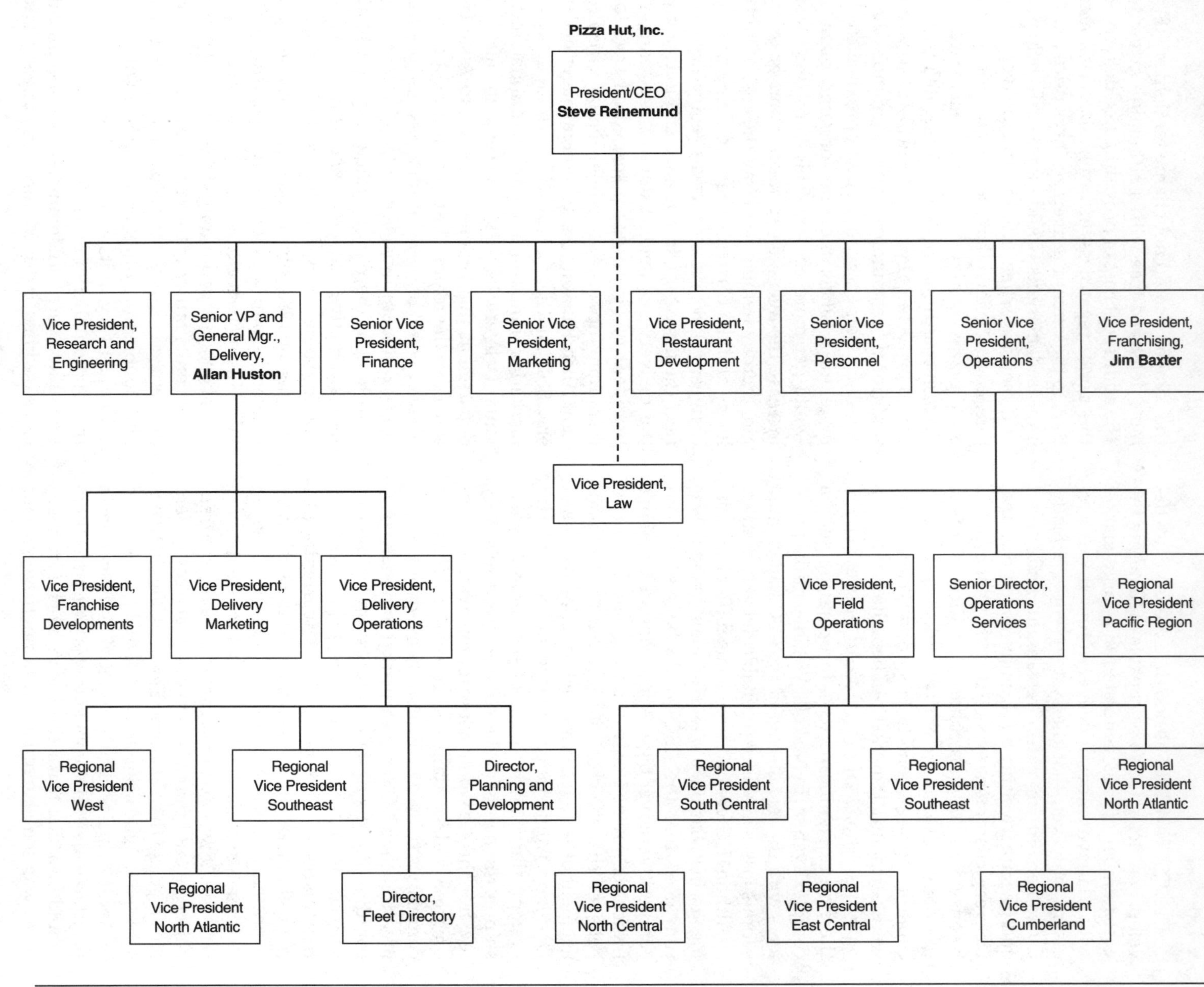

EXHIBIT 5
Open Pizza Hut System Traditional Restaurants and Devliery Units[a]

	Company-Owned		Franchisee-Owned		
	Traditional Restaurants	*Delivery-only Units*	*Traditional Restaurants*[b]	*Retrofit*	*Delivery-only Units*
August 1984	2,011	11	2,089	70	15
December 1984	2,025	16	2,137	98	20
August 1985	2,046	51	2,256	131	30
December 1985	2,004	78	2,352	162	46
August 1986	2,208	284	2,277	241	66
December 1986	2,173	361	2,395	292	96

[a]Domestic U.S. restaurants and delivery units only.
[b]Totals for franchisee-owned traditional restaurants include those restaurants retrofitted to provide delivery service.

were. The initial units opened were in markets with high levels of traditional restaurant penetration and high "per-store-average" (PSA) sales. A second group, opened later in 1986, were in low penetration and low per-store-average sales markets.

Throughout 1986, Pizza Hut managers on the traditional restaurant side of the business continued to be concerned about competition from the Pizza Hut delivery operation, as well as from Domino's. Huston and other managers in the delivery operation, however, believed that delivery was expanding the market by including people who would not go to a restaurant for pizza. They argued that consumers who ate pizza in restaurants and those who had pizza delivered sought very different benefits, and that delivery did not compete directly with traditional restaurants. Moreover, the adverse effects of Pizza Hut delivery units on traditional restaurant sales growth appeared to be most pronounced in markets where there was weak sales growth already; in strong markets the effect was short lived. As Reinemund noted in early 1986, "We do not yet know how great a factor this overlap will be. But what we do know is that in many cases our restaurant business has actually grown after our delivery units have entered the market." In the words of another senior Pizza Hut manager:

> While it is true that we often are serving the same customers, we are serving them on totally separate dining occasions. When we introduce delivery to a market, we get the business of customers who probably were ordering a competitor's pizza simply for the convenience of home delivery.

As for personnel, it was clear that needs of the delivery business were significantly different from those of the traditional restaurant business. Pizza Hut restaurant managers were trained to manage the "total customer experience" and, because of the isolation from customers, some restaurant managers did not think they would enjoy running a delivery-only unit. While many production and operation functions would overlap, store managers found it hard to see how career paths could cross over from traditional full-service restaurants to delivery units or vice versa. Moreover, moving as quickly as it had into new markets, Pizza Hut found it difficult to manage at the store level. Ninety percent of the people working in the delivery business were new, and delivery presented unfamiliar operational demands in the areas of driver management, trade area definition, and order taking.

THE FRANCHISEES' EXPERIENCE WITH DELIVERY

A few Pizza Hut franchisees had been offering delivery unofficially for 20 years. In the early 1980s, the company consistently attempted to dissuade franchisees from offering delivery. Nevertheless, the number of small-town franchisees delivering pizza to college dormitories and military bases from their traditional restaurants had begun to increase. In some isolated cases franchisees faced local competitive environments that they believed necessitated offering delivery. By 1982, about 25 franchisees operated delivery services from a total of about 75 standard eat-in restaurants.

Most franchisees that entered the delivery segment did so by retrofitting existing eat-in restaurants to allow for delivery "out the back door" (Exhibit 5 shows the number of franchisees owning retrofit and delivery-only units from 1984 to 1986). They found, however, that retrofitting significantly increased demands on the restaurant manager and required much greater local management skills. Because of operational bottlenecks, some franchisees lost money on the delivery business and ceased delivery operations. The company believed this supported its concept of opening separate delivery-only units.

Through 1985, the majority of Pizza Hut franchisees saw no reason for delivery. They faced little or no competition in their market from the major chains offering delivery, and were less interested in overall market share battles than the company seemed to be. Sixty-five percent of all franchised restaurants were in towns with populations under 50,000 people, and delivery in those rural areas was not as easy to justify economically as in more densely populated markets. In late 1985, when the company changed its position completely and began to encourage franchisees to open delivery-only units, most franchisees were not interested in doing so.

In November 1985, the company announced to franchisees that it interpreted franchise agreement development schedules to include delivery and, therefore, the company had the right to require franchisee development of delivery units in their markets. The company announced that it would not exercise that right for one-and-a-half years while it perfected the concept, but urged franchisees to begin developing delivery-only units immediately.

The franchise community's response was quick and clear. Most franchisees saw no reason to risk business in their eat-in restaurants by expanding into the delivery market. They denied that the development schedules allowed Pizza Hut to require them to open delivery units. They openly expressed their disagreement with the company's delivery concept, especially regarding upsizing (referred to by one franchisee as "up-pricing"). They also questioned the necessity of the computerized Customer Service Centers and the delivery-only units (some franchisees wanted to retrofit existing restaurants, and others wanted carry out allowed in the delivery units). Significant tension arose between the company and its franchisees. At a heated IPHFHA board meeting in December 1985, board members and Pizza Hut senior management recognized that they had been concentrating too much on each other and not enough on Domino's. They agreed to operate temporarily under a "yellow flag" plan (an automobile racing term referring to the period when each side continues to operate as before without either side trying to improve its relative position).

The company's upsizing concept continued to be a focal point of disagreement. Although Pizza Hut suggested prices, the franchisees were free to price their products as they pleased. The franchisees argued that, even though they had not increased prices as frequently as the company-owned restaurants had in past years, they were still at a price disadvantage when compared to the competition. This disadvantage was especially acute in the delivery business; franchisees believed that upsizing would exacerbate the problem because customers were conscious only of the absolute price of a small, medium, or large pizza and did not calculate price per square inch of the product.

The franchisees also wanted to know why Pizza Hut needed an expensive CSC system, if Domino's didn't have one. They felt that if delivery was necessary, the costs should be kept as low as possible. This meant simple phone ordering to each local restaurant, and delivery out of existing restaurants where feasible. It was important to franchisees that the system be as flexible as possible so that they could find local solutions to local problems.

The reorganization of Pizza Hut in early 1986, which provided for the delivery business to operate autonomously from the traditional restaurant business, raised another issue in the franchise community. Franchisees were concerned that while the company could afford to run the delivery and eat-in businesses separately, the franchisees did not have the resources for separate marketing and operations departments for the traditional restaurant and delivery business. The mismatch of organizational forms between company and franchisees was expected to create significant management difficulties. To make matters worse, the Pizza Hut national advertising account had been split in two within the advertising agency so that a separate group could begin working only on delivery. Many franchisees viewed the two businesses as one and were concerned that their separation would make coordination between delivery and eat-in even more difficult.

There was little consensus of opinion among the franchisees regarding the various elements of the company's delivery concept. There was, however, virtual unanimous franchisee concurrence that the existing franchise agreement did not cover delivery. In February 1986 Jim Baxter, who had been with Pizza Hut for almost 10 years, was appointed vice president of restaurant franchising and assumed the role of liaison between the company and franchisees. In May, newly appointed president Steve Reinemund accompanied Baxter to a series of regional meetings with the franchisees where Reinemund announced that the company no longer contended that the existing development agreement covered delivery. He also announced the company's intention to negotiate with the hoard of the IPHFHA to produce an amendment to the franchise agreement that would provide for systemwide entry into the delivery market. Reinemund suggested that the amendment would include incentives (e.g., reduced or no royalties for a certain time period on new delivery-only units) designed to make franchisee participation in the delivery segment more attractive. These incentives would be retroactive for any franchisee delivery-only units opened in the meantime. The amendment would take effect if franchisees representing 85% of the units approved it within a specified time period.

THE AUGUST FRANCHISEE MEETING

As the August 1986 franchisee meeting drew near, Pizza Hut management decided it was time to press again for the full involvement of all franchisees in systemwide entry into the delivery market. Pizza Hut operated delivery units in 16 markets, with a total of 284 company-owned units. The company had hired and trained over 10,000 people. The flagship Norfolk market, which had experienced difficulties, was now profitable. The first half-year results from the operating units were impressive, and Delivery General Manager Huston was confident that the company could make a good business case for delivery.

Huston and the delivery group gave an extremely upbeat presentation of the delivery data to franchisees at the August Meeting. Their purposes included

1. To convince franchisees that the time had come to give total support to the delivery effort
2. To "sell" the company's delivery concept to the franchisees
3. To successfully launch the amendment negotiation process that was to begin in earnest after the meeting

While many franchisees remained adamantly opposed to delivery, others were becoming convinced that they could, in fact, increase their overall income with delivery even if they would face decreased average margins. While the idea of delivery became more acceptable, however, there was still little support for the particulars of the company's delivery concept.

THE CURRENT SITUATION

As the negotiations for an amendment to the Franchise Agreement continued into the fall of 1986, competition in the delivery market intensified tremendously. Systemwide, Domino's increased advertising 100% over the previous year. Moreover, much of its advertising was specifically focused on the markets Pizza Hut was attempting to open for delivery. Domino's spent an average of 68% more on advertising in those markets than in its other markets. Moreover, Domino's had proven to be an able competitor with satisfied customers and an inexperienced but highly enthusiastic franchise system. They met Pizza Hut head-on in each market Pizza Hut entered by focusing on execution, quality, advertising, and price.

Discounting became even more prevalent in late 1986. Fifty percent of Domino's pizzas were sold on deal. Pantera's joined Little Caesar in offering two-for-one deals; Godfather's and Pizza Inn launched their own delivery services also with deep price discounts. Delivery proved to be much more price, coupon, and deal sensitive than the traditional restaurant business.

Of the 19 Pizza Hut company-controlled markets open in December 1986, three were profitable. At the unit level, of the 361 company-owned operating delivery units, 194 were profitable. Company-owned delivery units that had opened early that year performed well from both a sales and profit perspective. The fierce competitive environment in markets opened later that year, however, led to slower sales growth and greater operating losses than expected for those units. For example, in one market, per-store average weekly sales rose to $6,600 after three weeks. Domino's had responded with two-for-one deals for three months, and the per-store average weekly sales dropped to around $4,850. Moreover, in markets with greater than $8,000 per-store average weekly sales in traditional restaurants, Pizza Hut delivery units averaged $7,300; in markets where traditional per store average was less than $8,000, delivery units averaged only $4,225. Overall, the average weekly sales per delivery unit in December was $6,000.

Huston believed that some of the markets were overbuilt with delivery units, and that Pizza Hut was getting all the sales that could be expected from those units. The ratio of traditional restaurants to potential customers averaged 1 restaurant to 70,000 people, while the delivery units averaged 1 unit to 40,000 people.

Consumer research had shown that the standard Pizza Hut pizza served in the traditional restaurants was not as well suited to the delivery environment, causing quality to suffer. Pizza Hut research and development managers were confident that they could solve that problem by developing a new product designed especially for delivery. This would involve an entirely different production process than that used currently in the traditional restaurants.

Meanwhile, the number of franchisees who had introduced delivery was growing rapidly. Franchisees who in August had told Aaron that delivery would be "over their dead bodies" were inviting him to visit their delivery operations. Moreover, many franchisees who had introduced delivery were doing significantly better than the company-owned stores. Eighteen franchisees opened a total of 65 delivery-only units in 1986, bringing the overall total to 96. All but two units with over seven months experience were profitable. In addition, by December 1986, 292 traditional restaurants had been retrofitted by franchisees to provide delivery service. Because the delivery operations were co-mingled with the eat-in and carry out operation in the retrofitted restaurants, it was difficult to estimate their profitability, however, the franchisees were reported to be pleased with the results so far. The franchisees' success with delivery was attributed to the fact that they had developed markets where they were already strong and had carefully picked the trade areas with the highest potential. They had also priced more competitively, and only 20% had upsized. Most kept costs low by having phone orders go direct to each separate unit instead of using Customer Service Centers.

The winter franchisee meeting was scheduled for January, and Reinemund, Huston, and Baxter had less than a month to decide how to proceed. Before deciding what to do at that meeting, they wanted to review the overall strategy and likely profit impact on Pizza Hut of delivery.

CASE 15 | *Anheuser-Busch, Inc.*

In 1982 Anheuser-Busch (A-B) controlled 32 percent of the U.S. beer market and had clearly established itself as the ruler in the industry. The self-proclaimed "King of Beers" had successfully fought off a challenge by Miller, the second-largest brewer in the industry, to take over the throne. Several of the other top 10 companies in the industry were in trouble and seeking merger partners. They, therefore, presented no threat to the firmly placed crown of A-B, and A-B began seeking to capitalize on its competitor's turmoil.

August Busch III, chairman of A-B, felt very smug about his company's strong leadership position within the industry. He was confident that the company could "continue to dominate its rivals simply by redoubling its efforts—building huge and efficient breweries, spending heavily on advertising and promotion, maintaining price leadership where it holds commanding share, and cutting prices where needed to gain business." According to Dennis Long, president of A-B's Beer Division, "If you segment this country geographically, demographically, and by competitors, it gives you great confidence that there is still considerable room for us to grow."

A-B intended to increase its market share to 40 percent by 1990. It was seeking to increase its capacity 27 percent by means of a five-year capital expansion plan. This involved an investment of approximately $2 billion. A previous five-year expansion program costing $1.8 billion had increased the capacity of A-B by 50 percent. The major question facing A-B and its chairman was whether A-B would be able to achieve its objectives of increased market share and capacity in light of the decrease in beer consumption growth from 5 percent annually in the 1970s to less than 3 percent in 1982. This decrease was a direct result of the increased popularity of other beverages and a decrease in the number of 18- to 34-year-olds.

INDUSTRY BACKGROUND

Small-scale brewing in the United States began in 1633, when the first commercial brewery was founded in the Dutch colonial town of New Amsterdam, now New York City. It was not until the 1840s that large-scale brewing began to take place as a result of the introduction of a different type

This case was prepared as a basis for class discussion rather than to illustrate either effective or ineffective handling of an administrative situation.

of yeast from Germany. The 1870s saw the continued evolution of the beer industry when Louis Pasteur developed the process for controlling fermentation. This made the bottling of beer commercially feasible. During the 1900s, two events had a serious impact on the industry. These events were the results of regulatory and technological changes. The first, Prohibition, occurred in 1920, at a time when the industry consisted almost exclusively of local and regional brewers, numbering approximately 1500 brewers. When Prohibition was repealed in 1933, fewer than 800 of these brewers had survived. The second event, the introduction of commercial television, occurred in 1946. National advertising began to play an important role in determining market leadership. Television had given a definite edge to those brewers who could afford to advertise by placing their brand first in the consumer's mind.

EXHIBIT 1
Market Share in Beer Industry

Company	*Share in 1977*	*Share in 1981*
Anheuser-Busch	23.0%	30.3%
Miller	15.2	22.4
Schlitz	13.9	7.9
Pabst	10.1	7.5[a]
Heileman	3.9	7.8
Coors	8.0	7.4
Olympia	4.3	3.2
Stroh	3.8	5.0[b]
Schaefer	2.9	—
Carling National	2.6	—
Genesee	—	2.0
C. Schmidt	—	1.8
Other	12.3	4.7
Total	100.0%	100.0%

[a]Includes acquisition of Carling National.
[b]Includes acquisition of Schaefer.

Consolidation of the Industry

Over the past decade, the $10.5-billion beer industry had undergone considerable change. Consolidation had occurred as a result of the absorption by large brewers of many regional brewers. There were 92 breweries in 1970, and in 1982 that number had decreased to 43. In 1982, 95 percent of all the beer sold came from only 10 of these brewers, and 56 percent was accounted for by A-B and Miller. Exhibit 1 shows the largest brewers in 1977 and 1981.

This market dominance by A-B and Miller had drastically altered the industry. A-B and Miller paid their unionized employees more than the average wage in the industry, took advantage of economies of scale, and spent more than their competitors for advertising. They gained considerable control over the market as a result of their marketing expertise, an avalanche of money, and a great deal of animosity toward each other. The remaining brewers provided little challenge for the two leaders. The smaller brewers were suffering from such nightmares as ineffective production and pricing decisions, poor marketing, and continuous management turnover. As a result of their weak position, the smaller brewers had banded together. It had been necessary for several of them to merge in order to survive. In 1982 Stroh acquired Schlitz, and Pabst acquired Olympia Brewing. The long-run outlook for the industry was even greater consolidation.

It appeared that the beer industry was headed toward a controlled oligopoly, similar to that of the tobacco industry. Companies were dissuaded from entering the industry because of high entry costs and low-growth prospects. High entry costs involved two separate considerations: (a) the expense required to build marketing and production groups able to compete with A-B and Miller and (b) the expense and difficulty involved in competing, based on product differentiation. Product differentiation was necessary since price competition alone was not sufficient. However, small brewers were resorting to price cutting in an effort to simply maintain current market shares. This made the low-growth prospects of the industry very apparent. The only small brewer that could possibly compete with A-B and

Miller was G. Heileman because of its low-cost production facilities.

Along with a reduction in the number of brewers over the long run, it was expected that the number of brands would also decrease. However, this could be offset by new types of beer being offered to new market segments. If greater industry consolidation and stronger competition were to occur in the future, A-B and Miller could potentially benefit from it. A more stable industry would result in an end to the vicious price cutting of the past, and profits would be more easily achieved for the few firms remaining in the industry.

Market Shifts

The existing brewers sold different types of beer in all segments of the market. In order to continue expansion, new types of beer were continually being produced. The most recent opportunity for growth had come from the light segment. In the 1970s, only 3 percent of the total market was attributed to light beer. By 1982 light beer accounted for 15 percent of the total market with only 20 percent penetration. Three factors had contributed to the growth in this segment. First, the 25- to 34-year-old age group drank the greatest amount of diet soft drinks, and their health-conscious attitudes had had an effect on their beer drinking habits. Although the total population was growing at a rate of 1 percent annually, this age segment was forecast to grow at a 2 percent annual rate over the next five years. The second factor involved the increased importance of women in the light beer market. As a group, women appeared to prefer light beer. The third factor contributing to the growth of the light beer segment was advertising. In 1982 Miller held 60 percent of the light beer market; it had achieved its market leadership by appealing to the more weight-conscious drinker, such as the older male beer drinker.

Imports were another area in which the possibility for growth existed. In 1982 imported beer represented only 2.9 percent of total beer consumption. This market segment was expected to almost double in size by 1990. Competition in this area is a matter of taste and image. The leading imports were marketed by companies that were not involved with domestic beer products, but most of the larger domestic brewers sold at least one import. Major brewers obviously considered it important to be represented in all segments and regions of the beer market (see Exhibit 2).

Market Segmentation

To be successful in the national market, three types of strengths were required: marketing skill, product mix, and distribution. The current leaders in the national beer market, A-B and Miller, were strong in all three areas (see Exhibit 3). They possessed marketing expertise, powerful wholesaler networks, and broad product lines. The strength of their product lines was their focus on

EXHIBIT 2
Principal Brands of Major Brewers

Company	*Premium*	*Super*	*Light*	*Imported*
Anheuser-Busch	Budweiser	Michelob	Busweiser Light	Wurzburger Hofbrau
Miller	Miller High Life	Lowenbrau	Lite	Munich Oktoberfest
Schiltz	Schlitz	Erlanger	Schlitz Light Old Milwaukee Lite	
Pabst	Pabst Blue Ribbon	Andeker	Pabst Extra Lite	Fuerstenberg
Coors	Coors	Herman Joseph's 1868	Coors Light	Stella Arto
Heileman	Old Style Rainier	Special Export	[several entries]	Beck's

EXHIBIT 3
Strengths of Major Competitors in the Beer Industry in Three Key Areas

Company	*Distribution*	*Marketing Strength*	*Product Mix*
Anheuser-Busch	• Strongest in the industry. • Excellent unit volume increases.	• Superior—after the expenditure of considerable money, time, and effort. • Benefits to both unit volume and productivity.	• The best in the industry. • Something for everyone, but unit volume predominantly in the most profitable segment. • A plus for productivity.
Miller (Philip Morris)	• Far superior to the industry average. • Promotes good unit volume growth.	• Deepest pockets in the industry. • Proven skill. • Benefits to both unit volume and productivity.	• Limited but concentrated in the most profitable segment. • A plus for productivity.
Heileman	• Very strong in some areas and weak in most others. • Unit growth at industry average or slightly better.	• Limited financial strength but very efficient with the dollars it spends. • Makes it a viable competitor in the industry.	• Limited in the most profitable; very strong in the least profitable. • No impact on productivity.
Coors	Deteriorating in traditional markets; weak in new markets. • Continuing declines in unit volume.	• Thus far, underwhelming. • Both unit volume and productivity declining.	• Limited but concentrated in the most profitable segments. • A potential but unrealizable plus for productivity.
Pabst	• Weak and getting weaker. • Continuing declines in unit volume.	• Ineffective and low budget. • Effecting declines in both unit volume and productivity.	• Concentrated in the least profitable segments. • No impact on productivity.

Source: Prudential-Bache's *Brewery Industry Outlook,* March 10, 1983.

the high-margin and high-growth light, premium, and super-premium beer segments. In 1982 A-B and Miller held 56 percent of the market, and it was projected that by the end of the decade they would hold 70 percent. Consolidation had accelerated because many small competitors were unable to execute effective marketing programs. It was obvious from this that marketing prowess was necessary for success. Product mix was important because the value of the product mix must be greater than the summed values of the individual products, otherwise referred to as synergy. If this is not the case, it would be cost prohibitive to introduce a brand. Effective distribution was also a necessary ingredient to success. There was a tendency among consumers to purchase the brand sold in their neighborhood tavern. In order to capture these on-premise sales, effective distribution was essential. Although distribution strength varied from segment to segment, A-B was strongest in distribution overall.

As mentioned above, imported beer represented a mere 2.9 percent of the market in 1982. This market segment had grown slowly over the preceding five years but was expected to grow to

5 percent by 1990. Importers continued to expand their markets by introducing new types of beers to appeal to different segments of the drinking-age population (e.g., Amstel Light). Heineken controlled 30 percent of the imported beer market and Molson controlled 20 percent, but recently these brewers had been losing part of their market share to Beck, Moosehead, and Labatt. The major U.S. producers had only recently begun to market one or more types of imported beers. Imported beers had a distinctive taste and were marketed to appeal to consumers who were inner-directed, upscale, and urban. The imported segment was the sole segment of the total beer market that could experience a sales slowdown when the economy decelerated.

The smaller brewers also marketed beer that had a distinctive taste. These brewers tended to sell on a regional basis, staying in well-defined areas close to home. They specialized in lower-priced beers and controlled 10 percent of the total beer market in 1982. The number of small, local, family-owned breweries had decreased, and it was expected that this trend would continue. Between 1970 and 1980 this market declined substantially in size. As a result of increased fixed costs, many of these brewers had been unable to afford to continue in business on their own. With those that were able to survive, one of the key factors had been community pride and interest in the local brewery.

Competition

There are three areas in which brewers compete with one another: packaging, advertising, and price. Packaging provides brewers with a method of segmentation. Packaging choices include the traditional 12-ounce six-pack in bottles or cans; 20-ounce cans; 40-ounce bottles; 7-ounce eight-pack in bottles or cans; 12-ounce twelve pack in bottles or cans; and various keg sizes. During 1981, 59 percent of the total beer consumed was from cans, 9 percent was from returnable bottles, and 32 percent was from nonreturnable bottles. The use of returnable bottles had increased significantly since 1981 as a result of the passage of deposit laws in 19 state.

Over the past decade, advertising had become the major marketing tool. Since 1977, the advertising expenditures of the major brewers had been growing by more than 12 percent annually. Effective advertising had increased brand loyalties. There was an understanding among brewers to advertise in a legal and morally responsible manner. In order to promote the image of being socially responsible, brewers sponsored many public service commercials involving the subjects of teenage pregnancy and drunk driving. They did not show minors, intoxicated people, or the actual consumption of beer in their advertising. There were several market segments that were important targets of advertising campaigns. These included college students, sports fans, and ethnic groups. The brewers attempted to instill brand loyalty in college students by sending representatives to the campuses (Schlitz) or by sponsoring activities with promotional samples (Budweiser). The Hispanic market was large and important. To appeal to this market segment, Coors used actors of Hispanic background in its advertising, and A-B used a Spanish advertising agency to promote Michelob.

As new products were introduced, they were being targeted directly toward certain market segments. This was achieved mainly through advertising campaigns. Miller Lite was targeted toward older men; Michelob 7-ounce bottles were targeted toward 24- to 35-year-old women. In all the advertisements, focus was placed on identification with males, females, or couples. Beer is an extremely image-oriented product, and advertising campaigns were using a new emphasis. Instead of promoting beer just as a beverage that goes with a simple, relaxed lifestyle, the focus was on beer as a reward for a job well done. In these commercials, beer was the reward after a hard day's work or for winning at a sport. Humor was often injected into the commercials. Advertising played an important role in the beer industry, and it gave those brewers who could afford it a definite competitive advantage.

Price was no longer the important marketing tool it once was. It had lost its competitive importance. The emphasis had shifted to media. Pricing policies now depended upon product positioning. Brewers sold a number of price-sensitive brands, including super-premium, premium, popular-priced, light, and generic beer. It was expected that the premium, super-premium, and light brands would seek annual price increases of 6–7 percent compared with the smaller increases of 3–5 percent sought by the popular-priced brands.

Environmental Factors Affecting the Beer Industry

There were certain economic and demographic factors that affected the beer industry. Two of these factors were the unpredictability of changes in consumer tastes and preferences, and the effect of extended recessionary forces. If the demand for beer were to weaken substantially, this could result in an overcapacity in the industry. Other factors were increased beer consumption by women and the health-conscious attitude regarding lightness and moderation. The potential impact of these factors would be a favoring of beer over distilled spirits that would provide opportunity for enlargement and further segmentation of the beer market. A final factor encompassed all future movements in consumer economics and demographics. One of these forecasted trends was an increase of 20 percent in the 25- to 44-year-old age group by 1987. This age group had a greater amount of discretionary income, tended to eat out more frequently, and was more likely to entertain at home. Another forecasted trend involved the primary beer drinking age segment. The 18- to 24-year-old age group was expected to decrease in size. These projected trends would not be beneficial to the beer industry.

There were also regulatory factors that affected the beer industry. These included stricter litter control requirements, additional legislation requiring bottle deposits, the raising of the drinking age, and increases in the excise tax. If brewers were required to make alterations in their packaging and methods of distribution, the possible result would be increased costs and, therefore, lower profit margins. This also might result if additional legislation were passed requiring bottle deposits. Raising the drinking age would result in a shrinking of the number of 18- to 24-year-olds who could legally drink, which would also negatively affect brewers' profits. If there were a flat increase in the excise tax, this could lead to a redistribution of profits. The hardest hit by the increase, on a percentage basis, would be popular-priced and generic beers. This could lead consumers to believe that the price differential among brands was narrowing and, therefore, cause them to change to more expensive beers. This might prove devastating to the small regional brewers who specialized in lower-priced beers. The granting of permission for territorial agreements between wholesalers would also affect the beer industry. The provision of exclusive regional rights would widen the gap between the strong and the weak wholesalers.

Industry Financial and Operating Performance

In the past, the financial success of brewers had paralleled their performance in marketing, distribution, and product mix. The brewers who had displayed strength in these three areas had gained increasing control over the beer market, whereas the weaker performers had been losing market share.

Even though the gap between the strong and weak brewers had been widening, most brewers' profit margins had been hurt by the price wars of the past. This had somewhat limited flexibility in pricing. As a result, several other components of profitability had become important. These were productivity, unit volume, and gross margin. Productivity could be increased through changes to more favorable product mixes. There had been a shift to brands that had growth opportunities and/or appealing gross profit margins. The gross profit margin of each beer segment and its three- to five-year growth within each segment are shown in Exhibit 4.

Both A-B and Miller had focused their product lines on the fast-growing and high-margin light, premium, and super-premium market segments. Light beer was a good brand to market since it was usually less costly to produce, sold at a premium, had a high profit margin, and was, therefore, more profitable than other brands. In 1982, another factor of productivity, operating rate, did not look good for most of the producers in the industry. The average operating rate for the industry was 75 percent of capacity, far below the optimum rate of 90 to 95 percent. A-B was the only brewer with strength in this area; its plants were operating at approximately 98 percent of capacity.

The second important component of profitability was unit volume; the higher the unit volume the greater the profitability. Since a flattening of beer consumption trends was forecast, the ability of individual brewers to increase their unit volume would depend upon several factors. These included their capacity to finance strong marketing programs and the presence of strong distribution systems.

The third component of profitability was gross margin, which is equal to sales minus cost of goods sold. This figure represented the maximum amount that could be spent on marketing and administrative expenditures without incurring an operating loss. Past and projected industry gross profit is shown in Exhibit 5. The industry gross profit per barrel, excluding A-B and Miller, equaled only two-thirds that of A-B. It was not within the financial means of most brewers to reach a competitive level of marketing since this would necessitate a substantial increase in spending. There was apparently a dichotomy in the industry that could be expressed as "The rich get richer and the not-so-rich are lucky to keep running in place." In summation, higher gross margins represented more available funds for marketing expenditures. This in turn led to increased market share and sales, the results of which were greater volume and productivity, and, therefore, increased profitability.

The factors that would affect the future performance of the industry were a slow-growth environment, recession, and the cost outlook. The first factor, a slow-growth environment, would necessitate that even more emphasis be placed on increasing productivity and unit volume. Recession, the second factor, would have an impact upon certain brands of beer, the brands marketed to the people most affected by a recession. A good example of this is Miller High Life, which is strongly marketed toward blue-collar workers. Lastly, the outlook for costs was that (a) the costs

EXHIBIT 4
Financial Perspectives of Different Types of Beer

Beer Segment	*Gross Profit Margin*	*Three- to Five-Year Growth*	*Current Share*
Popular-priced beers	13%	(6)%	30%
Premium-priced beers	20	4	37
Light beers	24	11	15
Super-premium beers	33	8	7
Imports	NA	10	6
Specialty	25	10	5
Total			100%

Source: Prudential-Bache's *Brewery Industry Outlook,* March 10, 1983.

EXHIBIT 5
Past and Estimated Future Changes in Industry Gross Profit (Profit and Barrelage in Millions)

	1972	*1977*	*1982*	*1987*
Industry				
Total barrelage	131.8	156.9	180.0	209.0
Total gross profit	$1,479.5	$1,915.5	$2,454.5	$3,224.2
Gross profit/barrel	$11.23	$12.21	$13.64	$15.43
Anheuser-Busch				
Total barrelage	26.5	36.6	59.1	86.6
Total gross profit	$392.6	$571.1	$976.1	$1,555.7
Gross profit/barrel	$14.82	$15.60	$16.52	$17.96
Miller				
Total barrelage	5.3	24.2	39.3	54.5
Total gross profit	$71.6	$368.2	$580.7	$865.7
Gross profit/barrel	$13.51	$15.21	$14.78	$15.88
Industry—Less Bud and Miller				
Total barrelage	100.0	96.1	81.6	67.9
Total gross profit	$1,015.3	$976.2	$897.7	$802.8
Gross profit/barrel	$10.15	$10.96	$11.00	$11.82

Source: Prudential-Bache's *Brewery Industry Outlook,* March 10, 1983.

of raw materials and packaging would increase at a rate lower than that of inflation and that (b) advertising would not exceed an annual growth rate of 12 percent. Such a favorable cost outlook would enable brewers to keep operating margins within a 3 to 5 percent increase. Exhibit 6 presents a breakdown of the costs of the major brewers.

ANHEUSER-BUSCH PERSPECTIVES

Company Background

A-B was founded in 1852. Its corporate headquarters are in St. Louis, Missouri. The present chairman is August Busch III, a fourth-generation brewer. In 1957 A-B took the industry leadership away from Schlitz and has held this leadership position ever since. During that period, A-B has had to fend off challenges from both Schlitz and Miller. By the 1970s, A-B had grown so contented that even a challenge by Schlitz did not elicit any response. The brewer was running out of beer every summer and saw no need to market aggressively. The challenge by Schlitz failed only as a result of several marketing blunders that cost Schlitz many loyal customers. It was a challenge by Miller, acquired in 1969–70 by Philip Morris, Inc., that posed a definite threat to the leadership position of A-B and prompted it to act. A-B was in the middle of an awkward transition of management when Miller attacked, but what made mat-

EXHIBIT 6
Estimated Cost Breakdown for Major Brewers

Packaging	50%
Raw materials	14
Labor	12
Marketing	8
All other	16
Total	100%

Source: Prudential-Bache's *Brewery Industry Outlook,* March 10, 1983.

ters considerably worse was a strike the summer season of 1976 that kept its beer off the shelves during the summer season of 1976. In retaliation, A-B made an all-out effort to defeat Miller and successfully retained its leadership position. The war between A-B and Miller badly crippled the rest of the brewers in the industry, who were constantly struggling to survive.

Since 1976, A-B has increased its number of brands from three to eight to target all market segments. Busch and Natural Light are marketed as popular-priced brands, Budweiser and Budweiser Light as premium brands, and Michelob, Michelob Light, Michelob Dark, and an import, Wurzberger, as super-premium brands. All of its brands are backed by heavy advertising and promotion expenditures. The amount spent by A-B on media rose 170 percent, to $145 million, between 1977 and 1982. A-B was outspending all other brewers in the sponsoring of sporting events. In 1982 it sponsored 98 professional and 310 college sports events and successfully bid $10 million for beer sponsorship of the 1984 Summer Olympics.

Brewers have used "image" advertising to position their products ever since advertising was first employed, but its use has been on the rise in the past few years. The original targeted beer segment of Budweiser had a strong, rugged image and, therefore, from the beginning, Budweiser had been associated with the Clydesdale horses. A team of these horses pulled the original Budweiser wagon, but their use had become primarily ceremonial. The type of people now drinking Budweiser were higher-income, middle-aged individuals, more likely to be men and less likely to be minorities. In order to attract a broader market, including women, minorities, and older and younger people, A-B established a new campaign to promote Budweiser based on the slogan "This Bud's for you." The overall consumption of Budweiser tended to be evenly distributed geographically. As a result, it did not face the same problem as Miller High Life, which tended to be skewed geographically toward the economically depressed areas of the country. Exhibit 7 presents the estimated media costs of Budweiser, Miller High Life, and Schlitz in 1973, 1977, and 1981.

A-B marketed three light beers, Budweiser Light, Michelob Light, and Natural Light. These three brands were marketed toward the pre-

EXHIBIT 7

Estimated Media Costs per Barrel of Different Brands of Beer (Media and Barrelage in Millions)

				Five-Year Growth	
	1973	*1977*	*1981*	*73–77*	*77–81*
Budweiser					
Total media	$7.2	$22.7	$42.6	33.3%	17.0%
Total barrelage	22.5	25.7	37.6	3.4	10.0
Media/barrel	$0.32	$0.88	$1.13	28.8	6.5
Miller High Life					
Total media	$8.2	$14.6	$37.6	15.5	26.7
Total barrelage	6.4	16.7	24.0	27.1	9.5
Media/barrel	$1.28	$0.87	$1.57	(9.2)	15.9
Schlitz					
Total media	$10.3	$19.0	$17.6	16.5	(1.9)
Total barrelage	17.5	16.2	8.0	(1.9)	(16.1)
Media/barrel	$0.59	$1.17	$2.20	18.7	17.1

mium, super-premium, and mid-price market segments, respectively. When Budweiser Light was introduced in 1982, it met with unexpected success. This brand emphasized sports and was marketed with a sport-oriented theme, "Bring out your best. . . ." Budweiser Light was targeted toward the heavy beer drinker who was athletic and active, whereas Miller Lite was targeted toward the older male beer drinker who was weight conscious.

Busch, a popular-priced beer, was targeted toward the free-spirited man. Promotional campaigns for this brand were geared toward the hard-working blue-collar employee who headed to the mountains for relaxation. The super-premium market segment was dominated by Michelob, an A-B brand, and close behind was Lowenbrau, a Miller brand. There had been a slowing in the growth of this market segment. The new promotional campaign for Michelob Light targeted white-collar men and women who entertained, belonged to country clubs, and could afford to spend a little more for a special occasion beer. This campaign centered on heritage, tradition, quality, and distinctiveness. A-B, with its many expenditures on advertising, closely followed by Miller, was the leader of the industry.

Wholesalers have high fixed expenses as a result of the large capital outlays required to purchase trucks, etc. Therefore, a wholesaler depends on volume sales for profit and concentrates effort upon the brands that offer the greatest volume. It can be seen in Exhibit 8 that A-B and Miller had greater volume than competing brewers. A-B achieved product distribution through a network of 950 wholesalers and was reputed to have the most effective network of wholesalers in the industry. A-B had provided considerable support to its wholesalers, including the establishment of in-depth training seminars on financial management and warehousing. Wholesaler performance was evaluated on the basis of the frequency with which calls were made upon accounts, the weekly and monthly sales of all beers, and several other factors. It was normal for an A-B wholesaler to hold from 12 to more than 20 days' inventory, depending on the season. With a high inventory turnover rate, a wholesaler was able to generate profits much more quickly. The effective wholesaler system of A-B proved invaluable since it was forecast that, in the future, the fight between the brewers would be focused at the wholesaler level.

EXHIBIT 8
Average Case Volume per Brand per Distributor for Different Brewers

Anheuser-Busch	859,000
Miller	637,000
Heileman	108,000
Coors	438,000
Stroh/Schlitz	280,000
Pabst	154,000
Industry average	541,000
Industry average less A-B	405,000

Source: Prudential-Bache's *Brewery Industry Outlook,* March 10, 1983.

Company Financial and Operating Performance

A-B's many interests include baking operations, snack foods, transportation services, a baseball franchise, and real estate development. Despite these other interests, A-B's beer operations dominate its revenue base. The beer operations accounted for approximately 85 percent of revenue in 1982. As of June 1982, A-B controlled 31.4 percent of the U.S. beer market. It controlled 29.8 percent in 1981, 28.2 percent in 1980, and 23 percent in 1977 (see Exhibit 9). This was an increase in market share of 37 percent over a five-year period. The volume of beer sold by A-B also increased significantly over these five years. Between 1977 and 1982, beer volume rose from $36 million to $59.1 million, an increase of 64 percent. In 1981 A-B had total sales of $3.8 billion, and its

EXHIBIT 9
Top Brewer's Volume Share of Market, 1965–85 (in Millions of 31-Gallon Barrels)

	1965	*1975*	*1978*	*1979*	*1980*	*1981*	*1982E*	*1985E*
% Market Share								
Anheuser-Busch	11.7%	23.4%	25.1%	26.8%	28.2%	29.8%	32.0%	34.5%
Miller	3.7	8.6	18.9	20.7	21.0	22.0	22.0	23.6
Heileman	1.0	3.0	4.3	6.5	7.5	7.7	7.8	8.8
Schlitz	8.5	15.5	11.8	9.7	8.4	7.8	7.5	6.9
Stroh-Schaefer	—	7.3	6.2	5.6	5.5	5.0	4.8	5.2
Pabst	8.1	10.4	9.3	8.7	8.5	7.4	6.6	5.5
Coors	3.6	7.9	7.6	7.5	7.8	7.3	6.8	6.8
Olympia	—	4.4	4.0	3.5	3.4	3.1	2.9	2.5
All Others	63.4	19.4	12.8	10.9	9.7	9.9	9.7	6.2
A-B and Miller	15.4	32.0	44.0	47.5	49.2	51.9	54.0	58.1
% Point Change in Annual Market Share								
Anheuser-Busch	—	+1.2	+0.6	+1.7	+1.4	+1.6	+2.2	+0.8
Miller	—	+0.5	+3.4	+1.8	+0.3	+1.0	0.0	+0.5
Heileman	—	+0.2	+0.4	+2.2	+1.0	+0.2	+0.1	+0.3
Schlitz	—	+0.7	−1.2	−2.1	−1.3	−0.6	−0.4	−0.1
Stroh-Schaefer	—	—	−0.3	−0.6	−0.1	−0.5	−0.1	+0.1
Pabst	—	+0.2	−0.4	−0.6	−0.2	−1.1	−0.8	−0.4
Coors	—	+0.4	−0.1	−0.1	+0.3	−0.5	+0.4	−0.0
Olympia	—	—	−0.1	−0.5	−0.1	−0.3	−0.2	−0.?
All Others	—	−3.2	−2.2	−1.9	−1.1	+0.2	−0.2	−1.2
A-B and Miller	—	+1.7	+4.0	+3.5	+1.7	+2.6	+2.1	+1.4
Industry volume	100.8	150.3	165.8	172.6	177.9	812.8	185.0	207.5
Anheuser-Busch	11.8	35.2	41.6	46.2	50.2	54.5	59.3	71.5
Miller	3.7	12.9	31.3	35.8	37.3	40.3	40.7	49.0
Heileman	1.0	4.5	7.1	11.2	13.3	14.0	14.5	18.3
Schlitz	8.6	23.3	19.6	16.8	15.0	14.3	13.8	14.5
Stroh-Schaefer	—	11.0	10.2	9.6	9.7	9.1	8.8	10.8
Pabst	8.2	15.7	15.4	15.1	15.1	13.5	12.3	11.0
Coors	3.6	11.9	12.6	12.9	13.8	13.3	12.5	14.1
Olympia	—	6.6	6.7	6.0	6.1	5.7	5.3	5.2
Total Top Six	36.9	103.5	127.6	138.0	144.7	149.9	153.1	178.4
% Market Share of Top Six	36.6%	68.9%	77.0%	80.0%	81.3%	82.0%	82.8%	86.0%
% Share of A-B and Miller	15.4%	32.0%	44.0%	47.5%	49.2%	51.9%	54.1%	58.1%

Source: Advertising Age, December 24, 1983.
E = Estimated

profit for the year was $217.4 million. Exhibit 10 presents the financial and operating performance of A-B over a five-year period.

Over this five-year period, A-B had experienced an increase in sales and profits of 111 percent and 136 percent, respectively. It had a unit profitability of approximately $3.59 per barrel of beer sold, greater than that of the rest of the industry. Although it was forecast that total market earnings would increase by 15 to 20 percent in 1983, it was projected that A-B earnings would increase by 30 to 40 percent. As a result of its profit

EXHIBIT 10
Anheuser-Busch, Inc.
Five-Year Composite Summary of Financial Performance (in Million of Dollars)

	1978	*1979*	*1980*	*1981*	*1982*	*Industry Comparison (1982)*
Volume (7.2% growth)	41.6	46.2	50.2	54.5	59.1	1–2% Growth
Sales	$2259.6	$2775.9	$3295.4	$3847.2	$4576.6	$7297.9
Profit margin	4.9%	5.2%	5.2%	5.7%	6.3%	5.1%
Capital expenditures	228.7	432.3	590.0	421.3	350.0E	NA
Capitalization	36.1%	35.8%	43.2%	42.4%	33.9%*	NA
Interest coverage	8.1x	6.5x	4.0x	3.9x	4.0x	NA

Source: Information provided by Anheuser-Busch, Inc.
*6 monts ended June 30, 1982.

leadership in the industry, A-B had price elasticity.

A-B had experienced operating and financial success as a result of both productivity gains and unit volume increases. It had spent more than $2 billion over the past five years on a program to increase capacity. This had both expanded and upgraded the cost-effectiveness of the A-B plants. Over the next five years, A-B intended to invest another $2 billion in order to increase capacity from 62 million barrels to over 75 million. A significant portion of these funds was likely to be internally generated. A-B recently acquired the second-largest domestic baker, Campbell-Taggert, which should result in an increase in the amount of funds generated internally.

A-B had successfully positioned its products in the high-margin and fast-growing beer segments. It had also employed an aggressive marketing strategy.As a result, A-B, had achieved increases in unit volume that were greater than the growth in industry sales. Over the next five years, it was projected that annual unit growth for A-B would be 8 to 10 percent. This is shown in Exhibit 11. The exhibit also shows projected annual unit growth for five other companies and breaks down each of their market shares among the brands they offer. In order to obtain operating flexibility, A-B had also employed vertical integration. Many of the processes involved in the manufacturing of beer were carried on in-house at the A-B facilities. These included barley malting, metalized paper printing, and can manufacturing. Although A-B was putting considerable effort into expansion, other brewers were attempting to increase their return on investment by restricting capacity.

Expansion

In the 1970s, A-B was unsuccessful in its efforts to market root beer and a low-alcohol lemon-lime drink. As a result of these past failures, the company was moving into new areas more cautiously. Also, A-B had teamed up with partners for certain ventures. It had recently moved into the rapidly expanding "wine on tap" business with a partner, LaMont Winery, Inc. In this business, A-B was marketing larger kegs that distributed white, red, and rosé wines under the Master Cellars brand name. A-B had most recently expanded through diversification into the snack food business. Its Eagle Snacks were being dis-

EXHIBIT 11
Growth Potential of Different Brewers (Three to Five Years Out)

	Projected Annual Unit Growth	*Estimated Current Market Share*	*Projected Net Price Increase Realized by Company*
Anheuser-Busch	8–10%	32%	6–7%
Budweiser		22	
Budweiser Light		1	
Michelob		5	
Michelob Light		2	
Busch		1	
Natural Light		1	
Miller	6–8%	22%	6–7%
Miller		11	
Lite		9	
Lowenbrau		2	
Stroh/Schlitz (privately held)	3–5%	12%	4–6%
Stroh		5	
Old Milwaukee		4	
Schlitz		3	
Heileman	3–5%	8%	4–6%
Major Brand			
Old Style and numerous other brands including Blatz, Carling, Black Label, and Tuborg			
Coors	Declines	7%	6–7%
Coors		5	
Coors Light		2	
Herman Joseph's		NF	
George Killian		NF	
Pabst	Declines	7%	4%
Pabst			
Pabst Light			
Andeker		NF	
Henry Weinhard			

Source: Prudential-Bache's *Brewery Industry Outlook,* March 10, 1983.
NF = Not forecastable.

tributed nationwide through bars and convenience stores. The company's latest offering in the beer market was Budweiser Light. It was hoped that this brand would succeed in denting Miller's 60 percent share of the light beer market where Michelob Light and Natural Light had failed. The Budweiser Light brand was backed by substantial financial support, $40–$50 million.

In planning the future expansion of A-B, August Busch III had several strategic alternatives to consider. These could be divided into two categories: those involving beer operations and those involving nonbeer operations. Within the beer operations category there were several possible alternatives for expansion, including the light beer segment, acquisitions, European markets, divestitures, the Eastern bloc, and the 3.2 beer segment. There was definitely opportunity for expansion through the light beer segment because it was estimated that the potential for market penetration was at least 35 percent and currently penetration was only 20 percent. It would also be possible for A-B to expand through the acquisition of smaller brewers. The disadvantage of A-B of acquiring smaller brewers would be that most of these brewers tended to concentrate on unique market segments that would be too small or uneconomical for A-B to serve. Therefore, these acquisitions might offer few advantages. However, it might prove necessary to acquire some smaller brewers in order to stop them from banding together and establishing a third power in the industry.

Another way in which A-B could promote expansion was through European markets. It would be beneficial for A-B to explore and evaluate untapped European markets. The question mark in this alternative was whether A-B brands would be able to compete successfully against the heavier, fuller European brands. It could also prove beneficial to A-B to divest its Natural Light brand of beer, which had proved to be unsuccessful. In 1982 this brand was lowered in price when selling to supermarket accounts, since this was where consumers were extremely price sensitive. It appeared that the consumer was not attracted to A-B's idea of a "natural" beer as A-B had expected. There was potential for further expansion if A-B divested its Natural Light brand and used these brewing facilities for the production of Budweiser Light.

Another possible alternative for A-B was to put a vigorous effort into pursuing "Eastern" markets. It appeared that the Japanese were extremely attracted to products that project "Western" culture. The Japanese company that marketed Suntory whiskey was promoting the product in California to encourage its projection of a "Western" image so that it would be accepted in Japan. An aggressive marketing effort in this area of the world should promote the expansion of A-B. Expansion could also be promoted through pursuit of the 3.2 beer market segment. This variety of beer has half the alcohol, and thus half the calories, of regular beer. The only problem with pursuing this market segment was that it could affect the sales of light beer, which also has fewer calories than regular beer.

The other category of alternatives through which expansion could be achieved involved nonbeer operations. The major questions concerning Eagle Snacks and their potential for expansion involved the growth of the junk food market, how the product could be differentiated, and whether or not the product could obtain a significant part of the retail business, considering Frito-Lay's market domination. A-B could potentially expand through growth in the snack food business.

The other area through which A-B could expand was wine and spirits. Exhibit 12 compares the 1982 consumption of various liquids, such as beer, wine, spirits, etc. A-B had already moved into the "wine on tap" business with a partner. There were a number of other possibilities in this area it could explore. One of these possibilities involved determining the feasibility of acquiring a

EXHIBIT 12

1982 Liquid Consumption in the U.S. (Gallons per Capita)

Soft drinks	40.1
Coffee	26.1
Beer	24.4
Milk	20.5
Tea	6.3
Powdered drinks	NA
Juices	6.6
Spirits	1.9
Wines	2.3
Bottled water	2.2
Water	46.1
Total	176.5

Source: Beverage Industry, May 23, 1983.

winery and taking advantage of A-B's strengths in distribution and marketing. Another possibility involved exploring the potential for developing a product to compete with "Club Cocktails," currently being marketed by Heublein, Inc. A-B has great potential for further expansion since its strengths allow it to diversify. It has many possibilities to consider for future expansion.

To sum up, the future outlook for A-B is good. Its facilities were operating at 98 percent of capacity, and the brewer was confident that it could maintain its dominance in the industry. August Busch III was not fazed by slowing beer consumption and was confident that A-B could achieve its objectives of increased market share and capacity. If the company continued its aggressive marketing strategy and capitalized upon its ability to diversify and expand in other areas, there appeared to be no reason why it would not achieve its objectives.

CASE 16 | *Springboard Software, Inc.*

> Springboard produces and markets high quality, high value software products to satisfy the educational and productivity needs of consumers and students in the home and educational marketplaces.
>
> The company has traditionally produced and continues to produce educational products characterized as aids to help children learn specific curriculums. We are now emphasizing, however, products which help people access data, organize data, understand data and make wonderful, effective presentations of data.

These remarks, made by John Paulson, Chairman and Chief Executive Officer of Springboard Software, Inc., in January, 1986, summarized his company's primary activities. Springboard had undergone many changes since its founding over three years earlier as had the industry as a whole. The company had produced several educational products which had been or were currently on the industry's best-seller lists. Substantial growth did not begin for the company, however, until the February, 1985 release of THE NEWSROOM, software which made possible the creation of a small newspaper with a personal computer. The success of this product dramatically expanded the options available to Springboard's management. The most intriguing choice facing John Paulson and Springboard Software early in January, 1986 was whether to enter the business segment and, if so, how.

COMPANY BACKGROUND

Springboard Software, Inc. (formerly Counterpoint Software, Inc.) was engaged in the business of developing, marketing and selling high quality educational and productivity software products for the home and school marketplaces. Prior to founding the company, John Paulson had been a music teacher in the Wayzata Public School system. Paulson taught himself computer programming while still a teacher. His first computer program was written for his own children and was designed to help them learn basic skills through a

This case was prepared by Professor Natalie Tabb Taylor, Babson College as a basis for classroom discussion rather than to illustrate either effective or ineffective handling of a managerial situation. It is reproduced here by permission of the North American Case Research Association.

series of nine activities. Paulson was careful to design the product so that it would not frustrate children, but would give them a feeling of satisfaction and accomplishment:

> Young children are seldom in control of anything. A well designed software program, however, can put them in charge of their computer activities. This helps them develop confidence in themselves and their ability to participate in the world.

The user interface and sound pedagogical principles of this first program made it very effective and popular with children. Paulson decided to market it under the name EARLY GAMES FOR YOUNG CHILDREN and assigned it a retail price of $29.95. His first customer was Dayton's, Minneapolis' largest department store. Although the product was not professionally packaged, Dayton's made an initial purchase of twelve units. Sales to consumers were brisk and Dayton's began a cycle of reordering.

Encouraged by similar experiences with other retail stores, Paulson decided to quit teaching, seek funding and start an educational software company. The company was incorporated on August 24, 1982, with an initial capitalization of $40,000. Using a color photo of his daughter on the front, Paulson repackaged EARLY GAMES, hired two telephone salesmen and got a list of all the registered Apple dealers in America. In September, 1982 he mailed free sample products to every Apple dealer and had the salesmen follow up with telephone calls a few days later. Even though initial orders were small—between one and ten units—the company began shipping product in October. By December, EARLY GAMES was the number-two Apple educational software product in the country. The company broke even in 1982 with sales of $87,000.

In 1983 Springboard added IBM, Atari, Tandy and Commodore versions of EARLY GAMES to its product line. Four new titles with translations for various machine formats were also added. New packaging was developed and the company began a small advertising campaign. Sales for this first full year in operation reached $750,000.

In August of 1983 Cherry Tree Ventures, a Minneapolis venture firm, invested approximately $250,000 in Springboard to help it with cash flow problems and to position it for additional venture capital investments in 1984. At this time, the company's board of directors decided to hire a professional, experienced manager to function as CEO so that Paulson could focus his efforts on product development. An executive search was undertaken and an individual with a strong marketing background was found who became CEO in 1984.

The results of 1984 were not good, however. The company focused its efforts on developing relationships with the mass merchants at the expense of its established channels of distribution, the computer specialty stores. As part of this plan, a considerable amount of money was spent on advertising, packaging and promoting the growing Springboard line of products to consumers. These expenditures were funded by an additional $2 million of venture capital. Even though five new programs were added to the company's product line in 1984, Springboard lost $1.6 million on roughly $1 million in sales. The company began to experience severe problems with cash flow.

In February of 1985, Paulson's product development team released THE NEWSROOM. It was an immediate and unqualified success, even though it was launched without a single consumer ad or any promotion. Shortly thereafter, John Paulson resumed his position as Chief Executive Officer.

INDUSTRY AND COMPETITION

The microcomputer software industry had experienced dramatic growth in its less than ten years in existence. However, during 1985, the rate of growth slowed. Software sales tended to track the activity of related hardware. Personal computer hardware sales had been in a slump throughout

1985. Industry experts attributed the slowdown to a number of factors, including:

- a glut in hardware suppliers and products;
- saturation in the business and home market segments;
- potential buyers waiting for new generations of machines; and
- the need for new applications software.

The market for micro software was subject to rapid changes in technology. In order to succeed, a firm had to be able (1) to create innovative new products reflecting technological changes in hardware and software as well as customer needs and (2) to translate current products into newly accepted hardware formats in order to gain and maintain market share. By 1986, the supply of software products exceeded demand. Retail shelf space was limited; hence competition intensified as increased emphasis was placed on price concessions, brand recognition, advertising and dealer merchandising.

Rapid sales growth attracted a number of different players into the software industry. Hardware manufacturers such as IBM, Apple, Commodore and Atari had integrated backward into software development. As hardware prices decreased and equipment became increasingly indistinguishable to consumers, software was becoming the primary means of adding value. Apple, for example, bundled a word processing program and graphics program with every Macintosh it sold. Software helped manufacturers differentiate their hardware from competitors' offerings.

Certain companies whose primary activities were in other industries had diversified into the software industry as well. Book publishers, for example, had entered the education market in order to capitalize on their established contacts and channels of distribution.

A separate group of companies competed in software only and were referred to as independents or third-party software houses. Independent software companies tended to be privately held and functioned either as developers or publishers. Developers wrote programs which they licensed to publishers. Most publishers licensed programs and provided whatever expertise and resources were required to bring programs to market. Few were involved in both development and publishing. Most began as publishers, but increased competition forced them into development only or else drove them out of business altogether. The industry was currently undergoing a shakeout. Management believed more casualties would occur in the near future, creating potential opportunities for the surviving publishers.

While there were approximately 3,500 companies competing in the software industry, Springboard had roughly fifty direct competitors in the home and school market. No single company competed directly with Springboard's product line on a title-by-title basis. Sales figures for competitors were difficult to get, since the majority of these companies were privately owned. Competitor profiles, prepared by Springboard personnel, can be found in Appendix A. Additional information about the industry can be found in the report, Microcomputer Applications Software Industry—1986.[1]

PRODUCTS

In the first two years of its history, Springboard produced educational products for children. By 1986, the emphasis had shifted to products designed to help people of all ages become more productive in their lives at home and at school.

The cornerstone of Springboard's product development philosophy was product usefulness. As John Paulson explained:

> Many of our competitors have entered this marketplace with a callous disregard for the consumer's wants and needs. They have often underestimated both the intelligence of the consumer and the importance of the technology. Humans are tool users, after

[1]*Case Research Journal*, Spring 1988, p. 25.

all, and the computer is the most important, versatile tool ever created. To market products which exploit consumers' naivete and superficial curiosity is counterproductive indeed. The quick sale may be made, but eventually the consumer will realize that money has been spent on something that is not useful. It will be some time before that consumer considers buying software again.

Furthermore, the growth of computer penetration is slowed considerably by those who market poorly conceptualized software that does not represent a real value to the consumer. When a potential computer buyer investigates the available software, he or she is often reassured that there is no persuasive reason to own a computer. It may be months, even years before that consumer bothers to investigate a computer purchase again. And when the consumer does return to the computer store, the first question will still be "Why do I need a computer?" It is up to the software developers and marketers to provide compelling reasons.

That is why each and every product Springboard produces is, first and foremost, very useful. Each product takes advantage of the computer's unique capabilities to help people do things they want to do in ways more efficient, more effective and more satisfying than they could possibly do without the computer. Every Springboard program provides an excellent reason for having a computer.

By yearend 1985, Springboard had a total of thirteen program titles, most of which were available in different machine formats. Exhibit 1 provides information about Springboard's product line. Three of the titles listed were about to be discontinued because they did not represent the level of sophistication exhibited by the other products in terms of concept, design or execution.

By September, 1985, THE NEWSROOM had become the best-selling home computer program in the U.S., according to the Softsel Hot List, the in-

EXHIBIT 1
Springboard Product Series and Titles as of November 1985

Series/Titles	*Date of Introduction*	*Suggested Age Group*	*Suggested Retail*
Early Games Series			
Early Games for Young Children	Sept. 1982	$2\frac{1}{2}$–6	\$34.95
Stickers	March 1984	4–12	\$34.95
Easy as ABC	June 1984	3–6	\$39.95
*Music Maestro	May 1983	4–10	\$34.95
*Make a Match	Sept. 1983	$2\frac{1}{2}$–6	\$29.95
Skill Builders Series			
Piece of Cake Math	Sept. 1983	7–13	\$34.95
Fraction Factory	Sept. 1983	8–14	\$29.95
Creative Path Series			
Rainbow Painter	June 1984	4 and up	\$34.95
The Newsroom	Feb. 1985		\$59.95
Clip Art Collection, Vol. I	June 1985		\$29.95
Puzzle Master	Sept. 1984	4 and up	\$34.95
Mask Parade	Sept. 1984	4–12	\$39.95
Family Series			
*Quizagon	June 1984	Teens and adults	\$44.95

Source: Company.
*Soon to be discontinued.

dustry's guide to best-selling software programs at the wholesale level. In October, this program tied for places nine through fourteen at 2% in terms of unit market share of leading titles, regardless of category, as shown in the third graph in Exhibit 2. By 1985 yearend, THE NEWSROOM and related programs accounted for roughly three-quarters of Springboard's unit sales.

The second largest contributor to sales was EARLY GAMES FOR YOUNG CHILDREN, Paulson's first program. Sold primarily into the home market for use by pre-schoolers, EARLY GAMES had been identified in 1985 by the *Wall Street Journal* as the nation's fourth best seller in microcomputer educational software.

The company stood behind every title it sold with a guarantee which was rarely found in the industry: If a consumer was not satisfied for any reason, the product could be returned directly to Springboard for a full refund. To date, returns totaled less than 1% of sales.

CUSTOMER MARKETS

Roughly 75% of Springboard's sales were made to the home market primarily through computer specialty stores. Most of the remainder were to schools, either through educational distributors or local retail outlets. Approximately 5% of sales were through exclusive distribution agreements in different countries of the world.

During 1985, management determined that Springboard did not have the resources to effectively penetrate the education market. As a result, the company entered into a licensing agreement with Scholastic Software, Inc. to distribute a special school edition of THE NEWSROOM in the USA and Canada. Under this arrangement, Scholastic would produce a school package containing a teacher's guide and backup disks, capabilities which Springboard did not possess. Packaged in a Scholastic box, the title of the program and the name Springboard would be prominently displayed. Scholastic would sell the school edition for $75.

EXHIBIT 2
Springboard Software, Inc.
October, 1985 Market Share by Publisher and by Title

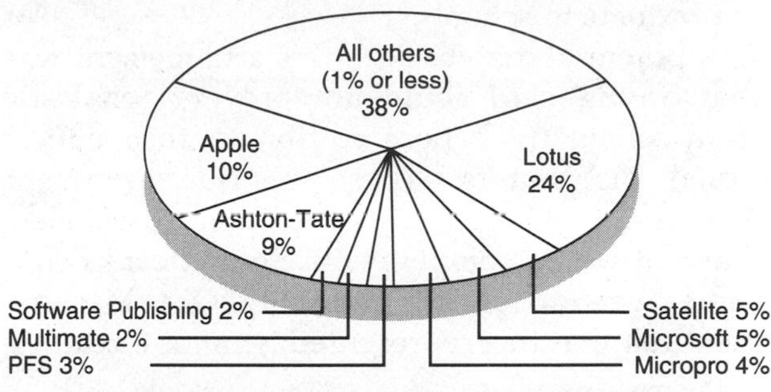

(a) Dollar Share among the Leading Publishers—October
(9 Publishers with shares higher than one percent)

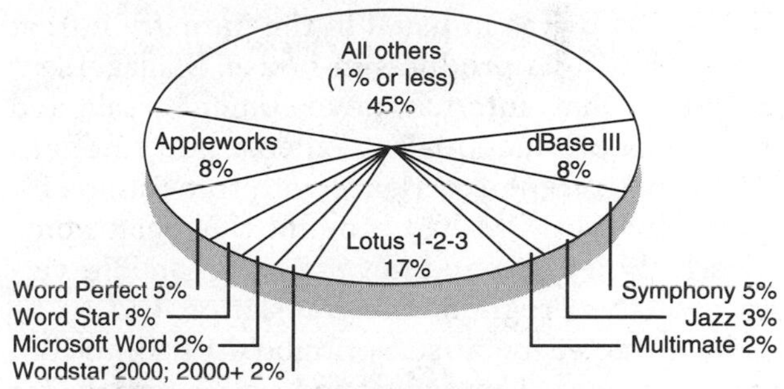

(b) Dollar Share among the Leading Titles—October
(10 Titles with shares higher than one percent)

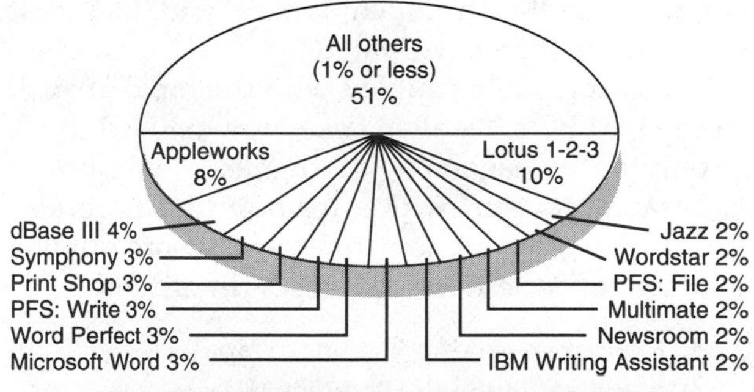

(c) Unit Share among the Leading Titles—October
(14 Titles with shares higher than one percent)

Scholastic had an excellent reputation in the industry. Other noted companies had entered into similar arrangements with them. Intentional Educations, for instance, had licensed a Scholasticized version of its hit program BANK STREET WRITER. Additionally, Scholastic had a large direct sales force that was already selling a variety of products to schools.

A potential drawback to this arrangement was that Springboard could not prevent Scholastic from selling the school edition to their educational distributors. Those distributors might eventually sell the school edition to retailers where it would compete with Springboard's consumer version of THE NEWSROOM. Management felt that this represented a minor threat.

EXHIBIT 3
Springboard Software, Inc.
Home and Personal Computer Yearend Installed Base, 1982–1984 (000 Units)

	1982	*1982*	*1984*
Apple II/IIe/IIc	500	900	2,000
Apple Macintosh	—	—	265
IBM PC/XT/AT	700	1,300	2,200
IBM PCjr	—	275	175
Commodore 64	1,100	1,500	3,100
Commodore 128	—	—	—
All others*	800	1,200	2,700
Total	3,100	5,175	10,540

Source: Marketing Technology, January 1985.
*Includes Radio Shack TRS 80, Tandy 1000/1200/2000, Atari.

PRODUCT DEVELOPMENT

Springboard was unusual in the industry in that it developed its products in-house. Management believed that internal development facilitated control of product quality, expense and schedule. The firm's recent experience with translations for THE NEWSROOM had brought this point home clearly. When demand developed for an IBM version of the program, the translation had to be subcontracted because Springboard had no IBM programmers. Commissioned in February for March delivery, the translation was not completed until late July. Bringing this translation to market had taken much longer and had cost much more than anticipated.

This experience coupled with the rapid growth in the IBM PC's installed base, shown in Exhibit 3, prompted management to augment its in-house programming staff with a team of IBM programmers. Management continued to explore outside sources for certain new products in order to:

1. Expand its product line more rapidly
2. Reduce product development risk
3. Encourage cross fertilization of ideas
4. Develop specific expertise within certain organizations

Springboard was also unusual in the industry in that it had proprietary code which allowed for the electronic transfer of graphics between incompatible IBM, Apple II, Macintosh and Commodore computers. Since educational products tended to be graphics oriented, this capability dramatically reduced the resources required to translate programs from one machine to another. As Paulson explained:

> Springboard has this unusual capability because it has an extraordinarily skilled and dedicated product development team. State-of-the-art programmers are supported by a staff of experienced computer artists and child development specialists. The programmers have displayed a remarkable ability to adapt to different machines as required by the marketplace.

All Springboard products were written in assembly code. Although use of higher-level languages reduced product development time, Springboard products tended to require assembly code in order to maximize the limited capabilities of popular computers. A program as advanced as THE NEWSROOM, for instance, could not be developed for the 64K Apple II computer in Pascal, C, Forth or any other compiled language. While use of assembly language increased product development time, it also made it more difficult for competitors to imitate Springboard's programs.

Another characteristic of the code developed for Springboard products was its evolutionary nature. Each product under development presented programming challenges which, when solved, provided a stepping stone to the next product. The programmers had methodically developed a library of software tools which could easily be adapted to specific program needs, thereby reducing product development time for future products. As a result, Springboard's existing product line represented a progression in programming capabilities which was marked by what was referred to internally as generations. In addition, current programs provided revenues to help fund programs under development.

In program development, Paulson placed top priority on developing families of products with the same relationship as a razor to razor blades:

> THE NEWSROOM, for example, is a powerful graphics/text presentation program that comes with over 600 wonderful, useful pieces of clip art. The number 600 is an interesting one in that it represents a real value to the consumer. Yet, after using THE NEWSROOM for a while, the consumer realized that this amount of clip art has only whetted his or her appetite. That's why we are developing the CLIP ART COLLECTION. To date, we have released CLIP ART COLLECTION VOLUME I and are thinking about releasing a VOLUME II featuring business clip art. VOLUME I sells very well, second only to THE NEWSROOM.
>
> Our ability to transfer graphics between incompatible computers electronically makes our razor blades very attractive. Once the art has been created, it takes only hours to make it available on all machine formats. Furthermore, as we continue to market high quality applications programs which use clip art, a larger and larger installed base of users will be purchasing the CLIP ART COLLECTION.

Springboard created products for proven hardware only. New computer brands and models had to establish a significant user base before management would allocate resources to support them.

PRODUCTION

Springboard subcontracted disk duplication and product packaging. The company currently had several suppliers. Management preferred to pay a slight premium for duplication and packaging in order to work with local suppliers.

Management had evaluated and expected to continue to evaluate the benefits of integrating backward into disk duplication. Disk duplication was not considered to be technically difficult, but experienced individuals were required to oversee this kind of operation. Bulk disks, for instance, required special handling. Duplication had to take place in a climate-controlled room, equipped with special air purifiers. Although prices were dropping, duplication equipment was still very expensive. Packaging was a separate operation, requiring specialized equipment, and tended to be labor intensive.

There appeared to be a trend towards in-house duplication among the larger software companies. Most of Springboard's direct competitors, however, did not perform their own disk duplication. Springboard's management felt that the economies of scale were not yet available to make backward integration superior to present supplier arrangements.

The company leased approximately 5,000 square feet of office space for an annual rental of approximately $96,000 in a Minneapolis suburb. The lease was to expire in 1988. The company's executive, marketing, product development and operations were located at these facilities.

MARKETING AND DISTRIBUTION

A key conclusion of the early 1984 business plan was that Springboard should shift emphasis to the mass volume retailer (MVR) channel of distribution. As a result, a mass marketing strategy was developed. This strategy was fashioned after Spinnaker Software's, the industry's fastest growing educational software company at the time. Spinnaker was the first company to apply sophisticated consumer marketing techniques in selling micro software. This approach bought them a considerable amount of shelf space in such major U.S. MVR's as Sears, K-Mart, and Toys R Us.

As a result of adopting a similar strategy, Springboard began to neglect its traditional distributor and computer specialty store channels of distribution. An example of this neglect was the manner in which the company changed its name from Counterpoint to Springboard. Retailers were not effectively communicated with so as to be able to make the connection between the two names. They mistakenly thought Counterpoint had gone out of business. Springboard was simply a new company they had never heard of. The result was a dramatic decrease in shelf space for Springboard's existing products and minimal access for its new products.

Financial results for 1984 did not meet expectations. Gross sales of well over $3 million were forecast for the year; actual sales barely reached $1 million. Paulson believed the shortfall was created primarily by the unwise and unsuccessful shift to the MVR channel of distribution as well as callous handling of existing accounts and ineffective use of resources. Springboard had considerably less distribution in the fourth quarter (the peak season) of 1984 than it had enjoyed in 1983.

Springboard's disappointing performance was masked somewhat by the problems suffered by the industry as a whole. Research firms had predicted a 100% increase in 1984 educational software sales whereas only 60% growth actually occurred. Spinnaker, for example, posted $15 million in sales, a fraction of the $50+ million its management had projected for the year. As a result, the ability of mass merchants to sell software and the effectiveness of large ad budgets and mass marketing techniques in general became topics of debate in the industry.

When Paulson took over again as CEO in 1985, he steered the company back to its original distribution channels. The computer specialty store, that purchased from the company's wholesale distributor customers, was once again the focus of Springboard's marketing and sales team efforts. Paulson had not ruled out the Spinnaker strategy entirely, however. As he explained:

> At this time, the big dollar marketing approach to consumer software is not leading to success. It can achieve moderate sales levels, but only at the sacrifice of profitability. Word of mouth from an army of satisfied customers is far more effective than a large ad budget. This may change in the future, however. It is important that we continue to evaluate just exactly what marketing techniques are effective and how much capital they require.

The company continued to support its dominant mode of distribution, wholesale distributors, as it attempted to expand into large chains of computer specialty stores. Management was cautiously testing distribution through certain MVRs as well as new forms of distribution such as electronic distribution and direct marketing. Springboard's international distribution strategy was to expand through the use of agents and licensing agreements. The company's top four customers accounted for 18%, 15%, 14% and 12% respectively of total gross sales volume during 1985.

FINANCE

Springboard had net sales of $889,750 and a $1.6 million net loss in 1984, the most recent year for which information was available. Unaudited financial results for the first nine months of fiscal 1985 indicated that the company was profitable on $3.1 million in net sales. See Exhibits 4 and 5 for historical and recent financial information for the company. While final results were not yet in, yearend 1985 sales were expected to approach the six million dollar mark.

Springboard made a small public offering in Minnesota in 1983, which was exempt from SEC requirements for public financial reporting under Regulation A because of its small size and the limited number of shares sold. Roughly 8% of the 1.6 million shares currently outstanding were traded publicly through a second-tier Minneapolis broker who made a market in the stock. Shares

EXHIBIT 4
Springboard Software, Inc.
Balance Sheet 1982–1984

	1984	*1983*	*1982*
Assets			
Current assets			
Cash and cash equivalents	$ 408,469	$ 73,206	$ 14,372
Accounts receivable, less allowance for doubtful accounts: 1984—23,953; 1983—$10,000	354,455	273,252	35,561
Inventories	153,605	112,505	7,387
Prepaid expenses	74,882	1,286	478
Total current assets	991,411	460,249	54,798
Certificate of deposit	150,000	—	—
Property and equipment at cost	227,849	30,737	1,333
Less: Accumulated Depreciation	(39,635)	(4,904)	(45)
	188,214	25,833	1,288
Product rights	—	1,229	2,364
	$1,329,625	$487,311	$58,450
Liabilities and Shareholders' Equity			
Current liabilities			
Accounts payable	$ 221,293	$154,438	$1,048
Working capital bank loan	154,608	—	—
Current portion of long-term debt	37,500	—	—
Accrued liabilities			
Payroll and taxes withheld	12,857	31,162	9,762
Vacation Pay	10,372	2,515	—
Other	56,230	2,423	—
Total current liabilities	493,220	190,538	10,810
Long-term debt less current portion	103,125	—	—
Total liabilities	596,345	190,538	10,810
Commitments			
Shareholders' equity			
Convertible preferred	83,737	14,000	—
Common stock	7,850	5,350	4,100
Additional paid-in capital	2,363,490	384,654	43,400
Retained earnings (deficit)	(1,721,797)	(107,231)	140
Total equity	733,280	296,773	47,640
	$1,329,625	$487,311	$58,450

Source: Company annual report.

EXHIBIT 5
Springboard Software, Inc.
Statement of Operations Years Ended December 31, 1984, 1983 and from August 24, 1982, through December 31, 1982

	1984	*1983*	*1982*
Gross revenue	$1,017,773	$766,100	$87,062
Less: sales returns*	128,123	42,452	—
Net revenue	889,650	723,648	87,062
Cost of sales	471,874	232,337	20,589
Gross profit*	417,874	491,311	66,473
Percent to net sales	47.0%	67.9%	76.4%
Operating expenses			
Marketing	816,967	—	—
Sales	264,631	282,062	31,565
General and administrative	490,628	231,665	18,358
Research and development	411,967	92,290	16,645
Interest expense	35,473	—	—
Other	12,774	(7,335)	(235)
Total operating expenses	2,032,440	598,682	66,333
Net profit (loss) before income tax	1,614,566)	107,371)	140
Income tax expense	—	—	—
Net profit (loss)	$(1,614,566)	$(107,371)	$ 140
Net loss per common share	$ (2.92)	$ (.22)	$ .00
Weighted average common shares outstanding	552,077	493,333	400,833

1985 Press Release

Minneapolis, October 18, 1985—Springboard Software Inc. announced net sales figures for the first three quarters of this year to be $3,066,000. Net sales for the same period last year were $501,000.

Unaudited financial results for the first nine months indicate the company is profitable.

Source: Company.

had traded in the $2 to $3 range over the last year. As of January, 1986, the company's major shareholders with their respective holdings were as follows:

Cherry Tree Venture Capital	30%
Former Chairman and CEO	15%
V. Suarez, private investor	10%
John Paulson	4%

The company currently had a $1.0 million total credit line, comprised of a $150,000 term loan on fixed assets and a $850,000 formula-based working capital loan. Springboard had paid no dividends to date.

ORGANIZATIONAL STRUCTURE AND MANAGEMENT PHILOSOPHY

During 1985, three full-time employees were added to the company—two for the newly created Customer Support group and one for the Marketing Department. By January, 1986, Springboard had twenty-four employees in total as shown in Exhibit 6. Contractors were hired to augment certain capabilities in advertising, public relations and production. Although the company had experienced a lot of change in its short history, Paulson felt confident about the personnel and Springboard's outlook:

> The most important, wonderful asset of Springboard is the people. The management team is experienced, competent and dedicated. This is critical since Springboard is in a constant state of change. The growth rate of the company and of the industry in general requires that management respond appropriately to a variety of problems and opportunities.
>
> All of the employees are capable and share a common commitment. It is not unusual to hear people talking at lunch about ways they can improve efficiency or solve a problem. They know they can freely discuss their feelings about what the company is doing and share their ideas and suggestions with management.
>
> It is my job to make certain that everyone understands and appreciates the importance of their unique roles within the company, how their responsibilities interrelate and how much the company values their participation. From the very beginning I have insisted that all employees participate in the company's Incentive Stock Option Plan. I want all of our goals and hopes to be harmonious. I will work hard to insure that everyone who is contributing to our success will share fairly in its rewards.
>
> Springboard is not, after all, a factory. It is not buildings or disks or cash flow. Our most important asset is our people. We depend upon them for the expertise, insight and creativity that success demands. And they deliver. They are determined to

EXHIBIT 6
Springboard Organizational Chart, January 1986

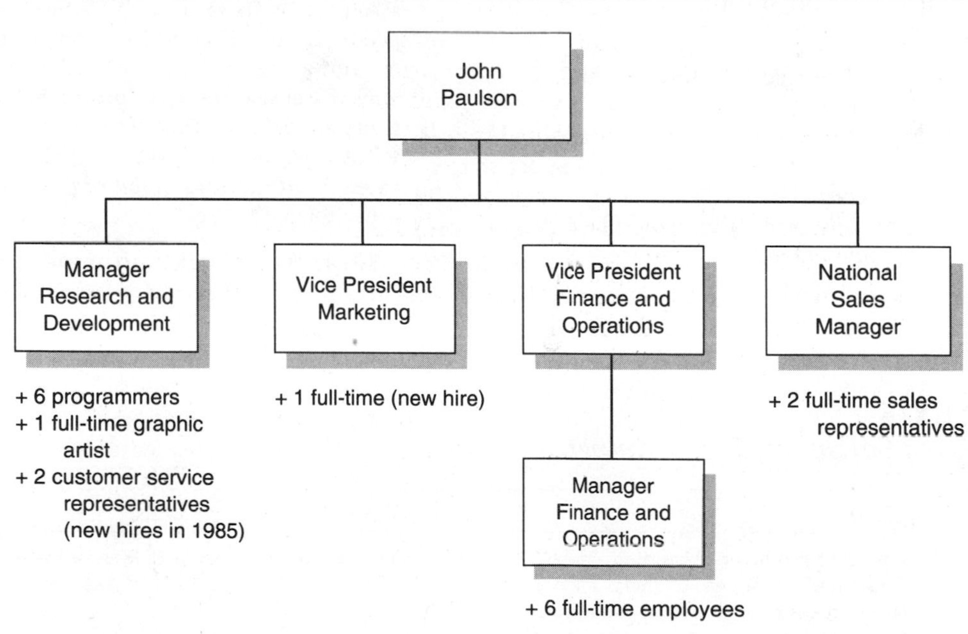

Source: Company.

transform programs into best-selling products, problems into worthwhile opportunities, and Springboard into one of the most respected leaders of this fascinating industry.

FUTURE EXPANSION PLANS

By January, 1986, although home and school remained Springboard's primary markets, management was considering creating business editions for certain titles. Paulson described the situation in this way:

> Because productivity titles are more useful to a wide variety of people, they have the potential of being sold into the business marketplace. THE NEWSROOM, for instance, is the most popular program currently being sold in schools in America, as well as being a best-seller to the home market. We anticipated sales into each of these markets when we developed the program. The interest of the business world in THE NEWSROOM, however, came as a surprise. It has many capabilities business people want to have.

Paulson felt that sales of this program into the business market would be inhibited by the following factors:

1. The packaging featured a picture of a high school newspaper
2. The clip art included was not business oriented
3. The price point was too low to get the support of business retail outlets
4. The program copy protection would be considered to be inconvenient

This situation required careful consideration, however, for it was likely to be repeated with other productivity programs currently under development, which, when completed, would represent a new generation of Springboard products.

A separate issue to be addressed was the disappointing sales performance of some of the company's other programs which Paulson perceived to be of superior quality to competitive offerings. In Paulson's words:

> Although EARLY GAMES continues to sell well and THE NEWSROOM is a tremendous success, other titles are not reaching their sales potential. MASK PARADE, RAINBOW PAINTER, STICKERS and PUZZLE MASTER are all outstanding products but they do not sell as well as they should. EASY AS ABC, for instance, is often cited by dealers, teachers and parents as the best alphabet program on the market, but it is consistently outsold by competing products which are nowhere near as good. Increasing the sales of these particular titles is one of the important challenges facing Springboard management.
>
> Our overall challenge is how to best use limited dollars to sell Springboard products. Is it possible to promote the company brand or is it safer to promote specific titles? How can management protect the strong growth of THE NEWSROOM and related products and still develop sales for the titles which are not achieving their potential? What is the best way to release the new products? What role does trade advertising play? How should it be balanced with consumer ads? What monies should be dedicated to promotions, point of purchase displays and other related tactics?

With these thoughts in mind, Paulson turned his attention to the 1986 report on the Microcomputer Applications Software Industry.

APPENDIX A
Springboard Software, Inc.: Competitor Profiling

Name	*Spinnaker*	*Broderbind*
Generic strategy	• Low-cost producer—branding • Breadth of line/access to shelf • 60% in mass retail—first on the scene • Price sensitive • Pre-emptive shelf space managers	• Focused on basic needs of less sophisticated users

Name	*Spinnaker*	*Broderbind*
Strengths	• First mover/shelf control • Strong marketing management • Strong financing • Diverse line • Many offerings • Bid ad dollars = reviews • Continuity in marketplace • Slick marketeers • Have executed a plan • Videotape concept supports MVR strength	• "Hot" products—item merchants • 30% MVR (C64 version of Print Shop), 70% specialty • Product strategy = Apple hit to C64 • Royalty strategy (reduced royalty % of revenues from 33% to 28%) • Reduced administrative costs from 21% to 13%—Talent spotters • Probably attract free-lance authors • Not promotional or price oriented • International dealings, good connection with Japan and MSX • First mover in "genres"—"Good enough" product/user accessible • 20% tech → 80% need of consumer
Weaknesses	• Defective disks and programs • Lost First Software • MVR want hits, not full line • Dependent on MVR—working capital in channel (no controls) • Weak quality image in schools especially • Dependent on C64 base • Inconsistent quality/appeal due to unrelated authors/sources—not highly thought of in traditional channels of distribution	• Marketing not POS • Milk products • Need items • Lack of franchise on names • Second-rate packaging • Apple is 60% of sales, IBM only 16%
General information		• 1984 sales of $11M, net income of $500K • Discount (55%); terms (30 days); freight (FOB headquarters; no coop; defective (return for replacement only); stock bal (10% of purchases over last 120 days) • Policies set in stone, they do not bargain and are tough to work with • Sales management left 3/85; company run by finance people • Order fulfillment good but takes 3–4 weeks • Support distributors, do not sell direct • Produce home and personal productivity programs under $100 • Games account for 20% of sales • Planning product line based on hobbies and pursuits • Bought Synapse in 1984 for $450K, may be looking for others

Name	*Random House*	*CBS Software*
Generic strategy	• Differentiated • Educational (mostly), some productivity and entertainment • High price	• Differentiated • Entertainment, education

Name	*Random House*	*CBS Software*
Strengths	• Strong financing • Great licenses: Peanuts, Garfield, Potatoe Head • Both in house programming as well as external licensing • 8 new programs in 1984; expect 18 new titles in 1985 • Division for school market: internal sales staff and packaging • Sell Handleman two titles . . . is this a strength?	• Financial strength • Offers extremely good terms • Ability to market to the consumer (entertainment business) • Name recognition • @ 37 titles—breadth of line • Strong distribution (retail service reps—good or bad?) • Licensed famous characters like Big Bird • Ads in *Time, Newsweek, People* • Promotions: Buy Felony and get another title free plus $5 refund • Parent and associated companies
Weaknesses	• No major hits • Not currently selling Softsel • Heavy reliance on education (starting to do utilities/entertainment) • Me-too packaging • Me-too marketing • Weak in IBM format	• Trying to be all things to all people • Maybe too big, not in tune with pulse of the industry • Service • No big winners in product line • Small presence at CES—are they getting out of business? • Rumored to be losing money • High return rate, low satisfaction • MVR is 50% of business, schools 10% • Specialty stores declining (40%) • Me-too packaging • Focus on C64 and Atari—changing to IBM, Apple • Licenses are costly
General information	• Division formed in 1982 • Dominant format is Apple, some C64, weak in IBM PC	• Main sales team has been fired • Planning ad shift towards schools • Changing to S.A.T. types and home productivity • Outside sales reps may start calling on large school districts

Name	*Davidson and Associates*	*EPYX*
Generic strategy	• Focused	• Differentiated • Entertainment and utility products
Strengths	• Focused on basic skills (utility) • All five products sell well (3 on charts) • Weak marketing works • Little known about them	• Profitable in April and May • Licenses: Barbie Dolls, G.I. Joe, Hotwheels, Olympics, etc. • Have been able to choose their distribution channels • Hot product (Fastload for C64)
Weaknesses	• Only five products • Original product is cash cow (3 yrs old) • Questionable product development capability • Packaging/marketing *appears* weak	• Lost $500,000 in 1984 • Computer specialty stores generate only 40% of revenue • Mass merchants generate 60% • Heavy reliance on entertainment software (starting to do utilities) • Packaging (me-too)

Name	*Davidson and Associates*	*EPYX*
		• Marketing (me-too) • Primarily C64 revenues (trying to change to Apple/IBM) • Probably pay heavy fees for licenses and royalties • Uphill battle to change image from entertainment to anything better

General information	• Founded 1982
	• 1983 sales = $750,000
	• 1984 sales = $2,500,000
		• Founded in 1978 as Automated Simulations Inc.
		• Name change to EPYX in 1983
		• Product philosophy according to Bob Botch, marketing director, is to slow down new product intros because of slower growth rate of home computer market:
		  • new products require more planning
		  • increased support for products
		  • used to sell entertainment but now concentrating on utility products
		  • expanding line to include high end machines
		• Used to intro 25 titles per year, now down to 10–15. They will only support the best-selling titles.
		• Botch thinks Apple and IBM computers have more active users and longer life cycles
		• Most successful product is Fastload for C64 (retail of $30–$40): initially represented 50% of sales, now represents 15%. Thus they plan to release more hardware/software utilities as well as home productivity.

Name	*Houghton Mifflin*	*Hayden*
Generic strategy	• Focused • "The 150 year old software company" . . . selling as an old established school book publisher (American Heritage Dictionary & Iowa Test of Basic Skills)	• "Throw a lot of titles at the wall and see what sticks" (50+ titles in a wide range of software categories; education, business, entertainment and productivity)
Strengths	• Well recognized and highly regarded by its market (schools) • Money • Solid and deep penetration of the school market • Good, consistent image in the product line . . . packaged by well defined series • Reasonable and stable pricing (c. $39.95) • Established line of reps to schools • Relatively alone in an unusual niche . . . business education (DO MORE Series; instructional aids to PFS, Lotus & Multiplan)	• Diverse line going in the largest segments of the market (education, business, entertainment and productivity) • Strong representation in the MAC world with five bestsellers "out of the chute;" Ensemble, I Know It's Here Somewhere, Hayden Speller (all MAC only, business and productivity bestsellers), and Sargon III and Music Works (MAC conversion from Apple) • 8 bestsellers in all of the categories mentioned: Ensemble, I Know It's Here Somewhere, Hayden Speller, Sargon III, Music Works, Score Improvement System (Mac), Holy Grail • Company name recognition • Established channel through reps to retailers

Name	*Houghton Mifflin*	*Hayden*
Weaknesses	• Limited distribution . . . almost 100% to schools through reps . . . SoftKat is an exclusive and their only access to the consumer market via retail . . . very weak distribution at the retail level • No bestsellers • Software such a nominal part of their business . . . may account for the relatively low profile in the industry and to the consumer • Depends entirely on outside sources for software development and conversion • Very limited promotional material . . . advertising restricted to school magazines • Drill and practice type software uninspired	• Rely almost entirely on reps • Lack of branding or consistent image throughout product line . . . confusing and weak packaging • Maybe cash poor (Consumer Electronics Show (CES) was financially hard on them and a "complete bust") • Dependent on outside for virtually all software development/conversion • Educational line is graphically dry and not at all their best performer . . . emphasizing the productivity and business software
General information		

Name	*Grolier Electronic Publishing, Inc.*

Generic strategy	• Differentiated . . . GEP's goal is to utilize electronic media to deliver information and educational programs in a timely, unique manner in ways that have never before been possible
	• Currently participates in several market niches:
	  • productivity (spread sheets, database, graphs)
	  • interactive adult computer adventure programs
	  • educational (pre/elem levels) NEW 6-85

Strengths	• GEP is a subsidiary of Grolier, Inc. (the world's leading publisher of encyclopedias) • Good management team with emphasis in publishing and microcomputer software sales and marketing • Strong financial backing from parent company • Product line has 20 titles (Apple/IBM/Comm 64) • Retail pricing mostly $30–$40 range • Has comprehensive advertising plan to support sales • Introduced "Miss Mouse" and "Ryme Land" reading readiness software for kids (4–7) • Can leverage "Grolier" name and reputation for quality educational materials
Weaknesses	• GEP was started in 1982 . . . just entered the software field in 1984 • Majority of the programs were just released and many are scheduled for release in next few months • No products on the hit lists yet
General information	

CASE 17 | *Mr. Jax Fashion Inc.*

It was 6:30 A.M., Monday, January 16, 1989; dawn had not yet broken on the Vancouver skyline and Louis Eisman, President of Mr. Jax Fashion Inc., was sitting at his desk-pondering opportunities for future growth. Growth had been an important objective for Eisman and the other principal shareholder, Joseph Segal. Initially the company had focused on the professional/career women's dresses, suits and coordinates market, but by 1986 it had virtually saturated its ability to grow in this Canadian market segment. Growth was then sought through the acquisition of 4 companies: a woolen textile mill and 3 apparel manufacturing companies. The result of this decade-long growth was that the company had become the sixth largest apparel manufacturer in Canada.

In the future, Eisman felt continued growth would require a modified approach. A particularly good growth option appeared to be expansion into the U.S. market. The window for U.S. growth seemed very favorable for Mr. Jax over the next several years. Good growth was forecast in the women's career/professional market, Mr. Jax's principal market segment, and the recently ratified Free Trade Agreement (FTA) would provide an excellent low tariff environment for expansion into the U.S. Yet, Eisman wanted to ensure that the appropriate growth strategy was selected because he was certain that, if the right approach was taken, Mr. Jax could be a major international apparel company by the end of the next decade.

THE INDUSTRY

The apparel industry was divided into a variety of market segments based upon gender, type of garment and price points. Based on price points, the women's segments ranged from low-priced unexceptional to runway fashion segments. Low-priced segments competed on a low-cost manufacturing capability while the higher-quality segments competed on design and marketing capabilities. In fact, companies in the higher-priced segments often subcontracted out manufacturing because it required a different skill base.

The professional/career women's segment ranged from the medium to medium-high price points. During the late 1970's and early 1980's, this segment had experienced strong growth due to the demographic growth in career-oriented, professional women. In the U.S., it had grown by 50% annually during the first half of the 1980's, but had slowed to about 20% in 1988, and experts predicted that by the mid-1990's growth would drop to the rate of GNP growth. The U.S. professional/career women's segment was estimated to be $2 billion in 1988. The Canadian market was estimated to be one tenth this size and growth was expected to emulate that in the U.S. market. Yet, the exact timing of the slowing of growth was difficult to predict because of the extreme cyclicality in the fashion industry.

Competition

Some of the more prominent Canada-based companies competing in the professional/career women's segment included:

- *Jones New York of Canada*, a marketing subsidiary of a U.S.-based fashion company, was thought to share the leadership position with Mr. Jax in the Canadian professional/career women's market.

This case was written by Professors C. Patrick Woodcock and J. Michael Geringer, with the assistance of Professor H. Crookell as a basis for class discussion only. Some of the data and figures presented represent estimations by the authors rather than by management or the company. Figures are in Canadian dollars unless otherwise stated.

The company focused exclusively on marketing clothes to this market segment. Manufacturing was contracted out to Asian companies.

- *The Monaco Group* had become a major Canadian designer and retailer of men's and women's fashions during the 1980's. By 1988, the company had sales of $21 million and a rate of return on capital of over 20%. It designed its own fashion lines and merchandised them through its own retail outlets as well as major department stores. Manufacturing was contracted to Asian companies. Recently, the company had been purchased by Dylex Inc., a large Canada-based retail conglomerate with 2,000 retail apparel stores located in both Canada and the U.S.
- *Nygard International Ltd.*, with revenues of over $200 million, was Canada's largest apparel manufacturer. Approximately one-third of its sales and production were located in the U.S. This company had historically focused on lower-priced clothing, but it had hired away Mr. Jax's former designer to create the Peter Nygard Signature Collection, a fashion line aimed at the professional/career women's market. This new line had been out for only six months and sales were rumored to be moderate.

Additional competition in this Canadian segment included a wide variety of U.S. and European imports. These companies generally manufactured garments in Asia and marketed them in Canada through independent Canadian sales agents. Historically, most had concentrated their marketing resources on the rapidly growing U.S. market, yet many had captured a significant share of the Canadian market based upon strong international brand recognition.

Prominent U.S.-based competition included the following companies:

- *Liz Claiborne* was the originator of the professional/career women's fashion look. This company, started in 1976, grew tremendously during the late 1970's and early 1980's and by 1988 it had sales in excess of $1.2 billion (U.S.). Claiborne generally competed on price and brand recognition, a strategy copied by many of the larger companies in this segment. To keep prices low, Claiborne contracted out manufacturing to low-cost manufacturers, 85% of which were Asian. The company's large size allowed it to wield considerable influence over these manufacturing relationships. Recently, the company had diversified into retailing.
- *J.H. Collectibles*, a Milwaukee-based company, had one of the more unique strategies in this segment. It produced slightly upscale products emphasizing quality and delivery. It owned manufacturing facilities in Wisconsin and Missouri and had sales of $200 million (U.S.).
- *Jones of New York*, the parent company of Jones New York of Canada, was a major competitor in the U.S. market. In fact, the majority of its $200 million (U.S.) in sales was derived from this market.
- *Evan-Picone* was a U.S.-based apparel designer and marketer which had become very successful in the slightly older professional/career women's market. This company also contracted out its manufacturing function and had annual sales in excess of $200 million (U.S.).

In addition, there were a myriad of other apparel designers, marketers and manufacturers competing in this segment. They included such companies as Christian Dior, Kasper, Pendleton, Carole Little, Susan Bristol, J.G. Hooke, Ellen Tracy, Anne Klein II, Perry Ellis, Adrienne Vittadini, Tahari, Harvé Bernard, Norma Kamali, Philippe Adec, Gianni Sport, Regina Porter and Herman Geist.

Profitability in this segment had been excellent. Liz Claiborne led profitability in the apparel industry with a 5-year average return on equity of 56% and a 12-month return of 45%. J.H. Collectibles had averaged over 40% return on equity during the last 5 years. This compared to an average return on equity in the overall apparel industry of 12.5% in the U.S. and 16% in Canada during the past 5 years.

Distribution

The selection and maintenance of retail distribution channels had become a very important consideration for apparel manufacturers in the 1980's. The retail industry had gone through a particularly bad year in 1988, although the professional/

career women's segment had been relatively profitable. Overall demand had declined and retail analysts were predicting revenue increases of only 1% to 2% in 1989, which paled beside the 6% to 7% growth experienced in the mid-1980's. The consensus was that high interest rates and inflation as well as somewhat stagnant demand levels were suppressing overall profitability in this industry. In addition, the industry appeared to be moving into a period of consolidation, resulting in a shift in power from the designers to the retailers.

To counter the retailers' increasing power, some apparel designers had been vertically integrating into retailing. The attractiveness of this option was based on controlling the downstream distribution channel activities and thus enabling an apparel company to aggressively pursue increased market share. The principal components for success in the retail apparel industry were location, brand awareness and superior purchasing skills. The apparel companies which had integrated successfully into retailing were the more market-oriented firms such as Benetton and Esprit.

The Free Trade Agreement

Historically, developed nations had protected their textile and clothing industries through the imposition of relatively high tariffs and import quotas. Tariffs for apparel imported into Canada averaged 24.5% and 22.5% into the U.S. while tariffs for worsted woolen fabrics, one of the principal ingredients for Mr. Jax's products, were 22.5% into Canada and 40% into the U.S. Import quotas were used to further limit the ability of developing country manufacturers to import into either country. Despite these obstacles, Canadian apparel imports had grown from 20% to 30% of total shipments during the 1980's, most of which came from developing countries. Shipments from the U.S. represented an estimated $200 million in 1988 while Canadian manufacturers exported approximately $70 million to the U.S.

The Free Trade Agreement (FTA) would alter trade restrictions in North America considerably. Over the next 10 years, all clothing and textile tariffs would be eliminated between Canada and the U.S., but stringent "rules of origin" would apply. To qualify, goods not only had to be manufactured in North America, but they also had to utilize raw materials (i.e., yarn, in the case of textiles, and fabric, in the case of apparel) manufactured in North America. Unfortunately, these "rules of origin" favoured U.S. apparel manufacturers as 85% of the textiles they used were sourced in the U.S. while Canadian manufacturers utilized mostly imported textiles. To ameliorate this disadvantage, a clause was appended to the agreement which allowed Canadians to export $500 million worth of apparel annually into the U.S. which was exempt from the "rules of origin" but would have a 50% Canadian value-added content. There was much speculation as to how this exemption would be allocated in approximately 5 years when demand was projected to exceed the exemption limit. Experts expected that companies which successfully demonstrated the competitive ability to export into the U.S. would have first rights to these exceptions.

Many industry experts had contemplated the consequences of the FTA and there was some agreement that in the short-term the FTA would most severely impact the lower-priced apparel segments in Canada because of the economies of scale which existed in the U.S. market (i.e., the average U.S. apparel manufacturer was 10 times larger than its Canadian counterpart). Yet, long-term prospects for all segments were restrained because most experts agreed that the industry was slowly being pressured by the Canadian government to become internationally competitive. The question was when international negotiations would eliminate more of the protection afforded to the industry. It was with this concern that Eisman had been continuously pushing the company to become a major international fashion designer and manufacturer.

Overall, Eisman considered the FTA a mixed blessing. Competition in Canada would increase moderately over time, but he felt that the lower tariff rates and the company's high-quality, in-house woolen mill presented a wonderful competitive advantage and opportunity for potential expansion into the U.S. market.

MR. JAX FASHIONS

In 1979, a venture capital company owned by Joseph Segal acquired a sleepy Vancouver-based apparel manufacturer having $3 million in sales, 70% of which was in men's wear. Segal immediately recruited Mr. Louis Eisman, a well-known women's fashion executive, who proceeded to drop the men's clothing line and aggressively refocus the company on the career/professional women's market segment.

Eisman appreciated the importance of design and for the first 3 years he designed all of the new fashion lines. In 1982, he recruited an up-and-coming young Canadian fashion designer, yet he continued to influence the direction of designs considerably. He traveled to Europe for approximately 2 months annually to review European fashion design trends and procure quality fabrics appropriate for the upcoming fashion season. He personally reviewed all designs. The combined women's fashion knowledge and designing abilities provided Mr. Jax with a high-quality, classically designed product which differentiated it from most other Canadian competition. In 1989, the designer resigned and Eisman recruited a New York–based fashion designer, Ron Leal. Leal had excellent design experience in several large U.S.-based design houses and, unlike the previous designer, he brought considerable U.S. market experience and presence.

Eisman's energy and drive were also critical in establishing the merchandising and distribution network. He personally developed relationships with many of the major retailers. He hired and developed sales agents, in-house sales staff, and in 1983, recruited Jackie Clabon who subsequently became VP–Marketing and Sales. The sales staff were considered to be some of the best in the industry. Clabon's extensive Canadian sales and merchandising experience combined with Eisman's design and marketing strength provided Mr. Jax with considerable managerial depth in these critical activities.

Initially, acceptance by Eastern fashion buyers was cool. The fashion "establishment" was highly skeptical of this Vancouver-based apparel designer and manufacturer. Thus, Eisman focused on smaller independent retail stores which were more easily swayed in their purchasing decisions and, as Mr. Jax gained a reputation for high-quality, classical design and excellent service, larger retail chains started to place orders. By 1988, Mr. Jax's products were sold in over 400 department and specialty stores across Canada. Major customers included The Bay, Eaton's, Holt Renfrew and Simpson's and, although initial marketing efforts were aimed at the smaller retailer, the majority of Mr. Jax's sales were now to the larger retail chains. The apparel lines were sold through a combination of sales agents and in-house salespersons. Ontario and Quebec accounted for 72% of its sales. In addition, two retail stores had recently been established in Vancouver and Seattle; the Vancouver store was very profitable but the Seattle store was very unprofitable.

Many industry experts felt that Mr. Jax's product line success could be attributed directly to Eisman. He was known for his energy and brashness, as well as his creativity and knowledge of the women's fashion market. In his prior merchandising and marketing experience, he had developed an intuitive skill for the capricious women's apparel market. This industry was often considered to be one of instinct rather than rationality. Eisman was particularly good at design, merchandising and marketing. He worked very closely with these departments, often getting involved in the smallest details. As Eisman said, "It is the details that make the difference in our business." Although Eisman concentrated a great deal of his effort and time on these functions, he also attempted to provide guidance to production. The production function had been important in providing the service advantage Mr. Jax held over imports. By 1988, Mr. Jax's professional/career women's fashion lines accounted for $25 million in revenues and $3 million in net income (see Exhibit 1).

Diversification through Acquisitions

In 1986, Segal and Eisman took Mr. Jax public, raising in excess of $17 million although they both retained one-third equity ownership. The newly raised capital was used to diversify growth through the acquisition of 4 semi-related companies.

In 1986, *Surrey Classics Manufacturing Ltd.*, a family owned Vancouver-based firm, was purchased for $2 million. This company was principally a manufacturer of lower-priced women's apparel and coats. The acquisition was initially made with the objective of keeping the company an autonomous unit. However, the previous owner and his management team adapted poorly to their subordinated position within the Mr. Jax organization and, upon expiration of their non-competition clauses, they resigned and started a competing company. Unfortunately, sales began to decline rapidly because of this new competition and the absence of managerial talent. To stem the losses, a variety of designers were hired under contract. However, Surrey's poor cash flow could not support the required promotional campaigns and the new fashion lines fared poorly, resulting in mounting operating losses.

In late 1988, Eisman reassigned Mr. Jax's VP-Finance as interim manager of Surrey Classics. As Eisman stated, "the company needed a manager who knew the financial priorities in the industry and could maximize the effectiveness of the company's productive capacity." Several administrative functions were transferred to Mr. Jax, including design, pattern making, sizing and scaling operations. Marketing and production continued to be independent operations housed in a leased facility just outside of Vancouver. Surrey Classics now produced a diversified product line which included Highland Queen, a licensed older women's line of woolen apparel, and Jaki Petite, a Mr. Jax fashion line patterned for smaller women. During this turnaround, Eisman himself provided the required industry specific management skills, which demanded a considerable amount of his time and attention. Presently, Eisman kept in daily contact and was involved in most major decisions. During this time Surrey's revenues had declined from $12 million in 1986 to $10.8 million in 1988 and net income had dropped from $100 thousand in 1986 to a loss of approximately $2 million in 1988. Eisman felt that in the next 2 years Surrey's operations would have to be rationalized into Mr. Jax's to save on overhead costs.

West Coast Woolen Mills Ltd. was a 40-year-old family-owned and Vancouver-based worsted woolen mill. Mr. Jax acquired the company for $2.2 million in 1987. Eisman was able to retain most of the previous management, all of whom had skills quite unique to the industry. West Coast marketed fabric to customers across Canada. In 1986, its sales were $5 million, profits were nil and its estimated capacity was $10 million annually. The company was the smallest of three worsted woolen mills in Canada, and in the U.S. there were about 18 worsted woolen manufacturers, several of which involved divisions of some of the largest textile manufacturing companies in the world.

Both Mr. Jax and West Coast had mutually benefitted from this acquisition. The affiliation allowed Mr. Jax to obtain control of fabric production scheduling, design and quality. In particular, Mr. Jax had been able to significantly reduce order lead times for fabric produced at this subsidiary, although the effects of this on West Coast had not been studied. West Coast benefitted from increased capital funding which had allowed it to invest in new equipment and technology, both important attributes in such a capital-intensive industry. These investments supported the company's long-term strategic objective of becoming the highest quality, most design-conscious worsted woolen mill in North America. This objective had already been reached in Canada.

Mr. Jax was presently fulfilling 30% to 40% of its textile demands through West Coast. The re-

EXHIBIT 1
Mr. Jax Fashion Inc.

Income Statement (000's)

Year	*1981*	*1982*	*1983*	*1984*	*1985*	*1986*	*1987 (9 months)*	*1988*
Sales	4,592	4,315	5,472	7,666	13,018	24,705	53,391	72,027
Cost of sales	2,875	2,803	3,404	4,797	7,885	14,667	38,165	49,558
Gross profit	1,717	1,512	2,068	2,869	5,133	10,038	15,226	22,469
Selling & gen. admin.	1,172	1,117	1,458	1,898	2,434	4,530	9,071	18,175
Income from operations	545	395	610	971	2,699	5,508	6,155	4,294
Other income	22	25	25	10	16	564	418	117
Loss from discontinued operation								(554)
Income before taxes	567	420	635	981	2,715	6,072	6,573	3,857
Income Taxes								
Current	150	194	285	432	1,251	2,874	2,746	1,825
Deferred	47	2	(5)	28	24	57	245	(195)
Net income	370	224	355	521	1,440	3,141	3,582	2,227
Share price range						$7.5–$11	$8–$18	$7.5–$14

Balance Sheet (000's)

	1981	*1982*	*1983*	*1984*	*1985*	*1986*	*1987*	*1988*
Current Assets								
Short-term investments	—	—	—	—	—	5,027	1,794	495
Accounts receivable	709	874	961	1,697	2,974	6,430	16,133	14,923
Inventories	464	474	684	736	1,431	3,026	15,431	16,914
Prepaid expenses	11	15	20	22	201	398	404	293
Income taxes recoverable	—	—	—	—	—	—	—	1,074
Prop., plant & equip.	318	349	424	572	795	4,042	7,789	13,645
Other assets	—	—	—	—	—	273	526	513
Total assets	1,502	1,712	2,089	3,027	5,401	22,196	42,077	47,857
Current Liabilities								
Bank indebtedness	129	356	114	351	579	575	1,788	4,729
Accounts payable	490	435	678	963	1,494	3,100	4,893	6,934
Income taxes payable	126	58	86	153	809	1,047	546	
Deferred taxes	84	86	81	109	133	217	462	267
Shareholder Equity								
Share equity	127	7	13	5	4	12,252	26,577	26,577
Retained earnings	546	770	1,125	1,446	2,347	5,005	7,811	9,350
Total liabilities	1,502	1,712	2,097	3,027	5,401	22,196	42,077	47,857

Note: In 1987, the accounting year end was changed from February 1988 to November 1987. This made the 1987 accounting year 9 months in duration.

Years 1981 to 1984 were estimated from Change in Financial Position Statements.

mainder was being sourced in Europe. By 1988, West Coast's revenues were $6.5 million and profitability was at the break-even point.

In 1987, Mr. Jax acquired *Olympic Pant and Sportswear Co. Ltd.* and *Canadian Sportswear Co. Ltd.*, both privately owned companies, for $18.3 million. The former management, excluding owners, was retained in both of these Winnipeg-based companies.

Olympic manufactured lower-priced men's and boys pants and outerwear as well as some women's sportswear. Canadian Sportswear manufactured low-priced women's and girls outerwear and coats. Canadian Sportswear was also a certified apparel supplier to the Canadian Armed Forces and, although these types of sales made up a minority of its revenue base, such a certification provided the company with a small but protected market niche. The disparity in target markets and locations between these companies and Mr. Jax dictated that they operate largely independently. The expected synergies were limited to a few corporate administrative functions such as finance and systems management.

Combined revenues for these companies had declined from $35 million in 1986 to $30 million in 1988. Both of these companies had remained profitable during this period, although profits had declined. In 1988, combined net income was $1.2 million. Management blamed declining revenues on increased competition and a shortage of management because of the previous owner's retirement.

The Corporation's Present Situation

Diversification had provided the company with excellent growth, but it had also created problems. The most serious was the lack of management control over the now diversified structure (Exhibit 2). By 1988, it had become quite clear that without the entrepreneurial control and drive of the previous owners, the companies were not as competitive as they had been prior to their acquisition. Therefore in late 1988, Eisman recruited a new CFO, Judith Madill, to coordinate a corporate control consolidation program. Madill had extensive accounting and corporate reorganization experience, but had limited operating experience in an entrepreneurial environment such as the fashion industry. Madill suggested that corporate personnel, financial, and systems management departments be established to integrate and aid in the management of the subsidiaries. Eisman was not completely convinced this was the right approach. He had always maintained that one of Mr. Jax's competitive strengths was its flexibility and rapid response time. He thought that increased administrative overhead would restrict this entrepreneurial characteristic in the company and that extra costs would severely restrict future expansion opportunities. Thus, he had limited the overhead expansion to 2 industrial accountants for the next year.

Consolidation was also occurring in the existing organization. Eisman was presently trying to recruit a vice president of production. Mr. Jax had never officially had such a position and, unfortunately, recruiting a suitable candidate was proving to be difficult. The problem was that there were relatively few experienced apparel manufacturing executives in North America. Furthermore, Vancouver was not an attractive place for fashion executives because it, not being a fashion center, would isolate him or her from future employment opportunities, and higher salaries as well as lower taxes tended to keep them in the U.S. Yet, a manager of production was badly needed to coordinate the internal production consolidation program. Originally, production had been located in an old 22,000 square foot facility. By 1986, it had grown to 48,000 square feet located in 4 buildings throughout Vancouver. Production flow encompassed the typical apparel industry operational tasks (see Exhibit 3). However, the division of tasks between buildings made production planning and scheduling very difficult. Production problems slowly accumulated between 1986 and 1988. The problems not only restricted capacity, but also caused customer service to deteriorate from an excellent shipment rate of

EXHIBIT 2
Mr. Jax Organizational Chart

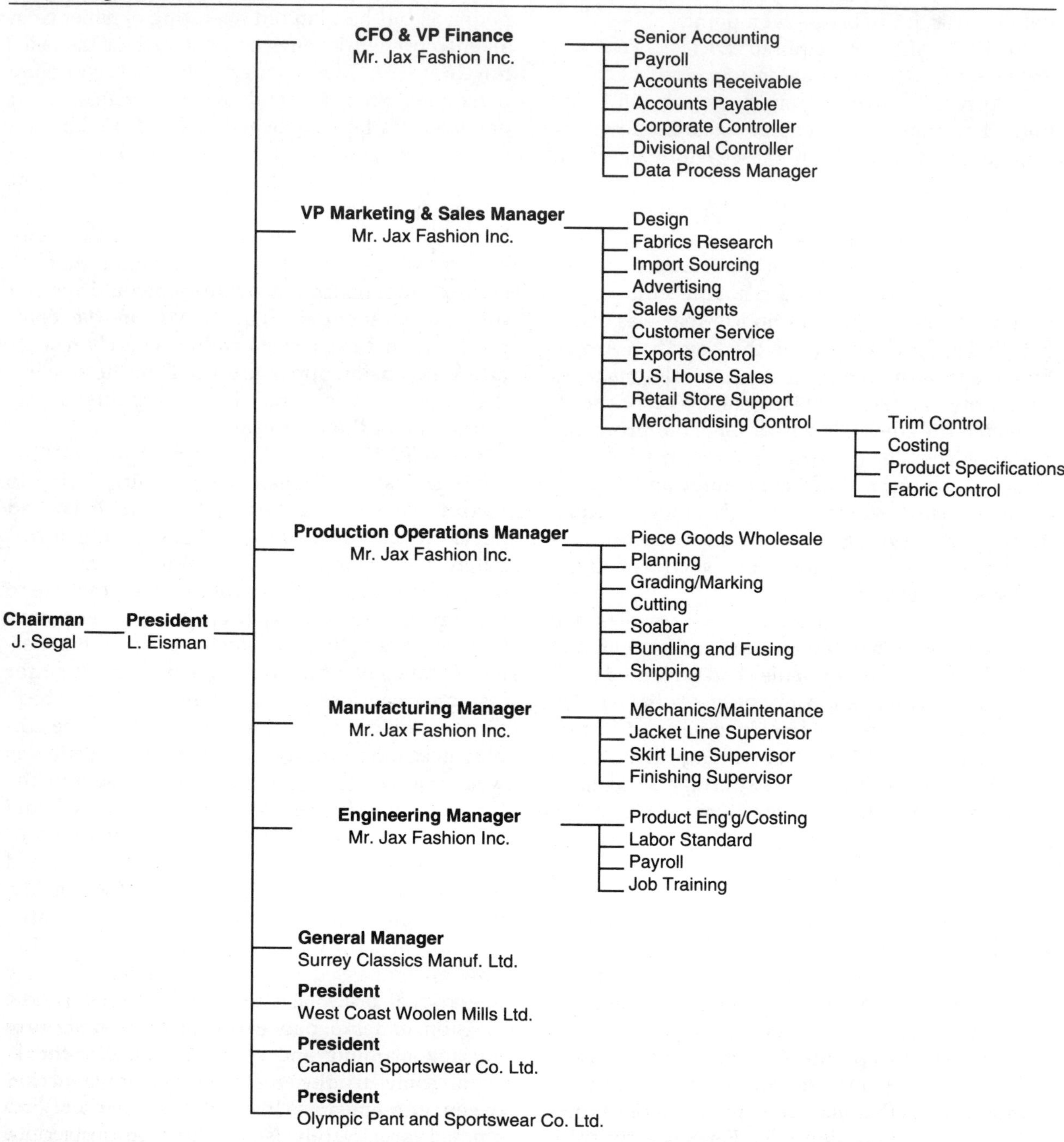

EXHIBIT 3
Production Flowchart

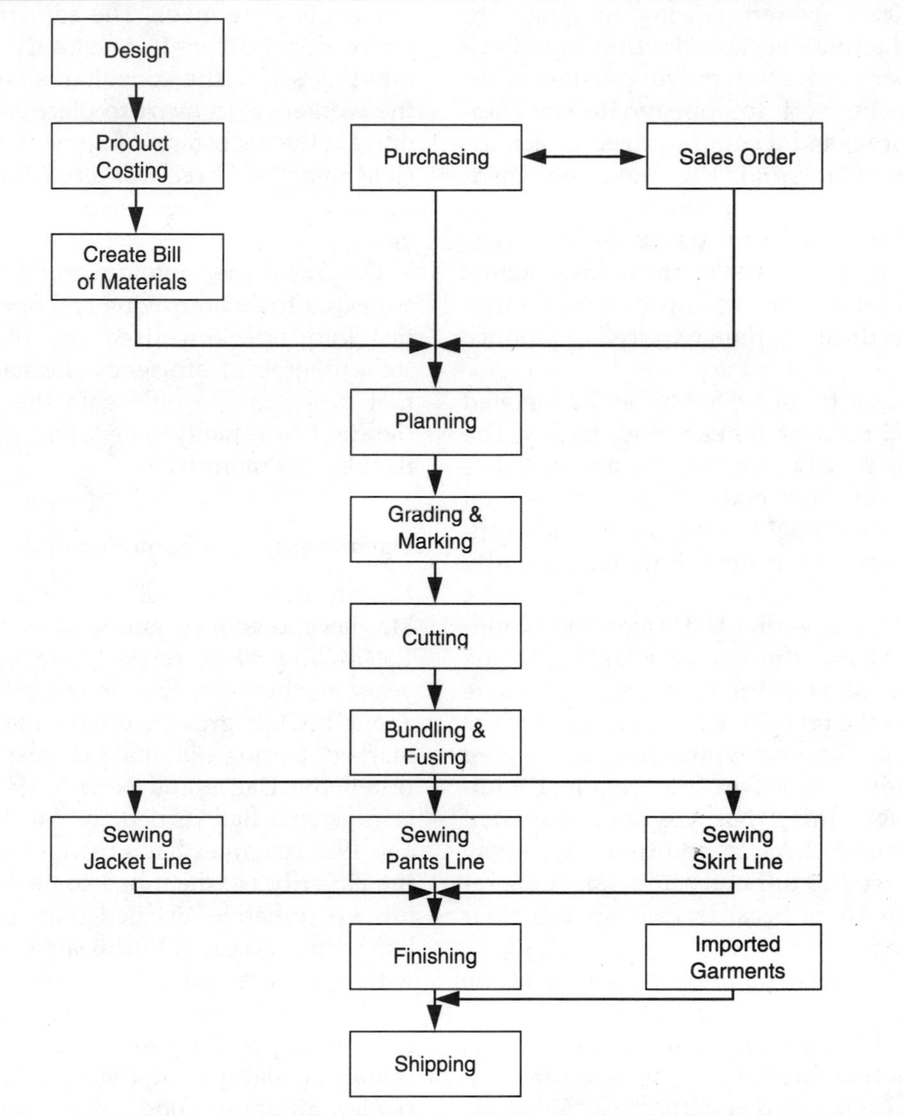

approximately 95% of orders to recently being sometimes below the industry average of 75%. Mr. Jax's ability to ship had been a key to their growth strategy in Canada. Normally, apparel manufacturers met between 70% and 80% of their orders, but Mr. Jax had built a reputation for shipping more than 90% of orders.

Consolidation had begun in the latter part of 1987. An old building in downtown Vancouver was acquired and renovated. The facility incorporated some of the most modern production equipment available. In total, the company had spent approximately $3.5 million on upgrading production technology. Equipment in the new facility included a $220,000 Gerber automatic cloth cutting machine to improve efficiency and reduce waste; $300,000 of modern sewing equipment to improve productivity and production capacity; a $200,000 Gerber production moving system to automatically move work to appropriate work stations as required; and a computerized design assistance system to integrate the above equipment (i.e., tracking in-process inventory, scheduling, planning and arranging and sizing cloth patterns for cutting). The objectives of these investments were to lower labor content, improve production capacity and reduce the time required to produce a garment.

In the last quarter of 1988, Mr. Jax had moved into this newly renovated head office facility. The building, which was renovated by one of Italy's leading architects, represented an architectural marvel with its skylights and soaring atriums. The production department had just recently settled into its expansive space. However, the move had not gone without incident. The equipment operators had difficulties adapting to the new machines. Most of the workers had become accustomed to the repetitive tasks required of the old technology. The new equipment was forcing them to retrain themselves and required additional effort; something that was not appreciated by many of the workers. In addition, the largely Asian work force had difficulty understanding retraining instructions because English was their second language.

To further facilitate the implementation of the consolidation program, an apparel production consultant had been hired. The consultant was using time-motion studies to reorganize and improve task efficiency and effectiveness. An example of a problem which had resulted from the move was the need for integration between the overall production planning, task assignment, worker remuneration and the new Gerber production moving system, if effective operation was desired. If these elements were not integrated, the new system would in fact slow production. Unfortunately, this integration had not been considered until after the move and the machine subsequently had to be removed until adjustments were made. The adjustments required converting workers from a salary base to a piece rate pay scale. The consultants were training all the workers to convert to piece rate work and to operate the necessary equipment in the most efficient manner. Three workers were being trained per week. The conversion was expected to take 2 years.

Despite these ongoing problems, production appeared to be improving and operational activities were now organized and coordinated with some degree of efficiency. Eisman was hopeful that production would gain the upper hand in the fight to remedy scheduling problems within the next six months.

Opportunities For Future Growth

Despite problems such as those detailed above, Mr. Jax's revenues and profits had grown by 1,500% and 500%, respectively, over the past 8 years. Furthermore, Eisman was extremely positive about further growth opportunities in the U.S. market. During the past 2 years, Eisman had tested the Dallas and New York markets. Local sales agents had carried the Mr. Jax fashion line and 1988 revenues had grown to $1 million (U.S.), the majority of which had come from Dallas. Follow-up research revealed that retail purchasers liked the "classical European styling combined with the North American flair."

This initial success had been inspiring but it had also exposed Eisman to the difficulties of entering the highly competitive U.S. market. In particular, attaining good sales representation and excellent service, both of which were demanded by U.S. retailers, would be difficult to achieve. Securing first-class sales representation required having either a strong market presence or a promising promotional program. In addition, Mr. Jax had found U.S. retailers to be extremely onerous in their service demands. These demands were generally a result of the more competitive retail environment. Demands were particularly stringent for smaller apparel suppliers because of their nominal selling power. These demands ranged from very low wholesale prices to extremely fast order-filling and re-stocking requirements. Eisman recognized that Mr. Jax would have to establish a focused, coordinated and aggressive marketing campaign to achieve its desired objectives in this market.

Eisman had studied two alternate approaches to entering the U.S. market. One approach involved establishing a retailing chain while the other involved starting a U.S.-based wholesale distribution subsidiary responsible for managing the aggressive promotional and sales campaign required.

Establishing a retail chain would require both new capital and skills. Capital costs, including leasehold improvements and inventory, would be initially very high and an administrative infrastructure as well as a distribution and product inventorying system would have to be established. Yet, starting a retail chain did have benefits. The retail approach would provide controllability, visibility and rapid market penetration. It was the approach taken by many of the aggressive apparel companies in the women's professional/career market segment, such as Liz Claiborne, Benetton and Esprit. Furthermore, Mr. Jax's marketing strength fit well with this strategic approach. Experts estimated that the initial capital required would be about $10 million to open up the first 30 stores, and then cost $300,000 per outlet thereafter. Sales revenues would grow to between $300,000 and $750,000 per outlet, depending upon the location, after 2 to 5 years. Operating margins on apparel stores were slightly less than 10%. Experts felt that within 5 years the company could possibly open 45 outlets; 5 the first year and 10 each year thereafter. In summary, this option would entail the greatest financial risk, but it would also have the greatest potential return.

The alternative approach was to establish a U.S. distribution subsidiary. This alternative would require capital and more of the same skills the company had developed in Canada. In general, the company would have to set up one or more showrooms throughout the U.S. The location of the showrooms would be critical to the approach eventually implemented. Exhibit 4 illustrates regional apparel buying habits in North America.

A wholesale distribution approach could be carried out in one of two ways; either on a regional or national basis. A regional approach would involve focusing on the smaller regional retail stores. These stores tended to attract less competitive attention because of the higher sales expense-to-revenue ratio inherent in servicing these accounts. The approach required the new distributor to provide good-quality fashion lines and service the accounts in a better manner than established suppliers. An advantage to this approach was that regional retailers demanded fewer and smaller price concessions compared to the larger national chains. The obstacles to this approach included the large sales force required and the superior service capability. Even though Mr. Jax had utilized this strategy successfully in Canada, success was not assured in the U.S. because of the very competitive environment. These factors made this approach both difficult to implement and slow relative to other approaches. Experts estimated fixed costs to average $1 million annually per region, of which 75% would be advertising and 25% other promotional costs. Additional operating costs would consist of sales commissions (7% of sales) and administrative overhead costs (see below). Revenues would be dependent upon many factors, but an initial annual growth rate of $1 million annually within each region was considered attainable over the next 5 years. In summary, this approach would minimize Mr. Jax's risk exposure, but it would also minimize the short-term opportunities.

The national approach was also a viable option. The greatest challenge in a national strategy would be the difficulty in penetrating well-established buyer/seller relationships. Floor space was expensive and national chains and department

EXHIBIT 4
North American Apparel Consumption by Region

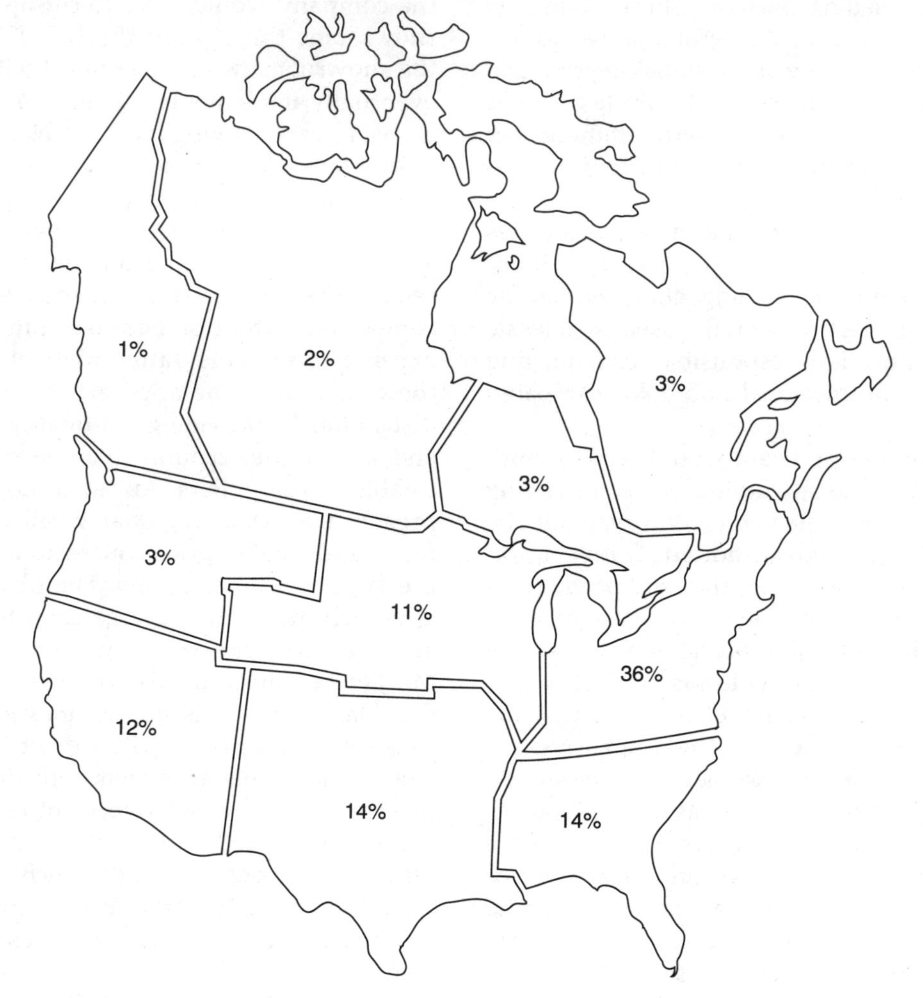

Source: U.S. & Canadian Governments.

stores tended to buy conservatively, sticking with the more reputable suppliers who they knew could produce a salable product and service large orders. They also tended to demand low prices and rapid re-order terms. In summary, the national approach provided significant entry barriers, but it also provided the greatest potential for market share growth. Clearly, if economies of scale and competitive advantage in the larger North American context was the desired goal, this had to be the eventual strategy.

The principal costs of this approach would be the advertising and promotional expenses. National apparel companies had advertising expenditures of many millions of dollars. In discussions with Eisman, industry advertising executives had recommended an advertising expenditure of between $3 and $5 million annually in the first 3 years and then, if successful, increasing it by $1 million annually in the next 2 successive years. Additional operating costs would be required for sales commissions (7% of sales) and administrative overhead (see below). The results of this approach were very uncertain and two outcomes were possible. If the approach was successful, Eisman expected that 1 or 2 accounts grossing $1 to $2 million annually could be captured in the first 2 years. Eisman then felt the sales would expand to about $5 million in the third year and increase by $5 million annually for the next 2 successive years. However, if the expected quality, design or service requirements were not sustained, sales would probably decline in the third year to that of the first year and then virtually disappear thereafter.

Both the national and regional approaches would require an infrastructure. Depending upon the approach taken, the head office could be located in a number of places. If a national approach was taken, Mr. Jax would have to locate in one of the major U.S. apparel centers (e.g., New York or California). Eisman estimated that the national approach would require a full-time Director of U.S. Operations immediately, while the regional approach could delay this hiring until required. Such a managing director would require extensive previous experience in the industry and be both capable and compatible with Mr. Jax's marketing, operating and strategic approach. To ensure top-quality candidates, Eisman felt that a signing bonus of at least $100,000 would have to be offered. The remuneration would be tied to sales growth and volume, but a continued minimum salary guarantee might be necessary until the sales reached some minimum volume. In addition, a full-time sales manager would be required. Eisman estimated that the subsidiary's administrative expense would be $500,000 if a regional approach was taken, versus $1 million for a national approach in both cases. Overhead costs would then escalate by approximately $0.5 million annually for the first 5 years.

Eisman had now studied the U.S. growth options for over 6 months. He felt a decision had to be made very soon, otherwise the company would forfeit the time window over which market growth opportunities clearly existed. The new FTA environment and the growth in the professional/career women's market segment were strong incentives, and delaying the decision would only increase the costs as well as the possibility of failure. Eisman realized the decision was critical to the company's evolution toward its ultimate goal of becoming a major international fashion company. The challenge was deciding which approach to take, as well as the sequencing and timing of the subsequent actions.

CASE 18 | *Sterling Marking Products Inc.*

On November 27, 1988, Jan d'Ailly, the 29-year-old International Marketing manager for Sterling Marking Products of London, Ontario, was reviewing his options with regards to selling the

Mark Maker embosser in the United Kingdom. He had identified possibilities for licensing, exporting, joint venture, and acquisition. Jan was expected to make his recommendations at tomorrow's International Marketing Committee meeting.

In addition to the U.K. market, a larger question loomed. The Mark Maker, which had captured over 60% of the Canadian embosser market in just two years, was starting to attract attention from dealers around the world. He had received inquiries from firms in Australia, Japan, Sweden, Italy, France, Barbados, Spain and Indonesia. These firms were interested in selling and in some cases manufacturing the Mark Maker. How, thought Jan, should Sterling move on these world wide opportunities?

EMBOSSERS AND THE EMBOSSER MARKET

Used to imprint seals on corporate, legal and certain government documents, embossers had been around for hundreds of years. Since that time, the only significant innovations were the developments of a pocket seal and the Mark Maker. Throughout the world, lawyers, corporations, and consumers had purchased seals for either legal requirements or personal reasons such as embossing their name on books and documents to show ownership or make them look more official. In countries where the legal system was based on English common law, an embosser was frequently a legal requirement for notary publics (lawyers who authenticated documents). Currently 90% of Mark Makers were purchased by lawyers and corporations. The fact that embossers appealed to business and consumers alike made any country in the world a potential market for embossers. Exhibit 1 outlines per capita GNP, population, basis of law (common, civil and so forth), and where available, statistics on lawyers and incorporations for 31 countries.

In 1986, the Canadian legal embosser market was estimated to be $1.5 million per year. While an embosser was not a legal requirement for companies, almost all the 70,000 incorporations and 20,000 corporate name changes per year resulted in embosser sales, with the remaining sales accounted for by those new lawyers who decided to become notary publics. Most embosser sales were accounted for by the traditional desk seal.

Throughout most of the world, the process of producing and selling embossers was similar (Exhibit 2). The embosser was composed of two parts: a sub-assembly, which was the actual body, and a die, which contained the text and graphic to be imprinted on documents. The die was then placed in the sub-assembly. Sub-assemblies were typically manufactured by national firms with metal working expertise. Within Canada, five firms produced most embosser bodies. Embosser die production was more diffused with a proliferation of small regional die manufacturers.

The actual sale of a complete embosser (sub-assembly and die) occurred through either product suppliers or service suppliers. Product suppliers (e.g., legal stationers) stocked products, such as incorporation kits, and other supplies required by lawyers. Service firms, such as name search houses, were usually employed by lawyers to assist in the incorporation process. Typically, these firms, as part of their service, provided an embosser.

An embosser sale resulted for one of two reasons: (1) a firm approached a lawyer to help them incorporate; or, (2) a lawyer became a notary public and required a seal. In both cases, the lawyer would then approach either a product supplier or a service firm (if the lawyer was using the particular service) and request an embosser. The product and services suppliers had two avenues for supplying embossers: they could purchase the sub-assembly, contract out the die manufacturing to one of the regional die suppliers, assemble the complete unit and then sell it to the lawyer; or, they could purchase the sub-assembly, produce the die internally, and then assemble the embosser.

Throughout the world, the legal seal industry had remained stagnant. While the number of

EXHIBIT 1
Sterling Marking Products Inc.
International Markets—Selected Information

Country	*Population (000,000's)*	*Per Capita GNP 1987*	*Notary*	*Number of Lawyers*	*Yearly Increase in Lawyers and Incorporations*	*Basis of Law*
Argentina	30	2,130	Yes			Civil
Australia	16	10,840	Yes	16,077		Common
Bangladesh	101	150	Yes			Common
Brazil	135	1,640	Yes			Civil
Canada	25	13,670	Yes		82,000	Common
China	1,041	310		12,000		Other
Colombia	28	1,320	Yes			Civil
Egypt	47	680	State*			Civil
France	55	9,550	Yes			Civil
Germany, Fed	61	10,940	Yes	30,510		Civil
India	765	110	Yes	200,000		Common
Indonesia	162	530	Yes			Civil
Iran	45	NA	Yes			Other
Italy	57	6,520				Civil
Japan	121	11,330	Yes	82,042		Both
Kuwait	1	14,270				Other
Mexico	79	2,080	Yes			Civil
Nigeria	100	760	Yes			Both
Norway	4	13,890	State*	2,000		Civil
Pakistan	95	380	Yes			Common
Philippines	55	600	Yes			Both
Poland	37	2,120	State*			Other
South Africa	32	2,010	Yes			Common
Spain	39	4,366	Yes			Civil
Sweden	12	6,421		2,000		Common
Switzerland	10	16,380	Yes			Both
Thailand	51	830				Both
Turkey	49	1,130	Yes			Civil
U.K.	56	8,390	Yes		200,000	Common
U.S.A.	239	16,400	Yes		820,000	Common
U.S.S.R.	277	NA	Yes	127,000		Other

*In these countries, notarization of documents is the responsibility of state bureaucratic officials and not lawyers.

models had grown, there had been very little innovation for 50 years. Three factors had contributed to this: the legal profession had accepted the problems associated with the seal; most of the die manufacturers were small, without funds for product development; and, for the larger firms, embosser sales were typically not the dominant product, thus there was little incentive for them to undertake embosser research and development. The combination of these factors resulted in a deterioration in the function of embossers such that it ceased to be an image product. The once proud seal became a commodity purchased on the basis of price alone.

EXHIBIT 2
The Process of Embosser Manufacturing and Sales in the Legal Market

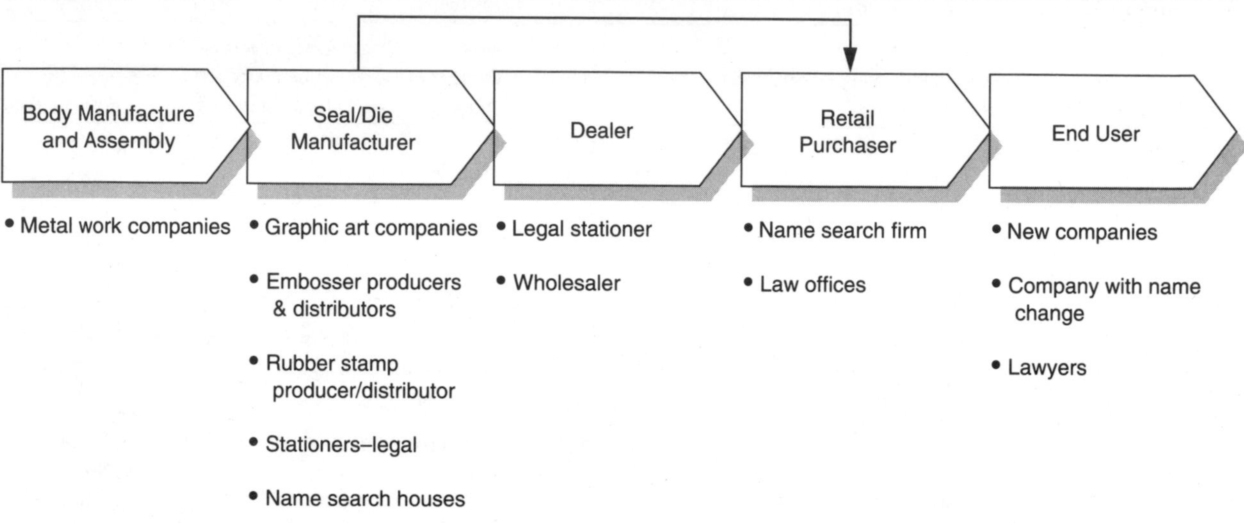

In many cases, medium and large manufacturers in the embosser industry also produced rubber stamp products. The rubber stamp industry had higher margins and was more competitive than was the embosser industry. Much innovative product and process R&D had occurred for rubber stamps. While rubber stamps and embossers were both used for marking purposes, until recently, the products were complements and not competitors. However, in some countries where corporations did not require an embossing seal, firms were starting to purchase rubber stamps, to stamp their corporate seal on documents, rather than the harder-to-use embosser.

THE MARK MAKER

Sterling Marking Products Inc. was founded in 1945 by Warren R. Schram, initially as a one-man rubber stamp company, in London, Ontario. Under Warren Schram's leadership and focus on customer service, Sterling developed a committed dealer network almost 1,000 strong. In 1976 Mr Schram's son, Bob, a University of Western Ontario MBA who had worked at Sterling for eleven years (since he was 19), acquired the business. At that time, Sterling's primary focus was still on the production and sale of rubber stamp products. In 1981, Bob Schram, Sam Hassan (Controller) and Cam Fink (General Manager) decided that the time was right to strike out into a new area. In the past, Sterling's embosser involvement consisted of supplying customers with assembled embossers. Since the sub-assembly was not manufactured by Sterling, their only value-adding activity was the actual assembly of the embosser and the manufacturing of the die. In management's view, all Sterling offered was an easily copied service. They decided that getting into embosser production and supply made strategic sense as it increased Sterling's independence. Bob, Sam and Cam thrashed about whether the new embosser should be a new, bold, innovative design or the old, traditional desk seal but with some of its flaws corrected.

Bob wanted his firm to bring back the prestige in the embosser. The suppliers believed that lawyers wanted to buy the lowest-cost items, regardless of utility or prestige. Bob felt that this assumption was inappropriate: "Lawyers buy BMW's and have large offices; prestige must be important to them." However, to try and develop a new, more functional, and prestigious embosser could be dangerous. Failure on an innovative design could damage their credibility with the employees, which the new management team was trying to establish. There were some significant benefits: they would learn about plastic molding and how to manage new product development. Further, if they succeeded, the nature of competition could shift from a commodity-like product dominated by small firms to a differentiated, product market dominated by one large firm, Sterling.

As a first step, Sterling applied for and received a $30,000 grant from the Ontario Provincial government to underwrite Mark Makers industrial design. To help in the design Bob conducted interviews with lawyers in which they were asked what they would like in a seal. From these discussions, and an analysis of other problems which he had identified with desk and pocket seals, Bob obtained an idea of the product features required in the new seal (Exhibit 3). Sterling then turned the design over to an industrial design consultant.

By the end of 1981, after extensive meetings with Bob and Cam, the consultant returned with the completed design, molds and tooling required to produce the Mark Maker. A meeting was subsequently held in which the product was shown to Sterling management. Bob assembled the Mark Maker, and to his horror discovered that "it would not even emboss toilet paper."

Employees were already questioning the young management team's initial decision to develop the Mark Maker. At the same time a poor economic climate was affecting Sterling profits. Bob felt that attention was better spent focusing on Sterling's current problems, rather than on developing the Mark Maker. For the next 30 days management discussed possible modifications for the Mark Maker—subsequently the project was shelved.

By the end of 1982, attention started to shift back to the Mark Maker. Management felt that perhaps they were too hasty in their abandonment of the project. Since they already had the basic design and the tooling for Mark Maker, they could develop the product internally. Cam Fink hired Anthony Gentelle (a Fanshawe College industrial design student). Willy Brandt, an independent mold maker was contracted to help in the mold design, and DuPont Canada Inc. was brought in to help select the appropriate materials for the Mark Maker. Cam and Anthony met after work for over a year, attempting to correct the flaws in the initial Mark Maker. By October 1984 the project which had taken five years and $400,000 to develop was finished. All that was left was to apply for a patent and then enter the new product on the market.

Sterling was proud of the Mark Maker. It weighed less than one pound and was trim. The weight and durability had arisen from using DuPont "Delrin" acetal resin and glass reinforced "Zytel" nylon resin. It had a collapsible handle in nylon which could lie flat at the push of a button, making the unit 13.5 centimeters long, 7 centimeters high and 5.4 centimeters wide (small enough to fit into a briefcase). Its impression quality was tested to 25,000 embossing operations and with the handle serving as a lever, the manual force needed to exert pressure on the die and achieve a clear impression was reduced. The parts were injection molded so that the assembly could be quickly snapped together. While Sterling would own the molds and tooling, sub-assembly production was contracted out to Willy Brandt's firm, Exacu Mould Inc. in London.

In December 1984, Sterling entered the product on the market. The sub-assembly was priced at $8.05 allowing Sterling a 50% profit. Competitor products were sold for $6.50 but Sterling felt that if they met this price, the ensuing 25% profit was insufficient to justify the investment. Further, it was felt that the Mark Maker's superior features should allow for a price premium.

Mark Maker orders were encouraging. In the first year (1985) 40,793 Mark Maker sub-assemblies were sold. Unfortunately, Sterling learned

EXHIBIT 3
Sterling Marking Products Inc.
Features of the Mark Maker and Competing Products (All prices are in $U.S. from Blumberg Catalog)

Advantages	Disadvantages
Mark Maker: $29.95	

• On-line ordering system
  • ease of ordering
  • accuracy
  • speed of delivery
• Plastic impression quality
• Modern appearance
• Ease of use
• Durability
• Easy to read index system
• Non-skid/non-mark pads
• Easy to use handle mechanism
	• Non-changeable dies
	• Non-reversible dies
	• Die size limitation
	• High sub-assembly cost
	• Will not fit in corporate registration binder

Pocket Seal: $19.00–$30.00	
• Compact—fits in corporate registration binder • Light weight • Inexpensive • Proven market acceptance (80% of the U.S. market) • Rotating die set • Various die sizes available	• Poor impression quality • Hard to use • Looks cheap • No indexing possible • Short throat
Traditional Desk Seal: $25.00–$35.00	
• Various die sizes available • Good-quality impression • Recognized as the classic • Special intricate logo capability	• Impression is inconsistent • Heavy • Akward to use • Non-interchangeable • Non-reversible • Frames crack • Not easily stored • Hard to transport • Sharp metal edges

Source: Advantages and disadvantages from Sterling records.

that many Mark Makers were gathering dust on the shelves of the legal stationers and name search houses. Sterling identified two primary reasons for the poor results: changing the image of the embosser from a commodity-like product to a differentiated one required more direct sales than dealers had used in the past; and, as Sterling only sold the sub-assemblies, they had no control over die production, and unfortunately, most of the dies were not manufactured to the rigorous specifications set out by Sterling. The inferior dies were damaging Mark Maker's credibility in the market.

As dealers were unwilling to change their die production processes, Sterling realized that they had to somehow convince their customers to exit the lucrative seal production aspect of their business and allow Sterling to sell them both the Mark Maker sub-assembly and the die.

At the same time that this problem was developing, Sterling's computer systems/services division was implementing a program which interfaced the computer with the typesetter. This initiative, started around 1981, was not related to Mark Maker. Rather, it was an attempt to increase the efficiency of stamp making operations by standardizing activities and automating production. Cam, Sam and Bob realized that with some modifications, the program could be used for on-line ordering and production of the Mark Maker. Customers would be supplied with terminals and modems (approximate cost $1,000) which would be used to dial into Sterling's computers in London using telephone lines, and enter the text for their embosser. The host computer could then communicate with the production computer engraving systems which would then output the text for the die. Getting the client to enter the text directly into the system virtually assured error free final text. In the past, some errors had occurred as a result of operators entering the client's text from the order form incorrectly. The on-line text outputting processes would also result in improved quality and lowered production costs. A by-product of the automated text processes could be that as part of the same run, text could be output which could be used to manufacture a brass identification plate. Previously, customers used a piece of paper placed in a plastic window on top of the Mark Maker for identification purposes.

Management felt that increased quality and service would help convince the majority of their customers who manufactured the dies to relinquish die production and make the customer captive to the Sterling system. However, Sterling realized that the major hurdle for getting dealers to relinquish production of the die was the price and speed of delivery. Die production, though only a small part of most of Sterling's customers' business, was nonetheless extremely profitable with margins of 50%. Sterling found a price which maintained most of their customers' old profit. In addition, Sterling endeavored to provide dealers with sales support (marketing literature and sales incentives). The new Mark Maker, which cost Sterling $6.64 in labor and materials ($5.01 for the sub-assembly and $1.63 for the die), $1.75 for shipping and $2.00 for selling and computer allocation, was retailed at $34.95 with wholesale volume discounts of up to 55%. Direct sales could be made to lawyers at the full list price of $34.95, however, this was not encouraged as it would put them in competition with their primary customers (legal stationers and name search houses). To ensure that dealers did not produce their own dies for the Mark Maker, Sterling limited sub-assembly sales to 20% of a customer's order. Sam Hassan felt that this was a necessary but high-risk decision as it precluded Sterling from selling only sub-assemblies as they had in the past.

In 1986, 22,948 assembled Mark Makers had been sold ($424,359) and five of Sterling's largest customers were using the on-line ordering system. In 1987, 41,287 units were sold ($712,332). 1988 sales were forecasted to be 58,705 ($1,004,415)—67% of all Canadian embosser sales. And with its gross margin of $8.63 per unit and a forecasted $6.63 per unit contribution after allocated expenses, Mark Maker was the number one product for Sterling. Mark Maker had become so entrenched in the Canadian market that it was becoming more difficult to find the old metal desk seal sub-assemblies in Canada. Few sales went to the traditional stationer houses (the bulk of the 1,000 dealer network developed by Warren Schram). 90% of sales went to a new type of customer: the legal stationer and law firms.

True to their initial objectives, Sterling had managed to change the competitive dynamic of the Canadian embosser market. Smaller regional die manufacturing firms were being pushed out of the business, the product was losing its commodity-like status, and metal sub-assembly manufacturing (which was dominated by American firms) was dying out. The only competitive reaction had been by Marque D'Or, a rival of Sterling's in Quebec. In response to the introduction of the Mark Maker, Marque D'Or had lowered their price for the old metal seal. However in the past month, Marque D'Or had begun to place more orders with Sterling as their largest customer had requested the Mark Maker. Sterling management felt that with this latest development in Quebec and recent inroads in Western Canada, it was conceivable that Mark Maker would have a 90% market share within the next few years.

The innovativeness of the Mark Maker was widely recognized. In 1986, the Mark Maker received two awards: a design Engineering Achievement Award at the Plast-ex show in Toronto; and the Federal Government's Award for Excellence in industrial design.

Despite this success, and lack of competitor reaction, management decided to continually innovate Mark Maker's product and service to discourage competitors. While the product and its design was patented for the next 15 years in Canada, U.S. and the European Economic Community, any modification, such as a different handle mechanism, would allow a competitor to legally duplicate the Mark Maker concept. However, the on-line ordering system could be difficult to replicate.

STERLING MARKING PRODUCTS INC.—1988

Sterling operated its production facility and head office in London, Ontario, with sales offices in London, Toronto and Windsor. Directly employing 141 people, Sterling offered a variety of products and services (Exhibit 4) which were divided into four operating segments: (1) Stationer items—rubber stamps, signs and markers; (2) Industrial marking systems—code dating; (3) Graphics—artwork, commercial printing and typesetting; and (4) data management and printing real estate books.

Many of these products were developed by Sterling. However, most of the industrial sales products such as high-speed label makers and line coding machines had been developed by other firms with Sterling holding the Canadian distribution rights.

This diversified product line arose from the visions of Bob Schram (42), Cam Fink (32) and Sam Hassan (42). Bob Schram's commitment to customer service and desire for innovation led him to seek ways to increase the utility of products. He often discussed new product ideas with customers, suppliers and employees. Sam's main interests were in computer technology. When he joined Sterling in 1978 he had a vision of a firm with unique computer capabilities. To help realize this, he formed a relationship with Ultimate Computers, a value-added resaler of computer hardware. Cam joined Sterling in 1981 after working for a firm which supplied automotive products to General Motors. Cam brought with him a focus on production efficiency. He saw Sterling making thousands of "somethings" efficiently, thereby reaping the benefits of economies of scale.

One of the by-products of these visions was the development of Sterling's computer skill advantage. The original purpose of the computer technology was to assist in processing and storing transactions. The custom nature of Sterling's marking products activity (e.g., stamps are personalized) created a tremendous paper burden in the organization as each sale generated its own order form. As Sterling grew, so did the number of individual orders. By 1980, it had reached the stage that the processing of transactions had become a costly and time consuming part of the production process. Sterling realized that without an efficient method of processing transactions, future growth would be limited, thus, they looked towards computers.

In 1980, Sterling bought their computer system. As they spent time developing administrative applications for the system and learned more about

EXHIBIT 4
Sterling Marking Products Inc.
Product Overview

Products	*Distribution*	*Strengths*
Marking Device & Stationery Products		
• Legal & Consumer Markmaker Embosser® • Rubber & Perma Stamps • Dating & Numbering Devices • Signage Systems • Desk Plates (Badges)	• Large consumer customer base • Direct mail programs • Major national accounts	• Loyal customers • Strong customer service • Unique on-line computer integrated manufacturing system
Industrial Products Group		
• Date Coding Application (Mechanical & Computer Spray Jet Machines) • Shipping Supplies • Steel Type & Punches • Mechanical Presses	• Large consumer customer base • Regional sales force based in Toronto, London, Windsor & Niagara Peninsula • Dealers	• Application responsive sales & manufacturing group • Worldwide product sourcing
Graphics Product Group		

• Commercial Artwork & Typesetting
• Printing Plates
  • Corrugated Cartons
  • Tape & Label
  • Flexo for Poly Bags
• Bingo Plates & Computer Programs
• Printing
  • MLS Directories
  • Direct Mail Brochures
	• National sales effort
	• Large consumer customer base
	• Major national accounts (Labatts)
		• Outstanding responsive sales & manufacturing capability to satisfy customer requests
		• Superior technical capability

Computer Systems/Services		
• Hardware selected from a wide range of vendors which support our Ultimate Operating System Specialty Software • Bingo Programs • MLS on-line system • Dealer on-line system incorporating our proprietary computer integrated manufacturing software driving typesetting and N/C computerized engraving output • Real Estate Broker systems for administrative function and on-line enquiries	• Companywide sales & marketing effort • Satisfied customers including 11 Real Estate Boards • On-line sales through our consumer customer & dealers	• Superior Operating System offering excellent migration flexibility of software • Creative, responsive sales & programming staff • Unique programs for typesetting output & data manipulation

the computer's capabilities, they started to realize that the computer could also be used for production and product development purposes. For example, the data manipulation routines used for order information coupled with the typesetting expertise garnished from the production of stamps could also be used to produce data base systems for real estate agents. All that was needed was some efficient searching routines. As well, the on-line production system would, if interfaced with the real estate data base, result in a cost effective method for printing the Real Estate books. In 1986 MLS database products and real estate book production was added to Sterling's business lines. In September 1988, this lucrative area had attracted contracts from 14 real estate boards in Canada. Other products and services arose from this technological edge such as on-line ordering and production. Another innovative extension was the production of Bingo cards. A program was developed which would design Bingo cards. The program determined the number of cards to produce based on hall sizes, output the printing plates and designed the bingo cards such that no card had a higher probability of hitting "BINGO" than any other.

The company also focused attention on improving production processes. Sterling's quality standards were fast being adopted by the larger firms in the industry. However, most firms could not keep up with Sterling's process innovations. Without Sterling's level of expertise, most were unable to progress much beyond the technology and processes of the 1960's.

Product and process innovation were viewed as a principal task for Sterling. The impetus behind this was a desire for growth. Sterling viewed themselves as a potential future IBM in terms of size. But the focus on growth, innovation and service had to be balanced with management's deep concern for employee well being. Schram felt that employees were the key to Sterling's success.

One of the primary objectives for the organization was to increase the satisfaction of employees and managers. Consideration of these and other intangible benefits was so important that Sam Hassan's job was not to merely look at return on investment but to rationalize investment on the basis of its long term benefit to the company. Sterling's investment decision criteria focused on the investment's effect in terms of the learning benefits of the investment, the impact of investment failure on both the employees' respect for management and overall operations and what the employees would think of management for undertaking the investment. Financial considerations (e.g., ROI), while being important, were usually of secondary status.

The focus on innovation, service and employee well being led to an adaptable, flexible organization, the result of which was dramatic increases in sales and profits. Between 1983 and 1987, sales increased 73% going from $4.6 million to $8 million, with 1988 sales estimated to be $10 million (Exhibit 5).

MANAGING GROWTH

Management's primary concern was the management of growth. They felt that what had "made" Sterling was its identity—a focus on innovation and a 40-year-old service ethic. Maintaining the sense of commitment and an environment where "it was fun to come up with something that benefits the customer" would be difficult. In recruiting they sought individuals like themselves. They looked for people who could "share the vision." Salaries were low but Sterling offered would-be employees opportunities for growth. An apprenticeship period was served by most new management employees (with the exception of marketing) where the individual was expected to develop informal leadership in the organization. Titles were meaningless and new hires were expected to work their way slowly into management, gaining respect from other employees and distinguishing themselves as leaders. New hires who were not able to earn the respect of employees would not last long. Management personnel were seldom given a clear role, direction, or authority.

EXHIBIT 5
Sterling Marking Products Inc.
Selected Financial and Corporate Information

	1983	*1984*	*1985*	*1986*	*1987*	*1988**
Mark Maker Sales			(subs)	(complete units)		
Units			40,793	22,948	41,287	58,705
$000's			343	424	712	1,004
Gross margin ($000's)					428	615
Contribution ($000's)					224	402
Employees						
Full time	106	103	120	122	130	
Part time		9	11	6	11	
Sales ($000's)	4,598	5,369	6,536	7,285	7,971	
Debt/equity	2.13	1.57	1.24	1.16	1.06	

*Estimate.

ORGANIZATIONAL STRUCTURE

While Sterling had explored the possibility of many different structures, they maintained the simple structure of the past, with most major decisions being made by Bob Schram after receiving input from various employees. Recently, the three senior managers had begun a process of adding more management employees, thereby removing themselves strictly from day-to-day operations and instead allowing them to focus on longer range strategic issues. Despite this, the three senior managers continued to work six to seven days a week.

The structure was undergoing other transformations. Attempts were being made to divisionalize Sterling's product groups. For example, Jan d'Ailly was put in charge of marketing for all marking devices. However, as one employee stated: "We see ourselves in the longer run going towards a divisional structure, but given the current dynamic of Sterling and its success, it is hard to get any sort of structure, functional or divisional."

Sterling's international activities were coordinated by the international marketing department, and the international marketing committee. The international marketing committee consisted of Jan, Sam, Cam, Bob, Rick Verette (Operations Manager), Vince Lebano (a representative of the Ontario Provincial government), and was chaired by Mel Dear, an ex-3M sales executive who was now a private consultant. The committee met every two to four weeks to discuss all aspects of international operations. The committee used a broad definition of international, which included any sales outside of Ontario.

Jan d'Ailly was hired as the one-man international marketing department in 1986, shortly after completing his MBA at the University of Western Ontario. Jan had worked in France, Taiwan, Australia, and South Africa and spoke English, Dutch, French and Mandarin. Consistent with Sterling's focus on customer service, Jan was hired more to provide customer support than to make sales. In fact, Jan did not have previous sales experience prior to joining Sterling. It was Jan's job to identify foreign markets for Sterling's products and to help out foreign customers. Since joining Sterling, Jan's time had been devoted to the Mark Maker. He had personally conducted market research trips to the United States and United Kingdom and was also involved in selecting Blumberg to introduce the Mark Maker into the United States.

THE UNITED KINGDOM TRIPS

Three market research trips had been made to the United Kingdom. These trips yielded information on the U.K. embosser market as well as information on labour availability, and information pertinent to Sterling's other products. Exhibit 6 presents a portion of Sterling's market study. The last trip was in November 1988. Jan together with Cam, Warren Schram and a consultant went to the United Kingdom for one week. The purpose of this trip was to confirm Sterling's perceptions of the U.K. market, and to investigate alternative modes for competing in the United Kingdom. The information in this section is based on the results of these research trips.

The United Kingdom was the only European country where seals were a legal requirement for corporations. Thus, all of the 100,000–120,000 incorporations, 50,000 corporate name changes and 12,000 new lawyers per year required embossers. This provided a fertile ground for embosser sales. The U.K. Government had recently indicated that an embossed seal might not be legally required in the future. Similar to Canada, sales were dominated by the traditional desk seal (approximately 50% of all sales). The major buyers of seals were lawyers and accountants who purchased some 70% of all seals, primarily for their incorporation clients.

Unlike Canada, the major embosser manufacturers were fully integrated. The largest manufacturers of both dies and embosser sub-assemblies were Jordan and Bolson. Much of Jordan's sales were to their own name search houses. In recent years, some of these were expressing displeasure at this arrangement as they wanted the flexibility to select embossers. The largest market shares of the seal production market were held by Bolson's (50%) and Jordan and Sons (28%).

85% of legal seals were handled through company formation agents. Similar to the service firms in Canada, formation agents were hired by lawyers to assist in incorporations. These agents also provided an embosser as part of their service; thus, if Sterling was to seriously compete in the U.K. market they would have to either usurp Jordan's production, or supply Bolson's customers. The major agents were Jordan and Sons (26% share of seal sales), Stanley Davis (13%), and London Law (10%).

The relationship between the seal producers and formation agents was one of great loyalty. Jordan and Sons purchased their seals from Jordan's, while Stanley Davis purchased from Bolson's.

Pocket seals were priced at £5.50 and desk seals at £7.50 (prices in Pounds Sterling—1 pound sterling = \$2.10 Canadian; \$1 U.S. = \$1.22 Canadian). Similar to Canada, the quality of the seals was poor.

THE CURRENT SITUATION

Jan looked again at his notes on the United Kingdom. Several possibilities existed. They could continue exporting sub-assemblies to Jordan. In 1984/85 Sterling had sold 5,000 Mark Maker sub-assemblies to Jordan. They were originally to be a distributor for Mark Maker, however, due to problems in die manufacturing and weak sales efforts, not only were sales low, but there was some concern that the Mark Maker was developing a bad reputation. Jordan had recently improved the quality, developed an effective on-line production system and was manufacturing high-quality dies. This, coupled with placing the Mark Maker prominently in their brochure, resulted in 3,000 Mark Makers being sold in the past year. Jordan was interested in continuing their relationship with Sterling, but they wanted to produce the dies themselves.

Perhaps, thought Jan, Sterling could export the finished product. Duty was only 4.6%, the value-added tax (a tax levied at each stage of production) was 15%, and overnight courier costs were \$7.50 per Mark Maker (the minimum courier charge was \$60). Meeting U.K. demands would be no problem. Sterling could produce 168,000 Mark Makers with seals per year out of its London, Ontario, plant, 250,000 if they added a third shift.

EXHIBIT 7

Sterling Marking Products Inc.

Market Size		*Rubber Stamp Market*	
Company registrations	100,000 } Range to 170,000	MacFarlane—$22,000,000	35%–50%
Name changes	50,000 }	Mark C. Brown	?10%
Vehicle testing stations	10,000 best guess	William Jones Clifton	?5%–10%
Personnel embossers	12,000 Jones Clifton	40–60 smaller firms	
Total market	172,000 seals/year Work with 680 per day	Said no one is making any money	

Structure of the Legal Seal Market

Seal Production			*Name Search Houses*			*End Users*		
Jordan's	48000	28%	Jordan's (A group of small houses)	45000	26%	Lawyers	60000	35%
Bolsom's	84000	49%	Stanley Davis	22500	13%	Accountants	60000	35%
			London Law	17200	10%			
Western			Smaller Houses	65300	38%			
Pro Marketing	21000	12%	(All less than Stanley Davis)			Private legal	30000	17%
City Seals			Rubber Stamp Companies					
	153000	89%		150000	87%	Vehicle testing stations	10000	6%
Jones Clifton	18000	10%	Retailers, Wholesalers			Consumers	12000	7%
			Direct Mail	22000	12%			
			Rubber Stamp Man.					
			MBF Clansman	?				
Totals	172000	100%		172000	100%		172000	100%

- Price competitive.
- Generally very low-quality seals.
- Seals delivered to name search houses or mailed direct to end users.

- As a whole, a very fragmented market.
- Heavy price competition: "Cheaper is Better."
- Jordan's seen as a leader in the industry, higher priced, and maintains a whole database and reporting business.
- Stanley Davis determined to catch Jordan's.

Source: Company report on the U.K. market.

Alternatively, Sterling could use licensing. MBF McFarlane, a UK-based rubber stamp manufacturer, had expressed an interest in this possibility. Maybe, thought Jan, all MBF wants is Sterling's computer technology and to keep Sterling from marketing other products there. In fact, MBF had visited Sterling in the spring of 1988 and in their recent catalogue claimed to have computer ordering capability.

Perhaps, Sterling could purchase one of the seal producers or construct their own branch. Labour availability was not a problem. Martyn Wright, a director of production with Jordan, had expressed a strong interest in leaving Jordan and heading up a Sterling operation in the United Kingdom. Martyn felt that Sterling could purchase Jordan's seal operations and tie the computer typesetting business into Jordan's production facility. Alternatively, Sterling could build their own branch. A 60,000 Mark Maker per year plant required two employees and $50,000 in equipment. This included the on-line ordering and production systems, and the software. Administrative support, rent and the employee salaries were estimated at $5,000 per month.

Jan tried to elicit management opinion on the various entry mode options. They saw Mark Maker as a product which could open foreign market doors for Sterling, thereby paving the way for the introduction of Sterling's other products. Unfortunately, senior management were not in total agreement on the appropriate entry modes required to attain these objectives. One of the managers believed that greater profits could be attained by licensing the product to a U.K. manufacturer. He felt that Sterling should be focusing its attention at developing new products and a stronger sales organization, not spreading resources thinner by getting involved in an overseas branch. Another senior manager felt that providing there was a reasonable chance of success in the United Kingdom, it would be in Sterling's best interest to have a branch there. This manager envisioned creating five branch plants with sales offices each year over the next five years. Each branch would control $1 million in yearly sales. Branch plants in the United States and United Kingdom were essential for the realization of this plan. He also felt that Sterling had developed a culture of innovation and risk taking. Accepting a licensing agreement would send the wrong message to employees.

Management was unsure of Sterling's ability to manage a foreign branch. They had experienced difficulties in managing the Windsor and Toronto offices and thought a branch overseas would pose even greater difficulties. They were considering putting a production and sales branch in Montreal within the next few years as a test of Sterling's ability to manage a foreign operation.

Another more recent experience was Sterling's recent foray into the United States. On May 1, 1988, Julius Blumberg Inc. (a U.S. legal stationer) was made Sterling's exclusive sales agent for the United States for a seven-month period, after which Sterling would have the option of appointing other agents. Under this arrangement, Blumberg would not produce the seal; rather, they would send their customers' orders to Sterling who would produce the seal and then ship both the seal and sub-assembly to the appropriate Blumberg office. It was felt that the market presence of Blumberg and a guarantee of featuring the Mark Maker in their catalogue would result in substantial U.S. sales. Jan looked back over the past five months. Overall sales had been disappointing (under 100 units per week). However, Sterling had learned much about the U.S. market from this experience. Jan felt that the low sales could have resulted from using the traditional passive approach to selling embossers. A catalogue could not impress upon customers the advantages of the Mark Maker over other embossers. Jan suspected that some direct promotion was required. During the past year, he had travelled to Blumberg offices in Albany, New York, and Texas. During these visits, he had tried to convince the salespeople to use a more direct sales approach. As an incentive, he offered them one dollar for each Mark Maker sold. The results of these visits were impressive. For example, in Albany, prior to Jan's visit, Mark Maker sales averaged 5 per week; shortly after his visit, sales increased to 70 per week. Blumberg felt that the direct approach was inappropriate and instructed their salesforce to tone down the sales approach, subsequently, sales dropped to their old levels.

The same problem had occurred in Canada. However, when the legal stationers started using more aggressive sales techniques and Sterling started dropping into legal offices to show them the Mark Maker, sales increased dramatically.

Jan looked over the U.K. market report again: how to decide? and how fast to move? More fundamentally, should they do anything with respect to the United Kingdom without first developing a broad approach to international markets?

CASE 19 | *Nike, Inc.*

During the fall of 1982, the Nike Company was recognized generally as one of the phenomenal success stories of the recent decade. From its small base in 1972, by 1981 the firm had blossomed into a $450,000,000 giant and expected sales to reach $650,000,000 in 1982. It had passed Adidas in the United States and held an estimated 30 percent of the American market. Most Nike executives were confident that a $1 billion sales year was imminent. Although the company owed much of its success to a vibrant management team, it was also very much the brainchild of a remarkable entrepreneur, Phil Knight, who still served as president, CEO, and major stockholder.

The Company's incredible growth rate was not without its problems. As Phil Knight reflected:

> There has been a severe overload on marketing compounded by our need to organize for new opportunities as our old products and markets mature. We are geared to handle existing lines where we have 30% or 40% of the market. But how about new areas which must be developed, like leisure products, international, the children's line, clothing and cleated shoes? I question whether our existing approaches can successfully pioneer these many opportunity areas, particularly given the increase in competition and changes in consumer habits.

THE INDUSTRY

Nike competed in two industries: sports and athletic shoes; and also sportswear. Each of these categories was estimated to exceed $10 billion in 1982 sales. Starting from its running heritage, Nike had branched out rapidly into an assortment of other sports (tennis, soccer, basketball, etc.) as well as leisure ("look-like") markets. Running, still the company's wellhead, was essentially an American phenomenon, though it had been copied in varying degrees elsewhere. By 1980, however, the running boom showed signs of leveling off. In the words of Phil Knight: "We see only a couple more years of strong growth in running

---

This case was written by Professor Robert T. Davis. Reprinted with permission of Stanford University Graduate School of Business.

shoes in the United States, though we are sure fitness is here to stay."

Because of the industry's evolution, there was a wide range of competitors and strategies. In running, for example, there were Adidas (the largest firm in total worldwide sales), Puma, Converse Rubber, Pony International, Asics (Tiger brand), New Balance, and Brooks (acquired by Wolverine in 1982), to mention the most obvious. Reliable data about these competitors was sketchy because many were either privately owned or divisions of larger companies. Moreover, market share estimates were based primarily on one commercial service that regularly surveyed 200 specialty retailers for competitive comparisons. Omitted from their sample were discounters, mass merchandisers, and most large department stores.

The market segments were diverse. In addition to the serious runners, the interested student might distinguish the faddist, the casual exerciser, the trend follower, the price buyer, the leisure-time devotee, the amateur sportsman, the high-fashion, status-conscious user, and any other number of variants. In recent months some observers felt that color coordination (between shoes and clothing) was a coming consumer preference. Indeed, one competitor (New Balance) had succeeded in drawing favorable comments about its grey, light brown, burgundy, and navy colors early in 1982. This same firm had recently increased its margins to the trade (to 55% compared to Nike's 48%–50%), upped its innovation rate, and put heavy emphasis on the specialty retailers. These actions appeared to have increased that firm's penetration of the innovator segment.

The clothing business was even more fragmented, consisting of thousands of designers, cutters, finishers, stylists, knitters, weavers, and so forth. Raw materials ranged from cotton and wool to a great variety of synthetics and blends. In the relevant world of Nike, the key actors were such competitors as Levi Strauss, Head, Adidas, and hundreds of prestige designers (e.g., Pierre Cardin, Bill Blass). There were, in addition, many retailer brands such as Brooks Brothers, Saks and I. Magnin.

During the '60s and '70s, Levi Strauss grew spectacularly on the basis of its "Western-cowboy" look and, thanks partly to the well-publicized acceptance by James Dean and Marlon Brando, jeans became the uniform for every self-respecting teenager or young adult. By 1980, however, there was some speculation that "the look" was about to shift to a new life-style—the fit, the jock, the athlete-winner. If this shift materialized, the implications were great for the trade.

It was also reasonably obvious that traditional manufacturer labels in fashion merchandise were under siege by the aforementioned designer labels. Large numbers of department stores and mass merchandisers were trying to gain distinction handling such "prestige" labels and the use of the "boutique look" within their stores. It almost seemed that there were two fundamental strategies at work—the price-oriented mass market appeal and the high-income status appeal. The distinction between these two was somewhat clouded by the adoption of prestige labels by the more aggressive mass merchandisers. Even Sears, Roebuck had relaxed its policy of carrying only house labels.

Adidas, Head, and Nike represented firms that had expanded into clothing from "hardware lines" (that is, shoes), whereas Levi Strauss experimented, not too successfully, with shoes. All of these firms, of course, vied for the same basic distribution system. At the retail level, the outlets could be classified as mass merchandisers (Sears), discounters (Marshalls and Mervyn's), department and specialty stores (R.H. Macy and I. Magnin), and a wide variety of small independents (sporting goods, shoe stores, running stores). These outlets could be reached through company salesmen, manufacturers' representatives, distributors, or even direct mail. Adidas, for example, covered the United States with four independent distributors; Levi Strauss used company salesmen; Nike employed manufacturers' representatives; and Sears, Roebuck sold direct through mail order and/or retail stores.

Nike's niche in the industry was substantial. The firm appealed to the market on the basis of quality, technical innovation, and high performance, all of which attracted the serious runner. This acceptance by the experts was the lever to open up the mass markets. The product diffused into the channels starting with the high-performance specialists and spread into the mass outlets on the basis of this "expert" endorsement. Nike had also been aggressive in product line extensions (such as leisure shoes and clothing). Whether or not to introduce a second label was a topic being discussed by senior management.

NIKE ORGANIZATION

One of the distinguishing characteristics of the company was its informal organization. From its beginning, Nike had been run as a small operation by a close-knit group of top managers. Most of them were sports enthusiasts and athletes and thus understood and appreciated the Nike line. A surprisingly large percentage also had legal or accounting backgrounds. But, as Phil Knight explained, "We mostly want people who are company experts, not functional experts." Problem solving, not specific technical knowledge, was the valued skill.

The organization chart, which is reproduced below, is therefore deceptive. It portrays the formal pieces of the organization, but not the way it works:

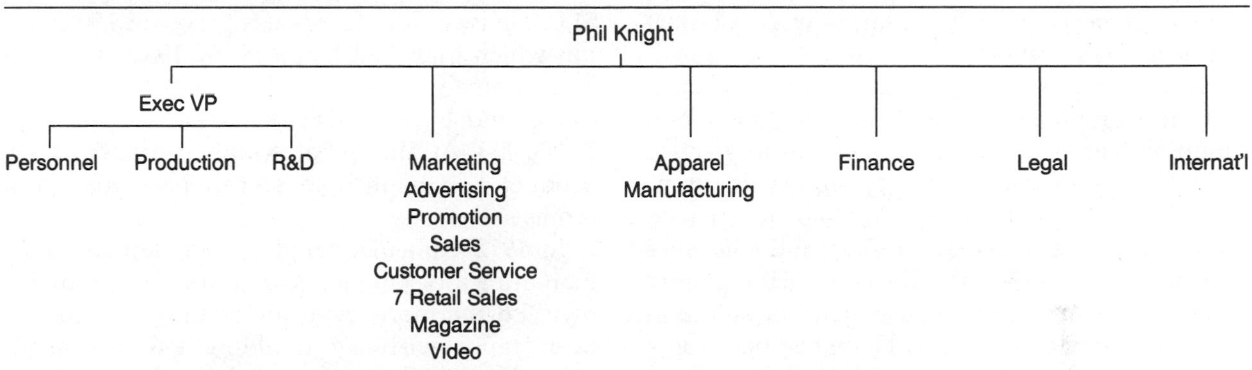

Because apparel was a relatively new product line, it was still associated with footwear marketing (the same sales reps, for example, were involved), though sourcing and product development were separately handled.

Management assignments across functions were normal. One senior manager had moved from legal to R&D, to lobbying, to marketing, and there were other equally dramatic assignment changes. Territorial imperatives were held to a minimum and such words as budgeting, planning, and control were dirty ones—even though the company did have working systems. The emphasis was upon informality, willingness to change, experimentation, and mutual decision making. The Friday Club was the chief management tool of the company. This group of 11 top managers[1] was called together regularly, as Phil Knight laughingly described, "to shout at each other." The meetings were open and informal and everyone contributed with enthusiasm his ideas

[1]These included in 1982: Chairman, Executive Vice President, Vice Presidents of Apparel, Finance, Production, Chief Counsel, Manager MIS, Vice President International, Director of Marketing, Theasurer, and Manager Far East Operation.

and solutions. Phil Knight played the catalyst role in eliciting ideas and in meshing the various personalities. There were no functional restrictions. The informality of these sessions was evident on one occasion when a visitor commented that Nike management "was a shambles." The next day at a follow-up meeting, each executive wore a T-shirt that said, "It's a shambles."

Even though the Friday Club was a key decision-making group, it wasn't as omnipotent as it might appear. In the first place, it was in practice a floating group with varying degrees of autonomy. There were five so-called old-timers who were really "the chairman's office" and who were considered the ultimate decision-making unit. The Friday Club itself could expand or shrink in size depending on the issue. There had been some meetings, to illustrate, at which over 30 managers participated. Perhaps more important was the fact that reporting to these senior executives was "conventional" organizational hierarchy. Marketing, to select one example, included research and advertising components while manufacturing had plant and quality assurance managers. The unique aspects of the Nike organization were the degree of mobility, the generalist perspective of the senior group, and the participative decision-making style.

HISTORY

Knight's enthusiasm for sports started early, and by his senior year in high school he was already an accomplished runner who had caught the eye of Bill Bowerman, the track and field coach at the University of Oregon. Knight attended that school and then received his MBA from Stanford in 1962. For one of his term papers, the budding entrepreneur developed an idea for a new business. He knew that running shoes were dominated by two German firms, Adidas and Puma, and he wondered why the Japanese couldn't do in shoes what they had already done in TV and cameras. After graduation from Stanford, Knight joined a CPA firm in Portland, Oregon, but as a sideline decided to import and sell Japanese running shoes. He traveled to Japan and contracted with Onitsuka to supply him with their Tiger line, as their exclusive agent for the 13 western states. He also persuaded his former track coach to join in the venture. Between them they invested $1,000 in inventory for shoes that cost $3.50 a pair but which they sold for $9.95. By 1966 the fledgling company had branched out to the East Coast, and by 1971 sales had reached just over $1,000,000. At this point Knight broadened his product line to include soccer, basketball, and tennis shoes.

In 1972 Onitsuka sought more control of its marketing and Knight decided to strike out on his own. Furthermore, even though his growth had been rapid—virtually doubling every year—it was still a small company and Knight was hard-pressed to obtain adequate financing. For each purchase, he had to put up a letter of credit that would tie up his credit for approximately 90 days. As luck would have it, he read a *Fortune* magazine article suggesting that Japanese trading companies could, among other things, extend credit on flexible terms, though at a slight premium. A few inquiries unearthed Nissho-Iwai, the sixth-largest trading company in Japan, and Knight and Nissho-Iwai soon agreed to a deal. Through Nissho-Iwai, Knight also acquired some manufacturing contacts who agreed to produce shoes to Nike's specifications.

The Nissho-Iwai deal gave Nike an important financial and business ally that made subsequent rapid growth possible. By putting up the necessary letters of credit every month, Nissho-Iwai freed Nike to concentrate on operating matters. In fact, the trading company went well beyond the strict limits of the agreement and gave Nike much needed flexibility. Nissho-Iwai served, furthermore, as the financial and administrative intermediary between Nike and the contract manufacturers. During these same early days, Phil established a strong Accounts Receivable group, which managed to keep receivables in line despite the explosive growth in sales.

The development of these contract manufacturers was an early preoccupation of top management. A traditional problem in the leisure shoe industry had been the lack of dependable supply and delivery, particularly for the retailers. Knight saw this as an opportunity. He first tied up a considerable percentage of the available shoe capacity in Japan and later in Taiwan and Korea. These vendors were delighted to supply such a fast-growing and profitable customer. By 1982 the company's production was centered in 28 plants, and over 80% of this production was in Taiwan and Korea. There were three plants in the United States. Knight also introduced a futures program for retailers, whereby the company guaranteed the price and delivery terms for any retailer who ordered six months in advance. The system worked as follows:

Illustrative Data	*Event*	*Elapsed Time*
March 30	Retailer places order with Nike (order is noncancelable by the retailer & guaranteed by Nike)	0
April 15	Nike places order with NIAC (Nisso-Iwai American Corp.)	15 days
April 25	NIAC orders from the plant	25 days
July 30	Plant completes manufacturing and ships order	120 days
September 1	Shoes come to warehouse in Seattle, Boston, or Memphis	150 days
September 15	Shoes shipped to retailer	165 days

Since 65% of the orders followed this sequence, the futures program in effect served as a planning device by giving Nike reasonably accurate sales forecasts and shipment schedules. By 1982 monthly shipments were averaging 4.5 million pair. The other 35% of the orders were placed by the dealers on a "when needed" basis. Delivery, in this second case, was not guaranteed.

Production costs were low and flexible but quality was high because all output was made to Nike specifications and the firm maintained its own quality control staff at each plant. In fact, the first expatriate employee was assigned to Taiwan in 1976. The table below summarizes the cost buildup from a hypothetical $1 manufacturing base:

Cost Buildup	
Cost to manufacturer (for a Korean plant)	$1.00
Price from Nissho-Iwai Corp. (Japan)	1.04
Price from Nissho-Iwai, U.S. (this is Nike cost)	1.08 + interest (near prime)
Price to the retail store	1.60
Price to the consumer	2.80–3.00

As one of the early employees of the firm said: "Product control is our forte." Indeed, the plants had considerable product flexibility and could easily handle volume swings of 25%–35%. The three U.S. plants were useful as a backup to the overseas contractors.

INNOVATION

Another early focus of Nike management was product innovation. Bowerman, for example, was a particularly creative individual who contributed the famous "waffle sole" (though at the expense of his wife's waffle iron). In fact, when Nike originally split from the Onitsuka group, the founders took with them two important product innovations that they had developed on their own time. Management's interest in innovation was so high that in 1974, while still small, the firm bought a factory in Exeter, New Hampshire, and dedicated it to R&D. This group subsequently developed a number of major innovations, including the airsole, the nylon top, and the full-cushioned mid-sole.

Innovation, in practice, was a constant give-and-take between marketing, production, and Exeter. For example, as marketing identified new product needs, it asked Exeter to conduct extensive research and testing in design and biomechanics.

Phil Knight was an important innovator in an even broader sense—not only in product but also in several aspects of the operations. He was described by one colleague as "farsighted and alert to new opportunities." To be specific, Knight foresaw the desirability of expanding production out of Japan, the opportunity in a guaranteed retailer delivery system, the potential of manufacturing in China, and the advantages of working with a trading company instead of a bank. Moreover, he anticipated a number of market changes and moved his company into other sports shoes (basketball, court, cleated, etc.), a children's line, non-athletic leisure and work shoes, and clothing. The firm's early concentration on running represented superb timing (either by luck or brilliant deduction) and positioned Nike in the consumer's mind as "a running company."

MARKETING

The marketing program was developed over several years. To start, the company hired sales representatives who, of necessity, were new, enthusiastic, hardworking shoe amateurs. They were supervised by East Coast and West Coast field managers. The number of representatives was gradually increased and their territories decreased, until in 1982 there were 28 representative organizations employing 180 salespeople. Some carried other lines; some did not. But all had thrived under Nike and depended upon the firm for their well-being. Sales were so large that representative commissions averaged 2½% instead of the more traditional 6%.

The representatives sold to 8,000 retailers who operated 13,000 outlets. Almost 2,500 of these outlets were classified as mass merchandisers, 2,500 specialty (i.e., running) stores, 1,500 sporting goods, and the rest shoe stores and miscellaneous. The premier mass merchandiser for Nike was J.C. Penney, which was added in 1977 before Nike was particularly well-known. (Adidas elected to go through J.C. Penney in 1981.) Quite obviously, the distribution system was effective and covered a wide range of clientele—from low-end to high-end specialty. Furthermore, the Nike line, priced between $19.95 and $70, was broad enough to accommodate each segment. These relatively few dealers who sold primarily the top of the line to the serious, innovative runners were handled through a "Torch program" and received special attention. For all dealers, Nike offered a number of special inducements: a generous 46% margin, guaranteed prices and delivery, and a coordinated program of promotions, advertising, training, and sponsorships. As between footwear and apparel, the retail stores employed by Nike split out as follows: Shoes only 25%; Apparel only 25%; Both 50%.

Nike also owned and operated seven retail stores. Their volume of $4 million was minor, but they were regarded as valuable training centers. There were no expansion plans.

The distribution story was different overseas where Nike was just beginning to expand. In Europe the jogging boom had not yet taken off, though Nike expected that it would. Adidas and Puma dominated the European distribution system and concentrated on the huge soccer market. These German competitors would not be easy to replace, particularly since their loss of market in the United States. As one industry executive stated: "Adidas and Puma will let the other American companies do whatever they want in Europe because they're not much of a threat. But after what Nike did to them in the U.S., they simply will not let themselves be embarrassed in their own backyards." It would not be easy for Nike to gain dealers whose livelihood depended on Adidas and Puma.

Japan was an easier target. Not only did the Japanese perceive American products as high quality, but also Nike had had years of contact with that market. England was another attractive market. Nike acquired its distributorships and also opened a manufacturing plant there to permit inexpensive access to the European markets.

Nike's promotion and advertising strategy was another ingredient of its success. The company, to start, employed a pull, not a push, approach built around its distinctive "swoosh" trademark. Its recent $18 million budget was spent as follows:

25% Product advertising in such vertical publications as *Running* and *The Runner*—stressing general concepts like cushioning and shoe weight.

Point-of-sale devices such as a retailer poster program, the use of technical tags and brochures, and dealer clinics.

25% Dealer co-op advertising where Nike would match the dealers' advertising outlays up to a specified limit.

50% Promotions that included free goods and/or cash payment to about 2,500 athletes as well as the sponsorship of selected athletic events (including a women's pro-tennis circuit).

The critical part of Nike's selling approach was the endorsement by these athletic "heroes." From the firm's first endorsers—Steve Prefontaine and Geoff Petrie—the list grew to include 40% of the players in the National Basketball Association, a large percentage of the top runners, and such individual stars as John McEnroe, Sebastian Coe and Dan Fouts. As one of the Nike managers said: "These athletes are our promotional team."

The effectiveness of Nike's strategies was reflected in their financial statements. (See Exhibits 1 and 2.)

CURRENT CONCERNS

Obviously, Nike had been a tremendous success. Nonetheless, size created its own problems and caused Phil Knight to review, more specifically, some of the important marketing issues.

The channels, as a case in point, represented one such area of concern. To quote from a company document:

> Given the present management's obsession with increased "numbers," it is not surprising that we are witnessing an increased emphasis on self-service in branded footwear retail sales. You need only look as far as the local G.I. Joe's, J.C.Penney, Meir & Frank, or Athletic Shoe Factory Outlet to see why the technical portion of our line is so badly misunderstood. In self-service retail outlets, you are hard pressed to find any sales help, let alone well-informed assistance from users of athletic footwear. Perhaps it is a function of our stagnant economy, but every retailer is talking about how to reduce his "selling costs" by employing mass merchant mentality, i.e., read *Proportionally Fewer Customer Service-Oriented Retail Outlets* to intelligently sell our technical line.
>
> With a significantly smaller and diminishing percentage of our products being sold in specialty or Torch accounts, it is no wonder that our reputation is being redefined in the consumer's mind with descriptive phrases such as, "Low-End, Non-Technical, Pricepoint and Promotional." The bulk of our sales volume is now attributable to dealers who are providing less and less point-of-purchase information about how our shoes perform to customers as retailers strive for more volume and fine tune their selling efficiency. The result of this shift in selling technique and brand identity puts increased pressure on Nike to pre-sell our products while making the shoes easily visible and recognizable as high-quality, innovative products.
>
> In the midst of the recent frenzied growth of mass consumption of branded athletic footwear, there has developed a reaction among both the more technically aware and prestige-seeking, affluent consumers to distinguish themselves from the pack. With increased discretionary buying power, these consumers are demanding high-tech products and are willing to "pay a little more to get just what I

EXHIBIT 1
Nike, Inc.

Profit and Loss Summaries

	1981	*1980*	*1979*
Revenues	457,742	269,775	149,830
Cost of sales	328,133	196,683	103,466
Selling and administrative	60,953	39,810	22,815
Interest	17,859	9,144	4,569
Other	92	107	(443)
Income before taxes	50,705	24,031	19,423
Taxes	24,750	11,526	9,700
Net income	25,955	12,505	9,723
Earnings per share	1.52	.77	.58

Breakdown of Sales

	1981	*1980*	*1979*
Domestic footwear	398,852	245,100	143,400
Domestic apparel	33,108	8,100	2,200
Foreign sales	25,782	16,575	4,230
Total	457,742	269,775	149,830

wanted." This is the segment of the market we have ignored and, as a result, have been losing to New Balance, Tiger, and Saucony. If Nike is going to continue to have mass volume sales and retain a strong share of the high-end sales, it is obvious we need to segment the product line and distinguish the product in this market so that it appeals to the high-tech, affluent consumers.

The High-Tech segment of the branded market is becoming substantially more crowded with new products and new brands. This is particularly true of running flats. Avia, for example, is gearing its entire entrance into the technical branded segments of the athletic footwear market with advertising and packaging that connotes high technology and new design innovations. Advanced technologies (materials, construction techniques) are creating a more confusing product environment for consumers to make buying decisions in. The expanded array of products and advertised product features, each (Puma, New Balance, Tiger) claiming to perform breakthroughs in sports research, is making our brand prey to slick (well-segmented) marketing strategies.

Of particular note was the recent incursion by some mass merchandisers into the high end of the shoe market. Mervyn's, to be specific, in early 1982 sold 300 pairs of Nike's newest technical product at very low prices. Nike received the income, to be sure, but was unable to capitalize in the consumer's mind on the technical advantage of the new product. To the consumer, it was only a price deal.

Another matter of worry had to do with individual responsibilities as opposed to company-wide responsibilities. Size had increased the breadth and depth of the various lines. For example, there were over 200 shoe types alone. But, as no one was responsible for any one line, this led to a lack of focus and attention to details in several lines. Moreover, as implied earlier,

EXHIBIT 2
Nike, Inc.

Balance Sheet

	May 31, 1981	*May 31, 1980*
Cash	1,792	1,827
Accounts receivable	87,236	63,861
Inventories	120,229	55,941
Deferred taxes	1,300	135
Prepaid expenses	2,487	2,151
Current assets	213,044	123,915
Property, plant, equipment	23,845	14,193
Accumulated depreciation	(7,673)	(4,027)
Other assets	1,073	534
Total assets	230,289	134,615
Liabilities		
Current portion of debt	6,620	3,867
Notes payable	61,190	36,500
Accounts payable	42,492	36,932
Accrued liabilities	15,401	10,299
Income taxes payable	12,654	6,693
Current liabilities	138,357	94,291
Long term debt	8,611	11,268
Common stock	28,600*	71
Retained earnings	54,721	28,985
Total liabilities	230,289	134,615

*In 1981 Nike went public with the sale of 1,360,000 shares of common stock, with Knight retaining 51% of the outstanding shares.

there were few formal lines of communication and very little hierarchy between managers and locations. And finally, in Phil's opinion, the company was relying on too few key people who were close friends and saw the company as fun more than as a business.

It was within this special environment that Phil was considering his possible moves. It was not easy to trade off more control and formality against the current organizational culture. And yet he was very much aware that the market's and his own company's evolution required a new look at how to organize for growth.

Although he had thought about the implications and was well aware that there were other choices, Knight thought he might ask the Friday Club to consider the implications of eight alternatives:

1. Do Nothing

Knight was sensitive to the real possibility that any kind of significant move might "spoil" the existing ambiance. After all, the organization had worked and had evolved a number of valuable attributes—informality, dynamism, and flexibility. Moreover, there was a minimum of territorial imperative within Nike: managers were not expected to build walls around their piece of the operation. On the contrary, open teamwork was expected. Over time, it was not surprising that the culture of the firm was well understood. The nuances of day by day interaction were as well developed as small talk between husband and wife.

Knight also considered it valuable that the footwear and apparel operations had been closely associated. Even though production for each was individually supervised, the marketing and sales were interdependent. The sales reps, to be specific, carried both lines.

It should be recognized, finally, that the organization with its functional orientation (namely marketing and manufacturing) focused upon these broad skills rather than separate products and markets. Presumably the functions would receive greater focus and hence deliver a higher level of generic expertise.

2. Divisionalize (and Decentralize) by Product Category

But size and rapid growth still bothered Knight: could the old informality continue?

One alternative format might be:

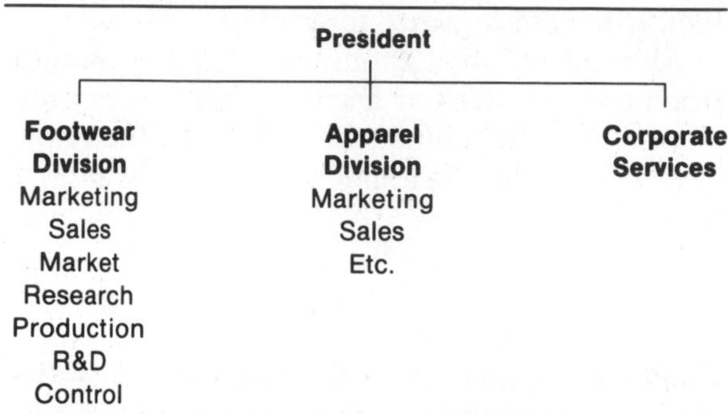

Each division would be a profit center and control a number of key activities. If this option were accepted, there remained a number of knotty questions:

a. Which activities would you assign to the divisions and which to corporate?
b. Would you totally separate footwear and apparel and, if so, how would you handle the salesforce?
c. Would the corporate services respond to divisional requests or initiate the requests?

3. Organize by Channel

Since there were two levels of buyers, customers (or the retailers) and consumers, why not two levels of organization? The advertising and promotional efforts would be directed at consumer segments while the in-store selling and other channel efforts would be directed at retail segments.

Thus, one might consider:

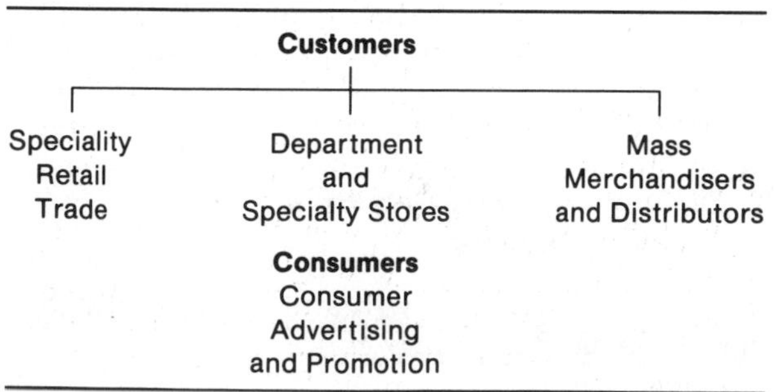

Such an orientation would recognize the power of the trade and the need to comprehend the needs and strategies of each major retail type.

There would be, of course, some tough problems such as duplicate product managers since the channels are not mutually exclusive in their choice of products. This organizational variation would marry footwear and apparel, which would facilitate the use of a single salesforce. Unfortunately the distribution of retail outlets between shoes and apparel might cause complications.

Maybe the biggest problem would be that of finding executives sufficiently skilled in retail operations to make everything work.

4. Organize by Markets or Segments

This variation would be a further recognition that consumer segmentation is primary. Perhaps there should be geographic "operations" such as Nike East, West, South, and North. This orientation already existed to the extent that there was an International and Domestic operation.

There were, needless to say, other segmentation alternatives such as demography, income, or application (runners vs. spectators).

5. Fragment the Marketing Function

This approach would permit the various marketing activities (research, sales, advertising, etc.) to specialize and develop as "service centers" for the operations. The other extreme would be to pool all of these pieces into a centrally directed marketing department.

6. Product Management System

An illustration of this orientation might include:

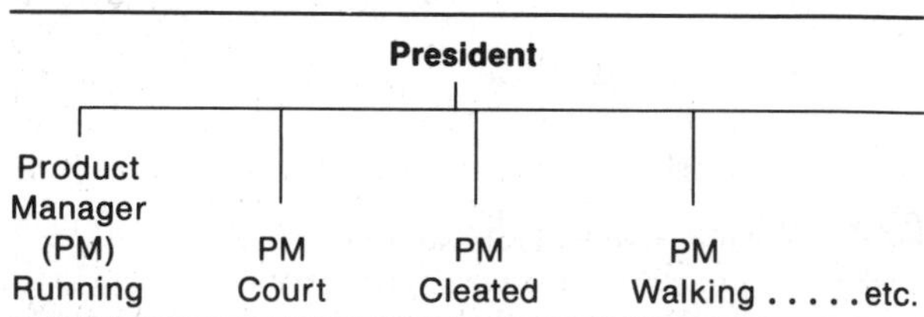

Each PM would be similar to a division manager but would probably have fewer responsibilities and be responsible primarily for the marketing mix.

In traditional product management systems, the manager has no direct authority over the separate business activities, rather the PM serves as a strategist, coordinator, and persuader who gets the job done through the efforts of others. One of the problems associated with this form of organization is to identify and develop young managers able to assume considerable responsibility without much authority.

7. Split the Marketing Group into "Established Businesses" and "New Opportunities"

Knight recognized that this organizational variation was a bit unorthodox, but he was intrigued with its recognition of two fundamental skills: old and new businesses. Whether such a split should include all the activities of the business or just selected ones, such as sales, R&D, and advertising, was an open question.

8. Establish "Task Forces" to Handle Critical Problem Areas As They Arise

The comforting aspect of this alternative was that it was reasonably similar to the present policy of "throwing" people at problems. The concept of a series of task forces, however, was a bit more formal but had the potential danger of developing a "keep-your-hands-off" attitude among the teams.

Task forces, nevertheless, did reinforce the company's flexible approach to management and would permit the firm to concentrate on critical issues. The question might be raised, however, that task forces might be difficult to coordinate: the results might be a series of discrete, although separately effective, decisions.

CASE 20 | *The Rise and Fall of Boise Cascade's Building Materials Centers*

In 1956, Robert V. Hansberger proceeded to transform a tiny Idaho lumber company into a powerful international conglomerate. His method was simple: He recruited top Harvard and Stanford MBAs to seek out merger and acquisition opportunities; then he let them manage what they amassed in an atmosphere virtually free from job descriptions, rigid reporting relationships, inflexible policies, and other formalities.

Companies comprised of saw mills and timber stands were among Hansberger's earliest acquisitions en route to building what became the Boise Cascade Corporation. But many of the acquired firms also owned lumber yards, which seemed

This case was prepared by Professor Erhard Karlheinz Valentin, Weber State College as the basis for classroom discussion rather than to illustrate either effective or ineffective handling of a managerial situation. It is reproduced here by permission of the North American Case Research Association and the author.

unprofitable and, hence, were to be sold. However, Pete O'Neill, one of Hansberger's prized young MBAs, convinced his boss to prune rather than liquidate. O'Neill got his wish and quickly turned the hodgepodge into the Building Materials Distribution Division (BMD).

BMD, which generated over 90 percent of its sales by serving professional building contractors and lumber dealers, became profitable as soon as O'Neill took charge. His rewards were approval to acquire facilities in California, Missouri, Virginia, and the Carolinas and promotions, in rapid succession, to vice president (1971) and senior vice president (1972). Operations east of the Rocky Mountains were disappointments, however, and were sold in 1977, leaving approximately 25 outlets. Nevertheless, top management had big plans for BMD: (1) More facilities were to be added, and (2) consumers engaged in do-it-yourself home improvement projects were to be targeted very aggressively. By 1980, BMD had grown to more than 100 outlets capable of serving both consumers and commercial customers. But what top management thought was a sure-fire extension of the division's core business soon turned into a nightmare and, ultimately, BMD's demise.

What went wrong? Opinions vary. For example, Bill Cowling, who was president of what was once Weyerhaeuser's Dixieline home improvement chain, suggested "Boise Cascade, like many of these other building products conglomerates that got into retailing, never understood the business." As if to confirm Cowling's assessment, Weyerhaeuser divested itself of Dixieline a month after his remarks appeared in the trade press. George McCown, who succeeded O'Neill in 1976, believed "the company demonstrated a 'fundamental schizophrenia' toward the need to centralize and standardize"; and Bill Van Note, a former BMD merchandising manager, claimed "There's a misconception that Boise Cascade was in retailing." In reality, he continued, the company was most interested in pushing its lumber and plywood through captive distribution. "We may have been the fourth or fifth largest chain," he said, "but we had a few stores here, a few stores there."[1]

Others blamed the prolonged nation-wide housing slump and upper management's eagerness to get into retailing without knowing anything about it. A former administrative assistant to BMD's general manager observed that everyone seemed so preoccupied with financial projections that no one ever asked how BMD would secure a competitive advantage.

BACKGROUND

The Hansberger Era

By 1970, Bob Hansberger and his young apprentices had made 35 acquisitions; and sales figures, which approached $2 billion, matched or surpassed those of major competitors, including Georgia-Pacific, Weyerhaeuser, International Paper, U.S. Plywood-Champion, and Johns Manville. However, Boise Cascade, headquartered in Boise, Idaho, dominated none of its markets. Instead, Hansberger focused on building what he called a broad-based forest products company, which, in addition to manufacturing and distributing products made directly from trees, included real estate development, urban renewal, mobile home manufacturing, modular housing, Princess Cruises (parent company of television's "Love Boat"), and the magazine *Psychology Today*.

When asked about the common thread among the firm's diverse endeavors, Hansberger called it an "idea company."[2] Boise Cascade's competitive advantage, he intimated, was rooted in the innate and expertly developed abilities of its executives. He believed they could recognize and capitalize on opportunities in virtually any industry.

---

[1]For a variety of conjectures, including those quoted in this paragraph, see John Caulfield, "Boise Sells Its California Stores," *National Home Center News*, October 21, 1985, pp. 1, 89.
[2]"Cinderella," *Forbes*, November 15, 1972, p. 72.

Yet during the early 1970s, the firm incurred write-offs and operating losses near $500 million, which were attributable mostly to real estate development ventures gone awry. As investors became aware of Boise Cascade's difficulties, the firm's common stock began to plummet from a high above 80 in 1969 toward a low of $8\frac{1}{4}$ in 1973. Moreover, in 1972, stockholders voted to replace Bob Hansberger with John Ferry, one of the first MBAs to join Hansberger's team. Under Ferry, Boise Cascade retrenched and divested itself of virtually all businesses not directly involved in manufacturing or distributing forest products.

BMD's Early Years[3]

Forging BMD from a jumble of unwanted lumber yards, as noted earlier, was Pete O'Neill's idea. The division's impressive operating results in 1969 and 1970 impressed top management, which not only promoted O'Neill, then in his early 30s, but also increased his responsibilities. By the end of 1972, as shown in Exhibit 1, he was in charge of the four divisions that collectively became known as the Timber and Building Materials Group: (1) BMD; (2) Manufactured Housing, including Kingsberry Homes and other modular housing operations; (3) Raygold Cabinets; and (4) Wood Products Marketing.

BMD, Manufactured Housing, and Raygold accounted for nearly 30 percent of Boise Cascade's 1972 sales and nearly 20 percent of its operating income. The combined 1972 before-tax ROI was 31.8 percent. Wood Products Marketing, the sales office responsible for selling all output from the firm's lumber, plywood, and particle board mills, was assigned to O'Neill because top management hoped he could effect a higher degree of vertical integration between the mills and BMD.[4]

BMD operated both wholesale branches and building materials centers. The latter became known simply as BMCs. The wholesale branches sold to independent lumber yards serving contractors and consumers and to the company-owned BMCs. The BMCs supplied mostly professional building contractors, but also served farmers, ranchers, and consumers to varying degrees. In 1972, BMD's facilities were located as shown in Exhibit 2.

Customer segment and gross margin breakdowns by region are given in Exhibit 3. The *consumer* category is comprised of retail sales to the general public and anyone who does not fit one of the other categories. In the Southern California Region (in essence, the San Diego vicinity) most consumer sales were made to urban home owners engaged in home repair and remodeling projects. However, in the Northwest Region, farmers and ranchers accounted for a substantial portion of sales recorded in the "consumer" column. Sales made by BMCs to professional building contractors are categorized as *builder sales*. The *dealer sales* category covers all wholesale transactions between wholesale branches and customers other than the BMCs. *Direct sales* are transactions coordinated by wholesale branches that result in direct shipments from mills to customers. *Intra-company sales* are actually intra-division sales made by wholesale branches to BMCs.

Expectations for 1974–1978

Shortly after being promoted to senior vice president, O'Neill placed Dan Hogan, then in his mid-40's, in charge of BMD. Hogan had managed a wholesale outlet in Salt Lake City, Utah, for many years before it was acquired by Boise Cascade and briefly managed the Northwest Region. By 1974, the year he became a vice president, Hogan had become something of a folk hero. His gruff manner and grassroots wisdom endeared him to O'Neill and to most of his subordinates, who saw him much as he saw himself: tough, but fair, earthy, and, most of all, pragmatic. Although Hogan had earned his bachelor's degree in business administration from the University of Utah, in

[3]During its early existence, BMD was called BM&S, i.e., Building Materials and Services.

[4]Financial data for Wood Products Marketing are unavailable.

EXHIBIT 1
Summary Chart of Organization: Late 1972

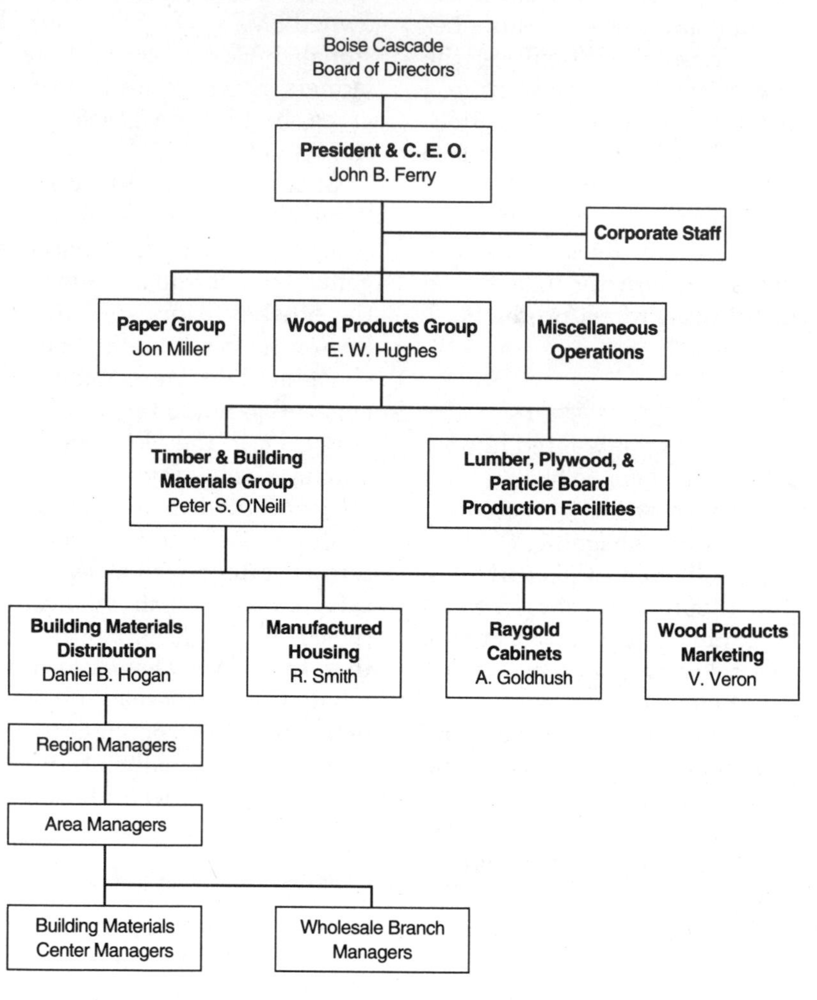

many ways, he was the antithesis of the young MBAs that ran so many of Boise Cascade's divisions.

As part of the annual planning process, group and division heads were required to formulate business plans covering the upcoming five-year period. In July of 1973, O'Neill and Hogan completed theirs. BMD's strengths, they noted, lay in supplying dealers and medium to large builders. Consumer sales accounted for little more than 5 percent of BMD's revenues. Though retailing operations in the San Diego area and, to some extent, in the Northwest Region had been successful, O'Neill felt BMD lacked retailing expertise. On the other hand, he was aware consumer demand was growing rapidly. He concluded that, even though it would be impractical to expand the divisions's retailing activities via internal

EXHIBIT 2
Locations of BMD Facilities, 1972

		Customer Segment Served		
		Builders	*Consumers*	*Dealers*
Northwest Region				
Washington:	Bellevue	X	X	
	Kennewick	X	X	
	Renton			X
	Spokane			X
	Yakima			X
Idaho:	Boise	X	X	
	Emmett	X	X	
	Gooding	X	X	
	Homedale	X	X	
	Idaho Falls	X	X	
	Payette	X	X	
	Rexburg	X	X	
	Rupert	X	X	
	Boise			X
	Idaho Falls			X
	Twin Falls			X
Utah:	Layton	X	X	
	Ogden	X	X	
	Provo	X	X	
	Tooele	X	X	
	Salt Lake City			X
Montana:	Billings			X
	Denver			X
Northern California Region				
California:	Healdsburg	X		
Southern California Region				
California:	National City	X		
	Tustin	X		
	Chula Vista	X	X	
	La Jolla	X	X	
	Point Loma	X	X	
	Pacific Beach	X	X	
	San Diego		X	
St. Louis Region				
Missouri:	St. Louis	X		X
South Atlantic Region				
N. Carolina:	Charlotte	X		
	Greensboro	X		
	Raleigh	X		
Virginia:	Newport News	X		
	Springfield	X		X
Delaware:	Georgetown	X		X

EXHIBIT 3
Sales and Gross Margins by Region and Customer Type: 1972 Sales (in $000)

			Dealer			
	Consumer	*Builder*	*Yard*	*Direct*	*Intra-Company*	*Total*
Northwest	7,768	18,182	37,172	37,135	8,743	109,000
No. Calif.		16,576		641	1,271	18,488
So. Calif.	3,113	38,142	10,261		2,359	53,875
St. Louis	1,171	8,771	1,731			11,673
So. Atlantic		29,444		6,947	782	37,173
Total	12,052	111,115	49,164	44,723	13,155	230,209
Gross Margin (%)						
Northwest	19	18	15	5	9	12*
No. Calif.		19		9	17	18
So. Calif.	24	19	11		10	18
St. Louis	31	23	17			23
So. Atlantic		20		7	7	17
Weighted Mean	21	19	14	5	10	15

*Gross margins in this column are weighted means.

growth, expansion by acquisition was a definite possibility that should be examined from time to time.

The main thrust of BMD's five-year plan was to be the continuation of previous endeavors of proven merit. Specifically, O'Neill and Hogan proposed an $80-million acquisition program and a $28-million internal expansion and rejuvenation effort. As shown in Exhibit 4, they expected acquisitions to produce $363 million in annual sales and $22 million in annual profit by 1978; and internal programs, they thought, would yield $78 million in sales and $8.3 million in profit by the end of the planning period. O'Neill and Hogan supported their projections largely by citing past performance. They pointed out BMD achieved sales and profit increases of 539 and 804 percent, respectively, between 1968 and 1973 while maintaining an average ROI of 24.2 percent. Moreover, sales and profits from the original base (mainly the Northwest Region, see Exhibit 2) increased by 160 and 554 percent, respectively.

According to the plan, the following criteria were to be applied in evaluating acquisition candidates: (1) annual sales volume should be in the $10–50 million range; (2) the population should be growing rapidly; (3) Boise Cascade's mills should be able to serve acquired outlets profitably; (4) key personnel should be willing to stay on; and (5) it should be possible to manage acquisitions from an existing base. The Northeast and the Northcentral states were identified as prime shipping and growth areas.[5]

It was stated in one section of the plan that whether acquisitions consisted of wholesale branches or builder yards mattered very little. Moreover, O'Neill believed any acquisition to be a good deal at the right price.

Other portions of the plan touched on vertical integration and fabrication opportunities that might be enhanced by placing greater emphasis on retailing. Coordination between Wood Prod-

[5]Most Boise Cascade lumber was grown inland, which made it much lighter than coastal lumber and cheaper to ship. Transportation cost savings accrued to Boise Cascade, not the customer; therefore, lumber could be sold more profitably in certain distant markets than in those surrounding the mills.

EXHIBIT 4
Financial Summary of BMD's 1973–1978 Business Plan (in $000)

	1973	*1974*	*1975*	*1976*	*1977*	*1978*
1972 Base Operations						
Sales	284,058	257,858	255,280	268,555	285,743	292,315
Income	17,175	12,367	12,764	14,502	16,573	17,539
Net cash flow	17,797	13,876	13,092	13,529	15,570	17,195
R.O.I.	35.7%	28.8%	29.9%	32.5%	35.6%	36.3%
Increment from Acquisitions						
Sales		80,000	118,800	208,300	265,900	362,700
Income		3,840	5,940	11,248	15,422	21,762
Net cash flow		(15,940)	(1,250)	(6,766)	6,556	3,025
R.O.I.		19.4%	23.2%	25.0%	28.6%	30.0%
Increment from Internal Expansion						
Sales		8,000	20,000	36,500	56,000	78,000
Income		835	2,119	3,872	5,943	8,282
Net cash flow		(2,298)	(1,931)	(1,128)	293	2,515
R.O.I.		26.7%	29.5%	31.8%	33.3%	35.1%
Total						
Sales	284,058	345,858	394,080	513,355	607,643	733,015
Income	17,175	17,042	20,823	29,622	37,938	47,583
Net cash flow	17,797	(4,362)	9,911	5,635	22,419	22,735
R.O.I.	35.7%	25.9%	27.1%	29.1%	32.1%	32.9%

ucts Marketing and other divisions within O'Neill's group, especially BMD, was stressed. In 1972, BMD purchased $70 million of Boise Cascade manufactured products, which accounted for 39 percent of BMD's total purchases and approximately 20 percent of the physical volume of Boise Cascade's mills.

Subsequent Developments

Top management launched its own corporate-wide search for opportunities in 1974 that soon led to BMD and the dramatic revision of O'Neill's business plan.

The McKinsey Report

In 1974, John Ferry hired a small team of consultants from McKinsey and Company's San Francisco office to evaluate Boise Cascade's various business units and the relationships among them. Assisted by a small internal planning staff, the consultants scrutinized BMD's operations and prospects for nearly four years. In their final report, issued in April of 1978, they recommended aggressive expansion and placing particular emphasis on retailing such that consumer sales would account for roughly 40 percent of the division's revenues and half of its gross profits. However, by the time McKinsey's final report was printed, efforts were well under way (based on informal preliminary findings) to turn all BMCs into facilities capable of serving consumers as well as contractors.

The report noted that operating efficiencies would be realized insofar as contractors and consumers would be served largely from a common inventory and from common facilities and that expansion would increase captive demand for Boise Cascade's lumber, plywood, and other manufactured products. But higher margins, less cyclicality, and a surge in do-it-yourself home improvement activity were cited as the main reasons for becoming more involved in retailing. These claims were documented and translated into impressive sales, income, and ROI projections.

Primary emphasis was to be placed on constructing and acquiring Type B BMCs. Type B BMCs were defined as facilities serving metropolitan areas of moderate size with solid builder and retail sales potential. Type A and Type C facilities, in contrast, were situated in rural and in large metropolitan markets, respectively. Some facilities that existed at the time are classified in Exhibit 5.

The listed Type C BMCs were all in the San Diego area and were designed to serve the contractor and the DIY segments equally. However, the physical facilities dedicated purely to contractor operations consisted largely of an order desk. Shipments to contractors' job sites were made from a single large central facility. Hence, contractor inventories were minimized, delivery vehicles were used more efficiently, and the BMCs could be built on fairly small parcels of land in attractive locations. The five San Diego BMCs were very similar in appearance and carried identical merchandise. In other words, retailing operations in the San Diego area were highly standardized and centrally managed. None of BMD's other operations were configured this way.

The McKinsey report went on to advocate modernization of BMD's information system and increased standardization and administrative centralization. Uniformity, the report maintained, would reduce the cost of selecting store sites, designing stores, training personnel, merchandising, advertising, and purchasing. But it stopped short of recommending a specific organizational structure that would empower a division-level staff to dictate to the BMCs. Top management and McKinsey knew such a recommendation would unhinge Dan Hogan and every manager down to the BMCs.

The McKinsey report also stated that two channels served the consumer market: (1) home

EXHIBIT 5

1977 Consumer Sales as a Percentage of Total Sales by Type of Facility

Type A	%	*Type B*	%	*Type C*	%
Tooele, UT	8	Meridian, ID	6	El Cajon, CA	36
Gooding, ID	16	Orem, UT	7	Oceanside, CA	39
Homedale, ID	20	Layton, UT	8	South Bay, CA	45
Payette, ID	30	Garland, TX	8	Poway, CA	48
Rexburg, ID	33	Pocatello, ID	10	Pacific Beach, CA	56
Rupert, ID	38	Oklahoma City, OK	11		
Emmett, ID	40	Springdale, AK	12		
		Bellevue, WA	13		
		Tulsa, OK	15		
		Kenewick, WA	15		
		Idaho Falls, ID	20		
		Point Loma, CA	28		
		Ogden, UT	30		
		Merced, CA	40		
Weighted Means					
Consumer sales	25%		16%		45%
ROI	32%		42%		86%
Retail floor (sq. ft.)	3,085		4,102		9,590

Source: Internal Boise Cascade documents.

centers, which cater almost exclusively to consumers; and (2) lumber and building materials yards, such as Boise Cascade's, which also target building contractors. On the surface, it would appear the two channels compete directly, but in fact, the consultants maintained, they coexist profitably in many places. The three BMCs with the most home center competitors, they pointed out, had the highest ROIs for 1977.

The following market selection criteria were enumerated: (1) the market must be comprised of a sufficient number of households to support retail sales, (2) the new home market must be growing steadily, (3) the BMC should face little competition from other lumber and building materials outlets (excluding home centers), and (4) repair and remodeling potential should be significant. Accordingly, the percentage of household heads under 45 years of age, the percentage of households with above average incomes, and the rate of housing turnover should be high.

Site selection criteria, too, were sketched out. For example, stores were to be located on the perimeter of the city and on the side showing the most growth. The importance of zoning laws, drive-by traffic, visibility, distance from other lumber yards, and various other factors were noted as well. Moreover, consumer sales potential originating from within a three mile radius had to exceed $2 million for Type B and C BMCs. Estimates of potential consumer sales were to be made using the "Gobar formula."

The Gobar Formula

What became known as the Gobar formula was essentially a retail gravitation model developed by the consulting firm Alfred Gobar and Associates.[6] Parameter estimates (i.e., estimates of regression coefficients) were based on research conducted for BMD in 1976 in the San Diego area. However, because markets are highly idiosyncratic, Gobar cautioned against using parameter estimates based on data gathered in one city to evaluate store sites in another. Hogan did not understand the merit of such advice and, hence, chose to ignore it. The Hillsboro, Oregon, BMC was among several unprofitable outlets built on sites selected using the Gobar formula (with the San Diego parameter estimates). It was on the edge of a large tract on which, BMD eventually discovered, no homes were to be built until the year 2000. Moreover, even though the facility could be seen from a main commuter highway, access was very awkward, and delivery trucks often got stuck in traffic. This BMC struggled for 18 months, then it was closed.

The New Frontier

By 1978, all facilities comprising the South Atlantic and the St. Louis regions (see Exhibit 2) had been sold because they continually performed below BMD's expectations and employees were not very receptive to Boise Cascade's policies and management style. Yet, shortly after selling these units, three major acquisitions were undertaken. First, the 18-unit Independent Lumber Company of Colorado was acquired in 1978. In mid-1979, 61 operating units located in Texas (46), Oklahoma (10), and Kansas (5) were bought for more than $50 million from Lone Star Industries; and finally, five units located in Washington and Oregon were bought late in 1979. Additionally, a few smaller acquisitions were made, and several units were built during the late 1970s and the early 1980s.

In 1981, more than 100 BMCs and 15 wholesale branches comprised BMD. Some BMCs were located along prime retail strips, while others were located much less favorably. Retail floor space ranged from 2,000 to 25,000 sq. ft.

The New Frontiersman

O'Neill resigned in 1976 after it became apparent he had made several poor acquisitions and would

[6]For details concerning gravitation and other site selection models, see Gary L. Lilien and Philip Kotler, *Marketing Decision Making: A Model-Building Approach*, New York: Harper & Row, 1983, pp. 454-462.

not become Boise Cascade's next president. Most of his responsibilities were turned over to George McCown, then a 41-year-old senior vice president with a bachelor's degree in engineering from Stanford and an MBA degree from Harvard. McCown had spent several years liquidating Boise Cascade's real estate developments and was eager to get into operations.

Whereas Hogan and O'Neill had great respect for each other, Hogan found McCown brash and arrogant. Hogan had little confidence in McCown's ideas and was uncomfortable with the emphasis his new boss and others in upper management placed on retailing and all that came with it, particularly standardization and centralization. Local managers, Hogan maintained, are in the best position to know their markets and, therefore, should be allowed to run their facilities without interference. However, Hogan considered vigorous opposition insubordinate; consequently, he was more inclined to grumble and procrastinate than protest openly about decisions not to his liking.

By early 1978, Hogan had been persuaded to create the position of division merchandising manager and to hire Bob Moutrie to fill it. Two purchasing agents, and later a third, reported to Moutrie. However, the bargain struck between Hogan and higher management was such that the division merchandising manager was given no direct line authority. In essence, he was an advisor to Hogan and the region, area, and BMC managers. Nevertheless, he was held accountable for retailing results.

The BMC managers insisted they needed ultimate control over their operations because Moutrie was unfamiliar with local conditions. On the other hand, Moutrie argued that leaving virtually all decisions in the hands of local managers made it impossible to develop effective programs or to realize economies of scale. Every successful retailing chain, he contended, relies on central staffs, not store-level management, to make purchasing, merchandising, and promotion decisions. Decentralized management, Moutrie thought, would jeopardize the entire retailing venture. Much bickering ensued until Moutrie left Boise Cascade in 1980.

BMD's search for a new merchandising manager lasted more than a year. But in 1981, Bill Van Note accepted the position. He was competent, direct, and, to Hogan's chagrin, unafraid to speak out. However, much as Moutrie, Van Note considered centralization vital and soon discovered Hogan vehemently opposed it. Tensions mounted between Hogan and Van Note, culminating in the latter's departure after less than six months on the job. Next came Ed Savage, Van Note's former boss and former president of Moore's, a successful Eastern building materials chain. Savage left in 1985 to become president of Lumbermen's, a chain headquartered in Shelton, Washington.

The Retreat

BMD's performance deteriorated to the point that all but the most essential staff positions were eliminated in May of 1982. Efforts to develop an up-to-date information system were halted entirely, even though hefty sums had been spent on systems consulting services provided by Management Horizons, Inc., and more than a dozen systems specialists had been hired and moved to Boise during the previous year or two. Operating results for the first six months of 1982 are shown in Exhibit 6.

By late 1985, only 22 BMCs and nine wholesale branches were left; the rest had been sold or closed. Lowe's bought 23 BMCs located in Texas and Oklahoma for $50 million in early 1985. Lowe's could have bought more stores, but found no others worth buying. Given the chance to "cherry pick" from the 10 Houston BMCs, Lowe's concluded "there are no cherries in Houston . . . only the pits."[7] Later in 1985, BMD divested itself of the Southern California Region; and in 1987, the remaining BMCs were sold.

[7]See Philip M. Perry, "Boise Retrenches," *National Home Center News*, February 25, 1985, p. 86.

EXHIBIT 6
Operating Results for the First Half of 1982 (in $000)

	Gross Sales	Net Sales	Profit	Investment
Idaho area	34,437	30,192	(96)	18,199
Utah area	19,882	16,105	(56)	11,636
Colorado area	56,470	45,936	(175)	29,213
Regional overhead			(581)	(577)
Rocky Mountain region	110,788	92,233	(908)	58,012
Pacific Northwest area	46,669	40,653	(190)	16,259
Northern California area	10,645	9,829	(917)	7,493
Southern California area	48,546	41,188	(1,272)	18,968
Regional overhead			(852)	(84)
West Coast region	105,860	91,671	(3,231)	42,636
Central Texas area	17,008	16,939	822	9,004
Dallas/Ft. Worth area	32,530	25,919	669	15,276
Houston area	31,267	29,797	464	18,393
Oklahoma/Kansas area	23,909	23,556	709	13,211
Regional overhead			(1,170)	858
South central region	104,714	96,211	1,492	56,742
BMD division overhead			(2,105)	
Intangible amorization			(169)	4,565

APPENDIX A
A Note on Building Materials Outlets

Independents sell more than 60 percent of all building materials; and only four chains have market shares greater than 1 percent. In contrast, general merchandise discount chains account for more than 90 percent of that sector's sales; and five major discounters account for nearly 50 percent. Yet, several chains catering substantially to consumers are steadily increasing market shares. Payless Cashways, for instance, grew from 78 stores in 1980 to 194 by the end of 1987.

Though classification schemes are far from uniform, most, but not all, building materials retailers can be categorized as builder- or consumer-oriented. Builder yards often started out serving professional contractors and showed little interest in consumers until the do-it-yourself movement caught on in the 1970s. Since consumer sales generally produced higher gross margins and were much less cyclical than contractor sales, many old-time lumber yards were given quick face lifts to make them more appealing to consumers. Typically, larger and brighter signs were installed, interiors were redecorated, floor space was expanded, merchandise assortments were augmented, and the power of advertising was discovered.

But while trying to attract consumers, such yards also tried to retain their builder clientele and generally expected much (though sometimes less than half) of their sales volume to come from the home builder segment. Builders usually are contacted periodically by an outside sales force, buy on account, are quoted lower prices than consumers, are served from a special desk, and often have a special entrance. Outlets of this type usually are located in industrial rather than prime retailing areas.

Among the consumer-oriented outlets, warehouse stores grew most rapidly in the 1980s. Typically, these no-frills operations move into stores abandoned by other retailers, contain up to 100,000 sq. ft. of retail floor space, and carry more than 20,000 items. Home Depot Inc., founded in 1978 by three very astute former executives with other home improvement chains, was the innovator and became the most successful.

The label "home center" usually is applied to outlets that sell little to home building contractors, but may cater to professional remodelers. According to *Home Center Magazine's 1984 Profile of the Home Center Market Summary Report*, a home center is any store that carries hardware, lumber and/or plywood, interior wall paneling and/or moulding and, in addition, carries several, though not all, related items such as tools, floor coverings, electrical and/or plumbing products, lawn and garden products, and automotive supplies.[8] The typical warehouse store, according to this definition, is simply a subspecies of home centers.

On the demand side, the surge in do-it-yourself activity in the 1970s has been attributed to favorable demographic, economic, and psychological factors. Among other things, the 25–44 age group grew very rapidly; new housing became very expensive; labor costs skyrocketed; and American values increasingly embraced independence and self-help. *Building Supply & Home Centers* estimated that, by 1990, American's homeowners would spend $73 billion for the modernization and repair of their homes. However, in a more recent report published in the September, 1986, issue of *Home Center Magazine* some doubt was cast on earlier projections for 1990, and discomforting parallels between building materials retailing and the grocery industry were drawn. Specifically, it was noted that indicators, such as excess capacity in some geographic markets and declining profit margins, suggested home centers have entered the mature phase of the retail life cycle. The Commerce Department's estimates of residential upkeep expenditures, which include labor as well as materials purchased, are shown in Exhibit A-1 along with the number of total private housing starts.

EXHIBIT A-1
Residential Upkeep Expenditures and Housing Starts

Year	*Residential Upkeep ($Billions)*	*Total Private Housing Starts (Thousands of Units)*
1971	16.2	2,052
1972	17.5	2,356
1973	18.5	2,945
1974	21.1	1,338
1975	25.2	1,160
1976	29.0	1,538

[8] *1984 Profile of the Home Center Market: Summary Report, Home Center Magazine*, p. 2.

CASE 21 | *Johnson Controls, Inc.*

Market, product, and organization dynamics can be explained, in both quantitative and qualitative terms, by a product life cycle graph. This analysis can provide an historical synopsis of important

This case was prepared by Tracy K. Short, planning analyst, Systems and Services Division, Johnson Controls, Inc., Milwaukee. Appeared in "Industrial Product Life Cycle Analysis," *Planning Review*, November, 1985, pp. 18–23.

strategic decisions, including those of the competition. It can show how external factors lead to the success or failure of a specific strategy. And it can be used as a benchmark in determining future marketing actions and in monitoring success. Life cycle analysis gives an industrial company a very important record of marketing and strategy achievements—and a very potent competitive weapon as well.

Product Life Cycle Theory (PLC) was introduced more than thirty years ago. Basically, it plots unit sales (or unit profits) against time to determine the evolutionary stages in the life cycle of a product (Fig. 1). This information can prove invaluable in planning marketing and product strategies.

While there's an intuitive and logical appeal to this concept, as well as an elegant simplicity, not many industrial companies really understand how to develop and apply life cycle analysis because:

- PLC research has largely focused on consumer durable and nondurable applications, and very few industrial models have been developed.
- Many industrial companies lack the marketing resources to utilize and effectively implement PLC strategies.
- Managers need to make assessments of market conditions before making any predictions about product or market strategies.
- Most industries don't record the kind of information on product introductions and profitability that the PLC model requires.
- Industrial products tend to have extended life spans, and slower, more conservative markets. This makes monitoring PLC changes frustrating.
- The environment in which industrial products are sold is more difficult to manage than the consumer goods environment.

JOHNSON CONTROLS

Despite many of these difficulties, Johnson Controls, Inc. developed a successful life cycle process in order to study the product and market dynamics of building automation systems (BAS).

Established in 1885 by Warren Johnson, the inventor of the first electric room thermostat, Johnson Controls was first a leader in temperature control technology and in recent years in building control technology. The company is now a major multinational organization with nearly 30,000 employees. With net sales of over $1.4 billion in 1984, Johnson Controls ranks among the top 300 companies in the *Fortune* ratings. On the international level, Johnson Controls has participated in the construction of more buildings worldwide than any other company. Its Systems & Services

FIGURE 1
Classical Product Life Cycle Stages

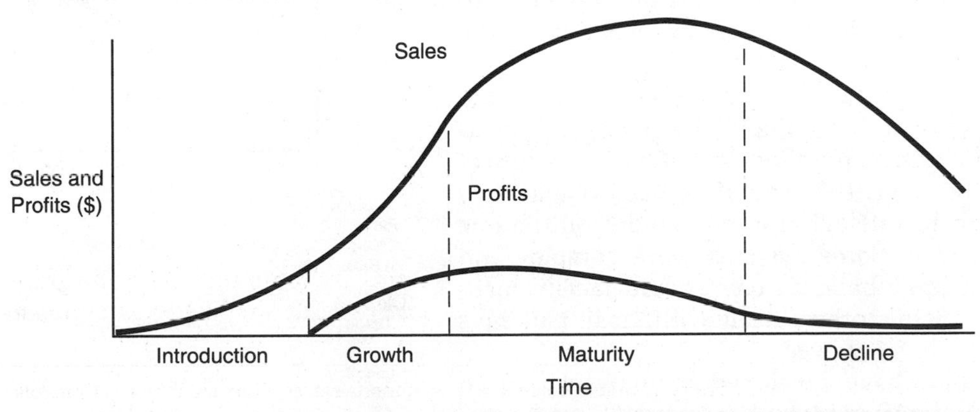

Division is one of the three major influences in the building controls industry.

Johnson Controls' building automation system (BAS) products offer state-of-the-art technology to control and maximize energy use in the heating, cooling, ventilation, fire safety, security, lighting, communications, and maintenance of nonresidential buildings.

DEVELOPING A FRAMEWORK

Developing a PLC framework is a very creative endeavor. Many more factors than unit sales and time come into play. Although Johnson Controls' model worked well for their purposes, different approaches may be more appropriate for other industrial firms. The key is flexibility. The process used in developing the life cycle scenario at Johnson Controls involved five steps:

- Building a quantitative model
- Identifying general product life cycle issues
- Generating solutions
- Determining the critical strategic issues
- Implementing the solutions

Building a Quantitative Model

Marketing research, sales reports, factory operations reports, pricing and financial data, and organizational charts were analyzed in great detail to develop a preliminary PLC model showing unit sales over time. Very often, past product sales information was difficult to obtain, especially in the desired form.

Classifying the various BAS products into manageable and meaningful life cycle groups was also difficult. A number of systems were introduced between 1965 and 1982, each one a functional or technological improvement on the one preceding it. Some systems were complex and handled large building energy and facility management while others dealt with small buildings and were less involved.

We could have developed an analysis for each individual BAS product. However, the most practical solution seemed to lie in grouping the products on a technological basis:

- Three of the early systems were based on hardware technology. These systems constituted one product life cycle family called the T-6000 group.
- The next group of systems were based on the development of computerized centralization, providing not only basic energy management control but also increased building management capabilities. These products could be easily categorized into a second life cycle family, identified as the JC/80 group.
- The third life cycle family included systems based on further improvements in computer technology, and most importantly, in improved computer hierarchical design that permitted greater distributed processing, increased system functionality, and facility management capability. This family was labeled the JC/85 group.

Figure 2 shows the product life cycle for the T-6000 BAS family. Basic models such as these were also developed for the JC/80 and JC/85 families. A large model showing BAS unit sales from 1965 through 1984 was also mapped out to enable us to analyze the overlaps between the three families better.

FIGURE 2
T-6000 Series Product Life Cycle Stages

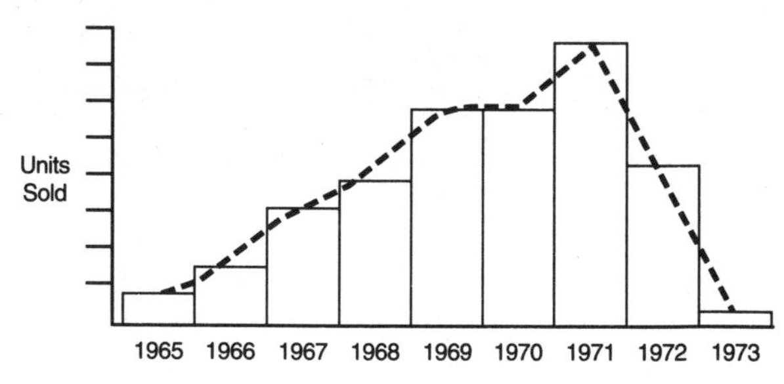

Percent Change in Sales	43.8	51.5	15.4	32.8	0	25.6	(44.9)	(83.7)
Life Cycle Stage	Introduction and Growth			Maturity			Decline	
Length of Stage	3 Years			3 Years			2 Years	

Life cycle stages were identified by studying the rate of change in units sold. Introductory and growth stages are theoretically identified by a fast increase in sales. A mature stage is indicated by slowing sales. And decline is shown by a negative growth rate. Determining the PLC stages of a product group were based largely on collective experience since it's rarely possible to be exact.

Identifying the Issues

Once we had the model, we could begin to ask the crucial questions that would pinpoint problem areas:

- Can we really establish the present and past life cycle positions of BAS products?
- What are the key environmental issues in the industry and how do they affect BAS markets and products (e.g., energy costs and nonresidential building construction)?
- How do the internal relationships between functional areas of the company (marketing, development, manufacturing) affect PLCs?
- Who are Johnson Controls' most important competitors? What products do they offer? What's their marketing strategy? How does this influence building automation system PLCs?
- What are the reasons for the peaks and valleys in the PLC curve?
- What technological developments are influencing the BAS life cycle?
- How are the company's marketing strategies affecting sales—including pricing, promotion, and placement?

Because of their qualitative nature, the resolution of these issues was not clear. No sooner do you come to grips with a previously undefined parameter than you discover even more hazy sub-issues lurking beneath it. After considerable study, we decided to use an interviewing process.

Generating Solutions

We conducted nineteen individual interviews with management and staff professionals in research and development, marketing, manufacturing, finance, and sales to generate explanations of the life cycle trends. We selected these people on the basis of their tenure in the company and their experience, past and present, with BAS products. The interviews were open-ended, with no leading questions.

The interviewing process proved to be very effective. The respondents were presented with the three quantitative PLC models for each BAS product family and were asked to explain what they saw happening at various junctures on the curves. Specifically, they were asked to described product developments, introductions, and transitions; pricing strategy; advertising strategy; planning efforts; organizational influences; and the impact of competition and external factors on sales over time.

We used the content analysis technique, popularized by John Naisbitt in *Megatrends,* to identify trends, issues, and key factors. Figure 3 shows one way the responses were grouped, analyzed, and related to changes in the U.S. economy from 1965 through 1978. Similar content analyses related Johnson Controls' BAS sales to changes in the competition, and in the construction and energy industries.

FIGURE 3
Comparison: Company X* Sales to the Economy

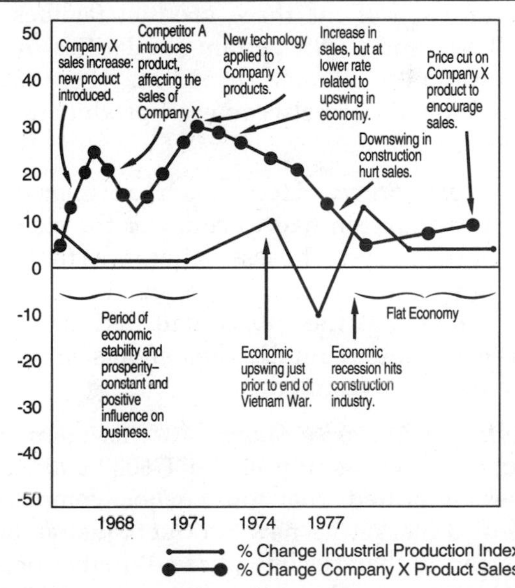

*Company X—fictitious data.

Determining Critical Strategic Issues

At this point, definite patterns in crucial life cycle issues began to emerge. These were issues that had had the most impact on BAS sales in the past and would probably continue to affect sales in the future. Basically, they involved:

- Products offered and technology used
- Prices
- Market position
- Overall marketing strategy
- Promotional emphasis
- Competitive influences

Table 2 shows one analysis technique we used to relate critical issues to the product life cycle stages of the T-6000 family. A similar analysis was also done for the JC/80 and JC/85 families. The information in Table 2 was based on the theoretical life cycle premises shown in Table 1. Of course, in real life, not all products follow these guidelines. For example, at Johnson Controls the introductory and growth stages of BAS products were often indiscernible and could be combined, leaving only three PLC stages to contend with instead of four.

Within each of the three product families, T-6000, JC/80, and JC/85, certain similarities in life cycle responses became apparent. There were also commonalities between each product family by life cycle stage.

Introductory Stage. Here, each new product family introduction had to consider the element of pent-up demand. The lesson here was for Johnson Controls to properly anticipate this demand—as well as the subsequent periods of decline—in order to minimize their effects on profits and return on investment.

Growth and Maturity Stage. At this point, the product life cycle study of the T-6000 and JC/80 families indicated that our major competitor seemed to market its new products just as ours were nearing their decline phase. Whether or not this was a planned strategy on the part of the competition, it indicated that we needed to develop a new strategy to protect our position, one that allowed us to introduce the industry's newest product ahead of the competition. This kind of forward planning will help us pin down the life cycle of our existing products more accurately, which will also allow us to maximize our profits without losing ground while simultaneously developing and introducing our new products.

The competition was very adept at using pricing and promotional weapons to their advantage. Although we viewed the competitive product as less capable from a technical standpoint, customers believed they were getting the best product. This was because the competition's advertising campaign leaned heavily on such emotional appeals as prestige—being first to install a system like this.

During the mid-seventies Johnson Controls successfully protected its maturing product position by developing a group of systems—part of the larger JC/80 family—that allowed our customers to upgrade as their needs dictated. We built our strategy on superior, user-friendly, upgradable products, a strong advertising campaign, and a well-thought-out market positioning strategy that allowed us to continue to generate profits from our maturing JC/80 product family.

Today, we're trying to be even more successful in managing our product lines to achieve maximum return on investment while guarding against competitive marketing initiatives and product campaigns.

Decline Stage. We noticed that the sales for each BAS product family decreased very rapidly to only a few units over a 24-month period at this stage. This always coincided with the introduction of a new JCI product. Although we could make up for lost sales with the increased earnings of the new product, we realized that had the decline of the old product been managed more slowly, overall sales might have been even better. We could be putting ourselves at risk by not avoiding the premature death of a successfully

TABLE 1
Classical Strategies Associated with Product Life Cycle Stages

	Product Life Cycle Stage			
Effects and Responses	*Introduction*	*Growth*	*Maturity*	*Decline*
Competition	• None of importance (if leader).	• Some emulators (if leader).	• More rivals as profits increase for product/market.	• Fewer rivals due to shakeout of weak product offerings.
Overall strategy	• Market establishment; focus on early adopters.	• Market penetration; focus on followers and find new markets. • If follower, concentrate on segment that can be dominated.	• Defense of market/product position; check the inroads of competition. • Hold share by improving quality, increasing sales effort, and advertising.	• Prepare to remove product from market. • Achieve and secure any possible benefits. • Maximize cash flow by reducing investment, advertising, development.
Profits	• Negligible because of high production, development, and marketing costs.	• Reach peak levels as a result of high prices and growing demand.	• Increasing competition will cut into margins and ultimately reduce profits.	• Declining volume pushes costs up to levels that eliminate profits entirely.
Prices	• Set higher than in later stages because of development and introductory costs.	• Begin to reduce prices to discourage new competitors and to build share as growth matures. • If follower, keep prices below leader.	• Prices will decline and then stabilize as more substitute products become available and product differentiation diminishes.	• Further decline in prices.
Marketing and advertising	• Advertising and marketing expenditures should be high relative to sales compared with mature products.	• Expenditures remain high relative to expenditure rates of established products, but will start to decline in relation to sales because of rapid sales volume growth.	• Marketing and advertising expenditures to sales ratio will decline substantially because of reduced margins and demand.	• Further decline in expenditures.
Distribution	• To select customers who will buy and can refer product to others.	• Intensify efforts to gain share. • More broad-based application.	• Intensify efforts to defend share.	• Eliminate unprofitable efforts.

TABLE 2
T-6000 Series Product Life Cycle Effects and Responses*

	1965–1968		1969–1970	1970–1972
Effects and Responses	*Introduction*	*Growth*	*Maturity*	*Decline*
Industry technology available	System format English language and control center capabilities available.		Coax cable expandability and digital transmission available.	• Fire and security applications developed for use with BAS. • Microprocessor technology available.
Competition	Competitor A not a threat.		Competitor A introduces new product using latest technology.	Competitor A threatens with a strong marketing & sales program.
JCI market strategy	T-6000 system introduced (first industry BAS).	T-6000 upgraded to increase market penetration.	T-6000 upgraded as defense to Competitor A.	Phased out T-6000's to introduce next generation system—JC/80.
JCI product distribution	Systems sold on a job-by-job basis—applications varied by job.			Branch distribution of BAS improved.
Pricing	Information unavailable.	Information unavailable.	Competitor A priced below JCI.	Competitor A priced below JCI.
JCI organization	Company building on computer and electronics experience.		• Select engineering group responsible for T-6000 sales and service • Regions primarily responsible for design and operation.	

*Information is generalized to protect JCI confidentiality.

maturing product, especially in a rapidly growing, technically sophisticated market.

This information allowed us to develop a set of rules-of-thumb for marketing managers to use in future strategic planning efforts. Table 3 shows possible strategies for the maturity and decline phases of the T-6000 family.

There's no one model that can be used by all businesses all the time in studying product life cycles. Even at Johnson Controls, the life cycle study approach for new products will be somewhat different. In some cases, such a study may simply prove too difficult. On the other hand, different lines of products that are related in function and technology can be grouped together. This turned out to be the most productive avenue to study BAS product life cycles at Johnson Controls.

IMPLEMENTING THE SOLUTIONS

The BAS product life cycle study took approximately six months to complete. One of its immediate benefits was that it paved the way for a related market study done soon after. According to

TABLE 3
T-6000 Possible Life Cycle Strategies

Maturity
1968–1971

- Increase market penetration.
- Defend established markets.
- Secure profits as soon as possible and cut costs.

Product
Selective addition of new features.

Price
High to take advantage of demand.

Placement
In key market segments.

Promotion
Create buyer preference.
Differentiate from competition.

Decline
1971–1973

- Milk all possible benefits.
- Prepare for removal or adaptation.
- Cut internal-support costs.

Product
No more features.

Price
Low to moderate to recover any possible profit.

Placement
Selective—phase out unprofitable segments.

Promotion
Minimal expense to cut costs.

William P. Lydon, Manager of Future Product Planning, "The study provided key information for a more comprehensive study of BAS products, which included further life cycles analysis, market segmentation analysis, market potential estimation, and a technology forecast."

Lee Fiegel, Director of Strategic Planning at the corporate level, felt that "the PLC study provided information that could aid marketing and product managers in setting cost and life cycle limitations on current products." Joel H. Richmond, now Manager of BAS Marketing Support Services, used the information in just that way. He developed a pricing scenario that allowed for recouping developing and marketing costs of existing software for the maturing DFMS product line without killing it with a new DFMS software introduction. According to Richmond, "Before we did the PLC analysis it was difficult to price existing software incrementally with newly developed software."

The PLC study reemphasized the importance of identifying the strategies appropriate to the different stages of a product's life span. Many manufacturers have a difficult time doing this, partly for reasons discussed above, but also because there's often a tug of war between marketing and R&D.

Mike McLean, Manager of BAS Marketing, felt that "the PLC study helped marketing maintain a balance between the desires of the sales force and engineering development. Sales is always vying for the latest feature of product—the one they lost the last sale over—while engineering is always pushing to redesign, do it better, or make the product more sophisticated."

The PLC study helped give us perspective on such questions as:

- Does the product need a face lift?
- Should the product be discontinued? If so, when?
- Will advertising help?
- How long before we need to invest in a new design?

The PLC study was especially critical in identifying and establishing the historical opportunities and threats facing Johnson Controls, the prevailing competitive strategies, and how the company's strategies met these challenges.

CASE 22 | *Lonetown Press*

Lonetown Press was opened in January, 1982, to provide a highly personalized contract printing service to artists and others devoted to hand printed lithography as a fine art medium. Founded by Randy Folkman, a master printer with eight years of experience, the company was capitalized for about $30,000 of Randy's money, which was used for the purchase of a Griffen Press and printing materials and supplies. Lonetown was located about 40 miles north of New York City in Fairfield County of southwestern Connecticut.

Randy planned to operate as a one-man shop at least for the first year. As a master printer and occasional artist in his own right, he had worked at Redvale Press, a private printing studio for the two years prior to founding Lonetown. Before that he was employed for two years at a studio in New York City and for four years at a print shop in Houston, Texas. While in Texas he completed his hand printing apprenticeship under the supervision of a Tamarind-trained master printer.

Randy wanted to work primarily at his printing and was especially interested in working with up and coming artists. Over the long term he wanted Lonetown to become recognized as a quality, highly personalized shop. At the same time, Randy hoped to pay himself fairly and make some profits as well as learn more about how prints are distributed. Otherwise he did not want to become overly involved in what he saw as the business or "financial" side of Lonetown.

With the founding of Lonetown Press, Randy realized he would have to determine what price to charge and how to quote prices. He contacted an accountant with whom he shared his background and knowledge of the business.

HAND PRINTED LITHOGRAPHY

Artists are attracted to hand printed lithography because of its mystique, the quantity of images that are produced, and the technical results the medium offers. Lithographs are created by drawing on a stone or plate with pencils, crayons or other materials with which artists are familiar. With a variety of surfaces and materials available the medium is versatile for artists who can easily visualize from the drawing the resulting prints or graphics, as they are called in the trade. The development of hand printed lithography in the United States is described by Antreasian and Adams:

> Although the principles of lithography are in essence simple, the technical processes involved in the printing of fine lithographs are exceptionally complex. For this reason, artists wishing to make lithographs have, since the early years of the nineteenth century, worked in collaboration with master lithographic printers: Gericault with Hullmandel and Villain, Redon with Blanchard and Clot, Picasso and Braque with Mourlot and Desjobert.
>
> Any lithograph printed from a stone or plate conceived and executed by the artist is an original lithograph, whether it is printed by the artist himself or by a collaborating printer. Until late in the nineteenth century, lithographs were rarely signed in pencil, and individual impressions were seldom numbered. Since that time, however, it has become customary for artists to sign and number each impression, attesting in this way both to the authenticity of the print and to its quality. Often, prints made in a lithographic workshop also bear the printer's bindstamp or chop. Like the artist's signature, this mark attests to the quality of the work.
>
> Original lithographs are normally printed in limited editions, although the size of the edition may

This case was prepared by Professor Fred W. Kniffin of the University of Connecticut, with the assistance of Amy Erlanger, as a basis for class discussion rather than to illustrate either effective or ineffective handling of an administrative situation.

> vary over a wide range. In the United States, artists' editions characteristically range from ten to one hundred; in Europe, editions of two hundred or more are not uncommon. The limiting of editions is due not so much to technical considerations as to intention. The artist may wish as a matter of principle to limit editions of his work, or he may wish to avoid an undue commitment of time or money to a single edition . . .
>
> By 1960, lithographic workshops had all but disappeared in this country. There were few master printers, and it was only with the greatest difficulty that an artist might engage himself in lithography. As a result, few of the major artists working in the United States made lithographs during the 1940s and 1950s.
>
> In 1960, Tamarind Lithography Workshop was established in Los Angeles under a grant from the Ford Foundation for the primary purpose of providing a new stimulus to the art of the lithograph in the United States. Since 1960, a number of professional lithographic workshops have opened throughout the country, many of them staffed by artisans trained at Tamarind. The lithographic workshops maintained at art schools and university art departments have likewise increased in number and, under the influence of the Tamarind program, have greatly improved in quality. Now, in the United States as well as in Europe, the artist again finds it possible to work in collaboration with skilled printers, and in these circumstances American Lithography has enjoyed a notable renaissance.

While hand printed graphics drawn by an artists were considered original art, they were priced lower than original canvasses and were therefore generally more affordable. With lower prices than canvasses the sales of hand printed lithographs held up well in periods of recession when sales of the total art market were predictably slower.

Prices for hand printed lithographs varied from $30.00 to $10,000 for modern prints; older prints of old masters were even higher. An artist whose canvasses commanded $20,000 might sell his hand printed graphics for $1,000 each. Typical prices for 22 × 30 inch prints ranged anywhere from $150 to $500 depending upon the artists, printer and where they were purchased.

Consumers acquired prints from art galleries, publishing houses and auctions and from other individuals such as dealers, interior decorators, artists and printers. Corporate art buyers often purchased graphics for their headquarters and other executive office buildings.

The publisher of a print is anyone who pays for the printing costs of an edition. Publishers may be galleries or publishing houses, or individuals such as dealers, artists or printers. When not the artist, the publisher pays the artist a flat fee and after paying the printing costs owns all the prints except those few retained by the printer and the artist.

In response to an inquiry from Lonetown's accountant a master printer stated that in his experience graphics or print galleries operated on a 50% markup from their selling price to the consumer. Of the costs that galleries paid publishers for prints he estimated that artists' fees accounted for 25% and printing costs another 25% with the balance going to publishers. On this basis, a print offered by a gallery to retail at $2,000 to the buyer entailed total printing costs of $250.

THE INDUSTRY AND LONETOWN PRESS

The hand printed lithography business in the United States had perhaps a half dozen major print shops that generally did their own publishing. These major shops usually employed four or more printers while the balance of the industry of 50 or so shops were one or two printer operations. There were probably less than sixty print shops in the U.S. accepting hand printed lithography work in 1982. Recent price schedules of the Tamarind Institute and two printing companies are shown in Exhibits 1, 2, and 3.

For at least some of their business most shops co-published. This involved a negotiation of charges in which the printer accepted some number of copies of the artist's edition in exchange for the printer's services. For example, Lonetown Press might retain 10 to 25 copies of a 50 print edition in lieu of the costs for printing

EXHIBIT 1
Typical Prices for Lithographic Printing

Effective 1 January 1982

The total cost of an edition is the *base charge,* plus the *impression charge,* plus *surcharges* (if any), plus the *cost of paper.* Paper will be billed at the most recent price paid by Tamarind with an allowance for care and shipping. The dimensions of a lithograph (paper size) are also a factor in determination of price. Tamarind's prices for printing are established in four groups, according to dimensions, and show the *maximum size* allowed for that price category. Prices for lithographs larger than 30 by 40 inches will be estimated upon request.

Base Charges

The *base charges* (per edition) include the services of Tamarind's professional staff, all costs related to graining of stones or plates, lithographic materials used in making drawings, materials and papers used in proofing, such proofing as is reasonable and necessary to arrive at a *bon à tirer* impression, the printing of the first ten proofs and/or impressions (however they may be designated), curating services, tissues and wrapping materials (packing for shipment, if desired, is billed separately).

	Size *15 by 22 in.* *38 by 56 cm.*	*Size* *19 by 25 in.* *49 by 64 cm.*	*Size* *22 by 30 in.* *56 by 76 cm.*	*Size* *30 by 40 in.* *76 by 102 cm.*
One color	$140.00	$200.00	$240.00	$340.00
Two colors	320.00	390.00	450.00	580.00
Three colors	450.00	530.00	600.00	750.00
Four colors	560.00	640.00	710.00	900.00
Five colors	660.00	740.00	820.00	1,050.00
Six colors	760.00	880,00	930.00	1,200.00

Impression Charges

The first ten proofs and/or impressions are included in the base charge; no charge is made for proofs and/or impressions rejected because of technical imperfections, or for proofs or impressions which become the property of the collaborating printers or of Tamarind. The following charges apply to all other impressions, however they may be designated:

	Size *15 by 22 in.* *38 by 56 cm.*	*Size* *19 by 25 in.* *49 by 64 cm.*	*Size* *22 by 30 in.* *56 by 76 cm.*	*Size* *30 by 40 in.* *76 by 102 cm.*
One color	$6.00	$7.00	$8.00	$10.00
Two colors	12.00	14.00	16.00	20.00
Three colors	18.00	21.00	24.00	30.00
Four colors	23.00	25.00	27.00	33.00
Five colors	27.00	29.00	31.00	36.00
Six colors	31.00	33.00	35.00	39.00

EXHIBIT 1
continued

Surcharges

Stone charges:	At sizes below 22 by 30 there is no price differential for work on stone. Surcharges for stone begin at 22 by 30 inches ($40.00) and increase proportional to size: the surcharge for use of our largest stone (36 by 52 inches) is $165.00.
Blended inking:	A surcharge will be added for use of blended or split inking. The charge is determined by the complexity of the blend; it will never be less than 10% and may be up to double the impression charge.
Curatorial services:	When the design of a print requires special curatorial services (as examples, tearing to a template, cutting to irregular shapes, applying metallic leaf, etc.) surcharges will be added proportional to the time required.
Technical processes:	Use of all standard lithographic drawing materials and processes is included in the base charge, including direct drawing on stones or plates or through transfer methods. For use of photographic processes and such special techniques as image reversal, printing on chine colle, etc., surcharges will be added proportional to the time required.

Examples

The cost of editions of 50 impressions of single-color lithographs at sizes 19 by 25 inches and 22 by 30 inches printed from stone on Rives BFK, would be calculated as follows:

	19 by 25 in.	*22 by 30 in.*
Base charge	$200.00	$240.00
Surcharge for stone	0	40.00
Impression charge (50%*)	350.00*	400.00*
Paper charges	50.00	50.00
Total:	$600.00	$730.00

*This figure may be adjusted depending upon the number of trial and/or color trial proofs.

Abandoned Projects

On occasion, an artist reaches a decision to abandon a project without printing an edition. In that event, Tamarind will refund a portion of the base charges, as follows:

1. If the project is abandoned prior to processing and proofing of the plates and/or stones, Tamarind's total charge will be the sum of $100.00, plus any surcharges for stone, plus $25 for each metal plate (or small stone) used. The remainder will be refunded or applied to another project.
2. If the project is abandoned during or at the end of a first proofing session (a session in which all of the printing elements are proofed, one upon another), Tamarind's total charge will be the sum of the surcharges for stone, and 75% of the base charge. The remainder will be refunded or applied to another project.
3. If a project is abandoned at any point beyond the end of the first proofing session (as defined above), the full base charge will be paid

PAYMENT OF ONE-HALF THE TOTAL ESTIMATED CHARGES
IS DUE BEFORE WORK IS BEGUN.
THE BALANCE IS DUE UPON DELIVERY OF THE EDITION.

EXHIBIT 2
Vermont Graphics, Inc.***

Price List
September, 1980
Proofing Charges (price including all materials)

Colors/Runs	*15 x 22*	*22 x 30*	*29 x 41*
One	$78.25	$117.20	$156.25
Two	148.50	219.00	281.25
Three	219.00	320.25	406.25
Four	289.00	422.00	531.25
Five	359.00	535.50	656.25
Six	516.00	750.00	937.50
Seven	600.00	872.00	1087.50
Eight	684.50	828.00	1237.50
Nine	768.75	1015.65	1387.50
Ten	853.00	1237.50	1537.50

Printing Charges per Impression

Colors/Runs	*15 x 22*	*22 x 30*	*29 x 41*
One	$7.75	$10.25	$13.30
Two	14.50	18.50	23.70
Three	21.00	27.00	34.30
Four	27.75	35.50	44.80
Five	34.50	52.75	55.30
Six	49.00	62.70	79.00
Seven	57.00	72.75	91.50
Eight	65.18	82.80	103.25
Nine	73.20	93.00	116.75
Ten	81.00	103.00	129.50

*Disguised name.

EXHIBIT 3
Oklahoma Print Shop***

Price List
For 22″ x 30″ Size
50 Prints
June, 1982
Proofing Charges

Colors/Runs	
One	$120.00
Two	170.00
Three	235.00
Four	285.00
Five	350.00
Six	420.00
Seven	495.00
Eight	575.00
Nine	665.00
Ten	735.00

Printing Charges per Impression

Colors/Runs	
One	$7.20
Two	10.80
Three	16.80
Four	21.60
Five	25.20
Six	28.80
Seven	32.40
Eight	36.00
Nine	39.60
Ten	43.20

*Disguised name.

services rendered. In this situation the artist would not incur an outlay for printing and Lonetown would assume responsibility for selling the graphics to compensate for the printing. A variation on co-publishing occurred when printers gave discounts in exchange for a part of the edition. These types of agreements were believed to be particularly appealing to up and coming artists to whom Randy wished to cater.

Lonetown's accountant had developed estimates of both annual and per job costs for the shop, since she was thinking of adding a markup to labor and/or material costs as the basis for creating a price schedule. Randy however was somewhat skeptical of this approach because he had concerns about pricing too high or too low in relation to competition. He wanted to price high enough to be taken seriously, but low enough to attract initial business. The accountant figured business expenses would run $11,000 annually, not including Randy's salary needs of $30,000 per year.

Lonetown Press Annual Expenses	
Public relations (personal entertainment)	$3,000
Advertising	2,000
Travel expenses	2,000
Depreciation	1,300
Lawyer & accountant fees	1,000
Insurance, electricity, heat	1,000
Property taxes	700
Total	$11,000

In addition to the master printer's labor hours, cost estimates that could be directly traced to each job were:

5-Color—50 Print Edition

Item	*Cost*
Standard paper	$175
Ink	10
Printing plates	95
Various chemicals	20
Total costs per job	$300

The most comfortable edition size for Lonetown Press was 50 prints; and editions over 200 prints were definitely less desirable. With editions of 150 and over the master printer in a one-person shop often encountered some tedium which could adversely affect the quality of his work.

At Lonetown the largest acceptable print was 30 × 40 inches since this was the maximum size that the Griffen Press could accommodate. Smaller paper sizes presented no problems.

Although four to five colors appealed most to Randy, the number of colors in a print was not of great importance. However, since each color in a print must be printed separately, printing additional colors required additional printing time.

A typical or average job for Lonetown might be a 5-color 22″ × 30″ edition of 50 prints. Randy felt that he could produce 25 such editions per year, or about one such edition every two weeks. Working at this rate would leave him barely sufficient time left over to consult with artists and galleries and do his bookkeeping and purchasing.

Randy felt confident about the long-term success of Lonetown; however, his immediate concern was quoting prices on several pending inquiries. He had decided that his price schedule should have separate prices for proofing and printing, prices for three sizes (18 × 24, 22 × 30, 30 × 40) and prices for one to ten colors. In addition, he wanted his price schedule to in some way reflect his preference for printing smaller editions.

CASE 23 | *Grasse Fragrances SA*

Grasse Fragrances, headquartered in Lyon, France, was the world's fourth largest producer of fragrances. Established in 1885, the company had grown from a small family owned business, selling fragrances to local perfume manufacturers, to a multinational enterprise with subsidiaries and agents in over 100 countries.

For Marketing Director Jean-Pierre Volet, the last few years had been devoted to building a strong headquarters marketing organization. In February 1989, however, he was returning to France after an extensive tour of Grasse sales offices and factories and a number of visits with key customers. As the Air France flight touched down in Lyon Airport, Jean-Pierre Volet was feeling very concerned about what he had learned on the trip. "Our sales force," he thought, "operates much as it did several years ago. If we're going to compete successfully in this new environment we have to completely rethink our sales force management practices."

THE FLAVOR AND FRAGRANCE INDUSTRY

Worldwide sales of essential oils, aroma chemicals and fragrance and flavor compounds were estimated to be around $5.5 billion in 1988.

Five major firms accounted for something like 50% of the industry's sales. The largest, International Flavors & Fragrances Inc. of New York, had 1988 sales of $839.5 million (up 76% from 1984), of which fragrances accounted for 62%. The company had plants in 21 countries and non-U.S. operations represented 70% of sales and 78% of operating profit.

Quest International, a wholly owned subsidiary of Unilever, was next in size, with sales estimated at $700 million, closely followed by The Givaudan Group, a wholly owned subsidiary of Hoffman-LaRoche, with sales of $536 million, and Grasse Fragrances with sales of $480 million. Firmenich, a closely held Swiss family firm, did not disclose results but 1987 sales were estimated at some $300 million.

Grasse produced only fragrances. Most major firms in the industry, however, produced both fragrances and flavors (i.e., flavor extracts and compounds mainly used in foods, beverages and pharmaceutical products). Generally, the products were very similar. The major difference was that the flavorist had to match his or her creations with their natural counterparts, such as fruits, meats, or spices, as closely as possible. On the other hand, the perfumer had the flexibility to use his or her imagination to create new fragrances. Perfumery was closely associated with fashion, encompassed a wide variety of choice and products had to be dermatologically safe. Development of flavors was more limited and products were required to meet strict toxicological criteria because the products were ingested.

Markets for Fragrances

While the use of perfumes is as old as history, it was not until the 19th century, when major advances were made in organic chemistry, that the fragrance industry emerged as it is known today. Focusing first on perfumes, use of fragrances expanded into other applications. In recent years manufacturers of soap, detergents and other household products had significantly increased their purchases of fragrances and have represented the largest single consumption category. Depending on the application, the chemical complexity of a particular fragrance and the quantity produced, prices could range from less than FF40 per kilogram to over FF4,000.[1]

Despite its apparent maturity the world market for fragrances was estimated to have grown at an average of 5–6% during the early 1980s and some estimates indicated that sales growth could increase even further during the last half of the decade. New applications supported these estimates. Microwave foods, for instance, needed additional flavorings to replicate familiar tastes that would take time to develop in a conventional oven. In laundry detergents, a significant fragrance market, the popularity of liquids provided a new stimulus to fragrance sales as liquid detergents needed more fragrance than did powders to achieve the desired aroma. Similarly, laundry detergents designed to remove odors as well as dirt also stimulated sales as they used more fragrance by volume.

[1]$1 = approximately FF6 in 1988.

The New Buying Behavior

Over time, buying behavior for fragrances, as well as markets, had changed significantly. Responsibility for the selection and purchase of fragrances became complex, particularly in large firms. R&D groups were expected to ensure the compatibility of the fragrance with the product under consideration; marketing groups were responsible for choosing a fragrance that gave the product a competitive edge in the market place, and purchasing groups had to obtain competitive prices and provide good deliveries.

Use of briefs (the industry term for a fragrance specification and request for quotation) became common. Typically, a brief would identify the general characteristics of the fragrance, the required cost parameters as well as an extensive description of the company's product and its intended strategy in the market place. Occasionally a fragrance producer would be sole sourced, generally for proprietary reasons. Usually, however, the customer would ask for at least two quotations, so competitive quotes were the norm.

GRASSE FRAGRANCES SA

Background

The company was founded in 1885 by Louis Piccard, a chemist, who had studied at the University of Lyon. He believed that progress in the field of organic chemistry could be used to develop a new industry—creating perfumes, as opposed to relying on nature. Using a small factory on the Siagne River near Grasse, the company soon became a successful supplier of fragrances to the leading perfume houses of Paris. Despite the interruptions by World Wars I and II, the company followed an early policy of international growth and diversification. Production and sales units were first established in Lyon, Paris and Rome. In the 1920s company headquarters were moved to Lyon. At that time the company entered the American market, first establishing a sales office and then a small manufacturing facility. Acquisitions were made in England, and subsequently the company established subsidiaries in Switzerland, Brazil, Argentina and Spain.

Faced with increased competition and large capital requirements for R&D, plant expansion and new product launches, the Piccard family decided to become a public company in 1968. Jacques Piccard, oldest son of the founder, was elected president and the family remained active in the management of the company. Assisted by the infusion of capital, Grasse was able to further expand its business activities in Europe, the United States, Latin America and the Far East.

In 1988 total sales were $450,000,000, up some 60% from 1984; 40% of sales came from Europe, 30% from North America, 10% from Latin America, 5% from Africa/Middle East and 15% from Asia/Pacific. In recent years the company's position had strengthened somewhat in North America.

By the end of 1988 the company had sales organizations or agents in 100 countries, laboratories in 18 countries, compounding facilities in 14 countries, chemical production centers in 3 countries and research centers in 3 countries. Employment was 2,500, of whom some 1,250 were employed outside France.

Products

In 1988, the company's main product lines were in two categories:

- Perfumery products used for perfumes, eau de cologne, eau de toilette, hair lotion, cosmetics, soaps, detergents, other household and industrial products
- Synthetics for perfume compounds, cosmetic specialties, sunscreening agents and preservatives for various industrial applications

According to Jacques Piccard:

> From the production side, flavors and fragrances are similar, although the creative and marketing approaches are quite different. So far we have elected

to specialize in just fragrances, but I think it's just a matter of time before we decide to get into flavors.

Following industry practice, Grasse divided its fragrances into four categories:

- Fine fragrances
- Toiletries and cosmetics
- Soaps and detergents
- Household and industrial

MARKETING AT GRASSE

In 1980, Jean-Pierre Volet was appointed Marketing Director, after a successful stint as country manager for the Benelux countries. At the time, the headquarters marketing organization was relatively small. Its primary role was to make sure the sales force had information on the company's products, send out samples of new perfumes that were developed in the labs, usually with little customer input, and handle special price or delivery requests. As Volet recalled:

> In the 1940s, 1950s and 1960s, most of our business was in fine fragrances, toiletries and cosmetics. Our customers tended to be small and focused on local markets. Our fragrance salesman would carry a suitcase of 5 gram samples, call on the customer, get an idea of what kind of fragrance the customer wanted and either leave a few samples for evaluation or actually write an order on the spot. It was a very personal kind of business. Buying decisions tended to be based on subjective impressions and the nature of the customer's relation with the salesman. Our headquarters marketing organization was designed to support that kind of of selling and buying. Today, however, we deal with large multinational companies who are standardizing their products across countries, and even regions, and who are using very sophisticated marketing techniques to guide their use of fragrances. Detergents and other household products represent an increasing share of the market. When I came to headquarters one of my important priorities was to structure a marketing organization which reflected this new environment.

In addition to the normal administrative activities such as field sales support, pricing and budgeting, Volet had built a fragrance creation group and a product management group. More recently he had established an international client coordination group. (The marketing organization in 1988 is shown in Exhibit 1.)

The fragrance creation group served as a bridge between the basic lab work and customer requirements. It also ran the company's fragrance training center, used to train both its own sales force and customer personnel in the application of fragrances. The product management group was organized in the four product categories. Product managers were expected to be knowledgeable about everything that was going on in their product category, worldwide, and to use their specialized knowledge to support field sales efforts as well as guide the creative people. It was Volet's plan that international client coordinators would coordinate sales efforts.

Field sales in France reported to Piccard through Raoul Salmon, who was also responsible for the activities of the company's agents used in countries where it did not have subsidiaries or branches. In recent years, use of agents had declined and it was the company's expectation that the decline would continue.

Outside France, field sales were the responsibility of Grasse country managers. In smaller countries country managers handled only sales, thus operating essentially as field sales managers. In other countries, where the company had manufacturing or other non-selling operations, the norm was to have a field sales manager reporting to the country manager. Although individual sales representatives reported to the field sales managers, it was understood that there was a dotted line relationship from the sales representatives to the ICCs and the product managers.

The company relied extensively on its field sales force for promotional efforts, customer relations and order getting activities. There were, however, two very different kinds of selling situations. As Salmon described them:

EXHIBIT 1
Partial Organizational Chart

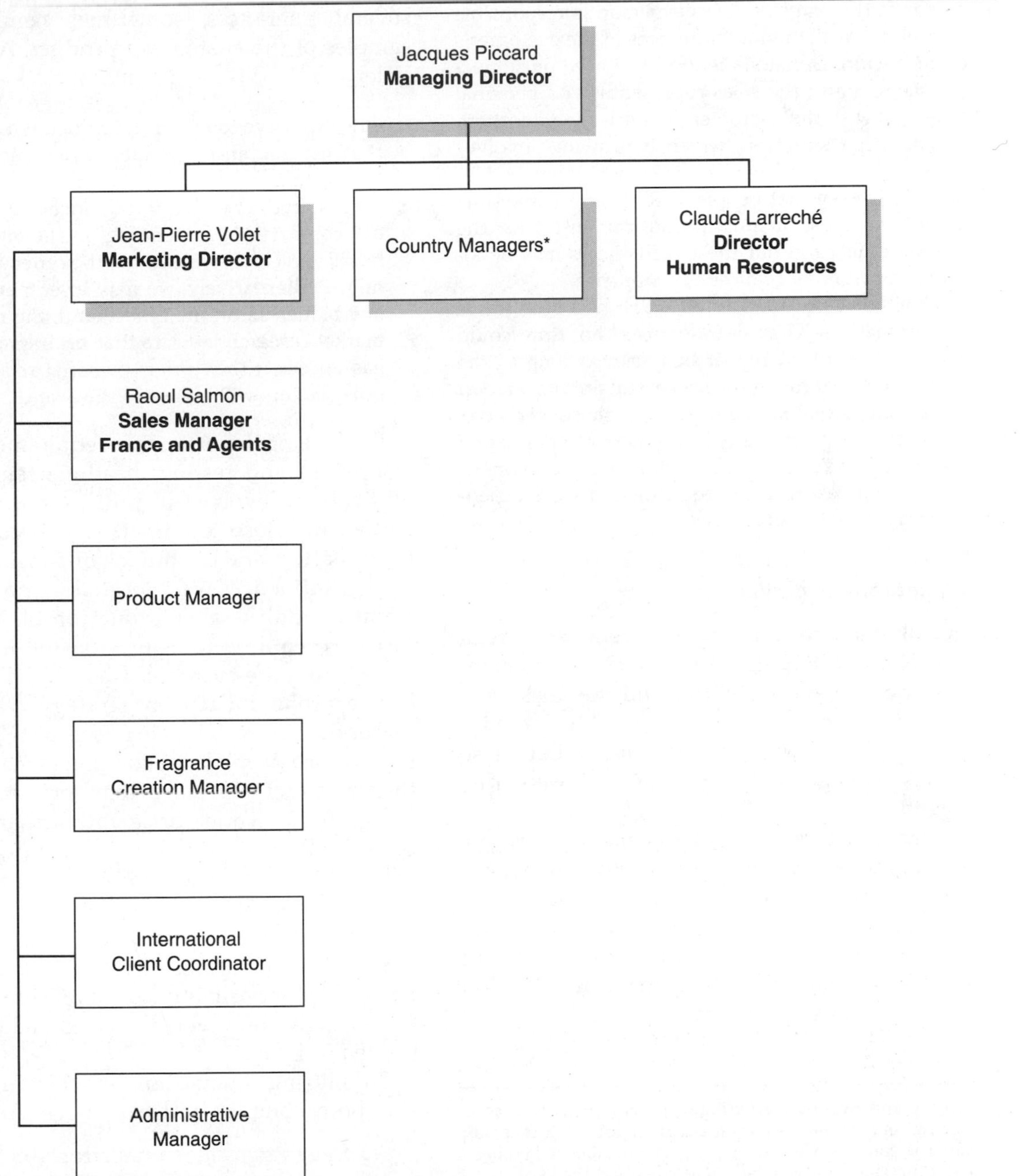

*Note: In France, all major functions (e.g., marketing, manufacturing, R&D) reported to Jacques Piccard. In most companies outside of France where the company did business, a subsidiary company was established, headed by a country manager. All company activities in each country reported to a country manager. In some countries, generally small, the company did business through agents who reported to Raoul Salmon.

There are still many customers, generally small-scale, who buy in the traditional way where the process is fairly simple. One salesperson is responsible for calling on all buying influences in the customer's organization. Decisions tend to be based on subjective factors and the sales representative's personal relations with the customer are critically important.

The other situation, which is growing, involves large and increasingly international customers. Not only do we see that people in R&D and marketing, as well as those in purchasing, can influence the purchase decision but these influencers may be located in a number of different countries.

In either case, once the decision had been made to purchase a Grasse fragrance, the firm could generally count on repeat business, as long as the customer's product was successful in the market place. On occasion, however, purchase decisions were revised, particularly if Grasse raised prices or if the customer's product came under strong competitive price pressure, thus requiring that a less expensive fragrance be considered.

The Quotation Procedure

For small orders the quotation procedure was relatively simple. Popular fragrances had established prices in every country and the sales force was expected to sell at these prices.[2] In some instances, price concessions were made but these required management approval and were discouraged.

For large orders it was the norm to develop a new fragrance. Increasingly, customers would provide Grasse with extensive information on their intended product and its marketing strategy, including the country, or countries, where the product would be sold. To make sure the fragrance fit the customer's intended marketing and product strategy, Grasse was expected to do market research in a designated pilot country on several fragrances, sometimes combined with samples of the customer's product. According to Volet:

> Once we have found or developed what we think is the best fragrance, we submit our quotation. Then the customer will do his own market research, testing his product with our fragrance and with those of our competitors. Depending on the outcome of the market research, we may get the order at a price premium. Alternatively, we may lose it, even if we are low bidder. If, on the other hand, the results of the market research indicate that no fragrance supplier has an edge, then price, personal relationships or other factors will influence the award.

Because of the extensive requirements for development and testing, headquarters in Grasse was always involved in putting a quotation together, and close coordination was vital between headquarters and the branch or subsidiary. When buying influences were located in more than one country, additional coordination of the sales effort was required to insure that information obtained from the customer was shared and also to insure a coherent account strategy.

Coordination of pricing was also growing in importance. Many large customers manufactured their products in more than one country and looked for a "world" price, rather than a country price. In these situations, country organizations were expected to take a corporate view of profits, sometimes at the expense of their own profit statements. The lead country (i.e., the country in which the purchasing decision would be made) had final responsibility for establishing the price. Increasingly, however, this price had to be approved in Lyon.

Submitting quotations in this environment was both complex and expensive. According to Volet:

> Receiving a brief from a customer starts a complex process. we immediately alert all our salespeople who call on various purchasing influences. Even

---

[2]Subject to approval by marketing headquarters, each Grasse producing unit established a transfer price for products sold outside the country. Country prices were established taking into account the country profit objectives and the local market conditions. Transfer prices were usually established for a year. Adjusting transfer prices for fluctuations in exchange rates was a matter of ongoing concern.

though the brief contains lots of information on what the customer wants we expect our salespeople to provide us with some additional information.

The next step is for our creative people to develop one or more fragrances which we believe will meet the customer's requirements. They are aided in this effort by our product managers who know what is going on with their products worldwide. If additional information is needed from the customer, our international client people will contact the appropriate salespeople.

After creating what we think is the right product, or products, we may conduct our own market research, in a country designated by the customer. This is usually done under the direction of our product manager, working closely with our market research people. Throughout this process, our sales force is expected to stay in close touch with the customer to give us any changes in his thinking or any competitive feedback. Based on the results of this effort, we then submit our proposal which gives the customer the price, samples and as much product information as possible.

With some customers, there is little further sales effort after they receive our quotation, and the buying decision is made "behind closed doors." In other instances, we may be asked to explain the results of our research or to discuss possible modifications in our product and, sometimes, in our price. Frequently we find that the customer is more concerned with our price policy (i.e., how firm the price is and for how long) than with the price quoted at the time of the brief.

When you make this kind of effort, you obviously hate to lose the order. On the other hand, even if we lose, the investment made in development work and market research is likely to pay off in winning another brief, either with the original customer or with another customer.

International Accounts

In 1988 about 50% of the firm's business came from some 40 international accounts. Looking to the future, it was expected that the number of international accounts would grow and some estimated that by 1994 as much as 80% of the firm's business would come from international accounts.

As of 1988, 18–20 international accounts were targeted for coordination by International Client Coordinators (ICCs) in Lyon. The principal responsibility of each ICC was to really know assigned customers on a worldwide basis and put that knowledge to use in coordinating work on a brief. The rest were followed in Lyon, but coordination was a subsidiary responsibility. In either case, it was the view at headquarters that coordination was critical. As Volet described it:

> We rely extensively on account teams. European teams may meet as often as once a quarter. Worldwide teams are more likely to meet annually. For designated accounts the ICC takes the lead role in organizing the meeting and, generally, coordinating sales efforts. For others the Parent Account Executive (the sales representative in the country selling the customer component with the greatest buying influence) plays the lead role. In these situations we hold the Parent Account Executive responsible for all the coordinating work. We also hold him responsible to be proactive and already working on the next brief long before we get a formal request.
>
> Here in Lyon we prepare extensive worldwide "bibles" on international accounts which are made available to all the members of the team. We also prepare quarterly project reports for team members. Our next step will be to computerize as much of this as possible.

Sales Management Practices

In 1988 sales force management practices were not standardized. Selection, compensation, training, organization, etc. were the responsibility of subsidiary management. Even so, a number of practices were similar.

Sales representatives tended to be compensated by a salary and bonus scheme. A typical minimum bonus was 1.5 month's salary, but could range up to 2.5 month's salary for excellent performance. The exact amount of the bonus was discretionary with sales management and could reward a number of factors.

Sales budgets were established from estimates made by sales representatives for direct orders (i.e., orders that would be placed by their assigned accounts). These estimates were developed from expectations of sales volume for fragrances currently being used by customers, in which case historical sales were the major basis for the estimate, and from estimates of sales of new fragrances. While historical sales of currently used fragrances were useful in predicting future sales, variations could occur. Sales activity of the customer's product was not totally predictable. In some instances, customers reopened a brief to competition, particularly where the customer was experiencing competitive cost pressures.

Predicting sales of new fragrances was even more difficult. Customers' plans were uncertain and the nature of the buying process made it difficult to predict the odds of success on any given transaction. Grasse Fragrances, nevertheless, relied heavily on these estimates. The sum of the estimates was expected to add up to the company budget for the coming year. When this was not the case, sales managers were expected to review their estimates and increase them appropriately.

The company had recently introduced, companywide, its own version of management by objectives. Each sales representative was expected to develop a personal set of objectives for negotiation with his or her sales manager. Formal account planning, however, had not been established, although some subsidiaries were starting the practice.

Sales training had two components. Product knowledge tended to be the responsibility of headquarters, relying heavily on the fragrance training center. Selling skills, however, were principally the responsibility of the subsidiary companies.

Selection practices were the most variable. Some subsidiaries believed that company and product knowledge were key to selling success and so tended to look inside the company for individuals who had the requisite company and product knowledge and who expressed an interest in sales work. Others believed that demonstrated selling skills were key and so looked outside the company for individuals with good selling track records, preferably in related industries.

SALES MANAGEMENT ISSUES

A number of sales management practices were of concern, both in headquarters and in the subsidiaries.

Influence Selling

Insuring appropriate effort on all buying influences was a major concern. According to Salmon:

> Our sales representatives understand the importance of influence selling, but we have no formal way of recognizing their efforts. A number of our large accounts, for instance, have their marketing groups located in Paris, and they have lots of influence on the buying decision. If we win the brief, however, purchasing is likely to take place in Germany or Spain or Holland, and my sales representative will not get any sales credit.

In a similar vein, Juan Rodriguez, sales manager for a group of countries in Latin America commented:

> We have a large account that does lots of manufacturing and purchasing in Latin America but does its R&D work in the US. The customer's people in Latin America tell us that without strong support from R&D in the US it is very difficult for them to buy our fragrances. The sales representative in New York is certainly aware of this but his boss is measured on profit, which can only come from direct sales in the US, so he's not enthusiastic about his sales representative spending a lot of time on influence business.

In some instances, the nature of the buying process resulted in windfalls for some sales representatives. Commenting on this aspect Salmon observed:

> It can work the other way as well. Our Spanish subsidiary recently received an order for 40 tons of a fragrance but the customer's decision to buy was to-

> tally influenced by sales representatives in Germany and Lyon. Needless to say, our Spanish subsidiary was delighted but the people in Germany and Lyon were concerned as to how their efforts would be recognized and rewarded.

While there was general recognition that influence selling was vital, it was not clear how it could be adequately measured and rewarded. As Salmon pointed out:

> In some instances (e.g., the order in Spain) we're pretty sure about the amount of influence exerted by those calling on marketing and R&D. In other instances, it is not at all clear. We have some situations where the sales representative honestly believes that his calls on, say, R&D are important but, in fact, they are not. At least not in our opinion. If we come up with the wrong scheme to measure influence, we could end up with a lot of wasted time and effort.

Incentive Compensation

Compensation practices were a matter of some concern. The salary component was established at a level designed to be competitive with similar sales jobs in each country. Annual raises had become the norm, with amounts based on performance, longevity and changes in responsibility. The bonus component was determined by the immediate manager, but there were concerns that bonuses had become automatic. Still further, some held the view that the difference between 1.5 and 2.5 times the monthly salary was not very motivating, even if bonus awards were more performance driven.

Whether merited or not, sales representatives expected some level of bonus, and there was concern that any change could cause morale problems. At the same time there was growing recognition of the increasing importance of team selling.

Overall responsibility for compensation practices was assigned to Claude Larreché, Director of Human Resources. According to Larreché:

> Some of our sales managers are interested in significantly increasing the incentive component of sales force compensation. It has been my view, however, that large incentive payments to the sales force could cause problems in other parts of our organization. Plus, there seems to be considerable variation in country practice with regard to incentive compensation. In the US, for instance, compensation schemes which combine a fixed, or salary, component and an incentive component, usually determined by sales relative to a quota, are common. To a lesser degree, we see some of this in Europe, and somewhat more in the south, but I'm not sure that we want to do something just because a lot of other companies are doing it.
>
> We're also thinking about some kind of team incentive or bonus. But this raises questions about who should be considered part of the team and how a team bonus should be allocated. Should the team be just the sales representatives, or should we include the ICCs? And what about the customer service people, without whom we wouldn't have a base of good performance to build on?
>
> Allocation is even more complicated. We're talking about teams comprised of people all around the world. I think it is only natural that the local manager will think that his sales representative made the biggest contribution, which could result in long arguments. One possibility would be for the team itself to allocate a bonus pool but I'm not sure how comfortable managers would be with such an approach.

Small Accounts

Despite the sales growth expected from international accounts, sales to smaller national accounts were expected to remain a significant part of the firm's revenues and, generally, had very attractive margins. According to one country sales manager:

> With the emphasis on international accounts, I'm concerned about how we handle our smaller single country accounts. Many of them still buy the way they did 10 and 20 years ago, although today we can select from over 30,000 fragrances. Our international accounts will probably generate 80% of our business in the years to come but the 20% we get from our smaller accounts is important and produces excel-

lent profits for the company. But I'm not sure that the kind of selling skills we need to handle international accounts are appropriate for the smaller accounts. Personal and long-term relationships are tremendously important to these accounts.

Language

In the early 1980s it had become apparent to Grasse management that French would not serve as the firm's common language. In most of its subsidiary countries, English was either the country language or the most likely second language. With considerable reluctance on the part of some French managers, it was decided that English would become the firm's official language. Personnel in the US and England, few of whom spoke a second language, welcomed the change. There were, however, a number of problems. As the Italian sales manager said:

> We understand the need for a common language when we bring in sales representatives from all over Europe or the world. And we understand that English is the "most common" language in the countries where we do business. All of my people understand that they will have to speak English in international account sales meetings. What they don't like, however, is that the Brits and the Americans tend to assume that they are smarter than the rest of us, simply because we can't express ourselves as fluently in English as they can. It's totally different when my people talk to someone from Latin America, or some other country, where English is their second language, too.
>
> A related problem is the attitudes people from one country have towards those of another. This goes beyond language. Frequently our people from northern Europe or North America will stereotype those of us from southern Europe or Latin America as disorganized or not business like. My people, on the other hand, see the northerners as inflexible and unimaginative. To some extent these views diminish after we get to know each other as individuals, but it takes time and there is always some underlying tension.

Language also influenced decisions on rotation of personnel. It was Volet's view that there should be movement between countries of sales managers and marketing personnel. Still further, he felt that sales representatives who aspired to promotion should also be willing to consider transfers to another country or to headquarters in Lyon. As he pointed out, however:

> Customer personnel in most of our international accounts speak English. Hence there is a temptation to feel that English language competency is the only requirement when considering reassignment of sales personnel. In fact, if we were to transfer a sales representative who spoke only English to Germany, for instance, he would be received politely the first time, but from then on it would be difficult for him to get an appointment with the customer. It has been our experience that our customers want to do business in their own language, even if they speak English fluently.
>
> An exception might be an international account whose parent is British and which transfers a lot of British personnel to another country. Even here, however, there will be lots of people in the organization for whom English is not a native tongue.
>
> Therefore, we require that our salespeople speak the language of the country and are comfortable with the country culture. Local people meet this requirement. The real issue is getting all, or most, of our people to be comfortable in more than one language and culture.

Sales Training

One of the most perplexing issues was what, if any, changes to make with regard to sales training. At headquarters there was considerable sentiment for standardization. As Volet put it:

> I really don't see that much difference in selling from one country to another. Of course, personal relations may be more important in, say, Latin America or the Middle East than in Germany but I think that as much as 80–85% of the selling job can be harmonized. In addition, it's my view that our international accounts expect us to have a standardized

> sales approach. Sales training, therefore, should be something we can do centrally at Lyon.

This view was supported by those in human resources. According to Claude Larreché:

> We no longer see ourselves as a collection of individual companies that remit profits to Lyon and engage in occasional technology transfer. Our view of the future is that we are a global company that must live in a world of global customers and markets. I think this means we must have a Grasse Fragrance culture that transcends national boundaries, including a common sales approach, i.e., this is the way Grasse approaches customers, regardless of where they are located. A key element in establishing such a culture is sales training here in Lyon.

Others disagreed with this point of view, however. Perhaps the most vociferous was the US sales manager:

> I understand what Jean-Pierre and Claude are saying and I support the notion of a common company culture. The fact is, however, that selling is different in the US than in other parts of the world. Not long ago we transferred a promising sales representative from Sweden to our office in Chicago. His sales approach, which was right for Sweden, was very relaxed and he had to make some major adjustments to fit the more formal and fast paced approach in Chicago. I don't see how a sales training program in Lyon can be of much help. Plus, the cost of sending people to Lyon comes out of my budget, and this would really hit my country manager's profits.
>
> In fact, I think we ought to have more flexibility with regard to all our sales management practices.

As Jean-Pierre Volet waited for his bag at the Lyon Airport, he wondered how far he should go in making changes with regard to the sales force. There were some limits on what he could do. He could not, for instance, change the basic structure of the company, i.e., the country manager form of organization, and he would have to get support from the country managers for his changes. Whatever he did would be controversial, but he was convinced some changes were necessary.

Name Index

Subject Index